STRUCTURE
AND
MEANING

HOUGHTON MIFFLIN COMPANY · BOSTON

Atlanta Dallas Geneva, Ill. Hopewell, N.J. Palo Alto London

Anthony Dubé, UNIVERSITY OF ARKANSAS
AT LITTLE ROCK

John Karl Franson, UNIVERSITY OF MAINE
AT FARMINGTON

Russell E. Murphy, UNIVERSITY OF ARKANSAS
AT LITTLE ROCK

James W. Parins, UNIVERSITY OF ARKANSAS
AT LITTLE ROCK

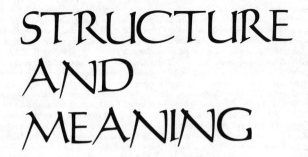

STRUCTURE AND MEANING

AN INTRODUCTION TO LITERATURE

Library of Congress Catalog Card Number: 75-31038

ISBN: 0-395-21967-1

CREDITS

Samuel Allen (Paul Vesey). "In My Father's House," from *Ivory Tusks* (1968). Reprinted by permission of Samuel Allen.   Robert Anderson. *Tea and Sympathy*. Copyright 1953 by Robert Anderson. Reprinted by permission of Random House, Inc. CAUTION: Professionals and amateurs are hereby warned that *Tea and Sympathy*, being fully protected under the copyright laws of the United States, the British Empire including the Dominion of Canada, and all other countries of the Copyright Union, is subject to royalty. All rights including professional, amateur, motion picture, recitation, lecturing, public reading, radio and television broadcasting, and the rights of translation into foreign languages, are strictly reserved. Particular emphasis is laid on the question of readings, permission for which must be obtained in writing from the Author's representative. All inquiries should be addressed to the Author's representative, Liebling-Wood, 551 Fifth Avenue, New York, N.Y., 10017.   Sherwood Anderson. "I Want to Know Why," from *The Smart Set* (November 1919) and *The Triumph of the Egg*, ed. B. W. Huebsch. Copyright 1921 by B. W. Huebsch. Copyright renewed 1948 by Eleanor C. Anderson. Reprinted by permission of Harold Ober Associates Incorporated.   Anonymous. "Epitaph on a Dentist" and "There was a young man of Bengal," from *The Oxford Book of Light Verse*, ed. W. H. Auden (1938). Reprinted by permission of The Clarendon Press, Oxford.   W. H. Auden. "Musée des Beaux Arts." Copyright 1940 and renewed 1968 by W. H. Auden. Reprinted from *Collected Shorter Poems 1927–1957*, by W. H. Auden, by permission of Random House, Inc., and Faber and Faber Limited.   James Baldwin. "Sonny's Blues." Copyright © 1957 by James Baldwin. Originally appeared in *Partisan Review*. Reprinted from *Going to Meet the Man* by James Baldwin with permission of The Dial Press, Inc.   Imamu Amiri Baraka (LeRoi Jones). "In Memory of Radio," from *Preface to a Twenty Volume Suicide Note* by LeRoi Jones. Copyright © 1961 by LeRoi Jones. Reprinted by permission of Corinth Books. "A Poem for Black Hearts," from *Black Magic Poetry 1961–1967*. Copyright © 1969 by LeRoi Jones. Reprinted by permission of the publisher, The Bobbs-Merrill Company, Inc.   Gwendolyn Brooks. "kitchenette building," from *The World of Gwendolyn Brooks*. Copyright 1945 by Gwendolyn Brooks Blakely. Reprinted by permission of Harper & Row, Publishers, Inc.   Ed Bullins. *The Electronic Nigger*. Reprinted with permission of Farrar, Straus & Giroux, Inc. from *New American Plays*, Volume III, ed. William Hoffman. Copyright © 1968 by Ed Bullins. Copyright © 1970 by Hill and Wang, Inc.   Raymond Carver. "Photograph of My Father in His Twenty-second Year." Copyright © 1970, 1975 by Raymond Carver. Used by permission of the author.   Padde Chayefsky. *Marty*. Copyright © 1955 by Paddy Chayefsky. Reprinted by permission of Simon and Schuster, Inc.   e.e. cummings. "next to of course god america i," copyright 1926 by Horace Liveright, renewed 1954 by E. E. Cummings; "in Just-," copyright 1923, 1951 by E. E. Cummings; "anyone lived in a pretty how town," copyright 1940 by E. E. Cummings, renewed 1968 by Marion Morehouse Cummings; "pity this busy monster, manunkind," copyright 1944 by E. E. Cummings, renewed 1972 by Nancy Andrews. Reprinted from *Complete Poems 1913–1962* by E. E. Cummings by permission of Harcourt Brace Jovanovich, Inc.   Emily Dickinson. "I taste a liquor never brewed—," "Twas like a Maelstrom," "I Heard a Fly buzz—when I died—," and "Because I could not stop for Death." Reprinted by permission of the publishers and the Trustees of Amherst College from Thomas H. Johnson, Editor, *The Poems of Emily Dickinson*, Cambridge, Mass.: The Belknap Press of Harvard University Press. Copyright 1951, 1955 by the President and Fellows of Harvard College. "After great pain a formal feeling comes—." Copyright 1929, 1947 by Mary L. Hampson. Reprinted from *The Complete Poems of Emily Dickinson*, edited by Thomas H. Johnson, by permission of Little, Brown and Co. "I like to see it lap the Miles" and "I died for Beauty." Reprinted from *Poems*, by Emily Dickinson, edited by Martha Dickinson Bianchi and Alfred Leete Hampson, by permission of Little, Brown and Co.   Paul Dunbar. "The Debt" and "Promise." Reprinted by permission of Dodd, Mead & Company, Inc. from *The Complete Poems of Paul Laurence Dunbar*.   Richard Eberhart. "If I Could Only Live at the Pitch That Is Near Madness," from *Collected Poems, 1930–1960*. Copyright © 1960 by Richard Eberhart. Reprinted by permission of Oxford University Press and Chatto and Windus Ltd.   T. S. Eliot. "The Hippopotamus," "The Love Song of J. Alfred Prufrock," and *The Waste Land*, from *Collected Poems 1909–1962* by T. S. Eliot. Copyright 1936 by Harcourt Brace Jovanovich, Inc.; copyright 1963, 1964 by T. S. Eliot. Reprinted by permission of Harcourt Brace Jovanovich, Inc. and Faber and Faber Ltd. "Burnt Norton," from *Four Quartets*, from T. S. Eliot's *The Complete Poems and Plays: 1909–1950*. Reprinted by permission of Harcourt Brace Jovanovich, Inc. and

Drawings by Saul Steinberg.
Plot and theater illustrations by George M. Ulrich.

Contents

4 THEME OR MEANING 144

5 STYLE 195

Other Stories to Read

Poetry

1 DENOTATION 413

2 CONNOTATION 425

3 IMAGERY 438

4 FIGURATIVE LANGUAGE   455

5 RHYTHM AND METER   469

6 SOUND DEVICES AND STANZA PATTERNS 488

7 ALLUSION AND SYMBOL 507

8 THE SCHEME OF MEANING 533

Other Poems to Read

Drama

Preface

The purpose of *Structure and Meaning* is to provide a comprehensive introductory study of fiction, poetry, and drama for the beginning student of literature. Selections were carefully chosen for their enduring literary excellence, their wide range and variety of style and theme, their proven appeal to students, and their ability to evoke challenging responses to the human experience. Long stories and long poems are often neglected in texts like this, but a few are included here to represent the genres more adequately. The pedagogical design of *Structure and Meaning* and its supportive materials are intended to help you achieve a greater understanding and appreciation of these works of literature. The emphasis on structure—the way good authors choose, order, and express their meanings—can, after you have assimilated it, provide the tools for unlocking the rich storehouse of experience that fiction, poetry, and drama can provide for any reader. At the same time we have tried to produce a volume flexible enough in its organization to allow for the personal teaching style of your instructor. Throughout, we have kept our eyes steadily on the chief participants in the classroom—the average student, as well as the above-average, and the instructor.

First, with you the student in mind, we prepared the explanatory material in the chapters as clearly and concisely as possible. The exercises accompanying the selections generally progress from the less troublesome to the more demanding, and we have opted to reinforce what you learn in one chapter by continually referring to difficult or significant material in subsequent chapters. Most chapters contain short biographies, selected bibliographies, and suggested topics for writing; and the section of the volume entitled "Writing About Literature" provides you with additional guidance. This section includes student-written essays—some satisfactory, some good, some excellent—which, we hope, will help and encourage you, particularly if you are unaccustomed to writing about literature. The glossary furnishes ready access to definitions of literary terms discussed more fully in the text.

Secondly, the design of the book is intended to allow for—indeed encourage—varying styles of instruction. Each instructor should employ whatever approach best fits personal inclination and the needs of the students. The instructor may systematically explore the elements of each genre, focus on a topical or thematic approach, suggest questions, exercises, topics for writing, and critical essays from the bibliographies to stimulate discussion and initiate writing projects, or assign readings exclusively for pleasure.

We owe a great debt of gratitude to the reviewers for their indispensable criticism and valuable suggestions. These critics include James W. Culp, Texas Tech University; Marvin Garfinkel, Erie Community College; H. Leon Gatlin, University of North Carolina at Charlotte; R. E. Hoover, Iowa State University; Robert Tuttle, Portland State University.

For assistance in the preliminary stages of the book, we wish to thank our many friends and colleagues at Texas Christian University, Texas Tech University, University of Texas at Arlington, West Texas State University, East Texas State University, Sam Houston State University, and Arkansas State University.

We are also gateful to our secretaries, Joyce Kinkade and Linda Temple, for typing and research, to Paul Summerlin for his diagrams, and to Nan Jo Summerlin Dubé for a penetrating reading of the entire manuscript. Finally, we must indeed thank the many students who have made our work a pleasure.

A.D.
J.K.F.
R.E.M.
J.W.P.

STRUCTURE
AND
MEANING

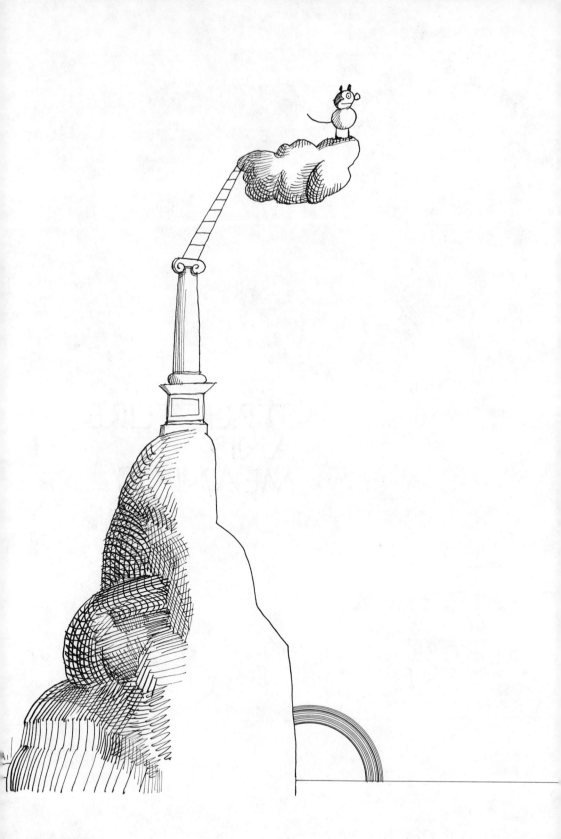

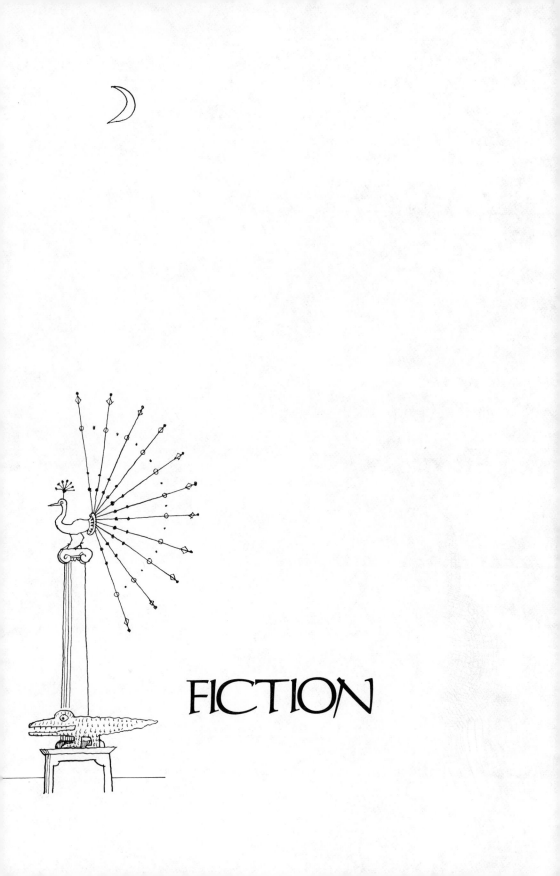

FICTION

Whated is fiction?

Fiction is man and woman (black, brown, white, red, yellow, and even green) being born, growing up, growing old, and dying; ideas, emotions, and imaginings; things seen, heard, smelled, touched, and felt; discord and harmony; the sweet and the sour; the beautiful and the horrible; the worlds of reality and the planets of fantasy; the present, the past, and the future; values to hold on to, dreams to reach for, and experiences—new, familiar, forgotten, undiscovered, or slipping through our hands—all this and much more.

A student often asks: "How can this make-believe stuff that I have to work so hard to figure out do me any good?" The next several pages will, it is hoped, offer some justification for our study of fiction.

On library shelves everywhere sit the thousand faces of fiction—what must be unequivocally a vast diversity of shapes, character, or charm. And somewhere in the crowd there is a type likely to catch each eye and engage each fancy.

Like any work of art, a work of fiction offers us a unique experience. A story is like a trip. It takes us from one place to another, delights us with scenes, people, and happenings, and returns us eagerly home again newly equipped for a more enriched existence. Like music, painting, drama, or poetry, *a story exists for one great purpose—to give us pleasure.* That is its real excuse for being, and is that not sufficient? The ways in which we derive genuine enjoyment from reading fiction are countless.

For some readers, pleasure comes from getting to know the strange, peculiar, and fascinating men and women who traverse our fictional stage and from reliving the memorable exploits of these characters. The entertainment may give pure joy, as is often the case in reading "escapist" literature, for examples, science fiction, tales of horror, and mysteries.

For others, especially the more practiced readers, pleasure comes from discovering the artistic skills of many writers: how they structure their diction and

5

syntax to make us think and feel in ways we had scarcely imagined before; how they manage their selection, arrangement, and emphasis of details to make comprehensible the human experience they wish to share with us. Serious fiction we can value not only for the enjoyment it gives but also for the understanding it communicates.

Stories offer us a vicarious experience, a way out of reality, a means of escape. This, to many of us, gives pleasure. As we read into a story, we seem to slip away quietly from the fixed, dull routines and pressures of daily living. Ironically, we are free from pain only momentarily. Peace of mind reigns but for an eye-wink. For as the author transports us to a distant place and acquaints us with new people, we lose ourselves and become involved (immediately) in the events of the story and the conflicts of others. We discover the frightening secret of buried treasure ("A Haunted House"); we try to understand the young boy offering a prayer for his father who has just brutally struck him down ("Counterparts"); and we experience what it is to be a poor, old, black woman in Mississippi, and we come to appreciate her capacity of self-sacrifice, endurance, and love ("A Worn Path").

Of course, a story does more for us than stop the real world. *It tenders companionship and solace.* Reading a story precludes our being alone with our moods of depression or feelings of inadequacy. We need not be companionless when we are confused, disillusioned, or unable to solve difficult problems. Instead, we can stroll through pages of fiction and find there—somewhere—someone with a name like ours who has faced the problems we face and felt the emotions we feel. This company is often a comfort to us.

A story also permits some insight into human behavior. And for many readers, the enlightenment affords pleasure. Many stories penetrate into the lives of characters with whom we identify. These stories also explore situations, problems, and concerns that we can appreciate. Often this experience translates meaning for us: it may tell us who we are and what we are about. In serious fiction we rarely observe a character in conflict without coming away with a moment of insight into some aspect of human nature, some understanding of life, or some added dimension of the psyche.

In the process of pondering and evaluating the significance of an experience—the figuring out of things important—we establish new relationships, expand our views, deepen our convictions, and discover new approaches or solutions to life's complexities. We may learn that tragedy and suffering make some men brothers ("The Open Boat"), that to deny commitment to anyone or anything is to deny one's sole opportunity to live fully and happily ("Flowering Judas").

The experience of reading fiction is a dynamic one. Emotionally and intellectually, we are different after reading a story. We have experienced something. If you are a person who yearns to enjoy life and *feel* deeply as well as *know* what this complex world is about, you will want to understand the motives of characters, you will want to sigh and smile and laugh and cry and rage with them—you will want to read fiction.

How many of us know so much that we have no need to read beyond text books, professional journals, and daily newspapers? Perhaps most of us cannot yet truthfully proclaim: "I know what life is about. I know about people and myself. I've read enough."

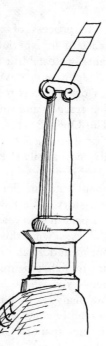

1 Plot

Plot is simply the story-line or action-line or conflict-line of a story. It is the sequence of interrelated actions and events that make up a story. It is what *happens* in fiction.

A simple summary of a conventional plot can be made in one sentence: Boy and girl meet (situation); boy and girl lose each other (complication); and boy and girl reclaim their love (resolution). A conventional plot can be illustrated by a diagram. The *introduction* sets the stage for the action that will follow; the *point of attack*

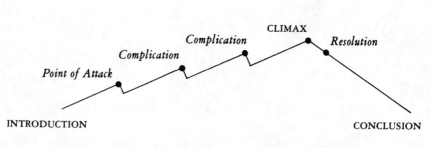

initiates the action, showing the main character in conflict with self, others, nature's forces, or social forces; the *complications* make the problem more difficult to solve; the *climax* presents the opposing forces at the apex of their struggle; the *resolution* settles the outcome of the conflict; and the *conclusion* terminates the action.

A more detailed description of a plot can be achieved by using an eight-point analysis and explaining each point in greater detail. Although this somewhat formal analysis has been used for so many years that it has become classic, it is applicable to the vast majority of the stories in this omnibus, even the most modern. And, of course, the eight points can be varied and rearranged.

Protagonist—the chief character

Prize—the protagonist's goal, objective, or purpose

Obstacle—the opposing force or forces

Point of Attack—the introduction of the problem (the conflict)

Complications—temporary hindrances

Climax—the point of highest emotional intensity

Resolution—the solving of the problem

Theme—the main point of the story

What happens in fiction happens to characters, and of all the characters in a story there is usually one whose fortunes we are most interested in—those of the *protagonist*. Man or woman, child or adult, he (or it might be she) is the main character who generally controls or forces most of the important action. One of many such characters is Leo Finkle in "The Magic Barrel." In his quest for love he encounters many difficulties, and we follow his struggle to the end of the story. We are indeed interested. Almost instantly we observe every move he makes; we want to know what will happen to him. We might be pained, happy, disappointed, touched by his sensitivity, or angered by his stupidity. Often his desires, his thoughts, his speeches, his actions become ours.

If we sympathize with the protagonist, we cheer as we might if a baseball pitcher were on the verge of completing a no-hit game. We want the protagonist to solve the problem, achieve the goal, or be victorious—whether probable or not. How can we not sympathize with Elisa ("The Chrysanthemums"), a lovely, young woman whose environment and situation have robbed her of feminine warmth and the kind of love that is obviously missing in her life? If, on the other hand, we do not sympathize with the protagonist, we may either loathe this character as we might a killer on the loose or care little for what happens. We have little or no sympathy for Farrington ("Counterparts"), who beats up his son for not having prepared supper, unless perhaps we can blame the mechanistic business world for his frustrations and loss of temper. But in a good short story, one thing is certain: we will identify with either the protagonist or the struggle and find ourselves interested in *what* happens and *why* it happens.

A protagonist wants something. That something sought or moved toward, sometimes unconsciously, is the *prize* or goal. So important is the prize to the protagonist that he or she will contend against strong opposition—even kill—to achieve it. Mr. Martin tries to outwit a coworker ("The Catbird Seat"); Macomber wants to prove his manhood or bravery ("The Short Happy Life of Francis Macomber"); and the boy inquires into the matter of ugliness in the world ("I Want to Know Why"). In some fiction the prize may be clear to the reader instantly; in other narratives it may become evident only at the conclusion of the story.

To be sure, there exists no story until *conflict* erupts, or until there is opposition to the desires of the protagonist. Conflict creates a story. It produces an obligatory clash between opposing forces.

Ordinarily, the protagonist fights against another character or group of characters, known as *antagonists.* For example, the protagonist may be a girl from the wrong side of the tracks who tries to prove herself a worthy prospect to the wealthy parents of the boy she loves. Sometimes the central character battles against the forces of nature, society, or fate: a man and his companions contend for survival, rowing a small boat against the maddened waves of a churning sea. Or the main character struggles against some aspect of himself: a man grapples to control a raging temper, which has already caused him to lose his job and his self-respect, and now threatens to incite him to commit murder.

Although we identify conflict chiefly as external or internal, physical or mental, generally it engages a combination of some or all of these struggles.

For conflict to exist, someone or something opposes the protagonist in the pursuit of the goal. This force (another character, society, environment, fate, or some aspect of the self), struggling to defeat the main character, is the *obstacle*.

More often than not, the forces in conflict clash in an incident that occurs early in the story. The earlier the better from the point of view of the reader's interest, for who will read far into a story or novel that exhibits no semblance of conflict? As soon as the reader has identified the protagonist, recognized the prize, and met the obstacle, the fuse of conflict, for all practical purposes, has been lit. This incident or initial complication, which introduces the conflict, we call the *point of attack*. In "Bartleby, the Scrivener" the conflict is introduced when the lawyer asks Bartleby to do something and he replies for the first time, "I prefer not to"; in "The Open Boat" the conflict is initiated the moment we are aware of the men's struggle to conquer the stormy seas and reach shore safely. Usually at this point in the story the reader asks, "Will the protagonist gain the prize?" This all-important question, to be asked several times as the plot develops and moves through several complications toward the climax, will not be answered until the resolution.

Whereas the obstacle remains in opposition to the protagonist throughout the action only to be removed, if removed at all, at the point of resolution, a *complication* normally subdues the protagonist or impedes progress toward the goal only temporarily.

When the men (men-protagonist) in their small craft struggle to make it safely to shore (survival-prize) against the antagonistic forces in nature (sea or fate-obstacle) and suddenly find their food and water supply exhausted, the latter discovery (in this story) only sets them back temporarily and therefore serves as a complication. Although their struggle has been made more difficult, nothing much has really changed. Survival is still possible. The protagonist will continue to battle nature's forces in an effort to reach shore.

Once the conflict has advanced through a series of complications, it reaches the point of highest emotional intensity—the *climax*. Purposely the action has moved toward this crucial scene in which the opposing forces confront each other. At this point the protagonist and the antagonist, or forces in conflict, stand at the height of their stuggle. Tension is high. For them it is the moment of truth. Here the reader asks the same question posed at the point of attack and at various moments of crises in the story—and for the last time—"Will the protagonist gain the prize?" During Macomber's final chase of the buffalo ("The Short Happy Life of Francis Macomber"), we may ask: "Will he bolt again or shoot to kill? Will he show himself to be a coward or a brave man?" Near the conclusion of the story, as the four weary men swim toward shore and survival ("The Open Boat"), we may ask: "Will they make it to shore?"

Once these questions have been answered, we have the *resolution* or dénouement, which presents the outcome of the conflict. Occasionally, the author offers no clear-cut resolution, giving the reader license to decide what really happens, but usually the problem is solved in one way or another. The protagonist wins or loses. He *does* make it to shore safely, or he drowns; the young woman from the bottom rung of the socioeconomic ladder *does* prove herself a worthy bride-to-be, or she does not; the raging man *does* suddenly come to grips with his problem, or he kills his best friend.

As the resolution settles a conflict or an argument, it may also shed light upon the meaning and significance of a story. The central meaning or thesis or premise or significance of a story we shall call *theme*. Theme is what the writer contends to be a truth or a principle about the human condition, communicated throughout the story. It may be expressed fully in an essay or tersely in the briefest of statements for the sake of review, as in the eight-point analysis. For example, "Suffering makes men brothers" may aptly express one of the major themes of "The Open Boat" or "A man may be pushed so far that he feels the need to retaliate" may fittingly point to the main theme of "The Catbird Seat."

Note in the following examples how a theme can change as the result of a different resolution. If the four men in their dinghy all survive their contest with the high seas, the author may be saying that we can conquer the forces of nature. If all the men drown, then the writer must be saying that we cannot defeat nature. If only one man out of four survives, then the author may be saying that our chances of survival against nature's forces are only slight. And, if the only man surviving happens to be the strongest of the group, the author may be saying that only the fittest survive; or if the one surviving is the weakest of the group, then the author may be telling us that people have little to do about what happens to them—they are controlled by fate. (For further details about theme, see Chapter 4.)

Of course, not every resolution emits a self-evident victory or defeat for the protagonist or sets meaning into perspective. Some stories are complex, dealing as they do with spiritual, psychological, or symbolic manifestations. The more complex the story, the more involuted its theme. However insignificant the meaning may appear to be, a good story says something.

After the resolution, what remains moves swiftly downward to the *conclusion*. Even these last few sentences often carry certain importance, for they may tie up loose ends or clarify meaning.

In addition to the elements of plot already examined, several other characteristics deserve the attention of the discriminating reader and are surely valuable to the student who seeks a better understanding and appreciation of the structure of plot.

A plot develops *chronologically* if the events unfold in precisely the order in which they occurred ("The Short Happy Life of Francis Macomber") or *retrospectively* (in a flashback) if the action shifts to something that happened earlier ("A Rose for Emily"). Rarely do modern fiction writers narrate the action in a strict chronological manner; instead they combine both techniques. Furthermore, to reveal some actions, writers use the *summary* method or the *dramatic* (scenic) method. An action revealed by means of summary usually covers long periods of time, and the summary reads like an historical report. The readers do not feel that they are observing the action ("Flowering Judas"). On the other hand, the action presented by the dramatic method generally focuses on more significant matter, enlarges its details, and heightens its effects with dialogue. Here the readers feel that what is happening is happening *now*, and they are seeing it all ("A Tree, a Rock, a Cloud").

A story also contains another kind of action that prepares us for a plunge into the tensions of the conflict. This is called *exposition*. Generally, it furnishes background information, introduces characters, and establishes setting. The information may be presented in a block at the beginning of a story or spread piecemeal throughout the story as needed.

Setting, which refers to time and place and all that time and place implies, is sometimes presented in the early pages of a story. But, when setting assumes a role larger than that of mere physical description, it is prominent throughout the story. Setting, among its several key functions, may set tone, mood, or atmosphere; shape conflict; reveal character; or contribute to the emotional, metaphorical, and overall significance of a story. Crane's vivid description of the sea in "The Open Boat" is so necessary to the action that the setting becomes, in essence, another character—the antagonist to the men in the dinghy; Eudora Welty's path, including all its barriers, not only shapes the physical conflict in "A Worn Path" but also casts light upon the social conflict present in the story.

Another important element of a story is *foreshadowing*, which the writer achieves by a particular speech, action, or symbol. To foreshadow is to suggest a more important future action, for example, the death of a small bird, suggesting the death of an important character. Foreshadowing serves any number of diverse functions, such as explaining motivation, heightening suspense, or insuring credibility. Consider the following incident:

Alone in his dimly lit study, a man sits at his desk, fidgeting. From a drawer he takes out a gun, and verifies that it is loaded. Suddenly without warning, a man enters the room. As the visitor approaches, the man at the desk quickly shoves the gun into his coat pocket. The visitor, we learn, is a business partner, unhappy over recent business failures. An argument erupts and the man at the desk pulls out his revolver and fires repeatedly into the body of his associate.

In this scene the presence of the gun before the entrance of the second character establishes the mood, creates suspense, and makes the killing plausible.

Closely connected to foreshadowing is the curiosity or anxiety we feel as we read on, disturbed and excited about what will happen next. This is called *suspense*.

The last term to be defined is *plausibility*. It may be described as that quality which makes us accept an action as true or makes us believe that it could happen.

The process of arranging events into a sequence, of selecting details, and of developing a story that communicates something can hardly be the result of an accident. On the contrary, every element in a story interracts with every other element to serve a precise purpose. Nothing is irrelevant or wasted. Each part develops logically and works intentionally with every other part to achieve the author's desired effects. This we call *artistic unity*. And every story worth reading again possesses this quality.

James Thurber (1894–1961)

Born in Columbus, Ohio, graduated from Ohio State University, he joined the staff of The New Yorker, *to which he contributed stories, essays, cartoons, and sketches for thirty-five years. Today his reputation remains secure as a foremost American humorist.* Fables For Our Time *(1940) and* A Thurber Carnival *(1945) contain some of his most famous short works.*

The Catbird Seat

Mr. Martin bought the pack of Camels on Monday night in the most crowded cigar store on Broadway. It was theatre time and seven or eight men were buying cigarettes. The clerk didn't even glance at Mr. Martin, who put the pack in his overcoat pocket and went out. If any of the staff at F & S had seen him buy the cigarettes, they would have been astonished, for it was generally known that Mr. Martin did not smoke, and never had. No one saw him.

It was just a week to the day since Mr. Martin had decided to rub out Mrs. Ulgine Barrows. The term "rub out" pleased him because it suggested nothing more than the correction of an error—in this case an error of Mr. Fitweiler. Mr. Martin had spent each night of the past week working out his plan and examining it. As he walked home now he went over it again. For the hundredth time he resented the element of imprecision, the margin of guesswork that entered into the business. The project as he had worked it out was casual and bold, the risks were considerable. Something might go wrong anywhere along the line. And therein lay the cunning of his scheme. No one would ever see in it the cautious, painstaking hand of Erwin Martin, head of the filing department at F & S, of whom Mr. Fitweiler had once said, "Man is fallible but Martin isn't." No one would see his hand, that is, unless it were caught in the act.

Sitting in his apartment, drinking a glass of milk, Mr. Martin reviewed his case against Mrs. Ulgine Barrows, as he had every night for seven nights. He began at the beginning. Her quacking voice and braying laugh had first profaned the halls of F & S on March 7, 1941 (Mr. Martin had a head for dates). Old Roberts, the personnel chief, had introduced her as the newly appointed special adviser to the president of the firm, Mr. Fitweiler. The woman had appalled Mr. Martin instantly, but he hadn't shown it. He had given her his dry hand, a look of studious concentration, and a faint smile. "Well," she had said, looking at the papers on his desk, "are you lifting the oxcart out of the ditch?" As Mr. Martin recalled that moment, over his milk, he squirmed slightly. He must keep his mind on her crimes as a special adviser, not on her peccadillos as a personality. This he found difficult to do, in spite of entering an objection and sustaining it. The faults of the woman as a woman kept chattering on in his mind like an unruly witness. She had, for almost two years now, baited him. In the halls, in the elevator, even in his own office, into which she romped now and then like a circus horse, she was constantly shouting these silly questions at him. "Are you lifting the oxcart out of the ditch? Are you tearing up the pea patch? Are you hollering down the rain barrel? Are you scraping around the bottom of the pickle barrel? Are you sitting in the catbird seat?"

It was Joey Hart, one of Mr. Martin's two assistants, who had explained what the gibberish meant. "She must be a Dodger fan," he had said. "Red Barber announces the Dodger games over the radio and he uses those expressions—picked 'em up down South." Joey had gone on to explain one or two. "Tearing up the pea patch" meant going on a rampage; "sitting in the catbird seat" meant sitting pretty, like a batter with three balls and no strikes on him. Mr. Martin dismissed all this with an effort. It had been annoying, it had driven him near to distraction, but he was too solid a man to be moved to murder by anything so childish. It was fortunate, he reflected as he passed on to the important charges against Mrs. Barrows, that he had stood up under it so well. He had maintained always an outward appearance of polite tolerance. "Why, I even believe you like the woman," Miss Paird, his other assistant, had once said to him. He had simply smiled.

A gavel rapped in Mr. Martin's mind and the case proper was resumed. Mrs. Ulgine Barrows stood charged with willful, blatant, and persistent attempts to destroy the efficiency and system of F &

S. It was competent, material, and relevant to review her advent and rise to power. Mr. Martin had got the story from Miss Paird, who seemed always able to find things out. According to her, Mrs. Barrows had met Mr. Fitweiler at a party, where she had rescued him from the embraces of a powerfully built drunken man who had mistaken the president of F & S for a famous retired Middle Western football coach. She had led him to a sofa and somehow worked upon him a monstrous magic. The aging gentleman had jumped to the conclusion there and then that this was a woman of singular attainments, equipped to bring out the best in him and in the firm. A week later he had introduced her into F & S as his special adviser. On that day confusion got its foot in the door. After Miss Tyson, Mr. Brundage, and Mr. Bartlett had been fired and Mr. Munson had taken his hat and stalked out, mailing in his resignation later, old Roberts had been emboldened to speak to Mr. Fitweiler. He mentioned that Mr. Munson's department had been "a little disrupted" and hadn't they perhaps better resume the old system there? Mr. Fitweiler had said certainly not. He had the greatest faith in Mrs. Barrows' ideas. "They require a little seasoning, a little seasoning, is all," he had added. Mr. Roberts had given it up. Mr. Martin reviewed in detail all the changes wrought by Mrs. Barrows. She had begun chipping at the cornices of the firm's edifice and now she was swinging at the foundation stones with a pickaxe.

Mr. Martin came now, in his summing up, to the afternoon of Monday, November 2, 1942—just one week ago. On that day, at 3 P.M., Mrs. Barrows had bounced into his office. "Boo!" she had yelled. "Are you scraping around the bottom of the pickle barrel?" Mr. Martin had looked at her from under his green eyeshade, saying nothing. She had begun to wander about the office, taking it in with her great, popping eyes. "Do you really need *all* these filing cabinets?" she had demanded suddenly. Mr. Martin's heart had jumped. "Each of these files," he had said, keeping his voice even, "plays an indispensable part in the system of F & S." She had brayed at him, "Well, don't tear up the pea patch!" and gone to the door. From there she had bawled, "But you sure have got a lot of fine scrap in here!" Mr. Martin could no longer doubt that the finger was on his beloved department. Her pickaxe was on the upswing, poised for the first blow. It had not come yet; he had received no blue memo from the enchanted Mr. Fitweiler bearing nonsensical instructions deriving from the obscene woman. But there was no doubt in Mr. Martin's mind that one would be forthcoming. He must act quickly. Already a precious week had gone by. Mr. Martin stood up in his living room, still holding his milk glass. "Gentlemen of the jury," he said to himself, "I demand the death penalty for this horrible person."

The next day Mr. Martin followed his routine, as usual. He polished his glasses more often and once sharpened an already sharp pencil, but not even Miss Paird noticed. Only once did he catch sight of his victim; she swept past him in the hall with a patronizing "Hi!" At five-thirty he walked home, as usual, and had a glass of milk, as usual. He had never drunk anything stronger in his life—unless you could count ginger ale. The late Sam Schlosser, the S of F & S, had praised Mr. Martin at a staff meeting several years before for his temperate habits. "Our most efficient worker neither drinks nor smokes," he had said. "The results speak for themselves." Mr. Fitweiler had sat by, nodding approval.

Mr. Martin was still thinking about that red-letter day as he walked over to the Schrafft's on Fifth Avenue near Forty-sixth Street. He got there, as he always did, at eight o'clock. He finished his dinner and the financial page of the *Sun* at a quarter to nine, as he always did. It was his custom after dinner to take a walk. This time he walked down Fifth Avenue at a casual pace. His gloved hands felt moist and warm, his forehead cold. He transferred the Camels from his overcoat to a jacket pocket. He wondered, as he did so, if they did not represent an unnecessary note of strain. Mrs. Barrows smoked only Luckies. It was his idea to puff a few puffs on a Camel (after the rubbing-out), stub it out in the ashtray holding her lipstick-stained Luckies, and thus drag a small red herring across the trail. Perhaps it was not a good idea. It would take time. He might even choke, too loudly.

Mr. Martin had never seen the house on West Twelfth Street where Mrs. Barrows lived, but he had a clear enough picture of it. Fortunately, she had bragged to everybody about her ducky first-floor apartment in the perfectly darling three-story red-brick. There would be no doorman or other attendants; just the tenants of the second and third floors. As he walked along, Mr. Martin realized that he would get there before nine-thirty. He had considered walking north on Fifth Avenue from Schrafft's to a point from which it would take him until ten o'clock to reach the house. At that hour people were less likely to be coming in or going out. But the procedure would have made an awkward loop in the straight thread of his casualness, and he had abandoned it. It was impossible to figure when people would be entering or leaving the house, anyway. There was a great risk at any hour. If he ran into anybody, he would simply have to place the rubbing-out of Ulgine Barrows in the inactive file forever. The same thing would hold true if there were someone in her apartment. In that case he would just say that he had been passing by, recognized her charming house, and thought to drop in.

It was eighteen minutes after nine when Mr. Martin turned into Twelfth Street. A man passed him, and a man and a woman, talking. There was no one within fifty paces when he came to the house, halfway down the block. He was up the steps and in the small vestibule in no time, pressing the bell under the card that said "Mrs. Ulgine Barrows." When the clicking in the lock started, he jumped forward against the door. He got inside fast, closing the door behind him. A bulb in a lantern hung from the hall ceiling on a chain seemed to give a monstrously bright light. There was nobody on the stair, which went up ahead of him along the left wall. A door opened down the hall in the wall on the right. He went toward it swiftly, on tiptoe.

"Well, for God's sake, look who's here!" bawled Mrs. Barrows, and her braying laugh rang out like the report of a shotgun. He rushed past her like a football tackle, bumping her. "Hey, quit shoving!" she said, closing the door behind them. They were in her living room, which seemed to Mr. Martin to be lighted by a hundred lamps. "What's after you?" she said. "You're as jumpy as a goat." He found he was unable to speak. His heart was wheezing in his throat. "I—yes," he finally brought out. She was jabbering and laughing as she started to help him off with his coat. "No, no," he said. "I'll put it here." He took it off and put it on a chair near the door. "Your hat and gloves, too," she said. "You're in a lady's house." He put his hat on top of the coat. Mrs. Barrows seemed larger than he had thought. He kept his gloves on. "I was passing by," he said. "I recognized—is there anyone here?" She laughed louder than ever. "No," she said, "we're all alone. You're as white as a sheet, you funny man. Whatever *has* come over you? I'll mix you a toddy." She started toward a door across the room. "Scotch-and-soda be all right? But say, you don't drink, do you?" She turned and gave him her amused look. Mr. Martin pulled himself together. "Scotch-and-soda will be all right," he heard himself say. He could hear her laughing in the kitchen.

Mr. Martin looked quickly around the living room for the weapon. He had counted on finding one there. There were andirons and a poker and something in a corner that looked like an Indian club. None of them would do. It couldn't be that way. He began to pace around. He came to a desk. On it lay a metal paper knife with an ornate handle. Would it be sharp enough? He reached for it and knocked over a small brass jar. Stamps spilled out of it and it fell to the floor with a clatter. "Hey," Mrs. Barrows yelled from the kitchen, "are you tearing up the pea patch?" Mr. Martin gave a strange laugh. Picking up the knife, he tried its point against his left wrist. It was blunt. It wouldn't do.

When Mrs. Barrows reappeared, carrying two high-balls, Mr. Martin, standing there with his gloves on, became acutely conscious of the fantasy he had wrought. Cigarettes in his pocket, a drink prepared for him—it was all too grossly improbable. It was more than that; it was impossible. Somewhere in the back of his mind a vague idea stirred, sprouted. "For heaven's sake, take off those gloves," said Mrs. Barrows. "I always wear them in the house," said Mr. Martin. The idea began to bloom, strange and wonderful. She put the glasses on a coffee table in front of a sofa and sat on the sofa. "Come over here, you odd little man," she said. Mr. Martin went over and sat beside her. It was difficult getting a cigarette out of the pack of Camels, but he managed it. She held a match for him, laughing. "Well," she said, handing him his drink, "this is perfectly marvellous. You with a drink and a cigarette."

Mr. Martin puffed, not too awkwardly, and took a gulp of the highball. "I drink and smoke all the time," he said. He clinked his glass against hers. "Here's nuts to that old windbag, Fitweiler," he said, and gulped again. The stuff tasted awful, but he made no grimace. "Really, Mr. Martin," she said, her voice and posture changing, "you are insulting our employer." Mrs. Barrows was now all special adviser to the president. "I am preparing a bomb," said Mr. Martin, "which will blow the old goat higher than hell." He had only had a little of the drink, which was not strong. It couldn't be that. "Do you take dope or something?" Mrs. Barrows asked coldly. "Heroin," said Mr. Martin. "I'll be coked to the gills when I bump that old buzzard off." "Mr. Martin!" she shouted, getting to her feet. "That will be all of that. You must go at once." Mr. Martin took another swallow of his drink. He tapped his cigarette out in the ashtray and put the pack of Camels on the coffee table. Then he got up. She stood glaring at him. He walked over and put on his hat and coat. "Not a word about this," he said, and laid an index finger against his lips. All Mrs. Barrows could bring out was "Really!" Mr. Martin put his hand on the doorknob. "I'm sitting in the catbird seat," he said. He stuck his tongue out at her and left. Nobody saw him go.

Mr. Martin got to his apartment, walking, well before eleven. No one saw him go in. He had two glasses of milk after brushing his teeth, and he felt elated. It wasn't tipsiness, because he hadn't been tipsy. Anyway, the walk had worn off all effects of the whiskey. He got in bed and read a magazine for a while. He was asleep before midnight.

Mr. Martin got to the office at eight-thirty the next morning, as usual. At a quarter to nine, Ulgine Barrows, who had never before arrived at work before ten, swept into his office. "I'm reporting to Mr. Fitweiler now!" she shouted. "If he turns you over to the police, it's no more than you deserve!" Mr. Martin gave her a look of shocked surprise. "I beg your pardon?" he said. Mrs. Barrows snorted and bounced out of the room, leaving Miss Paird and Joey Hart staring after her. "What's the matter with that old devil now?" asked Miss Paird. "I have no idea," said Mr. Martin, resuming his work. The other two looked at him and then at each other. Miss Paird got up and went out. She walked slowly past the closed door of Mr. Fitweiler's office. Mrs. Barrows was yelling inside, but she was not braying. Miss Paird could not hear what the woman was saying. She went back to her desk.

Forty-five minutes later, Mrs. Barrows left the president's office and went into her own, shutting the door. It wasn't until half an hour later that Mr. Fitweiler sent for Mr. Martin. The head of the filing department, neat, quiet, attentive, stood in front of the old man's desk. Mr. Fitweiler was pale and nervous. He took his glasses off and twiddled them. He made a small, bruffing sound in this throat. "Martin," he said, "you have been with us more than twenty years." "Twenty-two, sir," said Mr. Martin. "In that time," pursued the president, "your work and your—uh—manner have been exemplary." "I trust so, sir," said Mr. Martin. "I have understood, Martin," said Mr. Fitweiler, "that you have never taken a drink or smoked." "That is correct, sir," said Mr. Martin. "Ah, yes." Mr. Fitweiler polished his glasses. "You may describe what you did after leaving the office yesterday, Martin," he said. Mr. Martin allowed less than a second for his bewildered pause. "Certainly, sir," he said. "I walked home. Then I went to Schrafft's for dinner. Afterward I walked home again. I went to bed early, sir, and read a magazine for a while. I was asleep before eleven." "Ah, yes," said Mr. Fitweiler again. He was silent for a moment, searching for the proper words to say to the head of the filing department. "Mrs. Barrows," he said finally, "Mrs. Barrows has worked hard, Martin, very hard. It grieves me to report that she has suffered a severe breakdown. It has taken the form of a persecution complex accompanied by distressing hallucinations." "I am very sorry, sir," said Mr. Martin. "Mrs. Barrows is under the delusion," continued Mr. Fitweiler, "that you visited her last evening and behaved yourself in an—uh—unseemly manner." He raised his hand to silence Mr. Martin's little pained outcry. "It is the nature of these psychological diseases," Mr. Fitweiler said, "to fix upon the least likely and most innocent party as the—uh—source of persecution. These matters are not for the lay mind to grasp, Martin. I've just had my psychiatrist, Dr. Fitch, on the phone. He would not, of course, commit himself, but he made enough generalizations to substantiate my suspicions. I suggested to Mrs. Barrows, when she had completed her—uh—story to me this morning, that she visit Dr. Fitch, for I suspected a condition at once. She flew, I regret to say, into a rage, and demanded—uh—requested that I call you on the carpet. You may not know, Martin, but Mrs. Barrows had planned a reorganization of your department—subject to my approval, of course, subject to my approval. This brought you, rather than anyone else, to her mind—but again that is a phenomenon for Dr. Fitch and not for us. So, Martin, I am afraid Mrs. Barrows' usefulness here is at an end." "I am dreadfully sorry, sir," said Mr. Martin.

It was at this point that the door to the office blew open with the suddenness of a gas-main explosion and Mrs. Barrows catapulted through it. "Is the little rat denying it?" she screamed. "He can't get away with that!" Mr. Martin got up and moved discretely to a point beside Mr. Fitweiler's chair. "You drank and smoked at my apartment," she bawled at Mr. Martin, "and you know it! You called Mr. Fitweiler an old windbag and said you were going to blow him up when you got coked to the gills on your heroin!" She stopped yelling to catch her breath and a new glint came into her popping eyes. "If you weren't such a drab, ordinary little man," she said, "I think you'd planned it all. Sticking your tongue out, saying you were sitting in the catbird seat, because you thought no one would believe me when I told it! My God, it's really too perfect!" She brayed loudly and hysterically, and the fury was on her again. She glared at Mr. Fitweiler. "Can't you see how he has tricked us, you old fool? Can't you see his little game?" But Mr. Fitweiler had been surreptitiously pressing all the buttons under the top of his desk and employees of F & S began pouring into the room. "Stockton," said Mr. Fitweiler, "you and Fishbein will take Mrs. Barrows to her home. Mrs. Powell, you will go with them." Stockton, who had played a little football in high school, blocked Mrs. Barrows as she made for Mr. Martin. It took him and Fishbein together to force her out of the door into the hall, crowded with stenographers and office boys. She was still screaming imprecations at Mr. Martin, tangled and contradictory imprecations. The hubbub finally died out down the corridor.

"I regret that this has happened," said Mr. Fitweiler. "I shall ask you to dismiss it from your mind, Martin." "Yes, sir," said Mr. Martin, anticipating his chief's "That will be all" by moving to the door. "I will dismiss it." He went out and shut the door, and his step was light and quick in the hall. When he entered his department he had slowed down to his customary gait, and he walked quietly across the room to the W20 file, wearing a look of studious concentration.

Exercises   1. *List several of the more important incidents or actions that constitute the plot.*

2. *Who is the protagonist? Cite specific reasons for your choice. Identify the prize.*

3. *Who is the antagonist? Describe the conflict. Is the struggle primarily internal or external?*

4. *At what point in the story is the conflict surely introduced or positively known to the reader?*

5. *Point out a complication or two and explain why each is a complication.*

6. *Identify the climactic scene in the story. Tell why it is the climax.*

7. *Does the protagonist achieve the goal or not? Precisely where in the story do you find the resolution?*

8. *Underneath the comic surface, what serious point does the author make?*

Topics for Writing   1. *Either support or refute the plausibility of the story.*

2. *Write a narrative dealing with the experience of someone who is pushed around to the point of retaliation.*

3. *Write a plot summary.*

Selected Bibliography   *James Thurber*

Brady, C. A. "What Thurber Saw." *Commonweal*, 75 (December 8, 1961), 274–276.

Brandon, Henry. "Everybody Is Getting Very Serious: A Conversation with James Thurber." *New Republic*, 144 (May 15, 1961), 18.

Cooke, Alistair, ed. "James Thurber in Conversation with Alistair Cooke." *Atlantic Monthly*, 197 (August 1956), 36–40.

Cowley, Malcolm. "Salute to Thurber." *Saturday Review*, 44 (November 25, 1960), 14–18, 63–64.

Downing, Francis. "Thurber." *Commonweal*, 41 (March 9, 1945), 518–519.

Elias, Robert H. "James Thurber: The Primitive, the Innocent, and the Individual." *American Scholar*, 27 (Summer 1958), 355–363.

Holmes, Charles S. "James Thurber and the Art of Fantasy." *Yale Review*, 55 (October 1965), 17–33.

Morsberger, Robert E. *James Thurber*. New York: Twayne, 1964.

Franz Kafka (1883–1924)

Born in Prague of a middle-class Jewish family, he earned a doctorate in jurisprudence, fought in World War I, ruined his health, and died of tuberculosis. Against his wishes, his writings were published posthumously, gaining for him a reputation as a brilliant writer. His best-known works include The Castle, The Trial, Metamorphis, *and* The Penal Colony, *from which "A Hunger Artist" was translated by Edwin and Willa Muir. Max Brod, biographer and friend of Kafka, remarked, "If the angels made jokes in heaven, it would have to be in Franz Kafka's language."*

A Hunger Artist

During these last decades the interest in professional fasting has markedly diminished. It used to pay very well to stage such great performances under one's own management, but today that is quite impossible. We live in a different world now. At one time the whole town took a lively interest in the hunger artist; from day to day of his fast the excitement mounted; everybody wanted to see him at least once a day; there were people who bought season tickets for the last few days and sat from morning till night in front of his small barred cage; even in the nighttime there were visiting hours, when the whole effect was heightened by torch flares; on fine days the cage was set out in the open air, and then it was the children's special treat to see the hunger artist; for their elders he was often just a joke that happened to be in fashion, but the children stood open-mouthed, holding each other's hands for greater security, marveling at him as he sat there pallid in black tights, with his ribs sticking out so prominently, not even on a seat but down among straw on the ground, sometimes giving a courteous nod, answering questions with a constrained smile, or perhaps stretching an arm through the bars so that one might feel how thin it was, and then again withdrawing deep into himself, paying no attention to anyone or anything, not even to the all-important striking of the clock that was the only piece of furniture in his cage, but merely staring into vacancy with half-shut eyes, now and then taking a sip from a tiny glass of water to moisten his lips.

Besides casual onlookers, there were also relays of permanent watchers selected by the public, usually butchers, strangely enough, and it was their task to watch the hunger artist day and night, three of them at a time, in case he should have some secret recourse to nourishment. This was nothing but a formality, instituted to reassure the masses, for the initiates knew well enough that during his fast the artist would never in any circumstances, not even under forcible compulsion, swallow the smallest morsel of food; the honor of his profession forbade it. Not every watcher, of course, was capable of understanding this, there were often groups of night watchers who were very lax in carrying out their duties and deliberately huddled together in a retired corner to play cards with great absorption, obviously intending to give the hunger artist the chance of a little refreshment, which they supposed he could draw from some private hoard. Nothing annoyed the artist more than such watchers; they made him miserable; they made his fast seem unendurable; sometimes he mastered his feebleness sufficiently to sing during their watch for as long as he could keep going, to show them how unjust their suspicions were. But that was of little use; they only wondered at his cleverness in being able to fill his mouth even while singing. Much more to his taste were the watchers who sat close up to the bars, who were not content with the dim night lighting of the hall but focused him in the full glare of the electric pocket torch given them by the impresario. The harsh light did not trouble him at all, in any case he could never sleep properly, and he could always drowse a little, whatever the light, at any hour, even when the hall was thronged with noisy onlookers. He was quite happy at the prospect of spending a sleepless night with such watchers; he was ready to exchange jokes with them, to tell them stories out of his nomadic life, anything at all to keep them awake and demonstrate to them again that he had no eatables in his cage and that he was fasting as not one of them could fast. But his happiest moment was when the morning came and an enormous breakfast was brought them, at his expense, on which they flung themselves with the keen appetite of healthy men after a weary night of wakefulness. Of course there were people who argued that this breakfast was an unfair attempt to bribe the watchers, but that was going rather too far, and when they were invited to take on a night's vigil without a breakfast, merely for the sake of the cause, they made themselves scarce, although they stuck stubbornly to their suspicions.

Such suspicions, anyhow, were a necessary accompaniment to the profession of fasting. No one could possibly watch the hunger artist continuously, day and night, and so no one could produce first-hand evidence that the fast had really been rigorous and continuous; only the artist himself could know that, he was therefore bound to be the sole completely satisfied spectator of his own fast. Yet for other reasons he was never satisfied; it was not perhaps mere fasting that had brought him to such skeleton thinness that many people had regretfully to keep away from his exhibitions, because the sight of him was too much for them, perhaps it was dissatisfaction with himself that had worn him down. For he alone knew, what no other initiate knew, how easy it was to fast. It was the easiest thing in the world. He made no secret of this, yet people did not believe him, at the best they set him down as modest, most of them, however, thought he was out for publicity or else was some kind of cheat who found it easy to fast because he had discovered a way of making it easy, and then had the impudence to admit the fact, more or less. He had to put up with all that, and in the course of time had got used to it, but his inner dissatisfaction always rankled, and never yet, after any term of fasting—this must be granted to his credit—had he left the cage of his own free will. The longest period of fasting was fixed by his impresario at forty days, beyond that term he was not allowed to go, not even in great cities, and there was good reason for it, too. Experience had proved that for about forty days the interest of the public could be stimulated by a steadily increasing pressure of advertisement, but after that the town began to lose interest, sympathetic support began notably to fall off; there were of course local variations as between one town and another or one country and another, but as a general rule forty days marked the limit. So on the fortieth day the flower-bedecked cage was opened, enthusiastic spectators filled the hall, a military band played, two doctors entered the cage to measure the results of the fast, which were announced through a megaphone, and finally two young ladies appeared, blissful at having been selected for the honor, to help the hunger artist down the few steps leading to a small table on which was spread a carefully chosen invalid repast. And at this very moment the artist always turned stubborn. True, he would entrust his bony arms to the outstretched helping hands of the ladies bending over him, but stand up he would not. Why stop fasting at this particular moment, after forty days of it? He had held out for a long time, an illimitably long time; why stop now, when he was in his best fasting form, or rather, not yet quite in his best fasting form? Why should he be cheated of the fame he would get for fasting longer, for being not only the record hunger artist of all time, which presumably he was already, but for beating his own record by a performance beyond human imagination, since he felt that there were no limits to his capacity for fasting? His public pretended to admire him so much, why should it have so little patience with him; if he could endure fasting longer, why shouldn't the public endure it? Besides, he was tired, he was comfortable sitting in the straw, and now he was supposed to lift himself to his full height and go down to a meal the very thought of which gave him a nausea that only the presence of the ladies kept him from betraying, and even that with an effort. And he looked up into the eyes of the ladies who were apparently so friendly and in reality so cruel, and shook his head, which felt too heavy on its strengthless neck. But then there happened yet again what always happened. The impresario came forward, without a word—for the band made speech impossible—lifted his arms in the air above the artist, as if inviting Heaven to look down upon its creature here in the straw, this suffering martyr, which indeed he was, although in quite another sense; grasped him round the emaciated waist, with exaggerated caution, so that the frail condition he was in might be appreciated; and committed him to the care of the blenching ladies, not without secretly giving him a shaking so that his legs and body tottered and swayed. The artist now submitted completely; his head lolled on his breast as if it had landed there by chance; his body was hollowed out; his legs in a spasm of self-preservation clung close to each other at the knees, yet scraped on the ground as if it were not really solid ground, as if they were only trying to find solid ground; and the whole weight of his body, a featherweight after all, relapsed onto one of the ladies, who, looking round for help and panting a little—this post of honor was not at all what she had expected it to be—first stretched her neck as far as she could to keep her face at least free from contact with the artist, when finding this impossible, and her more fortunate companion not coming to her aid but merely holding extended on her own trembling hand the little bunch of knucklebones that was the artist's, to the great delight of the spectators burst into tears and had to be replaced by an attendant who had long been stationed in readiness. Then came the food, a little of which the impresario managed to get between the artist's lips, while he sat in a kind of half-fainting trance, to the accompaniment of cheerful patter designed to distract the public's attention from the artist's condition; after that, a toast was drunk to the public, supposedly prompted by a whisper from the artist in the impresario's ear; the band confirmed it with a mighty flourish, the spectators melted away, and no one had any cause to be dissatisfied with the proceedings, no one except the hunger artist himself, he only, as always.

So he lived for many years, with small regular intervals of recuperation, in visible glory, honored by the world, yet in spite of that troubled in spirit, and all the more troubled because no one would take his trouble seriously. What comfort could he possibly need? What more could he possibly wish for? And if some good-natured person, feeling sorry for him, tried to console him by pointing out that his melancholy was probably caused by fasting, it could happen, especially when he had been fasting for some time, that he reacted with an outburst of fury and to the general alarm began to shake the bars of his cage like a wild animal. Yet the impresario had a way of punishing these outbreaks which he rather enjoyed putting into operation. He would apologize publicly for the artist's behavior, which was only to be excused, he admitted, because of the irritability caused by fasting; a condition hardly to be understood by well-fed people; then by natural transition he went on to mention the artist's equally incomprehensible boast that he could fast for much longer than he was doing; he praised the high ambition, the good will, the great self-denial undoubtedly implicit in such a statement; and then quite simply countered it by bringing out photographs, which were also on sale to the public, showing the artist on the fortieth day of a fast lying in bed almost dead from exhaustion. This perversion of the truth, familiar to the artist though it was, always unnerved him afresh and proved too much for him. What was a consequence of the premature ending of his fast was here presented as the cause of it! To fight against this lack of understanding, against a whole world of nonunderstanding, was impossible. Time and again in good faith he stood by the bars listening to the impresario, but as soon as the photographs appeared he always let go and sank with a groan back on his straw, and the reassured public could once more come close and gaze at him.

A few years later when the witnesses of such scenes called them to mind, they often failed to understand themselves at all. For meanwhile the aforementioned change in public interest had set in; it seemed to happen almost overnight; there may have been profound causes for it, but who was going to bother about that; at any rate the pampered hunger artist suddenly found himself deserted one fine day by the amusement seekers, who went streaming past him to other more favored attractions. For the last time the impresario hurried him over half Europe to discover whether the old interest might still survive here and there; all in vain; everywhere, as if by secret agreement, a positive revulsion from professional fasting was in evidence. Of course it could not really have sprung up so suddenly as all that, and many premonitory symptoms which had not been sufficiently remarked or suppressed during the rush and glitter to success now came retrospectively to mind, but it was now too late to take any countermeasures. Fasting would surely come into fashion again at some future date, yet that was no comfort for those living in the present. What, then, was the hunger artist to do? He had been applauded by thousands in his time and could hardly come down to showing himself in a street booth at village fairs, and as for adopting another profession, he was not only too old for that but too fanatically devoted to fasting. So he took leave of the impresario, his partner in an unparalleled career, and hired himself to a large circus; in order to spare his own feelings he avoided reading the conditions of his contract.

A large circus with its enormous traffic in replacing and recruiting men, animals and apparatus can always find a use for people at any time, even for a hunger artist, provided of course that he does not ask too much, and in this particular case anyhow it was not only the artist who was taken on but his famous and long-known name as well, indeed considering the peculiar nature of his performance, which was not impaired by advancing age, it could not be objected that here was an artist past his prime, no longer at the height of his professional skill, seeking a refuge in some quiet corner of a circus; on the contrary, the hunger artist averred that he could fast as well as ever, which was entirely credible, he even alleged that if he were allowed to fast as he liked, and this was at once promised him without more ado, he could astound the world by establishing a record never yet achieved, a statement which certainly provoked a smile among the other professionals, since it left out of account the change in public opinion, which the hunger artist in his zeal conveniently forgot.

He had not, however, actually lost his sense of the real situation and took it as a matter of course that he and his cage should be stationed, not in the middle of the ring as a main attraction, but outside, near the animal cages, on a site that was after all easily accessible. Large and gaily painted placards made a frame for the cage and announced what was to be seen inside it. When the public came thronging out in the intervals to see the animals, they could hardly avoid passing the hunger artist's cage and stopping there for a moment, perhaps they might even have stayed longer had not those pressing behind them in the narrow gangway, who did not understand why they should be held up on their way toward the excitements of the menagerie, made it impossible for anyone to stand gazing quietly for any length of time. And that was the reason why the hunger artist, who had of course been looking forward to these visiting hours as the main achievement of his life, began instead to shrink from them. At first he could hardly wait for the intervals; it was exhilarating to watch the crowds come streaming his way, until only too soon—not even the most obstinate self-deception, clung to almost consciously, could hold out against the fact—the conviction was borne in upon him that these people, most of them, to judge from their actions, again and again, without exception, were all on their way to the menagerie. And the first sight of them from the distance remained the best. For when they reached his cage he was at once deafened by the storm of shouting and abuse that arose from the two contending factions, which renewed themselves continuously, of those who wanted to stop and stare at him—he soon began to dislike them more than the others—not out of real interest but only out of obstinate self-assertiveness, and those who wanted to go straight on to the animals. When the first great rush was past, the stragglers came along, and these, whom nothing could have prevented from stopping to look at him as long as they had breath, raced past with long strides, hardly even glancing at him, in their haste to get to the menagerie in time. And all too rarely did it happen that he had a stroke of luck, when some father of a family fetched up before him with his children, pointed a finger at the hunger artist and explained at length what the phenomenon meant, telling stories of earlier years when he himself had watched similar but much more thrilling performances, and the children, still rather uncomprehending, since neither inside nor outside school had they been sufficiently prepared for this lesson—what did they care about fasting?—yet showed by the brightness of their intent eyes that new and better times might be coming. Perhaps, said the hunger artist to himself many a time, things would be a little better if his cage were set not quite so near the menagerie. That made it too easy for people to make their choice, to say nothing of what he suffered from the stench of the menagerie, the animals' restlessness by night, the carrying past of raw lumps of flesh for the beasts of prey, the roaring at feeding times, which depressed him continually. But he did not dare to lodge a complaint with the management; after all, he had the animals to thank for the troops of people who passed his cage, among whom there might always be one here and there to take an interest in him, and who could tell where they might seclude him if he called attention to his existence and thereby to the fact that, strictly speaking, he was only an impediment on the way to the menagerie.

A small impediment, to be sure, one that grew steadily less. People grew familiar with the strange idea that they could be expected, in times like these, to take an interest in a hunger artist, and with this familiarity the verdict went out against him. He might fast as much as he could, and he did so; but nothing could save him now, people passed him by. Just try to explain to anyone the art of fasting! Anyone who has no feeling for it cannot be made to understand it. The fine placards grew dirty and illegible, they were torn down; the little notice board telling the number of fast days achieved, which at first was changed carefully every day, had long stayed at the same figure, for after the first few weeks even this small task seemed pointless to the staff; and so the artist simply fasted on and on, as he had once dreamed of doing, and it was no trouble to him, just as he had always foretold, but no one counted the days, no one, not even the artist himself, knew what records he was already breaking, and his heart grew heavy. And when once in a time some leisurely passer-by stopped, made merry over the old figure on the board and spoke of swindling, that was in its way the stupidest lie ever invented by indifference and inborn malice, since it was not the hunger artist who was cheating; he was working honestly, but the world was cheating him of his reward.

Many more days went by, however, and that too came to an end. An overseer's eye fell on the cage one day and he asked the attendants why this perfectly good cage should be left standing there unused with dirty straw inside it; nobody knew, until one man, helped out by the notice board, remembered about the hunger artist. They poked into the straw with sticks and found him in it. "Are you still fasting?" asked the overseer. "When on earth do you mean to stop?" "Forgive me, everybody," whispered the hunger artist; only the overseer, who had his ear to the bars, understood him. "Of course," said the overseer, and tapped his forehead with a finger to let the attendants know what state the man was in, "we forgive you." "I always wanted you to admire my fasting," said the hunger artist. "We do admire it," said the overseer, affably. "But you shouldn't admire it," said the hunger artist. "Well, then we don't admire it," said the overseer, "but why shouldn't we admire it?" "Because I have to fast, I can't help it," said the hunger artist. "What a fellow you are," said the overseer, "and why can't you help it?" "Because," said the hunger artist, lifting his head a little and speaking, with his lips pursed, as if for a kiss, right into the overseer's ear, so that no syllable might be lost, "because I couldn't find the food I liked. If I had found it, believe me, I should have made no fuss and stuffed myself like you or anyone else." These were his last words, but in his dimming eyes remained the firm though no longer proud persuasion that he was still continuing to fast.

"Well, clear this out now!" said the overseer, and they buried the hunger artist, straw and all. Into the cage they put a young panther. Even the most insensitive felt it refreshing to see this wild creature leaping around the cage that had so long been dreary. The panther was all right. The food he liked was brought him without hesitation by the attendants; he seemed not even to miss his freedom; his noble body, furnished almost to the bursting point with all that it needed, seemed to carry freedom around with it too; somewhere in his jaws it seemed to lurk; and the joy of life streamed with such ardent passion from his throat that for the onlookers it was not easy to stand the shock of it. But they braced themselves, crowded round the cage, and did not want ever to move away.

Exercises   *1. What does the protagonist represent? What does he seek?*

2. Who opposes him and why? What, then, is the conflict?

3. Give a brief eight-point analysis of the story. (Refer to the introduction.)

4. Critics have suggested several interpretations: they see the hunger artist as representative of artists, humanity, and Christ. Does your choice of what the hunger artist represents alter the protagonist's prize or conflict?

5. The public attitude toward the artist and his sacrifice changes from hollow respect to complete disinterest. Explain the spectators' keen interest in the panther. What does the panther represent?

6. Account for the reader's sympathy for the hunger artist.

7. How is the protagonist defeated? Why is he defeated?

8. What truth or principle about the human condition has the author expressed in this story?

<table>
<tr><td>Topics for
Writing</td><td>1. What contributes to the complexity of the story?</td></tr>
</table>

Topics for Writing

1. What contributes to the complexity of the story?

2. Select one interpretation of the story and defend your point of view with sufficient details from the story.

3. Summarize the plot.

Selected Bibliography

Franz Kafka

Arendt, Hannah. "Franz Kafka: A Revaluation." *Partisan Review*, 11 (Fall 1944), 412–422.

Asher, J. A. "Turning-Points in Kafka's Stories." *Modern Language Review*, 57 (January 1962), 47–52.

Camus, Albert. "Hope and the Absurd in the Work of Franz Kafka." In *The Myth of Sisyphus and Other Essays*, trans. Justin O'Brien. New York: Alfred A. Knopf, 1955, pp. 124–138.

Carrouges, Michel. *Kafka versus Kafka*, trans. Emmet Parker. University, Ala.: University of Alabama Press, 1968.

Collignon, Jean. "Kafka's Humor." *Yale French Studies*, 16 (Winter 1955–1956), 53–62.

Emrich, Wilhelm. *Franz Kafka: A Critical Study of His Writings*, trans. Sheema Zeben Buehne. New York: Frederick Ungar Publishing, 1968.

Flores, Angel, ed. *The Kafka Problem*. New York: New Directions, 1946.

——— and Homer Swander, eds. *Franz Kafka Today*. Madison: The University of Wisconsin Press, 1958.

Foulkes, A. P. *The Reluctant Pessimist: A Study of Franz Kafka*. The Hague: Mouton, 1967.

Greenberg, Martin. *The Terror of Art: Kafka and Modern Literature*. New York and London: Basic Books, 1968.

Janouch, Gustav. *Conversations with Kafka: Notes and Reminiscences*, trans. Goronwy Rees. London: Derek Verschoyle, 1953.

Moyer, Patricia. "Time and the Artist in Kafka and Hawthorne." *Modern Fiction Studies*, 4 (Winter 1958–1959), 295–306.

Neider, Charles. *The Frozen Sea: A Study of Franz Kafka*. New York: Oxford University Press, 1948.

Osborne, Charles. *Kafka*. New York: Barnes & Noble, 1967.

Politzer, Heinz. "Franz Kafka's Language." *Modern Fiction Studies*, 8 (Spring 1962), 16–22.

———. *Franz Kafka: Parable and Paradox*. Ithaca: Cornell University Press, 1962.

Sandbank, S. "Structures of Paradox in Kafka." *Modern Language Quarterly*, 28 (December 1967), 462–472.

Seyppel, Joachim H. "The Animal Theme and Totemism in Franz Kafka." *Literature and Psychology*, 4 (September 1954), 49–63.

Spilka, Mark. *Dickens and Kafka: A Mutual Interpretation*. Bloomington: Indiana University Press, 1963.

Stallman, Robert W. "Kafka's Cage." *Accent*, 8 (Winter 1948), 117–125.

Warren, Austin. *Rage for Order: Essays in Criticism*. Chicago: The University of Chicago Press, 1948.

Waterman, Arthur E. "Kafka's 'The Hunger Artist,'" *CEA*, 23, iii (1960–1961), 9.

Wilson, Edmund. "A Dissenting Opinion of Kafka." *New Yorker*, 23 (July 26, 1947), 58, 61–64.

Bernard Malamud (1914–   )

Born and reared in Brooklyn, educated at City College of New York (B.A., 1936) and Columbia University (M.A., 1942), he taught high school in Brooklyn, later in Harlem, then college at Oregon State University before joining the faculty at Bennington College in 1961 as a writer-in-residence. The Magic Barrel (1958), a collection of short stories, won him a National Book Award, and his novel The Fixer earned him a Pulitzer Prize in 1967. He writes about suffering, endurance, compassion, and love.

The Magic Barrel

Not long ago there lived in uptown New York, in a small, almost meager room, though crowded with books, Leo Finkle, a rabbinical student in the Yeshivah University. Finkle, after six years of study, was to be ordained in June and had been advised by an acquaintance that he might find it easier to win himself a congregation if he were married. Since he had no present prospects of marriage, after two tormented days of turning it over in his mind, he called in Pinye Salzman, a marriage broker whose two-line advertisement he had read in the *Forward*.

The matchmaker appeared one night out of the dark fourth-floor hallway of the graystone rooming house where Finkle lived, grasping a black, strapped portfolio that had been worn thin with use. Salzman, who had been long in the business, was of slight but dignified build, wearing an old hat, and an overcoat too short and tight for him. He smelled frankly of fish, which he loved to eat, and although he was missing a few teeth, his presence was not displeasing, because of an amiable manner curiously contrasted with mournful eyes. His voice, his lips, his wisp of beard, his bony fingers were animated, but give him a moment of repose and his mild blue eyes revealed a depth of sadness, a characteristic that put Leo a little at ease although the situation, for him, was inherently tense.

He at once informed Salzman why he had asked him to come, explaining that his home was in Cleveland, and that but for his parents, who had married comparatively late in life, he was alone in the world. He had for six years devoted himself almost entirely to his studies, as a result of which, understandably, he had found himself without time for a social life and the company of young women. Therefore he thought it the better part of trial and error—of embarrassing fumbling—to call in an experienced person to advise him on these matters. He remarked in passing that the function of the marriage broker was ancient and honorable, highly approved in the Jewish community, because it made practical the necessary without hindering joy. Moreover, his own parents had been brought together by a matchmaker. They had made, if not a financially profitable marriage—since neither had possessed any worldly goods to speak of—at least a successful one in the sense of their everlasting devotion to each other. Salzman listened in embarrassed surprise, sensing a sort of apology. Later, however, he experienced a glow of pride in his work, an emotion that had left him years ago, and he heartily approved of Finkle.

The two went to their business. Leo had led Salzman to the only clear place in the room, a table near a window that overlooked the lamp-lit city. He seated himself at the matchmaker's side but facing him, attempting by an act of will to suppress the unpleasant tickle in his throat. Salzman eagerly unstrapped his portfolio and removed a loose rubber band from a thin packet of much-handled cards. As he flipped through them, a gesture and sound that physically hurt Leo, the student pretended not to see and gazed steadfastly out the window. Although it was still February, winter was on its last legs, signs of which he had for the first time in years begun to notice. He now observed the round white moon, moving high in the sky through a cloud menagerie, and watched with half-open mouth as it penetrated a huge hen, and dropped out of her like an egg laying itself. Salzman, though pretending through eyeglasses he had just slipped on to be engaged in scanning the writing on the cards, stole occasional glances at the young man's distinguished face, noting with pleasure the long, severe scholar's nose, brown eyes heavy with learning, sensitive yet ascetic lips, and a certain, almost hollow quality of the dark cheeks. He gazed around at shelves upon shelves of books and let out a soft, contented sigh.

When Leo's eyes fell upon the cards, he counted six spread out in Salzman's hand.

"So few?" he asked in disappointment.

"You wouldn't believe me how much cards I got in my office," Salzman replied. "The drawers are already filled to the top, so I keep them now in a barrel, but is every girl good for a new rabbi?"

Leo blushed at this, regretting all he had revealed of himself in a curriculum vitae he had sent to Salzman. He had thought it best to acquaint him with his strict standards and specifications, but in having done so, felt he had told the marriage broker more than was absolutely necessary.

He hesitantly inquired, "Do you keep photographs of your clients on file?"

"First comes family, amount of dowry, also what kind promises," Salzman replied, unbuttoning his tight coat and settling himself in the chair. "After comes pictures, rabbi."

"Call me Mr. Finkle. I'm not yet a rabbi."

Salzman said he would, but instead called him doctor, which he changed to rabbi when Leo was not listening too attentively.

Salzman adjusted his horn-rimmed spectacles, gently cleared his throat and read in an eager voice the contents of the top card:

"Sophie P. Twenty four year. Widow one year. No children. Educated high school and two years college. Father promises eight thousand dollars. Has wonderful wholesale business. Also real estate. On the mother's side comes teachers, also one actor. Well known on Second Avenue."

Leo gazed up in surprise. "Did you say a widow?"

"A widow don't mean spoiled, rabbi. She lived with her husband maybe four months. He was a sick boy she made a mistake to marry him."

"Marrying a widow has never entered my mind."

"This is because you have no experience. A widow, especially if she is young and healthy like this girl, is a wonderful person to marry. She will be thankful to you the rest of her life. Believe me, if I was looking now for a bride, I would marry a widow."

Leo reflected, then shook his head.

Salzman hunched his shoulders in an almost imperceptible gesture of disappointment. He placed the card down on the wooden table and began to read another:

"Lily H. High school teacher. Regular. Not a substitute. Has savings and new Dodge car. Lived in Paris one year. Father is successful dentist thirty-five years. Interested in professional man. Well Americanized family. Wonderful opportunity.

"I knew her personally," said Salzman. "I wish you could see this girl. She is a doll. Also very intelligent. All day you could talk to her about books and theyater and what not. She also knows current events."

"I don't believe you mentioned her age?"

"Her age?" Salzman said, raising his brows. "Her age is thirty-two years."

Leo said after a while, "I'm afraid that seems a little too old."

Salzman let out a laugh. "So how old are you, rabbi?"

"Twenty-seven."

"So what is the difference, tell me, between twenty-seven and thirty-two? My own wife is seven years older than me. So what did I suffer?—Nothing. If Rothschild's a daughter wants to marry you, would you say on account her age, no?"

"Yes," Leo said dryly.

Salzman shook off the no in the yes. "Five years don't mean a thing. I give you my word that when you will live with her for one week you will forget her age. What does it mean five years—that she lived more and knows more than somebody who is younger? On this girl, God bless her, years are not wasted. Each one that it comes makes better the bargain."

"What subject does she teach in high school?"

"Languages. If you heard the way she speaks French, you will think it is music. I am in the business twenty-five years, and I recommend her with my whole heart. Believe me, I know what I'm talking, rabbi."

"What's on the next card?" Leo said abruptly.

Salzman reluctantly turned up the third card:

"Ruth K. Nineteen years. Honor student. Father offers thirteen thousand cash to the right bridegroom. He is a medical doctor. Stomach specialist with marvelous practice. Brother in law owns own garment business. Particular people."

Salzman looked as if he had read his trump card.

"Did you say nineteen?" Leo asked with interest.

"On the dot."

"Is she attractive?" He blushed. "Pretty?"

Salzman kissed his finger tips. "A little doll. On this I give you my word. Let me call the father tonight and you will see what means pretty."

But Leo was troubled. "You're sure she's that young?"

"This I am positive. The father will show you the birth certificate."

"Are you positive there isn't something wrong with her?" Leo insisted.

"Who says there is wrong?"

"I don't understand why an American girl her age should go to a marriage broker."

A smile spread over Salzman's face.

"So for the same reason you went, she comes."

Leo flushed. "I am pressed for time."

Salzman, realizing he had been tactless, quickly explained. "The father came, not her. He wants she should have the best, so he looks around himself. When we will locate the right boy he will introduce him and encourage. This makes a better marriage than if a young girl without experience takes for herself. I don't have to tell you this."

"But don't you think this young girl believes in love?" Leo spoke uneasily.

Salzman was about to gaffaw but caught himself and said soberly, "Love comes with the right person, not before."

Leo parted dry lips but did not speak. Noticing that Salzman had snatched a glance at the next card, he cleverly asked, "How is her health?"

"Perfect," Salzman said, breathing with difficulty. "Of course, she is a little lame on her right foot from an auto accident that it happened to her when she was twelve years, but nobody notices on account she is so brilliant and also beautiful."

Leo got up heavily and went to the window. He felt curiously bitter and upbraided himself for having called in the marriage broker. Finally, he shook his head.

"Why not?" Salzman persisted, the pitch of his voice rising.

"Because I detest stomach specialists."

"So what do you care what is his business? After you marry her do you need him? Who says he must come every Friday night in your house?"

Ashamed of the way the talk was going, Leo dismissed Salzman, who went home with heavy, melancholy eyes.

Though he had felt only relief at the marriage broker's departure, Leo was in low spirits the next day. He explained it as arising from Salzman's failure to produce a suitable bride for him. He did not care for his type of clientele. But when Leo found himself hesitating whether to seek out another matchmaker, one more polished than Pinye, he wondered if it could be—his protestations to the contrary, and although he honored his father and mother—that he did not, in essence, care for the matchmaking institution? This thought he quickly put out of mind yet found himself still upset. All day he ran around in the woods—missed an important appointment, forgot to give out his laundry, walked out of a Broadway cafeteria without paying and had to run back with the ticket in his hand; had even not recognized his landlady in the street when she passed with a friend and courteously called out, "A good evening to you, Doctor Finkle." By nightfall, however, he had regained sufficient calm to sink his nose into a book and there found peace from his thoughts.

Almost at once there came a knock on the door. Before Leo could say enter, Salzman, commercial cupid, was standing in the room. His face was gray and meager, his expression hungry, and he looked as if he would expire on his feet. Yet the marriage broker managed, by some trick of the muscles, to display a broad smile.

"So good evening. I am invited?"

Leo nodded, disturbed to see him again, yet unwilling to ask the man to leave.

Beaming still, Salzman laid his portfolio on the table. "Rabbi, I got for you tonight good news."

"I've asked you not to call me rabbi. I'm still a student."

"Your worries are finished. I have for you a first-class bride."

"Leave me in peace concerning this subject." Leo pretended lack of interest.

"The world will dance at your wedding."

"Please, Mr. Salzman, no more."

"But first must come back my strength," Salzman said weakly. He fumbled with the portfolio straps and took out of the leather case an oily paper bag, from which he extracted a hard, seeded roll and a small, smoked white fish. With a quick motion of his hand he stripped the fish out of its skin and began ravenously to chew. "All day in a rush," he muttered.

Leo watched him eat.

"A sliced tomato you have maybe?" Salzman hesitantly inquired.

"No."

The marriage broker shut his eyes and ate. When he had finished he carefully cleaned up the crumbs and rolled up the remains of the fish, in the paper bag. His spectacled eyes roamed the room until he discovered, amid some piles of books, a one-burner gas stove. Lifting his hat he humbly asked, "A glass tea you got, rabbi?"

Conscience-stricken, Leo rose and brewed the tea. He served it with a chunk of lemon and two cubes of lump sugar, delighting Salzman.

After he had drunk his tea, Salzman's strength and good spirits were restored.

"So tell me, rabbi," he said amiably, "you considered some more the three clients I mentioned yesterday?"

"There was no need to consider."

"Why not?"

"None of them suits me."

"What then suits you?"

Leo let it pass because he could give only a confused answer.

Without waiting for a reply, Salzman asked, "You remember this girl I talked to you—the high school teacher?"

"Age thirty-two?"

But, surprisingly, Salzman's face lit in a smile. "Age twenty-nine."

Leo shot him a look. "Reduced from thirty-two?"

"A mistake," Salzman avowed. "I talked today with the dentist. He took me to his safety deposit box and showed me the birth certificate. She was twenty-nine years last August. They made her a party in the mountains where she went for her vacation. When her father spoke to me the first time I forgot to write the age and I told you thirty-two, but now I remember this was a different client, a widow."

"The same one you told me about? I thought she was twenty-four?"

"A different. Am I responsible that the world is filled with widows?"

"No, but I'm not interested in them, nor for that matter, in school teachers."

Salzman pulled his clasped hands to his breast. Looking at the ceiling he devoutly exclaimed, "Yiddishe kinder, what can I say to somebody that he is not interested in high school teachers? So what then you are interested?"

Leo flushed but controlled himself.

"In what else will you be interested," Salzman went on, "if you not interested in this fine girl that she speaks four languages and has personally in the bank ten thousand dollars? Also her father guarantees further twelve thousand. Also she has a new car, wonderful clothes, talks on all subjects, and she will give you a first-class home and children. How near do we come in our life to paradise?"

"If she's so wonderful, why wasn't she married ten years ago?"

"Why?" said Salzman with a heavy laugh. "—Why? Because she is *partikiler*. This is why. She wants the *best*."

Leo was silent, amused at how he had entangled himself. But Salzman had aroused his interest in Lily H., and he began seriously to consider calling on her. When the marriage broker observed how intently Leo's mind was at work on the facts he had supplied, he felt certain they would soon come to an agreement.

Late Saturday afternoon, conscious of Salzman, Leo Finkle walked with Lily Hirschorn along Riverside Drive. He walked briskly and erectly, wearing with distinction the black fedora he had that morning taken with trepidation out of the dusty hat box on his closet shelf, and the heavy black Saturday coat he had thoroughly whisked clean. Leo also owned a walking stick, a present from a distant relative, but quickly put temptation aside and did not use it. Lily, petite and not unpretty, had on something signifying the approach of spring. She was au courant, animatedly, with all sorts of subjects, and he weighed her words and found her surprisingly sound—score another for Salzman, whom he uneasily sensed to be somewhere around, hiding perhaps high in a tree along the street, flashing the lady signals with a pocket mirror; or perhaps a cloven-hoofed Pan, piping nuptial ditties as he danced his invisible way before them, strewing wild buds on the walk and purple grapes in their path, symbolizing fruit of a union, though there was of course still none.

Lily startled Leo by remarking, "I was thinking of Mr. Salzman, a curious figure, wouldn't you say?"

Not certain what to answer, he nodded.

She bravely went on, blushing, "I for one am grateful for his introducing us. Aren't you?"

He courteously replied, "I am."

"I mean," she said with a little laugh—and it was all in good taste, or at least gave the effect of being not in bad—"do you mind that we came together so?"

He was not displeased with her honesty, recognizing that she meant to set the relationship aright, and understanding that it took a certain amount of experience in life, and courage, to want to do it quite that way. One had to have some sort of past to make that kind of beginning.

He said that he did not mind. Salzman's function was traditional and honorable—valuable for what it might achieve, which, he pointed out, was frequently nothing.

Lily agreed with a sigh. They walked on for a while and she said after a long silence, again with a nervous laugh, "Would you mind if I asked you something a little bit personal? Frankly, I find the subject fascinating." Although Leo shrugged, she went on half embarrassedly, "How was it that you came to your calling? I mean was it a sudden passionate inspiration?"

Leo, after a time, slowly replied, "I was always interested in the Law."

"You saw revealed in it the presence of the Highest?"

He nodded and changed the subject. "I understand that you spent a little time in Paris, Miss Hirschorn?"

"Oh, did Mr. Salzman tell you, Rabbi Finkle?" Leo winced but she went on, "It was ages ago and almost forgotten. I remember I had to return for my sister's wedding."

And Lily would not be put off. "When," she asked in a trembly voice, "did you become enamored of God?"

He stared at her. Then it came to him that she was

talking not about Leo Finkle, but of a total stranger, some mystical figure, perhaps even passionate prophet that Salzman had dreamed up for her—no relation to the living or dead. Leo trembled with rage and weakness. The trickster had obviously sold her a bill of goods, just as he had him, who'd expected to become acquainted with a young lady of twenty-nine, only to behold, the moment he laid eyes upon her strained and anxious face, a woman past thirty-five and aging rapidly. Only his self control had kept him this long in her presence.

"I am not," he said gravely, "a talented religious person," and in seeking words to go on, found himself possessed by shame and fear. "I think," he said in a strained manner, "that I came to God not because I loved Him, but because I did not."

This confession he spoke harshly because its unexpectedness shook him.

Lily wilted. Leo saw a profusion of loaves of bread go flying like ducks high over his head, not unlike the winged loaves by which he had counted himself to sleep last night. Mercifully, then, it snowed, which he would not put past Salzman's machinations.

He was infuriated with the marriage broker and swore he would throw him out of the room the minute he reappeared. But Salzman did not come that night, and when Leo's anger had subsided, an unaccountable despair grew in its place. At first he thought this was caused by his disappointment in Lily, but before long it became evident that he had involved himself with Salzman without a true knowledge of his own intent. He gradually realized—with an emptiness that seized him with six hands— that he had called in the broker to find him a bride because he was incapable of doing it himself. This terrifying insight he had derived as a result of his meeting and conversation with Lily Hirschorn. Her probing questions had somehow irritated him into revealing—to himself more than her—the true nature of his relationship to God, and from that it had come upon him, with shocking force, that apart from his parents, he had never loved anyone. Or perhaps it went the other way, that he did not love God so well as he might, because he had not loved man. It seemed to Leo that his whole life stood starkly revealed and he saw himself for the first time as he truly was— unloved and loveless. This bitter but somehow not fully unexpected revelation brought him to a point of panic, controlled only by extraordinary effort. He covered his face with his hands and cried.

The week that followed was the worst of his life. He did not eat and lost weight. His beard darkened and grew ragged. He stopped attending seminars and almost never opened a book. He seriously considered leaving the Yeshivah, although he was deeply troubled at the thought of the loss of all his years of study—saw them like pages torn from a book, strewn over the city—and at the devastating effect of this decision upon his parents. But he had lived without knowledge of himself, and never in the Five Books and all the Commentaries—mea culpa—had the truth been revealed to him. He did not know where to turn, and in all this desolating loneliness there was no *to whom*, although he often thought of Lily but not once could bring himself to go downstairs and make the call. He became touchy and irritable, especially with his landlady, who asked him all manner of personal questions; on the other hand, sensing his own disagreeableness, he waylaid her on the stairs and apologized abjectly, until mortified, she ran from him. Out of this, however, he drew the consolation that he was a Jew and that a Jew suffered. But gradually, as the long and terrible week drew to a close, he regained his composure and some idea of purpose in life: to go on as planned. Although he was imperfect, the ideal was not. As for his quest of a bride, the thought of continuing afflicted him with anxiety and heartburn, yet perhaps with this new knowledge of himself he would be more successful than in the past. Perhaps love would now come to him and a bride to that love. And for this sanctified seeking who needed a Salzman?

The marriage broker, a skeleton with haunted eyes, returned that very night. He looked, withal, the picture of frustrated expectancy—as if he had steadfastly waited the week at Miss Lily Hirschorn's side for a telephone call that never came.

Casually coughing, Salzman came immediately to the point: "So how did you like her?"

Leo's anger rose and he could not refrain from chiding the matchmaker: "Why did you lie to me, Salzman?"

Salzman's pale face went dead white, the world had snowed on him.

"Did you not state that she was twenty-nine?" Leo insisted.

"I give you my word—"

"She was thirty-five, if a day. *At least* thirty-five."

"Of this don't be too sure. Her father told me—"

"Never mind. The worst of it was that you lied to her."

"How did I lie to her, tell me?"

"You told her things about me that weren't true. You made me out to be more, consequently less than I am. She had in mind a totally different person, a sort of semi-mystical Wonder Rabbi."

"All I said, you was a religious man."

"I can imagine."

Salzman sighed. "This is my weakness that I have," he confessed. "My wife says to me I shouldn't be a salesman, but when I have two fine people that they would be wonderful to be married, I am so happy that I talk too much." He smiled wanly. "This is why Salzman is a poor man."

Leo's anger left him. "Well, Salzman, I'm afraid that's all."

The marriage broker fastened hungry eyes on him.

"You don't want any more a bride?"

"I do," said Leo, "but I have decided to seek her in a different way. I am no longer interested in an arranged marriage. To be frank, I now admit the necessity of premarital love. That is, I want to be in love with the one I marry."

"Love?" said Salzman, astounded. After a moment he remarked, "For us, our love is our life, not for the ladies. In the ghetto they—"

"I know, I know," said Leo. "I've thought of it often. Love, I have said to myself, should be a by-product of living and worship rather than its own end. Yet for myself I find it necessary to establish the level of my need and fulfill it."

Salzman shrugged but answered, "Listen, rabbi, if you want love, this I can find for you also. I have such beautiful clients that you will love them the minute your eyes will see them."

Leo smiled unhappily. "I'm afraid you don't understand."

But Salzman hastily unstrapped his portfolio and withdrew a manila packet from it.

"Pictures," he said, quickly laying the envelope on the table.

Leo called after him to take the pictures away, but as if on the wings of the wind, Salzman had disappeared.

March came. Leo had returned to his regular routine. Although he felt not quite himself yet—lacked energy—he was making plans for a more active social life. Of course it would cost something, but he was an expert in cutting corners; and when there were no corners left he would make circles rounder. All the while Salzman's pictures had lain on the table, gathering dust. Occasionally as Leo sat studying, or enjoying a cup of tea, his eyes fell on the manila envelope, but he never opened it.

The days went by and no social life to speak of developed with a member of the opposite sex—it was difficult, given the circumstances of his situation. One morning Leo toiled up the stairs to his room and stared out the window at the city. Although the day was bright his view of it was dark. For some time he watched the people in the street below hurrying along and then turned with a heavy heart to his little room. On the table was the packet. With a sudden relentless gesture he tore it open. For a half-hour he stood by the table in a state of excitement, examining the photographs of the ladies Salzman had included. Finally, with a deep sigh he put them down. There were six, of varying degrees of attractiveness, but look at them long enough and they all became Lily Hirschorn: all past their prime, all starved behind bright smiles, not a true personality in the lot. Life, despite their frantic yoohooings, had passed them by; they were pictures in a briefcase that stank of fish. After a while, however, as Leo attempted to return the photographs into the envelope, he found in it another, a snapshot of the type taken by a machine for a quarter. He gazed at it a moment and let out a cry.

Her face deeply moved him. Why, he could at first not say. It gave him the impression of youth—spring flowers, yet age—a sense of having been used to the bone, wasted; this came from the eyes, which were hauntingly familiar, yet absolutely strange. He had a vivid impression that he had met her before, but try as he might he could not place her although he could almost recall her name, as if he had read it in her own handwriting. No, this couldn't be; he would have remembered her. It was not, he affirmed, that she had an extraordinary beauty—no, though her face was attractive enough; it was that *something* about her moved him. Feature for feature, even some of the ladies of the photographs could do better; but she leaped forth to his heart—had *lived*, or wanted to—more than just wanted, perhaps regretted how she had lived—had somehow deeply suffered: it could be seen in the depths of those reluctant eyes, and from the way the light enclosed and shone from her, and within her, opening realms of possibility: this was her own. Her he desired. His head ached and eyes narrowed with the intensity of his gazing, then as if an obscure fog had blown up in the mind, he experienced fear of her and was aware that he had received an impression, somehow, of evil. He shuddered, saying softly, it is thus with us all. Leo brewed some tea in a small pot and sat sipping it without sugar, to calm himself. But before he had finished drinking, again with excitement he examined the face and found it good: good for Leo Finkle. Only such a one could understand him and help him seek whatever he was seeking. She might, perhaps, love him. How she had happened to be among the discards in Salzman's barrel he could never guess, but he knew he must urgently go find her.

Leo rushed downstairs, grabbed up the Bronx telephone book, and searched for Salzman's home address. He was not listed, nor was his office. Neither was he in the Manhattan book. But Leo remembered having written down the address on a slip of paper after he had read Salzman's advertisement in the "personals" column of the *Forward*. He ran up to his room and tore through his papers, without luck. It was exasperating. Just when he needed the matchmaker he was nowhere to be found. Fortunately Leo remembered to look in his wallet. There on a card he found his name written and a Bronx address. No phone number was listed, the reason—Leo now recalled—he had originally communicated with Salzman by letter. He got on his coat, put a hat on over his skull cap and hurried to the subway station. All the way to the far end of the Bronx he sat on the edge of his seat. He was more than once tempted to take out the picture and see if the girl's face was as he remembered it, but he refrained, allowing the snapshot to remain in his inside coat pocket, content to have her so close. When the train pulled into the station he was waiting at the door and bolted out. He quickly located the street Salzman had advertised. The building he sought was less than a block from the subway, but it was not an office building, nor even a loft, nor a store in which one could rent office space. It was a very old tenement house. Leo found Salzman's name in pencil on a soiled tag under the bell and climbed three dark flights to his apartment. When he knocked, the door was opened by a thin, asthmatic, gray-haired woman, in felt slippers.

"Yes?" she said, expecting nothing. She listened without listening. He could have sworn he had seen her, too, before but knew it was an illusion.

"Salzman—does he live here? Pinye Salzman," he said, "the matchmaker?"

She stared at him a long minute. "Of course."

He felt embarrassed. "Is he in?"

"No." Her mouth, though left open, offered nothing more.

"The matter is urgent. Can you tell me where his office is?"

"In the air." She pointed upward.

"You mean he has no office?" Leo asked.

"In his socks."

He peered into the apartment. It was sunless and dingy, one large room divided by a half-open curtain, beyond which he could see a sagging metal bed. The near side of the room was crowded with rickety chairs, old bureaus, a three-legged table, racks of cooking utensils, and all the apparatus of a kitchen. But there was no sign of Salzman or his magic barrel, probably also a figment of the imagination. An odor of frying fish made Leo weak to the knees.

"Where is he?" he insisted. "I've got to see your husband."

At length she answered, "So who knows where he is? Every time he thinks a new thought he runs to a different place. Go home, he will find you."

"Tell him Leo Finkle."

She gave no sign she had heard.

He walked downstairs, depressed.

But Salzman, breathless, stood waiting at his door.

Leo was astounded and overjoyed. "How did you get here before me?"

"I rushed."

"Come inside."

They entered. Leo fixed tea, and a sardine sandwich for Salzman. As they were drinking he reached behind him for the packet of pictures and handed them to the marriage broker.

Salzman put down his glass and said expectantly, "You found somebody you like?"

"Not among these."

The marriage broker turned away.

"Here is the one I want." Leo held forth the snapshot.

Salzman slipped on his glasses and took the picture into his trembling hand. He turned ghastly and let out a groan.

"What's the matter?" cried Leo.

"Excuse me. Was an accident this picture. She isn't for you."

Salzman frantically shoved the manila packet into his portfolio. He thrust the snapshot into his pocket and fled down the stairs.

Leo, after momentary paralysis, gave chase and cornered the marriage broker in the vestibule. The landlady made hysterical outcries but neither of them listened.

"Give me back the picture, Salzman."

"No." The pain in his eyes was terrible.

"Tell me who she is then."

"This I can't tell you. Excuse me."

He made to depart, but Leo, forgetting himself, seized the matchmaker by his tight coat and shook him frenziedly.

"Please," sighed Salzman. *"Please."*

Leo ashamedly let him go. "Tell me who she is," he begged. "It's very important for me to know."

"She is not for you. She is a wild one—wild, without shame. This is not a bride for a rabbi."

"What do you mean wild?"

"Like an animal. Like a dog. For her to be poor was a sin. This is why to me she is dead now."

"In God's name, what do you mean?"

"Her I can't introduce to you," Salzman cried.

"Why are you so excited?"

"Why, he asks," Salzman said, bursting into tears. "This is my baby, my Stella, she should burn in hell."

Leo hurried up to bed and hid under the covers. Under the covers he thought his life through. Although he soon fell asleep he could not sleep her out of his mind. He woke, beating his breast. Though he prayed to be rid of her, his prayers went unanswered. Through days of torment he endlessly struggled not to love her; fearing success, he escaped it. He then concluded to convert her to goodness, himself to God. The idea alternately nauseated and exalted him.

He perhaps did not know that he had come to a final decision until he encountered Salzman in a Broadway cafeteria. He was sitting alone at a rear table, sucking the bony remains of a fish. The marriage broker appeared haggard, and transparent to the point of vanishing.

Salzman looked up at first without recognizing him. Leo had grown a pointed beard and his eyes were weighted with wisdom.

"Salzman," he said, "love has at last come to my heart."

"Who can love from a picture?" mocked the marriage broker.

"It is not impossible."

"If you can love her, then you can love anybody. Let me show you some new clients that they just sent me their photographs. One is a little doll."

"Just her I want," Leo murmured.

"Don't be a fool, doctor. Don't bother with her."

"Put me in touch with her, Salzman," Leo said humbly. "Perhaps I can be of service."

Salzman had stopped eating and Leo understood with emotion that it was now arranged.

Leaving the cafeteria, he was, however, afflicted by a tormenting suspicion that Salzman had planned it all to happen this way.

Leo was informed by letter that she would meet him on a certain corner, and she was there one spring night, waiting under a street lamp. He appeared, carrying a small bouquet of violets and rosebuds. Stella stood by the lamp post, smoking. She wore white with red shoes, which fitted his expectations, although in a troubled moment he had imagined the dress red, and only the shoes white. She waited uneasily and shyly. From afar he saw that her eyes—clearly her father's—were filled with desperate innocence. He pictured, in her, his own redemption. Violins and lit candles revolved in the sky. Leo ran forward with flowers outthrust.

Around the corner, Salzman, leaning against a wall, chanted prayers for the dead.

Exercises

1. Review the major action of the story as it affects both Leo and Salzman.

2. For what is Leo searching early in the story? How does his search change?

3. What happens in the meeting between Leo and Lily Hirschorn? What does this crisis reveal about Leo?

4. Cite two or three complications that temporarily restrain Leo's progress.

5. At what exact point in the story is the obstacle removed, thereby allowing Leo to gain his prize? Specifically, what does he achieve?

6. Discuss the principal theme of the story.

7. How does the concluding scene contribute to a fuller understanding of the story?

8. What purpose might be served by the supernatural elements, the many ironies and ambiguities, especially in the ending of the story?

Topics for Writing

1. Draw a diagram that illustrates the plot line (refer to the introduction), and explain each point in detail.

2. Describe the nature and development of Leo's quest, how it changes and develops from the beginning to the end.

3. Using several important events in the plot, explain how each grows logically from something else and works purposely to achieve artistic unity.

4. Explain Salzman as both saint and sinner.

5. Compare and/or contrast Leo's quest with that of the hunger artist.

Selected Bibliography

Bernard Malamud

Alter, Robert. "Bernard Malamud: Jewishness as Metaphor." In *After The Tradition: Essays on Modern Jewish Writing.* New York: E. P. Dutton & Co., 1969, pp. 116–130.

Bellman, Samuel Irving. "Women, Children, and Idiots First: The Transformation Psychology of Bernard Malamud." *Critique*, 7 (Winter 1964–1965), 123–138.

Bluefarb, Sam. "Bernard Malamud: The Scope of Caricature." *English Journal*, 53 (May 1964), 319–326, 335.

Friedman, Alan Warren. "Bernard Malamud: The Hero as Schnook." *Southern Review* 4 n.s. (October 1968), 927–944.

Richman, Sidney. *Bernard Malamud.* New York: Twayne Publishers, 1966.

Rovit, Earl H. "Bernard Malamud and the Jewish Literary Tradition." *Critique*, 3 (Winter–Spring, 1960), 3–10.

Solotaroff, Theodore. "Bernard Malamud's Fiction: The Old Life and the New." *Commentary*, 33 (March 1962), 197–204.

Weiss, Samuel. "Passion and Purgation in Bernard Malamud." *University of Wisconsin Review*, 2, i (1966), 93–99.

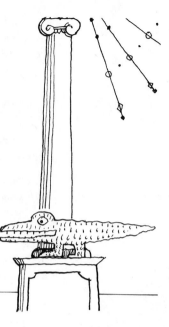

2 Character

Characters are people who make things happen in fiction. Although the writer reveals one character more completely than another or designates a larger function for one than for another, we should get to know them all rather well, however significant or trivial their roles. For the study of character will surely delight us and enlighten us.

In a broad sense, we can readily identify two main types of characters: one is three-dimensional and the other is one-dimensional. The first the author delineates more fully as a round, dynamic, or developing character, revealed chiefly in the dramatic mode. The second the author sketches simply as a flat, stock or stereotyped, static or underdeveloping character, disclosed either by the dramatic or by the summary method. Every character is important because each performs a role in the process of exhibiting life and examining the human condition.

In the short story the three-dimensional character is

usually the protagonist and/or the antagonist, for at best there is room for only two fully developed characters in so few pages. Short-story writers therefore focus sharply on a small moment in life and on relatively few aspects of character. By no means will they show us or tell us everything there is to know about a central character. Instead they will select judiciously those representative details intended to reveal *who* and *what* that character is, *how* and *why* that character acts thus. It is then the responsibility of the reader to sift out those "revealing" details in order to arrive at a total picture.

Let us examine the three dimensions of a major character. First, there are physical attributes: young, old, short, tall, slim, or obese; beautiful, handsome, big-eared, or freckled. Physical make-up can influence character in many ways. It may change attitudes, color outlook on life, deepen convictions, create tolerance, recklessness, or superstition. The star center on the basketball team is sure to hold certain attitudes different from those of the clumsy clod. The young lady with a brace on her leg is likely to develop real frustrations not shared by most of her friends.

Second, a three-dimensional character possesses a background: parents who are poor, rich, happy, or miserable; friends, enemies, talents, skills, hobbies, habits, likes, and dislikes. In reaching for an understanding of character it matters a great deal if she was reared in an orphanage or at home, if he slept in a crowded, bug-infested room or in the private suite of a mansion, if she was loved, neglected, or merely tolerated. Any of these influences can in some manner affect character and life-style.

Third, a principal character has a dimension that we will call the character's psychology. It refers to the traits, emotions, and behavior patterns that characterize a person as an individual. Impressions and influences from the past (for example, heredity and environment) make the character exactly what he or she is and do precisely what he or she does. These influences give birth to ambition in some people and kill it in others; they make one person's disposition easy-going, another's temperament contentious; they produce introverted and extroverted personalities; they beget frustrations and disappointments; and they engender obsessions, neuroses, manias, and phobias.

Only as we try to understand the complex nature of a character's physiological, sociological, and psychological make-up, can we expect to know why a woman poisons her lover and lives with his carcass in the adjoining room for forty years ("A Rose for Emily"), or why a young rabbinical student finds his true dedication to and love for God only after having fallen in love with a prostitute ("The Magic Barrel").

Nearly always the three-dimensional character is a *dynamic* or developing character. The person changes, is not static, is not the same person at the end of the story as at the beginning. The conflict through which the character moves brings about a lasting change in personality, basic values, or concept of human nature. Elisa ("The Chrysanthemums"), after her experience with the peddler, has perhaps gained strength of character and is now more easily able to accept her life with a husband who has proven insensitive to her womanly needs. The young boy ("I Want to Know Why"), discovering his good friend Jerry Tilford in the arms of a prostitute, concludes that a man is sometimes not as beautiful as a horse. He has been disillusioned; he has found ugliness, prejudices, and false values in the adult world. He is growing up. And Mabel ("The Horse Dealer's Daughter") is regenerated through a baptism of love. Whatever the change, whether it be a dislodgement of settled beliefs, a discovery, a revelation, or a new awareness, a dynamic character emerges out of conflict with a new set of eyes, never again to see the world as he or she once saw it.

Ordinarily, the author chooses to disclose the more important phases of the three-dimensional character by the dramatic method, that is, using action, as in drama, to give information and provide details. Often from these actions, then, we are able to deduce the reasons for thought and behavior. Thus, the artist creates a lifelike character who becomes real for us on the printed page.

Not nearly as fully developed is the one-dimensional character, the flat, stock, or stereotyped person, whom the author depicts fairly simply. The flat character is drawn with only surface facts and details; the stock or stereotyped character (the braggart, the bully, the mad scientist, the absent-minded professor) is sketched lightly with one or two easily recognizable personality traits that tend to dominate the character. There is little depth to the portrayal of a minor character. We learn virtually nothing about family or background; and behavior is familiar or predictable. About that character we are given as much information as the author deems necessary for the immediate, well-intentioned purpose. That purpose may be to provide a contrast to another character, to furnish a clue to a motive behind an action, or to present another view of an argument; there are many possibilities. Such characters are Ginger Nut, Nippers, and Turkey ("Bartleby, the Scrivener"); Farrington's wife Ada and his son Tom ("Counterparts"); Miss Churm, Jack Hawley, and Oronte ("The Real Thing"); Lily Hirschorn ("The Magic Barrel"); and Bildad ("I Want to Know Why"). Minor characters generally remain static. Rarely will they revise their essential natures or beliefs. Unmoved by the major conflict, minor characters remain the same people at the end of the story that they were at the beginning. The author has revealed the purpose through the dramatic method or through the summary method, by direct discussion or description.

A standard requirement of good fiction is that a character be convincing—and believable as a human being. We must believe that what is said and done might well be what a friend or neighbor would say or do confronted with the same problem or caught in a similar predicament. Characters, like people, sometimes behave foolishly and incredibly, but however unusual or fantastic their actions, we are convinced of their reality if the character performing the act responds to clearly identifiable, legitimate motivation, with actions that consistently obey the laws of that particular character's own being.

Characters act as they do for reasons. *Motivation* is the term we give for these reasons. Mabel, despairing over the loss of her father, the break-up of the family, and the bleakness of her future, attempts suicide by drowning ("The Horse Dealer's Daughter"). Having been severely reprimanded by his boss and having been defeated publicly at Indian wrestling, Farrington comes home to an unprepared supper and, in a fit of temper, strikes his son with a stick ("Counterparts").

To obey the laws of their own being, characters must behave according to the dictates of their own established natures. This quality of character is known as *consistency*. Characters will change only when adequate stimuli induce a change. Laura ("Flowering Judas"), incapable of committing herself to a human being or an idea, can only give herself half-heartedly to Braggioni's revolution, the dogmas of her church, the teaching of Indian children, and the political prisoners. She is consistent with her nature, saying "no" to everyone and everything, even to death. So is Emily ("A Rose for Emily") true to her nature. She sits with "her upright torso motionless as that of an idol," resisting change and stubbornly holding onto the Grierson family tradition of honor and pride.

Authors create every conceivable type of character, pattern of thought, breed of attitude, and kind of emotion all in the name of humanity, our fears, our hopes, our loves, our failures, our madness, and our perpetual search for truth. How can we do less than try to understand those characters and ourselves?

John Steinbeck (1902-1968)

Born in Salinas, California, the setting of many of his stories and novels, he studied briefly at Stanford University and worked at a variety of jobs—ranch hand, fruit-picker, laboratory assistant, house-painter—before settling down to a prolific writing career. His most notable fiction includes Of Mice and Men *(1937) and* The Grapes of Wrath *(1939), for which he reaped a Pulitzer Prize. He also received the Nobel Prize for Literature in 1962. His short story "The Chrysanthemums," rated excellent by the critics, is further considered a perfect study of character.*

The Chrysanthemums

The high grey-flannel fog of winter closed off the Salinas Valley from the sky and from all the rest of the world. On every side it sat like a lid on the mountains and made of the great valley a closed pot. On the broad, level land floor the gang plows bit deep and left the black earth shining like metal where the shares had cut. On the foothill ranches across the Salinas River, the yellow stubble fields seemed to be bathed in pale cold sunshine, but there was no sunshine in the valley now in December. The thick willow scrub along the river flamed with sharp and positive yellow leaves.

It was a time of quiet and of waiting. The air was cold and tender. A light wind blew up from the southwest so that the farmers were mildly hopeful of a good rain before long; but fog and rain do not go together.

Across the river, on Henry Allen's foothill ranch there was little work to be done, for the hay was cut and stored and the orchards were plowed up to receive the rain deeply when it should come. The cattle on the higher slopes were becoming shaggy and rough-coated.

Elisa Allen, working in her flower garden, looked down across the yard and saw Henry, her husband, talking to two men in business suits. The three of them stood by the tractor shed, each man with one foot on the side of the little Fordson. They smoked cigarettes and studied the machine as they talked.

Elisa watched them for a moment and then went back to her work. She was thirty-five. Her face was lean and strong and her eyes were as clear as water. Her figure looked blocked and heavy in her gardening costume, a man's black hat pulled low down over her eyes, clod-hopper shoes, a figured print dress almost completely covered by a big corduroy apron with four big pockets to hold the snips, the trowel and scratcher, the seeds and the knife she worked with. She wore heavy leather gloves to protect her hands while she worked.

She was cutting down the old year's chrysanthemum stalks with a pair of short and powerful scissors. She looked down toward the men by the tractor shed now and then. Her face was eager and mature and handsome; even her work with the scissors was over-eager, over-powerful. The chrysanthemum stems seemed too small and easy for her energy.

She brushed a cloud of hair out of her eyes with the back of her glove, and left a smudge of earth on her cheek in doing it. Behind her stood the neat white farm house with red geraniums close-banked around it as high as the windows. It was a hard-swept looking little house, with hard-polished windows, and a clean mud-mat on the front steps.

Elisa cast another glance toward the tractor shed. The strangers were getting into their Ford coupe. She took off a glove and put her strong fingers down into the forest of new green chrysanthemum sprouts that were growing around the old roots. She spread the leaves and looked down among the close-growing stems. No aphids were there, no sowbugs or snails or cutworms. Her terrier fingers destroyed such pests before they could get started.

Elisa started at the sound of her husband's voice. He had come near quietly, and he leaned over the wire fence that protected her flower garden from cattle and dogs and chickens.

"At it again," he said. "You've got a strong new crop coming."

Elisa straightened her back and pulled on the gardening glove again. "Yes. They'll be strong this coming year." In her tone and on her face there was a little smugness.

"You've got a gift with things," Henry observed. "Some of those yellow chrysanthemums you had this year were ten inches across. I wish you'd work out in the orchard and raise some apples that big."

Her eyes sharpened. "Maybe I could do it, too. I've a gift with things, all right. My mother had it. She could stick anything in the ground and make it grow. She said it was having planters' hands that knew how to do it."

"Well, it sure works with flowers," he said.

"Henry, who were those men you were talking to?"

"Why, sure, that's what I came to tell you. They were from the Western Meat Company. I sold those thirty head of three-year-old steers. Got nearly my own price, too."

"Good," she said. "Good for you."

"And I thought," he continued, "I thought how it's Saturday afternoon, and we might go to Salinas for dinner at a restaurant, and then to a picture show—to celebrate, you see."

"Good," she repeated. "Oh, yes. That will be good."

Henry put on his joking tone. "There's fights tonight. How'd you like to go to the fights?"

"Oh, no," she said breathlessly. "No, I wouldn't like fights."

"Just fooling, Elisa. We'll go to a movie. Let's see. It's two now. I'm going to take Scotty and bring down those steers from the hill. It'll take us maybe two hours. We'll go in town about five and have dinner at the Cominos Hotel. Like that?"

"Of course I'll like it. It's good to eat away from home."

"All right, then. I'll go get up a couple of horses."

She said, "I'll have plenty of time to transplant some of these sets, I guess."

She heard her husband calling Scotty down by the barn. And a little later she saw the two men ride up the pale yellow hillside in search of the steers.

There was a little square sandy bed kept for rooting the chrysanthemums. With her trowel she turned the soil over and over, and smoothed it and patted it firm. Then she dug ten parallel trenches to receive the sets. Back at the chrysanthemum bed she pulled out the little crisp shoots, trimmed off the leaves of each one with her scissors and laid it on a small orderly pile.

A squeak of wheels and plod of hoofs came from the

road. Elisa looked up. The country road ran along the dense bank of willows and cottonwoods that bordered the river, and up this road came a curious vehicle, curiously drawn. It was an old spring-wagon, with a round canvas top on it like the cover of a prairie schooner. It was drawn by an old bay horse and a little grey-and-white burro. A big stubble-bearded man sat between the cover flaps and drove the crawling team. Underneath the wagon, between the hind wheels, a lean and rangy mongrel dog walked sedately. Words were painted on the canvas, in clumsy, crooked letters. "Pots, pans, knives, sisors, lawn mores, Fixed." Two rows of articles, and the triumphantly definitive "Fixed" below. The black paint had run down in little sharp points beneath each letter.

Elisa, squatting on the ground, watched to see the crazy, loose-jointed wagon pass by. But it didn't pass. It turned into the farm road in front of her house, crooked old wheels skirling and squeaking. The rangy dog darted from between the wheels and ran ahead. Instantly the two ranch shepherds flew out at him. Then all three stopped, and with stiff and quivering tails, with taut straight legs, with ambassadorial dignity, they slowly circled, sniffing daintily. The caravan pulled up to Elisa's wire fence and stopped. Now the newcomer dog, feeling out-numbered, lowered his tail and retired under the wagon with raised hackles and bared teeth.

The man on the wagon seat called out, "That's a bad dog in a fight when he gets started."

Elisa laughed. "I see he is. How soon does he generally get started?"

The man caught up her laughter and echoed it heartily. "Sometimes not for weeks and weeks," he said. He climbed stiffly down, over the wheel. The horse and the donkey drooped like unwatered flowers.

Elisa saw that he was a very big man. Although his hair and beard were greying, he did not look old. His worn black suit was wrinkled and spotted with grease. The laughter had disappeared from his face and eyes the moment his laughing voice ceased. His eyes were dark, and they were full of the brooding that gets in the eyes of teamsters and of sailors. The calloused hands he rested on the wire fence were cracked, and every crack was a black line. He took off his battered hat.

"I'm off my general road, ma'am," he said. "Does this dirt road cut over across the river to the Los Angeles highway?"

Elisa stood up and shoved the thick scissors in her apron pocket. "Well, yes, it does, but it winds around and then fords the river. I don't think your team could pull through the sand."

He replied with some asperity, "It might surprise you what them beasts can pull through."

"When they get started?" she asked.

He smiled for a second. "Yes. When they get started."

"Well," said Elisa, "I think you'll save time if you go back to the Salinas road and pick up the highway there."

He drew a big finger down the chicken wire and made it sing. "I ain't in any hurry, ma'am. I go from Seattle to San Diego and back every year. Takes all my time. About six months each way. I aim to follow nice weather."

Elisa took off her gloves and stuffed them in the apron pocket with the scissors. She touched the under edge of her man's hat, searching for fugitive hairs. "That sounds like a nice kind of a way to live," she said.

He leaned confidentially over the fence. "Maybe you noticed the writing on my wagon. I mend pots and sharpen knives and scissors. You got any of them things to do?"

"Oh, no," she said quickly. "Nothing like that." Her eyes hardened with resistance.

"Scissors is the worst thing," he explained. "Most people just ruin scissors trying to sharpen 'em, but I know how. I got a special tool. It's a little bobbit kind of thing, and patented. But it sure does the trick."

"No. My scissors are all sharp."

"All right, then. Take a pot," he continued earnestly, "a bent pot, or a pot with a hole. I can make it like new so you don't have to buy no new ones. That's a saving for you."

"No," she said shortly. "I tell you I have nothing like that for you to do."

His face fell to an exaggerated sadness. His voice took on a whining undertone. "I ain't had a thing to do today. Maybe I won't have no supper tonight. You see I'm off my regular road. I know folks on the highway clear from Seattle to San Diego. They save their things for me to sharpen up because they know I do it so good and save them money."

"I'm sorry," Elisa said irritably. "I haven't anything for you to do."

His eyes left her face and fell to searching the ground. They roamed about until they came to the chrysanthemum bed where she had been working. "What's them plants, ma'am?"

The irritation and resistance melted from Elisa's face. "Oh, those are chrysanthemums, giant whites and yellows. I raise them every year, bigger than anybody around here."

"Kind of a long-stemmed flower? Looks like a quick puff of colored smoke?" he asked.

"That's it. What a nice way to describe them."

"They smell kind of nasty till you get used to them," he said.

"It's a good bitter smell," she retorted, "not nasty at all."

He changed his tone quickly. "I like the smell myself."

"I had ten-inch blooms this year," she said.

The man leaned farther over the fence. "Look. I know a lady down the road a piece, has got the nicest garden you ever seen. Got nearly every kind of flower but no chrysanthemums. Last time I was mending a copper-bottom washtub for her (that's a hard job but I do it good), she said to me, 'If you ever run acrost some nice chrysanthemums I wish you'd try to get me a few seeds.' That's what she told me."

Elisa's eyes grew alert and eager. "She couldn't have known much about chrysanthemums. You *can* raise them from seed, but it's much easier to root the little sprouts you see there."

"Oh," he said. "I s'pose I can't take none to her, then."

"Why yes you can," Elisa cried. "I can put some in damp sand, and you can carry them right along with you. They'll take root in the pot if you keep them damp. And then she can transplant them."

"She'd sure like to have some, ma'am. You say they're nice ones?"

"Beautiful," she said. "Oh, beautiful." Her eyes shone. She tore off the battered hat and shook out her dark pretty hair. "I'll put them in a flower pot, and you can take them right with you. Come into the yard."

While the man came through the picket gate Elisa ran excitedly along the geranium-bordered path to the back of the house. And she returned carrying a big red flower pot. The gloves were forgotten now. She kneeled on the ground by the starting bed and dug up the sandy soil with her fingers and scooped it into the bright new flower pot. Then she picked up the little pile of shoots she had prepared. With her strong fingers she pressed them into the sand and tamped around them with her knuckles. The man stood over her. "I'll tell you what to do," she said. "You remember so you can tell the lady."

"Yes, I'll try to remember."

"Well, look. These will take root in about a month. Then she must set them out, about a foot apart in good rich earth like this, see?" She lifted a handful of dark soil for him to look at. "They'll grow fast and tall. Now remember this. In July tell her to cut them down, about eight inches from the ground."

"Before they bloom?" he asked.

"Yes, before they bloom." Her face was tight with eagerness. "They'll grow right up again. About the last of September the buds will start."

She stopped and seemed perplexed. "It's the budding that takes the most care," she said hesitantly. "I don't know how to tell you." She looked deep into his eyes, searchingly. Her mouth opened a little, and she seemed to be listening. "I'll try to tell you," she said. "Did you ever hear of planting hands?"

"Can't say I have, ma'am."

"Well, I can only tell you what it feels like. It's when you're picking off the buds you don't want. Everything goes right down into your fingertips. You watch your fingers work. They do it themselves. You can feel how it is. They pick and pick the buds. They never make a mistake. They're with the plant. Do you see? Your fingers and the plant. You can feel that, right up your arm. They know. They never make a mistake. You can feel it. When you're like that you can't do anything wrong. Do you see that? Can you understand that?"

She was kneeling on the ground looking up at him. Her breast swelled passionately.

The man's eyes narrowed. He looked away self-consciously. "Maybe I know," he said. "Sometimes in the night in the wagon there—"

Elisa's voice grew husky. She broke in on him. "I've never lived as you do, but I know what you mean. When the night is dark—why, the stars are sharp-pointed, and there's quiet. Why, you rise up and up! Every pointed star gets driven into your body. It's like that. Hot and sharp and—lovely."

Kneeling there, her hand went out toward his legs in the greasy black trousers. Her hesitant fingers almost touched the cloth. Then her hand dropped to the ground. She crouched low like a fawning dog.

He said, "It's nice, just like you say. Only when you don't have no dinner, it ain't."

She stood up then, very straight, and her face was ashamed. She held the flower pot out to him and placed it gently in his arms. "Here. Put it in your wagon, on the seat, where you can watch it. Maybe I can find something for you to do."

At the back of the house she dug in the can pile and found two old and battered aluminum saucepans. She carried them back and gave them to him. "Here, maybe you can fix these."

His manner changed. He became professional. "Good as new I can fix them." At the back of his wagon he set a little anvil, and out of an oily tool box dug a small machine hammer. Elisa came through the gate to watch him while he pounded out the dents in the kettles. His mouth grew sure and knowing. At a difficult part of the work he sucked his under-lip.

"You sleep right in the wagon?" Elisa asked.

"Right in the wagon, ma'am. Rain or shine I'm dry as a cow in there."

"It must be nice," she said. "It must be very nice. I wish women could do such things."

"It ain't the right kind of a life for a woman."

Her upper lip raised a little, showing her teeth. "How do you know? How can you tell?" she said.

"I don't know, ma'am," he protested. "Of course I

don't know. Now here's your kettles, done. You don't have to buy no new ones."

"How much?"

"Oh, fifty cents'll do. I keep my prices down and my work good. That's why I have all them satisfied customers up and down the highway."

Elisa brought him a fifty-cent piece from the house and dropped it in his hand. "You might be surprised to have a rival some time. I can sharpen scissors, too. And I can beat the dents out of little pots. I could show you what a woman might do."

He put his hammer back in the oily box and shoved the little anvil out of sight. "It would be a lonely life for a woman, ma'am, and a scarey life, too, with animals creeping under the wagon all night." He climbed over the singletree, steadying himself with a hand on the burro's white rump. He settled himself in the seat, picked up the lines. "Thank you kindly, ma'am," he said. "I'll do like you told me; I'll go back and catch the Salinas road."

"Mind," she called, "if you're long in getting there, keep the sand damp."

"Sand, ma'am? . . . Sand? Oh, sure. You mean around the chrysanthemums. Sure I will." He clucked his tongue. The beasts leaned luxuriously into their collars. The mongrel dog took his place between the back wheels. The wagon turned and crawled out the entrance road and back the way it had come, along the river.

Elisa stood in front of her wire fence watching the slow progress of the caravan. Her shoulders were straight, her head thrown back, her eyes half-closed, so that the scene came vaguely into them. Her lips moved silently, forming the words "Good-bye—good-bye." Then she whispered, "That's a bright direction. There's a glowing there." The sound of her whisper startled her. She shook herself free and looked about to see whether anyone had been listening. Only the dogs had heard. They lifted their heads toward her from their sleeping in the dust, and then stretched out their chins and settled asleep again. Elisa turned and ran hurriedly into the house.

In the kitchen she reached behind the stove and felt the water tank. It was full of hot water from the noonday cooking. In the bathroom she tore off her soiled clothes and flung them into the corner. And then she scrubbed herself with a little block of pumice, legs and thighs, loins and chest and arms, until her skin was scratched and red. When she had dried herself she stood in front of a mirror in her bedroom and looked at her body. She tightened her stomach and threw out her chest. She turned and looked over her shoulder at her back.

After a while she began to dress, slowly. She put on her newest underclothing and her nicest stockings and the dress which was the symbol of her prettiness. She worked carefully on her hair, penciled her eyebrows and rouged her lips.

Before she was finished she heard the little thunder of hoofs and the shouts of Henry and his helper as they drove the red steers into the corral. She heard the gate bang shut and set herself for Henry's arrival.

His step sounded on the porch. He entered the house calling, "Elisa, where are you?"

"In my room, dressing. I'm not ready. There's hot water for your bath. Hurry up. It's getting late."

When she heard him splashing in the tub, Elisa laid his dark suit on the bed, and shirt and socks and tie beside it. She stood his polished shoes on the floor beside the bed. Then she went to the porch and sat primly and stiffly down. She looked toward the river road where the willow-line was still yellow with frosted leaves so that under the high grey fog they seemed a thin band of sunshine. This was the only color in the grey afternoon. She sat unmoving for a long time. Her eyes blinked rarely.

Henry came banging out of the door, shoving his tie inside his vest as he came. Elisa stiffened and her face grew tight. Henry stopped short and looked at her. "Why—why, Elisa. You look so nice!"

"Nice? You think I look nice? What do you mean by 'nice'?"

Henry blundered on. "I don't know. I mean you look different, strong and happy."

"I am strong? Yes, strong. What do you mean 'strong'?"

He looked bewildered. "You're playing some kind of a game," he said helplessly. "It's a kind of a play. You look strong enough to break a calf over your knee, happy enough to eat it like a watermelon."

For a second she lost her rigidity. "Henry! Don't talk like that. You didn't know what you said." She grew complete again. "I'm strong," she boasted. "I never knew before how strong."

Henry looked down toward the tractor shed, and when he brought his eyes back to her, they were his own again. "I'll get out the car. You can put on your coat while I'm starting."

Elisa went into the house. She heard him drive to the gate and idle down his motor, and then she took a long time to put on her hat. She pulled it here and pressed it there. When Henry turned the motor off she slipped into her coat and went out.

The little roadster bounced along on the dirt road by the river, raising the birds and driving the rabbits into the brush. Two cranes flapped heavily over the willow-line and dropped into the river-bed.

Far ahead on the road Elisa saw a dark speck. She knew.

She tried not to look as they passed it, but her eyes would not obey. She whispered to herself sadly, "He might have thrown them off the road. That wouldn't have been much trouble, not very much. But he kept the pot," she explained. "He had to keep the pot. That's why he couldn't get them off the road."

The roadster turned a bend and she saw the caravan ahead. She swung full around toward her husband so she could not see the little covered wagon and the mismatched team as the car passed them.

In a moment it was over. The thing was done. She did not look back.

She said loudly, to be heard above the motor, "It will be good, tonight, a good dinner."

"Now you're changed again," Henry complained. He took one hand from the wheel and patted her knee. "I ought to take you in to dinner oftener. It would be good for both of us. We get so heavy out on the ranch."

"Henry," she asked, "could we have wine at dinner?"

"Sure we could. Say! That will be fine."

She was silent for a while; then she said, "Henry, at those prize fights, do the men hurt each other very much?"

"Sometimes a little, not often. Why?"

"Well, I've read how they break noses, and blood runs down their chests. I've read how the fighting gloves get heavy and soggy with blood."

He looked around at her. "What's the matter, Elisa? I didn't know you read things like that." He brought the car to a stop, then turned to the right over the Salinas River bridge.

"Do any women ever go to the fights?" she asked.

"Oh, sure, some. What's the matter, Elisa? Do you want to go? I don't think you'd like it, but I'll take you if you really want to go."

She relaxed limply in the seat. "Oh, no. No. I don't want to go. I'm sure I don't." Her face was turned away from him. "It will be enough if we can have wine. It will be plenty." She turned up her coat collar so he could not see that she was crying weakly—like an old woman.

Exercises   *1. What impression does Steinbeck create with his initial physical description of Elisa? How does environment affect her?*

2. Cite one or two incidents, dramatically presented, that unveil some aspect of Elisa's character.

3. What is the significance of Elisa's thoughtful preparation for the trip to town?

4. What is Elisa's conflict? How is it resolved?

5. What role does the tinker play?

6. Has the experience of conflict produced any permanent change in Elisa? If so, discuss the change.

7. How much do we know about Henry? Is he a dynamic or static character? What function does he serve?

8. Explain the meaning of the following episodes: (a) Shortly after having met the peddler, Elisa removes her gloves, searches for displaced hairs under her man's hat, and moves about with palpitating excitement. (b) After the tinker leaves, Elisa tears off her soiled clothes and scrubs herself until her skin is scratched and red. (c) "I'm strong," she boasted [addressing Henry]. "I never knew before how strong."

Topics for Writing

1. Discuss the significance of the chrysanthemums in Elisa's life.

2. Interpret the story from the thematic point of view either of suppressed femininity or of lost experience.

3. Explain Henry's insensitivity to Elisa's problem.

4. Portray the character of Elisa.

Selected Bibliography

John Steinbeck

Calverton, V. F. "Steinbeck, Hemingway, and Faulkner." *Modern Quarterly*, 11 (1939), 36–44.

Carpenter, F. I. "John Steinbeck: American Dreamer." *Sewanee Review*, 26 (1941), 454–467.

Champney, Freeman. "John Steinbeck, Californian." *Antioch Review*, 7 (1947), 345–362.

Davis, Elmer. "The Steinbeck Country." *Saturday Review of Literature*, 24 (September 1938), 11.

Gibbs, L. R. "John Steinbeck, Moralist." *Antioch Review*, 2 (1942), 172–184.

McMahan, Elizabeth E. " 'The Chrysanthemums': Study of a Woman's Sexuality." *Modern Fiction Studies*, 14 (1968), 453–458.

Marcus, Mordecai. "The Lost Dream of Sex and Childbirth in 'The Chrysanthemums.'" *Modern Fiction Studies*, 11 (1965), 54–58.

Noonan, Gerald. "A Note on 'The Chrysanthemums.'" *Modern Fiction Studies*, 15 (1969), 542.

Osborne, William R. "The Texts of Steinbeck's 'The Chrysanthemums.'" *Modern Fiction Studies*, 12 (1966), 479–484.

William Faulkner *(1897–1962)*

Born in New Albany, Mississippi, he spent most of his life in the pine-hill country of Oxford, where, on his favorite park bench in the square, he sat on Saturdays and exchanged old tales with all willing participants, most of them farmers. The premier American writer of the twentieth century, so adjudged by many critics, won a Pulitzer Prize for A Fable *(1955), another Pulitzer Prize for* The Reivers *(posthumously awarded in 1963), and a Nobel Prize (1949). Other important works are* The Sound and the Fury *(1929),* As I Lay Dying *(1930),* Light in August *(1932), and* The Mansion *(1959). From his famous Nobel Prize speech comes this often-quoted pronouncement: "I believe that man will not merely endure: he will prevail."*

A Rose for Emily

1

When Miss Emily Grierson died, our whole town went to her funeral: the men through a sort of respectful affection for a fallen monument, the women mostly out of curiosity to see the inside of her house, which no one save an old manservant—a combined gardener and cook—had seen in at least ten years.

It was a big, squarish frame house that had once been white, decorated with cupolas and spires and scrolled balconies in the heavily lightsome style of the seventies, set on what had once been our most select street. But garages and cotton gins had encroached and obliterated even the august names of that neighborhood, only Miss Emily's house was left, lifting its stubborn and coquettish decay above the cotton wagons and the gasoline pumps—an eyesore among eyesores. And now Miss Emily had gone to join the representatives of those august names where they lay in the cedar-bemused cemetery among the ranked and anonymous graves of Union and Confederate soldiers who fell at the battle of Jefferson.

Alive, Miss Emily had been a tradition, a duty, and a care; a sort of hereditary obligation upon the town, dating from that day in 1894 when Colonel Sartoris, the mayor—he who fathered the edict that no Negro woman should appear on the streets without an apron—remitted her taxes, the dispensation dating from the death of her father on into perpetuity. Not that Miss Emily would have accepted charity. Colonel

Sartoris invented an involved tale to the effect that Miss Emily's father had loaned money to the town, which the town, as a matter of business, preferred this way of repaying. Only a man of Colonel Sartoris' generation and thought could have invented it, and only a woman could have believed it.

When the next generation, with its more modern ideas, became mayors and aldermen, this arrangement created some little dissatisfaction. On the first of the year they mailed her a tax notice. February came, and there was no reply. They wrote her a formal letter, asking her to call at the sheriff's office at her convenience. A week later the mayor wrote her himself, offering to call or to send his car for her, and received in reply a note on paper of an archaic shape, in a thin, flowing calligraphy in faded ink, to the effect that she no longer went out at all. The tax notice was also enclosed, without comment.

They called a special meeting of the Board of Aldermen. A deputation waited upon her, knocked at the door through which no visitor had passed since she ceased giving china-painting lessons eight or ten years earlier. They were admitted by the old Negro into a dim hall from which a stairway mounted into still more shadow. It smelled of dust and disuse—a close, dank smell. The Negro led them into the parlor. It was furnished in heavy, leather-covered furniture. When the Negro opened the blinds of one window, they could see that the leather was cracked; and when they sat down, a faint dust rose sluggishly about their thighs, spinning with slow motes in the single sun-ray. On a tarnished gilt easel before the fireplace stood a crayon portrait of Miss Emily's father.

They rose when she entered—a small, fat woman in black, with a thin gold chain descending to her waist and vanishing into her belt, leaning on an ebony cane with a tarnished gold head. Her skeleton was small and spare; perhaps that was why what would have been merely plumpness in another was obesity in her. She looked bloated, like a body long submerged in motionless water, and of that pallid hue. Her eyes, lost in the fatty ridges of her face, looked like two small pieces of coal pressed into a lump of dough as they moved from one face to another while the visitors stated their errand.

She did not ask them to sit. She just stood in the door and listened quietly until the spokesman came to a stumbling halt. Then they could hear the invisible watch ticking at the end of the gold chain.

Her voice was dry and cold. "I have no taxes in Jefferson. Colonel Sartoris explained it to me. Perhaps one of you can gain access to the city records and satisfy yourselves."

"But we have. We are the city authorities, Miss Emily. Didn't you get a notice from the sheriff, signed by him?"

"I received a paper, yes," Miss Emily said. "Perhaps he considers himself the sheriff. . . . I have no taxes in Jefferson."

"But there is nothing on the books to show that, you see. We must go by the—"

"See Colonel Sartoris. I have no taxes in Jefferson."

"But, Miss Emily—"

"See Colonel Sartoris." (Colonel Sartoris had been dead almost ten years.) "I have no taxes in Jefferson. Tobe!" The Negro appeared. "Show these gentlemen out."

2

So she vanquished them, horse and foot, just as she had vanquished their fathers thirty years before about the smell. That was two years after her father's death and a short time after her sweetheart—the one we believed would marry her—had deserted her. After her father's death she went out very little; after her sweetheart went away, people hardly saw her at all. A few ladies had the temerity to call, but were not received, and the only sign of life about the place was the Negro man—a young man then—going in and out with a market basket.

"Just as if a man—any man—could keep a kitchen properly," the ladies said; so they were not surprised when the smell developed. It was another link between the gross, teeming world and the high and mighty Griersons.

A neighbor, a woman, complained to the mayor, Judge Stevens, eighty years old.

"But what will you have me do about it, madam?" he said.

"Why, send her word to stop it," the woman said. "Isn't there a law?"

"I'm sure that won't be necessary," Judge Stevens said. "It's probably just a snake or a rat that nigger of hers killed in the yard. I'll speak to him about it."

The next day he received two more complaints, one from a man who came in diffident deprecation. "We really must do something about it, Judge. I'd be the last one in the world to bother Miss Emily, but we've got to do something." That night the Board of Aldermen met—three graybeards and one younger man, a member of the rising generation.

"It's simple enough," he said. "Send her word to have her place cleaned up. Give her a certain time to do it in, and if she don't . . ."

"Dammit, sir," Judge Stevens said, "will you accuse a lady to her face of smelling bad?"

So the next night, after midnight, four men crossed Miss Emily's lawn and slunk about the house like burglars, sniffing along the base of the brickwork and at the cellar openings while one of them performed a regular sowing motion with his hand out of a sack slung from his shoulder. They broke open the cellar door and sprinkled lime there, and in all the outbuildings. As they recrossed the lawn, a window that had been dark was lighted and Miss Emily sat in it, the light behind her, and her upright torso motionless as that of an idol. They crept quietly across the lawn and into the shadow of the locusts that lined the street. After a week or two the smell went away.

That was when people had begun to feel really sorry for her. People in our town, remembering how old lady Wyatt, her great-aunt, had gone completely crazy at last, believed that the Griersons held themselves a little too high for what they really were. None of the young men were quite good enough for Miss Emily and such. We had long thought of them as a tableau: Miss Emily a slender figure in white in the background, her father a spraddled silhouette in the foreground, his back to her and clutching a horsewhip, the two of them framed by the back-flung front door. So when she got to be thirty and was still single, we were not pleased exactly, but vindicated; even with insanity in the family she wouldn't have turned down all of her chances if they had really materialized.

When her father died, it got about that the house was all that was left to her; and in a way, people were glad. At last they could pity Miss Emily. Being left alone, and a pauper, she had become humanized. Now she too would know the old thrill and the old despair of a penny more or less.

The day after his death all the ladies prepared to call at the house and offer condolence and aid, as is our custom. Miss Emily met them at the door, dressed as usual and with no trace of grief on her face. She told them that her father was not dead. She did that for three days, with the ministers calling on her, and the doctors, trying to persuade her to let them dispose of the body. Just as they were about to resort to law and force, she broke down, and they buried her father quickly.

We did not say she was crazy then. We believed she had to do that. We remembered all the young men her father had driven away, and we knew that with nothing left, she would have to cling to that which had robbed her, as people will.

3

She was sick for a long time. When we saw her again, her hair was cut short, making her look like a girl, with a vague resemblance to those angels in colored church windows—sort of tragic and serene.

The town had just let the contracts for paving the sidewalks, and in the summer after her father's death they began the work. The construction company came with niggers and mules and machinery, and a foreman named Homer Barron, a Yankee—a big, dark, ready man, with a big voice and eyes lighter than his face. The little boys would follow in groups to hear him cuss the niggers, and the niggers singing in time to the rise and fall of picks. Pretty soon he knew everybody in town. Whenever you heard a lot of laughing anywhere about the square, Homer Barron would be in the center of the group. Presently we began to see him and

Miss Emily on Sunday afternoons driving in the yellow-wheeled buggy and the matched team of bays from the livery stable.

At first we were glad that Miss Emily would have an interest, because the ladies all said, "Of course a Grierson would not think seriously of a Northerner, a day laborer." But there were still others, older people, who said that even grief could not cause a real lady to forget *noblesse oblige*—without calling it *noblesse oblige*. They just said, "Poor Emily. Her kinsfolk should come to her." She had some kin in Alabama; but years ago her father had fallen out with them over the estate of old lady Wyatt, the crazy woman, and there was no communication between the two families. They had not even been represented at the funeral.

And as soon as the old people said, "Poor Emily," the whispering began. "Do you suppose it's really so?" they said to one another. "Of course it is. What else could . . ." This behind their hands; rustling of craned silk and satin behind jalousies closed upon the sun of Sunday afternoon as the thin, swift clop-clop-clop of the matched team passed: "Poor Emily."

She carried her head high enough—even when we believed that she was fallen. It was as if she demanded more than ever the recognition of her dignity as the last Grierson; as if it had wanted that touch of earthiness to reaffirm her imperviousness. Like when she bought the rat poison, the arsenic. That was over a year after they had begun to say "Poor Emily," and while the two female cousins were visiting her.

"I want some poison," she said to the druggist. She was over thirty then, still a slight woman, though thinner than usual, with cold, haughty black eyes in a face the flesh of which was strained across the temples and about the eyesockets as you imagine a lighthouse-keeper's face ought to look. "I want some poison," she said.

"Yes, Miss Emily. What kind? For rats and such? I'd recom—"

"I want the best you have. I don't care what kind."

The druggist named several. "They'll kill anything up to an elephant. But what you want is—"

"Arsenic," Miss Emily said. "Is that a good one?"

"Is . . . arsenic? Yes, ma'am. But what you want—"

"I want arsenic."

The druggist looked down at her. She looked back at him, erect, her face like a strained flag. "Why, of course," the druggist said. "If that's what you want. But the law requires you to tell what you are going to use it for."

Miss Emily just stared at him, her head tilted back in order to look him eye for eye, until he looked away and went and got the arsenic and wrapped it up. The Negro delivery boy brought her the package; the druggist didn't come back. When she opened the package at home there was written on the box, under the skull and bones: "For rats."

4

So the next day we all said, "She will kill herself"; and we said it would be the best thing. When she had first begun to be seen with Homer Barron, we had said, "She will marry him." Then we said, "She will persuade him yet," because Homer himself had remarked—he liked men, and it was known that he drank with the younger men in the Elk's Club—that he was not a marrying man. Later we said, "Poor Emily," behind the jalousies as they passed on Sunday afternoon in the glittering buggy, Miss Emily with her head high and Homer Barron with his hat cocked and a cigar in his teeth, reins and whip in a yellow glove.

Then some of the ladies began to say that it was a disgrace to the town and a bad example to the young people. The men did not want to interfere, but at last the ladies forced the Baptist minister—Miss Emily's people were Episcopal—to call upon her. He would never divulge what happened during that interview, but he refused to go back again. The next Sunday they again drove about the streets, and the following day the minister's wife wrote to Miss Emily's relations in Alabama.

So she had blood-kin under her roof again and we sat back to watch developments. At first nothing happened. Then we were sure that they were to be married. We learned that Miss Emily had been to the jeweler's and ordered a man's toilet set in silver, with the letters H.B. on each piece. Two days later we learned that she had bought a complete outfit of men's clothing, including a nightshirt, and we said, "They are married." We were really glad. We were glad because the two female cousins were even more Grierson than Miss Emily had ever been.

So we were not surprised when Homer Barron—the streets had been finished some time since—was gone. We were a little disappointed that there was not a public blowing-off, but we believed that he had gone on to prepare for Miss Emily's coming, or to give her a chance to get rid of the cousins. (By that time it was a cabal, and we were all Miss Emily's allies to help circumvent the cousins.) Sure enough, after another week they departed. And, as we had expected all along, within three days Homer Barron was back in town. A neighbor saw the Negro man admit him at the kitchen door at dusk one evening.

And that was the last we saw of Homer Barron. And of Miss Emily for some time. The Negro man went in and out with the market basket, but the front door remained closed. Now and then we would see her at a window for a moment, as the men did that night when they sprinked the lime, but for almost six months she did not appear on the streets. Then we knew that this was to be expected too; as if that quality of her father which had thwarted her woman's life so many times had been too virulent and too furious to die.

When we next saw Miss Emily, she had grown fat and her hair was turning gray. During the next few years it grew grayer and grayer until it attained an even pepper-and-salt iron-gray, when it ceased turning. Up to the day of her death at seventy-four it was still that vigorous iron-gray, like the hair of an active man.

From that time on her front door remained closed, save for a period of six or seven years, when she was about forty, during which she gave lessons in china-painting. She fitted up a studio in one of the downstairs rooms, where the daughters and granddaughters of Colonel Sartoris' contemporaries were sent to her with the same regularity and in the same spirit that they were sent on Sundays with a twenty-five cent piece for the collection plate. Meanwhile her taxes had been remitted.

Then the newer generation became the backbone and the spirit of the town, and the painting pupils grew up and fell away and did not send their children to her with boxes of color and tedious brushes and pictures cut from the ladies' magazines. The front door closed upon the last one and remained closed for good. When the town got free postal delivery Miss Emily alone refused to let them fasten the metal numbers above her door and attach a mailbox to it. She would not listen to them.

Daily, monthly, yearly we watched the Negro grow grayer and more stooped, going in and out with the market basket. Each December we sent her a tax notice, which would be returned by the post office a week later, unclaimed. Now and then we would see her in one of the downstairs windows—she had evidently shut up the top floor of the house—like the carven torso of an idol in a niche, looking or not looking at us, we could never tell which. Thus she passed from generation to generation—dear, inescapable, impervious, tranquil, and perverse.

And so she died. Fell ill in the house filled with dust and shadows, with only a doddering Negro man to wait on her. We did not even know she was sick; we had long since given up trying to get any information from the Negro. He talked to no one, probably not even to her, for his voice had grown harsh and rusty, as if from disuse.

She died in one of the downstairs rooms, in a heavy walnut bed with a curtain, her gray head propped on a pillow yellow and moldy with age and lack of sunlight.

5

The Negro met the first of the ladies at the front door and let them in, with their hushed, sibilant voices and their quick, curious glances, and then he disappeared. He walked right through the house and out the back and was not seen again.

The two female cousins came at once. They held the funeral on the second day, with the town coming to look at Miss Emily beneath a mass of bought flowers, with the crayon face of her father musing profoundly above the bier and the ladies sibilant and macabre; and the very old men—some in their brushed Confederate uniforms—on the porch and the lawn, talking of Miss Emily as if she had been a contemporary of theirs, believing that they had danced with her and courted her perhaps, confusing time with its mathematical progression, as the old do, to whom all the past is not a diminishing road, but, instead, a huge meadow which no winter ever quite touches, divided from them now by the narrow bottle-neck of the most recent decade of years.

Already we knew that there was one room in that region above stairs which no one had seen in forty years, and which would have to be forced. They waited until Miss Emily was decently in the ground before they opened it.

The violence of breaking down the door seemed to fill this room with pervading dust. A thin, acrid pall as of the tomb seemed to lie everywhere upon this room decked and furnished as for a bridal: upon the valance curtains of faded rose color, upon the rose-shaded lights, upon the dressing table, upon the delicate array of crystal and the man's toilet things backed with tarnished silver, silver so tarnished that the monogram was obscured. Among them lay a collar and tie, as if they had just been removed, which, lifted, left upon the surface a pale crescent in the dust. Upon a chair hung the suit, carefully folded; beneath it the two mute shoes and the discarded socks.

The man himself lay in the bed.

For a long while we just stood there, looking down at the profound and fleshless grin. The body had apparently once lain in the attitude of an embrace, but now the long sleep that outlasts love, that conquers even the grimace of love, had cuckolded him. What was left of him, rotted beneath what was left of the nightshirt, had become inextricable from the bed in which he lay; and upon him and upon the pillow beside him lay that even coating of the patient and biding dust.

Then we noticed that in the second pillow was the indentation of a head. One of us lifted something from it, and leaning forward, that faint and invisible dust dry and acrid in the nostrils, we saw a long strand of iron-gray hair.

Exercises
1. *Discuss the conflict and how it is resolved.*

2. *Describe Miss Emily's personality. What kind of person is she?*

3. *Detail both the physical and historical setting of the story. To what extent do they influence Miss Emily?*
4. *What social and psychological forces have helped shape Miss Emily's character?*

5. *Explain the credibility of her psychotic behavior. Why does she act the way she does?*

6. *What details of Miss Emily's environment, personality, and behavior lead you to an understanding of the meaning of the story?*

7. *In a few sentences summarize the meaning of the story.*

8. *What is Homer Barron's function in the story?*

Topics for Writing

1. *Examine Faulkner's basic attitude toward the declining Southern aristocratic tradition as expressed in this story.*

2. *Illustrate Faulkner's elaborate handling of time.*

3. *Explain the past as a character in the story.*

4. *Write an essay depicting Miss Emily as a tragic figure.*

Selected Bibliography

William Faulkner

Adams, Richard P. "The Apprenticeship of William Faulkner." *Tulane Studies in English*, 12 (1962), 113–156.

————. *Faulkner: Myth and Motion*. Princeton: Princeton University Press, 1968.

Arthos, John. "Ritual and Humor in the Writing of William Faulkner." *Accent*, 9 (1948), 17–30.

Bowling, Lawrence E. "Faulkner and the Theme of Innocence." *Kenyon Review*, 20 (1958), 466–487.

Brooks, Cleanth. "William Faulkner: Vision of Good and Evil." In *The Hidden God: Studies in Hemingway, Faulkner, Yeats, Eliot, and Warren*. New Haven and London: Yale University Press, 1963, pp. 22–43.

Clements, Arthur L., and Sister Mary Bride. "Faulkner's 'A Rose for Emily.'" *Explicator*, 20 (1962), 78.

Going, W. T. "Faulkner's 'A Rose for Emily.'" *Explicator*, 16 (1958), 27.

Grenier, Cynthia. "The Art of Fiction: An Interview with William Faulkner—September, 1955." *Accent*, 16 (1956), 167–177.

Hagopian, John V., and Martin Dolch. "Faulkner's 'A Rose for Emily.'" *Explicator*, 22 (1964), 68.

Hoffman, Frederick J., and Olga W. Vickery, eds. *William Faulkner: Three Decades of Criticism*. Lansing: Michigan State University Press, 1960.

Howell, Elmo. "Faulkner's 'A Rose for Emily.'" *Explicator*, 19 (1961), 26.

Johnson, C. W. M. "Faulkner's 'A Rose for Emily.'" *Explicator*, 6 (1948), 45.

Litz, Walton. "William Faulkner's Moral Vision." *Southwest Review*, 37 (1952), 200–209.

Slatoff, Walter J. *Quest For Failure: A Study of William Faulkner.* Ithaca: Cornell University Press, 1960.

Stein, Jean. "The Art of Fiction XII: William Faulkner." *Paris Review*, 4 (1956), 28–52.

Waggoner, Hyatt H. *William Faulkner: From Jefferson to The World.* Lexington: University of Kentucky Press, 1959.

Warren, Robert Penn, ed. *Faulkner: A Collection of Critical Essays.* Englewood Cliffs, N. J.: Prentice-Hall, 1966.

Watkins, Floyd C. "The Structure of 'A Rose for Emily.'" *Modern Language Notes*, 69 (1954), 508–510.

West, R. B. "Atmosphere and Theme in Faulkner's 'A Rose for Emily.'" *Perspective*, 2 (1949), 239–245.

———. "Faulkner's 'A Rose for Emily.'" *Explicator*, 7 (1948), 8.

Herman Melville *(1819–1891)*

Born in New York City, he shipped out to sea as a cabin boy at the age of eighteen, returned to the mainland to try his hand at several odd jobs, ran away again on a whaling ship, but deserted the crew to spend time among the island natives. About his exotic adventures he wrote two novels, Typee *(1846) and* Omoo *(1847), which immediately established his reputation as a writer.* Moby Dick *(1851), now considered his chef-d'oeuvre, was in its first printing a commercial failure.* Pierre *(1852) was a critical disaster. Publishing only an occasional novel and some poetry, he spent his last twenty-five years as Deputy Inspector for Customs in New York City. At the time of his death he was all but forgotten as a writer. But* Billy Budd, *found in a trunk of manuscripts and published posthumously in 1924, rescued him from near oblivion.*

Bartleby, the Scrivener

I am a rather elderly man. The nature of my avocations, for the last thirty years, has brought me into more than ordinary contact with what would seem an interesting and somewhat singular set of men, of whom, as yet, nothing, that I know of, has ever been written—I mean, the law-copyists, or scriveners. I have known very many of them, professionally and privately, and, if I pleased, could relate divers histories, at which good-natured gentlemen might smile, and sentimental souls might weep. But I waive the biographies of all other scriveners, for a few passages in the life of Bartleby, who was a scrivener, the strangest I ever saw, or heard of. While, of other law-copyists, I might write the complete life, of Bartleby nothing of that sort can be done. I believe that no materials exist, for a full and satisfactory biography of this man. It is an irreparable loss to literature. Bartleby was one of those beings of whom nothing is ascertainable, except from the original sources, and, in his case, those are very small. What my own astonished eyes saw of Bartleby, *that* is all I know of him, except, indeed, one vague report, which will appear in the sequel.

Ere introducing the scrivener, as he first appeared to me, it is fit I make some mention of myself, my *employes*, my business, my chambers, and general surroundings; because some such description is indispensable to an adequate understanding of the chief character about to be presented. Imprimis: I am a man who, from his youth upwards, has been filled with a profound conviction that the easiest way of life is the best. Hence, though I belong to a profession proverbially energetic and nervous, even to turbulence, at times, yet nothing of that sort have I ever suffered to invade my peace. I am one of those unambitious lawyers who never addresses a jury, or in any way draws down public applause; but, in the cool tranquillity of a snug retreat, do a snug business among rich men's bonds, and mortgages, and title-deeds. All who know me, consider me an eminently *safe* man. The last John Jacob Astor, a personage little given to poetic enthusiasm, had no hesitation in pronouncing my first grand point to be prudence; my next, method. I do not speak it in vanity, but simply record the fact, that I was not unemployed in my profession by the late John Jacob Astor; a name which, I admit, I love to repeat; for it hath a rounded and orbicular sound to it, and rings like unto bullion. I will freely add, that I was not insensible to the late John Jacob Astor's good opinion.

Some time prior to the period at which this little history begins, my avocations had been largely increased. The good old office, now extinct in the State of New York, of a Master in Chancery, had been conferred upon me. It was not a very arduous office, but very pleasantly remunerative. I seldom lose my temper; much more seldom indulge in dangerous indignation at wrongs and outrages; but, I must be permitted to be rash here, and declare, that I consider the sudden and violent abrogation of the office of Master in Chancery, by the new Constitution, as a ——— premature act; inasmuch as I had counted upon a life-lease of the profits, whereas I only received those of a few short years. But this is by the way.

My chambers were up stairs, at No. ——— Wall Street. At one end, they looked upon the white wall of the interior of a spacious sky-light shaft, penetrating the building from top to bottom.

This view might have been considered rather tame than otherwise, deficient in what landscape painters call "life." But, if so, the view from the other end of my chambers offered, at least, a contrast, if nothing more. In that direction, my windows commanded an unobstructed view of a lofty brick wall, black by age and everlasting shade; which wall required no spy-glass to bring out its lurking beauties, but, for the benefit of all near-sighted spectators, was pushed up to within ten feet of my window panes. Owing to the great height of the surrounding buildings, and my chambers being on the second floor, the interval between this wall and mine not a little resembled a huge square cistern.

   At the period just preceding the advent of Bartleby, I had two copyists in my employment, and a promising lad as an office-boy. First, Turkey; second, Nippers; third, Ginger Nut. These may seem names, the like of which are not usually found in the Directory. In truth, they were nicknames, mutually conferred upon each other by my three clerks, and were deemed expressive of their respective persons or characters. Turkey was a short, pursy Englishman, of about my own age—that is, somewhere not far from sixty. In the morning, one might say, his face was of a fine florid hue, but after twelve o'clock, meridian—his dinner hour—it blazed like a grate full of Christmas coals; and continued blazing—but, as it were, with a gradual wane—till six o'clock, P.M., or thereabouts; after which, I saw no more of the proprietor of the face, which, gaining its meridian with the sun, seemed to set with it, to rise, culminate, and decline the following day, with the like regularity and undiminished glory. There are many singular coincidences I have known in the course of my life, not the least among which was the fact, that, exactly when Turkey displayed his fullest beams from his red and radiant countenance, just then, too, at that critical moment, began the daily period when I considered his business capacities as seriously disturbed for the remainder of the twenty-four hours. Not that he was absolutely idle, or averse to business, then; far from it. The difficulty was, he was apt to be altogether too energetic. There was a strange, inflamed, flurried, flighty recklessness of activity about him. He would be incautious in dipping his pen into his inkstand. All his blots upon my documents were dropped there after twelve o'clock, meridian. Indeed, not only would he be reckless, and sadly given to making blots in the afternoon, but, some days, he went further, and was rather noisy. At such times, too, his face flamed with augmented blazonry, as if cannel coal had been heaped on anthracite. He made an unpleasant racket with his chair; spilled his sand-box; in mending his pens, impatiently split them all to pieces, and threw them on the floor in a sudden passion; stood up, and leaned over his table, boxing his papers about in a most indecorous manner, very sad to behold in an elderly man like him. Nevertheless, as he was in many ways a most valuable person to me, and all the time before twelve o'clock, meridian, was the quickest, steadiest creature, too, accomplishing a great deal of work in a style not easily to be matched—for these reasons, I was willing to overlook his eccentricities, though, indeed, occasionally, I remonstrated with him. I did this very gently, however, because, though the civilest, nay, the blandest and most reverential of men in the morning, yet, in the afternoon, he was disposed, upon provocation, to be slightly rash with his tongue—in fact, insolent. Now, valuing his morning services as I did, and resolved not to lose them—yet, at the same time, made uncomfortable by his inflamed ways after twelve o'clock—and being a man of peace, unwilling by my admonitions to call forth unseemly retorts from him, I took upon me, one Saturday noon (he was always worse on Saturdays) to hint to him, very kindly, that, perhaps, now that he was growing old, it might be well to abridge his labors; in short, he need not come to my chambers after twelve o'clock, but, dinner over, had best go home to his lodgings, and rest himself till tea-time. But no; he insisted upon his afternoon devotions. His countenance became intolerably fervid, as he oratorically assured me—gesticulating with a long ruler at the other end of the room—that if his services in the morning were useful, how indispensable, then, in the afternoon?

"With submission, sir," said Turkey, on this occasion. "I consider myself your right-hand man. In the morning I but marshal and deploy my columns; but in the afternoon I put myself at their head, and gallantly charge the foe, thus"—and he made a violent thrust with the ruler.

"But the blots, Turkey," intimated I.

"True; but, with submission, sir, behold these hairs! I am getting old. Surely, sir, a blot or two of a warm afternoon is not to be severely urged against gray hairs. Old age—even if it blot the page—is honorable. With submission, sir, we *both* are getting old."

This appeal to my fellow-feeling was hardly to be resisted. At all events, I saw that go he would not. So, I made up my mind to let him stay, resolving, nevertheless, to see to it that, during the afternoon, he had to do with my less important papers.

Nippers, the second on my list, was a whiskered, sallow, and, upon the whole, rather piratical-looking young man, of about five and twenty. I always deemed him the victim of two evil powers— ambition and indigestion. The ambition was evinced by a certain impatience of the duties of a mere copyist, an unwarrantable usurpation of strictly professional affairs, such as the original drawing up of legal documents. The indigestion seemed betokened in an occasional nervous testiness and grinning irritability, causing the teeth to audibly grind together over mistakes committed in copying; unnecessary maledictions, hissed, rather than spoken, in the heat of business; and especially by a continual discontent with the height of the table where he worked. Though of a very ingenious mechanical turn, Nippers could never get this table to suit him. He put chips under it, blocks of various sorts, bits of pasteboard, and at last went so far as to attempt an exquisite adjustment, by final pieces of folded blotting-paper. But no invention would answer. If, for the sake of easing his back, he brought the table lid at a sharp angle well up towards his chin, and wrote there like a man using the steep roof of a Dutch house for his desk, then he declared that it stopped the circulation in his arms. If now he lowered the table to his waistbands, and stooped over it in writing, then there was a sore aching in his back. In short, the truth of the matter was, Nippers knew not what he wanted. Or, if he wanted anything, it was to be rid of a scrivener's table altogether. Among the manifestations of his diseased ambition was a fondness he had for receiving visits from certain ambiguous-looking fellows in seedy coats, whom he called his clients. Indeed, I was aware that not only was he, at times, considerable of a ward-politician, but he occasionally did a little business at the Justices' courts, and was not unknown on the steps of the Tombs. I have good reason to believe, however, that one individual who called upon him at my chambers, and who, with a grand air, he insisted was his client, was no other than a dun, and the alleged title-deed, a bill. But, with all his failings, and the annoyances he caused me, Nippers, like his compatriot Turkey, was a very useful man to me; wrote a neat, swift hand; and, when he chose, was not deficient in a gentlemanly sort of deportment. Added to this, he always dressed in a gentlemanly sort of way; and so; incidentally, reflected credit upon my chambers. Whereas, with respect to Turkey, I had much ado to keep him from being a reproach to me. His clothes were apt to look oily, and smell of eating-houses. He wore his pantaloons very loose and baggy in summer. His coats were execrable; his hat not to be handled. But while the hat was a thing of indifference to me, inasmuch as his natural civility and deference, as a dependent Englishman, always led him to doff it the moment he entered the room, yet his coat was another matter. Concerning his coats, I reasoned with him; but with no effect. The truth was, I suppose, that a man with so small an income could not afford to sport such a lustrous face and a lustrous coat at one and the same time. As Nippers once observed, Turkey's money went chiefly for red ink. One winter day, I presented Turkey with a highly respectable-looking coat of my own—a padded gray coat, of a most comfortable warmth, and which buttoned straight up from the knee to the neck. I thought Turkey would appreciate the favor, and abate his rashness and obstreperousness of afternoons. But no; I verily believe that buttoning himself up in so downy and blanket-like a coat had a pernicious effect upon him—upon the same principle that too much oats are bad for horses. In fact, precisely as a rash, restive horse is said to feel his oats, so Turkey felt his coat. It made him insolent. He was a man whom prosperity harmed.

Though, concerning the self-indulgent habits of Turkey, I had my own private surmises, yet, touching Nippers, I was well persuaded that, whatever might be his faults in other respects, he was, at least, a temperate young man. But, indeed, nature herself seemed to have been his vintner, and, at his birth, charged him so thoroughly with an irritable, brandy-like disposition, that all subsequent potations were needless. When I consider how, amid the stillness of my chambers, Nippers would sometimes impatiently rise from his seat, and stooping over his table, spread his arms wide apart, seize the whole desk, and move it, and jerk it, with a grim, grinding motion on the floor, as if the table were a perverse voluntary agent, intent on thwarting and vexing him. I plainly perceive that, for Nippers, brandy-and-water were altogether superflous.

It was fortunate for me that, owing to its peculiar cause—indigestion—the irritability and consequent nervousness of Nippers were mainly observable in the morning, while in the afternoon he was comparatively mild. So that, Turkey's paroxysms only coming on about twelve o'clock, I never had to do with their eccentricities at one time. Their fits relieved each other, like guards. When Nippers's was on, Turkey's was off; and *vice versa*. This was a good natural arrangement, under the circumstances.

Ginger Nut, the third on my list, was a lad, some twelve years old. His father was a car-man, ambitious of seeing his son on the bench instead of a cart, before he died. So he sent him to my office, as student at law, errand-boy, cleaner and sweeper, at the rate of one dollar a week. He had a little desk to himself, but he did not use it much. Upon inspection, the drawer exhibited a great array of the shells of various sorts of nuts. Indeed, to this quick-witted youth, the whole noble science of the law was contained in a nut-shell. Not the least among the employments of Ginger Nut, as well as one which he discharged with the most alacrity, was his duty as cake and apple purveyor for Turkey and Nippers. Copying law-papers being proverbially a dry, husky sort of business, my two scriveners were fain to moisten their mouths very often with Spitzenbergs, to be had at the numerous stalls nigh the Custom House and Post Office. Also, they sent Ginger Nut very frequently for that peculiar cake—small, flat, round, and very spicy—after which he had been named by them. Of a cold morning, when business was but dull, Turkey would gobble up scores of these cakes, as if they were mere wafers—indeed, they sell them at the rate of six or eight for a penny—the scrape of his pen blending with the crunching of the crisp particles in his mouth. Of all the fiery afternoon blunders and flurried rashnesses of Turkey, was his once moistening a ginger-cake between his lips, and clapping it on to a mortgage, for a seal. I came within an ace of dismissing him then. But he mollified me by making an oriental bow, and saying—

"With submission, sir, it was generous of me to find you in stationery on my own account."

Now my original business—that of a conveyancer and title hunter, and drawer-up of recondite documents of all sorts—was considerably increased by receiving the master's office. There was now great work for scriveners. Not only must I push the clerks already with me, but I must have additional help.

In answer to my advertisement, a motionless young man one morning stood upon my office threshold, the door being open, for it was summer. I can see that figure now—pallidly neat, pitiably respectable, incurably forlorn! It was Bartleby.

After a few words touching his qualifications, I engaged him, glad to have among my corps of copyists a man of so singularly sedate an aspect, which I thought might operate beneficially upon the flighty temper of Turkey, and the fiery one of Nippers.

I should have stated before that ground glass folding-doors divided my premises into two parts, one of which was occupied by my scriveners, the other by myself. According to my humor, I threw open these doors, or closed them. I resolved to assign Bartleby a corner by the folding-doors, but on my side of them, so as to have this quiet man within easy call, in case any trifling thing was to be done. I placed his desk close up to a small side-window in that part of the room, a window which originally had afforded a lateral view of certain grimy back-yards and bricks, but which, owing to subsequent erections, commanded at present no view at all, though it gave some light. Within three feet of the panes was a wall, and the light came down from far above, between two lofty buildings, as from a very small opening in a dome. Still further to a satisfactory arrangement, I procured a high green folding screen, which might entirely isolate Bartleby from my sight, though not remove him from my voice. And thus, in a manner, privacy and society were conjoined.

At first, Bartleby did an extraordinary quantity of writing. As if long famishing for something to copy, he seemed to gorge himself on my documents. There was no pause for digestion. He ran a day and night line, copying by sun-light and by candle-light. I should have been quite delighted with his application, had he been cheerfully industrious. But he wrote on silently, palely, mechanically.

It is, of course, an indispensable part of a scrivener's business to verify the accuracy of his copy, word by word. Where there are two or more scriveners in an office, they assist each other in this examination, one reading from the copy, the other holding the original. It is a very dull, wearisome, and lethargic affair. I can readily imagine that, to some sanguine temperaments, it would be altogether intolerable. For example, I cannot credit that the mettlesome poet, Byron, would have contentedly sat down with Bartleby to examine a law document of, say five hundred pages, closely written in a crimpy hand.

Now and then, in the haste of business, it had been my habit to assist in comparing some brief document myself, calling Turkey or Nippers for this purpose. One object I had, in placing Bartleby so handy to me behind the screen, was, to avail myself of his services on such trivial occasions. It was on the third day, I think, of his being with me, and before any necessity had arisen for having his own writing examined, that, being much hurried to complete a small affair I had in hand, I abruptly called to Bartleby. In my haste and natural expectancy of instant compliance, I sat with my head bent over the original on my desk, and my right hand sideways, and somewhat nervously extended with the copy, so that, immediately upon emerging from his retreat, Bartleby might snatch it and proceed to business without the least delay.

In this very attitude did I sit when I called to him,

rapidly stating what it was I wanted him to do—namely, to examine a small paper with me. Imagine my surprise, nay, my consternation, when, without moving from his privacy, Bartleby, in a singularly mild, firm voice, replied, "I would prefer not to."

I sat awhile in perfect silence, rallying my stunned faculties. Immediately it occurred to me that my ears had deceived me, or Bartleby had entirely misunderstood my meaning. I repeated my request in the clearest tone I could assume; but in quite as clear a one came the previous reply, "I would prefer not to."

"Prefer not to," echoed I, rising in high excitement, and crossing the room with a stride. "What do you mean? Are you moon-struck? I want you to help me compare this sheet here—take it," and I thrust it towards him.

"I would prefer not to," said he.

I looked at him steadfastly. His face was leanly composed; his gray eye dimly calm. Not a wrinkle of agitation rippled him. Had there been the least uneasiness, anger, impatience or impertinence in his manner; in other words, had there been anything ordinarily human about him, doubtless I should have violently dismissed him from the premises. But as it was, I should have as soon thought of turning my pale plaster-of-paris bust of Cicero out of doors. I stood gazing at him awhile, as he went on with his own writing, and then reseated myself at my desk. This is very strange, thought I. What had one best do? But my business hurried me. I concluded to forget the matter for the present, reserving it for my future leisure. So calling Nippers from the other room, the paper was speedily examined.

A few days after this, Bartleby concluded four lengthy documents, being quadruplicates of a week's testimony taken before me in my High Court of Chancery. It became necessary to examine them. It was an important suit, and great accuracy was imperative. Having all things arranged, I called Turkey, Nippers, and Ginger Nut, from the next room, meaning to place the four copies in the hands of my four clerks, while I should read from the original. Accordingly, Turkey, Nippers, and Ginger Nut had taken their seats in a row, each with his document in his hand, when I called to Bartleby to join this interesting group.

"Bartleby! quick, I am waiting."

I heard a slow scrape of his chair legs on the uncarpeted floor, and soon he appeared standing at the entrance of his hermitage.

"What is wanted?" said he, mildly.

"The copies, the copies," said I, hurriedly. "We are going to examine them. There"—and I held towards him the fourth quadruplicate.

"I would prefer not to," he said, and gently disappeared behind the screen.

For a few moments I was turned into a pillar of salt,

standing at the head of my seated column of clerks. Recovering myself, I advanced towards the screen, and demanded the reason for such extraordinary conduct.

"*Why* do you refuse?"

"I would prefer not to."

With any other man I should have flown outright into a dreadful passion, scorned all further words, and thrust him ignominiously from my presence. But there was something about Bartleby that not only strangely disarmed me, but, in a wonderful manner, touched and disconcerted me. I began to reason with him.

"These are your own copies we are about to examine. It is labor saving to you, because one examination will answer for your four papers. It is common usage. Every copyist is bound to help examine his copy. Is it not so? Will you not speak? Answer!"

"I prefer not to," he replied in a flutelike tone. It seemed to me that, while I had been addressing him, he carefully revolved every statement that I made; fully comprehended the meaning; could not gainsay the irresistible conclusion, but, at the same time, some paramount consideration prevailed with him to reply as he did.

"You are decided, then, not to comply with my request—a request made according to common usage and common sense?"

He briefly gave me to understand, that on that point my judgment was sound. Yes: his decision was irreversible.

It is not seldom the case that, when a man is browbeaten in some unprecedented and violently unreasonable way, he begins to stagger in his own plainest faith. He begins, as it were, vaguely to surmise that, wonderful as it may be, all the justice and all the reason is on the other side. Accordingly, if any disinterested persons are present, he turns to them for some reinforcement of his own faltering mind.

"Turkey," said I, "what do you think of this? Am I not right?"

"With 'submission, sir," said Turkey, in his blandest tone, "I think that you are."

"Nippers," said I, "what do you think of it?"

"I think I should kick him out of the office."

(The reader, of nice perceptions, will here perceive that, it being morning, Turkey's answer is couched in polite and tranquil terms, but Nippers replies in ill-tempered ones. Or, to repeat a previous sentence, Nippers's ugly mood was on duty, and Turkey's off.)

"Ginger Nut," said I, willing to enlist the smallest suffrage in my behalf, "what do you think of it?"

"I think, sir, he's a little *luny*," replied Ginger Nut, with a grin.

"You hear what they say," said I, turning towards the screen, "come forth and do your duty."

But he vouchsafed no reply. I pondered a moment in

sore perplexity. But once more business hurried me. I determined again to postpone the consideration of this dilemma to my future leisure. With a little trouble we made out to examine the papers without Bartleby, though at every page or two Turkey deferentially dropped his opinion, that this proceeding was quite out of the common; while Nippers, twitching in his chair with a dyspeptic nervousness, ground out, between his set teeth, occasional hissing maledictions against the stubborn oaf behind the screen. And for his (Nippers's) part, this was the first and the last time he would do another man's business without pay.

Meanwhile Bartleby sat in his hermitage, oblivious to everything but his own peculiar business there.

Some days passed, the scrivener being employed upon another lengthy work. His late remarkable conduct led me to regard his ways narrowly. I observed that he never went to dinner; indeed, that he never went anywhere. As yet I had never, of my personal knowledge, known him to be outside of my office. He was a perpetual sentry in the corner. At about eleven o'clock though, in the morning, I noticed that Ginger Nut would advance toward the opening in Bartleby's screen, as if silently beckoned thither by a gesture invisible to me where I sat. The boy would then leave the office, jingling a few pence, and reappear with a handful of ginger-nuts, which he delivered in the hermitage, receiving two of the cakes for his trouble.

He lives, then, on ginger-nuts, thought I; never eats a dinner, properly speaking; he must be a vegetarian, then; but no! he never eats even vegetables, he eats nothing but ginger-nuts. My mind then ran on in reveries concerning the probable effects upon the human constitution of living entirely on ginger-nuts. Ginger-nuts are so called, because they contain ginger as one of their peculiar constituents, and the final flavoring one. Now, what was ginger? A hot, spicy thing. Was Bartleby hot and spicy? Not at all. Ginger, then, had no effect upon Bartleby. Probably he preferred it should have none.

Nothing so aggravates an earnest person as a passive resistance. If the individual so resisted be of a not inhumane temper, and the resisting one perfectly harmless in his passivity, then, in the better moods of the former, he will endeavor charitably to construe to his imagination what proves impossible to be solved by his judgment. Even so, for the most part, I regarded Bartleby and his ways. Poor fellow! thought I, he means no mischief; it is plain he intends no insolence; his aspect sufficiently evinces that his eccentricities are involuntary. He is useful to me. I can get along with him. If I turn away, the chances are he will fall in with some less-indulgent employer, and then he will be rudely treated, and perhaps driven forth miserably to starve. Yes. Here I can cheaply purchase a delicious self-approval. To befriend Bartleby; to humor him in his strange willfulness, will cost me little or nothing, while I lay up in my soul what will eventually prove a sweet morsel for my conscience. But this mood was not invariable with me. The passiveness of Bartleby sometimes irritated me. I felt strangely goaded on to encounter him in new opposition—to elicit some angry spark from him answerable to my own. But, indeed, I might as well have essayed to strike fire with my knuckles against a bit of Windsor soap. But one afternoon the evil impulse in me mastered me, and the following little scene ensued:

"Bartleby," said I, "when those papers are all copied, I will compare them with you."

"I would prefer not to."

"How? Surely you do not mean to persist in that mulish vagary?"

No answer.

I threw open the folding-doors near by, and, turning upon Turkey and Nippers, exclaimed:

"Bartleby a second time says, he won't examine his papers. What do you think of it, Turkey?"

It was afternoon, be it remembered. Turkey sat glowing like a brass boiler; his bald head steaming; his hands reeling among his blotted papers.

"Think of it?" roared Turkey; "I think I'll just step behind his screen, and black his eyes for him!"

So saying, Turkey rose to his feet and threw his arms into a pugilistic position. He was hurrying away to make good his promise, when I detained him, alarmed at the effect of incautiously rousing Turkey's combativeness after dinner.

"Sit down, Turkey," said I, "and hear what Nippers has to say. What do you think of it, Nippers? Would I not be justified in immediately dismissing Bartleby?"

"Excuse me, that is for you to decide, sir. I think his conduct quite unusual, and, indeed, unjust, as regards Turkey and myself. But it may only be a passing whim."

"Ah," exclaimed I, "you have strangely changed your mind, then—you speak very gently of him now."

"All beer," cried Turkey; "gentleness is effects of beer—Nippers and I dined together to-day. You see how gentle I am, sir. Shall I go and black his eyes?"

"You refer to Bartleby, I suppose. No, not to-day, Turkey," I replied; "pray, put up your fists."

I closed the doors, and again advanced towards Bartleby. I felt additional incentives tempting me to my fate. I burned to be rebelled against again. I remembered that Bartleby never left the office.

"Bartleby," said I, "Ginger Nut is away; just step around to the Post Office, won't you? (it was but a three minutes' walk), and see if there is anything for me."

"I would prefer not to."

"You *will* not?"

"I *prefer* not."

I staggered to my desk, and sat there in a deep study. My blind inveteracy returned. Was there any other thing in which I could procure myself to be ignominiously repulsed by this lean, penniless wight?—my hired clerk? What added thing is there, perfectly reasonable, that he will be sure to refuse to do?

"Bartleby!"

No answer.

"Bartleby," in a louder tone.

No answer.

"Bartleby," I roared.

Like a very ghost, agreeable to the laws of magical invocation, at the third summons, he appeared at the entrance of his hermitage.

"Go to the next room, and tell Nippers to come to me."

"I prefer not to," he respectfully and slowly said, and mildly disappeared.

"Very good, Bartleby," said I, in a quiet sort of serenely-severe self-possessed tone, intimating the unalterable purpose of some terrible retribution very close at hand. At the moment I half intended something of the kind. But upon the whole, as it was drawing towards my dinner-hour, I thought it best to put on my hat and walk home for the day, suffering much from perplexity and distress of mind.

Shall I acknowledge it? The conclusion of this whole business was, that it soon became a fixed fact of my chambers, that a pale young scrivener, by the name of Bartleby, had a desk there; that he copied for me at the usual rate of four cents a folio (one hundred words); but he was permanently exempt from examining the work done by him, that duty being transferred to Turkey and Nippers, out of compliment, doubtless, to their superior acuteness; moreover, said Bartleby was never, on my account, to be dispatched on the most trivial errand of any sort; and that even if entreated to take upon him such a matter, it was generally understood that he would "prefer not to"—in other words, that he would refuse point-blank.

As days passed on, I became considerably reconciled to Bartleby. His steadiness, his freedom from all dissipation, his incessant industry (except when he chose to throw himself into a standing revery behind his screen), his great stillness, his unalterableness of demeanor under all circumstances, made him a valuable acquisition. One prime thing was this—*he was always there*—first in the morning, continually through the day, and the last at night. I had a singular confidence in his honesty. I felt my most precious papers perfectly safe in his hands. Sometimes, to be sure, I could not, for the very soul of me, avoid falling into sudden spasmodic passions with him. For it was exceeding difficult to bear in mind all the time those strange peculiarities, privileges, and unheard of exemptions, forming the tacit stipulations on Bartleby's part under which he remained in my office. Now and then, in the eagerness of dispatching pressing business, I would inadvertently summon Bartleby, in a short, rapid tone, to put his finger, say, on the incipient tie of a bit of red tape with which I was about compressing some papers. Of course, from behind the screen the usual answer, "I prefer not to," was sure to come; and then, how could a human creature, with the common infirmities of our nature, refrain from bitterly exclaiming upon such perverseness—such unreasonableness. However, every added repulse of this sort which I received only tended to lessen the probability of my repeating the inadvertence.

Here it must be said, that according to the custom of most legal gentlemen occupying chambers in densely-populated law buildings, there were several keys to my door. One was kept by a woman residing in the attic, which person weekly scrubbed and daily swept and dusted my apartments. Another was kept by Turkey for convenience sake. The third I sometimes carried in my own pocket. The fourth I knew not who had.

Now, one Sunday morning I happened to go to Trinity Church, to hear a celebrated preacher, and finding myself rather early on the ground I thought I would walk around to my chambers for a while. Luckily I had my key with me; but upon applying it to the lock, I found it resisted by something inserted from the inside. Quite surprised, I called out; when to my consternation a key was turned from within; and thrusting his lean visage at me, and holding the door ajar, the apparition of Bartleby appeared, in his shirt sleeves, and otherwise in a strangely tattered deshabille, saying quietly that he was sorry, but he was deeply engaged just then, and—preferred not admitting me at present. In a brief word or two, he moreover added, that perhaps I had better walk around the block two or three times, and by that time he would probably have concluded his affairs.

Now, the utterly unsurmised appearance of Bartleby, tenanting my law-chambers of a Sunday morning, and with his cadaverously gentlemanly *nonchalance*, yet withal firm and self-possessed, had such a strange effect upon me, that incontinently I slunk away from my own door, and did as desired. But not without sundry twinges of impotent rebellion against the mild effrontery of this unaccountable scrivener. Indeed, it was his wonderful mildness chiefly, which not only disarmed me, but unmanned me as it were. For I consider that one, for the time, is a sort of unmanned when he tranquilly permits his hired clerk to dictate to him, and order him away from his own premises. Furthermore, I was full of uneasiness as to what Bartleby could possibly be doing in my office in his shirt sleeves, and in an otherwise dismantled condition of a Sunday morning. Was anything amiss going on? Nay, that was out of the question. It was not to be thought of for a moment that Bartleby was an immoral person. But what could he be doing there?—copying? Nay again, whatever might be his eccentricities, Bartleby was an eminently decorous person. He would be the last man to sit down to his desk in any state approaching to nudity. Besides, it was Sunday; and there was something about Bartleby that forbade the supposition that he would by any secular occupation violate the proprieties of the day.

Nevertheless, my mind was not pacified; and full of a restless curiosity, at last I returned to the door. Without hindrance I inserted my key, opened it, and entered. Bartleby was not to be seen. I looked round anxiously, peeped behind his screen; but it was very plain that he was gone. Upon more closely examining the place, I surmised that for an indefinite period Bartleby must have ate, dressed, and slept in my office, and that, too without plate, mirror, or bed. The cushioned seat of a rickety old sofa in one corner bore the faint impress of a lean, reclining form. Rolled away under his desk, I found a blanket; under the empty grate, a blacking box and brush; on a chair, a tin basin, with soap and a ragged towel; in a newspaper a few crumbs of ginger-nuts and a morsel of cheese. Yes, thought I, it is evident enough that Bartleby has been making his home here, keeping bachelor's hall all by himself. Immediately then the thought came sweeping across me, what miserable friendlessness and loneliness are here revealed! His poverty is great; but his solitude, how horrible! Think of it. Of a Sunday, Wall Street is deserted as Petra; and every night of every day it is an emptiness. This building, too, which of week-days hums with industry and life, at nightfall echoes with sheer vacancy, and all through Sunday is forlorn. And here Bartleby makes his home; sole spectator of a solitude which he has seen all populous—a sort of innocent and transformed Marius brooding among the ruins of Carthage!

For the first time in my life a feeling of over-powering stinging melancholy seized me. Before, I had never experienced aught but a not unpleasing sadness. The bond of a common humanity now drew me irresistibly to gloom. A fraternal melancholy! For both I and Bartleby were sons of Adam. I remembered the bright silks and sparkling faces I had seen that day, in gala trim, swan-like sailing down the Mississippi of Broadway; and I contrasted them with the pallid copyist, and thought to myself, Ah, happiness courts the light, so we deem the world is gay; but misery hides aloof, so we deem that misery there is none. These sad fancyings—chimeras, doubtless, of a sick and silly brain—led on to other and more special thoughts, concerning the eccentricities of Bartleby. Presentiments of strange discoveries hovered round me. The scrivener's pale form appeared to me laid out, among uncaring strangers, in its shivering winding sheet.

Suddenly I was attracted by Bartleby's closed desk, the key in open sight left in the lock.

I mean no mischief, seek the gratification of no heartless curiosity, thought I; besides, the desk is mine, and its contents, too, so I will make bold to look within. Everything was methodically arranged, the papers smoothly placed. The pigeon holes were deep, and removing the files of documents, I groped into their recesses. Presently I felt something there, and dragged it out. It was an old bandanna handkerchief, heavy and knotted. I opened it, and saw it was a savings bank.

I now recalled all the quiet mysteries which I had noted in the man. I remembered that he never spoke but to answer; that, though at intervals he had considerable time to himself, yet I had never seen him reading—no, not even a newspaper; that for long periods he would stand looking out, at his pale window behind the screen, upon the dead brick wall; I was quite sure he never visited any refectory or eating house; while his pale face clearly indicated that he never drank beer like Turkey, or tea and coffee even, like other men; that he never went anywhere in particular that I could learn; never went out for a walk, unless, indeed, that was the case at present; that he had declined telling who he was, or whence he came, or whether he had any relatives in the world; that though so thin and pale, he never complained of ill health. And more than all, I remembered a certain unconscious air of pallid—how shall I call it?—of pallid haughtiness, say, or rather an austere reserve about him, which had positively awed me into my tame compliance with his eccentricities, when I had feared to ask him to do the slightest incidental thing for me, even though I might know, from his long-continued motionlessness, that behind his screen he must be standing in one of those dead-wall reveries of his.

Revolving all these things, and coupling them with the recently discovered fact, that he made my office his constant abiding place and home, and not forgetful of his morbid moodiness; revolving all these things, a prudential feeling began to steal over me. My first emotions had been those of pure melancholy and sincerest pity; but just in proportion as the forlornness of Bartleby grew and grew to my imagination, did that same melancholy merge into fear, that pity into repulsion. So true it is, and so terrible, too, that up to a certain point the thought or sight of misery enlists our best affections; but, in certain special cases, beyond that point it does not. They err who would assert that invariably this is owing to the inherent selfishness of the human heart. It rather proceeds from a certain hopelessness of remedying excessive and organic ill. To a sensitive being, pity is not seldom pain. And when at last it is perceived that such pity cannot lead to effectual succor, common sense bids the soul be rid of it. What I saw that morning persuaded me that the scrivener was the victim of innate and incurable disorder. I might give alms to his body; but his body did not pain him; it was his soul that suffered, and his soul I could not reach.

I did not accomplish the purpose of going to Trinity Church that morning. Somehow, the things I had seen disqualified me for the time from church-going. I walked homeward, thinking what I would do with Bartleby. Finally, I resolved upon this—I would put certain calm questions to him the next morning, touching his history, etc., and if he declined to answer them openly and unreservedly (and I supposed he would prefer not), then to give him a twenty dollar bill over and above whatever I might owe him, and tell him his services were no longer required; but that if in any other way I could assist him, I would be happy to do so, especially if he desired to return to his native place, wherever that might be, I would willingly help to defray the expenses. Moreover, if, after reaching home, he found himself at any time in want of aid, a letter from him would be sure of a reply.

The next morning came.

"Bartleby," said I, gently calling to him behind his screen.

No reply.

"Bartleby," said I, in a still gentler tone, "come here; I am not going to ask you to do anything you would prefer not to do—I simply wish to speak to you."

Upon this he noiselessly slid into view.

"Will you tell me, Bartleby, where you were born?"

"I would prefer not to."

"Will you tell me *anything* about yourself?"

"I would prefer not to."

"But what reasonable objection can you have to speak to me? I feel friendly towards you."

He did not look at me while I spoke, but kept his glance fixed upon my bust of Cicero, which, as I then sat, was directly behind me, some six inches above my head.

"What is your answer, Bartleby," said I, after waiting a considerable time for a reply, during which his countenance remained immovable, only there was the faintest conceivable tremor of the white attenuated mouth.

"At present I prefer to give no answer," he said, and retired into his hermitage.

It was rather weak in me I confess, but his manner, on this occasion, nettled me. Not only did there seem to lurk in it a certain calm disdain, but his perverseness seemed ungrateful, considering the undeniable good usage and indulgence he had received from me.

Again I sat ruminating what I should do. Mortified as I was at his behavior, and resolved as I had been to dismiss him when I entered my office, nevertheless I strangely felt something superstitious knocking at my heart, and forbidding me to carry out my purpose, and denouncing me for a villain if I dared to breathe one bitter word against this forlornest of mankind. At last, familiarly drawing my chair behind his screen, I sat down and said: "Bartleby, never mind, then, about revealing your history; but let me entreat you, as a friend, to comply as far as may be with the usages of this office. Say now, you will help to examine papers to-morrow or next day: in short, say now, that in a day or two you will begin to be a little reasonable:—say so, Bartleby."

"At present I would prefer not to be a little reasonable," was his mildly cadaverous reply.

Just then the folding-doors opened, and Nippers approached. He seemed suffering from an unusually bad night's rest, induced by severer indigestion than common. He overheard those final words of Bartleby.

"*Prefer not*, eh?" gritted Nippers—"I'd *prefer* him, if I were you, sir," addressing me—"I'd *prefer* him; I'd give him preferences, the stubborn mule! What is it sir, pray, that he *prefers* not to do now?"

Bartleby moved not a limb.

"Mr. Nippers," said I, "I'd prefer that you would withdraw for the present."

Somehow, of late, I had got into the way of involuntarily using this word "prefer" upon all sorts of not exactly suitable occasions. And I trembled to think that my contact with the scrivener had already and seriously affected me in a mental way. And what further and deeper aberration might it not yet produce? This apprehension had not been without efficacy in determining me to summary measures.

As Nippers, looking very sour and sulky, was departing, Turkey blandly and deferentially approached.

"With submission, sir," said he, "yesterday I was thinking about Bartleby here, and I think that if he would but prefer to take a quart of good ale every day, it would do much towards mending him, and enabling him to assist in examining his papers."

"So you have got the word, too," said I, slightly excited.

"With submission, what word, sir?" asked Turkey, respectfully crowding himself into the contracted space behind the screen, and by so doing, making me jostle the scrivener. "What word, sir?"

"I would prefer to be left alone here," said Bartleby, as if offended at being mobbed in his privacy.

"*That's* the word, Turkey," said I—"*that's* it."

"Oh, *prefer*? oh yes—queer word. I never use it myself. But, sir, as I was saying, if he would but prefer—"

"Turkey," interrupted I, "you will please withdraw."

"Oh, certainly, sir, if you prefer that I should."

As he opened the folding-door to retire, Nippers at his desk caught a glimpse of me, and asked whether I would prefer to have a certain paper copied on blue paper or white. He did not in the least roguishly accent the word prefer. It was plain that it involuntarily rolled from his tongue. I thought to myself, surely I must get rid of a demented man, who already has in some degree turned the tongues, if not the heads of myself and clerks. But I thought it prudent not to break the dismission at once.

The next day I noticed that Bartleby did nothing but stand at his window in his dead-wall revery. Upon asking him why he did not write, he said that he had decided upon doing no more writing.

"Why, how now? what next?" exclaimed I, "do no more writing?"

"No more."

"And what is the reason?"

"Do you not see the reason for yourself?" he indifferently replied.

I looked steadfastly at him, and perceived that his eyes looked dull and glazed. Instantly it occurred to me, that his unexampled diligence in copying by his dim window for the first few weeks of his stay with me might have temporarily impaired his vision.

I was touched. I said something in condolence with him. I hinted that of course he did wisely in abstaining from writing for a while; and urged him to embrace that opportunity of taking wholesome exercise in the open air. This, however, he did not do. A few days after this, my other clerks being absent, and being in a great hurry to dispatch certain letters by the mail, I thought that, having nothing else earthly to do, Bartleby would surely be less inflexible than usual, and carry these letters to the post-office. But he blankly declined. So, much to my inconvenience, I went myself.

Still added days went by. Whether Bartleby's eyes improved or not, I could not say. To all appearance, I thought they did. But when I asked him if they did, he vouchsafed no answer. At all events, he would do no copying. At last, in reply to my urgings, he informed me that he had permanently given up copying.

"What!" exclaimed I; "suppose your eyes should get entirely well—better than ever before—would you not copy then?"

"I have given up copying," he answered, and slid aside.

He remained as ever, a fixture in my chamber. Nay—if that were possible—he became still more of a fixture than before. What was to be done? He would do nothing in the office; why should he stay there? In plain fact, he had now become a millstone to me; not only useless as a necklace, but afflictive to bear. Yet I was sorry for him. I speak less than truth when I say that, on his own account, he occasioned me uneasiness. If he would but have named a single relative or friend, I would instantly have written, and urged their taking the poor fellow away to some convenient retreat. But he seemed alone, absolutely alone in the universe. A bit of wreck in the mid Atlantic. At length, necessities connected with my business tyrannized over all other considerations. Decently as I could, I told Bartleby that in six days time he must unconditionally leave the office. I warned him to take measures, in the interval, for procuring some other abode. I offered to assist him in this endeavor, if he himself would but take the first step towards a removal. "And when you finally quit me, Bartleby," added I, "I shall see that you go not away entirely unprovided. Six days from this hour, remember."

At the expiration of that period, I peeped behind the screen, and lo! Bartleby was there.

I buttoned up my coat, balanced myself; advanced

slowly towards him, touched his shoulder, and said, "The time has come; you must quit this place; I am sorry for you; here is money; but you must go."

"I would prefer not," he replied, with his back still towards me.

"You *must*."

He remained silent.

Now I had an unbounded confidence in this man's common honesty. He had frequently restored to me sixpences and shillings carelessly dropped upon the floor, for I am apt to be very reckless in such shirt-button affairs. The proceeding, then, which followed will not be deemed extraordinary.

"Bartleby," said I, "I owe you twelve dollars on account; here are thirty-two; the odd twenty are yours—Will you take it?" and I handed the bills towards him.

But he made no motion.

"I will leave them here, then," putting them under a weight on the table. Then taking my hat and cane and going to the door, I tranquilly turned and added—"After you have removed your things from these offices, Bartleby, you will of course lock the door—since every one is now gone for the day but you—and if you please, slip your key underneath the mat, so that I may have it in the morning. I shall not see you again; so good-by to you. If, hereafter, in your new place of abode, I can be of any service to you, do not fail to advise me by letter. Good-by, Bartleby, and fare you well."

But he answered not a word; like the last column of some ruined temple, he remained standing mute and solitary in the middle of the otherwise deserted room.

As I walked home in a pensive mood, my vanity got the better of my pity. I could not but highly plume myself on my masterly management in getting rid of Bartleby. Masterly I call it, and such it must appear to any dispassionate thinker. The beauty of my procedure seemed to consist in its perfect quietness. There was no vulgar bullying, no bravado of any sort, no choleric hectoring, and striding to and fro across the apartment, jerking out vehement commands for Bartleby to bundle himself off with his beggarly traps. Nothing of the kind. Without loudly bidding Bartleby depart—as an inferior genius might have done—I *assumed* the ground that depart he must; and upon that assumption built all I had to say. The more I thought over my procedure, the more I was charmed with it. Nevertheless, next morning, upon awakening, I had my doubts—I had somehow slept off the fumes of vanity. One of the coolest and wisest hours a man has, is just after he awakes in the morning. My procedure seemed as sagacious as ever—but only in theory. How it would prove in practice— there was the rub. It was truly a beautiful thought to have assumed Bartleby's departure; but, after all, that assumption was simply my own, and none of Bartleby's. The great point was, not whether I had assumed that he would quit me, but whether he would prefer so to do. He was more a man of preferences than assumptions.

After breakfast, I walked down town, arguing the probabilities *pro* and *con*. One moment I thought it would prove a miserable failure, and Bartleby would be found all alive at my office as usual; the next moment it seemed certain that I should find his chair empty. And so I kept veering about. At the corner of Broadway and Canal Street, I saw quite an excited group of people standing in earnest conversation.

"I'll take odds he doesn't," said a voice as I passed.

"Doesn't go?—done!" said I, "put up your money."

I was instinctively putting my hand in my pocket to produce my own, when I remembered that this was an election day. The words I had overheard bore no reference to Bartleby, but to the success or non-success of some candidate for the mayoralty. In my intent frame of mind, I had, as it were, imagined that all Broadway shared in my excitement, and were debating the same question with me. I passed on, very thankful that the uproar of the street screened my momentary absent-mindedness.

As I had intended, I was earlier than usual at my office door. I stood listening for a moment. All was still. He must be gone. I tried the knob. The door was locked. Yes, my procedure had worked to a charm; he indeed must be vanished. Yet a certain melancholy mixed with this: I was almost sorry for my brilliant success. I was fumbling under the door mat for the key, which Bartleby was to have left there for me, when accidentally my knee knocked against a panel, producing a summoning sound, and in response a voice came to me from within—"Not yet; I am occupied."

It was Bartleby.

I was thunderstuck. For an instant I stood like the man who, pipe in mouth, was killed one cloudless afternoon long ago in Virginia, by summer lightning; at his own warm open window he was killed, and remained leaning out there upon the dreamy afternoon, till some one touched him, when he fell.

"Not gone!" I murmured at last. But again obeying that wondrous ascendancy which the inscrutable scrivener had over me, and from which ascendancy, for all my chafing, I would not completely escape, I slowly went down stairs and out into the street, and while walking round the block, considered what I should next do in this unheard-of perplexity. Turn the man out by an actual thrusting I could not; to drive him away by calling him hard names would not do; calling in the police was an unpleasant idea; and yet, permit him to enjoy his cadaverous triumph over me—this, too, I could not think of. What was to be done? or, if nothing could be done, was there anything further that I could *assume* in the matter? Yes, as before I had prospectively assumed that Bartleby would depart, so now I might retrospectively assume that departed he was. In the legitimate carrying out of this assumption, I might enter my office in a great hurry, and pretending not to see Bartleby at all, walk straight against him as if he were air. Such a proceeding would in a singular degree have the appearance of a home-thrust. It was hardly possible that Bartleby could withstand such an application of the doctrine of assumptions. But upon second thoughts the success of the plan seemed rather dubious. I resolved to argue the matter over with him again.

"Bartleby," said I, entering the office, with a quietly severe expression, "I am seriously displeased. I am pained, Bartleby. I had thought better of you. I had imagined you of such a gentlemanly organization, that in any delicate dilemma a slight hint would suffice—in short, an assumption. But it appears I am deceived. Why," I added, unaffectedly starting, "you have not even touched that money yet," pointing to it, just where I had left it the evening previous.

He answered nothing.

"Will you, or will you not, quit me?" I now demanded in a sudden passion, advancing close to him.

"I would prefer *not* to quit you," he replied, gently emphasizing the *not*.

"What earthly right have you to stay here? Do you pay any rent? Do you pay my taxes? Or is this property yours?"

He answered nothing.

"Are you ready to go on and write now? Are your eyes recovered? Could you copy a small paper for me this morning? or help examine a few lines? or step round to the post-office? In a word, will you do anything at all, to give a coloring to your refusal to depart the premises?"

He silently retired into his hermitage.

I was now in such a state of nervous resentment that I thought it but prudent to check myself at present from further demonstrations. Bartleby and I were alone. I remembered the tragedy of the unfortunate Adams and the still more unfortunate Colt in the solitary office of the latter; and how poor Colt, being dreadfully incensed by Adams, and imprudently permitting himself to get wildly excited, was at unawares hurried into his fatal act—an act which certainly no man could possibly deplore more than the actor himself. Often it had occurred to me in my ponderings upon the subject, that had that altercation taken place in the public street, or at a private residence, it would not have terminated as it did. It was the circumstance of being alone in a solitary office, up stairs, of a building entirely unhallowed by humanizing domestic associations—an uncarpeted office, doubtless, of a dusty, haggard sort of appearance—this it must have been, which greatly helped to enhance the irritable desperation of the hapless Colt.

But when this old Adam of resentment rose in me and tempted me concerning Bartleby, I grappled him and threw him. How? Why, simply by recalling the divine injunction: "A new commandment give I unto you, that ye love one another." Yes, this it was that saved me.

Aside from higher considerations, charity often operates as a vastly wise and prudent principle—a great safeguard to its possessor: Men have committed murder for jealousy's sake, and anger's sake, and hatred's sake, and selfishness' sake, and spiritual pride's sake; but no man, that ever I heard of, ever committed a diabolical murder for sweet charity's sake. Mere self-interest, then, if no better motive can be enlisted, should, especially with high-tempered men, prompt all beings to charity and philanthropy. At any rate, upon the occasion in question, I strove to drown my exasperated feelings towards the scrivener by benevolently construing his conduct. Poor fellow, poor fellow! thought I, he don't mean anything; and besides, he has seen hard times, and ought to be indulged.

I endeavored, also, immediately to occupy myself, and at the same time to comfort my despondency. I tried to fancy, that in the course of the morning, at such time as might prove agreeable to him, Bartleby, of his own free accord, would emerge from his hermitage and take up some decided line of march in the direction of the door. But no. Half-past twelve o'clock came; Turkey began to glow in the face, overturn his inkstand, and become generally obstreperous; Nippers abated down into quietude and courtesy; Ginger Nut munched his noon apple; and Bartleby remained standing at his window in one of his profoundest dead-wall reveries. Will it be credited? Ought I to acknowledge it? That afternoon I left the office without saying one further word to him.

Some days now passed, during which, at leisure intervals I looked a little into "Edwards on the Will," and "Priestly on Necessity." Under the circumstances, those books induced a salutary feeling. Gradually I slid into the persuasion that these troubles of mine, touching the scrivener, had been all predestinated from eternity, and Bartleby was billeted upon me for some mysterious purpose of an allwise Providence, which it was not for a mere mortal like me to fathom. Yes, Bartleby, stay there behind your screen, thought I; I shall persecute you no more; you are harmless and noiseless as any of these old chairs; in short, I never feel so private as when I know you are here. At last I see it, I feel it; I penetrate to the predestinated purpose of my life. I am content. Others may have loftier parts to enact; but my mission in this world, Bartleby, is to furnish you with office-room for such period as you may see fit to remain.

I believe that this wise and blessed frame of mind would have continued with me, had it not been for the unsolicited and uncharitable remarks obtruded upon me by my professional friends who visited the rooms. But thus it often is, that the constant friction of illiberal minds wears out at last the best resolves of the more generous. Though to be sure, when I reflected upon it, it was not strange that people entering my office should be struck by the peculiar aspect of the unaccountable Bartleby, and so be tempted to throw out some sinister observations concerning him. Sometimes an attorney, having business with me, and calling at my office, and finding no one but the scrivener there, would undertake to obtain some sort of precise information from him touching my whereabouts; but without heeding his idle talk, Bartleby would remain standing immovable in the middle of the room. So after contemplating him in that position for a time, the attorney would depart, no wiser than he came.

Also, when a reference was going on, and the room full of lawyers and witnesses, and business driving fast, some deeply-occupied legal gentleman present, seeing Bartleby wholly unemployed, would request him to run round to his (the legal gentleman's) office and fetch some papers for him. Thereupon, Bartleby would tranquilly decline, and yet remain idle as before. Then the lawyer would give a great stare, and turn to me. And what could I say? At last I was made aware that all through the circle of my professional acquaintance, a whisper of wonder was running round, having reference to the strange creature I kept at my office. This worried me very much. And as the idea came upon me of his possibly turning out a long-lived man, and keep occupying my chambers, and denying my authority; and perplexing my visitors; and scandalizing my professional reputation; and casting a general gloom over the premises; keeping soul and body together to the last upon his savings (for doubtless he spent but half a dime a day), and in the end perhaps outlive me, and claim possession of my office by right of his perpetual occupancy: as all these dark anticipations crowded upon me more and more, and my friends continually intruded their relentless remarks upon the apparition in my room; a great change was wrought in me. I resolved to gather all my faculties together, and forever rid me of this intolerable incubus.

Ere revolving any complicated project, however, adapted to this end, I first simply suggested to Bartleby the propriety of his permanent departure. In a calm and serious tone, I commended the idea to his careful and mature consideration. But, having taken three days to meditate upon it, he apprised me, that his original determination remained the same; in short, that he still preferred to abide with me.

What shall I do? I now said to myself, buttoning up my coat to the last button. What shall I do? what ought I to do? what does conscience say I *should* do with this man, or, rather, ghost. Rid myself of him, I must; go, he shall. But how? You will not thrust him, the poor, pale, passive mortal—you will not thrust such a helpless creature out of your door? you will not dishonor yourself by such cruelty? No, I will not, I cannot do that. Rather would I let him live and die here, and then mason up his remains in the wall. What, then, will you do? For all your coaxing, he will not budge. Bribes he leaves under your own paperweight on your table; in short, it is quite plain that he prefers to cling to you.

Then something severe, something unusual must be done. What! surely you will not have him collared by a constable, and commit his innocent pallor to the common jail? And upon what ground could you procure such a thing to be done?—a vagrant, is he? What! he a vagrant, a wanderer, who refuses to budge? It is because he will *not* be a vagrant, then, that you seek to count him *as* a vagrant. That is too absurd.

No visible means of support: there I have him. Wrong again: for indubitably he *does* support himself, and that is the only unanswerable proof that any man can show of his possessing the means so to do. No more, then. Since he will not quit me, I must quit him. I will change my offices; I will move elsewhere, and give him fair notice, that if I find him on my new premises I will then proceed against him as a common trespasser.

Acting accordingly, next day I thus addressed him: "I find these chambers too far from the City Hall; the air is unwholesome. In a word, I propose to remove my offices next week, and shall no longer require your services. I tell you this now, in order that you may seek another place."

He made no reply, and nothing more was said.

On the appointed day I engaged carts and men, proceeded to my chambers, and, having but little furniture, everything was removed in a few hours. Throughout, the scrivener remained standing behind the screen, which I directed to be removed the last thing. It was withdrawn; and, being folded up like a huge folio, left him the motionless occupant of a naked room. I stood in the entry watching him a moment, while something from within me upbraided me.

I re-entered, with my hand in my pocket—and—and my heart in my mouth.

"Good-by, Bartleby; I am going—good-by, and God some way bless you; and take that," slipping something in his hand. But it dropped upon the floor, and then—strange to say—I tore myself from him whom I had so longed to be rid of.

Established in my new quarters, for a day or two I kept the door locked, and started at every footfall in the passages. When I returned to my rooms, after any little absence, I would pause at the threshold for an instant, and attentively listen, ere applying my key. But these fears were needless. Bartleby never came nigh me.

I thought all was going well, when a perturbed-looking stranger visited me, inquiring whether I was the person who had recently occupied rooms at No.—Wall Street.

Full of forebodings, I replied that I was.

"Then, sir," said the stranger, who proved a lawyer, "you are responsible for the man you left there. He refuses to do any copying; he refuses to do anything; he says he prefers not to; and he refuses to quit the premises."

"I am very sorry, sir," said I, with assumed tranquillity, but an inward tremor, "but, really, the man you allude to is nothing to me—he is no relation or apprentice of mine, that you should hold me responsible for him."

"In mercy's name, who is he?"

"I certainly cannot inform you. I know nothing about him. Formerly I employed him as a copyist; but he has done nothing for me now for some time past."

"I shall settle him, then—good morning, sir."

Several days passed, and I heard nothing more; and, though I often felt a charitable prompting to call at the place and see poor Bartleby, yet a certain squeamishness, of I know not what, withheld me.

All is over with him, by this time, thought I, at last, when, through another week, no further intelligence reached me. But, coming to my room the day after, I found several persons waiting at my door in a high state of nervous excitement.

"That's the man—here he comes," cried the foremost one, whom I recognized as the lawyer who had previously called upon me alone.

"You must take him away, sir, at once," cried a portly person among them, advancing upon me, and whom I knew to be the landlord of No.—Wall Street. "These gentlemen, my tenants, cannot stand it any longer; Mr. B———," pointing to the lawyer, "has turned him out of his room, and he now persists in haunting the building generally, sitting upon the banisters of the stairs by day, and sleeping in the entry by night. Everybody is concerned; clients are leaving the offices; some fears are entertained of a mob; something you must do, and that without delay."

Aghast at this torrent, I fell back before it, and would fain have locked myself in my new quarters. In vain I persisted that Bartleby was nothing to me—no more than to any one else. In vain—I was the last person known to have anything to do with him, and they held me to the terrible account. Fearful, then, of being exposed in the papers (as one person present obscurely threatened), I considered the matter, and, at length, said, that if the lawyer would give me a confidential interview with the scrivener, in his (the lawyer's) own room, I would, that afternoon, strive my best to rid them of the nuisance they complained of.

Going up stairs to my old haunt, there was Bartleby silently sitting upon the banister at the landing.

"What are you doing here, Bartleby?" said I.

"Sitting upon the banister," he mildly replied.

I motioned him into the lawyer's room, who then left us.

"Bartleby," said I, "are you aware that you are the cause of great tribulation to me, by persisting in occupying the entry after being dismissed from the office?"

No answer.

"Now one of two things must take place. Either you must do something, or something must be done to you. Now what sort of business would you like to engage in? Would you like to re-engage in copying for some one?"

"No; I would prefer not to make any change."

"Would you like a clerkship in a dry-goods store?"

"There is too much confinement about that. No, I would not like a clerkship; but I am not particular."

"Too much confinement," I cried, "why you keep yourself confined all the time!"

"I would prefer not to take a clerkship," he rejoined, as if to settle that little item at once.

"How would a bar-tender's business suit you? There is no trying of the eye-sight in that."

"I would not like it at all; though, as I said before, I am not particular."

His unwonted wordiness inspirited me. I returned to the charge.

"Well, then, would you like to travel through the country collecting bills for the merchants? That would improve your health."

"No, I would prefer to be doing something else."

"How, then, would going as a companion to Europe, to entertain some young gentleman with your conversation—how would that suit you?"

"Not at all. It does not strike me that there is anything definite about that. I like to be stationary. But I am not particular."

"Stationary you shall be, then," I cried, now losing all patience, and, for the first time in all my exasperating connection with him, fairly flying into a passion. "If you do not go away from these premises before night, I shall feel bound—indeed, I *am* bound—to—to—to quit the premises myself!" I rather absurdly concluded, knowing not with what possible threat to try to frighten his immobility into compliance. Despairing of all further efforts, I was precipitately leaving him, when a final thought occurred to me—one which had not been wholly unindulged before.

"Bartleby," said I, in the kindest tone I could assume under such exciting circumstances, "will you go home with me now—not to my office, but my dwelling—and remain there till we can conclude upon some convenient arrangement for you at our leisure? Come, let us start now, right away."

"No: at present I would prefer not to make any change at all."

I answered nothing; but, effectually dodging every one by the suddenness and rapidity of my flight, rushed from the building, ran up Wall Street towards Broadway, and jumping into the first omnibus, was soon removed from pursuit. As soon as tranquillity returned, I distinctly perceived that I had now done all that I possibly could, both in respect to the demands of the landlord and his tenants, and with regard to my own desire and sense of duty, to benefit Bartleby, and shield him from rude persecution. I now strove to be entirely care-free and quiescent; and my conscience justified me in the attempt; though, indeed, it was not so successful as I could have wished. So fearful was I of being again hunted out by the incensed landlord and his exasperated tenants, that, surrendering my business to Nippers, for a few days, I drove about the upper part of the town and through the suburbs, in my rockaway; crossed over to Jersey City and Hoboken, and paid fugitive visits to Manhattanville and Astoria. In fact, I almost lived in my rockaway for the time.

When again I entered my office, lo, a note from the landlord lay upon the desk. I opened it with trembling hands. It informed me that the writer had sent to the police, and had Bartleby removed to the Tombs as a vagrant. Moreover, since I knew more about him than any one else, he wished me to appear at that place, and make a suitable statement of the facts. These tidings had a conflicting effect upon me. At first I was indignant; but, at last, almost approved. The landlord's energetic, summary disposition, had led him to adopt a procedure which I do not think I would have decided upon myself; and yet, as a last resort, under such peculiar circumstances, it seemed the only plan.

As I afterwards learned, the poor scrivener, when told that he must be conducted to the Tombs, offered not the slightest obstacle, but, in his pale, unmoving way, silently acquiesced.

Some of the compassionate and curious bystanders joined the party; and headed by one of the constables arm in arm with Bartleby, the silent procession filed its way through all the noise, and heat, and joy of the roaring thoroughfares at noon.

The same day I received the note, I went to the Tombs, or, to speak more properly, the Halls of Justice. Seeking the right officer, I stated the purpose of my call, and was informed that the individual I described was, indeed, within. I then assured the functionary that Bartleby was a perfectly honest man, and greatly to be compassionated, however, unaccountably eccentric. I narrated all I knew, and closed by suggesting the idea of letting him remain in as indulgent confinement as possible, till something less harsh might be done—though, indeed, I hardly knew what. At all events, if nothing else could be decided upon, the alms-house must receive him. I then begged to have an interview.

Being under no disgraceful charge, and quite serene and harmless in all his ways, they had permitted him freely to wander about the prison, and, especially, in the inclosed grass-platted yards thereof. And so I found him there, standing all alone in the quietest of the yards, his face towards a high wall, while all around, from the narrow slits of the jail windows, I thought I saw peering out upon him the eyes of murderers and thieves.

"Bartleby!"

"I know you," he said, without looking round—"and I want nothing to say to you."

"It was not I that brought you here, Bartleby," said I, keenly pained at his implied suspicion. "And to you, this should not be so vile a place. Nothing reproachful attaches to you by being here. And see, it is not so sad a place as one might think. Look, there is the sky, and here is the grass."

"I know where I am," he replied, but would say nothing more, and so I left him.

As I entered the corridor again, a broad meat-like man, in an apron, accosted me, and, jerking his thumb over his shoulder, said—"Is that your friend?"

"Yes."

"Does he want to starve? If he does, let him live on the prison fare, that's all."

"Who are you?" asked I, not knowing what to make of such an unofficially speaking person in such a place.

"I am the grub-man. Such gentlemen as have friends here, hire me to provide them with something good to eat."

"Is this so?" said I, turning to the turnkey.

He said it was.

"Well, then," said I, slipping some silver into the grub-man's hands (for so they called him), "I want you to give particular attention to my friend there; let him have the best dinner you can get. And you must be as polite to him as possible."

"Introduce me, will you?" said the grub-man, looking at me with an expression which seemed to say he was all impatience for an opportunity to give a specimen of his breeding.

Thinking it would prove of benefit to the scrivener, I acquiesced; and, asking the grub-man his name, went up with him to Bartleby.

"Bartleby, this is a friend; you will find him very useful to you."

"Your sarvant, sir, your sarvant," said the grub-man, making a low salutation behind his apron. "Hope you find it pleasant here, sir; nice grounds—cool apartments—hope you'll stay with us sometime—try to make it agreeable. What will you have for dinner to-day?"

"I prefer not to dine to-day," said Bartleby, turning away. "It would disagree with me; I am unused to dinners." So saying, he slowly moved to the other side of the inclosure, and took up a position fronting the dead-wall.

"How's this?" said the grub-man, addressing me with a stare of astonishment. "He's odd, ain't he?"

"I think he is a little deranged," said I, sadly.

"Deranged? deranged is it? Well, now, upon my word, I thought that friend of yourn was a gentleman forger; they are always pale and genteel-like, them forgers. I can't help pity 'em—can't help it, sir. Did you know Monroe Edwards?" he added, touchingly, and paused. Then, laying his hand piteously on my shoulder, sighed, "he died of consumption at Sing-Sing. So you weren't acquainted with Monroe?"

"No, I was never socially acquainted with any forgers. But I cannot stop longer. Look to my friend yonder. You will not lose by it. I will see you again."

Some few days after this, I again obtained admission to the Tombs, and went through the corridors in quest of Bartleby; but without finding him.

"I saw him coming from his cell not long ago," said a turnkey, "may be he's gone to loiter in the yards."

So I went in that direction.

"Are you looking for the silent man?" said another turnkey, passing me. "Yonder he lies—sleeping in the yard there. 'Tis not twenty minutes since I saw him lie down."

The yard was entirely quiet. It was not accessible to the common prisoners. The surrouding walls, of amazing thickness, kept off all sounds behind them. The Egyptian character of the masonry weighed upon me with its gloom. But a soft imprisoned turf grew under foot. The heart of the eternal pyramids, it seemed, wherein, by some strange magic, through the clefts, grass-seed, dropped by birds, had sprung.

Strangely huddled at the base of the wall, his knees drawn up, and lying on his side, his head touching the cold stones, I saw the wasted Bartleby. But nothing stirred. I paused; then went close up to him; stooped over, and saw that his dim eyes were open; otherwise he seemed profoundly sleeping. Something prompted me to touch him. I felt his hand, when a tingling shiver ran up my arm and down my spine to my feet.

The round face of the grub-man peered upon me now. "His dinner is ready. Won't he dine to-day, either? Or does he live without dining?"

"Lives without dining," said I, and closed the eyes.

"Eh!—He's asleep, ain't he?"

"With kings and counselors," murmured I.

There would seem little need for proceeding further in this history. Imagination will readily supply the meagre recital of poor Bartleby's interment. But, ere parting with the reader, let me say, that if this little narrative has sufficiently interested him, to awaken curiosity as to who Bartleby was, and what manner of life he led prior to the present narrator's making his acquaintance, I can only reply, that in such curiosity I fully share, but am wholly unable to gratify it. Yet here I hardly know whether I should divulge one little item of rumor, which came to my ear a few months after the scrivener's decease. Upon what basis it rested, I could never ascertain; and hence, how true it is I cannot now tell. But, inasmuch as this vague report has not been without a certain suggestive interest to me, however sad, it may prove the same with some others; and so I will briefly mention it. The report was this: that Bartleby had been a subordinate clerk in the Dead Letter Office at Washington, from which he had been suddenly removed by a change in the administration. When I think over this rumor, hardly can I express the emotions which seize me. Dead letters! does it not sound like dead men? Conceive a man by nature and misfortune prone to a pallid hopelessness, can any business seem more fitted to heighten it than that of continually handling these dead letters, and assorting them for the flames? For by the cart-load they are annually burned. Sometimes from out the folded paper the pale clerk takes a ring—the finger it was meant for, perhaps, moulders in the grave; a bank-note sent in swiftest charity—he whom it would relieve, nor eats nor hungers any more; pardon for those who died despairing; hope for those who died unhoping; good tidings for those who died stifled by unrelieved calamities. On erands of life, these letters speed to death.

Ah, Bartleby! Ah, humanity!

Exercises

1. *Prepare a solid case either for Bartleby or for the narrator as the protagonist.*

2. *Which character, Bartleby or the narrator, would you judge to be the more fully developed and dynamic character?*

3. *How does the narrator withdraw, more or less, from his world? How does Bartleby disturb the lawyer's "safe" world?*

4. *When Bartleby says, "I would prefer not to," what precisely is he doing? What is his chief motivation? Is his behavior consistent?*

5. *Trace the stages of Bartleby's development from the beginning of his isolation, through his withdrawal, to his death.*

6. *How does the final paragraph shed light on the characterizations of both Bartleby and the lawyer?*

7. *Ginger Nut, Nippers, and Turkey are minor characters. What constitutes their somewhat stereotyped nature? What functions do they have?*

8. *What comment on the meaning of life does the story suggest?*

Topics for Writing

1. *Render a valid interpretation based on one of the following topics: (a) personal v. social responsibilities; (b) self-values v. societal values; (c) nonconformity v. conformity; (d) creative world v. business world.*

2. *Consider Bartleby as the lawyer's other self.*

3. *Describe Bartleby as a quiet rebel.*

Selected Bibliography

Herman Melville

Abcarian, Richard. "The World of Love and the Spheres of Fright: Melville's 'Bartleby the Scrivener.'" *Studies in Short Fiction*, 1 (1964), 207–215.

Chase, Richard. *Herman Melville: A Critical Study*. (New York: Macmillan, 1949), pp. 143–149.

Eliot, Alexander. "Melville and Bartleby." *Furioso*, 3 (1947), 11–21.

Felheim, Marvin. "Meaning and Structure in 'Bartleby.'" *College English*, 23 (1962), 369–370, 375–376.

Fogle, Richard. "Melville's 'Bartleby': Absolution, Predestination, and Free Will." *Tulane Studies in English*, 4 (1954), 27–42.

Gardner, John. "Bartleby: Art and Social Commitment." *Philological Quarterly*, 43 (1964), 87–98.

Marcus, Mordecai. "Melville's Bartleby as a Psychological Double." *College English*, 23 (1962), 365–368.

Marx, Leo. "Melville's Parable of the Walls." *Sewanee Review*, 61 (1953), 602–627.

Oliver, E. S. "A Second Look at 'Bartleby.'" *College English*, 11 (1945), 431–439.

Spector, Robert Donald. "Melville's 'Bartleby' and the Absurd." *Nineteenth Century Fiction*, 16 (1961), 175–177.

Springer, Norman. "Bartleby and the Terror of Limitation." *PMLA*, 53 (1965), 410–418.

Widner, Kingsley. "The Negative Affirmation: Melville's 'Bartleby.'" *Modern Fiction Studies*, 7 (1962), 276–286.

3 Point of View

We observe the action of a story through the eyes and mind of the person or the community of characters the author designates to tell the story. This awareness through which we view the unfolding of events we call *point of view*.

For looking at a situation, the potential vantage points and their combinations are many, but generally a story can be told from one of four basic positions: the omniscient point of view, the limited omniscient point of view, the first-person point of view, and the dramatic point of view.

The *omniscient* point of view, sometimes called panoramic, shifting, or multiple, employs a narrator speaking in the third person, who knows just about all there is to know about each character and event in the story.

The all-knowing raconteur can disclose as much or as little about the backgrounds, the trials, the failures, the successes, the prejudices, the loves, and the hates of as few or as many of the characters as the author permits; omniscience allows entry to the minds of some or all of the characters, revealing what the author wishes to about their innermost thoughts and feelings.

Through the omniscient narrator writers are freed to move at will about the arena of conflict. They may easily shift consciousness from one character to another and viewpoint from the subjective to the objective. They may choose to conjecture on the significance of certain events and to pass judgment on the behavior of one or all of the characters. Such Godlike omnipresence and omniscience allows authors optimum visibility, scope, and freedom.

The following excerpt illustrates the omniscient point of view. Note the periodic shifts from the objective to the subjective points of view and the fact that we not only take cognizance of the action through the perspective of each character, but also that we have access to their consciousness, thus allowing a communication of their most secret attitudes and emotions.

Gordon J. Taylor, a tall, angry, meticulously dressed advertising executive, walked resolutely up the busy street, glanced about irritably, and pushed his large frame through the door into a pawn shop.

Behind the counter, an undersized, beggarly looking, cigar-chewing clerk stood undisturbed, glued to a radio blaring with a twitter of emotional excitement—produced apparently by a killing.

Apprized finally of the customer's interest in guns, the pawnbroker dawdled toward the gentleman.

"What's your handle, mister?" the clerk asked, glaring at the stranger as if he were a rank criminal.

"What?" Gordon asked, his thoughts lingering nervously on the painful events just passed.

"Your handle—your name?" the clerk insisted. He began to lose patience.

"Taylor . . . Gordon J.," he answered, still preoccupied with the matter of his wife and partner.

"Your racket—what do you do with the gems?" the pawnbroker asked shrewdly, determined to trap his man.

"Salesman." Gordon feared this line of questioning.

"In or outer?" the clerk persisted, barely concealing his contempt.

Gordon trembled. He could take it no longer. "Why all the questions?"

The pawnbroker, seizing what he felt was a capital opportunity to close the matter at hand, uttered sharply, "You want a gun or not?"

Gordon's need being absolute, he replied with apologetic nervousness.

"I don't appreciate this third-degree business."

"Listen, buster," the clerk said, taking the remark as a personal affront, "what kinda place you think we run here? We're legit. We can't sell no weapons to every joker that comes off the street. How do I know you ain't gonna pull a sheist or knock off somebody? That's why the questions, see. We gotta know an' the cops gotta know."

"The police?" Gordon asked, visibly shaken and doing a bad job of trying to hide his inner disturbance.

"Yeah, they wanna know. They wanna know make, serial number, who buys, why, address an' proof," the clerk said authoritatively. "You got some I.D.?"

The *limited omniscient* point of view, also known as the selective, or the limited, third person, uses a third-person narrator and limits our perception to that of a single character, who may be the protagonist, a minor character, or an outside observer. We invade only one mind and no other. By empowering us to see the action through the senses of only one person, the author draws us more intimately into that one character and those discoveries and experiences. Limited omniscience also produces a marked sense of realism and gives the story a semblance of built-in unity.

The following version of the earlier excerpt exemplifies the limited omniscient point of view, which clearly restricts our perspective to a single character's consciousness, that of the pawnbroker's. What the clerk sees and feels we see and feel, no more, no less. We admit to absolutely no knowledge of Gordon's inner thoughts.

"What's your handle, mister?" the clerk asked, glaring at the stranger as if he were a rank criminal.

"What?" Gordon asked.

"Your handle—your name?" the clerk insisted. He began to lose patience.

"Taylor . . . Gordon J."

"Your racket—what do you do with the gems?" the pawnbroker asked shrewdly, determined to trap his man.

"Salesman."

"In or outer?" the clerk persisted, barely concealing his contempt.

"Why all the questions?"

The pawnbroker, seizing what he felt was a capital opportunity to close the matter at hand, uttered sharply, "You want a gun or not?"

"I don't appreciate this third-degree business."

"Listen, buster," the clerk said, taking the remark as a personal affront, "what kinda place you think we run here? We're legit. We can't sell no weapons to every joker that comes off the street. How do I know you ain't gonna pull a sheist or knock off somebody? That's why the questions, see. We gotta know an' the cops gotta know."

"The police?"

"Yeah, they wanna know. They wanna know make, serial number, who buys, why, address an' proof," the clerk said authoritatively. "You got some I.D.?"

The *first-person*, or personal, point of view, which possesses many of the attributes of the limited omniscient, engages a protagonist, a minor character, or an outside observer to tell its story in "I" narration. Further, it establishes an intimate relationship between the narrator and the reader, gains for us a transcendent feeling of reality, and—by virtue of its single, consistent outlook—produces a natural unity.

Though we have access to the consciousness of one character, as in limited omniscient, here in the first-person point of view we are limited strictly to what the "I" narrator sees, thinks, and feels. We are confined to one character's reporting, views, and commentaries, however biased the editorializing may be.

As an outside observer, the first-person narrator gains in reliability because of noninvolvement in the events of the story. He is apt to be more objective than a first-person narrator character who, because of involvement in the action, tends to display prejudicial judgment. However, a first-person narrator character, especially a protagonist, is likely to invoke our empathy and involve us more intimately in the action. The gains and losses produced by this point of view are obvious.

Finally, after what must have been thirty minutes of grunts for attention, the dripping cigar wafted toward me.

"What's your handle, mister?" he asked, accusing me with his large, black, piercing eyes.

I immediately took a dislike to him. For one thing, I failed to understand his English; for another, I thought he was a stupid, little man.

"What?" I asked, my thoughts still lingering nervously on the painful events just passed.

"Your handle—your name?" he insisted, in as rude a manner as one could expect from an idiot.

"Taylor . . . Gordon J.," I answered, thinking it wiser to give him my real name.

"Your racket—what do you do with the gems?" he asked.

"Salesman," I said quickly, dismissing the line of questioning, which I did not at all like.

"In or outer?" he persisted.

I could take it no longer. I was afraid. He might find out more than he needed to know.

"Why all the questions?" I asked.

"You want a gun or not?"

I found myself at the mercy of this undaunted fool. I surely needed a gun, I thought.

"I don't appreciate this third-degree business," I told him.

That really jarred him. He took it as a personal attack on his integrity. What integrity? For a minute I imagined he was going to punch me in the mouth. He was mad; but he soon cooled off.

"Listen, buster," he said, "what kinda place you think we run here? We're legit. We can't sell no weapons to every joker that comes off the street. How do I know you ain't gonna pull a sheist or knock off somebody? That's why the questions, see. We gotta know an' the cops gotta know."

"The police?" I asked, visibly shaken and trying to conceal my anxiety.

"Yeah, they wanna know. They wanna know make, serial number, who buys, why, address an' proof," the little man said. "You got some I.D.?"

FOUR BASIC POSITIONS OF POINT OF VIEW

	Omniscient	Limited Omniscient
Voice	Third-person pronouns *he, she* mostly; first-person pronoun rarely	Third person pronouns
Consciousness	Access to consciousness of more than one character, perhaps all	Access to consciousness of one character
Position and Presence	Story told through eyes of outside observer whose presence is immense	Story told through eyes of outside observer, protagonist, or minor character whose presence dominates
Reliability	Reliable as implied author's voice	Reliable when observer used; less reliable when character used
Usage in Modern Fiction	Most infrequently used	Most frequently used
Other Features	1. allows maximum scope and flexibility 2. permits author intrusions, editorials, evaluations, and comments 3. creates distance between reader and characters	1. promotes sense of realism 2. allows author comments 3. establishes intimate relationship between reader and characters 4. achieves ready structural unity 5. combines scope of omniscient and immediacy of first-person narration

First-Person	Dramatic	
First-person pronouns *I, my, mine,* etc.	Third person pronouns	*Voice*
Access to consciousness of *own self*	Access to consciousness of *no* character	*Consciousness*
Story told through eyes of outside observer, protagonist, or minor character whose presence dominates	Story told through eyes of outside observer whose presence is near invisible	*Position and Presence*
Reliable when observer used; less reliable when character used	Reliable when "teller" remains neutral	*Reliability*
Frequently used	Recent development	*Usage in Modern Fiction*
1. promotes sense of realism 2. allows author comments 3. establishes intimate relationship between reader and characters 4. achieves ready structural unity	1. permits optimum flexibility 2. forbids author comments 3. places reader in position of spectator 4. allows action to move swiftly	*Other Features*

"Yes," I answered, haughtily displaying my awesome collection of credit cards. At long last I had my gun. And I knew it.

In the *dramatic* point of view, also referred to as the objective or the scenic, the author prepares the characters, issues them their lines, abandons the stage, and disappears into the wings. The narrator simply tells a story objectively, leaving the actors to emote and readers to discover for themselves what experience they may feel.

Because there is no access to the consciousness of any character, we must view everything from outside the story, as a spectator at the theater watches a play, through the externals of developing physical action, the appearance or description of the characters and their speech. We see only what is happening and hear only what is being spoken. Consequently, we must rely almost exclusively on our own powers of deductive reasoning to grasp the full meaning of the story.

The dramatic point of view presents an action that moves swiftly and gives the impression of immediacy. More than any other viewpoint, it affords the most objective insight into the characters and events of a story and purveys the greatest illusion of reality.

The next segment illustrates the dramatic point of view. Observe the differences in effects between this and other modes of narration.

"What's your handle, mister?" the clerk asked.
"What?"
"Your handle—your name?"
"Taylor . . . Gordon J."
"Your racket—what do you do with the gems?"
"Salesman."
"In or outer?"
"Why all the questions?"
"You want a gun or not?"
"I don't appreciate this third-degree business."
"Listen, buster," the clerk said, "what kinda place you think we run here? We're legit. We can't sell no weapons to every joker that comes off the street. How do I know you ain't gonna pull a sheist or knock off somebody? That's why the questions, see. We gotta know an' the cops gotta know."

"The police?" Gordon asked.

"Yeah, they wanna know. They wanna know make, serial number, who buys, why, address an' proof," the clerk said. "You got some I.D.?"

As frequently as one finds an author who adheres strictly to a single basic point of view, one discovers another who prefers to mix his own salmagundi. Almost certainly the creative writer will select a point of view or a mixture of two or three best suited to serve the artistic design or complement the materials being used.

An ability to distinguish between the various positions from which one views character and action should be important to the reader. Perhaps more importantly, the reader ought to ascertain what special effects a particular viewpoint achieves as well as explain why one approach can better accommodate an author's plan than another.

Carson McCullers (1917–1967)

Née Smith in Columbus, Georgia, she attended Columbia and New York University. At the age of twenty-three she published her first novel, The Heart Is a Lonely Hunter *(1940); later she wrote* A Member of the Wedding *(1946), which she subsequently adapted for the stage, and for which she won the Drama Critics Circle Award in 1950. She also received the International Publishers Prize in 1963. Paul Engle, distinguished poet and critic, calls "A Tree, a Rock, a Cloud" a perfect short story.*

A Tree, a Rock, a Cloud

It was raining that morning, and still very dark. When the boy reached the streetcar café he had almost finished his route and he went in for a cup of coffee. The place was an all-night café owned by a bitter and stingy man called Leo. After the raw, empty street, the café seemed friendly and bright: along the counter there were a couple of soldiers, three spinners from the cotton mill, and in a corner a man who sat hunched over with his nose and half his face down in a beer mug. The boy wore a helmet such as aviators wear. When he went into the café he unbuckled the chin strap and raised the right flap up over his pink little ear; often as he drank his coffee someone would speak to him in a friendly way. But this morning Leo did not look into his face and none of the men were talking. He paid and was leaving the café when a voice called out to him:

"Son! Hey Son!"

He turned back and the man in the corner was crooking his finger and nodding to him. He had brought his face out of the beer mug and he seemed suddenly very happy. The man was long and pale, with a big nose and faded orange hair.

"Hey Son!"

The boy went toward him. He was an undersized boy of about twelve, with one shoulder drawn higher than the other because of the weight of the paper sack. His face was shallow, freckled, and his eyes were round child eyes.

"Yeah Mister?"

The man laid one hand on the paper boy's shoulders, then grasped the boy's chin and turned his face slowly from one side to the other. The boy shrank back uneasily.

"Say! What's the big idea?"

The boy's voice was shrill; inside the café it was suddenly very quiet.

The man said slowly, "I love you."

All along the counter the men laughed. The boy, who had scowled and sidled away, did not know what to do. He looked over the counter at Leo, and Leo watched him with a weary, brittle jeer. The boy tried to laugh also. But the man was serious and sad.

"I did not mean to tease you, Son," he said. "Sit down and have a beer with me. There is something I have to explain."

Cautiously, out of the corner of his eye, the paper boy questioned the men along the counter to see what he should do. But they had gone back to their beer or their breakfast and did not notice him. Leo put a cup of coffee on the counter and a little jug of cream.

"He is a minor," Leo said.

The paper boy slid himself up onto the stool. His ear beneath the upturned flap of the helmet was very small and red. The man was nodding at him soberly. "It is important," he said. Then he reached in his hip pocket and brought out something which he held up in the palm of his hand for the boy to see.

"Look very carefully," he said.

The boy stared, but there was nothing to look at very carefully. The man held in his big, grimy palm a photograph. It was the face of a woman, but blurred, so that only the hat and the dress she was wearing stood out clearly.

"See?" the man asked.

The boy nodded and the man placed another picture in his palm. The woman was standing on the beach in a bathing suit. The suit made her stomach very big, and that was the main thing you noticed.

"Got a good look?" He leaned over closer and finally asked: "You ever seen her before?"

The boy sat motionless, staring slantwise at the man. "Not so I know of."

"Very well." The man blew on the photographs and put them back into his pocket. "That was my wife."

"Dead?" the boy asked.

Slowly the man shook his head. He pursed his lips as though about to whistle and answered in a long-drawn way: "Nuuu—" he said. "I will explain."

The beer on the counter before the man was in a large brown mug. He did not pick it up to drink. Instead he bent down and, putting his face over the rim, he rested there for a moment. Then with both hands he tilted the mug and sipped.

"Some night you'll go to sleep with your big nose in a mug and drown," said Leo. "Prominent transient drowns in beer. That would be a cute death."

The paper boy tried to signal to Leo. While the man was not looking he screwed up his face and worked his mouth to question soundlessly: "Drunk?" But Leo only raised his eyebrows and turned away to put some pink strips of bacon on the grill. The man pushed the mug away from him, straightened himself, and folded his loose crooked hands on the counter. His face was sad as he looked at the paper boy. He did not blink, but from time to time the lids closed down with delicate gravity over his pale green eyes. It was nearing dawn and the boy shifted the weight of the paper sack.

"I am talking about love," the man said. "With me it is a science."

The boy half slid down from the stool. But the man raised his forefinger, and there was something about him that held the boy and would not let him go away.

"Twelve years ago I married the woman in the photograph. She was my wife for one year, nine months, three days, and two nights. I loved her. Yes. . . . " He tightened his blurred, rambling voice and said again: "I loved her. I thought also that she loved me. I was a railroad engineer. She had all home comforts and luxuries. It never crept into my brain that she was not satisfied. But do you know what happened?"

"Mgneeow!" said Leo.

The man did not take his eyes from the boy's face. "She left me. I came in one night and the house was empty and she was gone. She left me."

"With a fellow?" the boy asked.

Gently the man placed his palm down on the counter. "Why naturally, Son. A woman does not run off like that alone."

The café was quiet, the soft rain black and endless in the street outside. Leo pressed down the frying bacon with the prongs of his long fork. "So you have been chasing the floozie for eleven years. You frazzled old rascal!"

For the first time the man glanced at Leo. "Please don't be vulgar. Besides, I was not speaking to you." He turned back to the boy and said in a trusting and secretive undertone. "Let's not pay any attention to him. O.K.?"

The paper boy nodded doubtfully.

"It was like this," the man continued. "I am a person who feels many things. All my life one thing after another has impressed me. Moonlight. The leg of a pretty girl. One thing after another. But the point is that when I had enjoyed anything there was a peculiar sensation as though it was laying around loose in me. Nothing seemed to finish itself up or fit in with the other things. Women? I had my portion of them. The same. Afterwards laying around loose in me. I was a man who had never loved."

Very slowly he closed his eyelids, and the gesture was like a curtain drawn at the end of a scene in a play. When he spoke again his voice was excited and the words came fast—the lobes of his large, loose ears seemed to tremble.

"Then I met this woman. I was fifty-one years old and she always said she was thirty. I met her at a filling station and we were married within three days. And do you know what it was like? I just can't tell you. All I had ever felt was gathered together around this woman. Nothing lay around loose in me any more but was finished up by her."

The man stopped suddenly and stroked his long nose. His voice sank down to a steady and reproachful undertone: "I'm not explaining this right. What happened was this. There were these beautiful feelings and loose little pleasures inside me. And this woman was something like an assembly line for my soul. I run these little pieces of myself through her and I come out complete. Now do you follow me?"

"What was her name?" the boy asked.

"Oh," he said. "I called her Dodo. But that is immaterial."

"Did you try to make her come back?"

The man did not seem to hear. "Under the circumstances you can imagine how I felt when she left me."

Leo took the bacon from the grill and folded two strips of it between a bun. He had a gray face, with slitted eyes, and a pinched nose saddled by faint blue shadows. One of the mill workers signaled for more coffee and Leo poured it. He did not give refills on coffee free. The spinner ate breakfast there every morning, but the better Leo knew his customers the stingier he treated them. He nibbled his own bun as though he grudged it to himself.

"And you never got hold of her again?"

The boy did not know what to think of the man, and his child's face was uncertain with mingled curiosity and doubt. He was new on the paper route; it was still strange to him to be out in the town in the black, queer early morning.

"Yes," the man said. "I took a number of steps to get her back. I went around trying to locate her. I went to Tulsa where she had folks. And to Mobile. I went to every town she had ever mentioned to me, and I hunted down every man she had formerly been connected with. Tulsa, Atlanta, Chicago, Cheehaw, Memphis. . . . For the better part of two years I chased around the country trying to lay hold of her."

"But the pair of them had vanished from the face of the earth!" said Leo.

"Don't listen to him," the man said confidentially. "And also just forget those two years. They are not important. What matters is that around the third year a curious thing begun to happen to me."

"What?" the boy asked.

The man leaned down and tilted his mug to take a sip of beer. But as he hovered over the mug his nostrils fluttered slightly; he sniffed the staleness of the beer and did not drink. "Love is a curious thing to begin with. At first I thought only of getting her back. It was a kind of mania. But then as time went on I tried to remember her. But do you know what happened?"

"No," the boy said.

"When I laid myself down on a bed and tried to think about her my mind became a blank. I couldn't see her. I would take out her pictures and look. No good. Nothing doing. A blank. Can you imagine it?"

"Say Mac!" Leo called down the counter. "Can you imagine this bozo's mind a blank!"

Slowly, as though fanning away flies, the man waved his hand. His green eyes were concentrated and fixed on the shallow little face of the paper boy.

"But a sudden piece of glass on a sidewalk. Or a nickel tune in a music box. A shadow on a wall at night. And I would remember. It might happen in a street and I would cry or bang my head against a lamppost. You follow me?"

"A piece of glass . . ." the boy said.

"Anything. I would walk around and I had no power of how and when to remember her. You think you can put up a kind of shield. But remembering don't come to a man face forward—it corners around sideways. I was at the mercy of everything I saw and heard. Suddenly instead of me combing the countryside to find her she begun to chase me around in my very soul. *She* chasing *me*, mind you! And in my soul.''

The boy asked finally: "What part of the country were you in then?"

"Ooh," the man groaned. "I was a sick mortal. It was like smallpox. I confess, Son, that I boozed. I fornicated. I committed any sin that suddenly appealed to me. I am loath to confess it but I will do so. When I recall that period it is all curdled in my mind, it was so terrible."

The man leaned his head down and tapped his forehead on the counter. For a few seconds he stayed bowed over in this position, the back of his stringy neck covered with orange furze, his hands with their long warped fingers held palm to palm in an attitude of prayer. Then the man straightened himself; he was smiling and suddenly his face was bright and tremulous and old.

"It was in the fifth year that it happened," he said. "And with it I started my science."

Leo's mouth jerked with a pale, quick grin. "Well none of we boys are getting any younger," he said. Then with sudden anger he balled up a dishcloth he was holding and threw it down hard on the floor. "You draggle-tailed old Romeo!"

"What happened?" the boy asked.

The old man's voice was high and clear: "Peace," he answered.

"Huh?"

"It is hard to explain scientifically, Son," he said. "I guess the logical explanation is that she and I had fleed around from each other for so long that finally we just got tangled up together and lay down and quit. Peace. A queer and beautiful blankness. It was spring in Portland and the rain came every afternoon. All evening I just stayed there on my bed in the dark. And that is how the science came to me."

The windows in the streetcar were pale blue with light. The two soldiers paid for their beers and opened the door—one of the soldiers combed his hair and wiped off his muddy puttees before they went outside. The three mill workers bent silently over their breakfasts. Leo's clock was ticking on the wall.

"It is this. And listen carefully. I meditated on love and reasoned it out. I realized what is wrong with us. Men fall in love for the first time. And what do they fall in love with?"

The boy's soft mouth was partly open and he did not answer.

"A woman," the old man said, "Without science, with nothing to go by, they undertake the most dangerous and sacred experience in God's earth. They fall in love with a woman. Is that correct, Son?"

"They start at the wrong end of love. They begin at the

climax. Can you wonder it is so miserable? Do you know how men should love?"

The old man reached over and grasped the boy by the collar of his leather jacket. He gave him a gentle little shake and his green eyes gazed down unblinking and grave.

"Son, do you know how love should be begun?"

The boy sat small and listening and still. Slowly he shook his head. The old man leaned closer and whispered:

"A tree. A rock. A cloud."

It was still raining outside in the street: a mild, gray, endless rain. The mill whistle blew for the six o'clock shift and the three spinners paid and went away. There was no one in the café but Leo, the old man, and the little paper boy.

"The weather was like this in Portland," he said. "At the time my science was begun. I meditated and I started very cautious. I would pick up something from the street and take it home with me. I bought a goldfish and I concentrated on the goldfish and I loved it. I graduated from one thing to another. Day by day I was getting this technique. On the road from Portland to San Diego—"

"Aw shut up!" screamed Leo suddenly. "Shut up! Shut up!"

The old man still held the collar of the boy's jacket; he was trembling and his face was earnest and bright and wild. "For six years now I have gone around by myself and built up my science. And now I am a master. Son. I can love anything. No longer do I have to think about it even. I see a street full of people and a beautiful light comes in me. I watch a bird in the sky. Or I meet a traveler on the road. Everything, Son. And anybody. All stranger and all loved! Do you realize what a science like mine can mean?"

The boy held himself stiffly, his hands curled tight around the counter edge. Finally he asked: "Did you ever really find that lady?"

"What? What say, Son?"

"I mean," the boy asked timidly. "Have you fallen in love with a woman again?"

The old man loosened his grasp on the boy's collar. He turned away and for the first time his green eyes had a vague and scattered look. He lifted the mug from the counter, drank down the yellow beer. His head was shaking slowly from side to side. Then finally he answered: "No, Son. You see that is the last step in my science. I go cautious. And I am not quite ready yet."

"Well!" said Leo. "Well well well!"

The old man stood in the open doorway. "Remember," he said. Framed there in the gray damp light of the early morning he looked shrunken and seedy and frail. But his smile was bright.

"Remember I love you," he said with a last nod. And the door closed quietly behind him.

The boy did not speak for a long time. He pulled down the bangs on his forehead and slid his grimy little forefinger around the rim of his empty cup. Then without looking at Leo he finally asked:

"Was he drunk?"

"No," said Leo shortly.

The boy raised his clear voice higher. "Then was he a dope fiend?"

"No."

The boy looked up at Leo, and his flat little face was desperate, his voice urgent and shrill. "Was he crazy? Do you think he was a lunatic?" The paper boy's voice dropped suddenly with doubt. "Leo? Or not?"

But Leo would not answer him. Leo had run a night café for fourteen years, and he held himself to be a critic of craziness. There were the town characters and also the transients who roamed in from the night. He knew the manias of all of them. But he did not want to satisfy the questions of the waiting child. He tightened his pale face and was silent.

So the boy pulled down the right flap of his helmet and as he turned to leave he made the only comment that seemed safe to him, the only remark that could not be laughed down and despised:

"He sure has done a lot of traveling."

Exercises   *1. The boy enters the café, which "seemed friendly and bright," from the outside world, where "it was raining that morning, and still very dark." Make clear the significance of the contrasting play of light and dark.*

2. Discover what attitude toward love the story expresses.

3. Reveal the theme of the story and its connection to the title.

4. Discuss the effectiveness of the telling of the story through the narrator's point of view. Why cannot the transient, Leo, or the boy narrate the story?

5. Precisely what is the transient trying to do? Does he achieve his goal? Why or why not?

6. What is Leo's function? Why does the boy turn to Leo for his answers? Why does Leo refuse to answer the boy?

7. Are the three main characters dynamic? Does anyone change or experience a moment of illumination?

8. Prepare an eight-point analysis of the story.

1. *Interpret the transient's system of scientific love.*

2. *Write a short story from the objective point of view dramatizing an event in your adolescent life that you feel has profoundly influenced your outlook or changed your character.*

3. *Explain why this particular story is best told through the dramatic point of view.*

Carson McCullers

Baldanza, Frank. "Plato in Dixie." *Georgia Review,* 12 (1958), 151–167.

Evans, Oliver. "The Case of Carson McCullers." *Georgia Review,* 18 (1964), 40–45.

———. "The Achievement of Carson McCullers." *English Journal,* 51 (1962), 301–308.

Folk, Barbara Nauer. "The Sad Sweet Music of Carson McCullers." *Georgia Review,* 16 (1962), 202–209.

Graner, Lawrence. "Carson McCullers." *University of Minnesota Pamphlets on American Writers* (84). Minneapolis: University of Minnesota Press, 1969.

Griffith, Albert J. "Carson McCullers' Myth of the Sad Cafe." *Georgia Review,* 21 (1957), 46–56.

Hamilton, Alice. "Loneliness and Alienation: The Life and Works of Carson McCullers." *Dalhousie Review,* 50 (1970), 215–229.

Hart, Jane. "Carson McCullers, Pilgrim of Loneliness." *Georgia Review,* 11 (1957), 53–58.

Hassan, Ihab H. "Carson McCullers: The Alchemy of Love and Aesthetics of Pain." *Modern Fiction Studies,* 5 (1959–60), 311–326.

Hughes, Catherine. "A World of Outcasts." *Commonweal,* 13 (October 1961), 73–75.

Phillips, Robert S. "Painful Love: Carson McCullers' Parable." *Southwest Review,* 51 (1966), 80–86.

Sherwood Anderson (1876–1941)

Born in Camden, Ohio, he quit school at the age of fourteen, worked at a variety of jobs, served in the Spanish-American War, was graduated from Wittenberg Academy, wrote copy for an advertising firm, and later founded, as well as managed, a paint factory. Driven by a passion to write, he abandoned the paint business, his wife, and three children and moved to Chicago, where he embarked on a new career and made friends with the so-called Chicago Renaissance group (Carl Sandburg, Theodore Dreiser, Vachel Lindsay, among them). His early works gained little recognition, but Winesburg, Ohio (1919), a collection of short stories, brought him widespread éclat.

I Want to Know Why

We got up at four in the morning, that first day in the east. On the evening before we had climbed off a freight train at the edge of town, and with the true instinct of Kentucky boys had found our way across town and to the race track and the stables at once. Then we knew we were all right. Hanley Turner right away found a nigger we knew. It was Bildad Johnson who in the winter works at Ed Becker's livery barn in our home town, Beckersville. Bildad is a good cook as almost all our niggers are and of course he, like everyone in our part of Kentucky who is anyone at all, likes the horses. In the spring Bildad begins to scratch around. A nigger from our country can flatter and wheedle anyone into letting him do most anything he wants. Bildad wheedles the stable men and the trainers from the horse farms in our country around Lexington. The trainers come into town in the evening to stand around and talk and maybe get into a poker game. Bildad gets in with them. He is always doing little favors and telling about things to eat, chicken browned in a pan, and how is the best way to cook sweet potatoes and corn bread. It makes your mouth water to hear him.

When the racing season comes on and the horses go to the races and there is all the talk on the streets in the evenings about the new colts, and everyone says when they are going over to Lexington or to the spring meeting at Churchill Downs or to Latonia, and the horsemen that have been down to New Orleans or maybe at the winter meeting at Havana in Cuba come home to spend a week before they start out again, at such a time when everything talked about in Beckersville is just horses and nothing else and the outfits start out and horse racing is in every breath of air you breathe, Bildad shows up with a job as cook for some outfit. Often when I think about it, his always going all season to the races and working in the livery barn in the winter where horses are and where men like to come and talk about horses, I wish I was a nigger. It's a foolish thing to say, but that's the way I am about being around horses, just crazy. I can't help it.

Well, I must tell you about what we did and let you in

on what I'm talking about. Four of us boys from Beckersville, all whites and sons of men who live in Beckersville regular, made up our minds we were going to the races, not just to Lexington or Louisville, I don't mean, but to the big eastern track we were always hearing our Beckersville men talk about, to Saratoga. We were all pretty young then. I was just turned fifteen and I was the oldest of the four. It was my scheme. I admit that and I talked the others into trying it. There was Hanley Turner and Henry Rieback and Tom Tumberton and myself. I had thirty-seven dollars I had earned during the winter working nights and Saturdays in Enoch Myer's grocery. Henry Rieback had eleven dollars and the others, Hanley and Tom, had only a dollar or two each. We fixed it all up and laid low until the Kentucky spring meetings were over and some of our men, the sportiest ones, the ones we envied the most, had cut out—then we cut out, too.

I won't tell you the trouble we had beating our way on freights and all. We went through Cleveland and Buffalo and other cities and saw Niagra Falls. We bought things there, souvenirs and spoons and cards and shells with pictures of the falls on them for our sisters and mothers, but thought we had better not send any of the things home. We didn't want to put the folks on our trail and maybe be nabbed.

We got into Saratoga as I said at night and went to the track. Bildad fed us up. He showed us a place to sleep in hay over a shed and promised to keep still. Niggers are all right about things like that. They won't squeal on you. Often a white man you might meet, when you had run away from home like that, might appear to be all right and give you a quarter or a half dollar or something, and then go right and give you away. White men will do that, but not a nigger. You can trust them. They are squarer with kids. I don't know why.

At the Saratoga meeting that year there were a lot of men from home. Dave Williams and Arthur Mulford and Jerry Myers and others. Then there was a lot from Louisville and Lexington Henry Rieback knew but I didn't. They were professional gamblers and Henry Rieback's father is one too. He is what is called a sheet writer and goes away most of the year to tracks. In the winter when he is home in Beckersville he don't stay there much but goes away to cities and deals faro. He is a nice man and generous, is always sending Henry presents, a bicycle and a gold watch and a boy scout suit of clothes and things like that.

My own father is a lawyer. He's all right, but don't make much money and can't buy me things and anyway I'm getting so old now I don't expect it. He never said nothing to me against Henry, but Hanley Turner and Tom Tumberton's fathers did. They said to their boys that money so come by is no good and they didn't want their boys brought up to hear gamblers' talk and be thinking about such things and maybe embrace them.

That's all right and I guess the men know what they are talking about, but I don't see what it's got to do with Henry or with horses either. That's what I'm writing this story about. I'm puzzled. I'm getting to be a man and want to think straight and be O.K., and there's something I saw at the race meeting at the eastern track I can't figure out.

I can't help it, I'm crazy about thoroughbred horses. I've always been that way. When I was ten years old and saw I was growing to be big and couldn't be a rider I was so sorry I nearly died. Harry Hellinfinger in Beckersville, whose father is Postmaster, is grown up and too lazy to work, but likes to stand around in the street and get up jokes on boys like sending them to a hardware store for a gimlet to bore square holes and other jokes like that. He played one on me. He told me that if I would eat half a cigar I would be stunted and not grow any more and maybe could be a rider. I did it. When father wasn't looking I took a cigar out of his pocket and gagged it down some way. It made me awful sick and the doctor had to be sent for, and then it did no good. I kept right on growing. It was a joke. When I told what I had done and why most fathers would have whipped me but mine didn't.

Well, I didn't get stunted and didn't die. It serves Harry Hellinfinger right. Then I made up my mind I would like to be a stable boy, but had to give that up too. Mostly niggers do that work and I knew father wouldn't let me go into it. No use to ask him.

If you've never been crazy about thoroughbreds it's because you've never been around where they are much and don't know any better. They're beautiful. There isn't anything so lovely and clean and full of spunk and honest and everything as some race horses. On the big horse farms that are all around our town Beckersville there are tracks and the horses run in the early morning. More than a thousand times I've got out of bed before daylight and walked two or three miles to the tracks. Mother wouldn't of let me go but father always says, "Let him alone." So I got some bread out of the bread box and some butter and jam, gobbled it and lit out.

At the tracks you sit on the fence with men, whites and niggers, and they chew tobacco and talk, and then the colts are brought out. It's early and the grass is covered with shiny dew and in another field a man is plowing and they are frying things in a shed where the track niggers sleep, and you know how a nigger can giggle and laugh and say things that make you laugh. A white man can't do it and some niggers can't but a track nigger can every time.

And so the colts are brought out and some are just galloped by stable boys, but almost every morning on a big track owned by a rich man who lives maybe in New York, there are always, nearly every morning, a few colts and some of the old race horses and geldings and mares that are cut loose.

It brings a lump up into my throat when a horse runs. I don't mean all horses but some. I can pick them nearly every time. It's in my blood like in the blood of race track niggers and trainers. Even when they just go slop-jogging along with a little nigger on their backs I can tell a winner. If my throat hurts and it's hard for me to swallow, that's him.

He'll run like Sam Hill when you let him out. If he don't win every time it'll be a wonder and because they've got him in a pocket behind another or he was pulled or got off bad at the post or something. If I wanted to be a gambler like Henry Rieback's father I could get rich. I know I could and Henry says so too. All I would have to do is wait 'til that hurt comes when I see a horse and then bet every cent. That's what I would do if I wanted to be a gambler, but I don't.

When you're at the tracks in the morning—not the race tracks but the training tracks around Beckersville—you don't see a horse, the kind I've been talking about, very often, but it's nice anyway. Any thoroughbred, that is sired right and out of a good mare and trained by a man that knows how, can run. If he couldn't what would he be there for and not pulling a plow?

Well, out of the stables they come and the boys are on their backs and it's lovely to be there. You hunch down on top of the fence and itch inside you. Over in the sheds the niggers giggle and sing. Bacon is being fried and coffee made. Everything smells lovely. Nothing smells better than coffee and manure and horses and niggers and bacon frying and pipes being smoked out of doors on a morning like that. It just gets you, that's what it does.

But about Saratoga. We was there six days and not a soul from home seen us and everything came off just as we wanted it to, fine weather and horses and races and all. We beat our way home and Bildad gave us a basket with fried chicken and bread and other eatables in it, and I had eighteen dollars when we got back to Beckersville. Mother jawed and cried but Pop didn't say much. I told everything we done except one thing. I did and saw that alone. That's what I'm writing about. It got me upset. I think about it at night. Here it is.

At Saratoga we laid up nights in the hay in the shed Bildad had showed us and ate with the niggers early and at night when the race people had all gone away. The men from home stayed mostly in the grandstand and betting field, and didn't come out around the places where the horses are kept except to the paddocks just before a race when the horses are saddled. At Saratoga they don't have paddocks under an open shed as at Lexington and Churchill Downs and other tracks down in our country, but saddle the horses right out in an open place under trees on a lawn as smooth and nice as Banker Bohon's front yard here in Beckersville. It's lovely. The horses are sweaty and nervous and shine and the men come out and smoke cigars and look at them and the trainers are there and the owners, and your heart thumps so you can hardly breathe.

Then the bugle blows for post and the boys that ride come running out with their silk clothes on and you run to get a place by the fence with the niggers.

I always am wanting to be a trainer or owner, and at the risk of being seen and caught and sent home I went to the paddocks before every race. The other boys didn't but I did.

We got to Saratoga on a Friday and on Wednesday the next week the big Mullford Handicap was to be run. Middlestride was in it and Sunstreak. The weather was fine and the track fast. I couldn't sleep the night before.

What had happened was that both these horses are the kind it makes my throat hurt to see. Middlestride is long and looks awkward and is a gelding. He belongs to Joe Thompson, a little owner from home who only has a half dozen horses. The Mullford Handicap is for a mile and Middlestride can't untrack fast. He goes away slow and is always way back at the half, then he begins to run and if the race is a mile and a quarter he'll just eat up everything and get there.

Sunstreak is different. He is a stallion and nervous and belongs on the biggest farm we've got in our country, the Van Riddle place that belongs to Mr. Van Riddle of New York. Sunstreak is like a girl you think about sometimes but never see. He is hard all over and lovely too. When you look at his head you want to kiss him. He is trained by Jerry Tillford who knows me and has been good to me lots of times, lets me walk into a horse's stall to look at him close and other things. There isn't anything as sweet as that horse. He stands at the post quiet and not letting on, but he is just burning up inside. Then when the barrier goes up he is off like his name, Sunstreak. It makes you ache to see him. It hurts you. He just lays down and runs like a bird dog. There isn't anything I ever see run like him except Middlestride when he gets untracked and stretches himself.

Gee! I ached to see that race and those two horses run, ached and dreaded it too. I didn't want to see either of our horses beaten. We had never sent a pair like that to the races before. Old men in Beckersville said so and the niggers said so. It was a fact.

Before the race I went over to the paddocks to see. I looked a last look at Middlestride, who isn't such a much standing in a paddock that way, then I went to see Sunstreak.

It was his day. I knew when I see him. I forgot all about being seen myself and walked right up. All the men from Beckersville were there and no one noticed me except Jerry Tillford. He saw me and something happened. I'll tell you about that.

I was standing looking at that horse and aching. In some way, I can't tell how, I knew just how Sunstreak felt inside. He was quiet and letting the niggers rub his legs and Mr. Van Riddle himself put the saddle on, but he was just a raging torrent inside. He was like the water in the river at Niagara Falls just before it goes plunk down. That horse wasn't thinking about running. He don't have to think about that. He was just thinking about holding himself back 'til the time for the running came. I knew that. I could just in a way see right inside him. He was going to do some awful running and I knew it. He wasn't bragging or letting on much or prancing or making a fuss, but just waiting. I knew it and Jerry Tillford his trainer knew. I looked up and then that man and I looked into each other's eyes. Something happened to me. I guess I loved the man as much as I did the horse because he knew what I knew. Seemed to me there wasn't anything in the world but that man and the horse and me. I cried and Jerry Tillford had a shine in his eyes. Then I came away to the fence to wait for the race. The horse was better than me, more steadier, and now I know better than Jerry. He was the quietest and he had to do the running.

Sunstreak ran first of course and he busted the world's record for a mile. I've seen that if I never see anything more. Everything came out just as I expected. Middlestride got left at the post and was way back and closed up to be second, just as I knew he would. He'll get a world's record too some day. They can't skin the Beckersville country on horses.

I watched the race calm because I knew what would happen. I was sure. Hanley Turner and Henry Rieback and Tom Tumberton were all more excited than me.

A funny thing had happened to me. I was thinking about Jerry Tillford the trainer and how happy he was all through the race. I liked him that afternoon even more than I ever liked my own father. I almost forgot the horses thinking that way about him. It was because of what I had seen in his eyes as he stood in the paddocks beside Sunstreak before the race started. I knew he had been watching and working with Sunstreak since the horse was a baby colt, had taught him to run and be patient and when to let himself out and not to quit, never. I knew that for him it was like a mother seeing her child do something brave or wonderful. It was the first time I ever felt for a man like that.

After the race that night I went out from Tom and Hanley and Henry. I wanted to be by myself and I wanted to be near Jerry Tillford if I could work it. Here is what happened.

The track in Saratoga is near the edge of town. It is all polished up and trees around, the evergreen kind, and grass and everything painted and nice. If you go past the track you get to a hard road made of asphalt for automobiles, and if you go along this for a few miles there is a road turns off to a little rummy-looking farm house set in a yard.

That night after the race I went along that road because I had seen Jerry and some other men go that way in an automobile. I didn't expect to find them. I walked for a ways and then sat down by a fence to think. It was the direction they went in. I wanted to be as near Jerry as I could. I felt close to him. Pretty soon I went up the side road—I don't know why—and came to the rummy farm house. I was just lonesome to see Jerry, like wanting to see your father at night when you were a young kid. Just then an automobile came along and turned in. Jerry was in it and Henry Rieback's father, and Arthur Bedford from home, and Dave Williams and two other men I didn't know. They got out of the car and went into the house, all but Henry Rieback's father who quarreled with them and said he wouldn't go. It was only about nine o'clock, but they were all drunk and the rummy-looking farm house was a place for bad women to stay in. That's what it was. I crept up along a fence and looked through a window and saw.

It's what gives me the fantods. I can't make it out. The women in the house were all ugly mean-looking women, not nice to look at or be near. They were homely too, except one who was tall and looked a little like the gelding Middlestride, but not clean like him, but with a hard ugly mouth. She had red hair. I saw everything plain. I got up by an old rose bush by an open window and looked. The women had on loose dresses and sat around in chairs. The men came in and some sat on the women's laps. The place smelled rotten and there was rotten talk, the kind a kid hears around a livery stable in a town like Beckersville in the winter but don't ever expect to hear talked when there are women around. It was rotten. A nigger wouldn't go into such a place.

I looked at Jerry Tillford. I've told you how I had the feeling about him on account of his knowing what was going on inside of Sunstreak in the minute before he went to the post for the race in which he made a world's record.

Jerry bragged in that bad woman house as I know Sunstreak wouldn't never have bragged. He said that he made that horse, that it was him that won the race and made the record. He lied and bragged like a fool. I never heard such silly talk.

And then, what do you suppose he did! He looked at the woman in there, the one that was lean and hard-mouthed and looked a little like the gelding Middlestride, but not clean like him, and his eyes began to shine just as they did when he looked at me and at Sunstreak in the paddocks at the track in the afternoon. I stood there by the window—gee!—but I wished I hadn't gone away from the tracks, but had stayed with the boys and the niggers and the horses. The tall rotten-looking woman was between us just as Sunstreak was in the paddocks in the afternoon.

Then, all of a sudden, I began to hate that man. I wanted to scream and rush in the room and kill him. I never had such a feeling before. I was so mad clean through that I cried and my fists were doubled up so my finger nails cut my hands.

And Jerry's eyes kept shining and he waved back and forth, and then he went and kissed that woman and I crept away and went back to the tracks and to bed and didn't sleep hardly any, and then next day I got the other kids to start home with me and never told them anything I seen.

I been thinking about it ever since. I can't make it out. Spring has come again and I'm nearly sixteen and go to the tracks mornings same as always, and I see Sunstreak and Middlestride and a new colt named Strident I'll bet will lay them all out, but no one thinks so but me and two or three niggers.

But things are different. At the tracks the air don't taste as good or smell as good. It's because a man like Jerry Tillford, who knows what he does, could see a horse like Sunstreak run, and kiss a woman like that the same day. I can't make it out. Darn him, what did he want to do like that for? I keep thinking about it and it spoils looking at horses and smelling things and hearing niggers laugh and everything. Sometimes I'm so mad about it I want to fight someone. It gives me the fantods. What did he do it for? I want to know why.

Exercises

1. *What kind of person is the narrator? When is he reliable? When is he not?*

2. *Through the first-person narrator the author manages to establish an intimate relationship between the reader and the characters. How does he accomplish this feat?*

3. *Is the boy a static or dynamic character? What is his dilemma? How is sympathy for him achieved?*

4. *What significant aspect of adolescent life does the story deal with? Briefly express the theme.*

5. *Discuss the implications of the title of the story and the meaning of the boy's final statement.*

6. *What exactly does the boy want to know?*

7. *For what purpose does the author give admirable human qualities to the horses?*

8. *Characterize Bildad. Explain his role in the story.*

Topics for
Writing

1. *Appreciate the plight of the young, naive boy who inevitably loses his innocence in the course of discovering evil in the world.*

2. *Write a comparison that points to the similarities and differences in the characters of the two boys in "A Tree, a Rock, a Cloud" and "I Want to Know Why."*

3. *Enumerate the advantages of the first-person-protagonist point of view as used in this story.*

Selected
Bibliography

Sherwood Anderson

Flanagan, J. T. "The Permanence of Sherwood Anderson." *Southwest Review*, 35 (1970), 170–177.

Gold, Herbert. "The Purity and Cunning of Sherwood Anderson." *Hudson Review*, 10 (1957–58), 548–557.

Howe, Irving. "Sherwood Anderson: An American as Artist." *Kenyon Review*, 13 (1951), 193–203.

O'Connor, Frank. *The Lonely Voice: A Study of the Short Story.*

Cleveland and New York: World Publishing, 1963, pp. 39–41.

Sherbo, Arthur. "I Want to Know Why and Brooks and Warren." *College English*, 15 (1954), 350–351.

Trilling, Lionel. *The Liberal Imagination.* New York: Viking Press, 1950, pp.23–33.

Weber, Brom. "Anderson and 'The Essence of Things.' " *Sewanee Review*, 59 (1951), 678–692.

White, Ray Lewis, ed. *The Achievement of Sherwood Anderson: Essays in Criticism.* Chapel Hill: University of North Carolina Press, 1966.

Winther, S. K. "The Aura of Loneliness in Sherwood Anderson." *Modern Fiction Studies*, 5 (1959), 145–152.

D. H. Lawrence (1885–1930)

Born in Nottinghamshire, England, the son of a coal miner and a schoolteacher, he studied at Nottingham University, endured for a time a clerical job, and taught school. Disenchanted, he forsook England and traveled extensively in search of the perfect life. Later, returning to England, he wrote essays, poetry, short stories, novels, and travel books. His best known novels, Sons and Lovers *(1913),* Women in Love *(1920),* The Fox *(1922), and* Lady Chatterley's Lover *(1928) were treated harshly by several critics as pornographic matter. Most critics agree, however, in calling "The Horse Dealer's Daughter" one of the most remarkable love stories in all literature.*

The Horse Dealer's Daughter

"Well, Mabel, and what are you going to do with yourself?" asked Joe, with foolish flippancy. He felt quite safe himself. Without listening for an answer, he turned aside, worked a grain of tobacco to the tip of his tongue and spat it out. He did not care about anything, since he felt safe himself.

The three brothers and the sister sat round the desolate breakfast table, attempting some sort of desultory consultation. The morning's post had given the final tap to the family fortune, and all was over. The dreary dining-room itself, with its heavy mahogany furniture, looked as if it were waiting to be done away with.

But the consultation amounted to nothing. There was a strange air of ineffectuality about the three men, as they sprawled at table, smoking and reflecting vaguely on their own condition. The girl was alone, a rather short, sullen-looking young woman of twenty-seven. She did not share the same life as her brothers. She would have been good-looking, save for the impassive fixity of her face, "bull-dog," as her brothers called it.

There was a confused tramping of horses' feet outside. The three men all sprawled round in their chairs to watch. Beyond the dark holly-bushes that separated the strip of lawn from the highroad, they could see a cavalcade of shire horses swinging out of their own yard, being taken for exercise. This was the last time. These were the last horses that would go through their hands. The young men watched with critical, callous look. They were all frightened at the collapse of their lives, and the sense of disaster in which they were involved left them no inner freedom.

Yet they were three fine, well-set fellows enough. Joe, the eldest, was a man of thirty-three, broad and handsome in a hot, flushed way. His face was red, he twisted his black mustache over a thick finger, his eyes were shallow and restless. He had a sensual way of uncovering his teeth when he laughed, and his bearing was stupid. Now he watched the horses with a glazed look of helplessness in his eyes, a certain stupor of downfall.

The great draught-horses swung past. They were tied head to tail, four of them, and they heaved along to where a lane branched off from the highroad, planting their great hoofs floutingly in the fine black mud, swinging their great rounded haunches sumptuously, and trotting a few sudden steps as they were led into the lane, round the corner. Every movement showed a massive, slumbrous strength, and a stupidity which held them in subjection. The groom at the head looked back, jerking the leading rope. And the cavalcade moved out of sight up the lane, the tail of the last horse, bobbed up tight and stiff, held out taut from the swinging great haunches as they rocked behind the hedges in a motion-like sleep.

Joe watched with glazed hopeless eyes. The horses were almost like his own body to him. He felt he was done for now. Luckily he was engaged to a woman as old as himself, and therefore her father, who was steward of a neighboring estate, would provide him with a job. He would marry and go into harness. His life was over, he would be a subject animal now.

He turned uneasily aside, the retreating steps of the horses echoing in his ears. Then, with foolish restlessness, he reached for the scraps of bacon-rind from the plates, and making a faint whistling sound, flung them to the terrier that lay against the fender. He watched the dog swallow them, and waited till the creature looked into his eyes. Then a faint grin came on his face, and in a high, foolish voice he said:

"You won't get much more bacon, shall you, you little bitch?"

The dog faintly and dismally wagged its tail, then lowered its haunches, circled round, and lay down again.

There was another helpless silence at the table. Joe sprawled uneasily in his seat, not willing to go till the family conclave was dissolved. Fred Henry, the second brother, was erect, clean-limbed, alert. He had watched the passing of the horses with more *sang-froid*. If he was an animal, like Joe, he was an animal which controls, not one which is controlled. He was master of any horse, and he carried himself with a well-tempered air of mastery. But he was not master of the situations of life. He pushed his coarse brown mustache upwards, off his lip, and glanced irritably at his sister, who sat impassive and inscrutable.

"You'll go and stop with Lucy for a bit, shan't you?" he asked. The girl did not answer.

"I don't see what else you can do," persisted Fred Henry.

"Go as a skivvy," Joe interpolated laconically.

The girl did not move a muscle.

"If I was her, I should go in for training for a nurse," said Malcolm, the youngest of them all. He was the baby of the family, a young man of twenty-two, with a fresh, jaunty *museau*.

But Mabel did not take any notice of him. They had talked at her and round her for so many years, that she hardly heard them at all.

The marble clock on the mantelpiece softly chimed the half-hour, the dog rose uneasily from the hearthrug and looked at the party at the breakfast table. But still they sat on in ineffectual conclave.

"Oh, all right," said Joe suddenly, apropos of nothing. "I'll get a move on."

He pushed back his chair, straddled his knees with a downward jerk, to get them free, in horsey fashion, and went to the fire. Still he did not go out of the room; he was curious to know what the others would do or say. He began to charge his pipe, looking down at the dog and saying, in a high, affected voice:

"Going wi' me? Going wi' me are ter? Tha'rt goin' further than that counts on just now, dost hear?"

The dog faintly wagged its tail, the man stuck out his jaw and covered his pipe with his hands, and puffed intently, losing himself in the tobacco, looking down all the while at the dog with an absent brown eye. The dog looked at him in mournful distrust. Joe stood with his knees stuck out, in real horsey fashion.

"Have you had a letter from Lucy?" Fred Henry asked his sister.

"Last week," came the neutral reply.

"And what does she say?"

There was no answer.

"Does she *ask* you to go and stop there?" persisted Fred Henry.

"She says I can if I like."

"Well, then, you'd better. Tell her you'll come on Monday."

This was received in silence.

"That's what you'll do then, is it?" said Fred Henry, in some exasperation.

But she made no answer. There was a silence of futility and irritation in the room. Malcolm grinned fatuously.

"You'll have to make up your mind between now and next Wednesday," said Joe loudly, "or else find yourself lodgings on the curbstone."

The face of the young woman darkened, but she sat on immutable.

"Here's Jack Fergusson!" exclaimed Malcolm, who was looking aimlessly out of the window.

"Where?" exclaimed Joe, loudly.

"Just gone past."

"Coming in?"

Malcolm craned his neck to see the gate.

"Yes," he said.

There was a silence. Mabel sat on like one condemned, at the head of the table. Then a whistle was heard from the kitchen. The dog got up and barked sharply. Joe opened the door and shouted:

"Come on."

After a moment a young man entered. He was muffled up in overcoat and a purple woolen scarf, and his tweed cap, which he did not remove, was pulled down on his head. He was of medium height, his face was rather long and pale, his eyes looked tired.

"Hello, Jack! Well, Jack!" exclaimed Malcolm and Joe. Fred Henry merely said "Jack!"

"What's doing?" asked the newcomer, evidently addressing Fred Henry.

"Same. We've got to be out by Wednesday. —Got a cold?"

"I have—got it bad, too."

"Why don't you stop in?"

"*Me* stop in? When I can't stand on my legs, perhaps I shall have a chance." The young man spoke huskily. He had a slight Scotch accent.

"It's a knock-out, isn't it," said Joe boisterously, "if a doctor goes round croaking with a cold. Looks bad for the patients, doesn't it?"

The young doctor looked at him slowly.

"Anything the matter with *you*, then?" he asked sarcastically.

"Not as I know of. Damn your eyes, I hope not. Why?"

"I thought you were very concerned about the patients, wondered if you might be one yourself."

"Damn it, no, I've never been patient to no flaming doctor, and hope I never shall be," returned Joe.

At this point Mabel rose from the table, and they all seemed to become aware of her existence. She began putting the dishes together. The young doctor looked at her, but did not address her. He had not greeted her. She went out of the room with the tray, her face impassive and unchanged.

"When are you off then, all of you?" asked the doctor.

"I'm catching the eleven-forty," replied Malcolm. "Are you goin' down wi' th' trap, Joe?"

"Yes, I've told you I'm going down wi' th' trap, haven't I?"

"We'd better be getting her in then. So long, Jack, if I don't see you before I go," said Malcolm, shaking hands.

He went out, followed by Joe, who seemed to have his tail between his legs.

"Well, this is the devil's own," exclaimed the doctor, when he was left alone with Fred Henry. "Going before Wednesday, are you?"

"That's the orders," replied the other.

"Where, to Northampton?"

"That's it."

"The devil!" exclaimed Fergusson, with quiet chagrin.

And there was silence between the two.

"All settled up, are you?" asked Fergusson.

"About."

There was another pause.

"Well, I shall miss yer, Freddy boy," said the young doctor.

"And I shall miss thee, Jack," returned the other.

"Miss you like hell," mused the doctor.

Fred Henry turned aside. There was nothing to say. Mabel came in again, to finish clearing the table.

"What are *you* going to do, then, Miss Pervin?" asked Fergusson. "Going to your sister's, are you?"

Mabel looked at him with her steady, dangerous eyes, that always made him uncomfortable, unsettling his superficial ease.

"No," she said.

"Well, what in the name of fortune *are* you going to do? Say what you *mean* to do," cried Fred Henry, with futile intensity.

But she only averted her head, and continued her work. She folded the white table-cloth, and put on the chenille cloth.

"The sulkiest bitch that ever trod!" muttered her brother.

But she finished her task with perfectly impassive face, the young doctor watching her interestedly all the while. Then she went out.

Fred Henry stared after her, clenching his lips, his blue eyes fixing in sharp antagonism, as he made a grimace of sour exasperation.

"You could bray her into bits, and that's all you'd get out of her," he said in a small, narrowed tone.

The doctor smiled faintly.

"What's she *going* to do, then?" he asked.

"Strike me if *I* know!" returned the other.

There was a pause. Then the doctor stirred.

"I'll be seeing you to-night, shall I?" he said to his friend.

"Ay—where's it to be? Are we going over to Jessdale?"

"I don't know. I've got such a cold on me. I'll come round to the Moon and Stars, anyway."

"Let Lizzie and May miss their night for once, eh?"

"That's it—if I feel as I do now."

"All's one—"

The two young men went through the passage and down to the back door together. The house was large, but it was servantless now, and desolate. At the back was a small bricked house-yard, and beyond that a big square, graveled fine and red, and having stables on two sides. Sloping, dank, winter-dark fields stretched away on the open sides.

But the stables were empty. Joseph Pervin, the father of the family, had been a man of no education, who had become a fairly large horse dealer. The stables had been full of horses, there was a great turmoil and come-and-go of horses and of dealers and grooms. Then the kitchen was full of servants. But of late things had declined. The old man had married a second time, to retrieve his fortunes. Now he was dead and everything was gone to the dogs, there was nothing but debt and threatening.

For months, Mabel had been servantless in the big house, keeping the home together in penury for her ineffectual brothers. She had kept house for ten years. But previously, it was with unstinted means. Then, however brutal and coarse everything was, the sense of money had kept her proud, confident. The men might be foul-mouthed, the women in the kitchen might have bad reputations, her brothers might have illegitimate children. But so long as there was money, the girl felt herself established, and brutally proud, reserved.

No company came to the house, save dealers and coarse

men. Mabel had no associates of her own sex, after her sister went away. But she did not mind. She went regularly to church, she attended to her father. And she lived in the memory of her mother, who had died when she was fourteen, and whom she had loved. She had loved her father, too, in a different way, depending upon him, and feeling secure in him, until at the age of fifty-four he married again. And then she had set hard against him. Now he had died and left them all hopelessly in debt.

She had suffered badly during the period of poverty. Nothing, however, could shake the curious sullen, animal pride that dominated each member of the family. Now, for Mabel, the end had come. Still she would not cast about her. She would follow her own way just the same. She would always hold the keys of her own situation. Mindless and persistent, she endured from day to day. Why should she think? Why should she answer anybody? It was enough that this was the end, and there was no way out. She need not pass any more darkly along the main street of the small town, avoiding every eye. She need not demean herself any more, going into the shops and buying the cheapest food. This was at an end. She thought of nobody, not even of herself. Mindless and persistent, she seemed in a sort of ecstasy to becoming nearer to her fulfillment, her own glorification, approaching her dead mother, who was glorified.

In the afternoon she took a little bag, with shears and sponge and a small scrubbing brush, and went out. It was a gray, wintry day, with saddened, dark-green fields and an atmosphere blackened by the smoke of foundries not far off. She went quickly, darkly along the causeway, heeding nobody, through the town to the churchyard.

There she always felt secure, as if no one could see her, although as a matter of fact she was exposed to the stare of everyone who passed along under the churchyard wall. Nevertheless, once under the shadow of the great looming church, among the graves, she felt immune from the world, reserved within the thick churchyard wall as in another country.

Carefully she clipped the grass from the grave, and arranged the pinky-white, small chrysanthemums in the tin cross. When this was done, she took an empty jar from a neighboring grave, brought water, and carefully, most scrupulously sponged the marble headstone and the coping-stone.

It gave her sincere satisfaction to do this. She felt in immediate contact with the world of her mother. She took minute pains, went through the park in a state bordering on pure happiness, as if in performing this task she came into a subtle, intimate connection with her mother. For the life she followed here in the world was far less real than the world of death she inherited from her mother.

The doctor's house was just by the church. Fergusson, being a mere hired assistant, was slave to the countryside. As he hurried now to attend to the outpatients in the surgery, glancing across the graveyard with his quick eye, he saw the girl at her task at the grave. She seemed so intent and remote, it was like looking into another world. Some mystical element was touched in him. He slowed down as he walked, watching her as if spellbound.

She lifted her eyes, feeling him looking. Their eyes met. And each looked away again at once, each feeling, in some way, found out by the other. He lifted his cap and passed on down the road. There remained distinct in his consciousness, like a vision, the memory of her face, lifted from the tombstone in the churchyard, and looking at him with slow, large, portentous eyes. It *was* portentous, her face. It seemed to mesmerize him. There was a heavy power in her eyes which laid hold of his whole being, as if he had drunk some powerful drug. He had been feeling weak and done before. Now the life came back into him, he felt delivered from his own fretted, daily self.

He finished his duties at the surgery as quickly as might be, hastily filling up the bottle of the waiting people with cheap drugs. Then, in perpetual haste, he set off again to visit several cases in another part of his round, before teatime. At all times he preferred to walk if he could, but particularly when he was not well. He fancied the motion restored him.

The afternoon was falling. It was gray, deadened, and wintry, with a slow, moist, heavy coldness sinking in and deadening all the faculties. But why should he think or notice? He hastily climbed the hill and turned across the dark-green fields, following the black cinder-track. In the distance, across a shallow dip in the country, the small town was clustered like smoldering ash, a tower, a spire, a heap of low, raw, extinct houses. And on the nearest fringe of the town, sloping into the dip, was Oldmeadow, the Pervins' house. He could see the stables and the outbuildings distinctly, as they lay towards him on the slope. Well, he would not go there many more times! Another resource would be lost to him, another place gone: the only company he cared for in the alien, ugly little town he was losing. Nothing but work, drudgery, constant hastening from dwelling to dwelling among the colliers and the iron-workers. It wore him out, but at the same time he had a craving for it. It was a stimulant to him to be in the homes of the working people, moving as it were through the innermost body of their life. His nerves were excited and gratified. He could come so near, into the very lives of the rough, inarticulate, powerfully emotional men and women. He grumbled, he said he hated the hellish hole. But as a matter of fact it excited him, the contact with the rough, strongly-feeling people was a stimulant applied direct to his nerves.

Below Oldmeadow, in the green, shallow, soddened hollow of fields, lay a square, deep pond. Roving across the landscape, the doctor's quick eye detected a figure in black passing through the gate of the field, down towards the pond. He looked again. It would be Mabel Pervin. His mind suddenly became alive and attentive.

Why was she going down there? He pulled up on the

path on the slope above, and stood staring. He could just make sure of the small black figure moving in the hollow of the failing day. He seemed to see her in the midst of such obscurity, that he was like a clairvoyant, seeing rather with the mind's eye than with ordinary sight. Yet he could see her positively enough, while he kept his eye attentive. He felt, if he looked away from her, in the thick, ugly falling dusk, he would lose her altogether.

He followed her minutely as she moved, direct and intent, like something transmitted rather than stirring in voluntary activity, straight down the field towards the pond. There she stood on the bank for a moment. She never raised her head. Then she waded slowly into the water.

He stood motionless as the small black figure walked slowly and deliberately towards the center of the pond, very slowly, gradually moving deeper into the motionless water, and still moving forward as the water got up to her breast. Then he could see her no more in the dusk of the dead afternoon.

"There!" he exclaimed. "Would you believe it?"

And he hastened straight down, running over the wet, soddened fields, pushing through the hedges, down into the depression of callous wintry obscurity. It took him several minutes to come to the pond. He stood on the bank, breathing heavily. He could see nothing. His eyes seemed to penetrate the dead water. Yes, perhaps that was the dark shadow of her black clothing beneath the surface of the water.

He slowly ventured into the pond. The bottom was deep, soft clay, he sank in, and the water clasped dead cold round his legs. As he stirred he could smell the cold, rotten clay that fouled up into the water. It was objectionable in his lungs. Still, repelled and yet not heeding, he moved deeper into the pond. The cold water rose over his thighs, over his loins, upon his abdomen. The lower part of his body was all sunk in the hideous cold element. And the bottom was so deeply soft and uncertain, he was afraid of pitching with his mouth underneath. He could not swim, and was afraid.

He crouched a little, spreading his hands under the water and moving them round, trying to feel for her. The dead cold pond swayed upon his chest. He moved again, a little deeper, and again, with his hands underneath, he felt all around under the water. And he touched her clothing. But it evaded his fingers. He made a desperate effort to grasp it.

And so doing he lost his balance and went under, horribly, suffocating in the foul earthy water, struggling madly for a few moments. At last, after what seemed an eternity, he got his footing, rose again into the air and looked around. He gasped, and knew he was in the world. Then he looked at the water. She had risen near him. He grasped her clothing, and drawing her nearer, turned to take his way to land again.

He went very slowly, carefully, absorbed in the slow progress. He rose higher, climbing out of the pond. The water was now only about his legs; he was thankful, full of relief to be out of the clutches of the pond. He lifted her and staggered onto the bank, out of the horror of wet, gray clay.

He laid her down on the bank. She was quite unconscious and running with water. He made the water come from her mouth, he worked to restore her. He did not have to work very long before he could feel the breathing begin again in her; she was breathing naturally. He worked a little longer. He could feel her live beneath his hands; she was coming back. He wiped her face, wrapped her in his overcoat, looked round into the dim, dark-gray world, then lifted her and staggered down the bank and across the fields.

It seemed an unthinkably long way, and his burden so heavy he felt he would never get to the house. But at last he was in the stableyard, and then in the house-yard. He opened the door and went into the house. In the kitchen he laid her down on the hearthrug, and called. The house was empty. But the fire was burning in the grate.

Then again he kneeled to attend to her. She was breathing regularly, her eyes were wide open and as if conscious, but there seemed something missing in her look. She was conscious in herself, but unconscious of her surroundings.

He ran upstairs, took blankets from a bed, and put them before the fire to warm. Then he removed her saturated, earthy-smelling clothing, rubbed her dry with a towel, and wrapped her naked in the blankets. Then he went into the dining-room, to look for spirits. There was a little whisky. He drank a gulp himself, and put some into her mouth.

The effect was instantaneous. She looked full into his face, as if she had been seeing him for some time, and yet had only just become conscious of him.

"Dr. Fergusson?" she said.

"What?" he answered.

He was divesting himself of his coat, intending to find some dry clothing upstairs. He could not bear the smell of the dead, clayey water, and he was mortally afraid for his own health.

"What did I do?" she asked.

"Walked into the pond," he replied. He had begun to shudder like one sick, and could hardly attend to her. Her eyes remained full on him, he seemed to be going dark in his mind, looking back at her helplessly. The shuddering became quieter in him, his life came back in him, dark and unknowing, but strong again.

"Was I out of my mind?" she asked, while her eyes were fixed on him all the time.

"Maybe, for the moment," he replied. He felt quiet, because his strength had come back. The strange fretful strain had left him.

"Am I out of my mind now?" she asked.

"Are you?" he reflected a moment. "No," he answered truthfully, "I don't see that you are." He turned his face aside. He was afraid now, because he felt dazed, and felt dimly that her power was stronger than his, in this issue. And she continued to look at him fixedly all the time. "Can you tell me where I shall find some dry things to put on?" he asked.

"Did you dive into the pond for me?" she asked.

"No," he answered. "I walked in. But I went in overhead as well."

There was silence for a moment. He hesitated. He very much wanted to go upstairs to get into dry clothing. But there was another desire in him. And she seemed to hold him. His will seemed to have gone to sleep, and left him, standing there slack before her. But he felt warm inside himself. He did not shudder at all, though his clothes were sodden on him.

"Why did you?" she asked.

"Because I didn't want you to do such a foolish thing," he said.

"It wasn't foolish," she said, still gazing at him as she lay on the floor, with a sofa cushion under her head. "It was the right thing to do. *I* knew best, then."

"I'll go and shift these wet things," he said. But still he had not the power to move out of her presence, until she sent him. It was as if she had the life of his body in her hands, and he could not extricate himself. Or perhaps he did not want to.

Suddenly she sat up. Then she became aware of her own immediate condition. She felt the blankets about her, she knew her own limbs. For a moment it seemed as if her reason were going. She looked round, with wild eye, as if seeking something. He stood still with fear. She saw her clothing lying scattered.

"Who undressed me?" she asked, her eyes resting full and inevitable on his face.

"I did," he replied, "to bring you round."

For some moments she sat and gazed at him awfully, her lips parted.

"Do you love me, then?" she asked.

He only stood and stared at her, fascinated. His soul seemed to melt.

She shuffled forward on her knees, and put her arms round him, round his legs, as he stood there, pressing her breasts against his knees and thighs, clutching him with strange, convulsive certainty, pressing his thighs against her, drawing him to her face, her throat, as she looked up at him with flaring, humble eyes of transfiguration, triumphant in first possession.

"You love me," she murmured, in strange transport, yearning and triumphant and confident. "You love me. I know you love me, I know."

And she was passionately kissing his knees, through the

wet clothing, passionately and indiscriminately kissing his knees, his legs, as if unaware of everything.

He looked down at the tangled wet hair, the wild, bare, animal shoulders. He was amazed, bewildered, and afraid. He had never thought of loving her. He had never wanted to love her. When he rescued her and restored her, he was a doctor, and she was a patient. He had had no single personal thought of her. Nay, this introduction of the personal element was very distasteful to him, a violation of his professional honor. It was horrible to have her there embracing his knees. It was horrible. He revolted from it, violently. And yet—and yet—he had not the power to break away.

She looked at him again, with the same supplication of powerful love, and that same transcendent, frightening light of triumph. In view of the delicate flame which seemed to come from her face like a light, he was powerless. And yet he had never intended to love her. He had never intended. And something stubborn in him could not give way.

"You love me," she repeated, in a murmur of deep, rhapsodic assurance. "You love me."

Her hands were drawing him, drawing him down to her. He was afraid, even a little horrified. For he had, really, no intention of loving her. Yet her hands were drawing him towards her. He put out his hand quickly to steady himself, and grasped her bare shoulder. A flame seemed to burn the hand that grasped her soft shoulder. He had no intention of loving her: his whole will was against his yielding. It was horrible. And yet wonderful was the touch of her shoulders, beautiful the shining of her face. Was she perhaps mad? He had a horror of yielding to her. Yet something in him ached also.

He had been staring away at the door, away from her. But his hand remained on her shoulder. She had gone suddenly very still. He looked down at her. Her eyes were now wide with fear, with doubt, the light was dying from her face, a shadow of terrible grayness was returning. He could not bear the touch of her eyes' question upon him, and the look of death behind the question.

With an inward groan he gave way, and let his heart yield towards her. A sudden gentle smile came on his face. And her eyes, which never left his face, slowly, slowly filled with tears. He watched the strange water rise in her eyes, like some slow fountain coming up. And his heart seemed to burn and melt away in his breast.

He could not bear to look at her any more. He dropped on his knees and caught her head with his arms and pressed her face against his throat. She was very still. His heart, which seemed to have broken, was burning with a kind of agony in his breast. And he felt her slow, hot tears wetting his throat. But he could not move.

He felt the hot tears wet his neck and the hollows of his neck, and he remained motionless, suspended through one of man's eternities. Only now it had become indispensable to him to have her face pressed close to him; he could never let her go again. He could never let her head go away from the close clutch of his arm. He wanted to remain like that forever, with his heart hurting him in a pain that was also life to him. Without knowing, he was looking down on her damp, soft brown hair.

Then, as it were suddenly, he smelt the horrid stagnant smell of that water. And at the same moment she drew away from him and looked at him. Her eyes were wistful and unfathomable. He was afraid of them, and he fell to kissing her, not knowing what he was doing. He wanted her eyes not to have that terrible, wistful, unfathomable look.

When she turned her face to him again, a faint delicate flush was glowing, and there was again dawning that terrible shining of joy in her eyes, which really terrified him, and yet which he now wanted to see, because he feared the look of doubt still more.

"You love me?" she said, rather faltering.

"Yes." The word cost him a painful effort. Not because it wasn't true. But because it was too newly true, the *saying* seemed to tear open again his newly-torn heart. And he hardly wanted it to be true, even now.

She lifted her face to him, and he bent forward and kissed her on the mouth, gently, with the one kiss that is an eternal pledge. And as he kissed her his heart strained again in his breast. He never intended to love her. But now it was over. He had crossed over the gulf to her, and all that he had left behind had shriveled and become void.

After the kiss, her eyes again slowly filled with tears. She sat still, away from him, with her face drooped aside, and her hands folded in her lap. The tears fell very slowly. There was complete silence. He too sat there motionless and silent on the hearthrug. The strange pain of his heart that was broken seemed to consume him. That he should love her? That this was love! That he should be ripped open in this way!— Him, a doctor!—How they would all jeer if they knew!—It was agony to him to think they might know.

In the curious naked pain of the thought he looked again to her. She was sitting there drooped into a muse. He saw a tear fall, and his heart flared hot. He saw for the first time that one of her shoulders was quite uncovered, one arm bare, he could see one of her small breasts; dimly, because it had become almost dark in the room.

"Why are you crying?" he asked, in an altered voice.

She looked up at him, and behind her tears the consciousness of her situation for the first time brought a dark look of shame to her eyes.

"I'm not crying, really," she said, watching him half frightened.

He reached his hand, and softly closed it on her bare arm.

"I love you! I love you!" he said in a soft, low, vibrating voice, unlike himself.

She shrank, and dropped her head. The soft, penetrating grip of his hand on her arm distressed her. She looked up at him.

"I want to go," she said. "I want to go and get you some dry things."

"Why?" he said. "I'm all right."

"But I want to go," she said. "And I want you to change your things."

He released her arm, and she wrapped herself in the blanket, looking at him rather frightened. And still she did not rise.

"Kiss me," she said wistfully.

He kissed her, but briefly, half in anger.

Then, after a second, she rose nervously, all mixed up in the blanket. He watched her in her confusion, as she tried to extricate herself and wrap herself up so that she could walk. He watched her relentlessly, as she knew. And as she went, the blanket trailing, and as he saw a glimpse of her feet and her white leg, he tried to remember her as she was when he had wrapped her in the blanket. But then he didn't want to remember, because she had been nothing to him then, and his nature revolted from remembering her as she was when she was nothing to him.

A tumbling, muffled noise from within the dark house startled him. Then he heard her voice:—"There are clothes." He rose and went to the foot of the stairs, and gathered up the garments she had thrown down. Then he came back to the fire, to rub himself down and dress. He grinned at his own appearance, when he had finished.

The fire was sinking, so he put on coal. The house was now quite dark, save for the light of a street-lamp that shone in faintly from beyond the holly trees. He lit the gas with matches he found on the mantelpiece. Then he emptied the pockets of his own clothes, and threw all his wet things in a heap into the scullery. After which he gathered up her sodden clothes, gently, and put them in a separate heap on the copper-top in the scullery.

It was six o'clock on the clock. His own watch had stopped. He ought to go back to the surgery. He waited, and still she did not come down. So he went to the foot of the stairs and called:

"I shall have to go."

Almost immediately he heard her coming down. She had on her best dress of black voile, and her hair was tidy, but still damp. She looked at him—and in spite of herself, smiled.

"I don't like you in those clothes," she said.

"Do I look a sight?" he answered.

They were shy of one another.

"I'll make you some tea," she said.

"No, I must go."

"Must you?" And she looked at him again with the wide, strained, doubtful eyes. And again, from the pain of his breast, he knew how he loved her. He went and bent to kiss her, gently, passionately, with his heart's painful kiss.

"And my hair smells so horrible," she murmured in distraction. "And I'm so awful, I'm so awful! Oh, no, I'm too awful." And she broke into bitter, heartbroken sobbing. "You can't want to love me, I'm horrible."

"Don't be silly, don't be silly," he said, trying to comfort her, kissing her, holding her in his arms. "I want you, I want to marry you, we're going to be married, quickly, quickly—tomorrow if I can."

But she only sobbed terribly, and cried:

"I feel awful. I feel awful. I feel I'm horrible to you."

"No, I want you, I want you," was all he answered, blindly, with that terrible intonation which frightened her almost more than her horror lest he should *not* want her.

3. *Identify the point of view used in the story and comment on its appropriateness to the author's purpose and effects.*

4. *Detail what you believe would be gained or lost were the story told from Dr. Fergusson's point of view.*

Selected
Bibliography   D. H. Lawrence

Amon, Frank. "D. H. Lawrence and the Short Story." In *The Achievement of D. H. Lawrence*, ed. Frederick J. Hoffman and Harry T. Moore. Norman: University of Oklahoma Press, 1953, pp. 222–234.

Ford, George H. *Double Measure: A Study of the Novels and Stories of D. H. Lawrence.* New York: Holt, Rinehart and Winston, 1965.

Frye, Northrop. "The Archetypes of Literature." *Kenyon Review*, 13 (1951), 92–110.

Junkins, Donald. "D. H. Lawrence's 'The Horse Dealer's Daughter.'" *Studies in Short Fiction*, 6 (1969), 210–212.

O'Connor, Frank. *The Lonely Voice: A Study of the Short Story.* Cleveland and New York: World Publishing, 1963, pp. 143–155.

Spilka, Mark. *The Love Ethic of D. H. Lawrence.* Bloomington: Indiana University Press, 1955.

Tedlock, E. W. *D. H. Lawrence, Artist & Rebel.* Albuquerque: University of New Mexico Press, 1963.

Vickery, John B. "Myth and Ritual in the Shorter Fiction of D. H. Lawrence." *Modern Fiction Studies*, 5 (1959), 65–82.

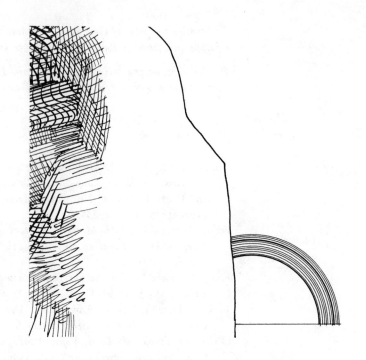

4 Theme or Meaning

Not every story imparts a world-shattering, philosophical pronouncement; not every story delivers a sermonette from which one can glean a moral or a lesson. But, to be sure, every serious, intelligent story that demands catechizing—a persistent, searching questioning—pulsates at its center with a living, unifying theme.

Each story so qualified has something to say. Call it, if you will, main idea, central insight, thesis, premise, statement, judgment, opinion, or meaning; but the preferred critical term is *theme.*

Theme makes a comment about some aspect of life, expresses a truth about human affairs, or conveys an insight into character. Theme frames the controlling idea, the underlying meaning of a story.

Interpretative fiction (and each story in this text fits the description) does more than exhibit personality, pose a problem, create a mood of despair, promise the reader a vicarious thrill, make him chuckle or shed a tear. It supports a view, an idea, or an attitude toward something. And as long as fiction deals with love and fear and suffering and hope, so long will these stories have something to say about love and fear and suffering and hope.

Occasionally an author will state the theme more or less explicitly, somewhere in the action through the voice of an articulate character or narrator, who acts as the spokesman. Crane points to at least two possible interpretations in the statements made by characters and the narrator in "The Open Boat." One of these assertions, appearing at the beginning of section 3, reads: "It would be difficult to describe the subtle brotherhood of men that was here established on the seas." By expressing this universal truth about human nature here and throughout the narrative, Crane leads us to infer that tragedy and suffering contribute to our common humanity. A second possible meaning can be deduced from the characters' changing attitudes toward nature. The refrain in section 4 that begins with "If I am going to drown . . ." and is again repeated at the beginning of section 6 recapitulates Crane's condemnation of the "old ninny-woman Fate" for gross mismanagement of human fortunes and for not regarding human beings as important. But more often than not, at least in modern fiction, readers must discover the theme for themselves, synthesizing meaning by inference, much as they complete the picture of the protagonist. To arrive at theme, every element of the short story—plot, character, point of view, and even title—should be consulted, for each contributes its portion to the total thematic communication of the story.

Search for meaning is hardly a free-for-all for message hunting. Surely not all stories cope with the matter of good versus evil. We must therefore guard against relying on supposed facts, details, and notions extraneous to the story or leapfrogging to conclusions that derive from personal experience. Interpretation, to be whole and valid, must emerge from the story itself and take into account all the significant events, relationships, and details we can perceive. A story is an organic whole in which all the parts serve that whole. Total interpretation is possible only with total analysis. However, prominent actions or notable details, perhaps a set of symbols, allusions, or pattern of imagery, may direct us easily toward meaning.

Consider, for example, the three key incidents in

"The Magic Barrel." Remember Leo's crisis that follows the Lily Hirshorn encounter. After that meeting Leo's attitude toward God and his concept of love and marriage change. Then re-examine the final scene, which produces at least two significant actions. First, Salzman's chant for the "dead." Who has died? Salzman? Or has something died in Leo or Stella? Second, Leo's reaction to the sight of Stella, posing as a prostitute against a lamppost. Leo sees in her eyes "desperate innocence" and his own redemption. In a sense, Leo is ordained here in this scene with Stella.

The urge to love and be loved is, in D. H. Lawrence's view, the ruling obsession of man; the absence, denial, or loss of love he pictures as one of the most pernicious forces in life. This attitude permeates much of his work, including "The Horse Dealer's Daughter." To arrive at theme in this story, we need to discover the significance of the incident at the pond in which Dr. Fergusson rescues Mabel from drowning. This action brings together these two lonely people. Love transfigures both their lives. Therein lies the central meaning of the story.

Many of Joyce's stories contain *epiphanies*, which we may define as moments of awareness, revelation, or insight for the reader and sometimes for the characters in the story. An epiphany is usually an isolated, intense moment that occurs near the end of a story. If there is an epiphany for the reader in "Counterparts," it would be in the beating of the child by the father. What meaning does this incident convey to you?

Another significant action is Macomber's final chase of the buffalo in "The Short Happy Life of Francis Macomber." If we can believe Hemingway when he labels Macomber a coward, then the act of bravery serves to initiate Macomber into manhood.

As significant events furnish clues to meaning, so do many details. For example, the flowers in "The Chrysanthemums" represent more than the color and beauty lacking in Elisa's appearance. To some readers they may symbolize female potency or creativity, which in Elisa's situation has been suppressed. We need only to watch her raise and handle the chrysanthemums with such loving care to determine that they are perhaps substitutes for the children this strong young woman never had.

Similarly, the wall motif in "Bartleby, the Scrivener" may offer some insight into one of the many possible interpretations of the story. The physical walls play a dominant role in the main action. So do the metaphorical walls, produced by Bartleby's everlasting "I prefer not to" and his withdrawals from the established system, which further alienate him from his fellow man.

The topic of "A Tree, a Rock, a Cloud" is love. Before the man finds love, his life was disorganized and purposeless; after he finds love, his life takes on order and meaning. In the narrative the man tries to share his "science of love" with the young newspaper boy. Surely, then, one of the major themes of the story must relate to the matter of love.

Occasionally, titles will offer us hints toward understanding an author's purpose and meaning in fiction. The title "A Hunger Artist" is indeed revealing if we understand what a hunger artist is. The artist fasts. The example he sets by the sacrifice he makes, the crowd rejects. They misunderstand him; they ignore him, preferring instead the pleasure and excitement the panther provides. Is the theme, then, a commentary on spiritual sterility in our time? Or could the theme be an indictment of a society that fails to appreciate art or artists?

The title "Flowering Judas" provides still another clue to the meaning of that story. Who is Judas? Why a flowering Judas? Laura, like Judas, betrays rather than loves. She rejects the love of Braggioni, the young captain, the youth, and Eugenio. She is incapable of committing herself to love—sexual, social, or religious. She betrays the ideal of love. Denying everything, she affirms nothing. She betrays herself. Katherine Anne Porter sums up Laura's conflict: Laura "is not at home in the world"; "she has been irreparably betrayed by the disunion between her way of living and her feeling of what life should be."

Readers will not usually fall upon an easy course or best approach to discovering theme. Each story boasts an exclusive soul, an individual style, and an emphasis all its own. In one story plot may provide the best insight. What is the story "A Worn Path" about? Pain, courage, endurance, and love? "A Worn Path" provides the path on which old Phoenix must journey as she struggles to reach a clinic that will supply her with the medicine necessary to keep her grandson alive.

During the course of that journey she seeks the power to go on—to live and endure for one more day. Everywhere complications threaten her: the hill, the thorns, the log, the barbed wire, the ditch. But Phoenix overcomes each obstacle. She makes it with patience, resourcefulness, hope, and courage, all of which she has gained through the power of love. She has the love of her dying grandson and he has her love. What comment about love, courage, or endurance can you make from this brief summary?

What is "The Catbird Seat" story about? A battle between the sexes in which the male triumphs? A man who has been pushed to the limit so that he feels he must retaliate? A tidy Mr. Martin, who has a mind that operates like a filing cabinet, considers himself efficient. However, Mr. Fitweiler, convinced that Martin's office needs overhauling, hires Mrs. Barrows as an efficiency expert. After due consideration, Martin decides to "rub her out." In a mock trial he acts as Mrs. Barrows' judge, jury, and executioner. She tells the truth about Martin's crazy, out-of-character behavior; but she is not believed. Instead Mrs. Barrows is considered irrational and fired from her job. What comment about human nature can you make from this synopsis?

Perhaps setting in "A Rose for Emily" might give us a key to one of its important themes. The physical and historical setting of this story, the picture of the Grierson house as a shrine to former Southern aristocratic grandeur in the context of a complex set of attitudes toward a declining tradition, must for us lead to a conclusion about a way of life that has disappeared.

In another story character may furnish the most understanding. Knowing *who* the young boy is and *what* he is in "I Want to Know Why" will indeed suggest possibilities of themes. The young boy is an idealist, immature and sensitive. He loves horses and begins to question certain accepted values of the adult world. The boy wants to know why parents place an "off limits" sign on race tracks because gambling goes on there; the boy wants to know what standard gives blacks inferior positions in society; the boy wants to know why adults have prejudices and false values; and the boy wants to know why his close friend Jerry Tillford, who loves beauty (horses), would lie and embrace ugliness (the girl) and not "think straight and be O.K." Is

Anderson in this story suggesting prerequisites to grow-ing up?

Another workable approach to theme involves a review of the answers posed by the eight-point analysis mentioned in the opening chapter. Especially should the thoughtful reader know the protagonist, explore the conflict, and determine the outcome of the story. What kind of person is the central character? What is he or she contesting for or against? What forces resist him? Does he realize his goal or not? Why or why not? Do you find a change in him at the conclusion of the story? Is he the wiser for his experience? This kind of questioning will unearth facts and particulars certain to lead to challenging responses to the human experience and to the central meaning of the story.

We might consider using this approach to "The Chrysanthemums" for the purpose of arriving at theme. Nearly everything in this story serves the function of characterizing Elisa. The setting of Salinas Valley, ob-viously a man's domain, separates Elisa from the rest of the world and heightens her sense of isolation. Her man-ly garb hides her femininity. The environment molds her character. Early in the story, when Elisa cuts down the old chrysanthemum stalks, Steinbeck describes her as a young woman of great energy. She is gardening, handling chrysanthemums with adoring care, instead of rearing children. The peddler also exposes Elisa's character. He flirts with her. His youthfulness and carefree life attract her. She reacts by removing her masculine mask. She feels like a woman again and reaches out toward him. But he breaks the spell and later discards her gift of the flowers. Elisa's husband also contributes to the total characterization. He is insensitive to her feminine needs and fails to grasp her potential. The fifth and sixth paragraphs convey the idea of this unrealized potential within her.

Elisa's major conflict is clearly within herself. The struggle is between her desire to express her feminine potential or womanliness and her resigned acceptance of her present way of life in the masculine world of the valley. The resolution shows Elisa accepting her life for what it is but with a tear on her face—with some regret.

When a writer expends much energy delineating a central figure and gives her or him an urgent problem to solve, the emphasis invariably converges upon that character and that dilemma. Logically speaking, should it not follow that the central significance of a story— whatever it is the author is trying to tell us—must emanate from that same source? If theme has any connection at all with the protagonist, as surely it must, then what that character says, thinks, and does converts to one of the author's chief concerns; and it should be ours.

Let us imagine a situation in which the author attacks the problem of a racially mixed marriage. Naturally, having chosen the subject matter, the author will make some observations for or against this kind of union. If the resolution points to imminent wedlock, the author approves and forces us to recall the reasons given throughout the story that support this position. If, on the other hand, the dénouement indicates a repudiation or broken engagement, the author disapproves and calls for a review of certain incidents and speeches predetermined to disclose objections. In James's "The Real Thing" the resolution itself points to a conclusion from which we might state the following theme: real things (or real people) are fit subjects for artists and their art but only insofar as the artists are permitted the use of their imaginations to reshape or recreate the original model.

Theme exists in fiction because characters live in a world like ours and face problems like ours. We hate, love, suffer, and die; and we, all of us, at one time or another, contemplate the nature of man and woman, life and death and what lies beyond, good and evil, reality and fantasy, and the existence of God.

Many of these concerns relate to universal human experience and consequently invade the domain of fiction repeatedly. Some of the better-known themes recurring frequently in serious fiction are: (1) Love heals or gives new life. (2) Evil corrupts. (3) Fate controls man's destiny. (4) Man cannot escape his past. (5) One cannot solve real-world problems with dream-world solutions.

Note the subject-verb mode of expression. Someone or something executes an action. "Disillusionment," though pointing to the topic of "I Want to Know Why," fails miserably as a statement of the story's theme. "Scientific naturalism" makes its presence felt in "The Open Boat," but the phrase completely misses the mark as a crystallization of meaning. "The nature of art" is a matter much discussed in "The Real Thing," but again there is no clear assertion of theme.

Learn to express the theme of a story in one sentence. Such an oversimplification of meaning is by no means whole and conclusive, but it serves satisfactorily the aim of quick indentification, and it may give the perceptive reader a point from which to penetrate more deeply into the story's meaning.

Stephen Crane *(1871–1900)*

Born in Newark, N.J., the fourteenth child of a Methodist minister, he attended Lafayette College and Syracuse University for two years before capitulating to a life crammed with extensive travel, vast experience, and prodigious literary achievements. He wrote for newspapers, lived in New York's Bowery, slept in flophouses, and eloped with the madam of a bawdy house. His first novel, Maggie: A Girl of the Streets *(1893), considered the first naturalistic American novel, he published at his own expense because no publisher would print it. His next book,* The Red Badge of Courage *(1895), brought him sudden fame. This novel and two short stories, "The Blue Hotel" and "The Open Boat," are established classics in American literature.*

The Open Boat
A Tale Intended To Be After the Fact. Being the Experience of Four Men from the Sunk Steamer "Commodore."

1

None of them knew the color of the sky. Their eyes glanced level, and were fastened upon the waves that swept toward them. These waves were of the hue of slate, save for the tops, which were of foaming white, and all of the men know the colors of the sea. The horizon narrowed and widened, and dipped and rose, and at all times its edge was jagged with waves that seemed thrust up in points like rocks. Many a man ought to have a bath-tub larger than the boat which here rode upon the sea.

These waves were most wrongfully and barbarously abrupt and tall, and each froth-top was a problem in small-boat navigation.

The cook squatted in the bottom and looked with both eyes at the six inches of gunwale which separated him from the ocean. His sleeves were rolled over his fat forearms, and the two flaps of his unbuttoned vest dangled as he bent to bail out the boat. Often he said: "Gawd! That was a narrow clip." As he remarked it he invariably gazed eastward over the broken sea.

The oiler, steering with one of the two oars in the boat, sometimes raised himself suddenly to keep clear of water that swirled in over the stern. It was a thin little oar and it seemed often ready to snap.

The correspondent, pulling at the other oar, watched the waves and wondered why he was there.

The injured captain, lying in the bow, was at this time buried in that profound dejection and indifference which comes, temporarily at least, to even the bravest and most enduring when, willy nilly, the firm fails, the army loses, the ship goes down. The mind of the master of a vessel is rooted deep in the timbers of her, though he commands for a day or a decade, and this captain had on him the stern impression of a scene in the greys of dawn of seven turned faces, and later a stump of a top-mast with a white ball on it that slashed to and fro at the waves, went low and lower, and down. Thereafter there was something strange in his voice. Although steady, it was deep with mourning, and of a quality beyond oration or tears.

"Keep 'er a little more south, Billie," said he.

" 'A little more south,' sir," said the oiler in the stern.

A seat in this boat was not unlike a seat upon a bucking broncho, and by the same token, a broncho is not much smaller. The craft pranced and reared, and plunged like an animal. As each wave came, and she rose for it, she seemed like a horse making at a fence outrageously high. The manner of her scramble over these walls of water is a mystic thing, and, moreover, at the top of them were ordinarily these problems in white water, the foam racing down from the summit of each wave, requiring a new leap, and a leap from the air. Then, after scornfully bumping a crest, she would slide, and race, and splash down a long incline, and arrive bobbing and nodding in front of the next menace.

A singular disadvantage of the sea lies in the fact that after successfully surmounting one wave you discover that there is another behind it just as important and just as nervously anxious to do something effective in the way of swamping boats. In a ten-foot dingey one can get an idea of the resources of the sea in the line of waves that is not probable to the average experience which is never at sea in a dingey. As each slatey wall of water approached, it shut all else from the view of the men in the boat, and it was not difficult to imagine that this particular wave was the final outburst of the ocean, the last effort of the grim water. There was a terrible grace in the move of the waves, and they came in silence, save for the snarling of the crests.

In the wan light, the faces of the men must have been grey. Their eyes must have glinted in strange ways as they gazed steadily astern. Viewed from a balcony, the whole thing would doubtless have been weirdly picturesque. But the men in the boat had no time to see it, and if they had had leisure there were other things to occupy their minds. The sun swung steadily up the sky, and they knew it was broad day because the color of the sea changed from slate to emerald-green, streaked with amber lights, and the foam was like tumbling snow. The process of the breaking day was unknown to them. They were aware only of this effect upon the color of the waves that rolled toward them.

In disjointed sentences the cook and the correspondent argued as to the difference between a life-saving station and a house of refuge. The cook had said: "There's a house of refuge just north of the Mosquito Inlet Light, and as soon as they see us, they'll come off in their boat and pick us up."

"As soon as who see us?" said the correspondent.

"The crew," said the cook.

"Houses of refuge don't have crews," said the correspondent. "As I understand them, they are only places where clothes and grub are stored for the benefit of shipwrecked people. They don't carry crews."

"Oh, yes, they do," said the cook.

"No, they don't," said the correspondent.

"Well, we're not there yet, anyhow," said the oiler, in the stern.

"Well," said the cook, "perhaps it's not a house of refuge that I'm thinking of as being near Mosquito Inlet Light. Perhaps it's a life-saving station."

"We're not there yet," said the oiler, in the stern.

2

As the boat bounced from the top of each wave, the wind tore through the hair of the hatless men, and as the craft plopped her stern down again the spray splashed past them. The crest of each of these waves was a hill, from the top of which the men surveyed, for a moment, a broad tumultuous expanse, shining and wind-riven. It was probably splendid. It was probably glorious, this play of the free sea, wild with lights of emerald and white and amber.

"Bully good thing it's an on-shore wind," said the cook. "If not, where would we be? Wouldn't have a show."

"That's right," said the correspondent.

The busy oiler nodded his assent.

Then the captain, in the bow, chuckled in a way that

expressed humor, contempt, tragedy, all in one. "Do you think we've got much of a show now, boys?" said he.

Whereupon the three were silent, save for a trifle of hemming and hawing. To express any particular optimism at this time they felt to be childish and stupid, but they all doubtless possessed this sense of the situation in their mind. A young man thinks doggedly at such times. On the other hand, the ethics of their condition was decidedly against any open suggestion of hopelessness. So they were silent.

"Oh, well," said the captain, soothing his children, "we'll get ashore all right."

But there was that in his tone which made them think, so the oiler quoth: "Yes! If this wind holds!"

The cook was bailing: "Yes! If we don't catch hell in the surf."

Canton flannel gulls flew near and far. Sometimes they sat down on the sea, near patches of brown seaweed that rolled on the waves with a movement like carpets on a line in a gale. The birds sat comfortably in groups, and they were envied by some in the dingey, for the wrath of the sea was no more to them than it was to a covey of prairie chickens a thousand miles inland. Often they came very close and stared at the men with black bead-like eyes. At these times they were uncanny and sinister in their unblinking scrutiny, and the men hooted angrily at them, telling them to be gone. One came, and evidently decided to alight on the top of the captain's head. The bird flew parallel to the boat and did not circle, but made short sidelong jumps in the air in chicken-fashion. His black eyes were wistfully fixed upon the captain's head. "Ugly brute," said the oiler to the bird. "You look as if you were made with a jack-knife." The cook and the correspondent swore darkly at the creature. The captain naturally wished to knock it away with the end of the heavy painter; but he did not dare do it, because anything resembling an emphatic gesture would have capsized this freighted boat, and so with his open hand, the captain gently and carefully waved the gull away. After it had been discouraged from the pursuit the captain breathed easier on account of his hair, and others breathed easier because the bird struck their minds at this time as being somehow grewsome and ominous.

In the meantime the oiler and the correspondent rowed. And also they rowed.

They sat together in the same seat, and each rowed an oar. Then the oiler took both oars; then the correspondent took both oars; then the oiler; then the correspondent. They rowed and they rowed. The very ticklish part of the business was when the time came for the reclining one in the stern to take his turn at the oars. By the very last star of truth, it is easier to steal eggs from under a hen than it was to change seats in the dingey. First the man in the stern slid his hand along the thwart and moved with care, as if he were of Sèvres. Then the man in the rowing seat slid his hand along the other thwart. It was all done with the most extraordinary care. As the two sidled past each other, the whole party kept watchful eyes on the coming wave, and the captain cried: "Look out now! Steady there!"

The brown mats of seaweed that appeared from time to time were like islands, bits of earth. They were traveling, apparently, neither one way nor the other. They were, to all intents, stationary. They informed the men in the boat that it was making progress slowly toward the land.

The captain, rearing cautiously in the bow, after the dingey soared on a great swell, said that he had seen the lighthouse at Mosquito Inlet. Presently the cook remarked that he had seen it. The correspondent was at the oars then, and for some reason he too wished to look at the lighthouse, but his back was toward the far shore and the waves were important, and for some time he could not seize an opportunity to turn his head. But at last there came a wave more gentle than the others, and when at the crest of it he swiftly scoured the western horizon.

"See it?" said the captain.

"No," said the correspondent slowly, "I didn't see anything."

"Look again," said the captain. He pointed. "It's exactly in that direction."

At the top of another wave, the correspondent did as he was bid, and this time his eyes chanced on a small still thing on the edge of the swaying horizon. It was precisely like the point of a pin. It took an anxious eye to find a lighthouse so tiny.

"Think we'll make it, captain?"

"If this wind holds and the boat don't swamp, we can't do much else," said the captain.

The little boat, lifted by each towering sea, and splashed viciously by the crests, made progress that in the absence of seaweed was not apparent to those in her. She seemed just a wee thing wallowing, miraculously top-up, at the mercy of five oceans. Occasionally, a great spread of water, like white flames, swarmed into her.

"Bail her, cook," said the captain serenely.

"All right, captain," said the cheerful cook.

3

It would be difficult to describe the subtle brotherhood of men that was here established on the seas. No one said that it was so. No one mentioned it. But it dwelt in the boat, and each man felt it warm him. They were a captain, an oiler, a cook, and a correspondent, and they were friends, friends in a more curiously iron-bound degree than may be common. The hurt captain, lying against the water-jar in the bow, spoke always in a low voice and calmly, but he could never command a more ready and swiftly obedient crew than the motley three of the dingey. It was more than a mere recognition of what was best for the common safety. There was surely in it a quality that was personal and heartfelt. And after this devotion to the commander of the boat there was this comradeship that the correspondent, for instance, who had been taught to be cynical of men, knew even at the time was the best experience of his life. But no one said that it was so. No one mentioned it.

"I wish we had a sail," remarked the captain. "We might try my overcoat on the end of an oar and give you two boys a chance to rest." So the cook and the correspondent held the mast and spread wide the overcoat. The oiler steered, and the little boat made good way with her new rig. Sometimes the oiler had to scull sharply to keep a sea from breaking into the boat, but otherwise sailing was a success.

Meanwhile the lighthouse had been growing slowly larger. It had now almost assumed color, and appeared like a little grey shadow on the sky. The man at the oars could not be prevented from turning his head rather often to try for a glimpse of this little grey shadow.

At last, from the top of each wave the men in the tossing boat could see land. Even as the lighthouse was an upright shadow on the sky, this land seemed but a long black shadow on the sea. It certainly was thinner than paper. "We must be about opposite New Smyrna," said the cook, who had coasted this shore often in schooners. "Captain, by the way, I believe they abandoned that life-saving station there about a year ago."

"Did they?" said the captain.

The wind slowly died away. The cook and the correspondent were not now obliged to slave in order to hold high the oar. But the waves continued their old impetuous swooping at the dingey, and the little craft, no longer under way, struggled woundily over them. The oiler or the correspondent took the oars again.

Shipwrecks are *à propos* of nothing. If men could only train for them and have them occur when the men had reached pink condition, there would be less drowning at sea. Of the four in the dingey none had slept any time worth mentioning for two days and two nights previous to embarking in the dingey, and in the excitement of clambering about the deck of a foundering ship they had also forgotten to eat heartily.

For these reasons, and for others, neither the oiler nor the correspondent was fond of rowing at this time. The correspondent wondered ingenuously how in the name of all that was sane could there be people who thought it amusing to row a boat. It was not an amusement; it was a diabolical punishment, and even a genius of mental aberrations could never conclude that it was anything but a horror to the muscles and a crime against the back. He mentioned to the boat in general how the amusement of rowing struck him, and the weary-faced oiler smiled in full sympathy. Previously to the foundering, by the way, the oiler had worked double-watch in the engine-room of the ship.

"Take her easy, now, boys," said the captain. "Don't spend yourselves. If we have to run a surf you'll need all your strength, because we'll sure have to swim for it. Take your time."

Slowly the land arose from the sea. From a black line it became a line of black and a line of white, trees and sand. Finally, the captain said that he could make out a house on the shore. "That's the house of refuge, sure," said the cook. "They'll see us before long, and come out after us."

The distant lighthouse reared high. "The keeper ought to be able to make us out now, if he's looking through a glass," said the captain. "He'll notify the life-saving people."

"None of those other boats could have got ashore to give word of the wreck," said the oiler, in a low voice. "Else the lifeboat would be out hunting us."

Slowly and beautifully the land loomed out of the sea. The wind came again. It had veered from the north-east to the south-east. Finally, a new sound struck the ears of the men in the boat. It was the low thunder of the surf on the shore. "We'll never be able to make the lighthouse now," said the captain. "Swing her head a little more north, Billie," said he.

"'A little more north,' sir," said the oiler.

Whereupon the little boat turned her nose once more down the wind, and all but the oarsman watched the shore grow. Under the influence of this expansion doubt and direful apprehension was leaving the minds of the men. The management of the boat was still most absorbing, but it could not prevent a quiet cheerfulness. In an hour, perhaps, they would be ashore.

Their backbones had become thoroughly used to balancing in the boat, and they now rode this wild colt of a dingey like circus men. The correspondent thought that he had been drenched to the skin, but happening to feel in the top pocket of his coat, he found therein eight cigars. Four of them were soaked with sea-water; four were perfectly scathless. After a search, somebody produced three dry matches, and thereupon the four waifs rode impudently in their little boat, and with an assurance of an impending rescue shining in their eyes, puffed at the big cigars and judged well and ill of all men. Everybody took a drink of water.

4

"Cook," remarked the captain, "there don't seem to be any signs of life about your house of refuge."

"No," replied the cook. "Funny they don't see us!"

A broad stretch of lowly coast lay before the eyes of the men. It was of dunes topped with dark vegetation. The roar of the surf was plain, and sometimes they could see the white lip of a wave as it spun up the beach. A tiny house was blocked out black upon the sky. Southward, the slim lighthouse lifted its little gray length.

Tide, wind, and waves were swinging the dingey northward. "Funny they don't see us," said the men.

The surf's roar was here dulled, but its tone was,

nevertheless, thunderous and mighty. As the boat swam over the great rollers, the men sat listening to this roar. "We'll swamp sure," said everybody.

It is fair to say here that there was not a life-saving station within twenty miles in either direction, but the men did not know this fact, and in consequence they made dark and opprobrious remarks concerning the eyesight of the nation's life-savers. Four scowling men sat in the dingey and surpassed records in the invention of epithets.

"Funny they don't see us."

The lightheartedness of a former time had completely faded. To their sharpened minds it was easy to conjure pictures of all kinds of incompetency and blindness and, indeed, cowardice. There was the shore of the populous land, and it was bitter and bitter to them that from it came no sign.

"Well," said the captain, ultimately, "I suppose we'll have to make a try for ourselves. If we stay out here too long, we'll none of us have strength left to swim after the boat swamps."

And so the oiler, who was at the oars, turned the boat straight for the shore. There was a sudden tightening of muscle. There was some thinking.

"If we don't all get ashore—" said the captain. "If we don't all get ashore, I suppose you fellows know where to send news of my finish?"

They then briefly exchanged some addresses and admonitions. As for the reflections of the men, there was a great deal of rage in them. Perchance they might be formulated thus: "If I am going to be drowned—if I am going to be drowned—if I am going to be drowned, why in the name of the seven mad gods who rule the sea, was I allowed to come thus far and contemplate sand and trees? Was I brought here merely to have my nose dragged away as I was about to nibble the sacred cheese of life? It is preposterous. If this old ninny-woman, Fate, cannot do better than this, she should be deprived of the management of men's fortunes. She is an old hen who knows not her intention. If she has decided to drown me, why did she not do it in the beginning and save me all this trouble? The whole affair is absurd. . . . But no, she cannot mean to drown me. She dare not drown me. She cannot drown me. Not after all this work." Afterward the man might have had an impulse to shake his fist at the clouds: "Just you drown me, now, and then hear what I call you!"

The billows that came at this time were more formidable. They seemed always just about to break and roll over the little boat in a turmoil of foam. There was a preparatory and long growl in the speech of them. No mind unused to the sea would have concluded that the dingey could ascend these sheer heights in time. The shore was still afar. The oiler was a wily surfman. "Boys," he said swiftly, "she won't live three minutes more, and we're too far out to swim. Shall I take her to sea again, captain?"

"Yes! Go ahead!" said the captain.

This oiler, by a series of quick miracles, and fast and steady oarsmanship, turned the boat in the middle of the surf and took her safely to sea again.

There was a considerable silence as the boat bumped over the furrowed sea to deeper water. Then somebody in gloom spoke. "Well, anyhow, they must have seen us from the shore by now."

The gulls went in slanting flight up the wind toward the grey desolate east. A squall, marked by dingy clouds, and clouds brick-red, like smoke from a burning building, appeared from the south-east.

"What do you think of those life-saving people? Ain't they peaches?"

"Funny they haven't seen us."

"Maybe they think we're out here for sport! Maybe they think we're fishin'. Maybe they think we're damned fools."

It was a long afternoon. A changed tide tried to force them southward, but the wind and wave said northward. Far ahead, where coastline, sea, and sky formed their mighty angle, there were little dots which seemed to indicate a city on the shore.

"St. Augustine?"

The captain shook his head. "Too near Mosquito Inlet."

And the oiler rowed, and then the correspondent rowed. Then the oiler rowed. It was a weary business. The human back can become the seat of more aches and pains than are registered in books for the composite anatomy of a regiment. It is a limited area, but it can become the theatre of innumerable muscular conflicts, tangles, wrenches, knots, and other comforts.

"Did you ever like to row, Billie?" asked the correspondent.

"No," said the oiler. "Hang it!"

When one exchanged the rowing-seat for a place in the bottom of the boat, he suffered a bodily depression that caused him to be careless of everything save an obligation to wiggle one finger. There was cold sea-water swashing to and fro in the boat, and he lay in it. His head, pillowed on a thwart, was within an inch of the swirl of a wave crest, and sometimes a particularly obstreperous sea came in-board and drenched him once more. But these matters did not annoy him. It is almost certain that if the boat had capsized he would have tumbled comfortably out upon the ocean as if he felt sure that it was a great soft mattress.

"Look! There's a man on the shore!"

"Where?"

"There! See 'im? See 'im?"

"Yes, sure! He's walking along."

"Now he's stopped. Look! He's facing us!"

"He's waving at us!"

"So he is! By thunder!"

"Ah, now we're all right! Now we're all right! There'll be a boat out here for us in half-an-hour."

"He's going on. He's running. He's going up to that house there."

The remote beach seemed lower than the sea, and it required a searching glance to discern the little black figure. The captain saw a floating stick and they rowed to it. A bath-towel was by some weird chance in the boat, and tying this on the stick, the captain waved it. The oarsman did not dare turn his head, so he was obliged to ask questions.

"What's he doing now?"

"He's standing still again. He's looking, I think. . . . There he goes again. Toward the house. . . . Now he's stopped again."

"Is he waving at us?"

"No, not now! He was, though."

"Look! There comes another man!"

"He's running."

"Look at him go, would you."

"Why, he's on a bicycle. Now he's met the other man. They're both waving at us. Look!"

"There comes something up the beach."

"What the devil is that thing?"

"Why, it looks like a boat."

"Why, certainly, it's a boat."

"No; it's on wheels."

"Yes, so it is. Well, that must be the life-boat. They drag them along shore on a wagon."

"That's the life-boat sure."

"No, by—, it's—it's an omnibus."

"I tell you it's a life-boat."

"It is not! It's an omnibus. I can see it plain. See? One of these big hotel omnibuses."

"By thunder, you're right. It's an omnibus, sure as fate. What do you suppose they are doing with an omnibus? Maybe they are going around collecting the life-crew, hey?"

"That's it, likely. Look! There's a fellow waving a little black flag. He's standing on the steps of the omnibus. There come those other two fellows. Now they're all talking together. Look at the fellow with the flag. Maybe he ain't waving it!"

"That ain't a flag, is it? That's his coat: Why, certainly, that's his coat."

"So it is; it's his coat. He's taken it off and is waving it around his head. But would you look at him swing it!"

"Oh, say, there isn't any life-saving station there. That's just a winter-resort hotel omnibus that has brought over some of the boarders to see us drown."

"What's that idiot with the coat mean? What's he signaling, anyhow?"

"It looks as if he were trying to tell us to go north. There must be a life-saving station up there."

"No; he thinks we're fishing. Just giving us a merry hand. See? Ah, there, Willie."

"Well, I wish I could make something out of those signals. What do you suppose he means?"

"He don't mean anything; he's just playing."

"Well, if he'd just signal us to try the surf again, or to go to sea and wait, or go north, or go south, or go to hell, there would be some reason in it. But look at him! He just stands there and keeps his coat revolving like a wheel. The ass!"

"There come more people."

"Now there's quite a mob. Look! Isn't that a boat?"

"Where? Oh, I see where you mean. No, that's no boat."

"That fellow is still waving his coat."

"He must think we like to see him do that. Why don't he quit it? It don't mean anything."

"I don't know. I think he is trying to make us go north. It must be that there's a life-saving station there somewhere."

"Say, he ain't tired yet. Look at 'im wave!"

"Wonder how long he can keep that up. He's been revolving his coat ever since he caught sight of us. He's an idiot. Why aren't they getting men to bring a boat out? A fishing boat—one of those big yawls—could come out here all right. Why don't he do something?"

"Oh, it's all right now."

"They'll have a boat out here for us in less than no time, now that they've seen us."

A faint yellow tone came into the sky over the low land. The shadows on the sea slowly deepened. The wind bore coldness with it, and the men began to shiver.

"Holy smoke!" said one, allowing his voice to express his impious mood, "if we keep on monkeying out here! If we've got to flounder out here all night!"

"Oh, we'll never have to stay here all night! Don't you worry. They've seen us now, and it won't be long before they'll come chasing out after us."

The shore grew dusky. The man waving a coat blended gradually into this gloom, and it swallowed in the same manner the omnibus and the group of people. The spray, when it dashed uproariously over the side, made the voyagers shrink and swear like men who were being branded.

"I'd like to catch the chump who waved the coat. I feel like soaking him one, just for luck."

Why? What did he do?''

"Oh, nothing, but then he seemed so damned cheerful."

In the meantime the oiler rowed, and then the correspondent rowed, and then the oiler rowed. Gray-faced and bowed forward, they mechanically, turn by turn, plied the leaden oars. The form of the lighthouse had vanished from the southern horizon, but finally a pale star appeared, just lifting from the sea. The streaked saffron in the west passed before the all-merging darkness, and the sea to the east was black. The land had vanished, and was expressed only by the low and drear thunder of the surf.

"If I am going to be drowned—if I am going to be drowned—if I am going to be drowned, why, in the name of the seven mad gods who rule the sea, was I allowed to come thus far and contemplate sand and trees? Was I brought here merely to have my nose dragged away as I was about to nibble the sacred cheese of life?"

The patient captain, drooped over the water-jar, was sometimes obliged to speak to the oarsman.

"Keep her head up! Keep her head up!"

"Keep her head up, sir." The voices were weary and low.

This was surely a quiet evening. All save the oarsman lay heavily and listlessly in the boat's bottom. As for him, his eyes were just capable of noting the tall black waves that swept forward in a most sinister silence, save for an occasional subdued growl of a crest.

The cook's head was on a thwart, and he looked without interest at the water under his nose. He was deep in other scenes. Finally he spoke. "Billie," he murmured dreamfully, "what kind of pie do you like best?"

5

"Pie!" said the oiler and the correspondent, agitatedly. "Don't talk about those things, blast you!"

"Well," said the cook, "I was just thinking about ham sandwiches, and—"

A night on the seas in an open boat is a long night. As darkness settled finally, the shine of the light, lifting from the sea in the south, changed to full gold. On the northern horizon a new light appeared, a small bluish gleam on the edge of the waters. These two lights were the furniture of the world. Otherwise there was nothing but waves.

Two men huddled in the stern, and distances were so magnificent in the dinghy that the rower was enabled to keep his feet partly warm by thrusting them under his companions. Their legs indeed extended far under the rowing-seat until they touched the feet of the captain forward. Sometimes, despite the efforts of the tired oarsman, a wave came piling into the boat, an icy wave of the night, and the chilling water soaked them anew. They would twist their bodies for a moment and groan, and sleep the dead sleep once more, while the water in the boat gurgled about them as the craft rocked.

The plan of the oiler and the correspondent was for one to row until he lost the ability, and then arouse the other from his sea-water couch in the bottom of the boat.

The oiler plied the oars until his head drooped forward and the overpowering sleep blinded him; and he rowed yet afterward. Then he touched a man in the bottom of the boat, and called his name. "Will you spell me for a little while?" he said meekly.

"Sure, Billie," said the correspondent, awaking and dragging himself to a sitting position. They exchanged places carefully, and the oiler, cuddling down in the sea-water at the cook's side, seemed to go to sleep instantly.

The particular violence of the sea had ceased. The waves came without snarling. The obligation of the man at the oars was to keep the boat headed so that the tilt of the rollers would not capsize her, and to preserve her from filling when the crests rushed past. The black waves were silent and hard to be seen in the darkness. Often one was almost upon the boat before the oarsman was aware.

In a low voice the correspondent addressed the captain. He was not sure that the captain was awake, although this iron man seemed to be always awake. "Captain, shall I keep her making for that light north, sir?"

The same steady voice answered him. "Yes. Keep it about two points off the port bow."

The cook had tied a life-belt around himself in order to get even the warmth which this clumsy cork contrivance could donate, and he seemed almost stove-like when a rower, whose teeth invariably chattered wildly as soon as he ceased his labor, dropped down to sleep.

The correspondent, as he rowed, looked down at the two men sleeping underfoot. The cook's arm was around the oiler's shoulders, and, with their fragmentary clothing and haggard faces, they were the babes of the sea—a grotesque rendering of the old babes in the wood.

Later he must have grown stupid at his work, for suddenly there was a growling of water, and a crest came with a roar and a swash into the boat, and it was a wonder that it did not set the cook afloat in his life-belt. The cook continued to sleep, but the oiler sat up, blinking his eyes and shaking with the new cold.

"Oh, I'm awful sorry, Billie," said the correspondent, contritely.

"That's all right, old boy," said the oiler, and lay down again and was asleep.

Presently it seemed that even the captain dozed, and the correspondent thought that he was the one man afloat on all the oceans. The wind had a voice as it came over the waves, and it was sadder than the end.

There was a long, loud swishing astern of the boat, and a gleaming trail of phosphorescence, like blue flame, was furrowed on the black waters. It might have been made by a monstrous knife.

Then there came a stillness, while the correspondent breathed with the open mouth and looked at the sea.

Suddenly there was another swish and another long flash of bluish light, and this time it was alongside the boat, and might almost have been reached with an oar. The correspondent saw an enormous fin speed like a shadow through the water, hurling the crystalline spray and leaving the long glowing trail.

The correspondent looked over his shoulder at the captain. His face was hidden, and he seemed to be asleep. He looked at the babes of the sea. They certainly were asleep. So, being bereft of sympathy, he leaned a little way to one side and swore softly into the sea.

But the thing did not then leave the vicinity of the boat. Ahead or astern, on one side or the other, at intervals long or short, fled the long sparkling streak, and there was to be heard the whiroo of the dark fin. The speed and power of the thing was greatly to be admired. It cut the water like a gigantic and keen projectile.

The presence of this biding thing did not affect the man with the same horror that it would if he had been a picnicker. He simply looked at the sea dully and swore in an undertone.

Nevertheless, it is true that he did not wish to be alone with the thing. He wished one of his companions to awake by chance and keep him company with it. But the captain hung motionless over the water-jar, and the oiler and the cook in the bottom of the boat were plunged in slumber.

6

"If I am going to be drowned—if I am going to be drowned—if I am going to be drowned, why, in the name of the seven mad gods who rule the sea, was I allowed to come thus far and contemplate sand and trees?"

During this dismal night, it may be remarked that a man would conclude that it was really the intention of the seven mad gods to drown him, despite the abominable injustice of it. For it was certainly an abominable injustice to drown a man who had worked so hard, so hard. The man felt it would be a crime most unnatural. Other people had drowned at sea since galleys swarmed with painted sails, but still—

When it occurs to a man that nature does not regard him as important, and that she feels she would not maim the universe by disposing of him, he at first wishes to throw bricks at the temple, and he hates deeply the fact that there are no bricks and no temples. Any visible expression of nature would surely be pelleted with his jeers.

Then, if there be no tangible thing to hoot, he feels, perhaps, the desire to confront a personification and indulge in pleas, bowed to one knee, and with hands supplicant, saying, "Yes, but I love myself."

A high cold star on a winter's night is the word he feels that she says to him. Thereafter he knows the pathos of his situation.

The men in the dinghy had not discussed these matters, but each had, no doubt, reflected upon them in silence and according to his mind. There was seldom any expression upon their faces save the general one of complete weariness. Speech was devoted to the business of the boat.

To chime the notes of his emotion, a verse mysteriously entered the correspondent's head. He had even forgotten that he had forgotten this verse, but it suddenly was in his mind.

> A soldier of the Legion lay dying in Algiers;
> There was a lack of woman's nursing, there was dearth
>   of woman's tears;
> But a comrade stood beside him, and he took that
>   comrade's hand.
> And he said, "I never more shall see my own, my native
>   land."

In his childhood the correspondent had been made acquainted with the fact that a soldier of the Legion lay dying in Algiers, but he had never regarded it as important. Myriads of his school-fellows had informed him of the soldier's plight, but the dinning had naturally ended by making him perfectly indifferent. He had never considered it his affair that a soldier of the Legion lay dying in Algiers, nor had it appeared to him as a matter for sorrow. It was less to him than the breaking of a pencil's point.

Now, however, it quaintly came to him as a human, living thing. It was no longer merely a picture of a few throes in the breast of a poet, meanwhile drinking tea and warming his feet at the grate; it was an actuality—stern, mournful, and fine.

The correspondent plainly saw the soldier. He lay on the sand with his feet out straight and still. While his pale left hand was upon his chest in an attempt to thwart the going of his life, the blood came between his fingers. In the far Algerian distance, a city of low square forms was set against a sky that was faint with the last sunset hues. The correspondent, plying the oars and dreaming of the slow and slower movements of the lips of the soldier, was moved by a profound and perfectly impersonal comprehension. He was sorry for the soldier of the Legion who lay dying in Algiers.

The thing which had followed the boat and waited had evidently grown bored at the delay. There was no longer to be heard the slash of the cutwater, and there was no longer the flame of the long trail. The light in the north still glimmered, but it was apparently no nearer to the boat. Sometimes the beam of the surf rang in the correspondent's ears, and he turned the craft seaward then and rowed harder. Southward, some one had evidently built a watch-fire on the beach. It was too low and too far to be seen, but it made a shimmering, roseate reflection upon the bluff back of it, and this could be discerned from the boat. The wind came stronger, and sometimes a wave suddenly raged out like a mountain-cat, and there was to be seen the sheen and sparkle of a broken crest.

The captain, in the bow, moved on his water-jar and sat erect. "Pretty long night," he observed to the correspondent. He looked at the shore. "Those life-saving people take their time."

"Did you see that shark playing around?"

"Yes, I saw him. He was a big fellow, all right."

"Wish I had known you were awake."

Later the correspondent spoke into the bottom of the boat.

"Billie!" There was a slow and gradual disentanglement. "Billie, will you spell me?"

"Sure," said the oiler.

As soon as the correspondent touched the cold, comfortable sea-water in the bottom of the boat and had huddled close to the cook's life-belt he was deep in sleep, despite the fact that his teeth played all the popular airs. This sleep was so good to him that it was but a moment before he heard a voice call his name in a tone that demonstrated the last stages of exhaustion. "Will you spell me?"

"Sure, Billie."

The light in the north had mysteriously vanished, but the correspondent took his course from the wide-awake captain.

Later in the night they took the boat farther out to sea, and the captain directed the cook to take one oar at the stern and keep the boat facing the seas. He was to call out if he should hear the thunder of the surf. This plan enabled the oiler and the correspondent to get respite together. "We'll give those boys a chance to get into shape again," said the captain. They curled down and, after a few preliminary chatterings and trembles, slept once more the dead sleep. Neither knew they had bequeathed to the cook the company of another shark, or perhaps the same shark.

As the boat caroused on the waves, spray occasionally bumped over the side and gave them a fresh soaking, but this had no power to break their repose. The ominous slash of the wind and the water affected them as it would have affected mummies.

"Boys," said the cook, with the notes of every reluctance in his voice, "she's drifted in pretty close. I guess one of you had better take her to sea again." The correspondent, aroused, heard the crash of the toppled crests.

As he was rowing, the captain gave him some whisky and water, and this steadied the chills out of him. "If I ever get ashore and anybody shows me even a photograph of an oar—"

At last there was a short conversation.

"Billie! . . . Billie, will you spell me?"

"Sure," said the oiler.

7

When the correspondent again opened his eyes, the sea and the sky were each of the gray hue of the dawning. Later, carmine and gold was painted upon the waters. The morning appeared finally, in its splendor, with a sky of pure blue, and the sunlight flamed on the tips of the waves.

On the distant dunes were set many little black cottages, and a tall white windmill reared above them. No man, nor dog, nor bicycle appeared on the beach. The cottages might have formed a deserted village.

The voyagers scanned the shore. A conference was held in the boat. "Well," said the captain, "if no help is coming, we might better try a run through the surf right away. If we stay out here much longer we will be too weak to do anything for ourselves at all." The others silently acquiesced in this reasoning. The boat was headed for the beach. The correspondent wondered if none ever ascended the tall wind-tower, and if then they never looked seaward. This tower was a giant, standing with its back to the plight of the ants. It represented in a degree, to the correspondent, the serenity of nature amid the struggles of the individual—nature in the wind, and nature in the vision of men. She did not seem cruel to him then, nor beneficent, nor treacherous, nor wise. But she was indifferent, flatly indifferent. It is, perhaps, plausible that a man in this situation, impressed with the unconcern of the universe, should see the innumerable flaws of his life and have them taste wickedly in his mind and wish for another chance. A distinction between right and wrong seems absurdly clear to him, then, in this new ignorance of the grave-edge, and he understands that if he were given another opportunity he would mend his conduct and his words, and be better and brighter during an introduction or at a tea.

"Now, boys," said the captain, "she is going to swamp sure. All we can do is to work her in as far as possible, and then when she swamps, pile out and scramble for the beach. Keep cool now, and don't jump until she swamps sure."

The oiler took the oars. Over his shoulders he scanned the surf. "Captain," he said, "I think I'd better bring her about, and keep her head-on to the seas, and back her in."

"All right, Billie," said the captain. "Back her in."

The oiler swung the boat then, and seated in the stern, the cook and the correspondent were obliged to look over their shoulders to contemplate the lonely and indifferent shore.

The monstrous inshore rollers heaved the boat high until the men were again enabled to see the white sheets of water scudding up the slanted beach. "We won't get in very close," said the captain. Each time a man could wrest his attention from the rollers, he turned his glance toward the shore, and in the expression of the eyes during this contemplation there was a singular quality. The correspondent, observing the others, knew that they were not afraid, but the full meaning of their glances was shrouded.

As for himself, he was too tired to grapple fundamentally with the fact. He tried to coerce his mind into thinking of it, but the mind was dominated at this time by the muscles, and the muscles said they did not care. It merely occurred to him that if he should drown it would be a shame.

There were no hurried words, no pallor, no plain agitation. The men simply looked at the shore. "Now, remember to get well clear of the boat when you jump," said the captain.

Seaward the crest of a roller suddenly fell with a thunderous crash, and the long white comber came roaring down upon the boat.

"Steady now," said the captain. The men were silent. They turned their eyes from the shore to the comber and waited. The boat slid up the incline, leaped at the furious top, bounced over it, and swung down the long back of the wave. Some water had been shipped, and the cook bailed it out.

But the next crest crashed also. The tumbling, boiling flood of white water caught the boat and whirled it almost perpendicular. Water swarmed in from all sides. The correspondent had his hands on the gunwale at this time, and when the water entered at that place he swiftly withdrew his fingers, as if he objected to wetting them.

The little boat, drunken with this weight of water, reeled and snuggled deeper into the sea.

"Bail her out, cook! Bail her out!" said the captain.

"All right, Captain," said the cook.

"Now, boys, the next one will do for us sure," said the oiler. "Mind to jump clear of the boat."

The third wave moved forward, huge, furious, implacable. It fairly swallowed the dinghy, and almost simultaneously the men tumbled into the sea. A piece of life-belt had lain in the bottom of the boat, and as the correspondent went overboard he held this to his chest with his left hand.

The January water was icy, and he reflected immediately that it was colder than he had expected to find it off the coast of Florida. This appeared to his dazed mind as a fact important enough to be noted at the time. The coldness of the water was sad; it was tragic. This fact was somehow mixed and confused with his opinion of his own situation so that it seemed almost a proper reason for tears. The water was cold.

When he came to the surface he was conscious of little but the noisy water. Afterward he saw his companions in the sea. The oiler was ahead in the race. He was swimming strongly and rapidly. Off to the correspondent's left, the cook's great white and corked back bulged out of the water; and in the rear the captain was hanging with his one good hand to the keel of the overturned dinghy.

There is a certain immovable quality to a shore, and the correspondent wondered at it amid the confusion of the sea.

It seemed also very attractive; but the correspondent knew that it was a long journey, and he paddled leisurely. The piece of life-preserver lay under him, and sometimes he whirled down the incline of a wave as if he were on a hand-sled.

But finally he arrived at a place in the sea where travel was beset with difficulty. He did not pause swimming to inquire what manner of current had caught him, but there his progress ceased. The shore was set before him like a bit of scenery on a stage, and he looked at it, and understood with his eyes each detail of it.

As the cook passed, much farther to the left, the captain was calling to him, "Turn over on your back, cook! Turn over on your back and use the oar."

"All right, sir," The cook turned on his back, and, paddling with an oar, went ahead as if he were a canoe.

Presently the boat also passed to the left of the correspondent, with the captain clinging with one hand to the keel. He would have appeared like a man raising himself to look over a board fence if it were not for the extraordinary gymnastics of the boat. The correspondent marveled that the captain could still hold to it.

They passed on nearer to shore—the oiler, the cook, the captain—and following them went the water-jar, bouncing gaily over the seas.

The correspondent remained in the grip of this strange new enemy, a current. The shore, with its white slope of sand and its green bluff, topped with little silent cottages, was spread like a picture before him. It was very near to him then, but he was impressed as one who, in a gallery, looks at a scene from Brittany or Algiers.

He thought: "I am going to drown? Can it be possible? Can it be possible? Can it be possible?" Perhaps an individual must consider his own death to be the final phenomenon of nature.

But later a wave perhaps whirled him out of this small deadly current, for he found suddenly that he could again make progress toward the shore. Later still he was aware that the captain, clinging with one hand to the keel of the dinghy, had his face turned away from the shore and toward him, and was calling his name. "Come to the boat! Come to the boat!"

In his struggle to reach the captain and the boat, he reflected that when one gets properly wearied drowning must really be a comfortable arrangement—a cessation of hostilities accompanied by a large degree of relief; and he was glad of it, for the main thing in his mind for some moments had been horror of the temporary agony; he did not wish to be hurt.

Presently he saw a man running along the shore. He was undressing with most remarkable speed. Coat, trousers, shirt, everything flew magically off him.

"Come to the boat!" called the captain.

"All right, Captain." As the correspondent paddled, he saw the captain let himself down to bottom and leave the boat. Then the correspondent performed his one little marvel of the voyage. A large wave caught him and flung him with ease and supreme speed completely over the boat and far beyond it. It struck him even then as an event in gymnastics and a true miracle of the sea. An overturned boat in the surf is not a plaything to a swimming man.

The correspondent arrived in water that reached only to his waist, but his condition did not enable him to stand for more than a moment. Each wave knocked him into a heap, and the under-tow pulled at him.

Then he saw the man who had been running and undressing, and undressing and running, come bounding into the water. He dragged ashore the cook, and then waded towards the captain, but the captain waved him away, and sent him to the correspondent. He was naked, naked as a tree in winter, but a halo was about his head, and he shone like a saint. He gave a strong pull, and a long drag, and a bully heave at the correspondent's hand. The correspondent, schooled in the minor formulae, said: "Thanks, old man." But suddenly the man cried: "What's that?" He pointed a swift finger. The correspondent said: "Go."

In the shallows, face downward, lay the oiler. His forehead touched sand that was periodically, between each wave, clear of the sea.

The correspondent did not know all that transpired afterward. When he achieved safe ground he fell, striking the sand with each particular part of his body. It was as if he had dropped from a roof, but the thud was grateful to him.

It seemed that instantly the beach was populated with men with blankets, clothes, and flasks, and women with coffeepots and all the remedies sacred to their minds. The welcome of the land to the men from the sea was warm and generous, but a still and dripping shape was carried slowly up the beach, and the land's welcome for it could only be the different and sinister hospitality of the grave.

When it came night, the white waves paced to and fro in the moonlight, and the wind brought the sound of the great sea's voice to the men on shore, and they felt that they could then be interpreters.

1. *Ascertain what you judge to be the chief emphasis of each of the seven parts of Crane's story. Consider plot, character, or theme.*

2. *Who is the protagonist? What is the conflict?*

3. *What can be inferred from the fact that the oiler, seemingly the fittest, drowns?*

4. *Identify Crane's shifting point of view.*

5. *What is the correspondent's early attitude toward the dying Algerian soldier? What motivates his change of feelings?*

6. *Gulls flew near the dinghy. At first the men envied these creatures, but later they considered "somehow grewsome and ominous" the gull that alighted atop the Captain's head. Why?*

7. *Interpret the meaning of: (a) the naked rescuer; (b) the survivors hearing "the sound of the great sea's voice" and feeling that "they could then be interpreters"; (c) the correspondent describing the comradeship of the four shipwrecked men as "the best experience in his life."*

8. *The four men hold to what view of nature at the beginning of the story? To what view have they converted at the end?*

9. *How does the resolution help you in arriving at the theme? State the theme.*

Topics for Writing

1. *Trace the characters' view of nature.*

2. *Compare man's condition in life to that of "man" in a ten-foot dinghy on the menacing sea.*

3. *Excerpting supporting details from the story, substantiate the premise that tragedy and suffering make men brothers.*

4. *Defend the contention that "The Open Boat" is a good example of naturalistic fiction.*

Selected Bibliography

Stephen Crane

Adams, Richard P. "Naturalistic Fiction: 'The Open Boat.'" *Tulane Studies in English,* 4 (1954), 137–146.

Berryman, John. "Commentary." In *The Arts of Reading* by Ralph Ross, John Berryman, and Allen Tate. New York: Thomas Y. Crowell Co., 1960, pp. 279–288.

Brennan, Joseph X. "Stephen Crane and the Limits of Irony." *Criticism*, 11 (1969), 183–200.

Buitenhuis, Peter. "The Essentials of Life." *Modern Fiction Studies*, 5 (1959), 243–250.

Burns, Landon C. "On 'The Open Boat.'" *Studies in Short Fiction*, 3 (1966), 455–457.

Colvert, James B. "Style and Meaning in Stephen Crane: *The Open Boat.*" *Texas Studies in English*, 37 (1958), 34–45.

Garnett, Edward. "Stephen Crane and His Work." In *Friday Nights*. New York: Alfred A. Knopf, 1922, pp. 201–217.

Gibson, Donald B. *The Fiction of Stephen Crane.* Carbondale and Edwardsville: Southern Illinois University Press, 1968.

Gordon, Caroline. "Stephen Crane." *Accent*, 9 (1949), 72.

Griffith, Clark. "Stephen Crane and the Ironic Last Word." *Philological Quarterly*, 47 (1968), 83–91.

Hagemann, E. R. "Crane's 'Real' War in His Short Stories." *American Quarterly*, 8 (1956), 356–367.

Kwiat, Joseph J. "Stephen Crane and Painting." *American Quarterly*, 4 (1952), 331–338.

Labor, Earle. "Crane and Hemingway: Anatomy of Trauma." *Renascence*, 11 (1959), 189–196.

Leaver, Florence. "Isolation in the Work of Stephen Crane." *South Atlantic Quarterly*, 61 (1962), 521–532.

Marcus, Mordecai. "The Three-Fold View of Nature in 'The Open Boat.'" *Philological Quarterly*, 41 (1962), 511–515.

Metzger, Charles R. "Realistic Devices in Stephen Crane's 'The Open Boat.'" *Midwest Quarterly*, 4 (1962), 47–54.

Meyers, Robert. "Crane's 'The Open Boat.'" *Explicator*, 21 (1963), 60.

Parks, Edd Winfield. "Crane's 'The Open Boat.'" *Nineteenth-Century Fiction*, 8 (1953), 77.

Randel, William. "The Cook in 'The Open Boat.'" *American Literature*, 34 (1962), 405–411.

Roth, Russell. "A Tree in Winter: The Short Fiction of Stephen Crane." *New Mexico Quarterly*, 23 (1953), 188–196.

Stallman, R. W. "Crane's Short Stories." In *The Houses That James Built and Other Literary Studies.* Lansing: Michigan State University Press, 1961, pp. 103–110.

Stein, William Bysshe. "Stephen Crane's *Homo Absurdus.*" *Bucknell Review*, 8 (1959), 168–188.

Walcutt, Charles Child. "Stephen Crane: Naturalist and Impressionist." In *American Literary Naturalism: A*

Divided Stream. Minneapolis: University of Minnesota Press, 1956, pp. 66–86.

James Joyce *(1882–1941)*

Born in Dublin, he attended Jesuit schools, was graduated from University College, taught languages in a Berlitz school, and left Ireland to live for the rest of his life on the Continent. Near blindness and great difficulty getting his work published failed to curtail his writing activities. His best known works are: Dubliners *(1914), a collection of short stories;* A Portrait of the Artist as a Young Man *(1916);* Ulysses *(1922), originally banned in England and the United States; and* Finnegans Wake *(1939). Today he is ranked as one of the great writers of his age.*

Counterparts

The bell rang furiously and, when Miss Parker went to the tube, a furious voice called out in a piercing North of Ireland accent:

"Send Farrington here!"

Miss Parker returned to her machine, saying to a man who was writing at a desk:

"Mr. Alleyne wants you upstairs."

The man muttered "*Blast* him!" under his breath and pushed back his chair to stand up. When he stood up he was tall and of great bulk. He had a hanging face, dark wine-coloured, with fair eyebrows and moustache: his eyes bulged forward slightly and the whites of them were dirty. He lifted up the counter and, passing by the clients, went out of the office with a heavy step.

He went heavily upstairs until he came to the second landing, where a door bore a brass plate with the inscription *Mr. Alleyne*. Here he halted, puffing with labour and vexation, and knocked. The shrill voice cried:

"Come in!"

The man entered Mr. Alleyne's room. Simultaneously Mr. Alleyne, a little man wearing goldrimmed glasses on a clean-shaven face, shot his head up over a pile of documents. The head itself was so pink and hairless it seemed like a large egg reposing on the papers. Mr. Alleyne did not lose a moment:

"Farrington? What is the meaning of this? Why have I always to complain of you? May I ask you why you haven't made a copy of that contract between Bodley and Kirwan? I told you it must be ready by four o'clock."

"But Mr. Shelley said, sir—"

"*Mr. Shelley said, sir.* . . . Kindly attend to what I say and not to what *Mr. Shelley says, sir.* You have always some excuse or another for shirking work. Let me tell you that if the contract is not copied before this evening I'll lay the matter before Mr. Crosbie. . . . Do you hear me now?"

"Yes, sir."

"Do you hear me now? . . . Ay and another little matter! I might as well be talking to the wall as talking to you. Understand once for all that you get a half an hour for your lunch and not an hour and a half. How many courses do you want, I'd like to know. . . . Do you mind me now?"

"Yes, sir."

Mr. Alleyne bent his head again upon his pile of papers. The man stared fixedly at the polished skull which directed the affairs of Crosbie & Alleyne, gauging its fragility. A spasm of rage gripped his throat for a few moments and then passed, leaving after it a sharp sensation of thirst. The man recognised the sensation and felt that he must have a good night's drinking. The middle of the month was passed and, if he could get the copy done in time, Mr. Alleyne might give him an order on the cashier. He stood still, gazing fixedly at the head upon the pile of papers. Suddenly, Mr. Alleyne began to upset all the papers, searching for something. Then, as if he had been unaware of the man's presence till that moment, he shot up his head again, saying:

"Eh? Are you going to stand there all day? Upon my word, Farrington, you take things easy!"

"I was waiting to see . . ."

"Very good, you needn't wait to see. Go downstairs and do your work."

The man walked heavily towards the door and, as he went out of the room, he heard Mr. Alleyne cry after him that if the contract was not copied by evening Mr. Crosbie would hear of the matter.

He returned to his desk in the lower office and counted the sheets which remained to be copied. He took up his pen and dipped it in the ink but he continued to stare stupidly at the last words he had written: *In no case shall the said Bernard Bodley be* . . . The evening was falling and in a few minutes they would be lighting the gas: then he could write. He felt that he must slake the thirst in his throat. He stood up from his desk and, lifting the counter as before, passed out of the office. As he was passing out the chief clerk looked at him inquiringly.

"It's all right, Mr. Shelley," said the man, pointing with his finger to indicate the objective of his journey.

The chief clerk glanced at the hat-rack, but, seeing the row complete, offered no remark. As soon as he was on the landing the man pulled a shepherd's plain cap out of his pocket, put it on his head and ran quickly down the rickety stairs. From the street door he walked on furtively on the inner side of the path towards the corner and all at once dived into a doorway. He was now safe in the dark snug O'Neill's shop, and, filling up the little window that looked into the bar with his inflamed face, the colour of dark wine or dark meat, he called out:

"Here, Pat, give us a g.p., like a good fellow."

The curate brought him a glass of plain porter. The man drank it at a gulp and asked for a caraway seed. He put his penny on the counter and, leaving the curate to grope for it in the gloom, retreated out of the snug as furtively as he had entered it.

Darkness, accompanied by a thick fog, was gaining upon the dusk of February and the lamps in Eustace Street had been lit. The man went up by the houses until he reached the door of the office, wondering whether he could finish his copy in time. On the stairs a moist pungent odour of perfumes saluted his nose: evidently Miss Delacour had come while he was out in O'Neill's. He crammed his cap back again into his pocket and re-entered the office, assuming an air of absent-mindedness.

"Mr. Alleyne has been calling for you," said the chief clerk severely. "Where were you?"

The man glanced at the two clients who were standing at the counter as if to intimate that their presence prevented him from answering. As the clients were both male the chief clerk allowed himself a laugh.

"I know that game," he said. "Five times in one day is a little bit. . . . Well, you better look sharp and get a copy of our correspondence in the Delacour case for Mr. Alleyne."

This address in the presence of the public, his run upstairs and the porter he had gulped down so hastily confused the man and, as he sat down at his desk to get what was required, he realised how hopeless was the task of finishing his copy of the contract before half past five. The dark damp night was coming and he longed to spend it in the bars, drinking with his friends amid the glare of gas and the clatter of glasses. He got out the Delacour correspondence and passed out of the office. He hoped Mr. Alleyne would not discover that the last two letters were missing.

The moist pungent perfume lay all the way up to Mr. Alleyne's room. Miss Delacour was a middle-aged woman of Jewish appearance. Mr. Alleyne was said to be sweet on her or on her money. She came to the office often and stayed a long time when she came. She was sitting beside his desk now in an aroma of perfumes, smoothing the handle of her umbrella and nodding the great black feather in her hat. Mr. Alleyne had swivelled his chair round to face her and thrown his right foot jauntily upon his left knee. The man put the correspondence on the desk and bowed respectfully but neither Mr. Alleyne nor Miss Delacour took any notice of his bow. Mr. Alleyne tapped a finger on the correspondence and then flicked it towards him as if to say: *That's all right: you can go.*

The man returned to the lower office and sat down again at his desk. He stared intently at the incomplete phrase: *In no case shall the said Bernard Bodley be . . .* and thought how strange it was that the last three words began with the same letter. The chief clerk began to hurry Miss Parker, saying she would never have the letters typed in time for post. The man listened to the clicking of the machine for a few minutes and then set to work to finish his copy. But his head was not clear and his mind wandered away to the glare and rattle of the public-house. It was a night for hot punches. He struggled on with his copy, but when the clock struck five he had still fourteen pages to write. Blast it! He couldn't finish it in time. He longed to execrate aloud, to bring his fist down on something violently. He was so enraged that he wrote *Bernard Bernard* instead of *Bernard Bodley* and had to begin again on a clean sheet.

He felt strong enough to clear out the whole office single-handed. His body ached to do something, to rush out and revel in violence. All the indignities of his life enraged him. . . . Could he ask the cashier privately for an advance? No, the cashier was no good, no damn good: he wouldn't give an advance. . . . He knew where he would meet the boys; Leonard and O'Halloran and Nosey Flynn. The barometer of his emotional nature was set for a spell of riot.

His imagination had so abstracted him that his name was called twice before he answered. Mr. Alleyne and Miss Delacour were standing outside the counter and all the clerks had turned round in anticipation of something. The man got up from his desk. Mr. Alleyne began a tirade of abuse, saying that two letters were missing. The man answered that he knew nothing about them, that he had made a faithful copy. The tirade continued: it was so bitter and violent that the man could hardly restrain his fist from descending upon the head of the manikin before him.

"I know nothing about any other two letters," he said stupidly.

"*You—know—nothing.* Of course you know nothing," said Mr. Alleyne. "Tell me," he added, glancing first for approval to the lady beside him, "do you take me for a fool? Do you think me an utter fool?"

The man glanced from the lady's face to the little egg-shaped head and back again; and, almost before he was aware of it, his tongue had found a felicitous moment:

"I don't think sir," he said, "that that's a fair question to put to me."

There was a pause in the very breathing of the clerks. Everyone was astounded (the author of the witticism no less than his neighbours) and Miss Delacour, who was a stout amiable person, began to smile broadly. Mr. Alleyne flushed to the hue of a wild rose and his mouth twitched with a dwarf's passion. He shook his fist in the man's face till it seemed to vibrate like the knob of some electric machine:

"You impertinent ruffian! You impertinent ruffian! I'll make short work of you! Wait till you see! You'll apologise to me for your impertinence or you'll quit the office instanter! You'll quit this, I'm telling you, or you'll apologise to me!"

He stood in a doorway opposite the office watching to see if the cashier would come out alone. All the clerks passed out and finally the cashier came out with the chief clerk. It was no use trying to say a word to him when he was with the chief clerk. The man felt that his position was bad enough. He had been obliged to offer an abject apology to Mr. Alleyne for his impertinence but he knew what a hornet's nest the office would be for him. He could remember the way in which Mr. Alleyne had hounded little Peake out of the office in order to make room for his own nephew. He felt savage and thirsty and revengeful, annoyed with himself and with everyone else. Mr. Alleyne would never give him an hour's rest; his life would be a hell to him. He had made a proper fool of himself this time. Could he not keep his tongue in his cheek? But they had never pulled together from the first, he and Mr. Alleyne, ever since the day Mr. Alleyne had overheard him mimicking his North of Ireland accent to amuse Higgins and Miss Parker: that had been the beginning of it. He might have tried Higgins for the money, but sure Higgins never had anything for himself. A man with two establishments to keep up, of course he couldn't. . . .

He felt his great body again aching for the comfort of the public-house. The fog had begun to chill him and he wondered could he touch Pat in O'Neill's. He could not touch him for more than a bob—and a bob was no use. Yet he must get money somewhere or other: he had spent his last penny for the g.p. and soon it would be too late for getting money anywhere. Suddenly, as he was fingering his watch-chain, he thought of Terry Kelly's pawn-office in Fleet Street. That was the dart! Why didn't he think of it sooner?

He went through the narrow alley of Temple Bar quickly, muttering to himself that they could all go to hell because he was going to have a good night of it. The clerk in Terry Kelly's said *A crown!* but the consignor held out for six shillings; and in the end the six shillings was allowed him literally. He came out of the pawn-office joyfully, making a little cylinder of the coins between his thumb and fingers. In Westmoreland Street the footpaths were crowded with young men and women returning from business and ragged urchins ran here and there yelling out the names of the evening editions. The man passed through the crowd, looking on the spectacle generally with proud satisfaction and staring masterfully at the office-girls. His head was full of the noises of tram-gongs and swishing trolleys and his nose already sniffed the curling fumes of punch. As he walked on he preconsidered the terms in which he would narrate the incident to the boys:

"So, I just looked at him—coolly, you know, and looked at her. Then I looked back at him again—taking my time, you know. 'I don't think that that's a fair question to put to me,' says I."

Nosey Flynn was sitting up in his usual corner of Davy Byrne's and, when he heard the story, he stood Farrington a half-one, saying it was as smart a thing as ever he heard. Farrington stood a drink in his turn. After a while O'Halloran and Paddy Leonard came in and the story was repeated to them. O'Halloran stood tailors of malt, hot, all round and told the story of the retort he had made to the chief clerk when he was in Callan's of Fownes's Street; but, as the retort was after the manner of the liberal shepherds in the eclogues, he had to admit that it was not as clever as Farrington's retort. At this Farrington told the boys to polish off that and have another.

Just as they were naming their poisons who should come in but Higgins! Of course he had to join in with the others. The men asked him to give his version of it, and he did so with great vivacity for the sight of five small hot whiskies was very exhilarating. Everyone roared laughing when he showed the way in which Mr. Alleyne shook his fist in Farrington's face. Then he imitated Farrington, saying, *"And here was my nabs, as cool as you please,"* while Farrington looked at the company out of his heavy dirty eyes, smiling and at times drawing forth stray drops of liquor from his moustache with the aid of his lower lip.

When that round was over there was a pause. O'Halloran had money but neither of the other two seemed to have any; so the whole party left the shop somewhat regretfully. At the corner of Duke Street Higgins and Nosey Flynn bevelled off to the left while the other three turned back towards the city. Rain was drizzling down on the cold streets and, when they reached the Ballast Office, Farrington suggested the Scotch House. The bar was full of men and loud with the noise of tongues and glasses. The three men pushed past the whining match-sellers at the door and formed a little party at the corner of the counter. They began to exchange stories. Leonard introduced them to a young fellow named Weathers who was performing at the Tivoli as an acrobat and knockabout *artiste*. Farrington stood a drink all round. Weathers said he would take a small Irish and Apollinaris. Farrington, who had definite notions of what was what, asked the boys would they have an Apollinaris too; but the boys told Tim to make theirs hot. The talk became theatrical. O'Halloran stood a round and then Farrington stood another round, Weathers protesting that the hospitality was too Irish. He promised to get them in behind the scenes and introduce them to some nice girls. O'Halloran said that he and Leonard would go, but that Farrington wouldn't go because he was a married man; and Farrington's heavy dirty eyes leered at the company in token that he understood he was being chaffed. Weathers made them all have just one little tincture at his expense and promised to meet them later on at Mulligan's in Poolbeg Street.

When the Scotch House closed they went round to Mulligan's. They went into the parlour at the back and O'Halloran ordered small hot specials all round. They were all beginning to feel mellow. Farrington was just standing another round when Weathers came back. Much to Farrington's relief he drank a glass of bitter this time. Funds were getting low but they had enough to keep them going. Presently two young women with big hats and a young man in a check suit came in and sat at a table close by. Weathers saluted them and told the company that they were out of the Tivoli. Farrington's eyes wandered at every moment in the direction of one of the young women. There was something striking in her appearance. An immense scarf of peacock-blue muslin was wound round her hat and knotted in a great bow under her chin; and she wore bright yellow gloves, reaching to the elbow. Farrington gazed admiringly at the plump arm which she moved very often and with much grace; and when, after a little time, she answered his gaze he admired still more her large dark brown eyes. The oblique staring expression in them fascinated him. She glanced at him once or twice and, when the party was leaving the room, she brushed against his chair and said *"O, pardon!"* in a London accent. He watched her leave the room in the hope that she would look back at him, but he was disappointed. He cursed his want of money and cursed all the rounds he had stood, particularly all the whiskies and Apollinaris which he had stood to Weathers. If there was one thing that he hated it was a sponge. He was so angry that he lost count of the conversation of his friends.

When Paddy Leonard called him he found that they were talking about feats of strength. Weathers was showing his biceps muscle to the company and boasting so much that the other two had called on Farrington to uphold the national honour. Farrington pulled up his sleeve accordingly and showed his biceps muscle to the company. The two arms were examined and compared and finally it was agreed to have a trial of strength. The table was cleared and the two men rested their elbows on it, clasping hands. When Paddy Leonard said *"Go!"* each was to try to bring down the other's hand to the table. Farrington looked very serious and determined.

The trial began. After about thirty seconds Weathers brought his opponent's hand slowly down on to the table. Farrington's dark wine-coloured face flushed darker still with anger and humiliation at having been defeated by such a stripling.

"You're not to put the weight of your body behind it. Play fair," he said.

"Who's not playing fair?" said the other.

"Come on again. The two best out of three."

The trial began again. The veins stood out on Farrington's forehead, and the pallor of Weather's complexion changed to peony. Their hands and arms trembled under the stress. After a long struggle Weathers again brought his opponent's hand slowly on to the table. There was a murmur of applause from the spectators. The curate, who was standing beside the table, nodded his red head towards the victor and said with stupid familiarity:

"Ah! that's the knack!"

"What the hell do you know about it?" said Farrington fiercely, turning on the man. "What do you put in your gab for?"

"Sh, sh!" said O'Halloran, observing the violent expression of Farrington's face. "Pony up, boys. We'll have just one little smahan more and then we'll be off."

A very sullen-faced man stood at the corner of O'Connell Bridge waiting for the little Sandymount tram to take him home. He was full of smouldering anger and revengefulness. He felt humiliated and discontented; he did not even feel drunk; and he had only twopence in his pocket. He cursed everything. He had done for himself in the office, pawned his watch, spent all his money; and he had not even got drunk. He began to feel thirsty again and he longed to be back again in the hot reeking public-house. He had lost his reputation as a strong man, having been defeated twice by a mere boy. His heart swelled with fury and, when he thought of the woman in the big hat who had brushed against him and said *Pardon!* his fury nearly choked him.

His tram let him down at Shelbourne Road and he steered his great body along in the shadow of the wall of the barracks. He loathed returning to his home. When he went in by the side-door he found the kitchen empty and the kitchen fire nearly out. He bawled upstairs:

"Ada! Ada!"

His wife was a little sharp-faced woman who bullied her husband when he was sober and was bullied by him when he was drunk. They had five children. A little boy came running down the stairs.

"Who is that?" said the man, peering through the darkness.

"Me, pa."

"Who are you? Charlie?"

"No, pa. Tom."

"Where's your mother?"

"She's out at the chapel."

"That's right. . . . Did she think of leaving any dinner for me?"

"Yes, pa. I—"

"Light the lamp. What do you mean by having the place in darkness? Are the other children in bed?"

The man sat down heavily on one of the chairs while the little boy lit the lamp. He began to mimic his son's flat accent, saying half to himself: *"At the chapel. At the chapel, if you please!"* When the lamp was lit he banged his fist on the table and shouted:

"What's for my dinner?"

"I'm going . . . to cook it, pa," said the little boy.

The man jumped up furiously and pointed to the fire.

"On that fire! You let the fire out! By God, I'll teach you to do that again!"

He took a step to the door and seized the walking-stick which was standing behind it.

"I'll teach you to let the fire out!" he said, rolling up his sleeve in order to give his arm free play.

The little boy cried *"O, pa!"* and ran whimpering round the table, but the man followed him and caught him by the coat. The little boy looked about him wildly but, seeing no way of escape, fell upon his knees.

"Now, you'll let the fire out the next time!" said the man, striking at him vigorously with the stick. "Take that, you little whelp!"

The boy uttered a squeal of pain as the stick cut his thigh. He clasped his hands together in the air and his voice shook with fright.

"O, pa!" he cried. "Don't beat me, pa! And I'll . . . I'll say a *Hail Mary* for you. . . . I'll say a *Hail Mary* for you, pa, if you don't beat me. . . . I'll say a *Hail Mary*. . . ."

Exercises

1. Comment upon the significance of the title. Identify several of the "counterparts" in the story.

2. Explain the roles of Mr. Alleyne, Farrington's wife Ada, and his son Tom. How is each frustrated?

3. Characterize Farrington. What are his faults?

4. Describe his conflict. Does he experience a moment of revelation?

5. What motivates Farrington to strike his son? Why does the boy offer to say a "Hail Mary" for his father?

6. What important statement about the human condition does the story make? What important events and details lead you to this conclusion?

7. Explore the hypothesis that nothing significant happens in the story.

1. *Discover the causes and effects of Farrington's brutality.*

2. *Delineate Farrington from one of the following descriptions: (a) a frustrated brute; (b) a victim of circumstances; (c) a tiny screw in a machine; (d) a self-indulgent, self-pitying fool.*

3. *Express the theme of the story.*

Selected
Bibliography

James Joyce

Beck, Warren. *Joyce's Dubliners: Substance, Vision, and Art.* Durham, N. C.: Duke University Press, 1969.

Friedrich, Gerhard. "The Gnomonic Clue to James Joyce's *Dubliners.*" *Modern Language Notes*, 72 (June 1957), 421–424.

———. "The Perspective of Joyce's *Dubliners.*" *College English*, 26 (March 1965), 421–426.

Ghiselin, Brewster. "The Unity of Joyce's *Dubliners.*" *Accent*, 16 (Spring 1956), 75–88. Part II (Summer 1956), 196–213.

Givens, Seon, ed. *James Joyce: Two Decades of Criticism.* New York: Vanguard Press, 1948.

Hart, Clive, ed. *James Joyce's Dubliners: Critical Essays.* New York: Viking Press, 1969.

Kenner, Hugh. *Dublin's Joyce.* Bloomington: Indiana University Press, 1956.

Pound, Ezra. "*Dubliners* and Mr. James Joyce." In *Pound/Joyce: The Letters of Ezra Pound to James Joyce, with Pound's Essays on Joyce*, ed. Forrest Read. New York: A New Directions Paperbook, 1967, pp. 27–30.

Walzl, Florence L. "Pattern on Paralysis in Joyce's *Dubliners*: A Study of the Original Framework." *College English*, 22 (January 1961), 221–228.

Katherine Anne Porter (1894–   )

Born in Indian Creek, Texas, a descendant of Daniel Boone, reared in Texas and Louisiana, educated in convent schools, she eloped at the age of sixteen and became a newspaper woman at the age of twenty-one. She spent the early 1920s in Mexico;

and, except for teaching stints at several universities, including Stanford, Michigan, and Virginia, she lived for the rest of her life in Paris. She is widely known for two collections of short fiction: Flowering Judas and Other Stories *(1930)* and Pale Horse, Pale Rider *(1939). Her only novel,* Ship of Fools *(1961), was an instant success. Among the large number of gifted American women writers, many critics consider her the most accomplished.*

Flowering Judas

Braggioni sits heaped upon the edge of a straight-backed chair much too small for him, and sings to Laura in a furry, mournful voice. Laura has begun to find reasons for avoiding her own house until the latest possible moment, for Braggioni is there almost every night. No matter how late she is, he will be sitting there with a surly, waiting expression, pulling at his kinky yellow hair, thumbing the strings of his guitar, snarling a tune under his breath. Lupe the Indian maid meets Laura at the door, and says with a flicker of a glance towards the upper room, "He waits."

Laura wishes to lie down, she is tired of her hairpins and the feel of her long tight sleeves, but she says to him, "Have you a new song for me this evening?" If he says yes, she asks him to sing it. If he says no, she remembers his favorite one, and asks him to sing it again. Lupe brings her a cup of chocolate and a plate of rice, and Laura eats at the small table under the lamp, first inviting Braggioni, whose answer is always the same: "I have eaten, and besides, chocolate thickens the voice."

Laura says, "Sing, then," and Braggioni heaves himself into song. He scratches the guitar familiarly as though it were a pet animal, and sings passionately off key, taking the high notes in a prolonged painful squeal. Laura, who haunts the markets listening to the ballad singers, and stops every day to hear the blind boy playing his reed-flute in Sixteenth of September Street, listens to Braggioni with pitiless courtesy, because she dares not smile at his miserable performance. Nobody dares to smile at him. Braggioni is cruel to everyone, with a kind of specialized insolence, but he is so vain of his talents, and so sensitive to slights, it would require a cruelty and vanity greater than his own to lay a finger on the vast cureless wound of his self-esteem. It would require courage, too, for it is dangerous to offend him, and nobody has this courage.

Braggioni loves himself with such tenderness and amplitude and eternal charity that his followers—for he is a leader of men, a skilled revolutionist, and his skin has been punctured in honorable warfare—warm themselves in the reflected glow, and say to each other:

"He has a real nobility, a love of humanity raised above mere personal affections." The excess of this self-love has flowed out, inconveniently for her, over Laura who, with so many others, owes her comfortable situation and her salary to him. When he is in a very good humour, he tells her, "I am tempted to forgive you for being a *gringa. Gringita!*" and Laura, burning, imagines herself leaning forward suddenly, and with a sound back-handed slap wiping the suety smile from his face. If he notices her eyes at these moments he gives no sign.

She knows what Braggioni would offer her, and she must resist tenaciously without appearing to resist, and if she could avoid it she would not admit even to herself the slow drift of his intention. During these long evenings which have spoiled a long month for her, she sits in her deep chair with an open book on her knees, resting her eyes on the consoling rigidity of the printed page when the sight and sound of Braggioni singing threaten to identify themselves with all her remembered afflictions and to add their weight to her uneasy premonitions of the future. The gluttonous bulk of Braggioni has become a symbol of her many disillusions, for a revolutionist should be lean, animated by heroic faith, a vessel of abstract virtues. This is nonsense, she knows it now and is ashamed of it. Revolution must have leaders, and leadership is a career for energetic men. She is, her comrades tell her, full of romantic error, for what she defines as cynicism in them is merely "a developed sense of reality." She is almost too willing to say, "I am wrong, I suppose I don't really understand the principles," and afterward she makes a secret truce with herself, determined not to surrender her will to such expedient logic. But she cannot help feeling that she has been betrayed irreparably by the disunion between her way of living and her feeling of what life should be, and at times she is almost contented to rest in this sense of grievance as a private store of consolation. Sometimes she wishes to run away, but she stays. Now she longs to fly out of this room, down the narrow stairs, and into the street where the houses lean together like conspirators under a single mottled lamp, and leave Braggioni singing to himself.

Instead she looks at Braggioni, frankly and clearly, like a good child who understands the rules of behavior. Her knees cling together under sound blue serge, and her round white collar is not purposely nun-like. She wears the uniform of an idea, and has renounced vanities. She was born Roman Catholic, and in spite of her fear of being seen by someone who might make a scandal of it, she slips now and again into some crumbling little church, kneels on the chilly stone, and says a Hail Mary on the gold rosary she bought in Tehuantepec. It is no good and she ends by examining the altar with its tinsel flowers and ragged brocades, and feels tender about the battered doll-shape of some male saint whose white, lace-trimmed drawers hang limply around his ankles below the hieratic dignity of his velvet robe. She has encased herself in a set of principles derived from her early training, leaving no detail of gesture or of personal taste untouched, and for this reason she will not wear lace made on machines. This is her private heresy, for in her special group the machine is sacred, and will be the salvation of the workers. She loves fine lace, and there is a tiny edge of fluted cobweb on this collar, which is one of twenty precisely alike, folded in blue tissue paper in the upper drawer of her clothes chest.

Braggioni catches her glance solidly as if he had been waiting for it, leans forward, balancing his paunch between his spread knees, and sings with tremendous emphasis, weighing his words. He has, the song relates, no father and no mother, nor even a friend to console him; lonely as a wave of the sea he comes and goes, lonely as a wave. His mouth opens round and yearns sideways, his balloon cheeks grow oily with the labour of song. He bulges marvellously in his expensive garments. Over his lavender collar, crushed upon a purple necktie, held by a diamond hoop: over his ammunition belt of tooled leather worked in silver, buckled cruelly around his gasping middle: over the tops of his glossy yellow shoes Braggioni swells with ominous ripeness, his mauve silk hose stretched taut, his ankles bound with the stout leather thongs of his shoes.

When he stretches his eyelids at Laura she notes again that his eyes are the true tawny yellow cat's eyes. He is rich, not in money, he tells her, but in power, and this power brings with it the blameless ownership of things, and the right to indulge his love of small luxuries. "I have a taste for the elegant refinements," he said once, flourishing a yellow silk handkerchief before her nose; "smell that? It is Jockey Club, imported from New York." Nonetheless he is wounded by life. He will say so presently. "It is true everything turns to dust in the hand, to gall on the tongue." He sighs and his leather belt creaks like a saddle girth. "I am disappointed in everything as it comes. Everything." He shakes his head. "You, poor thing, you will be disappointed too. You are born for it. We are more alike than you realize in some things. Wait and see. Some day you will remember what I have told you, you will know that Braggioni was your friend."

Laura feels a slow chill, a purely physical sense of danger, a warning in her blood that violence, mutilation, a shocking death, wait for her with lessening patience. She has translated this fear into something homely, immediate, and sometimes hesitates before crossing the street. "My personal fate is nothing, except as the testimony of a mental attitude," she reminds herself, quoting from some forgotten philosophic primer, and is sensible enough to add, "Anyhow, I shall not be killed by an automobile if I can help it."

"It may be true I am as corrupt, in another way, as Braggioni," she thinks in spite of herself, "as callous, as incomplete," and if this is so, any kind of death seems preferable. Still she sits quietly, she does not run. Where could she go? Uninvited she has promised herself to this place; she can no longer imagine herself as living in another country, and there is no pleasure in remembering her life before she came here.

Precisely what is the nature of this devotion, its true

motives, and what are its obligations? Laura cannot say. She spends part of her days in Xochimilco, near by, teaching Indian children to say in English, "The cat is on the mat." When she appears in the class room they crowd about her with smiles on their wise, innocent clay-colored faces, crying, "Good morning, my titcher!" in immaculate voices, and they make of her desk a fresh garden of flowers every day.

During her leisure she goes to union meetings and listens to busy important voices quarreling over tactics, methods, internal politics. She visits the prisoners of her own political faith in their cells, where they entertain themselves with counting cockroaches, repenting of their indiscretions, composing their memoirs, writing out manifestoes and plans for their comrades who are still walking about free, hands in pockets, sniffing fresh air. Laura brings them food and cigarettes and a little money, and she brings messages disguised in equivocal phrases from the men outside who dare not set foot in the prison for fear of disappearing into the cells kept empty for them. If the prisoners confuse night and day, and complain, "Dear little Laura, time doesn't pass in this infernal hole, and I won't know when it is time to sleep unless I have a reminder," she brings them their favorite narcotics, and says in a tone that does not wound them with pity, "Tonight will really be night for you," and though her Spanish amuses them, they find her comforting, useful. If they lose patience and all faith, and curse the slowness of their friends in coming to their rescue with money and influence, they trust her not to repeat everything, and if she inquires, "Where do you think we can find money, or influence?" they are certain to answer, "Well, there is Braggioni, why doesn't he do something?"

She smuggles letters from headquarters to men hiding from firing squads in back streets in mildewed houses, where they sit in tumbled beds and talk bitterly as if all Mexico were at their heels, when Laura knows positively they might appear at the band concert in the Alameda on Sunday morning, and no one would notice them. But Braggioni says, "Let them sweat a little. The next time they may be careful. It is very restful to have them out of the way for a while." She is not afraid to knock on any door in any street after midnight, and enter in the darkness, and say to one of these men who is really in danger: "They will be looking for you—seriously—tomorrow morning after six. Here is some money from Vicente. Go to Vera Cruz and wait."

She borrows money from the Roumanian agitator to give to his bitter enemy the Polish agitator. The favor of Braggioni is their disputed territory, and Braggioni holds the balance nicely, for he can use them both. The Polish agitator talks love to her over café tables, hoping to exploit what he believes is her secret sentimental preference for him, and he gives her misinformation which he begs her to repeat as the solemn truth to certain persons. The Roumanian is more adroit. He is generous with his money in all good causes, and lies to her with an air of ingenuous candor, as if he were her good friend and confidant. She never repeats anything they may say. Braggioni never asks questions. He has other ways to discover all that he wishes to know about them.

Nobody touches her, but all praise her grey eyes, and the soft, round under lip which promises gayety, yet is always grave, nearly always firmly closed: and they cannot understand why she is in Mexico. She walks back and forth on her errands, with puzzled eyebrows, carrying her little folder of drawings and music and school papers. No dancer dances more beautifully than Laura walks, and she inspires some amusing, unexpected ardours, which cause little gossip, because nothing comes of them. A young captain who had been a soldier in Zapata's army attempted, during a horseback ride near Cuernavaca, to express his desire for her with the noble simplicity befitting a rude folk-hero: but gently, because he was gentle. This gentleness was his defeat, for when he alighted, and removed her foot from the stirrup, and essayed to draw her down into his arms, her horse, ordinarily a tame one, shied fiercely, reared and plunged away. The young hero's horse careered blindly after his stable-mate, and the hero did not return to the hotel until rather late that evening. At breakfast he came to her table in full charro dress, grey buckskin jacket and trousers with strings of silver buttons down the leg, and he was in a humorous, careless mood. "May I sit with you?" and "You are a wonderful rider. I was terrified that you might be thrown and dragged. I should never have forgiven myself. But I cannot admire you enough for your riding!"

"I learned to ride in Arizona," said Laura.

"If you will ride with me again this morning, I promise you a horse that will not shy with you," he said. But Laura remembered that she must return to Mexico City at noon.

Next morning the children made a celebration and spent their playtime writing on the blackboard, "We lov ar ticher," and with tinted chalks they drew wreaths of flowers around the words. The young hero wrote her a letter: "I am a very foolish, wasteful, impulsive man. I should have first said I love you, and then you would not have run away. But you shall see me again." Laura thought, "I must send him a box of colored crayons," but she was trying to forgive herself for having spurred her horse at the wrong moment.

A brown, shock-haired youth came and stood in her patio one night and sang like a lost soul for two hours, but Laura could think of nothing to do about it. The moonlight spread a wash of gauzy silver over the clear spaces of the garden, and the shadows were cobalt blue. The scarlet blossoms of the judas tree were dull purple, and the names of the colors repeated themselves automatically in her mind, while she watched, not the boy, but his shadow, fallen like a dark garment across the fountain rim, trailing in the water. Lupe came silently and whispered expert counsel in her ear: "If you will throw him one little flower, he will sing another song or two and go away." Laura threw the flower, and he sang a last song and went away with the flower tucked in the band of his hat. Lupe said, "He is one of the organizers of the Typographers Union, and before that he sold corridos in the Merced market, and before that, he came from Guanajuato, where I was born. I would not trust any man, but I trust least those from Guanajuato."

She did not tell Laura that he would be back again the next night, and the next, nor that he would follow her at a certain fixed distance around the Merced market, through the Zocolo, up Francisco I. Madero Avenue, and so along the Paseo de la Reforma to Chapultepec Park, and into the Philosopher's Footpath, still with that flower withering in his hat, and an indivisible attention in his eyes.

Now Laura is accustomed to him, it means nothing except that he is nineteen years old and is observing a convention with all propriety, as though it were founded on a law of nature, which in the end it might well prove to be. He is beginning to write poems which he prints on a wooden press, and he leaves them stuck like handbills in her door. She is pleasantly disturbed by the abstract, unhurried watchfulness of his black eyes which will in time turn easily towards another object. She tells herself that throwing the flower was a mistake, for she is twenty-two years old and knows better; but she refuses to regret it, and persuades herself that her negation of all external events as they occur is a sign that she is gradually perfecting herself in the stoicism she strives to cultivate against that disaster she fears, though she cannot name it.

She is not at home in the world. Every day she teaches children who remain strangers to her, though she loves their tender round hands and their charming opportunist savagery. She knocks at unfamiliar doors not knowing whether a friend or a stranger shall answer, and even if a known face emerges from the sour gloom of that unknown interior, still it is the face of a stranger. No matter what this stranger says to her, nor what her message to him, the very cells of her flesh reject knowledge and kinship in one monotonous word. No. No. No. She draws her strength from this one holy talismanic word which does not suffer her to be led into evil. Denying everything, she may walk anywhere in safety, she looks at everything without amazement.

No, repeats this firm unchanging voice of her blood; and she looks at Braggioni without amazement. He is a great man, he wishes to impress this simple girl who covers her great round breasts with thick dark cloth, and who hides long, invaluably beautiful legs under a heavy skirt. She is almost thin except for the incomprehensible fullness of her breasts, like a nursing mother's, and Braggioni, who considers himself a judge of women, speculates again on the puzzle of her notorious virginity, and takes the liberty of speech which she permits without a sign of modesty, indeed, without any sort of sign, which is disconcerting.

"You think you are so cold, *gringita!* Wait and see. You will surprise yourself some day! May I be there to advise you!" He stretches his eyelids at her, and his ill-humored cat's eyes waver in a separate glance for the two points of light marking the opposite ends of a smoothly drawn path between the swollen curve of her breasts. He is not put off by that blue serge, nor by her resolutely fixed gaze. There is all the time in the world. His cheeks are bellying with the wind of song. "O girl with the dark eyes," he sings, and reconsiders. "But yours are not dark. I can change all that. O girl with the green eyes, you have stolen my heart away!" Then his mind wanders to the song, and Laura feels the weight of his attention being shifted elsewhere. Singing thus, he seems harmless, he is quite harmless, there is nothing to do but sit patiently and say "No," when the moment comes. She draws a full breath, and her mind wanders also, but not far. She dares not wander too far.

Not for nothing has Braggioni taken pains to be a good revolutionist and a professional lover of humanity. He will never die of it. He has the malice, the cleverness, the wickedness, the sharpness of wit, the hardness of heart, stipulated for loving the world profitably. *He will never die of it.* He will live to see himself kicked out from his feeding trough by other hungry world-saviors. Traditionally he must sing in spite of his life which drives him to bloodshed, he tells Laura, for his father was a Tuscany peasant who drifted to Yucatan and married a Maya woman: a woman of race, an aristocrat. They gave him the love and knowledge of music, thus: and under the rip of his thumbnail, the strings of the instrument complain like exposed nerves.

Once he was called Delgadito by all the girls and married women who ran after him; he was so scrawny all his bones showed under his thin cotton clothing, and he could squeeze his emptiness to the very backbone with his two hands. He was a poet and the revolution was only a dream then; too many women loved him and sapped away his youth, and he could never find enough to eat anywhere, anywhere! Now he is a leader of men, crafty men who whisper in his ear, hungry men who wait for hours outside his office for a word with him, emaciated men with wild faces who waylay him at the street gate with a timid "Comrade, let me tell you . . ." and they blow the foul breath from their empty stomachs in his face.

He is always sympathetic. He gives them handfuls of small coins from his own pocket, he promises them work, there will be demonstrations, they must join the unions and attend the meetings, above all they must be on the watch for spies. They are closer to him than his own brothers, without them he can do nothing—until tomorrow, comrade!

Until tomorrow. "They are stupid, they are lazy, they are treacherous, they would cut my throat for nothing," he says to Laura. He has good food and abundant drink, he hires an automobile and drives in the Paseo on Sunday morning, and enjoys plenty of sleep in a soft bed beside a wife who dares not disturb him; and he sits pampering his bones in easy billows of fat, singing to Laura, who knows and thinks these things about him. When he was fifteen, he tried to drown himself because he loved a girl, his first love, and she laughed at him. "A thousand women have paid for that," and his tight little mouth turns down at the corners. Now he perfumes his hair with Jockey Club, and confides to Laura: "One woman is really as good as another for me, in the dark. I prefer them all."

His wife organizes unions among the girls in the cigarette factories, and walks in picket lines, and even speaks at meetings in the evening. But she cannot be brought to acknowledge the benefits of true liberty. "I tell her I must have my freedom, net. She does not understand my point of view." Laura has heard this many times. Braggioni scratches the guitar and meditates. "She is an instinctively virtuous woman, pure gold, no doubt of that. If she were not, I should lock her up, and she knows it."

His wife, who works so hard for the good of the factory girls, employs part of her leisure lying on the floor weeping because there are so many women in the world, and only one husband for her, and she never knows where nor when to look for him. He told her: "Unless you can learn to cry when I am not here, I must go away for good." That day he went away and took a room at the Hotel Madrid.

It is this month of separation for the sake of higher principles that has been spoiled not only for Mrs. Braggioni, whose sense of reality is beyond criticism, but for Laura, who feels herself bogged in a nightmare. Tonight Laura envies Mrs. Braggioni, who is alone, and free to weep as much as she pleases about a concrete wrong. Laura has just come from a visit to the prison, and she is waiting for tomorrow with a bitter anxiety as if tomorrow may not come, but time may be caught immovably in this hour, with herself transfixed, Braggioni singing on forever, and Eugenio's body not yet discovered by the guard.

Braggioni says: "Are you going to sleep?" Almost before she can shake her head, he begins telling her about the May-day disturbances coming on in Morelia, for the Catholics hold a festival in honor of the Blessed Virgin, and the Socialists celebrate their martyrs on that day. "There will be two independent processions, starting from either end of town, and they will march until they meet, and the rest depends . . ." He asks her to oil and load his pistols. Standing up, he unbuckles his ammunition and spreads it laden across her knees. Laura sits with the shells slipping through the cleaning cloth dipped in oil, and he says again he cannot understand why she works so hard for the revolutionary idea unless she loves some man who is in it. "Are you not in love with someone?" "No," says Laura. "And no one is in love with you?" "No." "Then it is your own fault. No woman need go begging. Why, what is the matter with you? The legless beggar woman in the Alameda has a perfectly faithful lover. Did you know that?"

Laura peers down the pistol barrel and says nothing, but a long, slow faintness rises and subsides in her; Braggioni curves his swollen fingers around the throat of the guitar and softly smothers the music out of it, and when she hears him again he seems to have forgotten her, and is speaking in the hypnotic voice he uses when talking in small rooms to a listening, close-gathered crowd. Some day this world, now seemingly so composed and eternal, to the edges of every sea shall be merely a tangle of gaping trenches, or crashing walls and broken bodies. Everything must be torn from its accustomed place where it has rotted for centuries, hurled skyward and distributed, cast down again clean as rain, without separate identity. Nothing shall survive that the stiffened hands of poverty have created for the rich and no one shall be left alive except the elect spirits destined to procreate a new world cleansed of cruelty and injustice, ruled by benevolent anarchy: "Pistols are good, I love them, cannon are even better, but in the end I pin my faith to good dynamite," he concludes, and strokes the pistol lying in her hands. "Once I dreamed of destroying this city, in case it offered resistance to General Ortiz, but it fell into his hands like an overripe pear."

He is made restless by his own words, rises and stands waiting. Laura holds up the belt to him: "Put that on and go kill somebody in Morelia, and you will be happier," she says softly. The presence of death in the room makes her bold. "Today, I found Eugenio going into a stupor. He refused to allow me to call the prison doctor. He had taken all the tablets I had brought him yesterday. He said he took them because he was bored."

"He is a fool, and his death is his own business," says Braggioni, fastening his belt carefully.

"I told him if he had waited only a little while longer, you would have got him set free," says Laura. "He said he did not want to wait."

"He is a fool and we are well rid of him," says Braggioni, reaching for his hat.

He goes away. Laura knows his mood has changed, she will not see him any more for a while. He will send word when he needs her to go on errands into strange streets, to speak to the strange faces that will appear, like clay masks with the power of human speech, to mutter their thanks to Braggioni for his help. Now she is free, and she thinks, I must run while there is time. But she does not go.

Braggioni enters his own house where for a month his wife has spent many hours every night weeping and tangling her hair upon her pillow. She is weeping now, and she weeps more at the sight of him, the cause of all her sorrows. He looks about the room. Nothing is changed, the smells are good and familiar, he is well acquainted with the woman who comes toward him with no reproach except grief on her face. He says to her tenderly: "You are so good, please don't cry any more, you dear good creature." She says, "Are you tired, my angel? Sit here and I will wash your feet." She brings a bowl of water, and kneeling, unlaces his shoes, and when from her knees she raises her sad eyes under her blackened lids, he is sorry for everything, and bursts into tears. "Ah, yes, I am hungry, I am tired, let us eat something together," he says, between sobs. His wife leans her head on his arm and says, "Forgive me!" and this time he is refreshed by the solemn, endless rain of her tears.

Laura takes off her serge dress and puts on a white linen nightgown and goes to bed. She turns her head a little to one side, and lying still, reminds herself that it is time to sleep. Numbers tick in her brain like little clocks, soundless doors close of themselves around her. If you would sleep, you must not remember anything, the children will say tomorrow, good morning, my teacher, the poor prisoners who come every day bring flowers to their jailor. 1-2-3-4-5—it is monstrous to confuse love with revolution, night with day, life with death—ah, Eugenio!

The tolling of the midnight bell is a signal, but what does it mean? Get up, Laura, and follow me: come out of your sleep, out of your bed, out of this strange house. What are you doing in this house? Without a word, without fear she rose and reached for Eugenio's hand, but he eluded her with a sharp, sly smile and drifted away. This is not all, you shall see—Murderer, he said, follow me, I will show you a new country, but it is far away and we must hurry. No, said Laura, not unless you take my hand, no; and she clung first to the stair rail, and then to the topmost branch of the Judas tree that bent down slowly and set her upon the earth, and then to the rocky ledge of a cliff, and then to the jagged wave of a sea that was not water but a desert of crumbling stone. Where are you taking me, she asked in wonder but without fear. To death, and it is a long way off, and we must hurry, said Eugenio. No, said Laura, not unless you take my hand. Then eat these flowers, poor prisoner, said Eugenio in a voice of pity, take and eat: and from the Judas tree he stripped the warm bleeding flowers, and held them to her lips. She saw that his hand was fleshless, a cluster of small white petrified branches, and his eye sockets were without light, but she ate the flowers greedily for they satisfied both hunger and thirst. Murderer! said Eugenio, and Cannibal! This is my body and my blood. Laura cried No! and at the sound of her own voice, she awoke trembling, and was afraid to sleep again.

Exercises　　*1. This story more than any other so far studied develops largely through the summary method, that is, we are informed directly by statement, as opposed to the dramatic method. What is gained and lost by this approach to story-telling?*

2. Comment on the function in the story of Eugenio and Braggioni's wife.

3. Describe Laura's inner conflict. How does Laura's physical description suggest her inner conflict? Why is Laura incapable of loving anyone or anything?

4. State the theme of the story, and explain how it is revealed.

5. *The story contains several religious parallels and references. Why are they perverted?*

6. *Discuss Laura's dream and the purpose it serves.*

Topics for Writing

1. *Using evidence from the story, compare and contrast the characters of Laura and Braggioni.*

2. *Judas Iscariot, it is said, hanged himself from a judas or redbud tree. Enumerate examples of "flowering" betrayals in the story and justify their appropriateness to the theme.*

3. *Examine Laura as a Judas figure, explaining her betrayal as a denial of herself and Eugenio.*

Selected Bibliography

Katherine Anne Porter

Allen, Charles. "Katherine Anne Porter: Psychology as Art." *Southwest Review*, 41 (1956), 227–229.

Baker, Howard. "The Upward Path: Notes of the Work of Katherine Anne Porter." *Southern Review*, 4 n.s. (1968), 1–19.

Curley, Daniel. "Katherine Anne Porter: The Larger Plan." *Kenyon Review*, 25 (1963), 671–695.

Hartley, Lodwick. "Katherine Anne Porter." *Sewanee Review*, 48 (1940), 206–216.

Hendrick, George. *Katherine Anne Porter.* New York: Twayne Publishers, 1965.

Johnson, James William. "Another Look at Katherine Anne Porter." *Virginia Quarterly Review*, 36 (1960), 598–613.

Marsden, Malcolm M. "Love as Threat in Katherine Anne Porter's Fiction." *Twentieth Century Literature*, 13 (1967), 29–38.

Mooney, Harry John, Jr. *The Fiction and Criticism of Katherine Anne Porter*, rev. ed. Pittsburgh: University of Pittsburgh Press, 1962.

Nance, William L. *Katherine Anne Porter and the Art of Rejection.* Chapel Hill: University of North Carolina Press, 1964.

Porter, Katherine Anne. "Introduction." *In Flowering Judas and Other Stories.* New Work: The Modern Library, 1940, n.p.

Poss, S. H. "Variations on a Theme in Four Stories of Katherine Anne Porter." *Twentieth Century Literature*, 4 (1958), 21–29.

Ryan, Marjorie. "*Dubliners* and the Stories of Katherine Anne Porter." *American Literature*, 31 (1960), 464–473.

Schwartz, Edward. "The Fictions of Memory." *Southwest Review*, 45 (1960), 204–215.

Warren, Robert Penn. "Irony with a Center: Katherine Anne Porter." In *Selected Essays*. New York: Random House, 1958, pp. 136–156.

———. "Uncorrupted Consciousness: The Stories of Katherine Anne Porter." *Yale Review*, 55 (1965), 280–290.

Welty, Eudora. "The Eye of the Story." *Yale Review*, 55 (1965), 265–274.

West, Ray B., Jr. "Katherine Anne Porter: Symbol and Theme in 'Flowering Judas.'" *Accent*, 7 (1947), 182–188.

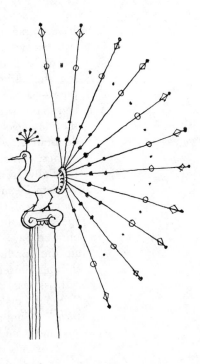

5 Style

Every writer, impelled by experience and imagination, evolves a fictional personality and an individualized way of telling a story. *Style* is the author's own distinct manner of writing; it is the "how" of what the author says and does with the materials. Style differentiates one author from another.

Broadly speaking style comprises a writer's every technique and each application of language. In addition to such aspects of language as diction, syntax, dialogue, imagery, allusion, tone, irony, and symbol (to list a few), style includes all the elements explored in previous chapters, in fact, every *travail*—every bit of business a writer transacts in a story: development of plot, delineation of characters, execution of point of view, and treatment of theme.

A narrower definition of style describes it as all matter dealing with language.

Diction The author's choice of words can ordinarily be classified as either formal or informal. One author's diction may have a grandiloquence all its own: high-born words, an esoteric vocabulary, a rhetoric flavored with foreign words, a speech richly connotative, a language producing the ultimate effects of poetry with all its trappings—simile, metaphor, alliteration, personification, and so on. Another writer's diction may lean heavily on the language of everyday discourse, a rhetoric largely denotative, words more popular than learned, dialects, clichés, and slang expressions.

Fully aware of the illimitable power of words, William Dean Howells, American editor-critic-novelist friend of Mark Twain, explored the remoter regions of speech, indulging in high-flown diction and ornate phraseology. He has one character "striving to propitiate the conductor by a dastardly amiability"; another shifting himself from one foot to another "with saltatory briskness"; and others uttering such expressions as "I would make a *point d'appui*," "I'm a *huite de mon siècle*," "I am not a mere *doppelgänger*," "*sotto voce* to her husband," and "O Parthian Shaft!"

Not only did Howells flavor his diction with foreign words and phrases; he also used certain opaque, abstract, overweighted English words that deny easy reference to human experience. The following stage directions, extracted from one of Howells's plays, provides a representative sampling of his elegant mode of expression.

The closing circle of his arms involves her and clasps her to his heart, from which beneficent shelter she presently exiles herself a pace or two and stands with either hand pressed against his breast while her eyes dwell with rapture on his face.

A more informal, less eloquent, style would perhaps indicate preferences for such words as *learned* or *smart* over the formal *erudite*; for *stout* or *fat* instead of *corpulent* or *obese*; for *drunk*, the slang *smashed* or *plastered* over *inebriated*; for *cop* or *fuzz* instead of *police officer* or *gendarme*.

Note Anderson's simple vocabulary, which is most fitting to the subject matter and to the character of the young boy narrating the events ("I Want to Know Why"):

There isn't anything so lovely and clean and full of spunk and honest and everything as some race horses.

After watching Jerry Tillford kissing the "tall rot-ten-looking woman" in the "bad woman house," the boy narrates: "Then, all of a sudden, I began to hate that man. I wanted to scream and rush in the room and kill him."

Connotation

Another attribute of diction is connotation, which goes beyond dictionary definition and means the implied or suggested other meaning of a word.

For example, *slender* and *emaciated* mean approximately the same, denotatively speaking, but how sharply different are their connotative meanings! *Slender* suggests someone slight of frame in a polite and graceful manner, but *emaciated* implies a wasting away of the body and is not at all attractive.

When, referring to Laura ("Flowering Judas"), the storyteller says, "Nobody touches her," she is not speaking merely in the literal, physical sense. She intimates that Laura is unaffected, truly unmoved by the experiences in her life. The children she teaches daily remain strangers to her; she goes to church but negates a serious commitment to religion; she delivers letters and narcotics to soldiers in prison but disallows a personal involvement in the revolution; and though valued for her feminine charms by the male animal, she cannot give herself to any man.

Syntax

Sentence structure or the arrangement of words in sentences provides another distinctive instrument of a writer's style. Sentences may be long and complex, make use of balance, parallel, and periodic structures. Balance is exemplified by this line:

To err is human, to forgive divine.

Alexander Pope

Parallel structure characterizes this sentence:

The mess boy had started them already, lifting the bottles out of the canvas cooling bags that sweated wet in the wind, that blew through the trees, that shaded the tents.

Ernest Hemingway

Periodic structure (that is, putting the most important words just before the closing period) gives emphasis here:

197   FICTION: STYLE

On the breast of her gown, in red cloth, surrounded with an elaborate embroidery and fantastic flourishes of gold thread, appeared the letter A.

Nathaniel Hawthorne

In other instances, sentences are short and employ the simplest pattern of construction.

Two writers with sharply contrasting styles are Ernest Hemingway and Henry James. Observe the obvious differences in their diction and syntax in the two following sentences:

The car was going a wild forty-five miles an hour across the open and as Macomber watched, the buffalo got bigger and bigger until he could see the gray, hairless, scabby look of one huge bull and how his neck was a part of his shoulders and the shiny black of his horns as he galloped a little behind the others that were strung out in that steady plunging gait; and then, the car swaying as though it had just jumped a road, they drew up close and he could see the plunging hugeness of the bull, and the dust in his sparsely haired hide, the wide boss of horn and his outstretched, wide-nostrilled muzzle, and he was raising his rifle when Wilson shouted, "Not from the car, you fool!" and he had no fear, only hatred of Wilson, while the brakes clamped on and the car skidded, plowing sideways to an almost stop and Wilson was out on one side and he on the other, stumbling as his feet hit the still speeding by of the earth, and then he was shooting at the bull as he moved away, hearing the bullets whunk into him, emptying his rifle at him as he moved steadily away, finally remembering to get his shots forward into the shoulder, and as he fumbled to re-load, he saw the bull was down.

I hadn't then visited his country, nor was I proficient in his tongue; but as he was not so meanly constituted—what Italian is?—as to depend only on that member for expression he conveyed to me, in familiar but graceful mimicry, that he was in search of exactly the employment in which the lady before me was engaged.

Hemingway's sentence is certainly much the longer, but if you examine it, you will find familiar, concrete, monosyllabic words and short, direct, uncomplicated clauses that could have been short, independent sentences but instead are joined by the connective *and*. At the opposite extreme is a style that employs a rather formal vocabulary and a long, complex sentence structure habitually interrupted by modification and qualification. Further reading of Hemingway and James only reinforces the characteristic stylistic differences.

Dialogue   The speech of characters, used profusely by some authors and sparingly by others, serves to advance action, explain motivation, and reveal thoughts and feelings. It is commonly described as natural, lively, stilted, witty, or dull. Unquestionably, speech must be appropriate to the region, profession or trade, character, and state of mind of the speaker.

Anderson ("I Want to Know Why") clearly employs the speech mannerisms of a fifteen-year-old boy in 1919.

Gee! I ached to see that race and those two horses run, ached and dreaded it too.

Malamud ("The Magic Barrel") captures the Yiddish speech patterns.

I have for you a first-class bride.

Yiddishe kinder, what can I say to somebody that he is not interested in high school teachers? So what then you are interested?

Eudora Welty ("A Worn Path") recreates the dialect of an old Mississippi black woman.

"Old woman," she said to herself, "that black dog come up out of the weeds to stall you off, and now there he sitting on his fine tail, smiling at you."

Allusion   Allusions are general or specific hints or references to persons, places, events, or objects that exist outside the time and space framework of a story. Authors use allusions to support their views or heighten the meaning of character and action. Their chief sources are the Bible, mythology, literature, and history.

Joyce ("Counterparts") refers indirectly to the Seven Deadly Sins, as they apply to the characterization of Farrington, to the Irish characters, and to the

199   Fiction: Style

places of his Dublin. McCullers ("A Tree, a Rock, a Cloud") hints at Coleridge's "The Rime of the Ancient Mariner," in which the mariner's message to the wedding guest parallels the transient's message to the boy. Porter ("Flowering Judas") alludes to numerous biblical and religious concepts. Her story contains an abundant religious vocabulary (faith, devotion, heresy) and ample references to passages in the New Testament, though twisted out of their original meaning (Laura's everlasting *No*, the foot-washing, the communion).

Tone Tone identifies or describes an author's attitude toward material and audience. Toward subject matter and reader the writer may feel humorous, nostalgic, affectionate, serious, melancholy, sarcastic, elated, angry, or as many other variations as there are emotions. As the painter conveys tone with shades of color and light, so the writer conveys tone with choice of words and their arrangement in sentences.

Can you easily identify the tone of each of the following three excerpts? What specific words, phrases, and clauses contribute to your discovery?

Mr. Martin could no longer doubt that the finger was on his beloved department. Her pickaxe was on the upswing, poised for the first blow. It had not come yet; he had received no blue memo from the enchanted Mr. Fitweiler bearing nonsensical instructions deriving from the obscene woman. . . . Mr. Martin stood up in his living room, still holding his milk glass. "Gentlemen of the jury," he said to himself, "I demand the death penalty for this horrible person."

James Thurber

The three brothers and the sister sat round the desolate breakfast table, attempting some sort of desultory consultation. The morning's post had given the final tap to the family fortune, and all was over. The dreary dining-room itself, with its heavy mahogany furniture, looked as if it were waiting to be done away with.

D. H. Lawrence

And when once in a time some leisurely passer-by stopped, made merry over the old figure on the board and spoke of swindling, that was in its way the stupidest lie ever invented by indifference and inborn malice, since it was not the hunger artist who was cheating; he was working honestly, but the world was cheating him of his reward.

Franz Kafka

Irony Irony often plays an important role in fiction. It is a simple, economical device by which a writer can suggest tone or meaning without elaborate explanations. It is at once incongruous and involves the opposite of what one expects.

In *verbal irony* a speaker says one thing but means another. When Mr. Fitweiler ("The Catbird Seat") tells Mr. Martin that Mrs. Barrows has "worked hard" and "suffered a severe breakdown," Martin says, "I am very sorry, sir." Ironically, he says the opposite of what he surely feels.

In *dramatic irony* we the reader, as witnesses to an action, know the truth regarding that incident about which the characters involved in the incident remain ignorant. When Laura ("Flowering Judas") denies everyone and everything, she in effect denies herself everything.

In *situation irony* a discrepancy exists between what one expects and what actually happens. When Leo ("The Magic Barrel"), a theological student, sees in Stella, a prostitute, "his own redemption"; when Miss Emily ("A Rose for Emily") sleeps for years with her dead lover in a bridal room that is really a tomb; and when both Mabel and Dr. Ferguson ("The Horse Dealer's Daughter") are given new life after their "baptism" in the cold, dead, rotten, clay-fouled water of the pond—then we have an ironical situation.

Porter's story ("Flowering Judas") is indeed heavy with irony, religious allusions, and symbols, sometimes perverted to achieve the author's special effects. Recall Laura's nightmarish dream: There is the washing of the feet of the "new Christ." This Christ, "fleshless and without light," does not forgive Laura but calls her a "murderer." Not the bread and wine provide for this communion, but the bleeding flowers from the Judas tree, which are made to satisfy both the eating of the body and the drinking of the blood in a cannibalistic ritual. And this communion leads not to life but to death.

Imagery   Very much part of fiction and not the sole property of
poetry, imagery is a word, group of words, or a
sentence that evokes a picture in our minds. Whether
literal or figurative, imagery communicates experience
with increased originality and vividness. In fiction the
most common types of imagery are simile, metaphor,
and personification.

All three types appear at least twice in the following
metaphorical selection ("The Open Boat"). How
many similes and examples of personification can you
discover in Crane's paragraph?

A seat in this boat was not unlike a seat upon a bucking
broncho, and, by the same token, a broncho is not
much smaller. The craft pranced and reared, and
plunged like an animal. As each wave came, and she
rose for it, she seemed like a horse making a fence
outrageously high. The manner of her scramble over
these walls of water is a mystic thing, and, moreover, at
the top of them were ordinarily these problems in white
water, the foam racing down from the summit of each
wave, requiring a new leap, and a leap from the air.
Then, after scornfully bumping a crest, she would
incline, and arrive bobbing and nodding in front of the
next menace.

Especially in "The Open Boat" does Crane use
personification to intensify the effects of his imagery:
"the lighthouse had been growing slowly larger"; later
"The distant lighthouse reared high"; and "Slowly and
beautifully the land loomed out of the sea." He also
gives the wind a voice, he compares Fate to an "old
ninny-woman," and (toward the end of the story) he
describes nature as not "cruel; nor beneficent, nor
treacherous, nor wise" but "indifferent."

Symbolism   Like imagery, symbols work economically to heighten
the meaning of a story by means of suggestion. A
symbol is a word, an object, a place, a person, or an
incident that stands for itself as well as for something
else. A symbol, then, is both itself and something more
significant than itself.

Symbols abound in many of our stories. Some we
may miss; some we may misinterpret; and some the
writer may not have consciously selected. But if sym-

bols are present, if they fit the context of a story, and if they are central to its meaning—they serve.

Frequently names of people and places serve as symbols. Phoenix ("A Worn Path") symbolizes love, endurance, immortality, and even perhaps Christ. Titles also represent larger meanings. "A Worn Path" suggests, at least to an older person, the much traveled road of life and all its trials and tribulations. "A Tree, a Rock, a Cloud" incorporates the transient's message concerning the science of love. How like a blossoming traitor is Laura ("Flowering Judas") when she betrays everyone, including herself! Why should Faulkner ("A Rose for Emily") offer Emily a *rose*, a symbol of love? Does not the pond become a place of baptism in "The Horse Dealer's Daughter," a story described as a symbol of rebirth?

In "The Chrysanthemums" Steinbeck uses an opulence of sexual imagery and color to represent the passionate desires of Elisa: the sharp-pointed stars "driven into the body—hot and sharp and—lovely," the *blood* that comes from broken noses at fights, the scratching her skin *red* after scrubbing herself once the tinker has gone, and the *wine* that will suffice.

And finally the young newspaper boy in "A Tree, a Rock, a Cloud" enters a cafe "friendly and bright" from the outside, where it is raining and dark. Symbolically the boy enters a place where enlightenment is possible, where an important lesson in life can be learned. He comes from the outside world, a place unenlightened, gloomy, and perhaps even sinister. At the beginning of the story the boy "raised the right flap up over his pink little ear" perhaps to hear something significant; at the end of the story, the boy "pulled down the right flap of his helmet," which signals the end of the transient's sermonet.

All of the components of style cohere to form an organic whole; each element has a valence, a capacity to unite, react, and interact with other elements to achieve an author's artistic design and purpose. The title joins the setting, which connects with the protagonist, who merges with the conflict, which links with the climax, which ties in with the resolution, which ultimately communicates experience and meaning with the aid of the shape and texture of words and the structure of sentences. No part is slight. Remove one and you will discover a fault—unity damaged, meaning lost, a character out of character—an experience opposed to an author's artistic intentions and less enriching to the reader.

Ernest Hemingway *(1899–1961)*

Born in Oak Park, Illinois, he was a boxer, a football player, a fisherman, a hunter, an ambulance driver, a reporter, an expatriate with Gertrude Stein, Ezra Pound, Sherwood Anderson, and F. Scott Fitzgerald, a friend of movie and sports celebrities, a drinker, a writer, a winner of the Pulitzer Prize (1953) and the Nobel Prize (1954), and a suicide. His most famous among many short stories is "The Killers" (1927). His most important major works are The Sun Also Rises *(1926),* A Farewell to Arms *(1929),* For Whom the Bell Tolls *(1940), and* The Old Man and the Sea *(1952). No American writer has produced so great an impact on the world of fiction.*

The Short Happy Life of Francis Macomber

It was now lunch time and they were all sitting under the double green fly of the dining tent pretending that nothing had happened.

"Will you have lime juice or lemon squash?" Macomber asked.

"I'll have a gimlet," Robert Wilson told him.

"I'll have a gimlet too. I need something," Macomber's wife said.

"I suppose it's the thing to do," Macomber agreed. "Tell him to make three gimlets."

The mess boy had started them already, lifting the bottles out of the canvas cooling bags that sweated wet in the wind that blew through the trees that shaded the tents.

"What had I ought to give them?" Macomber asked.

"A quid would be plenty," Wilson told him. "You don't want to spoil them."

"Will the headman distribute it?"

"Absolutely."

Francis Macomber had, half an hour before, been carried to his tent from the edge of the camp in triumph on the arms and shoulders of the cook, the personal boys, the skinner and the porters. The gun-bearers had taken no part in the demonstration. When the native boys put him down at the door of his tent, he had shaken all their hands, received their congratulations, and then gone into the tent and sat on the bed until his wife came in. She did not speak to him when she came in and he left the tent at once to wash his face and hands in the portable wash basin outside and go over to the dining tent to sit in a comfortable canvas chair in the breeze and the shade.

"You've got your lion," Robert Wilson said to him, "and a damned fine one too."

Mrs. Macomber looked at Wilson quickly. She was an extremely handsome and well-kept woman of the beauty and social position which had, five years before, commanded five thousand dollars at the price of endorsing, with photographs, a beauty product which she had never used. She had been married to Francis Macomber for eleven years.

"He is a good lion, isn't he?" Macomber said. His wife looked at him now. She looked at both these men as though she had never seen them before.

One, Wilson, the white hunter, she knew she had never truly seen before. He was about middle height with sandy hair, a stubby mustache, a very red face and extremely cold blue eyes with faint white wrinkles at the corners that grooved merrily when he smiled. He smiled at her now and she looked away from his face at the way his shoulders sloped in the loose tunic he wore with the four big cartridges held in loops where the left breast pocket should have been, at his big brown hands, his old slacks, his very dirty boots and back to his red face again. She noticed where the baked red of his face stopped in a white line that marked the circle left by his Stetson hat that hung now from one of the pegs of the tent pole.

"Well, here's to the lion," Robert Wilson said. He smiled at her again and, not smiling, she looked curiously at her husband.

Francis Macomber was very tall, very well built if you did not mind that length of bone, dark, his hair cropped like an oarsman, rather thin-lipped, and was considered handsome. He was dressed in the same sort of safari clothes that Wilson wore except that his were new, he was thirty-five years old, kept himself very fit, was good at court games, had a number of big-game fishing records, and had just shown himself, very publicly, to be a coward.

"Here's to the lion," he said. "I can't ever thank you for what you did."

Margaret, his wife, looked away from him and back to Wilson.

"Let's not talk about the lion," she said.

Wilson looked over at her without smiling and now she smiled at him.

"It's been a very strange day," she said. "Hadn't you ought to put your hat on even under the canvas at noon? You told me that, you know."

"Might put it on," said Wilson.

"You know you have a very red face, Mr. Wilson," she told him and smiled again.

"Drink," said Wilson.

"I don't think so," she said. "Francis drinks a great deal, but his face is never red."

"It's red today," Macomber tried a joke.

"No," said Margaret. "It's mine that's red today. But Mr. Wilson's is always red."

"Must be racial," said Wilson. "I say, you wouldn't like to drop my beauty as a topic, would you?"

"I've just started on it."

"Let's chuck it," said Wilson.

"Conversation is going to be so difficult," Margaret said.

"Don't be silly, Margot," her husband said.

"No difficulty," Wilson said. "Got a damn fine lion."

Margot looked at them both and they both saw that she was going to cry. Wilson had seen it coming for a long time and he dreaded it. Macomber was past dreading it.

"I wish it hadn't happened. Oh, I wish it hadn't happened," she said and started for her tent. She made no noise of crying but they could see that her shoulders were shaking under the rose-colored, sun-proofed shirt she wore.

"Women upset," said Wilson to the tall man. "Amounts to nothing. Strain on the nerves and one thing'n another."

"No," said Macomber. "I suppose that I rate that for the rest of my life now."

"Nonsense. Let's have a spot of the giant killer," said Wilson. "Forget the whole thing. Nothing to it anyway."

"We might try," said Macomber. "I won't forget what you did for me though."

"Nothing," said Wilson. "All nonsense."

So they sat there in the shade where the camp was pitched under some wide-topped acacia trees with a boulder-strewn cliff behind them, and a stretch of grass that ran to the bank of a boulder-filled stream in front with forest beyond it, and drank their just-cool lime drinks and avoided one another's eyes while the boys set the table for lunch. Wilson could tell that the boys all knew about it now and when he saw Macomber's personal boy looking curiously at his master while he was putting dishes on the table he snapped at him in Swahili. The boy turned away with his face blank.

"What were you telling him?" Macomber asked.

"Nothing. Told him to look alive or I'd see he got about fifteen of the best."

"What's that? Lashes?"

"It's quite illegal," Wilson said. "You're supposed to fine them."

"Do you still have them whipped?"

"Oh, yes. They could raise a row if they chose to complain. But they don't. They prefer it to the fines."

"How strange!" said Macomber.

"Not strange, really," Wilson said. "Which would you rather do? Take a good birching or lose your pay?"

Then he felt embarrassed at asking it and before Macomber could answer he went on, "We all take a beating every day, you know, one way or another."

This was no better. "Good God," he thought. "I am a diplomat, aren't I?"

"Yes, we take a beating," said Macomber, still not looking at him. "I'm awfully sorry about that lion business. It doesn't have to go any further, does it? I mean no one will hear about it, will they?"

"You mean will I tell it at the Mathaiga Club?" Wilson looked at him now coldly. He had not expected this. So he's a bloody four-letter man as well as a bloody coward, he thought. I rather liked him too until today. But how is one to know about an American?

"No," said Wilson. "I'm a professional hunter. We never talk about our clients. You can be quite easy on that. It's supposed to be bad form to ask us not to talk though."

He had decided now that to break would be much easier. He would eat, then, by himself and could read a book with his meals. They would eat by themselves. He would see them through the safari on a very formal basis—what was it the French called it? Distinguished consideration—and it would be a damn sight easier than having to go through this emotional trash. He'd insult him and make a good clean break. Then he could read a book with his meals and he'd still be drinking their whisky. That was the phrase for it when a safari went bad. You ran into another white hunter and you asked, "How is everything going?" and he answered, "Oh, I'm still drinking their whisky," and you knew everything had gone to pot.

"I'm sorry," Macomber said and looked at him with his American face that would stay adolescent until it became middle-aged, and Wilson noted his crew-cropped hair, fine eyes only faintly shifty, good nose, thin lips and handsome jaw. "I'm sorry I didn't realize that. There are lots of things I don't know."

So what could he do, Wilson thought. He was all ready
to break it off quickly and neatly and here the beggar was apologizing after
he had just insulted him. He made one more attempt. "Don't worry
about me talking," he said. "I have a living to make. You know in Africa
no woman ever misses her lion and no white man ever bolts."

"I bolted like a rabbit," Macomber said.

Now what in hell were you going to do about a man who
talked like that, Wilson wondered.

Wilson looked at Macomber with his flat, blue,
machine-gunner's eyes and the other smiled back at him. He had a pleasant
smile if you did not notice how his eyes showed when he was hurt.

"Maybe I can fix it up on buffalo," he said. "We're
after them next, aren't we?"

"In the morning if you like," Wilson told him. Per-
haps he had been wrong. This was certainly the way to take it. You most
certainly could not tell a damned thing about an American. He was all for
Macomber again. If you could forget the morning. But, of course, you
couldn't. The morning had been about as bad as they come.

"Here comes the Memsahib," he said. She was walk-
ing over from her tent refreshed and cheerful and quite lovely. She had a
very perfect oval face, so perfect that you expected her to be stupid. But
she wasn't stupid, Wilson thought, no, not stupid.

"How is the beautiful red-faced Mr. Wilson? Are you
feeling better, Francis, my pearl?"

"Oh, much," said Macomber.

"I've dropped the whole thing," she said, sitting down
at the table. "What importance is there to whether Francis is any good at
killing lions? That's not his trade. That's Mr. Wilson's trade. Mr. Wilson
is really very impressive killing anything. You do kill anything, don't
you?"

"Oh, anything," said Wilson. "Simply anything."
They are, he thought, the hardest in the world; the hardest, the cruelest,
the most predatory and the most attractive and their men have softened or
gone to pieces nervously as they have hardened. Or is it that they pick men
they can handle? They can't know that much at the age they marry, he
thought. He was grateful that he had gone through his education on
American women before now because this was a very attractive one.

"We're going after buff in the morning," he told her.

"I'm coming," she said.

"No, you're not."

"Oh, yes, I am. Mayn't I, Francis?"

"Why not stay in camp?"

"Not for anything," she said. "I wouldn't miss something like today for anything."

When she left, Wilson was thinking, when she went off
to cry, she seemed a hell of a fine woman. She seemed to understand, to

realize, to be hurt for him and for herself and to know how things really stood. She is away for twenty minutes and now she is back, simply enamelled in that American female cruelty. They are the damnedest women. Really the damnedest.

"We'll put on another show for you tomorrow," Francis Macomber said.

"You're not coming," Wilson said.

"You're very mistaken," she told him. "And I want *so* to see you perform again. You were lovely this morning. That is if blowing things' heads off is lovely."

"Here's the lunch," said Wilson. "You're very merry, aren't you?"

"Why not? I didn't come out here to be dull."

"Well, it hasn't been dull," Wilson said. He could see the boulders in the river and the high bank beyond with the trees and he remembered the morning.

"Oh, no," she said. "It's been charming. And tomorrow. You don't know how I look forward to tomorrow."

"That's eland he's offering you," Wilson said.

"They're the big cowy things that jump like hares, aren't they?"

"I suppose that describes them," Wilson said.

"It's very good meat," Macomber said.

"Did you shoot it, Francis?" she asked.

"Yes."

"They're not dangerous, are they?"

"Only if they fall on you," Wilson told her.

"I'm so glad."

"Why not let up on the bitchery just a little, Margot," Macomber said, cutting the eland steak and putting some mashed potato, gravy and carrot on the down-turned fork that tined through the piece of meat.

"I suppose I could," she said, "since you put it so prettily."

"Tonight we'll have champagne for the lion," Wilson said. "It's a bit too hot at noon."

"Oh, the lion," Margot said. "I'd forgotten the lion!"

So, Robert Wilson thought to himself, she *is* giving him a ride, isn't she? Or do you suppose that's her idea of putting up a good show? How should a woman act when she discovers her husband is a bloody coward? She's damn cruel but they're all cruel. They govern, of course, and to govern one has to be cruel sometimes. Still, I've seen enough of their damn terrorism.

"Have some more eland," he said to her politely.

That afternoon, late, Wilson and Macomber went out in the motor car with the native driver and the two gun-bearers. Mrs.

Macomber stayed in the camp. It was too hot to go out, she said, and she was going with them in the early morning. As they drove off Wilson saw her standing under the big tree, looking pretty rather than beautiful in her faintly rosy khaki, her dark hair drawn back off her forehead and gathered in a knot low on her neck, her face as fresh, he thought, as though she were in England. She waved to them as the car went off through the swale of high grass and curved around through the trees into the small hills of orchard bush.

In the orchard bush they found a herd of impala, and leaving the car they stalked one old ram with long, wide-spread horns and Macomber killed it with a very creditable shot that knocked the buck down at a good two hundred yards and sent the herd off bounding wildly and leaping over one another's backs in long, leg-drawn-up leaps as unbelievable and as floating as those one makes sometimes in dreams.

"That was a good shot," Wilson said. "They're a small target."

"Is it a worth-while head?" Macomber asked.

"It's excellent," Wilson told him. "You shoot like that and you'll have no trouble."

"Do you think we'll find buffalo tomorrow?"

"There's a good chance of it. They feed out early in the morning and with luck we may catch them in the open."

"I'd like to clear away the lion business," Macomber said. "It's not very pleasant to have your wife see you do something like that."

I should think it would be even more unpleasant to do it, Wilson thought, wife or no wife, or to talk about having done it. But he said, "I wouldn't think about that any more. Any one could be upset by his first lion. That's all over."

But that night after dinner and a whisky and soda by the fire before going to bed, as Francis Macomber lay on his cot with the mosquito bar over him and listened to the night noises it was not all over. It was neither all over nor was it beginning. It was there exactly as it happened with some parts of it indelibly emphasized and he was miserably ashamed at it. But more than shame he felt cold, hollow fear in him. The fear was still there like a cold slimy hollow in all the emptiness where once his confidence had been and it made him feel sick. It was still there with him now.

It had started the night before when he had wakened and heard the lion roaring somewhere up along the river. It was a deep sound and at the end there were sort of coughing grunts that made him seem just outside the tent, and when Francis Macomber woke in the night to hear it he was afraid. He could hear his wife breathing quietly, asleep. There was no one to tell he was afraid, nor to be afraid with him, and, lying alone, he did not know the Somali proverb that says a brave man is always frightened three times by a lion; when he first sees his track, when he first hears him roar and when he first confronts him. Then while they were eating breakfast by lantern light out in the dining tent, before the sun was up, the lion roared again and Francis thought he was just at the edge of camp.

"Sounds like an old-timer," Robert Wilson said, looking up from his kippers and coffee. "Listen to him cough."

"Is he very close?"

"A mile or so up the stream."

"Will we see him?"

"We'll have a look."

"Does his roaring carry that far? It sounds as though he were right in camp."

"Carries a hell of a long way," said Robert Wilson. "It's strange the way it carries. Hope he's a shootable cat. The boys said there was a very big one about here."

"If I get a shot, where should I hit him," Macomber asked, "to stop him?"

"In the shoulders," Wilson said. "In the neck if you can make it. Shoot for bone. Break him down."

"I hope I can place it properly," Macomber said.

"You shoot very well," Wilson told him. "Take your time. Make sure of him. The first one in is the one that counts."

"What range will it be?"

"Can't tell. Lion has something to say about that. Won't shoot unless it's close enough so you can make sure."

"At under a hundred yards?" Macomber asked.

Wilson looked at him quickly.

"Hundred's about right. Might have to take him a bit under. Shouldn't chance a shot at much over that. A hundred's a decent range. You can hit him wherever you want at that. Here comes the Memsahib."

"Good morning," she said. "Are we going after that lion?"

"As soon as you deal with your breakfast," Wilson said. "How are you feeling?"

"Marvellous," she said. "I'm very excited."

"I'll just go and see that everything is ready," Wilson went off. As he left the lion roared again.

"Noisy beggar," Wilson said. "We'll put a stop to that."

"What's the matter, Francis?" his wife asked him.

"Nothing," Macomber said.

"Yes, there is," she said. "What are you upset about?"

"Nothing," he said.

"Tell me," she looked at him. "Don't you feel well?"

"It's that damned roaring," he said. "It's been going on all night, you know."

"Why didn't you wake me," she said. "I'd love to have heard it."

"I've got to kill the damned thing," Macomber said, miserably.

"Well, that's what you're out here for, isn't it?"

"Yes. But I'm nervous. Hearing the thing roar gets on my nerves."

"Well then, as Wilson said, kill him and stop his roaring."

"Yes, darling," said Francis Macomber. "It sounds easy, doesn't it?"

"You're not afraid, are you?"

"Of course not. But I'm nervous from hearing him roar all night."

"You'll kill him marvellously," she said. "I know you will. I'm awfully anxious to see it."

"Finish your breakfast and we'll be starting."

"It's not light yet," she said. "This is a ridiculous hour."

Just then the lion roared in a deep-chested moaning, suddenly guttural, ascending vibration that seemed to shake the air and ended in a sigh and a heavy, deep-chested grunt.

"He sounds almost here," Macomber's wife said.

"My God," said Macomber. "I hate that damned noise."

"It's very impressive."

"Impressive. It's frightful."

Robert Wilson came up then carrying his short, ugly, shockingly big-bored .505 Gibbs and grinning.

"Come on," he said. "Your gun-bearer has your Springfield and the big gun. Everything's in the car. Have you solids?"

"Yes."

"I'm ready," Mrs. Macomber said.

"Must make him stop that racket," Wilson said. "You get in front. The Memsahib can sit back here with me."

They climbed into the motor car and, in the gray first daylight, moved off up the river through the trees. Macomber opened the breech of his rifle and saw he had metal-cased bullets, shut the bolt and put the rifle on safety. He saw his hand was trembling. He felt in his pocket for more cartridges and moved his fingers over the cartridges in the loops of his tunic front. He turned back to where Wilson sat in the rear seat of the doorless, box-bodied motor car beside his wife, them both grinning with excitement, and Wilson leaned forward and whispered,

"See the birds dropping. Means the old boy has left his kill."

On the far bank of the stream Macomber could see, above the trees, vultures circling and plummeting down.

"Chances are he'll come to drink along here," Wilson whispered. "Before he goes to lay up. Keep an eye out."

They were driving slowly along the high bank of the stream which here cut deeply to its boulder-filled bed, and they wound in and out through big trees as they drove. Macomber was watching the opposite bank when he felt Wilson take hold of his arm. The car stopped.

"There he is," he heard the whisper. "Ahead and to the right. Get out and take him. He's a marvellous lion."

Macomber saw the lion now. He was standing almost broadside, his great head up and turned toward them. The early morning breeze that blew toward them was just stirring his dark mane, and the lion looked huge, silhouetted on the rise of bank in the gray morning light, his shoulders heavy, his barrel of a body bulking smoothly.

"How far is he?" asked Macomber, raising his rifle.

"About seventy-five. Get out and take him."

"Why not shoot from where I am?"

"You don't shoot them from cars," he heard Wilson saying in his ear. "Get out. He's not going to stay there all day."

Macomber stepped out of the curved opening at the side of the front seat, onto the step and down onto the ground. The lion still stood looking majestically and coolly toward this object that his eyes only showed in silhouette, bulking like some super-rhino. There was no man smell carried toward him and he watched the object, moving his great head a little from side to side. Then watching the object, not afraid, but hesitating before going down the bank to drink with such a thing opposite him, he saw a man figure detach itself from it and he turned his heavy head and swung away toward the cover of the trees as he heard a cracking crash and felt the slam of a .30–06 220-grain solid bullet that bit his flank and ripped in sudden hot scalding nausea through his stomach. He trotted, heavy, big-footed, swinging wounded full-bellied, through the trees toward the tall grass and cover, and the crash came again to go past him ripping the air apart. Then it crashed again and he felt the blow as it hit his lower ribs and ripped on through, blood sudden hot and frothy in his mouth, and he galloped toward the high grass where he could crouch and not be seen and make them bring the crashing thing close enough so he could make a rush and get the man that held it.

Macomber had not thought how the lion felt as he got out of the car. He only knew his hands were shaking and as he walked away from the car it was almost impossible for him to make his legs move. They were stiff in the thighs, but he could feel the muscles fluttering. He raised the rifle, sighted on the junction of the lion's head and shoulders and pulled the trigger. Nothing happened though he pulled until he thought his finger would break. Then he knew he had the safety on and as he lowered the rifle to move the safety over he moved another frozen pace forward, and the lion seeing his silhouette now clear of the silhouette of the car, turned and started off at a trot, and, as Macomber fired, he heard a whunk that meant that the bullet was home; but the lion kept on going. Macomber shot again and every one saw the bullet throw a spout of dirt beyond the trotting lion. He shot again, remembering to lower his aim, and they all heard the bullet hit, and the lion went into a gallop and was in the tall grass before he had the bolt pushed forward.

Macomber stood there feeling sick at his stomach, his hands that held the Springfield still cocked, shaking, and his wife and Robert Wilson were standing by him. Beside him too were the two gun-bearers chattering in Wakamba.

"I hit him," Macomber said. "I hit him twice."

"You gut-shot him and you hit him somewhere forward," Wilson said without enthusiasm. The gun-bearers looked very grave. They were silent now.

"You may have killed him," Wilson went on. "We'll have to wait a while before we go in to find out."

"What do you mean?"

"Let him get sick before we follow him up."

"Oh," said Macomber.

"He's a hell of a fine lion," Wilson said cheerfully. "He's gotten into a bad place though."

"Why is it bad?"

"Can't see him until you're on him."

"Oh," said Macomber.

"Come on," said Wilson. "The Memsahib can stay here in the car. We'll go to have a look at the blood spoor."

"Stay here, Margot," Macomber said to his wife. His mouth was very dry and it was hard for him to talk.

"Why?" she asked.

"Wilson says to."

"We're going to have a look," Wilson said. "You stay here. You can see even better from here."

"All right."

Wilson spoke in Swahili to the driver. He nodded and said, "Yes, Bwana."

Then they went down the steep bank and across the stream, climbing over and around the boulders and up the other bank, pulling up by some projecting roots, and along it until they found where the lion had been trotting when Macomber first shot. There was dark blood on the short grass that the gun-bearers pointed out with grass stems, and that ran away behind the river bank trees.

"What do we do?" asked Macomber.

"Not much choice," said Wilson. "We can't bring the car over. Bank's too steep. We'll let him stiffen up a bit and then you and I'll go in and have a look for him."

"Can't we set the grass on fire?" Macomber asked.

"Too green."

"Can't we send beaters?"

Wilson looked at him appraisingly. "Of course we can," he said. "But it's just a touch murderous. You see we know the lion's wounded. You can drive an unwounded lion—he'll move on ahead of a noise—but a wounded lion's going to charge. You can't see him until you're right on him. He'll make himself perfectly flat in cover you wouldn't think would hide a hare. You can't very well send boys in there to that sort of a show. Somebody bound to get mauled."

"What about the gun-bearers?"

"Oh, they'll go with us. It's their *shauri*. You see, they signed on for it. They don't look too happy though, do they?"

"I don't want to go in there," said Macomber. It was out before he knew he'd said it.

"Neither do I," said Wilson very cheerily. "Really no choice though." Then, as an afterthought, he glanced at Macomber and saw suddenly how he was trembling and the pitiful look on his face.

"You don't have to go in, of course," he said. "That's what I'm hired for, you know. That's why I'm so expensive."

"You mean you'd go in by yourself? Why not leave him there?"

Robert Wilson, whose entire occupation had been with the lion and the problem he presented, and who had not been thinking about Macomber except to note that he was rather windy, suddenly felt as though he had opened the wrong door in a hotel and seen something shameful.

"What do you mean?"

"Why not just leave him?"

"You mean pretend to ourselves he hasn't been hit?"

"No. Just drop it."

"It isn't done."

"Why not?"

"For one thing, he's certain to be suffering. For another, some one else might run onto him."

"I see."

"But you don't have to have anything to do with it."

"I'd like to," Macomber said. "I'm just scared, you know."

"I'll go ahead when we go in," Wilson said, "with Kongoni tracking. You keep behind me and a little to one side. Chances are we'll hear him growl. If we see him we'll both shoot. Don't worry about anything. I'll keep you backed up. As a matter of fact, you know, perhaps you'd better not go. It might be much better. Why don't you go over and join the Memsahib while I just get it over with?''

"No, I want to go."

"All right," said Wilson. "But don't go in if you don't want to. This is my *shauri* now, you know."

"I want to go," said Macomber.

They sat under a tree and smoked.

"Want to go back and speak to the Memsahib while we're waiting?" Wilson asked.

"No."

"I'll just step back and tell her to be patient."

"Good," said Macomber. He sat there, sweating under his arms, his mouth dry, his stomach hollow feeling, wanting to find courage to tell Wilson to go on and finish off the lion without him. He could not know that Wilson was furious because he had not noticed the state he was in earlier and sent him back to his wife. While he sat there Wilson came up. "I have your big gun," he said. "Take it. We've given him time, I think. Come on."

Macomber took the big gun and Wilson said:

"Keep behind me and about five yards to the right and do exactly as I tell you." Then he spoke in Swahili to the two gun-bearers who looked the picture of gloom.

"Let's go," he said.

"Could I have a drink of water?" Macomber asked. Wilson spoke to the older gun-bearer, who wore a canteen on his belt, and the man unbuckled it, unscrewed the top and handed it to Macomber, who took it noticing how heavy it seemed and how hairy and shoddy the felt covering was in his hand. He raised it to drink and looked ahead at the high grass with the flat-topped trees behind it. A breeze was blowing toward them and the grass rippled gently in the wind. He looked at the gun-bearer and he could see the gun-bearer was suffering too with fear.

Thirty-five yards into the grass the big lion lay flattened out along the ground. His ears were back and his only movement was a slight twitching up and down of his long, black-tufted tail. He had turned at bay as soon as he had reached this cover and he was sick with the wound through his full belly, and weakening with the wound through his lungs that brought a thin foamy red to his mouth each time he breathed. His flanks were wet and hot and flies were on the little openings the solid bullets had made in his tawny hide, and his big yellow eyes, narrowed with hate, looked straight ahead, only blinking when the pain came as he breathed, and his claws dug in the soft baked earth. All of him, pain, sickness, hatred and all of his remaining strength, was tightening into an absolute concentration for a rush. He could hear the men talking and he waited, gathering all of himself into this preparation for a charge as soon as the men would come into the grass. As he heard their voices his tail stiffened to twitch up and down, and, as they came into the edge of the grass, he made a coughing grunt and charged.

Kongoni, the old gun-bearer, in the lead watching the blood spoor, Wilson watching the grass for any movement, his big gun ready, the second gun-bearer looking ahead and listening, Macomber close to Wilson, his rifle cocked, they had just moved into the grass when Macomber heard the blood-choked coughing grunt, and saw the swishing rush in the grass. The next thing he knew he was running; running wildly, in panic in the open, running toward the stream.

He heard the *ca-ra-wong!* of Wilson's big rifle, and again in a second crashing *carawong!* and turning saw the lion, horrible-looking now, with half his head seeming to be gone, crawling toward Wilson in the edge of the tall grass while the red-faced man worked the bolt on the short ugly rifle and aimed carefully as another blasting *carawong!* came from the muzzle, and the crawling, heavy, yellow bulk of the lion stiffened and the huge, mutilated head slid forward and Macomber, standing by himself in the clearing where he had run, holding a loaded rifle, while two black men and a white man looked back at him in contempt, knew the lion was dead. He came toward Wilson, his tallness all seeming a naked reproach, and Wilson looked at him and said:

"Want to take pictures?"

"No," he said.

That was all any one had said until they reached the motor car. Then Wilson had said:

"Hell of a fine lion. Boys will skin him out. We might as well stay here in the shade."

Macomber's wife had not looked at him nor he at her and he had sat by her in the back seat with Wilson sitting in the front seat. Once he had reached over and taken his wife's hand without looking at her and she had removed her hand from his. Looking across the stream to where the gun-bearers were skinning out the lion he could see that she had been able to see the whole thing. While they sat there his wife had reached forward and put her hand on Wilson's shoulder. He turned and she had leaned forward over the low seat and kissed him on the mouth.

"Oh, I say," said Wilson, going redder than his natural baked color.

"Mr. Robert Wilson," she said. "The beautiful red-faced Mr. Robert Wilson."

Then she sat down beside Macomber again and looked away across the stream to where the lion lay, with uplifted, white-muscled, tendon-marked naked forearms, and white bloating belly, as the black men fleshed away the skin. Finally the gun-bearers brought the skin over, wet and heavy, and climbed in behind with it, rolling it up before they got in, and the motor car started. No one had said anything more until they were back in camp.

That was the story of the lion. Macomber did not know how the lion had felt before he started his rush, nor during it when the unbelievable smash of the .505 with a muzzle velocity of two tons had hit him in the mouth, nor what kept him coming after that, when the second ripping crash had smashed his hind quarters and he had come crawling on toward the crashing, blasting thing that had destroyed him. Wilson knew something about it and only expressed it by saying, "Damned fine lion," but Macomber did not know how Wilson felt about things either. He did not know how his wife felt except that she was through with him.

His wife had been through with him before but it never lasted. He was very wealthy, and would be much wealthier, and he knew she would not leave him ever now. That was one of the few things that he really knew. He knew about that, about motor cycles—that was earliest—about motor cars, about duck-shooting, about fishing, trout, salmon and big-sea, about sex in books, many books, too many books, about all court games, about dogs, not much about horses, about hanging on to his money, about most of the other things his world dealt in, and about his wife not leaving him. His wife had been a great beauty and she was still a great beauty in Africa, but she was not a great enough beauty any more at home to be able to leave him and better herself and she knew it and he knew it. She had missed the chance to leave him and he knew it. If he had been better with women she would probably have started to worry about him getting another new, beautiful wife; but she knew too much about him to worry about him either. Also, he had always had a great tolerance which seemed the nicest thing about him if it were not the most sinister.

All in all they were known as a comparatively happily married couple, one of those whose disruption is often rumored but never occurs, and as the society columnist put it, they were adding more than a spice of *adventure* to their much envied and ever-enduring *Romance* by a *Safari* in what was known as *Darkest Africa* until the Martin Johnsons lighted it on so many silver screens where they were pursuing *Old Simba* the lion, the buffalo, *Tembo* the elephant and as well collecting specimens for the Museum of Natural History. This same columnist had reported them *on the verge* at least three times in the past and they had been. But they always made it up. They had a sound basis of union. Margot was too beautiful for Macomber to divorce her and Macomber had too much money for Margot ever to leave him.

It was now about three o'clock in the morning and Francis Macomber, who had been asleep a little while after he had stopped thinking about the lion, wakened and then slept again, woke suddenly, frightened in a dream of the bloody-headed lion standing over him, and listening while his heart pounded, he realized that his wife was not in the other cot in the tent. He lay awake with that knowledge for two hours.

At the end of that time his wife came into the tent, lifted her mosquito bar and crawled cozily into bed.

"Where have you been?" Macomber asked in the darkness.

"Hello," she said. "Are you awake?"

"Where have you been?"

"I just went out to get a breath of air."

"You did, like hell."

"What do you want me to say, darling?"

"Where have you been?"

"Out to get a breath of air."

"That's a new name for it. You *are* a bitch."

"Well, you're a coward."

"All right," he said. "What of it?"

"Nothing as far as I'm concerned. But please let's not talk, darling, because I'm very sleepy."

"You think that I'll take anything."

"I know you will, sweet."

"Well, I won't."

"Please, darling, let's not talk. I'm so very sleepy."

"There wasn't going to be any of that. You promised there wouldn't be."

"Well, there is now," she said sweetly.

"You said if we made this trip that there would be none of that. You promised."

"Yes, darling. That's the way I meant it to be. But the trip was spoiled yesterday. We don't have to talk about it, do we?"

"You don't wait long when you have an advantage, do you?"

"Please let's not talk. I'm so sleepy, darling."

"I'm going to talk."

"Don't mind me then, because I'm going to sleep." And she did.

At breakfast they were all three at the table before daylight and Francis Macomber found that, of all the many men that he had hated, he hated Robert Wilson the most.

"Sleep well?" Wilson asked in his throaty voice, filling a pipe.

"Did you?"

"Topping," the white hunter told him.

You bastard, thought Macomber, you insolent bastard.

So she woke him when she came in, Wilson thought, looking at them both with his flat, cold eyes. Well, why doesn't he keep his wife where she belongs? What does he think I am, a bloody plaster saint? Let him keep her where she belongs. It's his own fault.

"Do you think we'll find buffalo?" Margot asked, pushing away a dish of apricots.

"Chance of it," Wilson said and smiled at her. "Why don't you stay in camp?"

"Not for anything," she told him.

"Why not order her to stay in camp?" Wilson said to Macomber.

"You order her," said Macomber coldly.

"Let's not have any ordering, nor," turning to Macomber, "any silliness, Francis," Margot said quite pleasantly.

"Are you ready to start?" Macomber asked.

"Any time," Wilson told him. "Do you want the Memsahib to go?"

"Does it make any difference whether I do or not?"

The hell with it, thought Robert Wilson. The utter complete hell with it. So this is what it's going to be like. Well, this is what it's going to be like, then.

"Makes no difference," he said.

"You're sure you wouldn't like to stay in camp with her yourself and let me go out and hunt the buffalo?" Macomber asked.

"Can't do that," said Wilson. "Wouldn't talk rot if I were you."

"I'm not talking rot. I'm disgusted."

"Bad word, disgusted."

"Francis, will you please try to speak sensibly!" his wife said.

"I speak too damned sensibly," Macomber said. "Did you ever eat such filthy food?"

"Something wrong with the food?" asked Wilson quietly.

"No more than with everything else."

"I'd pull yourself together, laddybuck," Wilson said very quietly. "There's a boy waits at table that understands a little English."

"The hell with him."

Wilson stood up and puffing on his pipe strolled away, speaking a few words in Swahili to one of the gun-bearers who was standing waiting for him. Macomber and his wife sat on at the table. He was staring at his coffee cup.

"If you make a scene I'll leave you, darling," Margot said quietly.

"No, you won't."

"You can try it and see."

"You won't leave me."

"No," she said. "I won't leave you and you'll behave yourself."

"Behave myself? That's a way to talk. Behave myself."

"Yes. Behave yourself."

"Why don't *you* try behaving?"

"I've tried it so long. So very long."

"I hate that red-faced swine," Macomber said. "I loathe the sight of him."

"He's really *very* nice."

"Oh, *shut up*," Macomber almost shouted. Just then the car came up and stopped in front of the dining tent and the driver and the two gun-bearers got out. Wilson walked over and looked at the husband and wife sitting there at the table.

"Going shooting?" he asked.

"Yes," said Macomber, standing up. "Yes."

"Better bring a woolly. It will be cool in the car," Wilson said.

"I'll get my leather jacket," Margot said.

"The boy has it," Wilson told her. He climbed into the front with the driver and Francis Macomber and his wife sat, not speaking, in the back seat.

Hope the silly beggar doesn't take a notion to blow the back of my head off, Wilson thought to himself. Women *are* a nuisance on safari.

The car was grinding down to cross the river at a pebbly ford in the gray daylight and then climbed, angling up the steep bank, where Wilson had ordered a way shovelled out the day before so they could reach the parklike wooded rolling country on the far side.

It was a good morning, Wilson thought. There was a heavy dew and as the wheels went through the grass and low bushes he could smell the odor of the crushed fronds. It was an odor like verbena and he liked this early morning smell of the dew, the crushed bracken and the look of the tree trunks showing black through the early morning mist, as the car made its way through the untracked, parklike country. He had put the two in the back seat out of his mind now and was thinking about buffalo. The buffalo that he was after stayed in the daytime in a thick swamp where it was impossible to get a shot, but in the night they fed out into an open stretch of country and if he could come between them and their swamp with the car, Macomber would have a good chance at them in the open. He did not want to hunt buff with Macomber in thick cover. He did not want to hunt buff or anything else with Macomber at all, but he was a professional hunter and he had hunted with some rare ones in his time. If they got buff today there would only be rhino to come and the poor man would have gone through his dangerous game and things might pick up. He'd have nothing more to do with the woman and Macomber would get over that too. He must have gone through plenty of that before by the look of things. Poor beggar. He must have a way of getting over it. Well, it was the poor sod's own bloody fault.

He, Robert Wilson, carried a double size cot on safari

to accommodate any windfalls he might receive. He had hunted for a certain clientele, the international, fast, sporting set, where the women did not feel they were getting their money's worth unless they had shared that cot with the white hunter. He despised them when he was away from them although he liked some of them well enough at the time, but he made his living by them; and their standards were his standards as long as they were hiring him.

They were his standards in all except the shooting. He had his own standards about the killing and they could live up to them or get some one else to hunt them. He knew, too, that they all respected him for this. This Macomber was an odd one though. Damned if he wasn't. Now the wife. Well, the wife. Yes, the wife. Hm, the wife. Well he'd dropped all that. He looked around at them. Macomber sat grim and furious. Margot smiled at him. She looked younger today, more innocent and fresher and not so professionally beautiful. What's in her heart God knows, Wilson thought. She hadn't talked much last night. At that it was a pleasure to see her.

The motor car climbed up a slight rise and went on through the trees and then out into a grassy prairie-like opening and kept in the shelter of the trees along the edge, the driver going slowly and Wilson looking carefully out across the prairie and all along its far side. He stopped the car and studied the opening with his field glasses. Then he motioned to the driver to go on and the car moved slowly along, the driver avoiding wart-hog holes and driving around the mud castles ants had built. Then, looking across the opening, Wilson suddenly turned and said,

"By God, there they are!"

And looking where he pointed, while the car jumped forward and Wilson spoke in rapid Swahili to the driver, Macomber saw three huge, black animals looking almost cylindrical in their long heaviness, like big black tank cars, moving at a gallop across the far edge of the open prairie. They moved at a stiff-necked, stiff bodied gallop and he could see the upswept wide black horns on their heads as they galloped heads out; the heads not moving.

"They're three old bulls," Wilson said. "We'll cut them off before they get to the swamp."

The car was going a wild forty-five miles an hour across the open and as Macomber watched, the buffalo got bigger and bigger until he could see the gray, hairless, scabby look of one huge bull and how his neck was a part of his shoulders and the shiny black of his horns as he galloped a little behind the others that were strung out in that steady plunging gait; and then, the car swaying as though it had just jumped a road, they drew up close and he could see the plunging hugeness of the bull, and the dust in his sparsely haired hide, the wide boss of horn and his outstretched, wide-nostrilled muzzle, and he was raising his rifle when Wilson shouted, "Not from the car, you fool!" and he had no fear, only hatred of Wilson, while the brakes clamped on and the car skidded, plowing sideways to an almost stop and Wilson was out on one side and he on the other, stumbling as his feet hit the still speeding-by of the earth, and then he was shooting at the bull as he moved away, hearing the bullets whunk into him, emptying his rifle at him as he moved steadily away, finally remembering to get his shots forward into the shoulder, and as he fumbled to re-load, he saw the bull was down. Down on his knees, his big head tossing, and seeing the other two still galloping he shot at the leader and hit him. He shot again and missed and he heard the *carawonging* roar as Wilson shot and saw the leading bull slide forward onto his nose.

"Get that other," Wilson said. "Now you're shoot-ing!"

But the other bull was moving steadily at the same gallop and he missed, throwing a spout of dirt, and Wilson missed and the dust rose in a cloud and Wilson shouted, "Come on. He's too far!" and grabbed his arm and they were in the car again, Macomber and Wilson hanging on the sides and rocketing swayingly over the uneven ground, drawing up on the steady, plunging, heavy-necked, straight-moving gallop of the bull.

They were behind him and Macomber was filling his rifle, dropping shells onto the ground, jamming it, clearing the jam, then they were almost up with the bull when Wilson yelled "Stop," and the car skidded so that it almost swung over and Macomber fell forward onto his feet, slammed his bolt forward and fired as far forward as he could aim into the galloping, rounded black back, aimed and shot again, then again, and the bullets, all of them hitting, had no effect on the buffalo that he could see. Then Wilson shot, the roar deafening him, and he could see the bull stagger. Macomber shot again, aiming carefully, and down he came, onto his knees.

"All right," Wilson said. "Nice work. That's the three."

Macomber felt a drunken elation.

"How many times did you shoot?" he asked.

"Just three," Wilson said. "You killed the first bull. The biggest one. I helped you finish the other two. Afraid they might have got into cover. You had them killed. I was just mopping up a little. You shot damn well."

"Let's go to the car," said Macomber. "I want a drink."

"Got to finish off that buff first," Wilson told him. The buffalo was on his knees and he jerked his head furiously and bellowed in pig-eyed, roaring rage as they came toward him.

"Watch he doesn't get up," Wilson said. Then, "Get a little broadside and take him in the neck just behind the ear."

Macomber aimed carefully at the center of the huge,

jerking, rage-driven neck and shot. At the shot the head dropped forward.

"That does it," said Wilson. "Got the spine. They're a hell of a looking thing, aren't they?"

"Let's get the drink," said Macomber. In his life he had never felt so good.

In the car Macomber's wife sat very white faced. "You were marvellous, darling," she said to Macomber. "What a ride."

"Was it rough?" Wilson asked.

"It was frightful. I've never been more frightened in my life."

"Let's all have a drink," Macomber said.

"By all means," said Wilson. "Give it to the Memsahib." She drank the neat whisky from the flask and shuddered a little when she swallowed. She handed the flask to Macomber who handed it to Wilson.

"It was frightfully exciting," she said. "It's given me a dreadful headache. I didn't know you were allowed to shoot them from cars though."

"No one shot from cars," said Wilson coldly.

"I mean chase them from cars."

"Wouldn't ordinarily," Wilson said. "Seemed sporting enough to me though while we were doing it. Taking more chance driving that way across the plain full of holes and one thing and another than hunting on foot. Buffalo could have charged us each time we shot if he liked. Gave him every chance. Wouldn't mention it to any one though. It's illegal if that's what you mean."

"It seemed very unfair to me," Margot said, "chasing those big helpless things in a motor car."

"Did it?" said Wilson.

"What would happen if they heard about it in Nairobi?"

"I'd lose my licence for one thing. Other unpleasantness," Wilson said, taking a drink from the flask. "I'd be out of business."

"Really?"

"Yes, really."

"Well," said Macomber, and he smiled for the first time all day. "Now she has something on you."

"You have such a pretty way of putting things, Francis," Margot Macomber said. Wilson looked at them both. If a four-letter man marries a five-letter woman, he was thinking, what number of letters would their children be? What he said was, "We lost a gun-bearer. Did you notice it?"

"My God, no," Macomber said.

"Here he comes," Wilson said. "He's all right. He must have fallen off when we left the first bull."

Approaching them was the middle-aged gun-bearer, limping along in his knitted cap, khaki tunic, shorts and rubber sandals, gloomy-faced and disgusted looking. As he came up he called out to Wilson in Swahili and they all saw the change in the white hunter's face.

"What does he say?" asked Margot.

"He says the first bull got up and went into the bush," Wilson said with no expression in his voice.

"Oh," said Macomber blankly.

"Then it's going to be just like the lion," said Margot, full of anticipation.

"It's not going to be a damned bit like the lion," Wilson told her. "Did you want another drink, Macomber?"

"Thanks, yes," Macomber said. He expected the feeling he had had about the lion to come back but it did not. For the first time in his life he really felt wholly without fear. Instead of fear he had a feeling of definite elation.

"We'll go and have a look at the second bull," Wilson said. "I'll tell the driver to put the car in the shade."

"What are you going to do?" asked Margaret Macomber.

"Take a look at the buff," Wilson said.

"I'll come."

"Come along."

The three of them walked over to where the second buffalo bulked blackly in the open, head forward on the grass, the massive horns swung wide.

"He's a very good head," Wilson said. "That's close to a fifty-inch spread."

Macomber was looking at him with delight.

"He's hateful looking," said Margot. "Can't we go into the shade?"

"Of course," Wilson said. "Look," he said to Macomber, and pointed. "See that patch of bush?"

"Yes."

"That's where the first bull went in. The gun-bearer said when he fell off the bull was down. He was watching us helling along and the other two buff galloping. When he looked up there was the bull up and looking at him. Gun-bearer ran like hell and the bull went off slowly into that bush."

"Can we go in after him now?" asked Macomber eagerly.

Wilson looked at him appraisingly. Damned if this isn't a strange one, he thought. Yesterday he's scared sick and today he's a ruddy fire eater.

"No, we'll give him a while."

"Let's please go into the shade," Margot said. Her face was white and she looked ill.

They made their way to the car where it stood under a single, wide-spreading tree and all climbed in.

"Chances are he's dead in there," Wilson remarked. "After a little we'll have a look."

Macomber felt a wild unreasonable happiness that he had never known before.

"By God, that was a chase," he said. "I've never felt any such feeling. Wasn't it marvellous, Margot?"

"I hated it."

"Why?"

"I hated it," she said bitterly. "I loathed it."

"You know I don't think I'd ever be afraid of anything again," Macomber said to Wilson. "Something happened in me after we first saw the buff and started after him. Like a dam bursting. It was pure excitement."

"Cleans out your liver," said Wilson. "Damn funny things happen to people."

Macomber's face was shining. "You know something did happen to me," he said. "I feel absolutely different."

His wife said nothing and eyed him strangely. She was sitting far back in the seat and Macomber was sitting forward talking to Wilson who turned sideways talking over the back of the front seat.

"You know, I'd like to try another lion," Macomber said. "I'm really not afraid of them now. After all, what can they do to you?"

"That's it," said Wilson. "Worst one can do is kill you. How does it go? Shakespeare. Damned good. See if I can remember. Oh, damned good. Used to quote it to myself at one time. Let's see. 'By my troth, I care not; a man can die but once; we owe God a death and let it go which way it will he that dies this year is quit for the next.' Damned fine, eh?"

He was very embarrassed, having brought out this thing he had lived by, but he had seen men come of age before and it always moved him. It was not a matter of their twenty-first birthday.

It had taken a strange chance of hunting, a sudden precipitation into action without opportunity for worrying beforehand, to bring this about with Macomber, but regardless of how it had happened it had most certainly happened. Look at the beggar now, Wilson thought. It's that some of them stay little boys so long, Wilson thought. Sometimes all their lives. Their figures stay boyish when they're fifty. The great American boy-men. Damned strange people. But he liked this Macomber now. Damned strange fellow. Probably meant the end of cuckoldry too. Well, that would be a damned good thing. Damned good thing. Beggar had probably been afraid all his life. Don't know what started it. But over now. Hadn't had time to be afraid with the buff. That and being angry too. Motor car too. Motor cars made it familiar. Be a damn fire eater now.

He'd seen it in the war work the same way. More of a change than any loss of virginity. Fear gone like an operation. Something else grew in its place. Main thing a man had. Made him into a man. Women knew it too. No bloody fear.

From the far corner of the seat Margaret Macomber looked at the two of them. There was no change in Wilson. She saw Wilson as she had seen him the day before when she had first realized what his great talent was. But she saw the change in Francis Macomber now.

"Do you have that feeling of happiness about what's going to happen?" Macomber asked, still exploring his new wealth.

"You're not supposed to mention it," Wilson said, looking in the other's face. "Much more fashionable to say you're scared. Mind you, you'll be scared too, plenty of times."

"But you *have* a feeling of happiness about action to come?"

"Yes," said Wilson. "There's that. Doesn't do to talk too much about all this. Talk the whole thing away. No pleasure in anything if you mouth it up too much."

"You're both talking rot," said Margot. "Just because you've chased some helpless animals in a motor car you talk like heroes."

"Sorry," said Wilson. "I have been gassing too much." She's worried about it already, he thought.

"If you don't know what we're talking about why not keep out of it?" Macomber asked his wife.

"You've gotten awfully brave, awfully suddenly," his wife said contemptuously, but her contempt was not secure. She was very afraid of something.

Macomber laughed, a very natural hearty laugh. "You know I *have*," he said. "I really have."

"Isn't it sort of late?" Margot said bitterly. Because she had done the best she could for many years back and the way they were together now was no one person's fault.

"Not for me," said Macomber.

Margot said nothing but sat back in the corner of the seat.

"Do you think we've given him time enough?" Macomber asked Wilson cheerfully.

"We might have a look," Wilson said. "Have you any solids left?"

"The gun-bearer has some."

Wilson called in Swahili and the older gun-bearer, who was skinning out one of the heads, straightened up, pulled a box of solids out of his pocket and brought them over to Macomber, who filled his magazine and put the remaining shells in his pocket.

"You might as well shoot the Springfield," Wilson said. "You're used to it. We'll leave the Mannlicher in the car with the

Memsahib. Your gun-bearer can carry your heavy gun. I've this damned cannon. Now let me tell you about them." He had saved this until the last because he did not want to worry Macomber. "When a buff comes he comes with his head high and thrust straight out. The boss of the horns covers any sort of a brain shot. The only shot is straight into the nose. The only other shot is into his chest or, if you're to one side, into the neck or the shoulders. After they've been hit once they take a hell of a lot of killing. Don't try anything fancy. Take the easiest shot there is. They've finished skinning out that head now. Should we get started?"

He called to the gun-bearers, who came up wiping their hands, and the older one got into the back.

"I'll only take Kongoni," Wilson said. "The other can watch to keep the birds away."

As the car moved slowly across the open space toward the island of brushy trees that ran in a tongue of foliage along a dry water course that cut the open swale, Macomber felt his heart pounding and his mouth was dry again, but it was excitement, not fear.

"Here's where he went in," Wilson said. Then to the gun-bearer in Swahili, "Take the blood spoor."

The car was parallel to the patch of bush. Macomber, Wilson and the gun-bearer got down. Macomber, looking back, saw his wife, with the rifle by her side, looking at him. He waved to her and she did not wave back.

The brush was very thick ahead and the ground was dry. The middle-aged gun-bearer was sweating heavily and Wilson had his hat down over his eyes and his red neck showed just ahead of Macomber. Suddenly the gun-bearer said something in Swahili to Wilson and ran forward.

"He's dead in there," Wilson said. "Good work," and he turned to grip Macomber's hand and as they shook hands, grinning at each other, the gun-bearer shouted wildly and they saw him coming out of the bush sideways, fast as a crab, and the bull coming, nose out, mouth tight closed, blood dripping, massive head straight out, coming in a charge, his little pig eyes bloodshot as he looked at them. Wilson, who was ahead, was kneeling shooting, and Macomber, as he fired, unhearing his shot in the roaring of Wilson's gun, saw fragments like slate burst from the huge boss of the horns, and the head jerked, he shot again at the wide nostrils and saw the horns jolt again and fragments fly, and he did not see Wilson now and, aiming carefully, shot again with the buffalo's huge bulk almost on him and his rifle almost level with the on-coming head, nose out, and he could see the little wicked eyes and the head started to lower and he felt a sudden white-hot, blinding flash explode inside his head and that was all he ever felt.

Wilson had ducked to one side to get in a shoulder shot. Macomber had stood solid and shot for the nose, shooting a touch high each time and hitting the heavy horns, splintering and chipping them like hitting a slate roof, and Mrs. Macomber, in the car, had shot at the buffalo with the 6.5 Mannlicher as it seemed about to gore Macomber and had hit her husband about two inches up and a little to one side of the base of his skull.

Francis Macomber lay now, face down, not two yards from where the buffalo lay on his side and his wife knelt over him with Wilson beside her.

"I wouldn't turn him over," Wilson said.

The woman was crying hysterically.

"I'd get back in the car," Wilson said. "Where's the rifle?"

She shook her head, her face contorted. The gun-bearer picked up the rifle.

"Leave it as it is," said Wilson. Then "Go get Abdulla so that he may witness the manner of the accident."

He knelt down, took a handkerchief from his pocket, and spread it over Francis Macomber's crew-cropped head where it lay. The blood sank into the dry, loose earth.

Wilson stood up and saw the buffalo on his side, his legs out, his thinly-haired belly crawling with ticks. "Hell of a good bull," his brain registered automatically. "A good fifty inches, or better. Better." He called to the driver and told him to spread a blanket over the body and stay by it. Then he walked over to the motor car where the woman sat crying in the corner.

"That was a pretty thing to do," he said in a toneless voice. "He *would* have left you too."

"Stop it," she said.

"Of course it's an accident," he said. "I know that."

"Stop it," she said.

"Don't worry," he said. "There will be a certain amount of unpleasantness but I will have some photographs taken that will be very useful at the inquest. There's the testimony of the gun-bearers and the driver too. You're perfectly all right."

"Stop it," she said.

"There's a hell of a lot to be done," he said. "And I'll have to send a truck off to the lake to wireless for a plane to take the three of us into Nairobi. Why didn't you poison him? That's what they do in England."

"Stop it. Stop it. Stop it," the woman cried.

Wilson looked at her with his flat blue eyes.

"I'm through now," he said. "I was a little angry. I'd begun to like your husband."

"Oh, please stop it," she said. "Please, please stop it."

"That's better," Wilson said. "Please is much better. Now I'll stop."

1. Discuss Hemingway's use of point of view and what it accomplishes.

2. What is the purpose of the shift into the lion's consciousness? What may be lost by the use of this device?

3. How is Wilson, the mentor; Macomber, the student; and Margot, the destroyer?

4. To what extent is dialogue used? How would you describe it?

5. Cite several examples of irony.

6. For what good reason, if any, must Macomber die?

7. Why does Wilson charge Margot with deliberately murdering her husband?

8. State your idea of what the major theme is.

9. Read the following Hemingway excerpts and comment on their effectiveness.

(a) He was very wealthy, and would be much wealthier, and he knew she would not leave him ever now. That was one of the few things that he really knew. He knew about that, about motor cycles—that was earliest—about motor cars, about duck-shooting, about fishing, trout, salmon and big-sea, about sex in books, many books, too many books, about all court games, about dogs, not much about horses, about hanging on to his money, about most of the other things his world dealt in, and about his wife not leaving him.

(b) This Macomber was an odd one though. Damned if he wasn't. Now the wife. Well, the wife. Yes, the wife. Hm, the wife.

(c) "whonk"; "ca-ra-wong"; "carawonging."

Topics for Writing

1. Analyze point of view in "The Short Happy Life of Francis Macomber."

2. Describe Hemingway's style. Focus sharply on three of the nine aspects described in Chapter 5 (for example, diction, syntax, and dialogue).

3. This story has been judged technically brilliant. Defend this position.

4. Discuss the relationship between point of view, character, conflict, and theme.

Ernest Hemingway

Atkins, John. *The Art of Ernest Hemingway: His Work and Personality.* London: Peter Nevill, 1952.

Baker, Carlos, ed. *Hemingway and His Critics: An International Anthology.* New York: Hill and Wang, 1961.

———. *Hemingway: The Writer As Artist.* 3d ed. Princeton: Princeton University Press, 1963.

———. *Ernest Hemingway: A Life Story.* New York: Charles Scribner's Sons, 1969.

Beaver, Joseph. "Technique in Hemingway." *College English,* 14 (1953), 325–328.

Beck, Warren. "The Shorter Happy Life of Mrs. Macomber." *Modern Fiction Studies,* 4 (1955), 28–37.

Burnam, Tom. "Primitivism and Masculinity in the Work of Hemingway." *Modern Fiction Studies,* 1 (1955), 20–24.

Carpenter, Frederic I. "Hemingway Achieves the Fifth Dimension." *PMLA,* 69 (1954), 711–718.

Colvert, James B. "Ernest Hemingway's Morality in Action." *American Literature,* 27 (1955), 372–385.

DeFalco, Joseph. *The Hero in Hemingway's Short Stories.* Pittsburgh: University of Pittsburgh Press, 1963.

Graham, John. "Ernest Hemingway: The Meaning of Style." *Modern Fiction Studies,* 6 (1960–61), 298–313.

Gurko, Leo. *Ernest Hemingway and the Pursuit of Heroism.* New York: Thomas Y. Crowell, 1968.

Halliday, E.M. "Hemingway's Ambiguity: Symbolism and Irony." *American Literature,* 28 (1956), 1–22.

Hart, Robert C. "Hemingway on Writing." *College English,* 18 (1957), 314–320.

Hemphill, George. "Hemingway and James." *Kenyon Review,* 11 (1940), 50–60.

Hoffman, Frederick J. "No Beginning and No End: Hemingway and Death." *Essays in Criticism,* 3 (1953), 73–84.

Levin, Harry. "Observations on the Style of Ernest Hemingway." *Kenyon Review,* 13 (1951), 581–609.

Plimpton, George. "The Art of Fiction XXI: Ernest Hemingway." *Paris Review,* 5 (1958), 61–89.

Rosenfeld, Isaac. "A Farewell to Hemingway." *Kenyon Review,* 13 (1951), 147–155.

West, Ray. "Ernest Hemingway: The Failure of Sensibility." *Sewanee Review,* 53 (1945), 120–135.

Young, Philip. *Ernest Hemingway: A Reconsideration.* Rev. ed. University Park and London: Pennsylvania State University Press, 1966.

Henry James *(1843–1916)*

*Born in New York City into an extraordinary family—his
father was a distinguished religious philosopher and his
brother was a noted psychologist and philosopher—he embarked on a literary career in his late twenties, settling first in
Paris where he associated with such famous novelists as
Turgenev, Flaubert, de Maupassant, and Zola, then moving
to England where he lived as an American citizen until the
year of his death. First fame came with his short novel* Daisy
Miller *(1876). He wrote several important full-length novels,
among them* The American *(1877),* Washington Square
(1880), Portrait of a Lady *(1881), and* The Ambassadors
(1883).

The Real Thing

1

When the porter's wife, who used to answer the
house-bell, announced "A gentleman and a lady, sir," I had, as I often had
in those days—the wish being father to the thought—an immediate vision
of sitters. Sitters my visitors in this case proved to be; but not in the sense I
should have preferred. There was nothing at first however to indicate that
they mightn't have come for a portrait. The gentleman, a man of fifty, very
high and very straight, with a moustache slightly grizzled and a dark grey
walking-coat admirably fitted, both of which I noted professionally—I don't
mean as a barber or yet as a tailor—would have struck me as a celebrity if
celebrities often were striking. It was a truth of which I had for some time
been conscious that a figure with a good deal of frontage was, as one might
say, almost never a public institution. A glance at the lady helped to
remind me of this paradoxical law: she also looked too distinguished to be a
"personality." Moreover one would scarcely come across two variations
together.

Neither of the pair immediately spoke—they only
prolonged the preliminary gaze suggesting that each wished to give the
other a chance. They were visibly shy; they stood there letting me take
them in—which, as I afterwards perceived, was the most practical thing
they could have done. In this way their embarrassment served their cause.
I had seen people painfully reluctant to mention that they desired anything
so gross as to be represented on canvas; but the scruples of my new friends
appeared almost insurmountable. Yet the gentleman might have said "I

should like a portrait of my wife," and the lady might have said "I should like a portrait of my husband." Perhaps they weren't husband and wife—this naturally would make the matter more delicate. Perhaps they wished to be done together—in which case they ought to have brought a third person to break the news.

"We come from Mr. Rivet," the lady finally said with a dim smile that had the effect of a moist sponge passed over a "sunk" piece of painting, as well as of a vague allusion to vanished beauty. She was as tall and straight, in her degree, as her companion, and with ten years less to carry. She looked as sad as a woman could look whose face was not charged with expression; that is her tinted oval mask showed waste as an exposed surface shows friction. The hand of time had played over her freely, but to an effect of elimination. She was slim and stiff, and so well-dressed, in dark blue cloth, with lappets and pockets and buttons, that it was clear she employed the same tailor as her husband. The couple had an indefinable air of prosperous thrift—they evidently got a good deal of luxury for their money. If I was to be one of their luxuries it would behoove me to consider my terms.

"Ah Claude Rivet recommended me?" I echoed; and I added that it was very kind of him, though I could reflect that, as he only painted landscape, this wasn't a sacrifice.

The lady looked very hard at the gentleman, and the gentleman looked round the room. Then staring at the floor a moment and stroking his moustache, he rested his pleasant eyes on me with the remark: "He said you were the right one."

"I try to be, when people want to sit."

"Yes, we should like to," said the lady anxiously.

"Do you mean together?"

My visitors exchanged a glance. "If you could do anything with *me* I suppose it would be double," the gentleman stammered.

"Oh yes, there's naturally a higher charge for two figures than for one."

"We should like to make it pay," the husband confessed.

"That's very good of you," I returned, appreciating so unwonted a sympathy—for I supposed he meant pay the artist.

A sense of strangeness seemed to dawn on the lady. "We mean for the illustrations—Mr. Rivet said you might put one in."

"Put in—an illustration?" I was equally confused.

"Sketch her off, you know," said the gentleman, colouring.

It was only then that I understood the service Claude Rivet had rendered me; he had told them how I worked in black-and-white, for magazines, for storybooks, for sketches of contemporary life and consequently had copious employment for models. These things were true, but it was not less true—I may confess it now; whether because the aspiration was to lead to everything or to nothing I leave the reader to guess—that I couldn't get the honours, to say nothing of the emoluments, of a great painter of portraits out of my head. My "illustrations" were my potboilers; I looked to a different branch of art—far and away the most interesting it had always seemed to me—to perpetuate my fame. There was no shame in looking to it also to make my fortune; but that fortune was by so much further from being made from the moment my visitors wished to be "done" for nothing. I was disappointed; for in the pictorial sense I had immediately *seen* them. I had seized their type—I had already settled what I would do with it. Something that wouldn't absolutely have pleased them, I afterwards reflected.

"Ah you're—you're—a?" I began as soon as I had mastered my surprise. I couldn't bring out the dingy word "models": it seemed so little to fit the case.

"We haven't had much practice," said the lady.

"We've got to *do* something, and we've thought that an artist in your line might perhaps make something of us," her husband threw off. He further mentioned that they didn't know many artists and that they had gone first, on the off-chance—he painted views of course, but sometimes put in figures; perhaps I remembered—to Mr. Rivet, whom they had met a few years before at a place in Norfolk where he was sketching.

"We used to sketch a little ourselves," the lady hinted.

"It's very awkward, but we absolutely *must* do something," her husband went on.

"Of course we're not so *very* young," she admitted with a wan smile.

With the remark that I might as well know something more about them the husband had handed me a card extracted from a neat new pocket-book—their appurtenances were all of the freshest—and inscribed with the words "Major Monarch." Impressive as these words were they didn't carry my knowledge much further; but my visitor presently added: "I've left the army and we've had the misfortune to lose our money. In fact our means are dreadfully small."

"It's awfully trying—a regular strain," said Mrs. Monarch.

They evidently wished to be discreet—to take care not to swagger because they were gentlefolk. I felt them willing to recognise this as something of a drawback, at the same time that I guessed at an underlying sense—their consolation in adversity—that they *had* their points. They certainly had; but these advantages struck me as preponderantly social; such for instance as would help to make a drawing-room look well. However, a drawing-room was always, or ought to be, a picture.

In consequence of his wife's allusion to their age Major Monarch observed: "Naturally it's more for the figure that we thought of going in. We can still hold ourselves up." On the instant I saw that the figure was indeed their strong point. His "naturally" didn't sound vain, but it lighted up the question. "*She* has the best one," he continued, nodding at his wife with a pleasant after-dinner absence of circumlocution. I could only reply, as if we were in fact sitting over our wine, that this didn't prevent his own from being very good; which led him in turn to make answer: "We thought that if you ever have to do people like us we might be something like it. *She* particularly—for a lady in a book, you know."

I was so amused by them that, to get more of it, I did my best to take their point of view; and though it was an embarrassment to find myself appraising physically, as if they were animals on hire or useful blacks, a pair whom I should have expected to meet only in one of the relations in which criticism is tacit, I looked at Mrs. Monarch judicially enough to be able to exclaim after a moment with conviction: "Oh yes, a lady in a book!" She was singularly like a bad illustration.

"We'll stand up, if you like," said the Major; and he raised himself before me with a really grand air.

I could take his measure at a glance—he was six feet two and a perfect gentleman. It would have paid any club in process of formation and in want of a stamp to engage him at a salary to stand in the principal window. What struck me at once was that in coming to me they had rather missed their vocation; they could surely have been turned to better account for advertising purposes. I couldn't of course see the thing in detail, but I could see them make somebody's fortune—I don't mean their own. There was something in them for a waistcoat-maker, an hotel-keeper or a soap-vendor. I could imagine "We always use it" pinned on their bosoms with the greatest effect; I had a vision of the brilliancy with which they would launch a table d'hote.

Mrs. Monarch sat still, not from pride but from shyness, and presently her husband said to her: "Get up, my dear, and show how smart you are." She obeyed, but she had no need to get up to show it. She walked to the end of the studio and then came back blushing, her fluttered eyes on the partner of her appeal. I was reminded of an incident I had accidentally had a glimpse of in Paris—being with a friend there, a dramatist about to produce a play, when an actress came to him to ask to be entrusted with a part. She went through her paces before him, walked up and down as Mrs. Monarch was doing. Mrs. Monarch did it quite as well, but I abstained from applauding. It was very odd to see such people apply for such poor pay. She looked as if she had ten thousand a year. Her husband had used the word that described her: she was in the London current jargon essentially and typically "smart." Her figure was, in the same order of ideas, conspicuously and irreproachably "good." For a woman of her age her waist was surprisingly small; her elbow moreover had the orthodox crook. She held her head at the conventional angle, but why did she come to *me*? She ought to have tried on jackets at a big shop. I feared my visitors were not only destitute but "artistic"—which would be a great complication. When she sat down again I thanked her, observing that what a draughtsman most valued in his model was the faculty of keeping quiet.

"Oh *she* can keep quiet," said Major Monarch. Then he added jocosely: "I've always kept her quiet."

"I'm not a nasty fidget, am I?" It was going to wring tears from me, I felt, the way she hid her head, ostrich-like, in the other broad bosom.

The owner of this expanse addressed his answer to me. "Perhaps it isn't out of place to mention—because we ought to be quite business-like, oughtn't we?—that when I married her she was known as the Beautiful Statue."

"Oh dear!" said Mrs. Monarch ruefully.

"Of course I should want a certain amount of expression," I rejoined.

"Of *course!*"—and I had never heard such unanimity.

"And then I suppose you know that you'll get awfully tired."

"Oh we *never* get tired!" they eagerly cried.

"Have you had any kind of practice?"

They hesitated—they looked at each other. "We've been photographed—*immensely,*" said Mrs. Monarch.

"She means the fellows have asked us themselves," added the Major.

"I see—because you're so good-looking."

"I don't know what they thought, but they were always after us."

"We always got our photographs for nothing," smiled Mrs. Monarch.

"We might have brought some, my dear," her husband remarked.

"I'm not sure we have any left. We've given quantities away," she explained to me.

"With our autographs and that sort of thing," said the Major.

"Are they to be got in the shops?" I enquired as a harmless pleasantry.

"Oh yes, *hers*—they used to be."

"Not now," said Mrs. Monarch, with her eyes on the floor.

2

I could fancy the "sort of thing" they put on the presentation copies of their photographs, and I was sure they wrote a beautiful hand. It was odd how quickly I was sure of everything that concerned them. If they were now so poor as to have to earn shillings and pence they could never have had much of a margin. Their good looks had been their capital, and they had good-humouredly made the most of the career that this resource marked out for them. It was in their faces, the blankness, the deep intellectual repose of the twenty years of country-house visiting that had given them pleasant intonations. I could see the sunny drawing-rooms, sprinkled with periodicals she didn't read, in which Mrs. Monarch had continuously sat; I could see the wet shrubberies in which she had walked, equipped to admiration for either exercise. I could see the rich covers the Major had helped to shoot and the wonderful garments in which, late at night, he repaired to the smoking-room to talk about them. I could imagine their leggings and waterproofs, their knowing tweeds and rugs, their rolls of sticks and cases of tackle and neat umbrellas; and I could evoke the exact appearance of their servants and the compact variety of their luggage on the platforms of country stations.

They gave small tips, but they were liked; they didn't do anything themselves, but they were welcome. They looked so well everywhere; they gratified the general relish for stature, complexion and "form." They knew it without fatuity or vulgarity, and they respected themselves in consequence. They weren't superficial; they were thorough and kept themselves up—it had been their line. People with such a taste for activity had to have some line. I could feel how even in a dull house they could have been counted on for the joy of life. At present something had happened—it didn't matter what, their little income had grown less, it had grown least—and they had to do something for pocket-money. Their friends could like them, I made out, without liking to support them. There was something about them that represented credit—their clothes, their manners, their type; but if credit is a large empty pocket in which an occasional chink reverberates, the chink at least must be audible. What they wanted of me was to help to make it so. Fortunately they had no children—I soon divined that. They would also perhaps wish our relations to be kept secret: this was why it was "for the figure"—the reproduction of the face would betray them.

I liked them—I felt, quite as their friends must have done—they were so simple; and I had no objection to them if they would suit. But somehow with all their perfections I didn't easily believe in them. After all they were amateurs, and the ruling passion of my life was the detestation of the amateur. Combined with this was another perversity—an innate preference for the represented subject over the real one: the defect of the real one was so apt to be a lack of representation. I like things that appeared; then one was sure. Whether they *were* or not was a subordinate and almost always a profitless question. There were other considerations, the first of which was that I already had two or three recruits in use, notably a young person with big feet, in alpaca, from Kilburn, who for a couple of years had come to me regularly for my illustrations and with whom I was still—perhaps ignobly—satisfied. I frankly explained to my visitors how the case stood, but they had taken more precautions than I supposed. They had reasoned out their opportunity, for Claude Rivet had told them of the projected *édition de luxe* of one of the writers of our day—the rarest of the novelists—who, long neglected by the multitudinous vulgar and dearly prized by the attentive (need I mention Philip Vincent?), had had the happy fortune of seeing, late in life, the dawn and then the full light of a higher criticism; an estimate in which on the part of the public there was something really of expiation. The edition preparing, planned by a publisher of taste, was practically an act of high reparation; the wood-cuts with which it was to be enriched were the homage of English art to one of the most independent representatives of English letters. Major and Mrs. Monarch confessed to me they had hoped I might be able to work *them* into my branch of the enterprise. They knew I was to do the first of the books, "Rutland Ramsay," but I had to make clear to them that my participation in the rest of the affair—this first book was to be a test—must depend on the satisfaction I should give. If this should be limited my employers would drop me with scarce common forms. It was therefore a crisis for me, and naturally I was making special preparations, looking about for new people, should they be necessary, and securing the best types. I admitted however that I should like to settle down to two or three good models who would do for everything.

"Should we have often to—a—put on special clothes?" Mrs. Monarch timidly demanded.

"Dear yes—that's half the business."

"And should we be expected to supply our own costumes?"

"Oh no; I've got a lot of things. A painter's models put on—or put off—anything he likes."

"And you mean—a—the same?"

"The same?"

Mrs. Monarch looked at her husband again.

"Oh she was just wondering," he explained, "if the costumes are in *general* use." I had to confess that they were, and I mentioned further that some of them—I had a lot of genuine greasy last-century things—had served their time, a hundred years ago, on living world-stained men and women; on figures not perhaps so far removed, in that vanished world, from *their* type, the Monarchs', *quoi!* of a breeched and bewigged age. "We'll put on anything that *fits*," said the Major.

"Oh I arrange that—they fit in the pictures."

"I'm afraid I should do better for the modern books. I'd come as you like," said Mrs. Monarch.

"She has got a lot of clothes at home: they might do for contemporary life," her husband continued.

"Oh I can fancy scenes in which you'd be quite natural." And indeed I could see the slipshod rearrangements of stale properties—the stories I tried to produce pictures for without the exasperation of reading them—whose sandy tracts the good lady might help to people. But I had to return to the fact that for this sort of work—the daily mechanical grind—I was already equipped: the people I was working with were fully adequate.

"We only thought we might be more like *some* characters," said Mrs. Monarch mildly, getting up.

Her husband also rose; he stood looking at me with a dim wistfulness that was touching in so fine a man. "Wouldn't it be rather a pull sometimes to have—a—to have—?" He hung fire; he wanted me to help him by phrasing what he meant. But I couldn't—I didn't know. So he brought it out awkwardly: "The *real* thing; a gentleman, you know, or a lady." I was quite ready to give a general assent—I admitted that there was a great deal in that. This encouraged Major Monarch to say, following up his appeal with an unacted gulp: "It's awfully hard—we've tried everything." The gulp was communicative; it proved too much for his wife. Before I knew it Mrs. Monarch had dropped again upon a divan and burst into tears. Her husband sat down beside her, holding one of her hands; whereupon she quickly dried her eyes with the other, while I felt embarrassed as she looked up at me. "There isn't a confounded job I haven't applied for—waited for—prayed for. You can fancy we'd be pretty bad first. Secretaryships and that sort of thing? You might as well ask for a peerage. I'd be *anything*—I'm strong; a messenger or a coal-heaver. I'd put on a gold-laced cap and open carriage-doors in front of the haberdasher's; I'd hang about a station to carry portmanteaux; I'd be a postman. But they won't *look* at you; there are thousands as good as yourself already on the ground. *Gentlemen*, poor beggars, who've drunk their wine, who've kept their hunters!"

I was as reassuring as I knew how to be, and my visitors were presently on their feet again while, for the experiment, we agreed on an hour. We were discussing it when the door opened and Miss Churm came in with a wet umbrella. Miss Churm had to take the omnibus to Maida Vale and then walk half a mile. She looked a trifle blowsy and slightly splashed. I scarcely ever saw her come in without thinking afresh how odd it was that, being so little in herself, she should yet be so much in others. She was a meagre little Miss Churm, but was such an ample heroine of romance. She was only a freckled cockney, but she could represent everything, from a fine lady to a shepherdess; she had the faculty as she might have had a fine voice or long hair. She couldn't spell and she loved beer, but she had two or three "points," and practice, and a knack, and mother-wit, and a whimsical sensibility, and a love of the theatre, and seven sisters, and not an ounce of respect, especially for the *h*. The first thing my visitors saw was that her umbrella was wet, and in their spotless perfection they visibly winced at it. The rain had come on since their arrival.

"I'm all in a soak; there *was* a mess of people in the 'bus. I wish you lived near a stytion," said Miss Churm. I requested her to get ready as quickly as possible, and she passed into the room in which she always changed her dress. But before going out she asked me what she was to get into this time.

"It's the Russian princess, don't you know?" I answered; "the one with the 'golden eyes,' in black velvet, for the long thing in the *Cheapside*."

"Golden eyes? I *say!*" cried Miss Churm, while my companions watched her with intensity as she withdrew. She always arranged herself, when she was late, before I could turn round; and I kept my visitors a little on purpose, so that they might get an idea, from seeing her, what would be expected of themselves. I mentioned that she was quite my notion of an excellent model—she was really very clever.

"Do you think she looks like a Russian princess?" Major Monarch asked with lurking alarm.

"When I make her, yes."

"Oh if you have to *make* her—!" he reasoned, not without point.

"That's the most you can ask. There are so many who are not makeable."

"Well, now, *here's* a lady"—and with a persuasive smile he passed his arm into his wife's—"who's already made!"

"Oh I'm not a Russian princess," Mrs. Monarch protested a little coldly. I could see she had known some and didn't like them. There at once was a complication of a kind I never had to fear with Miss Churm.

This young lady came back in black velvet—the gown was rather rusty and very low on her lean shoulders—and with a Japanese fan in her red hands. I reminded her that in the scene I was doing she had to look over some one's head. "I forget whose it is; but it doesn't matter. Just look over a head."

"I'd rather look over a stove," said Miss Churm; and she took her station near the fire. She fell into position, settled herself into a tall attitude, gave a certain backward inclination to her head and a certain forward droop to her fan, and looked, at least to my prejudiced sense, distinguished and charming, foreign and dangerous. We left her looking so while I went downstairs with Major and Mrs. Monarch.

"I believe I could come about as near it as that," said Mrs. Monarch.

"Oh you think she's shabby, but you must allow for the alchemy of art."

However, they went off with an evident increase of comfort founded on their demonstrable advantage in being the real thing. I could fancy them shuddering over Miss Churm. She was very droll about them when I went back, for I told her what they wanted.

"Well, if *she* can sit I'll tyke to book-keeping," said my model.

"She's very ladylike," I replied as an innocent form of aggravation.

"So much the worse for *you*. That means she can't turn round."

"She'll do for the fashionable novels."

"Oh yes, she'll *do* for them!" my model humorously declared. "Ain't they bad enough without her?" I had often sociably denounced them to Miss Churm.

3

It was for the elucidation of a mystery in one of these works that I first tried Mrs. Monarch. Her husband came with her, to be useful if necessary—it was sufficiently clear that as a general thing he would prefer to come with her. At first I wondered if this were for "propriety's" sake—if he were going to be jealous and meddling. The idea was too tiresome, and if it had been confirmed it would speedily have brought our acquaintance to a close. But I soon saw there was nothing in it and that if he accompanied Mrs. Monarch it was—in addition to the chance of being wanted—simply because he had nothing else to do. When they were separate his occupation was gone and they never *had* been separate. I judged rightly that in their awkward situation their close union was their main comfort and that this union had no weak spot. It was a real marriage, an encouragement to the hesitating, a nut for pessimists to crack. Their address was humble—I remember afterwards thinking it had been the only thing about them that was really professional—and I could fancy the lamentable lodgings in which the Major would have been left alone. He could sit there more or less grimly with his wife—he couldn't sit there anyhow without her.

He had too much tact to try and make himself agreeable when he couldn't be useful; so when I was too absorbed in my work to talk he simply sat and waited. But I liked to hear him talk—it made my work, when not interrupting it, less mechanical, less special. To listen to him was to combine the excitement of going out with the economy of staying at home. There was only one hindrance—that I seemed not to know any of the people this brilliant couple had known. I think he wondered extremely, during the term of our intercourse, whom the deuce I *did* know. He hadn't a stray sixpence of an idea to fumble for, so we didn't spin it very fine; we confined ourselves to questions of leather and even of liquor—saddlers and breeches-makers and how to get excellent claret cheap—and matters like "good trains" and the habits of small game. His lore on these last subjects was astonishing—he managed to interweave the station-master with the ornithologist. When he couldn't talk about greater things he could talk cheerfully about smaller, and since I couldn't accompany him into reminiscences of the fashionable world he could lower the conversation without a visible effort to my level.

So earnest a desire to please was touching in a man who

could so easily have knocked one down. He looked after the fire and had an opinion on the draught of the stove without my asking him, and I could see that he thought many of my arrangements not half knowing. I remember telling him that if I were only rich I'd offer him a salary to come and teach me how to live. Sometimes he gave a random sigh of which the essence might have been: "Give me even such a bare old barrack as *this*, and I'd do something with it!" When I wanted to use him he came alone; which was an illustration of the superior courage of women. His wife could bear her solitary second floor, and she was in general more discreet; showing by various small reserves that she was alive to the propriety of keeping our relations markedly professional—not letting them slide into sociability. She wished it to remain clear that she and the Major were employed, not cultivated, and if she approved of me as a superior, who could be kept in his place, she never thought me quite good enough for an equal.

She sat with great intensity, giving the whole of her mind to it, and was capable of remaining for an hour almost as motionless as before a photographer's lens. I could see she had been photographed often, but somehow the very habit that made her good for that purpose unfitted her for mine. At first I was extremely pleased with her ladylike air, and it was a satisfaction, on coming to follow her lines, to see how good they were and how far they could lead the pencil. But after a little skirmishing I began to find her too insurmountably stiff; do what I would with it my drawing looked like a photograph or a copy of a photograph. Her figure had no variety of expression—she herself had no sense of variety. You may say that this was my business and was only a question of placing her. Yet I placed her in every conceivable position and she managed to obliterate their differences. She was always a lady certainly, and into the bargain was always the same lady. She was the real thing, but always the same thing. There were moments when I rather writhed under the serenity of her confidence that she *was* the real thing. All her dealings with me and all her husband's were an implication that this was lucky for *me*. Meanwhile I found myself trying to invent types that approached her own, instead of making her own transform itself—in the clever way that was not impossible for instance to poor Miss Churm. Arrange as I would and take the precautions I would, she always came out, in my pictures, too tall—landing me in the dilemma of having represented a fascinating woman as seven feet high, which (out of respect perhaps to my own very much scantier inches) was far from my idea of such a personage.

The case was worse with the Major—nothing I could do would keep *him* down, so that he became useful only for the representation of brawny giants. I adored variety and range, I cherished human accidents, the illustrative note; I wanted to characterise closely, and the thing in the world I most hated was the danger of being ridden by a type. I had quarreled with some of my friends about it; I had parted company with them for maintaining that one *had* to be, and that if the type was beautiful—witness Raphael and Leonardo—the servitude was only a gain. I was neither Leonardo nor Raphael—I might only be a presumptuous young modern searcher; but I held that everything was to be sacrificed sooner than character. When they claimed that the obsessional form could easily *be* character I retorted, perhaps superficially, "Whose?" It couldn't be everybody's—it might end in being nobody's.

After I had drawn Mrs. Monarch a dozen times I felt surer even than before that the value of such a model as Miss Churm resided precisely in the fact that she had no positive stamp, combined of course with the other fact that what she did have was a curious and inexplicable talent for imitation. Her usual appearance was like a curtain which she could draw up at request for a capital performance. This performance was simply suggestive; but it was a word to the wise—it was vivid and pretty. Sometimes even I thought it, though she was plain herself, too insipidly pretty; I made it a reproach to her that the figures drawn from her were monotonously (*bêtement*, as we used to say) graceful. Nothing made her more angry; it was so much her pride to feel she could sit for characters that had nothing in common with each other. She would accuse me at such moments of taking away her "reputytion."

It suffered a certain shrinkage, this queer quantity, from the repeated visits of my new friends. Miss Churm was greatly in demand, never in want of employment, so I had no scruple in putting her off occasionally, to try them more at my ease. It was certainly amusing at first to do the real thing—it was amusing to do Major Monarch's trousers. They *were* the real thing, even if he did come out colossal. It was amusing to do his wife's back hair—it was so mathematically neat—and the particular "smart" tension of her tight stays. She lent herself especially to positions in which the face was somewhat averted or blurred; she abounded in ladylike back views and *profils perdus.* When she stood erect she took naturally one of the attitudes in which court-painters represent queens and princesses; so that I found myself wondering whether, to draw out this accomplishment, I couldn't get the editor of the *Cheapside* to publish a really royal romance, "A Tale of Buckingham Palace." Sometimes however the real thing and the make-believe came into contact; by which I mean that Miss Churm, keeping an appointment or coming to make one on days when I had much work in hand, encountered her invidious rivals. The encounter was not on their part, for they noticed her no more than if she had been the housemaid; not from intentional loftiness, but simply because as yet, professionally, they didn't know how to fraternise, as I could imagine they would have liked—or at least that the Major would. They couldn't talk about the omnibus—they always walked; and they didn't know what else to try—she wasn't interested in good trains or cheap claret. Besides, they must have felt—in the air—that she was amused at them, secretly derisive of their ever knowing how. She wasn't a person to conceal the limits of her faith if she had had a chance to show them. On the other hand Mrs. Monarch didn't think her tidy; for why else did she take pains to say to me—it was going out of the way, for Mrs. Monarch—that she didn't like dirty women?

One day when my young lady happened to be present with my other sitters—she even dropped in, when it was convenient, for a chat—I asked her to be so good as to lend a hand in getting tea, a service with which she was familiar and which was one of a class that, living as I did in a small way, with slender domestic resources, I often appealed to my models to render. They liked to lay hands on my property, to break the sitting, and sometimes the china—it made them feel Bohemian. The next time I saw Miss Churm after this incident she surprised me greatly by making a scene about it—she accused me of having wished to humiliate her. She hadn't resented the outrage at the time, but had seemed obliging and amused, enjoying the comedy of asking Mrs. Monarch, who sat vague and silent, whether she would have cream and sugar, and putting an exaggerated simper into the question. She had tried intonations—as if she too wished to pass for the real thing—till I was afraid my other visitors would take offence.

Oh they were determined not to do this, and their touching patience was the measure of their great need. They would sit by the hour, uncomplaining, till I was ready to use them; they would come back on the chance of being wanted and would walk away cheerfully if it failed. I used to go to the door with them to see in what magnificent order they retreated. I tried to find other employment for them—I introduced them to several artists. But they didn't "take," for reasons I could appreciate, and I became rather anxiously aware that after such disappointments they fell back upon me with a heavier weight. They did me the honour to think me most *their* form. They weren't romantic enough for the painters, and in those days there were few serious workers in black-and-white. Besides, they had an eye to the great job I had mentioned to them—they had secretly set their hearts on supplying the right essence for my pictorial vindication of our fine novelist. They knew that for this undertaking I should want no costume-effects, none of the frippery of past ages—that it was a case in which everything would be contemporary and satirical and presumably genteel. If I could work them into it their future would be assured, for the labour would of course be long and the occupation steady.

One day Mrs. Monarch came without her husband—she explained his absence by his having had to go to the City. While she sat there in her usual relaxed majesty there came at the door a knock which I immediately recognised as the subdued appeal of a model out of work. It was followed by the entrance of a young man whom I at once saw to be a foreigner and who proved in fact an Italian acquainted with no English word but my name, which he uttered in a way that made it seem to include all others. I hadn't then visited his country, nor was I proficient in his tongue; but as he was not so meanly constituted—what Italian is?—as to depend only on that member for expression he conveyed to me, in familiar but graceful mimicry, that he was in search of exactly the employment in which the lady before me was engaged. I was not struck with him at first, and while I continued to draw I dropped few signs of interest or encouragement. He stood his ground however—not importunately, but with a dumb dog-like fidelity in his eyes that amounted to innocent impudence, the manner of a devoted servant—he might have been in the house for years—unjustly suspected. Suddenly it struck me that this very attitude and expression made a picture; whereupon I told him to sit down and wait till I should be free. There was another picture in the way he obeyed me, and I observed as I worked that there were others still in the way he looked wonderingly, with his head thrown back, about the high studio. He might have been crossing himself in Saint Peter's. Before I finished I said to myself "The fellow's a bankrupt orange-monger, but a treasure."

When Mrs. Monarch withdrew he passed across the room like a flash to open the door for her, standing there with the rapt pure gaze of the young Dante spellbound by the young Beatrice. As I never insisted, in such situations, on the blankness of the British domestic, I reflected that he had the making of a servant—and I needed one, but couldn't pay him to be only that—as well as of a model; in short I resolved to adopt my bright adventurer if he would agree to officiate in the double capacity. He jumped at my offer, and in the event my rashness—for I had really known nothing about him—wasn't brought home to me. He proved a sympathetic though a desultory ministrant, and had in a wonderful degree the *sentiment de la pose.* It was uncultivated, instinctive, a part of the happy instinct that had guided him to my door and helped him to spell out my name on the card nailed to it. He had had no other introduction to me than a guess, from the shape of my high north window, seen outside, that my place was a studio and that as a studio it would contain an artist. He had wandered to England in search of fortune, like other itinerants, and had embarked, with a partner and a small green hand-cart, on the sale of penny ices. The ices had melted away and the partner had dissolved in their train. My young man wore tight yellow trousers with reddish stripes and his name was Oronte. He was sallow but fair, and when I put him into some old clothes of my own he looked like an Englishman. He was as good as Miss Churm, who could look, when requested, like an Italian.

4

I thought Mrs. Monarch's face slightly convulsed when, on her coming back with her husband, she found Oronte installed. It was strange to have to recognise in a scrap of a lazzarone a competitor to her magnificent Major. It was she who scented danger first, for the Major was anecdotically unconscious. But Oronte gave us tea, with a hundred eager confusions—he had never been concerned in so queer a process—and I think she thought better of me for having at last an "establishment." They saw a couple of drawings that I had made of the establishment, and Mrs. Monarch hinted that it never would have struck her he had sat for them.

"Now the drawings you make from *us*, they look exactly like us," she reminded me, smiling in triumph; and I recognised that this was indeed just their defect. When I drew the Monarchs I couldn't anyhow get away from them—get into the character I wanted to represent; and I hadn't the least desire my model should be discoverable in my picture. Miss Churm never was, and Mrs. Monarch thought I hid her, very properly, because she was vulgar; whereas if she was lost it was only as the dead who got to heaven are lost—in the gain of an angel the more.

By this time I had got a certain start with "Rutland Ramsay," the first novel in the great projected series; that is I had produced a dozen drawings, several with the help of the Major and his wife, and I had sent them in for approval. My understanding with the publishers, as I have already hinted, had been that I was to be left to do my work, in this particular case, as I liked, with the whole book committed to me; but my connexion with the rest of the series was only contingent. There were moments when, frankly, it *was* a comfort to have the real thing under one's hand; for there were characters in "Rutland Ramsay" that were very much like it. There were people presumably as erect as the Major and women of as good a fashion as Mrs. Monarch. There was a great deal of country-house life—treated, it is true, in a fine fanciful ironical generalised way—and there was a considerable implication of knickerbockers and kilts. There were certain things I had to settle at the outset; such things for instance as the exact appearance of the hero and the particular bloom and figure of the heroine. The author of course gave me a lead, but there was a margin for interpretation. I took the Monarchs into my confidence, I told them frankly what I was about, I mentioned my embarrassments and alternatives. "Oh take *him*!" Mrs. Monarch murmured sweetly, looking at her husband; and "What could you want better than my wife?" the Major enquired with the comfortable candour that now prevailed between us.

I wasn't obliged to answer these remarks—I was only obliged to place my sitters. I wasn't easy in mind, and I postponed a little timidly perhaps the solving of my question. The book was a large canvas, the other figures were numerous, and I worked off at first some of the episodes in which the hero and the heroine were not concerned. When once I had set *them* up I should have to stick to them—I couldn't make my young man seven feet high in one place and five feet nine in another. I inclined on the whole to the latter measurement, though the Major more than once reminded me that *he* looked about as young as any one. It was indeed quite possible to arrange him, for the figure, so that it would have been difficult to detect his age. After the spontaneous Oronte had been with me a month, and after I had given him to understand several times over that his native exuberance would presently constitute an insurmountable barrier to our further intercourse, I waked to a sense of his heroic capacity. He was only five feet seven, but the remaining inches were latent. I tried him almost secretly at first, for I was really rather afraid of the judgement my other models would pass on such a choice. If they regarded

Miss Churm as little better than a snare what would they think of the representation by a person so little the real thing as an Italian street-vendor of a protagonist formed by a public school?

If I went a little in fear of them it wasn't because they bullied me, because they had got an oppressive foothold, but because in their really pathetic decorum and mysteriously permanent newness they counted on me so intensely. I was therefore very glad when Jack Hawley came home: he was always of such good counsel. He painted badly himself, but there was no one like him for putting his finger on the place. He had been absent from England for a year; he had been somewhere—I don't remember where—to get a fresh eye. I was in a good deal of dread of any such organ, but we were old friends; he had been away for months and a sense of emptiness was creeping into my life. I hadn't dodged a missile for a year.

He came back with a fresh eye, but with the same old black velvet blouse, and the first evening he spent in my studio we smoked cigarettes till the small hours. He had done no work himself, he had only got the eye; so the field was clear for the production of my little things. He wanted to see what I had produced for the *Cheapside*, but he was disappointed in the exhibition. That at least seemed the meaning of two or three comprehensive groans which, as he lounged on my big divan, his leg folded under him, looking at my latest drawings, issued from his lips with the smoke of the cigarette.

"What's the matter with you?" I asked.

"What's the matter with *you*?"

"Nothing save that I'm mystified."

"You are indeed. You're quite off the hinge. What's the meaning of this new fad?" And he tossed me, with visible irreverence, a drawing in which I happened to have depicted both my elegant models. I asked if he didn't think it good, and he replied that it struck him as execrable, given the sort of thing I had always represented myself to him as wishing to arrive at; but I let that pass—I was so anxious to see exactly what he meant. The two figures in the picture looked colossal, but I supposed this was *not* what he meant, inasmuch as, for aught he knew to the contrary, I might have been trying for some such effect. I maintained that I was working exactly in the same way as when he last had done me the honour to tell me I might do something some day. "Well, there's a screw loose somewhere," he answered; "wait a bit and I'll discover it." I depended upon him to do so: where else was the fresh eye? But he produced at last nothing more luminous than "I don't know—I don't like your types." This was lame for a critic who had never consented to discuss with me anything but the question of execution, the direction of strokes and the mystery of values.

"In the drawings you've been looking at I think my types are very handsome."

"Oh they won't do!"

"I've been working with new models."

"I see you have. *They* won't do."

"Are you very sure of that?"

"Absolutely—they're stupid."

"You mean *I* am—for I ought to get round that."

"You *can't*—with such people. Who are they?"

I told him, so far as was necessary, and he concluded heartlessly: *"Ce sont des gens qu'il faut mettre à la porte."*

"You've never seen them; they're awfully good"—I flew to their defence.

"Not seen them? Why all this recent work of yours drops to pieces with them. It's all I want to see of them."

"No one else has said anything against it—the *Cheapside* people are pleased."

"Every one else is an ass, and the *Cheapside* people the biggest asses of all. Come, don't pretend at this time of day to have pretty illusions about the public, especially about publishers and editors. It's not for *such* animals you work—it's for those you know, *coloro che sanno*; so keep straight for *me* if you can't keep straight for yourself. There was a certain sort of thing you used to try for—and a very good thing it was. But this twaddle isn't *in* it." When I talked with Hawley later about "Rutland Ramsay" and its possible successors he declared that I must get back into my boat again or I should go to the bottom. His voice in short was the voice of warning.

I noted the warning, but I didn't turn my friends out of doors. They bored me a good deal; but the very fact that they bored me admonished me not to sacrifice them—if there was anything to be done with them—simply to irritation. As I look back at this phase they seem to me to have pervaded my life not a little. I have a vision of them as most of the time in my studio, seated against the wall on an old velvet bench to be out of the way, and resembling the while a pair of patient courtiers in a royal ante-chamber. I'm convinced that during the coldest weeks of the winter they held their ground because it saved them fire. Their newness was losing its gloss, and it was impossible not to feel them objects of charity. Whenever Miss Churm arrived they went away, and after I was fairly launched in "Rutland Ramsay" Miss Churm arrived pretty often. They managed to express to me tacitly that they supposed I wanted her for the low life of the book, and I let them suppose it, since they had attempted to study the work—it was lying about the studio—without discovering that it dealt only with the highest circles. They had dipped into the most brilliant of our novelists without deciphering many passages. I still took an hour from them, now and again, in spite of Jack Hawley's warning: it would be time enough to dismiss them, if dismissal should be necessary, when the rigour of the season was over. Hawley had made their acquaintance—he had met them at my fireside—and thought them a ridiculous pair. Learning that he was a painter they tried to approach him, to show him too that they were the real thing; but he looked at them, across the big room, as if they were miles away: they were a compendium of everything he most objected to in the social system of his country. Such people as that, all convention and patent-leather, with ejaculations that stopped conversation, had no business in a studio. A studio was a place to learn to see, and how could you see through a pair of feather-beds?

The main inconvenience I suffered at their hands was that at first I was shy of letting it break upon them that my artful little servant had begun to sit to me for "Rutland Ramsay." They knew I had been odd enough—they were prepared by this time to allow oddity to artists—to pick a foreign vagabond out of the streets when I might have had a person with whiskers and credentials; but it was some time before they learned how high I rated his accomplishments. They found him in an attitude more than once, but they never doubted I was doing him as an organ-grinder. There were several things they never guessed, and one of them was that for a striking scene in the novel, in which a footman briefly figured, it occurred to me to make use of Major Monarch as the menial. I kept putting this off, I didn't like to ask him to don the livery—besides the difficulty of finding a livery to fit him. At last, one day late in the winter, when I was at work on the despised Oronte, who caught one's idea on the wing, and was in the glow of feeling myself go very straight, they came in, the Major and his wife, with their society laugh about nothing (there was less and less to laugh at); came in like country-callers—they always reminded me of that—who have walked across the park after church and are presently persuaded to stay to luncheon. Luncheon was over, but they could stay to tea—I knew they wanted it. The fit was on me, however, and I couldn't let my ardour cool and my work wait, with the fading daylight, while my model prepared it. So I asked Mrs. Monarch if she would mind laying it out—a request which for an instant brought all the blood to her face. Her eyes were on her husband's for a second, and some mute telegraphy passed between them. Their folly was over the next instant; his cheerful shrewdness put an end to it. So far from pitying their wounded pride, I must add, I was moved to give it as complete a lesson as I could. They bustled about together and got out the cups and saucers and made the kettle boil. I know they felt as if they were waiting on my servant, and when the tea was prepared I said: "He'll have a cup, please—he's tired." Mrs. Monarch brought him one where he stood, and he took it from her as if he had been a gentleman at a party squeezing a crush-hat with an elbow.

Then it came over me that she had made a great effort for me—made it with a kind of nobleness—and that I owed her a compensation. Each time I saw her after this I wondered what the compensation could be. I couldn't go on doing the wrong thing to oblige them. Oh it *was* the wrong thing, the stamp of the work for which they sat—Hawley was not the only person to say it now. I sent in a large number of the drawings I had made for "Rutland Ramsay," and I received a warning that was more to the point than Hawley's. The artistic adviser of the house for which I was working was of opinion that many of my illustrations were not what had been looked for. Most of these illustrations were the subjects in which the Monarchs had figured. Without going into the question of what *had* been looked for, I had to face the fact that at this rate I shouldn't get the other books to do. I hurled myself in despair on Miss Churm—I put her through all her paces. I not only adopted Oronte publicly as my hero, but one morning when the Major looked in to see if I didn't require him to finish a *Cheapside* figure for which he had begun to sit the week before, I told him I had changed my mind—I'd do the drawing from my man. At this my visitor turned pale and stood looking at me. "Is *he* your idea of an English gentleman?" he asked.

I was disappointed, I was nervous, I wanted to get on with my work; so I replied with irritation: "Oh my dear Major—I can't be ruined for *you!*"

It was a horrid speech, but he stood another moment—after which, without a word, he quitted the studio. I drew a long breath, for I said to myself that I shouldn't see him again. I hadn't told him definitely that I was in danger of having my work rejected, but I was vexed at his not having felt the catastrophe in the air, read with me the moral of our fruitless collaboration, the lesson that in the deceptive atmosphere of art even the highest respectability may fail of being plastic.

I didn't owe my friends money, but I did see them again. They reappeared together three days later, and, given all the other facts, there was something tragic in that one. It was a clear proof they could find nothing else in life to do. They had threshed the matter out in a dismal conference—they had digested the bad news that they were not in for the series. If they weren't useful to me even for the *Cheapside* their function seemed difficult to determine, and I could only judge at first that they had come, forgivingly, decorously, to take a last leave. This made me rejoice in secret that I had little leisure for a scene; for I had placed both my other models in position together and I was pegging away at a drawing from which I hoped to derive glory. It had been suggested by the passage in which Rutland Ramsay, drawing up a chair to Artemisia's piano-stool, says extraordinary things to her while she ostensibly fingers out a difficult piece of music. I had done Miss Churm at the piano before—it was an attitude in which she knew how to take on an absolutely poetic grace. I wished the two figures to "compose" together with intensity, and my little Italian had entered perfectly into my conception. The pair were vividly before me, the piano had been pulled out; it was a charming show of blended youth and murmured love, which I had only to catch and keep. My visitors stood and looked at it, and I was friendly to them over my shoulder.

They made no response, but I was used to silent company and went on with my work, only a little disconcerted—even though exhilarated by the sense that *this* was at least the ideal thing—at not having got rid of them after all. Presently I heard Mrs. Monarch's sweet voice beside or rather above me: "I wish her hair were a little better done." I looked up and she was staring with a strange fixedness at Miss Churm, whose back was turned to her. "Do you mind my just touching it?" she went on—a question which made me spring up for an instant as with the instinctive fear that she might do the young lady a harm. But she quieted me with a glance I shall never forget—I confess I should like to have been able to paint *that*—and went for a moment to my model. She spoke to her softly, laying a hand on her shoulder and bending over her; and as the girl, understanding, gratefully assented, she disposed her rough curls, with a few quick passes, in such a way as to make Miss Churm's head twice as charming. It was one of the most heroic personal services I've ever seen rendered. Then Mrs. Monarch turned away with a low sigh and, looking about her as if for something to do, stooped to the floor with a noble humility and picked up a dirty rag that had dropped out of my paint-box.

The Major meanwhile had also been looking for something to do, and, wandering to the other end of the studio, saw before him my breakfast-things neglected, unremoved. "I say, can't I be useful *here?*" he called out to me with an irrepressible quaver. I assented with a laugh that I fear was awkward, and for the next ten minutes, while I worked, I heard the light clatter of china and the tinkle of spoons and glass. Mrs. Monarch assisted her husband—they washed up my crockery, they put it away. They wandered off into my little scullery, and I afterwards found that they had cleaned my knives and that my slender stock of plate had an unprecedented surface. When it came over me, the latent eloquence of what they were doing, I confess that my drawing was blurred for a moment—the picture swam. They had accepted their failure, but they couldn't accept their fate. They had bowed their heads in bewilderment to the perverse and cruel law in virtue of which the real thing could be so much less precious than the unreal; but they didn't want to starve. If my servants were my models, then my models might be my servants. They would reverse the parts—the others would sit for the ladies and gentlemen and *they* would do the work. They would still be in the studio—it was an intense dumb appeal to me not to turn them out. "Take us on," they wanted to say—"we'll do *anything*."

My pencil dropped from hand; my sitting was spoiled and I got rid of my sitters who were also evidently rather mystified and awestruck. Then, alone with the Major and his wife I had a most uncomfortable moment. He put their prayer into a single sentence: "I say, you know—just let *us* do for you, can't you?" I couldn't—it was dreadful to see them emptying my slops; but I pretended I could, to oblige them, for about a week. Then I gave them a sum of money to go away, and I never saw them again. I obtained the remaining books, but my friend Hawley repeats that Major and Mrs. Monarch did me a permanent harm, got me into false ways. If it be true I'm content to have paid the price—for the memory.

Exercises
1. *What are the functions of Miss Churm and Oronte?*

2. *Cite a few examples of irony that shed light on meaning.*

3. *What forces are in conflict?*

4. *What does Jack Hawley represent?*

5. *How does the narrator compromise himself as artist?*

6. *What does the concluding sentence reveal?*

7. *In what artistic sense is the "unreal" more desirable than "the real thing"? State the theme.*

8. *Read the following excerpts and comment on James's diction and syntax.*

(a) I was so amused by them that, to get more of it, I did my best to take their point of view; and though it was an embarrassment to find myself appraising physically, as if they were animals on hire or useful blacks, a pair whom I should have expected to meet only in one of the relations in which criticism is tacit, I looked at Mrs. Monarch judicially enough to be able to exclaim after a moment with conviction: "Oh yes, a lady in a book!" She was singularly like a bad illustration.

(b) "their type, the Monarchs', *quoi!* of a breeched and bewigged age."

(c) "portmanteaux"; "omnibus"; "blowsy"; "profils perdus"; "appurtenances"; "circumlocution"; "coloro che sanno."

Topics for
Writing
1. *Formulate an artistic theory based exclusively on the facts, details, and events in "The Real Thing."*

2. *Write an essay contrasting the styles of Hemingway and James.*

Selected
Bibliography

Henry James

Andreas, Osborn. *Henry James and the Expanding Horizon: A Study of the Meaning and Basic Themes of James's Fiction.* Seattle: University of Washington Press, 1948.
Beach, Joseph Warren. *The Method of Henry James.* Enl. and

corr. ed. Philadelphia: Albert Saifer: Publisher, 1954.
(Originally published 1918.)

Berkelman, Robert. "Henry James' 'The Real Thing.'"
University of Kansas City Review, 26 (1960), 121–126.

Daiches, David. "Sensibility and Technique: Preface to a
Critique." *Kenyon Review*, 5 (1943), 569–579.

Dupee, Frederick W., ed. *The Question of Henry James: A
Collection of Critical Essays.* New York: Holt, Rinehart
and Winston, 1945.

————. *Henry James.* New York: William Sloane Associates,
1951. (Rev. ed. Garden City, N.Y.: Doubleday, 1956.)

Edel, Leon. *Henry James.* 5 vols. Philadelphia: J. P. Lippin-
cott, 1953–1969.

Gale, Robert L. *The Caught Image: Figurative Language in the
Fiction of Henry James.* Chapel Hill: University of North
Carolina Press, 1964.

Jefferson, D. W. *Henry James and the Modern Reader.* New
York: St. Martin's Press, 1964, pp. 146–163.

Labor, Earle. "James' 'The Real Thing': Three Levels of
Meaning." *College English*, 23 (1962), 376–378.

Lainoff, Seymour. "A Note on Henry James' 'The Real
Thing.'" *Modern Language Notes*, 71 (1956), 192–193.

McCarthy, Harold T. *Henry James: The Creative Process.* New
York: Thomas Yoseloff, 1958.

Matthiessen, F. O. *Henry James: The Major Phase.* New
York: Oxford University Press, 1944.

Munson, Gorham. "The Real Thing: A Parable for Writers
of Fiction." *University of Kansas City Review*, 16 (1950),
261–264.

Reilly, Robert J. "Henry James and the Morality of Fiction."
American Literature, 39 (1967), 1–30.

Short, R. W. "The Sentence Structure of Henry James."
American Literature, 18 (1946), 71–88.

Stone, Edward. *The Battle and the Books: Some Aspects of Henry
James.* Athens: Ohio University Press, 1964.

Vaid, Krishna Baldev. *Technique in the Tales of Henry James.*
Cambridge, Mass.: Harvard University Press, 1964.

Ward, J. A. *The Imagination of Disaster: Evil in the Fiction of
Henry James.* Lincoln: University of Nebraska Press,
1961.

Eudora Welty *(1909-   )*

Born in Jackson, Mississippi, where she still resides, she attended Mississippi State College for Women, the University of Wisconsin, and Columbia University. For brief periods she worked in radio, advertising, and journalism. Although best known for her short stories, which have appeared in such magazines as Harper's Bazaar, *the* Southern Review, *and the* Atlantic Monthly, *she received the Pulitzer Prize (1973) for her novel* The Optimist's Daughter.

A Worn Path

It was December—a bright frozen day in the early morning. Far out in the country there was an old Negro woman with her head tied in a red rag, coming along a path through the pinewoods. Her name was Phoenix Jackson. She was very old and small and she walked slowly in the dark pine shadows, moving a little from side to side in her steps, with the balanced heaviness and lightness of a pendulum in a grandfather clock. She carried a thin, small cane made from an umbrella, and with this she kept tapping the frozen earth in front of her. This made a grave and persistent noise in the still air, that seemed meditative, like the chirping of a solitary little bird.

She wore a dark striped dress reaching down to her shoetops, and an equally long apron of bleached sugar sacks, with a full pocket; all neat and tidy, but every time she took a step she might have fallen over her shoe-laces, which dragged from her unlaced shoes. She looked straight ahead. Her eyes were blue with age. Her skin had a pattern all its own of numberless branching wrinkles and as though a whole little tree stood in the middle of her forehead, but a golden color ran underneath, and the two knobs of her cheeks were illuminated by a yellow burning under the dark. Under the red rag her hair came down on her neck in the frailest of ringlets, still black, and with an odor like copper.

Now and then there was a quivering in the thicket. Old Phoenix said, "Out of my way, all you foxes, owls, beetles, jack rabbits, coons, and wild animals! . . . Keep out from under these feet, little bobwhites. . . . Keep the big wild hogs out of my path. Don't let none of those come running my direction. I got a long way." Under her small black-freckled hand her cane, limber as a buggy whip, would switch at the brush as if to rouse up any hiding things.

On she went. The woods were deep and still. The sun

made the pine needles almost too bright to look at, up where the wind rocked. The cones dropped as light as feathers. Down in the hollow was the mourning dove—it was not too late for him.

The path ran up a hill. "Seems like there is chains about my feet, time I get this far," she said, in the voice of argument old people keep to use with themselves. "Something always take a hold on his hill—pleads I should stay."

After she got to the top she turned and gave a full, severe look behind her where she had come. "Up through pines," she said at length. "Now down through oaks."

Her eyes opened their widest and she started down gently. But before she got to the bottom of the hill a bush caught her dress.

Her fingers were busy and intent, but her skirts were full and long, so that before she could pull them free in one place they were caught in another. It was not possible to allow the dress to tear. "I in the thorny bush," she said. "Thorns, you doing your appointed work. Never want to let folks pass—no sir. Old eyes thought you was a pretty little green bush."

Finally, trembling all over, she stood free, and after a moment dared to stoop for her cane.

"Sun so high!" she cried, leaning back and looking, while the thick tears went over her eyes. "The time getting all gone here."

At the foot of this hill was a place where a log was laid across the creek.

"Now comes the trial," said Phoenix.

Putting her right foot out, she mounted the log and shut her eyes. Lifting her skirt, levelling her cane fiercely before her, like a festival figure in some parade, she began to march across. Then she opened her eyes and she was safe on the other side.

"I wasn't as old as I thought," she said.

But she sat down to rest. She spread her skirts on the bank around her and folded her hands over her knees. Up above her was a tree in a pearly cloud of mistletoe. She did not dare to close her eyes, and when a little boy brought her a little plate with a slice of marble-cake on it she spoke to him. "That would be acceptable," she said. But when she went to take it there was just her own hand in the air.

So she left that tree, and had to go through a barbed-wire fence. There she had to creep and crawl, spreading her knees and stretching her fingers like a baby trying to climb the steps. But she talked loudly to herself: she could not let her dress be torn now, so late in the day, and she could not pay for having her arm or her leg sawed off if she got caught fast where she was.

At last she was safe through the fence and risen up out in the clearing. Big dead trees, like black men with one arm, were standing in the purple stalks of the withered cotton field. There sat a buzzard.

"Who you watching?"

In the burrow she made her way along.

"Glad this not the season for bulls," she said, looking sideways, "and the good Lord made his snakes to curl up and sleep in the winter. A pleasure I don't see no two-headed snake coming around that tree, where it come once. It took a while to get by him, back in the summer."

She passed through the old cotton and went into a field of dead corn. It whispered and shook, and was taller than her head. "Through the maze now," she said, for there was no path.

Then there was something tall, black, and skinny there, moving before her.

At first she took it for a man. It could have been a man dancing in the field. But she stood still and listened, and it did not make a sound. It was as silent as a ghost.

"Ghost," she said sharply, "who be you the ghost of? For I have heard of nary death close by."

But there was no answer, only the ragged dancing in the wind.

She shut her eyes, reached out her hand, and touched a sleeve. She found a coat and inside that an emptiness, cold as ice.

"You scarecrow," she said. Her face lighted. "I ought to be shut up for good," she said with laughter. "My senses is gone. I too old. I the oldest people I ever know. Dance, old scarecrow," she said, "while I dancing with you."

She kicked her foot over the furrow, and with mouth drawn down shook her head once or twice in a little strutting way. Some husks blew down and whirled in streamers about her skirts.

Then she went on, parting her way from side to side with the cane, through the whispering field. At last she came to the end, to a wagon track, where the silver grass blew between the red ruts. The quail were walking around like pullets, seeming all dainty and unseen.

"Walk pretty," she said. "This the easy place. This the easy going."

She followed the track, swaying through the quiet bare fields, through the little strings of trees silver in their dead leaves, past cabins silver from weather, with the doors and windows boarded shut, all like old women under a spell sitting there. "I walking in their sleep," she said, nodding her head vigorously.

In a ravine she went where a spring was silently flowing through a hollow log. Old Phoenix bent and drank. "Sweetgum makes the water sweet," she said, and drank more. "Nobody knows who made this well, for it was here when I was born."

The track crossed a swampy part where the moss hung as white as lace from every limb. "Sleep on, alligators, and blow your bubbles." Then the track went into the road.

Deep, deep the road went down between the high green-colored banks. Overhead the live-oaks met, and it was as dark as a cave.

A black dog with a lolling tongue came up out of the weeds by the ditch. She was meditating, and not ready, and when he came at her she only hit him a little with her cane. Over she went in the ditch, like a little puff of milk-weed.

Down there, her senses drifted away. A dream visited her, and she reached her hand up, but nothing reached down and gave her a pull. So she lay there and presently went to talking. "Old woman," she said to herself, "that black dog came up out of the weeds to stall you off, and now there he sitting on his fine tail, smiling at you."

A white man finally came along and found her—a hunter, a young man, with his dog on a chain.

"Well, Granny!" he laughed. "What are you doing there?"

"Lying on my back like a June-bug waiting to be turned over, mister," she said, reaching up her hand.

He lifted her up, gave her a swing in the air, and set her down, "Anything broken, Granny?"

"No sir, them old dead weeds is springy enough," said Phoenix, when she had got her breath. "I thank you for your trouble."

"Where do you live, Granny?" he asked, while the two dogs were growling at each other.

"Away back yonder, sir, behind the ridge. You can't even see it from here."

"On your way home?"

"No, sir, I going to town."

"Why, that's too far! That's as far as I walk when I come out myself, and I get something for my trouble." He patted the stuffed bag he carried, and there hung down a little closed claw. It was one of the bobwhites, with its beak hooked bitterly to show it was dead. "Now you go on home, Granny!"

"I bound to go to town, mister," said Phoenix. "The time come around."

He gave another laugh, filling the whole landscape. "I know you colored people! Wouldn't miss going to town to see Santa Claus!"

But something held Old Phoenix very still. The deep lines in her face went into a fierce and different radiation. Without warning she had seen with her own eyes a flashing nickel fall out of the man's pocket on to the ground.

"How old are you, Granny?" he was saying.

"There is no telling, mister," she said, "no telling."

Then she gave a little cry and clapped her hands, and

said, "Git on away from here, dog! Look! Look at that dog!" She laughed as if in admiration. "He ain't scared of nobody. He a big black dog." She whispered, "Sick him!"

"Watch me get rid of that cur," said the man. "Sick him, Pete! Sick him!"

Phoenix heard the dogs fighting and heard the man running and throwing sticks. She even heard a gunshot. But she was slowly bending forward by that time, further and further forward, the lids stretched down over her eyes, as if she were doing this in her sleep. Her chin was lowered almost to her knees. The yellow palm of her hand came out from the fold of her apron. Her fingers slid down and along the ground under the piece of money with the grace and care they would have in lifting an egg from under a sitting hen. Then she slowly straightened up, she stood erect, and the nickel was in her apron pocket. A bird flew by. Her lips moved. "God watching me the whole time. I come to stealing."

The man came back, and his own dog panted about them. "Well, I scared him off that time," he said, and then he laughed and lifted his gun and pointed it at Phoenix.

She stood straight and faced him.

"Doesn't the gun scare you?" he said, still pointing it.

"No, sir, I seen plenty go off closer by, in my day, and for less than what I done," she said, holding utterly still.

He smiled, and shouldered the gun. "Well, Granny," he said, "you must be a hundred years old and scared of nothing. I'd give you a dime if I had any money with me. But you take my advice and stay home, and nothing will happen to you."

"I bound to go on my way, mister," said Phoenix. She inclined her head in the red rag. Then they went in different directions, but she could hear the gun shooting again and again over the hill.

She walked on. The shadows hung from the oak trees to the road like curtains. Then she smelled wood-smoke, and smelled the river, and she saw a steeple and the cabins on their steep steps. Dozens of little black children whirled around her. There ahead was Natchez shining. Bells were ringing. She walked on.

In the paved city it was Christmas time. There were red and green electric lights strung and crisscrossed everywhere, and all turned on in the daytime. Old Phoenix would have been lost if she had not distrusted her eyesight and depended on her feet to know where to take her.

She paused quietly on the sidewalk, where people were passing by. A lady came along in the crowd, carrying an armful of red-, green-, and silver-wrapped presents; she gave off perfume like the red roses in hot summer, and Phoenix stopped her.

"Please, missy, will you lace up my shoe?" She held up her foot.

"What do you want, Grandma?"

"See my shoe," said Phoenix. "Do all right for out in the country, but wouldn't look right to go in a big building."

"Stand still then, Grandma," said the lady. She put her packages down carefully on the sidewalk beside her and laced and tied both shoes tightly.

"Can't lace 'em with a cane," said Phoenix. "Thank you, missy. I doesn't mind asking a nice lady to tie up my shoe when I gets out on the street."

Moving slowly and from side to side, she went into the stone building and into a tower of steps, where she walked up and around and around until her feet knew to stop.

She entered a door, and there she saw nailed up on the wall the document that had been stamped with the gold seal and framed in the gold frame which matched the dream that was hung up in her head.

"Here I be," she said. There was a fixed and ceremonial stiffness over her body.

"A charity case, I suppose," said an attendant who sat at the desk before her.

But Phoenix only looked above her head. There was sweat on her face; the wrinkles shone like a bright net.

"Speak up, Grandma," the woman said. "What's your name? We must have your history, you know. Have you been here before? What seems to be the trouble with you?"

Old Phoenix only gave a twitch to her face as if a fly were bothering her.

"Are you deaf?" cried the attendant.

But then the nurse came in.

"Oh, that's just old Aunt Phoenix," she said. "She doesn't come for herself—she has a little grandson. She makes these trips just as regular as clockwork. She lives away back off the Old Natchez Trace." She bent down. "Well, Aunt Phoenix, why don't you just take a seat? We won't keep you standing after your long trip." She pointed.

The old woman sat down, bolt upright in the chair.

"Now, how is the boy?" asked the nurse.

Old Phoenix did not speak.

"I said, how is the boy?"

But Phoenix only waited and stared straight ahead, her face very solemn and withdrawn into rigidity.

"Is his throat any better?" asked the nurse. "Aunt Phoenix, don't you hear me? Is your grandson's throat any better since the last time you came for the medicine?"

With her hand on her knees, the old woman waited, silent, erect and motionless, just as if she were in armor.

"You mustn't take up our time this way, Aunt Phoenix," the nurse said. "Tell us quickly about your grandson, and get it over. He isn't dead, is he?"

At last there came a flicker and then a flame of comprehension across her face, and she spoke.

"My grandson. It was my memory had left me. There I sat and forgot why I made my long trip."

"Forgot?" The nurse frowned. "After you came so far?"

Then Phoenix was like an old woman begging a dignified forgiveness for waking up frightened in the night. "I never did go to school—I was too old at the Surrender," she said in a soft voice. "I'm an old woman without an education. It was my memory fail me. My little grandson, he is just the same, and I forgot it in the coming."

"Throat never heals, does it?" said the nurse, speaking in a loud, sure voice to Old Phoenix. By now she had a card with something written on it, a little list. "Yes. Swallowed lye. When was it—January—two—three years ago—"

Phoenix spoke unasked now. "No, missy, he not dead, he just the same. Every little while his throat begin to close up again, and he not able to swallow. He not get his breath. He not able to help himself. So the time come around, and I go on another trip for the soothing-medicine."

"All right. The doctor said as long as you came to get it you could have it," said the nurse. "But it's an obstinate case."

"My little grandson, he sit up there in the house all wrapped up, waiting by himself," Phoenix went on. "We is the only two left in the world. He suffer and it don't seem to put him back at all. He got a sweet look. He going to last. He wear a little patch quilt and peep out, holding his mouth open like a little bird. I remembers so plain now. I not going to forget him again, no, the whole enduring time. I could tell him from all the others in creation."

"All right." The nurse was trying to hush her now. She brought her a bottle of medicine. "Charity," she said, making a check mark in a book.

Old Phoenix held the bottle close to her eyes and then carefully put it into her pocket.

"I thank you," she said.

"It's Christmas time, Grandma," said the attendant. "Could I give you a few pennies out of my purse?"

"Five pennies is a nickel," said Phoenix stiffly.

"Here's a nickel," said the attendant.

Phoenix rose carefully and held out her hand. She received the nickel and then fished the other nickel out of her pocket and laid it beside the new one. She stared at her palm closely, with her head on one side.

Then she gave a tap with her cane on the floor.

"This is what come to me to do," she said. "I going to the store and buy my child a little windmill they sells, made out of paper. He going to find it hard to believe there such a thing in the world. I'll march myself back where he waiting, holding it straight up in this hand.''

She lifted her free hand, gave a little nod, turned round, and walked out of the doctor's office. Then her slow step began on the stairs, going down.

Exercises

1. *What is the protagonist's goal? What is the conflict?*

2. *Enumerate the various crises that threaten Phoenix along her journey and tell what they reveal about her character.*

3. *Comment on several aspects of Eudora Welty's style.*

4. *How does Phoenix's capacity of self-sacrifice, endurance, and love suggest the theme?*

5. *Along the worn path Phoenix is perceptive, imaginative, courageous, wise, and talkative, but at the clinic she is ceremonially stiff and reticent. What accounts for this change in behavior?*

6. *Discuss the implications of the episode with the hunter.*

7. *Herodotus in his* Histories *reveals the legend of a sacred bird with gold and red plumage named phoenix, which consumes itself by fire and renews itself out of its own ashes to return whole and young again each five hundred years to the Egyptian city of the sun. The mythical bird symbolizes the sun; its rebirth suggests immortality. How then is the black woman an appropriate symbol of the bird phoenix?*

8. *Interpret the Christmas symbolism in the story.*

9. *What is the central theme?*

Topics for Writing

1. *Describe the story's effectiveness as it derives chiefly from a blend of character, setting, and action.*

2. *View Phoenix as a Christ-figure.*

3. *Write an essay citing and discussing several aspects of Miss Welty's style.*

Selected Bibliography

Eudora Welty

Daniel, Robert. ''The World of Eudora Welty.'' *Hopkins Review*, 7 (1953), 49–58.

Glenn, Eunice. "Fantasy in the Fiction of Eudora Welty." *A Southern Vanguard*, ed. Allen Tate. New York: Prentice-Hall, 1947, pp. 78–91.

Hartley, Lodwick. "Proserpina and the Old Ladies." *Modern Fiction Studies*, 3 (1957–58), 350–354.

Hicks, Granville. "Eudora Welty." *College English*, 14 (1952), 69–76. Also in *English Journal*, 41 (1952), 461–468.

Isaacs, Neil D. "Life of Phoenix." *Sewanee Review*, 71 (1963), 75–81.

Jones, William M. "Name and Symbol in the Prose of Eudora Welty." *Southern Folklore Quarterly*, 22 (1958), 173–185.

Rubin, Louis D., Jr. "Two Ladies of the South." *Sewanee Review*, 63 (1955), 671–681.

Vande Kieft, Ruth M. *Eudora Welty*. New York: Twayne Publishers, 1962.

Warren, Robert Penn. "The Love and the Separateness in Miss Welty." *Kenyon Review*, 6 (1944), 246–259.

Welty, Eudora. "How I Write." *Virginia Quarterly*, 31 (1955), 240–251.

Other Stories to Read

Charles Waddell Chestnutt
(1856–1932)

The Goophered Grapevine

We alighted from the buggy, walked about the yard for a while, and then wandered off into the adjoining vineyard. Upon Annie's complaining of weariness I led the way back to the yard, where a pine log lying under the spreading elm afforded a shady though somewhat hard seat. One end of the log was already occupied by a venerable-looking colored man. He held on his knees a hat full of grapes, over which he was smacking his lips with great gusto; and a pile of grapeskins near him indicated that the performance was no new thing. We approached him at an angle from the rear, and were close to him before he perceived us. He respectfully rose as we drew near, and was moving away, when I begged him to keep his seat.

"Don't let us disturb you," I said. "There is plenty of room for us all."

He resumed his seat with some embarrassment. While he had been standing, I had observed that he was a tall man, and though slightly bowed by the weight of years, apparently quite vigorous. He was not entirely black, and this fact, together with the quality of his hair, which was about six inches long and very bushy, except on the top of his head, where he was quite bald, suggested a slight strain of other than Negro blood. There was a shrewdness in his eyes, too, which was not altogether African, and which, as we afterwards learned from experience, was indicative of a corresponding shrewdness in his character. He went on eating his grapes, but did not seem to enjoy himself quite so well as he had apparently done before he became aware of our presence.

"Do you live around here?" I asked, anxious to put him at his ease.

"Yas, suh, I lives des ober yander, behine de nex' san'hill, on de Lumberton plank-road."

"Do you know anything about the time when this vineyard was cultivated?"

"Lawd bless you, suh, I knows all about it. Dey ain' na'er a man in dis settlement w'at won' tell you ole Julius McAdoo 'uz bawn en raise' on dis yer same plantation. Is you de Norv'n gemman w'at's gwine ter buy de ole vimya'd?"

"I am looking at it," I replied; "but I dont know that I shall care to buy unless I can be reasonably sure of making something out of it."

"Well, suh, you is a stranger ter me, en I is a stranger to you, en we is bofe strangers ter one anudder, but 'f I 'uz in yo' place, I wouldn't buy dis vimya'd."

"Why not?" I asked.

"Well, I dunno whe'r you b'lieves in conj'in' er not—some er de w'ite folks don't, er says dey don't—but de truf er de matter is dat dis yer ole vimya'd is goophered."

"Is what?" I asked, not grasping the meaning of this unfamiliar word.

"Is goophered—cunju'd, bewitch'."

He imparted this information with such solemn earnestness and with such an air of confidential mystery that I felt somewhat interested, while Annie was evidently much impressed, and drew closer to me.

"How do you know it is bewitched?" I asked.

"I wouldn' spec' fer you ter b'lieve me 'less you know all 'bout de fac's. But ef you en young miss dere doan' min' lis'nin' ter a ole nigger run on a minute er two w'ile you er restin', I kin 'spain to you how it all happen'."

We assured him that we would be glad to hear how it all happened, and he began to tell us. At first the current of his memory—or imagination—seemed somewhat sluggish; but as his embarrassment wore off, his language flowed more freely, and the story acquired perspective and coherence. As he became more and more absorbed in the narrative, his eyes assumed a dreamy expression, and he seemed to lose sight of his auditors, and to be living over again in monologue his life on the old plantation.

"Ole Mars Dugul' McAdoo," he began, "bought dis place long many years befo' de wah, en I 'member well w'en he sot out all dis yer part er de plantation in scuppernon's. De vimes growed monst'us fas', en Mars Dugal' made a thousan' gallon er scuppernon' wine eve'y year.

"Now, ef dey's an'thing a nigger lub, nex' ter 'possum, en chick'n, en watermillyums, it's scuppernon's. Dey ain' nuffin dat kin stan' up side'n de scuppernon' fer sweetness; sugar aint a suckumstance ter scuppernon'. W'en de season is nigh 'bout ober, an de grapes begin ter swivel up des a little wid de wrinkles er ole age—we'n de skin git sof' en brown—den de scuppernon' make you smack yo' lip en roll yo' eye en wush fer mo'; so I reckon it ain' very 'stonishin' dat niggers lub scuppernon'.

"Dey wuz a sight er niggers in de naberhood er de vimya'd. Dere wuz ole Mars Henry Brayboy's niggers, en ole Mars Jeems McLean's niggers, en Mars Dugal's own niggers; den dey wuz a settlement er free niggers en po' buckrahs down by de Wim'l'ton Road, en Mars Dugal' had de only vimya'd in de naberhood. I reckon it ain' so much so nowadays, but befo' de wah, in slab'ry times, a nigger didn' mine goin' fi' er ten miles in a night w'en dey wuz sump'n good ter eat at de yuther een'.

"So atter a w'ile Mars Dugal' begin ter miss his scuppernon's. Co'se he 'cuse' de niggers er it, but dey all 'nied it ter de las'. Mars Dugal' sot spring guns en steel traps, en he en de oberseah sot up nights once't or twice't, tel one night Mars Dugal'—he 'uz a monst'us keerless man—got his leg shot full er cow-peas. But somehow er nudder dey couldn' nebber ketch none er de niggers. I dunner how it happen, but it happen des like I tell you, en de grapes kep' on a-goin' des de same.

"But bimeby ole Mars Dugal' fix' up a plan ter stop it. Dey wuz a cunjuh 'oman livin' down 'mongs' de free niggers on de Wim'l'ton Road, en all de darkies fum Rockfish ter Beaver Crick wuz feared er her. She could wuk de mos' powerfulles' kin' er goopher—could make people hab fits, er rheumatiz', er mak 'em des dwinel away en die; en dey say she went out ridin' de niggers at night, fer she wuz a witch 'sides bein' a cunjuh 'oman. Mars Dugal' hearn 'bout Aun' Peggy's doin's, en begun ter 'flect whe'r er no he couldn't git her ter he'p him keep de niggers off'n de grapevimes. One day in de spring er de year, ole miss pack' up a basket er chick'n en poun'cake, en a bottle er scuppernon' wine, en Mars Dugal' tuk it in his buggy en driv over ter Aun' Peggy's cabin. He tuk de basket in, en had a long talk wid Aun' Peggy.

"De nex' day Aun' Peggy come up ter de vimya'd. De niggers seed her slippin' 'round, en dey soon foun' out what she 'uz doin' dere. Mars Dugal' had hi'ed her ter goopher de grapevimes. She sa'ntered 'roun' 'mongs' de vimes, en tuk a leaf fum dis one, en a grape-hull fum dat one, en den a little twig fum here, en a little pinch er dirt fum dere—en put it all in a big black bottle, wid a snake's toof en a speckle hen's gall en some ha'rs fum a black cat's tail, en den fill' de bottle wid scuppernon' wine. W'en she got de goopher all ready en fix', she tuk 'n went out in de woods en buried it under de root uv a red oak tree, en den come back en tole one er de niggers she done goopher de grapevimes, en a'er a nigger w'at eat dem grapes 'ud be sho ter die inside'n twel' mont's.

"Atter dat de niggers let de scuppernon's 'lone, en Mars Dugal' didn' hab no 'casion ter fine no mo' fault; en de season wuz mos' gone, w'en a strange gemman stop at de plantation one night ter see Mars Dugal' on some business; en his coachman, seein' de scuppernon's growing so nice en sweet, slip 'roun' behine de smoke-house en et all de scuppernon's he could hole. Nobody didn' notice it at de time, but dat night, on de way home, de gemman's hoss runned away en kill' de coachman. W'en we hearn de noos, Aun' Lucy, de cook, she up'n say she seed de strange nigger eat'n' er de scuppernon's behine de smoke-house; en den we knowed de goopher had be'en er wukkin'. Den one er de nigger chilluns runned away fum de quarters one day, en got in de scuppernon's, en died de nex' week. White folks say he die' er de fevuh, but de niggers knowed it wuz de goopher. So you k'n be sho de darkies didn' hab much ter do wid dem scuppernon' vimes.

"W'en de scuppernon' season 'uz ober fer dat year, Mars Dugal' foun' he had made fifteen hund'ed gallon er wine; en one er de niggers hearn him laffin' wid de oberseah fit ter kill, en sayin' dem fifteen hund'ed gallon er wine wuz monst'us good intrus' on de ten dollars he laid out on de vimya'd. So I 'low ez he paid Aun' Peggy ten dollars fer to goopher de grapevimes.

"De goopher didn' wuk no mo' tel de nex summer, w'en 'long to'ds de middle er de season one er de fiel' han's died; en ez dat lef' Mars Dugal' sho't er han's, he went off ter town fer ter buy anudder. He fotch de noo nigger home wid 'im. He wuz er ole nigger, er de color er a gingy-cake, en ball ez a hossaple on de top er his head. He wuz a peart ole nigger, do', en could do a big day's wuk.

"Now it happen dat one er de niggers on de nex' plantation, one er ole Mars Henry Brayboy's niggers, had runned away de day befo', en tuk ter de swamp, en ole Mars Dugal' en some er de yether nabor w'ite folks had gone out wid dere guns en dere dogs fer ter he'p 'em hunt fer de nigger; en de han's on our own plantation wuz all so flusterated dat we fuhgot ter tell de noo han' 'bout de goopher on de scuppernon' vimes. Co'se he smell de grapes en see de vimes, an atter dahk de fus' thing he done wuz ter slip off ter de grapevimes 'doubt sayin' nuffin ter nobody. Nex' mawnin' he tole some er de niggers 'bout de fine bait er scuppernon' he et de night befo'.

"W'en dey tole 'im 'bout de goopher on de grapevines, he 'uz dat tarrified dat he turn pale, en look des like he gwine ter die right in his tracks. De oberseah come up en axed w'at 'uz de matter; en w'en dey tole 'im Henry been eatin' er de scuppernon's, en got de goopher on 'im, he gin Henry a big drink er w'iskey, en 'low dat de nex' rainy day he take 'im ober ter Aun' Peggy's, en see ef she wouldn' take de goopher off'n him, seein' ez he didnt know nuffin' erbout it tel he done et de grapes.

"Sho nuff, it rain de nex' day, en de oberseah went ober ter Aun' Peggy's wid Henry. En Aun' Peggy say dat bein' ez Henry didn' know 'bout de goopher, en et de grapes in ign'ance er de conseq'ences, she reckon she mought be able ter take de goopher off'n him. So she fotch out er bottle wid some cunjuh medicine in it, en po'd some out in a go'd fer Henry ter drink. He manage ter git it down; he say it tas'e like w'iskey wid sump'in bitter in it. She 'lowed dat 'ud keep de goopher off'n him tel de spring; but w'en de sap begin ter rise in de grapevimes he ha' ter come en see her ag'in, en she tell him w'at he's ter do.

"Nex' spring, w'en de sap commence' ter rise in de scuppernon' vime, Henry tuk a ham one night. Whar'd he git de ham? *I* doan know; dey wa'n't no hams on de plantation 'cep'n w'at 'uz in de smokehouse, but *I* never see Henry 'bout de smokehouse. But ez I wuz a-sayin', he tuk de ham ober ter Aun' Peggy's; en Aun' Peggy tole 'im dat w'en Mars Dugal' begin ter prune de grapevimes, he must go en take 'n scrape off de sap what it ooze ou'n de cut een's er de vimes, en 'n'int his ball head wid it; en ef he do dat once't a year de goopher wouldn't wuk agin 'im long ez he done it. En bein' ez he fotch her de ham, she fix' it so he kin eat all de scuppernon' he want.

"So Henry 'n'int his head wid de sap out'n de big grapevime des ha'w way 'twix de quarters en de big house, en de goopher nebber wuk agin him dat summer. But the beatenes' thing you eber see happen ter Henry. Up ter dat time he wuz ez ball ez a sweeten' 'tater, but des ez soon ez de young leaves begun ter come out on de grapevimes, de ha'r begun ter grew out on Henry's head, en by de middle er de summer he had de bigges' head er ha'r on de plantation. Befo' dat, Henry had tol'able good ha'r 'roun' de aidges, but soon ez de young grapes begun ter come, Henry's ha'r begun to quirl all up in little balls, des like dis yer reg'lar grapy ha'r, en by de time de grapes got ripe his head look des like a bunch er grapes. Combin' it didn' do no good; he wuk at it ha'f de night wid er Jim Crow, en think he git it straighten' out, but in de mawnin' de grapes 'ud be dere des de same. So he gin it up, en tried ter keep de grapes down by havin' his ha'r cut sho't.

"But dat wa'n't de quares' thing 'bout de goopher. When Henry come ter de plantation, he wuz gittin' a little ole and stiff in de j'ints. But dat summer he got des ez spry en libely ez any young nigger on de plantation; fac', he got so biggity dat Mars Jackson, de oberseah, ha' ter th'eaten ter whip 'im ef he didn' stop cuttin' up his didos en behave hisse'f. But de mos cur'ouses' thing happen' in de fall, when de sap begin ter go down in de grapevimes. Fus, when de grapes 'uz gethered, de knots begun ter straighten out'n Henry's ha'r; en w'en de leaves begin ter fall, Henry's har commence' ter drap out; en when de vimes 'uz bar, Henry's head wuz baller'n it wuz in de spring, en he begin ter git ole en stiff in de j'ints ag'in, en paid no mo' 'tention ter de gals dyoin' er de whole winter. En nex' spring, w'en he rub de sap on ag'in, he got young ag'in, en so soopl en libely dat none er de young niggers on de plantation couldn' jump, ner dance, ner hoe ez much cotton ez Henry. But in de fall er de year his grapes 'mence' ter straighten out, en his j'ints ter git stiff, en his ha'r drap off, en de rheumatiz begin ter wrastle wid 'im.

"Now, ef you'd 'a' knowed ole Mars Dugal' McAdoo, you'd 'a' knowed dat it ha' ter be a mighty rainy day when he couldn' fine sump'n fer his niggers ter do, en it ha' ter be a mighty little hole he couldn' crawl thoo, en ha'ter be a monst'us cloudy night when a dollar git by him in de dahkness; en w'en he see how Henry git young in de spring en ole in de fall, he 'lowed ter hisse'f ez how he could make mo' money out'n Henry dan by wukkin' him in de cotton-fiel'. 'Long de nex' spring, atter de sap 'mence' ter rise, en Henry 'n'int 'is head en sta'ted for ter git young en soopl, Mars Dugal' up'n tuk Henry ter down, en sole 'im fer fifteen hunder' dollars. Co'se de man w'at bought Henry didn' know nuffin' 'bout de goopher, en Mars Dugal' didn't see no 'casion fer ter tell 'im. Lon to'ds de fall, w'en de sap went down, Henry begin ter git ole ag'in same ez yuzhal, en his noo marster begin ter git skeered les'n he gwine ter lose his fifteen-hunder'-dollar nigger. He sent fer a mighty fine doctor, but de med'cine didn' 'pear ter do no good; de goopher had a good holt. Henry tole de doctor 'bout de goopher, but de doctor des laff at 'im.

"One day in de winter Mars Dugal' went ter town, en wuz santerin' 'long de Main Street, w'en who should he meet but Henry's noo master. Dey said 'Hoddy,' en Mars Dugal' ax 'im ter hab a seegyar; en atter dey run on awhile 'bout de craps en de weather, Mars Dugal' ax 'im, sorter keerless, like ez ef he des thought of it—

"'How you like de nigger I sole you las' spring?'
"Henry's marster shuck his head en knock de ashes off'n his seegyar.

"'Spec' I made a bag bahgin when I bought dat nigger. Henry done good wuk all de summer, but sence de fall set in he 'pears ter be sorter pinin' away. Dey ain't nuffin pertickler de matter wid 'im—leastways de doctor say so—'cep'n' a tech er de rheumatiz; but his ha'r is all fell out, en ef he don't pick up his strenk mighty soon, I spec' I'm gwine ter lose 'im.'

"Dey smoked on awhile, en bimbeby ole mars say, 'Well, a bahgin's a bahgin, but you en me is good fren's, en I doan wan' ter see you lose all de money you paid fer dat nigger; en ef w'at you say is so, en I ain't 'sputin' it, he ain't wuf much now. I spec's you wukked him too ha'd dis summer, er e'se de swamps down here don't agree wid de san'-hill nigger. So you des lemme know, en ef he gits any wusser, I'll be willin' ter gib yer five hund'ed dollars for 'im, en take my chances on his livin'.'

"Sho' nuff, when Henry begun ter draw up wid de rheumatiz en it look like he gwine ter die fer sho, his noo marster sen' fer Mars Dugal', en Mars Dugal' gin him what he promus, en brung Henry home ag'in. He tuk good keer uv 'im dyoin' er de winter—give 'im w'iskey ter rub his rheumatiz, en terbacker ter smoke, en all he want ter eat—'caze a nigger w'at he could make a thousan' dollars a year off'n didn' grow on eve'y huckleberry bush.

"Nex' spring, w'en de sap rise en Henry's ha'r commence' ter sprout, Mars Dugal' sole 'im ag'in, down in Robeson County dis time; en he kep' dat sellin' business up fer five year er mo'. Henry nebber say nuffin' bout de goopher ter his noo marsters, 'caze he know he gwine ter be tuk good keer uv de nex' winter, w'en Mars Dugal' buy him back. En Mars Dugal' made 'nuff money off'n Henry ter buy anudder plantation ober on Beaver Crick.

"But 'long 'bout de een 'er dat five year dey come a stranger ter stop at de plantation. De fus' day he 'uz here he went out wid Mars Dugal' en spent all de mawnin' lookin' ober de vimya'd, en atter dinner dey spent all de evenin' playin' kya'ds. De niggers soon 'skivver' dat he wuz a Yankee, en dat he come down ter Norf C'lina fer ter l'arn de w'ite folks how to raise grapes en make wine. He promus Mars Dugal' he c'd make de grapevimes b'ar twice't ez many grapes, en dat de noo winepress he wuz a-sellin' would make mo' d'n twice't ez many gallons er wine. En ole Mars Dugal' des drunk it all in, des 'peared ter be bewitch' wid dat Yankee. W'en de darkies see dat Yankee runnin' 'roun' de vimya'd en diggin' under de grapevimes, dey shuk dere heads, en 'lowed dat dey feared Mars Dugal' losin' his min'. Mars Dugal' had all de dirt dug away fum under de roots er all de scuppernon' vimes, en' let 'em stan' dat away fer a week er mo'. Den dat Yankee made de niggers fix up a mixtry er lime en ashes en manyo, en po' it 'roun' de roots er de grapevimes. Den he 'vise Mars Dugal' fer ter trim de vimes close't, en Mars Dugal' tuck 'n done eve'ything de Yankee tole him ter do. Dyoin' all er dis time, mine yer, dis yer Yankee wuz libbin' off'n de fat er de lan', at de big house, en playin, kya'ds wid Mars Dugal' eve'y night; en dey say Mars Dugal' los' mo'n a thousan' dollars dyoin' er de week dat Yankee wuz a-ruinin' de grapevimes.

'W'en de sap ris nex' spring, ole Henry 'n'inted his head ez yuzhal, en his ha'r mence' ter grow des de same ez it done eve'y year. De scuppernon' vimes growed monst's fas', en de leaves wuz greener en thicker dan dey eber be'n dyoin' my rememb'ance; en Henry's ha'r growed out thicker dan eber, en he 'peared ter git younger 'n younger, en soopler; en seein' ez he wuz sho't er han's dat spring, havin' tuk in consid'able noo groun', Mars Dugal' 'git de crap in en de cotton chop'. So he kep' Henry on de plantation.

"But 'long 'bout time fer de grapes ter come on de scuppernon' vimes, dey 'peared ter come a change ober 'em; de leaves witherd en swivel' up, en de young grapes turn' yaller, en bimeby eve'ybody on de plantation could see dat de whole vimya'd wuz dyin'. Mars Dugal' tuk'n water de vimes en done all he could, but 't wa'n no use; dat Yankee had done bus' de watermillyum. One time de vimes picked up a bit, en Mars Dugal' 'lowed dey wuz gwine ter come out ag'in; but dat

Yankee done dug too close under de roots, en prune de branches too close ter de vime, en all dat lime en ashes done burn de life out'm de vimes, en dey des kep' a-with'in' en a-swivelin'.

"All dis time de goopher wuz a-wukkin'. When de vimes sta'ted ter wither, Henry 'mence' ter complain er his rheumatiz; en when de leaves begin ter dry up, his ha'r 'mence' ter drap out. When de vimes fresh' up a bit, Henry'd git peart ag'in, en when de vimes wither' ag'in, Henry'd git ole ag'in, en des kep' gittin' mo' fitten fer nuffin; he des pined away, en pined away, en fin'ly tuk ter his cabin; en when de big vime whar he got de sap ter 'n'int his head withered en turned yaller en died, Henry died too—des went out sorter like a cannel. Dey didn't 'pear ter be nuffin de matter wid 'im, 'cep'n de rheumatiz, but his strenk des dwinel' away 'tel he didn' hab ernuff lef' ter draw his bref. De goopher had got de under holt, en th'owed Henry dat time fer good en all.

"Mars Dugal' tuk on might'ly 'bout losin' his vimes en his nigger in de same year; en he swo' dat ef he could git holt er dat Yankee he'd wear 'im ter a frazzle, en den chaw up de frazzle; en he'd done it, too, for Mars Dugal' 'uz a monst'us brash man w'en he once git started. He sot de vimy'd out ober ag'in, but it wuz th'ee er fo' year befo' de vimes got ter b'arin' any scuppernon's.

"W'en de wah broke out, Mars Dugal' raise' a comp'ny, en went off ter fight de Yankees. He say he wuz mighty glad wah come, en he des want ter kill a Yankee fer eve'y dollar he los' 'long er dat grape-raisin' Yankee. En I 'spec' he would 'a' done it, too, ef de Yankees hadn' s'picioned sump'en en killed him fus'. Atter de s'render, ole Miss move' ter town, de niggers all scattered 'way fum de plantation, en de vimya'd ain' be'n cultervated sence."

"Is that story true?" asked Annie doubtfully, but seriously, as the old man concluded his narrative.

"It's des ez true ez I'm a-settin' here, miss. Dey's a easy way ter prove it: I kin lead de way right ter Henry's grave ober yonder in de plantation burying'-groun'. En I tell yer w'at, marster, I wouldn' 'vise you to buy dis yer ole vimya'd, 'caze de goopher's on it, en dey ain' no tellin' w'en it's gwine ter crap out."

"But I thought you said all the old vines died."

"Dey did 'pear ter die, but a few un 'em come out ag'in, en is mixed in 'mongs' de yuthers. I ain' skeered ter eat de grapes 'caze I knows de old vimes fum de noo ones, but wid strangers dey ain' no tellin' w'at mought happen. I wouldn' 'vise yer ter buy dis vimya'd."

I bought the vineyard, nevertheless, and it has been for a long time in a thriving condition, and is often referred to by the local press as a striking illustration of the opportunities open to Northern capital in the development of Southern industries. The luscious scuppernong holds first rank among our grapes, though we cultivate a great many other varieties; and our income from grapes packed and shipped to the Northern markets is quite considerable. I have not noticed any developments of the goopher in the vineyard, although I have a mild suspicion that our colored assistants do not suffer from want of grapes during the season.

I found, when I bought the vineyard, that Uncle Julius had occupied a cabin on the place for many years, and derived a respectable revenue from the product of the neglected grapevines. This, doubtless, accounted for his advice to me not to buy the vineyard, though whether it inspired the goopher story I am unable to state. I believe, however, that the wages I paid him for his services as coachman, for I gave him employment in that capacity, were more than an equivalent for anything he lost by the sale of the vineyard.

Nathaniel Hawthorne (1804–1864)
My Kinsman, Major Molineux

After the kings of Great Britain had assumed the right of appointing the colonial governors, the measures of the latter seldom met with the ready and general approbation which had been paid to those of their predecessors, under the original charters. The people looked with most jealous scrutiny to the exercise of power which did not emanate from themselves, and they usually rewarded their rulers with slender gratitude for the compliances by which, in softening their instructions from beyond the sea, they had incurred the reprehension of those who gave them. The annals of Massachusetts Bay will inform us, that of six governors in the space of about forty years from the surrender of the old charter, under James II., two were imprisoned by a popular insurrection; a third, as Hutchinson inclines to believe, was driven from the province by the whizzing of a musket-ball; a fourth, in the opinion of the same historian, was hastened to his grave by continual bickerings with the House of Representatives; and the remaining two, as well as their successors, till the Revolution, were favored with few and brief intervals of peaceful sway. The inferior members of the court party, in times of high political excitement, led scarcely a more desirable life. These remarks may serve as a preface to the following adventures, which chanced upon a summer night, not far from a hundred years ago. The reader, in order to avoid a long and dry detail of colonial affairs, is requested to dispense with an account of the train of circumstances that had caused much temporary inflammation of the popular mind.

It was near nine o'clock of a moonlight evening, when a boat crossed the ferry with a single passenger, who had obtained his conveyance at that unusual hour by the promise of an extra fare. While he stood on the landing-place, searching in either pocket for the means of fulfilling his agreement, the ferryman lifted a lantern, by the aid of which, and the newly risen moon, he took a very accurate survey of the stranger's figure. He was a youth of barely eighteen years, evidently country-bred, and now, as it should seem, upon his first visit to town. He was clad in a coarse gray coat, well worn, but in excellent repair; his under garments were durably constructed of leather, and fitted tight to a pair of serviceable and well-shaped limbs; his stockings of blue yarn were the incontrovertible work of a mother or a sister; and on his head was a three-cornered hat, which in its better days had perhaps sheltered the graver brow of the lad's father. Under his left arm was a heavy cudgel formed of an oak sapling, and retaining a part of the hardened root; and his equipment was completed by a wallet, not so abundantly stocked as to incommode the vigorous shoulders on which it hung. Brown, curly hair, well-shaped features, and bright, cheerful eyes were nature's gifts, and worth all that art could have done for his adornment.

The youth, one of whose names was Robin, finally drew from his pocket the half of a little province bill of five shillings, which, in the depreciation in that sort of currency, did but satisfy the ferryman's demand, with the surplus of a sexangular piece of parchment, valued at three pence. He then walked forward into the town, with as light a step as if his day's journey had not already exceeded thirty miles, and with as eager an eye as if he were entering London city, instead of the little metropolis of a New England colony. Before Robin had proceeded far, however, it occurred to him that he knew not whither to direct his steps; so he paused, and looked up and down the narrow street, scrutinizing the small and mean wooden buildings that were scattered on either side.

"This low hovel cannot be my kinsman's dwelling," thought he, "nor yonder old house, where the moonlight enters at the broken casement; and truly I see none hereabouts that might be worthy of him. It would have been wise to inquire my way of the ferryman, and doubtless he would have gone with me, and earned a shilling from the Major for his pains. But the next man I meet will do as well."

He resumed his walk, and was glad to perceive that the street now became wider, and the houses more respectable in their appearance. He soon discerned a figure moving on moderately in advance, and hastened his steps to overtake it. As Robin drew nigh, he saw that the passenger was a man in years, with a full periwig of gray hair, a wide-skirted coat of dark cloth, and silk stockings rolled above his knees. He carried a long and polished cane, which he struck down perpendicularly before him at every step; and at regular intervals he uttered two successive hems, of a peculiarly solemn and sepulchral intonation. Having made these observations, Robin laid hold of the skirt of the old man's coat, just when the light from the open door and windows of a barber's shop fell upon both their figures.

"Good evening to you, honored sir," said he, making a

low bow, and still retaining his hold of the skirt. "I pray you tell me whereabouts is the dwelling of my kinsman, Major Molineux."

The youth's question was uttered very loudly; and one of the barbers, whose razor was descending on a well-soaped chin, and another who was dressing a Ramillies wig, left their occupations, and came to the door. The citizen, in the mean time, turned a long-favored countenance upon Robin, and answered him in a tone of excessive anger and annoyance. His two sepulchral hems, however, broke into the very centre of his rebuke, with most singular effect, like a thought of the cold grave obtruding among wrathful passions.

"Let go my garment, fellow! I tell you, I know not the man you speak of. What! I have authority, I have—hem, hem—authority; and if this be the respect you show for your betters, your feet shall be brought acquainted with the stocks by daylight, tomorrow morning!"

Robin released the old man's skirt, and hastened away, pursued by an ill-mannered roar of laughter from the barber's shop. He was at first considerably surprised by the result of his question, but, being a shrewd youth, soon thought himself able to account for the mystery.

"This is some country representative," was his conclusion, "who has never seen the inside of my kinsman's door, and lacks the breeding to answer a stranger civilly. The man is old, or verily—I might be tempted to turn back and smite him on the nose. Ah, Robin, Robin! even the barber's boys laugh at you for choosing such a guide! You will be wiser in time, friend Robin."

He now became entangled in a succession of crooked and narrow streets, which crossed each other, and meandered at no great distance from the water-side. The smell of tar was obvious to his nostrils, the masts of vessels pierced the moonlight above the tops of the buildings, and the numerous signs, which Robin paused to read, informed him that he was near the centre of business. But the streets were empty, the shops were closed, and lights were visible only in the second stories of a few dwelling-houses. At length, on the corner of a narrow lane, through which he was passing, he beheld the broad countenance of a British hero swinging before the door of an inn, whence proceeded the voices of many guests. The casement of one of the lower windows was thrown back, and a very thin curtain permitted Robin to distinguish a party at supper, round a well-furnished table. The fragrance of the good cheer steamed forth into the outer air, and the youth could not fail to recollect that the last remnant of his traveling stock of provision had yielded to his morning appetite, and that noon had found and left him dinnerless.

"Oh, that a parchment three-penny might give me a right to sit down at yonder table!" said Robin, with a sigh. "But the Major will make me welcome to the best of his victuals; so I will even step boldly in, and inquire my way to his dwelling."

He entered the tavern, and was guided by the murmur of voices and the fumes of tobacco to the public-room. It was a long and low apartment, with oaken walls, grown dark in the continual smoke, and a floor which was thickly sanded, but of no immaculate purity. A number of persons—the larger part of whom appeared to be mariners, or in some way connected with the sea—occupied the wooden benches, or leather-bottomed chairs, conversing on various matters, and occasionally lending their attention to some topic of general interest. Three or four little groups were draining as many bowls of punch, which the West India trade had long since made a familiar drink in the colony. Others, who had the appearance of men who lived by regular and laborious handicraft, preferred the insulated bliss of an unshared potation, and became more taciturn under its influence. Nearly all, in short, evinced a predilection for the Good Creature in some of its various shapes, for this is a vice to which, as Fast Day sermons of a hundred years ago will testify, we have a long hereditary claim. The only guests to whom Robin's sympathies inclined him were two or three sheepish countrymen, who were using the inn somewhat after the fashion of a Turkish caravansary; they had gotten themselves into the darkest corner of the room, and heedless of the Nicotian atmosphere, were supping on the bread of their own ovens, and the bacon cured in their own chimney-smoke. But though Robin felt a sort of brotherhood with these strangers, his eyes were attracted from them to a person who stood near the door, holding whispered conversation with a group of ill-dressed associates. His features were separately striking almost to grotesqueness, and the whole face left a deep impression on the memory. The forehead bulged out into a double prominence, with a vale between; the nose came boldly forth in an irregular curve, and its bridge was of more than a finger's breadth; the eyebrows were deep and shaggy, and the eyes glowed beneath them like fire in a cave.

While Robin deliberated of whom to inquire respecting his kinsman's dwelling, he was accosted by the innkeeper, a little man in a stained white apron, who had come to pay his professional welcome to the stranger. Being in the second generation from a French Protestant, he seemed to have inherited the courtesy of his parent nation; but no variety of circumstances was ever known to change his voice from the one shrill note in which he now addressed Robin.

"From the country, I presume, sir?" said he, with a profound bow. "Beg leave to congratulate you on your arrival, and trust you intend a long stay with us. Fine town here, sir, beautiful buildings, and much that may interest a stranger. May I hope for the honor of your commands in respect to supper?"

"The man sees a family likeness! The Rogue has guessed that I am related to the Major!" thought Robin, who had hitherto experienced little superfluous civility.

All eyes were now turned on the country lad, standing at the door, in his worn three-cornered hat, gray coat, leather breeches, and blue yarn stockings, leaning on an oaken cudgel, and bearing a wallet on his back.

Robin replied to the courteous innkeeper, with such an assumption of confidence as befitted the Major's relative. "My honest friend," he said, "I shall make it a point to patronize your house on some occasion, when"—here he could not help lowering his voice—"when I may have more than a parchment three-pence in my pocket. My present business," continued he, speaking with lofty confidence, "is merely to inquire my way to the dwelling of my kinsman, Major Molineux."

There was a sudden and general movement in the room, which Robin interpreted as expressing the eagerness of each individual to become his guide. But the innkeeper turned his eyes to a written paper on the wall, which he read, or seemed to read, with occasional recurrences to the young man's figure.

"What have we here?" said he, breaking his speech into little dry fragments. "'Left the house of the subscriber, bounden servant, Hezekiah Mudge,—had on, when he went away, gray coat, leather breeches, master's third-best hat. One pound currency reward to whosoever shall lodge him in any jail of the province.' Better trudge, boy; better trudge!"

Robin had begun to draw his hand towards the lighter end of the oak cudgel, but a strange hostility in every countenance induced him to relinquish his purpose of breaking the courteous innkeeper's head. As he turned to leave the room, he encountered a sneering glance from the bold-featured personage whom he had before noticed; and no sooner was he beyond the door, than he heard a general laugh, in which the innkeeper's voice might be distinguished, like the dropping of small stones into a kettle.

"Now, is it not strange," thought Robin, with his usual shrewdness,—"is it not strange that the confession of an empty pocket should outweigh the name of my kinsman, Major Molineux? Oh, if I had one of those grinning rascals in the woods, where I and my oak sapling grew up together, I would teach him that my arm is heavy though my purse be light!"

On turning the corner of the narrow lane, Robin found himself in a spacious street, with an unbroken line of lofty houses on each side, and a steepled building at the upper end, whence the ringing of a bell announced the hour of nine. The light of the moon, and the lamps from the numerous shop-windows, discovered people promenading on the pavement, and amongst them Robin hoped to recognize his hitherto inscrutable relative. The result of his former inquiries made him unwilling to hazard another, in a scene of such publicity, and he determined to walk slowly and silently up the street, thrusting his face close to that of every elderly gentleman, in search of the Major's lineaments. In his progress, Robin encountered many gay and gallant figures. Embroidered garments of showy colors, enormous periwigs, gold-laced hats, and silver-hilted swords glided past him and dazzled his optics. Travelled youths, imitators of the European fine gentlemen of the period, trod jauntily along, half dancing to the fashionable tunes which they hummed, and making poor Robin ashamed of his quiet and natural gait. At length, after many pauses to examine the gorgeous display of goods in the shop-windows, and after suffering some rebukes for the impertinence of his scrutiny into people's faces, the Major's kinsman found himself near the steepled building, still unsuccessful in his search. As yet, however, he had seen only one side of the thronged street; so Robin crossed, and continued the same sort of inquisition down the opposite pavement, with stronger hopes than the philosopher seeking an honest man, but with no better fortune. He had arrived about midway towards the lower end, from which his course began, when he overheard the approach of some one who struck down a cane on the flag-stones at every step, uttering, at regular intervals, two sepulchral hems.

"Mercy on us!" quoth Robin, recognizing the sound.

Turning a corner, which chanced to be close at his right hand, he hastened to pursue his researches in some other part of the town. His patience now was wearing low, and he seemed to feel more fatigue from his rambles since he crossed the ferry, than from his journey of several days on the other side. Hunger also pleaded loudly within him, and Robin began to balance the propriety of demanding, violently, and with lifted cudgel, the necessary guidance from the first solitary passenger whom he should meet. While a resolution to this effect was gaining strength, he entered a street of mean appearance, on either side of which a row of ill-built houses was straggling towards the harbor. The moonlight fell upon no passenger along the whole extent, but in the third domicile which Robin passed there was a half-opened door, and his keen glance detected a woman's garment within.

"My luck may be better here," said he to himself.

Accordingly, he approached the door, and beheld it shut closer as he did so; yet an open space remained, sufficing for the fair occupant to observe the stranger, without a corresponding display on her part. All that Robin could discern was a strip of scarlet petticoat, and the occasional sparkle of an eye, as if the moonbeams were trembling on some bright thing.

"Pretty mistress," for I may call her so with a good conscience, thought the shrewd youth, since I know nothing to the contrary,—"my sweet pretty mistress, will you be kind enough to tell me whereabouts I must see the dwelling of my kinsman, Major Molineux?"

Robin's voice was plaintive and winning, and the female, seeing nothing to be shunned in the handsome country youth, thrust open the door, and came forth into the moonlight. She was a dainty little figure, with a white neck, round arms, and a slender waist, at the extremity of which her scarlet petticoat jutted out over a hoop, as if she were standing in a balloon. Moreover, her face was oval and pretty, her hair dark beneath the little cap, and her bright eyes possessed a sly freedom, which triumphed over those of Robin.

"Major Molineux dwells here," said this fair woman.

Now, her voice was the sweetest Robin had heard that night, the airy counterpart of a stream of melted silver; yet he could not help doubting whether that sweet voice spoke Gospel truth. He looked up and down the mean street, and then surveyed the house before which they stood. It was a small, dark edifice of two stories, the second of which projected over the lower floor, and the front apartment had the aspect of a shop for petty commodities.

"Now, truly, I am in luck," replied Robin, cunningly, "and so indeed is my kinsman, the Major, in having so pretty a housekeeper. But I prithee trouble him to step to the door; I will deliver him a message from his friends in the country, and then go back to my lodgings at the inn."

"Nay, the Major has been abed this hour or more," said the lady of the scarlet petticoat; "and it would be to little purpose to disturb him tonight, seeing his evening draught was of the strongest. But he is a kindhearted man, and it would be as much as my life's worth to let a kinsman of his turn away from the door. You are the good old gentleman's very picture, and I could swear that was his rainy-weather hat. Also he has garments very much resembling those leather small-clothes. But come in, I pray, for I bid you hearty welcome in his name."

So saying, the fair and hospitable dame took our hero by the hand; and the touch was light, and the force was gentleness, and though Robin read in her eyes what he did not hear in her words, yet the slender-waisted woman in the scarlet petticoat proved stronger than the athletic country youth. She had drawn his half-willing footsteps nearly to the threshold, when the opening of a door in the neighborhood startled the Major's housekeeper, and, leaving the Major's kinsman, she vanished speedily into her own domicile. A heavy yawn preceded the appearance of a man, who, like the Moonshine of Pyramus and Thisbe, carried a lantern, needlessly aiding his sister luminary in the heavens. As he walked sleepily up the street, he turned his broad, dull face on Robin, and displayed a long staff, spiked at the end.

"Home, vagabond, home!" said the watchman, in accents that seemed to fall asleep as soon as they were uttered. "Home, or we'll set you in the stock by peep of day!"

"This is the second hint of the kind," thought Robin. "I wish they would end my difficulties, by setting me there to-night."

Nevertheless, the youth felt an instinctive antipathy towards the guardian of midnight order, which at first prevented him from asking his usual question. But just when the man was about to vanish behind the corner, Robin resolved not to lose the opportunity, and shouted lustily after him,—

"I say, friend! will you guide me to the house of my kinsman, Major Molineux?"

The watchman made no reply, but turned the corner

and was gone; yet Robin seemed to hear the sound of drowsy laughter stealing along the solitary street. At that moment, also, a pleasant titter saluted him from the open window above his head; he looked up, and caught the sparkle of a saucy eye; a round arm beckoned to him, and next he heard light footsteps descending the staircase within. But Robin, being of the household of a New England clergyman, was a good youth, as well as a shrewd one; so he resisted temptation, and fled away.

He now roamed desperately, and at random, through the town, almost ready to believe that a spell was on him, like that by which a wizard of his country had once kept three pursuers wandering, a whole winter night, within twenty paces of the cottage which they sought. The streets lay before him, strange and desolate, and the lights were extinguished in almost every house. Twice, however, little parties of men, among whom Robin distinguished individuals in outlandish attire, came hurrying along; but, though on both occasions they paused to address him, such intercourse did not at all enlighten his perplexity. They did but utter a few words in some language of which Robin knew nothing, and perceiving his inability to answer, bestowed a curse upon him in plain English and hastened away. Finally, the lad determined to knock at the door of every mansion that might appear worthy to be occupied by his kinsman, trusting that perseverance would overcome the fatality that had hiterto thwarted him. Firm in this resolve, he was passing beneath the walls of a church, which formed the corner of two streets, when, as he turned into the shade of its steeple, he encountered a bulky stranger, muffled in a cloak. The man was proceeding with the speed of earnest business, but Robin planted himself full before him, holding the oak cudgel with both hands across his body as a bar to further passage.

"Halt, honest man, and answer me a question," said he, very resolutely. "Tell me, this instant, whereabouts is the dwelling of my kinsman, Major Molineux!"

"Keep your tongue between your teeth, fool, and let me pass!" said a deep, gruff voice, which Robin partly remembered. "Let me pass, I say, or I'll strike you to the earth!"

"No, no, neighbor!" cried Robin, flourishing his cudgel, and then thrusting its larger end close to the man's muffled face. "No, no, I'm not the fool you take me for, nor do you pass till I have an answer to my question. Whereabouts is the dwelling of my kinsman, Major Molineux?"

The stranger, instead of attempting to force his passage, stepped back into the moonlight, unmuffled his face, and stared full into that of Robin.

"Watch here an hour, and Major Molineux will pass by," said he.

Robin gazed with dismay and astonishment on the unprecedented physiognomy of the speaker. The forehead with its double prominence, the broad hooked nose, the shaggy eyebrows, and fiery eyes were those which he had noticed at the inn, but the man's complexion had undergone a singular, or, more properly, a twofold change. One side of the face blazed an intense red, while the other was black as midnight, the division line being in the broad bridge of the nose; and a mouth which seemed to extend from ear to ear was black or red, in contrast to the color of the cheek. The effect was as if two individual devils, a fiend of fire and a fiend of darkness, had united themselves to form this infernal visage. The stranger grinned in Robin's face, muffled his parti-colored features, and was out of sight in a moment.

"Strange things we travellers see!" ejaculated Robin.

He seated himself, however, upon the steps of the church-door, resolving to wait the appointed time for his kinsman. A few moments were consumed in philosophical speculations upon the species of man who had just left him; but having settled this point shrewdly, rationally, and satisfactorily, he was compelled to look elsewhere for his amusement. And first he threw his eyes along the street. It was of more respectable appearance than most of those into which he had wandered, and the moon, creating, like the imaginative power, a beautiful strangeness in familiar objects, gave something of romance to a scene that might not have possessed it in the light of day. The irregular and often quaint architecture of the houses, some of whose roofs were broken into numerous little peaks, while others ascended, steep and narrow, into a single point, and others again were square; the pure snow-white of some of their complexions, the aged darkness of others, and the thousand sparklings, reflected from bright substances in the walls of many; these matters engaged Robin's attention for a while, and then began to grow wearisome. Next he endeavored to define the forms of distant objects, starting away, with almost ghostly indistinctness, just as his eye appeared to grasp them; and finally he took a minute survey of an edifice which stood on the opposite side of the street, directly in front of the church-door, where he was stationed. It was a large, square mansion, distinguished from its neighbors by a balcony, which rested on tall pillars, and by an elaborate Gothic window, communicating therewith.

"Perhaps this is the very house I have been seeking," thought Robin.

Then he strove to speed away the time, by listening to a murmur which swept continually along the street, yet was scarcely audible, except to an unaccustomed ear like his; it was a low, dull, dreamy sound, compounded of many noises, each of which was at too great a distance to be separately heard. Robin marvelled at this snore of a sleeping town, and marvelled more whenever its continuity was broken by now and then a distant shout, apparently loud where it originated. But altogether it was a sleep-inspiring sound, and, to shake off its drowsy influence, Robin arose, and climbed a window-frame, that he might view the interior of the church. There the moonbeams came trembling in, and fell down upon the deserted pews, and extended along the quiet aisles. A fainter yet more awful radiance was hovering around the pulpit, and one solitary ray had dared to rest upon the open page of the great Bible. Had nature, in that deep hour, become a worshipper in the house which man had builded? Or was that heavenly light the visible sanctity of the place,—visible because no earthly and impure feet were within the walls? The scene made Robin's heart shiver with a sensation of loneliness stronger than he had ever felt in the remotest depths of his native woods; so he turned away and sat down again before the door. There were graves around the church, and now an uneasy thought obtruded into Robin's breast. What if the object of his search, which had been so often and so strangely thwarted, were all the time mouldering in his shroud? What if his kinsman should glide through yonder gate, and nod and smile to him in dimly passing by?

"Oh that any breathing thing were here with me!" said Robin.

Recalling his thoughts from this uncomfortable track, he sent them over forest, hill, and stream, and attempted to imagine how that evening of ambiguity and weariness had been spent by his father's household. He pictured them assembled at the door, beneath the tree, the great old tree, which had been spared for its huge twisted trunk and venerable shade, when a thousand leafy brethren fell. There, at the going down of the summer sun, it was his father's custom to perform domestic worship, that the neighbors might come and join with him like brothers of the family, and that the wayfaring man might pause to drink at that fountain, and keep his heart pure by freshening the memory of home. Robin distinguished the seat of every individual of the little audience; he saw the good man in the midst, holding the Scriptures in the golden light that fell from the western clouds; he beheld him close the book and all rise up to pray. He heard the old thanksgivings for daily mercies, the old supplications for their continuance, to which he had so often listened in weariness, but which were now among his dear remembrances. He perceived the slight inequality of his father's voice when he came to speak of the absent one; he noted how his mother turned her face to the broad and knotted trunk; how his elder brother scorned, because the beard was rough upon his upper lip, to permit his features to be moved; how the younger sister drew down a low hanging branch before her eyes; and how the little one of all, whose sports had hitherto broken the decorum of the scene, understood the prayer for her playmate, and burst into clamorous grief. Then he saw them go in at the door; and when Robin would have entered also, the latch tinkled into its place, and he was excluded from his home.

"Am I here, or there?" cried Robin, starting; for all at once, when his thoughts had become visible and audible in a dream, the long, wide, solitary street shone out before him.

He aroused himself, and endeavored to fix his attention steadily upon the large edifice which he had surveyed before. But still his mind kept vibrating between fancy and reality; by turns, the pillars of the balcony lengthened into the tall, bare stems of pines, dwindled down to human figures, settled again into their true shape and size, and then commenced a new succession of changes. For a single moment, when he deemed himself awake, he could have sworn that a visage—one which he seemed to remember, yet could not absolutely name as his kinsman's—was looking towards him from the Gothic window. A deeper sleep wrestled with and nearly overcame him, but fled at the sound of footsteps along the opposite pavement. Robin rubbed his eyes, discerned a man passing at the foot of the balcony, and addressed him in a loud, peevish, and lamentable cry.

"Hallo, friend! must I wait here all night for my kinsman, Major Molineux?"

The sleeping echoes awoke, and answered the voice; and the passenger, barely able to discern a figure sitting in the oblique shade of the steeple, traversed the street to obtain a nearer view. He was himself a gentleman in his prime, of open, intelligent, cheerful, and altogether prepossessing countenance. Perceiving a country youth, apparently homeless and without friends, he accosted him in a tone of real kindness, which had become strange to Robin's ears.

"Well, my good lad, why are you sitting here?" inquired he. "Can I be of service to you in any way?"

"I'm afraid not, sir," replied Robin, despondingly; "yet I shall take it kindly, if you'll answer me a single question. I've been searching, half the night, for one Major Molineux; now, sir, is there really such a person in these parts, or am I dreaming?"

"Major Molineux! The name is not altogether strange to me," said the gentleman, smiling. "Have you any objection to telling me the nature of your business with him?"

Then Robin briefly related that his father was a clergyman, settled on a small salary, at a long distance back in the country, and that he and Major Molineux were brothers' children. The Major, having inherited riches, and acquired civil and military rank, had visited his cousin, in great pomp, a year or two before; had manifested much interest in Robin and an elder brother, and, being childless himself, had thrown out hints respecting the future establishment of one of them in life. The elder brother was destined to succeed to the farm which his father cultivated in the interval of sacred duties; it was therefore determined that Robin should profit by his kinsman's generous intentions, especially as he seemed to be rather the favorite, and was thought to possess other necessary endowments.

"For I have the name of being a shrewd youth," observed Robin, in this part of his story.

"I doubt not you deserve it," replied his new friend, good-naturedly; "but pray proceed."

"Well, sir, being nearly eighteen years old, and well grown, as you see," continued Robin, drawing himself up to his full height,

"I thought it high time to begin the world. So my mother and sister put me in handsome trim, and my father gave me half the remnant of his last year's salary, and five days ago I started for this place, to pay the Major a visit. But, would you believe it, sir! I crossed the ferry a little after dark, and have yet found nobody that would show me the way to his dwelling; only, an hour or two since, I was told to wait here, and Major Molineux would pass by."

"Can you describe the man who told you this?" inquired the gentleman.

"Oh, he was a very ill-favored fellow, sir," replied Robin, "with two great bumps on his forehead, a hook nose, fiery eyes; and, what struck me as the strangest, his face was of two different colors. Do you happen to know such a man, sir?"

"Not intimately," answered the stranger, "but I chanced to meet him a little time previous to your stopping me. I believe you may trust his word, and that the Major will very shortly pass through this street. In the mean time, as I have a singular curiosity to witness your meeting, I will sit down here upon the steps and bear you company."

He seated himself accordingly, and soon engaged his companion in animated discourse. It was but a brief continuance, however, for a noise of shouting, which had long been remotely audible, drew so much nearer that Robin inquired its cause.

"What may be the meaning of this uproar?" asked he. "Truly, if your town be always as noisy, I shall find little sleep while I am an inhabitant."

"Why, indeed, friend Robin, there do appear to be three or four riotious fellows abroad to-night," replied the gentleman. "You must not expect all the stillness of your native woods here in our streets. But the watch will shortly be at the heels of these lads and—"

"Ay, and set them in the stocks by peep of day," interrupted Robin, recollecting his own encounter with the drowsy lantern-bearer. "But, dear sir, if I may trust my ears, an army of watchmen would never make head against such a multitude of rioters. There were at least a thousand voices went up to make that one shout."

"May not a man have several voices, Robin, as well as two complexions?" said his friend.

"Perhaps a man may; but Heaven forbid that a woman should!" responded the shrewd youth, thinking of the seductive tones of the Major's housekeeper.

The sounds of a trumpet in some neighboring street now became so evident and continual, that Robin's curiosity was strongly excited. In addition to the shouts, he heard frequent bursts from many instruments of discord, and a wild and confused laughter filled up the intervals. Robin rose from the steps, and looked wistfully towards a point whither people seemed to be hastening.

"Surely some prodigious merry-making is going on,"

exclaimed he. "I have laughed very little since I left home, sir, and should be sorry to lose an opportunity. Shall we step round the corner by that darkish house, and take our share of the fun?"

"Sit down again, sit down, good Robin," replied the gentleman, laying his hand on the skirt of the gray coat. "You forget that we must wait here for your kinsman; and there is reason to believe that he will pass by, in the course of a very few moments."

The near approach of the uproar had now disturbed the neighborhood; windows flew open on all sides; and many heads, in the attire of the pillow, and confused by sleep suddenly broken, were protruded to the gaze of whoever had leisure to observe them. Eager voices hailed each other from house to house, all demanding the explanation, which not a soul could give. Half-dressed men hurried towards the unknown commotion, stumbling as they went over the stone steps that thrust themselves into the narrow foot-walk. The shouts, the laughter, and the tuneless bray, the antipodes of music, came onwards with increasing din, till scattered individuals, and then denser bodies, began to appear round a corner at the distance of a hundred yards.

"Will you recognize your kinsman, if he passes in this crowd?" inquired the gentleman.

"Indeed, I can't warrant it, sir; but I'll take my stand here, and keep a bright lookout," answered Robin, descending to the outer edge of the pavement.

A mighty stream of people now emptied into the street, and came rolling slowly towards the church. A single horseman wheeled the corner in the midst of them, and close behind him came a band of fearful wind-instruments, sending forth a fresher discord now that no intervening buildings kept it from the ear. Then a redder light disturbed the moonbeams, and a dense multitude of torches shone along the street, concealing, by their glare, whatever object they illuminated. The single horseman, clad in a military dress, and bearing a drawn sword, rode onward as the leader, and, by his fierce and variegated countenance, appeared like war personified; the red of one cheek was an emblem of fire and sword; the blackness of the other betokened the mourning that attends them. In his train were wild figures in the Indian dress, and many fantastic shapes without a model, giving the whole march a visionary air, as if a dream had broken forth from some feverish brain, and were sweeping visibly through the midnight streets. A mass of people, inactive, except as applauding spectators, hemmed the procession in; and several women ran along the sidewalk, piercing the confusion of heavier sounds with their shrill voices of mirth or terror.

"The double-faced fellow has his eye upon me," muttered Robin, with an indefinite but an uncomfortable idea that he was himself to bear a part in the pageantry.

The leader turned himself in the saddle, and fixed his glance full upon the country youth, as the steed went slowly by. When

Robin had freed his eyes from those fiery ones, the musicians were passing before him, and the torches were close at hand; but the unsteady brightness of the latter formed a veil which he could not penetrate. The rattling of wheels over the stones sometimes found its way to his ear, and confused traces of a human form appeared at intervals, and then melted into the vivid light. A moment more, and the leader thundered a command to halt: the trumpets vomited a horrid breath, and then held their peace; the shouts and laughter of the people died away, and there remained only a universal hum, allied to silence. Right before Robin's eyes was an uncovered cart. There the torches blazed the brightest, there the moon shone out like day, and there, in tar-and-feathery dignity, sat his kinsman, Major Molineux!

He was an elderly man, of large and majestic person, and strong, square features, betokening a steady soul; but steady as it was, his enemies had found means to shake it. His face was pale as death, and far more ghastly; the broad forehead was contracted in his agony, so that his eyebrows formed one grizzled line; his eyes were red and wild, and the foam hung white upon his quivering lip. His whole frame was agitated by a quick and continual tremor, which his pride strove to quell, even in those circumstances of overwhelming humiliation. But perhaps the bitterest pang of all was when his eyes met those of Robin; for he evidently knew him on the instant, as the youth stood witnessing the foul disgrace of a head grown gray in honor. They stared at each other in silence, and Robin's knees shook, and his hair bristled, with a mixture of pity and terror. Soon, however, a bewildering excitement began to seize upon his mind; the preceding adventures of the night, the unexpected appearance of the crowd, the torches, the confused din and the hush that followed, the spectre of his kinsman reviled by that great multitude,—all this, and, more than all, a perception of tremendous ridicule in the whole scene, affected him with a sort of mental inebriety. At that moment a voice of sluggish merriment saluted Robin's ears; he turned instinctively, and just behind the corner of the church stood the lantern-bearer, rubbing his eyes, and drowsily enjoying the lad's amazement. Then he heard a peal of laughter like the ringing of silvery bells; a woman twitched his arm, a saucy eye met his, and he saw the lady of the scarlet petticoat. A sharp, dry cachinnation appealed to his memory, and, standing on tiptoe in the crowd, with his white apron over his head, he beheld the courteous little innkeeper. And lastly, there sailed over the heads of the multitude a great, broad laugh, broken in the midst by two sepulchral hems; thus, "Haw, haw, haw,—hem, hem,—haw, haw, haw, haw!"

The sound proceeded from the balcony of the opposite edifice, and thither Robin turned his eyes. In front of the Gothic window stood the old citizen, wrapped in a wide gown, his gray periwig exchanged for a nightcap, which was thrust back from his forehead, and his silk stockings hanging about his legs. He supported himself on his polished cane in a fit of convulsive merriment, which manifested itself on his solemn old features like a funny inscription on a tombstone. Then Robin seemed to hear the voices of the barbers, of the guests of the inn, and of all who had made sport of him that night. The contagion was spreading among the multitude, when all at once, it seized upon Robin, and he set forth a shout of laughter that echoed through the street,—every man shook his sides, every man emptied his lungs, but Robin's shout was the loudest there. The cloud-spirits peeped from their silvery islands, as the congregated mirth went roaring up the sky! The Man in the Moon heard the far bellow. "Oho," quoth he, "the old earth is frolicsome to-night!"

When there was a momentary calm in that tempestuous sea of sound, the leader gave the sign, the procession resumed its march. On they went, like fiends that throng in mockery around some dead potentate, mighty no more, but majestic still in his agony. On they went, in counterfeited pomp, in senseless uproar, in frenzied merriment, trampling all on an old man's heart. On swept the tumult, and left a silent street behind.

"Well, Robin, are you dreaming?" inquired the gentleman, laying his hand on the youth's shoulder.

Robin started, and withdrew his arm from the stone post to which he had instinctively clung, as the living stream rolled by him. His cheek was somewhat pale, and his eye not quite as lively as in the earlier part of the evening.

"Will you be kind enough to show me the way to the ferry?" said he, after a moment's pause.

"You have, then, adopted a new subject of inquiry?" observed his companion, with a smile.

"Why, yes, sir," replied Robin, rather dryly. "Thanks to you, and to my other friends, I have at last met my kinsman, and he will scarce desire to see my face again. I begin to grow weary of a town life, sir. Will you show me the way to the ferry?"

"No, my good friend Robin,—not to-night, at least," said the gentleman. "Some few days hence, if you wish it, I will speed you on your journey. Or, if you prefer to remain with us, perhaps, as you are a shrewd youth, you may rise in the world without the help of your kinsman, Major Molineux."

Joseph Conrad (1857–1924)

The Secret Sharer

On my right hand there were lines of fishing stakes resembling a mysterious system of half-submerged bamboo fences, incomprehensible in its division of the domain of tropical fishes, and crazy of aspect as if abandoned forever by some nomad tribe of fishermen now gone to the other end of the ocean; for there was no sign of human habitation as far as the eye could reach. To the left a group of barren islets, suggesting ruins of stone walls, towers, and block-houses, had its foundations set in a blue sea that itself looked solid, so still and stable did it lie below my feet; even the track of light from the westering sun shone smoothly, without that animated glitter which tells of an imperceptible ripple. And when I turned my head to take a parting glance at the tug which had just left us anchored outside the bar, I saw the straight line of the flat shore joined to the stable sea, edge to edge, with a perfect and unmarked closeness, in one leveled floor half brown, half blue under the enormous dome of the sky. Corresponding in their insignificance to the islets of the sea, two small clumps of trees, one on each side of the only fault in the impeccable joint, marked the mouth of the river Meinam we had just left on the first preparatory stage of our homeward journey; and, far back on the inland level, a larger and loftier mass, the grove surrounding the great Paknam pagoda, was the only thing on which the eye could rest from the vain task of exploring the monotonous sweep of the horizon. Here and there gleams as of a few scattered pieces of silver marked the windings of the great river; and on the nearest of them, just within the bar, the tug steaming right into the land became lost to my sight, hull and funnel and masts, as though the impassive earth had swallowed her up without an effort, without a tremor. My eye followed the light cloud of her smoke, now here, now there, above the plain, according to the devious curves of the stream, but always fainter and farther away, till I lost it at last behind the miter-shaped hill of the great pagoda. And then I was left alone with my ship, anchored at the head of the Gulf of Siam.

She floated at the starting point of a long journey, very still in an immense stillness, the shadows of her spars flung far to the eastward by the setting sun. At that moment I was alone on her decks. There was not a sound in her—and around us nothing moved, nothing lived, not a canoe on the water, not a bird in the air, not a cloud in the sky. In this breathless pause at the threshold of a long passage we seemed to be measuring our fitness for a long and arduous enterprise, the appointed task of both our existences to be carried out, far from all human eyes, with only sky and sea for spectators and for judges.

There must have been some glare in the air to interfere with one's sight, because it was only just before the sun left us that my roaming eyes made out beyond the highest ridge of the principal islet of the group something which did away with the solemnity of perfect solitude. The tide of darkness flowed on swiftly; and with tropical suddenness a swarm of stars came out above the shadowy earth, while I lingered yet, my hand resting lightly on my ship's rail as if on the shoulder of a trusted friend. But, with all that multitude of celestial bodies staring down at one, the comfort of quiet communion with her was gone for good. And there were also disturbing sounds by this time—voices, footsteps forward; the steward flitted along the main deck, a busily ministering spirit; a hand bell tinkled urgently under the poop deck. . . .

I found my two officers waiting for me near the supper table, in the lighted cuddy. We sat down at once, and as I helped the chief mate, I said:

"Are you aware that there is a ship anchored inside the islands? I saw her mastheads above the ridge as the sun went down."

He raised sharply his simple face, overcharged by a terrible growth of whisker, and emitted his usual ejaculations: "Bless my soul, sir! You don't say so!"

My second mate was a sound-cheeked, silent young man, grave beyond his years, I thought; but as our eyes happened to meet I detected a slight quiver on his lips. I looked down at once. It was not my part to encourage sneering on board my ship. It must be said, too, that I knew very little of my officers. In consequence of certain events of no particular significance, except to myself, I had been appointed to the command only a fortnight before. Neither did I know much of the hands forward. All these people had been together for eighteen months or so, and my position was that of the only stranger on board. I mention this because it has some bearing on what is to follow. But what I felt most was my being a stranger to the ship; and if all the truth must be told, I was somewhat of a stranger to myself. The youngest man on board (barring the second mate), and untried as yet by a position of the fullest responsibility, I was willing to take the adequacy of the others for granted. They had simply to be equal to their tasks: but I wondered how far I should turn out faithful to that ideal conception of one's own personality every man sets up for himself secretly.

Meantime the chief mate, with an almost visible effect of collaboration on the part of his round eyes and frightful whiskers, was trying to evolve a theory of the anchored ship. His dominant trait was to take all things into earnest consideration. He was of a painstaking turn of mind. As he used to say, he "Liked to account to himself" for practically everything that came in his way, down to a miserable scorpion he had found in his cabin a week before. The why and the wherefore of that scorpion— how it got on board and came to select his room rather than the pantry (which was a dark place and more what a scorpion would be partial to), and how on earth it managed to drown itself in the inkwell of his writing desk—had exercised him infinitely. The ship within the islands was much more easily accounted for; and just as we were about to rise from the table he made his pronouncement. She was, he doubted not, a ship from home lately arrived. Probably she drew too much water to cross the bar except at the top of spring tides. Therefore she went into that natural harbor to wait for a few days in preference to remaining in an open roadstead.

"That's so," confirmed the second mate, suddenly, in his slightly hoarse voice. "She draws over twenty feet. She's the

Liverpool ship *Sephora* with a cargo of coal. Hundred and twenty-three days from Cardiff.''

We looked at him in surprise.

"The tugboat skipper told me when he came on board for your letters, sir,'' explained the young man. "He expects to take her up the river the day after tomorrow.''

After thus overwhelming us with the extent of his information he slipped out of the cabin. The mate observed regretfully that he "could not account for that young fellow's whims.'' What prevented him telling us all about it at once, he wanted to know.

I detained him as he was making a move. For the last two days the crew had had plenty of hard work, and the night before they had very little sleep. I felt painfully that I—a stranger—was doing something unusual when I directed him to let all hands turn in without setting an anchor watch. I proposed to keep on deck myself till one o'clock or thereabouts. I would get the second mate to relieve me at that hour.

"He will turn out the cook and the steward at four,'' I concluded, "and then give you a call. Of course at the slightest sign of any sort of wind we'll have the hands up and make a start at once.''

He concealed his astonishment. "Very well, sir.'' Outside the cuddy he put his head in the second mate's door to inform him of my unheard-of caprice to take a five hours' anchor watch on myself. I heard the other raise his voice incredulously: "What? The captain himself?'' Then a few more murmurs, a door closed, then another. A few moments later I went on deck.

My strangeness, which had made me sleepless, had prompted that unconventional arrangement, as if I had expected in those solitary hours of the night to get on terms with the ship of which I knew nothing, manned by men of whom I knew very little more. Fast alongside a wharf, littered like any ship in port with a tangle of unrelated things, invaded by unrelated shore people, I had hardly seen her yet properly. Now, as she lay cleared for sea, the stretch of her main deck seemed to me very fine under the stars. Very fine, very roomy for her size, and very inviting. I descended the poop and paced the waist, my mind picturing to myself the coming passage through the Malay Archipelago, down the Indian Ocean, and up the Atlantic. All its phases were familiar enough to me, every characteristic, all the alternatives which were likely to face me on the high seas—everything! . . . except the novel responsibility of command. But I took heart from the reasonable thought that the ship was like other ships, the men like other men, and that the sea was not likely to keep any special surprises expressly for my discomfiture.

Arrived at that comforting conclusion, I bethought myself of a cigar and went below to get it. All was still down there. Everybody at the after end of the ship was sleeping profoundly. I came out again on the quarter-deck, agreeably at ease in my sleeping suit on that warm breathless night, barefooted, a glowing cigar in my teeth, and, going forward, I was met by the profound silence of the fore end of the ship. Only as I passed the door of the forecastle I heard a deep, quiet, trustful sigh of some sleeper inside. And suddenly I rejoiced in the great security of the sea as compared with the unrest of the land, in my choice of that untempted life presenting no disquieting problems, invested with an elementary moral beauty by the absolute straightforwardness of its appeal and by the singleness of its purpose.

The riding light in the fore-rigging burned with a clear, untroubled, as if symbolic, flame, confident and bright in the mysterious shades of the night. Passing on my way aft along the other side of the ship, I observed that the rope side ladder, put over, no doubt, for the master of the tug when he came to fetch away our letters, had not been hauled in as it should have been. I became annoyed at this, for exactitude in small matters is the very soul of discipline. Then I reflected that I had myself peremptorily dismissed my officers from duty, and by my own act had prevented the anchor watch being formally set and things properly attended to. I asked myself whether it was wise ever to interfere with the established routine of duties even from the kindest of motives. My action might have made me appear eccentric. Goodness only knew how that absurdly whiskered mate would "account" for my conduct, and what the whole ship thought of that informality of their new captain. I was vexed with myself.

Not from compunction certainly, but, as it were mechanically, I proceeded to get the ladder in myself. Now a side ladder of that sort is a light affair and comes in easily, yet my vigorous tug, which should have brought it flying on board, merely recoiled upon my body in a totally unexpected jerk. What the devil! . . . I was so astounded by the immovableness of that ladder that I remained stock-still, trying to account for it to myself like that imbecile mate of mine. In the end, of course, I put my head over the rail.

The side of the ship made an opaque belt of shadow on the darkling glassy shimmer of the sea. But I saw at once something elongated and pale floating very close to the ladder. Before I could form a guess a faint flash of phosphorescent light, which seemed to issue suddenly from the naked body of a man, flickered in the sleeping water with the elusive, silent play of summer lightning in a night sky. With a gasp I saw revealed to my stare a pair of feet, the long legs, a broad livid back immersed right up to the neck in a greenish cadaverous glow. One hand, awash, clutched the bottom rung of the ladder. He was complete but for the head. A headless corpse! The cigar dropped out of my gaping mouth with a tiny plop and a short hiss quite audible in the absolute stillness of all things under heaven. At that I suppose he raised up his face, a dimly pale oval in the shadow of the ship's side. But even then I could only barely make out down there the shape of his black-haired head. However, it was enough for the horrid, frost-bound sensation which had gripped me about the chest to pass off. The moment of vain exclamations was past, too. I only climbed on the spare spar and leaned over the rail as far as I could, to bring my eyes nearer to that mystery floating alongside.

As he hung by the ladder, like a resting swimmer, the sea lightning played about his limbs at every stir; and he appeared in it ghastly, silvery, fishlike. He remained as mute as a fish, too. He made no motion to get out of the water, either. It was inconceivable that he should not attempt to come on board, and strangely troubling to suspect that perhaps he did not want to. And my first words were prompted by just that troubled incertitude.

"What's the matter?" I asked in my ordinary tone, speaking down to the face upturned exactly under mine.

"Cramp," it answered, no louder. Then slightly anxious, "I say, no need to call anyone."

"I was not going to," I said.

"Are you alone on deck?"

"Yes."

I had somehow the impression that he was on the point of letting go the ladder to swim away beyond my ken—mysterious as he came. But, for the moment, this being appearing as if he had risen from the bottom of the sea (it was certainly the nearest land to the ship) wanted only to know the time. I told him. And he, down there, tentatively:

"I suppose your captain's turned in?"

"I am sure he isn't," I said.

He seemed to struggle with himself, for I heard something like the low, bitter murmur of doubt. "What's the good?" His next words came out with a hesitating effort.

"Look here, my man. Could you call him out quietly?"

I thought the time had come to declare myself.

"*I* am the captain."

I heard a "By Jove!" whispered at the level of the water. The phosphorescence flashed in the swirl of the water all about his limbs, his other hand seized the ladder.

"My name's Leggatt."

The voice was calm and resolute. A good voice. The self-possession of that man had somehow induced a corresponding state in myself. It was very quietly that I remarked:

"You must be a good swimmer."

"Yes. I've been in the water practically since nine o'clock. The question for me now is whether I am to let go this ladder and go on swimming till I sink from exhaustion, or—to come on board here."

I felt this was no mere formula of desperate speech, but a real alternative in the view of a strong soul. I should have gathered from this that he was young; indeed, it is only the young who are ever confronted by such clear issues. But at the time it was pure intuition on my part. A mysterious communication was established already between us two—in the face of that silent, darkened tropical sea. I was young, too; young enough to make no comment. The man in the water began suddenly to climb up the ladder, and I hastened away from the rail to fetch some clothes.

Before entering the cabin I stood still, listening in the lobby at the foot of the stairs. A faint snore came through the closed door of the chief mate's room. The second mate's door was on the hook, but the darkness in there was absolutely soundless. He, too, was young and could sleep like a stone. Remained the steward, but he was not likely to wake up before he was called. I got a sleeping suit out of my room and, coming back on deck, saw the naked man from the sea sitting on the main hatch, glimmering white in the darkness, his elbows on his knees and his head in his hands. In a moment he had concealed his damp body in a sleeping suit of the same gray-stripe pattern as the one I was wearing and followed me like my double on the poop. Together we moved right aft, bare-footed, silent.

"What is it?" I asked in a deadened voice, taking the lighted lamp out of the binnacle, and raising it to his face.

"An ugly business."

He had rather regular features; a good mouth; light eyes under somewhat heavy, dark eyebrows; a smooth, square forehead; no growth on his cheeks; a small, brown mustache, and a well-shaped, round chin. His expression was concentrated, meditative, under the inspecting light of the lamp I held up to his face; such as a man thinking hard in solitude might wear. My sleeping suit was just right for his size. A well-knit young fellow of twenty-five at most. He caught his lower lip with the edge of white, even teeth.

"Yes," I said, replacing the lamp in the binnacle. The warm, heavy tropical night closed upon his head again.

"There's a ship over there," he murmured.

"Yes, I know. The *Sephora*. Did you know of us?"

"Hadn't the slighest idea. I am the mate of her—" He paused and corrected himself. "I should say I *was*."

"Aha! Something wrong?"

"Yes. Very wrong indeed. I've killed a man."

"What do you mean? Just now?"

"No, on the passage. Weeks ago. Thirty-nine south. When I say a man—"

"Fit of temper," I suggested, confidently.

The shadowy, dark head, like mine, seemed to nod imperceptibly above the ghostly gray of my sleeping suit. It was, in the night, as though I had been faced by my own reflection in the depths of a somber and immense mirror.

"A pretty thing to have to own up to for a Conway boy," murmured my double, distinctly.

"You're a Conway boy?"

"I am," he said, as if startled. Then, slowly . . .
"Perhaps you too—"

It was so; but being a couple of years older I had left before he joined. After a quick interchange of dates a silence fell; and I thought suddenly of my absurd mate with his terrific whiskers and the "Bless my soul—you don't say so" type of intellect. My double gave me an inkling of his thoughts by saying:

"My father's a parson in Norfolk. Do you see me before a judge and jury on that charge? For myself I can't see the necessity. There are fellows that an angel from heaven— And I am not that. He was one of those creatures that are just simmering all the time with a silly sort of wickedness. Miserable devils that have no business to live at all. He wouldn't do his duty and wouldn't let anybody else do theirs. But what's the good of talking! You know well enough the sort of ill-conditioned snarling cur—"

He appealed to me as if our experiences had been as identical as our clothes. And I knew well enough the pestiferous danger of such a character where there are no means of legal repression. And I knew well enough also that my double there was no homicidal ruffian. I did not think of asking him for details, and he told me the story roughly in brusque, disconnected sentences. I needed no more. I saw it all going on as though I were myself inside that other sleeping unit.

"It happened while we were setting a reefed foresail, at dusk. Reefed foresail! You understand the sort of weather. The only sail we had left to keep the ship running; so you may guess what it had been like for days. Anxious sort of job, that. He gave me some of his cursed insolence at the sheet. I tell you I was overdone with this terrific weather that seemed to have no end to it. Terrific, I tell you—and a deep ship. I believe the fellow himself was half crazed with funk. It was no time for gentlemanly reproof, so I turned round and felled him like an ox. He up and at me. We closed just as an awful sea made for the ship. All hands saw it coming and took to the rigging, but I had him by the throat, and went on shaking him like a rat, the men above us yelling, 'Look out! look out!' Then a crash as if the sky had fallen on my head. They say that for over ten minutes hardly anything was to be seen of the ship—just the three masts and a bit of the forecastle head and of the poop all awash driving along in a smother of foam. It was a miracle that they found us, jammed together behind the forebits. It's clear that I meant business, because I was holding him by the throat still when they picked us up. He was black in the face. It was too much for them. It seems they rushed us aft together, gripped as we were, screaming 'Murder!' like a lot of lunatics, and broke into the cuddy. And the ship running for her life, touch and go all the time, any minute her last in a sea fit to turn your hair gray only a-looking at it. I understand that the skipper, too, started raving like the rest of them. The man had been deprived of sleep for more than a week, and to have this sprung on him at the height of a furious gale nearly drove him out of his mind. I wonder they didn't fling me overboard after getting the carcass of their precious shipmate out of my fingers. They had rather a job to separate us, I've been told. A sufficiently fierce story to make an old judge and a respectable jury sit up a bit. The first thing I heard when I came to myself was the maddening howling of that endless gale, and on that the voice of the old man. He was hanging on to my bunk, staring into my face out of his sou'wester.

"'Mr. Leggatt, you have killed a man. You can act no longer as chief mate of this ship.'"

His care to subdue his voice made it sound monotonous. He rested a hand on the end of the skylight to steady himself with, and all that time did not stir a limb, so far as I could see. "Nice little tale for a quiet tea party," he concluded in the same tone.

One of my hands, too, rested on the end of the skylight; neither did I stir a limb, so far as I knew. We stood less than a foot from each other. It occurred to me that if old "Bless my soul—you don't say so" were to put his head up the companion and catch sight of us, he would think he was seeing double, or imagine himself come upon a scene of weird witchcraft; the strange captain having a quiet confabulation by the wheel with his own gray ghost. I became very much concerned to prevent anything of the sort. I heard the other's soothing undertone.

"My father's a parson in Norfolk," it said. Evidently he had forgotten he had told me this important fact before. Truly a nice little tale.

"You had better slip down into my stateroom now," I said, moving off stealthily. My double followed my movements; our bare feet made no sound; I let him in, closed the door with care, and, after giving a call to the second mate, returned on deck for my relief.

"Not much sign of any wind yet," I remarked when he approached.

"No, sir. Not much," he assented, sleepily, in his hoarse voice, with just enough deference, no more, and barely suppressing a yawn.

"Well, that's all you have to look out for. You have got your orders."

"Yes, sir."

I paced a turn or two on the poop and saw him take up his position face forward with his elbow in the rat-lines of the mizzen-rigging before I went below. The mate's faint snoring was still going on peacefully. The cuddy lamp was burning over the table on which stood a vase with flowers, a polite attention from the ships' provision merchant—the last flowers we should see for the next three months at the very least. Two bunches of bananas hung from the beam symmetrically, one on each side of the rudder casing. Everything was as before in the ship—except that two of her captain's sleeping suits were simultaneously in use, one motionless in the cuddy, the other keeping very still in the captain's stateroom.

It must be explained here that my cabin had the form of the capital letter L, the door being within the angle and opening into the short part of the letter. A couch was to the left, the bed-place to the right; my writing desk and the chronometers' table faced the door. But anyone opening it, unless he stepped right inside, had no view of what I call the long (or vertical) part of the letter. It contained some lockers surmounted by a bookcase; and a few clothes, a thick jacket or two, caps, oilskin coat, and such like, hung on hooks. There was at the bottom of that part a door opening into my bathroom, which could be entered also directly from the saloon. But that way was never used.

The mysterious arrival had discovered the advantage of this particular shape. Entering my room, lighted strongly by a big bulkhead lamp swung on gimbals above my writing desk, I did not see him anywhere till he stepped out quietly from behind the coats hung in the recessed part.

"I heard somebody moving about, and went in there at once," he whispered.

I, too, spoke under my breath.

"Nobody is likely to come in here without knocking and getting permission."

He nodded. His face was thin and the sunburn faded, as though he had been ill. And no wonder. He had been, I heard presently, kept under arrest in his cabin for nearly seven weeks. But there was nothing sickly in his eyes or in his expression. He was not a bit like me, really; yet, as we stood leaning over my bed-place, whispering side by side, with our dark heads together and our backs to the door, anybody bold enough to open it stealthily would have been treated to the uncanny sight of a double captain busy talking in whispers with his other self.

"But all this doesn't tell me how you came to hang on to our side ladder," I inquired, in the hardly audible murmurs we used, after he had told me something more of the proceedings on board the *Sephora* once the bad weather was over.

"When we sighted Java Head I had had time to think all those matters out several times over. I had six weeks of doing nothing else, and with only an hour or so every evening for a tramp on the quarter-deck."

He whispered, his arms folded on the side of my bed-place, staring through the open port. And I could imagine perfectly the manner of this thinking out—a stubborn if not a steadfast operation; something of which I should have been perfectly incapable.

"I reckoned it would be dark before we closed with the land," he continued, so low that I had to strain my hearing, near as we were to each other, shoulder touching shoulder almost. "So I asked to speak to the old man. He always seemed very sick when he came to see me—as if he could not look me in the face. You know, that foresail saved the ship. She was too deep to have run long under bare poles. And it was I that managed to set it for him. Anyway, he came. When I had him in my cabin—he stood by the door looking at me as if I had the halter around my neck already—I asked him right away to leave my cabin door unlocked at night while the ship was going through Sunda Straits. There would be the Java coast within two or three miles, off Angier Point. I wanted nothing more. I've had a prize for swimming my second year in the Conway."

"I can believe it," I breathed out.

"God only knows why they locked me in every night. To see some of their faces you'd have thought they were afraid I'd go about at night strangling people. Am I a murdering brute? Do I look it? By Jove! if I had been he wouldn't have trusted himself like that into my room. You'll say I might have chucked him aside and bolted out, there and then—it was dark already. Well, no. And for the same reason I wouldn't think of trying to smash the door. There would have been a rush to stop me at the noise, and I did not mean to get into a confounded scrimmage. Somebody else might have got killed—for I would not have broken out only to get chucked back, and I did not want any more of that work. He refused, looking more sick than ever. He was afraid of the men, and also of that old second mate of his who had been sailing with him for years—a gray-headed old humbug; and his steward, too, had been with him devil knows how long—seventeen years or more—a dogmatic sort of loafer who hated me like poison, just because I was the chief mate. No chief mate ever made more than one voyage in the *Sephora*, you know. Those two old chaps ran the ship. Devil only knows what the skipper wasn't afraid of (all his nerve went to pieces altogether in that hellish spell of bad weather we had)—of what the law would do to him—of his wife, perhaps. Oh, yes! she's on board. Though I don't think she would have meddled. She would have been only too glad to have me out of the ship in any way. The 'brand of Cain' business, don't you see. That's all right. I was ready enough to go off wandering on the face of the earth—and that was price enough to pay for an Abel of that sort. Anyhow, he wouldn't listen to me. 'This thing must take its course. I represent the law here.' He was shaking like a leaf. 'So you won't?' 'No!' 'Then I hope you will be able to sleep on that,' I said, and turned my back on him. 'I wonder that *you* can,' cries he, and locks the door.

"Well, after that, I couldn't. Not very well. That was three weeks ago. We have had a slow passage through the Java Sea; drifted about Carimata for ten days. When we anchored here they thought, I suppose, it was all right. The nearest land (and that's five miles) is the ship's destination; the consul would soon set about catching me; and there would have been no object in bolting to these islets there. I don't suppose there's a drop of water on them. I don't know how it was, but tonight that steward, after bringing me my supper, went out to let me eat it, and left the door unlocked. And I ate it—all there was, too. After I had finished I strolled out on the quarter-deck. I don't know that I meant to do anything. A breath of fresh air was all I wanted, I believe. Then a sudden temptation came over me. I kicked off my slippers and was in the water before I had made up my mind fairly. Somebody heard the splash and they raised an awful hullabaloo. 'He's gone! Lower the boats! He's committed suicide! No, he's swimming.' Certainly I was swimming. It's not so easy for a swimmer like me to commit suicide by drowning. I landed on the nearest islet before the boat left the ship's side. I heard them pulling about in the dark, hailing, and so on, but after a bit they gave up. Everything quieted down and the anchorage became as still as death. I sat down on a stone and began to think. I felt certain they would start searching for me at daylight. There was no place to hide on those stony things—and if there had been, what would have been the good? But now I was clear of that ship, I was not going back. So after a while I took off all my clothes, tied them up in a bundle with a stone inside, and dropped them in the deep water on the outer side of that islet. That was suicide enough for me. Let them think what they liked, but I didn't mean to drown myself. I meant to swim till I sank—but that's not the same thing. I struck out for another of these little islands, and it was from that one that I first saw your riding light. Something to swim for. I went on easily, and on the way I came upon a flat rock a foot or two above water. In the daytime, I dare say, you might make it out with a glass from your poop. I scrambled up on it and rested myself for a bit. Then I made another start. That last spell must have been over a mile.''

His whisper was getting fainter and fainter, and all the time he stared straight out through the porthole, in which there was not even a star to be seen. I had not interrupted him. There was something that made comment impossible in his narrative, or perhaps in himself; a sort of feeling, a quality, which I can't find a name for. And when he ceased, all I found was a futile whisper: "So you swam for our light?"

"Yes—straight for it. It was something to swim for. I couldn't see any stars low down because the coast was in the way, and I couldn't see the land, either. The water was like glass. One might have been swimming in a confounded thousand-feet deep cistern with no place for scrambling out anywhere; but what I didn't like was the notion of swimming round and round like a crazed bullock before I gave out; and as I didn't mean to go back . . . No. Do you see me being hauled back, stark naked, off one of these little islands by the scruff of the neck and fighting like a wild beast? Somebody would have got killed for certain, and I did not want any of that. So I went on. Then your ladder—"

"Why didn't you hail the ship?" I asked, a little louder.

He touched my shoulder lightly. Lazy footsteps came right over our heads and stopped. The second mate had crossed from the other side of the poop and might have been hanging over the rail, for all we knew.

"He couldn't hear us talking—could he?" My double breathed into my very ear, anxiously.

His anxiety was an answer, a sufficient answer, to the question I had put to him. An answer containing all the difficulty of that situation. I closed the porthole quietly, to make sure. A louder word might have been overheard.

"Who's that?" he whispered then.

"My second mate. But I don't know much more of the fellow than you do."

And I told him a little about myself. I had been appointed to take charge while I least expected anything of the sort, not quite a fortnight ago. I didn't know either the ship or the people. Hadn't had the time in port to look about me or size anybody up. And as to the crew, all they knew was that I was appointed to take the ship home. For the rest, I was almost as much of a stranger on board as himself, I said. And at the moment I felt it most acutely. I felt that it would take very little to make me a suspect person in the eyes of the ship's company.

He had turned about meantime; and we, the two strangers in the ship, faced each other in identical attitudes.

"Your ladder—" he murmured, after a silence. "Who'd have thought of finding a ladder hanging over at night in a ship anchored out here! I felt just then a very unpleasant faintness. After the life I've been leading for nine weeks, anybody would have got out of condition. I wasn't capable of swimming round as far as your rudder chains. And, lo and behold! there was a ladder to get hold of. After I gripped it I said to myself, "What's the good?' When I saw a man's head looking over I thought I would swim away presently and leave him shouting—in whatever language it was. I didn't mind being looked at. I—liked it. And then you speaking to me so quietly—as if you had expected me—made me a hold on a little longer. It had been a confounded lonely time—I don't mean while swimming. I was glad to talk a little to somebody that didn't belong to the *Sephora*. As to asking for the captain, that was a mere impulse. It could have been no use, with all the ship knowing about me and the other people pretty certain to be round here in the morning. I don't know—I wanted to be seen, to talk with somebody, before I went on. I don't know what I would have said. . . . 'Fine night, isn't it?' or something of the sort."

"Do you think they will be round here presently?" I asked with some incredulity.

"Quite likely," he said, faintly.

He looked extremely haggard all of a sudden. His head rolled on his shoulders.

"H'm. We shall see then. Meantime get into that bed," I whispered. "Want help? There."

It was a rather high bed-place with a set of drawers

underneath. This amazing swimmer really needed the lift I gave him by seizing his leg. He tumbled in, rolled over on his back, and flung one arm across his eyes. And then, with his face nearly hidden, he must have looked exactly as I used to look in that bed. I gazed upon my other self for a while before drawing across carefully the two green serge curtains which ran on a brass rod. I thought for a moment of pinning them together for greater safety, but I sat down on the couch, and once there I felt unwilling to rise and hunt for a pin. I would do it in a moment. I was extremely tired, in a peculiarly intimate way, by the strain of stealthiness, by the effort of whispering and the general secrecy of this excitement. It was three o'clock by now and I had been on my feet since nine, but I was not sleepy; I could not have gone to sleep. I sat there, fagged out, looking at the curtains, trying to clear my mind of the confused sensation of being in two places at once, and greatly bothered by an exasperating knocking in my head. It was a relief to discover suddenly that it was not in my head at all, but on the outside of the door. Before I could collect myself the words "Come in" were out of my mouth, and the steward entered with a tray, bringing in my morning coffee. I had slept, after all, and I was so frightened that I shouted, "This way! I am here, steward," as though he had been miles away. He put down the tray on the table next the couch and only then said, very quietly, "I can see you are here, sir." I felt him give me a keen look, but I dared not meet his eyes just then. He must have wondered why I had drawn the curtains of my bed before going to sleep on the couch. He went out, hooking the door open as usual.

I heard the crew washing decks above me. I knew I would have been told at once if there had been any wind. Calm, I thought, and I was doubly vexed. Indeed, I felt dual more than ever. The steward reappeared suddenly in the doorway. I jumped up from the couch so quickly that he gave a start.

"What do you want here?"

"Close your port, sir—they are washing decks."

"It is closed," I said, reddening.

"Very well, sir." But he did not move from the doorway and returned my stare in an extraordinary, equivocal manner for a time. Then his eyes wavered, all his expression changed, and in a voice unusually gentle, almost coaxingly:

"May I come in to take the empty cup away, sir?"

"Of course!" I turned my back on him while he popped in and out. Then I unhooked and closed the door and even pushed the bolt. This sort of thing could not go on very long. The cabin was as hot as an oven, too. I took a peep at my double, and discovered that he had not moved, his arm was still over his eyes; but his chest heaved; his hair was wet; his chin glistened with perspiration. I reached over him and opened the port.

"I must show myself on deck," I reflected.

Of course, theoretically, I could do what I liked, with

no one to say nay to me within the whole circle of the horizon; but to lock my cabin door and take the key away I did not dare. Directly I put my head out of the companion I saw the group of my two officers, the second mate barefooted, the chief mate in long india-rubber boots, near the break of the poop, and the steward halfway down the poop ladder talking to them eagerly. He happened to catch sight of me and dived, the second ran down on the main deck shouting some order or other, and the chief mate came to meet me, touching his cap.

There was a sort of curiosity in his eye that I did not like. I don't know whether the steward had told them that I was "queer" only, or downright drunk, but I know the man meant to have a good look at me. I watched him coming with a smile which, as he got into point-blank range, took effect and froze his very whiskers. I did not give him time to open his lips.

"Square the yards by lifts and braces before the hands go to breakfast."

It was the first particular order I had given on board that ship; and I stayed on deck to see it executed, too. I had felt the need of asserting myself without loss of time. That sneering young cub got taken down a peg or two on that occasion, and I also seized the opportunity of having a good look at the face of every foremast man as they filed past me to go to the after braces. At breakfast time, eating nothing myself, I presided with such frigid dignity that the two mates were only too glad to escape from the cabin as soon as decency permitted; and all the time the dual working of my mind distracted me almost to the point of insanity. I was constantly watching myself, my secret self, as dependent on my actions as my own personality, sleeping in that bed, behind that door which faced me as I sat at the head of the table. It was very much like being mad, only it was worse because one was aware of it.

I had to shake him for a solid minute, but when at last he opened his eyes it was in the full possession of his senses, with an inquiring look.

"All's well so far," I whispered. "Now you must vanish into the bathroom."

He did so, as noiseless as a ghost, and I then rang for the steward, and facing him boldly, directed him to tidy up my stateroom while I was having my bath—"and be quick about it." As my tone admitted of no excuses, he said, "Yes, sir," and ran off to fetch his dustpan and brushes. I took a bath and did most of my dressing, splashing, and whistling softly for the steward's edification, while the secret sharer of my life stood drawn up bolt upright in that little space, his face looking very sunken in daylight, his eyelids lowered under the stern, dark line of his eyebrows drawn together by a slight frown.

When I left him there to go back to my room the steward was finishing dusting. I sent for the mate and engaged him in some insignificant conversation. It was, as it were, trifling with the terrific character of his whiskers; but my object was to give him an opportunity for a good look at my cabin. And then I could at last shut, with a clear conscience, the door of my stateroom and get my double back into the recessed part. There was nothing else for it. He had to sit still on a small folding stool, half smothered by the heavy coats hanging there. We listened to the steward going into the bathroom out of the saloon, filling the water bottles there, scrubbing the bath, setting things to rights, whisk, bang, clatter—out again into the saloon—turn the key—click. Such was my scheme for keeping my second self invisible. Nothing better could be contrived under the circumstances. And there we sat: I at my writing desk ready to appear busy with some papers, he behind me, out of sight of the door. It would not have been prudent to talk in daytime; and I could not have stood the excitement of that queer sense of whispering to myself. Now and then, glancing over my shoulder, I saw him far back there, sitting rigidly on the low stool, his bare feet close together, his arms folded, his head hanging on his breast—and perfectly still. Anybody would have taken him for me.

I was fascinated by it myself. Every moment I had to glance over my shoulder. I was looking at him when a voice outside the door said:

"Beg pardon, sir."

"Well!" . . .I kept my eyes on him, and so, when the voice outside the door announced, "There's a ship's boat coming our way, sir." I saw him give a start—the first movement he had made for hours. But he did not raise his bowed head.

"All right. Get the ladder over."

I hesitated. Should I whisper something to him? But what? His immobility seemed to have been never disturbed. What could I tell him he did not know already? . . . Finally I went on deck.

The skipper of the *Sephora* had a thin red whisker all round his face, and the sort of complexion that goes with hair of that color; also the particular, rather smeary shade of blue in the eyes. He was not exactly a showy figure; his shoulders were high, his stature but middling— one leg slightly more bandy than the other. He shook hands, looking vaguely around. A spiritless tenacity was his main characteristic, I judged. I behaved with a politeness which seemed to disconcert him. Perhaps he was shy. He mumbled to me as if he were ashamed of what he was saying; gave his name (it was something like Archbold—but at this distance of years I hardly am sure), his ship's name, and a few other particulars of that sort, in the manner of a criminal making a reluctant and doleful confession. He had had terrible weather on the passage out—terrible—terrible—wife aboard, too.

By this time we were seated in the cabin and the steward brought in a tray with a bottle and glasses. "Thanks! No." Never took liquor. Would have some water, though. He drank two tumblerfuls.

Terrible thirsty work. Ever since daylight had been exploring the islands round his ship.

"What was that for—fun?" I asked, with an appearance of polite interest.

"No!" He sighed. "Painful duty."

As he persisted in his mumbling and I wanted my double to hear every word, I hit upon the notion of informing him that I regretted to say I was hard of hearing.

"Such a young man, too!" he nodded, keeping his smeary blue, unintelligent eyes fastened upon me. What was the cause of it—some disease? he inquired, without the least sympathy and as if he thought that, if so, I'd got no more than I deserved.

"Yes; disease," I admitted in a cheerful tone which seemed to shock him. But my point was gained, because he had to raise his voice to give me his tale. It is not worth while to record that version. It was just over two months since all this had happened, and he had thought so much about it that he seemed completely muddled as to its bearings, but still immensely impressed.

"What would you think of such a thing happening on board your own ship? I've had the *Sephora* for these fifteen years. I am a well-known shipmaster."

He was densely distressed—and perhaps I should have sympathized with him if I had been able to detach my mental vision from the unsuspected sharer of my cabin as though he were my second self. There he was on the other side of the bulkhead, four or five feet from us, no more, as we sat in the saloon. I looked politely at Captain Archbold (if that was his name), but it was the other I saw, in a gray sleeping suit, seated on a low stool, his bare feet close together, his arms folded, and every word said between us falling into the ears of his dark head bowed on his chest.

"I have been at sea now, man and boy, for seven-and-thirty years, and I've never heard of such a thing happening in an English ship. And that it should be my ship. Wife on board, too."

I was hardly listening to him.

"Don't you think," I said, "that the heavy sea which, you told me, came aboard just then might have killed the man? I have seen the sheer weight of a sea kill a man very neatly, by simply breaking his neck."

"Good God!" he uttered, impressively, fixing his smeary eyes on me. "The sea! No man killed by the sea ever looked like that." He seemed positively scandalized at my suggestion. And as I gazed at him, certainly not prepared for anything original on his part, he advanced his head close to mine and thrust his tongue out at me so suddenly that I couldn't help starting back.

After scoring over my calmness in this graphic way he nodded wisely. If I had seen the sight, he assured me, I would never forget it as long as I lived. The weather was too bad to give the corpse a proper sea burial. So next day at dawn they took it up on the poop, covering its face with a bit of bunting; he read a short prayer, and then, just as it was, in its oilskins and long boots, they launched it amongst those mountainous seas that seemed ready every moment to swallow up the ship herself and the terrified lives on board of her.

"That reefed foresail saved you," I threw in.

"Under God—it did," he exclaimed fervently. "It was by a special mercy, I firmly believe, that it stood some of those hurricane squalls."

"It was the setting of that sail which—" I began.

"God's own hand in it," he interrupted me. "Nothing less could have done it. I don't mind telling you that I hardly dared give the order. It seemed impossible that we could touch anything without losing it, and then our last hope would have been gone."

The terror of that gale was on him yet. I let him go on for a bit, then said, casually—as if returning to a minor subject:

"You were very anxious to give up your mate to the shore people, I believe?"

He was. To the law. His obscure tenacity on that point had in it something incomprehensible and a little awful; something, as it were, mystical, quite apart from his anxiety that he should not be suspected of "countenancing any doings of that sort." Seven-and-thirty virtuous years at sea, of which over twenty of immaculate command, and the last fifteen in the *Sephora*, seemed to have laid him under some pitiless obligation.

"And you know," he went on, groping shamefacedly amongst his feelings, "I did not engage that young fellow. His people had some interest with my owners. I was in a way forced to take him on. He looked very smart, very gentlemanly, and all that. But do you know—I never liked him, somehow. I am a plain man. You see, he wasn't exactly the sort for the chief mate of a ship like the *Sephora*."

I had become so connected in thoughts and impressions with the secret sharer of my cabin that I felt as if I, personally, were being given to understand that I, too, was not the sort that would have done for the chief mate of a ship like the *Sephora*. I had no doubt of it in my mind.

"Not at all the style of man. You understand," he insisted, superfluously, looking hard at me.

I smiled urbanely. He seemed at a loss for a while.

"I suppose I must report a suicide."

"Beg pardon?"

"Sui-cide! That's what I'll have to write to my owners directly I get in."

"Unless you manage to recover him before tomorrow," I assented, dispassionately. . . . "I mean, alive."

He mumbled something which I really did not catch, and I turned my ear to him in a puzzled manner. He fairly bawled:

"The land—I say, the mainland is at least seven miles off my anchorage."

"About that."

My lack of excitement, of curiosity, of surprise, of any sort of pronounced interest, began to arouse his distrust. But except for the felicitous pretense of deafness I had not tried to pretend anything. I had felt utterly incapable of playing the part of ignorance properly, and therefore was afraid to try. It is also certain that he had brought some ready-made suspicions with him, and that he viewed my politeness as a strange and unnatural phenomenon. And yet how else could I have received him? Not heartily! That was impossible for psychological reasons, which I need not state here. My only object was to keep off his inquiries. Surlily? Yes, but surliness might have provoked a point-blank question. From its novelty to him and from its nature, punctilious courtesy was the manner best calculated to restrain the man. But there was the danger of his breaking through my defense bluntly. I could not, I think, have met him by a direct lie, also for psychological (not moral) reasons. If he had only known how afraid I was of his putting my feelings of identity with the other to the test! But, strangely enough—(I thought of it only afterward)—I believe that he was not a little disconcerted by the reverse side of that weird situation, by something in me that reminded him of the man he was seeking—suggested a mysterious similitude to the young fellow he had distrusted and disliked from the first.

However that might have been, the silence was not very prolonged. He took another oblique step.

"I reckon I had no more than a two-mile pull to your ship. Not a bit more."

"And quite enough, too, in this awful heat," I said.

Another pause full of mistrust followed. Necessity, they say, is mother of invention, but fear, too, is not barren of ingenious suggestions. And I was afraid he would ask me point-blank for news of my other self.

"Nice little saloon, isn't it?" I remarked, as if noticing for the first time the way his eyes roamed from one closed door to the other. "And very well fitted out, too. Here, for instance," I continued, reaching over the back of my seat negligently and flinging the door open, "is my bathroom."

He made an eager movement, but hardly gave it a glance. I got up, shut the door of the bathroom, and invited him to have a look round, as if I were very proud of my accommodation. He had to rise and be shown round, but he went through the business without any raptures whatever.

"And now we'll have a look at my stateroom," I

declared, in a voice as loud as I dared to make it, crossing the cabin to the starboard side with purposely heavy steps.

He followed me in and gazed around. My intelligent double had vanished. I played my part.

"Very convenient—isn't it?"

"Very nice. Very comf . . ." He didn't finish, and went out brusquely as if to escape from some unrighteous wiles of mine. But it was not to be. I had been too frightened not to feel vengeful; I felt I had him on the run, and I meant to keep him on the run. My polite insistence must have had something menacing in it, because he gave in suddenly. And I did not let him off a single item; mate's room, pantry, storerooms, the very sail locker which was also under the poop—he had to look into them all. When at last I showed him out on the quarter-deck he drew a long, spiritless sigh, and mumbled dismally that he must really be going back to his ship now. I desired my mate, who had joined us, to see to the captain's boat.

The man of whiskers gave a blast on the whistle which he used to wear hanging round his neck, and yelled, "*Sephoras* away!" My double down there in my cabin must have heard, and certainly could not feel more relieved than I. Four fellows came running out from somewhere forward and went over the side, while my own men, appearing on deck too, lined the rail. I escorted my visitor to the gangway ceremoniously, and nearly overdid it. He was a tenacious beast. On the very ladder he lingered, and in that unique, guiltily conscientious manner of sticking to the point:

"I say . . . you . . . you don't think that—"

I covered his voice loudly:

"Certainly not. . . . I am delighted. Good-by."

I had an idea of what he meant to say, and just saved myself by the privilege of defective hearing. He was too shaken generally to insist, but my mate, close witness of that parting, looked mystified and his face took on a thoughtful cast. As I did not want to appear as if I wished to avoid all communication with my officers, he had the opportunity to address me.

"Seems a very nice man. His boat's crew told our chaps a very extraordinary story, if what I am told by the steward is true. I suppose you had it from the captain, sir?"

"Yes. I had a story from the captain."

"A very horrible affair—isn't it, sir?"

"It is."

"Beats all these tales we hear about murders in Yankee ships."

"I don't think it beats them. I don't think it resembles them in the least."

"Bless my soul—you don't say so! But of course I've no acquaintance whatever with American ships, not I, so I couldn't go against your knowledge. It's horrible enough for me. . . . But the queerest part is that these fellows seemed to have some idea the man was hidden aboard here. They had really. Did you ever hear of such a thing?"

"Preposterous—isn't it?"

We were walking to and fro athwart the quarter-deck. No one of the crew forward could be seen (the day was Sunday), and the mate pursued:

"There was some little dispute about it. Our chaps took offense. 'As if we would harbor a thing like that,' they said. 'Wouldn't you like to look for him in our coal hole?' Quite a tiff. But they made it up in the end. I suppose he did drown himself. Don't you, sir?"

"I don't suppose anything."

"You have no doubt in the matter, sir?"

"None whatever."

I left him suddenly. I felt I was producing a bad impression, but with my double down there it was most trying to be on deck. And it was almost as trying to be below. Altogether a nerve-trying situation. But on the whole I felt less torn in two when I was with him. There was no one in the whole ship whom I dared take into my confidence. Since the hands had got to know his story, it would have been impossible to pass him off for anyone else, and an accidental discovery was to be dreaded now more than ever. . . .

The steward being engaged in laying the table for dinner, we could talk only with our eyes when I first went down. Later in the afternoon we had a cautious try at whispering. The Sunday quietness of the ship was against us; the stillness of air and water around her was against us; the elements, the men were against us—everything was against us in our secret partnership; time itself—for this could not go on forever. The very trust in Providence was, I suppose, denied to his guilt. Shall I confess that this thought cast me down very much? And as to the chapter of accidents which counts for so much in the book of success, I could only hope that it was closed. For what favorable accident could be expected?

"Did you hear everything?" were my first words as soon as we took up our position side by side, leaning over my bed-place.

He had. And the proof of it was his earnest whisper, "The man told you he hardly dared to give the order."

I understood the reference to be to that saving foresail.

"Yes. He was afraid of it being lost in the setting."

"I assure you he never gave the order. He may think he did, but he never gave it. He stood there with me on the break of the poop after the maintopsail blew away, and whimpered about our last hope—positively whimpered about it and nothing else—and the night coming on! To hear one's skipper go on like that in such weather was enough to drive any fellow out of his mind. It worked me up into a sort of desperation. I just took it into my own hands and went away from him, boiling, and— But what's the use telling you? *You* know! . . . Do you think that if I had not been pretty fierce with them I should have got the men to do anything? Not it! The bosun perhaps? Perhaps! It wasn't a heavy sea—it was a sea gone mad! I suppose the end of the world will be something like that; and a man may have the heart to see it coming once and be done with it—but to have to face it day after day—I don't blame anybody. I was precious little better than the rest. Only—I was an officer of that old coal-wagon, anyhow—''

"I quite understand," I conveyed that sincere assurance into his ear. He was out of breath with whispering; I could hear him pant slightly. It was all very simple. The same strung-up force which had given twenty-four men a chance, at least, for their lives, had, in a sort of recoil, crushed an unworthy mutinous existence.

But I had no leisure to weigh the merits of the matter—footsteps in the saloon, a heavy knock. "There's enough wind to get under way with, sir." Here was the call of a new claim upon my thoughts and even upon my feelings.

"Turn the hands up," I cried through the door. "I'll be on deck directly."

I was going out to make the acquaintance of my ship. Before I left the cabin our eyes met—the eyes of the only two strangers on board. I pointed to the recessed part where the little campstool awaited him and laid my finger on my lips. He made a gesture—somewhat vague—a little mysterious, accompanied by a faint smile, as if of regret.

This is not the place to enlarge upon the sensations of a man who feels for the first time a ship move under his feet to his own independent word. In my case they were not unalloyed. I was not wholly alone with my command; for there was that stranger in my cabin. Or rather, I was not completely and wholly with her. Part of me was absent. That mental feeling of being in two places at once affected me physically as if the mood of secrecy had penetrated my very soul. Before an hour had elapsed since the ship had begun to move, having occasion to ask the mate (he stood by my side) to take a compass bearing of the Pagoda, I caught myself reaching up to his ear in whispers. I say I caught myself, but enough had escaped to startle the man. I can't describe it otherwise than by saying that he shied. A grave, preoccupied manner, as though he were in possession of some perplexing intelligence, did not leave him henceforth. A little later I moved away from the rail to look at the compass with such a stealthy gait that the helmsman noticed it—and I could not help noticing the unusual roundness of his eyes. These are trifling instances, though it's to no commander's advantage to be suspected of ludicrous eccentricities. But I was also more seriously affected. There are to a seaman certain words, gestures, that should in given conditions come as naturally, as instinctively as the winking of a menaced eye. A certain order should spring on to his lips without thinking; a certain sign should get itself made, so to speak, without reflection. But all unconscious alertness had abandoned me. I had to make an effort of will to recall myself back (from the cabin) to the conditions of the moment. I felt that I was appearing an irresolute commander to those people who were watching me more or less critically.

And, besides, there were the scares. On the second day out, for instance, coming off the deck in the afternoon (I had straw slippers on my bare feet) I stopped at the open pantry door and spoke to the steward. He was doing something there with his back to me. At the sound of my voice he nearly jumped out of his skin, as the saying is, and incidentally broke a cup.

"What on earth's the matter with you?" I asked, astonished.

He was extremely confused. "Beg your pardon, sir. I made sure you were in your cabin."

"You see I wasn't."

"No, sir. I could have sworn I had heard you moving in there not a moment ago. It's most extraordinary . . . very sorry, sir."

I passed on with an inward shudder. I was so identified with my secret double that I did not even mention the fact in those scanty, fearful whispers we exchanged. I suppose he had made some slight noise of some kind or other. It would have been miraculous if he hadn't at one time or another. And yet, haggard as he appeared, he looked always perfectly self-controlled, more than calm—almost invulnerable. On my suggestion he remained almost entirely in the bathroom, which, upon the whole, was the safest place. There could be really no shadow of an excuse for anyone ever wanting to go in there, once the steward had done with it. It was a very tiny place. Sometimes he reclined on the floor, his legs bent, his head sustained on one elbow. At others I would find him on the campstool, sitting in his gray sleeping suit and with his cropped dark hair like a patient, unmoved convict. At night I would smuggle him into my bed-place, and we would whisper together, with the regular footfalls of the officer of the watch passing and repassing over our heads. It was an infinitely miserable time. It was lucky that some tins of fine preserves were stowed in a locker in my stateroom; hard bread I could always get hold of; and so he lived on stewed chicken, pate de foie gras, asparagus, cooked oysters, sardines—on all sorts of abominable sham delicacies out of tins. My early morning coffee he always drank; and it was all I dared do for him in that respect.

Every day there was the horrible maneuvering to go through so that my room and then the bathroom should be done in the usual way. I came to hate the sight of the steward, to abhor the voice of that harmless man. I felt that it was he who would bring on the disaster of discovery. It hung like a sword over our heads.

The fourth day out, I think (we were then working down the east side of the Gulf of Siam, tack for tack, in light winds and smooth water)—the fourth day, I say, of this miserable juggling with the unavoidable, as we sat at our evening meal, that man, whose slightest movement I dreaded, after putting down the dishes ran up on deck busily.

This could not be dangerous. Presently he came down again; and then it appeared that he had remembered a coat of mine which I had thrown over a rail to dry after having been wetted in a shower which had passed over the ship in the afternoon. Sitting stolidly at the head of the table I became terrified at the sight of the garment on his arm. Of course he made for my door. There was no time to lose.

"Steward," I thundered. My nerves were so shaken that I could not govern my voice and conceal my agitation. This was the sort of thing that made my terrifically whiskered mate tap his forehead with his forefinger. I had detected him using that gesture while talking on deck with a confidential air to the carpenter. It was too far to hear a word, but I had no doubt that this pantomime could only refer to the strange new captain.

"Yes, sir," the pale-faced steward turned resignedly to me. It was this maddening course of being shouted at, checked without rhyme or reason, arbitrarily chased out of my cabin, suddenly called into it, sent flying out of his pantry on incomprehensible errands, that accounted for the growing wretchedness of his expression.

"Where are you going with that coat?"

"To your room, sir."

"Is there another shower coming?"

"I'm sure I don't know, sir. Shall I go up again and see, sir?"

"No! never mind."

My object was attained, as of course my other self in there would have heard everything that passed. During this interlude my two officers never raised their eyes off their respective plates; but the lip of that confounded cub, the second mate, quivered visibly.

I expected the steward to hook my coat on and come out at once. He was very slow about it; but I dominated my nervousness sufficiently not to shout after him. Suddenly I became aware (it could be heard plainly enough) that the fellow for some reason or other was opening the door of the bathroom. It was the end. The place was literally not big enough to swing a cat in. My voice died in my throat and I went stony all over. I expected to hear a yell of surprise and terror, and made a movement, but had not the strength to get on my legs. Everything remained still. Had my second self taken the poor wretch by the throat? I don't know what I would have done next moment if I had not seen the steward come out of my room, close the door, and then stand quietly by the sideboard.

Saved. I thought. But, no! Lost! Gone! He was gone!

I laid my knife and fork down and leaned back in my chair. My head swam. After a while, when sufficiently recovered to speak in a steady voice, I instructed my mate to put the ship round at eight o'clock himself.

"I won't come on deck," I went on. "I think I'll turn in, and unless the wind shifts I don't want to be disturbed before midnight. I feel a bit seedy."

"You did look middling bad a little while ago," the chief mate remarked without showing any great concern.

They both went out, and I stared at the steward clearing the table. There was nothing to be read on that wretched man's face. But why did he avoid my eyes I asked myself. Then I thought I should like to hear the sound of his voice.

"Steward!"

"Sir!" Startled as usual.

"Where did you hang up that coat?"

"In the bathroom, sir." The usual anxious tone. "It's not quite dry yet, sir."

For some time longer I sat in the cuddy. Had my double vanished as he had come? But of his coming there was an explanation, whereas his disappearance would be inexplicable. . . . I went slowly into my dark room, shut the door, lighted the lamp, and for a time dared not turn round. When at last I did I saw him standing bolt upright in the narrow recessed part. It would not be true to say I had a shock, but an irresistible doubt of his bodily existence flitted through my mind. Can it be, I asked myself, that he is not visible to other eyes than mine? It was like being haunted. Motionless, with a grave face, he raised his hands slightly at me in a gesture which meant clearly, "Heavens! what a narrow escape!" Narrow indeed. I think I had come creeping quietly as near insanity as any man who has not actually gone over the border. That gesture restrained me, so to speak.

The mate with the terrific whiskers was not putting the ship on the other tack. In the moment of profound silence which followed upon the hands going to their stations I heard on the poop his raised voice: "Hard alee!" and the distant shout of the order repeated on the maindeck. The sails, in that light breeze, made but a faint fluttering noise. It ceased. The ship was coming round slowly; I held my breath in the renewed stillness of expectation; one wouldn't have thought that there was a single living soul on her decks. A sudden brisk shout, "Mainsail haul!" broke the spell, and in the noisy cries and rush overhead of the men running away with the main brace we two, down in my cabin, came together in our usual position by the bed-place.

He did not wait for my question. "I heard him fumbling here and just managed to squat myself down in the bath," he whispered to me. "The fellow only opened the door and put his arm in to hang the coat up. All the same—"

"I never thought of that," I whispered back, even more appalled than before at the closeness of the shave, and marveling at that something unyielding in his character which was carrying him through so finely. There was no agitation in his whisper. Whoever was being driven distracted, it was not he. He was sane. And the proof of his sanity was continued when he took up the whispering again.

"It would never do for me to come to life again."

It was something that a ghost might have said. But what he was alluding to was his old captain's reluctant admission of the theory of suicide. It would obviously serve his turn—if I had understood at all the view which seemed to govern the unalterable purpose of his action.

"You must maroon me as soon as ever you can get amongst these islands off the Cambodje shore," he went on.

"Maroon you! We are not living in a boy's adventure tale," I protested. His scornful whispering took me up.

"We aren't indeed! There's nothing of a boy's tale in this. But there's nothing else for it. I want no more. You don't suppose I am afraid of what can be done to me? Prison or gallows or whatever they may please. But you don't see me coming back to explain such things to an old fellow in a wig and twelve respectable tradesmen, do you? What can they know whether I am guilty or not—or of *what* I am guilty, either? That's my affair. What does the Bible say? 'Driven off the face of the earth.' Very well. I am off the face of the earth now. As I came at night so I shall go."

"Impossible!" I murmured. "You can't."

"Can't? . . . Not naked like a soul on the Day of Judgment. I shall freeze on to this sleeping suit. The Last Day is not yet—and . . . you have understood thoroughly. Didn't you?"

I felt suddenly ashamed of myself. I may say truly that I understood—and my hesitation in letting that man swim away from my ship's side had been a mere sham sentiment, a sort of cowardice.

"It can't be done now till next night," I breathed out. "The ship is on the offshore tack and the wind may fail us."

"As long as I know that you understand," he whispered. "But of course you do. It's a great satisfaction to have got somebody to understand. You seem to have been there on purpose." And in the same whisper, as if we two whenever we talked had to say things to each other which were not fit for the world to hear, he added, "It's very wonderful."

We remained side by side talking in our secret way—but sometimes silent or just exchanging a whispered word or two at long intervals. And as usual he stared through the port. A breath of wind came now and again into our faces. The ship might have been moored in dock, so gently and on an even keel she slipped through the water, that did not murmur even at our passage, shadowy and silent like a phantom sea.

At midnight I went on deck, and to my mate's great surprise put the ship round on the other tack. His terrible whiskers flitted round me in silent criticism. I certainly should not have done it if it had been only a question of getting out of that sleepy gulf as quickly as possible. I believe he told the second mate, who relieved him, that it was a great want of judgment. The other only yawned. That intolerable cub shuffled about so sleepily and lolled against the rails in such a slack, improper fashion that I came down on him sharply.

"Aren't you properly awake yet?"

"Yes, sir! I am awake."

"Well, then, be good enough to hold yourself as if you were. And keep a lookout. If there's any current we'll be closing with some islands before daylight."

The east side of the gulf is fringed with islands, some solitary, others in groups. On the blue background of the high coast they seem to float on silvery patches of calm water, arid and gray, or dark green and rounded like clumps of evergreen bushes, with the larger ones, a mile or two long, showing the outlines of ridges, ribs of gray rock under the dark mantle of matted leafage. Unknown to trade, to travel, almost to geography, the manner of life they harbor is an unsolved secret. There must be villages—settlements of fishermen at least—on the largest of them, and some communication with the world is probably kept up by native craft. But all that forenoon, as we headed for them, fanned along by the faintest of breezes, I saw no sign of man or canoe in the field of the telescope I kept on pointing at the scattered group.

At noon I gave no orders for a change of course, and the mate's whiskers became much concerned and seemed to be offering themselves unduly to my notice. At last I said:

"I am going to stand right in. Quite in—as far as I can take her."

The stare of extreme surprise imparted an air of ferocity also to his eyes, and he looked truly terrific for a moment.

"We're not doing well in the middle of the gulf," I continued, casually. "I am going to look for the land breezes tonight."

"Bless my soul! Do you mean, sir, in the dark amongst the lot of all them islands and reefs and shoals?"

"Well—if there are any regular land breezes at all on this coast one must get close inshore to find them, mustn't one?"

"Bless my soul!" he exclaimed again under his breath. All that afternoon he wore a dreamy, contemplative appearance which in him was a mark of perplexity. After dinner I went into my stateroom as if I meant to take some rest. There we two bent our dark heads over a half-unrolled chart lying on my bed.

"There," I said. "It's got to be Koh-ring. I've been looking at it ever since sunrise. It has got two hills and a low point. It must be inhabited. And on the coast opposite there is what looks like the mouth of a biggish river—with some town, no doubt, not far up. It's the best chance for you that I can see."

"Anything. Koh-ring let it be."

He looked thoughtfully at the chart as if surveying chances and distances from a lofty height—and following with his eyes his own figure wandering on the blank land of Cochin China, and then passing off that piece of paper clean out of sight into uncharted regions. And it was as if the ship had two captains to plan her course for her. I had been so worried and restless running up and down that I had not had the patience to dress that day. I had remained in my sleeping suit, with straw slippers and a soft floppy hat. The closeness of the heat in the gulf had been most oppressive, and the crew were used to see me wandering in that airy attire.

"She will clear the south point as she heads now," I whispered into his ear. "Goodness only knows when, though, but certainly after dark. I'll edge her in to half a mile, as far as I may be able to judge in the dark—"

"Be careful," he murmured, warningly—and I realized suddenly that all my future, the only future for which I was fit, would perhaps go irretrievably to pieces in any mishap to my first command.

I could not stop a moment longer in the room. I motioned him to get out of sight and made my way on the poop. That unplayful cub had the watch. I walked up and down for a while thinking things out, then beckoned him over.

"Send a couple of hands to open the two quarter-deck ports," I said, mildly.

He actually had the impudence, or else so forgot himself in his wonder at such an incomprehensible order, as to repeat:

"Open the quarter-deck ports! What for, sir?"

"The only reason you need concern yourself about is because I tell you to do so. Have them open wide and fastened properly."

He reddened and went off, but I believe made some jeering remark to the carpenter as to the sensible practice of ventilating a ship's quarter-deck. I know he popped into the mate's cabin to impart the fact to him because the whiskers came on deck, as it were by chance, and stole glances at me from below—for signs of lunacy or drunkenness, I suppose.

A little before supper, feeling more restless than ever, I rejoined, for a moment, my second self. And to find him sitting so quietly was surprising, like something against nature, inhuman.

I developed my plan in a hurried whisper.

"I shall stand in as close as I dare and then put her round. I shall presently find means to smuggle you out of here into the sail locker, which communicates with the lobby. But there is an opening, a sort of square for hauling the sails out, which gives straight on the quarter-deck and which is never closed in fine weather, so as to give air to the sails. When the ship's way is deadened in stays and all the hands are aft at the main braces you shall have a clear road to slip out and get overboard through the open quarter-deck port. I've had them both fastened up. Use a rope's end to lower yourself into the water so as to avoid a splash—you know. It could be heard and cause some beastly complication."

He kept silent for a while, then whispered, "I understand."

"I won't be there to see you go," I began with an effort. "The rest . . . I only hope I have understood, too."

"You have. From first to last," and for the first time there seemed to be a faltering, something strained in his whisper. He caught hold of my arm, but the ringing of the supper bell made me start. He didn't though; he only released his grip.

After supper I didn't come below again till well past eight o'clock. The faint, steady breeze was loaded with dew; and the wet, darkened sails held all there was of propelling power in it. The night, clear and starry, sparkled darkly, and the opaque, lightless patches shifting slowly against the low stars were the drifting islets. On the port bow there was a big one more distant and shadowily imposing by the great space of sky it eclipsed.

On opening the door I had a back view of my very own self looking at a chart. He had come out of the recess and was standing near the table.

"Quite dark enough," I whispered.

He stepped back and leaned against my bed with a level, quiet glance. I sat on the couch. We had nothing to say to each other. Over our heads the officer of the watch moved here and there. Then I heard him move quickly. I knew what that meant. He was making for the companion; and presently his voice was outside my door.

"We are drawing in pretty fast, sir. Land looks rather close."

"Very well," I answered. "I am coming on deck directly."

I waited till he was gone out of the cuddy, then rose. My double moved too. The time had come to exchange our last whispers, for neither of us was ever to hear each other's natural voice.

"Look here!" I opened a drawer and took out three sovereigns. "Take this, anyhow. I've got six and I'd give you the lot, only I must keep a little money to buy some fruit and vegetables for the crew from native boats as we go through Sunda Straits."

He shook his head.

"Take it," I urged him, whispering desperately. "No one can tell what—"

He smiled and slapped meaningly the only pocket of the sleeping jacket. It was not safe, certainly. But I produced a large old silk handkerchief of mine, and tying the three pieces of gold in a corner, pressed it on him. He was touched, I suppose, because he took it at last and tied it quickly round his waist under the jacket, on his bare skin.

Our eyes met; several seconds elapsed, till, our glances still mingled, I extended my hand and turned the lamp out. Then I passed through the cuddy, leaving the door of my room wide open. . . . "Steward!"

He was still lingering in the pantry in the greatness of his zeal, giving a rub-up to a plated cruet stand the last thing before going to bed. Being careful not to wake up the mate, whose room was opposite, I spoke in an undertone.

He looked round anxiously. "Sir!"

"Can you get me a little hot water from the galley?"

"I am afraid, sir, the galley fire's been out for some time now."

"Go and see."

He fled up the stairs.

"Now," I whispered, loudly, into the saloon—too loudly, perhaps, but I was afraid I couldn't make a sound. He was by my side in an instant—the double captain slipped past the stairs—through the tiny dark passage . . . a sliding door. We were in the sail locker, scrambling on our knees over the sails. A sudden thought struck me. I saw myself wandering barefooted, bareheaded, the sun beating on my dark poll. I snatched off my floppy hat and tried hurriedly in the dark to ram it on my other self. He dodged and fended off silently. I wonder what he thought had come to me before he understood and suddenly desisted. Our hands met gropingly, lingered united in a steady, motionless clasp for a second. . . . No word was breathed by either of us when they separated.

I was standing quietly by the pantry door when the steward returned.

"Sorry, sir. Kettle barely warm. Shall I light the spirit lamp?"

"Never mind."

I came out on deck slowly. It was now a matter of conscience to shave the land as close as possible—for now he must go overboard whenever the ship was put in stays. Must! There could be no going back for him. After a moment I walked over to leeward and my heart flew into my mouth at the nearness of the land on the bow. Under any other circumstances I would not have held on a minute longer. The second mate had followed me anxiously.

I looked on till I felt I could command my voice.

"She will weather," I said then in a quiet tone.

"Are you going to try that, sir?" he stammered out incredulously.

I took no notice of him and raised my tone just enough to be heard by the helmsman.

"Keep her good full."

"Good full, sir."

The wind fanned my cheek, the sails slept, the world was silent. The strain of watching the dark loom of the land grow bigger and denser was too much for me. I had shut my eyes—because the ship must go closer. She must! The stillness was intolerable. Were we standing still?

When I opened my eyes the second view started my heart with a thump. The black southern hill of Koh-ring seemed to hang right over the ship like a towering fragment of the everlasting night. On that enormous mass of blackness there was not a gleam to be seen, not a sound to be heard. It was gliding irresistibly toward us and yet seemed already within reach of the hand. I saw the vague figures of the watch grouped in the waist, gazing in awed silence.

"Are you going on, sir?" inquired an unsteady voice at my elbow.

I ignored it. I had to go on.

"Keep her full. Don't check her way. That won't do now," I said warningly.

"I can't see the sails very well," the helmsman answered me, in strange, quavering tones.

Was she close enough? Already she was, I won't say in the shadow of the land, but in the very blackness of it, already swallowed up as it were, gone too close to be recalled, gone from me altogether.

"Give the mate a call," I said to the young man who stood at my elbow still as death. "And turn all hands up."

My tone had a borrowed loudness reverberated from the height of the land. Several voices cried out together: "We are all on deck, sir."

Then stillness again, with the great shadow gliding closer, towering higher, without a light, without a sound. Such a hush had fallen on the ship that she might have been a bark of the dead floating in slowly under the very gate of Erebus.

"My God! Where are we?"

It was the mate moaning at my elbow. He was thunderstruck, and as it were deprived of the moral support of his whiskers. He clapped his hands and absolutely cried out, "Lost!"

"Be quiet," I said sternly.

He lowered his tone, but I saw the shadowy gesture of his despair. "What are we doing here?"

"Looking for the land wind."

He made as if to tear his hair, and addressed me recklessly.

"She will never get out. You have done it, sir. I knew it'd end in something like this. She will never weather, and you are too close now to stay. She'll drift ashore before she's round. O my God!"

I caught his arm as he was raising it to batter his poor devoted head, and shook it violently.

"She's ashore already," he wailed, trying to tear himself away.

"Is she? . . . Keep good full there!"

"Good full, sir," cried the helmsman in a frightened, thin, child-like voice.

I hadn't let go the mate's arm and went on shaking it. "Ready about, do you hear? You go forward"—shake—"and stop there"—shake—"and hold your noise"—shake—"and see these head sheets properly overhauled"—shake, shake—shake.

And all the time I dared not look toward the land lest my heart should fail me. I released my grip at last and he ran forward as if fleeing for dear life.

I wondered what my double there in the sail locker thought of this commotion. He was able to hear everything—and perhaps he was able to understand why, on my conscience, it had to be thus close—no less. My first order "Hard alee!" re-echoed ominously under the towering shadow of Koh-ring as if I had shouted in a mountain gorge. And then I watched the land intently. In that smooth water and light wind it was impossible to feel the ship coming-to. No! I could not feel her. And my second self was making now ready to slip out and lower himself overboard. Perhaps he was gone already . . . ?

The great black mass brooding over our very mastheads began to pivot away from the ship's side silently. And now I forgot the secret stranger ready to depart, and remembered only that I was a total stranger to the ship. I did not know her. Would she do it? How was she to be handled?

I swung the mainyard and waited helplessly. She was perhaps stoppped, and her very fate hung in the balance, with the black mass of Koh-ring like the gate of the everlasting night towering over her taffrail. What would she do now? Had she way on her yet? I stepped to the side swiftly, and on the shadowy water I could see nothing except a faint phosphorescent flash revealing the glassy smoothness of the sleeping surface. It was impossible to tell—and I had not learned yet the feel of my ship. Was she moving? What I needed was something easily seen, a piece of paper, which I could throw overboard and watch. I had nothing on me. To run down for it I didn't dare. There was no time. All at once my strained, yearning stare distinguished a white object floating within a yard of the ship's side. White on the black water. A phosphorescent flash passed under it. What was that thing? . . . I recognized my own floppy hat. It must have fallen off his head . . . and he didn't bother. Now I had what I wanted—the saving mark for my eyes. But I hardly thought of my other self, now gone from the ship, to be hidden forever from all friendly faces, to be a fugitive and a vagabond on the earth, with no brand of the curse on his sane forehead to stay a slaying hand . . . too proud to explain.

And I watched the hat—the expression of my sudden pity for his mere flesh. It had been meant to save his homeless head from the dangers of the sun. And now—behold—it was saving the ship, by serving me for a mark to help out the ignorance of my strangeness. Ha! It was drifting forward, warning me just in time that the ship had gathered sternway.

"Shift the helm," I said in a low voice to the seaman standing still like a statue.

The man's eyes glistened wildly in the binnacle light as he jumped round to the other side and spun round the wheel.

I walked to the break of the poop. On the overshadowed deck all hands stood by the forebraces waiting for my order. The stars ahead seemed to be gliding from right to left. And all was so still in the world that I heard the quiet remark "She's round," passed in a tone of intense relief between two seamen.

"Let go and haul."

The foreyards ran round with a great noise, amidst cheery cries. And now the frightful whiskers made themselves heard giving various orders. Already the ship was drawing ahead. And I was alone with her. Nothing! no one in the world should stand now between us, throwing a shadow on the way of silent knowledge and mute affection, the perfect communion of a seaman with his first command.

Walking to the taffrail, I was in time to make out, on the very edge of a darkness thrown by a towering black mass like the very gateway of Erebus—yes, I was in time to catch an evanescent glimpse of my white hat left behind to mark the spot where the secret sharer of my cabin and of my thoughts, as though he were my second self, had lowered himself into the water to take his punishment: a free man, a proud swimmer striking out for a new destiny.

W. W. Jacobs *(1863–1943)*
The Monkey's Paw

Without, the night was cold and wet; but in the small parlor of Lakesnam Villa the blinds were drawn and the fire burned brightly. Father and son were at chess, the former, who possessed ideas about the game involving radical changes, putting his king into such sharp and unnecessary perils that it even provoked comment from the white-haired old lady knitting placidly by the fire.

"Hark at the wind," said Mr. White, who, having seen a fatal mistake after it was too late, was amiably desirous of preventing his son from seeing it.

"I'm listening," said the latter, grimly surveying the board as he stretched out his hand. "Check."

"I should hardly think that he'd come tonight," said his father, with his hand poised over the board.

"Mate," replied the son.

"That's the worst of living so far out," bawled Mr. White, with sudden and unlooked-for violence; "of all the beastly, slushy, out-of-the-way places to live in, this is the worst. Pathway's a bog, and the road's a torrent. I don't know what people are thinking about. I suppose because only two houses on the road are let they think it doesn't matter."

"Never mind, dear," said his wife soothingly; "perhaps you'll win the next one."

Mr. White looked up sharply, just in time to intercept a knowing glance between mother and son. The words died away on his lips, and he hid a guilty grin in his thin gray beard.

"There he is," said Herbert White as the gate banged to loudly and heavy footsteps came toward the door.

The old man rose with hospitable haste and, opening the door, was heard condoling with the new arrival. The new arrival also condoled with himself, so that Mrs. White said, "Tut, tut!" and coughed gently as her husband entered the room, followed by a tall burly man, beady of eye and rubicund of visage.

"Sergeant Major Morris," he said, introducing him.

The sergeant major shook hands and, taking the proffered seat by the fire, watched contentedly while his host got out whisky and tumblers and stood a small copper kettle on the fire.

At the third glass his eyes got brighter and he began to talk, the little family circle regarding with eager interest this visitor from distant parts as he squared his broad shoulders in the chair and spoke of strange scenes and doughty deeds, of wars and plagues and strange peoples.

"Twenty-one years of it," said Mr. White, nodding at his wife and son. "When he went away, he was a slip of a youth in the warehouse. Now look at him."

"He don't look to have taken much harm," said Mrs. White politely.

"I'd like to go to India myself," said the old man, "just to look round a bit, you know."

"Better where you are," said the sergeant major, shaking his head. He put down the empty glass and, sighing softly, shook it again.

"I should like to see those old temples and fakirs and jugglers," said the old man. "What was that you started telling me the other day about a monkey's paw or something, Morris?"

"Nothing," said the soldier hastily. "Leastways, nothing worth hearing."

"Monkey's paw?" said Mrs. White curiously.

"Well, it's just a bit of what you might call magic, perhaps," said the sergeant major offhandedly.

His three listeners leaned forward eagerly. The visitor absent-mindedly put his empty glass to his lips and then set it down again. His host filled it for him.

"To look at," said the sergeant major, fumbling in his pocket, "it's just an ordinary little paw, dried to a mummy."

He took something out of his pocket and proffered it. Mrs. White drew back with a grimace, but her son, taking it, examined it curiously.

"And what is there special about it?" inquired Mr. White as he took it from his son and, having examined it, placed it upon the table.

"It had a spell put on it by an old fakir," said the sergeant major, "a very holy man. He wanted to show that fate ruled people's lives, and that those who interfered with it did so to their sorrow. He put a spell on it so that three separate men could each have three wishes from it."

His manner was so impressive that his hearers were conscious that their light laughter jarred somewhat.

"Well, why don't you have three, sir?" said Herbert White cleverly.

The soldier regarded him in the way that middle age is wont to regard presumptuous youth. "I have," he said quietly, and his blotchy face whitened.

"And did you really have the three wishes granted?" asked Mrs. White.

"I did," said the sergeant major, and his glass tapped against his strong teeth.

"And has anybody else wished?" inquired the old lady.

"The first man had his three wishes, yes," was the reply. "I don't know what the first two were, but the third was for death. That's how I got the paw."

His tones were so grave that a hush fell upon the group.

"If you've had your three wishes, it's no good to you now, then, Morris," said the old man at last. "What do you keep it for?"

The soldier shook his head. "Fancy, I suppose," he said slowly. "I did have some idea of selling it, but I don't think I will. It has caused enough mischief already. Besides, people won't buy. They think it's a fairy tale, some of them, and those who do think anything of it want to try it first and pay me afterward."

"If you could have another three wishes," said the old man, eying him keenly, "would you have them?"

"I don't know," said the other. "I don't know."

He took the paw and, dangling it between his front finger and thumb, suddenly threw it upon the fire. White, with a slight cry, stooped down and snatched it off.

"Better let it burn," said the soldier solemnly.

"If you don't want it, Morris," said the old man, "give it to me."

"I won't," said his friend doggedly. "I threw it on the fire. If you keep it, don't blame me for what happens. Pitch it on the fire again, like a sensible man."

The other shook his head and examined his new possession closely. "How do you do it?" he inquired.

"Hold it up in your right hand and wish aloud," said the sergeant major, "but I warn you of the consequences."

"Sounds like the *Arabian Nights*," said Mrs. White as she rose and began to set the supper. "Don't you think you might wish for four pairs of hands for me?"

Her husband drew the talisman from his pocket, and then all three burst into laughter as the sergeant major, with a look of alarm on his face, caught him by the arm.

"If you must wish," he said gruffly, "wish for something sensible."

Mr. White dropped it back into his pocket and, placing chairs, motioned his friend to the table. In the business of supper the talisman was partly forgotten, and afterward the three sat listening in an enthralled fashion to a second installment of the soldier's adventures in India.

"If the tale about the monkey paw is not more truthful than those he has been telling us," said Herbert as the door closed behind their guest, just in time for him to catch the last train, "we shan't make much out of it."

"Did you give him anything for it, father?" inquired Mrs. White, regarding her husband closely.

"A trifle," said he, coloring slightly. "He didn't want it, but I made him take it. And he pressed me again to throw it away."

"Likely," said Herbert, with pretended horror. "Why, we're going to be rich, and famous, and happy. Wish to be an emperor, father, to begin with; then you can't be henpecked."

He darted round the table, pursued by the maligned Mrs. White armed with an antimacassar.

Mr. White took the paw from his pocket and eyed it dubiously. "I don't know what to wish for, and that's a fact," he said slowly. "It seems to me I've got all I want."

"If you only cleared the house, you'd be quite happy, wouldn't you," said Herbert, with his hand on his shoulder. "Well, wish for two hundred pounds, then; that'll just do it."

His father, smiling shamefacedly at his own credulity, held up the talisman as his son, with a solemn face somewhat marred by a wink at his mother, sat down at the piano and struck a few impressive chords.

"I wish for two hundred pounds," said the old man distinctly.

A fine crash from the piano greeted the words, interrupted by a shuddering cry from the old man. His wife and son ran toward him.

"It moved," he cried, with a glance of disgust at the object as it lay on the floor. "As I wished, it twisted in my hands like a snake."

"Well, I don't see the money," said his son as he picked it up and placed it on the table, "and I bet I never shall."

"It must have been your fancy, father," said his wife, regarding him anxiously.

He shook his head. "Never mind, though; there's no harm done, but it gave me a shock all the same."

They sat down by the fire again while the two men finished their pipes. Outside, the wind was higher than ever, and the old man started nervously at the sound of a door banging upstairs. A silence unusual and depressing settled upon all three, which lasted until the old couple rose to retire for the night.

"I expect you'll find the cash tied up in a big bag in the middle of your bed," said Herbert as he bade them good night, "and something horrible squatting up on top of the wardrobe watching you as you pocket your ill-gotten gains."

In the brightness of the wintry sun next morning as it streamed over the breakfast table, Herbert laughed at his fears. There was an air of prosaic wholesomeness about the room which it had lacked on the previous night, and the dirty, shriveled little paw was pitched on the sideboard with a carelessness which betokened no great belief in its virtues.

"I suppose all old soldiers are the same," said Mrs. White. "The idea of our listening to such nonsense! How could wishes be granted in these days? And if they could, how could two hundred pounds hurt you, father?"

"Might drop on his head from the sky," said the frivolous Herbert.

"Morris said the things happened so naturally," said his father, "that you might if you so wished attribute it to coincidence."

"Well, don't break into the money before I come back," said Herbert as he rose from the table. "I'm afraid it'll turn you into a mean, avaricious man, and we shall have to disown you."

His mother laughed, and following him to the door, watched him down the road, and returning to the breakfast table, was very happy at the expense of her husband's credulity. All of which did not prevent her from scurrying to the door at the postman's knock, nor prevent her from referring somewhat shortly to retired sergeant-majors of bibulous habits when she found that the post brought a tailor's bill.

321   W. W. JACOBS

"Herbert will have some more of his funny remarks, I expect, when he comes home," she said, as they sat at dinner.

"I dare say," said Mr. White, pouring himself out some beer; "but for all that, the thing moved in my hand; that I'll swear to."

"You thought it did," said the old lady soothingly.

"I say it did," replied the other. "There was no thought about it; I had just— What's the matter?"

His wife made no reply. She was watching the mysterious movements of a man outside, who, peering in an undecided fashion at the house, appeared to be trying to make up his mind to enter. In mental connection with the two hundred pounds, she noticed that the stranger was well dressed and wore a silk hat of glossy newness. Three times he paused at the gate, and then walked on again. The fourth time he stood with his hand upon it, and then with sudden resolution flung it open and walked up the path. Mrs. White at the same moment placed her hands behind her, and hurriedly unfastening the strings of her apron, put that useful article of apparel beneath the cushion of her chair.

She brought the stranger, who seemed ill at ease, into the room. He gazed furtively at Mrs. White, and listened in a preoccupied fashion as the old lady apologized for the appearance of the room, and her husband's coat, a garment which he usually reserved for the garden. She then waited as patiently as her sex would permit for him to broach his business, but he was at first strangely silent.

"I—was asked to call," he said at last, and stooped and picked a piece of cotton from his trousers. "I come from Maw and Meggins."

The old lady started. "Is anything the matter?" she asked breathlessly. "Has anything happened to Herbert? What is it? What is it?"

Her husband interposed. "There, there, mother," he said hastily. "Sit down, and don't jump to conclusions. You've not brought bad news, I'm sure, sir," and he eyed the other wistfully.

"I'm sorry—" began the visitor.

"Is he hurt?" demanded the mother.

The visitor bowed in assent. "Badly hurt," he said quietly, "but he is not in any pain."

"Oh, thank God!" said the old woman, clasping her hands. "Thank God for that! Thank—"

She broke off suddenly as the sinister meaning of the assurance dawned upon her and she saw the awful confirmation of her fears in the other's averted face. She caught her breath and, turning to her slower-witted husband, laid her trembling old hand upon his. There was a long silence.

"He was caught in the machinery," said the visitor at length, in a low voice.

"Caught in the machinery," repeated Mr. White, in a dazed fashion, "yes."

He sat staring blankly out at the window and, taking his wife's hand between his own, pressed it as he had been wont to do in their old courting days nearly forty years before.

"He was the only one left to us," he said, turning gently to the visitor. "It is hard."

The other coughed and, rising, walked slowly to the window. "The firm wished me to convey their sincere sympathy with you in your great loss," he said, without looking around. "I beg that you will understand I am only their servant and merely obeying orders."

There was no reply; the old woman's face was white, her eyes staring, and her breath inaudible; on her husband's face was a look such as his friend the sergeant might have carried into his first action.

"I was to say that Maw and Meggins disclaim all responsibility," continued the other. "They admit no liability at all, but in consideration of your son's services they wish to present you with a certain sum as compensation."

Mr. White dropped his wife's hand and, rising to his feet, gazed with a look of horror at his visitor. His dry lips shaped the words, "How much?"

"Two hundred pounds," was the answer.

Unconscious of his wife's shriek, the old man smiled faintly, put out his hands like a sightless man, and dropped, a senseless heap, to the floor.

In the huge new cemetery, some two miles distant, the old people buried their dead, and came back to a house steeped in shadow and silence. It was all over so quickly that at first they could hardly realize it, and remained in a state of expectation as though of something else to happen—something else which was to lighten this load, too heavy for old hearts to bear. But the days passed, and expectation gave place to resignation—the hopeless resignation of the old, sometimes miscalled apathy. Sometimes they hardly exchanged a word, for now they had nothing to talk about and their days were long to weariness.

It was about a week after that that the old man, waking suddenly in the night, stretched out his hand and found himself alone. The room was in darkness, and the sound of subdued weeping came from the window. He raised himself in bed and listened.

"Come back," he said tenderly. "You will be cold."

"It is colder for my son," said the old woman, and wept afresh.

The sound of her sobs died away on his ears. The bed was warm, and his eyes heavy with sleep. He dozed fitfully, and then slept until a sudden wild cry from his wife awoke him with a start.

"The monkey's paw!" she cried wildly. "The monkey's paw!"

He started up in alarm. "Where! Where is it? What's the matter?"

She came stumbling across the room toward him. "I want it," she said quietly. "You've not destroyed it?"

"It's in the parlor, on the bracket," he replied, marveling. "Why?"

She cried and laughed together and, bending over, kissed his cheek.

"I only just thought of it," she said hysterically. "Why didn't I think of it before? Why didn't you think of it?"

"Think of what?" he questioned.

"The other two wishes," she replied rapidly. "We've only had one."

"Was not that enough?" he demanded fiercely.

"No," she cried triumphantly; "we'll have one more. Go down and get it quickly, and wish our boy alive again."

The man sat up in bed and flung the bedclothes from his quaking limbs. "Good God, you are mad!" he cried, aghast.

"Get it," she panted; "get it quickly, and wish—Oh, my boy, my boy!"

Her husband struck a match and lit the candle. "Get back to bed," he said unsteadily. "You don't know what you are saying."

"We had the first wish granted," said the old woman feverishly. "Why not the second?"

"A coincidence," stammered the old man.

"Go and get it and wish," cried the old woman, and dragged him toward the door.

He went down in the darkness, and felt his way to the parlor and then to the mantelpiece. The talisman was in its place, and a horrible fear that the unspoken wish might bring his mutilated son before him ere he could escape from the room seized upon him, and he caught his breath as he found that he had lost the direction of the door. His brow cold with sweat, he felt his way round the table and groped along the wall until he found himself in the small passage with the unwholesome thing in his hand.

Even his wife's face seemed changed as he entered the room. It was white and expectant, and to his fears seemed to have an unnatural look upon it. He was afraid of her.

"Wish!" she cried, in a strong voice.

"It is foolish and wicked," he faltered.

"Wish!" repeated his wife.

He raised his hand. "I wish my son alive again."

The talisman fell to the floor, and he regarded it

shudderingly. Then he sank trembling into a chair as the old woman, with burning eyes, walked to the window and raised the blind.

He sat until he was chilled with the cold, glancing occasionally at the figure of the old woman peering through the window. The candle end, which had burnt below the rim of the china candlestick, was throwing pulsating shadows on the ceiling and walls, until, with a flicker larger than the rest, it expired. The old man, with an unspeakable sense of relief at the failure of the talisman, crept back to his bed, and a minute or two afterward the old woman came silently and apathetically beside him.

Neither spoke, but both lay silently listening to the ticking of the clock. A stair creaked, and a squeaky mouse scurried noisily through the wall. The darkness was oppressive and, after lying for some time screwing up his courage, the husband took the box of matches and, striking one, went downstairs for a candle.

At the foot of the stairs the match went out, and he paused to strike another, and at the same moment a knock, so quiet and stealthy as to be scarcely audible, sounded on the front door.

The matches fell from his hand. He stood motionless, his breath suspended until the knock was repeated. Then he turned and fled swiftly back to his room, and closed the door behind him. A third knock sounded through the house.

"*What's that?*" cried the old woman, starting up.

"A rat," said the old man, in shaking tones, "a rat. It passed me on the stairs."

His wife sat up in bed listening. A loud knock resounded through the house.

"It's Herbert!" she screamed. "It's Herbert!"

She ran to the door, but her husband was before her and, catching her by the arm, held her tightly.

"What are you going to do?" he whispered hoarsely.

"It's my boy; it's Herbert!" she cried, struggling mechanically. "I forgot it was two miles away. What are you holding me for? Let go. I must open the door."

"For God's sake don't let it in," cried the old man, trembling.

"You're afraid of your own son!" she cried, struggling. "Let me go. I'm coming, Herbert; I'm coming."

There was another knock, and another. The old woman with a sudden wrench broke free and ran from the room. Her husband followed to the landing, and called after her appealingly as she hurried downstairs. He heard the chain rattle back and the bottom bolt drawn slowly and stiffly from the socket. Then the old woman's voice, strained and panting.

"The bolt!" she cried loudly. "Come down. I can't reach it."

But her husband was on his hands and knees groping wildly on the floor in search of the paw. If he could only find it before the thing outside got in. A perfect fusillade of knocks reverberated through the house, and he heard the scraping of a chair as his wife put it down in the passage against the door. He heard the creaking of the bolt as it came slowly back, and at the same moment he found the monkey's paw and frantically breathed his third and last wish.

The knocking ceased suddenly, although the echoes of it were still in the house. He heard the chair drawn back and the door opened. A cold wind rushed up the staircase, and a long loud wail of disappointment and misery from his wife gave him courage to run down to her side and then to the gate beyond. The street lamp flickering opposite shone on a quiet and deserted road.

Richard Wright *(1908–1960)*
Almos' a Man

Dave struck out across the fields, looking homeward through paling light. Whut's the usa talkin' wid 'em niggers in the field? Anyhow, his mother was putting supper on the table. Them niggers can't understan' *nothing*. One of these days he was going to get a gun and practice shooting, then they can't talk to him as though he were a little boy. He slowed, looking at the ground. Shucks. Ah ain' scared-a them even ef they are bigger'n me! Aw, Ah know whut Ah'ma do . . . Ah'm going by ol' Joe's sto'n git that Sears Roebuck catlog'n look at them guns. Mabbe Ma will lemme buy one when she gits mah pay from ol' man Hawkins. Ah'ma beg her t'gimme some money. Ah'm ol' ernough to have gun. Ah'm seventeen. Almos' a man. He strode, feeling his long, loose-jointed limbs. Shucks, a man oughta hava little gun aftah he done worked hard all day. . . .

He came in sight of Joe's store. A yellow lantern glowed on the front porch. He mounted the steps and went through the screen door, hearing it bang behind him. There was a strong smell of coal oil and mackerel fish. He felt very confident until he saw fat Joe walk in through the rear door, then his courage began to ooze.

"Howdy, Dave! Whutcha want?"

"How yuh, Mistah Joe? Aw, Ah don' wanna buy nothing, Ah jus wanted t' see ef yuh'd lemme look at that ol' catlog erwhile."

"Sure! You wanna see it here?"

"Nawsuh. Ah wan's t' take it home wid me. Ah'll bring it back termorrow when Ah come in from the fiel's."

"Yu plannin' on buyin' something?"

"Yessuh."

"Your ma letting you have your own money now?"

"Shucks. Mistah Joe, Ah'm gittin' t' be a man like anybody else!"

Joe laughed and wiped his greasy white face with a red bandanna.

"Whut you plannin' on buyin'?"

Dave looked at the floor, scratched his head, scratched his thigh, and smiled. Then he looked up shyly.

"Ah'll tell yuh, Mistah Joe, ef yuh promise yuh won't tell."

"I promise."

"Waal, Ah'ma buy a gun."

"A gun? Whut you want with a gun?"

"Ah wanna keep it."

"You ain't nothing but a boy. You don't need a gun."

"Aw, lemme have the catlog, Mistah Joe. Ah'll bring it back."

Joe walked through the rear door. Dave was elated. He looked around at barrels of sugar and flour. He heard Joe coming back. He craned his neck to see if he were bringing the book. Yeah, he's got it! Gawddog, he's got it!

"Here; but be sure you bring it back. It's the only one I got."

"Sho', Mistah Joe."

"Say, if you wanna buy a gun, why don't you buy one from me? I gotta gun to sell."

"Will it shoot?"

"Sure it'll shoot."

"Whut kind is it?"

"Oh, it's kinda old. . . . A left-hand Wheeler. A pistol. A big one."

"Is it got bullets in it?"

"It's loaded."

"Kin Ah see it?"

"Where's your money?"

"Whut yuh wan' fer it?"

"I'll let you have it for two dollars."

"Just *two* dollars? Shucks, Ah could buy tha' when Ah git mah pay."

"I'll have it here when you want it."

"Awright, suh. Ah be in fer it."

He went through the door, hearing it slam again behind

him. Ah'ma git some money from Ma'n buy me a gun! Only *two* dollahs! He tucked the thick catalogue under his arm and hurried.

"Where yuh been, boy?" His mother held a steaming dish of black-eyed peas.

"Aw, Ma, Ah jus stopped down the road t' talk wid th' boys."

"Yuh know bettah than t' keep suppah waitin'."

He sat down, resting the catalogue on the edge of the table.

"Yuh git up from there and git to the well'n wash yo'se'f! Ah ain' feedin' no hogs in mah house!"

She grabbed his shoulder and pushed him. He stumbled out of the room, then came back to get the catalogue.

"Whut this?"

"Aw, Ma, it's jus'a catlog."

"Who yuh git it from?"

"From Joe, down at the sto'."

"Waal, tha's good. We kin use it around the house."

"Naw, Ma." He grabbed for it. "Gimme mah catlog, Ma."

She held onto it and glared at him.

"Quit hollerin' at me! Whut's wrong wid yuh? Yuh crazy?"

"But, Ma, please. It ain' mine! It's Joe's! He tol' me t' bring it back t'im termorrow."

She gave up the book. He stumbled down the back steps, hugging the thick book under his arm. When he had splashed water on his face and hands he groped back to the kitchen and fumbled in a corner for the towel. He bumped into a chair; it clattered to the floor. The catalogue sprawled at his feet. When he had dried his eyes he snatched up the book and held it again under his arm. His mother stood watching him.

"Now, ef yuh gonna acka fool over that ol' book, Ah'll take it a' burn it up."

"Naw, Ma, please,"

"Waal, set down'n be still!"

He sat and drew the oil lamp close. He thumbed page after page, unaware of the food his mother set on the table. His father came in. Then his small brother.

"Whutcha got there, Dave?" his father asked.

"Jus'a catlog," he answered, not looking up.

"Ywah, here they is!" His eyes glowed at blue and black revolvers. He glanced up, feeling sudden guilt. His father was watching him. He eased the book under the table and rested it on his knees. After the blessing was asked, he ate. He scooped up peas and swallowed fat meat without chewing. Buttermilk helped to wash it down.

He did not want to mention money before his father. He would do much better by cornering his mother when she was alone. He looked at his father uneasily out of the edge of his eye.

"Boy, how come yuh don't quit foolin' wid tha' book'n eat yo' suppah?"

"Yessuh."

"How yuh'n ol' man Hawkins gittin' erlong?"

"Suh?"

"Can't yuh hear? Why don' yuh lissen? Ah ast yuh how wuz yuh'n ol' man Hawkins gittin erlong?"

"Oh, swell, Pa. Ah plows mo' lan' than anybody over there."

"Waal, yuh oughta keep yo' min' on whut yuh doin'."

"Yessuh."

He poured his plate full of molasses and sopped at it slowly with a chunk of corn bread. When all but his mother had left the kitchen, he still sat and looked again at the guns in the catalogue. Lawd, ef Ah only had tha' pretty one! He could almost feel the slickness of the weapon with his fingers. If he had a gun like that he would polish it and keep it shining so it would never rust. N'Ah'd keep it loaded, by Gawd!

"Ma?"

"Hunh?"

"Ol man Hawkins give yuh mah money yit?"

"Yeah, but ain' no usa yuh thinkin' 'bout th'owin' nona it erway. Ah'm keepin' tha' money so's yuh kin have cloes t' go to school this winter."

He rose and went to her side with the open catalogue in his palms. She was washing dishes, her head bent low over a pan. Shyly he raised the open book. When he spoke his voice was husky, faint.

"Ma, Gawd knows Ah wan's one of these."

"One of whut?" she asked, not raising her eyes.

"One of *these*," he said again, not daring even to point.

She glanced up at the page, then at him with wide eyes.

"Nigger, is yuh gone plum crazy?"

"Aw, Ma——"

"Git outta here! Don't yuh talk t' me 'bout no gun! Yuh a fool!"

"Ma, Ah kin buy one fer *two* dollahs."

"Not ef Ah knows it yuh ain'!"

"But yuh promised me one——"

"Ah don' care whut Ah promised! Yuh ain' nothing but a boy yit!"

"Ma, ef yuh le' me buy one Ah'll *never* ast yuh fer nothing no mo'!"

"Ah tol' yuh t' git outta here! Yuh ain' gonna toucha

329   RICHARD WRIGHT

penny of tha' money fer no gun! Tha's how come Ah has Mistah Hawkins t' pay yo wages t' me, cause Ah knows yuh ain' got no sense.''

"But, Ma, we needa gun. Pa ain' got no gun. We needa gun in the house. Yuh kin never tell whut might happen.''

"Now don' yuh try to maka fool outta me, boy! Ef we did hava gun yuh wouldn't have it!''

He laid the catalogue down and slipped his arm around her waist.

"Aw, Ma, Ah done worked hard alla summer'n ain' ast yuh fer nothin', is Ah, now?''

"That whut yuh s'pose t' do!''

"But, Ma, Ah wan's a gun. Yuh kin lemme have two dollahs outta mah money. Please, Ma. I kin give it to Pa. . . . Please, Ma! Ah loves yuh, Ma.''

When she spoke her voice came soft and low.

"Whut yuh wan' wida gun, Dave? Yuh don' need no gun. Yuh'll git in trouble. N'ef yo' Pa jus' *thought* Ah let yuh have money t' buy a gun he'd hava fit.''

"Ah'll hide it, Ma, it ain' but two dollahs.''

"Lawd, chil, whut's wrong wid yuh?''

"Ain' nothing wrong, Ma. Ah'm almos' a man now. Ah wan's a gun.''

"Who gonna sell yuh a gun?''

"Ol' Joe at the sto'.''

"N' it don' cos but two dollahs?''

"Tha's all, Ma. Just two dollahs. Please, Ma.''

She was stacking the plates away; her hands moved slowly, reflectively. Dave kept an anxious silence. Finally she turned to him.

"Ah'll let yuh git tha' gun ef yuh promise me one thing.''

"Whut's tha', Ma?''

"Yuh bring it straight back t' *me*, yuh hear? It'll be fer Pa.''

"Yessum! Lemme go now, Ma.''

She stooped, turned slightly to one side, raised the hem of her dress, rolled down the top of her stocking, and came up with a slender wad of bills.

"Here,'' she said. "Lawd knows yuh don' need no gun. But yer pa does. Yuh bring it right back t' *me*, yuh hear? Ah'ma put it up. Now ef yuh don', Ah'ma have yuh Pa lick yuh so hard yuh won' ferget it.''

The first movement he made the following morning was to reach under his pillow for the gun. In the gray light of dawn he held it loosely, feeling a sense of power. Could kill a man wida gun like this. Kill anybody, black er white. And if he were holding his gun in his hand nobody could run over him; they would have to respect him. It was a big gun, with a long barrel and a heavy handle. He raised and lowered it in his hand, marveling at its weight.

He had not come straight home with it as his mother had asked; instead he had stayed out in the fields, holding the weapon in his hand, aiming it now and then at some imaginary foe. But he had not fired it; he had been afraid that his father might hear. Also he was not sure he knew how to fire it.

To avoid surrendering the pistol he had not come into the house until he knew that all were asleep. When his mother had tiptoed to his bedside late that night and demanded the gun he had first played possum; then he had told her that the gun was hidden outdoors, that he would bring it to her in the morning. Now he lay turning it slowly in his hands. He broke it, took out the cartridges, felt them, and then put them back.

He slid out of bed, got a long strip of old flannel from a trunk, wrapped the gun in it, and tied it to his naked thigh while it was still loaded. He did not go in to breakfast. Even though it was not yet daylight, he started for Jim Hawkins' plantation. Just as the sun was rising he reached the barns where the mules and plows were kept.

"Hey! That you, Dave?"

He turned. Jim Hawkins stood eying him suspiciously.

"What're yuh doing here so early?"

"Ah didn't know Ah wuz gittin' up so early, Mistah Hawkins. Ah wuz fixin' t' hitch up ol' Jenny'n take her t' the fiels."

"Good. Since you're here so early, how about plowing that stretch down by the woods?"

"Suits me, Mistah Hawkins."

"Okay. Go to it!"

He hitched Jenny to a plow and started across the fields. Hot dog! This was just what he wanted. If he could get down by the woods he could shoot his gun and nobody would hear. He walked behind the plow, hearing the traces creaking, feeling the gun tied tight to his thigh.

When he reached the woods he plowed two whole rows before he decided to take out the gun. Finally he stopped, looked in all directions, then untied the gun and held it in his hand. He turned to the mule and smiled.

"Know whut this is, Jenny? Naw, yuh wouldn't know! Yuh's jus'a ol' mule! Anyhow, this is a gun'n it kin shoot, by Gawd!"

He held the gun at arm's length. Whut t' hell, Ah'ma shoot this thing! He looked at Jenny again.

"Lissen here, Jenny! When Ah pull this ol' trigger Ah don' wan' yuh t' run'n acka fool now."

Jenny stood with head down, her short ears pricked straight. Dave walked off about twenty feet, held the gun far out from him, at arm's length, and turned his head. Hell, he told himself, Ah ain' afraid. The gun felt loose in his fingers; he waved it wildly for a moment. Then he shut his eyes and tightened his forefinger. *Bloom!* A report half deafened him and he thought his right hand was torn from his arm. He heard Jenny whinnying and galloping over the field and he found himself on his knees, squeezing his fingers hard between his legs. His hand was numb; he jammed it into his mouth, trying to warm it, trying to stop the pain. The gun lay at his feet. He did not quite know what had happened. He stood up and stared at the gun as though it were a live thing. He gritted his teeth and kicked the gun. Yuh almos' broke mah arm! He turned to look for Jenny; she was far over the field, tossing her head and kicking wildly.

"Hol' on there, ol' mule!"

When he caught up with her she stood trembling, walling her big white eyes at him. The plow was far away; the traces had broken. Then Dave stopped short, looking, not believing. Jenny was bleeding. Her left side was red and wet with blood. He went closer. Lawd have mercy! Wondah did Ah shoot this mule? He grabbed for Jenny's mane. She flinched, snorted, whirled, tossing her head.

"Hol' on now! Hol' on."

Then he saw the hole in Jenny's side, right between the ribs. It was round, wet, red. A crimson stream streaked down the front leg, flowing fast. Good Gawd! Ah wuzn't shootin' at tha mule. . . . He felt panic. He knew he had to stop that blood or Jenny would bleed to death. He had never seen so much blood in all his life. He ran the mule for half a mile, trying to catch her. Finally she stopped, breathing hard, stumpy tail half arched. He caught her mane and led her back to where the plow and gun lay. Then he stopped and grabbed handfuls of damp black earth and tried to plug the bullet hole. Jenny shuddered, whinnied, and broke from him.

"Hol' on! Hol' on now!"

He tried to plug it again, but blood came anyhow. His fingers were hot and sticky. He rubbed dirt hard into his palms, trying to dry them. Then again he attempted to plug the bullet hole, but Jenny shied away, kicking her heels high. He stood helpless. He had to do something. He ran at Jenny; she dodged him. He watched a red stream of blood flow down Jenny's leg and form a bright pool at her feet.

"Jenny . . . Jenny . . ." he called weakly.

His lips trembled. She's bleeding t' death! He looked in the direction of home, wanting to go back, wanting to get help. But he saw the pistol lying in the damp black clay. He had a queer feeling that if he only did something this would not be; Jenny would not be there bleeding to death.

When he went to her this time she did not move. She

stood with sleepy, dreamy eyes; and when he touched her she gave a low-pitched whinny and knelt to the ground, her front knees slopping in blood.

"Jenny . . . Jenny . . ." he whispered.

For a long time she held her neck erect; then her head sank, slowly. Her ribs swelled with a mighty heave and she went over.

Dave's stomach felt empty, very empty. He picked up the gun and held it gingerly between this thumb and forefinger. He buried it at the foot of a tree. He took a stick and tried to cover the pool of blood with dirt—but what was the use? There was Jenny lying with her mouth open and her eyes walled and glassy. He could not tell Jim Hawkins he had shot his mule. But he had to tell something. Yeah, Ah'll tell em Jenny started gittin' wiln fell on the joint of the plow. But that would hardly happen to a mule. He walked across the field slowly, head down.

It was sunset. Two of Jim Hawkins' men were over near the edge of the woods digging a hole in which to bury Jenny. Dave was surrounded by a knot of people; all of them were looking down at the dead mule.

"I don't see how in the world it happened," said Jim Hawkins for the tenth time.

The crowd parted and Dave's mother, father, and small brother pushed into the center.

"Where Dave?" his mother called.

"There he is," said Jim Hawkins.

His mother grabbed him.

"Whut happened, Dave? Whut yuh done?"

"Nothing."

"C'mon, boy, talk," his father said.

Dave took a deep breath and told the story he knew nobody believed.

"Waal," he drawled. "Ah brung ol' Jenny down here so's Ah could do mah plowin'. Ah plowed 'bout two rows, just like yuh see." He stopped and pointed at the long rows of upturned earth. "Then something musta been wrong wid ol' Jenny. She wouldn't ack right a-tall. She started snortin'n kickin' her heels. Ah tried to hol' her, but she pulled erway, rearn'n goin' on. Then when the point of the plow was stickin' up in the air, she swung erroun'n twisted herself back on it. . . . She struck herse'f'n started t' bleed. N' fo' Ah could do anything, she wuz dead."

"Did you ever hear of anything like that in all your life?" asked Jim Hawkins.

There were white and black standing in the crowd. They murmured. Dave's mother came close to him and looked hard into his face.

"Tell the truth, Dave," she said.

"Looks like a bullet hole ter me," said one man.

"Dave, whut yuh do wid tha' gun?" his mother asked.

The crowd surged in, looking at him. He jammed his hands into his pockets, shook his head slowly from left to right, and backed away. His eyes were wide and painful.

"Did he hava gun?" asked Jim Hawkins.

"By Gawd, Ah tol' yuh tha' wuz a *gun* wound," said a man, slapping his thigh.

His father caught his shoulders and shook him till his teeth rattled.

"Tell whut happened, yuh rascal! Tell whut——"

Dave looked at Jenny's stiff legs and began to cry.

"Whut yuh do wid tha' gun?" his mother asked.

"Whut wuz he doin' wida gun?" his father asked.

"Come on and tell the truth," said Hawkins. "Ain't nobody going to hurt you. . . ."

His mother crowded close to him.

"Did yuh shoot tha' mule, Dave?"

Dave cried, seeing blurred white and black faces.

"Ah-h d-din-n't g-g-go t-t' s-shoo-ot h-her . . . Ah s-s-swear off Gawd Ah-h d-din't . . . Ah wuz a-tryin' t' s-see ef the ol' g-g-gun would s-shoot——"

"Where yuh git the gun from?" his father asked.

"Ah got it from Joe, at the sto'."

"Where yuh git the money?"

"Ma give it t' me."

"He kept worryin' me, Bob. . . . Ah had t' . . . Ah tol' 'im t' bring the gun right back t' me. . . . It was fer yuh, the gun."

"But how yuh happen to shoot that mule?" asked Jim Hawkins.

"Ah wuzn't shootin' at the mule, Mistah Hawkins. The gun jumped when Ah pulled the trigger. . . . N' fo' Ah knowed anything Jenny wuz there a-bleedin'."

Somebody in the crowd laughed. Jim Hawkins walked close to Dave and looked into his face.

"Well, looks like you have bought you a mule, Dave."

"Ah swear fo' Gawd, Ah didn't go t' kill the mule, Mistah Hawkins!"

"But you killed her!"

All the crowd was laughing now. They stood on tiptoe and poked heads over one another's shoulders.

"Well, boy, looks like yuh done bought a dead mule! Hahaha!"

"Ain' tha' ershame."

"Hohohohoho."

Dave stood, head down, twisting his feet in the dirt.

"Well, you needn't worry about it, Bob," said Jim Hawkins to Dave's father. "Just let the boy keep on working and pay me two dollars a month."

"What yuh wan' fer yo' mule, Mistah Hawkins?"

Jim Hawkins screwed up his eyes.

"Fifty dollars."

"Whut yuh do wid tha' gun?" Dave's father demanded.

Dave said nothing.

"Yuh wan' me t' take a tree lim'n beat yuh till yuh talk!"

"Nawsuh!"

"Whut yuh do wid it?"

"Ah th'owed it erway."

"Where?"

"Ah . . . Ah th'owed it in the creek."

"Waal, c'mon home. N' firs' thing in the mawnin' git to that creek'n fin' tha' gun."

"Yessuh."

"Whut yuh pay fer it?"

"Two dollahs."

"Take tha' gun'n git yo' money back'n carry it t' Mistah Hawkins, yuh hear? N' don' fergit Ah'ma lam yo' black bottom good fer this! Now march yo'se'f on home, suh!"

Dave turned and walked slowly. He heard people laughing. Dave glared, his eyes welling with tears. Hot anger bubbled in him. Then he swallowed and stumbled on.

That night Dave did not sleep. He was glad that he had gotten out of killing the mule so easily, but he was hurt. Something hot seemed to turn over inside him each time he remembered how they had laughed. He tossed on his bed, feeling his hard pillow. N' Pa says he's gonna beat me. . . . He remembered other beatings, and his back quivered. Naw, naw, Ah sho' don' wan' 'im t' beat me tha' way no mo'. Damn 'em *all*! Nobody ever gave him anything. All he did was work. They treat me lika mule. . . . N' then they beat me. . . . He gritted his teeth. N' Ma had t' tell on me.

Well, if he had to, he would take old man Hawkins that two dollars. But that meant selling the gun. And he wanted to keep that gun. Fifty dollahs fer a dead mule.

He turned over, thinking of how he had fired the gun. He had an itch to fire it again. Ef other men kin shoota gun, by Gawd, Ah kin! He was still listening. Mebbe they all sleepin' now. . . . The house was still. He heard the soft breathing of his brother. Yes, now! He would go down and get that gun and see if he could fire it! He eased out of bed and slipped into overalls.

The moon was bright. He ran almost all the way to the edge of the woods. He stumbled over the ground, looking for the spot where he had buried the gun. Yeah, here it is. Like a hungry dog scratching for a bone he pawed it up. He puffed his black cheeks and blew dirt from the trigger and barrel. He broke it and found four cartridges unshot. He looked around; the fields were filled with silence and moonlight. He clutched the gun stiff and hard in his fingers. But as soon as he wanted to pull the trigger, he shut his eyes and turned his head. Naw, Ah can't shoot wid mah eyes closed'n mah head turned. With effort he held his eyes open; then he squeezed. *Blooooom!* He was stiff, not breathing. The gun was still in his hands. Dammit, he'd done it! He fired again. *Blooooom!* He smiled. *Blooooom! Blooooom! Click, click.* There! It was empty. If anybody could shoot a gun, he could. He put the gun into his hip pocket and started across the fields.

When he reached the top of a ridge he stood straight and proud in the moonlight, looking at Jim Hawkins' big white house, feeling the gun sagging in his pocket. Lawd, ef Ah had jus' one mo' bullet Ah'd taka shot at tha' house. Ah'd like t' scare ol' man Hawkins jus'a little. . . . Jus' enough t' let 'im know Dave Sanders is a man.

To his left the road curved, running to the tracks of the Illinois Central. He jerked his head, listening. From far off came a faint *hoooof-hoooof; hooof-hoooof; hoooof-hoooof.* . . . Tha's number eight. He took a swift look at Jim Hawkins' white house; he thought of Pa, of Ma, of his little brother, and the boys. He thought of the dead mule and heard *hoooof-hoooof; hooof-hoooof; hoooof-hoooof.* . . . He stood rigid. Two dollahs a mont'. Le's see now. . . . Tha' means it'll take 'bout two years. Shucks! Ah'll be dam!

He started down the road, toward the tracks. Yeah, here she comes! He stood beside the track and held himself stiffly. Here she comes, erroun' the ben'. . . . C'mon, yuh slowpoke! C'mon! He had his hand on his gun; something quivered in his stomach. Then the train thundered past, the gray and brown boxcars rumbling and clinking. He gripped the gun tightly; then he jerked his hand out of his pocket. Ah betcha Bill wouldn't do it! Ah betcha. . . . The cars slid past, steel grinding upon steel. Ah'm riding yuh ternight so he'p me Gawd! He was hot all over. He hesitated just a moment; then he grabbed, pulled atop of a car, and lay flat. He felt his pocket; the gun was still there. Ahead the long rails were glinting in moonlight, stretching away, away to somewhere, somewhere where he could be a man. . . .

James Baldwin *(1924–)*

Sonny's Blues

I read about it in the paper, in the subway, on my way to work. I read it, and I couldn't believe it, and I read it again. Then perhaps I just stared at it, at the newsprint spelling out his name, spelling out the story. I stared at it in the swinging lights of the subway car, and in the faces and bodies of the people, and in my own face, trapped in the darkness which roared outside.

It was not to be believed and I kept telling myself that, as I walked from the subway station to the high school. And at the same time I couldn't doubt it. I was scared, scared for Sonny. He became real to me again. A great block of ice got settled in my belly and kept melting there slowly all day long, while I taught my classes algebra. It was a special kind of ice. It kept melting, sending trickles of ice water all up and down my veins, but it never got less. Sometimes it hardened and seemed to expand until I felt my guts were going to come spilling out or that I was going to choke or scream. This would always be at a moment when I was remembering some specific thing Sonny had once said or done.

When he was about as old as the boys in my classes his face had been bright and open, there was a lot of copper in it; and he'd had wonderfully direct brown eyes, and great gentleness and privacy. I wondered what he looked like now. He had been picked up, the evening before, in a raid on an apartment downtown, for peddling and using heroin.

I couldn't believe it: but what I mean by that is that I couldn't find any room for it anywhere inside me. I had kept it outside me for a long time. I hadn't wanted to know. I had had suspicions, but I didn't name them, I kept putting them away. I told myself that Sonny was wild, but he wasn't crazy. And he'd always been a good boy, he hadn't ever turned hard or evil or disrespectful, the way kids can, so quick, so quick, especially in Harlem. I didn't want to believe that I'd ever see my brother going down, coming to nothing, all that light in his face gone out, in the condition I'd already seen so many others. Yet it had happened and here I was, talking about algebra to a lot of boys who might, every one of them for all I knew, be popping off needles every time they went to the head. Maybe it did more for them than algebra could.

I was sure that the first time Sonny had ever had horse, he couldn't have been much older than these boys were now. These boys, now, were living as we'd been living then, they were growing up with a rush and their heads bumped abruptly against the low ceiling of their actual possibilities. They were filled with rage. All they really knew were two darknesses, the darkness of their lives, which was now closing in on them, and the darkness of the movies, which had blinded them to that other darkness, and in which they now, vindictively, dreamed, at once more together than they were at any other time, and more alone.

When the last bell rang, the last class ended, I let out my breath. It seemed I'd been holding it for all that time. My clothes were wet—I may have looked as though I'd been sitting in a steam bath, all dressed up, all afternoon. I sat alone in the classroom a long time. I listened to the boys outside, downstairs, shouting and cursing and laughing. Their laughter struck me for perhaps the first time. It was not the joyous laughter which—God knows why—one associates with children. It was mocking and insular, its intent to denigrate. It was disenchanted, and in this, also, lay the authority of their curses. Perhaps I was listening to them because I was thinking about my brother and in them I heard my brother. And myself.

One boy was whistling a tune, at once very complicated and very simple, it seemed to be pouring out of him as though he were a bird, and it sounded very cool and moving through all that harsh, bright air, only just holding its own through all those other sounds.

I stood up and walked over to the window and looked down into the courtyard. It was the beginning of the spring and the sap was rising in the boys. A teacher passed through them every now and again, quickly, as though he or she couldn't wait to get out of that courtyard, to get those boys out of their sight and off their minds. I started collecting my stuff. I thought I'd better get home and talk to Isabel.

The courtyard was almost deserted by the time I got downstairs. I saw this boy standing in the shadow of a doorway, looking just like Sonny. I almost called his name. Then I saw that it wasn't Sonny, but somebody we used to know, a boy from around our block. He'd been Sonny's friend. He'd never been mine, having been too young for me, and, anyway, I'd never liked him. And now, even though he was a grown-up man, he still hung around that block, still spent hours on the street corners, was always high and raggy. I used to run into him from time to time and he'd often work around to asking me for a quarter or fifty cents. He always had some real good excuse, too, and I always gave it to him, I don't know why.

But now, abruptly, I hated him. I couldn't stand the way he looked at me, partly like a dog, partly like a cunning child. I wanted to ask him what the hell he was doing in the school courtyard.

He sort of shuffled over to me, and he said, "I see you got the papers. So you already know about it."

"You mean about Sonny? Yes, I already know about it. How come they didn't get you?"

He grinned. It made him repulsive and it also brought to mind what he'd looked like as a kid. "I wasn't there. I stay away from them people."

"Good for you." I offered him a cigarette and I

watched him through the smoke. "You come all the way down here just to tell me about Sonny?"

"That's right." He was sort of shaking his head and his eyes looked strange, as though they were about to cross. The bright sun deadened his damp dark brown skin and it made his eyes look yellow and showed up the dirt in his kinked hair. He smelled funky. I moved a little away from him and I said, "Well, thanks. But I already know about it and I got to get home."

"I'll walk you a little ways," he said. We started walking. There were a couple of kids still loitering in the courtyard and one of them said goodnight to me and looked strangely at the boy beside me.

"What're you going to do?" he asked me. "I mean, about Sonny?"

"Look. I haven't seen Sonny for over a year, I'm not sure I'm going to do anything. Anyway, what the hell *can* I do?"

"That's right," he said quickly, "ain't nothing you can do. Can't much help old Sonny no more, I guess."

It was what I was thinking and so it seemed to me he had no right to say it.

"I'm surprised at Sonny, though," he went on—he had a funny way of talking, he looked straight ahead as though he were talking to himself—"I thought Sonny was a smart boy, I thought he was too smart to get hung."

"I guess he thought so too," I said sharply, "and that's how he got hung. And now about you? You're pretty goddamn smart, I bet."

Then he looked directly at me, just for a minute. "I ain't smart," he said. "If I was smart, I'd have reached for a pistol a long time ago."

"Look. Don't tell *me* your sad story, if it was up to me, I'd give you one." Then I felt guilty—guilty, probably, for never having supposed that the poor bastard *had* a story of his own, much less a sad one, and I asked, quickly, "What's going to happen to him now?"

He didn't answer this. He was off by himself some place. "Funny thing," he said, and from his tone we might have been discussing the quickest way to get to Brooklyn, "when I saw the papers this morning, the first thing I asked myself was if I had anything to do with it. I felt sort of responsible."

I began to listen more carefully. The subway station was on the corner, just before us, and I stopped. He stopped, too. We were in front of a bar and he ducked slightly, peering in, but whoever he was looking for didn't seem to be there. The juke box was blasting away with something black and bouncy and I half watched the barmaid as she danced her way from the juke box to her place behind the bar. And I watched her face as she laughingly responded to something someone said to her, still keeping time to the music. When she smiled one saw the little girl, one sensed the doomed, still-struggling woman beneath the battered face of the semi-whore.

"I never *give* Sonny nothing," the boy said finally, "but a long time ago I come to school high and Sonny asked me how it felt." He paused, I couldn't bear to watch him, I watched the barmaid, and I listened to the music which seemed to be causing the pavement to shake. "I told him it felt great." The music stopped, the barmaid paused and watched the juke box until the music began again. "It did."

All this was carrying me some place I didn't want to go. I certainly didn't want to know how it felt. It filled everything, the people, the houses, the music, the dark, quicksilver barmaid, with menace; and this menace was their reality.

"What's going to happen to him now?" I asked again.

"They'll send him away some place and they'll try to cure him." He shook his head. "Maybe he'll even think he's kicked the habit. Then they'll let him loose"—he gestured, throwing his cigarette into the gutter. "That's all."

"What do you mean, that's *all*?"

But I knew what he meant.

"I *mean*, that's *all*." He turned his head and looked at me, pulling down the corners of his mouth. "Don't you know what I mean?" he asked, softly.

"How the hell *would* I know what you mean?" I almost whispered it, I don't know why.

"That's right," he said to the air, "how would *he* know what I mean?" He turned toward me again, patient and calm, and yet I somehow felt him shaking, shaking as though he were going to fall apart. I felt that ice in my guts again, the dread I'd felt all afternoon; and again I watched the barmaid, moving about the bar, washing glasses, and singing. "Listen. They'll let him out and then it'll just start all over again. That's what I mean."

"You mean—they'll let him out. And then he'll just start working his way back in again. You mean he'll never kick the habit. Is that what you mean?"

"That's right," he said, cheerfully. "*You* see what I mean."

"Tell me," I said at last, "why does he want to die? He must want to die, he's killing himself, why does he want to die?"

He looked at me in surprise. He licked his lips. "He don't want to die. He wants to live. Don't nobody want to die, ever."

Then I wanted to ask him—too many things. He could not have answered, or if he had, I could not have borne the answers, I started walking. "Well, I guess it's none of my business."

"It's going to be rough on old Sonny," he said. We reached the subway station. "This is your station?" he asked. I nodded. I took one step down. "Damn!" he said, suddenly. I looked up at him. He grinned again. "Damn it if I didn't leave all my money home. You ain't got a dollar on you, have you? Just for a couple of days, is all."

All at once something inside gave and threatened to come pouring out of me. I didn't hate him any more. I felt that in another moment I'd start crying like a child.

"Sure," I said. "Don't sweat." I looked in my wallet and didn't have a dollar, I only had a five. "Here," I said. "That hold you?"

He didn't look at it—he didn't want to look at it. A terrible closed look came over his face, as though he were keeping the number on the bill a secret from him and me. "Thanks," he said, and now he was dying to see me go. "Don't worry about Sonny. Maybe I'll write him or something."

"Sure," I said. "You do that. So long."

"Be seeing you," he said. I went on down the steps.

And I didn't write Sonny or send him anything for a long time. When I finally did, it was just after my little girl died, he wrote me back a letter which made me feel like a bastard.

Here's what he said:

> Dear brother,
> You don't know how much I needed to hear from you. I wanted to write you many a time but I dug how much I must have hurt you and so I didn't write. But now I feel like a man who's been trying to climb up out of some deep, real deep and funky hole and just saw the sun up there, outside. I got to get outside.
> I can't tell you much about how I got here. I mean I don't know how to tell you. I guess I was afraid of something or I was trying to escape from something and you know I have never been very strong in the head (smile). I'm glad Mama and Daddy are dead and can't see what's happened to their son and I swear if I'd known what I was doing I would never have hurt you so, you and a lot of other fine people who were nice to me and who believed in me.
> I don't want you to think it had anything to do with me being a musician. It's more than that. Or maybe less than that. I can't get anything straight in my head down here and I try not to think about what's going to happen to me when I get outside again. Sometime I think I'm going to flip and *never* get outside and sometime I think I'll come straight back. I tell you one thing, though, I'd rather blow my brains out than go through this again. But that's what they all say, so they

tell me. If I tell you when I'm coming to New York and if you could meet me, I sure would appreciate it. Give my love to Isabel and the kids and I was sure sorry to hear about little Gracie. I wish I could be like Mama and say the Lord's will be done, but I don't know it seems to me that trouble is the one thing that never does get stopped and I don't know what good it does to blame it on the Lord. But maybe it does some good if you believe it.

Your brother,
Sonny

Then I kept in constant touch with him and I sent him whatever I could and I went to meet him when he came back to New York. When I saw him many things I thought I had forgotten came flooding back to me. This was because I had begun, finally, to wonder about Sonny, about the life that Sonny lived inside. This life, whatever it was, had made him older and thinner and it had deepened the distant stillness in which he had always moved. He looked very unlike my baby brother. Yet, when he smiled, when we shook hands, the baby brother I'd never known looked out from the depths of his private life, like an animal waiting to be coaxed into the light.

"How you been keeping?" he asked me.

"All right. And you?"

"Just fine." He was smiling all over his face. "It's good to see you again."

"It's good to see you."

The seven years' difference in our ages lay between us like a chasm: I wondered if these years would ever operate between us as a bridge. I was remembering, and it made it hard to catch my breath, that I had been there when he was born; and I had heard the first words he had ever spoken. When he started to walk, he walked from our mother straight to me. I caught him just before he fell when he took the first steps he ever took in this world.

"How's Isabel?"

"Just fine. She's dying to see you."

"And the boys?"

"They're fine, too. They're anxious to see their uncle."

"Oh, come on. You know they don't remember me."

"Are you kidding? Of course they remember you."

He grinned again. We got into a taxi. We had a lot to say to each other, far too much to know how to begin.

As the taxi began to move, I asked, "You still want to go to India?"

He laughed. "You still remember that. Hell, no. This place is Indian enough for me."

"It used to belong to them," I said.

And he laughed again. "They damn sure knew what they were doing when they got rid of it."

Years ago, when he was around fourteen, he'd been all hipped on the idea of going to India. He read books about people sitting on rocks, naked, in all kinds of weather, but mostly bad, naturally, and walking barefoot through hot coals and arriving at wisdom. I used to say that it sounded to me as though they were getting away from wisdom as fast as they could. I think he sort of looked down on me for that.

"Do you mind," he asked, "if we have the driver drive alongside the park? On the west side—I haven't seen the city in so long."

"Of course not," I said. I was afraid that I might sound as though I were humoring him, but I hoped he wouldn't take it that way.

So we drove along, between the green of the park and the stony, lifeless elegance of hotels and apartment buildings, toward the vivid, killing streets of our childhood. These streets hadn't changed, though housing projects jutted up out of them now like rocks in the middle of a boiling sea. Most of the houses in which we had grown up had vanished, as had the stores from which we had stolen, the basements in which we had first tried sex, the rooftops from which we had hurled tin cans and bricks. But houses exactly like the houses of our past yet dominated the landscape, boys exactly like the boys we once had been found themselves smothering in these houses, came down into the streets for light and air and found themselves encircled by disaster. Some escaped the trap, most didn't. Those who got out always left something of themselves behind, as some animals amputate a leg and leave it in the trap. It might be said, perhaps, that I had escaped, after all, I was a school teacher; or that Sonny had, he hadn't lived in Harlem for years. Yet, as the cab moved uptown through streets which seemed, with a rush, to darken with dark people, and as I covertly studied Sonny's face, it came to me that what we both were seeking through our separate cab windows was that part of ourselves which had been left behind. It's always at the hour of trouble and confrontation that the missing member aches.

We hit 110th Street and started rolling up Lenox Avenue. And I'd known this avenue all my life, but it seemed to me again, as it had seemed on the day I'd first heard about Sonny's trouble, filled with a hidden menace which was its very breath of life.

"We almost there," said Sonny.

"Almost." We were both too nervous to say anything more.

We live in a housing project. It hasn't been up long. A few days after it was up it seemed uninhabitably new, now, of course, it's already rundown. It looks like a parody of the good, clean, faceless life—God knows the people who live in it do their best to make it a parody. The beat-looking grass lying around isn't enough to make their lives green, the hedges will never hold out the streets, and they know it. The big windows fool no one, they aren't big enough to make space out of no space. They don't bother with the windows, they watch the TV screen instead. The playground is most popular with the children who don't play at jacks, or skip rope, or roller skate, or swing, and they can be found in it after dark. We moved in partly because it's not too far from where I teach, and partly for the kids; but it's really just like the houses in which Sonny and I grew up. The same things happen, they'll have the same things to remember. The moment Sonny and I started into the house I had the feeling that I was simply bringing him back into the danger he had almost died trying to escape.

Sonny has never been talkative. So I don't know why I was sure he'd be dying to talk to me when supper was over the first night. Everything went fine, the oldest boy remembered him, and the youngest boy liked him, and Sonny had remembered to bring something for each of them; and Isabel, who is really much nicer than I am, more open and giving, had gone to a lot of trouble about dinner and was genuinely glad to see him. And she's always been able to tease Sonny in a way that I haven't. It was nice to see her face so vivid again and to hear her laugh and watch her make Sonny laugh. She wasn't, or anyway, she didn't seem to be, at all uneasy or embarrassed. She chatted as though there were no subject which had to be avoided and she got Sonny past his first, faint stiffness. And thank God she was there, for I was filled with that icy dread again. Everything I did seemed awkward to me, and everything I said sounded freighted with hidden meaning. I was trying to remember everything I'd heard about dope addiction and I couldn't help watching Sonny for signs. I wasn't doing it out of malice. I was trying to find out something about my brother. I was dying to hear him tell me he was safe.

"Safe!" my father grunted, whenever Mama suggested trying to move to a neighborhood which might be safer for children. "Safe, hell! Ain't no place safe for kids, nor nobody."

He always went on like this, but he wasn't, ever, really as bad as he sounded, not even on weekends, when he got drunk. As a matter of fact, he was always on the lookout for "something a little better," but he died before he found it. He died suddenly, during a drunken weekend in the middle of the war, when Sonny was fifteen. He and Sonny hadn't ever got on too well. And this was partly because Sonny was the apple of his father's eye. It was because he loved Sonny so much and was frightened for him, that he was always fighting with him. It doesn't do any good to fight with Sonny. Sonny just moves back, inside himself, where he can't be reached. But the principal reason that they never hit it off is that they were so much alike. Daddy was big and rough and loud-talking, just the opposite of Sonny, but they both had—that same privacy.

Mama tried to tell me something about this, just after Daddy died. I was home on leave from the army.

This was the last time I ever saw my mother alive. Just the same, this picture gets all mixed up in my mind with pictures I had of her when she was younger. The way I always see her is the way she used to be on a Sunday afternoon, say, when the old folks were talking after the big Sunday dinner. I always see her wearing pale blue. She'd be sitting on the sofa. And my father would be sitting in the easy chair, not far from her. And the living room would be full of church folks and relatives. There they sit, in chairs all around the living room, and the night is creeping up outside, but nobody knows it yet. You can see the darkness growing against the windowpanes and you hear the street noises every now and again, or maybe the jangling beat of a tambourine from one of the churches close by, but it's real quiet in the room. For a moment nobody's talking, but every face looks darkening, like the sky outside. And my mother rocks a little from the waist, and my father's eyes are closed. Everyone is looking at something a child can't see. For a minute they've forgotten the children. Maybe a kid is lying on the rug, half asleep. Maybe somebody's got a kid in his lap and is absent-mindedly stroking the kid's head. Maybe there's a kid, quiet and big-eyed, curled up in a big chair in the corner. The silence, the darkness coming, and the darkness in the faces frightens the child obscurely. He hopes that the hand which strokes his forehead will never stop—will never die. He hopes that there will never come a time when the old folks won't be sitting around the living room, talking about where they've come from, and what they've seen, and what's happened to them and their kinfolk.

But something deep and watchful in the child knows that this is bound to end, is already ending. In a moment someone will get up and turn on the light. Then the old folks will remember the children and they won't talk any more that day. And when light fills the room, the child is filled with darkness. He knows that everytime this happens he's moved just a little closer to that darkness outside. The darkness outside is what the old folks have been talking about. It's what they've come from. It's what they endure. The child knows that they won't talk any more because if he knows too much about what's happened to *them*, he'll know too much too soon, about what's going to happen to *him*.

The last time I talked to my mother, I remember I was restless. I wanted to get out and see Isabel. We weren't married then and we had a lot to straighten out between us.

There Mama sat, in black, by the window. She was humming an old church song, *Lord, you brought me from a long ways off.* Sonny was out somewhere. Mama kept watching the streets.

"I don't know," she said, "if I'll ever see you again, after you go off from here. But I hope you'll remember the things I tried to teach you."

"Don't talk like that," I said, and smiled. "You'll be here a long time yet."

She smiled, too, but she said nothing. She was quiet for a long time. And I said, "Mama, don't you worry about nothing. I'll be writing all the time, and you be getting the checks. . . ."

"I want to talk to you about your brother," she said, suddenly. "If anything happens to me he ain't going to have nobody to look out for him."

"Mama," I said, "ain't nothing going to happen to you *or* Sonny. Sonny's all right. He's a good boy and he's got good sense."

"It ain't a question of his being a good boy," Mama said, "nor of his having good sense. It ain't only the bad ones, nor yet the dumb ones that gets sucked under." She stopped, looking at me. "Your Daddy once had a brother," she said, and she smiled in a way that made me feel she was in pain. "You didn't never know that, did you?"

"No," I said, "I never knew that," and I watched her face.

"Oh, yes," she said, "your Daddy had a brother." She looked out of the window again. "I know you never saw your Daddy cry. But *I* did—many a time, through all these years."

I asked her, "What happened to his brother? How come nobody's ever talked about him?"

This was the first time I ever saw my mother look old.

"His brother got killed," she said, "when he was just a little younger than you are now. I knew him. He was a fine boy. He was maybe a little full of the devil, but he didn't mean nobody no harm."

Then she stopped and the room was silent, exactly as it had sometimes been on those Sunday afternoons. Mama kept looking out into the streets.

"He used to have a job in the mill," she said, "and, like all young folks, he just liked to perform on Saturday nights. Saturday nights, him and your father would drift around to different places, go to dances and things like that, or just sit around with people they knew, and your father's brother would sing, he had a fine voice, and play along with himself on his guitar. Well, this particular Saturday night, him and your father was coming home from some place, and they were both a little drunk and there was a moon that night, it was bright like day. Your father's brother was feeling kind of good, and he was whistling to himself, and he had his guitar slung over his shoulder. They was coming down a hill and beneath them was a road that turned off from the highway. Well, your father's brother, being always kind of frisky, decided to run down this hill, and he did, with that guitar banging and clanging behind him, and he ran across the road, and he was making water behind a tree. And your father was sort of amused at him and he was still coming down the hill, kind of slow. Then he heard a car motor and that same minute his brother stepped from behind the tree, into the road, in the moonlight. And he started to cross the road. And your father started to run down the hill, he says he don't know why. This car was full of white men. They was all drunk, and when they seen your father's brother they let out a great whoop and holler and they aimed the car straight at him. They was having fun, they just wanted to scare him, the way they do sometimes, you know. But they was drunk. And I guess the boy, being drunk, too, and scared, kind of lost his head. By the time he jumped it was too late. Your father says he heard his brother scream when the car rolled over him, and he heard the wood of that guitar when it give, and he heard them strings go flying, and he heard them white men shouting, and the car kept on a-going and it ain't stopped till this day. And, time your father got down the hill, his brother weren't nothing but blood and pulp."

Tears were gleaming on my mother's face. There wasn't anything I could say.

"He never mentioned it," she said, "because I never let him mention it before you children. Your Daddy was like a crazy man that night and for many a night thereafter. He says he never in his life seen anything as dark as that road after the lights of that car had gone away. Weren't nothing, weren't nobody on that road, just your Daddy and his brother and that busted guitar. Oh, yes. Your Daddy never did really get right again. Till the day he died he weren't sure but that every white man he saw was the man that killed his brother."

She stopped and took out her handkerchief and dried her eyes and looked at me.

"I ain't telling you all this," she said, "to make you scared or bitter or to make you hate nobody. I'm telling you this because you got a brother. And the world ain't changed."

I guess I didn't want to believe this. I guess she saw this in my face. She turned away from me, toward the window again, searching those streets.

"But I praise my Redeemer," she said at last, "that He called your Daddy home before me. I ain't saying it to throw no flowers at myself, but, I declare, it keeps me from feeling too cast down to know I helped your father get safely through this world. Your father always acted like he was the roughest, strongest man on earth. And everybody took him to be like that. But if he hadn't had *me* there—to see his tears!"

She was crying again. Still, I couldn't move. I said, "Lord, Lord, Mama, I didn't know it was like that."

"Oh, honey," she said, "there's a lot that you don't know. But you are going to find it out." She stood up from the window and came over to me. "You got to hold on to your brother," she said, "and don't let him fall, no matter what it looks like is happening to him and no matter how evil you gets with him. You going to be evil with him many a time. But don't you forget what I told you, you hear?"

"I won't forget," I said. "Don't you worry, I won't forget. I won't let nothing happen to Sonny."

My mother smiled as though she were amused at something she saw in my face. Then, "You may not be able to stop nothing from happening. But you got to let him know you's *there*."

Two days later I was married, and then I was gone. And I had a lot of things on my mind and I pretty well forgot my promise to Mama until I got shipped home on a special furlough for her funeral.

And, after the funeral, with just Sonny and me alone in the empty kitchen, I tried to find out something about him.

"What do you want to do?" I asked him.

"I'm going to be a musician," he said.

For he had graduated, in the time I had been away, from dancing to the juke box to finding out who was playing what, and what they were doing with it, and he had bought himself a set of drums.

"You mean, you want to be a drummer?" I somehow had the feeling that being a drummer might be all right for other people but not for my brother Sonny.

"I don't think," he said, looking at me very gravely, "that I'll ever be a good drummer. But I think I can play a piano."

I frowned. I'd never played the role of the older brother quite so seriously before, had scarcely ever, in fact, *asked* Sonny a damn thing. I sensed myself in the presence of something I didn't really know how to handle, didn't understand. So I made my frown a little deeper as I asked: "What kind of musician do you want to be?"

He grinned. "How many kinds do you think there are?"

"Be *serious*," I said.

He laughed, throwing his head back, and then looked at me. "I *am* serious."

"Well, then, for Christ's sake, stop kidding around and answer a serious question. I mean, do you want to be a concert pianist, you want to play classical music and all that, or—or what?" Long before I finished he was laughing again. "For Christ's *sake*, Sonny!"

He sobered, but with difficulty. "I'm sorry. But you sound so—*scared*!" and he was off again.

"Well, you may think it's funny now, baby, but it's not going to be so funny when you have to make your living at it, let me tell you *that*." I was furious because I knew he was laughing at me and I didn't know why.

"No," he said, very sober now, and afraid, perhaps, that he'd hurt me, "I don't want to be a classical pianist. That isn't what interests me. I mean"—he paused, looking hard at me, as though his eyes would help me to understand, and then gestured helplessly, as though perhaps his hand would help—"I mean, I'll have a lot of studying to do, and I'll have to study *everything*, but, I mean, I want to play *with*—jazz musicians." He stopped. "I want to play jazz," he said.

Well, the word had never before sounded as heavy, as real, as it sounded that afternoon in Sonny's mouth. I just looked at him and I was probably frowning a real frown by this time. I simply couldn't see why on earth he'd want to spend his time hanging around nightclubs, clowning around on bandstands, while people pushed each other around a dance floor. It seemed—beneath him, somehow. I had never thought about it before, had never been forced to, but I suppose I had always put jazz musicians in a class with what Daddy called "good-time people."

"Are you *serious?*"

"Hell, *yes*, I'm serious."

He looked more helpless than ever, and annoyed, and deeply hurt.

I suggested, helpfully: "You mean—like Louis Armstrong?"

His face closed as though I'd struck him. "No. I'm not talking about none of that old-time, down home crap."

"Well, look, Sonny, I'm sorry, don't get mad. I just don't altogether get it, that's all. Name somebody—you know, a jazz musician you admire."

"Bird."

"Who?"

"Bird! Charlie Parker! Don't they teach you nothing in the goddamn army?"

I lit a cigarette. I was surprised and then a little amused to discover that I was trembling. "I've been out of touch," I said. "You'll have to be patient with me. Now. Who's this Parker character?"

"He's just one of the greatest jazz musicians alive," said Sonny, sullenly, his hands in his pockets, his back to me. "Maybe *the* greatest," he added, bitterly, "that's probably why *you* never heard of him."

"All right," I said, "I'm ignorant. I'm sorry. I'll go out and buy all the cat's records right away, all right?"

"It don't," said Sonny, with dignity, "make no difference to me. I don't care what you listen to. Don't do me no favors."

I was beginning to realize that I'd never seen him so upset before. With another part of my mind I was thinking that this would probably turn out to be one of those things kids go through and that I shouldn't make it seem important by pushing it too hard. Still, I didn't think it would do any harm to ask: "Doesn't all this take a lot of time? Can you make a living at it?"

He turned back to me and half leaned, half sat, on the kitchen table. "Everything takes time," he said, "and—well, yes, sure, I can make a living at it. But what I don't seem to be able to make you understand is that it's the only thing I want to do."

"Well, Sonny," I said, gently, "you know people can't always do exactly what they *want* to do—"

"*No*, I don't know that," said Sonny, surprising me. "I think people *ought* to do what they want to do, what else are they alive for?"

"You getting to be a big boy," I said desperately, "it's time you started thinking about your future."

"I'm thinking about my future," said Sonny, grimly. "I think about it all the time."

I gave up. I decided, if he didn't change his mind, that we could always talk about it later. "In the meantime," I said, "you got to finish school." We had already decided that he'd have to move in with Isabel and her folks. I knew this wasn't the ideal arrangement because Isabel's folks are inclined to be dicty and they hadn't especially wanted Isabel to marry me. But I didn't know what else to do. "And we have to get you fixed up at Isabel's."

There was a long silence. He moved from the kitchen table to the window. "That's a terrible idea. You know it yourself."

"Do you have a *better* idea?"

He just walked up and down the kitchen for a minute. He was as tall as I was. He had started to shave. I suddenly had the feeling that I didn't know him at all.

He stopped at the kitchen table and picked up my cigarettes. Looking at me with a kind of mocking, amused defiance, he put one between his lips. "You mind?"

"You smoking already?"

He lit the cigarette and nodded, watching me through the smoke. "I just wanted to see if I'd have the courage to smoke in front of you." He grinned and blew a great cloud of smoke to the ceiling. "It was easy." He looked at my face. "Come on, now. I bet you was smoking at my age, tell the truth."

I didn't say anything but the truth was on my face, and he laughed. But now there was something very strained in his laugh. "Sure. And I bet that ain't all you was doing."

He was frightening me a little. "Cut the crap," I said. "We already decided that you was going to go and live at Isabel's. Now what's got into you all of a sudden?"

"*You* decided it," he pointed out. "*I* didn't decide nothing." He stopped in front of me, leaning against the stove, arms loosely folded. "Look, brother. I don't want to stay in Harlem no more, I really don't." He was very earnest. He looked at me, then over toward the kitchen window. There was something in his eyes I'd never seen before, some thoughtfulness, some worry all his own. He rubbed the muscle of one arm. "It's time I was getting out of here."

"Where do you want to *go*, Sonny?"

"I want to join the army. Or the navy, I don't care. If I say I'm old enough, they'll believe me."

Then I got mad. It was because I was so scared. "You

must be crazy. You goddamn fool, what the hell do you want to go and join the *army* for?"

"I just told you. To get out of Harlem."

"Sonny, you haven't even finished *school*. And if you really want to be a musician, how do you expect to study if you're in the *army*?"

He looked at me, trapped, and in anguish. "There's ways. I might be able to work out some kind of deal. Anyway, I'll have the G.I. Bill when I come out."

"*If* you come out." We stared at each other. "Sonny, please. Be reasonable. I know the setup is far from perfect. But we got to do the best we can."

"I ain't learning nothing in school," he said. "Even when I go ." He turned away from me and opened the window and threw his cigarette out into the narrow alley. I watched his back. "At least, I ain't learning nothing you'd want me to learn." He slammed the window so hard I thought the glass would fly out, and turned back to me. "And I'm sick of the stink of these garbage cans!"

"Sonny," I said, "I know how you feel. But if you don't finish school now, you're going to be sorry later that you didn't. I grabbed him by the shoulders. "And you only got another year. It ain't so bad. And I'll come back and I swear I'll help you do *whatever* you want to do. Just try to put up with it till I come back. Will you please do that? For me?"

He didn't answer and he wouldn't look at me.

"Sonny. You hear me?"

He pulled away. "I hear you. But you never hear anything *I* say."

I didn't know what to say to that. He looked out of the window and then back at me. "OK," he said, and sighed. "I'll try."

Then I said, trying to cheer him up a little, "They got a piano at Isabel's. You can practice on it."

And as a matter of fact, it did cheer him up for a minute. "That's right," he said to himself. "I forgot that." His face relaxed a little. But the worry, the thoughtfulness, played on it still, the way shadows play on a face which is staring into the fire.

But I thought I'd never hear the end of that piano. At first, Isabel would write me, saying how nice it was that Sonny was so serious about his music and how, as soon as he came in from school, or wherever he had been when he was supposed to be at school, he went straight to that piano and stayed there until suppertime. And, after supper, he went back to that piano and stayed there until everybody went to bed. He was at the piano all day Saturday and all day Sunday. Then he bought a record player and started playing records. He'd play one record over and over again, all day long sometimes, and he'd improvise along with it on the piano. Or he'd play one section of the record, one chord, one change, one progression, then he'd do it on the piano. Then back to the record. Then back to the piano.

Well, I really don't know how they stood it. Isabel finally confessed that it wasn't like living with a person at all, it was like living with sound. And the sound didn't make any sense to her, didn't make any sense to any of them—naturally. They began, in a way, to be afflicted by this presence that was living in their home. It was as though Sonny were some sort of god, or monster. He moved in an atmosphere which wasn't like theirs at all. They fed him and he ate, he washed himself, he walked in and out of their door; he certainly wasn't nasty or unpleasant or rude, Sonny isn't any of those things; but it was as though he were all wrapped up in some cloud, some fire, some vision all his own; and there wasn't any way to reach him.

At the same time, he wasn't really a man yet, he was still a child, and they had to watch out for him in all kinds of ways. They certainly couldn't throw him out. Neither did they dare to make a great scene about that piano because even they dimly sensed, as I sensed, from so many thousands of miles away, that Sonny was at that piano playing for his life.

But he hadn't been going to school. One day a letter came from the school board and Isabel's mother got it—there had, apparently, been other letters but Sonny had torn them up. This day, when Sonny came in, Isabel's mother showed him the letter and asked where he'd been spending his time. And she finally got it out of him that he'd been down in Greenwich Village, with musicians and other characters, in a white girl's apartment. And this scared her and she started to scream at him and what came up, once she began—though she denies it to this day—was what sacrifices they were making to give Sonny a decent home and how little he appreciated it.

Sonny didn't play the piano that day. By evening, Isabel's mother had calmed down but then there was the old man to deal with, and Isabel herself. Isabel says she did her best to be calm but she broke down and started crying. She says she just watched Sonny's face. She could tell, by watching him, what was happening with him. And what was happening was that they penetrated his cloud, they had reached him. Even if their fingers had been a thousand times more gentle than human fingers ever are, he could hardly help feeling that they had stripped him naked and were spitting on that nakedness. For he also had to see that his presence, that music, which was life or death to him, had been torture for them and that they had endured it, not at all for his sake, but only for mine. And Sonny couldn't take that. He can take it a little better today than he could then but he's still not very good at it, and frankly, I don't know anybody who is.

The silence of the next few days must have been louder

than the sound of all the music ever played since time began. One morning, before she went to work, Isabel was in his room for something and she suddenly realized that all of his records were gone. And she knew for certain that he was gone. And he was. He went as far as the navy would carry him. He finally sent me a postcard from some place in Greece and that was the first I knew that Sonny was still alive. I didn't see him any more until we were both back in New York and the war had long been over.

He was a man by then, of course, but I wasn't willing to see it. He came by the house from time to time, but we fought almost every time we met. I didn't like the way he carried himself, loose and dreamlike all the time, and I didn't like his friends, and his music seemed to be merely an excuse for the life he led. It sounded just that weird and disordered.

Then we had a fight, a pretty awful fight, and I didn't see him for months. By and by I looked him up, where he was living, in a furnished room in the Village, and I tried to make it up. But there were lots of people in the room and Sonny just lay on his bed, and he wouldn't come downstairs with me, and he treated these other people as though they were his family and I weren't. So I got mad and then he got mad, and then I told him that he might just as well be dead as live the way he was living. Then he stood up and he told me not to worry about him any more in life, that he *was* dead as far as I was concerned. Then he pushed me to the door and the other people looked on as though nothing were happening, and he slammed the door behind me. I stood in the hallway, staring at the door. I heard somebody laugh in the room and then the tears came to my eyes. I started down the steps, whistling to keep from crying, I kept whistling to myself, *You going to need me, baby, one of these cold, rainy days.*

I read about Sonny's trouble in the spring. Little Grace died in the fall. She was a beautiful little girl. But she only lived a little over two years. She died of polio and she suffered. She had a slight fever for a couple of days, but it didn't seem like anything and we just kept her in bed. And we would certainly have called the doctor, but the fever dropped, she seemed to be all right. So we thought it had just been a cold. Then, one day, she was up, playing, Isabel was in the kitchen fixing lunch for the two boys when they'd come in from school, and she heard Grace fall down in the living room. When you have a lot of children you don't always start running when one of them falls, unless they start screaming or something. And, this time, Grace was quiet. Yet, Isabel says that when she heard that *thump* and then that silence, something happened in her to make her afraid. And she ran to the living room and there was little Grace on the floor, all twisted up, and the reason she hadn't screamed was that she couldn't get her breath. And when she did scream, it was the worst sound, Isabel says, that she'd ever heard in all her life, and she still hears it sometimes in her dreams. Isabel will sometimes wake me up with a low, moaning, strangled sound and I have to be quick to awaken her and hold her to me and where Isabel is weeping against me seems a mortal wound.

I think I may have written Sonny the very day that little Grace was buried. I was sitting in the living room in the dark, by myself, and I suddenly thought of Sonny. My trouble made his real.

One Saturday afternoon, when Sonny had been living with us, or, anyway, been in our house, for nearly two weeks, I found myself wandering aimlessly about the living room, drinking from a can of beer, and trying to work up the courage to search Sonny's room. He was out, he was usually out whenever I was home, and Isabel had taken the children to see their grandparents. Suddenly I was standing still in front of the living room window, watching Seventh Avenue. The idea of searching Sonny's room made me still. I scarcely dared to admit to myself what I'd be searching for. I didn't know what I'd do if I found it. Or if I didn't.

On the sidewalk across from me, near the entrance to a barbecue joint, some people were holding an old-fashioned revival meeting. The barbecue cook, wearing a dirty white apron, his conked hair reddish and metallic in the pale sun, and a cigarette between his lips, stood in the doorway, watching them. Kids and older people paused in their errands and stood there, along with some older men and a couple of very tough-looking women who watched everything that happened on the avenue, as though they owned it, or were maybe owned by it. Well, they were watching this, too. The revival was being carried on by three sisters in black, and a brother. All they had were their voices and their Bibles and a tambourine. The brother was testifying and while he testified two of the sisters stood together, seeming to say, amen, and the third sister walked around with the tambourine outstretched and a couple of people dropped coins into it. Then the brother's testimony ended and the sister who had been taking up the collection dumped the coins into her palm and transferred them to the pocket of her long black robe. Then she raised both hands, striking the tambourine against the air, and then against one hand, and she started to sing. And the two other sisters and the brother joined in.

It was strange, suddenly, to watch, though I had been seeing these street meetings all my life. So, of course, had everybody else down there. Yet, they paused and watched and listened and I stood still at the window. *"Tis the old ship of Zion,"* they sang, and the sister with the tambourine kept a steady, jangling beat, *"it has rescued many a thousand!"* Not a soul under the sound of their voices was hearing this song for the first time, not one of them had been rescued. Nor had they seen much in the way of rescue work being done around them. Neither did they especially believe in the holiness of the three sisters and the brother, they knew too much about them, knew where they lived, and how. The woman with the tambourine, whose voice dominated the air, whose face was bright with joy, was divided by very little from the woman who stood watching her, a cigarette between her heavy, chapped lips, her hair a cuckoo's nest, her face scarred and swollen from many beatings, and her black eyes glittering like coal. Perhaps they both knew this, which was why, when, as rarely, they addressed each other, they addressed each other as Sister. As the singing filled the air the watching, listening faces underwent a change, the eyes focusing on something within; the music seemed to soothe a poison out of them; and the time seemed, nearly, to fall away from the sullen, belligerent, battered faces, as though they were fleeing back to their first condition, while dreaming of their last. The barbecue cook half shook his head and smiled, and dropped his cigarette and disappeared into his joint. A man fumbled in his pockets for change and stood holding it in his hand impatiently, as though he had just remembered a pressing appointment further up the avenue. He looked furious. Then I saw Sonny, standing on the edge of the crowd. He was carrying a wide, flat notebook with a green cover, and it made him look, from where I was standing, almost like a schoolboy. The coppery sun brought out the copper in his skin, he was very faintly smiling, standing very still. Then the singing stopped, the tambourine turned into a collection plate again. The furious man dropped in his coins and vanished, so did a couple of women, and Sonny dropped some change in the plate, looking directly at the woman with a little smile. He started across the avenue, toward the house. He has a slow, loping walk, something like the way Harlem hipsters walk, only he's imposed on this his own half-beat. I had never really noticed it before.

I stayed at the window, both relieved and apprehensive. As Sonny disappeared from my sight, they began singing again. And they were still singing when his key turned in the lock.

"Hey," he said.

"Hey, yourself. You want some beer?"

"No. Well, maybe." But he came up to the window and stood beside me, looking out. "What a warm voice," he said.

They were singing *If I could only hear my mother pray again!*

"Yes," I said, "and she can sure beat that tambourine."

"But what a terrible song," he said, and laughed. He dropped his notebook on the sofa and disappeared into the kitchen. "Where's Isabel and the kids?"

"I think they went to see their grandparents. You hungry?"

"No." He came back into the living room with his can of beer. "You want to come some place with me tonight?"

I sensed, I don't know how, that I couldn't possibly say no. "Sure. Where?"

He sat down on the sofa and picked up his notebook

and started leafing through it. "I'm going to sit in with some fellows in a joint in the Village."

"You mean, you're going to play, tonight?"

"That's right." He took a swallow of his beer and moved back to the window. He gave me a sidelong look. "If you can stand it."

"I'll try," I said.

He smiled to himself and we both watched as the meeting across the way broke up. The three sisters and the brother, heads bowed, were singing *God be with you till we meet again*. The faces around them were very quiet. Then the song ended. The small crowd dispersed. We watched the three women and the lone man walk slowly up the avenue.

"When she was singing before," said Sonny, abruptly, "her voice reminded me for a minute of what heroin feels like sometimes—when it's in your veins. It makes you feel sort of warm and cool at the same time. And distant. And—and sure." He sipped his beer, very deliberately not looking at me. I watched his face. "It makes you feel—in control. Sometimes you've got to have that feeling."

"Do you?" I sat down slowly in the easy chair.

"Sometimes." He went to the sofa and picked up his notebook again. "Some people do."

"In order," I asked, "to play?" And my voice was very ugly, full of contempt and anger.

"Well"—he looked at me with great, troubled eyes, as though, in fact, he hoped his eyes would tell me things he could never otherwise say—"they *think* so. And *if* they think so—!"

"And what do *you* think?" I asked.

He sat on the sofa and put his can of beer on the floor. "I don't know," he said, and I couldn't be sure if he were answering my question or pursuing his thoughts. His face didn't tell me. "It's not so much to *play*. It's to *stand* it, to be able to make it at all. On any level." He frowned and smiled: "In order to keep from shaking to pieces."

"But these friends of yours," I said, "they seem to shake themselves to pieces pretty goddamn fast."

"Maybe." He played with the notebook. And something told me that I should curb my tongue, that Sonny was doing his best to talk, that I should listen. "But of course you only know the ones that've gone to pieces. Some don't—or least they haven't *yet* and that's just about all *any* of us can say." He paused. "And then there are some who just live, really, in hell, and they know it and they see what's happening and they go right on. I don't know." He sighed, dropped the notebook, folded his arms. "Some guys, you can tell from the way they play, they on something *all* the time. And you can see that, well, it makes something real for them. But of course," he picked up his beer from the floor and sipped it and put the can down again, "they *want* to, too, you've got to see that. Even some of them that say they don't—*some*, not all."

"And what about you?" I asked—I couldn't help it. "What about you? Do *you* want to?"

He stood up and walked to the window and remained silent for a long time. Then he sighed. "Me," he said. Then: "While I was downstairs before, on my way here, listening to that woman sing, it struck me all of a sudden how much suffering she must have had to go through—to sing like that. It's *repulsive* to think you have to suffer that much."

I said: "But there's no way not to suffer—is there, Sonny?"

"I believe not," he said and smiled, "but that's never stopped anyone from trying." He looked at me. "Has it?" I realized, with this mocking look, that there stood between us, forever, beyond the power of time or forgiveness, the fact that I had held silence—so long!—when he had needed human speech to help him. He turned back to the window. "No, there's no way not to suffer. But you try all kinds of ways to keep from drowning in it, to keep on top of it, and to make it seem—well, like *you*. Like you did something, all right, and now you're suffering for it. You know?" I said nothing. "Well you know," he said, impatiently, "why *do* people suffer? Maybe it's better to do something to give it a reason, *any* reason."

"But we just agreed," I said, "that there's no way not to suffer. Isn't it better, then, just to—take it?"

"But nobody just takes it," Sonny cried, "that's what I'm telling you! *Everybody* tries not to. You're just hung up on the *way* some people try—it's not *your* way!"

The hair on my face began to itch, my face felt wet. "That's not true," I said, "that's not true. I don't give a damn what other people do, I don't even care how they suffer. I just care how *you* suffer." And he looked at me. "Please believe me," I said, "I don't want to see you—die—trying not to suffer."

"I won't," he said, flatly, "die trying not to suffer. At least, not any faster than anybody else."

"But there's no need," I said, trying to laugh, "is there? in killing yourself."

I wanted to say more, but I couldn't. I wanted to talk about will power and how life could be—well, beautiful. I wanted to say that it was all within; but was it? or, rather, wasn't that exactly the trouble? And I wanted to promise that I would never fail him again. But it would all have sounded—empty words and lies.

So I made the promise to myself and prayed that I would keep it.

"It's terrible sometimes, inside," he said, "that's what's the trouble. You walk these streets, black and funky and cold, and there's not really a living ass to talk to, and there's nothing shaking, and there's no way of getting it out—that storm inside. You can't talk it and you can't make love with it, and when you finally try to get with it and play it, you realize *nobody's* listening. So *you've* got to listen. You got to find a way to listen.''

And then he walked away from the window and sat on the sofa again, as though all the wind had suddenly been knocked out of him. "Sometimes you'll do *anything* to play, even cut your mother's throat.'' He laughed and looked at me. "Or your brother's.'' Then he sobered. "Or your own.'' Then: "Don't worry. I'm all right now and I think I'll *be* all right. But I can't forget—where I've been. I don't mean just the physical place I've been, I mean where I've *been*. And *what* I've been.''

"What have you been, Sonny?'' I asked.

He smiled—but sat sideways on the sofa, his elbow resting on the back, his fingers playing with his mouth and chin, not looking at me. "I've been something I didn't recognize, didn't know I could be. Didn't know anybody could be.'' He stopped, looking inward, looking helplessly young, looking old. "I'm not talking about it now because I feel *guilty* or anything like that—maybe it would be better if I did, I don't know. Anyway, I can't really talk about it. Not to you, not to anybody,'' and now he turned and faced me. "Sometimes, you know, and it was actually when I was most *out* of the world, I felt that I was in it, that I was *with* it, really, and I could play or I didn't really have to *play*, it just came out of me, it was there. And I don't know how I played, thinking about it now, but I know I did awful things, those times, sometime, to people. Or it wasn't that I *did* anything to them—it was that they weren't real.'' He picked up the beer can; it was empty; he rolled it between his palms: "And other times—well, I needed a fix, I needed to find a place to lean, I needed to clear a space to *listen*—and I couldn't find it, and I—went crazy, I did terrible things to *me*, I was terrible *for* me.'' He began pressing the beer can between his hands, I watched the metal begin to give. It glittered, as he played with it, like a knife, and I was afraid he would cut himself, but I said nothing. "Oh, well. I can never tell you. I was all by myself at the bottom of something, stinking and sweating and crying and shaking, and I smelled it, you know? *my* stink, and I thought I'd die if I couldn't get away from it and yet, all the same, I knew that everything I was doing was just locking me in with it. And I didn't know,'' he paused, still flattening the beer can, "I didn't know, I still *don't* know, something kept telling me that maybe it was good to smell your own stink, but I didn't think that *that* was what I'd been trying to do—and—who can stand it?'' and he abruptly dropped the ruined beer can, looking at me with a small, still smile, and then rose, walking to the window as though it were the lodestone rock. I watched his face, he watched the avenue. "I couldn't tell you when Mama died—but the reason I wanted to leave Harlem so bad was to get away from drugs. And then, when I ran away, that's what I was running from—really. When I came back, nothing had changed, *I* hadn't changed, I was just—older.'' And he stopped, drumming with his fingers on the windowpane. The sun had vanished, soon darkness would fall. I watched his face. "It can come again," he said, almost as though speaking to himself. Then he turned to me. "It can come again," he repeated. "I just want you to know that."

"All right," I said, at last. "So it can come again. All right."

He smiled, but the smile was sorrowful. "I had to try to tell you," he said.

"Yes," I said. "I understand that."

"You're my brother," he said, looking straight at me, and not smiling at all.

"Yes," I repeated, "yes. I understand that."

He turned back to the window, looking out. "All that hatred down there," he said, "all that hatred and misery and love. It's a wonder it doesn't blow the avenue apart."

We went to the only nightclub on a short, dark street, downtown. We squeezed through the narrow, chattering, jam-packed bar to the entrance of the big room, where the bandstand was. And we stood there for a moment, for the lights were very dim in this room and we couldn't see. Then, "Hello, boy," said a voice and an enormous black man, much older than Sonny or myself, erupted out of all that atmospheric lighting and put an arm around Sonny's shoulder. "I been sitting right here," he said, "waiting for you."

He had a big voice, too, and heads in the darkness turned toward us.

Sonny grinned and pulled a little away, and said, "Creole, this is my brother, I told you about him."

Creole shook my hand. "I'm glad to meet you, son," he said, and it was clear that he was glad to meet me *there*, for Sonny's sake. And he smiled, "You got a real musician in *your* family," and he took his arm from Sonny's shoulder and slapped him, lightly, affectionately, with the back of his hand.

"Well. Now I've heard it all," said a voice behind us. This was another musician, and a friend of Sonny's, a coal-black, cheerful-looking man, built close to the ground. He immediately began confiding to me, at the top of his lungs, the most terrible things about Sonny, his teeth gleaming like a lighthouse and his laugh coming up out of him like the beginning of an earthquake. And it turned out that everyone at the bar knew Sonny, or almost everyone; some were musicians, working there, or nearby, or not working, some were simply hangers-on, and some were there to hear Sonny play. I was introduced to all of them and they were all very polite to me. Yet, it was clear that, for them, I was only Sonny's brother. Here, I was in Sonny's world. Or, rather: his kingdom. Here, it was not even a question that his veins bore royal blood.

They were going to play soon and Creole installed me, by myself, at a table in a dark corner. Then I watched them, Creole, and the little black man, and Sonny, and the others, while they horsed around, standing just below the bandstand. The light from the bandstand spilled just a little short of them and, watching them laughing and gesturing and moving about, I had the feeling that they, nevertheless, were being most careful not to step into that circle of light too suddenly: that if they moved into the light too suddenly, without thinking, they would perish in flame. Then, while I watched, one of them, the small, black man, moved into the light and crossed the bandstand and started fooling around with his drums. Then—being funny and being, also, extremely ceremonious—Creole took Sonny by the arm and led him to the piano. A woman's voice called Sonny's name and a few hands started clapping. And Sonny, also being funny and being ceremonious, and so touched, I think, that he could have cried, but neither hiding it nor showing it, riding it like a man, grinned, and put both hands to his heart and bowed from the waist.

Creole then went to the bass fiddle and a lean, very bright-skinned brown man jumped up on the bandstand and picked up his horn. So there they were, and the atmosphere on the bandstand and in the room began to change and tighten. Someone stepped up to the microphone and announced them. Then there were all kinds of murmurs. Some people at the bar shushed others. The waitress ran around, frantically getting in the last orders, guys and chicks got closer to each other, and the lights on the bandstand, on the quartet, turned to a kind of indigo. Then they all looked different there. Creole looked about him for the last time, as though he were making certain that all his chickens were in the coop, and then he—jumped and struck the fiddle. And there they were.

All I know about music is that not many people ever really hear it. And even then, on the rare occasions when something opens within, and the music enters, what we mainly hear, or hear corroborated, are personal, private, vanishing evocations. But the man who creates the music is hearing something else, is dealing with the roar rising from the void and imposing order on it as it hits the air. What is evoked in him, then, is of another order, more terrible because it has no words, and triumphant, too, for that same reason. And his triumph, when he triumphs, is ours. I just watched Sonny's face. His face was troubled, he was working hard, but he wasn't with it. And I had the feeling that, in a way, everyone on the bandstand was waiting for him, both waiting for him and pushing him along. But as I began to watch Creole, I realized that it was Creole who held them all back. He had them on a short rein. Up there, keeping the beat with his whole body, wailing on the fiddle, with his eyes half closed, he was listening to everything, but he was listening to Sonny. He was having a dialogue with Sonny. He wanted Sonny to leave the shoreline and strike out for the deep water. He was Sonny's witness that deep water and drowning were not the same thing—he had been there, and he knew. And he wanted Sonny to know. He was waiting for Sonny to do the things on the keys which would let Creole know that Sonny was in the water.

And, while Creole listened, Sonny moved, deep within,

exactly like someone in torment. I had never before thought of how awful the relationship must be between the musician and his instrument. He has to fill it, this instrument, with the breath of life, his own. He has to make it do what he wants it to do. And a piano is just a piano. It's made out of so much wood and wires and little hammers and big ones, and ivory. While there's only so much you can do with it, the only way to find this out is to try; to try and make it do everything.

And Sonny hadn't been near a piano for over a year. And he wasn't on much better terms with his life, not the life that stretched before him now. He and the piano stammered, started one way, got scared, stopped; started another way, panicked, marked time, started again; then seemed to have found a direction, panicked again, got stuck. And the face I saw on Sonny I'd never seen before. Everything had been burned out of it, and, at the same time, things usually hidden were being burned in, by the fire and fury of the battle which was occurring in him up there.

Yet, watching Creole's face as they neared the end of the first set, I had the feeling that something had happened, something I hadn't heard. Then they finished, there was scattered applause, and then, without an instant's warning, Creole started into something else, it was almost sardonic, it was *Am I Blue.* And, as though he commanded, Sonny began to play. Something began to happen. And Creole let out the reins. The dry, low, black man said something awful on the drums, Creole answered, and the drums talked back. Then the horn insisted, sweet and high, slightly detached perhaps, and Creole listened, commenting now and then, dry, and driving, beautiful and calm and old. Then they all came together again, and Sonny was part of the family again. I could tell this from his face. He seemed to have found, right there beneath his fingers, a damn brand-new piano. It seemed that he couldn't get over it. Then, for awhile, just being happy with Sonny, they seemed to be agreeing with him that brand-new pianos certainly were a gas.

Then Creole stepped forward to remind them that what they were playing was the blues. He hit something in all of them, he hit something in me, myself, and the music tightened and deepened, apprehension began to beat the air. Creole began to tell us what the blues were all about. They were not about anything very new. He and his boys up there were keeping it new, at the risk of ruin, destruction, madness, and death, in order to find new ways to make us listen. For, while the tale of how we suffer, and how we are delighted, and how we may triumph is never new, it always must be heard. There isn't any other tale to tell, it's the only light we've got in all this darkness.

And this tale, according to that face, that body, those strong hands on those strings, has another aspect in every country, and a new depth in every generation. Listen, Creole seemed to be saying, listen. Now these are Sonny's blues. He made the little black man on the drums know it, and the bright, brown man on the horn. Creole wasn't trying any longer to get Sonny in the water. He was wishing him Godspeed. Then he stepped back, very slowly, filling the air with the immense suggestion that Sonny speak for himself.

Then they all gathered around Sonny and Sonny played. Every now and again one of them seemed to say, amen. Sonny's fingers filled the air with life, his life. But that life contained so many others. And Sonny went all the way back, he really began with the spare, flat statement of the opening phrase of the song. Then he began to make it his. It was very beautiful because it wasn't hurried and it was no longer a lament. I seemed to hear with what burning he had made it his, with what burning we had yet to make it ours, how we could cease lamenting. Freedom lurked around us and I understood, at last, that he could help us to be free if we would listen, that he would never be free until we did. Yet, there was no battle in his face now. I heard what he had gone through, and would continue to go through until he came to rest in earth. He had made it his: that long line, of which we knew only Mama and Daddy. And he was giving it back, as everything must be given back, so that, passing through death, it can live forever. I saw my mother's face again, and felt, for the first time, how the stones of the road she had walked on must have bruised her feet. I saw the moonlit road where my father's brother died. And it brought something else back to me, and carried me past it. I saw my little girl again and felt Isabel's tears again, and I felt my own tears begin to rise. And I was yet aware that this was only a moment, that the world waited outside, as hungry as a tiger, and that trouble stretched above us, longer than the sky.

Then it was over. Creole and Sonny let out their breath, both soaking wet, and grinning. There was a lot of applause and some of it was real. In the dark, the girl came by and I asked her to take drinks to the bandstand. There was a long pause, while they talked up there in the indigo light and after awhile I saw the girl put a Scotch and milk on top of the piano for Sonny. He didn't seem to notice it, but just before they started playing again, he sipped from it and looked toward me, and nodded. Then he put it back on top of the piano. For me, then, as they began to play again, it glowed and shook above my brother's head like the very cup of trembling.

Virginia Woolf (1882–1941)

A Haunted House

Whatever hour you woke there was a door shutting. From room to room they went, hand in hand, lifting here, opening there, making sure—a ghostly couple.

"Here we left it," she said. And he added, "Oh, but here too!" "It's upstairs," she murmured. "And in the garden," he whispered. "Quietly," they said, "or we shall wake them."

But it wasn't that you woke us. Oh, no. "They're looking for it; they're drawing the curtain," one might say, and so read on a page or two. "Now they've found it," one would be certain, stopping the pencil on the margin. And then, tired of reading, one might rise and see for oneself, the house all empty, the doors standing open, only the wood pigeons bubbling with content and the hum of the threshing machine sounding from the farm. "What did I come in here for? What did I want to find?" My hands were empty. "Perhaps its upstair then?" The apples were in the loft. And so down again, the garden still as ever, only the book had slipped into the grass.

But they had found it in the drawing room. Not that one could ever see them. The windowpanes reflected apples, reflected roses; all the leaves were green in the glass. If they moved in the drawing room, the apple only turned its yellow side. Yet, the moment after, if the door was opened, spread about the floor, hung upon the walls, pendant from the ceiling—what? My hands were empty. The shadow of a thrush crossed the carpet; from the deepest wells of silence the wood pigeon drew its bubble of sound. "Safe, safe, safe," the pulse of the house beat softly. "The treasure buried; the room . . ." the pulse stopped short. Oh, was that the buried treasure?

A moment later the light had faded. Out in the garden then? But the trees spun darkness for a wandering beam of sun. So fine, so rare, coolly sunk beneath the surface the beam I sought always burned behind the glass. Death was the glass; death was between us; coming to the woman first, hundreds of years ago, leaving the house, sealing all the windows; the rooms were darkened. He left it, left her, went North, went East, saw the stars turned in the Southern sky; sought the house, found it dropped beneath the Downs. "Safe, safe, safe," the pulse of the house beat gladly. "The Treasure yours."

The wind roars up the avenue. Trees stoop and bend this way and that. Moonbeams splash and spill wildly in the rain. But the beam of the lamp falls straight from the window. The candle burns stiff and still. Wandering through the house, opening the windows, whispering not to wake us, the ghostly couple seek their joy.

"Here we slept," she says. And he adds, "Kisses without number." "Waking in the morning—" "Silver between the trees—" "Upstairs—" "In the garden—" "When summer came—" "In winter snowtime—" "The doors go shutting far in the distance, gently knocking like the pulse of a heart.

Nearer they come; cease at the doorway. The wind falls, the rain slides silver down the glass. Our eyes darken; we hear no steps beside us; we see no lady spread her ghostly cloak. His hands shield the lantern. "Look," he breathes. "Sound asleep. Love upon their lips."

Stooping, holding their silver lamp above us, long they look and deeply. Long they pause. The wind drives straightly; the flame stoops slightly. Wild beams of moonlight cross both floor and wall, and, meeting, stain the faces bent; the faces pondering; the faces that search the sleepers and seek their hidden joy.

"Safe, safe, safe," the heart of the house beats proudly. "Long years—" he sighs. "Again you found me." "Here," she murmurs, "sleeping; in the garden reading; laughing, rolling apples in the loft. Here we left our treasure—" Stooping, their light lifts the lids upon my eyes. "Safe! safe! safe!" the pulse of the house beats wildly. Waking, I cry "Oh, is this *your* buried treasure? The light in the heart."

Langston Hughes (1902–1967)
On the Road

He was not interested in the snow. When he got off the freight, one early evening during the depression, Sargeant never even noticed the snow. But he must have felt it seeping down his neck, cold, wet, sopping in his shoes. But if you had asked him, he wouldn't have known it was snowing. Sargeant didn't see the snow, not even under the bright lights of the main street, falling white and flaky against the night. He was too hungry, too sleepy, too tired.

The Reverend Mr. Dorset, however, saw the snow when he switched on his porch light, opened the front door of his parsonage, and found standing there before him a big black man with snow on his face, a human piece of night with snow on his face—obviously unemployed.

Said the Reverend Mr. Dorset before Sargeant even realized he'd opened his mouth: "I'm sorry. No! Go right on down this street four blocks and turn to your left, walk up seven and you'll see the Relief Shelter. I'm sorry. No!" He shut the door.

Sargeant wanted to tell the holy man that he had already been to the Relief Shelter, been to hundreds of relief shelters during the depression years, the beds were always gone and supper was over, the place was full, and they drew the color line anyhow. But the minister said, "No," and shut the door. Evidently he didn't want to hear about it. And he *had* a door to shut.

The big black man turned away. And even yet he didn't see the snow, walking right into it. Maybe he sensed it, cold, wet, sticking to his jaws, wet on his black hands, sopping in his shoes. He stopped and stood on the sidewalk hunched over—hungry, sleepy, cold—looking up and down. Then he looked right where he was—in front of a church. Of course! A church! Sure, right next to a parsonage, certainly a church.

It had *two* doors.

Broad white steps in the night all snowy white. Two high arched doors with slender stone pillars on either side. And way up, a round lacy window with a stone crucifix in the middle and Christ on the crucifix in stone. All this was pale in the street lights, solid and stony pale in the snow.

Sargeant blinked. When he looked up, the snow fell into his eyes. For the first time that night he *saw* the snow. He shook his head. He shook the snow from his coat sleeves, felt hungry, felt lost, felt not lost, felt cold. He walked up the steps of the church. He knocked at the door. No answer. He tried the handle. Locked. He put his shoulder against the door and his long black body slanted like a ramrod. He pushed. With loud rhythmic grunts, like the grunts in a chain-gang song, he pushed against the door.

"I'm tired . . . Huh! . . . Hongry . . . Uh! . . . I'm sleepy . . . Huh! I'm cold . . . I got to sleep somewheres," Sargeant said. "This here is a church, ain't it? Well, uh!"

He pushed against the door.

Suddenly, with an undue cracking and screaking, the door began to give way to the tall black Negro who pushed ferociously against it.

By now two or three white people had stopped in the street, and Sargeant was vaguely aware of some of them yelling at him concerning the door. Three or four more came running, yelling at him.

"Hey!" they said. "Hey!"

"Uh-huh," answered the big tall Negro, "I know it's a white folks' church, but I got to sleep somewhere." He gave another lunge at the door. "Huh!"

And the door broke open.

But just when the door gave way, two white cops arrived in a car, ran up the steps with their clubs, and grabbed Sargeant. But Sargeant for once had no intention of being pulled or pushed away from the door.

Sargeant grabbed, but not for anything so weak as a broken door. He grabbed for one of the tall stone pillars beside the door, grabbed at it and caught it. And held it. The cops pulled and Sargeant pulled. Most of the people in the street got behind the cops and helped them pull.

"A big black unemployed Negro holding onto our church!" thought the people. "The idea!"

The cops began to beat Sargeant over the head, and nobody protested. But he held on.

And then the church fell down.

Gradually, the big stone front of the church fell down,

the walls and the rafters, the crucifix and the Christ. Then the whole thing fell down, covering the cops and the people with bricks and stones and debris. The whole church fell down in the snow.

Sargeant got out from under the church and went walking on up the street with the stone pillar on his shoulder. He was under the impression that he had buried the parsonage and the Reverend Mr. Dorset who said, "No!" So he laughed, and threw the pillar six blocks up the street and went on.

Sargeant thought he was alone, but listening to the *crunch, crunch, crunch* on the snow of his own footsteps, he heard other footsteps, too, doubling his own. He looked around, and there was Christ walking along beside him, the same Christ that had been on the cross on the church—still stone with a rough stone surface, walking along beside him just like he was broken off the cross when the church fell down.

"Well, I'll be dogged," said Sargeant. "This here's the first time I ever seed you off the cross."

"Yes," said Christ, crunching his feet in the snow. "You had to pull the church down to get me off the cross."

"You glad?" said Sargeant.

"I sure am," said Christ.

They both laughed.

"I'm a hell of a fellow, ain't I?" said Sargeant. "Done pulled the church down!"

"You did a good job," said Christ. "They have kept me nailed on a cross for nearly two thousand years."

"Whee-ee-e!" said Sargeant. "I know you are glad to get off."

"I sure am," said Christ.

They walked on in the snow. Sargeant looked at the man of stone.

"And you have been up there two thousand years?"

"I sure have," Christ said.

"Well, if I had a little cash," said Sargeant, "I'd show you around a bit."

"I been around," said Christ.

"Yeah, but that was a long time ago."

"All the same," said Christ, "I've been around."

They walked on in the snow until they came to the railroad yards. Saegeant was tired, sweating and tired.

"Where you goin'?" Sargeant said, stopping by the tracks. He looked at Christ. Sargeant said, "I'm just a bum on the road. How about you? Where you goin'?"

"God knows," Christ said, "but I'm leavin' here."

They saw the red and green lights of the railroad yard half veiled by the snow that fell out of the night. Away down the track they saw a fire in a hobo jungle.

"I can go there and sleep," Sargeant said.

"You can?"

"Sure," said Sargeant. "That place ain't got no doors."

Outside the town, along the tracks, there were barren trees and bushes below the embankment, snow-gray in the dark. And down among the trees and bushes there were makeshift houses made out of boxes and tin and old pieces of wood and canvas. You couldn't see them in the dark, but you knew they were there if you'd ever been on the road, if you had ever lived with the homeless and hungry in a depression.

"I'm side-tracking," Sargeant said. "I'm tired."

"I'm gonna make it on to Kansas City," said Christ.

"O.K.," Sargeant said. "So long!"

He went down into the hobo jungle and found himself a place to sleep. He never did see Christ no more. About 6:00 A.M. a freight came by. Sargeant scrambled out of the jungle with a dozen or so more hobos and ran along the track, grabbing at the freight. It was dawn, early dawn, cold and gray.

"Wonder where Christ is by now?" Sargeant thought. "He musta gone on way on down the road. He didn't sleep in this jungle."

Sargeant grabbed the train and started to pull himself up into a moving coal car, over the edge of a wheeling coal car. But strangely enough, the car was full of cops. The nearest cop rapped Sargeant soundly across the knuckles with his night stick. Wham! Rapped his big black hands for clinging to the top of the car. Wham! But Sargeant did not turn loose. He clung on and tried to pull himself into the car. He hollered at the top of his voice, "Damn it, lemme in this car!"

"Shut up," barked the cop. "You crazy coon!" He rapped Sargeant across the knuckles and punched him in the stomach. "You ain't out in no jungle now. This ain't no train. You in jail."

Wham! across his bare black fingers clinging to the bars of his cell. Wham! between the steel bars low down against his shins.

Suddenly Sargeant realized that he really was in jail. He wasn't on no train. The blood of the night before had dried on his face, his head hurt terribly, and a cop outside in the corridor was hitting him across the knuckles for holding onto the door, yelling and shaking the cell door.

"They musta took me to jail for breaking down the door last night," Sargeant thought, "that church door."

Sargeant went over and sat on a wooden bench against the cold stone wall. He was emptier than ever. His clothes were wet, clammy cold wet, and shoes sloppy with snow water. It was just about dawn. There he was, locked up behind a cell door, nursing his bruised fingers.

The bruised fingers were his, but not the *door*.

Not the *club*, but the fingers.

"You wait," mumbled Sargeant, black against the jail wall. "I'm gonna break down this door, too."

"Shut up—or I'll paste you one," said the cop.

"I'm gonna break down this door," yelled Sargeant as he stood up in his cell.

Then he must have been talking to himself because he said, "I wonder where Christ's gone? I wonder if he's gone to Kansas City?"

Flannery O'Connor *(1925–1964)*
A Good Man Is Hard to Find

The grandmother didn't want to go to Florida. She wanted to visit some of her connections in east Tennessee and she was seizing at every chance to change Bailey's mind. Bailey was the son she lived with, her only boy. He was sitting on the edge of his chair at the table, bent over the orange sports section of the *Journal*. "Now look here, Bailey," she said, "see here, read this," and she stood with one hand on her thin hip and the other rattling the newspaper at his bald head. "Here this fellow that calls himself The Misfit is aloose from the Federal Pen and headed toward Florida and you read here what it says he did to these people. Just you read it. I wouldn't take my children in any direction with a criminal like that aloose in it. I couldn't answer to my conscience if I did."

Bailey didn't look up from his reading so she wheeled around then and faced the children's mother, a young woman in slacks, whose face was as broad and innocent as a cabbage and was tied round with a green head-kerchief that had two points on the top like rabbit's ears. She was sitting on the sofa, feeding the baby his apricots out of a jar. "The children have been to Florida before," the old lady said. "You all ought to take them somewhere else for a change so they would see different parts of the world and be broad. They never have been to east Tennessee."

The children's mother didn't seem to hear her but the eight-year-old boy, John Wesley, a stocky child with glasses, said, "If you don't want to go to Florida, why dontcha stay at home?" He and the little girl, June Star, were reading the funny papers on the floor.

"She wouldn't stay at home to be queen for a day," June Star said without raising her yellow head.

"Yes, and what would you do if this fellow, The Misfit, caught you?" the grandmother asked.

"I'd smack his face," John Wesley said.

"She wouldn't stay at home for a million bucks," June Star said. "Afraid she'd miss something. She has to go everywhere we go."

"All right, Miss," the grandmother said. "Just remember that the next time you want me to curl your hair."

June Star said her hair was naturally curly.

The next morning the grandmother was the first one in the car, ready to go. She had her big black valise that looked like the head of a hippopotamus in one corner, and underneath it she was hiding a basket with Pitty Sing, the cat, in it. She didn't intend for the cat to be left alone in the house for three days because he would miss her too much and she was afraid he might brush against one of the gas burners and accidentally asphyxiate himself. Her son, Bailey, didn't like to arrive at a motel with a cat.

She sat in the middle of the back seat with John Wesley and June Star on either side of her. Bailey and the children's mother and the baby sat in front and they left Atlanta at eight forty-five with the mileage on the car at 55890. The grandmother wrote this down because she thought it would be interesting to say how many miles they had been when they got back. It took them twenty minutes to reach the outskirts of the city.

The old lady settled herself comfortably, removing her white cotton gloves and putting them up with her purse on the shelf in front of the back window. The children's mother still had on slacks and still had her head tied up in a green kerchief, but the grandmother had on a navy blue straw sailor hat with a bunch of white violets on the brim and a navy blue dress with a small white dot in the print. Her collars and cuffs were white organdy trimmed with lace and at her neckline she had pinned a purple spray of cloth violets containing a sachet. In case of an accident, anyone seeing her dead on the highway would know at once that she was a lady.

She said she thought it was going to be a good day for driving, neither too hot nor too cold, and she cautioned Bailey that the speed limit was fifty-five miles an hour and that the patrolmen hid themselves behind billboards and small clumps of trees and sped out after you before you had a chance to slow down. She pointed out interesting details of the scenery: Stone Mountain; the blue granite that in some places came up to both sides of the highway; the brilliant red clay banks slightly streaked with purple; and the various crops that made rows of green lace-work on the ground. The trees were full of silver-white sunlight and the meanest of them sparkled. The children were reading comic magazines and their mother had gone back to sleep.

"Let's go through Georgia fast so we won't have to look at it much," John Wesley said.

"If I were a little boy," said the grandmother, "I wouldn't talk about my native state that way. Tennessee has the mountains and Georgia has the hills."

"Tennessee is just a hillbilly dumping ground," John Wesley said, "and Georgia is a lousy state too."

"You said it," June Star said.

"In my time," said the grandmother, folding her thin veined fingers, "children were more respectful of their native states and their parents and everything else. People did right then. Oh look at the cute little pickaninny!" she said and pointed to a Negro child standing in the door of a shack. "Wouldn't that make a picture, now?" she asked and they all turned and looked at the little Negro out of the back window. He waved.

"He didn't have any britches on," June Star said.

"He probably didn't have any," the grandmother explained. "Little niggers in the country don't have things like we do. If I could paint, I'd paint that picture," she said.

The children exchanged comic books.

The grandmother offered to hold the baby and the children's mother passed him over the front seat to her. She set him on her knee and bounced him and told him about the things they were passing. She rolled her eyes and screwed up her mouth and stuck her leathery thin face into his smooth bland one. Occasionally he gave her a faraway smile. They passed a large cotton field with five or six graves fenced in the middle of it, like a small island. "Look at the graveyard!" the grandmother said, pointing it out. "That was the old family burying ground. That belonged to the plantation."

"Where's the plantation?" John Wesley asked.

"Gone With the Wind," said the grandmother. "Ha. Ha."

When the children finished all the comic books they had brought, they opened the lunch and ate it. The grandmother ate a peanut butter sandwich and an olive and would not let the children throw the box and the paper napkins out the window. When there was nothing else to do they played a game by choosing a cloud and making the other two guess what shape it suggested. John Wesley took one the shape of a cow and June Star guessed a cow and John Wesley said, no, an automobile, and June Star said he didn't play fair, and they began to slap each other over the grandmother.

The grandmother said she would tell them a story if they would keep quiet. When she told a story, she rolled her eyes and waved her head and was very dramatic. She said once when she was a maiden lady she had been courted by a Mr. Edgar Atkins Teagarden from Jasper, Georgia. She said he was a very good-looking man and a gentleman and that he brought her a watermelon every Saturday afternoon with his initials cut in it, E. A. T. Well, one Saturday, she said, Mr. Teagarden brought the watermelon and there was nobody at home and he left it on the front porch and returned in his buggy to Jasper, but she never got the watermelon, she said, because a nigger boy ate it when he saw the ini-

tials, E. A. T.! This story tickled John Wesley's funny bone and he giggled and giggled but June Star didn't think it was any good. She said she
wouldn't marry a man that just brought her a watermelon on Saturday. The grandmother said she would have done well to marry Mr.
Teagarden because he was a gentleman and had bought Coca-Cola stock
when it first came out and that he had died only a few years ago, a very
wealthy man.

They stopped at The Tower for barbecued sandwiches.
The Tower was a part stucco and part wood filling station and dance hall set
in a clearing outside of Timothy. A fat man named Red Sammy Butts ran it
and there were signs stuck here and there on the building and for miles up
and down the highway saying, TRY RED SAMMY'S FAMOUS BAR-
BEQUE. NONE LIKE FAMOUS RED SAMMY'S! RED SAM! THE
FAT BOY WITH THE HAPPY LAUGH. A VETERAN! RED
SAMMY'S YOUR MAN!

Red Sammy was lying on the bare ground outside The
Tower with his head under a truck while a gray monkey about a foot high,
chained to a small chinaberry tree, chattered nearby. The monkey sprang
back into the tree and got on the highest limb as soon as he saw the children
jump out of the car and run toward him.

Inside, The Tower was a long dark room with a counter
at one end and tables at the other and dancing space in the middle. They all
sat down at a board table next to the nickelodeon and Red Sam's wife, a tall
burnt-brown woman with hair and eyes lighter than her skin, came and took
their order. The children's mother put a dime in the machine and played
"The Tennessee Waltz," and the grandmother said that tune always made
her want to dance. She asked Bailey if he would like to dance but he only
glared at her. He didn't have a naturally sunny disposition like she did and
trips made him nervous. The grandmother's brown eyes were very bright.
She swayed her head from side to side and pretended she was dancing in her
chair. June Star said play something she could tap to so the children's
mother put in another dime and played a fast number and June Star stepped
out onto the dance floor and did her tap routine.

"Ain't she cute?" Red Sam's wife said, leaning over the
counter. "Would you like to come be my little girl?"

"No I certainly wouldn't," June Star said. "I wouldn't
live in a broken-down place like this for a million bucks!" and she ran back
to the table.

"Ain't she cute?" the woman repeated, stretching her
mouth politely.

"Aren't you ashamed?" hissed the grandmother.

Red Sam came in and told his wife to quit lounging on
the counter and hurry with these people's order. His khaki trousers
reached just to his hip bones and his stomach hung over them like a sack of
meal swaying under his shirt. He came over and sat down at a table nearby
and let out a combination sigh and yodel. "You can't win," he said. "You

can't win," and he wiped his sweating red face off with a gray handkerchief. "These days you don't know who to trust," he said. "Ain't that the truth?"

"People are certainly not nice like they used to be," said the grandmother.

"Two fellers come in here last week," Red Sammy said, "driving a Chrysler. It was a old beat-up car but it was a good one and these boys looked all right to me. Said they worked at the mill and you know I let them fellers charge the gas they bought? Now why did I do that?"

"Because you're a good man!" the grandmother said at once.

"Yes'm, I suppose so," Red Sam said as if he were struck with the answer.

His wife brought the orders, carrying the five plates all at once without a tray, two in each hand and one balanced on her arm. "It isn't a soul in this green world of God's that you can trust," she said. "And I don't count nobody out of that, not nobody," she repeated, looking at Red Sammy.

"Did you read about that criminal, The Misfit, that's escaped?" asked the grandmother.

"I wouldn't be a bit surprised if he didn't attack this place right here," said the woman. "If he hears about it being here, I wouldn't be none surprised to see him. If he hears it's two cent in the cash register, I wouldn't be a tall surprised if he . . ."

"That'll do," Red Sam said. "Go bring these people their Co'Colas," and the woman went off to get the rest of the order.

"A good man is hard to find," Red Sammy said. "Everything is getting terrible. I remember the day you could go off and leave your screen door unlatched. Not no more."

He and the grandmother discussed better times. The old lady said that in her opinion Europe was entirely to blame for the way things were now. She said the way Europe acted you would think we were made of money and Red Sam said it was no use talking about it, she was exactly right. The children ran outside into the white sunlight and looked at the monkey in the lacy chinaberry tree. He was busy catching fleas on himself and biting each one carefully between his teeth as if it were a delicacy.

They drove off again into the hot afternoon. The grandmother took cat naps and woke up every few minutes with her own snoring. Outside of Toombsboro she woke up and recalled an old plantation that she had visited in this neighborhood once when she was a young lady. She said the house had six white columns across the front and that there was an avenue of oaks leading up to it and two little wooden trellis arbors on either side in front where you sat down with your suitor after a stroll in the garden. She recalled exactly which road to turn off to get to it. She knew that Bailey would not be willing to lose any time looking at an old house, but the more she talked about it, the more she wanted to see it once again and find out if the little twin arbors were still standing. "There was a secret panel in this house," she said craftily, not telling the truth but wishing that she were, "and the story went that all the family silver was hidden in it when Sherman came through but it was never found . . ."

"Hey!" John Wesley said. "Let's go see it! We'll find it! We'll poke all the woodwork and find it! Who lives there? Where do you turn off at? Hey Pop, can't we turn off there?"

"We never have seen a house with a secret panel!" June Star shrieked. "Let's go to the house with the secret panel! Hey Pop, can't we go see the house with the secret panel!"

"It's not far from here, I know," the grandmother said. "It wouldn't take over twenty minutes."

Bailey was looking straight ahead. His jaw was as rigid as a horseshoe. "No," he said.

The children began to yell and scream that they wanted to see the house with the secret panel. John Wesley kicked the back of the front seat and June Star hung over her mother's shoulder and whined desperately into her ear that they never had any fun even on their vacation, that they could never do what THEY wanted to do. The baby began to scream and John Wesley kicked the back of the seat so hard that his father could feel the blows in his kidney.

"All right!" he shouted and drew the car to a stop at the side of the road. "Will you all shut up? Will you all just shut up for one second? If you don't shut up, we won't go anywhere."

"It would be very educational for them," the grand-mother murmured.

"All right," Bailey said, "but get this: this is the only time we're going to stop for anything like this. This is the one and only time."

"The dirt road that you have to turn down is about a mile back," the grandmother directed. "I marked it when we passed."

"A dirt road," Bailey groaned.

After they had turned around and were headed toward the dirt road, the grandmother recalled other points about the house, the beautiful glass over the front doorway and the candle-lamp in the hall. John Wesley said that the secret panel was probably in the fireplace.

"You can't go inside this house," Bailey said. "You don't know who lives there."

"While you all talk to the people in front, I'll run around behind and get in a window," John Wesley suggested.

"We'll all stay in the car," his mother said.

They turned onto the dirt road and the car raced roughly along in a swirl of pink dust. The grandmother recalled the times when there were no paved roads and thirty miles was a day's journey. The dirt road was hilly and there were sudden washes in it and sharp curves on dangerous embankments. All at once they would be on a hill, looking down over the blue tops of trees for miles around, then the next minute, they would be in a red depression with the dust-coated trees looking down on them.

"This place had better turn up in a minute," Bailey said, "or I'm going to turn around."

The road looked as if no one had traveled on it in months.

"It's not much farther," the grandmother said and just as she said it, a horrible thought came to her. The thought was so embarrassing that she turned red in the face and her eyes dilated and her feet jumped up, upsetting her valise in the corner. The instant the valise moved, the newspaper top she had over the basket under it rose with a snarl and Pitty Sing, the cat, sprang onto Bailey's shoulder.

The children were thrown to the floor and their mother, clutching the baby, was thrown out the door onto the ground; the old lady was thrown into the front seat. The car turned over once and landed right-side-up in a gulch on the side of the road. Bailey remained in the driver's seat with the cat—gray-striped with a broad white face and an orange nose—clinging to his neck like a caterpillar.

As soon as the children saw they could move their arms and legs, they scrambled out of the car, shouting, "We've had an ACCIDENT!" The grandmother was curled up under the dashboard, hoping she was injured so that Bailey's wrath would not come down on her all at once. The horrible thought she had had before the accident was that the house she had remembered so vividly was not in Georgia but in Tennessee.

Bailey removed the cat from his neck with both hands and flung it out the window against the side of a pine tree. Then he got out of the car and started looking for the children's mother. She was sitting against the side of the red gutted ditch, holding the screaming baby, but she only had a cut down her face and a broken shoulder. "We've had an ACCIDENT!" the children screamed in a frenzy of delight.

"But nobody's killed," June Star said with disappointment as the grandmother limped out of the car, her hat still pinned to her head but the broken front brim standing up at a jaunty angle and the violet spray hanging off the side. They all sat down in the ditch, except the children, to recover from the shock. They were all shaking.

"Maybe a car will come along," said the children's mother hoarsely.

"I believe I have an injured organ," said the grandmother, pressing her side, but no one answered her. Bailey's teeth were clattering. He had on a yellow sport shirt with bright blue parrots designed on it and his face was as yellow as the shirt. The grandmother decided that she would not mention that the house was in Tennessee.

The road was about ten feet above and they could see only the tops of the trees on the other side of it. Behind the ditch they were sitting in there were more woods, tall and dark and deep. In a few minutes they saw a car some distance away on top of a hill, coming slowly as if the occupants were watching them. The grandmother stood up and waved both arms dramatically to attract their attention. The car continued to come on slowly, disappeared around a bend and appeared again, moving even slower, on top of the hill they had gone over. It was a big black battered hearse-like automobile. There were three men in it.

It came to a stop just over them and for some minutes, the driver looked down with a steady expressionless gaze to where they were sitting, and didn't speak. Then he turned his head and muttered something to the other two and they got out. One was a fat boy in black trousers and a red sweat shirt with a silver stallion embossed on the front of it. He moved around on the right side of them and stood staring, his mouth partly open in a kind of loose grin. The other had on khaki pants and a blue striped coat and a gray hat pulled down very low, hiding most of his face. He came around slowly on the left side. Neither spoke.

The driver got out of the car and stood by the side of it, looking down at them. He was an older man than the other two. His hair was just beginning to gray and he wore silver-rimmed spectacles that gave him a scholarly look. He had a long creased face and didn't have on any shirt or undershirt. He had on blue jeans that were too tight for him and was holding a black hat and a gun. The two boys also had guns.

"We've had an ACCIDENT!" the children screamed.

The grandmother had the peculiar feeling that the bespectacled man was someone she knew. His face was as familiar to her as if she had known him all her life but she could not recall who he was. He moved away from the car and began to come down the embankment, placing his feet carefully so that he wouldn't slip. He had on tan and white shoes and no socks, and his ankles were red and thin. "Good afternoon," he said. "I see you all had you a little spill."

"We turned over twice!" said the grandmother.

"Oncet," he corrected. "We seen it happen. Try their car and see will it run, Hiram," he said quietly to the boy with the gray hat.

"What you got that gun for?" John Wesley asked. "Whatcha gonna do with that gun?"

"Lady," the man said to the children's mother, "would you mind calling them children to sit down by you? Children make me nervous. I want all you all to sit down right together there where you're at."

"What are you telling US what to do for?" June Star asked.

Behind them the line of woods gaped like a dark open mouth. "Come here," said their mother.

"Look here now," Bailey began suddenly, "we're in a predicament! We're in . . ."

The grandmother shrieked. She scrambled to her feet and stood staring. "You're The Misfit!" she said. "I recognized you at once!"

"Yes'm," the man said, smiling slightly as if he were pleased in spite of himself to be known, "but it would have been better for all of you, lady, if you hadn't of reckernized me."

Bailey turned his head sharply and said something to his mother that shocked even the children. The old lady began to cry and The Misfit reddened.

"Lady," he said, "don't you get upset. Sometimes a man says things he don't mean. I don't reckon he meant to talk to you thataway."

"You wouldn't shoot a lady, would you?" the grandmother said and removed a clean handkerchief from her cuff and began to slap at her eyes with it.

The Misfit pointed the toe of his shoe into the ground and made a little hole and then covered it up again. "I would hate to have to," he said.

"Listen," the grandmother almost screamed, "I know you're a good man. You don't look a bit like you have common blood. I know you must come from nice people!"

"Yes mam," he said, "finest people in the world." When he smiled he showed a row of strong white teeth. "God never made a finer woman than my mother and my daddy's heart was pure gold," he said. The boy with the red sweat shirt had come around behind them and was standing with his gun at his hip. The Misfit squatted down on the ground. "Watch them children, Bobby Lee," he said. "You know they make me nervous." He looked at the six of them huddled together in front of him and he seemed to be embarrassed as if he couldn't think of anything to say. "Ain't a cloud in the sky," he remarked, looking up at it. "Don't see no sun but don't see no cloud neither."

"Yes, it's a beautiful day," said the grandmother. "Listen," she said, "you shouldn't call yourself The Misfit because I know you're a good man at heart. I can just look at you and tell."

"Hush!" Bailey yelled. "Hush! Everybody shut up and let me handle this!" He was squatting in the position of a runner about to sprint forward but he didn't move.

"I pre-chate that, lady," The Misfit said and drew a little circle in the ground with the butt of his gun.

"It'll take a half a hour to fix this here car," Hiram called, looking over the raised hood of it.

"Well, first you and Bobby Lee get him and that little boy to step over yonder with you," The Misfit said, pointing to Bailey and

John Wesley. "The boys want to ask you something," he said to Bailey. "Would you mind stepping back in them woods there with them?"

"Listen," Bailey began, "we're in a terrible predicament! Nobody realizes what this is," and his voice cracked. His eyes were as blue and intense as the parrots on his shirt and he remained perfectly still.

The grandmother reached up to adjust her hat brim as if she were going to the woods with him but it came off in her hand. She stood staring at it and after a second she let it fall on the ground. Hiram pulled Bailey up by the arm as if he were assisting an old man. John Wesley caught hold of his father's hand and Bobby Lee followed. They went off toward the woods and just as they reached the dark edge, Bailey turned and supported himself against a gray naked pine trunk, he shouted, "I'll be back in a minute, Mamma, wait on me!"

"Come back this instant!" his mother shrilled but they all disappeared into the woods.

"Bailey Boy!" the grandmother called in a tragic voice but she found she was looking at The Misfit squatting on the ground in front of her. "I just know you're a good man," she said desperately. "You're not a bit common!"

"Nome, I ain't a good man," The Misfit said after a second as if he had considered her statement carefully, "but I ain't the worst in the world neither. My daddy said I was different breed of dog from my brothers and sisters. 'You know,' Daddy said, 'it's some that can live their whole life out without asking about it and it's others has to know why it is, and this boy is one of the latters. He's going to be into everything!'" He put on his black hat and looked up suddenly and then away deep into the woods as if he were embarrassed again. "I'm sorry I don't have on a shirt before you ladies," he said, hunching his shoulders slightly. "We buried our clothes that we had on when we escaped and we're just making do until we can get better. We borrowed these from some folks we met," he explained.

"That's perfectly all right," the grandmother said. "Maybe Bailey has an extra shirt in his suitcase."

"I'll look and see terrectly," The Misfit said.

"Where are they taking him?" the children's mother screamed.

"Daddy was a card himself," The Misfit said. "You couldn't put anything over on him. He never got in trouble with the Authorities though. Just had the knack of handling them."

"You could be honest too if you'd only try," said the grandmother. "Think how wonderful it would be to settle down and live a comfortable life and not have to think about somebody chasing you all the time."

The Misfit kept scratching in the ground with the butt of

his gun as if he were thinking about it. "Yes'm, somebody is always after you," he murmured.

The grandmother noticed how thin his shoulder blades were just behind his hat because she was standing up looking down on him. "Do you ever pray?" she asked.

He shook his head. All she saw was the black hat wiggle between his shoulder blades. "Nome," he said.

There was a pistol shot from the woods, followed closely by another. Then silence. The old lady's head jerked around. She could hear the wind move through the tree tops like a long satisfied insuck of breath. "Bailey Boy!" she called.

"I was a gospel singer for a while," The Misfit said. "I been most everything. Been in the arm service, both land and sea, at home and abroad, been twict married, been an undertaker, been with the railroads, plowed Mother Earth, been in a tornado, seen a man burnt alive oncet," and he looked up at the children's mother and the little girl who were sitting close together, their faces white and their eyes glassy; "I even seen a woman flogged," he said.

"Pray, pray," the grandmother began, "pray, pray . . ."

"I never was a bad boy that I remember of," The Misfit said in an almost dreamy voice, "but somewheres along the line I done something wrong and got sent to the penitentiary. I was buried alive," and he looked up and held her attention to him by a steady stare.

"That's when you should have started to pray," she said. "What did you do to get sent to the penitentiary that first time?"

"Turn to the right, it was a wall," The Misfit said, looking up again at the cloudless sky. "Turn to the left, it was a wall. Look up it was a ceiling, look down it was a floor. I forgot what I done, lady. I set there and set there, trying to remember what it was I done and I ain't recalled it to this day. Oncet in a while, I would think it was coming to me, but it never come."

"Maybe they put you in by mistake," the old lady said vaguely.

"Nome," he said. "It wasn't no mistake. They had the papers on me."

"You must have stolen something," she said.

The Misfit sneered slightly. "Nobody had nothing I wanted," he said. "It was a head-doctor at the penitentiary said what I had done was kill my daddy but I known that for a lie. My daddy died in nineteen ought nineteen of the epidemic flu and I never had a thing to do with it. He was buried in the Mount Hopewell Baptist churchyard and you can go there and see for yourself."

"If you would pray," the old lady said, "Jesus would help you."

"That's right," The Misfit said.

"Well then, why don't you pray?" she asked trembling with delight suddenly.

"I don't want no hep," he said. "I'm doing all right by myself."

Bobby Lee and Hiram came ambling back from the woods. Bobby Lee was dragging a yellow shirt with bright blue parrots in it.

"Throw me that shirt, Bobby Lee," The Misfit said. The shirt came flying at him and landed on his shoulder and he put it on. The grandmother couldn't name what the shirt reminded her of. "No, lady," The Misfit said while he was buttoning it up, "I found out the crime don't matter. You can do one thing or you can do another, kill a man or take a tire off his car, because sooner or later you're going to forget what it was you done and just be punished for it."

The children's mother had begun to making heaving noises as if she couldn't get her breath. "Lady," he asked, "would you and that little girl like to step off younder with Bobby Lee and Hiram and join your husband?"

"Yes, thank you," the mother said faintly. Her left arm dangled helplessly and she was holding the baby, who had gone to sleep, in the other. "Hep that lady up, Hiram," The Misfit said as she struggled to climb out of the ditch, "and Bobby Lee, you hold onto that little girl's hand."

"I don't want to hold hands with him," June Star said. "He reminds me of a pig."

The fat boy blushed and laughed and caught her by the arm and pulled her off into the woods after Hiram and her mother.

Alone with The Misfit, the grandmother found that she had lost her voice. There was not a cloud in the sky nor any sun. There was nothing around her but woods. She wanted to tell him that he must pray. She opened and closed her mouth several times before anything came out. Finally she found herself saying, "Jesus, Jesus," meaning Jesus will help you, but the way she was saying it, it sounded as if she might be cursing.

"Yes'm," The Misfit said as if he agreed. "Jesus thown everything off balance. It was the same case with Him as with me except He hadn't committed any crime and they could prove I had committed one because they had the papers on me. Of course," he said, "they never shown me my papers. That's why I sign myself now. I said long ago, you get you a signature and sign everything you do and keep a copy of it. Then you'll know what you done and you can hold up the crime to the punishment and see do they match and in the end you'll have something to prove you ain't been treated right. I call myself The Misfit," he said, "because I can't make what all I done wrong fit what all I gone through in punishment."

There was a piercing scream from the woods, followed

closely by a pistol report. "Does it seem right to you, lady, that one is punished a heap and another ain't punished at all?"

"Jesus!" the old lady cried. "You've got good blood! I know you wouldn't shoot a lady! I know you come from nice people! Pray! Jesus, you ought not to shoot a lady. I'll give you all the money I've got!"

"Lady," The Misfit said, looking beyond her far into the woods, "there never was a body that give the undertaker a tip."

There were two more pistol reports and the grandmother raised her head like a parched old turkey hen crying for water and called, "Bailey Boy, Bailey Boy!" as if her heart would break.

"Jesus was the only One that ever raised the dead," The Misfit continued, "and He shouldn't have done it. He thown everything off balance. If He did what He said, then it's nothing for you to do but thow away everything and follow Him, and if He didn't, then it's nothing for you to do but enjoy the few minutes you got left the best way you can—by killing somebody or burning down his house or doing some other meanness to him. No pleasure but meanness," he said and his voice had become almost a snarl.

"Maybe He didn't raise the dead," the old lady mumbled, not knowing what she was saying and feeling so dizzy that she sank down in the ditch with her legs twisted under her.

"I wasn't there so I can't say He didn't," The Misfit said. "I wisht I had of been there," he said, hitting the ground with his fist. "It ain't right I wasn't there because if I had of been there I would of known. Listen lady," he said in a high voice, "if I had of been there I would of known and I wouldn't be like I am now." His voice seemed about to crack and the grandmother's head cleared for an instant. She saw the man's face twisted close to her own as if he were going to cry and she murmured, "Why you're one of my babies. You're one of my own children!" She reached out and touched him on the shoulder. The Misfit sprang back as if a snake had bitten him and shot her three times through the chest. Then he put his gun down on the ground and took off his glasses and began to clean them.

Hiram and Bobby Lee returned from the woods and stood over the ditch, looking down at the grandmother who half sat and half lay in a puddle of blood and with her legs crossed under her like a child's and her face smiling up at the cloudless sky.

Without his glasses, The Misfit's eyes were red-rimmed and pale and defenseless-looking. "Take her off and thow her where you thown the others," he said, picking up the cat that was rubbing itself against his leg.

"She was a talker, wasn't she?" Bobby Lee said, sliding down the ditch with a yodel.

"She would of been a good woman," The Misfit said, "if it had been somebody there to shoot her every minute of her life."

"Some fun!" Bobby Lee said.

"Shut up, Bobby Lee," The Misfit said. "It's no real pleasure in life."

Philip Roth (1933-   )
Defender of the Faith

In May of 1945, only a few weeks after the fighting had ended in Europe, I was rotated back to the States, where I spent the remainder of the war with a training company at Camp Crowder, Missouri. Along with the rest of the Ninth Army, I had been racing across Germany so swiftly during the late winter and spring that when I boarded the plane, I couldn't believe its destination lay to the west. My mind might inform me otherwise, but there was an inertia of the spirit that told me we were flying to a new front, where we would disembark and continue our push eastward—eastward until we'd circled the globe, marching through villages along whose twisting, cobbled streets crowds of the enemy would watch us take possession of what, up to then, they'd considered their own. I had changed enough in two years not to mind the trembling of the old people, the crying of the very young, the uncertainty and fear in the eyes of the once arrogant. I had been fortunate enough to develop an infantryman's heart, which, like his feet, at first aches and swells but finally grows horny enough for him to travel the weirdest paths without feeling a thing.

Captain Paul Barrett was my C.O. in Camp Crowder. The day I reported for duty, he came out of his office to shake my hand. He was short, gruff, and fiery, and—indoors or out—he wore his polished helmet liner pulled down to his little eyes. In Europe, he had received a battlefield commission and a serious chest wound, and he'd been returned to the States only a few months before. He spoke easily to me, and at the evening formation he introduced me to the troops. "Gentlemen," he said, "Sergeant Thurston, as you know, is no longer with this company. Your new first sergeant is Sergeant Nathan Marx, here. He is a veteran of the European theatre, and consequently will expect to find a company of soldiers here, and not a company of *boys*."

I sat up late in the orderly room that evening, trying half-heartedly to solve the riddle of duty rosters, personnel forms, and morning reports. The Charge of Quarters slept with his mouth open on a mattress on the floor. A trainee stood reading the next day's duty roster, which was posted on the bulletin board just inside the screen door. It was a warm evening, and I could hear radios playing dance music over in the barracks. The trainee, who had been staring at me whenever he thought I wouldn't notice, finally took a step in my direction.

"Hey, Sarge—we having a G.I. party tomorrow night?" he asked. A G.I. party is a barracks cleaning.

"You usually have them on Friday nights?" I asked him.

"Yes," he said, and then he added mysteriously, "That's the whole thing."

"Then you'll have a G.I. party."

He turned away, and I heard him mumbling. His shoulders were moving and I wondered if he was crying.

"What's your name soldier?" I asked.

"He turned, not crying at all. Instead, his green-speckled eyes, long and narrow, flashed like fish in the sun. He walked over to me and sat on the edge of my desk. He reached out a hand. "Sheldon," he said.

"Stand on your feet, Sheldon."

Getting off the desk, he said, "Sheldon Grossbart." He smiled at the familiarity into which he'd led me.

"You against cleaning the barracks Friday night, Grossbart?" I said. "Maybe we shouldn't have G.I. parties. Maybe we should get a maid." My tone startled me. I felt I sounded like every top sergeant I had ever known.

"No, Sergeant." He grew serious, but with a seriousness that seemed to be only the stifling of a smile. "It's just—G.I. parties on Friday night, of all nights."

He slipped up onto the corner of the desk again—not quite sitting, but not quite standing, either. He looked at me with those speckled eyes flashing, and then made a gesture with his hand. It was very slight—no more than a movement back and forth of the wrist—and yet it managed to exclude from our affairs everything else in the orderly room, to make the two of us the center of the world. It seemed, in fact, to exclude everything even about the two of us except our hearts.

"Sergeant Thurston was one thing," he whispered, glancing at the sleeping C.Q., "but we thought that with you here things might be a little different."

"We?"

"The Jewish personnel."

"Why?" I asked, harshly. "What's on your mind?" Whether I was still angry at the "Sheldon" business, or now at something else, I hadn't time to tell, but clearly I was angry.

"We thought you—Marx, you know, like Karl Marx. The Marx Brothers. Those guys are all—M-a-r-x. Isn't that how *you* spell it, Sergeant?"

"M-a-r-x."

"Fishbein said—" He stopped. "What I mean to say,

Sergeant—" His face and neck were red, and his mouth moved but no words came out. In a moment, he raised himself to attention, gazing down at me. It was as though he had suddenly decided he could expect no more sympathy from me than from Thurston, the reason being that I was of Thurston's faith, and not his. The young man had managed to confuse himself as to what my faith really was, but I felt no desire to straighten him out. Very simply, I didn't like him.

When I did nothing but return his gaze, he spoke, in an altered tone. "You see, Sergeant," he explained to me, "Friday nights, Jews are supposed to go to services."

"Did Sergeant Thurston tell you you couldn't go to them when there was a G.I. party?"

"No."

"Did he say you had to stay and scrub the floors?"

"No, Sergeant."

"Did the Captain say you had to stay and scrub the floors?"

"That isn't it, Sergeant. It's the other guys in the barracks." He leaned toward me. "They think we're goofing off. But we're not. That's when Jews go to services, Friday night. We have to."

"Then go."

"But the other guys make accusations. They have no right."

"That's not the Army's problem, Grossbart. It's a personal problem you'll have to work out yourself."

"But it's un*fair*."

I got up to leave. "There's nothing I can do about it," I said.

Grossbart stiffened and stood in front of me. "But this is a matter of *religion*, sir."

"Sergeant," I said.

"I mean 'Sergeant,'" he said, almost snarling.

"Look, go see the chaplain. You want to see Captain Barrett, I'll arrange an appointment."

"No, no. I don't want to make trouble, Sergeant. That's the first thing they throw up to you. I just want my rights!"

"Damn it, Grossbart, stop whining. You have your rights. You can stay and scrub floors or you can go to shul—"

The smile swam in again. Spittle gleamed at the corners of his mouth. "You mean church, Sergeant."

"I mean shul, Grossbart!"

I walked past him and went outside. Near me, I heard the scrunching of a guard's boots on gravel. Beyond the lighted windows of the barracks, young men in T shirts and fatigue pants were sitting on their bunks, polishing their rifles. Suddenly there was a light rustling behind me. I turned and saw Grossbart's dark frame fleeing back to the barracks, racing to tell his Jewish friends that they were right—that, like Karl and Harpo, I was one of them.

The next morning, while chatting with Captain Barrett, I recounted the incident of the previous evening. Somehow, in the telling, it must have seemed to the Captain that I was not so much explaining Grossbart's position as defending it. "Marx, I'd fight side by side with a nigger if the fella proved to me he was a man. I pride myself," he said, looking out the window, "that I've got an open mind. Consequently, Sergeant, nobody gets special treatment here, for the good *or* the bad. All a man's got to do is prove himself. A man fires well on the range, I give him a weekend pass. He scores high in P.T., he gets a weekend pass. He *earns* it." He turned from the window and pointed a finger at me. "You're a Jewish fella, am I right, Marx?"

"Yes, sir."

"And I admire you. I admire you because of the ribbons on your chest. I judge a man by what he shows me on the field of battle, Sergeant. It's what he's got *here*," he said, and then, though I expected he would point to his heart, he jerked a thumb toward the buttons straining to hold his blouse across his belly. "Guts," he said.

"O.K., sir. I only wanted to pass on to you how the men felt."

"Mr. Marx, you're going to be old before your time if you worry about how the men feel. Leave that stuff to the chaplain—that's his business, not yours. Let's us train these fellas to shoot straight. If the Jewish personnel feels the other men are accusing them of goldbricking— well, I just don't know. Seems awfully funny that suddenly the Lord is calling so loud in Private Grossman's ear he's just got to run to church.

"Synagogue," I said.

"Synagogue is right, Sergeant. I'll write that down for handy reference. Thank you for stopping by."

That evening, a few minutes before the company gathered outside the orderly room for the chow information, I called the C.Q., Corporal Robert LaHill, in to see me. LaHill was a dark, burly fellow whose hair curled out of his clothes wherever it could. He had a glaze in his eyes that made one think of caves and dinosaurs. "LaHill," I said, "when you take the formation, remind the men that they're free to attend church services *whenever* they are held, provided they report to the orderly room before they leave the area."

LaHill scratched his wrist, but gave no indication that he'd heard or understood.

"LaHill," I said, "*church*. You remember? Church, priest, Mass, confession."

He curled one lip into a kind of smile; I took it for a signal that for a second he had flickered back up into the human race.

"Jewish personnel who want to attend services this

evening are to fall out in front of the orderly room at 1900," I said. Then, as an afterthought, I added, "By order of Captain Barrett."

A little while later, as the day's last light—softer than any I had seen that year—began to drop over Camp Crowder, I heard LaHill's thick, inflectionless voice outside my window: "Give me your ears, troopers. Toppie says for me to tell you that at 1900 hours all Jewish personnel is to fall out in front, here, if they want to attend the Jewish Mass."

At seven o'clock, I looked out the orderly-room window and saw three soldiers in starched khakis standing on the dusty quandrangle. They looked at their watches and fidgeted while they whispered back and forth. It was getting dimmer, and, alone on the otherwise deserted field, they looked tiny. When I opened the door, I heard the noises of the G.I. party coming from the surrounding barracks—bunks being pushed to the walls, faucets pounding water into buckets, brooms whisking at the wooden floors, cleaning the dirt away for Saturday's inspection. Big puffs of cloth moved round and round on the window-panes. I walked outside, and the moment my foot hit the ground I thought I heard Grossbart call to the others, " 'Ten-*hut!*' " Or maybe, when they all three jumped to attention, I imagined I heard the command.

Grossbart stepped forward. "Thank you, sir," he said.

" 'Sergeant,' Grossbart," I reminded him. "You call officers 'sir.' I'm not an officer. You've been in the Army three weeks—you know that."

He turned his palms out at his sides to indicate that, in truth, he and I lived beyond convention. "Thank you, anyway," he said.

"Yes," a tall boy behind him said. "Thanks a lot."

And the third boy whispered, "Thank you," but his mouth barely fluttered, so that he did not alter by more than a lip's movement his posture of attention.

"For what?" I asked.

Grossbart snorted happily. "For the announcement. The Corporal's announcement. It helped. It made it—"

"Fancier." The tall boy finished Grossbart's sentence.

Grossbart smiled. "He means formal, sir. Public," he said to me. "Now it won't seem as though we're just taking off—goldbricking because the work has begun."

"It was by order of Captain Barrett," I said.

"Aaah, but you pull a little weight," Grossbart said. "So we thank you." Then he turned to his companions. "Sergeant Marx, I want you to meet Larry Fishbein."

The tall boy stepped forward and extended his hand. I shook it. "You from New York?" he asked.

"Me, too." He had a cadaverous face that collapsed inward from his cheekbone to his jaw, and when he smiled—as he did at the news of our communal attachment—revealed a mouthful of bad teeth. He was blinking his eyes a good deal, as though he were fighting back tears. "What borough?" he asked.

I turned to Grossbart. "It's five after seven. What time are services?"

"Shul," he said, smiling, "is in ten minutes. I want you to meet Mickey Halpern. This is Nathan Marx, our sergeant."

The third boy hopped forward. "Private Michael Halpern." He saluted.

"Salute officers, Halpern," I said. The boy dropped his hand, and, on its way down, in his nervousness, checked to see if his shirt pockets were buttoned.

"Shall I march them over, sir?" Grossbart asked. "Or are you coming along?"

From behind Grossbart, Fishbein piped up. "Afterward, they're having refreshments. A ladies' auxiliary from St. Louis, the rabbi told us last week."

"The chaplain," Halpern whispered.

"You're welcome to come along," Grossbart said.

To avoid his plea, I looked away, and saw, in the windows of the barracks, a cloud of faces staring out at the four of us. "Hurry along, Grossbart," I said.

"O.K., then," he said. He turned to the others. "Double time, *march!*"

They started off, but ten feet away Grossbart spun around and, running backward, called to me, "Good *shabbus,* sir!" And then the three of them were swallowed into the alien Missouri dusk.

Even after they had disappeared over the parade ground, whose green was now a deep blue, I could hear Grossbart singing the double-time cadence, and as it grew dimmer and dimmer, it suddenly touched a deep memory—as did the slant of the light—and I was remembering the shrill sounds of a Bronx playground where, years ago, beside the Grand Concourse, I played on long spring evenings such as this. It was a pleasant memory for a young man so far from peace and home, and it brought so many recollections with it that I began to grow exceedingly tender about myself. In fact, I indulged myself in a reverie so strong that I felt as though a hand were reaching down inside me. It had to reach so very far to touch me! It had to reach past those days in the forests of Belgium, and past the dying I'd refused to weep over; past the nights in German farmhouses whose books we'd burned to warm us; past endless stretches when I had shut off all softness I might feel for my fellows, and had managed even to deny myself the posture of a conqueror—the swagger that I, as a Jew, might well have worn as my boots whacked against the rubble of Wesel, Münster, and Braunschweig.

But now one night noise, one rumor of home and time past, and memory plunged down through all I had anesthetized, and came to what I suddenly remembered was myself. So it was not altogether curious that, in search of more of me, I found myself following Grossbart's tracks to Chapel No. 3, where the Jewish services were being held.

I took a seat in the last row, which was empty. Two rows in front of me sat Grossbart, Fishbein, and Halpern, holding little white Dixie cups. Each row of seats was raised higher than the one in front of it, and I could see clearly what was going on. Fishbein was pouring the contents of his cup into Grossbart's, and Grossbart looked mirthful as the liquid made a purple arc between Fishbein's hand and his. In the glaring yellow light, I saw the chaplain standing on the platform at the front; he was chanting the first line of the responsive reading. Grossbart's prayer book remained closed on his lap; he was swishing the cup around. Only Halpern responded to the chant by praying. The fingers of his right hand were spread wide across the cover of his open book. His cap was pulled down low onto his brow, which made it round, like a *yarmulke*. From time to time, Grossbart wet his lips at the cup's edge; Fishbein, his long yellow face a dying light bulb, looked from here to there, craning forward to catch sight of the faces down the row, then of those in front of him, then behind. He saw me, and his eyelids beat a tattoo. His elbow slid into Grossbart's side, his neck inclined toward his friend, he whispered something, and then, when the congregation next responded to the chant, Grossbart's voice was among the others. Fishbein looked into his book now, too; his lips, however, didn't move.

Finally, it was time to drink the wine. The chaplain smiled down at them as Grossbart swigged his in one long gulp, Halpern sipped, meditating, and Fishbein faked devotion with an empty cup. "As I look down amongst the congregation"—the chaplain grinned at the word—"this night, I see many new faces, and I want to welcome you to Friday-night services here at Camp Crowder. I am Major Leo Ben Ezra, your chaplain." Though an American, the chaplain spoke deliberately— syllable by syllable, almost—as though to communicate, above all, with the lip readers in his audience. "I have only a few words to say before we adjourn to the refreshment room, where the kind ladies of the Temple Sinai, St. Louis, Missouri, have a nice setting for you."

Applause and whistling broke out. After another momentary grin, the chaplain raised his hands, palms out, his eyes flicking upward a moment, as if to remind the troops where they were and Who Else might be in attendance. In the sudden silence that followed, I thought I heard Grossbart cackle, "Let the goyim clean the floors!" Were those the words? I wasn't sure, but Fishbein, grinning, nudged Halpern. Halpern looked dumbly at him, then went back to his prayer book, which had been occupying him all through the rabbi's talk. One hand tugged at the black kinky hair that stuck out under his cap. His lips moved.

The rabbi continued. "It is about the food that I want to speak to you for a moment. I know, I know, I know," he intoned, wearily, "how in the mouths of most of you the *trafe* food tastes like ashes.

I know how you gag, some of you, and how your parents suffer to think of their children eating foods unclean and offensive to the palate. What can I tell you? I can only say, close your eyes and swallow as best you can. Eat what you must to live, and throw away the rest. I wish I could help more. For those of you who find this impossible, may I ask that you try and try, but then come to see me in private. If your revulsion is so great, we will have to seek aid from those higher up.''

A round of chatter rose and subsided. Then everyone sang ''Ain Kelohainu''; after all those years, I discovered, I still knew the words. Then, suddenly, the service over, Grossbart was upon me. ''Higher up? He means the General?''

''Hey, Shelly,'' Fishbein said, ''he means God.'' He smacked his face and looked at Halpern. ''How high can you go!''

''Sh-h-h!'' Grossbart said. ''What do you think, Sergeant?''

''I don't know,'' I said. ''You better ask the chaplain.''

''I'm going to. I'm making an appointment to see him in private. So is Mickey.''

Halpern shook his head. ''No, no, Sheldon—''

''You have rights, Mickey,'' Grossbart said. ''They can't push us around.''

''It's O.K.,'' said Halpern. ''It bothers my mother, not me.''

Grossbart looked at me. ''Yesterday he threw up. From the hash. It was all ham and God knows what else.''

''I have a cold—that was why,'' Halpern said. He pushed his *yarmulke* back into a cap.

''What about you, Fishbein?'' I asked. ''You kosher, too?''

He flushed. ''A little. But I'll let it ride. I have a very strong stomach, and I don't eat a lot anyway.'' I continued to look at him, and he held up his wrist to reinforce what he'd just said; his watch strap was tightened to the last hole, and he pointed that out to me.

''But services are important to you?'' I asked him.

He looked at Grossbart. ''Sure, sir.''

'' 'Sergeant.' ''

''Not so much at home,'' said Grossbart, stepping between us, ''but away from home it gives one a sense of his Jewishness.''

''We have to stick together,'' Fishbein said.

I started to walk toward the door; Halpern stepped back to make way for me.

''That's what happened in Germany,'' Grossbart was saying, loud enough for me to hear. ''They didn't stick together. They let themselves get pushed around.''

I turned. ''Look Grossbart. This is the Army, no summer camp.''

He smiled. "So?"

Halpern tried to sneak off, but Grossbart held his arm.

"Grossbart, how old are you?" I asked.

"Nineteen."

"And you?" I said to Fishbein.

"The same. The same month, even."

"And what about him?" I pointed to Halpern, who had by now made it safely to the door.

"Eighteen," Grossbart whispered. "But like he can't tie his shoes or brush his teeth himself. I feel sorry for him."

"I feel sorry for all of us, Grossbart," I said, "but just act like a man. Just don't overdo it."

"Overdo what, sir?"

"The 'sir' business, for one thing. Don't overdo that," I said.

I left him standing there. I passed by Halpern, but he did not look at me. Then I was outside, but, behind, I heard Grossbart call, "Hey, Mickey, my *leben*, come on back. Refreshments!"

"*Leben!*" My grandmother's word for me!

One morning a week later, while I was working at my desk, Captain Barrett shouted for me to come into his office. When I entered, he had his helmet liner squashed down so far on his head that I couldn't even see his eyes. He was on the phone, and when he spoke to me, he cupped one hand over the mouthpiece. "Who the hell is Grossbart?"

"Third platoon, Captain," I said. "A trainee."

"What's all this stink about food? His mother called a goddam congressman about the food." He uncovered his mouthpiece and slid his helmet up until I could see his bottom eyelashes. "Yes, sir," he said into the phone. "Yes, sir. I'm still here, sir. I'm asking Marx, here, right now—"

He covered the mouthpiece again and turned his head back toward me. "Lightfoot Harry's on the phone," he said, between his teeth. "This congressman calls General Lyman, who calls Colonel Sousa, who calls the Major, who calls me. They're just dying to stick this thing on me. Whatsa matter?" He shook the phone at me. "I don't feed the troops? What the hell is this?"

"Sir, Grossbart is strange—" Barrett greeted that with a mockingly indulgent smile. I altered my approach. "Captain, he's a very orthodox Jew, and so he's only allowed to eat certain foods."

"He throws up, the congressman said. Every time he eats something, his mother says, he throws up!"

"He's accustomed to observing the dietary laws, Captain."

"So why's his old lady have to call the White House?"

"Jewish parents, sir—they're apt to be more protective than you expect. I mean, Jews have a very close family life. A boy goes away from home, sometimes the mother is liable to get very upset. Probably the boy mentioned something in a letter, and his mother misinterpreted."

"I'd like to punch him one right in the mouth," the Captain said. "There's a goddam war on, and he wants a silver platter!"

"I don't think the boy's to blame, sir. I'm sure we can straighten it out by just asking him. Jewish parents worry—"

"*All* parents worry, for Christ's sake. But they don't get on their high horse and start pulling strings—"

I interrupted, my voice higher, tighter than before. "The home life, Captain, is very important—but you're right, it may sometimes get out of hand. It's a very wonderful thing, Captain, but because it's so close, this kind of thing . . ."

He didn't listen any longer to my attempt to present both himself and Lightfoot Harry with an explanation for the letter. He turned back to the phone. "Sir?" he said. "Sir—Marx, here, tells me Jews have a tendency to be pushy. He says he thinks we can settle it right here in the company. . . . Yes, sir. . . . I *will* call back, sir, soon as I can." He hung up. "Where are the men, Sergeant?"

"On the range."

With a whack on the top of his helmet, he crushed it down over his eyes again, and charged out of his chair. "We're going for a ride," he said.

The Captain drove, and I sat beside him. It was a hot spring day, and under my newly starched fatigues I felt as though my armpits were melting down onto my sides and chest. The roads were dry, and by the time we reached the firing range, my teeth felt gritty with dust, though my mouth had been shut the whole trip. The Captain slammed the brakes on and told me to get the hell out and find Grossbart.

I found him on his belly, firing wildly at the five-hundred-feet target. Waiting their turns behind him were Halpern and Fishbein. Fishbein, wearing a pair of rimless G.I. glasses I hadn't seen on him before, had the appearance of an old peddler who would gladly have sold you his rifle and the cartridges that were slung all over him. I stood back by the ammo boxes, waiting for Grossbart to finish spraying the distant targets. Fishbein straggled back to stand near me.

"Hello, Sergeant Marx," he said.

"How are you?" I mumbled.

"Fine, thank you. Sheldon's really a good shot."

"I didn't notice."

"I'm not so good, but I think I'm getting the hang of it now. Sergeant, I don't mean to, you know, ask what I shouldn't—" The boy stopped. He was trying to speak intimately, but the noise of the shooting forced him to shout at me.

"What is it?" I asked. Down the range, I saw Captain Barrett standing up in the jeep, scanning the line for me and Grossbart.

"My parents keep asking and asking where we're going," Fishbein said. "Everybody says the Pacific. I don't care, but my parents—if I could relieve their minds, I think I could concentrate more on my shooting."

"I don't know where, Fishbein. Try to concentrate anyway."

"Sheldon says you might be able to find out."

"I don't know a thing, Fishbein. You just take it easy, and don't let Sheldon—"

"*I'm* taking it easy, Sergeant. It's at home—"

Grossbart had finished on the line, and was dusting his fatigues with one hand. I called to him. "Grossbart, the Captain wants to see you."

He came toward us. His eyes blazed and twinkled. "Hi!"

"Don't point that goddam rifle!" I said.

"I wouldn't shoot you, Sarge," He gave me a smile as wide as a pumpkin, and turned the barrel aside.

"Damn you, Grossbart, this is no joke! Follow me."

I walked ahead of him, and had the awful suspicion that, behind me, Grossbart was *marching*, his rifle on his shoulder, as though he were a one-man detachment. At the jeep, he gave the Captain a rifle salute. "Private Sheldon Grossbart, sir."

"At ease, Grossman." The captain sat down, slid over into the empty seat, and, crooking a finger, invited Grossbart closer.

"Bart, sir. Sheldon Gross*bart*. It's a comman error."

Grossbart nodded at me; I understood, he indicated. I looked away just as the mess truck pulled up to the range, disgorging a half-dozen K.P.'s with rolled-up sleeves. The mess sergeant screamed at them while they set up the chow-line equipment.

"Grossbart, your mama wrote some congressman that we don't feed you right. Do you know that?" the Captain said.

"It was my father, sir. He wrote to Representative Franconi that my religion forbids me to eat certain foods."

"What religion is that, Grossbart?"

"Jewish."

"'Jewish, *sir*,'" I said to Grossbart.

"Excuse me, sir. Jewish, sir."

"What have you been living on?" the Captain asked. "You've been in the Army a month already. You don't look to me like you're falling to pieces."

"I eat because I have to, sir. But Sergeant Marx will testify to the fact that I don't eat one mouthful more than I need in order to survive."

"Is that so, Marx?" Barrett asked.

"I've never seen Grossbart eat, sir," I said.

"But you heard the rabbi," Grossbart said. "He told us what to do, and I listened."

The Captain looked at me. "Well, Marx?"

"I still don't know what he eats and doesn't eat, sir."

Grossbart raised his arms to plead with me, and it looked for a moment as though he were going to hand me his weapon to hold. "But, Sergeant—"

"Look, Grossbart, just answer the Captain's questions," I said sharply.

Barrett smiled at me, and I resented it. "All right, Grossbart," he said. "What is it you want? The little piece of paper? You want out?"

"No, sir. Only to be allowed to live as a Jew. And for the others, too."

"What others?"

"Fishbein, sir, and Halpern."

"They don't like the way we serve, either?"

"Halpern throws up, sir. I've seen it."

"I thought *you* throw up."

"Just once, sir. I didn't know the sausage was sausage."

"We'll give menus, Grossbart. We'll show training films about the food, so you can identify when we're trying to poison you."

Grossbart did not answer. The men had been organized into two long chow lines. At the tail end of one, I spotted Fishbein—or, rather, his glasses spotted me. They winked sunlight back at me. Halpern stood next to him, patting the inside of his collar with a khaki handkerchief. They moved with the line as it began to edge up toward the food. The mess sergeant was still screaming at the K.P.s. For a moment, I was actually terrified by the thought that somehow the mess sergeant was going to become involved in Grossbart's problem.

"Marx," the Captain said, "you're a Jewish fella—am I right?"

I played straight man. "Yes, sir."

"How long you been in the Army? Tell this boy."

"Three years and two months."

"A year in combat, Grossbart. Twelve goddam months in combat all through Europe. I admire this man." The Captain snapped a wrist against my chest. "Do you hear him peeping about the food? Do you? I want an answer, Grossbart. Yes or no."

"No, sir."

"And why not? He's a Jewish fella."

"Some things are more important to some Jews than other things to other Jews."

Barrett blew up. "Look, Grossbart. Marx, here, is a good man—a goddam hero. When you were in high school, Sergeant Marx was killing Germans. Who does more for the Jews—you, by throwing up over a lousy piece of sausage, a piece of first-cut meat, or Marx, by killing those Nazi bastards? If I was a Jew, Grossbart, I'd kiss this man's feet. He's a goddam hero, and *he* eats what we give him. Why do you have to cause trouble is what I want to know! What is it you're buckin' for—a discharge?"

"No, sir."

"I'm talking to a wall! Sergeant, get him out of my way." Barrett swung himself back into the driver's seat. "I'm going to see the chaplain." The engine roared, the jeep spun around in a whirl of dust, and the Captain was headed back to camp.

For a moment, Grossbart and I stood side by side, watching the jeep. Then he looked at me and said, "I don't want to start trouble. That's the first thing they toss up to us."

When he spoke, I saw that his teeth were white and straight, and the sight of them suddenly made me understand that Grossbart actually did have parents—that once upon a time someone had taken little Sheldon to the dentist. He was their son. Despite all the talk about his parents, it was hard to believe in Grossbart as a child, an heir—as related by blood to anyone, mother, father, or, above all, to me. This realization led me to another.

"What does your father do, Grossbart?" I asked as we started to walk back toward the chow line.

"He's a tailor."

"An American?"

"Now, yes. A son in the Army," he said, jokingly.

"And your mother?" I asked.

He winked. "A *ballabusta*. She practically sleeps with a dust-cloth in her hand."

"She's also an immigrant?"

"All she talks is Yiddish, still."

"And your father, too?"

"A little English. 'Clean,' 'Press,' 'Take the pants in.' That's the extent of it. But they're good to me."

"Then, Grossbart—" I reached out and stopped him. He turned toward me, and when our eyes met, his seemed to jump back, to shiver in their sockets. "Grossbart—you were the one who wrote that letter, weren't you?"

It took only a second or two for his eyes to flash happy

again. "Yes." He walked on, and I kept pace. "It's what my father *would* have written if he had known how. It was his name, though. *He* signed it. He even mailed it. I sent it home. For the New York postmark."

I was astonished, and he saw it. With complete seriousness, he thrust his right arm in front of me. "Blood is blood, Sergeant," he said, pinching the blue vein in his wrist.

"What the hell *are* you trying to do, Grossbart?" I asked. "I've seen you eat. Do you know that? I told the Captain I don't know what you eat, but I've seen you eat like a hound at chow."

"We work hard, Sergeant. We're in training. For a furnace to work, you've got to feed it coal."

"Why did you say in the letter that you threw up all the time?"

"I was really talking about Mickey there. I was talking *for* him. He would never write, Sergeant, though I pleaded with him. He'll waste away to nothing if I don't help. Sergeant, I used my name—my father's name—but it's Mickey, and Fishbein, too, I'm watching out for."

"You're a regular Messiah, aren't you?"

We were at the chow line now.

"That's a good one, Sergeant," he said, smiling. "But who knows? Who can tell? Maybe you're the Messiah—a little bit. What Mickey says is the Messiah is a collective idea. He went to Yeshiva, Mickey, for a while. He says *together* we're the Messiah. Me a little bit, you a little bit. You should hear that kid talk, Sergeant, when he gets going."

"Me a little bit, you a little bit," I said. "You'd like to believe that, wouldn't you, Grossbart? That would make everything so clean for you."

"It doesn't seem too bad a thing to believe, Sergeant. It only means we should all *give* a little, is all."

I walked off to eat my rations with the other noncoms.

Two days later, a letter addressed to Captain Barrett passed over my desk. It had come through the chain of command—from the office of Congressman Franconi, where it had been received, to General Lyman, to Colonel Sousa, to Major Lamont, now to Captain Barrett. I read it over twice. It was dated May 14th, the day Barrett had spoken with Grossbart on the rifle range.

> Dear Congressman:
> First let me thank you for your interest in behalf of my son, Private Sheldon Grossbart. Fortunately, I was able to speak with Sheldon on the phone the other night, and I think I've been able to solve our problem. He is, as I mentioned in my last letter, a very religious

boy, and it was only with the greatest difficulty that I could persuade him that the religious thing to do—what God Himself would want Sheldon to do—would be to suffer the pangs of religious remorse for the good of his country and all mankind. It took some doing, Congressman, but finally he saw the light. In fact, what he said (and I wrote down the words on a scratch pad so as never to forget), what he said was "I guess you're right, Dad. So many millions of my fellow-Jews gave up their lives to the enemy, the least I can do is live for a while minus a bit of my heritage so as to help end this struggle and regain for all the children of God dignity and humanity." That, Congressman, would make any father proud.

By the way, Sheldon wanted me to know—and pass on to you—the name of a soldier who helped him reach this decision: SERGEANT NATHAN MARX. Sergeant Marx is a combat veteran who is Sheldon's first sergeant. This man has helped Sheldon over some of the first hurdles he's had to face in the Army, and is in part responsible for Sheldon's changing his mind about the dietary laws. I know Sheldon would appreciate any recognition Marx could receive.

Thank you and good luck. I look forward to seeing your name on the next election ballot.

Respectfully,
Samuel E. Grossbart

Attached to the Grossbart communiqué was another, addressed to General Marshall Lyman, the post commander, and signed by Representative Charles E. Franconi of the House of Representatives. The communiqué informed General Lyman that Sergeant Nathan Marx was a credit to the U.S. Army and the Jewish people.

What was Grossbart's motive in recanting? Did he feel he'd gone too far? Was the letter a strategic retreat—a crafty attempt to strengthen what he considered our alliance? Or had he actually changed his mind, via an imaginary dialogue between Grossbart *père* and Grossbart *fils*? I was puzzled, but only for a few days—that is, only until I realized that, whatever his reasons, he had actually decided to disappear from my life; he was going to allow himself to become just another trainee. I saw him at inspection, but he never winked; at chow formations, but he never flashed me a sign. On Sundays, with the other trainees, he would sit around watching the noncoms' softball team, for which I pitched, but not once did he speak an unnecessary word to me. Fishbein and Halpern retreated, too—at Grossbart's command, I was sure. Apparently he had seen that wisdom lay in turning back before he plunged over into the ugliness of privilege undeserved. Our separation allowed me to forgive him our past encounters, and, finally, to admire him for his good sense.

Meanwhile, free of Grossbart, I grew used to my job and my administrative tasks. I stepped on a scale one day, and discovered I had truly become a noncombatant; I had gained seven pounds. I found patience to get past the first three pages of a book. I thought about the future more and more, and wrote letters to girls I'd known before the war. I even got a few answers. I sent away to Columbia for a Law School catalogue. I continued to follow the war in the Pacific, but it was not my war. I thought I could see the end, and sometimes, at night, I dreamed that I was walking on the streets of Manhattan—Broadway, Third Avenue, 116th Street, where I had lived the three years I attended Columbia. I curled myself around these dreams and I began to be happy.

And then, one Saturday, when everybody was away and I was alone in the orderly room reading a month-old copy of the *Sporting News*, Grossbart reappeared.

"You a baseball fan, Sergeant?"

I looked up. "How are you?"

"Fine," Grossbart said. "They're making a soldier out of me."

"How are Fishbein and Halpern?"

"Coming along," he said. "We've got no training this afternoon. They're at the movies."

"How come you're not with them?"

"I wanted to come over and say hello."

He smiled—a shy regular-guy smile, as though he and I well knew that our friendship drew its sustenance from unexpected visits, remembered birthdays, and borrowed lawnmowers. At first it offended me, and then the feeling was swallowed by the general uneasiness I felt at the thought that everyone on the post was locked away in a dark movie theatre and I was here alone with Grossbart. I folded up my paper.

"Sergeant," he said, "I'd like to ask a favor. It is a favor, and I'm making no bones about it."

He stopped, allowing me to refuse him a hearing—which, of course, forced me into a courtesy I did not intend. "Go ahead."

"Well, actually it's two favors."

I said nothing.

"The first one's about these rumors. Everybody says we're going to the Pacific."

"As I told your friend Fishbein, I don't know," I said. "You'll just have to wait to find out. Like everybody else."

"You think there's a chance of any of us going East?"

"Germany?" I said. "Maybe."

"I meant New York."

"I don't think so, Grossbart. Offhand."

"Thanks for the information, Sergeant," he said.

"It's not information, Grossbart. Just what I surmise."

"It certainly would be good to be near home. My parents—you know." He took a step toward the door and then turned back. "Oh, the other thing. May I ask the other?"

"What is it?"

"The other thing is—I've got relatives in St. Louis, and they say they'll give me a whole Passover dinner if I can get down there. God, Sergeant, that'd mean an awful lot to me."

I stood up. "No passes during basic, Grossbart."

"But we're off from now till Monday morning, Sergeant. I could leave the post and no one would even know."

"I'd know. You'd know."

"But that's all. Just the two of us. Last night, I called my aunt, and you should have heard her. 'Come—come,' she said. 'I got gefilte fish, *chrain*—the works!' Just a day, Sergeant. I'd take the blame if anything happened."

"The Captain isn't here to sign a pass."

"You could sign."

"Look, Grossbart—"

"Sergeant, for two months, practically, I've been eating *trafe* till I want to die."

"I thought you'd made up your mind to live with it. To be minus a little bit of heritage."

He pointed a finger at me. "You!" he said. "That wasn't for you to read."

"I read it. So what."

"That letter was addressed to a congressman."

"Grossbart, don't feed me any baloney. You *wanted* me to read it."

"Why are you persecuting me, Sergeant?"

"Are you kidding!"

"I've run into this before," he said, "but never from my own!"

"Get out of here, Grossbart! Get the hell out of my sight!"

He did not move. "Ashamed, that's what you are," he said. "So you take it out on the rest of us. They say Hitler himself was half a Jew. Hearing you, I wouldn't doubt it."

"What are you trying to do with me, Grossbart?" I asked him. "What are you after? You want me to give you special privileges, to change the food, to find out about your orders, to give you weekend passes."

"You even talk like a goy!" Grossbart shook his fist. "Is this just a weekend pass I'm asking for? Is a Seder sacred, or not?"

Seder! It suddenly occurred to me that Passover had been celebrated weeks before. I said so.

"That's right," he replied. "Who says no? A month ago—and I was in the field eating hash! And now all I ask is a simple favor. A Jewish boy I thought would understand. My aunt's willing to go out of her way—to make a Seder a month later. . . ." He turned to go, mumbling.

"Come back here!" I called. He stopped and looked at me. "Grossbart, why can't you be like the rest? Why do you have to stick out like a sore thumb?"

"Because I'm a Jew, Sergeant. I *am* different. Better, maybe not. But different."

"This is a war, Grossbart. For the time being *be* the same."

"I refuse."

"What?"

"I refuse. I can't stop being me, that's all there is to it." Tears came to his eyes. "It's a hard thing to be a Jew. But now I understand what Mickey says—it's a harder thing to stay one." He raised a hand sadly toward me. "Look at *you.*"

"Stop crying!"

"Stop this, stop that, stop the other thing! *You* stop, Sergeant. Stop closing your heart to your own!" And, wiping his face with his sleeve, he ran out the door. "The least we can do for one another—the least . . ."

An hour later, looking out of the window, I saw Grossbart headed across the field. He wore a pair of starched khakis and carried a little leather ditty bag. I went out into the heat of the day. It was quiet; not a soul was in sight except, over by the mess hall, four K.P.s sitting around a pan, sloped forward from their waists, gabbing and peeling potatoes in the sun.

"Grossbart!" I called.

He looked toward me and continued walking.

"Grossbart, get over here!"

He turned and came across the field. Finally, he stood before me.

"Where are you going?" I asked.

"St. Louis. I don't care."

"You'll get caught without a pass."

"So I'll get caught without a pass."

"You'll go to the stockade."

"I'm *in* the stockade." He made an about-face and headed off.

I let him go only a step or two. "Come back here," I said, and he followed me into the office, where I typed out a pass and signed the Captain's name, and my own initials after it.

He took the pass and then, a moment later, reached out and grabbed my hand. "Sergeant, you don't know how much this means to me."

"O.K.," I said. "Don't get in any trouble."

"I wish I could show you how much this means to me."

"Don't do me any favors. Don't write any more congressmen for citations."

He smiled. "You're right, I won't. But let me do something."

"Bring me a piece of that gefilte fish. Just get out of here."

"I will!" he said. "With a slice of carrot and a little horseradish. I won't forget."

"All right. Just show your pass at the gate. And don't tell *anybody*."

"I won't. It's a month late, but a good Yom Tov to you."

"Good Yom Tov, Grossbart," I said.

"You're a good Jew, Sergeant. You like to think you have a hard heart, but underneath you're a fine, decent man. I mean that."

Those last three words touched me more than any words from Grossbart's mouth had the right to. "All right, Grossbart," I said. "Now call me 'sir,' and get the hell out of here."

He ran out the door and was gone. I felt very pleased with myself; it was a great relief to stop fighting Grossbart, and it had cost me nothing. Barrett would never find out, and if he did, I could manage to invent some excuse. For a while, I sat at my desk comfortable in my decision. Then the screen door flew back and Grossbart burst in again. "Sergeant!" he said. Behind him I saw Fishbein and Halpern, both in starched khakis, both carrying ditty bags like Grossbart's.

"Sergeant, I caught Mickey and Larry coming out of the movies. I almost missed them."

"Grossbart—did I say tell no one?" I said.

"But my aunt said I could bring friends. That I should, in fact."

"*I'm* the Sergeant, Grossbart—not your aunt!"

Grossbart looked at me in disbelief. He pulled Halpern up by his sleeve. "Mickey, tell the Sergeant what this would mean to you."

Halpern looked at me and, shrugging, said, "A lot."

Fishbein stepped forward without prompting. "This would mean a great deal to me and my parents, Sergeant Marx."

"No!" I shouted.

Grossbart was shaking his head. "Sergeant, I could see you denying me, but how you can deny Mickey, a Yeshiva boy—that's beyond me."

"I'm not denying Mickey anything," I said. "You just pushed a little too hard, Grossbart. *You* denied him."

"I'll give him my pass, then," Grossbart said. "I'll give him my aunt's address and a little note. At least let him go."

In a second, he had crammed the pass into Halpern's pants pocket. Halpern looked at me, and so did Fishbein. Grossbart was at the door, pushing it open. "Mickey, bring me a piece of gefilte fish, at least," he said, and then he was outside again.

The three of us looked at one another, and then I said, "Halpern, hand that pass over."

He took it from his pocket and gave it to me. Fishbein had now moved to the doorway, where he lingered. He stood there for a moment with his mouth slightly open, and then he pointed to himself. "And me?" he asked.

His utter ridiculousness exhausted me. I slumped down in my seat and felt pulses knocking at the back of my eyes. "Fishbein," I said, "you understand I'm not trying to deny you anything, don't you? If it was my Army, I'd serve gefilte fish in the mess hall. I'd sell *kugel* in the PX, honest to God."

Halpern smiled.

"You understand, don't you, Halpern?"

"Yes, Sergeant."

"And you, Fishbein? I don't want enemies. I'm just like you—I want to serve my time and go home. I miss the same things you miss."

"Then, Sergeant," Fishbein said, "why don't you come, too?"

"Where?"

"To St. Louis. To Shelly's aunt. We'll have a regular Seder. Play hide the-matzo." He gave me a broad, black-toothed smile.

I saw Grossbart again, on the other side of the screen.

"Pst!" He waved a piece of paper. "Mickey, here's the address. Tell her I couldn't get away."

Halpern did not move. He looked at me, and I saw the shrug moving up his arms into his shoulders again. I took the cover off the typewriter and made out passes for him and Fishbein. "Go," I said. "The three of you."

I thought Halpern was going to kiss my hand.

That afternoon, in a bar in Joplin, I drank beer and listened with half an ear to the Cardinal game. I tried to look squarely at what I'd become involved in, and began to wonder if perhaps the struggle with Grossbart wasn't as much my fault as his. What was I that I had to *muster* generous feelings? Who was I to have been feeling so grudging, so tight-hearted? After all, I wasn't being asked to move the world. Had I a right, then, or a reason, to clamp down on Grossbart, when that meant

clamping down on Halpern, too? And Fishbein—that ugly, agreeable soul?
Out of the many recollections of my childhood that had tumbled over me
these past few days, I heard my grandmother's voice: "What are you
making a *tsimmes?*" It was what she would ask my mother when, say, I had
cut myself while doing something I shouldn't have done, and her daughter
was busy bawling me out. I needed a hug and a kiss, and my mother would
moralize. But my grandmother knew—mercy overrides justice. I should
have known it, too. Who was Nathan Marx to be such a penny pincher
with kindness? Surely, I thought, the Messiah himself—if He should ever
come—won't niggle over nickels and dimes. God willing, he'll hug and
kiss.

      The next day, while I was playing softball over on the
parade ground, I decided to ask Bob Wright, who was noncom in charge of
Classification and Assignment, where he thought our trainees would be sent
when their cycle ended, in two weeks. I asked casually, between innings,
and he said, "They're pushing them all into the Pacific. Shulman cut the
orders on your boys the other day."

      The news shocked me, as though I were the father of
Halpern, Fishbein, and Grossbart.

      That night, I was just sliding into sleep when someone
tapped on my door. "Who is it?" I asked.

      "Sheldon."

      He opened the door and came in. For a moment, I felt
his presence without being able to see him. "How was it?" I asked.

      He popped into sight in the near-darkness before me.
"Great, Sergeant," Then he was sitting on the edge of the bed. I sat up.

      "How about you?" he asked. "Have a nice week-
end?"

      "Yes."

      "The others went to sleep." He took a deep, paternal
breath. We sat silent for a while, and a homey feeling invaded my ugly little
cubicle; the door was locked, the cat was out, the children were safely in
bed.

      "Sergeant, can I tell you something? Personal?"

      I did not answer, and he seemed to know why. "Not
about me. About Mickey. Sergeant, I never felt for anybody like I feel for
him. Last night I heard Mickey in the bed next to me. He was crying so, it
could have broken your heart. Real sobs."

      "I'm sorry to hear that."

      "I had to talk to him to stop him. He held my hand,
Sergeant—he wouldn't let it go. He was almost hysterical. He kept saying
if he only knew where we were going. Even if he knew it *was* the Pacific,
that would be better than nothing. Just to know."

      Long ago, someone had taught Grossbart the sad rule
that only lies can get the truth. Not that I couldn't believe in the fact of
Halpern's crying: his eyes *always* seemed red-rimmed. But, fact or not, it

became a lie when Grossbart uttered it. He was entirely strategic. But then—it came with the force of indictment—so was I! There are strategies of aggression, but there are strategies of retreat as well. And so, recognizing that I myself had not been without craft and guile, I told him what I knew. "It is the Pacific."

He let out a small gasp, which was not a lie. "I'll tell him. I wish it was otherwise."

"So do I."

He jumped on my words. "You mean you think you could do something? A change, maybe?"

"No, I couldn't do a thing."

"Don't you know anybody over at C. and A.?"

"Grossbart, there's nothing I can do," I said. "If your orders are for the Pacific, then it's the Pacific."

"But Mickey—"

"Mickey, you, me—everybody, Grossbart. There's nothing to be done. Maybe the war'll end before you go. Pray for a miracle."

"But—"

"Good night, Grossbart." I settled back, and was relieved to feel the springs unbend as Grossbart rose to leave. I could see him clearly now; his jaw had dropped, and he looked like a dazed prize-fighter. I noticed for the first time a little paper bag in his hand.

"Grossbart," I smiled. "My gift?"

"Oh, yes, Sergeant. Here—from all of us." He handed me the bag. "It's egg roll."

"Egg roll?" I accepted the bag and felt a damp grease spot on the bottom. I opened it, sure that Grossbart was joking.

"We thought you'd probably like it. You know—Chinese egg roll. We thought you'd probably have a taste for—"

"Your aunt served egg roll?"

"She wasn't home."

"Grossbart, she invited you. You told me she invited you and your friends."

"I know," he said. "I just reread the letter. *Next* week."

I got out of bed and walked to the window. "Grossbart," I said. But I was not calling to him.

"What?"

"What are you, Grossbart? Honest to God, what are you?"

I think it was the first time I'd asked him a question for which he didn't have an immediate answer.

"How can you do this to people?" I went on.

"Sergeant, the day away did us all a world of good. Fishbein, you should see him, he *loves* Chinese food."

"But the Seder," I said.

"We took second best, Sergeant."

Rage came charging at me. I didn't sidestep. "Grossbart, you're a liar!" I said. "You're a schemer and a crook. You've got no respect for anything. Nothing at all. Not for me, for the truth—not even for poor Halpern! You use us all—"

"Sergeant, Sergeant, I feel for Mickey. Honest to God, I do. I *love* Mickey. I try—"

"You try! You feel!" I lurched toward him and grabbed his shirt front. I shook him furiously. "Grossbart, get out! Get out and stay the hell away from me. Because if I see you, I'll make your life miserable. *You understand that?*"

"Yes."

I let him free, and when he walked from the room, I wanted to spit on the floor where he had stood. I couldn't stop the fury. It engulfed me, owned me, till it seemed I could only rid myself of it with tears or an act of violence. I snatched from the bed the bag Grossbart had given me and, with all my strength, threw it out the window. And the next morning, as the men policed the area around the barracks, I heard a great cry go up from one of the trainees, who had been anticipating only his morning handful of cigarette butts and candy wrappers. "Egg roll!" he shouted. "Holy Christ, Chinese goddam egg roll!"

A week later, when I read the orders that had come down from C. and A., I couldn't believe my eyes. Every single trainee was to be shipped to Camp Stoneman, California, and from there to the Pacific—every trainee but one. Private Sheldon Grossbart. He was to be sent to Fort Monmouth, New Jersey. I read the mimeographed sheet several times. Dee, Farrell, Fishbein, Fuselli, Fylypowicz, Glinicki, Gromke, Gucwa, Halpern, Hardy, Helebrandt, right down to Anton Zygadlo—all were to be headed West before the month was out. All except Grossbart. He had pulled a string, and I wasn't it. I lifted the phone and called C. and A.

The voice on the other end said smartly, "Corporal Shulman, sir."

"Let me speak to Sergeant Wright."

"Who is this calling, sir?"

"Sergeant Marx."

And, to my surprise, the voice said, "*Oh!*" Then, "Just a minute, Sergeant."

Shulman's "*Oh!*" stayed with me while I waited for Wright to come to the phone. Why "*Oh!*"? Who was Shulman? And then, so simply, I knew I'd discovered the string that Grossbart had pulled. In fact, I could hear Grossbart the day he'd discovered Shulman in the PX, or in the bowling alley, or maybe even at services. "Glad to meet you. Where you from? Bronx? Me, too. Do you know So-and-So? And

So-and-So? Me, too! You work at C. and A.? Really? Hey, how's chances of getting East? Could you do something? Change something? Swindle, cheat, lie? We gotta help each other, you know. If the Jews in Germany . . ."

Bob Wright answered the phone. "How are you, Nate? How's the pitching arm?"

"Good. Bob, I wonder if you could do me a favor." I heard clearly my own words, and they so reminded me of Grossbart that I dropped more easily than I could have imagined into what I had planned. "This may sound crazy, Bob, but I got a kid here on orders to Monmouth who wants them changed. He had a brother killed in Europe, and he's hot to go to the Pacific. Says he'd feel like a coward if he wound up Stateside. I don't know, Bob—can anything be done? Put somebody else in the Monmouth slot?"

"Who?" he asked cagily.

"Anybody. First guy in the alphabet. I don't care. The kid just asked if something could be done."

"What's his name?"

"Grossbart, Sheldon."

Wright didn't answer.

"Yeah," I said. "He's a Jewish kid, so he thought I could help him out. You know."

"I guess I can do something," he finally said. "The Major hasn't been around here for weeks. Temporary duty to the golf course. I'll try, Nate, that's all I can say."

"I'd appreciate it, Bob. See you Sunday," And I hung up, perspiring.

The following day, the corrected orders appeared: Fishbein, Fuselli, Fylypowicz, Glinicky, Gromke, Grossbart, Gucwa, Halpern, Hardy . . . Lucky Private Harley Alton was to go to Fort Monmouth, New Jersey, where, for some reason or other, they wanted an enlisted man with infantry training.

After chow that night, I stopped back at the orderly room to straighten out the guard-duty roster. Grossbart was waiting for me. He spoke first.

"You son of a bitch!"

I sat down at my desk, and while he glared at me, I began to make the necessary alterations in the duty roster.

"What do you have against me?" he cried. "Against my family? Would it kill you for me to be near my father, God knows how many months he has left to him?"

"Why so?"

"His heart," Grossbart said. "He hasn't had enough troubles in a lifetime, you've got to add to them. I curse the day I ever met you, Marx! Shulman told me what happened over there. There's no limit to your anti-Semitism, is there? The damage you've done here isn't enough. You have to make a special phone call! You really want me dead!"

I made the last few notations in the duty roster and got up to leave. "Good night, Grossbart."

"You owe me an explanation!" He stood in my path.

"Sheldon, you're the one who owes explanations."

He scowled. "To *you*?"

"To me, I think so—yes. Mostly to Fishbein and Halpern."

"That's right, twist things around. I owe nobody nothing, I've done all I could do for them. Now I think I've got the right to watch out for myself."

"For each other we have to learn to watch out, Sheldon. You told me yourself."

"You call this watching out for me—what you did?"

"No. For all of us."

I pushed him aside and started for the door. I heard his furious breathing behind me, and it sounded like a steam rushing from an engine of terrible strength.

"You'll be all right," I said from the door. And, I thought, so would Fishbein and Halpern be all right, even in the Pacific, if only Grossbart continued to see—in the obsequiousness of the one, the soft spirituality of the other—some profit for himself.

I stood outside the orderly room, and I heard Grossbart weeping behind me. Over in the barracks, in the lighted windows, I could see the boys in their T shirts sitting on their bunks talking about their orders, as they'd been doing for the past two days. With a kind of quiet nervousness, they polished shoes, shined belt buckles, squared away underwear, trying as best they could to accept their fate. Behind me, Grossbart swallowed hard, accepting his. And then, resisting with all my will an impulse to turn and seek pardon for my vindictiveness, I accepted my own.

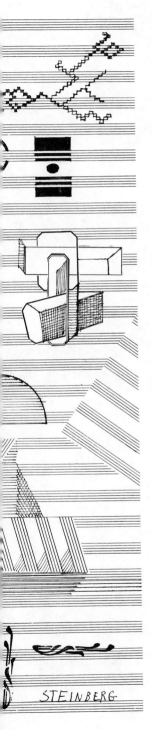

POETRY

STEINBERG

Some of us approach the study of poetry with happy anticipation. Others do so with apprehension, and some approach it with honest dread. Admittedly, the study of verse (or of any subject) can be downright unpleasant, especially if the instructor is not particularly interested in it or assigns material so difficult only the initiated will understand it. Unfortunately, not all instructors in literature recognize that the student beginning the serious study of poetry is seldom prepared to appreciate the intellectual puzzles that some poems contain; neither is the student likely to be enthusiastic about a poem ninety pages long, or a poem in dialect, or one bristling with outdated words. Often the student is able to make some sense out of such poems, but without enjoying the experience.

Even if you approach poetry with reservations, probably you can name a poem or two that you have enjoyed, possibly the lyrics of a popular song or a few lines of verse you cannot forget. If so, you demonstrate that poetry itself is alive and well even though the formal study of it in some situations is less than healthy. The major premise of *Structure and Meaning* is that literature exists to be enjoyed and therefore that if a particular poem and reader do not strike up a happy relationship, something basic is wrong with the poem, the reader, the instructor (if one is involved), or all three. There are a variety of ways a poem can please us. For instance, the poem may be humorous, like this anonymous limerick:

There was a young man of Bengal
Who went to a fancy-dress ball.
    He went just for fun
    Dressed up as a bun,
And a dog ate him up in the hall.

Or this inscription for the gravestone of a dentist:

Stranger, approach this spot with gravity;
John Brown is filling his last cavity.

409

We may enjoy a poem that invites us to think about ourselves, as do these lines from "Alone," attributed to Edgar Allen Poe (1809–1849):

From childhood's hour I have not been
As others were—I have not seen
As others saw—I could not bring
My passions from a common spring—
From the same source I have not taken
My sorrow—I could not awaken
My heart to joy at the same tone—
And all I lov'd—I lov'd alone.

Or about how precious life is:

Mark Van Doren   *(1894–1972)*

from Morning Worship

I wake and hear it raining.
Were I dead, what would I give
Lazily to lie here,
Like this, and live?

Or about what a kiss can mean:

Leigh Hunt   *(1784–1859)*

Rondeau

Jenny kissed me when we met,
    Jumping from the chair she sat in;
Time, you thief, who love to get
    Sweets into your list, put that in:
Say I'm weary, say I'm sad,
    Say that health and wealth have missed me,
Say I'm growing old, but add,
    Jenny kissed me.

Or about what it might be like to face death:

Emily Dickinson (1830–1886)

I heard a Fly buzz—when I died—

I heard a Fly buzz—when I died—
The Stillness in the Room
Was like the Stillness in the Air—
Between the Heaves of Storm—

The Eyes around—had wrung them dry—   5
And Breaths were gathering firm
For the last Onset—when the King
Be witnessed—in the Room—

I willed my Keepsakes—Signed away
What portion of me be   10
Assignable—and then it was
There interposed a Fly—

With Blue—uncertain stumbling Buzz—
Between the light—and me—
And then the Windows failed—and then   15
I could not see to see—

Often the subject matter alone arouses our interest, as these titles suggest:

The Seminole Village in Miami

beware   :   do not read this poem

A Noiseless Patient Spider

But whatever the poets' subjects, whatever their approaches and techniques, their work is meant to be enjoyed.

Naturally, the benefits derived from reading poetry include more than enjoyment and pleasure. Our outlook is broadened, our intellectual and emotional responses are sharpened and matured, and our understanding of ourselves and of others expanded and deepened. But these are fringe benefits, and if we fail to enjoy we will seldom return for more.

The aim of this section of *Structure and Meaning*, therefore, is to develop an enjoyment of poetry by presenting brief instruction in the art of poetry, illustrated with a wide variety of poems. As we read on, let us remember the introduction Robert Herrick (1591–1674) provided for his volume of poems:

The Argument of His Book

I sing of brooks, of blossoms, birds, and bowers;
Of April, May, of June, and July flowers.
I sing of Maypoles, hock-carts, wassails, wakes,
Of bridegrooms, brides, and of their bridal cakes.
I write of youth, of love, and have access
By these to sing of cleanly wantonness.
I sing of dews, of rains, and piece by piece
Of balm, of oil, of spice, and ambergris.
I sing of times trans-shifting, and I write
How roses first came red, and lilies white.
I write of groves, of twilights, and I sing
The court of Mab, and of the fairy king.
I write of hell; I sing (and ever shall)
Of heaven, and hope to have it after all.

I   Denotation

Once published, a poem becomes the reader's. For the difficulties inherent in many poems, we as readers can train ourselves to read intelligently and sensitively.

Thou sayest my lines are hard;
    And I the truth will tell;
They are both hard, and marred,
    If thou not readest them well.

Robert Herrick (1591–1674)

Because poetry is concentrated communication, individual words are often highly important. On a page of fiction, an unfamiliar word here and there will seldom hamper our understanding of the whole, but in a poem, a few unfamiliar words may obscure meaning and detract from our enjoyment. Of course, not all poetry contains difficult or unusual words, yet even if our recognition vocabulary is large, eventually we will encounter important words in poetry we do not know. Because these words may be crucial to the sense of the poem, we have the challenge of identifying their denotative (or dictionary) meanings. The aim of this chapter is to help you recognize and meet that challenge.

The most profitable way to approach an unfamiliar poem is to read it first in its entirety without stopping to puzzle over every unfamiliar word. Frequently the poem will clarify its own difficulties. Having read the entire poem, you should double back to clarify any important words that remain unfamiliar. With this in mind, consider the following poem:

Robert Frost *(1874–1963)*

Dust of Snow

> The way a crow
> Shook down on me
> The dust of snow
> From a hemlock tree
>
> Has given my heart
> A change of mood
> And saved some part
> Of a day I had rued.

Perhaps the word *rued* is not in your bag of words. But you need to know what it means if you are to understand what happens to the speaker of the poem, what "change of mood" he undergoes.

Exercises   1. In the poem, is a day I had rued *positive or negative?*

2. *What synonyms does* rued *suggest? After listing several, you should check a good college dictionary to confirm or correct your conclusions.*

3. *Although the incident with the crow may at first seem insignificant, obviously it had a powerful effect on the speaker. Why?*

In the next poem you may find more than one unfamiliar word, yet clues within the poem should make a dictionary unnecessary.

Raymond Carver (1938–)

Photograph of My Father in His Twenty-second Year

October. Here in this dank, unfamiliar kitchen
I study my father's embarrassed young man's face.
Sheepish grin, he holds in one hand a string
Of spiny yellow perch, in the other
A bottle of Carlsbad beer.　　　　　　　　　　　5

In jeans and denim shirt, he leans
Against the front fender of a Ford *circa* 1934.
He would like to pose bluff and hearty for his posterity,
Wear his old hat cocked over his ear, stick out his
　　tongue. . .
All his life my father wanted to be bold.　　　　10

But the eyes give him away, and the hands
That limply offer the string of dead perch
And the bottle of beer. Father, I loved you,
Yet how can I say thank you, I who cannot hold my
　　liquor either
And do not even know the places to fish?　　　　15

Exercise　　*Relying only on the poem itself, define the following words, giving in each case the hints within the poem that point to each word's denotation:* dank *kitchen,* sheepish *grin,* circa *1934,* bluff *and* hearty.

Although several words in the following poem are outdated (the poem was published in 1648), the context or situation of the poem resolves much of their difficulty. For instance, you may never have heard of *dandled*, yet after reading the poem you should have little difficulty defining it.

Robert Herrick *(1591–1674)*

The Vision

Sitting alone (as one forsook)
Close by a silver-shedding brook;
With hands held up to Love, I wept;
And after sorrows spent, I slept:
Then in a vision I did see   5
A glorious form appear to me:
A virgins face she had; her dresse
Was like a sprightly *Spartanesse.*
A silver bow with green silk strung,
Down from her comely shoulders hung: 10
And as she stood, the wanton air
Dandled the ringlets of her hair.
Her legs were such *Diana* shows,
When tuckt up she a hunting goes;
With buskins shortned to descrie   15
The happy dawning of her thigh:
Which when I saw, I made access
To kisse that tempting nakedness:
But she forbad me, with a wand
Of myrtle she had in her hand: 20
And chiding me, said, hence, remove,
Herrick, thou art too coarse to love.

Exercise   *Without a dictionary, define* dandled, comely, *and* buskins *as they are used by Herrick.*

The poem itself, then, is a valuable source of information about words you cannot define at first glance. Even though close reading of the poem may at first seem unnaturally slow, remember that good poetry unlocks its delicacies only to the patient and sensitive reader.

For unusual words that the poem itself fails to clarify, we usually turn to a good dictionary. Yet dictionary and context must be used together. A given word may have more than one denotation, in which case you must select what best fits the parts of speech (*care* for others is rare; they *care* for bears; a *Care* package on the stairs), or in short, the usage appropriate to the poem you are reading. The verse that follows comments on the mystery of death, and to perceive the details of the scene is to participate more fully in the poem.

Robert Frost *(1874–1963)*

The Rabbit-Hunter

Careless and still
The hunter lurks
With gun depressed,
Facing alone
The alder swamps   *5*
Ghastly snow-white.
And his hound works
In the offing there
Like one possessed,
And yelps delight   *10*
And sings and romps,
Bringing him on
The shadowy hare
For him to rend
And deal a death   *15*
That he nor it
(Nor I) have wit
To comprehend.

Exercises   *1. Give several denotations for* depressed, *then select the one most suitable here.*

2. From the context and your dictionary, formulate a brief description of alder swamps.

3. Locate the hound in the scene (what does in the offing *mean?).*

4. Give several denotations of rend *(verb), then select the one most suitable here; do the same for* wit.

The following poems also contain words unrecognized by average readers. In addition, the poems contain words that are recognizable, but are used in unusual ways.

John Crowe Ransom *(1888–1974)*

Bells for John Whiteside's Daughter

There was such speed in her little body,
And such lightness in her footfall,
It is no wonder her brown study
Astonishes us all.

Her wars were bruited in our high window.   *5*
We looked among orchard trees and beyond
Where she took arms against her shadow,
Or harried unto the pond

The lazy geese, like a snow cloud
Dripping their snow on the green grass,   *10*
Tricking and stopping, sleepy and proud,
Who cried in goose, Alas,

For the tireless heart within the little
Lady with rod that made them rise
From their noon apple-dreams and scuttle   *15*
Goose-fashion under the skies!

But now go the bells, and we are ready,
In one house we are sternly stopped
To say we are vexed at her brown study,
Lying so primly propped.   *20*

Exercises

1. *Why the* bells? *Tell what has happened to this girl and why the speaker and others are* in one house . . . sternly stopped. *Before answering, you may wish to consult a dictionary for* brown study.

2. *What are the* wars *for which the daughter takes* arms?

3. *From context and dictionary identify appropriate denotations for* bruited, harried, scuttle, *and* vexed.

Phyllis McGinley *(1905–   )*

Intimations of Mortality

On being told by the dentist that "this will be over soon"

Indeed, it will soon be over, I shall be done
    With the querulous drill, the forceps, the clove-
smelling cotton.
I can go forth into fresher air, into sun,
    This narrow anguish forgotten.

In twenty minutes or forty or half an hour,   *5*
    I shall be easy, and proud of my hard-got gold.
But your apple of comfort is eaten by worms, and
sour.
    Your consolation is cold.

This will not last, and the day will be pleasant after.
    I'll dine tonight with a witty and favorite friend. *10*
No doubt tomorrow I shall rinse my mouth with
laughter.
    And also that will end.

The handful of time that I am charily granted
    Will likewise pass, to oblivion duly apprenticed.
Summer will blossom and autumn be faintly enchanted.   *15*
    Then time for the grave, or the dentist.

Because you are shrewd, my man, and your hand is
clever,
    You must not believe your words have a charm to
spell me.
There was never a half of an hour that lasted forever.
    Be quiet. You need not tell me.   *20*

Exercises   *1. Give appropriate denotations for* querulous, anguish,
charily, oblivion, apprenticed, *and* shrewd.

2. We usually think of narrow *in terms of width. What does*
narrow anguish *mean in this poem?*

*3. State the dentist's admonition to his patient, and give the
patient's unspoken reply.*

4. Who is master of the situation? Why?

Many good poems will challenge your understanding, and if you approach poetry with an alert mind and a good dictionary, you will discover that the many worlds of poetry are more comprehensible, more fascinating, and the exploration more enjoyable than you may have thought. Yet even though individual words in a poem are important, a poem cannot be defined as the sum of its parts. Because it is much more than that, paraphrasing a poem should never become your ultimate goal, nor your final experience with the poem. Because good poetry is meant to be enjoyed, and not just understood, your understanding of the individual words and phrases of a poem should always be a means to an end, not the end itself.

Kenneth Rexroth (1905–)

The Mirror in the Woods

A mirror hung on the broken
Walls of an old summer house
Deep in the dark woods. Nothing
Ever moved in it but the
Undersea shadows of ferns,   5
Rhododendrons and redwoods.
Moss covered the frame. One day
The gold and glue gave way and
The mirror slipped to the floor.
For many more years it stood   10
On the shattered boards. Once in
A long time a wood rat would
Pass it by without ever
Looking in. At last we came,
Breaking the sagging door and   15
Letting in a narrow wedge
Of sunlight. We took the mirror
Away and hung it in my
Daughter's room with a barre before
It. Now it reflects ronds, escartes,   20
Relevés and arabesques.
In the old house the shadows,
The wood rats and moss work unseen.

Exercise   *A standard English dictionary probably will not identify*
            barre, rond (rond de jambe), escarte (écarté), or relevé,
            although a dictionary of ballet terms would. Without consult-
            ing a specialized dictionary, make an educated guess at what
            they describe, then look up the more common arabesque *in your*
            dictionary to see if you are close.

James Tate *(1943–   )*

Dark Street

So this is the dark street
where only an angel lives:
I never saw anything like it.
For the first time in a lifetime
I feel the burgeoning of wings   5
somewhere behind my frontal lobes.
So this is the dark street.
Did his lights come on,
or do I dream?
I never saw anything like it.   10

Even the trees' languorous leaves
look easy to touch.
So this is the dark street.
Here he comes now:
good afternoon, Father—   15
your handshake is so pleasing.
Brush the shards from my shoulders,
what lives we have ahead of us!
So this is the dark street.
I never saw anything like it.   20

Exercises   *1. Determine suitable denotations for* burgeoning *of* wings, *frontal* lobes, languorous *leaves, and* shards *on the* shoulders.

2. Knowing the words listed in the previous question should help you explain what is happening to the speaker. Consider the following questions, supporting your answers with evidence from the poem: (a) Is the speaker alive or dead? (b) Where might the dark street be? (c) Why might the leaves be languorous? (d) Who is the angel? Is he good or bad?

Sylvia Plath *(1932–1963)*

Black Rook in Rainy Weather

On the stiff twig up there
Hunches a wet black rook
Arranging and rearranging its feathers in the rain.
I do not expect miracle
Or an accident   5

To set the sight on fire
In my eye, nor seek
Any more in the desultory weather some design,
But let spotted leaves fall as they fall,
Without ceremony, or portent   10

Although, I admit, I desire,
Occasionally, some backtalk
From the mute sky, I can't honestly complain:
A certain minor light may still
Leap incandescent   15

Out of kitchen table or chair
As if a celestial burning took
Possession of the most obtuse objects now and then—
Thus hallowing an interval
Otherwise inconsequent   20

By bestowing largesse, honor,
One might say love. At any rate, I now walk
Wary (for it could happen
Even in this dull, ruinous landscape); skeptical,
Yet politic; ignorant   25

Of whatever angel may choose to flare
Suddenly at my elbow. I only know that a rook
Ordering its black feathers can so shine
As to seize my senses, haul
My eyelids up, and grant   30

A brief respite from fear
Of total neutrality. With luck,
Trekking stubborn through this season
Of fatigue, I shall
Patch together a content   35

Of sorts. Miracles occur,
If you care to call those spasmodic
Tricks of radiance miracles. The wait's begun again,
The long wait for the angel,
For that rare, random descent.   40

Exercises

1. *Relying on both the context and a good dictionary, determine the meaning of the following words:* desultory *weather,* portent, *a light* incandescent, celestial *burning,* obtuse *objects,* hallowing *an interval, an interval otherwise* inconsequent, *bestowing* largesse *(or largess),* politic, *a brief* respite, *and* spasmodic *tricks.*

2. *Distinguish between what the speaker expects from the scene and what the scene so far has provided.*

3. *With what frequency and regularity are the speaker's anticipations fulfilled?*

4. *Summarize the insight into so-called "poetic inspiration" supplied by the poem.*

Thomas Campion   *(1567–1620)*

from Two Books of Airs

Jack and Joan they think no ill,
But loving live, and merry still;
Do their weekdays' work, and pray
Devoutly on the holyday;
Skip and trip it on the green,   5
And help to choose the summer queen;
Lash out, at a country feast,
Their silver penny with the best.

Well can they judge of nappy ale,
And tell at large a winter tale;   10
Climb up to the apple loft.
And turn the crabs till they be soft.
Tib is all the father's joy,
And little Tom the mother's boy.
All their pleasure is content;   15
And care, to pay their yearly rent.

Joan can call by name her cows
And deck her windows with green boughs;
She can wreaths and tutties make,
And trim with plums a bridal cake.   20
Jack knows what brings gain or loss,
And his long flail can stoutly toss,
Makes the hedge, which others break,
And ever thinks what he doth speak.

Now, you courtly dames and knights,   *25*
That study only strange delights,
Though you scorn the home-spun gray
And revel in your rich array,
Though your tongues dissemble deep
And can your heads from danger keep,   *30*
Yet, for all your pomp and train,
Securer lives the silly swain.

Exercises

1. If any of the following words in this 1613 poem are unfamiliar, they can be found in most college dictionaries: nappy, crabs, flail, revel, dissemble, swain.

2. Is silly (in the last line) used in the modern sense (foolish, stupid)? If not, provide an appropriate denotation.

3. Lash out (line 7) and tutties (line 19) probably will not be defined in a standard dictionary, so you will need to consult the more comprehensive Oxford English Dictionary in your college library. When using this multivolume work, refer to the front of each volume for help with abbreviations, and observe that besides defining words, the OED provides historical examples of particular usages. This information can aid you in determining when a particular word was used in a particular sense. Give suitable denotations for lash out and tutty and the historical example closest to the date of the poem.

Topics for Writing

1. Although "Photograph of My Father in His Twenty-second Year" is about the speaker's father, it is also about the speaker himself. Compose an essay in which you describe what the poem reveals about him.

2. How does the speaker in "Photograph of My Father in His Twenty-second Year" really feel about his father? Write an essay in which you identify hints in the poem that help you answer this question.

3. Select a photograph of a person you know, and write an essay telling what the photograph reveals about that person. Hand in the photograph with your essay.

2 Connotation

A minor but often-quoted American poet, Edgar A. Guest (1881–1959), has a line that reads "It takes a heap o' livin' in a house t' make it home." Although not especially profound, his point does highlight an essential difference in meaning between two ordinary words, *house* and *home*. Both words denote a domicile or place of dwelling. For most of us, however, *home* is charged with emotional associations that the more plain word *house* lacks. *Home* suggests or *connotes* security, acceptance, and comfort, associations that (as Guest's line makes clear) arise from our experiences. A house, then, becomes a home only when we have participated in a variety of experiences within its walls. When we have done so, the word *home* brings to our minds those days, those weeks, those years. So when poets use *home*, they know that it will stimulate predictable feelings in most of their readers. If they try to communicate through such connotations, poets will usually use associations that are widely accepted, such as those clustered around *home*, rather than private associations or even associations understood only by a select group. As readers, on the other hand, we should guard against interpreting a word in terms of our own private connotations. If *home* to us has negative connotations—quarreling, say, or parental disapproval—we might misunderstand the intent of references like that in Guest's line unless we make an adjustment that allows for our own atypical experience.

By developing a sensitivity to connotations, we can participate more richly in poetry. Often the attitudes and feelings of the poem's speaker are shown by connotation, and for this reason, understanding the denotation of each word and of the whole poem is only a preliminary step toward a fuller experience. The next poem relies heavily on widely recognized connotations to communicate not only a surface meaning, but also the deeper emotions of those involved.

John Lennon (1940–   )
Paul McCartney (1942–   )

She's Leaving Home

Wednesday morning at five o'clock as the day begins
Silently closing her bedroom door
Leaving the note that she hoped would say more
She goes downstairs to the kitchen clutching her hand-
    kerchief
Quietly turning the backdoor key   5
Stepping outside she is free.
She (We gave her most of our lives) is leaving
    (Sacrificed most of our lives) home (We gave her
    everything money could buy)
She's leaving home after living alone
For so many years. Bye, bye.

Father snores as his wife gets into her dressing gown *11*
Picks up the letter that's lying there
Standing alone at the top of the stairs
She breaks down and cries to her husband
Daddy our baby's gone.
How would she treat us so thoughtlessly   *15*
How could she do this to me.
She (We never thought of ourselves) is leaving (Never a
    thought for ourselves) home (We struggled all of
    our lives to get by)
She's leaving home after living alone
For so many years. Bye, bye.

Friday morning at nine o'clock she is far away.   *20*
Waiting to keep the appointment she made
Meeting a man from the motor trade
She (What did we do that was wrong) is having (We
    didn't know what was wrong) fun (Fun is the one
    thing that money can't buy)
Something inside that was always denied
For so many years. Bye, bye.   *25*
She's leaving home bye bye.

In line 4, *clutching* means (literally) holding firmly, yet it suggests powerful emotions that holding firmly does not. A cook might hold an eggbeater *firmly,* but he would *clutch* the beater only if an intruder were at the backdoor. Because the situation in this poem is more emotional than beating an egg, *clutching* obviously is more appropriate than holding firmly. Furthermore, the word helps us sense the emotion of the situation: not the overly sentimental weeping at little or nothing, the feelings surrounding this incident are those of genuine anxiety and fear of the unknown. *Clutches* connotes violence too, clawlike violence (as in "the eagle *clutches* the rabbit"). In a desperate act to survive and (perhaps) to find herself, this lonesome girl struggles away from her prison into a frightening and unfamiliar freedom. The single word *clutching* conveys much of this feeling, and if we are not sensitive to the associations such words communicate, we may miss much of the depth the poem contains.

Exercises   *1. The parenthetical expressions in the poem reflect the point of view of the parents (chiefly the mother). What connotations in the passage* we gave her most of our lives *are absent in* we gave her most of our attention?

2. Are those connotations similar to, or different from, the connotations in these two passages: sacrificed most of our lives *and* we gave her everything money could buy?

3. Define what the parents have given of themselves.

4. Why have the authors chosen our baby *for line 14 instead of* our daughter, *or* our girl, *or* Jolina, *or even perhaps that* sneak?

The associations implied by many of the words in the following poem work together to create a unified feeling for the speaker's life.

Al Young *(1939–   )*

Lonesome in the Country

How much of me is sandwiches radio beer?
How much pizza traffic & neon messages?
I take thoughtful journeys to supermarkets,
philosophize about the newest good movie,
camp out at magazine racks & on floors,   5
catch humanity leering back in laundromats,
invent shortcuts by the quarter hour

There's meaning to all this itemization
& I'd do well to look for it in woodpiles
or in hills & springs or trees in the woods   10
instead of staying in the shack all the time
imagining too much
      falling asleep in old chairs

All that childhood I spent in farmhouses
& still cant tell one bush from another—   15
Straight wilderness would wipe me out
faster than cancer from cigarette smoke

Meantime my friends are out all day long
stomping thru the woods all big-eyed
& that's me walking the road afternoons   20
head in a book
    all that hilly sweetness wasting

Exercises *1. The speaker postulates an explanation for his inability to participate enthusiastically in the country. What is it?*

2. Define as closely as you can the type of city life he has led. To do so, concentrate on the connotations evoked by sandwiches, radio (in this age of TV), beer, pizza, traffic, and so on. For instance, why not hors d'oeuvres instead of sandwiches? Or why not color TV instead of radio, gin instead of beer?

Following is a humorous attempt to dispute the widely held connotation of the countryside as a place of romance, escape, freedom, an attempt to "correct" what the speaker believes are mistaken notions about the country.

Nathaniel Willis (1806–1867)

Love in a Cottage

They may talk of love in a cottage,
    And bowers of trellised vine—
Of nature bewitchingly simple,
    And milkmaids half divine;
They make talk of the pleasure of sleeping   5
    In the shade of a spreading tree,
And a walk in the fields at morning,
    By the side of a footstep free!

But give me a sly flirtation
    By the light of a chandelier—   10
With music to play in the pauses,
    And nobody very near;
Or a seat on a silken sofa,
    With a glass of pure old wine,
And mamma too blind to discover   15
The small white hand in mine.

Your love in a cottage is hungry,
    Your vine is a nest for flies—
Your milkmaid shocks the Graces,
    And simplicity talks of pies!   20
You lie down to your shady slumber
    And wake with a bug in your ear,
And your damsel that walks in the morning
    Is shod like a mountaineer.

True love is at home on a carpet,   25
    And mightily likes his ease—
And true love has an eye for a dinner,
    And starves beneath shady trees.
His wing is the fan of a lady,
    His foot's an invisible thing,   30
And his arrow is tipp'd with a jewel
    And shot from a silver string.

1. Although this poem and the preceding one are spoken by advocates of city life, their city lives differ widely. What are those differences?

2. The speaker above, while purporting to be realistic, plainly is biased. Do the details (chandeliers, music, silken sofa, pure old wine) *in his "perfect setting for love" have any negative connotations for you?*

3. Do you believe the poet praises or criticizes the speaker's concept of "love"?

4. How do you feel toward the speaker? Give evidence from the poem for these feelings. Do they have anything to do with connotations of words in the poem?

The Browning poem that follows has been called a perfect poem. The poet's careful selection of words highlights how effective a poem can be when the diction fits the situation and when connotations function harmoniously to create a unified experience for sensitive readers.

Robert Browning   *(1812–1889)*

Meeting at Night

1   The gray sea and the long black land;
   And the yellow half-moon large and low;
   And the startled little waves that leap
   In fiery ringlets from their sleep,
   As I gain the cove with pushing prow,
   And quench its speed i' the slushy sand.

2   Then a mile of warm sea-scented beach;
   Three fields to cross till a farm appears;
   A tap at the pane, the quick sharp scratch
   And blue spurt of a lighted match,
   And a voice less loud, through its joys and fears,
   Than the two hearts beating each to each!

Exercises

1. List the words and phrases the poet uses to suggest, either denotatively or connotatively, the sense of haste and urgency.

2. What words suggest fire, heat?

3. Identify the specific lines in which the poet fuses haste and heat into a single emotional sensation. What is that sensation?

4. Why are haste and heat appropriate connotations for this particular love situation?

Like the Browning poem, "An Absence of Nettles" relies heavily on connotation. As you read, observe how the poet has chosen words that reflect the speaker's viewpoint and attitude toward his task.

Robert Nye *(1939–)*

An Absence of Nettles

I like nettles, but I took
The cold scythe for your sake
To clean the way where you would walk
And make it possible
For your foreshadowed flowers.   5

An evening I worked there,
And another, longer; gripping
The ancient handles with a clumsy craft,
Swinging the rusty blade about my knees,
Crouched to listen to it.   10

The keen heads of nettles
Lopped without pity
Were raked and carried up
To a black-hearted bonfire;
The shaven earth was ready.   15

I pulled up such roots
As the hands can find,
And cast away pebbles;
Weeding and watering
My own grave.   20

But now—no flowers have come
To fit your shadows;
The earth will not accept
The seeds you sow. And who can care for
An absence of nettles, an ungrowing place?   25

1. *Define the speaker's feeling about the nettles before he is asked to cut them out, his feeling during the two evenings he performs the task, and his feeling afterwards.*

2. *To deepen your awareness of the speaker's feelings, consider the following: (a) He emphasizes that the scythe is* cold, ancient, rusty *and that he himself is* clumsy using it; *what connotations, therefore, arise from these adjectives that reflect his feelings after cutting the nettles? (b) What is suggested by his choosing to mention cutting the* heads *of the nettles and his description of the heads as* keen? *Check your dictionary for the denotation of* keen *as a verb; what relevance might that meaning have here? (c) Why does the poet use* lopped *rather than* cut off? *(d) Why not a* bright cleansing fire *instead of a* black-hearted bonfire?

3. *Now that you have defined the speaker's feelings, explain what you think he means by describing his task as* weeding and watering/My own grave.

Carol Lynn Pearson *(1939–   )*

Of Places Far

To me Istanbul
Was only a name,
Until a picture
You took
Of the Blue Mosque
Came.

I don't receive
Postcards from heaven
Showing Saint Peter
At prayer,
But, oh—that place
Is real enough,
Now that
You are there.

Exercise

The speaker does very little to identify the person being addressed in this poem. Yet because of the circumstances, the unidentified you *is replete with connotations. Delineate those connotations as you describe who the* you *of the poem is.*

Claude McKay (1890–1948)

The White House

Your door is shut against my tightened face,
And I am sharp as steel with discontent;
But I possess the courage and the grace
To bear my anger proudly and unbent.
The pavement slabs burn loose beneath my feet,
And passion rends my vitals as I pass,
A chafing savage, down the decent street,
Where boldly shines your shuttered door of glass.
Oh, I must search for wisdom every hour,
Deep in my wrathful bosom sore and raw,
And find in it the superhuman power
To hold me to the letter of your law!
Oh, I must keep my heart inviolate
Against the poison of your deadly hate.

Exercises

1. The title certainly is not devoid of connotations, particularly when we know that McKay is a black poet. Still, in order to be aware of the connotations that the poet wishes to communicate by the title and thereby to experience the impact of the speaker's discontent, what must you know about "The White House"?

2. Is the poem sufficiently clear to supply that information? Give evidence to support your answer.

John Keats (1795–1821)

To Sleep

O soft embalmer of the still midnight,
Shutting, with careful fingers and benign,
Our gloom-pleased eyes, embowered from the light,
Enshaded in forgetfulness divine;
O soothest Sleep! if so it please thee, close,
In midst of this thine hymn, my willing eyes,
Or wait the amen, ere thy poppy throws
Around my bed its lulling charities;
Then save me, or the passéd day will shine
Upon my pillow, breeding many woes;

Save me from curious conscience, that still lords
Its strength for darkness, burrowing like a mole;
Turn the key deftly in the oiléd wards,
And seal the hushéd casket of my soul.

1. Why would preserver *fail in place of* embalmer *in the first line above? And* container *for* casket *in the last line?*

2. Make a list of the words and phrases that in some way connote death. After each, describe briefly what associations it has for you.

3. To become more aware of the similarities between death and sleep that Keats alludes to, identify the words and phrases in your list that connote sleep as well as death.

4. Perhaps for most of us the word death, *and words associated with it, have mostly negative connotations. How would you classify Keats's connotations of death?*

5. With your answer to the previous question in mind, what do you believe the speaker in the poem wishes to gain? To lose? Include his allusions to death in your considerations.

John Milton (1608–1674)

On the Late Massacre in Piedmont

Avenge, O Lord, thy slaughtered saints, whose bones
Lie scattered on the Alpine mountains cold;
Ev'n them who kept thy truth so pure of old,
When all our fathers worshiped stocks and stones,
Forget not: in thy book record their groans
Who were thy sheep, and in their ancient fold
Slain by the bloody Piedmontese, that rolled
Mother with infant down the rocks. Their moans
The vales redoubled to the hills, and they
To Heav'n. Their martyred blood and ashes sow
O'er all th' Italian fields, where still doth sway
The triple Tyrant: that from these may grow
A hundredfold who, having learnt thy way,
Early may fly the Babylonian woe.

Exercises   1. *This poem describes the actual massacre of more than a thousand men, women, and children of a primitive Protestant sect living in the mountain villages of northern Italy. Identify words and phrases whose connotations reflect the Protestant Milton's feelings, and judging from those connotations, identify the extent of Milton's feeling about the event.*

2. *If Milton had favored the massacre, what substitutions might he have made for the words and phrases you listed above? In answering, observe how readily the connotations of a poet's diction communicate his attitudes.*

Dylan Thomas (1914–1953)

The hand that signed the paper felled a city

The hand that signed the paper felled a city;
Five sovereign fingers taxed the breath,
Doubled the globe of dead and halved a country;
These five kings did a king to death.

The mighty hand leads to a sloping shoulder,   *5*
The finger joints are cramped with chalk;
A goose's quill has put an end to murder
That put an end to talk.

The hand that signed the treaty bred a fever,
And famine grew, and locusts came;   *10*
Great is the hand that holds dominion over
Man by a scribbled name.

The five kings count the dead but do not soften
The crusted wound nor stroke the brow;
A hand rules pity as a hand rules heaven;   *15*
Hands have no tears to flow.

Exercises   1. *Whose hand signs* the paper *mentioned in the title and in line 1?*

2. *What is the nature of that paper? Would you identify it with the treaty of line 9? What, then,* felled a city?

3. *Identify* these five kings *of line 13, as well as* a king *(line 4).*

4. *What is the* murder *cited in line 7? To answer, consider what preceded that murder as well as what ended it.*

5. Describe in general terms what the poem is saying about the hand that . . . felled a city.

6. How does the speaker feel about that state of affairs? Give evidence of his feelings, showing the significance of emotional connotations that communicate the feeling.

7. In comparison with Milton's poem, is this poem more passionate? Give evidence to support your opinion.

Percy Bysshe Shelley *(1792–1822)*

Song to the Men of England

Men of England, wherefore plough
For the lords who lay ye low?
Wherefore weave with toil and care
The rich robes your tyrants wear?

Wherefore feed, and clothe, and save,   *5*
From the cradle to the grave,
Those ungrateful drones who would
Drain your sweat—nay, drink your blood?

Wherefore, Bees of England, forge
Many a weapon, chain, and scourge,   *10*
That these stingless drones may spoil
The forced produce of your toil?

Have ye leisure, comfort, calm,
Shelter, food, love's gentle balm?
Or what is it ye buy so dear   *15*
With your pain and with your fear?

The seed ye sow, another reaps;
The wealth ye find, another keeps;
The robes ye weave, another wears;
The arms ye forge, another bears.   *20*

Sow seed,—but let no tyrant reap;
Find wealth,—let no impostor heap;
Weave robes,—let not the idle wear;
Forge arms,—in your defence to bear.

Shrink to your cellars, holes, and cells;   *25*
In halls ye deck another dwells.
Why shake the chains ye wrought? Ye see
The steel ye tempered glance on ye.

With plough and spade, and hoe and loom,
Trace your grave, and build your tomb,   30
And weave your winding-sheet, till fair
England be your sepulchre.

Topics
for Writing

1. Discuss in an essay Shelley's use of connotation in "Song to the Men of England." What do you believe was his purpose in writing the poem?

2. How appropriate are the comparisons made between men and bees in "Song to the Men of England"? If you are unfamiliar with the details of a beehive and the specific functions of the queen, the workers, and the drones, consult an encyclopedia as an aid in evaluating the poet's references.

3 Imagery

Petrarch, a famous Italian poet of the fourteenth century, defined poetry as "a speaking Picture." His definition stresses the importance of images, suggesting that they are the very heart of poetic art. An *image* is a representation of sensory experience, and although an image is usually thought of as visual, literary critics extend the term to include all the senses: sight, sound, taste, smell, touch, temperature, distance, movement, and so forth. *Imagery* is any combination of these representations.

Undoubtedly many of the images from earlier poems in this book remain in your mind: the crow in the snow, the mirror in the woods, the black rook, the burning nettles, the blue mosque, the hushed casket of the soul. A moment's reflection will convince you that much of the delight of poetry comes from the vividness of its images. Imagery derives such life-giving power from its link with actual experience: an image stimulates the readers to recall their own experiences with that particular subject or sensation. In so doing, earlier

438

responses are aroused, and the resulting experience with the poem becomes intensely personal and emotionally complex. Consequently, the readers actually participate with the poet in the creation of poetic images, and their response (including enjoyment) depends heavily upon the extent of past experience.

Before examining the value of giving close attention to imagery, we should note important distinctions among types of images. Images can be either *literal* or *figurative*. Those that are *literal* involve no change in meaning:

> I saw a young snake glide
> Out of the mottle shade
> And hang, limp on a stone:
> A thin mouth, and a tongue
> Stayed, in the still air.

These opening lines from "Snake" by Theodore Roethke (1908–1963) contain images familiar to us all—a small snake emerging from a hiding place, its thin mouth, its extended and forked tongue. These descriptive words mean exactly—literally—what they say and are designed to control the readers' mental picture of the scene, as well as their response to the scene. What is the difference between these images and the image in the following lines about a disheartened soldier, from "London" by William Blake (1757–1827)?

> And the hapless Soldier's sigh
> Runs in blood down Palace walls.

Clearly this image, a "sigh" that "runs in blood" down walls, demands a shift in meaning. Literally a soldier's sigh is not a stream of blood, but such a comparison is useful to poets as they seek to communicate experience and ideas. The implied comparison in this example is a *metaphor* (discussed in the following chapter), and it fits into the general classification of *figurative language*. Whenever a poet tries to communicate through comparison, he almost always uses imagery. Examine the poem below for literal and figurative images.

William Butler Yeats (1865–1939)

The Lake Isle of Innisfree

> I will arise and go now, and go to Innisfree,
> And a small cabin build there, of clay and wattles
>   made:
> Nine bean-rows will I have there, a hive for the
>   honeybee,
> And live alone in the bee-loud glade.

And I shall have some peace there, for peace comes
    dropping slow,
Dropping from the veils of the morning to where the
    cricket sings;
There midnight's all a glimmer, and noon a purple
    glow,
And evening full of the linnet's wings.

I will arise and go now, for always night and day
I hear lake water lapping with low sounds by the
    shore;
While I stand on the roadway, or on the pavements
    grey,
I hear it in the deep heart's core.

Exercises   *1. Identify several literal and several figurative images.*

2. Which images appeal to the sense of sound?

*3. What is described more vividly, the place the speaker
wishes to go to or the place he now is?*

The third question draws attention to another important
distinction among images: besides literal or figurative, imagery can be *fixed*
or *free*. A *fixed image* is one in which the meaning and associations are
approximately the same for all readers. A young snake is a young snake, and
whoever reads Roethke's poem will visualize about the same scene. In
controlling our response by his use of fixed imagery, Roethke seeks to
create a fairly specific scene and a definable mood. Here is the entire
poem:

I saw a young snake glide
Out of the mottle shade
And hang, limp on a stone:
A thin mouth, and a tongue
Stayed, in the still air.

It turned; it drew away;
Its shadow bent in half;
It quickened, and was gone.

I felt my slow blood warm.
I longed to be that thing,
The pure, sensuous form.

And I may be, some time.

A fixed image helps readers feel secure. Because it is already formed, all they must do is respond. But often the poet uses fixed images to prepare for a later complexity in which readers are drawn into the unusual, the intricate, perhaps the inexplicable. Notice how this is the case in "Snake." When the speaker tells us that after the snake disappeared "I felt my slow blood warm," the poet is expressing a universal dislike for snakes. He has given us a picture of a serpent and has told us that he feels as we do about them. But then he ventures into a complexity in the last three lines, wherein he wishes, despite his fear of snakes, to be one. That idea suggests an image of the speaker as a serpent that may shock the readers. They probably will puzzle for awhile over reasons why the speaker's admiration of the *pure, sensuous form* prompts him to desire transformation and just why the speaker seems to have a certain time in mind when it might take place. Sustaining the readers throughout this complication, however, is a foundation of fixed images that makes them able to cope with the freer imagery at the end.

A *free image* is not so limited. It is open to various interpretations and values. It requires more of its readers: they must use their imaginations to a greater extent and probe rather than merely respond. Understandably, free imagery is particularly appropriate in existential verse, which invites each reader toward discovering identity and selfhood. As a consequence, readers may feel less comfortable with the task imposed by free imagery. Good poets are usually restrained in their use of it, because they recognize (as Roethke does in "Snake") that a concrete frame of reference, a definite picture, is needed, at least at the beginning of the poem.

As you read the following two poems, watch for *fixed* and *free* imagery, recognizing that there are varying degrees of each type.

John Hartford *(1937–   )*

I would not be here

I would not be here
If I hadn't been there
I wouldn't been there
if I hadn't just turned
on Wednesday the third   5
in the late afternoon
got to talking with George
who works out in the back
and only because
he was getting off early   10
to go see a man
at a Baker Street bookstore
with a rare first edition
of steamboats and cotton
a book he would never   15
have sought in the first place
had he not been inspired
by a fifth grade replacement
school teacher in Kirkwood
who was picked just at random   20
by some man on a school board
who couldn't care less
and she wouldn't been working
if not for her husband
who moved two months prior   25
to work in the office
of a man he had met
while he served in the army
and only because
they were in the same barracks   30
an accident caused
by a poorly made roster
mixed up on the desk
of a sergeant from Denver
who wouldn't be in   35
but for being in back
in a car he was riding
before he enlisted
that hit a cement truck
and killed both his buddies   40

but a back seat flew up there
and spared him from dying
and only because
of the fault of a workman
who forgot to turn screws   45
on a line up in Detroit
'cause he hollered at Sam
who was hateful that morning
hung over from drinking
alone at a tavern   50
because of a woman
he wished he'd not married
he met long ago
at a Jewish bar mitzvah
for the son of a man   55
who had moved there from Jersey
who managed the drugstore
that sold the prescription
that cured up the illness
he caught way last summer   60
he wouldn't have caught
except . . .

Exercises   1. *After telling (as well as you can) where* here *and* there *are (lines 1 and 2), describe the Wednesday* turn *the speaker mentions in line 4. How fixed or free are these images?*

2. *Do you think nearly everyone who reads this poem will see about the same picture of George and where he works? Why or why not?*

3. *How fixed or free is the image of the book George plans to buy? Be specific.*

4. *Would you classify as fixed or free the images of the substitute teacher, the sergeant, the workman, Sam, the drugstore manager?*

Samuel Allen (*Paul Vesey; 1927–*)

In My Father's House

A Reverie

In my father's house, when dusk had fallen
I was alone on the dim first floor
I sensed someone, a power, desirous
Of forcing the outer door.
            How shall I explain—   *5*

I bolted it securely
And was locking the inner when
Somehow I was constrained to turn
To see it quietly open again.

Transfixed before the panther night   *10*
My heart gave one tremendous bound
Paralyzed, my feet refused
The intervening ground.
            How shall I say—

I was in the house and dusk had fallen   *15*
I was alone on the earthen floor
I knew there was a power
Lurking beyond the door.

I bolted the outside
And was closing the inner when   *20*
I noticed the first had swung open again
My heart bound and I knew it would be upon me I
      rushed to the door
It came upon me out of the night and I rushed to the
      yard
If I could throw the ball the stone the spear in my
      hand
Against the wall my father would be warned but now
Their hands had fallen on me and they had taken me and
      I tried   *26*
To cry out but O I could not cry out and the cold grey
      waves
Came over me O stifling me and drowning me.

Exercises 1. *Are there any figurative images in this poem?*

2. *How fixed is the scene? Support your answer with evidence from the poem.*

3. *How fixed is the image of the* power *that assaults the speaker? How real to the speaker is that* power?

4. *Do you believe the poet intends us to interpret that* power *as real, supernatural, or psychological?*

5. *In addition to the visual imagery, what other sensory imagery can you locate?*

6. *How consistent with the mood of the poem is the imagery, both visual and nonvisual?*

Whenever a single image dominates an extended passage or an entire poem, that image is a *controlling image*. In this poem by John Keats (1795–1821), notice that although it includes many images, that of the hand exercises a powerful control over the others:

This Living Hand

> This living hand, now warm and capable
> Of earnest grasping, would, if it were cold
> And in the icy silence of the tomb,
> So haunt thy days and chill thy dreaming nights
> That thou wouldst wish thine own heart dry of blood
> So in my veins red life might stream again,
> And thou be conscience-calmed—see here it is—
> I hold it towards you.

If the poet groups similar images in a short passage, the concentration is an *image cluster*. Robert Graves (1895–   ) provides a concentration of images in the following poem. As you read it, identify a common denominator among the images. Observe also the foundation of fixed imagery that Graves provides to orient the reader, and the free imagery at the end.

Lost Love

His eyes are quickened so with grief,
He can watch a grass or leaf
Every instant grow; he can
Clearly through a flint wall see,
Or watch the startled spirit flee   5
From the throat of a dead man.
    Across two counties he can hear
And catch your words before you speak.
The woodlouse or the maggot's weak
Clamor rings in his sad ear,   10
And noise so slight it would surpass
Credence—drinking sound of grass,
Worm talk, clashing jaws of moth
Chumbling holes in cloth;
The groan of ants who undertake   15
Gigantic loads for honor's sake
(Their sinews creak, their breath comes thin);
Whir of spiders when they spin,
And minute whispering, mumbling, sighs
Of idle grubs and flies.   20
    This man is quickened so with grief,
He wanders god-like or like thief
Inside and out, below, above,
Without relief seeking lost love.

Finally, in addition to *controlling images* and *image clusters*, the reader should be aware that imagery often occurs in patterns. Modern literary criticism occasionally places heavy emphasis on such patterning as a key to the deeper meanings of the work. The verse below is rich in fixed imagery. As you read it, watch for *image patterns*, paying close attention to the relationship between imagery and action.

William Butler Yeats   (1865–1939)

The Song of Wandering Aengus

I went out to the hazel wood,
Because a fire was in my head,
And cut and peeled a hazel wand,
And hooked a berry to a thread;
And when white moths were on the wing,   5
And moth-like stars were flickering out,
I dropped the berry in a stream
And caught a little silver trout.

When I had laid it on the floor
I went to blow the fire aflame,   10
But something rustled on the floor,
And some one called me by my name:
It had become a glimmering girl
With apple blossom in her hair
Who called me by my name and ran   15
And faded through the brightening air.

Though I am old with wandering
Through hollow lands and hilly lands,
I will find out where she has gone,
And kiss her lips and take her hands;   20
And walk among long dappled grass,
And pluck till time and times are done
The silver apples of the moon,
The golden apples of the sun.

Exercises   1. *What does Aengus mean when he says that* a fire was in
my head *(line 2)? What do you think he desires as he goes to
the woods? How does fire play a part in his attempt to satisfy
his desire (stanza 2)? How does fire play a part in the
fulfillment that he wishes for at the end of the poem?*

2. *What connotations does* wand *have (line 3) that correlate
with the mood of the poem? After pointing out the noticeable
shift in the mood and the action of the poem, identify what you
think Aengus needs to bring back the* glimmering girl, *and
perhaps why he cannot find it.*

3. *If the fire imagery is closely associated with Aengus'
feelings, what is the silver imagery associated with? Consider
with care the pattern of silver imagery and how the poet uses
that color to unify the changing identities, finally in the last
two lines providing something of a fusion of the silver and the
gold. What do these two colors do for the poem as a whole?*

Questions about imagery that lead the reader to a fuller understanding of poetry are the focus of the exercises following the next group of poems: how does the imagery support the central idea? what illumination of the poem's meaning and the poem's effect is achieved by examining the images? Answers to these and other questions testify to the importance of imagery in the art of creating "speaking Pictures."

Sara Henderson Hay (1906–   )

For a Dead Kitten

Put the rubber mouse away,
Pick the spools up from the floor,
What was velvet-shod, and gay,
Will not want them any more.

What was warm, is strangely cold.
Whence dissolved the little breath?
How could this small body hold
So immense a thing as Death?

Exercises

1. What effect does the controlling image of the kitten have on the meaning of the poem as a whole?

2. How do the additional images, including those associated with the senses of touch, sound, motion, and temperature, support the controlling image?

3. Do you believe the poet expresses a universal attitude toward death?

Elinor Wylie (1885–1928)

Velvet Shoes

Let us walk in the white snow
    In a soundless space;
With footsteps quiet and slow,
    At a tranquil pace,
    Under veils of white lace.   5

I shall go shod in silk,
    And you in wool,
White as a white cow's milk,
    More beautiful
    Than the breast of a gull.   10

We shall walk through the still town
    In a windless peace;
We shall step upon white down,
    Upon silver fleece,
    Upon softer than these.   *15*

We shall walk in velvet shoes:
    Wherever we go
Silence will fall like dews
    On white silence below.
    We shall walk in the snow.   *20*

Exercises   *1. Point out images of color, sight, sound, motion, touch, and distance; then comment on the consistency among the images of each group and on the harmony of all the images to each other.*

2. Are all the images appropriate to the effect of the poem? In judging appropriateness, take into account the connotations of the images. For instance, the breast of a swan is as soft as that of a seagull; what connotations does the gull have that the swan does not? How effective are those connotations in this scene?

James Thomson   (1700–1748)

from Winter

As thus the snows arise, and, foul and fierce,
All Winter drives along the darken'd air,
In his own loose-revolving fields, the Swain
Disaster'd stands; sees other hills ascend,
Of unknown joyless brow; and other Scenes,   *5*
Of horrid prospect, shag the trackless plain:
Nor finds the river, nor the forest, hid
Beneath the formless wild; but wanders on
From hill to dale, still more and more astray;
Impatient flouncing through the drifted heaps,   *10*
Stung with the thoughts of Home; the thoughts of
    Home
Rush on his nerves, and call their vigour forth
In many a vain attempt. How sinks his soul!
What black despair, what horror fills his heart!
When for the dusky spot, which fancy feign'd   *15*
His tufted Cottage, rising through the snow,
He meets the roughness of the middle waste,
Far from the track and bless'd abode of man;
While round him Night resistless closes fast,

And every tempest, howling o'er his head,   20
Renders the savage wilderness more wild.
Then throng the busy shapes into his Mind,
Of cover'd pits, unfathomably deep,
A dire descent! beyond the power of frost;
Of faithless bogs; of precipices huge,   25
Smooth'd up with snow; and, what is land unknown,
What water, of the still unfrozen spring,
In the loose marsh or solitary lake,
Where the fresh fountain from the bottom boils.
These check his fearful steps; and down he sinks,   30
Beneath the shelter of the shapeless drift,
Thinking o'er all the bitterness of Death;
Mix'd with the tender anguish nature shoots
Through the wrung bosom of the dying man,
His wife, his children, and his friends unseen.   35
In vain for him the officious Wife prepares
The fire fair-blazing, and the vestment warm;
In vain his little Children, peeping out
Into the mingling storm, demand their sire,
With tears of artless innocence. Alas!   40
Nor wife, nor children more shall he behold,
Nor friends, nor sacred home. On every nerve
The deadly Winter seizes; shuts up sense;
And, o'er his inmost vitals creeping cold,
Lays him along the snows, a stiffen'd Corse,   45
Stretch'd out, and bleaching in the northern blast.

Exercises

1. Are most of the images in this passage fixed or free? Why do you think the poet fashioned them as he did? What, in short, seems to be his purpose?

2. Contrasting greatly with Wylie's picture of winter in "Velvet Shoes," this scene is packed with images that reflect particular human fears. Locate as many negative images as you can, then identify the fears that they help to communicate.

3. Generally we think of fear as a product of the mind and the emotions, fear of failure, for example, or fear of the unknown, fear of the future. Which of the farmer's fears relate to (or derive from) the senses and are communicated to us through imagery?

Gwendolyn Brooks *(1917–   )*

kitchenette building

We are things of dry hours and the involuntary plan,
Grayed in, and gray. "Dream" makes a giddy sound,
    not strong
Like "rent," "feeding a wife," "satisfying a man."

But could a dream send up through onion fumes
Its white and violet, fight with fried potatoes
And yesterday's garbage ripening in the hall,
Flutter, or sing an aria down these rooms

Even if we were willing to let it in,
Had time to warm it, keep it very clean,
Anticipate a message, let it begin?

We wonder. But not well! not for a minute!
Since Number Five is out of the bathroom now,
We think of lukewarm water, hope to get in it.

Exercises   *1. Point out the color images in this poem. What in the poem is each color associated with? Can you suggest an explanation for the poet's choices, taking into account the connotations that each color has and remembering that the poet is a woman?*

2. What effect do the smells in the poem have in "painting the Picture"? The sounds?

3. Label the fixed and the free images in the poem, giving a reason for the poet's choice to fix certain ones and leave others free. Does her choice seem to you a wise one?

Philip Freneau   *(1752–1832)*

The Indian Burying Ground

In spite of all the learned have said,
I still my old opinion keep;
The *posture*, that *we* give the dead,
Points out the soul's eternal sleep.

Not so the ancients of these lands—   5
The Indian, when from life released,
Again is seated with his friends,
And shares again the joyous feast.

His imaged birds, and painted bowl,
And venison, for a journey dressed.   *10*
Bespeak the nature of the soul,
ACTIVITY, that knows no rest.

His bow, for action ready bent,
And arrows, with a head of stone,
Can only mean that life is spent,   *15*
And not the old ideas gone.

Thou, stranger, that shalt come this way,
No fraud upon the dead commit—
Observe the swelling turf, and say
They do not *lie*, but here they *sit*.   *20*

Here still a lofty rock remains,
On which the curious eye may trace
(Now wasted, half, by wearing rains)
The fancies of a ruder race.

Here still an aged elm aspires,   *25*
Beneath whose far-projecting shade
(And which the shepherd still admires)
The children of the forest played!

There oft a restless Indian queen
(Pale *Shebah*, with her braided hair)   *30*
And many a barbarous form is seen
To chide the man that lingers there.

By midnight moons, o'er moistening dews,
In habit for the chase arrayed,
The hunter still the deer pursues,   *35*
The hunter and the deer, a shade!

And long shall timorous fancy see
The painted chief, and pointed spear,
And Reason's self shall bow the knee
To shadows and delusions here.   *40*

1. If words like venison, turf, rude race, habit, *and* a shade *are unfamiliar to you, check your dictionary for appropriate denotations.*

2. What concept or idea does the poet suggest in referring to the ancient Indian custom of burying the dead sitting up? What connotations implied by that position does the poet emphasize throughout the poem?

3. How are the elements of nature mentioned by the poet connected to the central idea of the poem?

4. Many images reinforce that central idea, and a few contrast with it. After pointing to the images in the latter category, tell what ideas they convey to you. Do you believe the poet intended those ideas to be expressed by the poem? How can you tell?

Wallace Stevens *(1879–1955)*

Anecdote of the Jar

I placed a jar in Tennessee,
And round it was, upon a hill.
It made the slovenly wilderness
Surround that hill.

The wilderness rose up to it,   5
And sprawled around, no longer wild.
The jar was round upon the ground
And tall and of a port in air.

It took dominion everywhere.
The jar was gray and bare.   10
It did not give of bird or bush,
Like nothing else in Tennessee.

1. Why and in what ways does the jar change the wilderness?

2. The meaning of lines 7–8 and of 11–12 may not be immediately clear to you. How would you paraphrase them?

3. How close is the relationship in this poem between image and meaning? Be specific, supporting your answer with evidence from the poem.

William Shakespeare *(1564–1616)*

Sonnet 73

That time of year thou mayst in me behold
When yellow leaves, or none, or few, do hang
Upon those boughs which shake against the cold,
Bare ruined choirs, where late the sweet birds sang.
In me thou see'st the twilight of such day   5
As after sunset fadeth in the west;
Which by and by black night doth take away,
Death's second self, that seals up all in rest.
In me thou see'st the glowing of such fire,
That on the ashes of his youth doth lie,   10
As the deathbed whereon it must expire,
Consumed with that which it was nourished by.
This thou perceiv'st, which makes thy love more
        strong,
To love that well which thou must leave ere long.

Exercises

1. What are the choirs *the speaker refers to (line 4)?*

2. Specify what black night *(line 7) takes away. Can you explain why the poet calls night* Death's second self *(line 8), and what* seals up all in rest *(line 8)?*

3. Explain the literal meaning of the fire-ashes-deathbed imagery (lines 9–12).

4. The central idea about the speaker's age and the hope he expresses in the final two lines are not complex. Why, then, do you think the poet seeks to communicate that theme through a series of related (and at times complex) images? In your answer define what these images do for you in terms of conveying that central idea.

Topics
for Writing

1. The imagery in "Lost Love" by Robert Graves reveals much about the mind of the man who has lost his love. Using the images, analyze the state of his mind in a brief essay.

2. Is the grief-stricken man in "Lost Love" god-like or like thief, or both (line 20)? In an essay present evidence to support your conclusion.

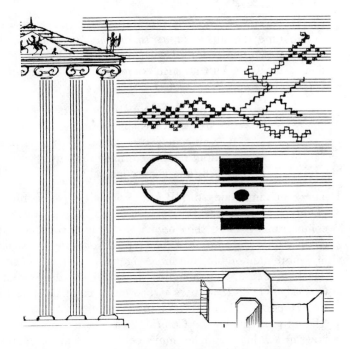

4 Figurative Language

Much poetic communication is achieved through comparisons, especially if the idea, the feeling, or the sensation to be communicated is a complex or an abstract one. When Henry Vaughan (1622–1695) attempts to describe his perceptions of eternity and of time, he does so by comparing them with subjects more imaginable:

from The World

I saw eternity the other night
Like a great ring of pure and endless light,
    All calm as it was bright;
And round beneath it, Time, in hours, days, years,
    Driven by the spheres,
Like a vast shadow moved, in which the world
    And all her train were hurled.

By giving to eternity the image of *a great ring* of light and to time the image of *a vast shadow*, Vaughan is able to achieve an effective communication of what he has thought and felt. A poem about time that begins with no such comparisons is "Burnt Norton" from *Four Quartets* by T. S. Eliot (1888–1965):

> Time present and time past
> Are both perhaps present in time future,
> And time future contained in time past.
> If all time is eternally present
> All time is unredeemable.

These opening lines of "Burnt Norton" do communicate, but not so readily nor so vividly as do Vaughan's; Eliot, however, does rely on comparisons later in the poem. Not only is communication aided when comparisons are employed, but the presentation is usually more interesting, more memorable, and more vigorous. Instead of a lifeless and abstract line like 'Cease, sad thoughts, that make me depressed,' Samuel Taylor Coleridge (1772–1834) uses a vivid image comparing his troubled thoughts to a serpent: "Hence, Viper thoughts, that coil about my mind" (from "Dejection: An Ode"). Coleridge was aware that we cannot easily imagine how his thoughts make him feel unless he compares his feeling to something more imaginable. Thus he relies on a serpent image to communicate the fearful and constricting sensation created in his mind by distressing thoughts.

These comparisons are part of *figurative language*—nonliteral language that employs such *figures of speech* as *antithesis, apostrophe, hyperbole, irony, metaphor, metonymy, personification, simile,* and *synecdoche.* Although we will deal with only four figures of speech in this chapter—*metaphor, simile, personification,* and *apostrophe*—all these terms are defined in the Glossary. Figures of speech are by no means peculiar to poetry. Because our language is by nature highly figurative, we employ figures of speech in nearly all types of communication. But because poets frequently seek to surprise us, to stimulate us, to create for us vivid pictures, and in general to lead us down avenues of awareness we have not experienced before, they rely heavily on figurative language.

A *metaphor* is a figure of speech implying an identification between two subjects belonging to different classes. Although the two subjects thus identified are essentially incompatible, the invitation to compare them stimulates our minds and senses to perceive similarities. The resulting perception often leads to new insight. Walt Whitman (1819–1892) used this kind of identification in attempting to communicate the solitary nature of the soul:

A Noiseless Patient Spider

A noiseless patient spider,
I marked where on a little promontory it stood isolated,
Marked how to explore the vacant vast surrounding,
It launched forth filament, filament, filament, out of
    itself,
Ever unreeling them, ever tirelessly speeding them.

And you O my soul where you stand,
Surrounded, detached, in measureless oceans of space,
Ceaselessly musing, venturing, throwing, seeking the
    spheres to connect them,
Till the bridge you will need be formed, till the ductile
    anchor hold,
Till the gossamer thread you fling catch somewhere, O
    my soul.

Exercises   *1. Despite the difference between the spider trying to anchor
its web and the soul trying to secure its place in the universe,
certain revealing likenesses between spider and man do exist.
Identify as many as you can.*

*2. Of what value is the metaphor in this poem? What does it
help the poet reveal that he could not reveal as well without it?*

3. Whitman calls the spider noiseless *and* patient. *Is he
then suggesting, figuratively, that all men, like the spider, seek
to understand their place in the universe and that all men are*
noiseless *and* patient *in that search? How do you know?*

*4. What evidence is there for classifying the poem as optimis-
tic or pessimistic?*

Following are two poems by Robert Herrick (1591–
1674). Even though both are on the same topic, they are different partly
because one makes use of a metaphor to characterize the infant, whereas
the other does not:

Upon A Child That Died

Here she lies, a pretty bud,
Lately made of flesh and blood,
Who as soon fell fast asleep
As her little eyes did peep.
Give her strewings, but not stir
The earth that lightly covers her.

Upon A Child

Here a pretty baby lies
Sung asleep with lullabies:
Pray be silent, and not stir
Th' easy earth that covers her.

Exercise   *Are there any metaphors in the second poem? Does the bud
metaphor in the first poem increase or diminish your appreciation
of the poem? In answering, explain as precisely as
possible how the metaphor effects your perception of the scene.*

In Herrick's first poem, the major subject or *tenor* is the
child and the secondary subject or *vehicle* is the flower bud. Whenever the
tenor and the vehicle correlate on more than one point, either explicitly or
by implication, the metaphor is called *extended* rather than simple. In
Herrick's first poem, the primary similarity between infant and bud is that
both are just beginning life. Yet other similarities are important as well:
both are pretty, both are delicate, both are scarcely open (the child's eyes
can hardly *peep*). Notice the implied points of similarity in the metaphor
from this poem by Edna St. Vincent Millay (1892–1950):

Hyacinth

I am in love with him to whom a hyacinth is dearer
Than I shall ever be dear.
On nights when the field-mice are abroad he cannot
     sleep:
He hears their narrow teeth at the bulbs of his hya-
     cinths.
But the gnawing at my heart he does not hear.

Plainly, the *gnawing* felt by the speaker is much like the gnawing of the
hyacinth bulbs by the mice: probably it is caused by many small incidents,
just as many mice gnaw the bulbs; apparently it occurs mostly at night, just
as the mice gnaw on the bulbs after dark; the gnawing may destroy her
heart, just as the mice destroy the bulbs; her heart is similar in shape to a
hyacinth bulb; and from it could grow a lovely relationship, just as the
richly scented hyacinth grows from the bulb.

Sometimes the poet will specify quite clearly many of
the correlations he wishes us to make in a metaphor. In these lines a poet
who endured periods of deep depression uses his metaphor this way to
convey his feelings about himself and the world.

William Cowper *(1731–1800)*

from The Task

I was a stricken deer, that left the herd
Long since; with many an arrow deep infixt
My panting side was charg'd when I withdrew
To seek a tranquil death in distant shades.
There was I found by one who had himself   5
Been hurt by th' archers. In his side he bore,
And in his hands and feet, the cruel scars.
With gentle force soliciting the darts,
He drew them forth, and heal'd, and bade me live.
Since then, with few associates, in remote   10
And silent woods I wander, far from those
My former partners of the peopled scene;
With few associates, and not wishing more.
Here much I ruminate, as much I may,
With other views of men and manners now   15
Than once, and others of a life to come.
I see that all are wand'rers, gone astray
Each in his own delusions; they are lost
In chase of fancied happiness, still woo'd
And never won. Dream after dream ensues;   20
And still they dream that they shall still succeed.
And still are disappointed. Rings the world
With the vain stir. I sum up half mankind,
And add two thirds of the remaining half,
And find the total of their hopes and fears   25
Dreams, empty dreams.

Exercises   *1. After identifying the tenor and the vehicle, point to as many subordinate similarities as you can.*

2. Of what value to us is the speaker's identification with the deer? Imagine the poem without the metaphor and draw a conclusion regarding the effect it has in the communication of these lines.

3. According to the speaker, who restored him to health? How do you know?

4. Summarize the speaker's conclusions about mankind. How does he relate them to the stricken deer metaphor?

Whenever a comparison between two unlike subjects is made by using *like, as, than, appears,* or *seems,* we call that figure of speech a *simile.* The simile and the metaphor have the same general purpose: to consider the tenor from the point of view of the vehicle in order to lead us toward a deeper understanding of both. Like metaphors, similes vary from simple to extended. Spenser's poem is constructed around an extended simile:

Edmund Spenser   *(1552?–1599)*

Sonnet 54

Of this world's theater in which we stay,
My love like the spectator idly sits,
Beholding me that all the pageants play,
Disguising diversely my troubled wits.
Sometimes I joy when glad occasion fits
And mask in mirth like to a comedy;
Soon after, when my joy to sorrow flits,
I wail and make my woes a tragedy.
Yet she beholding me with constant eye
Delights not in my mirth nor rues my smart;
But when I laugh she mocks, and when I cry
She laughs, and hardens evermore her heart.
What then can move her? If nor mirth nor moan,
She is no woman, but a senseless stone.

Occasionally the poet compares subjects that are radically different. Such eccentric and often ingenious comparisons, or *conceits,* are usually intended to shock us, forcing us to consider similarities we would probably never imagine on our own. John Donne (1572–1631) employs two conceits in these lines from "A Valediction: Forbidding Mourning":

Our two souls therefore, which are one,
   Though I must go, endure not yet
A breach, but an expansion,
   Like gold to airy thinness beat.

If they be two, they are two so   5
   As stiff twin compasses are two;
Thy soul, the fixed foot, makes no show
   To move, but doth, if th' other do.

And though it in the center sit,
   Yet when the other far doth roam,   10
It leans and hearkens after it,
   And grows erect, as that comes home.

Such wilt thou be to me, who must
　　Like th' other foot, obliquely run;
Thy firmness makes my circle just,　　　　　　　　*15*
　　And makes me end where I begun.

Exercises　　*1. How are the speaker and his wife (or lover) like gold to airy thinness beat? What insight into the speaker's feeling does the simile provide that would be absent if the simile were excluded?*

2. The speaker's feelings are also conveyed in the compass conceit. Summarize the meaning of the conceit, paying particular attention to the significance of lines 8, 12, 15–16.

　　　　Poets wishing to render more dramatic an inanimate object or an abstract concept may (as we have seen) compare it to something imaginable, like comparing time to a ring of light. Or instead of a plain metaphor, they may use *personification*, giving to the subject human characteristics with the purpose of turning the subject into a more vivid as well as a more comprehensible one. Just as a metaphor and a simile may vary from simple to extended, so may personification vary, from *slight* (in which the object retains most of its own qualities) to more *complete*. When Robert Browning (1812–1889) writes in "Childe Roland to the Dark Tower Came" that the sun "shot one grim / Red leer," he creates a slight personification by endowing the sun with the human ability to look down with malice. A more complete personification can be found in the following poem:

Denise Levertov　(1923–　　)

Scenes from the Life of the Peppertrees

1　　The peppertrees, the peppertrees!

Cats are stretching in the doorways,
sure of everything. It is morning.
　　But the peppertrees
stand aside in diffidence, with berries　　　　　　*5*
of modest red.
　　　　　　Branch above branch, an air
of lightness; of shadows
scattered lightly.
　　　　　　A cat　　　　　　　　　　　　　　*10*
closes upon its shadow.

Up and up goes the sun,
sure of everything.
    The peppertrees
        shiver a little. 15
Robust
and soot-black, the cat
leaps to a low branch. Leaves
close about him.

2   The yellow moon dreamily 20
tipping buttons of light
down among the leaves. Marimba,
marimba—from beyond the
black street.
           Somebody dancing, 25
somebody
      getting the hell
outta here. Shadows of cats
weave around the treetrunks,
the exposed knotty roots. 30

3   The man on the bed sleeping
defenseless. Look—
his bare long feet together
sideways, keeping each other
warm. And the foreshortened shoulders, 35
the head
barely visible. He is good.
Let him sleep.
         But the third peppertree
   is restless, twitching 40
thin leaves in the light
of afternoon. After a while
it walks over and taps
on the upstairs window with a bunch
of red berries. Will he wake? 45

Exercises

1. *In what ways are the peppertrees like people? Unlike people?*

2. *In an important sense the trees are unlike the cats and the sun in part 1. What is that major difference?*

3. *How might you connect that difference to the action of the third peppertree in part 3?*

4. *Why does a peppertree tap on the window?*

The most common personification involves an *apostrophe* in which something (usually absent) is addressed as though it were a person. John Donne opens "The Sun Rising" with an apostrophe in which the speaker rebukes the sun for interrupting his lovemaking:

John Donne   *(1572–1631)*

from The Sun Rising

> Busy old fool, unruly sun,
> Why dost thou thus,
> Through windows and through curtains call on us?
> Must to thy motions lovers' seasons run?
> Saucy pedantic wretch, go chide
> Late school boys and sour prentices,
> Go tell court huntsmen that the King will ride,
> Call country ants to harvest offices;
> Love, all alike, no season knows nor clime,
> Nor hours, days, months, which are the rags of time.

When inanimate objects are given human emotions, the personification is called the *pathetic fallacy*:

William Wordsworth   *(1770–1850)*

from Lines Written in Early Spring

> Through primrose tufts, in that green bower,
> The periwinkle trailed its wreaths;
> And 'tis my faith that every flower
> Enjoys the air it breathes.

When not handled with the delicacy Wordsworth exhibits here, the pathetic fallacy becomes unconvincing and even ludicrous. All figurative language, in fact, requires a skillful poet to render it appropriate, memorable, and illuminating. But we too must develop sensitivity to figures of speech if we are to be the recipients of what they offer in a poem. We must learn to explicate the metaphor and the simile by identifying the tenor and vehicle, discovering their relevant common characteristics, and identifying the effects produced. Just as the success of a figure of speech depends on how good the images are and how well the figure illuminates the poet's perceptions, so does the success of the poem for us depend in part on how sensitively we respond to those figures.

Denise Levertov (1923–)

The Victors

In June the bush we call
alder was heavy, listless,
its leaves studded with galls,

growing wherever we didn't
want it. We cut it   5
savagely, hunted it from the pasture, chopped it

away from the edge of the wood.
In July, still everywhere, it appeared
wearing green berries.

Anyway it must go. It takes   10
the light and air and the good of the earth
from flowers and young trees.

But now in August
its berries are red. Do the birds
eat them? Swinging   15

clusters of red, the hedges are full of them,
red-currant red, a graceful
ornament or a merry smile.

Exercises   *1. Who wins and who loses in this poem?*

2. Identify the use made of personification, telling which human characteristics are specified and which are implied.

William Shakespeare *(1564–1616)*

Sonnet 143

Lo, as a careful housewife runs to catch
One of her feathered creatures broke away,
Sets down her babe, and makes all swift dispatch
In pursuit of the thing she would have stay
Whilst her neglected child holds her in chase,
Cries to catch her whose busy care is bent
To follow that which flies before her face,
Not prizing her poor infant's discontent—
So runn'st thou after that which flies from thee
Whilst I thy babe chase thee afar behind.
But if thou catch thy hope, turn back to me,
And play the mother's part, kiss me, be kind.
So will I pray that thou mayst have thy "Will,"
If thou turn back and my loud crying still.

Exercises   *1. After identifying the tenor and the vehicle in this extended
simile, comment on the appropriateness of the vehicle for the
tenor.*

2. What effects are created by the comparison?

*3. Are the images fixed or free? How memorable are they?
How universal?*

John Milton *(1608–1674)*

from Paradise Lost

For now, and since first break of dawn, the fiend,
Mere serpent in appearance, forth was come,
And on his quest, where likeliest he might find
The only two of mankind, but in them
The whole included race, his purposed prey.   *5*
In bower and field he sought, where any tuft
Of grove or garden-plot more pleasant lay,
Their tendance or plantation for delight;
By fountain or by shady rivulet
He sought them both, but wished his hap might find
Eve separate; he wished, but not with hope   *11*
Of what so seldom chanced; when to his wish,
Beyond his hope, Eve separate he spies,
Veiled in a cloud of fragrance, where she stood,
Half spied, so thick the roses bushing round   *15*

About her glowed, oft stooping to support
Each flower of slender stalk, whose head though gay
Carnation, purple, azure, or specked with gold,
Hung drooping unsustained, them she upstays
Gently with myrtle band, mindless the while   20
Herself, though fairest unsupported flower,
From her best prop so far, and storm so nigh.

Exercises   *1. Once we have determined what Eve is doing as Satan
approaches her in Paradise, how might we explain the specific
point of comparison between tenor and vehicle?*

*2. In what other ways could Eve be considered a flower? In
your answer, take into account correlations between woman and
flower such as that suggested in line 5 as well as universally
recognized similarities.*

Jon Looney   *(1948–   )*

from **Dream**

All over
these hills are
the insides of
my father's head.

Exercises   *1. What is the tenor? the vehicle?*

*2. What does the title do for our understanding of the
tenor-vehicle relationship?*

Ishmael Reed   *(1938–   )*

beware   :   do not read this poem

tonite, thriller was
abt an ol woman, so vain she
surrounded herself w/
     many mirrors

it got so bad that finally she   5
locked herself indoors & her
whole life became the
     mirrors

one day the villagers broke
into her house, but she was too   10
swift for them. she disappeared
          into a mirror
each tenant who bought the house
after that, lost a loved one to
          the ol woman in the mirror: 15
          first a little girl
          then a young woman
          then the young woman/s husband

the hunger of this poem is legendary
it has taken in many victims   20
back off from this poem
it has drawn in yr feet
back off from this poem
it has drawn in yr legs

back off from this poem   25
it is a greedy mirror
you are into this poem from
          the waist down
nobody can hear you can they?
this poem has had you up to here   30
          belch
this poem aint got no manners
you can't call out frm this poem
relax now & go w/ this poem
move & roll on to this poem   35
do not resist this poem
this poem has yr eyes
this poem has his head
this poem has his arms
this poem has his fingers   40
this poem has his fingertips

this poem is the reader & the
reader this poem.
statistic: the us bureau of missing persons reports
              that in 1968 over 100,000 people disap-
              peared   45
              leaving no solid clues
                        nor trace   only
a space   in the lives of their friends

Exercises

1. *Through line 41, what is the tenor? The vehicle? How is that vehicle personified? What part does the ol woman play in the personification?*

2. *What action does the imagery suggest in lines 34–36, and how is that action connected with our reading of this poem (or any poem)?*

Alfred, Lord Tennyson *(1809–1892)*

Crossing the Bar

Sunset and evening star,
    And one clear call for me!
And may there be no moaning of the bar,
    When I put out to sea,

But such a tide as moving seems asleep,   5
    Too full for sound and foam,
When that which drew from out the boundless deep
    Turns again home.

Twilight and evening bell,
    And after that the dark!   10
And may there be no sadness of farewell,
    When I embark;

For tho' from out our bourne of Time and Place
    The flood may bear me far,
I hope to see my Pilot face to face   15
    When I have crost the bar.

Topics for Writing

1. *In Tennyson's "Crossing the Bar," is the sea an effective image to employ in connection with death? Write an essay on the poet's use of the sea, pointing to specific details in the poem that support your evaluation.*

2. *Write an essay in which you tell whether "Crossing the Bar" reflects faith in life after death.*

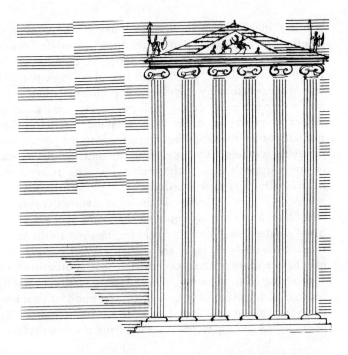

5 Rhythm and Meter

Students in literature classes often ask why we need to study rhythm and meter in poetry at all. They ask if it isn't all just confusing and if ultimately the study of technicalities doesn't stand in the way of our understanding what the poet meant to say. Questions of this kind really demand—and deserve—answers. Poets too have fostered such questions by their seeming casualness about organization and details. Byron and Dylan Thomas, for example, give the impression that they were able to sit down and, in a single burst of inspiration, produce a poem. Actually, they were great technicians who labored long and hard over what others might call irrelevant details in order to get their poems as near to perfect as they could be.

Maybe the best way to answer for ourselves questions about the need for the study of meter and other poetic devices is to be sure that we understand what poetry is. A poem has being as an entity, and this entity is made up of many parts. Poetry is not just an arrangement of words on paper. It is words in action, patterns of sounds and meanings and rhythms at work in our minds, whether the poem is recited aloud or read silently. These patterns show us, tell us, suggest to us objects and emotions, thoughts and moods. Poetry is the totality of all this, and not just one of its single parts. But to ignore any one of these is to deny ourselves complete understanding. Because rhythm and meter are parts of the total poem, we need to look carefully at this aspect of poetry in order to understand the sum. Rhythm and meter provide for us, then, another way of seeing the poem, another opportunity of seeing it whole. To understand the basics of the metrical side of poetry is not a difficult task. Although some unfamiliar nomenclature is used occasionally, it is easily mastered.

Nearly all language involves rhythm. Listen to a child chanting while skipping rope, to the auctioneer's melodic voice trying to drive up the price of an old cabinet, or even to the television newscaster reciting the day's events at six o'clock. While one type of spoken language may have a more pronounced rhythm than another type—a nursery rhyme, say, compared to the stock market report—still each has its own cadence or beat. The language of poetry is no exception: it contains a wide range of beats and rhythms, as varied as those we find in music. Read the following poem aloud and try to get a sense of the poem's rhythm:

Louis MacNeice *(1907–1963)*

Bagpipe Music

It's no go the merrygoround, it's no go the rickshaw,
All we want is a limousine and a ticket for the peep-
    show.
Their knickers are made of crêpe-de-chine, their shoes
    are made of python,
Their halls are lined with tiger rugs and their walls with
    heads of bison.

John MacDonald found a corpse, put it under the sofa,
Waited till it came to life and hit it with a poker,   6
Sold its eyes for souvenirs, sold its blood for whiskey,
Kept its bones for dumbbells to use when he was fifty.

It's no go the Yogi-man, it's no go Blavatsky,
All we want is a bank balance and a bit of skirt in a
    taxi.   10

Annie MacDougall went to milk, caught her foot in the
  heather,
Woke to hear a dance record playing of Old Vienna.
It's no go your maidenheads, it's no go your culture,
All we want is a Dunlop tire and the devil mend the
  puncture.

The Laird o' Phelps spent Hogmanay declaring he was
  sober,   *15*
Counted his feet to prove the fact and found he had one
  foot over.
Mrs. Carmichael had her fifth, looked at the job with
  repulsion,
Said to the midwife "Take it away; I'm through with
  overproduction."

It's no go the gossip column, it's no go the Ceilidh,
All we want is a mother's help and a sugar-stick for the
  baby.   *20*

Willie Murray cut his thumb, couldn't count the damage,
Took the hide of an Ayrshire cow and used it for a
  bandage.
His brother caught three hundred cran when the seas
  were lavish,
Threw the bleeders back in the sea and went upon the
  parish.

It's no go the Herring Board, it's no go the Bible, *25*
All we want is a packet of fags when our hands are idle.

It's no go the picture palace, it's no go the stadium,
It's no go the country cot with a pot of pink geraniums,
It's no go the Government grants, it's no go the
  elections,
Sit on your arse for fifty years and hang your hat on a
  pension.   *30*

It's no go my honey love, it's no go my poppet;
Work your hands from day to day, the winds will blow
  the profit.
The glass is falling hour by hour, the glass will fall
  forever,
But if you break the bloody glass you won't hold up the
  weather.

Exercises   *1. Would you say that the poem has a definite rhythm? Or is the beat illusive and hard to pin down?*

2. Does the poem seem to have a regular *rhythm?*

3. How do you account for any sense of rhythm you find in the poem?

Rhythm in poetry, or in any kind of language for that matter, depends on the relationship between stressed words and syllables and those which are unstressed. Stressed words or syllables are many times said to be accented, and the unstressed are referred to as being unaccented or slack. When the relationship between accented and slack syllables forms a regular pattern in a poem, we call it meter. Most poetry in English is metrical, although the rhythmic patterns in some poems are less obvious than the meter in others. Many poets, too, have experimented with meter, and the results are often unusual.

The first step in determining the meter of a poem is to locate the stresses. This process often comes naturally as you read poetry, expecially if it is read aloud, but sometimes it helps to exaggerate slightly. Read the following two poems and try to establish for yourself the rhythmic pattern of the verse. As you read, pencil in an accent mark over every stressed syllable.

A. E. Housman *(1859–1936)*

R. L. S.

Home is the sailor, home from sea:
   Her far-borne canvas furled
The ship pours shining on the quay
   The plunder of the world.

Home is the hunter from the hill:
   Fast in the boundless snare
All flesh lies taken at his will
   And every fowl of air.

'Tis evening on the moorland free,
   The starlit wave is still:
Home is the sailor from the sea,
   The hunter from the hill.

Henry David Thoreau *(1817–1862)*

Haze

Woof of the sun, ethereal gauze,
Woven of Nature's richest stuffs,
Visible heat, air-water and dry sea,
Last conquest of the eye;
Toil of the day displayed, sun-dust,
Aerial surf upon the shores of earth,
Ethereal estuary, frith of light,
Breakers of air, billows of heat,
Fine summer spray on inland seas;
Bird of the sun, transparent-winged
Owlet of noon, soft-pinioned,
From heath or stubble rising without song,
Establish thy serenity o'er the fields.

Exercises

1. Look at the accent marks you have made over the stressed syllables in "R.L.S." Do the marked syllables occur in any sort of pattern? What about the unaccented, or slack, syllables?

2. Which poem has the more regular meter? How can you tell?

3. Thoreau describes the haze as being ethereal gauze, aerial surf, *and* sun-dust, *an illusive and fleeting thing. Is the lack of a strong, regular beat compatible with this idea? How?*

When we analyze a line of poetry in order to determine its meter, we are said to be *scanning* the line. In scanning, we usually break the line down into groups of two or three syllables called *feet*. Theoretically, a line may have any number of feet, but usually poetry has from one to six or seven feet a line. These groups of syllables, for the most part, have one stressed syllable and one or more unstressed syllables. The position of the stressed syllable in relation to the unstressed theoretically remains the same, although frequently there are variations to this pattern to avoid monotony and to keep the meter from appearing to be forced.

There are four basic feet patterns in English poetry: the *iambic*, which consists of one unstressed syllable followed by a stressed one; the *trochaic*, a stressed syllable followed by an unstressed one; the *anapestic*, which is two unstressed and then a stressed syllable; and finally the *dactylic*, whose pattern is one stressed syllable followed by two unstressed. Here are some examples of metrically regular lines of poetry marked to show the stressed and unstressed syllables. The vertical lines separate the poetic feet:

Iambic   How rare/ly Rea/son guides / the stub/born Choice.
Samuel Johnson, "The Vanity of Human Wishes"

Trochaic   Golden / branch a/mong the / shadows
Alfred Tennyson, "To Virgil"

Anapestic   Twas the night / before Christ/mas, when all /

through the house
Clement Moore, "A Visit from Saint Nicholas"

Dactylic   Ye who be/lieve in af/fection that / hopes, and

en/dures, and is / patient
Henry Wadsworth Longfellow, "Evangeline"

Just as metrical feet are classified according to stress patterns, so are lines of poetry divided into types according to the number of feet they contain. A one-foot line we call *monometer*. Lines of two feet we call *dimeter*, of three feet *trimeter*, of four feet *tetrameter*, of five feet *pentameter*, of six feet *hexameter*. Each line of regular poetry, then, can be identified by, first, the type of foot which is dominant in it and, second, the number of feet in the line. Thus, after scanning the following line, we can identify it as iambic pentameter.

Forth reaching to the fruit, she plucked, she eat.
John Milton, Paradise Lost

This next line is in trochaic tetrameter.

Worlds on worlds are rolling ever.
Percy Bysshe Shelly, "Hellas"

The meter in a poem often reflects the theme, and in good poetry the sense and the form are harmonious. Consider the following poem by George Gordon, Lord Byron (1788–1824):

The Destruction of Sennacherib

1   The Assyrian came down like the wolf on the fold,
And his cohorts were gleaming in purple and gold;
And the sheen of their spears was like stars on the sea,
When the blue wave rolls nightly on deep Galilee.

2   Like the leaves of the forest when summer is green,   5
That host with their banners at sunset were seen:
Like the leaves of the forest when autumn hath blown,
That host on the morrow lay withered and strown.

3   For the Angel of Death spread his wings on the blast,
And breathed in the face of the foe as he passed;   10
And the eyes of the sleepers waxed deadly and chill,
And their hearts but once heaved, and forever grew
     still!

4   And there lay the steed with his nostril all wide,
But through it there rolled not the breath of his pride;
And the foam of his gasping lay white on the turf,   15
And cold as the spray of the rock-beating surf.

5   And there lay the rider distorted and pale,
With the dew on his brow, and the rust on his mail:
And the tents were all silent, the banners alone,
The lances unlifted, the trumpet unblown.   20

6   And the widows of Ashur are loud in their wail,
And the idols are broke in the temple of Baal;
And the might of the Gentile, unsmote by the sword,
Hath melted like snow in the glance of the Lord!

Exercises   *1. Scan the poem and identify the meter.*

2. This poem describes a great battle between armies of horsemen. How does the meter help in this description?

3. Discuss the simile in the last line of the fourth stanza. What effect does meter have on a comparison of this kind?

Strict adherence to a regular meter is not necessarily a sign of merit in a poem. In fact, a poet who writes in a regular meter and never varies from it is likely to be accused of being too monotonous and too dry. Most poets recognize this. John Milton, for instance, wrote *Paradise Lost*, an epic poem of over ten thousand lines, in iambic pentameter, but he was able, skillfully and for us happily, to vary his meter from the standard five foot pattern. Had he stuck stubbornly and tenaciously to his meter, the result would no doubt have been as sleep-provoking as any pill on the market, no matter how interesting and exciting the other aspects of the poem.

One of the primary functions meter serves is to establish a sense of anticipation in the reader's or listener's head. In our mind's ear we recognize the beat and expect this rhythm to continue, but if we are surprised by a sudden variation, the effect is often esthetically pleasing. The poet, like the musician, can startle us out of our ennui; for the most part, we enjoy this sensation. There are practical considerations, too. Sometimes a multisyllable word or phrase used in a poem has its own natural rhythm, which doesn't happen to fit into the meter of the poem. Trying to force the word or phrase into the metrical pattern would create an artificiality that would be heard immediately by the reader-listener. And this artificiality would destroy, to some extent, the integrity of the poem. In other cases, where the accent is placed determines the very meaning of the phrase. Thus, to insist in every case that the rhythmic pattern of the phrase must follow the poem's basic meter could alter the meaning and destroy or make ambiguous the sense of the line.

Therefore, variation from the standard meter is often necessary to preserve the meaning of the poem, to avoid artificiality and monotony, and to add the spice of surprise to our total appreciation of the poem. Read the following poem and then go back and scan it.

Thomas Wyatt (1503–1542)

If thou wilt mighty be

> If thou wilt mighty be, flee from the rage
>   Of cruel will, and see thou keep thee free
> From the foul yoke of sensual bondage;
>   For though thy empire stretch to Indian sea,
>   And for thy fear trembleth the fardest Thule,
> If thy desire have over thee the power,   6
> Subject then art thou and no governor.

If to be noble and high thy mind be moved,
    Consider well thy ground and thy beginning;
For he that hath each star in heaven fixed,   *10*
    And gives the moon her horns and her
    eclipsing,
    Alike hath made thee noble in his working;
So that wretched no way thou may be,
Except foul lust and vice do conquer thee.

    All were it so thou had a flood of gold   *15*
        Unto thy thirst, yet should it not suffice;
    And though with Indian stones, a thousand fold
        More precious than can thyself devise,
        Ycharged were thy back, thy covetise
And busy biting yet should never let   *20*
Thy wretched life, ne do thy death profet.

Exercises   1. *What is the meter?*

2. *Are there variations to the meter? Give some examples. Can you give reasons for having these variations? Do the variations detract from the poem? Why or why not?*

    So far we have been looking at poems that are fairly regular and can be scanned according to the standard accentual syllabic system we have discussed. Not all poetry, however, can be analyzed metrically according to this method. Poets do experiment and as a consequence have produced some unusual metric results, unusual at least for the time in which they were introduced. One of these experiments is called *free verse*, or in French, *vers libre*. This is not to be confused with *blank verse*, which is unrhymed iambic pentameter. The free-verse line does not conform to any predetermined configurations based on accents or syllables; it uses no conventional metrical devices. The result is that this kind of poetry, at least to some extent, resembles prose, except that the line remains the basic unit, rather than the sentence or the paragraph. Justifications for this kind of poetry include the claim that the poet is free to operate according to the demands of the subject or theme without the distraction of having to conform to any set meter. Several excellent poets, especially some of the modern or contemporary ones, have chosen to write free verse. The following is an example.

William Carlos Williams *(1883–1963)*

Queen-Ann's-Lace

Her body is not so white as
anemone petals nor so smooth—nor
so remote a thing. It is a field
of the wild carrot taking
the field by force; the grass   5
does not raise above it.
Here is no question of whiteness,
white as can be, with a purple mole
at the center of each flower.
Each flower is a hand's span   10
of her whiteness. Wherever
his hand has lain there is
a tiny purple blemish. Each part
is a blossom under his touch
to which the fibres of her being   15
stem one by one, each to its end,
until the whole field is a
white desire, empty, a single stem,
a cluster, flower by flower,
a pious wish to whiteness gone over—   20
or nothing.

Exercises   *1. Do you think that the absence of a regular meter detracts from or enhances the poem? Why?*

2. Does the poem have any rhythm at all? Why or why not?

In addition to developments like free verse, there have been many experiments with the theory of prosody, prosody being that very inexact science which studies metrics or versification. Ever since human beings have been creating poetry, it seems, they have been trying to articulate what it is exactly that makes poetry different from what is thought of as prose. One way of attempting to arrive at this definition over the years has been to try to develop a satisfactory theory of prosody. There have been many such trials and many explanations given for what principle the poetic line is based on. Some prosodists, as we have seen, contend that the scansion of a poetic line depends on discernible patterns based on the relationship between stressed and unstressed syllables. Others, such as the nineteenth-century poet Coventry Patmore, developed theories that revolved around the idea that a poetic line was based on time, much as the measure in music is based on isochronous intervals. Still others, basing their arguments on studies of classical Greek and Old English poetry, maintain that a poetic line is organized according to a fixed number of stressed syllables, the number of unstressed syllables being immaterial. Gerard Manley Hopkins, one of the great innovators in this area, developed a theory of prosody that he called Sprung Rhythm. The basis for the organization of the poetic line, Hopkins says, is a fixed number of stressed syllables in the line. Look at the following poem and see if you can tell how he organizes his lines.

Gerard Manley Hopkins *(1844–1889)*

The Windhover
To Christ Our Lord

I caught this morning morning's minion, kingdom
    of daylight's dauphin, dapple-dawn-drawn Falcon,
    in his riding
Of the rolling level underneath him steady air, and
    striding
High there, how he rung upon the rein of a wimpling
    wing
In his ecstasy! then off, off forth on swing,
    As a skate's heel sweeps smooth on a bow-bend:
    the hurl and gliding
    Rebuffed the big wind. My heart in hiding
Stirred for a bird,—the achieve of, the mastery of the
    thing!

Brute beauty and valour and act, oh, air, pride, plume,
    here
    Buckle! AND the fire that breaks from thee then, a
    billion
Times told lovelier, more dangerous, O my chevalier!

    No wonder of it: shéer plód makes plough down
    sillion
Shine, and blue-bleak embers, ah my dear,
    Fall, gall themselves, and gash gold-vermilion.

1. Is Hopkins' poetry identical to free verse? Why or why not?

2. Is Sprung Rhythm too sprung? Is it so unstructured that it ceases to be rhythmic at all? Defend your answer.

3. Does Hopkins' vocabulary seem to have anything to do with the way the line is organized?

It is important to remember that merit in poetry, like merit in all things, is determined by the evaluation of a total entity: we need to look at the poem from all sides and to respond to it in as many ways as we can before we make any final critical decisions about it. The meter and its interaction with the rest of the poem are only one facet of understanding and appreciating the work.

Read and scan the following poems. Identify their meter and tell if and why you think the meter is an integral part of the totality of the poem.

Thomas Hardy (1840–1928)

The Ruined Maid

"O'Melia, my dear, this does everything crown!
Who could have supposed I should meet you in Town?
And whence such fair garments, such prosperi-ty?"
"O didn't you know I'd been ruined?" said she.

"You left us in tatters, without shoes or socks,   *5*
Tired of digging potatoes, and spudding up docks;
And now you've gay bracelets and bright feathers
    three!"
"Yes: that's how we dress when we're ruined," said
    she.

"At home in the barton you said 'thee' and 'thou,'
And 'thik oon,' and 'theäs oon,' and 't'other'; but now
Your talking quite fits 'ee for high compa-ny!"   *11*
"Some polish is gained with one's ruin," said she.

"Your hands were like paws then, your face blue and
    bleak
But now I'm bewitched by your delicate cheek,
And your little gloves fit as on any la-dy!"   *15*
"We never do work when we're ruined," said she.

"You used to call home-life a hag-ridden dream,
And you'd sigh, and you'd sock; but at present you
    seem
To know not of megrims or melancho-ly!"
"True. One's pretty lively when ruined," said she. *20*

"I wish I had feathers, a fine sweeping gown,
And a delicate face, and could strut about Town!"
"My dear—a raw country girl, such as you be,
Cannot quite expect that. You ain't ruined," said
    she.

Exercises   *1. Identify the speakers. Would you expect two such persons to
address each other in such metrical language? Why do you
suppose Hardy has them do this?*

*2. Is the meter "forced" at times? Give specific examples.
Does this add or detract from the poem's effect? Why?*

Alfred, Lord Tennyson   *(1809–1892)*

Break, break, break

Break, break, break,
    On thy cold gray stones, O Sea!
And I would that my tongue could utter
    The thoughts that arise in me.

O, well for the fisherman's boy,   *5*
    That he shouts with his sister at play!
O, well for the sailor lad,
    That he sings in his boat on the bay!

And the stately ships go on
    To their haven under the hill;   *10*
But O for the touch of a vanished hand
    And the sound of a voice that is still!

Break, break, break,
    At the foot of thy crags, O Sea!
But the tender grace of a day that is dead   *15*
    Will never come back to me.

1. *What relationship does the meter have to the setting of the poem?*

2. *How is the setting—the seashore—appropriate to the theme—grief and death?*

3. *What opposites work against each other in the poem? How do they spotlight the idea of loss and mourning. What part does the rhythmic structure play in this struggle between opposites?*

Emily Dickinson *(1830–1886)*

I like to see it lap the Miles—

I like to see it lap the Miles—
And lick the Valleys up—
And stop to feed itself at Tanks—
And then—prodigious step

Around a Pile of Mountains—   5
And supercilious peer
In Shanties—by the sides of Roads—
And then a Quarry pare

To fit its sides
And crawl between   10
Complaining all the while
In horrid—hooting stanza—
Then chase itself down Hill—

And neigh like Boanerges—
Then—prompter than a Star   15
Stop—docile and omnipotent
At its own stable door—

Exercises   1. *What is the* it *referred to in the first line? Is there a central metaphor in the poem? What is it?*

2. *How does the meter relate to the theme and organizing metaphor of the poem?*

Henry Wadsworth Longfellow *(1807–1882)*

The tide rises, the tide falls

The tide rises, the tide falls,
The twilight darkens, the curlew calls,
Along the sea-sands damp and brown
The traveler hastens toward the town,
 And the tide rises, the tide falls.   5

Darkness settles on roofs and walls,
But the sea, the sea in the darkness calls;
The little waves, with their soft, white hands,
Efface the footprints in the sands,
 And the tide rises, the tide falls.   10

The morning breaks; the steeds in their stalls
Stamp and neigh, as the hostler calls;
The day returns, but nevermore
Returns the traveler to the shore,
 And the tide rises, the tide falls.   15

Exercises

1. What are the sea-sands *the traveler hastens upon? Who is the traveler? Why are the footprints erased, and why are we sure the traveler will never return?*

2. What is the role of time in this poem? Why is the first line repeated three times?

3. What can you say about the meter as it affects the total poem? Is it effective?

Christina Rossetti *(1830–1894)*

Song

When I am dead, my dearest,
 Sing no sad songs for me;
Plant thou no roses at my head,
 Nor shady cypress tree:
Be the green grass above me   5
 With showers and dewdrops wet:
And if thou wilt, remember,
 And if thou wilt, forget.

I shall not see the shadows,
    I shall not feel the rain;   *10*
I shall not hear the nightingale
    Sing on as if in pain:
And dreaming through the twilight
    That doth not rise nor set,
Haply I may remember,   *15*
    And haply may forget.

Exercises   *1. How does the meter serve to amplify the distinction between the two main elements of the theme, remembering and forgetting?*

2. How do particular objects mentioned in the poem contribute to the mood? Is the mood too contrived? Why or why not?

William Cowper (1731–1800)

Lines Written During a Period of Insanity

Hatred and vengeance, my eternal portion,
Scarce can endure delay of execution,
Wait, with impatient readiness, to seize my
            Soul in a moment.

Damned below Judas: more abhorred than he was,   *5*
Who for a few pence sold his holy Master.
Twice betrayed Jesus me, the last delinquent,
            Deems the profanest.

Man disavows, and Deity disowns me:
Hell might afford my miseries a shelter;   *10*
Therefore hell keeps her ever hungry mouths all
            Bolted against me.

Hard lot! encompassed with a thousand dangers;
Weary, faint, trembling with a thousand terrors;
I'm called, if vanquished, to receive a sentence   *15*
            Worse than Abiram's.

Him the vindictive rod of angry justice
Sent quick and howling to the center headlong;
I, fed with judgment, in a fleshly tomb, am
            Buried above ground.   *20*

Matthew Arnold   *(1822–1888)*

Dover Beach

The sea is calm tonight.
The tide is full, the moon lies fair
Upon the straits; on the French coast the light
Gleams and is gone; the cliffs of England stand,
Glimmering and vast, out in the tranquil bay.   5
Come to the window, sweet is the night-air!
Only, from the long line of spray
Where the sea meets the moon-blanched land,
Listen! you hear the grating roar
Of pebbles which the waves draw back, and fling,   10
At their return, up the high strand,
Begin, and cease, and then again begin,
With tremulous cadence slow, and bring
The eternal note of sadness in.

Sophocles long ago   15
Heard it on the Aegean, and it brought
Into his mind the turbid ebb and flow
Of human misery; we
Find also in the sound a thought,
Hearing it by this distant northern sea.   20

The Sea of Faith
Was once, too, at the full, and round earth's shore
Lay like the folds of a bright girdle furled.
But now I only hear
Its melancholy, long, withdrawing roar,   25
Retreating, to the breath
Of the night-wind, down the vast edges drear
And naked shingles of the world.

Ah, love, let us be true
To one another! for the world, which seems   *30*
To lie before us like a land of dreams,
So various, so beautiful, so new,
Hath really neither joy, nor love, nor light,
Nor certitude, nor peace, nor help for pain;
And we are here as on a darkling plain   *35*
Swept with confused alarms of struggle and flight,
Where ignorant armies clash by night.

Exercises   *1. What is the thought Arnold finds in the sound at line 19? Does the meter of the poem contribute to this thought? How?*

2. What did Sophocles hear long ago that Arnold now hears? What is cadence? What does cadence have to do with the theme of the poem?

Walt Whitman   (1819–1892)

Beat! beat! drums!

Beat! beat! drums! blow! bugles! blow!
Through the windows—through doors—burst like a
    ruthless force,
Into the solemn church, and scatter the congregation,
Into the school where the scholar is studying;
Leave not the bridegroom quiet—no happiness must he
    have now with his bride,   *5*
Nor the peaceful farmer any peace, ploughing his field
    or gathering his grain,
So fierce you whirr and pound you drums—so shrill you
    bugles blow.

Beat! beat! drums!—blow! bugles! blow!
Over the traffic of cities—over the rumble of wheels in
    the streets;
Are beds prepared for sleepers at night in the houses?
    no sleepers must sleep in those beds,   *10*
No bargainers' bargains by day—no brokers or specula-
    tors—would they continue?
Would the talkers be talking? would the singer attempt
    to sing?
Would the lawyer rise in the court to state his case
    before the judge?

Then rattle quicker, heavier drums—you bugles wilder
  blow.
Beat! beat! drums!—blow! bugles! blow!   15
Make no parley—stop for no expostulation,
Mind not the timid—mind not the weeper or prayer,
Mind not the old man beseeching the young man,
Let not the child's voice be heard, nor the mother's
  entreaties,
Make even the trestles to shake the dead where they lie
  awaiting the hearses,   20
So strong you thump O terrible drums—so loud you
  bugles blow.

Exercises

1. Is the poem more rhythmic than others you have read? Less rhythmic? Explain.

2. Whitman, it has been said, writes in cadences rather than in meter. From your perception of the rhythmic structure of this poem, attempt to distinguish between meter and cadence.

Topics for Writing

1. Scan a Shakespeare sonnet, noticing departures from iambic pentameter. Examine each variation and explain its purpose or effectiveness.

2. Examine a poem written in free verse, such as Whitman's "Beat! beat! drums!" or William Carlos Williams' "Queen-Ann's-Lace." Point out metrical symmetries that distinguish this writing from prose or show that the poem you have chosen does not differ significantly from a prose passage of your choice.

6 Sound Devices and Stanza Patterns

Since early childhood, most of us have been familiar with what rhyme is, although it undoubtedly took us some time consciously to know the definition: the correspondence of terminal sounds in words. We have all heard rhyming devices used in nursery rhymes and weather saws like this one:

Red sky at night—
Sailors' delight.
Red sky at morning—
Sailors' warning.

Rhyme is one of those devices involving the repetition of sound patterns that poets have used down through the years to make their poetry appealing to the reader's ear. There are many other sound devices poets use for emphasis, effect, and organization, like alliteration, assonance, and consonance, but these will be discussed later.

Rhyme is most noticeable, usually, when it occurs at the ends of the lines of a poem. In the following stanza, we have two rhymes, or what we for the sake of convenience call *a rhyme* and *b rhyme*.

I hear the noise about thy keel;	*a*
I hear the bell struck in the night:	*b*
I see the cabin window bright;	*b*
I see the sailor at the wheel.	*a*

In this stanza, from Tennyson's *In Memoriam*, we can see rhyme, or corresponding sounds at the ends of words, used to help organize the poetry. The poet has taken his *a* rhyme and his *b* rhyme and used them to organize his stanza vertically in the same way he uses meter to organize his poetry horizontally. The result is a tight, two-dimensionsal effect; the rhyme serves to hold together a section of the poem and give it unity.

Many different rhyming units are used in poetry. The simplest and one of the most popular is called the *couplet*. As the name implies, the couplet's organization depends upon the rhyming of words at the end of a pair of lines. For instance, these from William Blake's "Auguries of Innocence":

The Emmets Inch and Eagles Mile
Make Lame Philosophy to Smile

The heroic couplet is a refinement on this form. The *heroic couplet* consists of two iambic pentameter (see Chapter 5) rhymed lines that are end-stopped, that is, finish with a strong punctuation mark like a period or colon. Each line is usually balanced, with a caesura (a rest, a pause) somewhere in the middle. The couplets are called *heroic* because this form was widely used in the seventeenth and eighteenth centuries in English translations of classical epic or heroic poems as well as in mock heroic poems like "The Rape of the Lock." The following lines are organized into heroic couplets:

Thus man by his own strength to heaven
would soar,
And would not be obliged to God for more.
Vain wretched creature, how art thou misled,
To think thy wit these god-like notions bred!
These truths are not the product of thy mind,
But dropt from heaven and of a nobler kind.

John Dryden, "Religio Laici"

Rhyme is used to organize poetic units longer than couplets, as we have seen in the example from Tennyson. A *stanza* is the name for a group of lines organized into a regular pattern, usually involving both meter and rhyme. Stanzas are parts of a larger poetic structure, and their type depends on the total conception of the poem. Down through the years, many different types of stanzas have been used, and certain conventions or expectations have come to be associated with the various stanzaic patterns. The ballad stanza, for instance, is a familiar one to nearly everyone. Many of us have heard it since infancy:

> "Mistress Mary, quite contrary,
> How does your garden grow?"
> "With silver bells and cockle shells
> And pretty maids all in a row."

The *ballad stanza*, in its most widely used variation, has four lines—the first and third written in iambic tetrameter and the second and fourth in iambic trimeter. In this formation, often called *common meter*, the second and the fourth lines are rhymed. The ballad stanza, because its roots are in the folk songs and poems of the distant past, is most often used in narratives that deal with such topics as old legends, tragic love stories, and adventures of folk heroes. The form is also used in literary ballads like Coleridge's "The Rime of the Ancient Mariner," in which the poet intends to capture the feeling of an old folk legend, while writing an original serious poem of his own.

> About, about, in reel and rout   *a*
> The death-fires danced at night;   *b*
> The water, like a witch's oils,   *c*
> Burnt green, and blue and white.   *b*
>
> *Samuel Taylor Coleridge,*
> "The Rime of the Ancient Mariner"

The ballad stanza is also said to be a *quatrain*, a word referring to any stanza or poem of four lines. Other quatrains have a variety of meters and rhyme schemes. Two of the commoner types, the *elegiac stanza* and the *In Memoriam stanza*, are given here as examples:

> So once it would have been—'tis so no more;   *a*
> I have submitted to a new control: *b*
> A power is gone, which nothing can restore;   *a*
> A deep distress hath humanized my Soul.   *b*
>
> *William Wordsworth,* "Elegiac Stanzas"

> So now I sit here quite alone,   *a*
>   Blinded with tears; nor grieve for that,   *b*
>   For nought is left worth looking at   *b*
> Since my delightful land is gone.   *a*
>
> *Christina Rossetti,* "Shut Out"

Many poets are given to more complex stanzaic forms. Some of these forms were discovered in continental European literature and adapted to English, while others, like the Spenserian stanza, are native to England. The *Spenserian stanza*, ever since it was first used by Edmund Spenser in his *Faerie Queen* (1590), has come to be associated with voluptuousness of language and lushness of imagery. It is a nine-line stanza, with eight lines of iambic pentameter and a last line of iambic hexameter, called an Alexandrine. The rhyme scheme is *ababbcbcc*. The following is an example from *The Faerie Queen* (Book III, Canto IX, Stanza 1):

Redoubted knights, and honorable Dames,	*a*
To whom I levell all my labours end,	*b*
Right sore I feare, least with unworthy blames	*a*
This odious argument my rimes should shend,	*b*
Or ought your goodly patience offend,	*b*
Whiles of a wanton Lady I do write,	*c*
Which with her loose incontinence doth blend	*b*
The shyning glory of your soveraigne light,	*c*
And knighthood fowle defacéd by a faithlesse knight.	*c*

Another stanza form often used in English is *ottava rima*. Used widely in Italian romances, it has been adapted by various poets who write in English. The stanza consists of eight lines of iambic pentameter with a rhyme scheme of *ababab cc*. The concluding couplet provides an epigrammatical impact at the end of each stanza.

This may seem strange, but yet 'tis very common;	*a*
For instance—gentlemen, whose ladies take	*b*
Leave to o'erstep the written rights of Woman,	*a*
And break the——Which commandment is't they break?	*b*
(I have forgot the number, and think no man	*a*
Should rashly quote, for fear of a mistake;)	*b*
I say, when these same gentlemen are jealous,	*c*
They make some blunder, which their ladies tell us.	*c*

George Gordon, Lord Byron,
Don Juan, Canto I, Stanza 98

Rhyme royal is a stanza form used by Shakespeare and Chaucer among others. It consists of seven lines of iambic pentameter rhymed *ababbcc*.

Of heaven or hell I have no power to sing,	*a*
I cannot ease the burden of your fears,	*b*
Or make quick-coming death a little thing,	*a*
Or bring again the pleasure of past years,	*b*
Nor for my words shall ye forget your tears,	*b*
Or hope again for aught that I can say,	*c*
The idle singer of an empty day.	*c*

William Morris, "The Earthly Paradise"

A particularly fascinating stanza form is the *terza rima*. Used by Dante in *The Divine Comedy*, this three-line stanza rhymes *aba* and is in iambic pentameter. Each terza rima stanza interlocks with the next stanza by means of rhyme, and the result is a tight verse form which still allows for a progression of ideas.

The sun by now 'oer that horizon's rim	*a*
Was sinking, whose meridian circle stands	*b*
With its mid-arch above Jerusalem	*a*
While night, who wheels opposed to him, from sands	*b*
Of Ganges mounted with the Scales, whose weight	*c*
Drops in her hour of victory from her hands	*b*
So that, where we were, fair Aurora, late	*c*
Flushing from white to rose-vermilion,	*d*
Grew sallow with ripe age and matron state.	*c*

Dante, The Divine Comedy *(Sayers translation)*

Sometimes an entire poem, as distinguished from a stanza, has its own poetic form. An important one is the sonnet. The sonnet is a fourteen line poem written in iambic pentameter with one of two rhyme schemes. The *Petrarchan* (or *Italian*) sonnet is divided into two parts: an octave (eight-line stanza) usually rhymed *abbaabba* and a sestet (six-line stanza) rhyming much as the poet chooses. There is most often a rhetorical turn or shift between the octave and the sestet. A proposition is given or question is raised in the first eight lines, and then a solution or answer is presented in the sestet. Thus the octave prepares for the statement made by the sestet.

Dante Gabriel Rossetti (1828–1882)

A Sonnet *from* The House of Life

A Sonnet is a moment's monument,—	*a*
Memorial from the Soul's eternity	*b*
To one dead deathless hour. Look that it be,	*b*
Whether for lustral rite or dire portent,	*a*
Of its own arduous fulness reverent:	*a*
Carve it in ivory or in ebony,	*b*
As Day or Night may rule; and let Time see	*b*
Its flowering crest impearled and orient.	*a*
A Sonnet is a coin: its face reveals	*c*
The soul—its converse, to what Power 'tis due:	*d*
Whether for tribute to the august appeals	*c*
O Life, or dower in Love's high retinue,	*d*
It serve; or, 'mid the dark wharf's cavernous breath,	*e*
In Charon's palm it pay the toll to Death.	*e*

The *Shakespearean* (or *English* or *Elizabethan*) *sonnet* is divided into three quatrains and ends with a rhymed couplet.

William Shakespeare (1564–1616)

Sonnet 106

When in the chronicle of wasted time	*a*
I see descriptions of the fairest wights,	*b*
And beauty making beautiful old rhyme	*a*
In praise of ladies dead and lovely knights,	*b*
Then, in the blazon of sweet beauty's best,	*c*
Of hand, of foot, of lip, of eye, of brow,	*d*
I see their antique pen would have expressed	*c*
Even such a beauty as you master now.	*d*
So all their praises are but prophecies	*e*
Of this our time, all you prefiguring;	*f*
And, for they looked but with divining eyes,	*e*
They had not skill enough your worth to sing:	*f*
For we, which now behold these present days,	*g*
Have eyes to wonder, but lack tongues to praise.	*g*

Although the sonnet is a difficult and demanding form, it is used by many poets because it is concise and tight. Shakespeare's Sonnet 106, for instance, is a self-contained logical construction. The three quatrains take us from point to point until we reach the couplet, which furnishes the conclusion.

The *villanelle* is another familiar poetic form, although not as widely used as the sonnet. It is made up of five tercets (three-line stanzas) rhyming *aba*, with a quatrain at the end, rhyming *abaa*. In addition, certain lines are repeated: line 1 is repeated in lines 6, 12, and 18, while line 3 is repeated in 9, 15, and 19. The following is an example:

Dylan Thomas   *(1914–1953)*

Do not go gentle into that good night

Do not go gentle into that good night,
Old age should burn and rave at close of day;
Rage, rage against the dying of the light.

Though wise men at their end know dark is right,
Because their words had forked no lightning they   *5*
Do not go gentle into that good night.

Good men, the last wave by, crying how bright
Their frail deeds might have danced in a green bay,
Rage, rage against the dying of the light.

Wild men who caught and sang the sun in flight,   *10*
And learn, too late, they grieved it on its way,
Do not go gentle into that good night.

Grave men, near death, who see with blinding sight
Blind eyes could blaze like meteors and be gay,
Rage, rage against the dying of the light.   *15*

And you, my father, there on the sad height,
Curse, bless, me now with your fierce tears, I pray.
Do not go gentle into that good night.
Rage, rage against the dying of the light.

In addition to rhyme, there are other poetic devices that depend on the repetition of certain sound patterns. Rhyme, as we have seen, occurs when there is a duplication of sounds at the end of a word. *Alliteration* is the repetition of initial sounds in words, for instance *the weary way-worn wanderer*, or *daylight's dauphin, dapple-dawn-drawn Falcon*. Alliteration has played an important part in English poetry over the years and in fact served as the basis for organizing the poetic line in early English verse.

Today, alliteration is used to bring an appealing chiming effect to a poem. It is most often used in conjunction with other devices of sound like rhyme and assonance.

Assonance, too, relies on repeating sound patterns. Assonance is the close repetition of the same vowels followed by different consonants. Stephen Crane has examples in his poetry like *rolled over* and *"Champing and mouthing of hats."* *Consonance*, on the other hand, is the repetition of consonant sounds without a corresponding repetition of vowel sounds. Hopkins often uses this device in his poetry as when he uses the *r* sound in this following series of words: *original, spare, strange.* *Internal rhyme*, another of the poetic devices involving sound, is the repetition of terminal sounds in words, like *cat* and *rat*, when they occur within a line of poetry rather than at the end. *The flower's leaf, the sheaf of grain* is one example.

The sound devices, rhyme, alliteration, consonance, and assonance are all items in the poet's toolbox. Like skilled artisans, poets use these tools to create the best possible piece of work. Like cabinetmakers or stonemasons, they are always aware of the scope and limitations of each tool. The real master poet uses them accordingly.

Read the following poems and excerpts and first determine the stanza pattern or the poetic form. Then identify the devices of sound the poet uses to make a point, to spotlight or enhance an idea, or simply to make the poetry more appealing to our mind's ear.

John Keats *(1795–1821)*

from The Eve of St. Agnes

> Beyond a mortal man impassioned far
> At these voluptuous accents, he arose,
> Ethereal, flushed, and like a throbbing star
> Seen mid the sapphire heaven's deep repose;
> Into her dream he melted, as the rose
> Blendeth its odor with the violet—
> Solution sweet: meantime the frost-wind blows
> Like Love's alarum pattering the sharp sleet
> Against the windowpanes; St. Agnes' moon hath set.

Exercises   *1. What is the stanza pattern? Why do you think Keats chose this particular form?*

2. In "The Eve of St. Agnes" setting and mood are very important. From your reading of this stanza what is the setting and what is the mood the poet is trying to create?

3. How would you describe Keats's language in this poem?

Theodore Roethke *(1908–1963)*

The Waking

I wake to sleep, and take my waking slow.
I feel my fate in what I cannot fear.
I learn by going where I have to go.

We think by feeling. What is there to know?
I hear my being dance from ear to ear.   5
I wake to sleep, and take my waking slow.

Of those so close beside me, which are you?
God bless the Ground! I shall walk softly there,
And learn by going where I have to go.

Light takes the Tree; but who can tell us how?   10
The lowly worm climbs up a winding stair;
I wake to sleep, and take my waking slow.

Great Nature has another thing to do
To you and me; so take the lively air,
And, lovely, learn by going where to go.   15

This shaking keeps me steady. I should know.
What falls away is always. And is near.
I wake to sleep, and take my waking slow.
I learn by going where I have to go.

Exercises

1. Often critics discuss ambiguity in poetry, and many conclude that it is desirable. Discuss the ambiguity in this poem, especially in lines 1, 4, 16, and 17. Does the ambiguity interfere with the movement of thought in the poem? Why or why not?

2. What is the poetic form? Is this form appropriate to the theme and to any kind of logical progression you find? Explain.

Alfred, Lord Tennyson *(1809–1892)*

from In Memoriam A. H. H.
Obit. MDCCCXXXIII

Dark house, by which once more I stand
 Here in the long unlovely street,
 Doors, where my heart was used to beat
So quickly, waiting for a hand,

A hand that can be clasped no more—
 Behold me, for I cannot sleep,
 And like a guilty thing I creep
At earliest morning to the door.

He is not here; but far away
 The noise of life begins again,
 And ghastly through the drizzling rain
On the bald street breaks the blank day.

Anonymous

The Unquiet Grave

"The wind doth blow today, my love,
 And a few small drops of rain;
I never had but one true-love,
 In cold grave she was lain.

"I'll do as much for my true-love   5
 As any young man may;
I'll sit and mourn all at her grave
 For a twelvemonth and a day,"

The twelvemonth and a day being up,
 The dead began to speak: 10
"Oh who sits weeping on my grave,
 And will not let me sleep?"

" 'T is I, my love, sits on your grave,
 And will not let you sleep;
For I crave one kiss of your clay-cold lips, 15
 And that is all I seek."

"You crave one kiss of my clay-cold lips,
    But my breath smells earthly strong;
If you have one kiss of my clay-cold lips,
    Your time will not be long.   *20*

" 'T is down in yonder garden green,
    Love, where we used to walk,
The finest flower that e'er was seen
    Is withered to a stalk.

"The stalk is withered dry, my love,   *25*
    So will our hearts decay;
So make yourself content, my love,
    Till God calls you away."

Exercises   *1. These two poems were composed hundreds of years apart. Both deal with a perennial theme—the reaction to the death of a loved one. Compare and contrast the two reactions.*

2. Identify the stanzaic patterns and discuss their appropriateness to the totality of each poem. Remember that the Tennyson passage is part of a larger poem.

Percy Bysshe Shelley *(1792–1822)*

Ode to the West Wind

1   O wild West Wind, thou breath of Autumn's being,
Thou, from whose unseen presence the leaves dead
And driven, like ghosts from an enchanter fleeing,

Yellow, and black, and pale, and hectic red,
Pestilence-stricken multitudes: O thou,   *5*
Who chariotest to their dark .wintry bed

The wingéd seeds, where they lie cold and low,
Each like a corpse within its grave, until
Thine azure sister of the Spring shall blow

Her clarion o'er the dreaming earth, and fill   *10*
(Driving sweet buds like flocks to feed in air)
With living hues and odors plain and hill:

Wild Spirit, which art moving everywhere;
Destroyer and preserver; hear, oh, hear!

2   Thou on whose stream, mid the steep sky's
        commotion,   15
    Loose clouds like earth's decaying leaves are shed,
    Shook from the tangled boughs of Heaven and Ocean,

    Angels of rain and lightning: there are spread
    On the blue surface of thine aëry surge,
    Like the bright hair uplifted from the head   20

    Of some fierce Maenad, even from the dim verge
    Of the horizon to the zenith's height,
    The locks of the approaching storm. Thou dirge

    Of the dying year, to which this closing night
    Will be the dome of a vast sepulcher,   25
    Vaulted with all thy congregated might

    Of vapors, from whose solid atmosphere
    Black rain, and fire, and hail will burst: oh, hear!

3   Thou who didst waken from his summer dreams
    The blue Mediterranean, where he lay,   30
    Lulled by the coil of his crystálline streams,

    Beside a pumice isle in Baiae's bay,
    And saw in sleep old palaces and towers
    Quivering within the wave's intenser day,

    All overgrown with azure moss and flowers   35
    So sweet, the sense faints picturing them! Thou
    For whose path the Atlantic's level powers

    Cleave themselves into chasms, while far below
    The sea-blooms and the oozy woods which wear
    The sapless foliage of the ocean, know   40

    Thy voice, and suddenly grow gray with fear,
    And tremble and despoil themselves: oh, hear!

4   If I were a dead leaf thou mightest bear;
    If I were a swift cloud to fly with thee;
    A wave to pant beneath thy power, and share   45

    The impulse of thy strength, only less free
    Than thou, O uncontrollable! If even
    I were as in my boyhood, and could be

    The comrade of thy wanderings over Heaven,
    As then, when to outstrip thy skyey speed   50
    Scarce seem a vision; I would ne'er have striven

As thus with thee in prayer in my sore need.
Oh, lift me as a wave, a leaf, a cloud!
I fall upon the thorns of life! I bleed!

A heavy weight of hours has chained and bowed   *55*
One too like thee: tameless, and swift, and proud.

5   Make me thy lyre, even as the forest is:
What if my leaves are falling like its own!
The tumult of thy mighty harmonies

Will take from both a deep, autumnal tone,   *60*
Sweet though in sadness. Be thou, Spirit fierce,
My spirit! Be thou me, impetuous one!

Drive my dead thoughts over the universe
Like withered leaves to quicken a new birth!
And, by the incantation of this verse,   *65*

Scatter, as from an unextinguished hearth
Ashes and sparks, my words among mankind!
Be through my lips to unawakened earth

The trumpet of a prophecy! O Wind,
If Winter comes, can Spring be far behind?   *70*

Exercises   *1. There is a sense of movement or progression in the poem. How does the stanzaic pattern contribute to this progression?*

2. The seasons of the year play an important part in the poem as well as such natural phenomena as clouds, leaves, and the sea. Discuss these natural elements and show how they are integral to the theme.

Jonathan Swift (1667–1745)

A Description of a City Shower

Careful observers may foretell the hour
(By sure prognostics) when to dread a shower:
While rain depends, the pensive cat gives o'er
Her frolics, and pursues her tail no more.
Returning home at night, you'll find the sink   *5*
Strike your offended sense with double stink.
If you be wise, then go not far to dine;
You'll spend in coach hire more than save in wine.
A coming shower your shooting corns presage,
Old achés throb, your hollow tooth will rage.   *10*

Sauntering in coffeehouse is Dulman seen;
He damns the climate and complains of spleen.
  Meanwhile the South, rising with dabbled wings,
A sable cloud athwart the welkin flings,
That swilled more liquor than it could contain,   _15_
And, like a drunkard, gives it up again.
Brisk Susan whips her linen from the rope,
While the first drizzling shower is borne aslope:
Such is that sprinkling which some careless quean
Flirts on you from her mop, but not so clean: _20_
You fly, invoke the gods; then turning, stop
To rail; she singing, still whirls on her mop.
Not yet the dust had shunned the unequal strife,
But, aided by the wind, fought still for life,
And wafted with its foe by violent gust,   _25_
'Twas doubtful which was rain and which was dust.
Ah! where must needy poet seek for aid,
When dust and rain at once his coat invade?
Sole coat, where dust cemented by the rain
Erects the nap, and leaves a mingled stain.   _30_
  Now in contiguous drops the flood comes down,
Threatening with deluge this devoted town.
To shops in crowds the daggled females fly,
Pretend to cheapen goods, but nothing buy.
The Templar spruce, while every spout's abroach,   _35_
Stays till 'tis fair, yet seems to call a coach.
The tucked-up sempstress walks with hasty strides,
While streams run down her oiled umbrella's sides.
Here various kinds, by various fortunes led,
Commence acquaintance underneath a shed.   _40_
Triumphant Tories and desponding Whigs
Forget their feuds, and join to save their wigs.
Boxed in a chair the beau impatient sits,
While spouts run clattering o'er the roof by fits,
And ever and anon with frightful din   _45_
The leather sounds; he trembles from within.
So when Troy chairmen bore the wooden steed,
Pregnant with Greeks impatient to be freed
(Those bully Greeks who, as the moderns do,
Instead of paying chairmen, run them through),   _50_
Laocoön struck the outside with his spear,
And each imprisoned hero quaked for fear.
  Now from all parts the swelling kennels flow,
And bear their trophies with them as they go:
Filth of all hues and odors seem to tell   _55_
What street they sailed from, by their sight and smell.

They, as each torrent drives with rapid force,
From Smithfield or St. Pulchre's shape their course,
And in huge confluence joined at Snow Hill ridge,
Fall from the conduit prone to Holborn Bridge.   *60*
Sweepings from butchers' stalls, dung, guts, and blood,
Drowned puppies, stinking sprats, all drenched in mud,
Dead cats, and turnip tops, come tumbling down the
    flood.

Exercise   *In broad terms, we can say that realism is telling the story straight, rather than telling it as we want it to be. Given this definition, can we call Swift's poem a realistic one? What details can you point out to support your case?*

William Wordsworth *(1770–1850)*

I wandered lonely as a cloud

I wandered lonely as a cloud
That floats on high o'er vales and hills,
When all at once I saw a crowd,
A host, of golden daffodils;
Beside the lake, beneath the trees,   *5*
Fluttering and dancing in the breeze.

Continuous as the stars that shine
And twinkle on the milky way,
They stretched in never-ending line
Along the margin of a bay: *10*
Ten thousand saw I at a glance,
Tossing their heads in sprightly dance.

The waves beside them danced; but they
Outdid the sparkling waves in glee;
A poet could not but be gay,   *15*
In such a jocund company;
I gazed—and gazed—but little thought
What wealth the show to me had brought:

For oft, when on my couch I lie
In vacant or in pensive mood,   *20*
They flash upon that inward eye
Which is the bliss of solitude;
And then my heart with pleasure fills,
And dances with the daffodils.

1. *How does Wordsworth here synthesize two common stanza-ic patterns to create a third?*

2. *The poem contains musings on the perception and recollection of beauty. When is beauty most appreciated, according to the speaker in the poem? Isn't the bloom of daffodils transitory and fleeting? Of what value is such short-lived pleasure? Explain.*

John Keats *(1795–1821)*

Bright Star

Bright star, would I were steadfast as thou art—
    Not in lone splendor hung aloft the night
And watching, with eternal lids apart,
    Like nature's patient, sleepless Eremite,
The moving waters at their priestlike task
    Of pure ablution round earth's human shores,
Or gazing on the new soft fallen mask
    Of snow upon the mountains and the moors—
No—yet still steadfast, still unchangeable,
    Pillowed upon my fair love's ripening breast,
To feel forever its soft fall and swell,
    Awake forever in a sweet unrest,
Still, still to hear her tender-taken breath,
And so live ever—or else swoon to death.

1. *One word, as we know, may have many shades of meaning. Take the word* steadfast *in Keats's poem and discuss its possible denotative and connotative meanings.*

2. *What is the central metaphor? Does the form of the poem fit in with the major comparison that is being made? How?*

Geoffrey Chaucer *(ca. 1343–1400)*

Against Women Unconstant

Madame, for youre newefangelnesse,
Many a servant have ye put out of grace.
I take my leve of your unstedefastnesse,
For wel I woot, whil ye have lives space,
Ye can not love ful half yeer in a place,   *5*
To newe thing youre lust is ay so keene;
In stede of blew, thus may ye were al greene.

Right as a mirour nothing may enpresse,
But, lightly as it cometh, so mote it pace,
So fareth youre love, youre werkes bereth witnesse. *10*
Ther is no faith that may your herte enbrace;
But, as a wedercok, that turneth his face
With every wind, ye fare, and this is seene;
In stede of blew, thus may ye were al greene.

Ye might be shrined, for youre brotelnesse,   *15*
Bet than Dalida, Criseide or Candace;
For ever in chaunging stant youre sikernesse;
That tache may no wight fro your herte arace.
If ye lese oon, ye can wel twain purchace;
Al light for somer, ye woot wel what I mene,   *20*
In stede of blew, thus may ye were al greene.

Exercises

1. Keats here describes steadfastness as being a positive trait. Would Chaucer agree? Explain. Does Keats' definition of the word as it applies in the poem differ from that of Chaucer in his? Explain.

2. What is the stanza form in "Against Women Unconstant?"

Gerard Manley Hopkins *(1844–1889)*

Felix Randal

Felix Randal the farrier, O is he dead then? my duty all
    ended,
Who have watched his mould of man, big-boned and
    hardy-handsome
Pining, pining, till time when reason rambled in it and
    some
Fatal four disorders, fleshed there, all contended?

Sickness broke him. Impatient, he cursed at first, but
    mended
Being anointed and all; though a heavenlier heart began
    some
Months earlier, since I had our sweet reprieve and
    ransom
Tendered to him. Ah well, God rest him all road ever
    he offended!

This seeing the sick endears them to us, us too it
    endears.
My tongue had taught thee comfort, touch had
    quenched thy tears,
Thy tears that touched my heart, child, Felix, poor Felix
    Randal;
How far from then forethought of, all thy more boister-
    ous years,
When thou at the random grim forge, powerful amidst
    peers,
Didst fettle for the great grey drayhorse his bright and
    battering sandal!

Exercises   *1. What is the poetic form? Is there a shift of emphasis from the first part of the poem to the second?*

2. What devices of sound does Hopkins use? Do they provide emphasis? How?

3. What is the most powerful line in the poem? Why?

1. *Compare a Petrarchan sonnet and a Shakespearean sonnet
to show how structure controls content.*

2. *Examine the following passage from Pope's* Essay on
Criticism.

True ease in writing comes from art, not chance,
As those move easiest who have learned to dance.
'Tis not enough no harshness gives offense,
The sound must seem an echo to the sense:
Soft is the strain when Zephyr gently blows,
And the smooth stream in smoother numbers flows;
But when loud surges lash the sounding shore,
The hoarse, rough verse should like the torrent roar;
When Ajax strives some rock's vast weight to throw,
The line too labors, and the words move slow;
Not so, when swift Camilla scours the plain,
Flies o'er the unbending corn, and skims along the
  main.

*Show how the sound echoes the sense in this passage. What
structural limits has the poet imposed upon himself? Do the
restrictions of poetic form limit what the poet can say?*

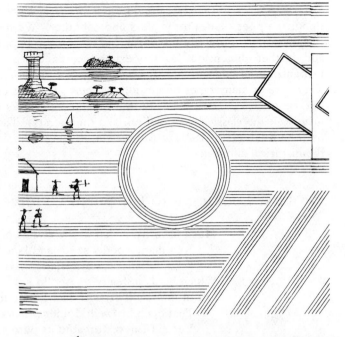

7 Allusion and Symbol

T. S. Eliot has said that the poet puts meaning in his poem "to satisfy one habit of the reader, to keep his mind diverted and quiet, while the poem does its work upon him: much as the imaginary burglar is always provided with a bit of nice meat for the house-dog." What Eliot is saying is that, while there may be more important things than meaning in poetry, we as readers have come to expect to find meaning in a poem and the good poet tries to satisfy our expectations. The poet has several ways of providing such meaning, and the best is usually the one that makes meaning as unobtrusive as possible. That is to say, the poet works by indirection. Rather than announcing the poem's "meaning" with a moral tag at the end, the poet drops clues throughout that lead us to discover the meaning on our own. The poem as meaningful statement becomes a game of the best sort, for it is a game we cannot lose. The more we understand how the poet develops meaning, then, the better we can enjoy the game each poem is.

One favorite device is *allusion*. While talking about one thing, the poet alludes to or plays upon another. We need not recognize the allusion to appreciate the poem, but it stands to reason that as allusions add further dimensions to the experience in the poem, so does our recognizing an allusion add dimensions to our experience of the poem. There are as many types of allusions as there are fields of human activity, but generally we can speak of four major categories of allusions: the historical, the classical, the biblical, and the literary. The following poem by John Keats (1795–1821) provides an interesting example of the first type, the historical allusion:

On First Looking into Chapman's Homer

Much have I traveled in the realms of gold,
    And many goodly states and kingdoms seen;
    Round many western islands have I been
Which bards in fealty to Apollo hold.
Oft of one wide expanse had I been told
    That deep-browed Homer ruled as his demesne;
    Yet did I never breathe its pure serene
Till I heard Chapman speak out loud and bold:
Then felt I like some watcher of the skies
    When a new planet swims into his ken;
Or like stout Cortez when with eagle eyes
    He stared at the Pacific—and all his men
Looked at each other with a wild surmise—
    Silent, upon a peak in Darien.

Because Keats's poem is about his reading George Chapman's Elizabethan translation of Homer's *Iliad*, we cannot really call those references to Apollo and Homer classical allusions; they are, rather, part of the announced subject of the poem. Where Keats does use an allusion is in his reference to an historical incident, the European discovery of the Pacific Ocean. By drawing a comparison between the "new world" that he has discovered in a book and an important moment in the discovery of the New World, Keats emphasizes his own excitement. We have to recognize the allusion, which simply requires that we know something of history. Once that recognition is made, we receive the added sense of the excitement that Keats must have felt, and because we make a "discovery" ourselves, we perhaps even share in that excitement.

Exercises *1. There can be no doubt that Keats is making an historical allusion in that reference to Cortez standing on a peak in Darien and staring at the Pacific, an ocean that until that moment had not existed for the European mind. However, Keats has his facts wrong. It was not Cortez but Balboa, another early Spanish explorer, who discovered the Pacific Ocean in 1513. How might Keats's mistake detract from the effectiveness of the allusion? How factually accurate should an historical allusion be?*

2. If we miss Keats's historical allusion altogether, does he still convey the measure of his excitement to us? By what device?

William Butler Yeats (1865–1939) is a poet especially renowned for using all manner of allusions in his poetry. Allusions to classical mythology, ancient and contemporary history and historical figures, the Old Testament and the New, and literature—sometimes his own earlier poems—abound in his poems, creating a fabric of reference and cross-reference so rich that we as readers find in them an endless source of fascination and discovery. The following poem is just one example:

Long-legged Fly

That civilization may not sink,
Its great battle lost,
Quiet the dog, tether the pony
To a distant post;
Our master Caesar is in the tent   5
Where the maps are spread,
His eyes fixed upon nothing,
A hand under his head.
Like a long-legged fly upon the stream
His mind moves upon silence.   10

That the topless towers be burnt
And men recall that face,
Move most gently if move you must
In this lonely place.
She thinks, part woman, three parts a child,   15
That nobody looks; her feet
Practice a tinker shuffle
Picked up on a street.
Like a long-legged fly upon the stream
Her mind moves upon silence.   20

That girls at puberty may find
The first Adam in their thought,
Shut the door of the Pope's chapel,
Keep those children out.
There on that scaffolding reclines   *25*
Michael Angelo.
With no more sound than the mice make
His hand moves to and fro.
Like a long-legged fly upon the stream
His mind moves upon silence.   *30*

We could argue that since "our master Caesar" is
mentioned in no specific historical context (for example, which of any
number of Roman Caesars does Yeats intend?), there is more of the
symbolic than the allusive in that reference. (We shall consider symbols
later.) But *the topless towers* that are to *be burnt* in the second stanza might
remind us of the burning towers of Troy. The destruction of Troy, we now
know, was an historical event, but we are further reminded of Homer's
Iliad, a classical work of literature that mythologized that historical event.
If we feel that we are letting ourselves get carried away by reading too much
into a single line, the next line— "And men recall that face"—assures us
that we are not wrong, but only if we catch the further allusion. It ought to
remind us of the beautiful Helen, for whom the Trojan War was fought.
Notice, however, that this is not only an historical allusion or simply a
classical allusion to Homer, in whose great poem Helen appears. The very
way in which Yeats phrases those two lines referring to Helen and the
destruction of Troy could remind us of another literary treatment of that
same theme. From Christopher Marlowe's *Doctor Faustus*, a play written in
the late sixteenth century, come these two lines:

> Was this the face that launched a thousand ships
> And burnt the topless towers of Ilium?

Those lines are spoken by Faustus when he beholds Helen, whose spirit the
Devil has summoned up for him. The main thing for us to notice is
how richly Yeats has combined historical, classical, and literary allusions in
a bare two lines of poetry. We as readers are given many points of entry
into his meaning, depending upon the extent of our knowledge of history
and our experiences with literature. Again, once we recognize the
allusions, even if only on one level, we can begin to work toward
understanding Yeats's meaning.

1. The first Adam, the Pope's chapel, and Michael Angelo appear in the third stanza. Are they allusions? If so, what type or types of allusions are they? How do they work one upon another to create meaning within the stanza?

2. Must we recognize the wealth of allusions in "Long-Legged Fly" to be able to interpret the meaning of that poem? How, for example, does Yeats provide us with a tool for understanding his meaning with that image of a long-legged fly upon a stream? That image is further presented to us as a simile. What comparisons are being made?

T. S. Eliot (1888–1965) is another poet who works extensively with allusion. He relies primarily upon literary allusions in much of his poetry, however, and while we cannot possibly deal with the vast extent of those allusions, we can examine one aspect of them. The more literature a people produces, the more opportunity there is for literary allusion. This holds true not only for Western literature as a whole, but for English literature in particular, which has a long and rich tradition behind it. One poem that captured the imagination of many later poets, including Eliot, follows.

Andrew Marvell (1621–1678)

To His Coy Mistress

Had we but world enough, and time,
This coyness, lady, were no crime.
We would sit down, and think which way
To walk, and pass our long love's day.
Thou by the Indian Ganges' side   5
Shoudst rubies find; I by the tide
Of Humber would complain. I would
Love you ten years before the flood,
And you should, if you please, refuse
Till the conversion of the Jews.   10
My vegetable love should grow
Vaster than empires and more slow;
An hundred years should go to praise
Thine eyes, and on thy forehead gaze;
Two hundred to adore each breast,   15
But thirty thousand to the rest;
An age at least to every part,
And the last age should show your heart.

For, lady, you deserve this state,
Nor would I love at lower rate.   20
    But at my back I always hear
Time's wingéd chariot hurrying near;
And yonder all before us lie
Deserts of vast eternity.
Thy beauty shall no more be found;   25
Nor, in thy marble vault, shall sound
My echoing song; then worms shall try
That long-preserved virginity,
And your quaint honor turn to dust,
And into ashes all my lust: 30
The grave's a fine and private place,
But none, I think, do there embrace.
    Now therefore, while the youthful hue
Sits on thy skin like morning glow,
And while thy willing soul transpires   35
At every pore with instant fires,
Now let us sport us while we may,
And now, like amorous birds of prey,
Rather at once our time devour
Than languish in his slow-chapped power.   40
Let us roll all our strength and all
Our sweetness up into one ball,
And tear our pleasures with rough strife
Through the iron gates of life:
Thus, though we cannot make our sun   45
Stand still, yet we will make him run.

Exercise   *There are biblical allusions in the Marvell poem. How many
can you identify? Discuss their significance.*

    "To His Coy Mistress" is a masterful and somewhat
ironic statement of an age-old poetic theme, the *carpe diem* motif. Quite
briefly, this motif deals with the questions of love and death, time's
passage, and, thus, what use we should make of what little time we have.
Once a statement as definitive as Marvell's is made, later poets can return to
it again and again in their own treatments of similar themes. Eliot does so
in the following poem.

The Love Song of J. Alfred Prufrock

S'io credesse che mia risposta fosse
A persona che mai tornasse al mondo,
Questa fiamma staria senza piu scosse.
Ma perciocche giammai di questo fondo
Non torno vivo alcun, s'i'odo il vero,
Senza tema d'infamia ti rispondo.

Let us go then, you and I,
When the evening is spread out against the sky
Like a patient etherized upon a table;
Let us go, through certain half-deserted streets,
The muttering retreats   5
Of restless nights in one-night cheap hotels
And sawdust restaurants with oyster-shells:
Streets that follow like a tedious argument
Of insidious intent
To lead you to an overwhelming question. . .   10
Oh, do not ask, "What is it?"
Let us go and make our visit.

In the room the women come and go
Talking of Michelangelo.

The yellow fog that rubs its back upon the window-
        panes   15
The yellow smoke that rubs its muzzle on the window-
        panes
Licked its tongue into the corners of the evening,
Lingered upon the pools that stand in drains,
Let fall upon its back the soot that falls from chimneys,
Slipped by the terrace, made a sudden leap,   20
And seeing that it was a soft October night,
Curled once about the house, and fell asleep.

And indeed there will be time
For the yellow smoke that slides along the street,
Rubbing its back upon the window-panes;   25
There will be time, there will be time
To prepare a face to meet the faces that you meet;
There will be time to murder and create,
And time for all the works and days of hands
That lift and drop a question on your plate;   30
Time for you and time for me,
And time yet for a hundred indecisions,
And for a hundred visions and revisions,
Before the taking of a toast and tea.

In the room the women come and go   *35*
Talking of Michelangelo.

And indeed there will be time
To wonder, "Do I dare?" and, "Do I dare?"
Time to turn back and descend the stair,
With a bald spot in the middle of my hair—   *40*
[They will say: "How his hair is growing thin!"]
My morning coat, my collar mounting firmly to the
    chin,
My necktie rich and modest, but asserted by a simple
    pin—
[They will say: "But how his arms and legs are thin!"]
Do I dare   *45*
Disturb the universe?
In a minute there is time
For decisions and revisions which a minute will reverse.

For I have known them all already, known them all:
Have known the evenings, mornings, afternoons,   *50*
I have measured out my life with coffee spoons;
I know the voices dying with a dying fall
Beneath the music from a farther room.
        So how should I presume?

And I have known the eyes already, known them
    all—   *55*
The eyes that fix you in a formulated phrase,
And when I am formulated, sprawling on a pin,
When I am pinned and wriggling on the wall,
Then how should I begin
To spit out all the butt-ends of my days and ways? *60*
        And how should I presume?

And I have known the arms already, known them all—
Arms that are braceleted and white and bare
[But in the lamplight, downed with light brown hair!]
Is it perfume from a dress   *65*
That makes me so digress?
Arms that lie along a table, or wrap about a shawl.
        And should I then presume?
        And how should I begin?

                    .   .   .   .   .

Shall I say, I have gone at dusk through narrow streets   70
And watched the smoke that rises from the pipes
Of lonely men in shirt-sleeves, leaning out of windows? . . .

I should have been a pair of ragged claws
Scuttling across the floors of silent seas.

. . . . .

And the afternoon, the evening, sleeps so peace-   75
    fully!
Smoothed by long fingers,
Asleep . . . tired . . . or it malingers,
Stretched on the floor, here beside you and me.
Should I, after tea and cakes and ices,
Have the strength to force the moment to its crisis? 80
But though I have wept and fasted, wept and prayed,
Though I have seen my head [grown slightly bald]
    brought in upon a platter,
I am no prophet—and here's no great matter;
I have seen the moment of my greatness flicker,
And I have seen the eternal Footman hold my coat, and
    snicker,   85
And in short, I was afraid.

And would it have been worth it, after all,
After the cups, the marmalade, the tea,
Among the porcelain, among some talk of you and me,
Would it have been worth while,   90
To have bitten off the matter with a smile,
To have squeezed the universe into a ball
To roll it toward some overwhelming question,
To say: "I am Lazarus, come from the dead,
Come back to tell you all, I shall tell you all"—   95
If one, settling a pillow by her head,
    Should say: "That is not what I meant at all.
    That is not it, at all."

And would it have been worth it, after all,
Would it have been worth while,   100
After the sunsets and the dooryards and the sprinkled
    streets,
After the novels, after the teacups, after the skirts that
    trail along the floor—
And this, and so much more?—
It is impossible to say just what I mean!

But as if a magic lantern threw the nerves in patterns on
    a screen: *105*
Would it have been worth while
If one, settling a pillow or throwing off a shawl,
And turning toward the window, should say:
    "That is not it at all,
    That is not what I meant, at all."   *110*

     . . . . .

No! I am not Prince Hamlet, nor was meant to be;
Am an attendant lord, one that will do
To swell a progress, start a scene or two,
Advise the prince; no doubt, an easy tool,
Deferential, glad to be of use,   *115*
Politic, cautious, and meticulous;
Full of high sentence, but a bit obtuse;
At times, indeed, almost ridiculous—
Almost, at times, the Fool.

I grow old . . . I grow old . . .   *120*
I shall wear the bottoms of my trousers rolled.

Shall I part my hair behind? Do I dare to eat a peach?
I shall wear white flannel trousers, and walk upon the
    beach.
I have heard the mermaids singing, each to each.

I do not think that they will sing to me.   *125*

I have seen them riding seaward on the waves
Combing the white hair of the waves blown back
When the wind blows the water white and black.

We have lingered in the chambers of the sea
By sea-girls wreathed with seaweed red and brown   *130*
Till human voices wake us, and we drown.

Exercises   *1. "The Love Song of J. Alfred Prufrock" obviously deals
with the question of love and time. Where in this unquestionably complex poem does Eliot allude to Marvell's poem on the
same theme? How does Eliot's use of Marvell comment on
Prufrock's dilemma? To answer that question, we must first
determine how Marvell's speaker "means" the statement, and
then whether or not Eliot intends us to take Prufrock as
meaning it in the same way. If he does not, we find literary
allusion being used for the purposes of irony.*

2. *There is also a reference to Lazarus in "Prufrock." What type of allusion does that reference constitute? What does it tell us about Prufrock's view of himself? How does Prufrock's idea of what the women's reaction would be give us still further insights into Prufrock's character?*

3. *Is the Michelangelo the women in "Prufrock" talk about the same Michael Angelo whom we met in Yeats's poem? If we find each poet making different use of the same historical figure, how does each poet nevertheless require that we have some general sense of who Michael Angelo is?*

Even the epigraph to "Prufrock" is a literary allusion. The verses are taken from Dante's *Inferno* (Canto XXVII, lines 61–66). Translated, they read:

> If I thought my answer were given
> To anyone who would ever return to the world,
> This flame would stand still without moving any further.
> But since never from this abyss
> Has anyone ever returned alive, if what I hear is true,
> Without fear of infamy I answer thee.

These words are spoken for Dante by Guido da Montefeltro, who is being punished in the Eighth Circle of Hell for giving false counsel. Though Eliot quotes the lines directly, on what grounds might we argue that they are actually a literary allusion, that is, a reference that we must recognize if it is to create meaning? How do those lines comment on the character of Prufrock? On the poem, "The Love Song of J. Alfred Prufrock"?

The following lines are from another Eliot poem, *The Waste Land* (lines 173–202):

> The river's tent is broken: the last fingers of leaf
> Clutch and sink into the wet bank. The wind
> Crosses the brown land, unheard. The nymphs are
>   departed.
> Sweet Thames, run softly, till I end my song.
> The river bears no empty bottles, sandwich papers,   5
> Silk handkerchiefs, cardboard boxes, cigarette ends
> Or other testimony of summer nights. The nymphs are
>   departed.
> And their friends, the loitering heirs of city directors;
> Departed, have left no addresses.
> By the waters of Leman I sat down and wept . . .   10
> Sweet Thames, run softly till I end my song,
> Sweet Thames, run softly, for I speak not loud or long.

But at my back in a cold blast I hear
The rattle of the bones, and chuckle spread from ear to
    ear.
A rat crept softly through the vegetation   *15*
Dragging its slimy belly on the bank
While I was fishing in the dull canal
On a winter evening round behind the gashouse
Musing upon the king my brother's wreck
And on the king my father's death before him.   *20*
White bodies naked on the low damp ground
And bones cast in a little low dry garret,
Rattled by the rat's foot only, year to year.
But at my back from time to time I hear
The sound of horns and motors, which shall bring *25*
Sweeney to Mrs. Porter in the spring.
O the moon shone bright on Mrs. Porter
And on her daughter
They wash their feet in soda water
Et O ces d'enfants, chantant dans la coupole!   *30*

Practically every other line in this single passage is a literary allusion, but we should now be able to recognize at least one. What is it, and how does it help us construct some meaning for the passage?

    By now, we might be led to conclude that poets ask a lot of us in their use of allusions, whatever their sources. They seem to demand a great deal of reading and a wide knowledge of our history and culture. It would be foolish to deny that with poets like Yeats and Eliot, that is precisely the point. To understand their poetry, we must have other experience in literature. Without that experience, such poetry is difficult, but not inaccessible, as we shall see in our discussion of the symbol. Some poets, however, make allusions that we can understand from watching television, listening to the radio, going to the movies, and keeping abreast of contemporary events.

Sylvia Plath   *(1932–1963)*

Daddy

You do not do, you do not do
Any more, black shoe
In which I have lived like a foot
For thirty years, poor and white,
Barely daring to breathe or Achoo.   *5*

Daddy, I have had to kill you.
You died before I had time—
Marble-heavy, a bag full of God,
Ghastly statue with one grey toe
Big as a Frisco seal   *10*

And a head in the freakish Atlantic
Where it pours bean green over blue
In the waters off beautiful Nauset.
I used to pray to recover you.
Ach, du.   *15*

In the German tongue, in the Polish town
Scraped flat by the roller
Of wars, wars, wars.
But the name of the town is common.
My Polack friend   *20*

Says there are a dozen or two.
So I never could tell where you
Put your foot, your root,
I never could talk to you.
The tongue stuck in my jaw.   *25*

It stuck in a barb wire snare.
Ich, ich, ich, ich,
I could hardly speak.
I thought every German was you.
And the language obscene   *30*

An engine, an engine
Chuffing me off like a Jew.
A Jew to Dachau, Auschwitz, Belsen.
I began to talk like a Jew.
I think I may well be a Jew.   *35*

The snows of the Tyrol, the clear beer of Vienna
Are not very pure or true.
With my gypsy ancestress and my weird luck
And my Taroc pack and my Taroc pack
I may be a bit of a Jew.   *40*

I have always been scared of *you*,
With your Luftwaffe, your gobbledygoo.
And your neat moustache
And your Aryan eye, bright blue,
Panzer-man, panzer-man, O You—   *45*

Not God but a swastika
So black no sky could squeak through.
Every woman adores a Fascist,
The boot in the face, the brute
Brute heart of a brute like you.   *50*

You stand at the blackboard, daddy,
In the picture I have of you,
A cleft in your chin instead of your foot
But no less a devil for that, no not
Any less the black man who   *55*

Bit my pretty red heart in two.
I was ten when they buried you.
At twenty I tried to die
And get back, back, back to you.
I thought even the bones would do.   *60*

But they pulled me out of the sack,
And they stuck me together with glue,
And then I knew what to do.
I made a model of you,
A man in black with a Meinkampf look   *65*

And a love of the rack and the screw.
And I said I do, I do.
So daddy, I'm finally through.
The black telephone's off at the root,
The voices just can't worm through.   *70*

If I've killed one man, I've killed two—
The vampire who said he was you
And drank my blood for a year,
Seven years, if you want to know.
Daddy, you can lie back now.   *75*

There's a stake in your fat black heart
And the villagers never liked you.
They are dancing and stamping on you.
They always *knew* it was you.
Daddy, daddy, you bastard, I'm through.   *80*

1. *What is Plath alluding to with her mention of* Dachau, Auschwitz, Belsen? *Identify the other allusions to the same historical events and discuss how they establish a basis of meaning in the poem.*

2. *Plath also talks about* a vampire *and* a stake in your fat black heart. *To what is she alluding? How does that mode of allusion comment upon the other allusions? What do both have to do with the fact that the poem is apparently addressed to her father?*

Imamu Amiri Baraka
(LeRoi Jones; 1934–   )

In Memory of Radio

Who has ever stopped to think of the divinity of Lamont
    Cranston?
(Only Jack Kerouac, that I know of: & me.
The rest of you probably had on WCBS and Kate
    Smith,
Or something equally unattractive.)

What can I say?   5
It is better to have loved and lost
Than to put linoleum in your living rooms?

Am I a sage or something?
Mandrake's hypnotic gesture of the week?
(Remember, I do not have the healing powers of Oral
    Roberts . . .   10
I cannot, like F. J. Sheen, tell you how to get saved &
    rich!
I cannot even order you to gaschamber satori like Hitler
    or Goody Knight

& Love is an evil word.
Turn it backwards/see, what I mean?
An evol word. & besides   15
Who understands it?
I certainly wouldn't like to go out on that kind of limb.

Saturday mornings we listened to *Red Lantern* & his
    undersea folk.
At 11, *Let's Pretend*/& we did/& I, the poet, still do,
    Thank God!

What was it he used to say (after the transformation,
    when he was safe   *20*
& invisible & the unbelievers couldn't throw stones?)
    "Heh, heh, heh,
Who knows what evil lurks in the hearts of men? The
    Shadow knows."

O, yes he does
O, yes he does.
An evil word it is,   *25*
This Love.

Exercises   *1. Baraka makes many open allusions to old radio programs
and to relatively recent celebrities. How many are related to
radio as a vehicle for entertainment? How are the others
connected with radio? How does Baraka use the first group to
comment on the second? What meaning is thus derived from
the poem?*

     *2. Some of Baraka's allusions, though they are all to events in
his own lifetime (within less than the last half century), may
seem as obscure to you as the allusions of Yeats and Eliot.
How do you account for that apparent obscurity? Does
Baraka imply an awareness of such a limitation to his
allusions?*

     If we were to define allusion in poetry now, we might
say that it is any reference in a poem to a piece of information or to an
experience that we as readers may have had. The poet has the right to
assume that the general reader has read parts of the Bible, is familiar with
other works of literature, and knows some bare-bone facts of history. At
the very least, that general reader goes to the movies, watches old movies
on television, listens to the radio, and reads the newspaper. Still, we might
argue, the poet *is* asking a lot, and the general reader is closer to the ideal
than any particular one of us is. There are, however, allusions that require
no more than that we are alive and reasonably well aware of the world
around us. When the poet refers to the sun and the moon, to the seasons,
to flowers and birds, trees, the sea or any number of other natural objects
or occurrences, the poet is, in a manner of speaking, "alluding" to them.
He or she expects us to bring our own experiences of nature to bear to
understand the poem. Because these natural phenomena, like some
historical and biblical figures, are common knowledge, we call them *symbols*
rather than allusions, which sometimes require specialized knowledge. For
our purposes, then, let us call a *symbol* an allusion to something or someone
whose significance has become a part of our common human and cultural
store.

The particular strength of a symbol as a poetic device lies partly in the fact that we do not need to be especially well informed or literary to appreciate it. Furthermore, while the symbol is suggestive, working more on implication (connotation) than explicit meaning (denotation), its strength lies also in our ability to identify it immediately for what it is, whether or not we all agree on its symbolic value or meaning. For example, if we turn back to Yeats's "Long-legged Fly," we find that *the Pope's chapel* and that image of Michael Angelo lying on a scaffold ask us to have some special knowledge of history. We have to know that Pope Julius II commissioned Michael Angelo to paint scenes from providential history on the ceiling of the Sistine Chapel and that Michael Angelo had to set up an elaborate scaffolding to do so. The references to *our master Caesar* and even to *the first Adam*, however, are hardly obscure to us as the inheritors of Judaic and Roman culture. Although those references are equally laden with meaning, that meaning is more symbolic than allusive in quality.

All we really need know to begin to interpret what Yeats means is that *the first Adam* is indeed the first Adam, the Adam of the Garden of Eden. All the significances that come to mind when each of us thinks of the story of Adam and Eve, the Garden, the Tree of the Knowledge of Good and Evil, the Temptation, the Fall, the expulsion from the Garden, and so forth are compacted into the one simple reference; and Yeats can so compress his meaning because Adam is a name immediately identifiable with the story of the Creation. The same holds true for *our master Caesar*. The word *Caesar* has become such a symbol for vast secular authority that both the Germans and Russians have used it as a title for their own secular leaders, the Kaiser and the Czar. With that one reference, Yeats again compresses an unlimited number of potential significances related to worldly power, the glory of kings, the responsibilities of leadership, the bounds of duty and allegiance, and, in addition, the transient nature of all secular states and leaders. Reconsidering Yeats's poem now, we should find its meaning becoming more accessible, though more open-ended as well. Because symbols compact their significances with an incredible intensity, we cannot easily reduce symbolic statement to any neat formulation of meaning, a prose paraphrase. Yeats himself called poetic symbolism "hints too subtle for the intellect," and we would do well to keep Yeats's warning in mind.

Exercises *1. We have discussed* the first Adam *as both allusion and symbol. How does it directly relate to Michael Angelo and the Sistine Chapel?*

2. In view of the foregoing discussion, how might both the long-legged fly and the stream in that poem be regarded as symbols? For what?

William Butler Yeats (1865–1939)

The Second Coming

Turning and turning in the widening gyre
The falcon cannot hear the falconer;
Things fall apart; the center cannot hold;
Mere anarchy is loosed upon the world,
The blood-dimmed tide is loosed, and everywhere   5
The ceremony of innocence is drowned;
The best lack all conviction, while the worst
Are full of passionate intensity.

Surely some revelation is at hand;
Surely the Second Coming is at hand;   10
The Second Coming! Hardly are those words out
When a vast image out of *Spiritus Mundi*
Troubles my sight: somewhere in sands of the desert
A shape with lion body and the head of a man,
A gaze blank and pitiless as the sun,   15
Is moving its slow thighs, while all about it
Reel shadows of the indignant desert birds.
The darkness drops again; but now I know
That twenty centuries of stony sleep
Were vexed to nightmare by a rocking cradle,   20
And what rough beast, its hour come round at last,
Slouches towards Bethlehem to be born?

Exercises   *1. Is "The Second Coming" referred to in this poem an
allusion or a symbol? Or does Yeats use it on both levels. If
so, where and how does its allusive quality become transformed
into a symbolic quality?*

*2. "The Second Coming" is a highly symbolic poem. Select
all the words and word-phrases out of the poem that seem to
imply more than they say or to stand for something else. You
might find yourself reducing the poem to nothing more than
verbs, adverbs, and conjunctions. To begin interpreting the
poem, then, reconstruct the possible significances of each
symbol, first, individually and, second, as they limit each
other.*

Symbols may be more easily identified than allusions,
but symbols trouble us for the very reason that we cannot fasten a single,
particular meaning to them. Still, within any given context, any one symbol
is somewhat limited in its significances by the other symbols within that

same context. Darkness, for example, can signify death, blindness, ignorance, superstition, intellectual intolerance, moral anarchy, and so on, that is, anything that is connotative of the absence of light. In "The Second Coming," however, *the darkness* that will drop again has all those significances and more because of the symbolic richness of that poem, which is filled with so many "hints too subtle for the intellect" that we may never be satisfied with the meaning we assign to it. The following poem is a fine example of how a variety of symbols (literal references with figurative values) also defines and limits the meanings of each other.

John Donne *(1572–1631)*

The Sun Rising

Busy old fool, unruly sun,
Why dost thou thus,
Through windows and through curtains call on us?
Must to thy motions lovers' seasons run?
Saucy pedantic wretch, go chide   5
Late schoolboys and sour prentices,
Go tell court huntsmen that the king will ride,
Call country ants to harvest offices;
Love, all alike, no season knows nor clime,
Nor hours, days, months, which are the rags of
time.   10

Thy beams, so reverend and strong
Why shouldst thou think?
I could eclipse and cloud them with a wink,
But that I would not lose her sight so long;
If her eyes have not blinded thine,   15
Look, and tomorrow late tell me,
Whether both th' Indias of spice and mine
Be where thou left'st them, or lie here with me.
Ask for those kings whom thou saw'st yesterday,
And thou shalt hear, all here in one bed lay.   20

She's all states, and all princes, I,
Nothing else is.
Princes do but play us; compared to this,
All honor's mimic, all wealth alchemy.

Thou, sun, art half as happy as we,   *25*
   In that the world's contracted thus;
Thine age asks ease, and since thy duties be
To warm the world, that's done in warming us.
Shine here to us, and thou art everywhere;
This bed thy center is, these walls, thy sphere.   *30*

Exercises   *1. Though Donne uses the poetic device of* apostrophe *in directly addressing the sun, he means the same bright object that we can see in the sky on any clear day. Still, does the sun in Donne's poem become a symbol? What is it a symbol of? How is it appropriate for Donne's purposes?*

2. Symbols, we should now realize, are always nouns or noun-phrases, that is, objects or persons or creatures or natural actions and occurrences ripe with meaning. It is because poets speak in metaphor *(that is, speak about one noun or object or action in comparison with another) that poetry continually pushes us into the realm of symbolic statement. Donne's metaphors are more familiar than Yeats's, but no less symbolic. Identify them and discuss their symbolic quality.*

Sometimes, too, the poet provides us with a translation, as it were, for the symbols. The poet may at first seem to be merely representing an object or group of objects, but then goes on to say something else that gives those former objects a symbolic quality. We looked at the following poem in the section on metaphor, but it is certainly worth further consideration.

Walt Whitman *(1819–1892)*

A Noiseless Patient Spider

A noiseless patient spider,
I mark'd where on a little promontory it stood isolated,
Mark'd how to explore the vacant vast surrounding,
It launch'd forth filament, filament, filament, out of
    itself,
Ever unreeling them, ever tirelessly speeding them.

And you O my soul where you stand,
Surrounded, detached, in measureless oceans of space,
Ceaselessly musing, venturing, throwing, seeking the
    spheres to connect them,
Till the bridge you will need be form'd, till the ductile
    anchor hold,
Till the gossamer thread you fling catch somewhere, O
    my soul.

Exercises
  1. How does the second stanza of the poem force us to regard the first stanza in a symbolic light? If, for example, the spider *and* promontory *of the first stanza become something more than a spider and a promontory after we have read the second, what do they become? What symbolic values would those two nouns have had without the balance provided by the second stanza?*

2. Study the second stanza closely. Its abstract quality may seem to be a direct statement. But consider words like soul, oceans of space, the bridge, the ductile anchor, *and* the gossamer thread. *How might you regard these words as symbols also?*

3. Whitman's poem is so beautifully structured and conceived that we can reverse the order of the stanzas. How does the symbolic structure of each comment upon and virtually anchor the symbolic structure of the other?

The following poem by Robert Frost (1874–1963) is a further example of how a poet relies on the symbolic or connotative values inherent in all words to imply meaning without foisting a particular meaning upon us.

Design

I found a dimpled spider, fat and white,
On a white heal-all, holding up a moth
Like a white piece of rigid satin cloth—
Assorted characters of death and blight
Mixed ready to begin the morning right,
Like the ingredients of a witches' broth—
A snow-drop spider, a flower like froth,
And dead wings carried like a paper kite.

What had that flower to do with being white,
The wayside blue and innocent heal-all?
What brought the kindred spider to that height,
Then steered the white moth thither in the night?
What but design of darkness to appall?—
If design govern in a thing so small.

Exercises

*1. In the first stanza, Frost uses three similes. How does
each, by equating one object or group of objects with another,
limit the symbolic quality of both sides of the poetic equation?*

*2. By the end of the first stanza, has Frost made us think of
the spider, the flower, and the moth as something more than a
spider, a flower, and a moth? If so, what have they become
in terms of their symbolic significances? Combined, do the
three objects have a greater symbolic quality than each has
separately?*

*3. Discuss the symbolic quality of Frost's darkness in
comparison with Yeats's in "The Second Coming." Discuss
Frost's use of the spider as symbol in comparison with
Whitman's in "A Noiseless Patient Spider." How does each
poet announce a symbolic quality to his statements? One thing
we must decide is whether "assorted characters of blight and
death" in the Frost poem is itself a symbolic statement, or a
direct statement of the meaning he wants us to derive from his
symbols.*

Edmund Spenser (ca. 1552–1599)

Sonnet 81

Fayre is my love, when her fayre golden heares,
With the loose wynd ye waving chance to marke:
Fayre when the rose in her red cheekes appeares,
Or in her eyes the fyre of love does sparke.
Fayre when her brest lyke a rich laden barke,
With pretious merchandize she forth doth lay:
Fayre when that cloud of pryde, which oft doth dark
Her goodly light with smiles she drives away.
But fayrest she, when so she doth display,
The gate with pearles and rubyes richly dight:
Throgh which her words so wise do make their way
To beare the message of her gentle spright.
The rest be works of natures wonderment,
But this the worke of harts astonishment.

William Shakespeare *(1564–1616)*

Sonnet 130

My mistress' eyes are nothing like the sun;
Coral is far more red than her lips' red;
If snow be white, why then her breasts are dun;
If hairs be wires, black wires grow on her head.
I have seen roses damasked, red and white,
But no such roses see I in her cheeks;
And in some perfumes is there more delight
Than in the breath that from my mistress reeks.
I love to hear her speak, yet well I know
That music hath a far more pleasing sound;
I grant I never saw a goddess go;
My mistress, when she walks, treads on the ground.
And yet, by heaven, I think my love as rare
As any she belied with false compare.

William Blake *(1757–1827)*

The Sick Rose

O Rose, thou art sick.
The invisible worm
That flies in the night
In the howling storm

Has found out thy bed
Of crimson joy,
And his dark secret love
Does thy life destroy.

Paul Laurence Dunbar *(1872–1906)*

Promise

I grew a rose within a garden fair,
And, tending it with more than loving care,
I thought how, with the glory of its bloom,
I should the darkness of my life illume;
And, watching, ever smiled to see the lusty bud
Drink freely in the summer sun to tinct its blood.

My rose began to open, and its hue
Was sweet to me as to it sun and dew;
I watched it taking on its ruddy flame
Until the day of perfect blooming came,
Then hasted I with smiles to find it blushing red—
Too late! Some thoughtless child had plucked my rose
    and fled!

John Crowe Ransom *(1888–1974)*

Piazza Piece

—I am a gentleman in a dustcoat trying
To make you hear. Your ears are soft and small
And listen to an old man not at all,
They want the young men's whispering and sighing.
But see the roses on your trellis dying
And hear the spectral singing of the moon;
For I must have my lovely lady soon,
I am a gentleman in a dustcoat trying.

—I am a lady young in beauty waiting
Until my truelove comes, and then we kiss.
But what gray man among the vines is this
Whose words are dry and faint as in a dream?
Back from my trellis, Sir, before I scream!
I am a lady young in beauty waiting.

William Carlos Williams *(1883–1963)*

The Rose

The rose is obsolete
but each petal ends in
an edge, the double facet
cementing the grooved
columns of air—The edge   *5*
cuts without cutting
meets—nothing—renews
itself in metal or porcelain—

wither? It ends—

But if it ends   *10*
the start is begun
so that to engage roses
becomes a geometry—

Sharper, neater, more cutting
figured in majolica—   *15*
the broken plate
glazed with a rose

Somewhere the sense
makes copper roses
steel roses—   *20*

The rose carried weight of love
but love is at an end—of roses
It is at the edge of the
petal that love waits

Crips, worked to defeat   *25*
laboredness—fragile
plucked, moist, half-raised
cold, precise, touching

What

The place between the petal's   *30*
edge and the

From the petal's edge a line starts
that being of steel
infinitely fine, infinitely
rigid penetrates   *35*

the Milky Way
without contact—lifting
from it—neither hanging
nor pushing—

The fragility of the flower   40
unbruised
penetrates space.

Exercise   *The rose is one of the most common poetic symbols in our culture
and one of the most enduring. Readers have not become tired of
hearing about roses, however, only because of the awareness of
good poets that the rose can fade just as surely as a poetic
symbol as the real flower can. Put simply, any symbol, because
its value rests in its commonality, can be overused. Thus, what
was once a discovery of vivid resemblances can lose its freshness
and vitality. In the actual beauty of the rose, its fragrance, its
fragility, its need for care and cultivation, its short life, and
even its protective thorns, poets have always found symbolic
equivalents to the facts of human youth and beauty, life and
love and death. Each of the preceding six poems presents us
with a rose; they are arranged chronologically. Having read
them as a unit, consider how each poet uses the rose as a
symbol. Does he use it in its traditional symbolic function, or
does he play games with that function? Does he deal with the
rose on a literal level, letting your awareness of its symbolic
qualities act upon you? Does he make you confront it as a
symbol, but then try to make you see new dimensions to its
enduring symbolic qualities? (The poems may be examined
profitably for other symbols as well.)*

Topics for   *1. Compare and contrast any two of the above poets' uses of the*
Writing   *rose as symbol.*

*2. Discuss how Eliot's use of Marvell in "The Love Song of J.
Alfred Prufrock" comments on Prufrock's character and his
possible dilemma.*

*3. Explicate either of the Yeats poems, using the symbolic
structure to determine meaning.*

*4. Compare and contrast Whitman's "A Noiseless Patient
Spider" and Frost's "Design," focusing on the symbolic value
each poet assigns to the spider.*

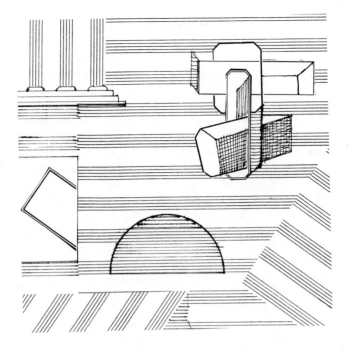

8 The Scheme of Meaning

"If *that's* what he meant, why didn't he say it?" Once a poem has been interpreted for us, this complaint is commonly leveled at a poet. What we never stop to consider is that perhaps *that* is not what the poet *meant* at all, nor do we consider that even if *that* is what was *meant*, the poet may have meant many other things as well and may have wanted to achieve many other effects besides a strictly intellectual one. We tend to regard the intellect as something apart from feelings and emotions, yet as we have seen in earlier chapters, poetry appeals to our senses and to our love of rhythm and musical harmony as much as it appeals to our logical minds. Finally, too, and in ways that are often difficult to talk about, it appeals to our feelings and our emotions. It can arouse us and depress us, cheer us up and agitate us, lull us into a sense of serenity, stir us, anger us, frustrate us. Not all of these effects are reducible to statements of meaning, and at this juncture we would be wise to recall Eliot's statement that meaning in poetry is intended to distract us while the poem does its work.

However, even with this kind of meaning, the poet can be a trickster who involves our minds on levels deeper than the purely intellectual. Poets love games, and because their medium is words, they especially love word games. We as readers want our meanings, and poets will provide them for us if we work hard enough. Still, as we saw in Chapter 7, after we have done all our work, how can we really be sure that the meaning we arrive at is the meaning intended? In point of fact, we cannot. Robert Frost says as much when he remarks that poetry is "the one permissible way of saying one thing and meaning another." Some poets go out of their way to do just that, and when they do we as readers have been moved into the cloudy realm of *irony*, *paradox*, and *ambiguity*. There we can become confused and frustrated until we find ourselves agitated into trying to make sense of something that seems to refuse to make sense. At such times we should really be reminded that even something as prosaic as meaning—a nice, pat, logical statement—is, in poetry, transformed into something rich and strange. Once we accept as much, we can begin to enjoy the aesthetic qualities of meaning in poetry, for poetry overlays everything, including our logical minds, with emotions and feelings.

The following poem is an innocuously pretty love lyric:

Christopher Marlowe *(1564–1593)*

The Passionate Shepherd to His Love

Come live with me and be my love,
And we will all the pleasures prove
That valleys, groves, hills, and fields,
Woods, or steepy mountain yields.

And we will sit upon the rocks,   5
Seeing the shepherds feed their flocks,
By shallow rivers to whose falls
Melodious birds sing madrigals.

And I will make thee beds of roses
And a thousand fragrant posies,   10
A cap of flowers, and a kirtle
Embroidered all with leaves of myrtle;

A gown made of the finest wool
Which from our pretty lambs we pull;
Fair lined slippers for the cold,   *15*
With buckles of the purest gold;

A belt of straw and ivy buds,
With coral clasps and amber studs:
And if these pleasures may thee move,
Come live with me, and be my love.   *20*

The shepherd swains shall dance and sing
For thy delight each May morning:
If these delights thy mind may move,
Then live with me and be my love.

We ought to feel that we would be belaboring the
obvious to interpret the meaning of Marlowe's poem. It is written in a
mode called *the pastoral*, which presumes that a summertime innocence can
be found in the lives that shepherds live. This particular shepherd promises
his love all sorts of pastoral delights to prove to her his love. If we find the
poem a bit too ideally idyllic, so did one of Marlowe's contemporaries, the
English explorer Sir Walter Raleigh, who wrote a poem of his own in
answer to Marlowe's shepherd.

Sir Walter Raleigh   *(ca. 1552–1618)*

The Nymph's Reply to the Shepherd

If all the world and love were young,
And truth in every shepherd's tongue,
These pretty pleasures might me move
To live with thee and be thy love.

Time drives the flocks from field to fold,   *5*
When rivers rage and rocks grow cold,
And Philomel becometh dumb;
The rest complains of cares to come.

The flowers do fade, and wanton fields
To wayward winter reckoning yields;   *10*
A honey tongue, a heart of gall,
Is fancy's spring, but sorrow's fall.

Thy gowns, thy shoes, thy beds of roses,
Thy cap, thy kirtle, and thy posies
Soon break, soon wither, soon forgotten—   *15*
In folly ripe, in reason rotten.

Thy belt of straw and ivy buds,
Thy coral clasps and amber studs,
All these in me no means can move
To come to thee and be thy love.   *20*

But could youth last and love still breed,
Had joys no date nor age no need,
Then these delights my mind might move
To live with thee and be thy love.

Offered an eternal summer of youth and love, Raleigh's
nymph reminds Marlowe's shepherd of the facts of life. Flowers fade,
winter comes, everything withers—including love and love's golden promise, the lover's promises. If we know the Marlowe poem, then the Raleigh
poem is for one thing an allusion and, paired with the Marlowe poem, an
ironic counterpoint to it. That is to say, for everything Marlowe's shepherd
promises, Raleigh's nymph counters with an opposite. The poem begins
with the statement "If all the world and love were young,/And truth in
every shepherd's tongue," but then goes on to prove that the world and
love are not young and, therefore, that shepherds are liars like everyone
else.

In the last stanza, however, hope is held out to the
shepherd:

But could youth last and love still breed
Had joys no date nor age no need,
Then these delights my mind might move
To live with thee and be thy love.

Here, then, we encounter an apparent paradox. Because the rest of the
poem has already shown us that the conditions of those first two lines are an
earthly impossibility, the nymph's own closing promise—the conditions on
which she will be the shepherd's love—is an absurdity. But the paradox is
only apparent, because its absurdity is just the point: the promises of love
are themselves absurdities, which make no sense in the real world. The
irony of the Raleigh poem compounds itself into paradox only to make that
paradox a part of the irony. One part of the poem contradicts the other
while at the same time the entire poem is contradicting Marlowe's, and all
we come out with at the end is a sense of the wide gap between the high
hopes of human aspirations and the cold realities of mortal experiences.

But now let us return to the Marlowe poem. We could
argue that whenever a poet is openly speaking in a voice clearly identified as
one other than his own, he may be speaking ironically. That is to say, in no
way can we call Christopher Marlowe the speaker in this poem: he has
clearly masked himself as a "passionate shepherd." Christopher Marlowe
was many things—a poet, a playwright, a secret agent, but he was never a
shepherd. Of course, the pastoral mode requires that the poet pretend to

be a shepherd, and Raleigh admits as much when he has the nymph reply to *the Shepherd*, not to Kit Marlowe.

Still, if we read the Marlowe poem very carefully, we may begin to suspect that Marlowe is as aware of the actual world's shortcomings as Raleigh's nymph would like the shepherd to be. For one obvious thing, the world the shepherd speaks of is carefully circumscribed to include only "valleys, groves, hills, and fields,/ Woods or steepy mountains." It may be a small point, but a great deal of the world—seas, deserts, cities, jungles—is left out. Again, however, the omission is in keeping with the pastoral mode. Who ever heard of a shepherd in a city or on the seas? But as we read on, we find another indication that the shepherd is something of a realist: he promises his love *fair lined slippers for the cold.* So, then, there is winter in this ideal world of his. While we cannot be sure the shepherd is aware of the implications of what he is saying, can we be sure that Marlowe is not? *A gown made of the finest wool* is also promised the nymph, but only at the expense of those *pretty lambs* whose wool will be pulled off. Pain and cold for them? Perhaps. And at the conclusion of the poem, when the shepherd promises that "swains shall dance and sing/For thy delight each May morning," a further question may come to mind. Although in another part of the pastoral convention May is the month of love, it is likely that a nymph as realistic as Raleigh's would catch the implication: What about the other 334 days of the year? Can we be sure that Marlowe was any less aware of his own poetry's implications? We cannot, of course, nor can we ask Christopher Marlowe his intentions.

What we can do is assign the discrepancies we have found to the nature of *ambiguity*: several possible meanings are implied within the same statement, and each meaning seems to expand on if not contradict the other. Like an optical illusion, the poem's meaning changes depending on how we look at it. Notice how this device is different from *irony*, when a statement is made that clearly means something else, and *paradox*, when a statement puzzles us by the very fact that it seems to be both sense and nonsense simultaneously. With paradox, indeed, its truth rests in its absurdity and our emotional struggle to force the apparently absurd to make logical sense.

All this has introduced you to three terms whose precise meanings are as elusive as the tricks of words and the mind from which they come. For example, the statements in Raleigh's poem are not in themselves ironic; they are ironic only in the context of Marlowe's poem, and that irony is compounded when we encounter the paradoxical about-face (which is only an apparent one) at the end of the Raleigh poem. The point to remember is that the more ambivalent the poet is about the true nature of the state of the world and man's and woman's place in it, the more the poet must function in irony, paradox, and ambiguity. As poetic devices, all they tell us is that the poet does not want us to be sure either. Instead, we are puzzled into the same sense of uncertainty, and that uncertainty of meaning can have as much emotional impact as a well-struck image or a startling metaphor. That is how meaning in poetry differs from meaning in expository prose: the further we look into the meaning of a poem, the less the poem allows us easy answers, and at its best it may actually force us to ask questions of ourselves and of our world.

Exercise   *Consider the fact that while* nymph *refers to a lovely woman, it can also refer to an immortal female spirit, particularly in the pastoral mode. Does that fact further confuse the issue behind Raleigh's "Reply"? Can we account for any confusions with one or more of the three devices currently being considered? (You might want to consult the Oxford English Dictionary for the various meanings that* nymph *had in Raleigh's time.)*

Because the religious impulse is usually a mixture of faith and doubt, religious poetry is especially ripe with an emotional ambivalence of statement disguised as meaning. Read the next three poems with this in mind.

John Donne *(1572–1631)*

Hymn to God My God, in My Sickness

Since I am coming to that holy room
    Where, with Thy choir of saints for evermore,
I shall be made Thy music; as I come
    I tune the instrument here at the door,
    And what I must do then, think here before.   *5*

Whilst my physicians by their love are grown
    Cosmographers, and I their map, who lie
Flat on this bed, that by them may be shown
    That this is my southwest discovery
    Per fretum febris, by these straits to die,   *10*

I joy, that in these straits, I see my West;
    For, though their currents yield return to none,
What shall my West hurt me? As West and East
    In all flat maps (and I am one) are one,
    So death doth touch the resurrection.   *15*

Is the Pacific Sea my home? Or are
    The Eastern riches? Is Jerusalem?
Anyan, and Mágellan, and Gíbraltar,
    All straits, and none but straits, are ways to them,
    Whether where Japhet dwelt, or Cham, or
    Shem.   *20*

We think that Paradise and Calvary,
  Christ's cross, and Adam's tree, stood in one place;
Look, Lord, and find both Adams met in me;
  As the first Adam's sweat surrounds my face,
  May the last Adam's blood my soul embrace.   *25*

So, in his purple wrapped, receive me, Lord;
  By these his thorns give me his other crown;
And, as to others' souls I preached Thy word,
  Be this my text, my sermon to mine own:
  Therefore that he may raise the Lord throws
  down.   *30*

Exercises   *1. How does Donne explain the paradox "death doth touch the resurrection"? You might first decide whether or not that statement is paradoxical.*

2. Is there irony in the question "Is the Pacific Sea my home?" Think of the metaphor Donne has established and of the word play often associated with ambiguity and irony.

3. The final line of the poem is irony that becomes paradox, and there is an ambiguity in the pronoun he. *What are the possible meanings that can be assigned to that single line? How are we prepared for that verse's conundrum by the entire last two stanzas, especially the paradox that* both Adams met in me?

4. In his purple wrapped? Whose purple? How wrapped? What purple? Can any of those questions be answered with a single definite response?

George Herbert   *(1593–1633)*

Virtue

Sweet day, so cool, so calm, so bright,
  The bridal of the earth and sky:
The dew shall weep thy fall tonight;
  For thou must die.

Sweet rose, whose hue, angry and brave,   *5*
  Bids the rash gazer wipe his eye:
Thy root is ever in its grave,
  And thou must die.

Sweet spring, full of sweet days and roses,
   A box where sweets compacted lie;   *10*
My music shows ye have your closes,
      And all must die.

Only a sweet and virtuous soul,
   Like seasoned timber, never gives;
But though the whole world turn to coal,   *15*
      Then chiefly lives.

Exercises   *1. How is it virtually a literal statement, once we account for the word play, that "the dew shall weep thy fall tonight"?*

2. Follow the development of the poem from stanza one through three. There is a clear pattern in the way the statement enlarges. What is that pattern? How does that pattern create ambiguity in the line "A box where sweets compacted lie"?

3. By the time Herbert calls the soul seasoned timber, *has he established an undertone of irony and paradox that virtually makes the statement true? What patterns of irony and paradox give the poem's final paradox—for the soul to live the world must die—a logic we cannot easily resist?*

Ben Jonson   *(1573–1637)*

A Hymn to God the Father

Hear me, O God!
A broken heart,
Is my best part;
Use still thy rod,
That I may prove   *5*
Therein thy love.

If thou hadst not
Been stern to me,
But left me free,
I had forgot   *10*
Myself and thee.

For sin's so sweet,
As minds ill bent
Rarely repent,
Until they meet   *15*
Their punishment.

Who more can crave
Than thou hast done,
That gav'st a Son,
To free a slave?   *20*
First made of naught,
With all since bought.

Sin, Death, and Hell,
His glorious Name
Quite overcame,   *25*
Yet I rebel,
And slight the same.

But I'll come in
Before my loss
Me farther toss,   *30*
As sure to win
Under his Cross.

Exercises   *1. Identify and discuss the paradox in the first stanza.*

2. Identify the allusion in the final stanza. How is there irony, and paradox then, in the words loss *and* toss? *The notion of winning something is double-edged as well. How? First you must determine how someone can paradoxically win and lose at the same time.*

Evidently, irony, paradox, and ambiguity are the devices by which the poet can pretend to provide a logical meaning to matters that otherwise remain mysterious and fraught with emotion. But because that logic is only apparent and is actually paradoxical, it is a meaning that arouses our feelings and emotions as surely as it tricks our minds.

Ben Jonson (1573–1637)

An Epitaph on Master Philip Gray

Reader, stay,
And if I had no more to say,
But here doth lie till the Last Day
All that is left of Philip Gray,
It might thy patience richly pay:
For if such men as he could die,
What surety of life have thou, and I?

Exercises *1. How might Jonson's epitaph richly pay our patience? Look for a pun on patience.*

2. How does the final couplet of the poem present an absurd situation? What emotion is aroused if you try to resolve that absurdity?

Not only the nature of love, or our religious strivings, or the mystery of death, which are all personal dilemmas, can be treated by the poet through irony and paradox; so too can social conditions. Regard the following pair of poems by William Blake (1757–1827).

Holy Thursday [I]

'Twas on a Holy Thursday, their innocent faces clean,
The children walking two & two, in red & blue & green,
Grey headed beadles walkd before with wands as white
    as snow,
Till into the high dome of Paul's they like Thames'
    waters flow.

O what a multitude they seemd, these flowers of
    London town!
Seated in companies they sit with radiance all their own.
The hum of multitudes was there, but multitudes of
    lambs,
Thousands of little boys & girls raising their innocent
    hands.

Now like a mighty wind they raise to heaven the voice
    of song,
Or like harmonious thunderings the seats of heaven
    among.
Beneath them sit the aged men, wise guardians of the
    poor;
Then cherish pity, lest you drive an angel from your
    door.

Holy Thursday [II]

Is this a holy thing to see,
In a rich and fruitful land,
Babes reducd to misery,
Fed with cold and usurous hand?

Is that trembling cry a song?   5
Can it be a song of joy?
And so many children poor?
It is a land of poverty!

And their sun does never shine,
And their fields and bleak & bare,   10
And their ways are fill'd with thorns;
It is eternal winter there.

For where-e'er the sun does shine,
And where-e'er rain does fall,
Babe can never hunger there,   15
Nor poverty the mind appall.

Exercises   *1. Once you have read "Holy Thursday [II]," can you ever
read "Holy Thursday [I]" again without catching a tongue-
in-cheek tone throughout it? Is that tone actually in the poem,
or is it the result of your having read the second poem in the
pair? For one thing, who are the* grey headed beadles *and
what are their* wands as white as snow?

*2. How does the final stanza of "Holy Thursday [II]" make
a straightforward statement that becomes ironical and paradoxical in the context of the entire poem?*

Percy Bysshe Shelley *(1792–1822)*

Ozymandias

I met a traveler from an antique land
Who said: Two vast and trunkless legs of stone
Stand in the desert . . . Near them, on the sand,
Half sunk, a shattered visage lies, whose frown,
And wrinkled lip, and sneer of cold command,
Tell that its sculptor well those passions read
Which yet survive, stamped on these lifeless things,
The hand that mocked them, and the heart that fed:
And on the pedestal these words appear:
"My name is Ozymandias, king of kings:
Look on my works, ye Mighty, and despair!"
Nothing beside remains. Round the decay
Of that colossal wreck, boundless and bare
The lone and level sands stretch far away.

1. What did Ozymandias mean by those words carved on the pedestal of his statue? What do those words mean so far as the "traveler from an antique land" is concerned?

2. How, in a sense, did the sculptor have the last laugh on Ozymandias? Shall something have a last laugh even on the sculptor? What paradox does the poem finally present?

Shelley purposely established a series of boxes within boxes in "Ozymandias": the speaker of the poem is telling us what the traveler told him, and the traveler has told him what it says on the base of the statue and what the scene around it looks like. But those words were ordered carved on the monument by Ozymandias centuries before when the surrounding scene no doubt looked different. The poem becomes a comment on the nature of irony in poetry: what people say in one context may come back to mock them centuries later, removed from the original context.

Robert Browning (1812–1889), through the device of the dramatic monologue, used a man's words in a similar way, but we are made to imagine the man in a live situation.

Andrea del Sarto
Called "The Faultless Painter"

But do not let us quarrel any more,
No, my Lucrezia; bear with me for once:
Sit down and all shall happen as you wish.
You turn your face, but does it bring your heart?
I'll work then for your friend's friend, never fear,   5
Treat his own subject after his own way,
Fix his own time, accept too his own price,
And shut the money into this small hand
When next it takes mine. Will it? tenderly?
Oh, I'll content him—but tomorrow, Love!   10
I often am much wearier than you think,
This evening more than usual, and it seems
As if—forgive now—should you let me sit
Here by the window with your hand in mine
And look a half-hour forth on Fiesole,   15
Both of one mind, as married people use,
Quietly, quietly the evening through
I might get up tomorrow to my work
Cheerful and fresh as ever. Let us try.
Tomorrow, how you shall be glad for this!   20
Your soft hand is a woman of itself,

And mine the man's bared breast she curls inside.
Don't count the time lost, neither; you must serve
For each of the five pictures we require:
It saves a model. So! keep looking so—   25
My serpenting beauty, rounds on rounds!
—How could you ever prick those perfect ears,
Even to put the pearl there! oh, so sweet—
My face, my moon, my everybody's moon,
Which everybody looks on and calls his,   30
And, I suppose, is looked on by in turn,
While she looks—no one's: very dear, no less.
You smile? why, there's my picture ready made,
There's what we painters call our harmony!
A common grayness silvers everything,   35
All in a twilight, you and I alike
—You, at the point of your first pride in me
(That's gone you know)—but I, at every point;
My youth, my hope, my art, being all toned down
To yonder sober pleasant Fiesole.   40
There's the bell clinking from the chapel-top;
That length of convent-wall across the way
Holds the trees safer, huddled more inside;
The last monk leaves the garden; days decrease,
And autumn grows, autumn in everything.   45
Eh? the whole seems to fall into a shape
As if I saw alike my work and self
And all that I was born to be and do,
A twilight-piece. Love, we are in God's hand.
How strange now, looks the life he makes us lead; 50
So free we seem, so fettered fast we are!
I feel he laid the fetter: let it lie!
This chamber for example—turn your head—
All that's behind us! You don't understand
Nor care to understand about my art,   55
But you can hear at least when people speak:
And that cartoon, the second from the door
—It is the thing, Love! so such things should be—
Behold Madonna! I am bold to say.
I can do with my pencil what I know,   60
What I see, what at bottom of my heart
I wish for, if I ever wish so deep—
Do easily, too—when I say, perfectly,
I do not boast, perhaps: yourself are judge,
Who listened to the Lagate's talk last week,   65
And just as much they used to say in France.
At any rate 'tis easy, all of it!

No sketches first, no studies, that's long past:
I do what many dream of, all their lives,
—Dream? strive to do, and agonize to do,   70
And fail in doing. I could count twenty such
On twice your fingers, and not leave this town,
Who strive—you don't know how the others strive
To paint a little thing like that you smeared
Carelessly passing with your robes afloat—   75
Yet do much less, so much less, Someone says,
(I know his name, no matter)—so much less!
Well, less is more, Lucrezia: I am judged.
There burns a truer light of God in them,
In their vexed beating stuffed and stopped-up brain, 80
Heart, or whate'er else, than goes on to prompt
This low-pulsed forthright craftsman's hand of mine.
Their works drop groundward, but themselves, I know,
Reach many a time a heaven that's shut to me,
Enter and take their place there sure enough,   85
Though they come back and cannot tell the world.
My works are nearer heaven, but I sit here.
The sudden blood of these men! at a word—
Praise them, it boils, or blame them, it boils too.
I, painting from myself and to myself,   90
Know what I do, am unmoved by men's blame
Or their praise either. Somebody remarks
Morello's outline there is wrongly traced,
His hue mistaken; what of that? or else,
Rightly traced and well ordered; what of that?   95
Speak as they please, what does the mountain care?
Ah, but a man's reach should exceed his grasp,
Or what's a heaven for? All is silver-gray
Placid and perfect with my art: the worse!
I know both what I want and what might gain,   100
And yet how profitless to know, to sigh
"Had I been two, another and myself,
Our head would have o'erlooked the world!"
     No doubt.
Yonder's a work now, of that famous youth
The Urbinate who died five years ago.   105
('Tis copied, George Vasari sent it me.)
Well, I can fancy how he did it all,
Pouring his soul, with kings and popes to see,
Reaching, that heaven might so replenish him,
Above and through his art—for it gives way;   110
That arm is wrongly put—and there again—
A fault to pardon in the drawing's lines,

Its body, so to speak: its soul is right,
He means right—that, a child may understand.
Still, what an arm! and I could alter it: 115
But all the play, the insight and the stretch—
Out of me, out of me! And wherefore out?
Had you enjoined them on me, given me soul,
We might have risen to Rafael, I and you!
Nay, Love, you did give all I asked, I think—   120
More than I merit, yes, by many times.
But had you—oh, with the same perfect brow,
And perfect eyes, and more than perfect mouth,
And the low voice my soul hears, as a bird
The fowler's pipe, and follows to the snare—   125
Had you, with these the same, but brought a mind!
Some women do so. Had the mouth there urged
"God and the glory! never care for gain.
The present by the future, what is that?
Live for fame, side by side with Agnolo!   130
"Rafael is waiting: up to God, all three!"
I might have done it for you. So it seems:
Perhaps not. All is as God over-rules.
Beside, incentives come from the soul's self;
The rest avail not. Why do I need you?   135
What wife had Rafael, or has Agnolo?
In this world, who can do a thing, will not;
And who would do it, cannot, I perceive:
Yet the will's somewhat—somewhat, too, the power—
And thus we half-men struggle. At the end,   140
God, I conclude, compensates, punishes.
'Tis safer for me, if the award be strict,
That I am something underrated here,
Poor this long while, despised, to speak the truth.
I dared not, do you know, leave home all day,   145
For fear of chancing on the Paris lords.
The best is when they pass and look aside;
But they speak sometimes; I must bear it all.
Well may they speak! That Francis, that first time,
And that long festal year at Fontainebleau!   150
I surely then could sometimes leave the ground,
Put on the glory, Rafael's daily wear,
In that humane great monarch's golden look—
One finger in his beard or twisted curl
Over his mouth's good mark that made the smile, 155
One arm about my shoulder, round my neck,
The jingle of his gold chain in my ear,
I painting proudly with his breath on me,

All his court round him, seeing with his eyes,
Such frank French eyes, and such a fire of souls   *160*
Profuse, my hand kept plying by those hearts—
And, best of all, this, this, this face beyond,
This in the background, waiting on my work,
To crown the issue with a last reward!
A good time, was it not, my kingly days?   *165*
And had you not grown restless . . . but I know—
'Tis done and past; 'twas right, my instinct said;
Too live the life grew, golden and not gray,
And I'm the weak-eyed bat no sun should tempt
Out of the grange whose four walls make his world.*170*
How could it end in any other way?
You called me, and I came home to your heart.
The triumph was—to reach and stay there; since
I reached it ere the triumph, what is lost?
Let my hands frame your face in your hair's gold,   *175*
You beautiful Lucrezia that are mine!
"Rafael did this, Andrea painted that;
The Roman's is the better when you pray,
But still the other's Virgin was his wife—"
Men will excuse me. I am glad to judge   *180*
Both pictures in your presence; clearer grows
My better fortune, I resolve to think.
For, do you know, Lucrezia, as God lives,
Said one day Agnolo, his very self,
To Rafael . . . I have known it all these years . . . *185*
(When the young man was flaming out his thoughts
Upon a palace-wall for Rome to see,
Too lifted up in heart because of it)
"Friend, there's a certain sorry little scrub
Goes up and down our Florence, none cares how, *190*
Who, were he set to plan and execute
As you are, pricked on by your popes and kings,
Would bring the sweat into that brow of yours!"
To Rafael's! And indeed the arm is wrong.
I hardly dare . . . yet, only you to see,   *195*
Give the chalk here—quick, thus the line should go!
Ay, but the soul! he's Rafael! rub it out!
Still, all I care for, if he spoke the truth,
(What he? why, who but Michel Agnolo?
Do you forget already words like those?)   *200*
If really there was such a chance, so lost,
Is, whether you're—not grateful—but more pleased.
Well, let me think so. And you smile indeed!
This hour has been an hour! Another smile?

If you would sit thus by me every night   205
I should work better, do you comprehend?
I mean that I should earn more, give you more.
See, it is settled dusk now; there's a star;
Morello's gone, the watch-lights show the wall,
The cue-owls speak the name we call them by.   210
Come from the window, love—come in, at last,
Inside the melancholy little house
We built to be so gay with. God is just.
King Francis may forgive me: oft at nights
When I look up from painting, eyes tired out,   215
The walls become illumined, brick from brick
Distinct, instead of mortar, fierce bright gold,
That gold of his I did cement them with!
Let us but love each other. Must you go?
That Cousin here again? he waits outside?   220
Must see you—you, and not with me? Those loans?
More gaming debts to pay? you smiled for that?
Well, let smiles buy me! have you more to spend?
While hand and eye and something of a heart
Are left me, work's my ware, and what's it worth? 225
I'll pay my fancy. Only let me sit
The gray remainder of the evening out,
Idle, you call it, and muse perfectly
How I could paint, were I but back in France,
One picture, just one more—the Virgin's face,   230
Not yours this time! I want you at my side
To hear them—that is, Michel Agnolo—
Judge all I do and tell you of its worth.
Will you? Tomorrow, satisfy your friend.
I take the subjects for his corridor,   235
Finish the portrait out of hand—there, there,
And throw him in another thing or two
If he demurs; the whole should prove enough
To pay for this same Cousin's freak. Beside,
What's better and what's all I care about,   240
Get you the thirteen scudi for the ruff!
Love, does that please you? Ah, but what does he,
The Cousin! what does he to please you more?
        I am grown peaceful as old age tonight.
I regret little, I would change still less.   245
Since there my past life lies, why alter it?
The very wrong to Francis! it is true
I took his coin, was tempted and complied,
And built this house and sinned, and all is said.
My father and my mother died of want.   250

Well, had I riches of my own? you see
How one gets rich! Let each one bear his lot.
They were born poor, lived poor, and poor they died:
And I have labored somewhat in my time
And not been paid profusely. Some good son   *255*
Paint my two hundred pictures—let him try!
No doubt, there's something strikes a balance. Yes,
You loved me quite enough, it seems tonight.
This must suffice me here. What would one have?
In heaven, perhaps, new chances, one more chance—
Four great walls in the New Jerusalem,   *261*
Meted on each side by the angel's reed,
For Leonard, Rafael, Agnolo and me
To cover—the three first without a wife,
While I have mine! So—still they overcome   *265*
Because there's still Lucrezia—as I choose.

Again the Cousin's whistle! Go, my Love.

Exercises   *1. "Andrea del Sarto" works on the principle of dramatic irony. The more the man talks about himself, the more we become aware of a situation of which he is not aware. What do you perceive to be del Sarto's value? What does he have pride in? How does he view the love of his wife Lucrezia? Does del Sarto's view of himself, his life's work, and his marriage jibe with what Browning suggests is the real situation? What might that real situation be?*

2. "Ah, but a man's reach should exceed his grasp,/Or what's a heaven for?" Now that you know who said that often-quoted aphorism and in what context it was said, what do you think of it as words of wisdom? Did Browning intend them that way?

3. Who is Lucrezia's Cousin?

Poets use irony, ambiguity, and paradox, then, to modulate meaning as surely as organists modulate sounds with the stops on the organ. Note, however, that we are not now talking about the sound of poetry, but about its sense. Yet that sense comes through a mode of sound, which we call *voice*, the tone of voice the poet uses in writing his poem. Obviously we do not hear the tone of the poet's voice; we feel it. Sometimes, like a mimic, the poet uses a variety of voices to create an irony of tone.

Thomas Hardy *(1840–1928)*

Ah, are you digging on my grave?

"Ah, are you digging on my grave,
　　My loved one?—planting rue?"
—"No: yesterday he went to wed
One of the brightest wealth has bred.
'It cannot hurt her now,' he said,　　　　　　*5*
　　'That I should not be true.'"

"Then who is digging on my grave?
　　My nearest dearest kin?"
—"Ah, no: they sit and think, 'What use!
What good will planting flowers produce?　　*10*
No tendance of her mound can loose
　　Her spirit from Death's gin.'"

"But some one digs upon my grave?
　　My enemy?—prodding sly?"
—"Nay: When she heard you had passed the Gate　*15*
That shuts on all flesh soon or late,
She thought you no more worth her hate,
　　And cares not where you lie."

"Then, who is digging on my grave?
　　Say—since I have not guessed!"　　　　　　*20*
—"O it is I, my mistress dear,
Your little dog, who still lives near,
And much I hope my movements here
　　Have not disturbed your rest?"

"Ah, yes! *You* dig upon my grave . . .　　　　*25*
　　Why flashed it not on me
That one true heart was left behind!
What feeling do we ever find
To equal among human kind
　　A dog's fidelity!"　　　　　　　　　　　　*30*

"Mistress, I dug upon your grave
　　To bury a bone, in case
I should be hungry near this spot
When passing on my daily trot.
I am sorry, but I quite forgot　　　　　　　　*35*
　　It was your resting-place."

1. How many voices are at work in this poem? How does the poem play those voices one against another to build toward one meaning and then undercut it.

2. The premise of this poem is so unobtrusive that we barely notice its absurdity. What is that premise? How is it absurd? How does the poet play on our emotions to reduce that absurdity to something of a truth?

The poet can also use his or her own lyric voice, but in a manner so intense that we find ourselves caught up by the force of intensely personal emotions.

Gerard Manley Hopkins *(1844–1889)*

No worst, there is none

No worst, there is none. Pitched past pitch of grief,
More pangs will, schooled at forepangs, wilder wring.
Comforter, where, where is your comforting?
Mary, mother of us, where is your relief?
My cries heave, herds-long; huddle in a main, a chief-
woe, world-sorrow; on an age-old anvil wince and
    sing—
Then lull, then leave off. Fury had shrieked 'No ling-
ering! Let me be fell: force I must be brief'.
O the mind, mind has mountains; cliffs of fall
Frightful, sheer, no-man-fathomed. Hold them cheap
May who ne'er hung there. Nor does long our small
Durance deal with that steep or deep. Here! creep,
Wretch, under a comfort serves in a whirlwind: all
Life death does end and each day dies with sleep.

Exercises *1. How does Hopkins play on the words* comforter, com-
forting, *and* comfort *until the final line transforms a fact (life ends in death) into a figurative statement (sleep is like death) into a spiritual truth? Is this irony, ambiguity, or paradox?*

2. Hopkins' poetry is difficult to "understand" unless we catch the tone his words establish. Read the poem out loud for its actual effect on the ear. Does the poem make more sense when you actually hear rather than read its voice?

The poet, too, can establish an irony of tone by speaking in a voice we are all too familiar with and thus often do not hear as well as we ought to.

e. e. cummings *(1894–1962)*

"next to of course god america i

"next to of course god america i
love you land of the pilgrims' and so forth oh
say can you see by the dawn's early my
country 'tis of centuries come and go
and are no more what of it we should worry
in every language even deafanddumb
thy sons acclaim your glorious name by gorry
by jingo by gee by gosh by gum
why talk of beauty what could be more beautiful than these heroic happy dead
who rushed like lions to the roaring slaughter
they did not stop to think they died instead
then shall the voice of liberty be mute?"

He spoke. And drank rapidly a glass of water

Exercises   *1. What voice is cummings mimicking here? How does he make that voice sound ridiculous? Does the speaker think he sounds ridiculous? What is the effect of the final line of the poem?*

2. Students love cummings because he uses no punctuation and capitalization and gets away with it. In this particular poem, how does the lack of those typographical indicators comment on the speaker? Who else does "not stop to think"? How can we tell?

Sometimes the poet speaks in a voice so urbane and conversational—or colloquial—that we listen for the pleasure of it, wondering all the while what the point is.

W. H. Auden *(1907–1973)*

Musée des Beaux Arts

About suffering they were never wrong,
The Old Masters: how well they understood
Its human position; how it takes place
While someone else is eating or opening a window or
    just walking dully along;
How, when the aged are reverently, passionately wait-
    ing   5
For the miraculous birth, there always must be
Children who did not specially want it to happen,
    skating
On a pond at the edge of the wood:
They never forgot
That even the dreadful martyrdom must run its
    course   10
Anyhow in a corner, some untidy spot
Where the dogs go on with their doggy life and the
    torturer's horse
Scratches its innocent behind on a tree.

In Breughel's *Icarus*, for instance: how everything turns
    away
Quite leisurely from the disaster; the ploughman
    may   15
Have heard the splash, the forsaken cry,
But for him it was not an important failure; the sun
    shone
As it had to on the white legs disappearing into the
    green
Water; and the expensive delicate ship that must have
    seen
Something amazing, a boy falling out of the sky,   20
Had somewhere to get to and sailed calmly on.

Exercises

*1. There are several allusions in this poem. Identify them and
discuss their significance.*

*2. Irony is established when the poet's tone of voice does not
match the subject matter talked about. How does that hold true
for this poem of Auden's? Is he making light of very serious
matters? How do the poet's colloquialisms deny us an attitude
of high seriousness and sentimentality?*

3. Because the poet is lecturing us in a pleasant sort of way, this is a fine poem to analyze strictly in terms of theme. Taking into account the poet's tone and word choices, discuss the theme of "Musée des Beaux Arts." Be sure you discuss what the poem means, and not what you would like it to mean.

As you can no doubt realize by now, a great many of the poems in earlier chapters can be just as profitably examined for the emotional qualities established by irony, paradox, and ambiguity and for the role that voice plays in establishing those poetic modes. Certainly Marvell's, Eliot's, Donne's, and Ransom's poems in the preceding chapter can all be reconsidered in the light of the material presented in this chapter. Furthermore, perhaps we are mindful by now that all manners and methods of poetic expression play their parts in establishing meaning in poetry. This final chapter was titled "The Scheme of Meaning" on purpose, of course. On one level the title is a pun, a weak species of ambiguity that may or may not work. But like the other puns we have seen, it is intended to point up something in the way of meaning. The devices dealt with in these last two chapters do indeed contribute a great share of the intellectual aspect of meaning in poetry. Nevertheless, despite how excitingly puzzling we may have found that intellectual meaning to be, poetry would be a rather cut and dried affair, more in the nature of brain teasers, if those devices were not used in conjunction with still other devices discussed in earlier chapters. To be sure, without as many poetic devices as possible acting in conjunction, we would not have those delightful combinations of *structure* and *meaning* that truly constitute poetry, and one way we can determine a good poem is to notice how many different appeals, emotional as well as intellectual, visual as well as aural, the particular poem makes to us.

In poetry, then, the scheme of meaning is just that. Whether we call it a bag of tricks or stock in trade or, more simply, a craft, the poet, as we have seen, has a wealth of devices to use in any attempt both to entertain and to instruct us, and the beauty of poetry has always been that it leavens the latter function with the former. We may miss a poem's meaning entirely, but we may still have had the pleasure of hearing the world with the poet's ears or seeing it with the poet's eyes. We should now be aware that the poet may have intended us to "miss" the meaning or may have meant other things as well.

As we learn to enjoy poetry, we learn to understand it, and we enjoy it by understanding how the poet works and how poetry works. Throughout these chapters, we have attempted to introduce both those aspects of an incredibly complex—and rich and rewarding—art. Like everything else in life, no device in poetry can work in isolation from any others. In Frost's "Design" and Shelley's "Ozymandias," for example, the *pattern* of the sonnet form adds immensely to the compact statement of each theme. *Ambiguity, irony,* and *paradox* would be unknown without *connotation*, for language would then have a scientific precision that would not allow for the marvelous factual imprecisions the world permits the poet. That all things seem to exist on both a *literal* and *figurative* level makes for *allusion* and *symbol*. We could go on, but the point is probably apparent by now. When studying poetry, we should bring to bear all that we have learned and experienced of it, for that is what the poet tries to bring to bear in composing the poetry for us.

Topics for Writing

1. Select from among the poems within this collection a poem in which the speaker is clearly not the poet. (The surest way to discover as much is to look for the use of quotation marks within the poem as in Hardy's "Ah, are you digging on my grave." Sometimes, too, a particular speaker is identified in the poem's title, as in the cases of Browning's "Andrea del Sarto" and Eliot's "The Love Song of J. Alfred Prufrock.") Once you have selected the poem, show how the poet manipulates the speaking voice to create irony and ambiguity, or different levels of meaning, within the poem.

2. Select a poem in which you find the poet punning. (The best test: if you think he is, he probably is.) Paying special attention to those puns, or ambiguous words and phrases, analyze the poem's meaning as it varies according to your reading of those same words and phrases.

3. Select a poem in which a serious subject—love, death, warfare—seems to be treated in a frivolous or at least whimsical manner. In discussing that poem, cite from it those lines that seem to you to prove that the poet is not being as serious as the subject might warrant. Consider too how effectively new or different meanings are thereby achieved.

Other Poems to Read

Anonymous

Barbara Allan

It was in and about the Martinmas time,
    When the green leaves were a-fallin',
That Sir John Graeme in the West Country
    Fell in love with Barbara Allan.

He sent his man down through the town   *5*
    To the place where she was dwellin':
"O haste and come to my master dear,
    Gin ye be Barbara Allan."

O slowly, slowly rase she up,
    To the place where he was lyin',   *10*
And when she drew the curtain by:
    "Young man, I think you're dyin'."

"O it's I'm sick, and very, very sick,
    And 'tis a' for Barbara Allan."
O the better for me ye sal never be,   *15*
    Though your heart's blood were a-spillin'."

"O dinna ye mind, young man," said she,
    "When ye the cups were fillin',
That ye made the healths gae round and round,
    And slighted Barbara Allan?"   *20*

He turned his face unto the wall,
    And death with him was dealin':
"Adieu, adieu, my dear friends all,
    And be kind to Barbara Allan."

And slowly, slowly, rase she up,   *25*
    And slowly, slowly left him;
And sighing said she could not stay,
    Since death of life had reft him.

She had not gane a mile but twa,
    When she heard the dead-bell knellin',   *30*
And every jow that the dead-bell ga'ed
    It cried, "Woe to Barbara Allan!"

"O mother, mother, make my bed,
    O make it soft and narrow:
Since my love died for me today,   *35*
    I'll die for him tomorrow."

Anonymous

Lord Randall

"Oh where ha'e ye been, Lord Randall my son?
O where ha'e ye been, my handsome young man?"
    "I ha'e been to the wild wood: mother, make my
    bed soon,
    For I'm weary wi' hunting, and fain wald lie down."

"Where gat ye your dinner, Lord Randall my son?   *5*
Where gat ye your dinner, my handsome young man?"
    "I dined wi' my true love; mother, make my bed
    soon,
    For I'm weary wi' hunting, and fain wald lie down."

"What gat ye to your dinner, Lord Randall my son?
What gat ye to your dinner, my handsome young
    man?"   *10*
    "I gat eels boiled in broo: mother, make my bed
    soon,
    For I'm weary wi' hunting and fain wald lie down."

"What became of your bloodhounds, Lord Randall my
son?
What became of your bloodhounds, my handsome
young man?"
"O they swelled and they died: mother, make my
bed soon,   15
For I'm weary wi' hunting and fain wald lie down."

"O I fear ye are poisoned, Lord Randall my son!
O I fear ye are poisoned, my handsome young man!"
"O yes, I am poisoned: mother, make my bed
soon,
For I'm sick at the heart, and I fain wald lie
down."   20

Anonymous

Weep you no more, sad fountains

Weep you no more, sad fountains!
        What need you flow so fast?
Look, how the snowy mountains
        Heaven's sun doth gently waste.
But my sun's heavenly eyes   5
        View not your weeping,
        That now lies sleeping
Softly, now softly lies
        Sleeping.

Sleep is a reconciling,   10
        A rest that peace begets.
Doth not the sun rise smiling
        When fair at even he sets?
Rest you then, rest, sad eyes,
        Melt not in weeping,   15
        While she lies sleeping
Softly, now softly lies
        Sleeping.

Anonymous

Sir Patrick Spens

The king sits in Dumferling toune,
　　Drinking the blude-reid wine:
"O whar will I get a guid sailor,
　　To sail this schip of mine?"

Up and spak an eldern knicht,　　　　　　　　5
　　Sat at the kings richt kne:
"Sir Patrick Spens is the best sailor
　　That sails upon the se."

The king has written a braid letter,
　　And signd it wi his hand,　　　　　　　　10
And sent it to Sir Patrick Spens,
　　Was walking on the sand.

The first line that Sir Patrick red,
　　A loud lauch lauched he;
The next line that Sir Patrick red,　　　　　15
　　The teir blinded his ee.

"O wha is this has don this deid,
　　This ill deid don to me,
To send me out this time o' the yeir,
　　To sail upon the se!　　　　　　　　　　20

"Mak hast, mak haste, my mirry men all,
　　Our guid schip sails the morne."
"Oh say na sae, my master deir,
　　For I feir a deadlie storme.

"Late late yestreen I saw the new moone,　25
　　Wi the auld moone in hir arme,
And I feir, I feir, my deir master,
　　That we will cum to harme."

O our Scots nobles wer richt laith
　　To weet their cork-heild schoone,　　　30
Bot lang owre a' the play wer playd,
　　Thait hats they swam aboone.

O lang, lang may their ladies sit,
　　Wi thair fans into their hand,
Or eir they se Sir Patrick Spens　　　　　35
　　Cum sailing to the land.

O lang, lang may the ladies stand,
    Wi thair gold kems in their hair,
Waiting for thair ain deir lords,
    For they'll se thame na mair.   *40*

Haf owre, half owre to Aberdour,
    It's fiftie fadom deip,
And thair lies guid Sir Patrick Spens,
    Wi the Scots lords at his feit.

Anonymous

Get Up and Bar the Door

It fell about the Martinmas time,
    And a gay time it was then,
When our good wife got puddings to make,
    And she's boild them in the pan.

The wind sae cauld blew south and north,   *5*
    And blew into the floor;
Quoth our goodman to our goodwife,
    "Gae out and bar the door."

"My hand is in my hussyfskap,
    Goodman, as ye may see;   *10*
An it shoud nae be barrd this hundred year,
    It's no be barrd for me."

They made a paction tween them twa,
    They made it firm and sure,
That the first word whaeer shoud speak,   *15*
    Shoud rise and bar the door.

Then by there came two gentlemen,
    At twelve oclock at night,
And they could neither see house nor hall,
    Nor coal nor candle-light.   *20*

"Now whether is this a rich man's house,
    Or whether is it a poor?"
But neer a word wad ane o them speak,
    For barring of the door.

And first they ate the white puddings,   *25*
    And then they ate the black;
Tho muckle thought the goodwife to hersel,
    Yet neer a word she spake.

Then said the one unto the other,
    "Here, man, tak ye my knife;   *30*
Do ye tak aff the auld man's beard,
    And I'll kiss the goodwife."

"But there's nae water in the house,
    And what shall we do than?"
"What ails ye at the pudding-broo,   *35*
    That boils into the pan?"

O up then started our goodman,
    An angry man was he:
"Will ye kiss my wife before my een,
    And scad me wi pudding-bree?"   *40*

Then up and started our goodwife,
    Gied three skips on the floor:
"Goodman, you've spoken the foremost word;
    Get up and bar the door."

Anonymous

Frankie and Johnny

Frankie and Johnny were lovers, great God how they
    could love!
Swore to be true to each other, true as the stars up
    above.
He was her man, but he done her wrong.

Frankie she was his woman, everybody knows.
She spent her forty dollars for Johnny a suit of clothes.
He was her man, but he done her wrong.   *6*

Frankie and Johnny went walking, Johnny in his brand
    new suit.
"O good Lawd," said Frankie, "but don't my Johnny
    look cute?"
He was her man, but he done her wrong.

Frankie went down to the corner, just for a bucket of
    beer.   *10*
Frankie said, "Mr. Bartender, has my loving Johnny
    been here?
He is my man, he wouldn't do me wrong."

"I don't want to tell you no story. I don't want to tell
    you no lie,
But your Johnny left here an hour ago with that lousy
    Nellie Blye.
He is your man, but he's doing you wrong."   *15*

Frankie went back to the hotel, she didn't go there for
    fun,
For under her red kimono she toted a forty-four gun.
He was her man, but he done her wrong.

Frankie went down to the hotel and looked in the
    window so high,
And there was her loving Johnny a-loving up Nellie
    Blye.   *20*
He was her man, but he was doing her wrong.

Frankie threw back her kimono, took out that old
    forty-four.
Root-a-toot-toot, three times she shot, right through
    the hardwood door.
He was her man, but he was doing her wrong.

Johnny grabbed off his Stetson, crying, "O Frankie
    don't shoot!"   *25*
Frankie pulled that forty-four, went root-a-toot-toot-
    toot-toot.
He was her man, but he done her wrong.

"Roll me over gently, roll me over slow,
Roll me on my right side, for my left side hurts me so,
I was her man, but I done her wrong."   *30*

With the first shot Johnny staggered, with the second
    shot he fell;
When the last bullet got him, there was a new man's
    face in hell.
He was her man, but he done her wrong.

"O, bring out your rubber-tired hearses, bring out your
    rubber-tired hacks;
Gonna take Johnny to the graveyard and ain't gonna
    bring him back.   *35*
He was my man, but he done me wrong."

563   ANONYMOUS

"O, put me in that dungeon, put me in that cell,
Put me where the northeast wind blows from the
    southeast corner of hell.
I shot my man, cause he done me wrong!"

Anonymous

On top of old Smoky

On top of old Smoky,
All cover'd with snow,
I lost my true lover,
For courtin' too slow.

A-courtin's a pleasure,   *5*
A-flirtin's a grief,
A false-hearted lover—
Is worse than a thief.

For a thief, he will rob you,
And take what you have,   *10*
But a false-hearted lover—
Sends you to your grave.

She'll hug you and kiss you,
And tell you more lies,
Than the ties on the railroad,   *15*
Or the stars in the skies.

Anonymous

The Power of Money

'Tis not the silver nor gold for itself
    That makes men adore it, but 'tis for its power:
For no man does dote upon pelf because pelf,
    But all court the lady in hope of her dower:
The wonders that now in our days we behold,   *5*
Done by the irresistible power of gold,
Our zeal, and our love, and allegiance do hold.

This purchaseth kingdoms, kings, scepters, and crowns;
    Wins battles, and conquers the conquerors bold;
Takes bulwarks, and castles, and cities, and towns,   *10*
    And our prime laws are writ in letters of gold;
'Tis this that our Parliament calls and creates,
Turns kings into keepers, and kingdoms to states,
And peopledoms these into highdoms translates.

This, plots can devise, and discover what they are;   *15*
    This, makes the great felons the lesser condemn;
This, sets those on the bench, that should stand at the
    bar,
    Who judge such as by right ought to execute them;
Gives the boisterous clown his unsufferable pride,
Makes beggars, and fools, and usurpers to ride,   *20*
Whiles ruin'd proprietors run by their side.

                    *   *   *

This makes your blue aprons Right Worshipful;
    And for this we stand bare, and before them do fall;
They leave their young heirs well fleeced with wool,
    Whom we must call squires, and then they pay
    all: *25*
Who with beggarly souls, though their bodies be gaudy,
Court the pale chambermaid, and nickname her a lady,
And for want of good wit, they do swear and talk
    bawdy.

This marriages makes, 'tis a center of love,
    It draws on the man, and it pricks up the
    woman   *30*
Birth, virtue, and parts no affection can move,
    Whilst this makes a lord stoop to the brat of a
    broom man;
This gives virtue and beauty to the lasses that you woo,
Makes women of all sorts and ages to do;
'Tis the soul of the world, and the worldling too.   *35*

This procures us whores, hawks, hounds and hares;
    'Tis this keeps your groom, and your groom keeps
    your gelding;
This built citizens wives, as well as wares;
    And this makes your coy lady so coming and
    yielding;   *39*
This buys us good sack, which revives like the spring,
'Tis this your poetical fancies do bring;
And this makes you as merry as we that do sing.

There is a lady sweet and kind

There is a lady sweet and kind,
Was never face so pleased my mind;
I did but see her passing by,
And yet I love her till I die.

Her gesture, motion, and her smiles,   *5*
Her wit, her voice, my heart beguiles,
Beguiles my heart, I know not why,
And yet I love her till I die.

Her free behavior, winning looks,
Will make a lawyer burn his books;   *10*
I touched her not, alas! not I,
And yet I love her till I die.

Had I her fast betwixt mine arms,
Judge you that think such sports were harms,
Were't any harm? no, no! fie, fie!   *15*
For I will love her till I die.

Should I remain confinèd there
So long as Phoebus in his sphere,
I to request, she to deny,
Yet would I love her till I die.   *20*

Cupid is wingèd and doth range,
Her country so my love doth change;
But change she earth, or change she sky,
Yet will I love her till I die.

Imamu Amiri Baraka
(LeRoi Jones; 1934–   )

A Poem for Black Hearts

For Malcolm's eyes, when they broke
the face of some dumb white man. For
Malcolm's hands raised to bless us
all black and strong in his image
of ourselves, for Malcolm's words   *5*

fire darts, the victor's tireless
thrusts, words hung above the world
change as it may, he said it, and
for this he was killed, for saying,
and feeling, and being/ change, all   *10*
collected hot in his heart, For Malcolm's
heart, raising us above our filthy cities,
for his stride, and his beat, and his address
to the grey monsters of the world, For Malcolm's
pleas for your dignity, black men, for your life,   *15*
black men, for the filling of your minds
with righteousness, For all of him dead and
gone and vanished from us, and all of him which
clings to our speech black god of our time.
For all of him, and all of yourself, look up,   *20*
black man, quit stuttering and shuffling, look up,
black man, quit whining and stooping, for all of him,
For Great Malcolm a prince of the earth,
    let nothing in us rest
until we avenge ourselves for his death, stupid
    animals   *25*
that killed him, let us never breathe a pure breath if
we fail, and white men call us faggots till the end of
the earth.

Thomas L. Beddoes   *(1803–1849)*

Song

How many times do I love thee, dear?
   Tell me how many thoughts there be
     In the atmosphere
     Of a new-fall'n year,
Whose white and sable hours appear
   The latest flake of Eternity—
So many times do I love thee, dear.

How many times do I love again?
   Tell me how many beads there are
     In a silver chain
     Of evening rain,
Unraveled from the tumbling main,
   And threading the eye of a yellow star—
So many times do I love again.

William Blake   *(1757–1827)*

A Poison Tree

I was angry with my friend:
I told my wrath, my wrath did end.
I was angry with my foe:
I told it not, my wrath did grow.

And I water'd it in fears,   5
Night & morning with my tears;
And I sunned it with smiles,
And with soft deceitful wiles.

And it grew both day and night,
Till it bore an apple bright;   10
And my foe beheld it shine,
And he knew that it was mine,

And into my garden stole
When the night had veil'd the pole:
In the morning glad I see   15
My foe outstretch'd beneath the tree.

The Little Black Boy

My mother bore me in the southern wild,
And I am black, but O! my soul is white;
White as an angel is the English child,
But I am black, as if bereaved of light.

My mother taught me underneath a tree,   5
And sitting down before the heat of day,
She took me on her lap and kissed me,
And, pointing to the east, began to say:

"Look on the rising sun: there God does live,
And gives his light, and gives his heat away;   10
And flowers and trees and beasts and men receive
Comfort in morning, joy in the noonday.

"And we are put on earth a little space,
That we may learn to bear the beams of love;
And these black bodies and this sunburnt face   15
Is but a cloud, and like a shady grove.

"For when our souls have learned the heat to bear,
The cloud will vanish; we shall hear his voice,
Saying: 'Come out from the grove, my love and care,
And round my golden tent like lambs rejoice.'"   *20*

Thus did my mother say, and kissed me;
And thus I say to little English boy:
When I from black and he from white cloud free,
And round the tent of God like lambs we joy,

I'll shade him from the heat, till he can bear   *25*
To lean in joy upon our Father's knee;
And then I'll stand and stroke his silver hair,
And be like him, and he will then love me.

The Tyger

Tyger! Tyger! burning bright
In the forests of the night,
What immortal hand or eye
Could frame thy fearful symmetry?

In what distant deeps or skies   *5*
Burnt the fire of thine eyes?
On what wings dare he aspire?
What the hand dare sieze the fire?

And what shoulder, & what art,
Could twist the sinews of thy heart?   *10*
And when thy heart began to beat,
What dread hand? & what dread feet?

What the hammer? what the chain?
In what furnace was thy brain?
What the anvil? what dread grasp   *15*
Dare its deadly terrors clasp?

When the stars threw down their spears,
And water'd heaven with their tears,
Did he smile his work to see?
Did he who made the Lamb make thee?   *20*

Tyger! Tyger! burning bright
In the forests of the night,
What immortal hand or eye,
Dare frame thy fearful symmetry?

Infant Sorrow

My mother groan'd! my father wept.
Into the dangerous world I leapt:
Helpless, naked, peping loud:
Like a fiend hid in a cloud.

Struggling in my father's hands,
Striving against my swadling bands,
Bound and weary I thought best
To sulk upon my mother's breast.

Elizabeth Barrett Browning *(1806–1861)*

How do I love thee?

How do I love thee? Let me count the ways.
I love thee to the depth and breadth and height
My soul can reach, when feeling out of sight
For the ends of Being and ideal Grace.
I love thee to the level of everyday's
Most quiet need, by sun and candle light.
I love thee freely, as men strive for Right;
I love thee purely, as they turn from Praise.
I love thee with the passion put to use
In my old griefs, and with my childhood's faith.
I love thee with a love I seemed to lose
With my lost saints—I love thee with the breath,
Smiles, tears, of all my life!—and, if God choose,
I shall but love thee better after death.

Robert Browning *(1812–1889)*

Love Among the Ruins

1   Where the quiet-colored end of evening smiles,
        Miles and miles
    On the solitary pastures where our sheep
        Half-asleep

Tinkle homeward through the twilight, stray or stop *5*
    As they crop—
Was the site once of a city great and gay
    (So they say),
Of our country's very capital, its prince
    Ages since *10*
Held his court in, gathered councils, wielding far
    Peace or war.

2   Now—the country does not even boast a tree,
    As you see,
To distinguish slopes of verdure, certain rills *15*
    From the hills
Intersect and give a name to (else they run
    Into one),
Where the domed and daring palace shot its spires
    Up like fires *20*
O'er the hundred-gated circuit of a wall
    Bounding all,
Made of marble, men might march on nor be pressed,
    Twelve abreast.

3   And such plenty and perfection, see, of grass *25*
    Never was!
Such a carpet as, this summertime, o'erspreads
    And embeds
Every vestige of the city, guessed alone,
    Stock or stone— *30*
Where a multitude of men breathed joy and woe
    Long ago;
Lust of glory pricked their hearts up, dread of shame
    Struck them tame;
And that glory and that shame alike, the gold *35*
    Bought and sold.

4   Now—the single little turret that remains
    On the plains,
By the caper overrooted, by the gourd
    Overscored, *40*
While the patching houseleek's head of blossom winks
    Through the chinks—
Marks the basement whence a tower in ancient time
    Sprang sublime,
And a burning ring, all round, the chariots traced *45*
    As they raced,
And the monarch and his minions and his dames
    Viewed the games.

5   And I know, while thus the quiet-colored eve
        Smiles to leave   *50*
To their folding, all our many-tinkling fleece
        In such peace,
And the slopes and rills in undistinguished gray
        Melt away—
That a girl with eager eyes and yellow hair   *55*
        Waits me there
In the turret whence the charioteers caught soul
        For the goal,
When the king looked, where she locks now,
        breathless, dumb
        Till I come.   *60*

6   But he looked upon the city, every side,
        Far and wide,
All the mountains topped with temples, all the glades'
        Colonnades,
All the causeys, bridges, aqueducts—and then,   *65*
        All the men!
When I do come, she will speak not, she will stand,
        Either hand
On my shoulder, give her eyes the first embrace
        Of my face,   *70*
Ere we rush, ere we extinguish sight and speech
        Each on each.

7   In one year they sent a million fighters forth
        South and north,
And they built their gods a brazen pillar high   *75*
        As the sky,
Yet reserved a thousand chariots in full force—
        Gold, of course,
Oh heart! oh blood that freezes, blood that burns!
        Earth's returns   *80*
For whole centuries of folly, noise, and sin!
        Shut them in,
With their triumphs and their glories and the rest!
        Love is best.

Respectability

1   Dear, had the world in its caprice
      Deigned to proclaim ''I know you both,
      Have recognized your plighted troth,
    Am sponsor for you: live in peace!''—
    How many precious months and years   5
      Of youth had passed, that speed so fast,
      Before we found it out at last,
    The world, and what it fears?

2   How much of priceless life were spent
      With men that every virtue decks,   10
      And women models of their sex,
    Society's true ornament—
    Ere we dared wander, nights like this,
      Through wind and rain, and watch the Seine,
      And feel the Boulevard break again   15
    To warmth and light and bliss?

3   I know! the world proscribes not love;
      Allows my fingers to caress
      Your lips' contour and downiness,
    Provided it supply a glove.   20
    The world's good word!—the Institute!
      Guizot receives Montalembert!
      Eh? Down the court three lampions flare:
    Put forward your best foot!

William Cullen Bryant *(1794–1878)*

Thanatopsis

    To him who in the love of Nature holds
Communion with her visible forms, she speaks
A various language; for his gayer hours
She has a voice of gladness, and a smile
And eloquence of beauty, and she glides   5
Into his darker musings, with a mild
And healing sympathy, that steals away
Their sharpness, ere he is aware. When thoughts
Of the last bitter hour come like a blight
Over thy spirit, and sad images   10

Of the stern agony, and shroud, and pall,
And breathless darkness, and the narrow house,
Make thee to shudder and grow sick at heart;—
Go forth, under the open sky, and list
To Nature's teachings, while from all around—   15
Earth and her waters, and the depths of air—
Comes a still voice—Yet a few days, and thee
The all-beholding sun shall see no more
In all his course; nor yet in the cold ground,
Where thy pale form was laid, with many tears,   20
Nor in the embrace of ocean, shall exist
Thy image. Earth, that nourished thee, shall claim
Thy growth, to be resolved to earth again,
And, lost each human trace, surrendering up
Thine individual being, shalt thou go   25
To mix forever with the elements,
To be a brother to the insensible rock
And to the sluggish clod, which the rude swain
Turns with his share, and treads upon. The oak
Shall send his roots abroad, and pierce thy mould.   30

 Yet not to thine eternal resting-place
Shalt thou retire alone, nor couldst thou wish
Couch more magnificent. Thou shalt lie down
With patriarchs of the infant world—with kings,
The powerful of the earth—the wise, the good,   35
Fair forms, and hoary seers of ages past,
All in one mighty sepulchre. The hills
Rock-ribbed and ancient as the sun,—the vales
Stretching in pensive quietness between;
The venerable woods—rivers that move   40
In majesty, and the complaining brooks
That make the meadows green; and, poured round all,
Old Ocean's gray and melancholy waste,—
Are but the solemn decorations all
Of the great tomb of man. The golden sun,   45
The planets, all the infinte host of heaven,
Are shining on the sad abodes of death,
Through the still lapse of ages. All that tread
The globe are but a handful to the tribes
That slumber in its bosom.—Take the wings   50
Of morning, pierce the Barcan wilderness,
Or lose thyself in the continuous woods
Where rolls the Oregon, and hears no sound,
Save his own dashings—yet the dead are there:
And millions in those solitudes, since first   55

The flight of years began, have laid them down
In their last sleep—the dead reign there alone.
So shalt thou rest, and what if thou withdraw
In silence from the living, and no friend
Take note of thy departure? All that breathe   *60*
Will share thy destiny. The gay will laugh
When thou are gone, the solemn brood of care
Plod on, and each one as before will chase
His favorite phantom; yet all these shall leave
Their mirth and their employments, and shall come *65*
And make their bed with thee. As the long train
Of ages glide away, the sons of men,
The youth in life's green spring, and he who goes
In the full strength of years, matron and maid,
The speechless babe, and the gray-headed man—   *70*
Shall one by one be gathered to thy side,
By those, who in their turn shall follow them.

    So live, that when thy summons comes to join
The innumerable caravan, which moves
To that mysterious realm, where each shall take   *75*
His chamber in the silent halls of death,
Thou go not, like the quarry-slave at night,
Scourged to his dungeon, but, sustained and soothed
By an unfaltering trust, approach thy grave,
Like one who wraps the drapery of his couch   *80*
About him, and lies down to pleasant dreams.

Robert Burns *(1759–1796)*

A Red, Red Rose

O, my luve is like a red, red rose,
    That's newly sprung in June.
O, my luve is like the melodie,
    That's sweetly played in tune.

As fair art thou, my bonie lass,   *5*
    So deep in luve am I,
And I will luve thee still, my dear,
    Till a' the seas gang dry.

Till a' the seas gang dry, my dear,
    And the rocks melt wi' the sun!   *10*
And I will luve thee still, my dear,
    While the sands o' life shall run.

And fare thee weel, my only luve,
    And fare thee weel a while!
And I will come again, my luve,   *15*
    Tho' it were ten thousand mile!

Holy Willie's Prayer

O Thou, wha in the heavens dost dwell,
Wha, as it pleases best thysel',
Sends ane to heaven and ten to hell,
    A' for thy glory,
And no for ony guid or ill   *5*
    They've done afore thee!

I bless and praise thy matchless might,
Whan thousands thou hast left in night,
That I am here afore thy sight,
    For gifts an' grace   *10*
A burnin' an' a shinin' light,
    To a' this place.

What was I, or my generation,
That I should get sic exaltation?
I, wha deserve most just damnation,   *15*
    For broken laws,
Sax thousand years 'fore my creation,
    Thro' Adam's cause.

When frae my mither's womb I fell,
Thou might hae plungéd me in hell,   *20*
To gnash my gums, to weep and wail,
    In burnin lakes,
Where damnéd devils roar and yell,
    Chained to their stakes;

Yet I am here a chosen sample,   *25*
To show thy grace is great and ample;
I'm here a pillar in thy temple,
    Strong as a rock,
A guide, a buckler, an example
    To a' thy flock.   *30*

O Lord, thou kens what zeal I bear,
When drinkers drink, and swearers swear.
And singin' there and dancin' here,
    Wi' great an' sma:
For I am keepit by thy fear   *35*
    Free frae them a'.

But yet, O Lord! confess I must
At times I'm fashed wi' fleshy lust;
An' sometimes too, wi' warldly trust,
    Vile self gets in;   *40*
But thou remembers we are dust,
    Defiled in sin.

O Lord! yestreen, thou kens, wi' Meg—
Thy pardon I sincerely beg;
O! may't ne'er be a livin' plague   *45*
    To my dishonour,
An' I'll ne'er lift a lawless leg
    Again upon her.

Besides I farther maun allow,
Wi' Lizzie's lass, three times I trow—   *50*
But, Lord, that Friday I was fou,
    When I cam near her,
Or else thou kens thy servant true
    Wad never steer her.

May be thou lets this fleshly thorn   *55*
Beset thy servant e'en and morn
Lest he owre high and proud should turn,
    That he's sae gifted;
If sae, thy hand maun e'en be borne,
    Until thou lift it.   *60*

Lord, bless thy chosen in this place,
For here thou hast a chosen race;
But God confound their stubborn face,
    And blast their name,
Wha bring thy elders to disgrace   *65*
    An' public shame.

Lord, mind Gawn Hamilton's deserts,
He drinks, an' swears, an' plays at cartes,
Yet has sae mony takin arts
    Wi' great an' sma',   *70*
Frae God's ain priest the people's hearts
    He steals awa'.

An' when we chastened him therefor,
Thou kens how he bred sic a splore
As set the warld in a roar   *75*
    O' laughin' at us;
Curse thou his basket and his store,
    Kail and potatoes.

Lord, hear my earnest cry an' pray'r,
Against that presbytery o' Ayr;   *80*
Thy strong right hand, Lord, make it bare
    Upo' their heads;
Lord, weigh it down, and dinna spare,
    For their misdeeds.

O Lord my God, that glib-tongued Aiken,   *85*
My very heart and soul are quakin',
To think how we stood sweatin, shakin,
    An' pissed wi' dread,
While he, wi' hingin lips and snakin,
    Held up his head.   *90*

Lord in the day of vengeance try him;
Lord, visit them wha did employ him,
And pass not in thy mercy by them,
    Nor hear their pray'r:
But, for thy people's sake, destroy them,   *95*
    And dinna spare.

But, Lord, remember me and mine
Wi' mercies temp'ral and divine,
That I for gear and grace may shine
    Excelled by nane,   *100*
And a' the glory shall be thine,
    Amen, Amen!

George Gordon, Lord Byron *(1788–1824)*

She walks in beauty

She walks in beauty, like the night
    Of cloudless climes and starry skies;
And all that's best of dark and bright
    Meet in her aspect and her eyes:
Thus mellow'd to that tender light   *5*
    Which heaven to gaudy day denies.

One shade the more, one ray the less,
    Had half impaired the nameless grace
Which waves in every raven tress,
    Or softly lightens o'er her face;   *10*
Where thoughts serenely sweet express
    How pure, how dear their dwelling-place.

And on that cheek, and o'er that brow,
    So soft, so calm, yet eloquent,
The smiles that win, the tints that glow,   *15*
    But tell of days in goodness spent,
A mind at peace with all below,
    A heart whose love is innocent!

Stanzas

When a Man Hath No Freedom to Fight for at Home

When a man hath no freedom to fight for at home,
    Let him combat for that of his neighbors;
Let him think of the glories of Greece and of Rome,
    And get knocked on his head for his labors.

To do good to mankind is the chivalrous plan,
    And is always as nobly requited;
Then battle for freedom wherever you can,
    And, if not shot or hanged, you'll get knighted.

Thomas Campion *(1567–1620)*

There is a garden in her face

There is a garden in her face,
Where roses and white lilies grow;
    A heav'nly paradise is that place,
Wherein all pleasant fruits do flow.
      There cherries grow which none may buy   *5*
      Till cherry-ripe themselves do cry.

Those cherries fairly do enclose
Of orient pearl a double row,
    Which when her lovely laughter shows,
They look like rosebuds filled with snow.   *10*
      Yet them nor peer nor prince can buy,
      Till cherry-ripe themselves do cry.

Her eyes like angels watch them still;
Her brows like bended bows do stand,
    Threat'ning with piercing frowns to kill   *15*
All that attempt with eye or hand
      Those sacred cherries to come nigh,
      Till cherry-ripe themselves do cry.

Henry Carey *(1687?–1743)*

The Ballad of Sally in Our Alley

Of all the girls that are so smart,
    There's none like pretty Sally;
She is the darling of my heart,
    And she lives in our alley:
There is no lady in the land   *5*
    Is half so sweet as Sally;
She is the darling of my heart,
    And she lives in our alley.

Her father he makes cabbage-nets,
    And through the streets does cry 'em;   *10*
Her mother she sells laces long,
    To such as please to buy 'em;

But sure such folks could ne'er beget
    So sweet a girl as Sally;
She is the darling of my heart,   15
    And she lives in our alley.

When she is by, I leave my work
    (I love her so sincerely);
My master comes, like any Turk,
    And bangs me most severely;   20
But let him bang his bellyful,
    I'll bear it all for Sally;
She is the darling of my heart,
    And she lives in our alley.

Of all the days that's in the week,   25
    I dearly love but one day,
And that's the day that comes betwixt
    A Saturday and Monday;
For then I'm dressed, all in my best,
    To walk abroad with Sally;   30
She is the darling of my heart,
    And she lives in our alley.

My master carries me to church,
    And often am I blamed,
Because I leave him in the lurch,   35
    As soon as text is named:
I leave the church in sermon time,
    And slink away to Sally;
She is the darling of my heart,
    And she lives in our alley.   40

When Christmas comes about again,
    O then I shall have money;
I'll hoard it up, and box and all
    I'll give it to my honey:
And would it were ten thousand pounds,   45
    I'd give it all to Sally;
She is the darling of my heart,
    And she lives in our alley.

My master and the neighbours all
    Make game of me and Sally,   50
And (but for her) I'd better be
    A slave, and row a galley:
But when my seven long years are out,
    O then I'll marry Sally!
O then we'll wed, and then we'll bed;   55
    But not in our alley!

Lewis Carroll *(1832–1898)*

"You are old, father William"

"You are old, father William," the young man said,
    "And your hair has become very white;
And yet you incessantly stand on your head—
    Do you think, at your age, it is right?"

"In my youth," father William replied to his son,   *5*
    "I feared it might injure the brain;
But now that I'm perfectly sure I have none,
    Why, I do it again and again."

"You are old," said the youth, "as I mentioned before,
    And have grown most uncommonly fat;   *10*
Yet you turned a back-somersault in at the door—
    Pray, what is the reason of that?"

"In my youth," said the sage, as he shook his grey
    locks,
    "I kept all my limbs very supple
By the use of this ointment—one shilling the box— *15*
    Allow me to sell you a couple."

"You are old," said the youth, "and your jaws are too
    weak
    For anything tougher than suet;
Yet you finished the goose, with the bones and the
    beak—
    Pray, how did you manage to do it?"   *20*

"In my youth," said his father, "I took to the law,
    And argued each case with my wife;
And the muscular strength, which it gave to my jaw,
    Has lasted the rest of my life."

"You are old," said the youth; "one would hardly
    suppose   *25*
    That your eye was as steady as ever;
Yet you balanced an eel on the end of your nose—
    What made you so awfully clever?"

"I have answered three questions, and that is enough,"
    Said his father; "don't give yourself airs!   *30*
Do you think I can listen all day to such stuff?
    Be off, or I'll kick you downstairs!"

John Clare *(1793–1864)*

I Am

I am—yet what I am, none cares or knows;
    My friends forsake me like a memory lost:
I am the self-consumer of my woes—
    They rise and vanish in oblivions host,
Like shadows in love frenzied stifled throes   5
    And yet I am, and live—like vapours tossed

Into the nothingness of scorn and noise,
    Into the living sea of waking dreams,
Where there is neither sense of life or joys,
    But the vast shipwreck of my life's esteems;   10
Even the dearest that I love the best
    Are strange—nay, rather, stranger than the rest.

I long for scenes where man hath never trod
    A place where woman never smiled or wept
There to abide with my Creator God,   15
    And sleep as I in childhood sweetly slept,
Untroubling and untroubled where I lie
    The grass below, above, the vaulted sky.

Arthur Clough *(1819–1861)*

"There is no God," the wicked saith

"There is no God," the wicked saith,
    "And truly it's a blessing,
For what he might have done with us
    It's better only guessing."

"There is no God," a youngster thinks,   5
    "Or really, if there may be,
He surely didn't mean a man
    Always to be a baby."

"There is no God, or if there is,"
    The tradesman thinks, "'twere funny   10
If he should take it ill in me
    To make a little money."

"Whether there be," the rich man says,
   "It matters very little,
For I and mine, thank somebody,   15
   Are not in want of victual."

Some others, also, to themselves
   Who scarce so much as doubt it,
Think there is none, when they are well,
   And do not think about it.   20

But country folks who live beneath
   The shadow of the steeple;
The parson and the parson's wife,
   And mostly married people;

Youths green and happy in first love,   25
   So thankful for illusion;
And men caught out in what the world
   Calls guilt, in first confusion;

And almost everyone when age,
   Disease, or sorrows strike him,   30
Inclines to think there is a God,
   Or something very like Him.

Samuel Taylor Coleridge *(1772–1834)*

Desire

Where true Love burns Desire is Love's pure flame;
It is the relex of our earthly frame,
That takes its meaning from the nobler part,
And but translates the language of the heart.

Epitaph

Stop, Christian passer-by! —Stop, child of God,
And read with gentle breast. Beneath this sod
A poet lies, or that which once seem'd he.
O, lift one thought in prayer for S. T. C.;
That he who many a year with toil of breath
Found death in life, may here find life in death!
Mercy for praise—to be forgiven for fame
He ask'd, and hoped, through Christ. Do thou the
   same!

Abraham Cowley *(1618–1667)*

The Wish

Well then; I now do plainly see,
This busy world and I shall ne'er agree;
The very honey of all earthly joy
    Does of all meats the soonest cloy;
    And they, methinks, deserve my pity   *5*
Who for it can endure the stings,
The crowd, and buzz, and murmurings
    Of this great hive, the city.

Ah, yet, ere I descend to the grave
May I a small house and large garden have!   *10*
And a few friends, and many books, both true,
    Both wise, and both delightful too!
    And since love ne'er will from me flee,
A mistress moderately fair,
And good as guardian angels are,   *15*
    Only beloved, and loving me!

O fountains, when in you shall I
Myself, eased of unpeaceful thoughts, espy?
O fields! O woods! when, when shall I be made
    The happy tenant of your shade?   *20*
    Here's the spring-head of pleasure's flood,
Here's wealthy Nature's treasury,
Where all the riches lie that she
    Has coined and stamped for good.

Pride and ambition here   *25*
Only in farfetched metaphors appear;
Here naught but winds can hurtful murmurs scatter,
    And naught but Echo flatter.
    The gods, when they descended, hither
From heaven did always choose their way;   *30*
And therefore we may boldly say
    That 'tis the way, too, thither.

How happy here should I
And one dear she live and, embracing, die!
She who is all the world, and can exclude   *35*
    In deserts, solitude.
    I should have then this only fear,
Lest men, when they my pleasures see,
Should hither throng to live like me,
    And so make a city here.   *40*

e. e. cummings *(1894–1962)*

pity this busy monster,manunkind

pity this busy monster,manunkind,

not. Progress is a comfortable disease:
your victim(death and life safely beyond)

plays with the bigness of his littleness
—electrons deify one razorblade
into a mountainrange;lenses extend

unwish through curving wherewhen till unwish
returns on its unself.
                          A world of made
is not a world of born—pity poor flesh

and trees,poor stars and stones,but never this
fine specimen of hypermagical

ultraomnipotence. We doctors know

a hopeless case if—listen: there's a hell
of a good universe next door;let's go

in Just-

in Just-
spring   when the world is mud-
luscious the little
lame balloonman

whistles   far   and wee   5

and eddieandbill come
running from marbles and
piracies and it's
spring

when the world is puddle-wonderful   10

the queer
old balloonman whistles
far   and   wee
and bettyandisbel come dancing

from hop-scotch and jump-rope and   *15*

it's
spring
and
    the

       goat-footed   *20*

balloonMan   whistles
far
and
wee

anyone lived in a pretty how town

anyone lived in a pretty how town
(with up so floating many bells down)
spring summer autumn winter
he sang his didn't he danced his did.

Women and men(both little and small)   *5*
cared for anyone not at all
they sowed their isn't they reaped their same
sun moon stars rain

children guessed(but only a few
and down they forgot as up they grew   *10*
autumn winter spring summer)
that noone loved him more by more

when by now and tree by leaf
she laughed his joy she cried his grief
bird by snow and stir by still   *15*
anyone's any was all to her

someones married their everyones
laughed their cryings and did their dance
(sleep wake hope and then)they
said their nevers they slept their dream   *20*

stars rain sun moon
(and only the snow can begin to explain
how children are apt to forget to remember
with up so floating many bells down)

587   E. E. CUMMINGS

one day anyone died i guess   *25*
(and noone stooped to kiss his face)
busy folk buried them side by side
little by little and was by was

all by all and deep by deep
and more by more they dream their sleep   *30*
noone and anyone earth by april
wish by spirit and if by yes.

Women and men(both dong and ding)
summer autumn winter spring
reaped their sowing and went their came   *35*
sun moon stars rain

Emily Dickinson   *(1830–1886)*

After great pain, a formal feeling comes—

After great pain, a formal feeling comes—
The Nerves sit ceremonious, like Tombs—
The stiff Heart questions was it He, that bore,
And Yesterday, or Centuries before?

The Feet, mechanical, go round—
Of Ground, or Air, or Ought—
A Wooden way
Regardless grown,
A Quartz contentment, like a stone—

This is the Hour of Lead—
Remembered, if outlived,
As Freezing persons, recollect the Snow—
First—Chill—then Stupor—then the letting go—

I died for Beauty—but was scarce

I died for Beauty—but was scarce
Adjusted in the Tomb
When One who died for Truth, was lain
In an adjoining Room—

He questioned softly "Why I failed"?
"For Beauty", I replied—
"And I—for Truth—Themself are One—
We Bretheren, are", He said—

And so, as Kinsmen, met a Night—
We talked between the Rooms—
Until the Moss had reached our lips—
And covered up—our names—

I taste a liquor never brewed—

I taste a liquor never brewed—
From Tankards scooped in Pearl—
Not all the Frankfort Berries
Yield such an Alcohol!

Inebriate of Air—am I—   5
And Debauchee of Dew—
Reeling—thro endless summer days—
From inns of Molten Blue—

When "Landlords" turn the drunken Bee
Out of the Foxglove's door—   10
When Butterflies—renounce their "drams"—
I shall but drink the more!

Till Seraphs swing their snowy Hats—
And Saints—to windows run—
To see the little Tippler   15
From Manzanilla come!

Because I could not stop for Death

Because I could not stop for Death,
He kindly stopped for me;
The carriage held but just ourselves
And Immortality.

We slowly drove, he knew no haste,   5
And I had put away
My labor, and my leisure too,
For his civility.

We passed the school where children played
At wrestling in a ring;   *10*
We passed the fields of gazing grain,
We passed the setting sun.

We paused before a house that seemed
A swelling of the ground;
The roof was scarcely visible,   *15*
The cornice but a mound.

Since then 'tis centuries; but each
Feels shorter than the day
I first surmised the horses' heads
Were toward eternity.   *20*

'Twas like a Maelstrom, with a notch

'Twas like a Maelstrom, with a notch,
That nearer, every Day,
Kept narrowing its boiling Wheel
Until the Agony

Toyed coolly with the final inch   *5*
Of your delirious Hem—
And you dropt, lost,
When something broke—
And let you from a Dream—

As if a Goblin with a Guage—   *10*
Kept measuring the Hours—
Until you felt your Second
Weight, helpless, in his Paws—

And not a Sinew—stirred—could help,
And sense was setting numb—   *15*
When God—remembered—and the Fiend
Let go, then, Overcome—

As if your Sentence stood—pronounced—
And you were frozen led
From Dungeon's luxury of Doubt   *20*
To Gibbets, and the Dead—

And when the Film had stitched your eyes
A Creature gasped "Reprieve"!
Which Anguish was the utterest—then—
To perish, or to live?   *25*

John Donne (1572–1631)

Death be not proud

Death be not proud, though some have called thee
Mighty and dreadfull, for, thou art not soe,
For, those, whom thou think'st, thou dost overthrow,
Die not, poore death, nor yet canst thou kill mee.
From rest and sleepe, which but thy pictures bee,
Much pleasure, then from thee, much more must
    flow,
And soonest our best men with thee doe goe,
Rest of their bones, and soules deliverie.
Thou art slave to Fate, Chance, kings, and desperate
    men
And dost with poyson, warre, and sicknesse dwell,
And poppie, or charmes can make us sleepe as well,
And better than thy stroake; why swell'st thou then?
One short sleepe past, wee wake eternally,
And death shall be no more; death, thou shalt die.

The Triple Fool

I am two fools, I know,
For loving, and for saying so
    In whining poetry.
But where's that wise man that would not be I
    If she would not deny?   5
Then as th' earth's inward, narrow, crooked lanes
Do purge sea water's fretful salt away,
    I thought if I could draw my pains
Through rhyme's vexation, I should them allay.
Grief brought to numbers cannot be so fierce,   10
For he tames it that fetters it in verse.

But when I have done so,
Some man, his art and voice to show,
    Doth set and sing my pain,
And by delighting many, frees again   15
    Grief, which verse did restrain.
To love and grief tribute of verse belongs,
But not of such as pleases when 'tis read;
    Both are increased by such songs,
For both their triumphs so are publishèd,   20
And I, which was two fools, do so grow three.
Who are a little wise, the best fools be.

Dregs

The fire is out, and spent the warmth thereof,
(This is the end of every song man sings!)
The golden wine is drunk, the dregs remain,
Bitter as wormwood and as salt as pain;
And health and hope have gone the way of love
Into the drear oblivion of lost things.
Ghosts go along with us until the end;
This was a mistress, this, perhaps, a friend.
With pale, indifferent eyes, we sit and wait
For the dropped curtain and the closing gate:
This is the end of all the songs man sings.

Michael Drayton   *(1563–1631)*

Since there's no help, come let us kiss and part

Since there's no help, come let us kiss and part;
Nay, I have done, you get no more of me,
And I am glad, yea glad with all my heart
That thus so cleanly I myself can free;
Shake hands forever, cancel all our vows,
And when we meet at any time again,
Be it not seen in either of our brows
That we one jot of former love retain.
Now at the last gasp of love's latest breath,
When, his pulse failing, passion speechless lies,
When faith is kneeling by his bed of death,
And innocence is closing up his eyes,
Now if thou wouldst, when all have given him over,
From death to life thou mightst him yet recover.

Paul Laurence Dunbar *(1872–1906)*

The Debt

This is the debt I pay
Just for one riotous day,
Years of regret and grief,
Sorrow without relief.

Pay it I will to the end—
Until the grave, my friend,
Gives me a true release—
Gives me the clasp of peace.

Slight was the thing I bought,
Small was the debt I thought,
Poor was the loan at best—
God! but the interest!

John Dryden *(1631–1700)*

A Song for St. Cecilia's Day

1   From harmony, from heavenly harmony
    This universal frame began;
    When Nature underneath a heap
    Of jarring atoms lay,
    And could not heave her head,   5
The tuneful Voice was heard from high,
    "Arise, ye more than dead."
Then cold and hot and moist and dry
    In order to their stations leap,
    And music's power obey.   10
From harmony, from heavenly harmony
    This universal frame began:
    From harmony to harmony
Through all the compass of the notes it ran,
The diapason closing full in Man.   15

2   What passion cannot music raise and quell?
        When Jubal struck the corded shell,
      His listening brethren stood around,
        And, wondering, on their faces fell
      To worship that celestial sound: *20*
Less than a God they thought there could not dwell
      Within the hollow of that shell,
        That spoke so sweetly and so well.
   What passion cannot music raise and quell?

3   The trumpet's loud clangor   *25*
        excites us to arms
      With shrill notes of anger
        And mortal alarms.
      The double, double, double beat
        Of the thund'ring drum   *30*
      Cries "Hark, the foes come;
   Charge, charge, 'tis too late to retreat."

4   The soft complaining flute
      In dying notes discovers
      The woes of hopeless lovers,   *35*
  Whose dirge is whispered by the warbling lute.

5   Sharp violins proclaim
   Their jealous pangs and desperation,
  Fury, frantic indignation,
  Depth of pains and height of passion,   *40*
      For the fair, disdainful dame.

6   But Oh! What art can teach,
      What human voice can reach,
      The sacred organ's praise?
    Notes inspiring holy love,   *45*
  Notes that wing their heavenly ways
      To mend the choirs above.

7 Orpheus could lead the savage race,
  And trees unrooted left their place,
      Sequaceous of the lyre;   *50*
  But bright Cecilia raised the wonder higher;
  When to her organ vocal breath was given,
  An angel heard and straight appeared,
      Mistaking earth for heaven.

Grand Chorus As from the power of sacred lays   55
                    The spheres began to move,
          And sung the great Creator's praise
                    To all the blest above;
          So when the last and dreadful hour
          This crumbling pageant shall devour,   60
          The trumpet shall be heard on high,
          The dead shall live, the living die,
          And music shall untune the sky.

Richard Eberhart (1904–   )

If I could only live at the pitch
that is near madness

If I could only live at the pitch that is near madness
When everything is as it was in my childhood
Violent, vivid, and of infinite possibility:
That the sun and the moon broke over my head.

Then I cast time out of the trees and fields,   5
Then I stood immaculate in the Ego;
Then I eyed the world with all delight,
Reality was the perfection of my sight.

And time has big handles on the hands,
Fields and trees a way of being themselves.   10
I saw battalions of the race of mankind
Standing stolid, demanding a moral answer.

I gave the moral answer and I died
And into a realm of complexity came
Where nothing is possible but necessity   15
And the truth wailing there like a red babe.

T. S. Eliot *(1888–1965)*

The Hippopotamus

Similiter et omnes revereantur Diaconos, ut mandatum Jesu Christi; et Episcopum, ut Jesum Christum, existentem filium Patris; Presbyteros autem, ut concilium Dei et conjunctionem Apostolorum. Sine his Ecclesia non vocatur; de quibus suadeo vos sic habeo.

S. IGNATII AD TRALLIANOS

And when this epistle is read among you, cause that it be read also in the church of the Laodiceans.

The broad-backed hippopotamus
Rests on his belly in the mud;
Although he seems so firm to us
He is merely flesh and blood.

Flesh and blood is weak and frail,   5
Susceptible to nervous shock;
While the True Church can never fail
For it is based upon a rock.

The hippo's feeble steps may err
In compassing material ends,   10
While the True Church need never stir
To gather in its dividends.

The 'potamus can never reach
The mango on the mango-tree;
But fruits of pomegranate and peach   15
Refresh the Church from over sea.

At mating time the hippo's voice
Betrays inflexions hoarse and odd,
But every week we hear rejoice
The Church, at being one with God.   20

The hippopotamus's day
Is passed in sleep; at night he hunts;
God works in a mysterious way—
The Church can sleep and feed at once.

I saw the 'potamus take wing   25
Ascending from the damp savannas,
And quiring angels round him sing
The praise of God, in loud hosannas.

Blood of the Lamb shall wash him clean
And him shall heavenly arms enfold,   30
Among the saints he shall be seen
Performing on a harp of gold.

He shall be washed as white as snow,
By all the martyr'd virgins kist,
While the True Church remains below   *35*
Wrapt in the old miasmal mist.

Robert Frost   *(1874–1963)*

The Road Not Taken

Two roads diverged in a yellow wood,
And sorry I could not travel both
And be one traveler, long I stood
And looked down one as far as I could
To where it bent in the undergrowth;   *5*

Then took the other, as just as fair,
And having perhaps the better claim,
Because it was grassy and wanted wear;
Though as for that, the passing there
Had worn them really about the same,   *10*

And both that morning equally lay
In leaves no step had trodden black.
Oh, I kept the first for another day!
Yet knowing how way leads on to way,
I doubted if I should ever come back.   *15*

I shall be telling this with a sigh
Somewhere ages and ages hence:
Two roads diverged in a wood, and I—
I took the one less traveled by,
And that has made all the difference.   *20*

Stopping by Woods on a Snowy Evening

Whose woods these are I think I know.
His house is in the village, though;
He will not see me stopping here
To watch his woods fill up with snow.

My little horse must think it queer   5
To stop without a farmhouse near
Between the woods and frozen lake
The darkest evening of the year.

He gives his harness bells a shake
To ask if there is some mistake.   10
The only other sound's the sweep
Of easy wind and downy flake.

The woods are lovely, dark, and deep,
But I have promises to keep,
And miles to go before I sleep,   15
And miles to go before I sleep.

Birches

When I see birches bend to left and right
Across the lines of straighter darker trees,
I like to think some boy's been swinging them.
But swinging doesn't bend them down to stay
As ice storms do. Often you must have seen them   5
Loaded with ice a sunny winter morning
After a rain. They click upon themselves
As the breeze rises, and turn many-colored
As the stir cracks and crazes their enamel.
Soon the sun's warmth makes them shed crystal shells
Shattering and avalanching on the snow crust—   11
Such heaps of broken glass to sweep away
You'd think the inner dome of heaven had fallen.
They are dragged to the withered bracken by the load,
And they seem not to break; though once they are
      bowed
                                                     15
So low for long, they never right themselves:
You may see their trunks arching in the woods
Years afterwards, trailing their leaves on the ground
Like girls on hands and knees that throw their hair
Before them over their heads to dry in the sun.   20
But I was going to say when Truth broke in
With all her matter of fact about the ice storm,

I should prefer to have some boy bend them
As he went out and in to fetch the cows—
Some boy too far from town to learn baseball,   *25*
Whose only play was what he found himself,
Summer or winter, and could play alone.
One by one he subdued his father's trees
By riding them down over and over again
Until he took the stiffness out of them,   *30*
And not one but hung limp, not one was left
For him to conquer. He learned all there was
To learn about not launching out too soon
And so not carrying the tree away
Clear to the ground. He always kept his poise   *35*
To the top branches, climbing carefully
With the same pains you use to fill a cup
Up to the brim, and even above the brim.
Then he flung outward, feet first, with a swish,
Kicking his way down through the air to the
        ground.   *40*
So was I once myself a swinger of birches.
And so I dream of going back to be.
It's when I'm weary of considerations,
And life is too much like a pathless wood
Where your face burns and tickles with the cobwebs *45*
Broken across it, and one eye is weeping
From a twig's having lashed across it open.
I'd like to get away from earth awhile
And then come back to it and begin over.
May no fate willfully misunderstand me   *50*
And half grant what I wish and snatch me away
Not to return. Earth's the right place for love:
I don't know where it's likely to go better.
I'd like to go by climbing a birch tree,
And climb black branches up a snow-white trunk *55*
Toward heaven, till the tree could bear no more,
But dipped its top and set me down again.
That would be good both going and coming back.
One could do worse than be a swinger of birches.

Robert Graves (1895–   )

A Slice of Wedding Cake

Why have such scores of lovely, gifted girls
    Married impossible men?
Simple self-sacrifice may be ruled out,
    And missionary endeavor, nine times out of ten.

Repeat "impossible men": not merely rustic,   5
    Foul-tempered or depraved
(Dramatic foils chosen to show the world
    How well women behave, and always have be-
    haved).

Impossible men: idle, illiterate,
    Self-pitying, dirty, sly,   10
For whose appearance even in City parks
    Excuses must be made to casual passers-by.

Has God's supply of tolerable husbands
    Fallen, in fact, so low?
Or do I always over-value woman   15
    At the expense of man?
              Do I?
                 It might be so.

Robert Greene (1560–1592)

Philomela's Ode

Sitting by a river's side,
Where a silent stream did glide,
Muse I did of many things
That the mind in quiet brings.
I 'gan think how some men deem   5
Gold their god, and some esteem
Honor is the chief content
That to man in life is lent,
And some others do contend
Quiet none like to a friend;   10
Others hold there is no wealth
Cómpared to a perfect health;

Some man's mind in quiet stands
When he is lord of many lands.
But I did sigh, and said all this   *15*
Was but a shade of perfect bliss;
And in my thoughts I did approve
Nought so sweet as is true love.
Love 'twixt lovers passeth these,
When mouth kisseth and heart 'grees,   *20*
With folded arms and lips meeting,
Each soul another sweetly greeting;
For by the breath the soul fleeteth,
And soul with soul in kissing meeteth.
If love be so sweet a thing,   *25*
That such happy bliss doth bring,
Happy is love's sugared thrall;
But unhappy maidens all,
Who esteem your virgin blisses
Sweeter than a wife's sweet kisses.   *30*
No such quiet to the mind
As true love with kisses kind!
But if a kiss prove unchaste,
Then is true love quite disgraced.
Though love be sweet, learn this of me: *35*
No love sweet but honesty.

Thom Gunn *(1929–   )*

Considering the Snail

The snail pushes through a green
night, for the grass is heavy
with water and meets over
the bright path he makes, where rain
has darkened the earth's dark. He   *5*
moves in a wood of desire,

pale antlers barely stirring
as he hunts. I cannot tell
what power is at work, drenched there
with purpose, knowing nothing.   *10*
What is a snail's fury? All
I think is that if later

I parted the blades above
the tunnel and saw the thin
trail of broken white across   *15*
litter, I would never have
imagined the slow passion
to that deliberate progress.

Thomas Hardy *(1840–1928)*

The Convergence of the Twain
Lines on the Loss of the "Titanic"

1 In a solitude of the sea
Deep from human vanity,
And the Pride of Life that planned her, stilly couches
she.

2 Steel chambers, late the pyres
Of her salamandrine fires,   *5*
Cold currents thrid, and turn to rhythmic tidal lyres.

3 Over the mirrors meant
To glass the opulent
The sea worm crawls—grotesque, slimed, dumb,
indifferent.

4 Jewels in joy designed   *10*
To ravish the sensuous mind
Lie lightless, all their sparkles bleared and black and
blind.

5 Dim moon-eyed fishes near
Gaze at the gilded gear
And query: "What does this vaingloriousness down
here?" . . .   *15*

6 Well: while was fashioning
This creature of cleaving wing,
The Immanent Will that stirs and urges everything

7 Prepared a sinister mate
For her—so gaily great—   *20*
A Shape of Ice, for the time far and dissociate.

8 And as the smart ship grew
   In stature, grace, and hue,
In shadowy silent distance grew the Iceberg too.

9 Alien they seemed to be: 25
   No mortal eye could see
The intimate welding of their later history,

10 Or sign that they were bent
   By paths coincident
On being anon twin halves of one august event, 30

11 Till the Spinner of the Years
   Said "Now!" And each one hears,
And consummation comes, and jars two hemispheres.

Seamus Heaney (1939–)

Poor Women in a City Church

The small wax candles melt to light,
Flicker in marble, reflect bright
Asterisks on brass candlesticks:
At the Virgin's altar on the right
Blue flames are jerking on wicks.   5

Old dough-faced women with black shawls
Drawn down tight kneel in the stalls.
Cold yellow candle-tongues, blue flame
Mince and caper as whispered calls
Take wing up to the Holy Name.   10

Thus each day in the sacred place
They kneel. Golden shrines, altar lace,
Marble columns and cool shadows
Still them. In the gloom you cannot trace
A wrinkle on their beeswax brows.   15

George Herbert *(1593–1633)*

The Windows

Lord, how can man preach thy eternal word?
  He is a brittle crazy glass,
Yet in thy temple thou dost him afford
  This glorious and transcendent place
  To be a window, through thy grace.   *5*

But when thou dost anneal in glass thy story,
  Making thy life to shine within
The holy preacher's, then the light and glory
  More rev'rend grows, and doth more win;
  Which else shows wat'rish, bleak, and thin.   *10*

Doctrine and life, colors and light in one,
  When they combine and mingle, bring
A strong regard and awe; but speech alone
  Doth vanish like a flaring thing,
  And in the ear, not conscience, ring.   *15*

The Agony

Philosophers have measured mountains,
Fathomed the depths of seas, of states, and kings,
Walked with a staff to heaven, and traced fountains;
  But there are two vast, spacious things,
The which to measure it doth more behoove,   *5*
Yet few there are that sound them: Sin and Love.

Who would know Sin, let him repair
Unto Mount Olivet; there shall he see
A man so wrung with pains that all his hair,
  His skin, his garments bloody be.   *10*
Sin is that press and vice which forceth pain
To hunt his cruel food through every vein.

Who knows not love, let him assay
And taste that juice which on the cross a pike
Did set again abroach; then let him say   *15*
  If ever he did taste the like.
Love is that liquor sweet and most divine,
Which my God feels as blood, but I as wine.

Discipline

Throw away Thy rod,
Throw away Thy wrath.
  O my God,
Take the gentle path.

For my heart's desire   5
Unto Thine is bent;
  I aspire
To a full consent.

Not a word or look
I affect to own,   10
  But by book,
And Thy book alone.

Though I fail, I weep;
Though I halt in pace,
  Yet I creep   15
To the throne of grace.

Then let wrath remove;
Love will do the deed,
  For with love
Stony hearts will bleed.   20

Love is swift of foot.
Love's a man of war,
  And can shoot,
And can hit from far.

Robert Herrick (1591–1674)

The Night-Piece, to Julia

Her eyes the glow-worm lend thee;
The shooting stars attend thee;
  And the elves also,
  Whose little eyes glow
Like the sparks of fire, befriend thee.   5

No will-o'-the-wisp mis-light thee;
Nor snake or slow-worm bite thee;
    But on, on thy way,
    Not making a stay,
Since ghost there's none to affright thee.   *10*

Let not the dark thee cumber;
What though the moon does slumber?
    The stars of the night
    Will lend thee their light,
Like tapers clear without number.   *15*

Then, Julia, let me woo thee,
Thus, thus to come unto me;
    And when I shall meet
    Thy silv'ry feet,
My soul I'll pour into thee.   *20*

Robert Hershon (1935–   )

The Cooper & Bailey Great London Circus

In 1876
The Cooper & Bailey Great London Circus
Sailing from *Tasmania* to *Australia*
Suffered *Grievous* Injuries
During A Storm of *Singular* Magnitude   *5*

The *Rhinoceros* and The *Lion*
And The *Alligator* and The *Silver Fox*
And The *Tattooed Mule* and The *Imitation*
Penguin and The *Whitewashed Elephant*
Were Among Those *Drowned*   *10*
In The *Bubbling* Pacific

Cunning James Bailey
Had The Waterlogged *Giraffe*
Stuffed by A Gentleman in Sydney
Its *Head* Equipped with A *Device*   *15*
That Made It *Nod* Slowly and Regularly
Wily Bailey
Showed The Beast in A *Darkened Cage*
And It *Appeared* to Be *Alive* Which Made
The *Australian* People   *20*

Very Very Happy
And So They *Remain* to This Day
A *Grand* Triumph for The *Grand* Bailey
Mourner of Rhino *Fisher* of Lion
Resurrector of Giraffe   25
The *Bold* and *Businesslike* Bailey
Who *Gave* The People What They *Wanted*
This Has Been A Demanding Quarter
For Your Company Sales Decreased 14
Percent over The Corresponding Period   30
A Year Ago Nevertheless
We Are Pleased To Tell You That
Net Earnings (There Was A Fire
In Ohio In Which Several Clowns
Burned Up) *More Than Held Their Own*   35
Hold Your Own Hold Her Own
Hold His Own Nod Your Head

Gerard Manley Hopkins *(1844–1889)*

God's Grandeur

The world is charged with the grandeur of God.
    It will flame out, like shining from shook foil;
    It gathers to a greatness, like the ooze of oil
Crushed. Why do men then now not reck his rod?
Generations have trod, have trod, have trod;
    And all is seared with trade; bleared, smeared with
    toil;
    And wears man's smudge and shares man's smell:
    the soil
Is bare now, nor can foot feel, being shod.

And for all this, nature is never spent;
    There lives the dearest freshness deep down
    things;
And though the last lights off the black West went
    Oh, morning, at the brown brink eastward,
    springs—
Because the Holy Ghost over the bent
    World broods with warm breast and with ah! bright
    wings.

Pied Beauty

Glory be to God for dappled things—
  For skies of couple-colour as a brinded cow;
    For rose-moles all in stipple upon trout that swim;
Fresh-firecoal chestnut-falls; finches' wings;
  Landscape plotted and pieced—fold, fallow, and plough;
    And all trades, their gear and tackle and trim.

All things counter, original, spare, strange;
  Whatever is fickle, freckled (who knows how?)
    With swift, slow; sweet, sour; adazzle, dim;
He fathers-forth whose beauty is past change: Praise him.

A. E. Housman   (1859–1936)

Oh, when I was in love with you

Oh, when I was in love with you,
  Then I was clean and brave,
And miles around the wonder grew
  How well did I behave.

And now the fancy passes by,
  And nothing will remain,
And miles around they'll say that I
  Am quite myself again.

Terence, this is stupid stuff

"Terence, this is stupid stuff:
You eat your victuals fast enough;
There can't be much amiss, 'tis clear,
To see the rate you drink your beer.
But oh, good Lord, the verse you make,   *5*
It gives a chap the belly-ache.
The cow, the old cow, she is dead;
It sleeps well, the horned head:
We poor lads, 'tis our turn now
To hear such tunes as killed the cow.   *10*
Pretty friendship 'tis to rhyme
Your friends to death before their time
Moping melancholy mad:
Come, pipe a tune to dance to, lad."

Why, if 'tis dancing you would be,   *15*
There's brisker pipes than poetry.
Say, for what were hop-yards meant,
Or why was Burton built on Trent?
Oh many a peer of England brews
Livelier liquor than the Muse,   *20*
And malt does more than Milton can
To justify God's ways to man.
Ale, man, ale's the stuff to drink
For fellows whom it hurts to think:
Look into the pewter pot   *25*
To see the world as the world's not.
And faith, 'tis pleasant till 'tis past:
The mischief is that 'twill not last.
Oh I have been to Ludlow fair
And left my necktie God knows where,   *30*
And carried half-way home, or near,
Pints and quarts of Ludlow beer:
Then the world seemed none so bad,
And I myself a sterling lad;
And down in lovely muck I've lain,   *35*
Happy till I woke again.
Then I saw the morning sky:
Heigho, the tale was all a lie;
The world, it was the old world yet,
I was I, my things were wet,   *40*
And nothing now remained to do
But begin the game anew.

609   A. E. HOUSMAN

Therefore, since the world has still
Much good, but much less good than ill,
And while the sun and moon endure   *45*
Luck's a chance, but trouble's sure,
I'd face it as a wise man would,
And train for ill and not for good.
'Tis true, the stuff I bring for sale
Is not so brisk a brew as ale: *50*
Out of a stem that scored the hand
I wrung it in a weary land.
But take it: if the smack is sour,
The better for the embittered hour;
It should do good to heart and head   *55*
When your soul is in my soul's stead;
And I will friend you, if I may,
In the dark and cloudy day.

There was a king reigned in the East:
There, when kings will sit to feast,   *60*
They get their fill before they think
With poisoned meat and poisoned drink.
He gathered all that springs to birth
From the many-venomed earth;
First a little, thence to more,   *65*
He sampled all her killing store;
And easy, smiling, seasoned sound,
Sate the king when healths went round.
They put arsenic in his meat
And stared aghast to watch him eat;   *70*
They poured strychnine in his cup
And shook to see him drink it up:
They shook, they stared as white's their shirt:
Them it was their poison hurt.
—I tell the tale that I heard told.   *75*
Mithridates, he died old.

To an Athlete Dying Young

The time you won your town the race
We chaired you through the market place;
Man and boy stood cheering by,
And home we brought you shoulder-high.

Today, the road all runners come,   *5*
Shoulder-high we bring you home,
And set you at your threshold down,
Townsman of a stiller town.

Smart lad, to slip betimes away
From fields where glory does not stay   *10*
And early though the laurel grows
It withers quicker than the rose.

Eyes the shady night has shut
Cannot see the record cut,
And silence sounds no worse than cheers   *15*
After earth has stopped the ears:

Now you will not swell the rout
Of lads that wore their honors out,
Runners whom renown outran
And the name died before the man.   *20*

So set, before its echoes fade,
The fleet foot on the sill of shade,
And hold to the low lintel up
The still defended challenge cup.

And round that early laureled head   *25*
Will flock to gaze the strengthless dead
And find unwithered on its curls
The garland briefer than a girl's.

Langston Hughes   *(1902–1967)*

Dream Deferred

What happens to a dream deferred?
Does it dry up
like a raisin in the sun?
Or fester like a sore—
And then run?

Does it stink like rotten meat?
Or crust and sugar over—
like a syrupy sweet?

Maybe it just sags
like a heavy load.

Or does it explode?

I, too, sing America

I, too, sing America.

I am the darker brother.
They send me to eat in the kitchen
When company comes,
But I laugh,   5
And eat well,
And grow strong.

Tomorrow,
I'll sit at the table
When company comes.   10
Nobody'll dare
Say to me,
"Eat in the kitchen,"
Then.

Besides,   15
They'll see how beautiful I am
And be ashamed—

I, too, am America.

Ted Hughes (1930–   )

A Disaster

There came news of a word.
Crow saw it killing men. He ate well.
He saw it bulldozing

Whole cities to rubble. Again he ate well.
He saw its excreta poisoning seas.   5
He became watchful.
He saw its breath burning whole lands
To dusty char.
He flew clear and peered.

The word oozed its way, all mouth,   10
Earless, eyeless.
He saw it sucking the cities
Like the nipples of a sow
Drinking out all the people
Till there were none left,   15
All digested inside the word.

Ravenous, the word tried its great lips
On the earth's bulge, like a giant lamprey—
There it started to suck.

But its effort weakened.   20
It could digest nothing but people.
So there it shrank, wrinkling weaker,
Puddling
Like a collapsing mushroom.
Finally, a drying salty lake.   25
Its era was over.
All that remained of it a brittle desert
Dazzling with the bones of earth's people

Where Crow walked and mused.

Randall Jarrell (1914–1965)

The Orient Express

One looks from the train
Almost as one looked as a child. In the sunlight
What I see still seems to me plain,
I am safe; but at evening
As the lands darken, a questioning   5
Precariousness comes over everything.

Once after a day of rain
I lay longing to be cold; and after a while
I was cold again, and hunched shivering
Under the quilt's many colors, gray   *10*
With the dull ending of the winter day.
Outside me there were a few shapes
Of chairs and tables, things from a primer;
Outside the window
There were the chairs and tables of the world. . . . *15*
I saw that the world
That had seemed to me the plain
Gray mask of all that was strange
Behind it—of all that *was*—was all.

But it is beyond belief.   *20*
One thinks, "Behind everything
An unforced joy, an unwilling
Sadness (a willing sadness, a forced joy)
Moves changelessly"; one looks from the train
And there is something, the same thing   *25*
Behind everything: all these little villages,
A passing woman, a field of grain,
The man who says good-bye to his wife—
A path through a wood full of lives, and the train
Passing, after all unchangeable   *30*
And not now ever to stop, like a heart—

It is like any other work of art.
It is and never can be changed.
Behind everything there is always
The unknown unwanted life.   *35*

Elizabeth Jennings (1926–   )

In Memory of Anyone Unknown to Me

At this particular time I have no one
Particular person to grieve for, though there must
Be Many, many unknown ones going to dust
Slowly, not remembered for what they have done
Or left undone. For these, then, I will grieve   *5*
Being impartial, unable to deceive.

How they lived or died is quite unknown,
And, by the fact gives my grief purity—
An important person quite apart from me
Or one obscure who drifted down alone.   *10*
Both or all I remember, have a place.
For these I never encountered face to face.

Sentiment will creep in. I cast it out
Wishing to give these classical repose,
No epitaph, no poppy and no rose   *15*
From me, and certainly no wish to learn about
The way they lived or died. In earth or fire
They are gone. Simply because they were human, I
    admire.

Ben Jonson *(1573–1637)*

Song: to Celia

Come, my Celia, let us prove,
While we can, the sports of love.
Time will not be ours for ever;
He, at length, our good will sever;
Spend not then his gifts in vain.   *5*
Suns that set may rise again;
But if once we lose this light,
'T is with us perpetual night.
Why should we defer our joys?
Fame and rumor are but toys.   *10*
Cannot we delude the eyes
Of a few poor household spies?
Or his easier ears beguile,
Thus removéd by our wile?
'T is no sin love's fruits to steal;   *15*
But the sweet theft to reveal,
To be taken, to be seen,
These have crimes accounted been.

John Keats (1795–1821)

To Autumn

Season of mists and mellow fruitfulness,
  Close bosom friend of the maturing sun:
Conspiring with him how to load and bless
  With fruit the vines that round the thatch-eaves run;
To bend with apples the mossed cottage-trees,   5
  And fill all fruit with ripeness to the core;
    To swell the gourd, and plump the hazel shells
With a sweet kernel; to set budding more,
  And still more, later flowers for the bees,
  Until they think warm days will never cease,   10
    For Summer has o'er-brimmed their clammy cells.

Who hath not seen thee oft amid thy store?
  Sometimes whoever seeks abroad may find
Thee sitting careless on a granary floor,
  Thy hair soft-lifted by the winnowing wind;   15
Or on a half-reaped furrow sound asleep,
  Drowsed with the fume of poppies, while thy hook
    Spares the next swath and all its twinèd flowers:
And sometimes like a gleaner thou dost keep,
  Steady thy laden head across a brook;   20
  Or by a cider-press, with patient look,
    Thou watchest the last oozings hours by hours.

Where are the songs of Spring? Ay, where are they?
  Think not of them, thou hast thy music too,—
While barrèd clouds bloom the soft-dying day,   25
  And touch the stubble-plains with rosy hue;
Then in a wailful choir the small gnats mourn
  Among the river sallows, borne aloft
    Or sinking as the light wind lives or dies;
And full-grown lambs loud bleat from hilly bourn;   30
  Hedge-crickets sing: and now with treble soft
  The red-breast whistles from a garden-croft;
    And gathering swallows twitter in the skies.

La Belle Dame sans Merci

Oh, what can ail thee, knight-at-arms,
    Alone and palely loitering?
The sedge has withered from the lake,
    And no birds sing.

Oh, what can ail thee, knight-at-arms,   *5*
    So haggard and so woe-begone?
The squirrel's granary is full,
    And the harvest's done.

I see a lily on thy brow,
    With anguish moist and fever dew;   *10*
And on thy cheeks a fading rose
    Fast withereth too.

"I met a lady in the meads,
    Full beautiful—a faery's child;
Her hair was long, her foot was light,   *15*
    And her eyes were wild.

"I made a garland for her head,
    And bracelets too, and fragrant zone;
She looked at me as she did love,
    And made sweet moan.   *20*

"I set her on my pacing steed;
    And nothing else saw all day long;
For sideways would she lean, and sing
    A faery's song.

"She found me roots of relish sweet,   *25*
    And honey wild, and manna-dew,
And sure in language strange she said,
    'I love thee true.'

"She took me to her elfin grot,
    And there she wept, and sighed full sore,   *30*
And there I shut her wild, wild eyes,
    With kisses four.

"And there she lullèd me asleep,
    And there I dreamed—ah! woe betide!—
The latest dream I ever dreamed   *35*
    On the cold hill side.

"I saw pale kings and princes too,
    Pale warriors, death-pale were they all,
They cried—'La Belle Dame sans Merci
    Hath thee in thrall!'   *40*

"I saw their starved lips in the gloam,
    With horrid warning gapèd wide;
And I awoke, and found me here
    On the cold hill's side.

"And this is why I sojourn here,   *45*
    Alone and palely loitering,
Though the sedge is withered from the lake,
    And no birds sing."

Ode on a Grecian Urn

1   Thou still unravish'd bride of quietness,
      Thou foster-child of silence and slow time,
    Sylvan historian, who canst thus express
      A flowery tale more sweetly than our rhyme:
    What leaf-fring'd legend haunts about thy shape   *5*
      Of deities or mortals, or of both,
        In Tempe or the dales of Arcady?
      What men or gods are these? What maidens loth?
    What mad pursuit? What struggle to escape?   *9*
        What pipes and timbrels? What wild ecstasy?

2   Heard melodies are sweet, but those unheard
      Are sweeter; therefore, ye soft pipes, play on;
    Not to the sensual ear, but, more endear'd,
      Pipe to the spirit ditties of no tone:
    Fair youth, beneath the trees, thou canst not leave   *15*
      Thy song, nor ever can those trees be bare;
        Bold Lover, never, never canst thou kiss,
    Though winning near the goal—yet, do not grieve;
      She cannot fade, though thou hast not thy bliss,
        For ever wilt thou love, and she be fair!   *20*

3   Ah, happy, happy boughs! that cannot shed
      Your leaves, nor ever bid the Spring adieu;
    And, happy melodist, unwearied,
      For ever piping songs for ever new;

More happy love! more happy, happy love!   25
    For ever warm and still to be enjoy'd,
        For ever panting, and for ever young;
All breathing human passion far above,
    That leaves a heart high-sorrowful and cloy'd,
        A burning forehead, and a parching tongue. 30

4   Who are these coming to the sacrifice?
    To what green altar, O mysterious priest,
Lead'st thou that heifer lowing at the skies,
    And all her silken flanks with garlands drest?
What little town by river or sea shore,   35
    Or mountain-built with peaceful citadel,
        Is emptied of this folk, this pious morn?
And, little town, thy streets for evermore
    Will silent be; and not a soul to tell
        Why thou art desolate, can e'er return.   40

5   O Attic shape! Fair attitude! with brede
    Of marble men and maidens overwrought,
With forest branches and the trodden weed;
    Thou, silent form, dost tease us out of thought
As doth eternity: Cold Pastoral!   45
    When old age shall this generation waste,
        Thou shalt remain, in midst of other woe
Than ours, a friend to man, to whom thou say'st,
    "Beauty is truth, truth beauty,"—that is all
        Ye know on earth, and all ye need to know. 50

Walter Savage Landor *(1775–1864)*

On His Own Death

Death stands above me, whispering low
    I know not what into my ear:
Of his strange language all I know
    Is, there is not a word of fear.

On His Seventy-Fifth Birthday

I strove with none, for none was worth my strife.
Nature I loved and, next to Nature, Art:
I warm'd both hands before the fire of life;
It sinks, and I am ready to depart.

Edward Lear *(1812–1888)*

Cold Are the Crabs

Cold are the crabs that crawl on yonder hills,
Colder the cucumbers that grow beneath,
And colder still the brazen chops that wreathe
The tedious gloom of philosophic pills!
For when the tardy film of nectar fills
The ample bowls of demons and of men,
There lurks the feeble mouse, the homely hen,
And there the porcupine with all her quills.
Yet much remains—to weave a solemn strain
That lingering sadly—slowly dies away,
Daily departing with departing day.
A pea-green gamut on a distant plain
When wily walruses in congress meet—
Such such is life—

Vachel Lindsay *(1879–1931)*

General William Booth Enters into Heaven
To be sung to the tune of "The Blood of the Lamb"
with indicated instruments

1   *(Bass drum beaten loudly.)*
Booth led boldly with his big bass drum,
(Are you washed in the blood of the Lamb?)
The saints smiled gravely, and they said, "He's come."
(Are you washed in the blood of the Lamb?)

Walking lepers followed, rank on rank,   5
Lurching bravos from the ditches dank,
Drabs from the alleyways and drug-fiends pale—
Minds still passion-ridden, soul-powers frail:—
Vermin-eaten saints with moldy breath
Unwashed legions with the ways of death—   10
(Are you washed in the blood of the Lamb?)

   (Banjos.)
Every slum had sent its half-a-score
The round world over. (Booth had groaned for more.)
Every banner that the wide world flies
Bloomed with glory and transcendent dyes.   15
Big-voiced lasses made their banjos bang!
Tranced, fanatical, they shrieked and sang;—
"Are you washed in the blood of the Lamb?"
Hallelujah! It was queer to see
Bull-necked convicts with that land make free!   20
Loons with trumpets blowed a blare, blare, blare—
On, on, upward thro' the golden air!
(Are you washed in the blood of the Lamb?)

2   *(Bass drum slower and softer.)*
Booth died blind, and still by faith he trod,
Eyes still dazzled by the ways of God.   25
Booth led boldly, and he looked the chief:
Eagle countenance in sharp relief,
Beard a-flying, air of high command
Unabated in that holy land.

   (Sweet flute music.)
Jesus came from out the Courthouse door,   30
Stretched His hands above the passing poor.
Booth saw not, but led his queer ones there
'Round and 'round the mighty Courthouse square.
Yet in an instant all that blear review
Marched on spotless, clad in raiment new.   35
The lame were straightened, withered limbs uncurled,
And blind eyes opened on a new sweet world.

   (Bass drum louder.)
Drabs and vixens in a flash made whole!
Gone was the weasel-head, the snout, the jowl!
Sages and sibyls now, and athletes clean,   40
Rulers of empires, and of forests green!

(Grand chorus of all instruments. Tambourines to the foreground.)
The hosts were sandaled and their wings were fire!
(Are you washed in the blood of the Lamb?)
But their noise played havoc with the angel-choir.
(Are you washed in the blood of the Lamb?)   45
Oh, shout Salvation! it was good to see
Kings and Princes by the Lamb set free.
The banjos rattled and the tambourines
Jing-jing-jingled in the hands of Queens!

(Reverently sung, no instruments.)
And when Booth halted by the curb for prayer   50
He saw his Master thro' the flag-filled air.
Christ came gently with a robe and crown
For Booth the soldier, while the throng knelt down.
He saw King Jesus. They were face to face,
And he knelt a-weeping in that holy place.   55
Are you washed in the blood of the Lamb?

Robert Lovelace *(1618–1658)*

To Lucasta, Going to the Wars

Tell me not, Sweet, I am unkind
That from the nunnery
Of thy chaste breast and quiet mind,
To war and arms I fly.

True, a new mistress now I chase,
The first foe in the field;
And with a stronger faith embrace
A sword, a horse, a shield.

Yet this inconstancy is such
As you too shall adore;
I could not love thee, Dear, so much,
Loved I not honor more.

Amy Lowell   *(1874–1925)*

Patterns

I walk down the garden-paths,
And all the daffodils
Are blowing; and the bright blue squills.
I walk down the patterned garden-paths
In my stiff, brocaded gown.   *5*
With my powdered hair and jewelled fan,
I too am a rare
Pattern. As I wander down
The garden-paths.

My dress is richly figured,   *10*
And the train
Makes a pink and silver stain
On the gravel, and the thrift
Of the borders.
Just a plate of current fashion,   *15*
Tripping by in high-heeled, ribboned shoes.
Not a softness anywhere about me,
Only whalebone and brocade.
And I sink on a seat in the shade
Of a lime-tree. For my passion   *20*
Wars against the stiff brocade.
The daffodils and squills
Flutter in the breeze
As they please.
And I weep;   *25*
For the lime-tree is in blossom
And one small flower has dropped upon my bosom.
And the plashing of waterdrops
In the marble fountain
Comes down the garden-paths.   *30*
The dripping never stops.
Underneath my stiffened gown
Is the softness of a woman bathing in a marble basin,
A basin in the midst of hedges grown
So thick, she cannot see her lover hiding,   *35*
But she guesses he is near,
And the sliding of the water
Seems the stroking of a dear
Hand upon her.
What is Summer in a fine brocaded gown!   *40*
I should like to see it lying in a heap upon the ground.
All the pink and silver crumpled up on the ground.

I would be the pink and silver as I ran along the paths,
And he would stumble after,
Bewildered by my laughter.   *45*
I should see the sun flashing from his sword-hilt and the
    buckles on his shoes.
I would choose
To lead him in a maze along the patterned paths,
A bright and laughing maze for my heavy-booted lover.
Till he caught me in the shade,   *50*
And the buttons of his waistcoat bruised my body as he
    clasped me
Aching, melting, unafraid.
With the shadows of the leaves and the sundrops,
And the plopping of the waterdrops,
All about us in the open afternoon—   *55*
I am very like to swoon
With the weight of this brocade,
For the sun sifts through the shade.

Underneath the fallen blossom
In my bosom,   *60*
Is a letter I have hid.
It was brought to me this morning by a rider from the
    Duke.
"Madam, we regret to inform you that Lord Hartwell
Died in action Thursday se'nnight."
As I read it in the white, morning sunlight,   *65*
The letters squirmed like snakes.
"Any answer, Madam?" said my footman.
"No," I told him.
"See that the messenger takes some refreshment.
No, no answer."   *70*
And I walked into the garden,
Up and down the patterned paths,
In my stiff, correct brocade.
The blue and yellow flowers stood up proudly in the
    sun,
Each one.   *75*
I stood upright too,
Held rigid to the pattern
By the stiffness of my gown.
Up and down I walked,
Up and down.   *80*

In a month he would have been my husband.
In a month, here underneath this lime,
We would have broke the pattern;
He for me, and I for him,
He as Colonel, I as Lady,   85
On this shady seat.
He had a whim
That sunlight carried blessing.
And I answered, "It shall be as you have said."
Now he is dead.   90

In Summer and in Winter I shall walk
Up and down
The patterned garden-paths
In my stiff, brocaded gown.
The squills and daffodils   95
Will give place to pillared roses, and to asters, and to
    snow.
I shall go
Up and down,
In my gown.
Gorgeously arrayed,   100
Boned and stayed.
And the softness of my body will be guarded from
    embrace
By each button, hook, and lace.
For the man who should loose me is dead,
Fighting with the Duke in Flanders,   105
In a pattern called a war.
Christ! What are patterns for?

John Lyly *(1554–1606)*

Cupid and My Campaspe

Cupid and my Campaspe played
At cards for kisses; Cupid paid.
He stakes his quiver, bow, and arrows,
His mother's doves and team of sparrows;
Loses them, too. Then down he throws
The coral of his lip, the rose
Growing on's cheek (but none knows how);
With these, the crystal of his brow,

And then the dimple of his chin:
All these did my Campaspe win.
At last he set her both his eyes;
She won, and Cupid blind did rise.
O Love, has she done this to thee?
What shall, alas! become of me?

Sandford Lyne *(1945–   )*

The Dog

The old, shade-baked dog bolted
off the porch,
the plowboys in a beat-up Chevy yelling
like wet flags, a towel
wrapped in the hubcap. By the time   *5*
the dog caught up, he looked
like an enraged sud, running on stilts.
With a mercy that expects greater gore
the boys held off
the acid-gun from his eyes.   *10*
His snarling teeth
clinched in on the towel, took the bait,
took on
down his whole length the spin
of the tire, like   *15*
a woodstock on a lathe, his head
wrapped turban-fashion like a splayed
Saracen. He felt every bone
snap and puncture
some inexpendable organ,   *20*
even for a dog.
When the towel worked loose
from the bloody
ornament of the smoking wheel, he did
not convulse or yelp,   *25*
or die. But standing
kneedeep in his dropping guts, he took
the middle
of the road, and waited.

When the car turned around, came back   *30*
in a whine, he
planted himself like an iron
pick, met the grill
face to face, sent
his whole insides up the hood, the windshield, like *35*
the world's biggest butterfly, blocked
the entire vision
of the onrushing earth, the shoulder,
ditch,
telephone pole, the   *40*
falling sky

in the kingdom of dog.

Archibald MacLeish (1892–   )

Ars Poetica

A poem should be palpable and mute
As a globed fruit,

Dumb
As old medallions to the thumb,

Silent as the sleeve-worn stone   *5*
Of casement ledges where the moss has grown—

A poem should be wordless
As the flight of birds.

A poem should be motionless in time
As the moon climbs,   *10*

Leaving, as the moon releases
Twig by twig the night-entangled trees,

Leaving, as the moon behind the winter leaves,
Memory by memory the mind—

A poem should be motionless in time   *15*
As the moon climbs.

A poem should be equal to:
Not true.

For all the history of grief
An empty doorway and a maple leaf.   *20*

For love
The leaning grasses and two lights above the sea—

A poem should not mean
But be.

You, Andrew Marvell

And here face down beneath the sun
And here upon earth's noonward height
To feel the always coming on
The always rising of the night:

To feel creep up the curving east   *5*
The earthly chill of dusk and slow
Upon those under lands the vast
And ever climbing shadow grow

And strange at Ecbatan the trees
Take leaf by leaf the evening strange   *10*
The flooding dark about their knees
The mountains over Persia change

And now at Kermanshah the gate
Dark empty and the withered grass
And through the twilight now the late   *15*
Few travelers in the westward pass

And Baghdad darken and the bridge
Across the silent river gone
And through Arabia the edge
Of evening widen and steal on   *20*

And deepen on Palmyra's street
The wheel rut in the ruined stone
And Lebanon fade out and Crete
High through the clouds and overblown

And over Sicily the air   *25*
Still flashing with the landward gulls
And loom and slowly disappear
The sails above the shadowy hulls

And Spain go under and the shore
Of Africa the gilded sand   *30*
And evening vanish and no more
The low pale light across that land

Nor now the long light on the sea:

And here face downward in the sun
To feel how swift how secretly   *35*
The shadow of the night comes on . . .

Louis MacNeice *(1907–1963)*

Sunday Morning

Down the road someone is practicing scales,
The notes like little fishes vanish with a wink of tails,
Man's heart expands to tinker with his car
For this is Sunday morning, Fate's great bazaar,
Regard these means as ends, concentrate on this Now,
And you may grow to music or drive beyond Hindhead
    anyhow,
Take corners on two wheels until you go so fast
That you can clutch a fringe or two of the windy past,
That you can abstract this day and make it to the week
    of time
A small eternity, a sonnet self-contained in rhyme.

But listen, up the road, something gulps, the church
    spire
Opens its eight bells out, skulls' mouths which will not
    tire
To tell how there is no music or movement which
    secures
Escape from the weekday time. Which deadens and
    endures.

Edgar Lee Masters *(1868–1950)*

Cassius Hueffer

They have chiseled on my stone the words:
"His life was gentle, and the elements so mixed in him
That nature might stand up and say to all the world,
This was a man."
Those who knew me smile
As they read this empty rhetoric.
My epitaph should have been:
"Life was not gentle to him,
And the elements so mixed in him
That he made warfare on life,
In the which he was slain."
While I lived I could not cope with slanderous tongues,
Now that I am dead I must submit to an epitaph
Graven by a fool!

Margaret Fuller Slack

I would have been as great as George Eliot
But for an untoward fate.
For look at the photograph of me made by Penniwit,
Chin resting on hand, and deep-set eyes—
Gray, too, and far-searching.   5
But there was the old, old problem:
Should it be celibacy, matrimony or unchastity?
Then John Slack, the rich druggist, wooed me,
Luring me with the promise of leisure for my novel,
And I married him, giving birth to eight children,   10
And had no time to write.
It was all over with me, anyway,
When I ran the needle in my hand
While washing the baby's things,
And died from lock-jaw, an ironical death.   15
Hear me, ambitious souls,
Sex is the curse of life!

Herman Melville (1819–1891)

The Maldive Shark

About the Shark, phlegmatical one,
Pale sot of the Maldive sea,
The sleek little pilot-fish, azure and slim,
How alert in attendance be.
From his saw-pit of mouth, from his charnel of maw 5
They have nothing of harm to dread,
But liquidly glide on his ghastly flank
Or before his Gorgonian head;
Or lurk in the port of serrated teeth
In white triple tiers of glittering gates,   10
And there find a haven when peril's abroad,
An asylum in jaws of the Fates!
They are friends; and friendly they guide him to prey,
Yet never partake of the treat—
Eyes and brains to the dotard lethargic and dull,   15
Pale ravener of horrible meat.

James Merrill (1926–   )

Laboratory Poem

Charles used to watch Naomi, taking heart
And a steel saw, open up turtles, live.
While she swore they felt nothing, he would gag
At blood, at the blind twitching, even after
The murky dawn of entrails cleared, revealing   5
Contours he knew, egg-yellows like lamps paling.

Well then. She carried off the beating heart
To the kymograph and rigged it there, a rag
In fitful wind, now made to strain, now stopped
By her solutions tonic or malign   10
Alternately in which it would be steeped.
What the heart bore, she noted on a chart,

For work did not stop only with the heart.
He thought of certain human hearts, their climb
Through violence into exquisite disciplines   15
Of which, as it now appeared, they all expired.
Soon she would fetch another and start over,
Easy in the presence of her lover.

Richard Messer (1938–   )

Shadows

My saw split living wood
into the light. A jay screamed
as the sun came loose
from the broken fingers of the leaves.

Underground, luminescent roots went black
like dangling nerves from a severed spine;
the great tree went blind, tripped
and fell straight out, face down
into its jumbled chips,
sucking its shadow in
like a last breath.

Then the hungry sunlight dropped
over the stump
and around my darkening shadow.

John Milton (1608–1674)

When I consider how my light is spent

When I consider how my light is spent,
    Ere half my days, in this dark world and wide,
    And that one Talent which is death to hide,
    Lodg'd with me useless, though my Soul more
    bent

To serve therewith my Maker, and present
    My true account, lest he returning chide;
    "Doth God exact day-labor, light denied,"
    I fondly ask; But patience to prevent
That murmur soon replies, "God doth not need
    Either man's work or his own gifts; who best
    Bear his mild yoke, they serve him best; his State
Is Kingly. Thousands at his bidding speed
    And post o'er Land and Ocean without rest:
    They also serve who only stand and wait."

How soon hath Time, the subtle thief of youth

How soon hath Time, the subtle thief of youth,
    Stol'n on his wing my three and twentieth year!
    My hasting days fly on with full career,
    But my late spring no bud or blossom show'th.
Perhaps my semblance might deceive the truth,
    That I to manhood am arriv'd so near,
    And inward ripeness doth much less appear,
    That some more timely-happy spirits endu'th.
Yet be it less or more, or soon or slow,
    It shall be still in strictest measure ev'n
    To that same lot, however mean or high,
Toward which Time leads me, and the will of Heav'n;
    All is, if I have grace to use it so,
    As ever in my great task-Master's eye.

Marianne Moore   *(1887–1972)*

Poetry

I, too, dislike it: there are things that are important
beyond all this fiddle.
    Reading it, however, with a perfect contempt for it,
    one discovers in
    it after all, a place for the genuine.
        Hands that can grasp, eyes
        that can dilate, hair that can rise   5
            if it must, these things are important not
            because a

high-sounding interpretation can be put upon them
but because they are
    useful. When they become so derivative as to
    become unintelligible,
    the same thing may be said for all of us, that we
        do not admire what   *10*
        we cannot understand: the bat
            holding on upside down or in quest of
            something to

eat, elephants pushing, a wild horse taking a roll, a
tireless wolf under
    a tree, the immovable critic twitching his skin
    like a horse that feels a flea, the base-
    ball fan, the statistician—   *15*
        nor is it valid
            to discriminate against 'business docu-
            ments and

school-books'; all these phenomena are important.
One must make a distinction
    however: when dragged into prominence by half
    poets, the result is not poetry,
    nor till the poets among us can be   *20*
        'literalists of
        the imagination'—above
            insolence and triviality and can present

for inspection, imaginary gardens with real toads in
them, shall we have
    it. In the meantime, if you demand on the one
    hand,   *25*
        the raw material of poetry in
        all its rawness and
        that which is on the other hand
            genuine, then you are interested in
            poetry.

Ogden Nash   *(1902–1971)*

Inter-Office Memorandum

The only people who should really sin
Are the people who can sin with a grin,
Because if sinning upsets you,
Why, nothing at all is what it gets you.
Everybody certainly ought to eschew all offences how-
    ever venial   5
As long as they are conscience's menial.
Some people suffer weeks of remorse after having
    committed the slightest peccadillo,
And other people feel perfectly all right after feeding
    their husbands arsenic or smothering their grand-
    mother with a pillow.
Some people are perfectly self-possessed about spend-
    ing their lives on the verge of delirium tremens,
And other people feel like hanging themselves on a
    coathook just because they took that extra cocktail
    and amused their fellow guests with recitations
    from the poems of Mrs. Hemans.   10
Some people calmly live a barnyard life because they
    find monogamy dull and arid,
And other people have sinking spells if they dance twice
    in an evening with a lady to whom they aren't
    married.
Some people feel forever lost if they are riding on a bus
    and the conductor doesn't collect their fare,
And other people ruin a lot of widows and orphans, and
    all they think is, Why there's something in this
    business of ruining widows and orphans, and they
    go out and ruin some more and get to be a
    millionaire.
Now it is not the purpose of this memorandum, or
    song,   15
To attempt to define the difference between right and
    wrong;
All I am trying to say is that if you are one of the
    unfortunates who recognize that such a difference
    exists,
Well, you had better oppose even the teensiest tempta-
    tion with clenched fists,
Because if you desire peace of mind it is all right to do
    wrong if it never occurs to you that it is wrong to do
    it,

Because you can sleep perfectly well and look the world
    in the eye after doing anything at all so long as you
    don't rue it,   *20*
While on the other hand nothing at all is any fun
So long as you yourself know it is something you
    shouldn't have done.
There is only one way to achieve happiness on this
    terrestrial ball,
And that is to have either a clear conscience, or none at
    all.

Bonaro W. Overstreet *(1902–   )*

John Doe, Jr.

Among the Missing . . .
I think he always was—
Only no one thought to mention it before . . .

He was the boy who didn't make the team
although, God knows, he tried: his were the fingers, *5*
always too eager, that always fumbled the ball.
He was the fellow
people forgot to invite when they planned a party.
After the party, once in a while, they would say,
"We should have invited John." But that was after;
and most of the time they did not think about it.   *11*
John thought about it: thought of the laughter and
    music.
He was the chap who dreamed that his loneliness
might somehow find in words a redemptive beauty:
the yearning youth who sent his poems and stories, *15*
bundled in hope, to editors—found them,
paired to rejection slips, in his mail-box later.

He was the man, defeated by diffidence,
who waited in line—and who did not get the job . . .
Only war had use for him, and only   *20*
long enough to lose him . . .
                Among the missing . . .

Wilfred Owen *(1893–1918)*

Greater Love

Red lips are not so red
    As the stained stones kissed by the English dead.
Kindness of wooed and wooer
Seems shame to their love pure.
O Love, your eyes lose lure   *5*
    When I behold eyes blinded in my stead!

Your slender attitude
    Trembles not exquisite like limbs knife skewed,
Rolling and rolling there
Where God seems not to care;   *10*
Till the fierce love they bear
    Cramps them in death's extreme decrepitude.

Your voice sings not so soft—
    Though even as wind murmuring through raftered
    loft—
Your dear voice is not dear,   *15*
Gentle, and evening clear,
As theirs whom none now hear,
    Now earth has stopped their piteous mouths that
    coughed.

Heart, you were never hot   *19*
    Nor large, nor full like hearts made great with shot;
And though your hand be pale,
Paler are all which trail
Your cross through flame and hail:
    Weep, you may weep, for you may touch them
    not.

Anthem for Doomed Youth

What passing-bells for these who die as cattle?
Only the monstrous anger of the guns.
Only the stuttering rifles' rapid rattle
Can patter out their hasty orisons.
No mockeries for them from prayers or bells,
Nor any voice of mourning save the choirs—
The shrill, demented choirs of wailing shells;
And bugles calling for them from sad shires.

What candles may be held to speed them all?
Not in the hands of boys, but in their eyes
Shall shine the holy glimmers of good-byes.
The pallor of girls' brows shall be their pall;
Their flowers the tenderness of patient minds,
And each slow dusk a drawing-down of blinds.

George Peek   *(1945–   )*

The Seminole Village in Miami

Annie Jim
           sat
by her sewing machine—

The breeze
           through   *5*
the chickee was moist and cool—

And her husband
                slept
with his wired, broken jaw.

The alligator   *10*
           had won
one round,
while the crowd cheered
and gasped
and focused their cameras.   *15*

Annie Jim
           still sits
by her sewing machine,

Creating
           Joseph's coat-of-many-colors   *20*
for tourists on the move.

Twenty dollars
                for part
of a family's soul.

Edgar Allan Poe *(1809–1849)*

The Raven

Once upon a midnight dreary, while I pondered, weak
and weary,
Over many a quaint and curious volume of forgotten
lore—
While I nodded, nearly napping, suddenly there came a
tapping,
As of some one gently rapping, rapping at my chamber
door.
" 'Tis some visitor," I muttered, "tapping at my
chamber door—   5
Only this and nothing more."

Ah, distinctly I remember it was in the bleak
December;
And each separate dying ember wrought its ghost upon
the floor.
Eagerly I wished the morrow;—vainly I had sought to
borrow
From my books surcease of sorrow—sorrow for the lost
Lenore—   10
For the rare and radiant maiden whom the angels name
Lenore—
Nameless *here* for evermore.

And the silken, sad, uncertain rustling of each purple
curtain
Thrilled me—filled me with fantastic terrors never felt
before;
So that now, to still the beating of my heart, I stood
repeating   15
" 'Tis some visitor entreating entrance at my chamber
door—
Some late visitor entreating entrance at my chamber
door:—
This it is and nothing more."

Presently my soul grew stronger; hesitating then no
    longer,
"Sir," said I, "or Madam, truly your forgiveness I
    implore;   20
But the fact is I was napping, and so gently you came
    rapping,
And so faintly you came tapping, tapping at my chamber
    door,
That I scarce was sure I heard you"—here I opened
    wide the door;—
    Darkness there and nothing more.

Deep into that darkness peering, long I stood there
    wondering, fearing,   25
Doubting, dreaming dreams no mortal ever dared to
    dream before;
But the silence was unbroken, and the stillness gave no
    token,
And the only word there spoken was the whispered
    word, "Lenore?"
Till I whispered, and an echo murmured back the word,
    "Lenore!"
    Merely this and nothing more.   30

Back into the chamber turning, all my soul within me
    burning,
Soon again I heard a tapping somewhat louder than
    before.
"Surely," said I, "surely that is something at my
    window lattice;
Let me see, then, what thereat is, and this mystery
    explore—
Let my heart be still a moment and this mystery
    explore;—   35
    'Tis the wind and nothing more!"

Open here I flung the shutter, when, with many a flirt
    and flutter,
In there stepped a stately Raven of the saintly days of
    yore;
Not the least obeisance made he; not a minute stopped
    or stayed he;
But, with mien of lord or lady, perched above my
    chamber door—   40
Perched upon a bust of Pallas just above my chamber
    door—
    Perched, and sat, and nothing more.

Then this ebony bird beguiling my sad fancy into
  smiling,
By the grave and stern decorum of the countenance it
  wore,
"Though thy crest be shorn and shaven, thou," I said,
  "art sure no craven,   45
Ghastly grim and ancient Raven wandering from the
  Nightly shore—
Tell me what thy lordly name is on the Night's Plutoni-
  an shore!"
  Quoth the Raven, "Nevermore."

Much I marvelled this ungainly fowl to hear discourse
  so plainly,
Though its answer little meaning—little relevancy
  bore;   50
For we cannot help agreeing that no living human being
Ever yet was blessed with seeing bird above his chamber
  door—
Bird or beast upon the sculptured bust above his
  chamber door,
  With such name as "Nevermore."

But the Raven, sitting lonely on the placid bust, spoke
  only   55
That one word, as if his soul in that one word he did
  outpour.
Nothing farther then he uttered—not a feather then he
  fluttered—
Till I scarcely more than muttered "Other friends have
  flown before—
On the morrow *he* will leave me, as my Hopes have
  flown before."
  Then the bird said "Nevermore."   60

Startled at the stillness broken by reply so aptly spoken,
"Doubtless," said I, "what it utters is its only stock and
  store
Caught from some unhappy master whom unmerciful
  Disaster
Followed fast and followed faster till his songs one
  burden bore—
Till the dirges of his Hope that melancholy burden
  bore   65
  Of 'Never-nevermore.'"

But the Raven still beguiling my sad fancy into smiling,
Straight I wheeled a cushioned seat in front of bird, and
    bust and door;
Then, upon the velvet sinking, I betook myself to
    linking
Fancy unto fancy, thinking what this ominous bird of
    yore—   *70*
What this grim, ungainly, ghastly, gaunt, and ominous
    bird of yore
    Meant in croaking "Nevermore."

This I sat engaged in guessing, but no syllable
    expressing
To the fowl whose fiery eyes now burned into my
    bosom's core;
This and more I sat divining, with my head at ease
    reclining   *75*
On the cushion's velvet lining that the lamp-light
    gloated o'er,
But whose velvet-violet lining with the lamp-light
    gloating o'er,
    She shall press, ah, nevermore!

Then, methought, the air grew denser, perfumed from
    an unseen censer
Swung by seraphim whose foot-falls tinkled on the
    tufted floor.   *80*
"Wretch," I cried, "thy God hath lent thee—by these
    angels he hath sent thee
Respite—respite and nepenthe from thy memories of
    Lenore;
Quaff, oh quaff this kind nepenthe and forget this lost
    Lenore!"
    Quoth the Raven "Nevermore."

"Prophet!" said I, "thing of evil!—prophet still, if bird
    or devil!—   *85*
Whether Tempter sent, or whether tempest tossed thee
    here ashore,
Desolate yet all undaunted, on this desert land
    enchanted—
On this home by Horror haunted—tell me truly, I
    implore—
Is there—*is* there balm in Gilead?—tell me—tell me, I
    implore!"
    Quoth the Raven "Nevermore."   *90*

"Prophet!" said I, "thing of evil!—prophet still, if bird
  or devil!
By that Heaven that bends above us—by that God we
  both adore—
Tell this soul with sorrow laden if, within the distant
  Aidenn,
It shall clasp a sainted maiden whom the angels named
  Lenore—
Clasp a rare and radiant maiden whom the angels name
  Lenore."   95
  Quoth the Raven "Nevermore."

"Be that word our sign of parting, bird or fiend!" I
  shrieked, upstarting—
"Get thee back into the tempest and the Night's
  Plutonian shore!
Leave no black plume as a token of that lie thy soul hath
  spoken!
Leave my loneliness unbroken!—quit the bust above
  my door!   100
Take thy beak from out my heart, and take thy form
  from off my door!"
  Quoth the Raven "Nevermore."

And the Raven, never flitting, still is sitting, *still* is
  sitting
On the pallid bust of Pallas just above my chamber
  door;
And his eyes have all the seeming of a demon's that is
  dreaming,   105
And the lamp-light o'er him streaming throws his
  shadow on the floor;
And my soul from out that shadow that lies floating on
  the floor
  Shall be lifted—nevermore!

Alexander Pope *(1688–1744)*

The Rape of the Lock
An Heroi-comical Poem

Nolueram, Belinda, tuos violare capillos; sed juvat hoc precibus me tribuisse tuis.

MARTIAL

Canto 1

What dire offense from amorous causes springs,
What mighty contests rise from trivial things,
I sing—This verse to Caryll, Muse! is due:
This, even Belinda may vouchsafe to view:
Slight is the subject, but not so the praise,   *5*
If she inspire, and he approve my lays.
    Say what strange motive, Goddess! could compel
A well-bred lord to assault a gentle belle?
Oh, say what stranger cause, yet unexplored,
Could make a gentle belle reject a lord?   *10*
In tasks so bold can little men engage,
And in soft bosoms dwells such mighty rage?
    Sol through white curtains shot a timorous ray,
And oped those eyes that must eclipse the day.
Now lapdogs give themselves the rousing shake,   *15*
And sleepless lovers just at twelve awake:
Thrice rung the bell, the slipper knocked the ground,
And the pressed watch returned a silver sound.
Belinda still her downy pillow pressed,
Her guardian Sylph prolonged the balmy rest: *20*
'Twas he had summoned to her silent bed
The morning dream that hovered o'er her head.
A youth more glittering than a birthnight beau
(That even in slumber caused her cheek to glow)
Seemed to her ear his winning lips to lay,   *25*
And thus in whispers said, or seemed to say:
    "Fairest of mortals, thou distinguished care
Of thousand bright inhabitants of air!
If e'er one vision touched thy infant thought,
Of all the nurse and all the priest have taught,   *30*
Of airy elves by moonlight shadows seen,
The silver token, and the circled green,
Or virgins visited by angel powers,
With golden crowns and wreaths of heavenly flowers,
Hear and believe! thy own importance know,   *35*
Nor bound thy narrow views to things below.

Some secret truths, from learned pride concealed,
To maids alone and children are revealed:
What though no credit doubting wits may give?
The fair and innocent shall still believe.   *40*
Know, then, unnumbered spirits round thee fly,
The light militia of the lower sky:
These, though unseen, are ever on the wing,
Hang o'er the box, and hover round the Ring.
Think what an equipage thou hast in air,   *45*
And view with scorn two pages and a chair.
As now your own, our beings were of old,
And once enclosed in woman's beauteous mold;
Thence, by a soft transition, we repair
From earthly vehicles to these of air.   *50*
Think not, when woman's transient breath is fled,
That all her vanities at once are dead:
Succeeding vanities she still regards,
And though she plays no more, o'erlooks the cards.
Her joy in gilded chariots, when alive,   *55*
And love of ombre, after death survive.
For when the Fair in all their pride expire,
To their first elements their souls retire:
The sprites of fiery termagants in flame
Mount up, and take a Salamander's name.   *60*
Soft yielding minds to water glide away,
And sip, with Nymphs, their elemental tea.
The graver prude sinks downward to a Gnome,
In search of mischief still on earth to roam.
The light coquettes in Sylphs aloft repair,   *65*
And sport and flutter in the fields of air.
      "Know further yet; whoever fair and chaste
Rejects mankind, is by some Sylph embraced:
For spirits, freed from mortal laws, with ease
Assume what sexes and what shapes they please.   *70*
What guards the purity of melting maids,
In courtly balls, and midnight masquerades,
Safe from the treacherous friend, the daring spark,
The glance by day, the whisper in the dark,
When kind occasion prompts their warm desires,   *75*
When music softens, and when dancing fires?
'Tis but their Sylph, the wise Celestials know,
Though Honor is the word with men below.
      "Some nymphs there are, too conscious of their
            face,
For life predestined to the Gnomes' embrace.   *80*

These swell their prospects and exalt their pride,
When offers are disdained, and love denied:
Then gay ideas crowd the vacant brain,
While peers, and dukes, and all their sweeping train,
And garters, stars, and coronets appear,   *85*
And in soft sounds, 'your Grace' salutes their ear.
'Tis these that early taint the female soul,
Instruct the eyes of young coquettes to roll,
Teach infant cheeks a bidden blush to know,
And little hearts to flutter at a beau.   *90*
    "Oft, when the world imagine women stray,
The Sylphs through mystic mazes guide their way,
Through all the giddy circle they pursue,
And old impertinence expel by new.
What tender maid but must a victim fall   *95*
To one man's treat, but for another's ball?
When Florio speaks what virgin could withstand,
If gentle Damon did not squeeze her hand?
With varying vanities, from every part,
They shift the moving toyshop of their heart;   *100*
Where wigs with wigs, with sword-knots sword-knots
    strive,
Beaux banish beaux, and coaches coaches drive.
This erring mortals levity may call;
Oh, blind to truth! the Sylphs contrive it all.
    "Of these am I, who thy protection claim,   *105*
A watchful sprite, and Ariel is my name.
Late, as I ranged the crystal wilds of air,
In the clear mirror of thy ruling star
I saw, alas! some dread event impend,
Ere to the main this morning sun descend,   *110*
But Heaven reveals not what, or how, or where:
Warned by the Sylph, O pious maid, beware!
This to disclose is all thy guardian can:
Beware of all, but most beware of Man!"
    He said; when Shock, who thought she slept too
    long,   *115*
Leaped up, and waked his mistress with his
    tongue.
'Twas then, Belinda, if report say true,
Thy eyes first opened on a billet-doux,
Wounds, charms, and ardors were no sooner read,
But all the vision vanished from thy head.   *120*
    And now, unveiled, the toilet stands displayed,
Each silver vase in mystic order laid.

First, robed in white, the nymph intent adores,
With head uncovered, the cosmetic powers.
A heavenly image in the glass appears;   125
To that she bends, to that her eyes she rears.
The inferior priestess, at her altar's side,
Trembling begins the sacred rites of pride.
Unnumbered treasures ope at once, and here
The various offerings of the world appear;   130
From each she nicely culls with curious toil,
And decks the goddess with the glittering spoil.
This casket India's glowing gems unlocks,
And all Arabia breathes from yonder box.
The tortoise here and elephant unite,   135
Transformed to combs, the speckled and the white.
Here files of pins extend their shining rows,
Puffs, powders, patches, Bibles, billet-doux.
Now awful Beauty put on all its arms;
The fair each moment rises in her charms,   140
Repairs her smiles, awakens every grace,
And calls forth all the wonders of her face;
Sees by degrees a purer blush arise,
And keener lightnings quicken in her eyes.
The busy Sylphs surround their darling care,   145
These set the head, and those divide the hair,
Some fold the sleeve, whilst others plait the gown;
And Betty's praised for labors not her own.

Canto 2   Not with more glories, in the ethereal plain,
The sun first rises o'er the purpled main,
Than, issuing forth, the rival of his beams
Launched on the bosom of the silver Thames.
Fair nymphs and well-dressed youths around her shone,
But every eye was fixed on her alone.   6
On her white breast a sparkling cross she wore,
Which Jews might kiss, and infidels adore.
Her lively looks a sprightly mind disclose,
Quick as her eyes, and as unfixed as those: 10
Favors to none, to all she smiles extends;
Oft she rejects, but never once offends.
Bright as the sun, her eyes the gazers strike,
And, like the sun, they shine on all alike.
Yet graceful ease, and sweetness void of pride,   15
Might hide her faults, if belles had faults to hide:
If to her share some female errors fall,
Look on her face, and you'll forget 'em all.

This nymph, to the destruction of mankind,
Nourished two locks which graceful hung behind   *20*
In equal curls, and well conspired to deck
With shining ringlets the smooth ivory neck.
Love in these labyrinths his slaves detains,
And mighty hearts are held in slender chains.
With hairy springes we the birds betray,   *25*
Slight lines of hair surprise the finny prey,
Fair tresses man's imperial race ensnare,
And beauty draws us with a single hair.

The adventurous Baron the bright locks admired,
He saw, he wished, and to the prize aspired.   *30*
Resolved to win, he meditates the way,
By force to ravish, or by fraud betray;
For when success a lover's toil attends,
Few ask if fraud or force attained his ends.

For this, ere Phoebus rose, he had implored   *35*
Propitious Heaven, and every power adored,
But chiefly Love—to Love an altar built,
Of twelve vast French romances, neatly gilt.
There lay three garters, half a pair of gloves,
And all the trophies of his former loves.   *40*
With tender billet-doux he lights the pyre,
And breathes three amorous sighs to raise the fire.
Then prostrate falls, and begs with ardent eyes
Soon to obtain, and long possess the prize:
The powers gave ear, and granted half his prayer,   *45*
The rest the winds dispersed in empty air.

But now secure the painted vessel glides,
The sunbeams trembling on the floating tides,
While melting music steals upon the sky,
And softened sounds along the waters die.   *50*
Smooth flow the waves, the zephyrs gently play,
Belinda smiled, and all the world was gay.
All but the Sylph—with careful thoughts oppressed,
The impending woe sat heavy on his breast.
He summons straight his denizens of air;   *55*
The lucid squadrons round the sails repair:
Soft o'er the shrouds aërial whispers breathe
That seemed but zephyrs to the train beneath.
Some to the sun their insect-wings unfold,
Waft on the breeze, or sink in clouds of gold.   *60*
Transparent forms too fine for mortal sight,
Their fluid bodies half dissolved in light,
Loose to the wind their airy garments flew,
Thin glittering textures of the filmy dew,

Dipped in the richest tincture of the skies,   *65*
Where light disports in ever-mingling dyes,
While every beam new transient colors flings,
Colors that change whene'er they wave their wings.
Amid the circle, on the gilded mast,
Superior by the head was Ariel placed;   *70*
His purple pinions opening to the sun,
He raised his azure wand, and thus begun:
    "Ye Sylphs and Sylphids, to your chief give ear!
Fays, Fairies, Genii, Elves, and Daemons, hear!
Ye know the spheres and various tasks assigned   *75*
By laws eternal to the aërial kind.
Some in the fields of purest ether play,
And bask and whiten in the blaze of day.
Some guide the course of wandering orbs on high,
Or roll the planets through the boundless sky.   *80*
Some less refined, beneath the moon's pale light
Pursue the stars that shoot athwart the night,
Or suck the mists in grosser air below,
Or dip their pinions in the painted bow,
Or brew fierce tempests on the wintry main,   *85*
Or o'er the glebe distill the kindly rain.
Others on earth o'er human race preside,
Watch all their ways, and all their actions guide:
Of these the chief the care of nations own,
And guard with arms divine the British Throne.   *90*
    "Our humbler province is to tend the Fair,
Not a less pleasing, though less glorious care:
To save the powder from too rude a gale,
Nor let the imprisoned essences exhale;
To draw fresh colors from the vernal flowers;   *95*
To steal from rainbows e'er they drop in showers
A brighter wash; to curl their waving hairs,
Assist their blushes, and inspire their airs;
Nay oft, in dreams invention we bestow,
To change a flounce, or add a furbelow.   *100*
    "This day black omens threat the brightest fair,
That e'er deserved a watchful spirit's care;
Some dire disaster, or by force or slight,
But what, or where, the Fates have wrapped in night:
Whether the nymph shall break Diana's law,   *105*
Or some frail china jar receive a flaw,
Or stain her honor or her new brocade,
Forget her prayers, or miss a masquerade,

Or lose her heart, or necklace, at a ball;
Or whether Heaven has doomed that Shock must fall.
Haste, then, ye spirits! to your charge repair: *111*
The fluttering fan be Zephyretta's care;
The drops to thee, Brillante, we consign;
And, Momentilla, let the watch be thine;
Do thou, Crispissa, tend her favorite Lock;   *115*
Ariel himself shall be the guard of Shock.
        "To fifty chosen Sylphs, of special note,
We trust the important charge, the petticoat;
Oft have we known that sevenfold fence to fail,
Though stiff with hoops, and armed with ribs of
        whale.   *120*
Form a strong line about the silver bound,
And guard the wide circumference around.
        "Whatever spirit, careless of his charge,
His post neglects, or leaves the fair at large,
Shall feel sharp vengeance soon o'ertake his sins,   *125*
Be stopped in vials, or transfixed with pins,
Or plunged in lakes of bitter washes lie,
Or wedged whole ages in a bodkin's eye;
Gums and pomatums shall his flight restrain,
While clogged he beats his silken wings in vain,   *130*
Or alum styptics with contracting power
Shrink his thin essence like a riveled flower:
Or, as Ixion fixed, the wretch shall feel
The giddy motion of the whirling mill,
In fumes of burning chocolate shall glow,   *135*
And tremble at the sea that froths below!"
        He spoke; the spirits from the sails descend;
Some, orb in orb, around the nymph extend;
Some thread the mazy ringlets of her hair;
Some hang upon the pendants of her ear: *140*
With beating hearts the dire event they wait,
Anxious, and trembling for the birth of Fate.

Canto 3   Close by those meads, forever crowned with
                flowers,
Where Thames with pride surveys his rising towers,
There stands a structure of majestic frame,
Which from the neighboring Hampton takes its name.
Here Britain's statesmen oft the fall foredoom   *5*
Of foreign tyrants and of nymphs at home;
Here thou, great Anna! whom three realms obey,
Dost sometimes counsel take—and sometimes tea.

Hither the heroes and the nymphs resort,
To taste awhile the pleasures of a court;   *10*
In various talk the instructive hours they passed,
Who gave the ball, or paid the visit last;
One speaks the glory of the British Queen,
And one describes a charming Indian screen;
A third interprets motions, looks, and eyes;   *15*
At every word a reputation dies.
Snuff, or the fan, supply each pause of chat,
With singing, laughing, ogling, and all that.
        Meanwhile, declining from the noon of day,
The sun obliquely shoots his burning ray;   *20*
The hungry judges soon the sentence sign,
And wretches hang that jurymen may dine;
The merchant from the Exchange returns in peace,
And the long labors of the toilet cease.
Belinda now, whom thirst of fame invites,   *25*
Burns to encounter two adventurous knights,
At ombre singly to decide their doom,
And swells her breast with conquests yet to come.
Straight the three bands prepare in arms to join,
Each band the number of the sacred nine.   *30*
Soon as she spreads her hand, the aërial guard
Descend, and sit on each important card:
First Ariel perched upon a Matadore,
Then each according to the rank they bore;
For Sylphs, yet mindful of their ancient race,   *35*
Are, as when women, wondrous fond of place.
        Behold, four Kings in majesty revered,
With hoary whiskers and a forky beard;
And four fair Queens whose hands sustain a flower,
The expressive emblem of their softer power;   *40*
Four Knaves in garbs succinct, a trusty band,
Caps on their heads, and halberts in their hand;
And parti-colored troops, a shining train,
Draw forth to combat on the velvet plain.
        The skillful nymph reviews her force with care;   *45*
"Let Spades be trumps!" she said, and trumps they
        were.
        Now move to war her sable Matadores,
In show like leaders of the swarthy Moors.
Spadillio first, unconquerable lord!
Led off two captive trumps, and swept the board.   *50*
As many more Manillio forced to yield,
And marched a victor from the verdant field.

Him Basto followed, but his fate more hard
Gained but one trump and one plebeian card.
With his broad saber next, a chief in years,   55
The hoary Majesty of Spades appears,
Puts forth one manly leg, to sight revealed,
The rest his many-colored robe concealed.
The rebel Knave, who dares his prince engage,
Proves that just victim of his royal rage.   60
Even mighty Pam, that kings and queens o'erthrew
And mowed down armies in the fights of loo,
Sad chance of war! now distitute of aid,
Falls undistinguished by the victor Spade.

    Thus far both armies to Belinda yield;   65
Now to the Baron fate inclines the field.
His warlike amazon her host invades,
The imperial consort of the crown of Spades.
The Club's black tyrant first her victim died,
Spite of his haughty mien and barbarous pride.   70
What boots the regal circle on his head,
His giant limbs, in state unwieldy spread?
That long behind he trails his pompous robe,
And of all monarchs only grasps the globe?

    The Baron now his Diamonds pours apace;   75
The embroidered King who shows but half his face,
And his refulgent Queen, with powers combined
Of broken troops an easy conquest find.
Clubs, Diamonds, Hearts, in wild disorder seen,
With throngs promiscuous strew the level green.   80
Thus when dispersed a routed army runs,
Of Asia's troops, and Afric's sable sons,
With like confusion different nations fly,
Of various habit, and of various dye,
The pierced battalions disunited fall   85
In heaps on heaps; one fate o'erwhelms them all.

    The Knave of Diamonds tries his wily arts,
And wins (oh, shameful chance!) the Queen of Hearts.
At this, the blood the virgin's cheek forsook,
A livid paleness spreads o'er all her look;   90
She sees, and trembles at the approaching ill,
Just in the jaws of ruin, and Codille,
And now (as oft in some distempered state)
On one nice trick depends the general fate.
An Ace of Hearts steps forth; the King unseen
Lurked in her hand, and mourned his captive Queen.
He springs to vengeance with an eager pace,
And falls like thunder on the prostrate Ace.

The nymph exulting fills with shouts the sky;
The walls, the woods, and long canals reply.   *100*
   O thoughtless mortals! ever blind to fate,
Too soon dejected, and too soon elate:
Sudden these honors shall be snatched away,
And cursed forever this victorious day.
   For lo! the board with cups and spoons is
       crowned,   *105*
The berries crackle, and the mill turns round;
On shining altars of Japan they raise
The silver lamp; the fiery spirits blaze:
From silver spouts the grateful liquors glide,
While China's earth receives the smoking tide.   *110*
At once they gratify their scent and taste,
And frequent cups prolong the rich repast.
Straight hover round the fair her airy band;
Some, as she sipped, the fuming liquor fanned,
Some o'er her lap their careful plumes displayed,   *115*
Trembling, and conscious of the rich brocade.
Coffee (which makes the politician wise,
And see through all things with his half-shut eyes)
Sent up in vapors to the Baron's brain
New stratagems, the radiant Lock to gain.   *120*
Ah, cease, rash youth! disist ere 'tis too late,
Fear the just Gods, and think of Scylla's fate!
Changed to a bird, and sent to flit in air,
She dearly pays for Nisus' injured hair!
   But when to mischief mortals bend their will,   *125*
How soon they find fit instruments of ill!
Just then, Clarissa drew with tempting grace
A two-edged weapon from her shining case:
So ladies in romance assist their knight,
Present the spear, and arm him for the fight.   *130*
He takes the gift with reverence, and extends
The little engine on his fingers' ends;
This just behind Belinda's neck he spread,
As o'er the fragrant steams she bends her head.
Swift to the Lock a thousand sprites repair,   *135*
A thousand wings, by turns, blow back the hair,
And thrice they twitched the diamond in her ear,
Thrice she looked back, and thrice the foe drew near.
Just in that instant, anxious Ariel sought
The close recesses of the virgin's thought;   *140*
As on the nosegay in her breast reclined,
He watched the ideas rising in her mind,

Sudden he viewed, in spite of all her art,
An earthly lover lurking at her heart.
Amazed, confused, he found his power expired,   *145*
Resigned to fate, and with a sigh retired.

    The Peer now spreads the glittering forfex wide,
To enclose the Lock; now joins it, to divide.
Even then, before the fatal engine closed,
A wretched Sylph too fondly interposed;   *150*
Fate urged the shears, and cut the Sylph in twain
(But airy substance soon unites again):
The meeting points the sacred hair dissever
From the fair head, forever, and forever!

    Then flashed the living lightning from her eyes,
And screams of horror rend the affrighted skies.   *156*
Not louder shrieks to pitying heaven are cast,
When husbands, or when lapdogs breathe their last;
Or when rich china vessels fallen from high,
In glittering dust and painted fragments lie!   *160*
"Let wreaths of triumph now my temples twine,"
The victor cried, "the glorious prize is mine!
While fish in streams, or birds delight in air,
Or in a coach and six the British Fair,
As long as *Atalantis* shall be read,   *165*
Or the small pillow grace a lady's bed,
While visits shall be paid on solemn days,
When numerous wax-lights in bright order blaze,
While nymphs take treats, or assignations give,
So long my honor, name, and praise shall live!   *170*
What Time would spare, from Steel receives its date,
And monuments, like men, submit to fate!
Steel could the labor of the Gods destroy,
And strike to dust the imperial towers of Troy;
Steel could the works of mortal pride confound,   *175*
And hew triumphal arches to the ground.
What wonder then, fair nymph! thy hairs should feel,
The conquering force of unresisted Steel?"

Canto 4   But anxious cares the pensive nymph oppressed,
And secret passions labored in her breast.
Not youthful kings in battle seized alive,
Not scornful virgins who their charms survive,
Not ardent lovers robbed of all their bliss,   *5*
Not ancient ladies when refused a kiss,
Not tyrants fierce that unrepenting die,
Not Cynthia when her manteau's pinned awry,

E'er felt such rage, resentment, and despair,
As thou, sad virgin! for thy ravished hair.   *10*
    For, that sad moment, when the Sylphs withdrew
And Ariel weeping from Belinda flew,
Umbriel, a dusky, melancholy sprite
As ever sullied the fair face of light,
Down to the central earth, his proper scene,   *15*
Repaired to search the gloomy Cave of Spleen.
    Swift on his sooty pinions flits the Gnome,
And in a vapor reached the dismal dome.
No cheerful breeze this sullen region knows,
The dreaded east is all the wind that blows.   *20*
Here in a grotto, sheltered close from air,
And screened in shades from day's detested glare,
She sighs forever on her pensive bed,
Pain at her side, and Megrim at her head.
    Two handmaids wait the throne: alike in place,   *25*
But differing far in figure and in face.
Here stood Ill-Nature like an ancient maid,
Her wrinkled form in black and white arrayed;
With store of prayers for mornings, nights, and noons,
Her hand is filled; her bosom with lampoons.   *30*
    There Affectation, with a sickly mien,
Shows in her cheek the roses of eighteen,
Practiced to lisp, and hang the head aside,
Faints into airs, and languishes with pride,
On the rich quilt sinks with becoming woe,   *35*
Wrapped in a gown, for sickness and for show.
The fair ones feel such maladies as these,
When each new nightdress gives a new disease.
    A constant vapor o'er the palace flies,
Strange phantoms rising as the mists arise;   *40*
Dreadful as hermit's dreams in haunted shades,
Or bright as visions of expiring maids.
Now glaring fiends, and snakes on rolling spires,
Pale specters, gaping tombs, and purple fires;
Now lakes of liquid gold, Elysian scenes,   *45*
And crystal domes, and angels in machines.
    Unnumbered throngs on every side are seen
Of bodies changed to various forms by Spleen.
Here living teapots stand, one arm held out,
One bent; the handle this, and that the spout: *50*
A pipkin there, like Homer's tripod, walks;
Here sighs a jar, and there a goose pie talks;
Men prove with child, as powerful fancy works,
And maids, turned bottles, call aloud for corks.

Safe passed the Gnome through this fantastic
    band,   55
A branch of healing spleenwort in his hand.
Then thus addressed the Power: "Hail, wayward
    Queen!
Who rule the sex to fifty from fifteen:
Parent of vapors and of female wit,
Who give the hysteric or poetic fit,   60
On various tempers act by various ways,
Make some take physic, others scribble plays;
Who cause the proud their visits to delay,
And send the godly in a pet to pray.
A nymph there is that all thy power disdains,   65
And thousands more in equal mirth maintains.
But oh! if e'er thy Gnome could spoil a grace,
Or raise a pimple on a beauteous face,
Like citron-waters matrons' cheeks inflame,
Or change complexions at a losing game;   70
If e'er with airy horns I planted heads,
Or rumpled petticoats, or tumbled beds,
Or caused suspicion when no soul was rude,
Or discomposed the headdress of a prude,
Or e'er to costive lapdog gave disease,   75
Which not the tears of brightest eyes could ease,
Hear me, and touch Belinda with chagrin:
That single act gives half the world the spleen."
    The Goddess with a discontented air
Seems to reject him though she grants his prayer. 80
A wondrous bag with both her hands she binds,
Like that where once Ulysses held the winds;
There she collects the force of female lungs,
Sighs, sobs, and passions, and the war of tongues.
A vial next she fills with fainting fears,   85
Soft sorrows, melting griefs, and flowing tears.
The Gnome rejoicing bears her gifts away,
Spreads his black wings, and slowly mounts to day.
    Sunk in Thalestris' arms the nymph he found,
Her eyes dejected and her hair unbound.   90
Full o'er their heads the swelling bag he rent,
And all the Furies issued at the vent.
Belinda burns with more than mortal ire,
And fierce Thalestris fans the rising fire.   94
"O wretched maid!" she spreads her hands, and cried
(While Hampton's echoes, "Wretched maid!" replied),

"Was it for this you took such constant care
The bodkin, comb, and essence to prepare?
For this your locks in paper durance bound,
For this with torturing irons wreathed around?   *100*
For this with fillets strained your tender head,
And bravely bore the double loads of lead?
Gods! shall the ravisher display your hair,
While the fops envy, and the ladies stare!
Honor forbid! at whose unrivaled shrine   *105*
Ease, pleasure, virtue, all, our sex resign.
Methinks already I your tears survey,
Already hear the horrid things they say,
Already see you a degraded toast,
And all your honor in a whisper lost!   *110*
How shall I, then, your helpless fame defend?
'Twill then be infamy to seem your friend!
And shall this prize, the inestimable prize,
Exposed through crystal to the gazing eyes,
And heightened by the diamond's circling rays,   *115*
On that rapacious hand forever blaze?
Sooner shall grass in Hyde Park Circus grow,
And wits take lodgings in the sound of Bow;
Sooner let earth, air, sea, to chaos fall,
Men, monkeys, lapdogs, parrots, perish all!"   *120*
       She said; then raging to Sir Plume repairs,
And bids her beau demand the precious hairs
(Sir Plume of amber snuffbox justly vain,
And the nice conduct of a clouded cane).
With earnest eyes, and round unthinking face,   *125*
He first the snuffbox opened, then the case,
And thus broke out—"My Lord, why, what the devil!
Zounds! damn the lock! 'fore Gad, you must be civil!
Plague on't! 'tis past a jest—nay prithee, pox!
Give her the hair"—he spoke, and rapped his box. *130*
       "It grieves me much," replied the Peer again,
"Who speaks so well should ever speak in vain.
But by this Lock, this sacred Lock I swear
(Which never more shall join its parted hair;
Which never more its honors shall renew,   *135*
Clipped from the lovely head where late it grew),
That while my nostrils draw the vital air,
This hand, which won it, shall forever wear."
He spoke, and speaking, in proud triumph spread
The long-contended honors of her head.   *140*

But Umbriel, hateful Gnome, forbears not so;
He breaks the vial whence the sorrows flow.
Then see! the nymph in beauteous grief appears,
Her eyes half languishing, half drowned in tears;
On her heaved bosom hung her drooping head,   *145*
Which with a sigh she raised, and thus she said:
    "Forever cursed be this detested day,
Which snatched my best, my favorite curl away!
Happy! ah, ten times happy had I been,
If Hampton Court these eyes had never seen!   *150*
Yet am not I the first mistaken maid,
By love of courts to numerous ills betrayed.
Oh, had I rather unadmired remained
In some lone isle, or distant northern land;
Where the gilt chariot never marks the way,   *155*
Where none learn ombre, none e'er taste bohea!
There kept my charms concealed from mortal eye,
Like roses that in deserts bloom and die.
What moved my mind with youthful lords to roam?
Oh, had I stayed, and said my prayers at home!   *160*
'Twas this the morning omens seemed to tell,
Thrice from my trembling hand the patch box fell;
The tottering china shook without a wind,
Nay, Poll sat mute, and Shock was most unkind!
A Sylph too warned me of the threats of fate,   *165*
In mystic visions, now believed too late!
See the poor remnants of these slighted hairs!
My hands shall rend what e'en thy rapine spares.
These in two sable ringlets taught to break,
Once gave new beauties to the snowy neck;   *170*
The sister lock now sits uncouth, alone,
And in its fellow's fate foresees its own;
Uncurled it hangs, the fatal shears demands,
And tempts once more thy sacrilegious hands.
Oh, hadst thou, cruel! been content to seize   *175*
Hairs less in sight, or any hairs but these!"

Canto 5   She said: the pitying audience melt in tears.
But Fate and Jove had stopped the Baron's ears.
In vain Thalestris with reproach assails,
For who can move when fair Belinda fails?
Not half so fixed the Trojan could remain,   *5*
While Anna begged and Dido raged in vain.
Then grave Clarissa graceful waved her fan;
Silence ensued, and thus the nymph began:

"Say why are beauties praised and honored most,
The wise man's passion, and the vain man's toast?   *10*
Why decked with all that land and sea afford,
Why angels called, and angel-like adored?
Why round our coaches crowd the white-gloved beaux,
Why bows the side box from its inmost rows?
How vain are all these glories, all our pains,   *15*
Unless good sense preserve what beauty gains;
That men may say when we the front box grace,
'Behold the first in virtue as in face!'
Oh! if to dance all night, and dress all day,
Charmed the smallpox, or chased old age away,   *20*
Who would not scorn what housewife's cares produce,
Or who would learn one earthly thing of use?
To patch, nay ogle, might become a saint,
Nor could it sure be such a sin to paint.
But since, alas! frail beauty must decay,   *25*
Curled or uncurled, since locks will turn to gray;
Since painted, or not painted, all shall fade,
And she who scorns a man must die a maid;
What then remains but well our power to use,
And keep good humor still whate'er we lose?   *30*
And trust me, dear, good humor can prevail
When airs, and flights, and screams, and scolding fail.
Beauties in vain their pretty eyes may roll;
Charms strike the sight, but merit wins the soul."

So spoke the dame, but no applause ensued;   *35*
Belinda frowned, Thalestris called her prude.
"To arms, to arms!" the fierce virago cries,
And swift as lightning to the combat flies.
All side in parties, and begin the attack;
Fans clap, silks rustle, and tough whalebones crack;   *40*
Heroes' and heroines' shouts confusedly rise,
And bass and treble voices strike the skies.
No common weapons in their hands are found,
Like Gods they fight, nor dread a mortal wound.
So when bold Homer makes the Gods engage,   *45*
And heavenly breasts with human passions rage;
'Gainst Pallas, Mars; Latona, Hermes arms;
And all Olympus rings with loud alarms:
Jove's thunder roars, heaven trembles all around,
Blue Neptune storms, the bellowing deeps resound: *50*
Earth shakes her nodding towers, the ground gives way,
And the pale ghosts start at the flash of day!
Triumphant Umbriel on a sconce's height
Clapped his glad wings, and sat to view the fight:

Propped on the bodkin spears, the sprites survey   55
The growing combat, or assist the fray.
    While through the press enraged Thalestris flies,
And scatters death around from both her eyes,
A beau and witling perished in the throng,
One died in metaphor, and one in song.   60
"O cruel nymph! a living death I bear,"
Cried Dapperwit, and sunk beside his chair.
A mournful glance Sir Fopling upwards cast,
"Those eyes are made so killing"—was his last.
Thus on Maeander's flowery margin lies   65
The expiring swan, and as he sings he dies.
    When bold Sir Plume had drawn Clarissa down,
Chloe stepped in, and killed him with a frown;
She smiled to see the doughty hero slain,
But, at her smile, the beau revived again.   70
    Now Jove suspends his golden scales in air,
Weighs the men's wits against the lady's hair;
The doubtful beam long nods from side to side;
At length the wits mount up, the hairs subside.
    See, fierce Belinda on the Baron flies,   75
With more than usual lightning in her eyes;
Nor feared the chief the unequal fight to try,
Who sought no more than on his foe to die.
    But this bold lord with manly strength endued,
She with one finger and a thumb subdued: 80
Just where the breath of life his nostrils drew,
A charge of snuff the wily virgin threw;
The Gnomes direct, to every atom just,
The pungent grains of titillating dust.
Sudden, with starting tears each eye o'erflows,   85
And the high dome re-echoes to his nose.
    "Now meet thy fate," incensed Belinda cried,
And drew a deadly bodkin from her side.
(The same, his ancient personage to deck,
Her great-great-grandsire wore about his neck,   90
In three seal rings; which after, melted down,
Formed a vast buckle for his widow's gown:
Her infant grandame's whistle next it grew,
The bells she jingled, and the whistle blew;
Then in a bodkin graced her mother's hairs,   95
Which long she wore, and now Belinda wears.)
    "Boast not my fall," he cried, "insulting foe!
Thou by some other shalt be laid as low.
Nor think to die dejects my lofty mind:
All that I dread is leaving you behind!   100

Rather than so, ah, let me still survive,
And burn in Cupid's flames—but burn alive."
    "Restore the Lock!" she cries; and all around
"Restore the Lock!" the vaulted roofs rebound.
Not fierce Othello in so loud a strain   105
Roared for the handkerchief that caused his pain.
But see how oft ambitious aims are crossed,
And chiefs contend till all the prize is lost!
The lock, obtained with guilt, and kept with pain,
In every place is sought, but sought in vain: 110
With such a prize no mortal must be blessed,
So Heaven decrees! with Heaven who can contest?
    Some thought it mounted to the lunar sphere,
Since all things lost on earth are treasured there.
There heroes' wits are kept in ponderous vases,   115
And beaux's in snuffboxes and tweezer cases.
There broken vows and deathbed alms are found,
And lovers' hearts with ends of riband bound,
The courtier's promises, and sick man's prayers,
The smiles of harlots, and the tears of heirs,   120
Cages for gnats, and chains to yoke a flea,
Dried butterflies, and tomes of casuistry.
    But trust the Muse—she saw it upward rise,
Though marked by none but quick, poetic eyes
(So Rome's great founder to the heavens withdrew,
To Proculus alone confessed in view);   126
A sudden star, it shot through liquid air,
And drew behind a radiant trail of hair.
Not Berenice's locks first rose so bright,
The heavens bespangling with disheveled light.   130
The Sylphs behold it kindling as it flies,
And pleased pursue its progress through the skies.
    This the beau monde shall from the Mall survey,
And hail with music its propitious ray.
This the blest lover shall for Venus take,   135
And send up vows from Rosamonda's Lake.
This Partridge soon shall view in cloudless skies,
When next he looks through Galileo's eyes;
And hence the egregious wizard shall foredoom
The fate of Louis, and the fall of Rome.   140
    Then cease, bright nymph! to mourn thy ravished
        hair,
Which adds new glory to the shining sphere!
Not all the tresses that fair head can boast,
Shall draw such envy as the Lock you lost.

For, after all the murders of your eye,   145
When, after millions slain, yourself shall die:
When those fair suns shall set, as set they must,
And all those tresses shall be laid in dust,
This Lock the Muse shall consecrate to fame,
And 'midst the stars inscribe Belinda's name.   150

Ezra Pound   (1885–1972)

Ballad of the Goodly Fere
Simon Zelotes Speaketh It Somewhile After the Crucifixion

Ha' we lost the goodliest fere o' all
For the priests and the gallows tree?
Aye lover he was of brawny men,
O' ships and the open sea.

When they came wi' a host to take Our Man   5
His smile was good to see,
"First let these go!" quo' our Goodly Fere,
"Or I'll see ye damned," says he.

Aye he sent us out through the crossed high spears
And the scorn of his laugh rang free,   10
"Why took ye not me when I walked about
Alone in the town?" says he.

Oh we drunk his "Hale" in the good red wine
When we last made company,
No capon priest was the Goodly Fere   15
But a man o' men was he.

I ha' seen him drive a hundred men
Wi' a bundle o' cords swung free,
That they took the high and holy house
For their pawn and treasury.   20

They'll no' get him a' in a book I think
Though they write it cunningly;
No mouse of the scrolls was the Goodly Fere
But aye loved the open sea.

If they think they ha' snared our Goodly Fere 25
They are fools to the last degree.
"I'll go to the feast," quo' our Goodly Fere,
"Though I go to the gallows tree."

"Ye ha' seen me heal the lame and blind,
And wake the dead," says he, 30
"Ye shall see one thing to master all:
'Tis how a brave man dies on the tree."

A son of God was the Goodly Fere
That bade us his brothers be.
I ha' seen him cow a thousand men. 35
I have seen him upon the tree.

He cried no cry when they drave the nails
And the blood gushed hot and free,
The hounds of the crimson sky gave tongue
But never a cry cried he. 40

I ha' seen him cow a thousand men
On the hills o' Galilee,
They whined as he walked out calm between,
Wi' his eyes like the grey o' the sea,

Like the sea that brooks no voyaging 45
With the winds unleashed and free,
Like the sea that he cowed at Genseret
Wi' twey words spoke' suddenly.

A master of men was the Goodly Fere,
A mate of the wind and sea, 50
If they think they ha' slain our Goodly Fere
They are fools eternally.

I ha' seen him eat o' the honey-comb
Sin' they nailed him to the tree.

John Crowe Ransom *(1888–1974)*

Here Lies a Lady

Here lies a lady of beauty and high degree.
Of chills and fever she died, of fever and chills,
The delight of her husband, her aunts, an infant of
  three,
And of medicos marvelling sweetly on her ills.

For either she burned, and her confident eyes would
  blaze,   5
And her fingers fly in a manner to puzzle their heads—
What was she making? Why, nothing; she sat in a maze
Of old scraps of laces, snipped into curious shreds—

Or this would pass, and the light of her fire decline
Till she lay discouraged and cold as a thin stalk white
  and blown,   10
And would not open her eyes, to kisses, to wine;
The sixth of these states was her last; the cold settled
  down.

Sweet ladies, long may ye bloom, and toughly I hope ye
  may thole,
But was she not lucky? In flowers and lace and
  mourning,
In love and great honour we bade God rest her soul 15
After six little spaces of chill, and six of burning.

Edwin Arlington Robinson *(1869–1935)*

Karma

Christmas was in the air and all was well
With him, but for a few confusing flaws
In divers of God's images. Because
A friend of his would neither buy nor sell,
Was he to answer for the axe that fell?
He pondered; and the reason for it was,
Partly, a slowly freezing Santa Clause
Upon the corner, with his beard and bell.

Acknowledging an improvident surprise,
He magnified a fancy that he wished
The friend whom he had wrecked were here again.
Not sure of that, he found a compromise;
And from the fullness of his heart he fished
A dime for Jesus who had died for man.

Richard Cory

Whenever Richard Cory went down town,
We people on the pavement looked at him:
He was a gentleman from sole to crown,
Clean favored, and imperially slim.

And he was always quietly arrayed,   5
And he was always human when he talked;
But still he fluttered pulses when he said,
"Good-morning," and he glittered when he walked.

And he was rich—yes, richer than a king—
And admirably schooled in every grace: 10
In fine, we thought that he was everything
To make us wish that we were in his place.

So on we worked, and waited for the light,
And went without the meat, and cursed the bread;
And Richard Cory, one calm summer night,   15
Went home and put a bullet through his head.

Theodore Roethke *(1908–1963)*

The Meadow Mouse

1   In a shoe box stuffed in an old nylon stocking
Sleeps the baby mouse I found in the meadow,
Where he trembled and shook beneath a stick
Till I caught him up by the tail and brought him in,
Cradled in my hand,   5
A little quaker, the whole body of him trembling,
His absurd whiskers sticking out like a cartoon-mouse,

His feet like small leaves,
Little lizard-feet,
Whitish and spread wide when he tried to struggle
    away,   *10*
Wriggling like a miniscule puppy.

Now he's eaten his three kinds of cheese and drunk
    from his bottle-cap watering-trough—
So much he just lies in one corner,
His tail curled under him, his belly big   *15*
As his head; his bat-like ears
Twitching, tilting toward the least sound.

Do I imagine he no longer trembles
When I come close to him?
He seems no longer to tremble.   *20*

2   But this morning the shoe-box house on the back porch
    is empty.
Where has he gone, my meadow mouse,
My thumb of a child that nuzzled in my palm?—
To run under the hawk's wing,
Under the eye of the great owl watching from the
    elm-tree,   *25*
To live by courtesy of the shrike, the snake, the
    tom-cat.

I think of the nestling fallen into the deep grass,
The turtle gasping in the dusty rubble of the highway,
The paralytic stunned in the tub, and the water rising,—
All things innocent, hapless, forsaken.   *30*

I Knew a Woman

I knew a woman, lovely in her bones,
When small birds sighed, she would sigh back at them;
Ah, when she moved, she moved more ways than one:
The shapes a bright container can contain!
Of her choice virtues only gods should speak,   *5*
Or English poets who grew up on Greek
(I'd have them sing in chorus, cheek to cheek).

How well her wishes went! She stroked my chin,
She taught me Turn, and Counter-turn, and Stand;
She taught me Touch, that undulant white skin;   *10*
I nibbled meekly from her proffered hand;

She was the sickle; I, poor I, the rake,
Coming behind her for her pretty sake
(But what prodigious mowing we did make).

Love likes a gander, and adores a goose: *15*
Her full lips pursed, the errant note to seize;
She played it quick, she played it light and loose;
My eyes, they dazzled at her flowing knees;
Her several parts could keep a pure repose,
Or one hip quiver with a mobile nose   *20*
(She moved in circles, and those circles moved).

Let seed be grass, and grass turn into hay:
I'm martyr to a motion not my own;
What's freedom for? To know eternity.
I swear she cast a shadow white as stone.   *25*
But who would count eternity in days?
These old bones live to learn her wanton ways:
(I measure time by how a body sways).

Dante Gabriel Rossetti (1828–1882)

The Blessed Damozel

The blessed damozel leaned out
    From the gold bar of heaven;
Her eyes were deeper than the depth
    Of waters stilled at even;
She had three lilies in her hand,   *5*
    And the stars in her hair were seven.

Her robe, ungirt from clasp to hem,
    No wrought flowers did adorn,
But a white rose of Mary's gift,
    For service meetly worn;   *10*
Her hair that lay along her back
    Was yellow like ripe corn.

Herseemed she scarce had been a day
    One of God's choristers;
The wonder was not yet quite gone   *15*
    From that still look of hers;
Albeit, to them she left, her day
    Had counted as ten years.

(To *one* it is ten years of years.
    . . . Yet now, and in this place,   *20*
Surely she leaned o'er me—her hair
    Fell all about my face. . . .
Nothing: the autumn fall of leaves.
    The whole year sets apace.)

It was the rampart of God's house   *25*
    That she was standing on;
By God built over the sheer depth
    The which is Space begun;
So high, that looking downward thence
    She scarce could see the sun.   *30*

It lies in heaven, across the flood
    Of ether, as a bridge.
Beneath, the tides of day and night
    With flame and darkness ridge
The void, as low as where this earth   *35*
    Spins like a fretful midge.

Around her, lovers, newly met
    'Mid deathless love's acclaims,
Spoke evermore among themselves
    Their heart-remembered names;   *40*
And the souls mounting up to God
    Went by her like thin flames.

And still she bowed herself and stooped
    Out of the circling charm;
Until her bosom must have made   *45*
    The bar she leaned on warm,
And the lilies lay as if asleep
    Along her bended arm.

From the fixed place of heaven she saw
    Time like a pulse shake fierce   *50*
Through all the worlds. Her gaze still strove
    Within the gulf to pierce
Its path; and now she spoke as when
    The stars sang in their spheres.

The sun was gone now; the curled moon   *55*
    Was like a little feather
Fluttering far down the gulf; and now
    She spoke through the still weather.
Her voice was like the voice the stars
    Had when they sang together.   *60*

(Ah, sweet! Even now, in that bird's song,
    Strove not her accents there,
Fain to be harkened? When those bells
    Possessed the midday air,
Strove not her steps to reach my side   *65*
    Down all the echoing stair?)

"I wish that he were come to me,
    For he will come," she said.
"Have I not prayed in heaven?—on earth,
    Lord, Lord, has he not prayed?   *70*
Are not two prayers a perfect strength?
    And shall I feel afraid?

"When round his head the aureole clings,
    And he is clothed in white,
I'll take his hand and go with him   *75*
    To the deep wells of light;
As unto a stream we will step down,
    And bathe there in God's sight.

"We two will stand beside that shrine,
    Occult, withheld, untrod,   *80*
Whose lamps are stirred continually
    With prayers sent up to God;
And see our old prayers, granted, melt
    Each like a little cloud.

"We two will lie i' the shadow of   *85*
    That living mystic tree
Within whose secret growth the Dove
    Is sometimes felt to be,
While every leaf that His plumes touch
    Saith His Name audibly.   *90*

"And I myself will teach to him,
    I myself, lying so,
The songs I sing here; which his voice
    Shall pause in, hushed and slow,
And find some knowledge at each pause,   *95*
    Or some new thing to know."

(Alas! We two, we two, thou say'st!
    Yea, one wast thou with me
That once of old. But shall God lift
    To endless unity   *100*
The soul whose likeness with thy soul
    Was but its love for thee?)

"We two," she said, "will seek the groves
    Where the lady Mary is,
With her five handmaidens, whose names   105
    Are five sweet symphonies,
Cecily, Gertrude, Magdalen,
    Margaret, and Rosalys.

"Circlewise sit they, with bound locks
    And foreheads garlanded;   110
Into the fine cloth white like flame
    Weaving the golden thread,
To fashion the birth-robes for them
    Who are just born, being dead.

"He shall fear, haply, and be dumb;   115
    Then will I lay my cheek
To his, and tell about our love,
    Not once abashed or weak;
And the dear Mother will approve
    My pride, and let me speak.   120

"Herself shall bring us, hand in hand,
    To Him round whom all souls
Kneel, the clear-ranged unnumbered heads
    Bowed with their aureoles;
And angels meeting us shall sing   125
    To their citherns and citoles.

"There will I ask of Christ the Lord
    Thus much for him and me—
Only to live as once on earth
    With Love, only to be,   130
As then awhile, forever now,
    Together, I and he."

She gazed and listened and then said,
    Less sad of speech than mild—
"All this is when he comes." She ceased.   135
    The light thrilled toward her, filled
With angels in strong, level flight.
    Her eyes prayed, and she smiled.

(I saw her smile.) But soon their path
    Was vague in distant spheres;   140
And then she cast her arms along
    The golden barriers,
And laid her face between her hands,
    And wept. (I heard her tears.)

Delmore Schwartz (1913–1966)

For Rhoda

Calmly we walk through this April's day,
Metropolitan poetry here and there,
In the park sit pauper and rentier,
The screaming children, the motor car
Fugitive about us, running away,   5
Between the worker and the millionaire
Number provides all distances,
It is Nineteen Thirty-Seven now,
Many great dears are taken away,
What will become of you and me   10
(This is the school in which we learn . . .)

Besides the photo and the memory?
(. . . that time is the fire in which we burn.)
(This is the school in which we learn . . .)
What is the self amid this blaze?   15
What am I now that I was then
Which I shall suffer and act again,
The theodicy I wrote in my high school days
Restored all life from infancy,
The children shouting are bright as they run   20
(This is the school in which they learn . . .)
Ravished entirely in their passing play!
(. . . that time is the fire in which they burn.)
Avid its rush, that reeling blaze!
Where is my father and Eleanor?   25
Not where are they now, dead seven years,
But what they were then?
                               No more? No more?
From Ninteen-Fourteen to the present day,
Bert Spira and Rhoda consume, consume
Not where they are now (where are they now?)   30
But what they were then, both beautiful;
Each minute bursts in the burning room,
The great globe reels in the solar fire,
Spinning the trivial and unique away.
(How all things flash! How all things flare!)   35
What am I now that I was then?
May memory restore again and again
The smallest color of the smallest day:
Time is the school in which we learn,
Time is the fire in which we burn.   40

Anne Sexton *(1928–1974)*

The Abortion

Somebody who should have been born
is gone.

Just as the earth puckered its mouth,
each bud puffing out from its knot,
I changed my shoes, and then drove south.   *5*

Up past the Blue Mountains, where
Pennsylvania humps on endlessly,
wearing, like a crayoned cat, its green hair,

its roads sunken in like a gray washboard;
where, in truth, the ground cracks evilly,   *10*
a dark socket from which the coal has poured,

Somebody who should have been born
is gone.

the grass as bristly and stout as chives,
and me wondering when the ground would break,   *15*
and me wondering how anything fragile survives;

up in Pennsylvania, I met a little man,
not Rumpelstiltskin, at all, at all . . .
he took the fullness that love began.

Returning north, even the sky grew thin   *20*
like a high window looking nowhere.
The road was as flat as a sheet of tin.

Somebody who should have been born
is gone.

Yes, woman, such logic will lead   *25*
to loss without death. Or say what you meant,
you coward . . . this baby that I bleed.

William Shakespeare *(1564–1616)*

Sonnet 18

Shall I compare thee to a summer's day?
Thou art more lovely and more temperate:
Rough winds do shake the darling buds of May,
And summer's lease hath all too short a date:
Sometime too hot the eye of heaven shines,
And often is his gold complexion dimmed;
And every fair from fair sometimes declines,
By chance or nature's changing course untrimmed;
But thy eternal summer shall not fade,
Nor lose possession of that fair thou owest;
Nor shall Death brag thou wander'st in his shade,
When in eternal lines to time thou growest:
So long as men can breathe, or eyes can see,
So long lives this, and this gives life to thee.

Sonnet 29

When, in disgrace with fortune and men's eyes,
I all alone beweep my outcast state,
And trouble deaf heaven with my bootless cries,
And look upon myself, and curse my fate,
Wishing me like to one more rich in hope,
Featured like him, like him with friends possessed,
Desiring this man's art and that man's scope,
With what I most enjoy contented least;
Yet in these thoughts myself almost despising,
Haply I think on thee—and then my state,
Like to the lark at break of day arising
From sullen earth, sings hymns at heaven's gate;
For thy sweet love remembered such wealth brings
That then I scorn to change my state with kings.

Karl Shapiro (1913–   )

University

To hurt the Negro and avoid the Jew
Is the curriculum. In mid-September
The entering boys, identified by hats,
Wander in a maze of mannered brick
    Where boxwood and magnolia brood   5
    And columns with imperious stance
    Like rows of ante-bellum girls
        Eye them, outlanders.

In whited cells, on lawns equipped for peace,
Under the arch, and lofty banister,   10
Equals shake hands, unequals blankly pass;
The exemplary weather whispers, "Quiet, quiet"
    And visitors on tiptoe leave
    For the raw North, the unfinished West,
    As the young, detecting an advantage,   15
        Practice a face.

Where, on their separate hill, the colleges,
Like manor houses of an older law,
Gaze down embankments on a land in fee,
The Deans, dry spinsters over family plate,   20
    Ring out the English name like coin,
    Humor the snob and lure the lout.
    Within the precincts of this world
        Poise is a club.

But on the neighboring range, misty and high,   25
The past is absolute: some luckless race
Dull with inbreeding and conformity
Wears out its heart, and comes barefoot and bad
    For charity or jail. The scholar
    Sanctions their obsolete disease;   30
    The gentleman revolts with shame
        At his ancestor.

And the true nobleman, once a democrat,
Sleeps on his private mountain. He was one
Whose thought was shapely and whose dream was
    broad;   35
This school he held his art and epitaph.
    But now it takes from him his name,
    Falls open like a dishonest look,
    And shows us, rotted and endowed,
        Its senile pleasure.   40

Drug Store

I do remember an apothecary,
And hereabouts 'a dwells

It baffles the foreigner like an idiom,
And he is right to adopt it as a form
Less serious than the living-room or bar;
    For it disestablishes the café,
Is a collective, and on basic country.   *5*

Not that it praises hygiene and corrupts
The ice-cream parlor and the tobacconist's
Is it a center; but that the attractive symbols
    Watch over puberty and leer
Like rubber bottles waiting for sick-use.   *10*

Youth comes to jingle nickels and crack wise;
The baseball scores are his, the magazines
Devoted to lust, the jazz, the Coca-Cola,
    The lending-library of love's latest.
He is the customer, he is heroized.   *15*

And every nook and cranny of the flesh
Is spoken to by packages with wiles.
"Buy me, buy me," they whimper and cajole;
    The hectic range of lipstick pouts,
Revealing the wicked and the simple mouth.   *20*

With scarcely any evasion in their eye
They smoke, undress their girls, exact a stance;
But only for a moment. The clock goes round;
    Crude fellowships are made and lost;
They slump in booths like rags, not even drunk. *25*

Percy Bysshe Shelley *(1792–1822)*

Mutability

1   The flower that smiles to-day
        To-morrow dies;
    All that we wish to stay
        Tempts and then flies.
    What is this world's delight?   *5*
    Lightning that mocks the night,
        Brief even as bright.

2   Virtue, how frail it is!
              Friendship how rare!
     Love, how it sells poor bliss   10
              For proud despair!
     But we, though soon they fall,
     Survive their joy, and all
              Which ours we call.

3   Whilst skies are blue and bright,   15
              Whilst flowers are gay,
     Whilst eyes that change ere night
              Make glad the day;
     Whilst yet the calm hours creep,
     Dream thou—and from thy sleep   20
              Then wake to weep.

Jon Silkin (1930–   )

Creatures

Shells are now found
Of creatures not still subsisting,
Chipped from the hardened mud under
Which oil lurks.

Men came with their chipped diamonds   5
And a pole with these smelted onto it
To bore rock. Oil broke out
Into the clear American air.

Barely noticed at the time
Among the soil screwed from   10
Above the crude useful oil,
Shells, about half an inch.
They were whorled, and chipped from
What they had been hardening in,
Falling through the glistening mud   15
They filled with the spiral
Wriggling creature gone from them.
It is a spiral horn, silent;
And shaped like an inert
Clammy-skinned spring.   20

They grew property:
An amnion, a house,
Their grave no more special,
No more particular than
A pattern, a repetition of curving   25
Continuous shape, for survival.

Robert Southey   *(1774–1843)*

The Cataract of Lodore

"How does the water
Come down at Lodore?"
My little boy ask'd me
Thus, once on a time;
And moreover he task'd me   5
To tell him in rhyme.
Anon at the word,
There first came one daughter
And then came another,
To second and third   10
The request of their brother,
And to hear how the water
Comes down at Lodore,
With its rush and its roar,
As many a time   15
They had seen it before.
So I told them in rhyme,
For of rhymes I had store:
And 'twas in my vocation
For their recreation   20
That so I should sing;
Because I was Laureate
To them and the King.

From its sources which well
In the tarn on the fell;   25
From its fountains
In the mountains,
Its rills and its gills;
Through moss and through brake,

It runs and it creeps   30
For awhile, till it sleeps
In its own little lake.
And thence at departing,
Awakening and starting,
It runs through the reeds   35
And away it proceeds,
Through meadow and glade,
In sun and in shade,
And through the wood-shelter,
Among crags in its flurry,   40
Helter-skelter,
Hurry-scurry.
Here it comes sparkling,
And there it lies darkling;
Now smoking and frothing   45
Its tumult and wrath in,
Till in this rapid race
On which it is bent,
It reaches the place
Of its steep descent.   50

The cataract strong
Then plunges along,
Striking and raging
As if a war waging
Its caverns and rocks among: 55
Rising and leaping,
Sinking and creeping,
Swelling and sweeping,
Showering and springing,
Flying and flinging,   60
Writhing and ringing,
Eddying and whisking,
Spouting and frisking,
Turning and twisting,
Around and around   65
With endless rebound!
Smiting and fighting,
A sight to delight in;
Confounding, astounding,
Dizzying and deafening the ear with its sound.   70

Collecting, projecting,
Receding and speeding,
And shocking and rocking,
And darting and parting,
And threading and spreading,   *75*
And whizzing and hissing,
And dripping and skipping,
And hitting and splitting,
And shining and twining,
And rattling and battling,   *80*
And shaking and quaking,
And pouring and roaring,
And waving and raving,
And tossing and crossing,
And flowing and going,   *85*
And running and stunning,
And foaming and roaming,
And dinning and spinning,
And dropping and hopping,
And working and jerking,   *90*
And guggling and struggling,
And heaving and cleaving,
And moaning and groaning;
And glittering and frittering,
And gathering and feathering,   *95*
And whitening and brightening,
And quivering and shivering,
And hurrying and skurrying,
And thundering and floundering;

Dividing and gliding and sliding,   *100*
And falling and brawling and sprawling,
And driving and riving and striving,
And sprinkling and twinkling and wrinkling,
And sounding and bounding and rounding,
And bubbling and troubling and doubling,   *105*
And grumbling and rumbling and tumbling,
And clattering and battering and shattering;

Retreating and beating and meeting and sheeting,
Delaying and straying and playing and spraying,
Advancing and prancing and glancing and dancing, *110*
Recoiling, turmoiling and toiling and boiling,
And gleaming and streaming and steaming and
    beaming,
And rushing and flushing and brushing and gushing,
And flapping and rapping and clapping and slapping,

And curling and whirling and purling and twirling, *115*
And thumping and plumping and bumping and
    jumping,
And dashing and flashing and splashing and clashing;
And so never ending, but always descending,
Sounds and motions forever and ever are blending,
All at once all o'er, with a mighty uproar; *120*
And this way the water comes down at Lodore.

Wallace Stevens (1879–1955)

Disillusionment of Ten O'Clock

The houses are haunted
By white night-gowns
None are green,
Or purple with green rings,
Or green with yellow rings, *5*
Or yellow with blue rings,
None of them are strange,
With socks of lace
And beaded ceintures.
People are not going *10*
To dream of baboons and periwinkles.
Only, here and there, an old sailor,
Drunk and asleep in his boots,
Catches tigers
In red weather. *15*

Thirteen Ways of Looking at a Blackbird

1   Among twenty snowy mountains,
    The only moving thing
    Was the eye of the blackbird.

2   I was of three minds,
    Like a tree *5*
    In which there are three blackbirds.

3   The blackbird whirled in the autumn winds.
    It was a small part of the pantomime.

4   A man and a woman
    Are one.
    A man and a woman and a blackbird
    Are one.

5   I do not know which to prefer,
    The beauty of inflections
    Or the beauty of innuendoes,
    The blackbird whistling
    Or just after.

6   Icicles filled the long window
    With barbaric glass.
    The shadow of the blackbird
    Crossed it, to and fro.
    The mood
    Traced in the shadow
    In indecipherable cause.

7   O thin men of Haddam,
    Why do you imagine golden birds?
    Do you not see how the blackbird
    Walks around the feet
    Of the women about you?

8   I know noble accents
    And lucid, inescapable rhythms;
    But I know, too,
    That the blackbird is involved
    In what I know.

9   When the blackbird flew out of sight,
    It marked the edge
    Of one of many circles.

10 At the sight of blackbirds
    Flying in a green light,
    Even the bawds of euphony
    Would cry out sharply.

11 He rode over Connecticut
    In a glass coach.
    Once, a fear pierced him,
    In that he mistook
    The shadow of his equipage
    For blackbirds.

12 The river is moving.
    The blackbird must be flying.

13   It was evening all afternoon.   50
          It was snowing
          And it was going to snow.
          The blackbird sat
          In the cedar-limbs.

Sir John Suckling (1609–1642)

A Soldier

I am a man of war and might,
And know thus much, that I can fight,
Whether I am in the wrong or right,
     Devoutly.

No woman under heaven I fear,   5
New oaths I can exactly swear,
And forty healths my brain will bear
     Most stoutly.

I cannot speak, but I can do
As much as any of our crew,   10
And, if you doubt it, some of you
     May prove me.

I dare be bold thus much to say,
If that my bullets do but play,
You would be hurt so night and day,   15
     Yet love me.

Edward Taylor (1642?–1729)

Housewifery

Make me, O Lord, Thy spinning-wheel complete.
    Thy holy Word my distaff make for me;
Make mine affections Thy swift flyers neat;
    And make my soul Thy holy spool to be;
    My conversation make to be Thy reel,   5
    And reel the yarn thereon spun of Thy wheel.

Make me Thy loom then; knit therein this twine;
　　And make Thy Holy Spirit, Lord, wind quills;
Then weave the web Thyself. The yarn is fine.
　　Thine ordinances make my fulling mills.　　　　　*10*
　　Then dye the same in heavenly colors choice,
　　All pinked with varnished flowers of paradise.

Then clothe therewith mine understanding, will,
　　Affections, judgment, conscience, memory,
My words and actions, that their shine may fill　　*15*
　　My ways with glory and Thee glorify.
　　Then mine apparel shall display before Ye
　　That I am clothed in holy robes for glory.

Henry Taylor *(1942–　　)*

Speech

1　I crouch over my radio
　　to tune in the President,
　　thinking how lucky I am
　　not to own a television.

2　Now the rich, cultivated voice　　　　　　*5*
　　with its cautious, measured pauses
　　fills my living room, fills
　　the wastebasket, the vase
　　on the mantel, the hurricane
　　lamps, and even fills　　　　　　　　　*10*
　　the antique pottery whiskey jug
　　beside the fireplace, nourishing
　　the dried flowers I have put in it.

3　"I had a responsibility,"
　　he says; the phrase pours　　　　　　　*15*
　　from the speaker like molasses,
　　flows to the rug, spreads
　　into a black, shining puddle,
　　slowly expands, covers
　　the rug with dark sweetness.　　　　　　*20*
　　It begins to draw flies;
　　they eat all the syrup
　　and clamor for more.

4 I can barely hear the speech
above the buzzing of their wings.   *25*
But the Commander-in-Chief
has the solution: another
phrase, sweeter, thicker,
blacker, oozes out
over my living room floor: *30*
"I have personal reasons
for wanting peace." This is more
than the flies will be able to eat;
they will stay quiet
for the rest of the speech.   *35*

5 Now, you are thinking, comes
the Good Part, the part
where the syrup proves poisonous
and kills all the flies.
My fellow Americans, that   *40*
is not at all what happened.
The flies grew fat on the phrases,
grew as large as bullfrogs.

6 They are everywhere in the house,
and the syrup continues   *45*
to feed and fatten them;
in the pottery whiskey jug,
sprouting new leaves and buds,
even the dried flowers thrive.

7 The speech   *50*
has been over for weeks now;
they go on eating
but they stay quiet
and seem peaceful enough.
At night, sometimes,   *55*
I can hear them
making soft liquid sounds
of contentment.

Alfred, Lord Tennyson *(1809–1892)*

Flower in the crannied wall

Flower in the crannied wall,
I pluck you out of the crannies.
I hold you here, root and all, in my hand,
Little flower—but *if* I could understand
What you are, root and all, and all in all,
I should know what God and man is.

Tears, Idle Tears

Tears, idle tears, I know not what they mean,
Tears from the depth of some divine despair
Rise in the heart, and gather to the eyes,
In looking on the happy autumn-fields,
And thinking of the days that are no more.   5

Fresh as the first beam glittering on a sail,
That brings our friends up from the underworld
Sad as the last which reddens over one
That sinks with all we love below the verge;
So sad, so fresh, the days that are no more.   10

Ah, sad and strange as in dark summer dawns
The earliest pipe of half-awakened birds
To dying ears, when unto dying eyes
The casement slowly grows a glimmering square;
So sad, so strange, the days that are no more.   15

Dear as remembered kisses after death,
And sweet as those by hopeless fancy feigned
On lips that are for others; deep as love,
Deep as first love, and wild with all regret;
O Death in Life, the days that are no more!   20

Dylan Thomas *(1914–1953)*

The Hunchback in the Park

The hunchback in the park
A solitary mister
Propped between trees and water
From the opening of the garden lock
That lets the trees and water enter   5
Until the Sunday somber bell at dark

Eating bread from a newspaper
Drinking water from the chained cup
That the children filled with gravel
In the fountain basin where I sailed my ship   10
Slept at night in a dog kennel
But nobody chained him up.

Like the park birds he came early
Like the water he sat down
And Mister they called Hey mister   15
The truant boys from the town
Running when he had heard them clearly
On out of sound

Past lake and rockery
Laughing when he shook his paper   20
Hunchbacked in mockery
Through the loud zoo of the willow groves
Dodging the park keeper
With his stick that picked up leaves.

And the old dog sleeper   25
Alone between nurses and swans
While the boys among willows
Made the tigers jump out of their eyes
To roar on the rockery stones
And the groves were blue with sailors   30

Made all day until bell time
A woman figure without fault
Straight as a young elm
Straight and tall from his crooked bones
That she might stand in the night   35
After the locks and chains

All night in the unmade park
After the railings and shrubberies
The birds the grass the trees the lake
And the wild boys innocent as strawberries   *40*
Had followed the hunchback
To his kennel in the dark.

Edward Thomas   (1878–1917)

The Gallows

There was a weasel lived in the sun
With all his family,
Till a keeper shot him with his gun
And hung him up on a tree,
Where he swings in the wind and rain,   *5*
In the sun and in the snow,
Without pleasure, without pain,
On the dead oak tree bough.

There was a crow who was no sleeper,
But a thief and a murderer   *10*
Till a very late hour; and this keeper
Made him one of the things that were,
To hang and flap in rain and wind,
In the sun and in the snow.
There are no more sins to be sinned   *15*
On the dead oak tree bough.

There was a magpie, too,
Had a long tongue and a long tail;
He could both talk and do—
But what did that avail?   *20*
He, too, flaps in the wind and rain
Alongside weasel and crow,
Without pleasure, without pain,
On the dead oak tree bough.

And many other beasts   25
And birds, skin, bone, and feather,
Have been taken from their feasts
And hung up there together,
To swing and have endless leisure
In the sun and in the snow,   30
Without pain, without pleasure,
On the dead oak tree bough.

Thomas Traherne (1637–1674)

Shadows in the Water

In unexperienced infancy
Many a sweet mistake doth lie:
Mistake though false, intending true;
A seeming somewhat more than view;
    That doth instruct the mind   5
    In things that lie behind,
And many secrets to us show
Which afterwards we come to know.

Thus did I by the water's brink
Another world beneath me think;   10
And while the lofty spacious skies
Reversèd there, abused mine eyes,
    I fancied other feet
    Came mine to touch or meet;
As by some puddle I did play   15
Another world within it lay.

Beneath the water people drowned,
Yet with another heaven crowned,
In spacious regions seemed to go
As freely moving to and fro: 20
    In bright and open space
    I saw their very face;
Eyes, hands, and feet they had like mine;
Another sun did with them shine.

'Twas strange that people there should walk, 25
And yet I could not hear them talk:
That through a little wat'ry chink,
Which one dry ox or horse might drink,
    We other worlds should see,
    Yet not admitted be; 30
And other confines there behold
Of light and darkness, heat and cold.

I called them oft, but called in vain;
No speeches we could entertain:
Yet did I there expect to find 35
Some other world, to please my mind.
    I plainly saw by these
    A new Antipodes,
Whom, though they were so plainly seen,
A film kept off that stood between. 40

By walking men's reversed feet
I chanced another world to meet;
Though it did not to view exceed
A phantom, 'tis a world indeed,
    Where skies beneath us shine, 45
    And earth by art divine
Another face presents below,
Where people's feet against ours go.

Within the regions of the air,
Compassed about with heavens fair, 50
Great tracts of land there may be found
Enriched with fields and fertile ground;
    Where many numerous hosts
    In those far distant coasts,
For other great and glorious ends 55
Inhabit, my yet unknown friends.

O ye that stand upon the brink,
Whom I so near me through the chink
With wonder see: what faces there,
Whose feet, whose bodies, do ye wear? 60
    I my companions see
    In you, another me.
They seemèd others, but are we;
Our second selves these shadows be.

Henry Vaughan *(1622–1695)*

The Book

Eternal God! Maker of all
That have lived here since the man's fall;
The Rock of Ages! in whose shade
They live unseen, when here they fade;

Thou knew'st this paper when it was   5
Mere seed, and after that but grass;
Before 'twas dressed or spun, and when
Made linen, who did wear it then:
What were their lives, their thoughts, and deeds,
Whether good corn or fruitless weeds.   10

    Thou knew'st this tree when a green shade
Covered it, since a cover made,
And where it flourished, grew, and spread,
As if it never should be dead.

    Thou knew'st this harmless beast when he   15
Did live and feed by Thy decree
On each green thing; then slept—well fed—
Clothed with this skin which now lies spread
A covering o'er this aged book;
Which makes me wisely weep, and look   20
On my own dust; mere dust it is,
But not so dry and clean as this.
Thou knew'st and saw'st them all, and though
Now scattered thus, dost know them so.

    O knowing, glorious Spirit! when   25
Thou shalt restore trees, beasts, and men,
When Thou shalt make all new again,
Destroying only death and pain,
Give him amongst Thy works a place
Who in them loved and sought Thy face!   30

Peter Viereck *(1916–   )*

Game Called on Account of Darkness

Once there was a friend.
He watched me from the sky.
Maybe he never lived at all.
Maybe too much friendship made him die.

When the gang played cops-and-robbers in the alley, 5
It was my friend who told me which were which,
Now he doesn't tell me any more.
(Which team am I playing for?)

My science teacher built a telescope
To show me every answer in the end.   10
I stared and stared at every star for hours.
I couldn't find my friend.

At Sunday School they said I breathe too much.
When I hold my breath within the under
Side of earth, they said I'll find my friend.   15
. . . I wonder.

He was like a kind of central heating
In the big cold house, and that was good.
One by one I have to chop my toys now,
As firewood.   20

Everytime I stood upon a crossroads,
It made me mad to feel him watch me choose.
I'm glad there's no more spying while I play.
Still, I'm sad he went away.

Edmund Waller *(1606–1687)*

On a Girdle

That which her slender waist confined
Shall now my joyful temples bind;
No monarch but would give his crown,
His arms might do what this has done.

It was my heaven's extremest sphere,
The pale which held that lovely deer;
My joy, my grief, my hope, my love,
Did all within this circle move.

A narrow compass, and yet there
Dwelt all that's good and all that's fair;
Give me but what this ribband bound,
Take all the rest the sun goes round!

Go, lovely rose

Go, lovely rose!
Tell her that wastes her time and me,
That now she knows,
When I resemble her to thee,
How sweet and fair she seems to be.   5

Tell her that's young,
And shuns to have her graces spied,
That hadst thou sprung
In deserts, where no men abide,
Thou must have uncommended died.   10

Small is the worth
Of beauty from the light retired;
Bid her come forth,
Suffer herself to be desired,
And not blush so to be admired.   15

Then die! that she
The common fate of all things rare
May read in thee;
How small a part of time they share
That are so wondrous sweet and fair!   20

Isaac Watts *(1674–1748)*

Crucifixion to the World by the Cross of Christ

When I survey the wondrous cross
On which the Prince of Glory died,
My richest gain I count but loss,
And pour contempt on all my pride.

Forbid it, Lord, that I should boast 5
Save in the death of Christ my God;
All the vain things that charm me most,
I sacrifice them to his blood.

See from his head, his hands, his feet,
Sorrow and Love flow mingled down; 10
Did e'er such Love and Sorrow meet?
Or thorns compose so rich a crown?

His dying crimson like a robe
Spreads o'er his body on the tree;
Then am I dead to all the globe, 15
And all the globe is dead to me.

Were the whole realm of Nature mine,
That were a present far too small;
Love so amazing, so divine,
Demands my soul, my life, my all. 20

Walt Whitman *(1819–1892)*

One's-self I sing

One's-self I sing, a simple separate person,
Yet utter the word Democratic, the word En-Masse.

Of physiology from top to toe I sing,
Not physiognomy alone nor brain alone is worthy for
the Muse,
I say the Form complete is worthier far,
The Female equally with the Male I sing.

Of Life immense in passion, pulse, and power,
Cheerful, for freest action form'd under the laws
    divine,
The Modern Man I sing.

When I heard the learn'd astronomer

When I heard the learn'd astronomer,
When the proofs, the figures, were ranged in columns
    before me,
When I was shown the charts and diagrams, to add,
    divide, and measure them,
When I sitting heard the astronomer where he lectured
    with much applause in the lecture-room,
How soon unaccountable I became tired and sick,
Till rising and gliding out I wander'd off by myself,
In the mystical moist night-air, and from time to time,
Look'd up in perfect silence at the stars.

To a Common Prostitute

Be composed—be at ease with me—I am Walt Whit-
    man, liberal and lusty as Nature,
Not till the sun excludes you do I exclude you,
Not till the waters refuse to glisten for you and the
    leaves to rustle for you, do my words refuse to
    glisten and rustle for you.
My girl I appoint with you an appointment, and I charge
    you that you make preparation to be worthy to
    meet me,
And I charge you that you be patient and perfect till I
    come.

Till then I salute you with a significant look that you do
    not forget me.

Native Moments

Native moments—when you come upon me—ah you
    are here now,
Give me now libidinous joys only,
Give me the drench of my passions, give me life coarse
    and rank,
To-day I go consort with Nature's darlings, to-night
    too,
I am for those who believe in loose delights, I share the
    midnight orgies of young men,
I dance with the dancers and drink with the drinkers,
The echoes ring with our indecent calls, I pick out some
    low person for my dearest friend,
He shall be lawless, rude, illiterate, he shall be one
    condemned by others for deeds done,
I will play a part no longer, why should I exile myself
    from my companions?
O you shunn'd persons, I at least do not shun you,
I come forthwith in your midst, I will be your poet,
I will be more to you than to any of the rest.

Richard Wilbur   *(1921–   )*

Juggler

A ball will bounce, but less and less. It's not
A light-hearted thing, resents its own resilience.
Falling is what it loves, and the earth falls
So in our hearts from brilliance,
Settles and is forgot.   5
It takes a sky-blue juggler with five red balls

To shake our gravity up. Whee, in the air
The balls roll round, wheel on his wheeling hands,
Learning the ways of lightness, alter to spheres
Grazing his finger ends,   10
Cling to their courses there,
Swinging a small heaven about his ears.

But a heaven is easier made of nothing at all
Than the earth regained, and still and sole within
The spin of worlds, with a gesture sure and noble   *15*
He reels that heaven in,
Landing it ball by ball,
And trades it all for a broom, a plate, a table.

Oh, on his toe the table is turning, the broom's
Balancing up on his nose, and the plate whirls   *20*
On the tip of the broom! Damn, what a show, we cry:
The boys stamp, and the girls
Shriek, and the drum booms
And all comes down, and he bows and says good-bye.

If the juggler is tired now, if the broom stands   *25*
In the dust again, if the table starts to drop
Through the daily dark again, and though the plate
Lies flat on the table top,
For him we batter our hands
Who has won for once over the world's weight.   *30*

Oscar Wilde   *(1854–1900)*

The Harlot's House

We caught the tread of dancing feet,
We loitered down the moonlit street,
And stopped beneath the harlot's house.

Inside, above the din and fray,
We heard the loud musicians play   *5*
The "Treues Liebes Herz" of Strauss.

Like strange mechanical grotesques,
Making fantastic arabesques,
The shadows raced across the blind.

We watched the ghostly dancers spin   *10*
To sound of horn and violin,
Like black leaves wheeling in the wind.

Like wire-pulled automatons,
Slim silhouetted skeletons
Went sidling through the slow quadrille.   *15*

They took each other by the hand,
And danced a stately saraband;
Their laughter echoed thin and shrill.

Sometimes a clockwork puppet pressed
A phantom lover to her breast,   20
Sometimes they seemed to try to sing.

Sometimes a horrible marionette
Came out, and smoked its cigarette
Upon the steps like a live thing.

Then, turning to my love, I said,   25
"The dead are dancing with the dead,
The dust is whirling with the dust."

But she—she heard the violin,
And left my side, and entered in:
Love passed into the house of lust.   30

Then suddenly the tune went false,
The dancers wearied of the waltz,
The shadows ceased to wheel and whirl.

And down the long and silent street,
The dawn, with silver-sandaled feet,   35
Crept like a frightened girl.

Requiescat

Tread lightly, she is near
        Under the snow,
Speak gently, she can hear
        The daisies grow.

All her bright golden hair   5
        Tarnished with rust,
She that was young and fair
        Fallen to dust.

Lily-like, white as snow,
        She hardly knew   10
She was a woman, so
        Sweetly she grew.

Coffin-board, heavy stone,
    Lie on her breast;
I vex my heart alone,
    She is at rest.   15

Peace, peace; she cannot hear
    Lyre or sonnet;
All my life's buried here.
    Heap earth upon it.   20

William Wordsworth *(1770–1850)*

The Solitary Reaper

Behold her, single in the field,
Yon solitary Highland Lass!
Reaping and singing by herself;
Stop here, or gently pass!
Alone she cuts and binds the grain,   5
And sings a melancholy strain;
O listen! for the Vale profound
Is overflowing with the sound.

No Nightingale did ever chaunt
More welcome notes to weary bands   10
Of travellers in some shady haunt
Among Arabian sands:
A voice so thrilling ne'er was heard
In spring-time from the Cuckoo-bird,
Breaking the silence of the seas   15
Among the farthest Hebrides.

Will no one tell me what she sings?—
Perhaps the plaintive numbers flow
For old, unhappy, far-off things,
And battles long ago: 20
Or is it some more humble lay,
Familiar matter of today?
Some natural sorrow, loss, or pain,
That has been, and may be again?

Whate'er the theme, the Maiden sang   *25*
As if her song could have no ending;
I saw her singing at her work,
And o'er the sickle bending;
I listened, motionless and still;
And, as I mounted up the hill,   *30*
The music in my heart I bore,
Long after it was heard no more.

The world is too much with us

The world is too much with us; late and soon,
Getting and spending, we lay waste our powers:
Little we see in Nature that is ours;
We have given our hearts away, a sordid boon!
This Sea that bares her bosom to the moon;
The winds that will be howling at all hours,
And are up-gathered now like sleeping flowers;
For this, for everything, we are out of tune;
It moves us not.—Great God! I'd rather be
A Pagan suckled in a creed outworn;
So might I, standing on this pleasant lea,
Have glimpses that would make me less forlorn;
Have sight of Proteus rising from the sea;
Or hear old Triton blow his wreathéd horn.

We Are Seven

—A simple Child,
That lightly draws its breath,
And feels its life in every limb,
What should it know of death?

I met a little cottage Girl: *5*
She was eight years old, she said;
Her hair was thick with many a curl
That clustered round her head.

She had a rustic, woodland air,
And she was wildly clad: *10*
Her eyes were fair, and very fair;
—Her beauty made me glad.

"Sisters and brothers, little Maid,
How many may you be?"
"How many? Seven in all," she said,   *15*
And wondering looked at me.

"And where are they? I pray you tell."
She answered , "Seven are we;
And two of us at Conway dwell,
And two are gone to sea.   *20*

"Two of us in the churchyard lie,
My sister and my brother;
And, in the churchyard cottage, I
Dwell near them with my mother."

"You say that two at Conway dwell,   *25*
And two are gone to sea,
Yet ye are seven! I pray you tell,
Sweet Maid, how this may be."

Then did the little Maid reply,
"Seven boys and girls are we;   *30*
Two of us in the churchyard lie,
Beneath the churchyard tree."

"You run about, my little Maid,
Your limbs they are alive;
If two are in the churchyard laid,   *35*
Then ye are only five."

"Their graves are green, they may be seen,"
The little Maid replied,
"Twelve steps or more from my mother's door,
And they are side by side.   *40*

"My stockings there I often knit,
My kerchief there I hem;
And there upon the ground I sit,
And sing a song to them.

"And often after sunset, sir,   *45*
When it is light and fair,
I take my little porringer,
And eat my supper there.

"The first that died was sister Jane;
In bed she moaning lay,   *50*
Till God released her of her pain;
And then she went away.

"So in the churchyard she was laid;
And, when the grass was dry,
Together round her grave we played,   55
My brother John and I.

"And when the ground was white with snow,
And I could run and slide,
My brother John was forced to go,
And he lies by her side."   60

"How many are you, then," said I,
"If they two are in heaven?"
Quick was the little Maid's reply,
"O master! we are seven."

"But they are dead; those two are dead!   65
Their spirits are in heaven!"
'Twas throwing words away; for still
The little Maid would have her will,
And said, "Nay, we are seven!"

DRAMA

STEINBERG

W hat is drama?

It is an acting out of a story by actors in front of an audience. Drama, like fiction and poetry, is a genre of literature. That is, when we contemplate its language as written, it is literature; but when we regard its language as spoken, it is theater.

Drama is simply one way of telling a story. All the elements of fiction—character, plot, conflict, exposition, complication, climax, resolution, and others—are also found in drama.

Playwrights share with the writers of fiction many of the problems growing out of the process of selecting the materials that they ultimately mold into their creations. All want to beget interesting, believable characters, exhibit a mighty struggle, present complications designed to ''thicken'' the plot, sustain interest, and give vent to some attitude toward the meaning of life.

But dramatic art is unique. Its uniqueness issues from the fact that action on stage unfolds and pulsates before our very eyes. The participants are not merely storybook people cast into conflict; they are real people contending against each other's passions and motives.

Conflict, of course, throbs at the center of every story, but the story dramatically enlivened on stage achieves a lifelikeness and intensity that fiction can only hope to accomplish. The playwright can be more direct and more powerful than the fiction writer. The playwright can present conflict with the intensity and immediacy of the present, as the fiction writer cannot do. In fiction, the events are reported to us as having already happened, and conversation represents what characters have already said. But in drama, the events are revealed to us as they unfold, and the dialogue is what characters are saying *now*. Watching or reading a play, we ''feel'' the action as it takes place. We are there. Only drama will bring us this close to characters and the significance of their actions.

For this vitality and power, missing in other literary forms, playwrights pay a price. They must, in fact, exchange several freedoms (available to fiction writers) for certain limitations.

Of necessity, playwrights fit their materials into a tight structure: they condense and compress their depiction of characters, their actions, and their speeches. At the other extreme, fiction writers, especially novelists, write a lengthy story that runs on a looser track: they may introduce long, descriptive passages, digressions, and many of the details that crowd our daily experiences.

Dramatists can waste no time. They must recount the story within the strict time frame alloted—what Shakespeare called "the two-hours' traffic of our stage." That time limit cannot usually exceed three hours. A telephone conversation, a duel, a lengthy argument, or a wedding ceremony that would consume fifteen minutes or longer in real life lasts but a few minutes on stage. Because playwrights must tell the story swiftly, they must make every action and every speech count, in fact, make it indispensable.

Further, playwrights are restricted by a single point of view, which is severely objective. They cannot, for instance, permit their own voices to be heard, commenting upon an event or character, explaining motivation, or interpreting the significance of an action, except through a character. By and large we infer meaning from what the characters do and say.

Another constraint is playwrights' near absolute dependence on dialogue to tell the story. Dialogue is everything to drama, whereas it is one means among several to fiction.

The effects the dramatist achieves have large appeal, for the drama enjoys the greatest popularity among all the arts, if we include the dramas presented on television to audiences of countless millions. More people saw a single performance of *Oedipus* on American television than have seen the thousands of performances given throughout the world since Sophocles wrote the drama 2400 years ago.

Drama appeals to us for no fewer reasons than fiction does. We enjoy drama first and foremost because it is entertaining and second because the world of make-believe affords us an opportunity to escape the monotony of the daily details of life. Further, we are witness to a story: our emotions are stirred and our sympathies are aroused. Also, we find companionship, perhaps comfort, and we may be enlightened. Finally, we take pleasure in great dramas as literary masterpieces for the stories playwrights tell, the ideas contained in them, or the beauty of the artistry.

Though the fullest enjoyment of a play may come from seeing it performed, pleasure and profit are surely gained by reading a drama. We as readers of drama accept an enormous responsibility. No other genre requires so much of us. We are at once the director, the set designer, the make-up man, all the actors, and sometimes the playwright. Any play that we read can live if brought to life in our imaginations. For us the rewards are great.

The reader of a play may gain a distinct advantage over the viewer, who, given the necessary speed and compression of the genre, may have missed some points. The viewer may also have fallen short of appreciating the playwright's many talents.

A sensitive, mature reading of plays augments our knowledge of drama, cultivates our taste, refines our critical posture, and perhaps even earns us the right to be counted among those intelligent and responsive members of an audience for which every playwright craves.

1 Plot

Plot is the sequence of interrelated actions and events that make up a story. By means of arrangement and emphasis the action stirs emotional power and promotes thematic significance. As it is true of fiction, so it is true of drama. The elements of plot are therefore common to each genre. But in drama, some need a different emphasis, and there are in addition new elements, considered the exclusive property of the dramatic form, that should be dealt with more fully.

Dramatic plots have a variety of structures. Most Greek tragedies (like *Oedipus*) have a simple, tightly knit plot and relatively few major characters. The following diagram illustrates the plot of a Greek drama:

TURNING POINT

Rising Action   *Falling Action*

EXPOSITION   CLIMAX

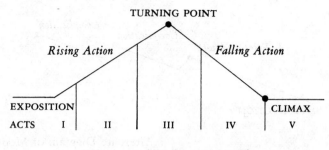

Diagram of Shakespearian Play

The *exposition* contains necessary background information; the *rising action* consists of the introduction and the heightening of the conflict; the *turning point* (also called *crisis*) refers to a high point in the action involving a decisive clash between opposing forces. At this point there is a change in the direction of the action; the main character or the antagonist is shown as having the upper hand; the *falling action* (although the adjective and the diagram are misleading us to think that there is a slackening off of interest) continues to advance the action with increased intensity; the *climax* refers to the point of highest emotional involvement for the audience.

At the opposite extreme, Elizabethan plays (like *Romeo and Juliet*) have several sets of characters who are energetically involved in a plethora of situations and complicated actions. The Shakespearian five-act play is diagramed above.

Modern drama fits no single formula. Its plot may be either simple or complex. The plot of a conventional modern play can be charted as at the bottom of this page, or, as an alternative, the plots of most conven-

Diagram of Modern Play

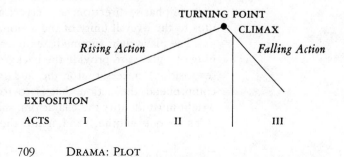

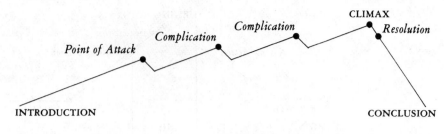

Alternate Diagram of Modern Play

tional modern dramas can be depicted as at the top of this page. The *introduction* (also called *exposition*) sets the stage for the action that will follow; the *point of attack* (also referred to as *inciting force*) initiates the action, showing the main character in conflict with nature's forces, social forces, others, or the self; the *complications* make the problem more difficult to solve; the *climax* presents the opposing forces at the apex of their struggle; the *resolution* (also called *dénouement*) settles the outcome of the conflict; and the *conclusion* (also referred to as *ending*) terminates the action.

The internal structure of a typical three-act play follows a fairly predictable pattern. Act One presents the preliminary exposition and introduces the characters and the main conflict (point of attack). Act Two advances the action forward through any number of complications with increasing suspense. Act Three raises the action to the highest point of emotional intensity (the climax) and then offers a solution to the major problem (the resolution). Plays constructed with scene divisions within acts or only with scenes, as in the case of *The Emperor Jones*, function in much the same manner. For the most part, the dramatist divides the action into these segments to indicate a passage of time or to show a change in setting or character. Acts or scenes each contain a segment of the action; each has its own emphasis, direction, and crisis; and each contributes to the overall unity of the action.

The playwright's immediate obligation at the beginning of a play is to provide the background information (exposition) necessary for the audience or reader to comprehend the action that is to follow. The playwright must identify the characters, show their relationships to one another, and ignite the fuse of conflict without undue delay. At the outset, *who* these characters are and *what* they are doing must be apparent. This exposition, sometimes called *antecedent action*, has actually preceded the beginning of the play. There was a time when Oedipus had not killed Laïos or married his mother; a time when the Capulets and the Montagues were not feuding; and a time when Doc had not become addicted to alcohol. All this antecedent action is important and, if the playwright is to avoid bewildering the audience, must be interjected early in the play.

The most direct kind of exposition the playwright achieves by making a direct statement to the audience. The vehicle of communication can be a prologue, a chorus, or a narrator. Each of these methods ordinarily sets the tone and atmosphere of the drama, provides background data about one or two main characters, and gives some notion of the nature of the conflict.

Sophocles, for example, in his prologue of seventy lines, reveals Oedipus suffering with the suppliants, who have come to beg their honored lord to rid the city of a devastating pestilence. In addition, we learn that Oedipus has already sent Creon, Iocastâ's brother, to consult the Oracle at Delphi and that he, Oedipus, will do everything the Oracle requires of him.

The shorter prologue in *Romeo and Juliet* centers on the poignant conflict—the cause of it and the end of it. The chorus informs us of an ancient grudge between two noble households, the breaking out anew of the feud, the untold suffering, the suicides of "a pair of star-cross'd lovers," and the end of hostilities.

Likewise, the soliloquy and the aside may be used to present exposition effectively. *Soliloquy* means "to speak alone." The speaker, alone on the stage, gives the appearance of talking to himself or herself, although he or she really addresses the audience with a lengthy speech that commonly reflects penetrating thoughts about his or her character. Similarly, the *aside*, which merely pretends at being a stage whisper, is really spoken directly to the audience or occasionally to some of the characters. Usually as terse as a single word or sentence, it comments on an action or a character.

Any one of these methods (prologue, chorus, narrator, soliloquy, aside) will accomplish the dramatist's purpose of imparting preliminary information, although today they are dismissed as outmoded and used infrequently.

To present early exposition indirectly the modern playwright customarily favors the use of a setting, an incident, or a conversation between two characters other than the protagonist and the antagonist.

Setting furnishes a great deal more material than one would reasonably expect: it gives the times in which the action takes place, sets tone and atmosphere, points to the conflict, mirrors the dispositions of characters, and presents innumerable other significant details. The first thing we see or read about in *Come Back, Little Sheba* is the setting. The play takes place in the 1920s. The scene we look at is this: an extremely cluttered, filthy living room, smoky glass curtains, a littered davenport, a dark, grimy kitchen, and a table piled high with dirty dishes left from yesterday's supper. This setting gives us much information about the inhabitants of the house and provides clues to the action.

Equally effective in transmitting information is a single incident, such as the opening street brawl between members of the feuding houses in *Romeo and Juliet*. It is this scene in which the fiery Tybalt, a Capulet, recognizes Romeo as a Montague, thus preparing us to anticipate a collision between Romeo and Tybalt.

No less revealing is the opening conversation in *Tea and Sympathy* between Lilly and Laura. In those few minutes of dialogue we are given the following information: Tom Lee is singing about "the joys of love"; he is the only boy in the boarding house who does not have an afternoon class; he is thinking (according to Lilly) what other boys are thinking about—sex; Laura is the only person Lilly can trust; Lilly expected Bill to remain a bachelor; she thought it would take a special kind of girl for him to marry; Laura spent a wonderful summer in Italy with Bill; Bill had given Laura a five-and-dime engagement ring; and Laura was once in the theater. From this conversation we can also safely deduce that Lilly is preoccupied with sex; she is distrustful even of her own husband, whom she fears; she is insincere; and that Laura (a contrasting figure) is not so preoccupied with boys and sex; she is honest, genteel, and more understanding of human nature.

Exposition is, of course, not limited to the beginnings of plays. Playwrights introduce background information throughout the play, whenever they deem it necessary. They only gradually complete the picture of the main characters, that is, reveal all that they want us to know about them—their experiences, their thoughts, and their motives. It is not until late in the play that we hear of Bill's own effeminate tendencies (*Tea and Sympathy*); of Doc's and Lola's premarital intimacies (*Come Back, Little Sheba*); of George's real hatred of Keller (*All My Sons*); and of Maurya's great losses to the sea—a husband, a husband's father, and all her six sons (*Riders to the Sea*).

To be sure, playwrights select judiciously, revealing only those specific details absolutely vital to our understanding of the play, and at precisely the right moment; consequently, the details that do get incorporated into the play are indeed significant. And, to serve their many purposes, dramatists use any number of expository devices, those already mentioned and, in addition, confidants, dumb shows, charts, slides, film, music, or whatever. The means by which playwrights disclose facts and details vary according to the times in which they write and the techniques they prefer.

There is a kind of tranquility in drama, at the beginning, before the action begins, and toward the end, after a solution is found (if one is found) for the main problem. Conflict disturbs this tranquility. It is what the plot is about—conflict is the essence of drama.

Conflict is described as the struggle of forces in opposition to each other, for example, human beings against human beings, human beings against society, environment, or fate, or human beings against some aspect of the self. It may also be defined as the *action* and *reaction* of characters or forces opposing each other. This view of conflict resembles a good tug-of-war. First one side gains an advantage, then the other. In between the tugs there are temporary moments of relaxation and adjustment. With the frantic last tug the climax is reached a few moments before the one side pulls down the other in defeat, at the point of resolution. And, if there is a standstill, there is no resolution. Conflict may be as simple as in *Marty*, as ambiguous as in *Oedipus*, as moral as in *All My Sons*, or as psychological as in *The Emperor Jones*. The conflict in *Marty* is between Marty and his feelings of inferiority; in *Oedipus* it is between man and the gods or fate; in *All My Sons* it is between Keller and his dreams of material success; in *The Emperor Jones* it is between Jones and his superstitions and fears.

A good approach to the analysis of conflict (or plot) is the use of the following eight-point formula:

Protagonist—the chief character

Prize—the goal

Obstacle—the opposing force or forces

Point of Attack—the introduction of the problem (conflict)

Complications—temporary hindrances

Climax—the moment of truth

Resolution—the solving of the problem

Theme—the main point of the story

In the face of conflict a character has a choice or several choices to make. A decision to act one way or another must inevitably be made. A major character whose decisions and actions generally force and control the main action is the *protagonist*. We may or may not sympathize, but we do identify with the protagonist or the problem, and we are eager to know what will happen. In most plays major characters are caught in decisive moments of conflict. They respond with action, seeking answers to perplexing questions, struggling to overcome difficulties, or wrestling to achieve something. What the protagonist seeks to achieve or overcome is called the *prize* or goal. The opposition— the someone (antagonist) or something (forces of nature, fate, the ethos of society, or warring internal passions) opposing the protagonist in the pursuit of the goal—we call the *obstacle*. No conflict exists without this opposition, which persists until the outcome is known at the end of the play.

Conflict, then, is made up of a protagonist who struggles against great odds (obstacle) to achieve a goal (prize). Once this situation becomes known to us, the dramatic story has really begun (point of attack). Oedipus (the protagonist) decides, whatever the cost, to cure the cause of the blight that infects Thebes (prize and point of attack). Once he has made that decision, and despite what the Oracle promises (gods or fate as obstacle), he refuses to alter his course, and disaster ensues.

Plot is constructed of the building blocks of *complications*. They are problems, difficulties, or changes that usually come up unexpectedly to impede temporarily the protagonist's progress toward the goal. Let us examine the complications that structure the plot of *Romeo and Juliet*.

1. Romeo, a Montague, and Juliet, a Capulet, whose families are engaged in a bitter feud, fall in love (initial complication or point of attack)

2. Romeo slays Tybalt

3. Romeo is consequently banished, thereby preventing the young lovers from seeing one another

4. Juliet's father insists that Juliet marry Paris

5. To avoid the impending nuptials, Juliet takes a magic potion that allows her to feign death

6. The letter disclosing the "death" plan fails to reach Romeo

7. On learning of Juliet's apparent death, Romeo goes to the burial vault where Juliet lies, imagines her to be dead, and so poisons himself

8. Juliet awakens to find her lover dead (final complication or climax)

9. She stabs herself, joining Romeo in death (resolution)

Through complications the action moves upward and forward toward the most crucial scene in the play, which we know as the *climax*. It is the point of highest emotional intensity. For the forces in opposition, at the apex of their struggle, it is the moment of truth.

What follows is the *resolution* or dénouement, which announces the outcome of the entire sequence of events. At this point something has been decided for or against the protagonist. The struggle is won, or it is lost. The resolution, which settles the conflict, may shed light upon the theme of the play. *Theme* is the point the playwright tries to make, the central meaning or significance of the drama.

GREEK THEATER AND STAGE

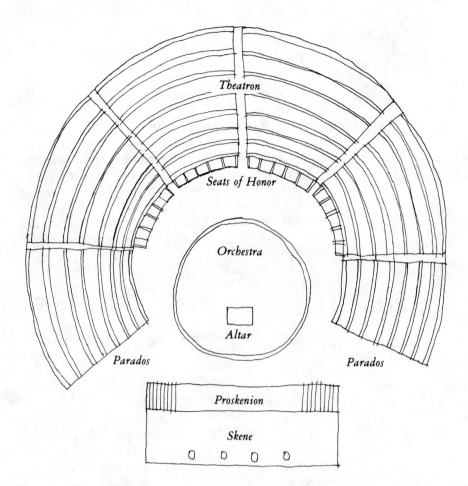

Theatron	Seating area for audience on hillside in open air
Seats of honor	Seating area for dignitaries, including priests and public officials
Orchestra	Stage or acting area and dancing place of chorus
Altar	Place for offering sacrifices
Parados	Points of entry and exit for chorus
Proskenion	Scenery, usually representing the front of a palace or temple (also called "proscenium")
Skene	Building with three doors used for background scenery, entrance and exit of actors; houses dressing rooms and stage machinery

Sophocles *(495–405 B.C.)*

Born at Colonus, near Athens, he learned to write tragedies from his tutor Aeschylus. He was a young man in his twenties when he first began to compete for prizes at drama festivals. Writing more than 120 plays, he won first prizes twenty-four times, a record unequaled by his master or by his successors. So enthusiastic were the Athenians about the plays of Sophocles that they bestowed on him the highest honor granted an Athenian citizen—they gave him the title of General. Critics consider Oedipus, the King *one of the greatest tragedies ever written. Other well-known Sophoclean dramas are* Antigone *and* Electra.

Oedipus Rex

An English Version by Dudley Fitts and Robert Fitzgerald

PERSONS REPRESENTED

OEDIPUS	MESSENGER
A PRIEST	SHEPHERD OF LAÏOS
CREON	SECOND MESSENGER
TEIRESIAS	CHORUS OF THEBAN
IOCASTE	ELDERS

THE SCENE: *Before the palace of Oedipus, King of Thebes. A central door and two lateral doors open onto a platform which runs the length of the façade. On the platform, right and left, are altars; and three steps lead down into the "orchestra," or chorus-ground. At the beginning of the action these steps are crowded by* SUPPLIANTS *who have brought branches and chaplets of olive leaves and who lie in various attitudes of despair.* OEDIPUS *enters*

PROLOGUE

OEDIPUS   My children, generations of the living
In the line of Kadmos, nursed at his ancient hearth:

Why have you strewn yourselves before these altars
In supplication, with your boughs and garlands?
The breath of incense rises from the city
With a sound of prayer and lamentation.

                                Children,
I would not have you speak through messengers,
And therefore I have come myself to hear you—
I, Oedipus, who bear the famous name.

                                            To a PRIEST

You, there, since you are eldest in the company,
Speak for them all, tell me what preys upon you,
Whether you come in dread, or crave some blessing:
Tell me, and never doubt that I will help you
In every way I can; I should be heartless
Were I not moved to find you suppliant here.

PRIEST   Great Oedipus, O powerful King of Thebes!
You see how all the ages of our people
Cling to your altar steps: here are boys
Who can barely stand alone, and here are priests
By weight of age, as I am a priest of God,
And young men chosen from those yet unmarried;
As for the others, all that multitude,
They wait with olive chaplets in the squares,
At the two shrines of Pallas, and where Apollo
Speaks in the glowing embers.

                              Your own eyes
Must tell you: Thebes is tossed on a murdering sea
And can not lift her head from the death surge.
A rust consumes the buds and fruits of the earth;
The herds are sick; children die unborn,
And labor is vain. The god of plague and pyre
Raids like detestable lightning through the city,
And all the house of Kadmos is laid waste,
All emptied, and all darkened: Death alone
Battens upon the misery of Thebes.

You are not one of the immortal gods, we know;
Yet we have come to you to make our prayer
As to the man surest in mortal ways
And wisest in the ways of God. You saved us
From the Sphinx, that flinty singer, and the tribute
We paid to her so long; yet you were never
Better informed than we, nor could we teach you:
It was some god breathed in you to set us free.

Therefore, O mighty King, we turn to you:
Find us our safety, find us a remedy,

Whether by counsel of the gods or men.
A king of wisdom tested in the past
Can act in a time of troubles, and act well.
Noblest of men, restore
Life to your city! Think how all men call you
Liberator for your triumph long ago;
Ah, when your years of kingship are remembered,
Let them not say *We rose, but later fell*—
Keep the State from going down in the storm!
Once, years ago, with happy augury,
You brought us fortune; be the same again!
No man questions your power to rule the land:
But rule over men, not over a dead city!
Ships are only hulls, citadels are nothing,
When no life moves in the empty passageways.

OEDIPUS   Poor children! You may be sure I know
All that you longed for in your coming here.
I know that you are deathly sick; and yet,
Sick as you are, not one is as sick as I.
Each of you suffers in himself alone
His anguish, not another's; but my spirit
Groans for the city, for myself, for you.

I was not sleeping, you are not waking me.
No, I have been in tears for a long while
And in my restless thought walked many ways.
In all my search, I found one helpful course,
And that I have taken: I have sent Creon,
Son of Menoikeus, brother of the Queen,
To Delphi, Apollo's place of revelation,
To learn there, if he can,
What act or pledge of mine may save the city.
I have counted the days, and now, this very day,
I am troubled, for he has overstayed his time.
What is he doing? He has been gone too long.
Yet whenever he comes back, I should do ill
To scant whatever hint the god may give.

PRIEST   It is a timely promise. At this instant
They tell me Creon is here.

OEDIPUS   O Lord Apollo!
May his news be fair as his face is radiant!

PRIEST   It could not be otherwise: he is crowned with bay,
The chaplet is thick with berries.

OEDIPUS   We shall soon know;
He is near enough to hear us now.

Enter CREON

O Prince:

Brother: son of Menoikeus:
What answer do you bring us from the god?

CREON   It is favorable. I can tell you, great afflictions
Will turn out well, if they are taken well.

OEDIPUS   What was the oracle? These vague words
Leave me still hanging between hope and fear.

CREON   Is it your pleasure to hear me with all these
Gathered around us? I am prepared to speak,
But should we not go in?

OEDIPUS   Let them all hear it.
It is for them I suffer, more than for myself.

CREON   Then I will tell you what I heard at Delphi.

In plain words
The god commands us to expel from the land of Thebes
An old defilement that it seems we shelter.
It is a deathly thing, beyond expiation.
We must not let it feed upon us longer.

OEDIPUS   What defilement? How shall we rid ourselves of it?

CREON   By exile or death, blood for blood. It was
Murder that brought the plague-wind on the city.

OEDIPUS   Murder of whom? Surely the god has named him?

CREON   My lord: long ago Laïos was our king,
Before you came to govern us.

OEDIPUS   I know:
I learned of him from others; I never saw him.

CREON   He was murdered; and Apollo commands us now
To take revenge upon whoever killed him.

OEDIPUS   Upon whom? Where are they? Where shall we find a clue
To solve that crime, after so many years?

CREON   Here in this land, he said.

                         If we make enquiry,
We may touch things that otherwise escape us.

OEDIPUS   Tell me: Was Laïos murdered in his house,
Or in the fields, or in some foreign country?

CREON   He said he planned to make a pilgrimage.
He did not come home again.

OEDIPUS   And was there no one,
No witness, no companion, to tell what happened?

CREON   They were all killed but one, and he got away
So frightened that he could remember one thing only.

OEDIPUS   What was that one thing? One may be the key
To everything, if we resolve to use it.

CREON   He said that a band of highwaymen attacked them,
Outnumbered them, and overwhelmed the King.

OEDIPUS   Strange, that a highwayman should be so daring—
    Unless some faction here bribed him to do it.
CREON   We thought of that. But after Laïos' death
    New troubles arose and we had no avenger.
OEDIPUS   What troubles could prevent your hunting down the killers?
CREON   The riddling Sphinx's song
    Made us deaf to all mysteries but her own.
OEDIPUS   Then once more I must bring what is dark to light.
    It is most fitting that Apollo shows,
    As you do, this compunction for the dead.
    You shall see how I stand by you, as I should,
    To avenge the city and the city's god,
    And not as though it were for some distant friend,
    But for my own sake, to be rid of evil.
    Whoever killed King Laïos might—who knows?—
    Decide at any moment to kill me as well.
    By avenging the murdered king I protect myself.
    Come, then, my children: leave the altar steps,
    Lift up your olive boughs!
                            One of you go
    And summon the people of Kadmos to gather here.
    I will do all that I can; you may tell them that.

                                            Exit a PAGE

    So, with the help of God,
    We shall be saved—or else indeed we are lost.
PRIEST   Let us rise, children. It was for this we came,
    And now the King has promised it himself.
    Phoibos has sent us an oracle; may he descend
    Himself to save and drive out the plague.

                    Exeunt OEDIPUS *and* CREON *into the palace by the central door.*
                    The PRIEST *and the* SUPPLIANTS *disperse R and L. After a short*
                    pause the CHORUS *enters the orchestra*

PARADOS   *Strophe One*

CHORUS   What is God singing in his profound
    Delphi of gold and shadow?
    What oracle for Thebes, the sunwhipped city?
    Fear unjoints me, the roots of my heart tremble.
    Now I remember, O Healer, your power, and wonder;
    Will you send doom like a sudden cloud, or weave it
    Like nightfall of the past?
    Speak, speak to us, issue of holy sound:
    Dearest to our expectancy: be tender!

Antistrophe One

Let me pray to Athenê, the immortal daughter of Zeus,
And to Artemis her sister
Who keeps her famous throne in the market ring,
And to Apollo, bowman at the far butts of heaven—

O gods, descend! Like three streams leap against
The fires of our grief, the fires of darkness;
Be swift to bring us rest!

As in the old time from the brilliant house
Of air you stepped to save us, come again!

Strophe Two

Now our afflictions have no end,
Now all our stricken host lies down
And no man fights off death with his mind;

The noble plowland bears no grain,
And groaning mothers can not bear—

See, how our lives like birds take wing,
Like sparks that fly when a fire soars,
To the shore of the god of evening.

Antistrophe Two

The plague burns on, it is pitiless,
Though pallid children laden with death
Lie unwept in the stony ways,

And old gray women by every path
Flock to the strand about the altars

There to strike their breasts and cry
Worship of Phoibos in wailing prayers:
Be kind, God's golden child!

Strophe Three

There are no swords in this attack by fire,
No shields, but we are ringed with cries.
Send the besieger plunging from our homes

Into the vast sea-room of the Atlantic
Or into the waves that foam eastward of Thrace—
For the day ravages what the night spares—

Destroy our enemy, lord of the thunder!
Let him be riven by lightning from heaven!

Antistrophe Three

Phoibos Apollo, stretch the sun's bowstring,
That golden cord, until it sing for us,
Flashing arrows in heaven!
       Artemis, Huntress,
Race with flaring lights upon our mountains!
O scarlet god, O golden-banded brow,
O Theban Bacchos in a storm of Maenads,

            Enter OEDIPUS, *C.*

Whirl upon Death, that all the Undying hate!
Come with blinding cressets, come in joy!

SCENE ONE

OEDIPUS Is this your prayer? It may be answered. Come,
  Listen to me, act as the crisis demands,
  And you shall have relief from all these evils.

  Until now I was a stranger to this tale,
  As I had been a stranger to the crime.
  Could I track down the murderer without a clue?
  But now, friends,
  As one who became a citizen after the murder,
  I make this proclamation to all Thebans:
  If any man knows by whose hand Laïos, son of Labdakos,
  Met his death, I direct that man to tell me everything,
  No matter what he fears for having so long withheld it.
  Let it stand as promised that no further trouble
  Will come to him, but he may leave the land in safety.

  Moreover: If anyone knows the murderer to be foreign,
  Let him not keep silent: he shall have his reward from me.
  However, if he does conceal it; if any man
  Fearing for his friend or for himself disobeys this edict,
  Hear what I propose to do:

  I solemnly forbid the people of this country,
  Where power and throne are mine, ever to receive that man

Or speak to him, no matter who he is, or let him
Join in sacrifice, lustration, or in prayer.
I decree that he be driven from every house,
Being, as he is, corruption itself to us: the Delphic
Voice of Zeus has pronounced this revelation.
Thus I associate myself with the oracle
And take the side of the murdered king.

As for the criminal, I pray to God—
Whether it be a lurking thief, or one of a number—
I pray that that man's life be consumed in evil and wretchedness.
And as for me, this curse applies no less
If it should turn out that the culprit is my guest here,
Sharing my hearth.
                              You have heard the penalty.
I lay it on you now to attend to this
For my sake, for Apollo's, for the sick
Sterile city that heaven has abandoned.
Suppose the oracle had given you no command:
Should this defilement go uncleansed for ever?
You should have found the murderer: your king,
A noble king, had been destroyed!
                              Now I,
Having the power that he held before me,
Having his bed, begetting children there
Upon his wife, as he would have, had he lived—
Their son would have been my children's brother,
If Laïos had had luck in fatherhood!
(But surely ill luck rushed upon his reign)—
I say I take the son's part, just as though
I were his son, to press the fight for him
And see it won! I'll find the hand that brought
Death to Labdakos' and Polydoros' child,
Heir of Kadmos' and Agenor's line.
And as for those who fail me,
May the gods deny them the fruit of the earth,
Fruit of the womb, and may they rot utterly!
Let them be wretched as we are wretched, and worse!

For you, for loyal Thebans, and for all
Who find my actions right, I pray the favor
Of justice, and of all the immortal gods.
CHORAGOS   Since I am under oath, my lord, I swear
    I did not do the murder, I can not name
    The murderer. Might not the oracle
    That has ordained the search tell where to find him?

OEDIPUS   An honest question. But no man in the world
     Can make the gods do more than the gods will.
CHORAGOS   There is one last expedient—
OEDIPUS   Tell me what it is.
     Though it seem slight, you must not hold it back.
CHORAGOS   A lord clairvoyant to the lord Apollo,
     As we all know, is the skilled Teiresias.
     One might learn much about this from him, Oedipus.
OEDIPUS   I am not wasting time:
     Creon spoke of this, and I have sent for him—
     Twice, in fact; it is strange that he is not here.
CHORAGOS   The other matter—that old report—seems useless.
OEDIPUS   Tell me. I am interested in all reports.
CHORAGOS   The King was said to have been killed by highwaymen.
OEDIPUS   I know. But we have no witnesses to that.
CHORAGOS   If the killer can feel a particle of dread,
     Your curse will bring him out of hiding!
OEDIPUS   No.
     The man who dared that act will fear no curse.

                              Enter the blind seer TEIRESIAS, *led by a* PAGE
CHORAGOS   But there is one man who may detect the criminal.
     This is Teiresias, this is the holy prophet
     In whom, alone of all men, truth was born.
OEDIPUS   Teiresias: seer: student of mysteries,
     Of all that's taught and all that no man tells,
     Secrets of Heaven and secrets of the earth:
     Blind though you are, you know the city lies
     Sick with plague; and from this plague, my lord,
     We find that you alone can guard or save us.

     Possibly you did not hear the messengers?
     Apollo, when we sent to him,
     Sent us back word that this great pestilence
     Would lift, but only if established clearly
     The identity of those who murdered Laïos.
     They must be killed or exiled.
                              Can you use
     Birdflight or any art of divination
     To purify yourself, and Thebes, and me
     From this contagion? We are in your hands.
     There is no fairer duty
     Than that of helping others in distress.
TEIRESIAS   How dreadful knowledge of the truth can be
     When there's no help in truth! I knew this well,
     But did not act on it: else I should not have come.
OEDIPUS   What is troubling you? Why are your eyes so cold?

TEIRESIAS   Let me go home. Bear your own fate, and I'll
    Bear mine. It is better so: trust what I say.
OEDIPUS   What you say is ungracious and unhelpful
    To your native country. Do not refuse to speak.
TEIRESIAS   When it comes to speech, your own is neither temperate
    Nor opportune. I wish to be more prudent.
OEDIPUS   In God's name, we all beg you—
TEIRESIAS   You are all ignorant.
    No; I will never tell you what I know.
    Now it is my misery; then, it would be yours.
OEDIPUS   What! You do know something, and will not tell us?
    You would betray us all and wreck the State?
TEIRESIAS   I do not intend to torture myself, or you.
    Why persist in asking? You will not persuade me.
OEDIPUS   What a wicked old man you are! You'd try a stone's
    Patience! Out with it! Have you no feeling at all?
TEIRESIAS   You call me unfeeling. If you could only see
    The nature of your own feelings . . .
OEDIPUS   Why,
    Who would not feel as I do? Who could endure
    Your arrogance toward the city?
TEIRESIAS   What does it matter!
    Whether I speak or not, it is bound to come.
OEDIPUS   Then, if "it" is bound to come, you are bound to tell me.
TEIRESIAS   No, I will not go on. Rage as you please.
OEDIPUS   Rage? Why not!
                And I'll tell you what I think:
    You planned it, you had it done, you all but
    Killed him with your own hands: if you had eyes,
    I'd say the crime was yours, and yours alone.
TEIRESIAS   So? I charge you, then,
    Abide by the proclamation you have made:
    From this day forth
    Never speak again to these men or to me;
    You yourself are the pollution of this country.
OEDIPUS   You dare say that! Can you possibly think you have
    Some way of going free, after such insolence?
TEIRESIAS   I have gone free. It is the truth sustains me.
OEDIPUS   Who taught you shamelessness? It was not your craft.
TEIRESIAS   You did. You made me speak. I did not want to.
OEDIPUS   Speak what? Let me hear it again more clearly.
TEIRESIAS   Was it not clear before? Are you tempting me?
OEDIPUS   I did not understand it. Say it again.
TEIRESIAS   I say that you are the murderer whom you seek.
OEDIPUS   Now twice you have spat out infamy. You'll pay for it!
TEIRESIAS   Would you care for more? Do you wish to be really angry?

OEDIPUS   Say what you will. Whatever you say is worthless.
TEIRESIAS   I say you live in hideous shame with those
    Most dear to you. You can not see the evil.
OEDIPUS   It seems you can go on mouthing like this for ever.
TEIRESIAS   I can, if there is power in truth.
OEDIPUS   There is:
    But not for you, not for you,
    You sightless, witless, senseless, mad old man!
TEIRESIAS   You are the madman. There is no one here
    Who will not curse you soon, as you curse me.
OEDIPUS   You child of endless night! You can not hurt me
    Or any other man who sees the sun.
TEIRESIAS   True: it is not from me your fate will come.
    That lies within Apollo's competence,
    As it is his concern.
OEDIPUS   Tell me:
    Are you speaking for Creon, or for yourself?
TEIRESIAS   Creon is no threat. You weave your own doom.
OEDIPUS   Wealth, power, craft of statesmanship!
    Kingly position, everywhere admired!
    What savage envy is stored up against these,
    If Creon, whom I trusted, Creon my friend,
    For this great office which the city once
    Put in my hands unsought—if for this power
    Creon desires in secret to destroy me!

    He has bought this decrepit fortune-teller, this
    Collector of dirty pennies, this prophet fraud—
    Why, he is no more clairvoyant than I am!
                                        Tell us:
    Has your mystic mummery ever approached the truth?
    When that hellcat the Sphinx was performing here,
    What help were you to these people?
    Her magic was not for the first man who came along:
    It demanded a real exorcist. Your birds—
    What good were they? or the gods, for the matter of that?
    But I came by,
    Oedipus, the simple man, who knows nothing—
    I thought it out for myself, no birds helped me!
    And this is the man you think you can destroy,
    That you may be close to Creon when he's king!
    Well, you and your friend Creon, it seems to me,
    Will suffer most. If you were not an old man,
    You would have paid already for your plot.
CHORAGOS   We can not see that his words or yours
    Have been spoken except in anger, Oedipus,

And of anger we have no need. How can God's will
Be accomplished best? That is what most concerns us.

TEIRESIAS   You are a king. But where argument's concerned
I am your man, as much a king as you.
I am not your servant, but Apollo's.
I have no need of Creon to speak for me.

Listen to me. You mock my blindness, do you?
But I say that you, with both your eyes, are blind:
You can not see the wretchedness of your life,
Nor in whose house you live, no, nor with whom.
Who are your father and mother? Can you tell me?
You do not even know the blind wrongs
That you have done them, on earth and in the world below.
But the double lash of your parents' curse will whip you
Out of this land some day, with only night
Upon your precious eyes.
Your cries then—where will they not be heard?
What fastness of Kithairon will not echo them?
And that bridal-descant of yours—you'll know it then,
The song they sang when you came here to Thebes
And found your misguided berthing.
All this, and more, that you can not guess at now,
Will bring you to yourself among your children.

Be angry, then. Curse Creon. Curse my words.
I tell you, no man that walks upon the earth
Shall be rooted out more horribly than you.

OEDIPUS   Am I to bear this from him?—Damnation
Take you! Out of this place! Out of my sight!

TEIRESIAS   I would not have come at all if you had not asked me.

OEDIPUS   Could I have told that you'd talk nonsense, that
You'd come here to make a fool of yourself, and of me?

TEIRESIAS   A fool? Your parents thought me sane enough.

OEDIPUS   My parents again!—Wait: who were my parents?

TEIRESIAS   This day will give you a father, and break your heart.

OEDIPUS   Your infantile riddles! Your damned abracadabra!

TEIRESIAS   You were a great man once at solving riddles.

OEDIPUS   Mock me with that if you like; you will find it true.

TEIRESIAS   It was true enough. It brought about your ruin.

OEDIPUS   But if it saved this town?

TEIRESIAS (to the PAGE)   Boy, give me your hand.

OEDIPUS   Yes, boy; lead him away.
                                             —While you are here
We can do nothing. Go; leave us in peace.

TEIRESIAS   I will go when I have said what I have to say.

How can you hurt me? And I tell you again:
The man you have been looking for all this time,
The damned man, the murderer of Laïos,
That man is in Thebes. To your mind he is foreignborn,
But it will soon be shown that he is a Theban,
A revelation that will fail to please.

                                        A blind man,
Who has his eyes now; a penniless man, who is rich now;
And he will go tapping the strange earth with his staff;
To the children with whom he lives now he will be
Brother and father—the very same; to her
Who bore him, son and husband—the very same
Who came to his father's bed, wet with his father's blood.

Enough. Go think that over.
If later you find error in what I have said,
You may say that I have no skill in prophecy.

                     Exit TEIRESIAS, *led by his* PAGE. OEDI-
                     PUS *goes into the palace*

ODE ONE   *Strophe One*

CHORUS   The Delphic stone of prophecies
    Remembers ancient regicide
    And a still bloody hand.
    That killer's hour of flight has come.
    He must be stronger than riderless
    Coursers of untiring wind,
    For the son of Zeus armed with his father's thunder
    Leaps in lightning after him;
    And the Furies follow him, the sad Furies.

     Antistrophe One

Holy Parnassos' peak of snow
Flashes and blinds that secret man,
That all shall hunt him down:
Though he may roam the forest shade
Like a bull gone wild from pasture
To rage through glooms of stone.
Doom comes down on him; flight will not avail him;
For the world's heart calls him desolate,
And the immortal Furies follow, for ever follow.

But now a wilder thing is heard
From the old man skilled at hearing Fate in the wingbeat of a bird.
Bewildered as a blown bird, my soul hovers and can not find
Foothold in this debate, or any reason or rest of mind.
But no man ever brought—none can bring
Proof of strife between Thebes' royal house,
Labdakos' line, and the son of Polybos;
And never until now has any man brought word
Of Laïos' dark death staining Oedipus the King.

Antistrophe Two

Divine Zeus and Apollo hold
Perfect intelligence alone of all tales ever told;
And well though this diviner works, he works in his own night;
No man can judge that rough unknown or trust in second sight,
For wisdom changes hands among the wise.
Shall I believe my great lord criminal
At a raging word that a blind old man let fall?
I saw him, when the carrion woman faced him of old,
Prove his heroic mind! These evil words are lies.

SCENE TWO

CREON   Men of Thebes:
    I am told that heavy accusations
    Have been brought against me by King Oedipus.

    I am not the kind of man to bear this tamely.

    If in these present difficulties
    He holds me accountable for any harm to him
    Through anything I have said or done—why, then,
    I do not value life in this dishonor.
    It is not as though this rumor touched upon
    Some private indiscretion. The matter is grave.
    The fact is that I am being called disloyal
    To the State, to my fellow citizens, to my friends.
CHORAGOS   He may have spoken in anger, not from his mind.
CREON   But did you not hear him say I was the one
    Who seduced the old prophet into lying?
CHORAGOS   The thing was said; I do not know how seriously.

CREON   But you were watching him! Were his eyes steady?
    Did he look like a man in his right mind?

CHORAGOS   I do not know.
    I can not judge the behavior of great men.
    But here is the King himself.

Enter OEDIPUS

OEDIPUS   So you dared come back.
    Why? How brazen of you to come to my house,
    You murderer!

                    Do you think I do not know
    That you plotted to kill me, plotted to steal my throne?
    Tell me, in God's name: am I coward, a fool,
    That you should dream you could accomplish this?
    A fool who could not see your slippery game?
    A coward, not to fight back when I saw it?
    You are the fool, Creon, are you not? hoping
    Without support or friends to get a throne?
    Thrones may be won or bought: you could do neither.

CREON   Now listen to me. You have talked; let me talk, too.
    You can not judge unless you know the facts.

OEDIPUS   You speak well: there is one fact; but I find it hard
    To learn from the deadliest enemy I have.

CREON   That above all I must dispute with you.

OEDIPUS   That above all I will not hear you deny.

CREON   If you think there is anything good in being stubborn
    Against all reason, then I say you are wrong.

OEDIPUS   If you think a man can sin against his own kind
    And not be punished for it, I say you are mad.

CREON   I agree. But tell me: what have I done to you?

OEDIPUS   You advised me to send for that wizard, did you not?

CREON   I did. I should do it again.

OEDIPUS   Very well. Now tell me:
    How long has it been since Laïos—

CREON   What of Laïos?

OEDIPUS   Since he vanished in that onset by the road?

CREON   It was long ago, a long time.

OEDIPUS   And this prophet,
    Was he practicing here then?

CREON   He was; and with honor, as now.

OEDIPUS   Did he speak of me at that time?

CREON   He never did;
    At least, not when I was present.

OEDIPUS   But . . . the enquiry?
    I suppose you held one?

CREON   We did, but we learned nothing.

OEDIPUS   Why did the prophet not speak against me then?

CREON   I do not know; and I am the kind of man
      Who holds his tongue when he has no facts to go on.
OEDIPUS   There's one fact that you know, and you could tell it.
CREON   What fact is that? If I know it, you shall have it.
OEDIPUS   If he were not involved with you, he could not say
      That it was I who murdered Laïos.
CREON   If he says that, you are the one that knows it!—
      But now it is my turn to question you.
OEDIPUS   Put your questions. I am no murderer.
CREON   First, then: You married my sister?
OEDIPUS   I married your sister.
CREON   And you rule the kingdom equally with her?
OEDIPUS   Everything that she wants she has from me.
CREON   And I am the third, equal to both of you?
OEDIPUS   That is why I call you a bad friend.
CREON   No. Reason it out, as I have done.
      Think of this first. Would any sane man prefer
      Power, with all a king's anxieties,
      To that same power and the grace of sleep?
      Certainly not I.
      I have never longed for the king's power—only his rights.
      Would any wise man differ from me in this?
      As matters stand, I have my way in everything
      With your consent, and no responsibilities.
      If I were king, I should be a slave to policy.

      How could I desire a scepter more
      Than what is now mine—untroubled influence?
      No, I have not gone mad; I need no honors,
      Except those with the perquisites I have now.
      I am welcome everywhere; every man salutes me,
      And those who want your favor seek my ear,
      Since I know how to manage what they ask.
      Should I exchange this ease for that anxiety?
      Besides, no sober mind is treasonable.
      I hate anarchy
      And never would deal with any man who likes it.

      Test what I have said. Go to the priestess
      At Delphi, ask if I quoted her correctly.
      And as for this other thing: if I am found
      Guilty of treason with Teiresias,
      Then sentence me to death! You have my word
      It is a sentence I should cast my vote for—
      But not without evidence!
                                    You do wrong
      When you take good men for bad, bad men for good.

A true friend thrown aside—why, life itself
Is not more precious!
                    In time you will know this well:
For time, and time alone, will show the just man,
Though scoundrels are discovered in a day.
CHORAGOS   This is well said, and a prudent man would ponder it.
    Judgments too quickly formed are dangerous.
OEDIPUS   But is he not quick in his duplicity?
    And shall I not be quick to parry him?
    Would you have me stand still, hold my peace, and let
    This man win everything, through my inaction?
CREON   And you want—what is it, then? To banish me?
OEDIPUS   No, not exile. It is your death I want,
    So that all the world may see what treason means.
CREON   You will persist, then? You will not believe me?
OEDIPUS   How can I believe you?
CREON   Then you are a fool.
OEDIPUS   To save myself?
CREON   In justice, think of me.
OEDIPUS   You are evil incarnate.
CREON   But suppose that you are wrong?
OEDIPUS   Still I must rule.
CREON   But not if you rule badly.
OEDIPUS   O city, city!
CREON   It is my city, too!
CHORAGOS   Now, my lords, be still. I see the Queen,
    Iocastê, coming from her palace chambers;
    And it is time she came, for the sake of you both.
    This dreadful quarrel can be resolved through her.

                                                    Enter IOCASTE

IOCASTE   Poor foolish men, what wicked din is this?
    With Thebes sick to death, is it not shameful
    That you should rake some private quarrel up?
    (*To* OEDIPUS) Come into the house.
                                —And you, Creon, go now:
    Let us have no more of this tumult over nothing.
CREON   Nothing? No, sister: what your husband plans for me
    Is one of two great evils: exile or death.
OEDIPUS   He is right.
                        Why, woman I have caught him squarely
    Plotting against my life.
CREON   No! Let me die
    Accurst if ever I have wished you harm!
IOCASTE   Ah, believe it, Oedipus!
    In the name of the gods, respect this oath of his
    For my sake, for the sake of these people here!

CHORAGOS   Open your mind to her, my lord. Be ruled by her, I beg
    you!
OEDIPUS   What would you have me do?
CHORAGOS   Respect Creon's word. He has never spoken like a fool,
    And now he has sworn an oath.
OEDIPUS   You know what you ask?
CHORAGOS   I do.
OEDIPUS   Speak on, then.
CHORAGOS   A friend so sworn should not be baited so,
    In blind malice, and without final proof.
OEDIPUS   You are aware, I hope, that what you say
    Means death for me, or exile at the least.

Strophe Two

CHORAGOS   No, I swear by Helios, first in Heaven!
                May I die friendless and accurst,
            The worst of deaths, if ever I meant that!
                It is the withering fields
                    That hurt my sick heart:
                Must we bear all these ills,
                    And now your bad blood as well?
OEDIPUS   Then let him go. And let me die, if I must,
    Or be driven by him in shame from the land of Thebes.
    It is your unhappiness, and not his talk,
    That touches me.
                As for him—
    Wherever he is, I will hate him as long as I live.
CREON   Ugly in yielding, as you were ugly in rage!
    Natures like yours chiefly torment themselves.
OEDIPUS   Can you not go? Can you not leave me?
CREON   I can.
    You do not know me; but the city knows me,
    And in its eyes I am just, if not in yours.

                                        Exit CREON

Antistrophe One

CHORAGOS   Lady Iocastê, did you not ask the King to go to his chambers?
IOCASTE   First tell me what has happened.

CHORAGOS   There was suspicion without evidence; yet it rankled
    As even false charges will.
IOCASTE   On both sides?
CHORAGOS   On both.
IOCASTE   But what was said?
CHORAGOS   Oh let it rest, let it be done with!
    Have we not suffered enough?
OEDIPUS   You see to what your decency has brought you:
    You have made difficulties where my heart saw none.

Antistrophe Two

CHORAGOS   Oedipus, it is not once only I have told you—
                  You must know I should count myself unwise
              To the point of madness, should I now forsake you—
                  You, under whose hand,
                      In the storm of another time,
                  Our dear land sailed out free.
                      But now stand fast at the helm!
IOCASTE   In God's name, Oedipus, inform your wife as well:
    Why are you so set in this hard anger?
OEDIPUS   I will tell you, for none of these men deserves
    My confidence as you do. It is Creon's work,
    His treachery, his plotting against me.
IOCASTE   Go on, if you can make this clear to me.
OEDIPUS   He charges me with the murder of Laïos.
IOCASTE   Has he some knowledge? Or does he speak from hearsay?
OEDIPUS   He could not commit himself to such a charge,
    But he has brought in that damnable soothsayer
    To tell his story.
IOCASTE   Set your mind at rest.
    If it is a question of soothsayers, I tell you
    That you will find no man whose craft gives knowledge
    Of the unknowable.
                      Here is my proof:

An oracle was reported to Laïos once
(I will not say from Phoibos himself, but from
His appointed ministers, at any rate)
That his doom would be death at the hands of his own son—
His son, born of his flesh and of mine!

Now, you remember the story: Laïos was killed
By marauding strangers where three highways meet;
But his child had not been three days in this world
Before the King had pierced the baby's ankles

And left him to die on a lonely mountainside.
Thus, Apollo never caused that child
To kill his father, and it was not Laïos' fate
To die at the hands of his son, as he had feared.
This is what prophets and prophecies are worth!
Have no dread of them.
                         It is God himself
Who can show us what he wills, in his own way.

OEDIPUS   How strange a shadowy memory crossed my mind,
    Just now while you were speaking; it chilled my heart.

IOCASTE   What do you mean? What memory do you speak of?

OEDIPUS   If I understand you, Laïos was killed
    At a place where three roads meet.

IOCASTE   So it was said;
    We have no later story.

OEDIPUS   Where did it happen?

IOCASTE   Phokis, it is called: at a place where the Theban Way
    Divides into the roads towards Delphi and Daulia.

OEDIPUS   When?

IOCASTE   We had the news not long before you came
    And proved the right to your succession here.

OEDIPUS   Ah, what net has God been weaving for me?

IOCASTE   Oedipus! Why does this trouble you?

OEDIPUS   Do not ask me yet.
    First, tell me how Laïos looked, and tell me
    How old he was.

IOCASTE   He was tall, his hair just touched
    With white; his form was not unlike your own.

OEDIPUS   I think that I myself may be accurst
    By my own ignorant edict.

IOCASTE   You speak strangely.
    It makes me tremble to look at you, my King.

OEDIPUS   I am not sure that the blind man can not see.
    But I should know better if you were to tell me—

IOCASTE   Anything—though I dread to hear you ask it.

OEDIPUS   Was the King lightly escorted, or did he ride
    With a large company, as a ruler should?

IOCASTE   There were five men with him in all: one was a herald;
    And a single chariot, which he was driving.

OEDIPUS   Alas, that makes it plain enough!
                                        But who—
    Who told you how it happened?

IOCASTE   A household servant,
    The only one to escape.

OEDIPUS   And is he still
    A servant of ours?

IOCASTE   No; for when he came back at last
And found you enthroned in the place of the dead king,
He came to me, touched my hand with his, and begged
That I would send him away to the frontier district
Where only the shepherds go—
As far away from the city as I could send him.
I granted his prayer; for although the man was a slave,
He had earned more than this favor at my hands.

OEDIPUS   Can he be called back quickly?

IOCASTE   Easily.
    But why?

OEDIPUS   I have taken too much upon myself
Without enquiry; therefore I wish to consult him.

IOCASTE   Then he shall come.

                          But am I not one also
To whom you might confide these fears of yours?

OEDIPUS   That is your right; it will not be denied you,
Now least of all; for I have reached a pitch
Of wild foreboding. Is there anyone
To whom I should sooner speak?
Polybos of Corinth is my father.
My mother is a Dorian: Meropê.
I grew up chief among the men of Corinth
Until a strange thing happened—
Not worth my passion, it may be, but strange.

At a feast, a drunken man maundering in his cups
Cries out that I am not my father's son!

I contained myself that night, though I felt anger
And a sinking heart. The next day I visited
My father and mother, and questioned them. They stormed,
Calling it all the slanderous rant of a fool;
And this relieved me. Yet the suspicion
Remained always aching in my mind;
I knew there was talk; I could not rest;
And finally, saying nothing to my parents,
I went to the shrine at Delphi.
The god dismissed my question without reply;
He spoke of other things.

                          Some were clear,
Full of wretchedness, dreadful, unbearable:
As, that I should lie with my own mother, breed
Children from whom all men would turn their eyes;
And that I should be my father's murderer.

I heard all this, and fled. And from that day
Corinth to me was only in the stars

Descending in that quarter of the sky,
As I wandered farther and farther on my way
To a land where I should never see the evil
Sung by the oracle. And I came to this country
Where, so you say, King Laïos was killed.

I will tell you all that happened there, my lady.

There were three highways
Coming together at a place I passed;
And there a herald came towards me, and a chariot
Drawn by horses, with a man such as you describe
Seated in it. The groom leading the horses
Forced me off the road at his lord's command;
But as this charioteer lurched over towards me
I struck him in my rage. The old man saw me
And brought his double goad down upon my head
As I came abreast.
                    He was paid back, and more!
Swinging my club in this right hand I knocked him
Out of his car, and he rolled on the ground.
                                        I killed him.

I killed them all.
Now if that stranger and Laïos were—kin,
Where is a man more miserable than I?
More hated by the gods? Citizen and alien alike
Must never shelter me or speak to me—
I must be shunned by all.
                    And I myself
Pronounced this malediction upon myself!

Think of it: I have touched you with these hands,
These hands that killed your husband. What defilement!

Am I all evil, then? It must be so,
Since I must flee from Thebes, yet never again
See my own countrymen, my own country,
For fear of joining my mother in marriage
And killing Polybos, my father.
                            Ah,
If I was created so, born to this fate,
Who could deny the savagery of God?

O holy majesty of heavenly powers!
May I never see that day! Never!
Rather let me vanish from the race of men
Than know the abomination destined me!

CHORAGOS   We too, my lord, have felt dismay at this.
    But there is hope: you have yet to hear the shepherd.
OEDIPUS   Indeed, I fear no other hope is left me.
IOCASTE   What do you hope from him when he comes?
OEDIPUS   This much:
    If his account of the murder tallies with yours,
    Then I am cleared.
IOCASTE   What was it that I said
    Of such importance?
OEDIPUS   Why, "marauders," you said,
    Killed the King, according to this man's story.
    If he maintains that still, if there were several,
    Clearly the guilt is not mine: I was alone.
    But if he says one man, singlehanded, did it,
    Then the evidence all points to me.
IOCASTE   You may be sure that he said there were several;
    And can he call back that story now? He can not.
    The whole city heard is as plainly as I.
    But suppose he alters some detail of it:
    He can not ever show that Laïos' death
    Fulfilled the oracle: for Apollo said
    My child was doomed to kill him; and my child—
    Poor baby!—it was my child that died first.

    No. From now on, where oracles are concerned,
    I would not waste a second thought on any.
OEDIPUS   You may be right.
                            But come: let someone go
    For the shepherd at once. This matter must be settled.
IOCASTE   I will send for him.
    I would not wish to cross you in anything,
    And surely not in this.—Let us go in.

                                Exeunt into the palace

ODE TWO   *Strophe One*

CHORUS   Let me be reverent in the ways of right,
    Lowly the paths I journey on;
    Let all my words and actions keep
    The laws of the pure universe
    From highest Heaven handed down.
    For Heaven is their bright nurse,
    Those generations of the realms of light;
    Ah, never of mortal kind were they begot,
    Nor are they slaves of memory, lost in sleep:
    Their Father is greater than Time, and ages not.

Antistrophe One

The tyrant is a child of Pride
Who drinks from his great sickening cup
Recklessness and vanity,
Until from his high crest headlong
He plummets to the dust of hope.
That strong man is not strong.
But let no fair ambition be denied;
May God protect the wrestler for the State
In government, in comely policy,
Who will fear God, and on His ordinance wait.

Strophe Two

Haughtiness and the high hand of disdain
Tempt and outrage God's holy law;
And any mortal who dares hold
No immortal Power in awe
Will be caught up in a net of pain:
The price for which his levity is sold.
Let each man take due earnings, then,
And keep his hands from holy things,
And from blasphemy stand apart—
Else the crackling blast of heaven
Blows on his head, and on his desperate heart;
Though fools will honor impious men,
In their cities no tragic poet sings.

Antistrophe Two

Shall we lose faith in Delphi's obscurities,
We who have heard the world's core
Discredited, and the sacred wood
Of Zeus at Elis praised no more?
The deeds and the strange prophecies
Must make a pattern yet to be understood.
Zeus, if indeed you are lord of all,
Throned in light over night and day,
Mirror this in your endless mind:
Our masters call the oracle
Words on the wind, and the Delphic vision blind!
Their hearts no longer know Apollo,
And reverence for the gods has died away.

SCENE THREE

Enter IOCASTE

IOCASTE Princes of Thebes, it has occurred to me
To visit the altars of the gods, bearing
These branches as a suppliant, and this incense.
Our King is not himself: his noble soul
Is overwrought with fantasies of dread,
Else he would consider
The new prophecies in the light of the old.
He will listen to any voice that speaks disaster,
And my advice goes for nothing.

She approaches the altar, R.

      To you, then, Apollo,
Lycean lord, since you are nearest, I turn in prayer.
Receive these offerings, and grant us deliverance
From defilement. Our hearts are heavy with fear
When we see our leader distracted, as helpless sailors
Are terrified by the confusion of their helmsman.

Enter MESSENGER

MESSENGER Friends, no doubt you can direct me:
Where shall I find the house of Oedipus,
Or, better still, where is the King himself?
CHORAGOS It is this very place, stranger; he is inside.
This is his wife and mother of his children.
MESSENGER I wish her happiness in a happy house,
Blest in all the fulfillment of her marriage.
IOCASTE I wish as much for you: your courtesy
Deserves a like good fortune. But now, tell me:
Why have you come? What have you to say to us?
MESSENGER Good news, my lady, for your house and your husband.
IOCASTE What news? Who sent you here?
MESSENGER   I am from Corinth.
The news I bring ought to mean joy for you,
Though it may be you will find some grief in it.
IOCASTE What is it? How can it touch us in both ways?
MESSENGER The people of Corinth, they say,
Intend to call Oedipus to be their king.
IOCASTE But old Polybos—is he not reigning still?
MESSENGER No. Death holds him in his sepulchre.
IOCASTE What are you saying? Polybos is dead?
MESSENGER If I am not telling the truth, may I die myself.
IOCASTE (*to a* MAIDSERVANT) Go in, go quickly; tell this to your master.

O riddlers of God's will, where are you now!
This was the man whom Oedipus, long ago,
Feared so, fled so, in dread of destroying him—
But it was another fate by which he died.

Enter OEDIPUS, *C.*

OEDIPUS   Dearest Iocastê, why have you sent for me?

IOCASTE   Listen to what this man says, and then tell me
What has become of the solemn prophecies.

OEDIPUS   Who is this man? What is his news for me?

IOCASTE   He has come from Corinth to announce your father's death!

OEDIPUS   Is it true, stranger? Tell me in your own words.

MESSENGER   I can not say it more clearly: the King is dead.

OEDIPUS   Was it by treason? Or by an attack of illness?

MESSENGER   A little thing brings old men to their rest.

OEDIPUS   It was sickness, then?

MESSENGER   Yes, and his many years.

OEDIPUS   Ah!
Why should a man respect the Pythian hearth, or
Give heed to the birds that jangle above his head?
They prophesied that I should kill Polybos,
Kill my own father; but he is dead and buried,
And I am here—I never touched him, never,
Unless he died of grief for my departure,
And thus, in a sense, through me. No. Polybos
Has packed the oracles off with him underground.
They are empty words.

IOCASTE   Had I not told you so?

OEDIPUS   You had; it was my faint heart that betrayed me.

IOCASTE   From now on never think of those things again.

OEDIPUS   And yet—must I not fear my mother's bed?

IOCASTE   Why should anyone in this world be afraid,
Since Fate rules us and nothing can be foreseen?
A man should live only for the present day.

Have no more fear of sleeping with your mother:
How many men, in dreams, have lain with their mothers!
No reasonable man is troubled by such things.

OEDIPUS   That is true; only—
If only my mother were not still alive!
But she is alive. I can not help my dread.

IOCASTE   Yet this news of your father's death is wonderful.

OEDIPUS   Wonderful. But I fear the living woman.

MESSENGER   Tell me, who is this woman that you fear?

OEDIPUS   It is Meropê, man; the wife of King Polybos.

MESSENGER   Meropê? Why should you be afraid of her?
OEDIPUS   An oracle of the gods, a dreadful saying.
MESSENGER   Can you tell me about it or are you sworn to silence?
OEDIPUS   I can tell you, and I will.

Apollo said through his prophet that I was the man
Who should marry his own mother, shed his father's blood
With his own hands. And so, for all these years
I have kept clear of Corinth, and no harm has come—
Though it would have been sweet to see my parents again.

MESSENGER   And is this the fear that drove you out of Corinth?
OEDIPUS   Would you have me kill my father?
MESSENGER   As for that
You must be reassured by the news I gave you.
OEDIPUS   If you could reassure me, I would reward you.
MESSENGER   I had that in mind, I will confess: I thought
I could count on you when you returned to Corinth.
OEDIPUS   No: I will never go near my parents again.
MESSENGER   Ah, son, you still do not know what you are doing—
OEDIPUS   What do you mean? In the name of God tell me!
MESSENGER   —If these are your reasons for not going home.
OEDIPUS   I tell you, I fear the oracle may come true.
MESSENGER   And guilt may come upon you through your parents?
OEDIPUS   That is the dread that is always in my heart.
MESSENGER   Can you not see that all your fears are groundless?
OEDIPUS   How can you say that? They are my parents, surely?
MESSENGER   Polybos was not your father.
OEDIPUS   Not my father?
MESSENGER   No more your father than the man speaking to you.
OEDIPUS   But you are nothing to me!
MESSENGER   Neither was he.
OEDIPUS   Then why did he call me son?
MESSENGER   I will tell you:
Long ago he had you from my hands, as a gift.
OEDIPUS   Then how could he love me so, if I was not his?
MESSENGER   He had no children, and his heart turned to you.
OEDIPUS   What of you? Did you buy me? Did you find me by chance?
MESSENGER   I came upon you in the crooked pass of Kithairon.
OEDIPUS   And what were you doing there?
MESSENGER   Tending my flocks.
OEDIPUS   A wandering shepherd?
MESSENGER   But your saviour, son, that day.
OEDIPUS   From what did you save me?
MESSENGER   Your ankles should tell you that.
OEDIPUS   Ah, stranger, why do you speak of that childhood pain?
MESSENGER   I cut the bonds that tied your ankles together.
OEDIPUS   I have had the mark as long as I can remember.

MESSENGER   That was why you were given the name you bear.

OEDIPUS   God! Was it my father or my mother who did it?
   Tell me!

MESSENGER   I do not know. The man who gave you to me
   Can tell you better than I.

OEDIPUS   It was not you that found me, but another?

MESSENGER   It was another shepherd gave you to me.

OEDIPUS   Who was he? Can you tell me who he was?

MESSENGER   I think he was said to be one of Laïos' people.

OEDIPUS   You mean the Laïos who was king here years ago?

MESSENGER   Yes; King Laïos; and the man was one of his herdsmen.

OEDIPUS   Is he still alive? Can I see him?

MESSENGER   These men here
   Know best about such things.

OEDIPUS   Does anyone here
   Know this shepherd that he is talking about?
   Have you seen him in the fields, or in the town?
   If you have, tell me. It is time things were made plain.

CHORAGOS   I think the man he means is that same shepherd
   You have already asked to see. Iocastê perhaps
   Could tell you something.

OEDIPUS   Do you know anything
   About him, Lady? Is he the man we have summoned?
   Is that the man this shepherd means?

IOCASTE   Why think of him?
   Forget this herdsman. Forget it all.
   This talk is a waste of time.

OEDIPUS   How can you say that,
   When the clues to my true birth are in my hands?

IOCASTE   For God's love, let us have no more questioning!
   Is your life nothing to you?
   My own is pain enough for me to bear.

OEDIPUS   You need not worry. Suppose my mother a slave,
   And born of slaves: no baseness can touch you.

IOCASTE   Listen to me, I beg you: do not do this thing!

OEDIPUS   I will not listen; the truth must be made known.

IOCASTE   Everything that I say is for your own good!

OEDIPUS   My own good
   Snaps my patience, then; I want none of it.

IOCASTE   You are fatally wrong! May you never learn who you are!

OEDIPUS   Go, one of you, and bring the shepherd here.
   Let us leave this woman to brag of her royal name.

IOCASTE   Ah, miserable!
   That is the only word I have for you now.
   That is the only word I can ever have.

                                        Exit into the palace.

CHORAGOS   Why has she left us, Oedipus? Why has she gone
    In such a passion of sorrow? I fear this silence:
    Something dreadful may come of it.
OEDIPUS   Let it come!
    However base my birth, I must know about it.
    The Queen, like a woman, is perhaps ashamed
    To think of my low origin. But I
    Am a child of Luck; I can not be dishonored.
    Luck is my mother; the passing months, my brothers,
    Have seen me rich and poor.
                                If this is so,
    How could I wish that I were someone else?
    How could I not be glad to know my birth?

ODE THREE   *Strophe*

CHORUS   If ever the coming time were known
    To my heart's pondering,
    Kithairon, now by Heaven I see the torches
    At the festival of the next full moon,
    And see the dance, and hear the choir sing
    A grace to your gentle shade:
    Mountain where Oedipus was found,
    O mountain guard of a noble race!
    May the god who heals us lend his aid,
    And let that glory come to pass
    For our king's cradling-ground.

        Antistrophe

    Of the nymphs that flower beyond the years,
    Who bore you, royal child,
    To Pan of the hills or the timberline Apollo,
    Cold in delight where the upland clears,
    Or Hermês for whom Kyllenê's heights are piled?
    Or flushed as evening cloud,
    Great Dionysos, roamer of mountains,
    He—was it he who found you there,
    And caught you up in his own proud
    Arms from the sweet god-ravisher
    Who laughed by the Muses' fountains?

SCENE FOUR

OEDIPUS   Sirs: though I do not know the man,
I think I see him coming, this shepherd we want:
He is old, like our friend here, and the men
Bringing him seem to be servants of my house.
But you can tell, if you have ever seen him.

Enter SHEPHERD *escorted by servants*

CHORAGOS   I know him, he was Laïos' man. You can trust him.

OEDIPUS   Tell me first, you from Corinth: is this the shepherd
We were discussing?

MESSENGER   This is the very man.

OEDIPUS (*to* SHEPHERD)   Come here. No, look at me. You must
answer
Everything I ask.—You belonged to Laïos?

SHEPHERD   Yes: born his slave, brought up in his house.

OEDIPUS   Tell me: what kind of work did you do for him?

SHEPHERD   I was a shepherd of his, most of my life.

OEDIPUS   Where mainly did you go for pasturage?

SHEPHERD   Sometimes Kithairon, sometimes the hills near-by.

OEDIPUS   Do you remember ever seeing this man out there?

SHEPHERD   What would he be doing there? This man?

OEDIPUS   This man standing here. Have you ever seen him before?

SHEPHERD   No. At least, not to my recollection.

MESSENGER   And that is not strange, my lord. But I'll refresh
His memory: he must remember when we two
Spent three whole seasons together, March to September,
On Kithairon or thereabouts. He had two flocks;
I had one. Each autumn I'd drive mine home
And he would go back with his to Laïos' sheepfold.—
Is this not true, just as I have described it?

SHEPHERD   True, yes; but it was all so long ago.

MESSENGER   Well, then: do you remember, back in those days
That you gave me a baby boy to bring up as my own?

SHEPHERD   What if I did? What are you trying to say?

MESSENGER   King Oedipus was once that little child.

SHEPHERD   Damn you, hold your tongue!

OEDIPUS   No more of that!
It is your tongue needs watching, not this man's.

SHEPHERD   My King, my Master, what is it I have done wrong?

OEDIPUS   You have not answered his question about the boy.

SHEPHERD   He does not know . . . He is only making trouble . . .

OEDIPUS   Come, speak plainly, or it will go hard with you.

SHEPHERD   In God's name, do not torture an old man!

OEDIPUS   Come here, one of you; bind his arms behind him.

SHEPHERD   Unhappy king! What more do you wish to learn?

OEDIPUS   Did you give this man the child he speaks of?

SHEPHERD   I did.

And I would to God I had died that very day.

OEDIPUS   You will die now unless you speak the truth.

SHEPHERD   Yet if I speak the truth, I am worse than dead.

OEDIPUS   Very well; since you insist upon delaying—

SHEPHERD   No! I have told you already that I gave him the boy.

OEDIPUS   Where did you get him? From your house? From somewhere
     else?

SHEPHERD   Not from mine, no. A man gave him to me.

OEDIPUS   Is that man here? Do you know whose slave he was?

SHEPHERD   For God's love, my King, do not ask me any more!

OEDIPUS   You are a dead man if I have to ask you again.

SHEPHERD   Then . . . Then the child was from the palace of Laïos.

OEDIPUS   A slave child? or a child of his own line?

SHEPHERD   Ah, I am on the brink of dreadful speech!

OEDIPUS   And I of dreadful hearing. Yet I must hear.

SHEPHERD   If you must be told, then . . .

                                        They said it was Laïos' child,
But it is your wife who can tell you about that.

OEDIPUS   My wife!—Did she give it to you?

SHEPHERD   My lord, she did.

OEDIPUS   Do you know why?

SHEPHERD   I was told to get rid of it.

OEDIPUS   An unspeakable mother!

SHEPHERD   There had been prophecies . . .

OEDIPUS   Tell me.

SHEPHERD   It was said that the boy would kill his own father.

OEDIPUS   Then why did you give him over to this old man?

SHEPHERD   I pitied the baby, my King,

And I thought that this man would take him far away
To his own country.

                        He saved him—but for what a fate!
For if you are what this man says you are,
No man living is more wretched than Oedipus.

OEDIPUS   Ah, God!

It was true!

        All the prophecies!

                    —Now,
O Light, may I look on you for the last time!
I, Oedipus,
Oedipus, damned in his birth, in his marriage damned,
Damned in the blood he shed with his own hand!

                                    He rushes into the palace

ODE FOUR   *Strophe One*

CHORUS   Alas for the seed of men.

What measure shall I give these generations
That breathe on the void and are void
And exist and do not exist?

Who bears more weight of joy
Than mass of sunlight shifting in images,
Or who shall make his thought stay on
That down time drifts away?

Your splendor is all fallen.

O naked brow of wrath and tears,
O change of Oedipus!
I who saw your days call no man blest—
Your great days like ghosts gone.

Antistrophe One

That mind was a strong bow.
Deep, how deep you drew it then, hard archer,
At a dim fearful range,
And brought dear glory down!

You overcame the stranger—
The virgin with her hooking lion claws—
And though death sang, stood like a tower
To make pale Thebes take heart.

Fortress against our sorrow!

Divine king, giver of laws,
Majestic Oedipus!
No prince in Thebes had ever such renown,
No prince won such grace of power.

Strophe Two

And now of all men ever known
Most pitiful is this man's story:
His fortunes are most changed, his state
Fallen to a low slave's
Ground under bitter fate.

O Oedipus, most royal one!
The great door that expelled you to the light

749   DRAMA: PLOT

Gave at night—ah, gave night to your glory:
As to the father, to the fathering son.

All understood too late.

How could that queen whom Laïos won,
The garden that he harrowed at his height,
Be silent when that act was done?

Antistrophe Two

But all eyes fail before time's eye,
All actions come to justice there.
Though never willed, though far down the deep past,
Your bed, your dread sirings,
Are brought to book at last.
Child by Laïos doomed to die,
Then doomed to lose that fortunate little death,
Would God you never took breath in this air
That with my wailing lips I take to cry:

For I weep the world's outcast.

I was blind, and now I can tell why:
Asleep, for you had given ease of breath
To Thebes, while the false years went by.

EXODUS

Enter, from the palace, SECOND MESSENGER

SECOND MESSENGER   Elders of Thebes, most honored in this land,
What horrors are yours to see and hear, what weight
Of sorrow to be endured, if, true to your birth,
You venerate the line of Labdakos!
I think neither Istros nor Phasis, those great rivers,
Could purify this place of the corruption
It shelters now, or soon must bring to light—
Evil not done unconsciously, but willed.

The greatest griefs are those we cause ourselves.
CHORAGOS   Surely, friend, we have grief enough already;
What new sorrow do you mean?
SECOND MESSENGER   The Queen is dead.
CHORAGOS   Iocastê? Dead? But at whose hand?
SECOND MESSENGER   Her own.
The full horror of what happened you can not know,

For you did not see it; but I, who did, will tell you
As clearly as I can how she met her death.

When she had left us,
In passionate silence, passing through the court,
She ran to her apartment in the house,
Her hair clutched by the fingers of both hands.
She closed the doors behind her; then, by that bed
Where long ago the fatal son was conceived—
That son who should bring about his father's death—
We heard her call upon Laïos, dead so many years,
And heard her wail for the double fruit of her marriage,
A husband by her husband, children by her child.

Exactly how she died I do not know:
For Oedipus burst in moaning and would not let us
Keep vigil to the end: it was by him
As he stormed the room that our eyes were caught.
From one to another of us he went, begging a sword,
Cursing the wife who was not his wife, the mother
Whose womb had carried his own children and himself.
I do not know: it was none of us aided him,
But surely one of the gods was in control!
For with a dreadful cry
He hurled his weight, as though wrenched out of himself,
At the twin doors: the bolts gave, and he rushed in.
And there we saw her hanging, her body swaying
From the cruel cord she had noosed about her neck.
A great sob broke from him, heartbreaking to hear,
As he loosed the rope and lowered her to the ground.

I would blot out from my mind what happened next!
For the King ripped from her gown the golden brooches
That were her ornament, and raised them, and plunged them down
Straight into his own eyeballs, crying, "No more,
No more shall you look on the misery about me,
The horrors of my own doing! Too long you have known
The faces of those whom I should never have seen,
Too long been blind to those for whom I was searching!
From this hour, go in darkness!" And as he spoke,
He struck at his eyes—not once, but many times;
And the blood spattered his beard,
Bursting from his ruined sockets like red hail.

So from the unhappiness of two this evil has sprung,
A curse on the man and woman alike. The old
Happiness of the house of Labdakos

Was happiness enough: where is it today?
It is all wailing and ruin, disgrace, death—all
The misery of mankind that has a name—
And it is wholly and for ever theirs.

CHORAGOS   Is he in agony still? Is there no rest for him?

SECOND MESSENGER   He is calling for someone to lead him to the gates
So that all the children of Kadmos may look upon
His father's murderer, his mother's—no,
I can not say it!

            And then he will leave Thebes,
Self-exiled, in order that the curse
Which he himself pronounced may depart from the house.
He is weak, and there is none to lead him,
So terrible is his suffering.

            But you will see:
Look, the doors are opening; in a moment
You will see a thing that would crush a heart of stone.

          The central door is opened; OEDIPUS, *blinded, is led in.*

CHORAGOS   Dreadful indeed for men to see.
Never have my own eyes
Looked on a sight so full of fear.

Oedipus!
What madness came upon you, what daemon

Leaped on your life with heavier
Punishment than a mortal man can bear?
No: I can not even
Look at you, poor ruined one.
And I would speak, question, ponder,
If I were able. No.
You make me shudder.

OEDIPUS   God. God.
Is there a sorrow greater?
Where shall I find harbor in this world?
My voice is hurled far on a dark wind.
What has God done to me?

CHORAGOS   Too terrible to think of, or to see.

Strophe One

OEDIPUS   O cloud of night,
Never to be turned away: night coming on,
I can not tell how: night like a shroud!

My fair winds brought me here.

            O God. Again
The pain of the spikes where I had sight,

The flooding pain
Of memory, never to be gouged out.
CHORAGOS   This is not strange.
You suffer it all twice over, remorse in pain,
Pain in remorse.

Antistrophe One

OEDIPUS   Ah dear friend
Are you faithful even yet, you alone?
Are you still standing near me, will you stay here,
Patient, to care for the blind?
                                        The blind man!
Yet even blind I know who it is attends me,
By the voice's tone—
Though my new darkness hide the comforter.
CHORAGOS   O fearful act!
What god was it drove you to rake black
Night across your eyes?

Strophe Two

OEDIPUS   Apollo. Apollo. Dear
Children, the god was Apollo.
He brought my sick, sick fate upon me.
But the blinding hand was my own!
How could I bear to see
When all my sight was horror everywhere?
CHORAGOS   Everywhere; that is true.
OEDIPUS   And now what is left?
Images? Love? A greeting even,
Sweet to the senses? Is there anything?
Ah, no, friends: lead me away.
Lead me away from Thebes.
                                        Lead the great wreck
And hell of Oedipus, whom the gods hate.
CHORAGOS   Your fate is clear, you are not blind to that.
Would God you had never found it out!

Antistrophe Two

OEDIPUS   Death take the man who unbound
My feet on that hillside
And delivered me from death to life! What life?
If only I had died,

This weight of monstrous doom
Could not have draggd me and my darlings down.
CHORAGOS   I would have wished the same.
OEDIPUS   Oh never to have come here
With my father's blood upon me! Never
To have been the man they call his mother's husband!
Oh accurst! Oh child of evil,
To have entered that wretched bed—

                                    the selfsame one!
More primal than sin itself, this fell to me.
CHORAGOS   I do not know how I can answer you.
You were better dead than alive and blind.
OEDIPUS   Do not counsel me any more. This punishment
That I have laid upon myself is just.
If I had eyes,
I do not know how I could bear the sight
Of my father, when I came to the house of Death,
Or my mother: for I have sinned against them both
So vilely that I could not make my peace
By strangling my own life.

                        Or do you think my children,
Born as they were born, would be sweet to my eyes?
Ah never, never! Nor this town with its high walls,
Nor the holy images of the gods.

                        For I,
Thrice miserable!—Oedipus, noblest of all the line
Of Kadmos, have condemned myself to enjoy
These things no more, by my own malediction
Expelling that man whom the gods declared
To be a defilement in the house of Laïos.
After exposing the rankness of my own guilt,
How could I look men frankly in the eyes?
No, I swear it,
If I could have stifled my hearing at its source,
I would have done it and made all this body
A tight cell of misery, blank to light and sound:
So I should have been safe in a dark agony
Beyond all recollection.

                        Ah Kithairon!
Why did you shelter me? When I was cast upon you,
Why did I not die? Then I should never
Have shown the world my execrable birth.

Ah Polybos! Corinth, city that I believed
The ancient seat of my ancestors: how fair
I seemed, your child! And all the while this evil

Was cancerous within me!

For I am sick
In my daily life, sick in my origin.

O three roads, dark ravine, woodland and way
Where three roads met: you, drinking my father's blood,
My own blood, spilled by my own hand: can you remember
The unspeakable things I did there, and the things
I went on from there to do?

O marriage, marriage!
The act that engendered me, and again the act
Performed by the son in the same bed—

Ah, the net
Of incest, mingling fathers, brothers, sons,
With brides, wives, mothers: the last evil
That can be known by men: no tongue can say
How evil!

No. For the love of God, conceal me
Somewhere far from Thebes; or kill me; or hurl me
Into the sea, away from men's eyes for ever.

Come, lead me. You need not fear to touch me.
Of all men, I alone can bear this guilt.

Enter CREON

CHORAGOS   We are not the ones to decide; but Creon here
  May fitly judge of what you ask. He only
  Is left to protect the city in your place.
OEDIPUS   Alas, how can I speak to him? What right have I
  To beg his courtesy whom I have deeply wronged?
CREON   I have not come to mock you, Oedipus,
  Or to reproach you, either.
  (*To* ATTENDANTS)   —You, standing there:
  If you have lost all respect for man's dignity,
  At least respect the flame of Lord Helios:
  Do not allow this pollution to show itself
  Openly here, an affront to the earth
  And Heaven's rain and the light of day. No, take him
  Into the house as quickly as you can.
  For it is proper
  That only the close kindred see his grief.
OEDIPUS   I pray you in God's name, since your courtesy
  Ignores my dark expectation, visiting
  With mercy this man of all men most execrable:
  Give me what I ask—for your good, not for mine.
CREON   And what is it that you would have me do?
OEDIPUS   Drive me out of this country as quickly as may be
  To a place where no human voice can ever greet me.

755   DRAMA: PLOT

CREON   I should have done that before now—only,
   God's will had not been wholly revealed to me.
OEDIPUS   But his command is plain: the parricide
   Must be destroyed. I am that evil man.
CREON   That is the sense of it, yes; but things are,
   We had best discover clearly what is to be done.
OEDIPUS   You would learn more about a man like me?
CREON   You are ready now to listen to the god.
OEDIPUS   I will listen. But it is to you
   That I must turn for help. I beg you, hear me.

   The woman in there—
   Give her whatever funeral you think proper:
   She is your sister.
                        —But let me go, Creon!
   Let me purge my father's Thebes of the pollution
   Of my living here, and go out to the wild hills,
   To Kithairon, that has won such fame with me,
   The tomb my mother and father appointed for me,
   And let me die there, as they willed I should.
   And yet I know
   Death will not ever come to me through sickness
   Or in any natural way: I have been preserved
   For some unthinkable fate. But let that be.
   As for my sons, you need not care for them.
   They are men, they will find some way to live.
   But my poor daughters, who have shared my table,
   Who never before have been parted from their father—
   Take care of them, Creon; do this for me.
   And will you let me touch them with my hands
   A last time, and let us weep together?
   Be kind, my lord,
   Great prince, be kind!
                        Could I but touch them,
   They would be mine again, as when I had my eyes.
                        Enter ANTIGONE *and* ISMENE, *attended*
   Ah, God!
   Is it my dearest children I hear weeping?
   Has Creon pitied me and sent my daughters?
CREON   Yes, Oedipus: I knew that they were dear to you
   In the old days, and know you must love them still.
OEDIPUS   May God bless you for this—and be a friendlier
   Guardian to you than he has been to me!

   Children, where are you?
   Come quickly to my hands: they are your brother's—

Hands that have brought your father's once clear eyes
To this way of seeing—

Ah dearest ones,

I had neither sight nor knowledge then, your father
By the woman who was the source of his own life!
And I weep for you—having no strength to see you—,
I weep for you when I think of the bitterness
That men will visit upon you all your lives.
What homes, what festivals can you attend
Without being forced to depart again in tears?
And when you come to marriageable age,
Where is the man, my daughters, who would dare
Risk the bane that lies on all my children?
Is there any evil wanting? Your father killed
His father; sowed the womb of her who bore him;
Engendered you at the fount of his own existence!
That is what they will say of you.

Then, whom

Can you ever marry? There are no bridegrooms for you,
And your lives must wither away in sterile dreaming.
O Creon, son of Menoikeus!
You are the only father my daughters have,
Since we, their parents, are both of us gone for ever.
They are your own blood: you will not let them
Fall into beggary and loneliness;
You will keep them from the miseries that are mine!
Take pity on them; see, they are only children,
Friendless except for you. Promise me this,
Great Prince, and give me your hand in token of it.

CREON clasps his right hand

Children:
I could say much, if you could understand me,
But as it is, I have only this prayer for you:
Live where you can, be as happy as you can—
Happier, please God, than God has made your father!

CREON   Enough. You have wept enough. Now go within.

OEDIPUS   I must; but it is hard.

CREON   Time eases all things.

OEDIPUS   But you must promise—

CREON   Say what you desire.

OEDIPUS   Send me from Thebes!

CREON   God grant that I may!

OEDIPUS   But since God hates me . . .

CREON   No, he will grant your wish.

OEDIPUS   You promise?

CREON   I can not speak beyond my knowledge.
OEDIPUS   Then lead me in.
CREON   Come now, and leave your children.
OEDIPUS   No! Do not take them from me!
CREON   Think no longer
     That you are in command here, but rather think
     How, when you were, you served your own destruction.

>   *Exeunt into the house all but the* CHORUS; *the* CHORAGOS *chants
>   directly to the audience*

CHORAGOS   Men of Thebes: look upon Oedipus.

This is the king who solved the famous riddle
And towered up, most powerful of men.
No mortal eyes but looked on him with envy,
Yet in the end ruin swept over him.
Let every man in mankind's frailty
Consider his last day; and let none
Presume on his good fortune until he find
Life, at his death, a memory without pain.

Exercises   1. *The five choral odes divide the drama into six distinct
parts. What does each contribute to the tight, well-knit
structure of the plot?*

2. *In addition to connecting the present action with the past
action, what other purposes does the prologue serve?*

3. *Discuss the function of the chorus.*

4. *The play concentrates not on Oedipus's patricide, regicide,
or incest, but on the most "dramatic" moment in his life.
What is that moment?*

5. *In what ways is Oedipus noble, admirable, or good?*

6. *What flaws in Oedipus's character contribute to his fall?*

7. *How is Oedipus responsible for his misfortunes? How is
Fate responsible?*

8. *The literal meaning of the name Oedipus is "swollen
foot," and the more liberal meaning is "on the track of
knowledge." How appropriate are these names to the character of Oedipus?*

9. *Explain the roles of Teiresias and Creon as contrasts to the
character of Oedipus.*

10. *What possible themes does the drama suggest?*

Topics for Writing

1. Discuss the crime of Laïos and Iocastê who, when abandoning their infant son, knowingly attempted to kill him.

2. The drama contains several clusters of imagery, all of them integrated with the theme. Show how the metaphors of vision and blindness bear on the theme.

3. Support the position of those critics who view Oedipus, the King *as one of the greatest tragedies in literature.*

Selected Bibliography

Sophocles

Adams, Sinclair M. *Sophocles the Playwright.* Toronto: University of Toronto Press, 1957.

Barstow, Marjorie. "Oedipus Rex: A Typical Greek Tragedy." *Classical Weekly*, October 5, 1912.

Bowra, C. M. *Sophoclean Tragedy.* Oxford: Oxford University Press, 1944.

Cameron, Alister. *The Identity of Oedipus the King: Five Essays on the Oedipus Tyrannus.* New York: New York University Press, 1968.

Carroll, J. P. "Some Remarks on the Questions in the *Oedipus Tyrannus.*" *Classical Journal*, 32 (April 1937), 406–416.

Cook, Albert. *Oedipus Rex: A Mirror for Greek Drama.* Belmont, Calif.: Wadsworth, 1963.

Cooper, Lane. *The Greek Genius and Its Influence.* Ithaca: Cornell University Press, 1952.

Earp, Frank R. *The Style of Sophocles.* New York: Russell & Russell, 1972.

Ehrenberg, V. *Sophocles and Pericles.* New York: Humanities Press, 1954.

Hembold, W. C. "The Paradox of the Oedipus." *American Journal of Philology*, 72 (1951), 239 ff.

Jebb, Sir Richard C. "The Age of Pericles." *Essays and Addresses.* Havertown, Pa.: Richard West, 1973.

Kirkwood, Gordon M. *A Study of Sophoclean Drama.* Ithaca: Johnson Reprint, 1958.

Kitto, Humphrey D. *Greek Tragedy: A Literary Study.* London: Methuen, 1950.

Knox, Bernard M. "The Date of the *Oedipus Tyrannus.*" *American Journal of Philology*, 77 (1956), 133–147.

———. *The Heroic Temper: Studies in Sophoclean Tragedy.* Berkeley: University of California Press, 1965.

John Millington Synge *(1871–1909)*

Born at Rathfarnam, near Dublin, of Protestant Irish landowner stock, he was graduated from Trinity College, studied music in Germany, wandered through Europe, and moved to Paris to embark upon a literary career. While there Synge became friendly with several writers, among them William Butler Yeats, who advised him to return to the Aran Islands for writing inspiration. This he did for the setting of Riders to the Sea *(1902), which many critics consider a perfect one-act play. His other highly successful but highly controversial play is* Playboy of the Western World *(1907). He died of a cancerous growth in his neck shortly before his intended marriage to an Abbey Theatre actress.*

Riders to the Sea

CHARACTERS

MAURYA, *an old woman*
BARTLEY, *her son*
CATHLEEN, *her daughter*
NORA, *a younger daughter*
MEN AND WOMEN

An island off the west of Ireland.

> *Cottage kitchen, with nets, oil-skins, spinning-wheel, some new boards standing by the wall, etc.* CATHLEEN, *a girl of about twenty, finishes kneading cake, and puts it down on the pot-oven by the fire; then wipes her hands, and begins to spin at the wheel.* NORA, *a young girl, puts her head in at the door.*

NORA (*in a low voice*)   Where is she?

CATHLEEN   She's lying down, God help her, and may be sleeping, if she's able.

> NORA *comes in softly, and takes a bundle from under her shawl*

CATHLEEN (*spinning the wheel rapidly*)   What is it you have?

NORA   The young priest is after bringing them. It's a shirt and a plain stocking were got off a drowned man in Donegal.

> CATHLEEN *stops her wheel with a sudden movement, and leans out to listen*

NORA   We're to find out if it's Michael's they are, some time herself will be down looking by the sea.

CATHLEEN   How would they be Michael's, Nora? How would he go the length of that way to the Far North?

NORA   The young priest says he's known the like of it. "If it's Michael's they are," says he, "you can tell herself he's got a clean burial by the grace of God, and if they're not his, let no one say a word about them, for she'll be getting her death," says he, "with crying and lamenting."

The door which NORA *half closed is blown open by a gust of wind*

CATHLEEN (*looking out anxiously*)   Did you ask him would he stop Bartley going this day with the horses to the Galway fair?

NORA   "I won't stop him," says he, "but let you not be afraid. Herself does be saying prayers half through the night, and the Almighty God won't leave her destitute," says he, "with no son living."

CATHLEEN   Is the sea bad by the white rocks, Nora?

NORA   Middling bad, God help us. There's a great roaring in the west, and it's worse it'll be getting when the tide's turned to the wind. (*She goes over to the table with the bundle*) Shall I open it now?

CATHLEEN   Maybe she'd wake up on us, and come in before we'd done. (*Coming to the table*) It's a long time we'll be, and the two of us crying.

NORA (*goes to the inner door and listens*)   She's moving about on the bed. She'll be coming in a minute.

CATHLEEN   Give me the ladder, and I'll put them up in the turf-loft, the way she won't know of them at all, and maybe when the tide turns she'll be going down to see would he be floating from the east.

They put the ladder against the gable of the chimney; CATHLEEN *goes up a few steps and hides the bundle in the turf-loft.* MAURYA *comes from the inner room*

MAURYA (*looking up at* CATHLEEN *and speaking querulously*)   Isn't it turf enough you have for this day and evening?

CATHLEEN   There's a cake baking at the fire for a short space (*throwing down the turf*) and Bartley will want it when the tide turns if he goes to Connemara.

NORA *picks up the turf and puts it round the pot-oven*

MAURYA (*sitting down on a stool at the fire*)   He won't go this day with the wind rising from the south and west. He won't go this day, for the young priest will stop him surely.

NORA   He'll not stop him, Mother, and I heard Eamon Simon and Stephen Pheety and Colum Shawn saying he would go.

MAURYA   Where is he itself?

NORA   He went down to see would there be another boat sailing in the week, and I'm thinking it won't be long till he's here now, for the tide's turning at the green head, and the hooker's tacking from the east.

CATHLEEN   I hear some one passing the big stones.

NORA (*looking out*)   He's coming now, and he in a hurry.

BARTLEY (*comes in and looks round the room; speaking sadly and quietly*)   Where is the bit of new rope, Cathleen, was bought in Connemara?

CATHLEEN (*coming down*)   Give it to him, Nora; it's on a nail by the white boards. I hung it up this morning, for the pig with the black feet was eating it.

NORA (*giving him a rope*)   Is that it, Bartley?

MAURYA   You'd do right to leave that rope, Bartley, hanging by the boards. (BARTLEY *takes the rope*) It will be wanting in this place, I'm telling you, if Michael is washed up tomorrow morning, or the next morning, or any morning in the week, for it's a deep grave we'll make him by the grace of God.

BARTLEY (*beginning to work with the rope*)   I've no halter the way I can ride down on the mare, and I must go now quickly. This is the one boat going for two weeks or beyond it, and the fair will be a good fair for horses I heard them saying below.

MAURYA   It's a hard thing they'll be saying below if the body is washed up and there's no man in it to make the coffin, and I after giving a big price for the finest white boards you'd find in Connemara. (*She looks round at the boards*)

BARTLEY   How would it be washed up, and we after looking each day for nine days, and a strong wind blowing a while back from the west and south?

MAURYA   If it wasn't found itself, that wind is raising the sea, and there was a star up against the moon, and it rising in the night. If it was a hundred horses, or a thousand horses you had itself, what is the price of a thousand horses against a son where there is one son only?

BARTLEY (*working at the halter, to* CATHLEEN)   Let you go down each day, and see the sheep aren't jumping in on the rye, and if the jobber comes you can sell the pig with the black feet if there is a good price going.

MAURYA   How would the like of her get a good price for a pig?

BARTLEY (*to* CATHLEEN)   If the west wind holds with the last bit of the moon let you and Nora get up weed enough for another cock for the kelp. It's hard set we'll be from this day with no one in it but one man to work.

MAURYA   It's hard set we'll be surely the day you're drownd'd with the rest. What way will I live and the girls with me, and I an old woman looking for the grave?

> BARTLEY *lays down the halter, takes off his old coat and puts on a newer one of the same flannel*

BARTLEY (*to* NORA)   Is she coming to the pier?

NORA (*looking out*)   She's passing the green head and letting fall her sails.

BARTLEY (*getting his purse and tobacco*)   I'll have half an hour to go down, and you'll see me coming again in two days, or in three days, or maybe in four days if the wind is bad.

MAURYA (*turning round to the fire, and putting her shawl over her head*)   Isn't it a hard and cruel man won't hear a word from an old woman, and she holding him from the sea?

CATHLEEN   It's the life of a young man to be going on the sea, and who would listen to an old woman with one thing and she saying it over?

BARTLEY (*taking the halter*)   I must go now quickly. I'll ride down on the red mare, and the gray pony'll run behind me. . . . The blessing of God on you. (*He goes out*)

MAURYA (*crying out as he is in the door*)   He's gone now, God spare us, and we'll not see him again. He's gone now, and when the black night is falling I'll have no son left me in the world.

CATHLEEN   Why wouldn't you give him your blessing and he looking round in the door? Isn't it sorrow enough is on every one in this house without your sending him out with an unlucky word behind him, and a hard word in his ear?

> MAURYA *takes up the tongs and begins raking the fire aimlessly without looking round*

NORA (*turning toward her*)   You're taking away the turf from the cake.

CATHLEEN (*crying out*)   The Son of God forgive us, Nora, we're after forgetting his bit of bread. (*She comes over to the fire*)

NORA   And it's destroyed he'll be going till dark night, and he after eating nothing since the sun went up.

CATHLEEN (*turning the cake out of the oven*)   It's destroyed he'll be, surely. There's no sense left on any person in a house where an old woman will be talking forever.

> MAURYA *sways herself on her stool*

CATHLEEN (*cutting off some of the bread and rolling it in a cloth; to* MAURYA)   Let you go down now to the spring well and give him this and he passing. You'll see him then and the dark word will be broken, and you can say "God speed you," the way he'll be easy in his mind.

MAURYA (*taking the bread*)   Will I be in it as soon as himself?

CATHLEEN   If you go now quickly.

MAURYA (*standing up unsteadily*)   It's hard set I am to walk.

CATHLEEN (*looking at her anxiously*)   Give her the stick, Nora, or maybe she'll slip on the big stones.

NORA   What stick?

CATHLEEN   The stick Michael brought from Connemara.

MAURYA (*taking a stick* NORA *gives her*)   In the big world the old people do be leaving things after them for their sons and children, but in this place it is the young men do be leaving things behind for them that do be old.

> *She goes out slowly.* NORA *goes over to the ladder*

CATHLEEN   Wait, Nora, maybe she'd turn back quickly. She's that sorry, God help her, you wouldn't know the thing she'd do.

NORA   Is she gone round by the bush?

CATHLEEN (*looking out*)   She's gone now. Throw it down quickly, for the Lord knows when she'll be out of it again.

NORA (*getting the bundle from the loft*)   The young priest said he'd be passing tomorrow, and we might go down and speak to him below if it's Michael's they are surely.

CATHLEEN (*taking the bundle*)   Did he say what way they were found?

NORA (*coming down*)   "There were two men," says he, "and they rowing round with poteen before the cocks crowed, and the oar of one of them caught the body, and they passing the black cliffs of the north."

CATHLEEN (*trying to open the bundle*)   Give me a knife, Nora, the string's perished with the salt water, and there's a black knot on it you wouldn't loosen in a week.

NORA (*giving her a knife*)   I've heard tell it was a long way to Donegal.

CATHLEEN (*cutting the string*)   It is surely. There was a man in here a while ago—the man sold us that knife—and he said if you set off walking from the rocks beyond, it would be seven days you'd be in Donegal.

NORA   And what time would a man take, and he floating?

> CATHLEEN *opens the bundle and takes out a bit of a stocking. They look at them eagerly*

CATHLEEN (*in a low voice*)   The Lord spare us, Nora! isn't it a queer hard thing to say if it's his they are surely?

NORA   I'll get his shirt off the hook the way we can put the one flannel on the other. (*She looks through some clothes hanging in the corner*) It's not with them, Cathleen, and where will it be?

CATHLEEN   I'm thinking Bartley put it on him in the morning, for his own shirt was heavy with the salt in it. (*Pointing to the corner*) There's a bit of a sleeve was of the same stuff. Give me that and it will do.

> NORA *brings it to her and they compare the flannel*

CATHLEEN   It's the same stuff, Nora; but if it is itself aren't there great rolls of it in the shops of Galway, and isn't it many another man may have a shirt of it as well as Michael himself?

NORA (*who has taken up the stocking and counted the stitches, crying out*)   It's Michael, Cathleen, it's Michael; God spare his soul, and what will herself say when she hears this story, and Bartley on the sea?

CATHLEEN (*taking the stocking*)   It's a plain stocking.

NORA   It's the second one of the third pair I knitted, and I put up threescore stitches, and I dropped four of them.

CATHLEEN (*counts the stitches*)   It's that number is in it. (*Crying out*) Ah, Nora, isn't it a bitter thing to think of him floating that way to the Far North, and no one to keen him but the black hags that do be flying on the sea?

NORA (*swinging herself round, and throwing out her arms on the clothes*)   And isn't it a pitiful thing when there is nothing left of a man who was a great rower and fisher, but a bit of an old shirt and a plain stocking?

CATHLEEN (*after an instant*)   Tell me is herself coming, Nora? I hear a little sound on the path.

NORA (*looking out*)   She is, Cathleen. She's coming up to the door.

CATHLEEN   Put these things away before she'll come in. Maybe it's easier she'll be after giving her blessing to Bartley, and we won't let on we've heard anything the time he's on the sea.

NORA (*helping* CATHLEEN *to close the bundle*)   We'll put them here in the corner.

> *They put them into a hole in the chimney corner.* CATHLEEN *goes back to the spinning-wheel*

NORA   Will she see it was crying I was?

CATHLEEN   Keep your back to the door the way the light'll not be on you.

> NORA *sits down at the chimney corner, with her back to the door.* MAURYA *comes in very slowly, without looking at the girls, and goes over to her stool at the other side of the fire. The cloth with the bread is still in her hand. The girls look at each other, and* NORA *points to the bundle of bread*

(*After spinning for a moment*)   You didn't give him his bit of bread?

> MAURYA *begins to keen softly, without turning round*

Did you see him riding down?

> MAURYA *goes on keening*

(*A little impatiently*) God forgive you; isn't it a better thing to raise your voice and tell what you seen, than to be making lamentation for a thing that's done? Did you see Bartley, I'm saying to you.

MAURYA (*with a weak voice*)   My heart's broken from this day.

CATHLEEN (*as before*)   Did you see Bartley?

MAURYA   I seen the fearfulest thing.

CATHLEEN (*leaves her wheel and looks out*)   God forgive you; he's riding the mare now over the green head, and the gray pony behind him.

MAURYA (*starts, so that her shawl falls back from her head and shows her white tossed hair. With a frightened voice*)   The gray pony behind him.

CATHLEEN (*coming to the fire*)   What is it ails you, at all?

MAURYA (*speaking very slowly*)   I've seen the fearfulest thing any person has seen, since the day Bride Dara seen the dead man with a child in his arms.

CATHLEEN AND NORA   Uah.

> *They crouch down in front of the old woman at the fire*

NORA   Tell us what it is you seen.

MAURYA   I went down to the spring well, and I stood there saying a prayer to myself. Then Bartley came along, and he riding on the red mare with the gray pony behind him. (*She puts up her hands, as if to hide something from her eyes*) The Son of God spare us, Nora!

CATHLEEN   What is it you seen?

MAURYA   I seen Michael himself.

CATHLEEN (*speaking softly*)   You did not, Mother; it wasn't Michael you seen, for his body is after being found in the Far North, and he's got a clean burial by the grace of God.

MAURYA (*a little defiantly*)   I'm after seeing him this day, and he riding and galloping. Bartley came first on the red mare; and I tried to say, "God speed you," but something choked the words in my throat. He went by quickly; and "the blessing of God on you," says he, and I could say nothing. I looked up then, and I crying, at the gray pony, and there was Michael upon it—with fine clothes on him, and new shoes on his feet.

CATHLEEN (*begins to keen*)   It's destroyed we are from this day. It's destroyed, surely.

NORA   Didn't the young priest say the Almighty God wouldn't leave her destitute with no son living?

MAURYA (*in a low voice, but clearly*)   It's little the like of him knows of the sea. . . . Bartley will be lost now, and let you call in Eamon and make me a good coffin out of the white boards, for I won't live after them. I've had a husband, and a husband's father, and six sons in this house—six fine men, though it was a hard birth I had with every one of them and they coming to the world—and some of them were found and some of them were not found, but they're gone now the lot of them. . . . There were Stephen, and Shawn, were lost in the great wind, and found after in the Bay of Gregory of the Golden Mouth, and carried up the two of them on the one plank, and in by that door.

> *She pauses for a moment, the girls start as if they heard something through the door that is half open behind them*

NORA (*in a whisper*)   Did you hear that, Cathleen? Did you hear a noise in the northeast?

CATHLEEN (*in a whisper*)   There's some one after crying out by the seashore.

MAURYA (*continues without hearing anything*)   There was Sheamus and his father, and his own father again, were lost in a dark night, and not a stick or sign was seen of them when the sun went up. There was Patch after was drowned out of a curagh that turned over. I was sitting here with Bartley, and he a baby, lying on my two knees, and I seen two women, and three women, and four women coming in, and they crossing themselves, and not saying a word. I looked out then, and there were men coming after them, and they holding a thing in the half of a red sail, and water dripping out of it—it was a dry day, Nora—and leaving a track to the door.

> *She pauses again with her hand stretched out toward the door. It opens softly and old women begin to come in, crossing themselves on the threshold, and kneeling down in front of the stage with red petticoats over their heads*

MAURYA (*half in a dream, to* CATHLEEN)   Is it Patch or Michael, or what is it at all?

CATHLEEN   Michael is after being found in the Far North, and when he is found there how could he be here in this place?

MAURYA   There does be a power of young men floating round in the sea, and what way would they know if it was Michael they had, or another man like him, for when a man is nine days in the sea, and the wind blowing, it's hard set his own mother would be to say what man was it.

CATHLEEN   It's Michael, God spare him, for they're after sending us a bit of his clothes from the Far North.

> *She reaches out and hands* MAURYA *the clothes that belonged to Michael.* MAURYA *stands up slowly, and takes them in her hands.* NORA *looks out*

NORA   They're carrying a thing among them and there's water dripping out of it and leaving a track by the big stones.

CATHLEEN (*in a whisper to the women who have come in*)   Is it Bartley it is?

ONE OF THE WOMEN   It is surely, God rest his soul.

> *Two younger women come in and pull out the table. Then men carry in the body of* BARTLEY, *laid on a plank, with a bit of a sail over it, and lay it on the table*

CATHLEEN (*to the women, as they are doing so*)   What way was he drowned?

ONE OF THE WOMEN   The gray pony knocked him into the sea, and he was washed out where there is a great surf on the white rocks.

> MAURYA *has gone over and knelt down at the head of the table. The women are keening softly and swaying themselves with a slow movement.* CATHLEEN *and* NORA *kneel at the other end of the table. The men kneel near the door*

MAURYA (*raising her head and speaking as if she did not see the people around her*)   They're all gone now, and there isn't anything more the sea can do to me. . . . I'll have no call now to be crying and praying when the wind breaks from the south, and you can hear the surf is in the east, and the surf is in the west, making a great stir with the two noises, and they hitting one on the other. I'll have no call now to be going down and getting Holy Water in the dark nights after Samhain, and I won't care what way the sea is when the other women will be keening. (*To* NORA) Give me the Holy Water, Nora, there's a small sup still on the dresser.

> NORA *gives it to her*

MAURYA (*drops Michael's clothes across Bartley's feet, and sprinkles the Holy Water over him*)   It isn't that I haven't prayed for you, Bartley, to the Almighty God. It isn't that I haven't said prayers in the dark night till you wouldn't know what I'd be saying; but it's a great rest I'll have now, and it's time surely. It's a great rest I'll have now, and great sleeping in the long nights after Samhain, if it's only a bit of wet flour we do have to eat, and maybe a fish that would be stinking. (*She kneels down again, crossing herself, and saying prayers under her breath*)

CATHLEEN (*to an old man*)   Maybe yourself and Eamon would make a coffin when the sun rises. We have fine white boards herself bought, God help her, thinking Michael would be found, and I have a new cake you can eat while you'll be working.

THE OLD MAN (*looking at the boards*)   Are there nails with them?

CATHLEEN   There are not, Colum; we didn't think of the nails.

ANOTHER MAN   It's a great wonder she wouldn't think of the nails, and all the coffins she's seen made already.

CATHLEEN   It's getting old she is, and broken.

> MAURYA *stands up again very slowly and spreads out the pieces of Michael's clothes beside the body, sprinkling them with the last of the Holy Water*

NORA (*in a whisper to* CATHLEEN)   She's quiet now and easy; but the day Michael was drowned you could hear her crying out from this to the spring well. It's fonder she was of Michael, and would any one have thought that?

CATHLEEN (*slowly and clearly*)   An old woman will be soon tired with anything she will do, and isn't it nine days herself is after crying and keening, and making great sorrow in the house?

MAURYA (*puts the empty cup mouth downwards on the table, and lays her hands together on Bartley's feet*)   They're all together this time, and the end is come. May the Almighty God have mercy on Bartley's soul, and on Michael's soul, and on the souls of Sheamus and Patch, and Stephen and Shawn; (*bending her head*) and may He have mercy on my soul, Nora, and on the soul of every one is left living in the world.

> She pauses, and the keen rises a little more loudly from the women, then sinks away

Michael has a clean burial in the Far North, by the grace of the Almighty God. Bartley will have a fine coffin out of the white boards, and a deep grave surely. What more can we want than that? No man at all can be living forever, and we must be satisfied.

> *She kneels down again and the curtain falls slowly*

Exercises   1. By what method does Synge present his preliminary exposition? What, specifically, do we learn?

2. The bundle of clothes that belong to Michael remain on stage throughout the play. What dramatic purpose is served by this device?

3. What is Bartley's dramatic function?

4. Give the eight-point analysis.

5. How is sympathy achieved for Maurya? What makes her a larger-than-life character?

6. The sea, as the central image of the play, should serve to focus and unify everything. Does it do this, and, if so, how?

7. What does the name Maurya (meaning "goddess of fate") contribute to meaning?

8. Disclose the irony in Maurya's final remarks.

9. *Who are the "riders to the sea"? How are they symbolically "riders to the sea"?*

10. *What comment on the human condition does the play make?*

Topics for Writing

1. *Critics have often referred to* Riders to the Sea *as a perfect one-act drama. Give your reasons for concurring with their statement.*

2. *Discover the ironies in the drama, and explain how they develop the central theme.*

3. *One critic has said that we are, all of us, "riders to the sea." In what ways?*

Selected Bibliography

John Millington Synge

Allison, Alexander W., ed. *Masterpieces of the Drama.* 2nd ed. New York: Macmillan, 1966. Pages 505–506.

Bauman, R. "John Millington Synge and Irish Folklore." *Southern Folklore Quarterly* 27 (December 1963), 267–279.

Beerbohm, Max. *Around Theatres.* New York: Simon and Schuster, 1954. Pages 314–319.

Bickley, Francis. *J. M. Synge and the Irish Dramatic Movement.* New York: Russell & Russell, 1968. Pages 34–37.

Boyd, Ernest. *Ireland's Literary Renaissance.* Totowa, New Jersey: Rowman & Littlefield, 1968. Pages 321–323.

Corkery, Daniel. *Synge and Anglo-Irish Literature.* New York: Russell & Russell, 1956. Pages 135–146.

Coxhead, Elizabeth. *J. M. Synge and Lady Gregory.* New York: British Book Center, 1962. Pages 14–16.

Currie, R. H., and M. Bryan. "*Riders to the Sea* Reappraised." *Texas Quarterly,* 11 (Winter 1968), 139–146.

Durbach, E. "Synge's Tragic Vision of the Old Mother and the Sea." *Modern Drama,* 14 (February 1972), 363–372.

Ganz, A. "J. M. Synge and the Drama of Art." *Modern Drama,* 10 (May 1967), 57–68.

Heilman, Robert B. *Tragedy and Melodrama.* New York: Doubleday, 1969. Pages 38–39, 40, 72, 80, 82.

Henn, T. R. *The Harvest of Tragedy.* London: Methuen, 1956. Pages 202–203.

Howe, P. P. *J. M. Synge, a Critical Study.* New York: Haskell House, 1968. Pages 51–60.

Malone, Andrew E. *The Irish Drama.* New York: B. Blom, 1965. Page 150.

2 Character

Characters in drama, like their fictional counterparts, divide into two broad categories. They are three-dimensional or one-dimensional.

Three-dimensional characters are developed fully, that is, as fully as is necessary to let us know them intimately. We know about physical attributes, background, drives, frustrations, and perhaps even the cut of clothes they fancy. These round (fully developed) characters are also known as *dynamic* (developing) characters, which means that, through the course of the action, they grow and change. Something in the conflict has touched them deeply so that at the final curtain they are different persons from the ones we met at the opening.

Unlike three-dimensional characters, whose complex nature demands full treatment, one-dimensional characters (flat, stock, or stereotyped) are sketched simply with one or two easily recognizable personality traits. They are *static* (flat) characters who rarely change their essential nature or beliefs. Generally, we can identify the "type" quickly.

To be sure, each character is important; each serves a function; and all must be convincing. Among the many aspects of character, none is more important in our evaluation than the quality of plausibility. By *plausibility* is meant that what a character says or does is believable. And words and actions are believable if the character is *consistent*, not, as the common phrase reminds us, "out of character," and if the motivation is adequate, that is, there are sufficient reasons within the characterization to account for words and actions.

Characters in plays resemble people in real life, and, like their living counterparts, manifest their personalities chiefly in what they do and in what they say. In plays, as in life, we further get to know people by observing the way they look, the gestures they make, the tone of voice they use, and the remarks others make about them. Thus, the playwright reveals the personality of characters by means of action, dialogue and—to a lesser degree—appearance and gesture.

Although the methods of characterization in fiction and drama are similar, two unmistakable differences are dictated by the limitations of the dramatic form.

First, the dramatic story, which imposes a time limitation on the playwright, forces the compression of delineations of characters and their actions. Unable to develop completely many of the characters, the dramatist makes use of any number of stock or type characters—the braggart, the dreamer, the fool, the liar, the do-gooder, the bumbler, the busy-body, and the like.

Second, because drama permits little or no access to the minds of characters, we as viewers or readers of drama must infer character. We must presuppose that we are hearing and seeing, in those selected moments of existence through which the characters pass, significant aspects of their innermost natures. It is indeed so. Every speech imparts something of the nature of the person "speaking," the person "spoken about," and sometimes the person "spoken to"; every action divulges something about the doer and the characters involved in or affected by that action. A dramatic action reveals character most prominently. Just as we learn something about people during the course of living, so we learn something about characters during the course of reading or seeing a play.

Juliet's suicide (*Romeo and Juliet*) not only reveals a great love for Romeo and an idealistic wish to join him in death but also an immaturity that drives a young girl swiftly to take her own life without any consideration of alternative solutions. Cathleen and Nora (*Riders to the Sea*), in hiding the bundle containing Michael's shirt and socks, exhibit deep concern and sympathy for Maurya's feelings. Lola (*Come Back, Little Sheba*) watches with fascination the lovemaking of Marie and Turk. The scene, which must function for Lola as an act of sublimation, unmasks for us a certain brashness in her character and suggests a lack of fulfillment in her relationship with Doc.

Another important source of character revelation can be found in what a particular character says. We form judgments about people based upon their opinions of others and their convictions about issues of concern to them.

The following, Marty's speech (*Marty*), clearly reveals his sensitive nature and his feelings of inferiority and failure with women.

Sooner or later, there comes a point in a man's life when he gotta face some facts, and one fact I gotta face is that whatever it is that women like, I ain't got it. I chased enough girls in my life. I went to enough dances. I got hurt enough. I don't wanna get hurt no more. I just called a girl this afternoon, and I got a real brush-off, boy. I figured I was past the point of being hurt, but that hurt. Some stupid woman who I didn't even wanna call up. She gave me the brush. That's the history of my life. I don't wanna go to the Waverly Ballroom because all that ever happened to me there was girls made me feel like I was a bug. I got feelings, you know. I had enough pain. No, thank you.

The next speech, delivered by Bill (*Tea and Sympathy*), shows us a man absorbed in his school, unduly concerned with what people think, and compelled to succeed.

This is something that touches me very closely. The name of the school, its reputation, the reputation of all of us here. I went here and my father before me, and one day I hope our children will come here, when we have them. And, of course, one day I hope to be headmaster.

From the following dialogue, spoken by the Emperor, we can infer that Jones *(The Emperor Jones)* is at least cocky, shrewd, and unafraid. We may further conclude that he values his importance immoderately and esteems himself superior to the natives.

Ain't a man's talkin' big what makes him big—long as he makes folks believe it? Sho', I talks large when I ain't got nothin' to back it up, but I ain't talkin' wild just de same. I knows I kin fool 'em—I *knows* it—and dat's backin' enough fo' my game. And ain't I got to learn deir lingo and teach some of dem English befo' I kin talk to 'em? Ain't dat wuk? You ain't never learned ary word er it, Smithers, in de ten years you been heah, dough yo' knows it's money in yo' pocket tradin' wid 'em if you does. But you'se too shiftless to take de trouble.

I'se got five lead bullets in dis gun good enuff fo' common bush niggers—and after dat I got de silver bullet left to cheat 'em out o' gittin me.

Does you think I'd slink out de back door like a common nigger? I'se Emperor yit, ain't I? And de Emperor Jones leaves de way he comes, and dat black trash don't dare stop him—not yit, leastways.

In judging character, however, *how* something is said may be just as valuable as *what* is said. The several occasions on which Oedipus *(Oedipus Rex)* reprimands Teiresias, Creon, Iocastê, and the shepherd for actions he disapproves present a king possessed of an easily loosened temper.

Another speech, which Doc lets loose upon Lola *(Come Back, Little Sheba)*, reveals a new side of his character that had not surfaced earlier. Before this scene, he was easy-going, tolerant, humble, and reverent; now he shows himself angry, tyrannical, scornful, and profane.

God damn you! Get away from that telephone. *(He chases her into the living room where she gets the couch between them)* That's right, phone! Tell the world I'm drunk.

Tell the whole damn world. Scream your head off, you fat slut. Holler till all the neighbors think I'm beatin' hell outuv you. Where's Bruce now—under Marie's bed? You got all fresh and pretty for him, didn't you? Combed your hair for once—you even washed the back of your neck and put on a girdle. You were willing to harness all that fat into one bundle.

What a character has to say about another character also tells us a great deal about the kind of people that populate our stage. Nora, referring to her mother, tells Cathleen: "She's quiet now and easy; but the day Michael was drowned you could hear her crying out from this to the spring well. It's fonder she was of Michael, and would any one have thought that?" Nora's statement adds another quality to Maurya's character: though Michael may have been her favorite son, she mourns Bartley just as much as she had for Michael.

With George's comments to Chris *(All My Sons)*, we begin to doubt Keller's innocence:

GEORGE And he's the kind of boss to let a hundred and twenty-one cylinder heads be repaired and shipped out of his shop without even knowing about it?

CHRIS He's that kind of boss.

GEORGE And that's the same Joe Keller who never left his shop without first going around to see that all the lights were out.

CHRIS *(with growing anger)* The same Joe Keller.

GEORGE The same man who knows how many minutes a day his workers spend in the toilet.

And Tom's disclosure exposes his father for what he is—a man who is obviously disappointed in a boy who is not a "regular fellow," that is, a football hero or reasonable facsimile; a man who does not seem to care to have his son around; and a man who is not really a father. "Last ten years I haven't been home, I mean really home. Summers my father packs me off to camps, and the rest of the time I've been at boarding schools." About Christmas and Easter vacations, Tom adds: "My father gets a raft of tickets to plays and concerts, and sends me and my aunt."

The physical appearance of a character may also add significance to the portrayal of character. Marty, who has difficulty getting dates with girls, sees himself as a fat, ugly, little man. Jones, at first, wears a light-blue uniform coat sprayed with brass buttons, heavy gold chevrons on his shoulders, gold braid on his collar and cuffs, bright red pants, laced boots with brass spurs, and a belt with a long-barreled, pearl-handled revolver in a holster—paraphernalia befitting his position as lord and master. Later in the play, when he has stripped himself down to a loin cloth, no longer is he Emperor, no longer is he master of his "self." And Lola makes her first appearance on stage appropriately dressed in a lumpy kimono and wearing dirty comfies on her feet.

Everything that happens in a play is important. The way a character eats, laughs, opens doors, or hangs up a telephone may divulge a trait of character, a motive, an attitude, or something else as revealing of inner nature. In *Come Back, Little Sheba*, Marie, dressed in a dainty negligee, skips into the kitchen with the ebullience that only youth can feel in the morning. What a contrast she presents to Lola! Even the gesture of nodding a head or poking a finger, the movement of lips into a smile or a grimace, may express an idea, an attitude, or an emotion.

In analyzing character it is important to ask *how* character is revealed. It is also important to determine *who* and *what* the characters are, *how* and *why* they act as they do.

MODERN PROSCENIUM THEATER AND STAGE

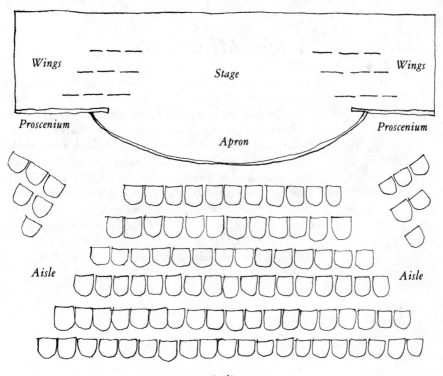

Stage	Main acting area, raised several feet above floor of audience. Size and outline of acting area is determined by placement of drops and other pieces of scenery
Wings	Parts of stage not used as acting area; house scenery and equipment and serve as entrances and exits for performers; lead to dressing rooms and other backstage facilities
Proscenium	Wall between stage and audience masking wings and flyloft; play is viewed through a large arch in the wall
Apron	Shallow area of stage projecting out from proscenium toward audience, used chiefly to achieve intimacy with audience
Audience	First-floor seating area, usually raked upward away from the stage; spectators also view play from boxes and balconies at the sides and back of the theater
Aisle	Entrance and exit for audience and occasionally for actors

Arthur Miller (1915-   )

Born in New York City, the son of a prosperous manufacturer, he was graduated from the University of Michigan, where he won the Avery Hopwood Prize for playwriting. Early in his career he wrote plays for the Federal Theatre Project, radio, and motion pictures and published two novels. All My Sons (1947) won the Drama Critics' Award, the Donaldson Award, and the Antoinette Perry Award. Death of a Salesman *(1949), widely acclaimed as one of the best serious dramas written by an American, won the Drama Critics' Award and a Pulitzer Prize. His other major plays are* The Crucible *(1953),* A View from the Bridge *(1956),* After the Fall *(1964), and* The Price *(1968).*

All My Sons

CHARACTERS

JOE KELLER	CHRIS KELLER
JIM BAYLISS	BERT
FRANK LUBEY	KATE KELLER
SUE BAYLISS	ANN
LYDIA LUBEY	GEORGE

ACT ONE   *The back yard of the Keller home in the outskirts of an American town. August of our era.*

The stage is hedged on right and left by tall, closely planted poplars which lend the yard a secluded atmosphere. Upstage is filled with the back of the house and its open, unroofed porch which extends into the yard some six feet. The house is two stories high and has seven rooms. It would have cost perhaps fifteen thousand in the early twenties when it was built. Now it is nicely painted, looks tight and comfortable, and the yard is green with sod, here and there plants whose season is gone. At the right, beside the house, the entrance of the driveway can be seen, but the poplars cut off view of its continuation downstage. In the left corner, downstage, stands the four-foot-high stump of a slender apple tree whose upper trunk and branches lie toppled beside it, fruit still clinging to its branches.

Downstage right is a small, trellised arbor, shaped like a sea shell, with a decorative bulb hanging from its forward-curving roof. Garden chairs and a table are scattered about. A garbage pail on the ground next to the porch steps, a wire leaf-burner near it.

ON THE RISE: *It is early Sunday morning.* JOE KELLER *is sitting in the sun reading the want ads of the Sunday paper, the other sections of which lie neatly on the ground beside him. Behind his back, inside the arbor,* DOCTOR JIM BAYLISS *is reading part of the paper at the table.*

KELLER *is nearing sixty. A heavy man of stolid mind and build, a business man these many years, but with the imprint of the machine-shop worker and boss still upon him. When he reads, when he speaks, when he listens, it is with the terrible concentration of the uneducated man for whom there is still wonder in many commonly known things, a man whose judgments must be dredged out of experience and a peasant-like common sense. A man among men.*

DOCTOR BAYLISS *is nearly forty. A wry self-controlled man, an easy talker, but with a wisp of sadness that clings even to his self-effacing humor.*

At curtain, JIM *is standing at left, staring at the broken tree. He taps a pipe on it, blows through the pipe, feels in his pockets for tobacco, then speaks.*

JIM   Where's your tobacco?

KELLER   I think I left it on the table.

> JIM *goes slowly to table in the arbor, finds a pouch, and sits there on the bench, filling his pipe*

Gonna rain tonight.

JIM   Paper says so?

KELLER   Yeah, right here.

JIM   Then it can't rain.

> FRANK LUBEY *enters, through a small space between the poplars.* FRANK *is thirty-two but balding. A pleasant, opinionated man, uncertain of himself, with a tendency toward peevishness when crossed, but always wanting it pleasant and neighborly. He rather saunters in, leisurely, nothing to do. He does not notice* JIM *in the arbor. On his greeting,* JIM *does not bother looking up*

FRANK   Hya.

KELLER   Hello, Frank. What's doin'?

FRANK   Nothin'. Walking off my breakfast. (*Looks up at the sky*) That beautiful? Not a cloud.

KELLER (*looking up*)   Yeah, nice.

FRANK   Every Sunday ought to be like this.

KELLER (*indicating the sections beside him*)   Want the paper?

FRANK   What's the difference, it's all bad news. What's today's calamity?

KELLER   I don't know, I don't read the news part any more. It's more interesting in the want ads.

FRANK   Why, you trying to buy something?

KELLER   No, I'm just interested. To see what people want, y'know? For instance, here's a guy is lookin' for two Newfoundland dogs. Now what's he want with two Newfoundland dogs?

FRANK   That is funny.

KELLER   Here's another one. Wanted—old dictionaries. High prices paid. Now what's a man going to do with an old dictionary?

FRANK   Why not? Probably a book collector.

KELLER   You mean he'll make a living out of that?

FRANK   Sure, there's a lot of them.

KELLER (*shaking his head*)   All the kind of business goin' on. In my day, either you were a lawyer, or a doctor, or you worked in a shop. Now—

FRANK   Well, I was going to be a forester once.

KELLER   Well, that shows you; in my day, there was no such thing. (*Scanning the page, sweeping it with his hand*) You look at a page like this you realize how ignorant you are. (*Softly, with wonder, as he scans page*) Psss!

FRANK (*noticing tree*)   Hey, what happened to your tree?

KELLER   Ain't that awful? The wind must've got it last night. You heard the wind, didn't you?

FRANK   Yeah, I got a mess in my yard, too. (*Goes to tree*) What a pity. (*Turning to* KELLER) What'd Kate say?

KELLER   They're all asleep yet. I'm just waiting for her to see it.

FRANK (*struck*)   You know?—it's funny.

KELLER   What?

FRANK   Larry was born in August. He'd been twenty-seven this month. And his tree blows down.

KELLER (*touched*)   I'm surprised you remember his birthday, Frank. That's nice.

FRANK   Well, I'm working on his horoscope.

KELLER   How can you make him a horoscope? That's for the future, ain't it?

FRANK   Well, what I'm doing is this, see. Larry was reported missing on November twenty-fifth, right?

KELLER   Yeah?

FRANK   Well, then, we assume that if he was killed it was on November twenty-fifth. Now, what Kate wants—

KELLER   Oh, Kate asked you to make a horoscope?

FRANK   Yeah, what she wants to find out is whether November twenty-fifth was a favorable day for Larry.

KELLER   What is that, favorable day?

FRANK   Well, a favorable day for a person is a fortunate day, according to his stars. In other words it would be practically impossible for him to have died on his favorable day.

KELLER   Well, was that his favorable day?—November twenty-fifth?

FRANK   That's what I'm working on to find out. It takes time! See, the point is, if November twenty-fifth was his favorable day, then it's completely possible he's alive somewhere, because—I mean it's possible. (*He notices* JIM *now.* JIM *is looking at him as though at an idiot. To* JIM—*with an uncertain laugh*) I didn't even see you.

KELLER (*to* JIM)   Is he talkin' sense?

JIM   Him? He's all right. He's just completely out of his mind, that's all.

FRANK (*peeved*)   The trouble with you is, you don't *believe* in anything.

JIM   And your trouble is that you believe in *anything*. *You* didn't see my kid this morning, did you?

FRANK   No.

KELLER   Imagine? He walked off with his thermometer. Right out of his bag.

JIM (*getting up*)   What a problem. One look at a girl and he takes her temperature. (*Goes to driveway, looks upstage toward street*)

FRANK   That boy's going to be a real doctor; he's smart.

JIM   Over my dead body he'll be a doctor. A good beginning, too.

FRANK   Why? It's an honorable profession.

JIM (*looking at him tiredly*)   Frank, will you stop talking like a civics book?

KELLER *laughs*

FRANK   Why, I saw a movie a couple of weeks ago, reminded me of you. There was a doctor in that picture—

KELLER   Don Ameche!

FRANK   I think it was, yeah. And he worked in his basement discovering things. That's what you ought to do; you could help humanity, instead of—

JIM   I would love to help humanity on a Warner Brothers salary.

KELLER (*pointing at him, laughing*)   That's very good, Jim.

JIM (*looking toward house*)   Well, where's the beautiful girl was supposed to be here?

FRANK (*excited*)   Annie came?

KELLER   Sure, sleepin' upstairs. We picked her up on the one o'clock train last night. Wonderful thing. Girl leaves here, a scrawny kid. Couple of years go by, she's a regular woman. Hardly recognized her, and she was running in and out of this yard all her life. That was a very happy family used to live in your house, Jim.

JIM   Like to meet her. The block can use a pretty girl. In the whole neighborhood there's not a damned thing to look at.

(SUE, JIM'S *wife, enters. She is rounding forty, an overweight woman who fears it. On seeing her* JIM *wryly adds*)

Except my wife, of course.

SUE (*in same spirit*)   Mrs. Adams is on the phone, you dog.

JIM (*to* KELLER)   Such is the condition which prevails—(*going to his wife*) my love, my light.

SUE   Don't sniff around me. (*Pointing to their house*) And give her a nasty answer. I can smell her perfume over the phone.

JIM   What's the matter with her now?

SUE   I don't know, dear. She sounds like she's in terrible pain—unless her mouth is full of candy.

JIM   Why don't you just tell her to lay down?

SUE   She enjoys it more when you tell her to lay down. And when are you going to see Mr. Hubbard?

JIM   My dear; Mr. Hubbard is not sick, and I have better things to do than to sit there and hold his hand.

SUE   It seems to me that for ten dollars you could hold his hand.

JIM (*to* KELLER)   If your son wants to play golf tell him I'm ready. Or if he'd like to take a trip around the world for about thirty years. (*He exits*)

KELLER   Why do you needle him? He's a doctor, women are supposed to call him up.

SUE   All I said was Mrs. Adams is on the phone. Can I have some of your parsley?

KELLER   Yeah, sure.

            She goes to parsley box and pulls some parsley.

     You were a nurse too long, Susie. You're too . . . too . . . realistic.

SUE (*laughing, pointing at him*)   Now you said it!

                    LYDIA LUBEY *enters. She is a robust, laughing girl of twenty-seven*

LYDIA   Frank, the toaster—(*Sees the others*) Hya.

KELLER   Hello!

LYDIA (*to* FRANK)   The toaster is off again.

FRANK   Well, plug it in, I just fixed it.

LYDIA (*kindly, but insistently*)   Please, dear, fix it back like it was before.

FRANK   I don't know why you can't learn to turn on a simple thing like a toaster! (*He exits*)

SUE (*laughing*)   Thomas Edison.

LYDIA (*apologetically*)   He's really very handy. (*She sees broken tree*) Oh, did the wind get your tree?

KELLER   Yeah, last night.

LYDIA   Oh, what a pity. Annie get in?

KELLER   She'll be down soon. Wait'll you meet her, Sue, she's a knockout.

SUE   I should've been a man. People are always introducing me to beautiful women. (*To* JOE) Tell her to come over later. I imagine she'd like to see what we did with her house. And thanks. (*She exits*)

LYDIA   Is she still unhappy, Joe?

KELLER   Annie? I don't suppose she goes around dancing on her toes, but she seems to be over it.

LYDIA   She going to get married? Is there anybody—?

KELLER   I suppose—say, it's a couple years already. She can't mourn a boy forever.

LYDIA   It's so strange—Annie's here and not even married. And I've got three babies. I always thought it'd be the other way around.

KELLER   Well, that's what a war does. I had two sons, now I got one. It changed all the tallies. In my day when you had sons it was an honor. Today a doctor could make a million dollars if he could figure out a way to bring a boy into the world without a trigger finger.

LYDIA   You know, I was just reading—

Enter CHRIS KELLER *from house, stands in doorway*

Hya, Chris.

FRANK *shouts from offstage*

FRANK   Lydia, come in here! If you want the toaster to work don't plug in the malted mixer.

LYDIA (*embarrassed, laughing*)   Did I?

FRANK   And the next time I fix something don't tell me I'm crazy! Now come in here!

LYDIA (*to* KELLER)   I'll never hear the end of this one.

KELLER (*calling to* FRANK)   So what's the difference? Instead of toast have a malted!

LYDIA   Sh! Sh! (*She exits, laughing*)

CHRIS *watches her off. He is thirty-two; like his father, solidly built, a listener. A man capable of immense affection and loyalty. He has a cup of coffee in one hand, part of a doughnut in the other.*

KELLER   You want the paper?

CHRIS   That's all right, just the book section. (*He bends down and pulls out part of paper on porch floor*)

KELLER   You're always reading the book section and you never buy a book.

CHRIS (*coming down to settee*)   I like to keep abreast of my ignorance. (*He sits on settee*)

KELLER   What is that, every week a new book comes out?

CHRIS   Lot of new books.

KELLER   All different.

CHRIS   All different.

KELLER *shakes his head, puts knife down on bench, takes oilstone up to the cabinet.*

KELLER   Psss! Annie up yet?

CHRIS   Mother's giving her breakfast in the dining room.

KELLER (*looking at broken tree*)   See what happened to the tree?

CHRIS (*without looking up*)   Yeah.

KELLER   What's Mother going to say?

BERT *runs on from driveway. He is about eight. He jumps on stool, then on* KELLER'S *back*

BERT   You're finally up.

KELLER (*swinging him around and putting him down*)   Ha! Bert's here! Where's Tommy? He's got his father's thermometer again.

BERT   He's taking a reading.

CHRIS   What!

BERT   But it's only oral.

KELLER   Oh, well, there's no harm in oral. So what's new this morning, Bert?

BERT   Nothin'. (*He goes to broken tree, walks around it*)

KELLER   Then you couldn't've made a complete inspection of the block. In the beginning, when I first made you a policeman you used to come in every morning with something new. Now, nothin's ever new.

BERT   Except some kids from Thirtieth Street. They started kicking a can down the block, and I made them go away because you were sleeping.

KELLER   Now you're talkin', Bert. Now you're on the ball. First thing you know I'm liable to make you a detective.

BERT (*pulling him down by the lapel and whispering in his ear*)   Can I see the jail now?

KELLER   Seein' the jail ain't allowed, Bert. You know that.

BERT   Aw, I betcha there isn't even a jail. I don't see any bars on the cellar windows.

KELLER   Bert, on my word of honor there's a jail in the basement. I showed you my gun, didn't I?

BERT   But that's a hunting gun.

KELLER   That's an arresting gun!

BERT   Then why don't you ever arrest anybody? Tommy said another dirty word to Doris yesterday, and you didn't even demote him.

KELLER *chuckles and winks at* CHRIS, *who is enjoying all this.*

KELLER   Yeah, that's a dangerous character, that Tommy. (*Beckons him closer*) What word does he say?

BERT (*backing away quickly in great embarrassment*)   Oh, I can't say that.

KELLER (*grabbing him by the shirt and pulling him back*)   Well, gimme an idea.

BERT   I can't. It's not a nice word.

KELLER   Just whisper it in my ear. I'll close my eyes. Maybe I won't even hear it.

BERT, *on tiptoe, puts his lips to* KELLER'S *ear, then in unbearable embarrassment steps back*

BERT   I can't, Mr. Keller.

CHRIS (*laughing*)   Don't make him do that.

KELLER   Okay, Bert. I take your word. Now go out, and keep both eyes peeled.

BERT (*interested*)   For what?

KELLER   For what! Bert, the whole neighborhood is depending on you. A policeman don't ask questions. Now peel them eyes!

BERT (*mystified, but willing*)   Okay. (*He runs off stage back of arbor*)

KELLER (*calling after him*)   And mum's the word, Bert.

BERT   About what?

KELLER   Just in general. Be v-e-r-y careful.

BERT (*nodding in bewilderment*)   Okay. (*He exits*)

KELLER (*laughing*)   I got all the kids crazy!

CHRIS   One of these days, they'll all come in here and beat your brains out.

KELLER   What's she going to say? Maybe we ought to tell her before she sees it.

CHRIS   She saw it.

KELLER   How could she see it? I was the first one up. She was still in bed.

CHRIS   She was out here when it broke.

KELLER   When?

CHRIS   About four this morning. (*Indicating window above them*) I heard it cracking and I woke up and looked out. She was standing right here when it cracked.

KELLER   What was she doing out here four in the morning?

CHRIS   I don't know. When it cracked she ran back into the house and cried in the kitchen.

KELLER   Did you talk to her?

CHRIS   No. I—I figured the best thing was to leave her alone. (*Pause*)

KELLER (*deeply touched*)   She cried hard?

CHRIS   I could hear her right through the floor of my room.

KELLER (*after slight pause*)   What was she doing out here at that hour? (CHRIS *silent. With an undertone of anger showing*) She's dreaming about him again. She's walking around at night.

CHRIS   I guess she is.

KELLER   She's getting just like after he died. (*Slight pause*) What's the meaning of that?

CHRIS   I don't know the meaning of it. (*Slight pause*) But I know one thing, Dad. We've made a terrible mistake with Mother.

KELLER   What?

CHRIS   Being dishonest with her. That kind of thing always pays off, and now it's paying off.

KELLER   What do you mean, dishonest?

CHRIS   You know Larry's not coming back and I know it. Why do we allow her to go on thinking that we believe with her?

KELLER   What do you want to do, argue with her?

CHRIS   I don't want to argue with her, but it's time she realized that nobody believes Larry is alive any more.

> KELLER *simply moves away, thinking, looking at the ground*

Why shouldn't she dream of him, walk the nights waiting for him? Do we contradict her? Do we say straight out that we have no hope any more? That we haven't had any hope for years now?

KELLER (*frightened at the thought*)   You can't say that to her.

CHRIS   We've got to say it to her.

KELLER   How're you going to prove it? Can you prove it?

CHRIS   For god's sake, three years! Nobody comes back after three years. It's insane.

KELLER   To you it is, and to me. But not to her. You can talk yourself blue in the face, but there's no body and there's no grave, so where are you?

CHRIS   Sit down, Dad. I want to talk to you.

KELLER looks at him searchingly a moment

KELLER   The trouble is the Goddam newspapers. Every month some boy turns up from nowhere, so the next one is going to be Larry, so—

CHRIS   All right, all right, listen to me. (*Slight pause.* KELLER *sits on settee*) You know why I asked Annie here, don't you?

KELLER (*he knows, but—*)   Why?

CHRIS   You know.

KELLER   Well, I got an an idea, but—What's the story?

CHRIS   I'm going to ask her to marry me. (*Slight pause.* KELLER *nods*)

KELLER   Well, that's only your business, Chris.

CHRIS   You know it's not only my business.

KELLER   What do you want me to do? You're old enough to know your own mind.

CHRIS (*asking, annoyed*)   Then it's all right, I'll go ahead with it?

KELLER   Well, you want to be sure Mother isn't going to—

CHRIS   Then it isn't just my business.

KELLER   I'm just sayin'—

CHRIS   Sometimes you infuriate me, you know that? Isn't it your business, too, if I tell this to Mother and she throws a fit about it? You have such a talent for ignoring things.

KELLER   I ignore what I gotta ignore. The girl is Larry's girl.

CHRIS   She's not Larry's girl.

KELLER   From Mother's point of view he is not dead and you have no right to take his girl. (*Slight pause*) Now you can go on from there if you know where to go, but I'm tellin' you I don't know where to go. See? I don't know. Now what can I do for you?

CHRIS   I don't know why it is, but every time I reach out for something I want, I have to pull back because other people will suffer. My whole bloody life, time after time after time.

KELLER   You're a considerate fella, there's nothing wrong in that.

CHRIS   To hell with that.

KELLER   Did you ask Annie yet?

CHRIS   I wanted to get this settled first.

KELLER   How do you know she'll marry you? Maybe she feels the same way Mother does?

CHRIS   Well, if she does, then that's the end of it. From her letters I think she's forgotten him. I'll find out. And then we'll thrash it out with Mother? Right? Dad, don't avoid me.

KELLER   The trouble is, you don't see enough women. You never did.

CHRIS   So what? I'm not fast with women.

KELLER   I don't see why it has to be Annie.

CHRIS   Because it is.

KELLER   That's a good answer, but it don't answer anything. You haven't seen her since you went to war. It's five years.

CHRIS   I can't help it. I know her best. I was brought up next door to her. These years when I think of someone for my wife, I think of Annie. What do you want, a diagram?

KELLER   I don't want a diagram . . . I—I'm— She thinks he's coming back, Chris. You marry that girl and you're pronouncing him dead. Now what's going to happen to Mother? Do you know? I don't! (*Pause*)

CHRIS   All right, then, Dad.

KELLER (*thinking* CHRIS *has retreated*)   Give it some more thought.

CHRIS   I've given it three years of thought. I'd hoped that if I waited, Mother would forget Larry and then we'd have a regular wedding and everything happy. But if that can't happen here, then I'll have to get out.

KELLER   What the hell is *this*?

CHRIS   I'll get out. I'll get married and live some place else. Maybe in New York.

KELLER   Are you crazy?

CHRIS   I've been a good son too long, a good sucker. I'm through with it.

KELLER   You've got a business here, what the hell is this?

CHRIS   The business! The business doesn't inspire me.

KELLER   Must you be inspired?

CHRIS   Yes. I like it an hour a day. If I have to grub for money all day long at least at evening I want it beautiful. I want a family, I want some kids, I want to build something I can give myself to. Annie is in the middle of that. Now . . . where do I find it?

KELLER   You mean—(*Goes to him*) Tell me something, you mean you'd leave the business?

CHRIS   Yes. On this I would.

KELLER (*after a pause*)   Well . . . you don't want to think like that.

CHRIS   Then help me stay here.

KELLER   All right, but—but don't think like that. Because what the hell did I work for? That's only for you, Chris, the whole shootin' match is for you!

CHRIS   I know that, Dad. Just you help me stay here.

KELLER (*putting a fist up to* CHRIS's *jaw*)   But don't think that way, you hear me?

CHRIS   I am thinking that way.

KELLER (*lowering his hand*)   I don't understand you, do I?

CHRIS   No, you don't. I'm a pretty tough guy.

KELLER   Yeah. I can see that.

> MOTHER *appears on porch. She is in her early fifties, a woman of uncontrolled inspirations and an overwhelming capacity for love*

MOTHER   Joe?

CHRIS (*going toward porch*)   Hello, Mom.

MOTHER (*indicating house behind her; to* KELLER)   Did you take a bag from under the sink?

KELLER   Yeah, I put it in the pail.

MOTHER   Well, get it out of the pail. That's my potatoes.

> CHRIS *bursts out laughing—goes up into alley*

KELLER (*laughing*)   I thought it was garbage.

MOTHER   Will you do me a favor, Joe? Don't be helpful.

KELLER   I can afford another bag of potatoes.

MOTHER   Minnie scoured that pail in boiling water last night. It's cleaner than your teeth.

KELLER   And I don't understand why, after I worked forty years and I got a maid, why I have to take out the garbage.

MOTHER   If you would make up your mind that every bag in the kitchen isn't full of garbage you wouldn't be throwing out my vegetables. Last time it was the onions.

> CHRIS *comes on, hands her bag*

KELLER   I don't like garbage in the house.

MOTHER   Then don't eat. (*She goes into the kitchen with bag*)

CHRIS   That settles you for today.

KELLER   Yeah, I'm in last place again. I don't know, once upon a time I used to think that when I got money again I would have a maid and my wife would take it easy. Now I got money, and I got a maid, and my wife is workin' for the maid. (*He sits in one of the chairs*)

> MOTHER *comes out on last line. She carries a pot of string beans*

MOTHER   It's her day off, what are you crabbing about?

CHRIS (*to* MOTHER)   Isn't Annie finished eating?

MOTHER (*looking around preoccupiedly at yard*)   She'll be right out. (*Moves*) That wind did some job on this place. (*Of the tree*) So much for that, thank God.

KELLER (*indicating chair beside him*)   Sit down, take it easy.

MOTHER (*pressing her hand to top of her head*)   I've got such a funny pain on the top of my head.

CHRIS   Can I get you an aspirin?

> MOTHER *picks a few petals off ground, stands there smelling them in her hand, then sprinkles them over plants*

MOTHER   No more roses. It's so funny . . . everything decides to happen at the same time. This month is his birthday; his tree blows down, Annie comes. Everything that happened seems to be coming back. I was just down the cellar, and what do I stumble over? His baseball glove. I haven't seen it in a century.

CHRIS   Don't you think Annie looks well?

MOTHER   Fine. There's no question about it. She's a beauty . . . I still don't know what brought her here. Not that I'm not glad to see her, but—

CHRIS   I just thought we'd all like to see each other again.

> MOTHER *just looks at him, nodding ever so slightly—almost as though admitting something*

And I wanted to see her myself.

MOTHER (*as her nods halt, to* KELLER)   The only thing is I think her nose got longer. But I'll always love that girl. She's one that didn't jump into bed with somebody else as soon as it happened with her fella.

KELLER (*as though that were impossible for Annie*)   Oh, what're you—?

MOTHER   Never mind. Most of them didn't wait till the telegrams were opened. I'm just glad she came, so you can see I'm not *completely* out of my mind. (*Sits, and rapidly breaks string beans in the pot*)

CHRIS   Just because she isn't married doesn't mean she's been mourning Larry.

MOTHER (*with an undercurrent of observation*)   Why then isn't she?

CHRIS (*a little flustered*)   Well . . . it could've been any number of things.

MOTHER (*directly at him*)   Like what, for instance?

CHRIS (*embarrassed, but standing his ground*)   I don't know. Whatever it is. Can I get you an aspirin?

> MOTHER *puts her hand to her head. She gets up and goes aimlessly toward the trees on rising*

MOTHER   It's not like a headache.

KELLER   You don't sleep, that's why. She's wearing out more bedroom slippers than shoes.

MOTHER   I had a terrible night. (*She stops moving*) I never had a night like that.

CHRIS (*looking at* KELLER)   What was it, Mom? Did you dream?

MOTHER   More, more than a dream.

CHRIS (*hesitantly*)   About Larry?

MOTHER   I was fast asleep, and— (*Raising her arm over the audience*) Remember the way he used to fly low past the house when he was in training? When we used to see his face in the cockpit going by? That's the way I saw him. Only high up. Way, way up, where the clouds are. He was so real I could reach out and touch him. And suddenly he started to fall. And crying, crying to me . . . Mom, Mom! I could hear him like he was in the room. Mom! . . . it was his voice! If I could touch him I knew I could stop him, if I could only— (*Breaks off, allowing her outstretched hand to fall*) I woke up and it was so funny— The wind . . . it was like the roaring of his engine. I came out here . . . I must've still been half asleep. I could hear that roaring like he was going by. The tree snapped right in front of me—and I like—came awake. (*She is looking at tree. She suddenly realizes something, turns with a reprimanding finger shaking slightly at* KELLER) See? We should never have planted that tree. I said so in the first place; it was too soon to plant a tree for him.

CHRIS (*alarmed*)   Too soon!

MOTHER (*angering*)   We rushed into it. Everybody was in such a hurry to bury him. I *said* not to plant it yet. (*To* KELLER) I *told* you to—!

CHRIS   Mother, Mother! (*She looks into his face*) The wind blew it down. What significance has that got? What are you talking about? Mother, please . . . Don't go through it all again, will you? It's no good, it doesn't accomplish anything. I've been thinking, y'know?—maybe we ought to put our minds to forgetting him?

MOTHER   That's the third time you've said that this week.

CHRIS   Because it's not right; we never took up our lives again. We're like at a railroad station waiting for a train that never comes in.

MOTHER (*pressing top of her head*)   Get me an aspirin, heh?

CHRIS   Sure, and let's break out of this, heh, Mom? I thought the four of us might go out to dinner a couple of nights, maybe go dancing out at the shore.

MOTHER   Fine. (*To* KELLER) We can do it tonight.

KELLER   Swell with me!

CHRIS   Sure, let's have some fun. (*To* MOTHER) You'll start with this aspirin. (*He goes up and into house with new spirit. Her smile vanishes*)

MOTHER (*with an accusing undertone*)   Why did he invite her here?

KELLER   Why does that bother you?

MOTHER   She's been in New York three and a half years, why all of a sudden—?

KELLER   Well, maybe—maybe he just wanted to see her.

MOTHER   Nobody comes seven hundred miles "just to see."

KELLER   What do you mean? He lived next door to the girl all his life, why shouldn't he want to see her again?

MOTHER *looks at him critically*

Don't look at me like that, he didn't tell me any more than he told you.

MOTHER (*—a warning and a question*)   He's not going to marry her.

KELLER   How do you know he's even thinking of it?

MOTHER   It's got that about it.

KELLER (*sharply watching her reaction*)   Well? So what?

MOTHER (*alarmed*)   What's going on here, Joe?

KELLER   Now listen, kid—

MOTHER (*avoiding contact with him*)   She's not his girl, Joe; she knows she's not.

KELLER   You can't read her mind.

MOTHER   Then why is she still single? New York is full of men, why isn't she married? (*Pause*) Probably a hundred people told her she's foolish, but she's waited.

KELLER   How do you know why she waited?

MOTHER   She knows what I know, that's why. She's faithful as a rock.

In my worst moments, I think of her waiting, and I know again that I'm right.

KELLER   Look, it's a nice day. What are we arguing for?

MOTHER (*warningly*)   Nobody in this house dast take her faith away, Joe. Strangers might. But not his father, not his brother.

KELLER (*exasperated*)   What do you want me to do? What do you want?

MOTHER   I want you to act like he's coming back. Both of you. Don't think I haven't noticed you since Chris invited her. I won't stand for any nonsense.

KELLER   But, Kate—

MOTHER   Because if he's not coming back, then I'll kill myself! Laugh. Laugh at me. (*She points to tree*) But why did that happen the very night she came back? Laugh, but there are meanings in such things. She goes to sleep in his room and his memorial breaks in pieces. Look at it; look. (*She sits on bench*) Joe—

KELLER   Calm yourself.

MOTHER   Believe with me, Joe. I can't stand all alone.

KELLER   Calm yourself.

MOTHER   Only last week a man turned up in Detroit, missing longer than Larry. You read it yourself.

KELLER   All right, all right, calm yourself.

MOTHER   You above all have got to believe, you—

KELLER (*rising*)   Why me above all?

MOTHER   Just don't stop believing.

KELLER   What does that mean, me above all?

BERT *comes rushing on*

BERT   Mr. Keller! Say, Mr. Keller . . . (*Pointing up driveway*) Tommy just said it again!

KELLER (*not remembering any of it*)   Said what? Who?

BERT   The dirty word.

KELLER   Oh. Well—

BERT   Gee, aren't you going to arrest him? I warned him.

MOTHER (*with suddenness*)   Stop that, Bert. Go home. (BERT *backs up, as she advances*) There's no jail here.

KELLER (*as though to say, "Oh-what-the-hell-let-him-believe-there-is"*)   Kate—

MOTHER (*turning on* KELLER *furiously*)   There's no jail here! I want you to stop that jail business!

He turns, shamed, but peeved

BERT (*past her to* KELLER)   He's right across the street.

MOTHER   Go home, Bert. (BERT *turns around and goes up driveway. She is shaken. Her speech is bitten off, extremely urgent*) I want you to stop that, Joe. That whole jail business!

KELLER (*alarmed, therefore angered*)   Look at you, look at you shaking.

MOTHER (*trying to control herself, moving about clasping her hands*)   I can't help it.

KELLER   What have I got to hide? What the hell is the matter with you, Kate?

MOTHER   I didn't say you had anything to hide, I'm just telling you to stop it! Now stop it! (*As* ANN *and* CHRIS *appear on porch.* ANN *is twenty-six, gentle but despite herself capable of holding fast to what she knows.* CHRIS *opens door for her*)

ANN   Hya, Joe! (*She leads off a general laugh that is not self-conscious because they know one another too well*)

CHRIS (*bringing* ANN *down, with an outstretched, chivalric arm*)   Take a breath of that air, kid. You never get air like that in New York.

MOTHER (*genuinely overcome with it*)   Annie, where did you get that dress!

ANN   I couldn't resist. I'm taking it right off before I ruin it. (*Swings around*) How's that for three weeks' salary?

MOTHER (*to* KELLER)   Isn't she the most—? (*To* ANN) It's gorgeous, simply gor—

CHRIS (*to* MOTHER)   No kidding, now, isn't she the prettiest gal you ever saw?

MOTHER (*caught short by his obvious admiration, she finds herself reaching out for a glass of water and aspirin in his hand, and—*)   You gained a little weight, didn't you, darling? (*She gulps pill and drinks*)

ANN   It comes and goes.

KELLER   Look how nice her legs turned out!

ANN (*as she runs to fence*)   Boy, the poplars got thick, didn't they?

KELLER *moves to setee and sits*

KELLER   Well, it's three years, Annie. We're gettin' old, kid.

MOTHER   How does Mom like New York?

ANN *keeps looking through trees*

ANN (*a little hurt*)   Why'd they take our hammock away?

KELLER   Oh, no, it broke. Couple of years ago.

MOTHER   What broke? He had one of his light lunches and flopped into it.

ANN (*laughs and turns back toward* JIM*'s yard*)   Oh, excuse me!

JIM *has come to fence and is looking over it. He is smoking a cigar.*
As she cries out, he comes on around on stage

JIM   How do you do. (*To* CHRIS) She looks very intelligent!

CHRIS   Ann, this is Jim—Doctor Bayliss.

ANN (*shaking* JIM*'s hand*)   Oh, sure, he writes a lot about you.

JIM   Don't you believe it. He likes everybody. In the battalion he was known as Mother McKeller.

ANN   I can believe it. You know—? (*To* MOTHER) It's so strange seeing him come out of that yard. (*To* CHRIS) I guess I never grew up. It almost seems that Mom and Pop are in there now. And you and my brother doing algebra, and Larry trying to copy my home-work. Gosh, those dear dead days beyond recall.

JIM   Well, I hope that doesn't mean you want me to move out?

SUE (*calling from offstage*)   Jim, come in here! Mr. Hubbard is on the phone!

JIM   I told you I don't want—

SUE (*commandingly sweet*)   Please, dear! Please!

JIM (*resigned*)   All right, Susie. (*Trailing off*) All right, all right . . . (*To* ANN) I've only met you, Ann, but if I may offer you a piece of advice— When you marry, never—even in your mind—never count your husband's money.

SUE (*from offstage*)   Jim?

JIM   At once! (*Turns and goes off*) At once. (*He exits*)

MOTHER (*—*ANN *is looking at her. She speaks meaningfully*)   I told her to take up the guitar. It'd be a common interest for them. (*They laugh*) Well, he loves the guitar!

> ANN, *as though to overcome* MOTHER, *becomes suddenly lively, crosses to* KELLER *on settee, sits on his lap*

ANN   Let's eat at the shore tonight! Raise some hell around here, like we used to before Larry went!

MOTHER (*emotionally*)   You think of him! You see? (*Triumphantly*) She thinks of him!

ANN (*with an uncomprehending smile*)   What do you mean, Kate?

MOTHER   Nothing. Just that you—remember him, he's in your thoughts.

ANN   That's a funny thing to say; how could I help remembering him?

MOTHER (*—it is drawing to a head the wrong way for her; she starts anew. She rises and comes to* ANN)   Did you hang up your things?

ANN   Yeah . . . (*To* CHRIS) Say, you've sure gone in for clothes. I could hardly find room in the closet.

MOTHER   No, don't you remember? That's Larry's room.

ANN   You mean . . . they're Larry's?

MOTHER   Didn't you recognize them?

ANN (*slowly rising, a little embarrassed*)   Well, it never occurred to me that you'd—I mean the shoes are all shined.

MOTHER   Yes, dear. (*Slight pause.* ANN *can't stop staring at her.* MOTHER *breaks it by speaking with the relish of gossip, putting her arm around* ANN *and walking with her*) For so long I've been aching for a nice conversation with you, Annie. Tell me something.

ANN   What?

MOTHER   I don't know. Something nice.

CHRIS (*wryly*)   She means do you go out much?

MOTHER   Oh, shut up.

KELLER   And are any of them serious?

MOTHER (*laughing, sits in her chair*)   Why don't you both choke?

KELLER   Annie, you can't go into a restaurant with that woman any more. In five minutes thirty-nine strange people are sitting at the table telling her their life story.

MOTHER   If I can't ask Annie a personal question—

KELLER   Askin' is all right, but don't beat her over the head. You're beatin' her, you're beatin' her. (*They are laughing*)

> ANN *takes pan of beans off stool, puts them on floor under chair and sits*

ANN (*to* MOTHER)   Don't let them bulldoze you. Ask me anything you like. What do you want to know, Kate? Come on, let's gossip.

MOTHER (*to* CHRIS *and* KELLER)   She's the only one is got any sense. (*To* ANN) Your mother—she's not getting a divorce, heh?

ANN   No, she's calmed down about it now. I think when he gets out they'll probably live together. In New York, of course.

MOTHER   That's fine. Because your father is still—I mean he's a decent man after all is said and done.

ANN   I don't care. She can take him back if she likes.

MOTHER   And you? You—(*shakes her head negatively*)—go out much? (*Slight pause*)

ANN (*delicately*)   You mean am I still waiting for him?

MOTHER   Well, no. I don't expect you to wait for him but—

ANN (*kindly*)   But that's what you mean, isn't it?

MOTHER   Well . . . yes.

ANN   Well, I'm not, Kate.

MOTHER (*faintly*)   You're not?

ANN   Isn't it ridiculous? You don't really imagine he's—?

MOTHER   I know, dear, but don't say it's ridiculous, because the papers were full of it; I don't know about New York, but there was half a page about a man missing even longer than Larry, and he turned up from Burma.

CHRIS (*coming to* ANN)   He couldn't have wanted to come home very badly, Mom.

MOTHER   Don't be so smart.

CHRIS   You can have a helluva time in Burma.

ANN (*rises and swings around in back of* CHRIS)   So I've heard.

CHRIS   Mother, I'll bet you money that you're the only woman in the country who after three years is still—

MOTHER   You're sure?

CHRIS   Yes, I am.

MOTHER   Well, if you're sure then you're sure. (*She turns her head away an instant*) They don't say it on the radio but I'm sure that in the dark at night they're still waiting for their sons.

CHRIS   Mother, you're absolutely—

MOTHER (*waving him off*)   Don't be so damned smart! Now stop it! (*Slight pause*) There are just a few things you *don't* know. All of you. And I'll tell you one of them, Annie. Deep, deep in your heart you've always been waiting for him.

ANN (*resolutely*)   No, Kate.

MOTHER (*with increasing demand*)   But deep in your heart, Annie!

CHRIS   She ought to know, shouldn't she?

MOTHER   Don't let them tell you what to think. Listen to your heart. Only your heart.

ANN   Why does your heart tell you he's alive?

MOTHER   Because he has to be.

ANN   But why, Kate?

MOTHER (*going to her*)   Because certain things have to be, and certain things can never be. Like the sun has to rise, it has to be. That's why there's God. Otherwise anything could happen. But there's God, so certain things can never happen. I would know, Annie—just like I knew the day he—(*indicates* CHRIS)—went into that terrible battle. Did he write me? Was it in the papers? No, but that morning I couldn't raise my head off the pillow. Ask Joe. Suddenly, I knew. I knew! And he was nearly killed that day. Ann, you *know* I'm right!

> ANN *stands there in silence, then turns trembling, going upstage*

ANN   No, Kate.

MOTHER   I have to have some tea.

> FRANK *appears, carrying ladder*

FRANK   Annie! (*Coming down*) How are you, gee whiz!

ANN (*taking his hand*)   Why, Frank, you're losing your hair.

KELLER   He's got responsibility.

FRANK   Gee whiz!

KELLER   Without Frank the stars wouldn't know when to come out.

FRANK (*laughs; to* ANN)   You look more womanly. You've matured. You—

KELLER   Take it easy, Frank, you're a married man.

ANN (*as they laugh*)   You still haberdashering?

FRANK   Why not? Maybe I too can get to be president. How's your brother? Got his degree, I hear.

ANN   Oh, George has his own office now!

FRANK   Don't say! (*Funereally*) And your dad? Is he—?

ANN (*abruptly*)   Fine. I'll be in to see Lydia.

FRANK (*sympathetically*)   How about it, does Dad expect a parole soon?

ANN (*with growing ill-ease*)   I really don't know, I—

FRANK (*staunchly defending her father for her sake*)   I mean because I feel, y'know, that if an intelligent man like your father is put in prison, there ought to be a law that says either you execute him, or let him go after a year.

CHRIS (*interrupting*)   Want a hand with that ladder, Frank?

FRANK (*taking cue*)   That's all right, I'll— (*Picks up ladder*) I'll finish the horoscope tonight, Kate. (*Embarrassed*) See you later, Ann, you look wonderful. (*He exits. They look at* ANN)

ANN (*to* CHRIS, *as she sits slowly on stool*)   Haven't they stopped talking about Dad?

CHRIS (*comes down and sits on arm of chair*)   Nobody talks about him any more.

KELLER (*rises and comes to her*)   Gone and forgotten, kid.

ANN   Tell me. Because I don't want to meet anybody on the block if they're going to—

CHRIS   I don't want you to worry about it.

ANN (*to* KELLER)   Do they still remember the case, Joe? Do they talk about you?

KELLER   The only one still talks about it is my wife.

MOTHER   That's because you keep on playing policeman with the kids. All their parents hear out of you is jail, jail, jail.

KELLER   Actually what happened was that when I got home from the penitentiary the kids got very interested in me. You know kids. I was—(*laughs*)—like the expert on the jail situation. And as time passed they got it confused and . . . I ended up a detective. (*Laughs*)

MOTHER   Except that *they* didn't get it confused. (*To* ANN) He hands out police badges from the Post Toasties boxes. (*They laugh*)

> ANN *rises and comes to* KELLER, *putting her arm around his shoulder*

ANN (*wondrously at them, happy*)   Gosh, it's wonderful to hear you laughing about it.

CHRIS   Why, what'd you expect?

ANN   The last thing I remember on this block was one word—"Murderers!" Remember that, Kate?—Mrs. Hammond standing in front of our house and yelling that word? She's still around, I suppose?

MOTHER   They're all still around.

KELLER   Don't listen to her. Every Saturday night the whole gang is playin' poker in this arbor. All the ones who yelled murderer takin' my money now.

MOTHER   Don't, Joe; she's a sensitive girl, don't fool her. (*To* ANN) They still remember about Dad. It's different with him. (*Indicates* JOE) He was exonerated, your father's still there. That's why I wasn't so enthusiastic about your coming. Honestly, I know how sensitive you are, and I told Chris, I said—

KELLER   Listen, you do like I did and you'll be all right. The day I come home, I got out of my car—but not in front of the house . . . on the corner. You should've been here, Annie, and you too, Chris; you'd-a seen something. Everybody knew I was getting out that day; the porches were loaded. Picture it now; none of them believed I was innocent. The story was, I pulled a fast one getting myself exonerated. So I get out of my car, and I walk down the street. But very slow. And with a smile. The beast! I was the beast; the guy who sold cracked cylinder heads to the Army Air Force; the guy who made twenty-one P-40s crash in Australia. Kid, walkin' down the street that day I was guilty as hell. Except I wasn't, and there was a court paper in my pocket to prove I wasn't, and I walked . . . past . . . the porches. Result? Fourteen months later I had one of the best shops in the state again, a respected man again; bigger than ever.

CHRIS (*with admiration*)   Joe McGuts.

KELLER (*now with great force*)   That's the only way you lick 'em is guts! (*To* ANN) The worst thing you did was to move away from here. You made it tough for your father when he gets out. That's why I tell you, I like to see him move back right on this block.

MOTHER (*pained*)   How could they move back?

KELLER   It ain't gonna end *till* they move back! (*To* ANN) Till people play cards with him again, and talk with him, and smile with him—you play cards with a man you know he can't be a murderer. And the next time you write him I like you to tell him just what I said.

ANN *simply stares at him*

You hear me?

ANN (*surprised*)   Don't you hold anything against him?

KELLER   Annie, I never believed in crucifying people.

ANN (*mystified*)   But he was your partner, he dragged you through the mud.

KELLER   Well, he ain't my sweetheart, but you gotta forgive, don't you?

ANN   You, either, Kate? Don't you feel any—?

KELLER (*to* ANN)   The next time you write Dad—

ANN   I don't write him.

KELLER (*struck*)   Well, every now and then you—

ANN (*a little shamed, but determined*)   No, I've *never* written to him. Neither has my brother. (*To* CHRIS) Say, do you feel this way, too?

CHRIS   He murdered twenty-one pilots.

KELLER   What the hell kinda talk is that?

MOTHER   That's not a thing to say about a man.

ANN   What else can you say? When they took him away I followed him, went to him every visiting day. I was crying all the time. Until the news came about Larry. Then I realized. It's wrong to pity a man like that. Father or no father, there's only one way to look at him. He knowingly shipped out parts that would crash an airplane. And how do you know Larry wasn't one of them?

MOTHER   I was waiting for that. (*Going to her*) As long as you're here, Annie, I want to ask you never to say that again.

ANN   You surprise me. I thought you'd be mad at him.

MOTHER   What your father did had nothing to do with Larry. Nothing.

ANN   But we can't know that.

MOTHER (*striving for control*)   As long as you're here!

ANN (*perplexed*)   But, Kate—

MOTHER   Put that out of your head!

KELLER   Because—

MOTHER (*quickly to* KELLER)   That's all, that's enough. (*Places her hand on her head*) Come inside now, and have some tea with me. (*She turns and goes up steps*)

KELLER (*to* ANN)   The one thing you—

MOTHER (*sharply*)   He's not dead, so there's no argument! Now come!

KELLER (*angrily*)   In a minute!

MOTHER *turns and goes into house*

Now look, Annie—

CHRIS   All right, Dad, forget it.

KELLER   No, she dasn't feel that way. Annie—

CHRIS   I'm sick of the whole subject, now cut it out.

KELLER   You want her to go on like this? (*To* ANN) Those cylinder heads went into P-40s only. What's the matter with you? You know Larry never flew a P-40.

CHRIS   So who flew those P-40s, pigs?

KELLER   The man was a fool, but don't make a murderer out of him. You got no sense? Look what it does to her! (*To* ANN) Listen, you gotta appreciate what was doin' in that shop in the war. The both of you! It was a madhouse. Every half hour the Major callin' for cylinder heads, they were whippin' us with the telephone. The trucks were hauling them away hot, damn near. I mean just try to see it human, see it human. All of a sudden a batch comes out with a crack. That happens, that's the business. A fine, hairline crack. All right, so—so he's a little man, your father, always scared of loud voices. What'll the Major say?—Half a day's production shot . . . . What'll I say? You know what I mean? Human. (*He pauses*) So he takes out his tools and he—covers over the cracks. All right—that's bad, it's wrong, but that's what a little man does. If I could have gone in that day I'd a told him—junk 'em, Steve, we can afford it. But alone he was afraid. But I know he meant no harm. He believed they'd hold up a hundred per cent. That's a mistake, but it ain't murder. You mustn't feel that way about him. You understand me? It ain't right.

ANN (*she regards him a moment*)   Joe, let's forget it.

KELLER   Annie, the day the news came about Larry he was in the next cell to mine—Dad. And he cried, Annie—he cried half the night.

ANN (*touched*)   He shoulda cried all night. (*Slight pause*)

KELLER (*almost angered*)   Annie, I do not understand why you—!

CHRIS (*breaking in—with nervous urgency*)   Are you going to stop it?

ANN   Don't yell at him. He just wants everybody happy.

KELLER (*clasps her around waist, smiling*)   That's my sentiments. Can you stand steak?

CHRIS   And champagne!

KELLER   Now you're operatin'! I'll call Swanson's for a table!. Big time tonight, Annie!

ANN   Can't scare me.

KELLER (*to* CHRIS, *pointing at* ANN)   I like that girl. Wrap her up. (*They laugh. Goes up porch*) You got nice legs, Annie! . . . I want to see everybody drunk tonight. (*Pointing to* CHRIS) Look at him, he's blushin'! (*He exits, laughing, into house*)

CHRIS (*calling after him*)   Drink your tea, Casanova. (*He turns to* ANN) Isn't he a great guy?

ANN   You're the only one I know who loves his parents.

CHRIS   I know. It went out of style, didn't it?

ANN (*with a sudden touch of sadness*)   It's all right. It's a good thing. (*She looks about*) You know? It's lovely here. The air is sweet.

CHRIS (*hopefully*)   You're not sorry you came?

ANN   Not sorry, no. But I'm—not going to stay.

CHRIS   Why?

ANN   In the first place, your mother as much as told me to go.

CHRIS   Well—

ANN   You saw that—and then you—you've been kind of—

CHRIS   What?

ANN   Well . . . kind of embarrassed ever since I got here.

CHRIS   The trouble is I planned on kind of sneaking up on you over a period of a week or so. But they take it for granted that we're all set.

ANN   I knew they would. Your mother anyway.

CHRIS   How did you know?

ANN   From *her* point of view, why else would I come?

CHRIS   Well . . . would you want to?

> ANN *still studies him*

I guess you know this is why I asked you to come.

ANN   I guess this is why I came.

CHRIS   Ann, I love you. I love you a great deal. (*Finally*) I love you.

> Pause. *She waits*

I have no imagination . . . that's all I know to tell you.

> ANN *is waiting, ready*

I'm embarrassing you. I didn't want to tell it to you here. I wanted some place we'd never been; a place where we'd be brand new to each other. . . . You feel it's wrong here, don't you? This yard, this chair? I want you to be ready for me. I don't want to win you away from anything.

ANN (*putting her arms around him*)   Oh, Chris, I've been ready a long, long time!

CHRIS   Then he's gone forever. You're sure.

ANN   I almost got married two years ago.

CHRIS   Why didn't you?

ANN   You started to write to me—(*Slight pause*)

CHRIS   You felt something that far back?

ANN   Every day since!

CHRIS   Ann, why didn't you let me know?

ANN   I was waiting for you, Chris. Till then you never wrote. And when you did, what did you say? You sure can be ambiguous, you know.

CHRIS (*looks toward house, then at her, trembling*)   Give me a kiss, Ann. Give me a—(*They kiss*) God, I kissed you, Annie, I kissed Annie. How long, how long I've been waiting to kiss you!

ANN   I'll never forgive you. Why did you wait all these years? All I've done is sit and wonder if I was crazy for thinking of you.

CHRIS   Annie, we're going to live now! I'm going to make you so happy. (*He kisses her, but without their bodies touching*)

ANN (*a little embarrassed*)   Not like that you're not.

CHRIS   I kissed you . . .

ANN   Like Larry's brother. Do it like you, Chris.

He breaks away from her abruptly

What is it, Chris?

CHRIS   Let's drive some place . . . I want to be alone with you.

ANN   No . . . what is it, Chris, your mother?

CHRIS   No—nothing like that.

ANN   Then what's wrong? Even in your letters, there was something ashamed.

CHRIS   Yes. I suppose I have been. But it's going from me.

ANN   You've got to tell me—

CHRIS   I don't know how to start. (*He takes her hand*)

ANN   It wouldn't work this way. (*Slight pause*)

CHRIS (*speaks quietly, factually at first*)   It's all mixed up with so many other things. . . . You remember, overseas, I was in command of a company?

ANN   Yeah, sure.

CHRIS   Well, I lost them.

ANN   How many?

CHRIS   Just about all.

ANN   Oh, gee!

CHRIS   It takes a little time to toss that off. Because they weren't just men. For instance, one time it'd been raining several days and this kid came to me, and gave me his last pair of dry socks. Put them in my pocket. That's only a little thing—but . . . that's the kind of guys I had. They didn't die; they killed themselves for each other. I mean that exactly; a little more selfish and they'd 've been here today. And I got an idea—watching them go down. Everything was being destroyed, see, but it seemed to me that one new thing was made. A kind of—responsibility. Man for man. You understand me?—To show that, to bring that onto the earth again like some kind of a monument and everyone would feel it standing there, behind him, and it would make a difference to him. (*Pause*) And then I came home and it was incredible. I—there was no meaning in it here; the whole thing to them was a kind of a—bus accident. I went to work with Dad, and that rat-race again. I felt—what you said—ashamed somehow. Because nobody was changed at all. It seemed to make suckers out of a lot of guys. I felt wrong to be alive, to open the bank-book, to drive the new car, to see the new refrigerator. I mean you can take those things out of a war, but when you drive that car you've got to know that it came out of the love a man can have for a man, you've got to be a little better because of that. Otherwise what you have is really loot, and there's blood on it. I didn't want to take any of it. And I guess that included you.

ANN And you still feel that way?

CHRIS I want you now, Annie.

ANN Because you mustn't feel that way any more. Because you have a right to whatever you have. Everything, Chris, understand that? To me, too . . . And the money, there's nothing wrong in your money. Your father put hundreds of planes in the air, you should be proud. A man should be paid for that . . .

CHRIS Oh Annie, Annie . . . I'm going to make a fortune for you!

KELLER (*offstage*) Hello . . . Yes. Sure.

ANN (*laughing softly*) What'll I do with a fortune?

They kiss. KELLER *enters from house*

KELLER (*thumbing toward house*) Hey, Ann, your brother—

They step apart shyly. KELLER *comes down, and wryly*

What is this, Labor Day?

CHRIS (*waving him away, knowing the kidding will be endless*) All right, all right.

ANN You shouldn't burst out like that.

KELLER Well, nobody told me it was Labor Day. (*Looks around*) Where's the hot dogs?

CHRIS (*loving it*) All right. You said it once.

KELLER Well, as long as I know it's Labor Day from now on, I'll wear a bell around my neck.

ANN (*affectionately*) He's so subtle!

CHRIS George Bernard Shaw as an elephant.

KELLER George!—hey, you kissed it out of my head—your brother's on the phone.

ANN (*surprised*) My brother?

KELLER Yeah, George. Long distance.

ANN What's the matter, is anything wrong?

KELLER I don't know, Kate's talking to him. Hurry up, she'll cost him five dollars.

ANN (*takes a step upstage, then comes down toward* CHRIS) I wonder if we ought to tell your mother yet? I mean I'm not very good in an argument.

CHRIS We'll wait till tonight. After dinner. Now don't get tense, just leave it to me.

KELLER What're you telling her?

CHRIS Go ahead, Ann.

With misgivings, ANN *goes up and into house*

We're getting married, Dad.

KELLER *nods indecisively*

Well, don't you say anything?

KELLER (*distracted*) I'm glad, Chris, I'm just—George is calling from Columbus.

CHRIS Columbus!

KELLER   Did Annie tell you he was going to see his father today?

CHRIS   No, I don't think she knew anything about it.

KELLER (*asking uncomfortably*)   Chris! You—you think you know her pretty good?

CHRIS (*hurt and apprehensive*)   What kind of a question?

KELLER   I'm just wondering. All these years George don't go to see his father. Suddenly he goes . . . and she comes here.

CHRIS   Well, what about it?

KELLER   It's crazy, but it comes to my mind. She don't hold nothin' against me, does she?

CHRIS (*angry*)   I don't know what you're talking about.

KELLER (*a little more combatively*)   I'm just talkin'. To his last day in court the man blamed it all on me; and this is his daughter. I mean if she was sent here to find out something?

CHRIS (*angered*)   Why? What is there to find out?

ANN (*on phone, offstage*)   Why are you so excited, George? What happened there?

KELLER   I mean if they want to open up the case again, for the nuisance value, to hurt us?

CHRIS   Dad . . . how could you think that of her?

ANN (*still on phone*)   But what did he say to you, for God's sake? } *Together*

KELLER   It couldn't be, heh. You know.

CHRIS   Dad, you amaze me . . .

KELLER (*breaking in*)   All right, forget it, forget it. (*With great force, moving about*) I want a clean start for you, Chris. I want a new sign over the plant—Christopher Keller, Incorporated.

CHRIS (*a little uneasily*)   J. O. Keller is good enough.

KELLER   We'll talk about it. I'm going to build you a house, stone, with a driveway from the road. I want you to spread out, Chris, I want you to use what I made for you. (*He is close to him now*) I mean, with joy, Chris, without shame . . . with joy.

CHRIS (*touched*)   I will, Dad.

KELLER (*with deep emotion*)   Say it to me.

CHRIS   Why?

KELLER   Because sometimes I think you're . . . ashamed of the money.

CHRIS   No, don't feel that.

KELLER   Because it's good money, there's nothing wrong with that money.

CHRIS (*a little frightened*)   Dad, you don't have to tell me this.

KELLER (*—with overriding affection and self-confidence now. He grips* CHRIS *by the back of the neck, and with laughter between his determined jaws*)   Look, Chris, I'll go to work on Mother for you. We'll get her so drunk tonight we'll all get married! (*Steps away, with a wide gesture of his arm*) There's gonna be a wedding, kid, like there never was seen! Champagne, tuxedos—!

He breaks off as ANN'S *voice comes out loud from the house where she is still talking on phone*

ANN   Simply because when you get excited you don't control yourself.

MOTHER *comes out of house*

. . . Well, what did he tell you for God's sake? (*Pause*) All right, come then. (*Pause*) Yes, they'll all be here. Nobody's running away from you. And try to get hold of yourself, will you? (*Pause*) All right, all right. Good-by.

There is a brief pause as ANN *hangs up receiver, then comes out of kitchen*

CHRIS   Something happen?

KELLER   He's coming here?

ANN   On the seven o'clock. He's in Columbus. (*To* MOTHER) I told him it would be all right.

KELLER   Sure, fine! Your father took sick?

ANN (*mystified*)   No, George didn't say he was sick. I—(*Shaking it off*) I don't know, I suppose it's something stupid, you know my brother— (*She comes to* CHRIS) Let's go for a drive, or something . . .

CHRIS   Sure. Give me the keys, Dad.

MOTHER   Drive through the park. It's beautiful now.

CHRIS   Come on, Ann. (*To them*) Be back right away.

ANN (*as she and* CHRIS *exit up driveway*)   See you.

MOTHER *comes down toward* KELLER, *her eyes fixed on him*

KELLER   Take your time. (*To* MOTHER) What does George want?

MOTHER   He's been in Columbus since this morning with Steve. He's gotta see Annie right away, he says.

KELLER   What for?

MOTHER   I don't know. (*She speaks with warning*) He's a lawyer now, Joe. George is a lawyer. All these years he never even sent a postcard to Steve. Since he got back from the war, not a postcard.

KELLER   So what?

MOTHER (*her tension breaking out*)   Suddenly he takes an airplane from New York to see him. An airplane!

KELLER   Well? So?

MOTHER (*trembling*)   Why?

KELLER   I don't read minds. Do you?

MOTHER   Why, Joe? What has Steve suddenly got to tell him that he takes an airplane to see him?

KELLER   What do I care what Steve's got to tell him?

MOTHER   You're sure, Joe?

KELLER (*frightened, but angry*)   Yes, I'm sure.

MOTHER (*sits stiffly in a chair*)   Be smart now, Joe. The boy is coming. Be smart.

KELLER (*desperately*)   Once and for all, did you hear what I said? I said I'm sure!

MOTHER (*nods weakly*)　All right, Joe. (*He straightens up*) Just . . . be smart.

> KELLER, *in hopeless fury, looks at her, turns around, goes up to porch and into house, slamming screen door violently behind him.* MOTHER *sits in chair downstage, stiffly, staring, seeing*

CURTAIN

ACT TWO　*As twilight falls, that evening.*

> *On the rise,* CHRIS *is discovered sawing the broken-off tree, leaving stump standing alone. He is dressed in good pants, white shoes, but without a shirt. He disappears with tree up the alley when* MOTHER *appears on porch. She comes down and stands watching him. She has on a dressing gown, carries a tray of grapejuice drink in a pitcher, and glasses with sprigs of mint in them.*

MOTHER (*calling up alley*)　Did you have to put on good pants to do that?
> *She comes downstage and puts tray on table in the arbor. Then looks around uneasily, then feels pitcher for coolness.* CHRIS *enters from alley brushing off his hands*

You notice there's more light with that thing gone?

CHRIS　Why aren't you dressing?

MOTHER　It's suffocating upstairs. I made a grape drink for Georgie. He always liked grape. Come and have some.

CHRIS (*impatiently*)　Well, come on, get dressed. And what's Dad sleeping so much for? (*He goes to table and pours a glass of juice*)

MOTHER　He's worried. When he's worried he sleeps. (*Pauses. Looks into his eyes*) We're dumb, Chris. Dad and I are stupid people. We don't know anything. You've got to protect us.

CHRIS　You're silly; what's there to be afraid of?

MOTHER　To his last day in court Steve never gave up the idea that Dad made him do it. If they're going to open the case again I won't live through it.

CHRIS　George is just a damn fool, Mother. How can you take him seriously?

MOTHER　That family hates us. Maybe even Annie—

CHRIS　Oh, now, Mother . . .

MOTHER　You think just because you like everybody, they like you!

CHRIS　All right, stop working yourself up. Just leave everything to me.

MOTHER　When George goes home tell her to go with him.

CHRIS (*noncommittally*)　Don't worry about Annie.

MOTHER　Steve is her father, too.

CHRIS　Are you going to cut it out? Now, come.

MOTHER (*going upstage with him*)　You don't realize how people can hate, Chris, they can hate so much they'll tear the world to pieces.

CHRIS   Look! She's dressed already. (*As he and* MOTHER *mount porch*) I've just got to put on a shirt.

ANN (*in a preoccupied way*)   Are you feeling well, Kate?

MOTHER   What's the difference, dear. There are certain people, y'know, the sicker they get the longer they live. (*She goes into house*)

CHRIS   You look nice.

ANN   We're going to tell her tonight.

CHRIS   Absolutely, don't worry about it.

ANN   I wish we could tell her now. I can't stand scheming. My stomach gets hard.

CHRIS   It's not scheming, we'll just get her in a better mood.

MOTHER (*offstage, in the house*)   Joe, are you going to sleep all day!

ANN (*laughing*)   The only one who's relaxed is your father. He's fast asleep.

CHRIS   I'm relaxed.

ANN   Are you?

CHRIS   Look. (*He holds out his hand and makes it shake*) Let me know when George gets here.

> *He goes into the house.* ANN *moves aimlessly, and then is drawn toward tree stump. She goes to it, hesitantly touches broken top in the hush of her thoughts. Offstage* LYDIA *calls "Johnny! Come get your supper!"* SUE *enters, and halts, seeing* ANN

SUE   Is my husband—?

ANN (*turns, startled*)   Oh!

SUE   I'm terribly sorry.

ANN   It's all right, I—I'm a little silly about the dark.

SUE (*looks about*)   It is getting dark.

ANN   Are you looking for your husband?

SUE   As usual. (*Laughs tiredly*) He spends so much time here, they'll be charging him rent.

ANN   Nobody was dressed so he drove over to the depot to pick up my brother.

SUE   Oh, your brother's in?

ANN   Yeah, they ought to be here any minute now. Will you have a cold drink?

SUE   I will, thanks.

> ANN *goes to table and pours*

My husband. Too hot to drive me to beach. Men are like little boys; for the neighbors they'll always cut the grass.

ANN   People like to do things for the Kellers. Been that way since I can remember.

SUE   It's amazing. I guess your brother's coming to give you away, heh?

ANN (*giving her drink*)   I don't know. I suppose.

SUE   You must be all nerved up.

ANN   It's always a problem getting yourself married, isn't it?

SUE   That depends on your shape, of course. I don't see why you should
        have had a problem.

ANN   I've had chances—

SUE   I'll bet. It's romantic . . . it's very unusual to me, marrying the
        brother of your sweetheart.

ANN   I don't know. I think it's mostly that whenever I need somebody
        to tell me the truth I've always thought of Chris. When he tells you
        something you know it's so. He relaxes me.

SUE   And he's got money. That's important, you know.

ANN   It wouldn't matter to me.

SUE   You'd be surprised. It makes all the difference. I married an
        intern. On my salary. And that was bad, because as soon as a woman
        supports a man he owes her something. You can never owe somebody
        without resenting them.

                    ANN *laughs*

        That's true, you know.

ANN   Underneath, I think the doctor is very devoted.

SUE   Oh, certainly. But it's bad when a man always sees the bars in front
        of him. Jim thinks he's in jail all the time.

ANN   Oh . . .

SUE   That's why I've been intending to ask you a small favor, Ann. It's
        something very important to me.

ANN   Certainly, if I can do it.

SUE   You can. When you take up housekeeping, try to find a place away
        from here.

ANN   Are you fooling?

SUE   I'm very serious. My husband is unhappy with Chris around.

ANN   How is that?

SUE   Jim's a successful doctor. But he's got an idea he'd like to do
        medical research. Discover things. You see?

ANN   Well, isn't that good?

SUE   Research pays twenty-five dollars a week minus laundering the hair
        shirt. You've got to give up your life to go into it.

ANN   How does Chris—

SUE *(with growing feeling)*   Chris makes people want to be better than it's
        possible to be. He does that to people.

ANN   Is that bad?

SUE   My husband has a family, dear. Every time he has a session with
        Chris he feels as though he's compromising by not giving up everything
        for research. As though Chris or anybody else isn't compromising. It
        happens with Jim every couple of years. He meets a man and makes a
        statue out of him.

ANN   Maybe he's right. I don't mean that Chris is a statue, but—

SUE   Now darling, you know he's not right.

ANN   I don't agree with you. Chris—

SUE   Let's face it, dear. Chris is working with his father, isn't he? He's taking money out of that business every week in the year.

ANN   What of it?

SUE   You ask me what of it?

ANN   I certainly do. (*She seems about to burst out*) You oughtn't cast aspersions like that, I'm surprised at you.

SUE   You're surprised at me!

ANN   He'd never take five cents out of that plant if there was anything wrong with it.

SUE   You know that.

ANN   I know it. I resent everything you've said.

SUE (*moving toward her*)   You know what I resent, dear?

ANN   Please, I don't want to argue.

SUE   I resent living next door to the Holy Family. It makes me look like a bum, you understand?

ANN   I can't do anything about that.

SUE   Who is he to ruin a man's life? Everybody knows Joe pulled a fast one to get out of jail.

ANN   That's not true!

SUE   Then why don't you go out and talk to people? Go on, talk to them. There's not a person on the block who doesn't know the truth.

ANN   That's a lie. People come here all the time for cards and—

SUE   So what? They give him credit for being smart. I do, too, I've got nothing against Joe. But if Chris wants people to put on the hair shirt let him take off his broadcloth. He's driving my husband crazy with that phony idealism of his, and I'm at the end of my rope on it!

> CHRIS *enters on porch, wearing shirt and tie now. She turns quickly, hearing. With a smile*

Hello, darling. How's Mother?

CHRIS   I thought George came.

SUE   No, it was just us.

CHRIS (*coming down to them*)   Susie, do me a favor, heh? Go up to Mother and see if you can calm her. She's all worked up.

SUE   She still doesn't know about you two?

CHRIS (*laughs a little*)   Well, she senses it, I guess. You know my mother.

SUE (*going up to porch*)   Oh, yeah, she's psychic.

CHRIS   Maybe there's something in the medicine chest.

SUE   I'll give her one of everything. (*On porch*) Don't worry about Kate; couple of drinks, dance her around a little . . . She'll love Ann. (*To* ANN) Because you're the female version of him.

> CHRIS *laughs*

Don't be alarmed, I said version. (*She goes into house*)

CHRIS   Interesting woman, isn't she?

ANN   Yeah, she's very interesting.

CHRIS   She's a great nurse, you know, she—

ANN (*in tension, but trying to control it*)   Are you still doing that?

CHRIS (*sensing something wrong, but still smiling*)   Doing what?

ANN   As soon as you get to know somebody you find a distinction for them. How do you know she's a great nurse?

CHRIS   What's the matter, Ann?

ANN   The woman hates you. She despises you!

CHRIS   Hey . . . What's hit you?

ANN   Gee, Chris—

CHRIS   What happened here?

ANN   You never— Why didn't you tell me?

CHRIS   Tell you what?

ANN   She says they think Joe is guilty.

CHRIS   What difference does it make what they think?

ANN   I don't care what they think, I just don't understand why you took the trouble to deny it. You said it was all forgotten.

CHRIS   I didn't want you to feel there was anything wrong in you coming here, that's all. I know a lot of people think my father was guilty, and I assumed there might be some question in your mind.

ANN   But I never once said I suspected him.

CHRIS   Nobody says it.

ANN   Chris, I know how much you love him, but it could never—

CHRIS   Do you think I could forgive him if he'd done that thing?

ANN   I'm not here out of a blue sky, Chris. I turned my back on my father, if there's anything wrong here now—

CHRIS   I know that, Ann.

ANN   George is coming from Dad, and I don't think it's with a blessing.

CHRIS   He's welcome here. You've got nothing to fear from George.

ANN   Tell me that . . . Just tell me that.

CHRIS   The man is innocent, Ann. Remember he was falsely accused once and it put him through hell. How would you behave if you were faced with the same thing again? Annie, believe me, there's nothing wrong for you here, believe me, kid.

ANN   All right, Chris, all right.

> *They embrace as* KELLER *appears quietly on porch.* ANN *simply studies him*

KELLER   Every time I come out here it looks like Playland!

> *They break and laugh in embarrassment*

CHRIS   I thought you were going to shave?

KELLER (*sitting on bench*)   In a minute. I just woke up, I can't see nothin'.

ANN   You looked shaved.

KELLER   Oh, no. (*Massages his jaw*) Gotta be extra special tonight. Big night, Annie. So how's it feel to be a married woman?

ANN (*laughs*)   I don't know, yet.

KELLER (*to* CHRIS)   What's the matter, you slippin'? (*He takes a little box of apples from under the bench as they talk*)

CHRIS   The great roué!

KELLER   What is that, roué?

CHRIS   It's French.

KELLER   Don't talk dirty. (*They laugh*)

CHRIS (*to* ANN)   You ever meet a bigger ignoramus?

KELLER   Well, somebody's got to make a living.

ANN (*as they laugh*)   That's telling him.

KELLER   I don't know, everybody's gettin' so Goddam educated in this country there'll be nobody to take away the garbage. (*They laugh*) It's gettin' so the only dumb ones left are the bosses.

ANN   You're not so dumb, Joe.

KELLER   I know, but you go into our plant, for instance. I got so many lieutenants, majors and colonels that I'm ashamed to ask somebody to sweep the floor. I gotta be careful I'll insult somebody. No kiddin'. It's a tragedy: you stand on the street today and spit, you're gonna hit a college man.

CHRIS   Well, don't spit.

KELLER (*breaks apple in half, passing it to* ANN *and* CHRIS)   I mean to say, it's comin' to a pass. (*He takes a breath*) I been thinkin', Annie . . . your brother, George. I been thinkin' about your brother George. When he comes I like you to *brooch* something to him.

CHRIS   Broach.

KELLER   What's the matter with brooch?

CHRIS (*smiling*)   It's not English.

KELLER   When I went to night school it was brooch.

ANN (*laughing*)   Well, in day school it's broach.

KELLER   Don't surround me, will you? Seriously, Ann . . . You say he's not well. George, I been thinkin', why should he knock himself out in New York with that cut-throat competition, when I got so many friends here; I'm very friendly with some big lawyers in town. I could set George up here.

ANN   That's awfully nice of you, Joe.

KELLER   No, kid, it ain't nice of me. I want you to understand me. I'm thinking of Chris. (*Slight pause*) See . . . this is what I mean. You get older, you want to feel that you—accomplished something. My only accomplishment is my son. I ain't brainy. That's all I accomplished. Now, a year, eighteen months, your father'll be a free man. Who is he going to come to, Annie? His baby. You. He'll come, old, mad, into your house.

ANN   That can't matter any more, Joe.

KELLER   I don't want that to come between us. (*Gestures between* CHRIS *and himself*)

ANN   I can only tell you that that could never happen.

KELLER   You're in love now, Annie, but believe me, I'm older than you and I know—a daughter is a daughter, and a father is a father. And it could happen. (*He pauses*) I like you and George to go to him in prison and tell him . . . "Dad, Joe wants to bring you into the business when you get out."

ANN (*surprised, even shocked*)   You'd have him as a partner?

KELLER   No, no partner. A good job. (*Pause. He sees she is is shocked, a little mystified. He gets up, speaks more nervously*) I want him to know, Annie . . . while he's sitting there I want him to know that when he gets out he's got a place waitin' for him. It'll take his bitterness away. To know you got a place . . . it sweetens you.

ANN   Joe, you owe him nothing.

KELLER   I owe him a good kick in the teeth, but he's your father.

CHRIS   Then kick him in the teeth! I don't want him in the plant, so that's that! You understand? And besides, don't talk about him like that. People misunderstand you!

KELLER   And I don't understand why she has to crucify the man.

CHRIS   Well, it's her father, if she feels—

KELLER   No, no.

CHRIS (*almost angrily*)   What's it to you? Why—?

KELLER (*—a commanding outburst in high nervousness*)   A father is a father! (*As though the outburst had revealed him, he looks about, wanting to retract it. His hand goes to his cheek*) I better—I better shave. (*He turns and a smile is on his face. To* ANN) I didn't mean to yell at you, Annie.

ANN   Let's forget the whole thing, Joe.

KELLER   Right. (*To* CHRIS) She's likeable.

CHRIS (*a little peeved at the man's stupidity*)   Shave, will you?

KELLER   Right again.

> As he turns to porch LYDIA comes hurrying from her house

LYDIA   I forgot all about it. (*Seeing* CHRIS *and* ANN) Hya. (*To* JOE) I promised to fix Kate's hair for tonight. Did she comb it yet?

KELLER   Always a smile, hey, Lydia?

LYDIA   Sure, why not?

KELLER (*going up on porch*)   Come on up and comb my Katie's hair.

> LYDIA *goes up on porch*

She's got a big night, make her beautiful.

LYDIA   I will.

KELLER (*holds door open for her and she goes into kitchen. To* CHRIS *and* ANN) Hey, that could be a song. (*He sings softly*)

> Come on up and comb my Katie's hair . . .
>
> Oh, come on up, 'cause she's my lady fair—

(*To* ANN) How's that for one year of night school? (*He continues singing as he goes into kitchen*)

> Oh, come on up, come on up, and comb my
> lady's hair—
>
> JIM BAYLISS *rounds corner of driveway, walking rapidly.* JIM *crosses to* CHRIS, *motions him and pulls him down excitedly.* KELLER *stands just inside kitchen door, watching them*

CHRIS   What's the matter? Where is he?

JIM   Where's your mother?

CHRIS   Upstairs, dressing.

ANN (*crossing to them rapidly*)   What happened to George?

JIM   I asked him to wait in the car. Listen to me now. Can you take some advice? (*They wait*) Don't bring him in here.

ANN   Why?

JIM   Kate is in bad shape, you can't explode this in front of her.

ANN   Explode what?

JIM   You know why he's here, don't try to kid it away. There's blood in his eye; drive him somewhere and talk to him alone.

> ANN *turns to go up drive, takes a couple of steps, sees* KELLER, *and stops. He goes quietly on into house*

CHRIS (*shaken, and therefore angered*)   Don't be an old lady.

JIM   He's come to take her home. What does that mean? (*To* ANN) You know what that means. Fight it out with him some place else.

ANN (*comes back down toward* CHRIS)   I'll drive . . . him somewhere.

CHRIS (*goes to her*)   No.

JIM   Will you stop being an idiot?

CHRIS   Nobody's afraid of him here. Cut that out!

> He starts for driveway, but is brought up short by GEORGE, who enters there. GEORGE is CHRIS's age, but a paler man, now on the edge of his self-restraint. He speaks quietly, as though afraid to find himself screaming. An instant's hesitation and CHRIS steps up to him, hand extended, smiling

CHRIS   Helluva way to do; what're you sitting out there for?

GEORGE   Doctor said your mother isn't well, I—

CHRIS   So what? She'd want to see you, wouldn't she? We've been waiting for you all afternoon.

> He puts his hand on GEORGE's arm, but GEORGE pulls away, coming across toward ANN

ANN (*touching his collar*)   This is filthy, didn't you bring another shirt?

> GEORGE breaks away from her, and moves down, examining the yard. Door opens, and he turns rapidly, thinking it is KATE, but it's SUE. She looks at him; he turns away and moves to fence. He looks over it at his former home. SUE comes downstage

SUE (*annoyed*)   How about the beach, Jim?

JIM   Oh, it's too hot to drive.

SUE   How'd you get to the station—Zeppelin?

CHRIS   This is Mrs. Bayliss, George. (*Calling, as* GEORGE *pays no attention, staring at house*) George! (GEORGE *turns*) Mrs. Bayliss.

SUE   How do you do.

GEORGE (*removing his hat*)   You're the people who bought our house, aren't you?

SUE   That's right. Come and see what we did with it before you leave.

GEORGE (*walks down and away from her*)   I liked it the way it was.

SUE (*after a brief pause*)   He's frank, isn't he?

JIM (*pulling her off*)   See you later. . . . Take it easy, fella. (*They exit*)

CHRIS (*calling after them*)   Thanks for driving him! (*Turning to* GEORGE) How about some grape juice? Mother made it especially for you.

GEORGE (*with forced appreciation*)   Good old Kate, remembered my grape juice.

CHRIS   You drank enough of it in this house. How've you been, George?—Sit down.

GEORGE (*keeps moving*)   It takes me a minute. (*Looking around*) It seems impossible.

CHRIS   What?

GEORGE   I'm back here.

CHRIS   Say, you've gotten a little nervous, haven't you?

GEORGE   Yeah, toward the end of the day. What're you, big executive now?

CHRIS   Just kind of medium. How's the law?

GEORGE   I don't know. When I was studying in the hospital it seemed sensible, but outside there doesn't seem to be much of a law. The trees got thick, didn't they? (*Points to stump*) What's that?

CHRIS   Blew down last night. We had it there for Larry. You know.

GEORGE   Why, afraid you'll forget him?

CHRIS (*starts for* GEORGE)   Kind of a remark is that?

ANN (*breaking in, putting a restraining hand on* CHRIS)   When did you start wearing a hat?

GEORGE (*discovers hat in his hand*)   Today. From now on I decided to look like a lawyer, anyway. (*He holds it up to her*) Don't you recognize it?

ANN   Why? Where—?

GEORGE   Your father's— He asked me to wear it.

ANN   How is he?

GEORGE   He got smaller.

ANN   Smaller?

GEORGE   Yeah, little. (*Holds out his hand to measure*) He's a little man. That's what happens to suckers, you know. It's good I went to him in time—another year there'd be nothing left but his smell.

CHRIS   What's the matter, George, what's the trouble?

GEORGE   The trouble? The trouble is when you make suckers out of people once, you shouldn't try to do it twice.

CHRIS   What does that mean?

GEORGE (*to* ANN)   You're not married yet, are you?

ANN   George, will you sit down and stop—?

GEORGE   Are you married yet?

ANN   No, I'm not married yet.

GEORGE   You're not going to marry him.

ANN   Why am I not going to marry him?

GEORGE   Because his father destroyed your family.

CHRIS   Now look, George . . .

GEORGE   Cut it short, Chris. Tell her to come home with me. Let's not argue, you know what I've got to say.

CHRIS   George, you don't want to be the voice of God, do you?

GEORGE   I'm—

CHRIS   That's been your trouble all your life, George, you dive into things. What kind of a statement is that to make? You're a big boy now.

GEORGE   I'm a big boy now.

CHRIS   Don't come bulling in here. If you've got something to say, be civilized about it.

GEORGE   Don't civilize me!

ANN   Shhh!

CHRIS (*ready to hit him*)   Are you going to talk like a grown man or aren't you?

ANN (*quickly, to forestall an outburst*)   Sit down, dear. Don't be angry, what's the matter?

He allows her to seat him, looking at her

Now what happened? You kissed me when I left, now you—

GEORGE (*breathlessly*)   My life turned upside down since then. I couldn't go back to work when you left. I wanted to go to Dad and tell him you were going to be married. It seemed impossible not to tell him. He loved you so much. (*He pauses*) Annie—we did a terrible thing. We can never be forgiven. Not even to send him a card at Christmas. I didn't see him once since I got home from the war! Annie, you don't know what was done to that man. You don't know what happened.

ANN (*afraid*)   Of course I know.

GEORGE   You can't know, you wouldn't be here. Dad came to work that day. The night foreman came to him and showed him the cylinder heads . . . they were coming out of the process with defects. There was something wrong with the process. So Dad went directly to the phone and called here and told Joe to come down right away. But the morning passed. No sign of Joe. So Dad called again. By this time he had over a hundred defectives. The Army was screaming for stuff and Dad didn't have anything to ship. So Joe told him . . . on the phone he told him to weld, cover up the cracks in any way he could, and ship them out.

CHRIS   Are you through now?

GEORGE (*surging up at him*)   I'm not through now! (*Back to ANN*) Dad was afraid. He wanted Joe there if he was going to do it. But Joe can't come down . . . He's sick. Sick! He suddenly gets the flu! Suddenly! But he promised to take responsibility. Do you understand what I'm saying? On the telephone you can't have responsibility! In a court you can always deny a phone call and that's exactly what he did. They knew he was a liar the first time, but in the appeal they believed that rotten lie and now Joe is a big shot and your father is the patsy. (*He gets up*) Now what're you going to do? Eat his food, sleep in his bed? Answer me; what're you going to do?

CHRIS   What're you going to do, George?

GEORGE   He's too smart for me, I can't prove a phone call.

CHRIS   Then how dare you come in here with that rot?

ANN   George, the court—

GEORGE   The court didn't know your father! But you know him. You know in your heart Joe did it.

CHRIS (*whirling him around*)   Lower your voice or I'll throw you out of here!

GEORGE   She knows. She knows.

CHRIS (*to* ANN)   Get him out of here, Ann. Get him out of here.

ANN   George, I know everything you've said. Dad told that whole thing in court, and they—

GEORGE (*—almost a scream*)   The court did not know him, Annie!

ANN   Shhh!—But he'll say anything, George. You know how quick he can lie.

GEORGE (*turning to* CHRIS, *with deliberation*)   I'll ask you something, and look me in the eye when you answer me.

CHRIS   I'll look you in the eye.

GEORGE   You know your father—

CHRIS   I know him well.

GEORGE   And he's the kind of boss to let a hundred and twenty-one cylinder heads be repaired and shipped out of his shop without even knowing about it?

CHRIS   He's that kind of boss.

GEORGE   And that's the same Joe Keller who never left his shop without first going around to see that all the lights were out.

CHRIS (*with growing anger*)   The same Joe Keller.

GEORGE   The same man who knows how many minutes a day his workers spend in the toilet.

CHRIS   The same man.

GEORGE   And my father, that frightened mouse who'd never buy a shirt without somebody along—that man would dare do such a thing on his own?

CHRIS   On his own. And because he's a frightened mouse this is another thing he'd do—throw the blame on somebody else because he's not man enough to take it himself. He tried it in court but it didn't work, but with a fool like you it works!

GEORGE   Oh, Chris, you're a liar to yourself!

ANN (*deeply shaken*)   Don't talk like that!

CHRIS (*sits facing* GEORGE)   Tell me, George. What happened? The court record was good enough for you all these years, why isn't it good now? Why did you believe it all these years?

GEORGE (*after a slight pause*)   Because you believed it. . . . That's the truth, Chris. I believed everything, because I thought you did. But today I heard it from his mouth. From his mouth it's altogether different than the record. Anyone who knows him, and knows your father, will believe it from his mouth. Your Dad took everything we have. I can't beat that. But she's one item he's not going to grab. (*He turns to* ANN) Get your things. Everything they have is covered with blood. You're not the kind of a girl who can live with that. Get your things.

CHRIS   Ann . . . you're not going to believe that, are you?

ANN (*goes to him*)   You know it's not true, don't you?

GEORGE   How can he tell you? It's his father. (*To* CHRIS) None of these things ever even cross your mind?

CHRIS   Yes, they crossed my mind. Anything can cross your mind!

GEORGE   *He knows*, Annie. He knows!

CHRIS   The voice of God!

GEORGE   Then why isn't your name on the business? Explain that to her!

CHRIS   What the hell has that got to do with—?

GEORGE   Annie, why isn't his name on it?

CHRIS   Even when I don't own it!

GEORGE   Who're you kidding? Who gets it when he dies? (*To* ANN) Open your eyes, you know the both of them, isn't that the first thing they'd do, the way they love each other?—J. O. Keller and Son?

> *Pause.* ANN *looks from him to* CHRIS

I'll settle it. Do you want to settle it, or are you afraid to?

CHRIS   What do you mean?

GEORGE   Let me go up and talk to your father. In ten minutes you'll have the answer. Or are you afraid of the answer?

CHRIS   I'm not afraid of the answer. I know the answer. But my mother isn't well and I don't want a fight here now.

GEORGE   Let me go to him.

CHRIS   You're not going to start a fight here now.

GEORGE (*to* ANN)   What more do you want!

> *There is a sound of footsteps in the house*

ANN (*turns her head suddenly toward house*)   Someone's coming.

CHRIS (*to George, quietly*)   You won't say anything now.

ANN   You'll go soon. I'll call a cab.

GEORGE   You're coming with me.

ANN   And don't mention marriage, because we haven't told her yet.

GEORGE   You're coming with me.

ANN   You understand? Don't—George, you're not going to start anything now! (*She hears footsteps*) Shsh!

> MOTHER *enters on porch. She is dressed almost formally; her hair is fixed. They are all turned toward her. On seeing* GEORGE *she raises both hands, comes down toward him*

MOTHER   Georgie, Georgie.

GEORGE (*—he has always liked her*)   Hello, Kate.

MOTHER (*cups his face in her hands*)   They made an old man out of you. (*Touches his hair*) Look, you're gray.

GEORGE (*—her pity, open and unabashed, reaches into him, and he smiles sadly*)   I know, I—

MOTHER   I told you when you went away, don't try for medals.

GEORGE (*laughs, tiredly*)   I didn't try, Kate. They made it very easy for me.

MOTHER (*actually angry*)   Go on. You're all alike. (*To* ANN) Look at him, why did you say he's fine? He looks like a ghost.

GEORGE (*relishing her solicitude*)   I feel all right.

MOTHER   I'm sick to look at you. What's the matter with your mother, why don't she feed you?

ANN   He just hasn't any appetite.

MOTHER   If he ate in my house he'd have an appetite. (*To* ANN) I pity your husband! (*To* GEORGE) Sit down. I'll make you a sandwich.

GEORGE (*—sits with an embarrassed laugh*)   I'm really not hungry.

MOTHER   Honest to God, it breaks my heart to see what happened to all the children. How we worked and planned for you, and you end up no better than us.

GEORGE (*with deep feeling for her*)   You . . . you haven't changed at all, you know that, Kate?

MOTHER   None of us changed, Georgie. We all love you. Joe was just talking about the day you were born and the water got shut off. People were carrying basins from a block away—a stranger would have thought the whole neighborhood was on fire! (*They laugh. She sees the juice. To* ANN) Why didn't you give him some juice!

ANN (*defensively*)   I offered it to him.

MOTHER (*scoffingly*)   You offered it to him! (*Thrusting glass into* GEORGE's *hand*) Give it to him! (*To* GEORGE, *who is laughing*) And now you're going to sit here and drink some juice . . . and look like something!

GEORGE (*sitting*)   Kate, I feel hungry already.

CHRIS (*proudly*)   She could turn Mahatma Ghandi into a heavyweight!

MOTHER (*to* CHRIS, *with great energy*)   Listen, to hell with the restaurant! I got a ham in the icebox, and frozen strawberries, and avocados, and—

ANN   Swell, I'll help you!

GEORGE   The train leaves at eight-thirty, Ann.

MOTHER (*to* ANN)   You're leaving?

CHRIS   No, Mother, she's not—

ANN (*breaking through it, going to* GEORGE)   You hardly got here; give yourself a chance to get acquainted again.

CHRIS   Sure, you don't even know us any more.

MOTHER   Well, Chris, if they can't stay, don't—

CHRIS   No, it's just a question of George, Mother, he planned on—

GEORGE (*gets up politely, nicely, for* KATE's *sake*)   Now wait a minute, Chris . . .

CHRIS (*smiling and full of command, cutting him off*)   If you want to go, I'll drive you to the station now, but if you're staying, no arguments while you're here.

MOTHER (*at last confessing the tension*)   Why should he argue? (*She goes to him. With desperation and compassion, stroking his hair*) Georgie and us have no argument. How could we have an argument, Georgie? We all got hit by the same lightning, how can you—? Did you see what happened to Larry's tree, Georgie? (*She has taken his arm, and unwillingly he moves across stage with her*) Imagine? While I was dreaming of him in the middle of the night, the wind came along and—

LYDIA *enters on porch. As soon as she sees him:*

LYDIA   Hey, Georgie! Georgie! Georgie! Georgie! Georgie! (*She comes down to him eagerly. She has a flowered hat in her hand, which* KATE *takes from her as she goes to* GEORGE)

GEORGE (*as they shake hands eagerly, warmly*)   Hello, Laughy. What'd you do, grow?

LYDIA   I'm a big girl now.

MOTHER   Look what she can do to a hat!

ANN (*to* LYDIA, *admiring the hat*)   Did you make that?

MOTHER   In ten minutes! (*She puts it on*)

LYDIA (*fixing it on her head*)   I only rearranged it.

GEORGE   You still make your own clothes?

CHRIS (*of* MOTHER)   Ain't she classy! All she needs now is a Russian wolfhound.

MOTHER (*moving her head*)   It feels like somebody is sitting on my head.

ANN   No, it's beautiful, Kate.

MOTHER (*kisses* LYDIA. *To* GEORGE)   She's a genius! You should've married her. (*They laugh*) This one can feed you!

LYDIA (*strangely embarrassed*)   Oh, stop that, Kate.

GEORGE (*to* LYDIA)   Didn't I hear you had a baby?

MOTHER   You don't hear so good. She's got three babies.

GEORGE (*a little hurt by it—to* LYDIA)   No kidding, three?

LYDIA   Yeah, it was one, two, three— You've been away a long time, Georgie.

GEORGE   I'm beginning to realize.

MOTHER (*to* CHRIS *and* GEORGE)   The trouble with you kids is you *think* too much.

LYDIA   Well, we think, too.

MOTHER   Yes, but not all the time.

GEORGE (*with almost obvious envy*)   They never took Frank, heh?

LYDIA (*a little apologetically*)   No, he was always one year ahead of the draft.

MOTHER   It's amazing. When they were calling boys twenty-seven Frank was just twenty-eight, when they made it twenty-eight he was just twenty-nine. That's why he took up astrology. It's all in when you were born, it just goes to show.

CHRIS   What does it go to show?

MOTHER (*to* CHRIS)   Don't be so intelligent. Some superstitions are very nice! (*To* LYDIA) Did he finish Larry's horoscope?

LYDIA   I'll ask him now, I'm going in. (*To* GEORGE, *a little sadly, almost embarrassed*) Would you like to see my babies? Come on.

GEORGE   I don't think so, Lydia.

LYDIA (*understanding*)   All right. Good luck to you, George.

GEORGE   Thanks. And to you . . . And Frank.

> She smiles at him, turns and goes off to her house. GEORGE *stands staring after her*

LYDIA (*as she runs off*)   Oh, Frank!

MOTHER (*reading his thoughts*)   She got pretty, heh?

GEORGE (*sadly*)   Very pretty.

MOTHER (*as a reprimand*)   She's beautiful, you damned fool!

GEORGE (*looks around longingly; and softly, with a catch in his throat*)   She makes it seem so nice around here.

MOTHER (*shaking her finger at him*)   Look what happened to you because you wouldn't listen to me! I told you to marry that girl and stay out of the war!

GEORGE (*laughs at himself*)   She used to laugh too much.

MOTHER   And you didn't laugh enough. While you were getting mad about Fascism Frank was getting into her bed.

GEORGE (*to* CHRIS)   He won the war, Frank.

CHRIS   All the battles.

MOTHER (*in pursuit of this mood*)   The day they started the draft, Georgie, I told you you loved that girl.

CHRIS (*laughs*)   And truer love hath no man!

MOTHER   I'm smarter than any of you.

GEORGE (*laughing*)   She's wonderful!

MOTHER   And now you're going to listen to me, George. You had big principles, Eagle Scouts the three of you; so now I got a tree, and this one—(*indicating* CHRIS)—when the weather gets bad he can't stand on his feet; and that big dope— (*pointing to* LYDIA's *house*) —next door who never reads anything but Andy Gump has three children and his house paid off. Stop being a philosopher, and look after yourself. Like Joe was just saying—you move back here, he'll help you get set, and I'll find you a girl and put a smile on your face.

GEORGE   Joe? Joe wants me here?

ANN (*eagerly*)   He asked me to tell you, and I think it's a good idea.

MOTHER   Certainly. Why must you make believe you hate us? Is that another principle?—that you have to hate us? You don't hate us, George, I know you, you can't fool me, I diapered you. (*Suddenly, to* ANN) You remember Mr. Marcy's daughter?

ANN (*laughing, to* GEORGE)   She's got you hooked already!

> GEORGE *laughs, is excited*

MOTHER   You look her over, George; you'll see she's the most beautiful—

CHRIS   She's got warts, George.

MOTHER (*to* CHRIS)   She hasn't got warts! (*To* GEORGE) So the girl has a little beauty mark on her chin—

CHRIS   And two on her nose.

MOTHER   You remember. Her father's the retired police inspector.

CHRIS   Sergeant, George.

MOTHER   He's a very kind man!

CHRIS   He looks like a gorilla.

MOTHER (*to* GEORGE)   He never shot anybody.

> *They all burst out laughing, as* KELLER *appears in doorway.*
> GEORGE *rises abruptly and stares at* KELLER, *who comes rapidly down to him*

KELLER (—*the laughter stops. With strained joviality*)   Well! Look who's here! (*Extending his hand*) Georgie, good to see ya.

GEORGE (*shaking hands—somberly*)   How're you, Joe?

KELLER   So-so. Gettin' old. You comin' out to dinner with us?

GEORGE   No, got to be back in New York.

ANN   I'll call a cab for you. (*She goes up into the house*)

KELLER   Too bad you can't stay, George. Sit down. (*To* MOTHER) He looks fine.

MOTHER   He looks terrible.

KELLER   That's what I said, you look terrible, George. (*They laugh*) I wear the pants and she beats me with the belt.

GEORGE   I saw your factory on the way from the station. It looks like General Motors.

KELLER   I wish it was General Motors, but it ain't. Sit down, George. Sit down. (*Takes cigar out of his pocket*) So you finally went to see your father, I hear?

GEORGE   Yes, this morning. What kind of stuff do you make now?

KELLER   Oh, little of everything. Pressure cookers, an assembly for washing machines. Got a nice, flexible plant now. So how'd you find Dad? Feel all right?

GEORGE (*searching* KELLER, *speaking indecisively*)   No, he's not well, Joe.

KELLER (*lighting his cigar*)   Not his heart again, is it?

GEORGE   It's everything, Joe. It's his soul.

KELLER (*blowing out smoke*)   Uh huh—

CHRIS   How about seeing what they did with your house?

KELLER   Leave him be.

GEORGE (*to* CHRIS, *indicating* KELLER)   I'd like to talk to him.

KELLER   Sure, he just got here. That's the way they do, George. A little man makes a mistake and they hang him by the thumbs; the big ones become ambassadors. I wish you'd-a told me you were going to see Dad.

GEORGE (*studying him*)   I didn't know you were interested.

KELLER   In a way, I am. I would like him to know, George, that as far as I'm concerned, any time he wants, he's got a place with me. I would like him to know that.

GEORGE   He hates your guts, Joe. Don't you know that?

KELLER   I imagined it. But that can change, too.

MOTHER   Steve was never like that.

GEORGE   He's like that now. He'd like to take every man who made money in the war and put him up against a wall.

CHRIS   He'll need a lot of bullets.

GEORGE   And he'd better not get any.

KELLER   That's a sad thing to hear.

GEORGE (*with bitterness dominant*)   Why? What'd you expect him to think of you?

KELLER (*—the force of his nature rising, but under control*)   I'm sad to see he hasn't changed. As long as I know him, twenty-five years, the man never learned how to take the blame. You know that, George.

GEORGE (*—he does*)   Well, I—

KELLER   But you do know it. Because the way you come in here you don't look like you remember it. I mean like in nineteen thirty-seven when we had the shop on Flood Street. And he damn near blew us all up with that heater he left burning for two days without water. He wouldn't admit that was his fault, either. I had to fire a mechanic to save his face. You remember that.

GEORGE   Yes, but—

KELLER   I'm just mentioning it, George. Because this is just another one of a lot of things. Like when he gave Frank that money to invest in oil stock.

GEORGE (*distressed*)   I know that, I—

KELLER (*driving in, but restrained*)   But it's good to remember those things, kid. The way he cursed Frank because the stock went down. Was that Frank's fault? To listen to him Frank was a swindler. And all the man did was give him a bad tip.

GEORGE (*gets up, moves away*)   I know those things . . .

KELLER   Then remember them, remember them.

> ANN *comes out of house*

There are certain men in the world who rather see everybody hung before they'll take blame. You understand me, George?

> *They stand facing each other,* GEORGE *trying to judge him*

ANN (*coming downstage*)   The cab's on its way. Would you like to wash?

MOTHER (*with the thrust of hope*)   Why must he go? Make the midnight, George.

KELLER   Sure, you'll have dinner with us!

ANN   How about it? Why not? We're eating at the lake, we could have a swell time.

A long pause, as GEORGE *looks at* ANN, CHRIS, KELLER, *then back to her*

GEORGE   All right.

MOTHER   Now you're talking.

CHRIS   I've got a shirt that'll go right with that suit.

MOTHER   Size fifteen and a half, right, George?

GEORGE   Is Lydia—? I mean—Frank and Lydia coming?

MOTHER   I'll get you a date that'll make her look like a— (*She starts upstage*)

GEORGE (*laughing*)   No, I don't want a date.

CHRIS   I know somebody just for you! Charlotte Tanner! (*He starts for the house*)

KELLER   Call Charlotte, that's right.

MOTHER   Sure, call her up.

            CHRIS *goes into house*

ANN   You go up and pick out a shirt and tie.

GEORGE (*stops, looks around at them and the place*)   I never felt at home any-where but here. I feel so— (*He nearly laughs, and turns away from them*) Kate, you look so young, you know? You didn't change at all. It . . . rings an old bell. (*Turns to* KELLER) You too, Joe, you're amazingly the same. The whole atmosphere is.

KELLER   Say, I ain't got time to get sick.

MOTHER   He hasn't been laid up in fifteen years.

KELLER   Except my flu during the war.

MOTHER   Huhh?

KELLER   My flu, when I was sick during . . . the war.

MOTHER   Well, sure . . . (*To* GEORGE) I mean except for that flu.

            GEORGE *stands perfectly still*

Well, it slipped my mind, don't look at me that way. He wanted to go to the shop but he couldn't lift himself off the bed. I thought he had pneumonia.

GEORGE   Why did you say he's never—?

KELLER   I know how you feel, kid, I'll never forgive myself. If I could've gone in that day I'd never allow Dad to touch those heads.

GEORGE   She said you've never been sick.

MOTHER   I said he was sick, George.

GEORGE (*going to* ANN)   Ann, didn't you hear her say—?

MOTHER   Do you remember every time you were sick?

GEORGE   I'd remember pneumonia. Especially if I got it just the day my partner was going to patch up cylinder heads . . . What happened that day, Joe?

            FRANK *enters briskly from driveway, holding Larry's horoscope in his hand. He comes to* KATE

FRANK   Kate! Kate!

MOTHER   Frank, did you see George?

FRANK (*extending his hand*)   Lydia told me, I'm glad to . . . you'll have to pardon me. (*Pulling* MOTHER *over*) I've got something amazing for you, Kate, I finished Larry's horoscope.

MOTHER   You'd be interested in this, George. It's wonderful the way he can understand the—

CHRIS (*entering from house*)   George, the girl's on the phone—

MOTHER (*desperately*)   He finished Larry's horoscope!

CHRIS   Frank, can't you pick a better time than this?

FRANK   The greatest men who ever lived believed in the stars!

CHRIS   Stop filling her head with that junk!

FRANK   Is it junk to feel that there's a greater power than ourselves? I've studied the stars of his life! I won't argue with you, I'm telling you. Somewhere in this world your brother is alive!

MOTHER (*instantly to* CHRIS)   Why isn't it possible?

CHRIS   Because it's insane.

FRANK   Just a minute now. I'll tell you something and you can do as you please. Just let me say it. He was supposed to have died on November twenty-fifth. But November twenty-fifth was his favorable day.

CHRIS   Mother!

MOTHER   Listen to him!

FRANK   It was a day when everything good was shining on him, the kind of day he should've married on. You can laugh at a lot of it, I can understand you laughing. But the odds are a million to one that a man won't die on his favorable day. That's known, that's known, Chris!

MOTHER   Why isn't it possible, why isn't it possible, Chris!

GEORGE (*to* ANN)   Don't you understand what she's saying? She just told you to go. What are you waiting for now?

CHRIS   Nobody can tell her to go.

A car horn is heard

MOTHER (*to* FRANK)   Thank you, darling, for your trouble. Will you tell him to wait, Frank?

FRANK (*as he goes*)   Sure thing.

MOTHER (*calling out*)   They'll be right out, driver!

CHRIS   She's not leaving, Mother.

GEORGE   You heard her say it, he's never been sick!

MOTHER   He misunderstood me, Chris!

CHRIS *looks at her, struck*

GEORGE (*to* ANN)   He simply told your father to kill pilots, and covered himself in bed!

CHRIS   You'd better answer him, Annie. Answer him.

MOTHER   I packed your bag, darling.

CHRIS   What?

MOTHER   I packed your bag. All you've got to do is close it.

ANN   I'm not closing anything. He asked me here and I'm staying till he tells me to go. (*To* GEORGE) Till Chris tells me!

CHRIS   That's all! Now get out of here, George!

MOTHER (*to* CHRIS)   But if that's how he feels—

CHRIS   That's all, nothing more till Christ comes, about the case or Larry as long as I'm here! (*To* GEORGE) Now get out of here, George!

GEORGE (*to* ANN)   You tell me. I want to hear you tell me.

ANN   Go, George!

> *They disappear up the driveway,* ANN *saying, "Don't take it that way, Georgie! Please don't take it that way"*

CHRIS (*turning to his mother*)   What do you mean, you packed her bag? How dare you pack her bag?

MOTHER   Chris—

CHRIS   How dare you pack her bag?

MOTHER   She doesn't belong here.

CHRIS   Then I don't belong here.

MOTHER   She's Larry's girl.

CHRIS   And I'm his brother and he's dead, and I'm marrying his girl.

MOTHER   Never, never in this world!

KELLER   You lost your mind?

MOTHER   You have nothing to say!

KELLER (*cruelly*)   I got plenty to say. Three and a half years you been talking like a maniac—

> MOTHER *smashes him across the face*

MOTHER   Nothing. You have nothing to say. Now I say. He's coming back, and everybody has got to wait.

CHRIS   Mother, Mother—

MOTHER   Wait, wait—

CHRIS   How long? How long?

MOTHER (*rolling out of her*)   Till he comes; forever and ever till he comes!

CHRIS (*as an ultimatum*)   Mother, I'm going ahead with it.

MOTHER   Chris, I've never said no to you in my life, now I say no!

CHRIS   You'll never let him go till I do it.

MOTHER   I'll never let him go and you'll never let him go!

CHRIS   I've let him go. I've let him go a long—

MOTHER (*with no less force, but turning from him*)   Then let your father go.

> *Pause.* CHRIS *stands transfixed*

KELLER   She's out of her mind.

MOTHER   Altogether! (*To* CHRIS, *but not facing them*) Your brother's alive, darling, because if he's dead, your father killed him. Do you understand me now? As long as you live, that boy is alive. God does not let a son be killed by his father. Now you see, don't you? Now you see. (*Beyond control, she hurries up and into house*)

KELLER (—CHRIS *has not moved. He speaks insinuatingly, questioningly*)   She's out of her mind.

CHRIS (*in a broken whisper*)   Then . . . you did it?

KELLER (*with the beginning of plea in his voice*)   He never flew a P-40—

CHRIS (*struck; deadly*)   But the others.

KELLER (*insistently*)   She's out of her mind. (*He takes a step toward* CHRIS, *pleadingly*)

CHRIS (*unyielding*)   Dad . . . you did it?

KELLER   He never flew a P-40, what's the matter with you?

CHRIS (*still asking, and saying*)   Then you did it. To the others.

> *Both hold their voices down*

KELLER (*afraid of him, his deadly insistence*)   What's the matter with you? What the hell is the matter with you?

CHRIS (*quietly, incredibly*)   How could you do that? How?

KELLER   What's the matter with you!

CHRIS   Dad . . . Dad, you killed twenty-one men!

KELLER   What, killed?

CHRIS   You killed them, you murdered them.

KELLER (*as though throwing his whole nature open before* CHRIS)   How could I kill anybody?

CHRIS   Dad! Dad!

KELLER (*trying to hush him*)   I didn't kill anybody!

CHRIS   Then explain it to me. What did you do? Explain it to me or I'll tear you to pieces!

KELLER (*horrified at his overwhelming fury*)   Don't, Chris, don't—

CHRIS   I want to know what you did, now what did you do? You had a hundred and twenty cracked engine-heads, now what did you do?

KELLER   If you're going to hang me then I—

CHRIS   I'm listening. God Almighty, I'm listening!

KELLER (*—their movements now are those of subtle pursuit and escape.* KELLER *keeps a step out of* CHRIS'*s range as he talks*)   You're a boy, what could I do! I'm in business, a man is in business; a hundred and twenty cracked, you're out of business; you got a process, the process don't work you're out of business; you don't know how to operate, your stuff is no good; they close you up, they tear up your contracts, what the hell's it to them? You lay forty years into a business and they knock you out in five minutes, what could I do, let them take forty years, let them take my life away? (*His voice cracking*) I never thought they'd install them. I swear to God. I thought they'd stop 'em before anybody took off.

CHRIS   Then why'd you ship them out?

KELLER   By the time they could spot them I thought I'd have the process going again, and I could show them they needed me and they'd let it go by. But weeks passed and I got no kick-back, so I was going to tell them.

CHRIS   Then why didn't you tell them?

KELLER   It was too late. The paper, it was all over the front page, twenty-one went down, it was too late. They came with handcuffs into the shop, what could I do? (*He sits on bench*) Chris . . . Chris, I did it for you, it was a chance and I took it for you. I'm sixty-one years old, when would I have another chance to make something for you? Sixty-one years old you don't get another chance, do ya?

CHRIS   You even knew they wouldn't hold up in the air.

KELLER   I didn't say that.

CHRIS   But you were going to warn them not to use them—

KELLER   But that don't mean—

CHRIS   It means you knew they'd crash.

KELLER   It don't mean that.

CHRIS   Then you *thought* they'd crash.

KELLER   I was afraid maybe—

CHRIS   You were afraid maybe! God in heaven, what kind of a man are you? Kids were hanging in the air by those heads. You knew that!

KELLER   For you, a business for you!

CHRIS (*with burning fury*)   For me! Where do you live, where have you come from? For me!—I was dying every day and you were killing my boys and you did it for me? What the hell do you think I was thinking of, the Goddam business? Is that as far as your mind can see, the business? What is that, the world—the business? What the hell do you mean, you did it for me? Don't you have a country? Don't you live in the world? What the hell are you? You're not even an animal, no animal kills his own, what are you? What must I do to you? I ought to tear the tongue out of your mouth, what must I do? (*With his fist he pounds down upon his father's shoulder. He stumbles away, covering his face as he weeps*) What must I do, Jesus God, what must I do?

KELLER   Chris . . . My Chris . . .

CURTAIN

ACT THREE   *Two o'clock the following morning,* MOTHER *is discovered on the rise, rocking ceaselessly in a chair, staring at her thoughts. It is an intense, slight, sort of rocking. A light shows from upstairs bedroom, lower floor windows being dark. The moon is strong and casts its bluish light.*

   Presently JIM, *dressed in jacket and hat, appears, and seeing her, goes up beside her.*

JIM   Any news?

MOTHER   No news.

JIM (*gently*)   You can't sit up all night, dear, why don't you go to bed?

MOTHER   I'm waiting for Chris. Don't worry about me, Jim, I'm perfectly all right.

JIM   But it's almost two o'clock.

MOTHER   I can't sleep. (*Slight pause*) You had an emergency?

JIM (*tiredly*)   Somebody had a headache and thought he was dying. (*Slight pause*) Half of my patients are quite mad. Nobody realizes how many people are walking around loose, and they're cracked as coconuts. Money. Money-money-money-money. You say it long enough it doesn't mean anything.

She smiles, makes a silent laugh

Oh, how I'd love to be around when that happens!

MOTHER (*shaking her head*)   You're so childish, Jim! Sometimes you are.

JIM (*looks at her a moment*)   Kate. (*Pause*) What happened?

MOTHER   I told you. He had an argument with Joe. Then he got in the car and drove away.

JIM   What kind of argument?

MOTHER   An argument, Joe . . . He was crying like a child, before.

JIM   They argued about Ann?

MOTHER (*after slight hesitation*)   No, not Ann. Imagine? (*Indicates lighted window above*) She hasn't come out of that room since he left. All night in that room.

JIM (*looks at window, then at her*)   What'd Joe do, tell him?

MOTHER (*stops rocking*)   Tell him what?

JIM   Don't be afraid, Kate, I know. I've always known.

MOTHER   How?

JIM   It occurred to me a long time ago.

MOTHER   I always had the feeling that in the back of his head, Chris . . . almost knew. I didn't think it would be such a shock.

JIM (*gets up*)   Chris would never know how to live with a thing like that. It takes a certain talent—for lying. You have it, and I do. But not him.

MOTHER   What do you mean . . . He's not coming back?

JIM   Oh, no, he'll come back. We all come back, Kate. These private little revolutions always die. The compromise is always made. In a peculiar way. Frank is right—every man does have a star. The star of one's honesty. And you spend your life groping for it, but once it's out it never lights again. I don't think he went very far. He probably just wanted to be alone to watch his star go out.

MOTHER   Just as long as he comes back.

JIM   I wish he wouldn't, Kate. One year I simply took off, went to New Orleans; for two months I lived on bananas and milk, and studied a certain disease. It was beautiful. And then she came, and she cried. And I went back home with her. And now I live in the usual darkness; I can't find myself; it's even hard sometimes to remember the kind of man I wanted to be. I'm a good husband; Chris is a good son—he'll come back.

KELLER *comes out on porch in dressing gown and slippers. He goes upstage—to alley.* JIM *goes to him*

JIM   I have a feeling he's in the park. I'll look around for him. Put her to bed, Joe; this is no good for what she's got. (JIM *exits up driveway*)

KELLER (*coming down*)   What does he want here?

MOTHER   His friend is not home.

KELLER (*comes down to her. His voice is husky*)   I don't like him mixing in so much.

MOTHER   It's too late, Joe. He knows.

KELLER (*apprehensively*)   How does he know?

MOTHER   He guessed a long time ago.

KELLER   I don't like that.

MOTHER (*laughs dangerously, quietly into the line*)   What you don't like.

KELLER   Yeah, what I don't like.

MOTHER   You can't bull yourself through this one, Joe, you better be smart now. This thing—this thing is not over yet.

KELLER (*indicating lighted window above*)   And what is she doing up there? She don't come out of the room.

MOTHER   I don't know, what is she doing? Sit down, stop being mad. You want to live? You better figure out your life.

KELLER   She don't know, does she?

MOTHER   She saw Chris storming out of here. It's one and one—she knows how to add.

KELLER   Maybe I ought to talk to her?

MOTHER   Don't ask me, Joe.

KELLER (*—almost an outburst*)   Then who do I ask? But I don't think she'll do anything about it.

MOTHER   You're asking me again.

KELLER   I'm askin' you. What am I, a stranger? I thought I had a family here. What happened to my family?

MOTHER   You've got a family. I'm simply telling you that I have no strength to think any more.

KELLER   You have no strength. The minute there's trouble you have no strength.

MOTHER   Joe, you're doing the same thing again; all your life whenever there's trouble you yell at me and you think that settles it.

KELLER   Then what do I do? Tell me, talk to me, what do I do?

MOTHER   Joe . . . I've been thinking this way. If he comes back—

KELLER   What do you mean "if"? He's comin' back!

MOTHER   I think if you sit him down and you—explain yourself. I mean you ought to make it clear to him that you know you did a terrible thing. (*Not looking into his eyes*) I mean if he saw that you realize what you did. You see?

KELLER   What ice does that cut?

MOTHER (*a little fearfully*)   I mean if you told him that you want to pay for what you did.

KELLER (*sensing . . . quietly*)   How can I pay?

MOTHER   Tell him—you're willing to go to prison. (*Pause*)

KELLER (*struck, amazed*)   I'm willing to—?

MOTHER (*quickly*)   You wouldn't go, he wouldn't ask you to go. But if you told him you wanted to, if he could feel that you wanted to pay, maybe he would forgive you.

KELLER   He would forgive me! For what?

MOTHER   Joe, you know what I mean.

KELLER   I don't know what you mean! You wanted money, so I made
     money. What must I be forgiven? You wanted money, didn't you?

MOTHER   I didn't want it that way.

KELLER   I didn't want it that way, either! What difference is it what you
     want? I spoiled the both of you. I should've put him out when he was
     ten like I was put out, and make him earn his keep. Then he'd know
     how a buck is made in this world. Forgiven! I could live on a quarter a
     day myself, but I got a family so I—

MOTHER   Joe, Joe . . . It don't excuse it that you did it for the family.

KELLER   It's got to excuse it!

MOTHER   There's something bigger than the family to him.

KELLER   Nothin' is bigger!

MOTHER   There is to him.

KELLER   There's nothin' he could do that I wouldn't forgive. Because
     he's my son. Because I'm his father and he's my son.

MOTHER   Joe, I tell you—

KELLER   Nothin's bigger than that. And you're goin' to tell him, you
     understand? I'm his father and he's my son, and if there's something
     bigger than that I'll put a bullet in my head!

MOTHER   You stop that!

KELLER   You heard me. Now you know what to tell him. (*Pause. He
     moves from her—halts*) But he wouldn't put me away though . . . He
     wouldn't do that . . . Would he?

MOTHER   He loved you, Joe, you broke his heart.

KELLER   But to put me away . . .

MOTHER   I don't know. I'm beginning to think we don't really know
     him. They say in the war he was such a killer. Here he was always
     afraid of mice. I don't know him. I don't know what he'll do.

KELLER   Goddam, if Larry was alive he wouldn't act like this. He
     understood the way the world is made. He listened to me. To him the
     world had a forty-foot front, it ended at the building line. This one,
     everything bothers him. You make a deal, overcharge two cents, and
     his hair falls out. He don't understand money. Too easy, it came too
     easy. Yes, sir. Larry. That was a boy we lost. Larry. Larry. (*He
     slumps on chair in front of her*) What am I gonna do, Kate?

MOTHER   Joe, Joe, please . . . You'll be all right, nothing is going to
     happen.

KELLER (*desperately, lost*)   For you, Kate, for both of you, that's all I ever
     lived for . . .

MOTHER   I know, darling, I know.

                              ANN *enters from house. They say nothing, waiting for her to speak*

ANN   Why do you stay up? I'll tell you when he comes.

KELLER (*rises, goes to her*)   You didn't eat supper, did you? (*To* MOTHER)
     Why don't you make her something?

MOTHER   Sure, I'll—

ANN   Never mind, Kate, I'm all right. (*They are unable to speak to each other*) There's something I want to tell you. (*She starts, then halts*) I'm not going to do anything about it.

MOTHER   She's a good girl! (*To* KELLER) You see? She's a—

ANN   I'll do nothing about Joe, but you're going to do something for me. (*Directly to* MOTHER) You made Chris feel guilty with me. Whether you wanted to or not, you've crippled him in front of me. I'd like you to tell him that Larry is dead and that you know it. You understand me? I'm not going out of here alone. There's no life for me that way. I want you to set him free. And then I promise you, everything will end, and we'll go away, and that's all.

KELLER   You'll do that. You'll tell him.

ANN   I know what I'm asking, Kate. You had two sons. But you've only got one now.

KELLER   You'll tell him.

ANN   And you've got to say it to him so he knows you mean it.

MOTHER   My dear, if the boy was dead, it wouldn't depend on my words to make Chris know it. . . . The night he gets into your bed, his heart will dry up. Because he knows and you know. To his dying day he'll wait for his brother! No, my dear, no such thing. You're going in the morning, and you're going alone. That's your life, that's your lonely life. (*She goes to porch, and starts in*)

ANN   Larry is dead, Kate.

MOTHER (*—she stops*)   Don't speak to me.

ANN   I said he's dead. I know! He crashed off the coast of China November twenty-fifth! His engine didn't fail him. But he died. I know . . .

MOTHER   How did he die? You're lying to me. If you know, how did he die?

ANN   I loved him. You know I loved him. Would I have looked at anyone else if I wasn't sure? That's enough for you.

MOTHER (*moving on her*)   What's enough for me? What're you talking about? (*She grasps* ANN's *wrists*)

ANN   You're hurting my wrists.

MOTHER   What are you talking about! (*Pause. She stares at* ANN *a moment, then turns and goes to* KELLER)

ANN   Joe, go in the house.

KELLER   Why should I—

ANN   Please go.

KELLER   Lemme know when he comes. (KELLER *goes into house*)

MOTHER (*as she sees* ANN *taking a letter from her pocket*)   What's that?

ANN   Sit down.

MOTHER *moves left to chair, but does not sit*

First you've got to understand. When I came, I didn't have any idea that Joe—I had nothing against him or you. I came to get married. I hoped . . . So I didn't bring this to hurt you. I thought I'd show it to you only if there was no other way to settle Larry in your mind.

MOTHER   Larry? (*Snatches letter from* ANN's *hand*)

ANN   He wrote it to me just before he—

> MOTHER *opens and begins to read letter*

I'm not trying to hurt you, Kate. You're making me do this, now remember you're— Remember. I've been so lonely, Kate . . . I can't leave here alone again.

> *A long, low moan comes from* MOTHER's *throat as she reads*

You made me show it to you. You wouldn't believe me. I told you a hundred times, why wouldn't you believe me!

MOTHER   Oh, my God . . .

ANN (*with pity and fear*)   Kate, please, please . . .

MOTHER   My God, my God . . .

ANN   Kate, dear, I'm so sorry . . . I'm so sorry.

> CHRIS *enters from driveway. He seems exhausted*

CHRIS   What's the matter—?

ANN   Where were you? . . . You're all perspired.

> MOTHER *doesn't move*

Where were you?

CHRIS   Just drove around a little. I thought you'd be gone.

ANN   Where do I go? I have nowhere to go.

CHRIS (*to* MOTHER)   Where's Dad?

ANN   Inside lying down.

CHRIS   Sit down, both of you. I'll say what there is to say.

MOTHER   I didn't hear the car . . .

CHRIS   I left it in the garage.

MOTHER   Jim is out looking for you.

CHRIS   Mother . . . I'm going away. There are a couple of firms in Cleveland, I think I can get a place. I mean, I'm going away for good. (*To* ANN *alone*) I know what you're thinking, Annie. It's true. I'm yellow. I was made yellow in this house because I suspected my father and I did nothing about it, but if I knew that night when I came home what I know now, he'd be in the district attorney's office by this time, and I'd have brought him there. Now if I look at him, all I'm able to do is cry.

MOTHER   What are you talking about? What else can you do?

CHRIS   I could jail him! I could jail him, if I were human any more. But I'm like everybody else now. I'm practical now. You made me practical.

MOTHER   But you have to be.

CHRIS   The cats in that alley are practical, the bums who ran away when we were fighting were practical. Only the dead ones weren't practical. But now I'm practical, and I spit on myself. I'm going away. I'm going now.

ANN (*going up to him*)   I'm coming with you.

CHRIS   No, Ann.

ANN   Chris, I don't ask you to do anything about Joe.

CHRIS   You do, you do.

ANN   I swear I never will.

CHRIS   In your heart you always will.

ANN   Then do what you have to do!

CHRIS   Do what? What is there to do? I've looked all night for a reason
to make him suffer.

ANN   There's reason, there's reason!

CHRIS   What? Do I raise the dead when I put him behind bars? Then
what'll I do it for? We used to shoot a man who acted like a dog, but
honor was real there, you were protecting something. But here? This
is the land of the great big dogs, you don't love a man here, you eat
him! That's the principle; the only one we live by—it just happened to
kill a few people this time, that's all. The world's that way, how can I
take it out on him? What sense does that make? This is a zoo, a zoo!

ANN (*to* MOTHER)   You know what he's got to do! Tell him!

MOTHER   Let him go.

ANN   I won't let him go. You'll tell him what he's got to do . . .

MOTHER   Annie!

ANN   Then I will!

> KELLER *enters from house.* CHRIS *sees him, goes down near arbor*

KELLER   What's the matter with you? I want to talk to you.

CHRIS   I've got nothing to say to you.

KELLER (*taking his arm*)   I want to talk to you!

CHRIS (*pulling violently away from him*)   Don't do that, Dad. I'm going to
hurt you if you do that. There's nothing to say, so say it quick.

KELLER   Exactly what's the matter? What's the matter? You got too
much money? Is that what bothers you?

CHRIS (*with an edge of sarcasm*)   It bothers me.

KELLER   If you can't get used to it, then throw it away. You hear me?
Take every cent and give it to charity, throw it in the sewer. Does that
settle it? In the sewer, that's all. You think I'm kidding? I'm tellin'
you what to do, if it's dirty then burn it. It's your money, that's not my
money. I'm a dead man, I'm an old dead man, nothing's mine. Well,
talk to me! What do you want to do!

CHRIS   It's not what I want to do. It's what you want to do.

KELLER   What should I want to do?

> CHRIS *is silent*

Jail? You want me to go to jail? If you want me to go, say so! Is that
where I belong? Then tell me so! (*Slight pause*) What's the matter,
why can't you tell me? (*Furiously*) You say everything else to me, say
that! (*Slight pause*) I'll tell you why you can't say it. Because you
know I don't belong there. Because you know! (*With growing emphasis
and passion, and a persistent tone of desperation*) Who worked for nothin'
in that war? When they work for nothin', I'll work for nothin'. Did

they ship a gun or a truck outa Detroit before they got their price? Is that clean? It's dollars and cents, nickels and dimes; war and peace, it's nickels and dimes, what's clean? Half the Goddam country is gotta go if I go! That's why you can't tell me.

CHRIS   That's exactly why.

KELLER   Then . . . why am *I* bad?

CHRIS   *I* know you're no worse than most men but I thought you were better. I never saw you as a man. I saw you as my father. (*Almost breaking*) I can't look at you this way, I can't look at myself!

> *He turns away, unable to face* KELLER. ANN *goes quickly to* MOTHER, *takes letter from her and starts for* CHRIS. MOTHER *instantly rushes to intercept her*

MOTHER   Give me that!

ANN   He's going to read it! (*She thrusts letter into* CHRIS's *hand*) Larry. He wrote it to me the day he died.

KELLER   Larry!

MOTHER   Chris, it's not for you. (*He starts to read*) Joe . . . go away . . .

KELLER (*mystified, frightened*)   Why'd she say, Larry, what—?

MOTHER (*desperately pushes him toward alley, glancing at* CHRIS)   Go to the street, Joe, go to the street! (*She comes down beside* KELLER) Don't, Chris . . . (*Pleading from her whole soul*) Don't tell him.

CHRIS (*quietly*)   Three and one half years . . . talking, talking. Now you tell me what you must do. . . . This is how he died, now tell me where you belong.

KELLER (*pleading*)   Chris, a man can't be a Jesus in this world!

CHRIS   I know all about the world. I know the whole crap story. Now listen to this, and tell me what a man's got to be! (*Reads*) "My dear Ann: . . ." You listening? He wrote this the day he died. Listen, don't cry. . . . Listen! "My dear Ann: It is impossible to put down the things I feel. But I've got to tell you something. Yesterday they flew in a load of papers from the States and I read about Dad and your father being convicted. I can't express myself. I can't tell you how I feel—I can't bear to live any more. Last night I circled the base for twenty minutes before I could bring myself in. How could he have done that? Every day three or four men never come back and he sits back there doing business. . . . I don't know how to tell you what I feel. . . . I can't face anybody. . . . I'm going out on a mission in a few minutes. They'll probably report me missing. If they do, I want you to know that you mustn't wait for me. I tell you, Ann, if I had him there now I could kill him—"

> KELLER *grabs letter from* CHRIS's *hand and reads it. After a long pause:*

Now blame the world. Do you understand that letter?

KELLER (*speaking almost inaudibly*)   I think I do. Get the car. I'll put on my jacket.

He turns and starts slowly for the house. MOTHER *rushes to intercept him*

MOTHER   Why are you going?   You'll sleep, why are you going?

KELLER   I can't sleep here.   I'll feel better if I go.

MOTHER   You're so foolish.   Larry was your son too, wasn't he?   You know he'd never tell you to do this.

KELLER (*looking at letter in his hand*)   Then what is this if it isn't telling me? Sure, he was my son.   But I think to him they were all my sons.   And I guess they were, I guess they were.   I'll be right down. (*Exits into house*)

MOTHER (*to* CHRIS, *with determination*)   You're not going to take him!

CHRIS   I'm taking him.

MOTHER   It's up to you, if you tell him to stay he'll stay.   Go and tell him!

CHRIS   Nobody could stop him now.

MOTHER   You'll stop him!   How long will he live in prison?   Are you trying to kill him?

CHRIS (*holding out letter*)   I thought you read this!

MOTHER (*of Larry, the letter*)   The war is over!   Didn't you hear?   It's over!

CHRIS   Then what was Larry to you?   A stone that fell into the water? It's not enough for him to be sorry.   Larry didn't kill himself to make you and Dad sorry.

MOTHER   What more can we be!

CHRIS   You can be better!   Once and for all you can know there's a universe of people outside and you're responsible to it, and unless you know that, you threw away your son because that's why he died.

> *A shot is heard in the house.   They stand frozen for a brief second.*
> CHRIS *starts for porch, pauses at step, turns to* ANN

CHRIS   Find Jim!

> *He goes on into the house and* ANN *runs up driveway.* MOTHER *stands alone, transfixed*

MOTHER (*softly, almost moaning*)   Joe . . . Joe . . . Joe . . . Joe . . .

> CHRIS *comes out of house, down to* MOTHER*'s arms*

CHRIS (*almost crying*)   Mother, I didn't mean to—

MOTHER   Don't dear.   Don't take it on yourself.   Forget now.   Live.

> CHRIS *stirs as if to answer*

Shhh . . . (*She puts his arms down gently and moves toward porch*)
Shhh . . . (*As she reaches porch steps she begins sobbing*)

CURTAIN

Exercises   *1. What precisely is the conflict?   How is it resolved?*

2. Identify several complications and explain why they are complications.

3. *Discover examples of necessary background information (exposition) presented throughout the play.*

4. *For the purpose of achieving suspense, Miller plants bits of information here and there, withholding the complete facts until later. Cite a few examples.*

5. *Locate several speeches that help depict Keller's character. Locate the principal actions that reveal the kind of person he really is.*

6. *Describe Joe Keller.*

7. *Contrast the character of Keller with that of his son Chris.*

8. *Account for Keller's suicide.*

Topics for Writing

1. *Choose a character you wish to analyze. Paying particular attention to speeches and to actions, tell who he or she is, what he or she is, and what motivates him or her.*

2. *Verify the plausibility and consistency of Keller's character in his important decisions that affect the main action, including the final act.*

3. *Explain how Keller attains total or partial self-awareness.*

Selected Bibliography

Arthur Miller

Boggs, W. Arthur. "*Oedipus* and *All My Sons*." *The Personalist*, 42 (1956), 555–560.

Murray, Edward. *Arthur Miller, Dramatist*. New York: Ungar, 1967. Pages 1–21.

Nourse, J. T. *Arthur Miller's Death of a Salesman and All My Sons*. New York: Monarch, 1965.

Wells, Arvin R. "The Living and the Dead in *All My Sons*." *Modern Drama*, 7 (1961–62), 46–51.

Yorks, Samuel A. "Joe Keller and His Sons." *Western Humanities Review* 13 (1964), 401–407.

Paddy Chayefsky *(1923–)*

Born in New York City into what he has called "a standard Jewish family with standard Jewish values," he attended City College of New York, studied at the Hollywood Actor's Lab, performed in night clubs, and wrote plays for radio and motion pictures. Holiday Song *(1952), adapted from a* Reader's Digest *story, brought him his first television success.* Marty *(1953) won awards for him and Rod Steiger, the first actor to portray Marty. The film version, which is the text used here, received many accolades, including Oscars for Ernest Borgnine as Best Actor and for its producers for the Best Film of 1955. His major works include* Bachelor Party *(1957), a teleplay;* The Goddess *(1957), a screenplay;* The Tenth Man *(1959), a play that enjoyed a long successful run on Broadway;* The Passion of Josef *(1964), a stage play about Stalin; and* The Americanization of Emily *(1969), a screenplay.*

Marty

CAST

MARTY PILLETTI	BARTENDER
CLARA DAVIS	TWENTY-YEAR-OLD
ANGIE	ITALIAN WOMAN
MOTHER	SHORT GIRL
AUNT CATHERINE	GIRL
VIRGINIA	YOUNG MOTHER
THOMAS	STAG
YOUNG MAN	FORTY-YEAR-OLD
CRITIC	

ACT ONE   FADE-IN: *A butcher shop in the Italian district of New York City. Actually, we fade in on a close-up of a butcher's saw being carefully worked through a side of beef, and we dolly back to show the butcher at work, and then the whole shop. The butcher is a mild-mannered, stout, short, balding young man of thirty-six. His charm lies in an almost indestructible good-natured amiability.*

   The shop contains three women customers. One is a YOUNG MOTHER *with a baby carriage. She is chatting with a second woman of about forty at the door. The customer being waited on at the moment is a stout, elderly* ITALIAN WOMAN *who is standing on tiptoe, peering over the white display counter, checking the butcher as he saws away*

ITALIAN WOMAN   Your kid brother got married last Sunday, eh, Marty?

MARTY (*absorbed in his work*)   That's right, Missus Fusari. It was a very nice affair.

ITALIAN WOMAN   That's the big tall one, the fellow with the mustache.

MARTY (*sawing away*)   No, that's my other brother Freddie. My other brother Freddie, he's been married four years already. He lives down on Quincy Street. The one who got married Sunday, that was my little brother Nickie.

ITALIAN WOMAN   I thought he was a big, tall, fat fellow. Didn't I meet him here one time? Big, tall, fat fellow, he tried to sell me life insurance?

MARTY (*sets the cut of meat on the scale, watches its weight register*)   No, that's my sister Margaret's husband Frank. My sister Margaret, she's married to the insurance salesman. My sister Rose, she married a contractor. They moved to Detroit last year. And my other sister, Frances, she got married about two and a half years ago in Saint John's Church on Adams Boulevard. Oh, that was a big affair. Well, Missus Fusari, that'll be three dollars, ninety-four cents. How's that with you?

> The ITALIAN WOMAN *produces an old leather change purse from her pocketbook and painfully extracts three single dollar bills and ninety-four cents to the penny and lays the money piece by piece on the counter*

YOUNG MOTHER (*calling from the door*)   Hey, Marty, I'm inna hurry.

MARTY (*wrapping the meat, calls amiably back*)   You're next right now, Missus Canduso.

> The old ITALIAN WOMAN *has been regarding* MARTY *with a baleful scowl*

ITALIAN WOMAN   Well, Marty, when you gonna get married? You should be ashamed. All your brothers and sisters, they all younger than you, and they married, and they got children. I just saw your mother inna fruit shop, and she says to me: "Hey, you know a nice girl for my boy Marty?" Watsa matter with you? That's no way. Watsa matter with you? Now, you get married, you hear me what I say?

MARTY (*amiably*)   I hear you, Missus Fusari.

> The old lady takes her parcel of meat, but apparently feels she still hasn't quite made her point

ITALIAN WOMAN   My son Frank, he was married when he was nineteen years old. Watsa matter with you?

MARTY   Missus Fusari, Missus Canduso over there, she's inna big hurry, and . . .

ITALIAN WOMAN   You be ashamed of yourself.

She takes her package of meat, turns, and shuffles to the door and exits. MARTY *gathers up the money on the counter, turns to the cash register behind him to ring up the sale*

YOUNG MOTHER   Marty, I want a nice big fat pullet, about four pounds. I hear your kid brother got married last Sunday.

MARTY   Yeah, it was a very nice affair, Missus Canduso.

YOUNG MOTHER   Marty, you oughtta be ashamed. All your kid brothers and sisters, married and have children. When you gonna get married?

> CLOSE-UP: MARTY. *He sends a glance of weary exasperation up to the ceiling. With a gesture of mild irritation, he pushes the plunger of the cash register. It makes a sharp ping.*

> DISSOLVE TO: *Close-up of television set. A baseball game is in progress. Camera pulls back to show we are in a typical neighborhood bar—red leatherette booths—a jukebox, some phone booths. About half the bar stools are occupied by neighborhood folk.* MARTY *enters, pads amiably to one of the booths where a young man of about thirty-odd already sits. This is* ANGIE. MARTY *slides into the booth across from* ANGIE. ANGIE *is a little wasp of a fellow. He has a newspaper spread out before him to the sports pages.* MARTY *reaches over and pulls one of the pages over for himself to read. For a moment the two friends sit across from each other, reading the sports pages. Then* ANGIE, *without looking up, speaks*

ANGIE   Well, what do you feel like doing tonight?

MARTY   I don't know, Angie. What do you feel like doing?

ANGIE   Well, we oughtta do something. It's Saturday night. I don't wanna go bowling like last Saturday. How about calling up that big girl we picked up inna movies about a month ago in the RKO Chester?

MARTY (*not very interested*)   Which one was that?

ANGIE   That big girl that was sitting in front of us with the skinny friend.

MARTY   Oh, yeah.

ANGIE   We took them home alla way out in Brooklyn. Her name was Mary Feeney. What do you say? You think I oughtta give her a ring? I'll take the skinny one.

MARTY   It's five o'clock already, Angie. She's probably got a date by now.

ANGIE   Well, let's call her up. What can we lose?

MARTY   I didn't like her, Angie. I don't feel like calling her up.

ANGIE   Well, what do you feel like doing tonight?

MARTY   I don't know. What do you feel like doing?

ANGIE   Well, we're back to that, huh? I say to you: "What do you feel like doing tonight?" And you say to me: "I don't know, what do you feel like doing?" And then we wind up sitting around your house with a couple of cans of beer, watching Sid Caesar on television. Well, I tell you what I feel like doing. I feel like calling up this Mary Feeney. She likes you.

> MARTY *looks up quickly at this*

MARTY   What makes you say that?

ANGIE   I could see she likes you.

MARTY   Yeah, sure.

ANGIE (*half rising in his seat*)   I'll call her up.

MARTY   You call her up for yourself, Angie. I don't feel like calling her up.

> ANGIE *sits down again. They both return to reading the paper for a moment. Then* ANGIE *looks up again*

ANGIE   Boy, you're getting to be a real drag, you know that?

MARTY   Angie, I'm thirty-six years old. I been looking for a girl every Saturday night of my life. I'm a little, short, fat fellow, and girls don't go for me, that's all. I'm not like you. I mean, you joke around, and they laugh at you, and you get along fine. I just stand around like a bug. What's the sense of kidding myself? Everybody's always telling me to get married. Get married. Get married. Don't you think I wanna get married? I wanna get married. They drive me crazy. Now, I don't wanna wreck your Saturday night for you, Angie. You wanna go somewhere, you go ahead. I don't wanna go.

ANGIE   Boy, they drive me crazy too. My old lady, every word outta her mouth, when you gonna get married?

MARTY   My mother, boy, she drives me crazy.

> ANGIE *leans back in his seat, scowls at the paper-napkin container.* MARTY *returns to the sports page. For a moment a silence hangs between them. Then . . .*

ANGIE   So what do you feel like doing tonight?

MARTY (*without looking up*)   I don't know. What do you feel like doing?

> *They both just sit,* ANGIE *frowning at the napkin container,* MARTY *at the sports page.*
>
> *The camera slowly moves away from the booth, looks down the length of the bar, up the wall, past the clock—which reads ten to five—and over to the television screen, where the baseball game is still going on.*
>
> DISSOLVE SLOWLY TO: *The television screen, now blank. The clock now reads a quarter to six.*
>
> *Back in the booth,* MARTY *now sits alone. In front of him are three empty beer bottles and a beer glass, half filled. He is sitting there, his face expressionless, but his eyes troubled. Then he pushes himself slowly out of the booth and shuffles to the phone booth; he goes inside, closing the booth door carefully after him. For a moment* MARTY *just sits squatly. Then with some exertion—due to the cramped quarters—he contrives to get a small address book out of his rear pants pocket. He slowly flips through it, finds the page he wants, and studies it, scowling; then he takes a dime from the change he has just received, plunks it into the proper slot, waits for a dial tone . . . then carefully dials a number. . . . He waits. He is*

> *beginning to sweat a bit in the hot little booth, and his chest begins to*
> *rise and fall deeply*

MARTY (*with a vague pretense at good diction*)   Hello, is this Mary Feeney?
. . . Could I please speak to Miss Mary Feeney? . . . Just tell her an
old friend . . . (*He waits again. With his free hand he wipes the gathering
sweat from his brow*) . . . Oh, hello there, is this Mary Feeney? Hello
there, this is Marty Pilletti. I wonder if you recall me . . . Well, I'm
kind of a stocky guy. The last time we met was inna movies, the RKO
Chester. You was with another girl, and I was with a friend of mine
name Angie. This was about a month ago . . .

> *The girl apparently doesn't remember him. A sort of panic begins to*
> *seize* MARTY. *His voice rises a little*

The RKO Chester on Payne Boulevard. You was sitting in front of us,
and we was annoying you, and you got mad, and . . . I'm the fellow
who works inna butcher shop . . . come on, you know who I am! . . .
That's right, we went to Howard Johnson's and we had hamburgers.
You hadda milk shake . . . Yeah, that's right. I'm the stocky one, the
heavy-set fellow. . . . Well, I'm glad you recall me, because I hadda
swell time that night, and I was just wondering how everything was with
you. How's everything? . . . That's swell . . . Yeah, well, I'll tell
you why I called . . . I was figuring on taking in a movie tonight, and I
was wondering if you and your friend would care to see a movie tonight
with me and my friend . . . (*his eyes are closed now*) Yeah, tonight. I
know it's pretty late to call for a date, but I didn't know myself till . . .
Yeah, I know, well how about . . . Yeah, I know, well maybe next
Saturday night. You free next Saturday night? . . . Well, how about
the Saturday after that? . . . Yeah, I know . . . Yeah . . . Yeah . . .
Oh, I understand, I mean . . .

> *He just sits now, his eyes closed, not really listening. After a moment*
> *he returns the receiver to its cradle and sits, his shoulders slack, his*
> *hands resting listlessly in the lap of his spotted white apron. . . .*
> *Then he opens his eyes, straightens himself, pushes the booth door*
> *open, and advances out into the bar. He perches on a stool across the*
> *bar from the* BARTENDER, *who looks up from his magazine*

BARTENDER   I hear your kid brother got married last week, Marty.

MARTY (*looking down at his hands on the bar*)   Yeah, it was a very nice affair.

BARTENDER   Well, Marty, when you gonna get married?

> MARTY *tenders the bartender a quick scowl, gets off his perch, and*
> *starts for the door—untying his apron as he goes*

MARTY   If my mother calls up, Lou, tell her I'm on my way home.

> DISSOLVE TO: *Marty's* MOTHER *and a young couple sitting*
> *around the table in the dining room of Marty's home. The young*
> *couple—we will soon find out—are* THOMAS, *Marty's cousin, and*
> *his wife,* VIRGINIA. *They have apparently just been telling the*
> *mother some sad news, and the three are sitting around frowning.*

*The dining room is a crowded room filled with chairs and
lamps, pictures and little statues, perhaps even a small grotto of little
vigil lamps. To the right of the dining room is the kitchen,
old-fashioned, Italian, steaming, and overcrowded. To the left of the
dining room is the living room, furnished in same fashion as the
dining room. Just off the living room is a small bedroom, which is
Marty's. This bedroom and the living room have windows looking
out on front. The dining room has windows looking out to side
alleyway. A stairway in the dining room leads to the second floor.*

The MOTHER *is a round, dark, effusive little woman*

MOTHER (*after a pause*)   Well, Thomas, I knew sooner or later this was
gonna happen. I told Marty, I said: "Marty, you watch. There's
gonna be real trouble over there in your cousin Thomas' house."
Because your mother was here, Thomas, you know?

THOMAS   When was this, Aunt Theresa?

MOTHER   This was one, two, three days ago. Wednesday. Because I
went to the fruit shop on Wednesday, and I came home. And I come
arounna back, and there's your mother sitting onna steps onna porch.
And I said: "Catherine, my sister, wadda you doing here?" And she
look uppa me, and she beganna cry.

THOMAS (*to his wife*)   Wednesday. That was the day you threw the milk
bottle.

MOTHER   That's right. Because I said to her: "Catherine, watsa matter?" And she said to me: "Theresa, my daughter-in-law, Virginia,
she just threw the milk bottle at me."

VIRGINIA   Well, you see what happen, Aunt Theresa . . .

MOTHER   I know, I know . . .

VIRGINIA   She comes inna kitchen, and she begins poking her head over
my shoulder here and poking her head over my shoulder there . . .

MOTHER   I know, I know . . .

VIRGINIA   And she begins complaining about this, and she begins complaining about that. And she got me so nervous, I spilled some milk I
was making for the baby. You see, I was making some food for the
baby, and . . .

MOTHER   So I said to her, "Catherine . . ."

VIRGINIA   So, she got me so nervous I spilled some milk. So she said:
"You're spilling the milk." She says: "Milk costs twenty-four cents a
bottle. Wadda you, a banker?" So I said: "Mama, leave me alone,
please. You're making me nervous. Go on in the other room and turn
on the television set." So then she began telling me how I waste
money, and how I can't cook, and how I'm raising my baby all wrong,
and she kept talking about these couple of drops of milk I spilt, and I
got so mad, I said: "Mama, you wanna see me really spill some milk?"
So I took the bottle and threw it against the door. I didn't throw it at
her. That's just something she made up. I didn't throw it anywheres
near her. Well, of course, alla milk went all over the floor. The whole

twenty-four cents. Well, I was sorry right away, you know, but she ran outta the house.

> *Pause*

MOTHER   Well, I don't know what you want me to do, Virginia. If you want me, I'll go talk to her tonight.

> THOMAS *and* VIRGINIA *suddenly frown and look down at their hands as if of one mind*

THOMAS   Well, I'll tell you, Aunt Theresa . . .

VIRGINIA   Lemme tell it, Tommy.

THOMAS   Okay.

VIRGINIA (*leaning forward to the* MOTHER)   We want you to do a very big favor for us, Aunt Theresa.

MOTHER   Sure.

VIRGINIA   Aunt Theresa, you got this big house here. You got four bedrooms upstairs. I mean, you got this big house just for you and Marty. All your other kids are married and got their own homes. And I thought maybe Tommy's mother could come here and live with you and Marty.

MOTHER   Well . . .

VIRGINIA   She's miserable living with Tommy and me, and you're the only one that gets along with her. Because I called up Tommy's brother, Joe, and I said: "Joe, she's driving me crazy. Why don't you take her for a couple of years?" And he said: "Oh, no!" I know I sound like a terrible woman . . .

MOTHER   No, Virginia, I know how you feel. My husband, may God bless his memory, his mother, she lived with us for a long time, and I know how you feel.

VIRGINIA (*practically on the verge of tears*)   I just can't stand it no more! Every minute of the day! Do this! Do that! I don't have ten minutes alone with my husband! We can't even have a fight! We don't have no privacy! Everybody's miserable in our house!

THOMAS   All right, Ginnie, don't get so excited.

MOTHER   She's right. She's right. Young husband and wife, they should have their own home. And my sister, Catherine, she's my sister, but I gotta admit, she's an old goat. And plenny-a times in my life I feel like throwing the milk bottle at her myself. And I tell you now, as far as I'm concerned, if Catherine wantsa come live here with me and Marty, it's all right with me.

> VIRGINIA *promptly bursts into tears*

THOMAS (*not far from tears himself, lowers his face*)   That's very nice-a you, Aunt Theresa.

MOTHER   We gotta ask Marty, of course, because this is his house too. But he's gonna come home any minute now.

VIRGINIA (*having mastered her tears*)   That's very nice-a you, Aunt Theresa.

MOTHER (*rising*)   Now, you just sit here. I'm just gonna turn onna small fire under the food. (*She exits into the kitchen*)

VIRGINIA (*calling after her*)   We gotta go right away because I promised the baby sitter we'd be home by six, and it's after six now . . .

> *She kind of fades out. A moment of silence.* THOMAS *takes out a cigarette and lights it*

THOMAS (*calling to his aunt in the kitchen*)   How's Marty been lately, Aunt Theresa?

MOTHER (*off in kitchen*)   Oh, he's fine. You know a nice girl he can marry? (*She comes back into the dining room, wiping her hands on a kitchen towel*) I'm worried about him, you know? He's thirty-six years old, gonna be thirty-seven in January.

THOMAS   Oh, he'll get married, don't worry, Aunt Theresa.

MOTHER (*sitting down again*)   Well, I don't know. You know a place where he can go where he can find a bride?

THOMAS   The Waverly Ballroom. That's a good place to meet girls, Aunt Theresa. That's a kind of big dance hall, Aunt Theresa. Every Saturday night, it's just loaded with girls. It's a nice place to go. You pay seventy-seven cents. It used to be seventy-seven cents. It must be about a buck and a half now. And you go in and you ask some girl to dance. That's how I met Virginia. Nice, respectable place to meet girls. You tell Marty, Aunt Theresa, you tell him: "Go to the Waverly Ballroom. It's loaded with tomatoes."

MOTHER (*committing the line to memory*)   The Waverly Ballroom. It's loaded with tomatoes.

THOMAS   Right.

VIRGINIA   You tell him, go to the Waverly Ballroom.

> *There is the sound of a door being unlatched off through the kitchen. The* MOTHER *promptly rises*

MOTHER   He's here.

> *She hurries into the kitchen. At the porch entrance to the kitchen,* MARTY *has just come in. He is closing the door behind him. He carries his butcher's apron in a bundle under his arm*

MARTY   Hello, Ma.

> *She comes up to him, lowers her voice to a whisper*

MOTHER (*whispers*)   Marty, Thomas and Virginia are here. They had another big fight with your Aunt Catherine. So they ask me, would it be all right if Catherine come to live with us. So I said, all right with me, but we have to ask you. Marty, she's a lonely old lady. Nobody wants her. Everybody's throwing her outta their house. . . .

MARTY   Sure, Ma, it's okay with me.

> *The* MOTHER'S *face breaks into a fond smile. She reaches up and pats his cheek with genuine affection*

MOTHER   You gotta good heart. (*Turning and leading the way back to the dining room.* THOMAS *has risen*) He says okay, it's all right Catherine comes here.

THOMAS   Oh, Marty, thanks a lot. That really takes a load offa my mind.

MARTY   Oh, we got plenny-a room here.

MOTHER   Sure! Sure! It's gonna be nice! It's gonna be nice! I'll come over tonight to your house, and I talk to Catherine, and you see, everything is gonna work out all right.

THOMAS   I just wanna thank you people again because the situation was just becoming impossible.

MOTHER   Siddown, Thomas, siddown. All right, Marty, siddown. . . .
          She exits into the kitchen.
                    MARTY *has taken his seat at the head of the table and is waiting to be served.* THOMAS *takes a seat around the corner of the table from him and leans across to him*

THOMAS   You see, Marty, the kinda thing that's been happening in our house is Virginia was inna kitchen making some food for the baby. Well, my mother comes in, and she gets Virginia so nervous, she spills a couple-a drops . . .

VIRGINIA (*tugging at her husband*)   Tommy, we gotta go. I promise the baby sitter six o'clock.

THOMAS (*rising without interrupting his narrative*)   So she starts yelling at Virginia, waddaya spilling the milk for. So Virginia gets mad . . .
          His wife is slowly pulling him to the kitchen door
          She says, "You wanna really see me spill milk?" So Virginia takes the bottle and she throws it against the wall. She's got a real Italian temper, my wife, you know that . . .
          He has been tugged to the kitchen door by now

VIRGINIA   Marty, I don't have to tell you how much we appreciate what your mother and you are doing for us.

THOMAS   All right, Marty, I'll see you some other time . . . I'll tell you all about it.

MARTY   I'll see you, Tommy.
          THOMAS *disappears into the kitchen after his wife*

VIRGINIA (*off, calling*)   Good-by, Marty!
          Close in on MARTY, *sitting at table*

MARTY   Good-by, Virginia! See you soon!
          He folds his hands on the table before him and waits to be served.
                    The MOTHER *enters from the kitchen. She sets the meat plate down in front of him and herself takes a chair around the corner of the table from him.* MARTY *without a word takes up his knife and fork and attacks the mountain of food in front of him. His mother sits quietly, her hands a little nervous on the table before her, watching him eat. Then . . .*

MOTHER   So what are you gonna do tonight, Marty?

MARTY   I don't know, Ma. I'm all knocked out. I may just hang arounna house.
          The MOTHER *nods a couple of times. There is a moment of silence. Then . . .*

MOTHER   Why don't you go to the Waverly Ballroom?
          This gives MARTY *pause. He looks up*

MARTY   What?

MOTHER   I say, why don't you go to the Waverly Ballroom? It's loaded with tomatoes.

MARTY regards his mother for a moment

MARTY   It's loaded with what?

MOTHER   Tomatoes.

MARTY (*snorts*)   Ha! Who told you about the Waverly Ballroom?

MOTHER   Thomas, he told me it was a very nice place.

MARTY   Oh, Thomas. Ma, it's just a big dance hall, and that's all it is. I been there a hundred times. Loaded with tomatoes. Boy, you're funny, Ma.

MOTHER   Marty, I don't want you hang arounna house tonight. I want you to go take a shave and go out and dance.

MARTY   Ma, when are you gonna give up? You gotta bachelor on your hands. I ain't never gonna get married.

MOTHER   You gonna get married.

MARTY   Sooner or later, there comes a point in a man's life when he gotta face some facts, and one fact I gotta face is that whatever it is that women like, I ain't got it. I chased enough girls in my life. I went to enough dances. I got hurt enough. I don't wanna get hurt no more. I just called a girl this afternoon, and I got a real brush-off, boy. I figured I was past the point of being hurt, but that hurt. Some stupid woman who I didn't even wanna call up. She gave me the brush. That's the history of my life. I don't wanna go to the Waverly Ballroom because all that ever happened to me there was girls made me feel like I was a bug. I got feelings, you know. I had enough pain. No, thank you.

MOTHER   Marty . . .

MARTY   Ma, I'm gonna stay home and watch Sid Caesar.

MOTHER   You gonna die without a son.

MARTY   So I'll die without a son.

MOTHER   Put on your blue suit . . .

MARTY   Blue suit, gray suit, I'm still a fat little man. A fat little ugly man.

MOTHER   You not ugly.

MARTY (*his voice rising*)   I'm ugly . . . I'm ugly! . . . I'm UGLY!

MOTHER   Marty . . .

MARTY (*crying aloud, more in anguish than in anger*)   Ma! Leave me alone! . . . (*He stands abruptly, his face pained and drawn. He makes half-formed gestures to his mother, but he can't find words at the moment. He turns and marches a few paces away, turns to his mother again*) Ma, waddaya want from me?! Waddaya want from me?! I'm miserable enough as it is! Leave me alone! I'll go to the Waverly Ballroom! I'll put onna blue suit and I'll go! And you know what I'm gonna get for my trouble? Heartache! A big night of heartache! (*He sullenly marches back to his seat, sits down, picks up his fork, plunges it into the lasagna, and stuffs a mouthful into his mouth; he chews vigorously for a moment. It is impossible to*

remain angry for long. After a while he is shaking his head and muttering)
Loaded with tomatoes . . . boy, that's rich . . .

> *He plunges his fork in again. Camera pulls slowly away from him*
> *and his mother, who is seated—watching him*

FADE OUT

ACT TWO   FADE IN: *Exterior, three-story building. Pan up to second floor . . . bright neon lights reading "Waverly Ballroom" . . . The large, dirty windows are open; and the sound of a fair-to-middling swing band whooping it up comes out.*

    DISSOLVE TO: *Interior, Waverly Ballroom—large dance floor crowded with jitterbugging couples, eight-piece combination hitting a loud kick. Ballroom is vaguely dark, made so by papier-mâché over the chandeliers to create alleged romantic effect. The walls are lined with stags and waiting girls, singly and in small murmuring groups. Noise and mumble and drone.*

    DISSOLVE TO: *Live shot—a row of stags along a wall. Camera is looking lengthwise down the row. Camera dollies slowly past each face, each staring out at the dance floor, watching in his own manner of hungry eagerness. Short, fat, tall, thin stags. Some pretend diffidence. Some exhibit patent hunger.*

    Near the end of the line, we find MARTY *and* ANGIE, *freshly shaved and groomed. They are leaning against the wall, smoking, watching their more fortunate brethren out on the floor.*

ANGIE   Not a bad crowd tonight, you know?

MARTY   There was one nice-looking one there in a black dress and beads, but she was a little tall for me.

ANGIE (*looking down past* MARTY *along the wall right into the camera*)   There's a nice-looking little short one for you right now.

MARTY (*following his gaze*)   Where?

ANGIE   Down there. That little one there.

> *The camera cuts about eight faces down, to where the girls are now standing. Two are against the wall. One is facing them, with her back to the dance floor. This last is the one* ANGIE *has in mind. She is a cute little kid, about twenty, and she has a bright smile on—as if the other two girls are just amusing her to death.*

MARTY   Yeah, she looks all right from here.

ANGIE   Well, go on over and ask her. You don't hurry up, somebody else'll grab her.

> MARTY *scowls, shrugs*

MARTY   Okay, let's go.

> *They slouch along past the eight stags, a picture of nonchalant unconcern. The three girls, aware of their approach, stiffen, and*

ANGIE *their chatter comes to a halt.* ANGIE *advances to one of the girls along the wall*

ANGIE   Waddaya say, you wanna dance?

The girl looks surprised—as if this were an extraordinary invitation to receive in this place—looks confounded at her two friends, shrugs, detaches herself from the group, moves to the outer fringe of the pack of dancers, raises her hand languidly to dancing position, and awaits ANGIE *with ineffable boredom.* MARTY, *smiling shyly, addresses the short girl*

MARTY   Excuse me, would you care for this dance?

The short girl gives MARTY *a quick glance of appraisal, then looks quickly at her remaining friend*

SHORT GIRL (*not unpleasantly*)   Sorry. I just don't feel like dancing just yet.

MARTY   Sure.

He turns and moves back past the eight stags, all of whom have covertly watched his attempt. He finds his old niche by the wall, leans there. A moment later he looks guardedly down to where the short girl and her friend are. A young, dapper boy is approaching the short girl. He asks her to dance. The short girl smiles, excuses herself to her friend, and follows the boy out onto the floor. MARTY *turns back to watching the dancers bleakly. A moment later he is aware that someone on his right is talking to him. . . . He turns his head. It is a young man of about twenty-eight*

MARTY   You say something to me?

YOUNG MAN   Yeah. I was just asking you if you was here stag or with a girl.

MARTY   I'm stag.

YOUNG MAN   Well, I'll tell you. I got stuck onna blind date with a dog, and I just picked up a nice chick, and I was wondering how I'm gonna get ridda the dog. Somebody to take her home, you know what I mean? I be glad to pay you five bucks if you take the dog home for me.

MARTY (*a little confused*)   What?

YOUNG MAN   I'll take you over, and I'll introduce you as an old army buddy of mine, and then I'll cut out. Because I got this chick waiting for me out by the hatcheck, and I'll pay you five bucks.

MARTY (*stares at the* YOUNG MAN)   Are you kidding?

YOUNG MAN   No, I'm not kidding.

MARTY   You can't just walk off onna girl like that.

The YOUNG MAN *grimaces impatiently and moves down the line of stags. . . .* MARTY *watches him, still a little shocked at the proposition. About two stags down, the* YOUNG MAN *broaches his plan to another* STAG. *This* STAG, *frowning and pursing his lips, seems more receptive to the idea. . . . The* YOUNG MAN *takes out a wallet and gives the* STAG *a five-dollar bill. The* STAG *detaches*

himself from the wall and, a little ill at ease, follows the YOUNG
MAN *back past* MARTY *and into the lounge.* MARTY *pauses a
moment and then, concerned, walks to the archway that separates the
lounge from the ballroom and looks in.*

*The lounge is a narrow room with a bar and booths. In contrast
to the ballroom, it is brightly lighted—causing* MARTY *to squint.*

In the second booth from the archway sits a GIRL, *about
twenty-eight. Despite the careful grooming that she has put into her
cosmetics, she is blatantly plain. The* YOUNG MAN *and the* STAG
are standing, talking to her. She is looking up at the YOUNG MAN,
*her hands nervously gripping her Coca-Cola glass. We cannot hear
what the* YOUNG MAN *is saying, but it is apparent that he is
introducing his new-found army buddy and is going through some
cock-and-bull story about being called away on an emergency. The*
STAG *is presented as her escort-to-be, who will see to it that she gets
home safely. The* GIRL *apparently is not taken in at all by this,
though she is trying hard not to seem affected.*

She politely rejects the STAG's *company and will get home by
herself, thanks for asking anyway. The* YOUNG MAN *makes a few
mild protestations, and then he and the* STAG *leave the booth and come
back to the archway from where* MARTY *has been watching the scene.
As they pass* MARTY, *we overhear a snatch of dialogue*

YOUNG MAN   . . . In that case, as long as she's going home alone, give
me the five bucks back. . . .

STAG   . . . Look, Mac, you paid me five bucks. I was willing. It's my five
bucks. . . .

They pass on. MARTY *returns his attention to the* GIRL. *She is
still sitting as she was, gripping and ungripping the glass of
Coca-Cola in front of her. Her eyes are closed. Then, with a little
nervous shake of her head, she gets out of the booth and stands—
momentarily at a loss for what to do next. The open fire doors leading
out onto the large fire escape catch her eye. She crosses to the fire
escape, nervous, frowning, and disappears outside.*

MARTY *stares after her, then slowly shuffles to the open
fire-escape doorway. It is a large fire escape, almost the size of a
small balcony. The* GIRL *is standing by the railing, her back to the
doorway, her head slunk on her bosom. For a moment* MARTY *is
unaware that she is crying. Then he notices the shivering tremors
running through her body and the quivering shoulders. He moves a
step onto the fire escape. He tries to think of something to say*

MARTY   Excuse me, Miss. Would you care to dance?

The GIRL *slowly turns to him, her face streaked with tears, her lip
trembling. Then, in one of those peculiar moments of simultaneous
impulse, she lurches to* MARTY *with a sob, and* MARTY *takes her to
him. For a moment they stand in an awkward embrace,* MARTY *a
little embarrassed, looking out through the doors to the lounge,*

wondering if anybody is seeing them. Reaching back with one hand, he closes the fire doors, and then, replacing the hand around her shoulder, he stands stiffly, allowing her to cry on his chest.

DISSOLVE TO: Exterior, apartment door. The MOTHER *is standing, in a black coat and a hat with a little feather, waiting for her ring to be answered. The door opens.* VIRGINIA *stands framed in the doorway*

VIRGINIA Hello, Aunt Theresa, come in.

The MOTHER *goes into the small foyer.* VIRGINIA *closes the door*

MOTHER (*in a low voice, as she pulls her coat off*) Is Catherine here?

VIRGINIA (*helps her off with coat, nods—also in a low voice*) We didn't tell her nothing yet. We thought we'd leave it to you. We thought you'd put it like how you were lonely, and why don't she come to live with you. Because that way it looks like she's doing you a favor, insteada we're throwing her out, and it won't be so cruel on her. Thomas is downstairs with the neighbors . . . I'll go call him.

MOTHER You go downstairs to the neighbors and stay there with Thomas.

VIRGINIA Wouldn't it be better if we were here?

MOTHER You go downstairs. I talk to Catherine alone. Otherwise, she's gonna start a fight with you.

A shrill, imperious woman's voice from an offstage room suddenly breaks into the muttered conference in the foyer

AUNT (*off*) Who's there?! Who's there?!

The MOTHER *heads up the foyer to the living room, followed by* VIRGINIA, *holding the* MOTHER's *coat*

MOTHER (*calls back*) It's me, Catherine! How you feel?

At the end of the foyer, the two sisters meet. The AUNT *is a spare, gaunt woman with a face carved out of granite. Tough, embittered, deeply hurt type of face*

AUNT Hey! What are you doing here?

MOTHER I came to see you. (*The two sisters quickly embrace and release each other*) How you feel?

AUNT I gotta pain in my left side and my leg throbs like a drum.

MOTHER I been getting pains in my shoulder.

AUNT I got pains in my shoulder, too. I have a pain in my hip, and my right arm aches so much I can't sleep. It's a curse to be old. How you feel?

MOTHER I feel fine.

AUNT That's nice.

Now that the standard greetings are over, AUNT CATHERINE *abruptly turns and goes back to her chair. It is obviously her chair. It is an old, heavy oaken chair with thick armrests. The rest of the apartment is furnished in what is known as "modern"—a piece from* House Beautiful *here, a piece from* Better Homes and Gardens *there.* AUNT CATHERINE *sits, erect and forbidding, in her chair.*

The MOTHER *seats herself with a sigh in a neighboring chair.*
VIRGINIA, *having hung the* MOTHER's *coat, now turns to the two
older woman. A pause*

VIRGINIA   I'm going downstairs to the Cappacini's. I'll be up inna little
while.

AUNT CATHERINE *nods expressionlessly.* VIRGINIA *looks at her
for a moment, then impulsively crosses to her mother-in-law*

VIRGINIA   You feel all right?

The old lady looks up warily, suspicious of this sudden solicitude

AUNT   I'm all right.

VIRGINIA *nods and goes off to the foyer. The two old sisters sit,
unmoving, waiting for the door to close behind* VIRGINIA. *Then the*
MOTHER *addresses herself to* AUNT CATHERINE

MOTHER   We gotta post card from my son, Nickie, and his bride this
morning. They're in Florida inna big hotel. Everything is very nice.

AUNT   That's nice.

MOTHER   Catherine, I want you come live with me in my house with
Marty and me. In my house, you have your own room. You don't
have to sleep onna couch inna living room like here.

The AUNT *looks slowly and directly at the* MOTHER

Catherine, your son is married. He got his own home. Leave him in
peace. He wants to be alone with his wife. They don't want no old
lady sitting inna balcony. Come and live with me. We will cook in the
kitchen and talk like when we were girls. You are dear to me, and you
are dear to Marty. We are pleased for you to come.

AUNT   Did they come to see you?

MOTHER   Yes.

AUNT   Did my son Thomas come with her?

MOTHER   Your son Thomas was there.

AUNT   Did he also say he wishes to cast his mother from his house?

MOTHER   Catherine, don't make an opera outta this. The three-a you
anna baby live in three skinny rooms. You are an old goat, and she has
an Italian temper. She is a good girl, but you drive her crazy. Leave
them alone. They have their own life.

The old AUNT *turns her head slowly and looks her sister square in the
face. Then she rises slowly from her chair*

AUNT (coldly)   Get outta here. This is my son's house. This is where I
live. I am not to be cast out inna street like a newspaper.

The MOTHER *likewise rises. The two old women face each other
directly*

MOTHER   Catherine, you are very dear to me. We have cried many times
together. When my husband died, I would have gone insane if it were
not for you. I ask you to come to my house because I can make you
happy. Please come to my house.

The two sisters regard each other. Then AUNT CATHERINE *sits
again in her oaken chair, and the* MOTHER *returns to her seat. The*

hardened muscles in the old AUNT's *face suddenly slacken, and she turns to her sister*

AUNT   Theresa, what shall become of me?

MOTHER   Catherine . . .

AUNT   It's gonna happen to you. Mark it well. These terrible years. I'm afraida look inna mirror. I'm afraid I'm gonna see an old lady with white hair, like the old ladies inna park, little bundles inna black shawl, waiting for the coffin. I'm fifty-six years old. What am I to do with myself? I have strength in my hands. I wanna cook. I wanna clean. I wanna make dinner for my children. I wanna be of use to somebody. Am I an old dog to lie in fronta the fire till my eyes close? These are terrible years, Theresa! Terrible years!

MOTHER   Catherine, my sister . . .

The old AUNT *stares, distraught, at the* MOTHER

AUNT   It's gonna happen to you! It's gonna happen to you! What will you do if Marty gets married?! What will you cook?! What happen to alla children tumbling in alla rooms?! Where is the noise?! It is a curse to be a widow! A curse! What will you do if Marty gets married?! What will you do?!

> *She stares at the* MOTHER—*her deep, gaunt eyes haggard and pained. The* MOTHER *stares back for a moment, then her own eyes close. The* AUNT *has hit home. The* AUNT *sinks back onto her chair, sitting stiffly, her arms on the thick armrests. The* MOTHER *sits hunched a little forward, her hands nervously folded in her lap*

(*Quietly*)   I will put my clothes inna bag and I will come to you tomorrow.

> *The camera slowly dollies back from the two somber sisters.*
> SLOW FADE-OUT.
> CUT TO: *Close-up, intimate,* MARTY *and the* GIRL *dancing cheek to cheek. Occasionally the heads of other couples slowly waft across the camera view, temporarily blocking out view of* MARTY *and the* GIRL. *Camera stays with them as the slow dance carries them around the floor. Tender scene*

GIRL   . . . The last time I was here the same sort of thing happened.

MARTY   Yeah?

GIRL   Well, not exactly the same thing. The last time I was up here about four months ago. Do you see that girl in the gray dress sitting over there?

MARTY   Yeah.

GIRL   That's where I sat. I sat there for an hour and a half without moving a muscle. Now and then, some fellow would sort of walk up to me and then change his mind. I just sat there, my hands in my lap. Well, about ten o'clock, a bunch of kids came in swaggering. They weren't more than seventeen, eighteen years old. Well, they swaggered down along the wall, leering at all the girls. I thought they were kind of cute . . . and as they passed me, I smiled at them. One of the kids looked at me and said: "Forget it, ugly, you ain't gotta chance." I burst out crying. I'm a big crier, you know.

MARTY   So am I.

GIRL   And another time when I was in college . . .

MARTY   I cry alla time. Any little thing. I can recognize pain a mile away. My brothers, my brother-in-laws, they're always telling me what a goodhearted guy I am. Well, you don't get goodhearted by accident. You get kicked around long enough you get to be a real professor of pain. I know exactly how you feel. And I also want you to know I'm having a very good time with you now and really enjoying myself. So you see, you're not such a dog as you think you are.

GIRL   I'm having a very good time too.

MARTY   So there you are. So I guess I'm not such a dog as I think I am.

GIRL   You're a very nice guy, and I don't know why some girl hasn't grabbed you off long ago.

MARTY   I don't know either. I think I'm a very nice guy. I also think I'm a pretty smart guy in my own way.

GIRL   I think you are.

MARTY   I'll tell you some of my wisdom which I thunk up on those nights when I got stood up, and nights like that, and you walk home thinking: "Watsa matter with me? I can't be that ugly." Well, I figure, two people get married, and they gonna live together forty, fifty years. So it's just gotta be more than whether they're good-looking or not. My father was a real ugly man, but my mother adored him. She told me that she used to get so miserable sometimes, like everybody, you know? And she says my father always tried to understand. I used to see them sometimes when I was a kid, sitting in the living room, talking and talking, and I used to adore my old man because he was so kind. That's one of the most beautiful things I have in my life, the way my father and my mother were. And my father was a real ugly man. So it don't matter if you look like a gorilla. So you see, dogs like us, we ain't such dogs as we think we are.

They dance silently for a moment, cheeks pressed against each other. Close-ups of each face

GIRL   I'm twenty-nine years old. How old are you?

MARTY   Thirty-six.

They dance silently, closely. Occasionally the heads of other couples sway in front of the camera, blocking our view of MARTY *and the* GIRL. *Slow, sweet dissolve.*

DISSOLVE TO: Interior, kitchen, MARTY's *home. Later that night. It is dark. Nobody is home. The rear porch door now opens, and the silhouettes of* MARTY *and the* GIRL *appear—blocking up the doorway*

MARTY   Wait a minute. Lemme find the light.

He finds the light. The kitchen is suddenly brightly lit. The two of them stand squinting to adjust to the sudden glare

I guess my mother ain't home yet. I figure my cousin Thomas and Virginia musta gone to the movies, so they won't get back till one o'clock, at least.

> *The* GIRL *has advanced into the kitchen, a little ill at ease, and is looking around.* MARTY *closes the porch door*

This is the kitchen.

GIRL   Yes, I know.

> MARTY *leads the way into the dining room*

MARTY   Come on inna dining room. (*He turns on the light in there as he goes. The* GIRL *follows him in*) Siddown, take off your coat. You want something to eat? We gotta whole halfa chicken left over from yesterday.

GIRL (*perching tentatively on the edge of a chair*)   No, thank you. I don't think I should stay very long.

MARTY   Sure. Just take off your coat a minute.

> *He helps her off with her coat and stands for a moment behind her, looking down at her. Conscious of his scrutiny, she sits uncomfortably, her breasts rising and falling unevenly.* MARTY *takes her coat into the dark living room. The* GIRL *sits patiently, nervously.* MARTY *comes back, sits down on another chair. Awkward silence*

So I was telling you, my kid brother Nickie got married last Sunday . . . That was a very nice affair. And they had this statue of some woman, and they had whisky spouting outta her mouth. I never saw anything so grand in my life. (*The silence falls between them again*) And watta meal. I'm a butcher, so I know a good hunka steak when I see one. That was choice filet, right off the toppa the chuck. A buck-eighty a pound. Of course, if you wanna cheaper cut, get rib steak. That gotta lotta waste on it, but it comes to about a buck and a quarter a pound, if it's trimmed. Listen, Clara, make yourself comfortable. You're all tense.

GIRL   Oh, I'm fine.

MARTY   You want me to take you home, I'll take you home.

GIRL   Maybe that would be a good idea.

> *She stands. He stands, frowning, a little angry—turns sullenly and goes back into the living room for her coat. She stands unhappily. He comes back and wordlessly starts to help her into her coat. He stands behind her, his hands on her shoulders. He suddenly seizes her, begins kissing her on the neck. Camera comes up quickly to intensely intimate close-up, nothing but the heads. The dialogue drops to quick, hushed whispers*

No, Marty, please . . .

MARTY   I like you, I like you, I been telling you all night I like you . . .

GIRL   Marty . . .

MARTY   I just wanna kiss, that's all . . .

> *He tries to turn her face to him. She resists*

GIRL   No . . .

MARTY   Please . . .

GIRL   No . . .

MARTY   Please . . .

GIRL   Marty . . .

> *He suddenly releases her, turns away violently*

MARTY (*crying out*)   All right! I'll take you home! All right! (*He marches a few angry paces away, deeply disturbed. Turns to her*) All I wanted was a lousy kiss! What am I, a leper or something?!

> *He turns and goes off into the living room to hide the flush of hot tears threatening to fill his eyes. The* GIRL *stands, herself on the verge of tears*

GIRL (*mutters, more to herself than to him*)   I just didn't feel like it, that's all.

> *She moves slowly to the archway leading to the living room.* MARTY *is sitting on the couch, hands in his lap, looking straight ahead. The room is dark except for the overcast of the dining-room light reaching in. The* GIRL *goes to the couch, perches on the edge beside him. He doesn't look at her*

MARTY   Well, that's the history of my life. I'm a little, short, fat, ugly guy. Comes New Year's Eve, everybody starts arranging parties, I'm the guy they gotta dig up a date for. I'm old enough to know better. Let me get a packa cigarettes, and I'll take you home.

> *He starts to rise, but doesn't . . . sinks back onto the couch, looking straight ahead. The* GIRL *looks at him, her face peculiarly soft and compassionate*

GIRL   I'd like to see you again, very much. The reason I didn't let you kiss me was because I just didn't know how to handle the situation. You're the kindest man I ever met. The reason I tell you this is because I want to see you again very much. Maybe, I'm just so desperate to fall in love that I'm trying too hard. But I know that when you take me home, I'm going to just lie on my bed and think about you. I want very much to see you again.

> MARTY *stares down at his hands in his lap*

MARTY (*without looking at her*)   Waddaya doing tomorrow night?

GIRL   Nothing.

MARTY   I'll call you up tomorrow morning. Maybe we'll go see a movie.

GIRL   I'd like that very much.

MARTY   The reason I can't be definite about it now is my Aunt Catherine is probably coming over tomorrow, and I may have to help out.

GIRL   I'll wait for your call.

MARTY   We better get started to your house because the buses only run about one an hour now.

GIRL   All right.

> *She stands*

MARTY   I'll just get a packa cigarettes.

> *He goes into his bedroom. We can see him through the doorway, opening his bureau drawer and extracting a pack of cigarettes. He*

comes out again and looks at the girl for the first time. They start to walk to the dining room. In the archway, MARTY *pauses, turns to the* GIRL

Waddaya doing New Year's Eve?

GIRL   Nothing.

They quietly slip into each other's arms and kiss. Slowly their faces part, and MARTY's *head sinks down upon her shoulder. He is crying. His shoulders shake slightly. The* GIRL *presses her cheek against the back of his head. They stand . . . there is the sound of the rear porch door being unlatched. They both start from their embrace. A moment later the* MOTHER's *voice is heard off in the kitchen*

MOTHER   Hallo! Hallo, Marty? (*She comes into the dining room, stops at the sight of the* GIRL) Hallo, Marty, when you come home?

MARTY   We just got here about fifteen minutes ago, Ma. Ma, I want you to meet Miss Clara Davis. She's a graduate of New York University. She teaches history in Benjamin Franklin High School.

This seems to impress the MOTHER

MOTHER   Siddown, siddown. You want some chicken? We got some chicken in the icebox.

GIRL   No, Mrs. Pilletti, we were just going home. Thank you very much anyway.

MOTHER   Well, siddown a minute. I just come inna house. I'll take off my coat. Siddown a minute. (*She pulls her coat off*)

MARTY   How'd you come home, Ma? Thomas give you a ride?

The MOTHER *nods*

MOTHER   Oh, it's a sad business, a sad business.

She sits down on a dining-room chair, holding her coat in her lap. She turns to the GIRL, *who likewise sits*

My sister Catherine, she don't get along with her daughter-in-law, so she's gonna come live with us.

MARTY   Oh, she's coming, eh, Ma?

MOTHER   Oh, sure. (*To the* GIRL) It's a very sad thing. A woman, fifty-six years old, all her life, she had her own home. Now, she's just an old lady, sleeping on her daughter-in-law's couch. It's a curse to be a mother, I tell you. Your children grow up and then what is left for you to do? What is a mother's life but her children? It is a very cruel thing when your son has no place for you in his home.

GIRL   Couldn't she find some sort of hobby to fill out her time?

MOTHER   Hobby! What can she do? She cooks and she cleans. You gotta have a house to clean. You gotta have children to cook for. These are the terrible years for a woman, the terrible years.

GIRL   You mustn't feel too harshly against her daughter-in-law. She also wants to have a house to clean and a family to cook for.

The MOTHER *darts a quick, sharp look at the* GIRL—*then looks back to her hands which are beginning to twist nervously*

MOTHER   You don't think my sister Catherine should live in her daughter-in-law's house?

GIRL   Well, I don't know the people, of course, but, as a rule, I don't think a mother-in-law should live with a young couple.

MOTHER   Where do you think a mother-in-law should go?

GIRL   I don't think a mother should depend so much upon her children for her rewards in life.

MOTHER   That's what it says in the book in New York University. You wait till you are a mother. It don't work out that way.

GIRL   Well, it's silly for me to argue about it. I don't know the people involved.

MARTY   Ma, I'm gonna take her home now. It's getting late, and the buses only run about one an hour.

MOTHER (*standing*)   Sure.

The GIRL *stands*

GIRL   It was very nice meeting you, Mrs. Pilletti. I hope I'll see you again.

MOTHER   Sure.

MARTY *and the* GIRL *move to the kitchen*

MARTY   All right, Ma. I'll be back in about an hour.

MOTHER   Sure.

GIRL   Good night, Mrs. Pilletti.

MOTHER   Good night.

> MARTY *and the* GIRL *exit into the kitchen. The* MOTHER *stands, expressionless, by her chair watching them go. She remains standing rigidly even after the porch door can be heard being opened and shut. The camera moves up to a close-up of the* MOTHER. *Her eyes are wide. She is staring straight ahead. There is fear in her eyes*

FADE OUT

ACT THREE   FADE-IN: *Film—close-up of church bells clanging away. Pan down church to see typical Sunday morning, people going up the steps of a church and entering. It is a beautiful June morning.*

> DISSOLVE TO: *Interior, Marty's bedroom—sun fairly streaming through the curtains.* MARTY *is standing in front of his bureau, slipping his arms into a clean white shirt. He is freshly shaved and groomed. Through the doorway of his bedroom we can see the* MOTHER *in the dining room, in a coat and hat, all set to go to Mass, taking the last breakfast plates away and carrying them into the kitchen. The camera moves across the living room into the dining room. The* MOTHER *comes out of the kitchen with a paper napkin and begins crumbing the table.*

> *There is a knock on the rear porch door. The* MOTHER *leaves*

her crumbling and goes into the kitchen. Camera goes with her. She opens the rear door to admit AUNT CATHERINE, *holding a worn old European carpetbag. The* AUNT *starts to go deeper into the kitchen, but the* MOTHER *stays her with her hand.*

MOTHER (*in low, conspiratorial voice*)   Hey, I come home from your house last night, Marty was here with a girl.

AUNT   Who?

MOTHER   Marty.

AUNT   Your son Marty?

MOTHER   Well, what Marty you think is gonna be here in this house with a girl?

AUNT   Were the lights on?

MOTHER   Oh, sure. (*Frowns suddenly at her sister*)   The girl is a college graduate.

AUNT   They're the worst. College girls are one step from the streets. They smoke like men inna saloon.

> *The* AUNT *puts her carpetbag down and sits on one of the wooden kitchen chairs. The* MOTHER *sits on another*

MOTHER   That's the first time Marty ever brought a girl to this house. She seems like a nice girl. I think he has a feeling for this girl.

> *At this moment a burst of spirited whistling emanates from* MARTY's *bedroom.*
>
> CUT TO: MARTY's *bedroom*—MARTY *standing in front of his mirror, buttoning his shirt or adjusting his tie, whistling a gay tune.*
>
> CUT BACK TO: *The two sisters, both their faces turned in the direction of the whistling. The whistling abruptly stops. The two sisters look at each other. The* AUNT *shrugs*

He been whistling like that all morning.

> *The* AUNT *nods bleakly*

AUNT   He is bewitched. You will see. Today, tomorrow, inna week, he's gonna say to you: "Hey, Ma, it's no good being a single man. I'm tired running around." Then he's gonna say: "Hey, Ma, wadda we need this old house? Why don't we sell this old house, move into a nicer parta town? A nice little apartment?"

MOTHER   I don't sell this house, I tell you that. This is my husband's house, and I had six children in this house.

AUNT   You will see. A couple-a months, you gonna be an old lady, sleeping onna couch in your daughter-in-law's house.

MOTHER   Catherine, you are a blanket of gloom. Wherever you go, the rain follows. Some day, you gonna smile, and we gonna declare a holiday.

> *Another burst of spirited whistling comes from* MARTY, *off. It comes closer, and* MARTY *now enters in splendid spirits, whistling away. He is slipping into his jacket*

MARTY (*ebulliently*)   Hello, Aunt Catherine! How are you? You going to Mass with us?

AUNT   I was at Mass two hours ago.

MARTY   Well, make yourself at home. The refrigerator is loaded with food. Go upstairs, take any room you want. It's beautiful outside, ain't it?

AUNT   There's a chill. Watch out, you catch a good cold and pneumonia.

MOTHER   My sister Catherine, she can't even admit it's a beautiful day.

> MARTY—*now at the sink, getting himself a glass of water—is examining a piece of plaster that has fallen from the ceiling*

MARTY (*examining the chunk of plaster in his palm*)   Boy, this place is really coming to pieces. (*Turns to* MOTHER) You know, Ma, I think, sometime we oughta sell this place. The plumbing is rusty— everything. I'm gonna have to replaster that whole ceiling now. I think we oughta get a little apartment somewheres in a nicer parta town. . . . You all set, Ma?

MOTHER   I'm all set.

> *She starts for the porch door. She slowly turns and looks at* MARTY, *and then at* AUNT CATHERINE—*who returns her look.* MOTHER *and* MARTY *exit.*
>
> DISSOLVE TO: *Church. The* MOTHER *comes out of the doors and down a few steps to where* MARTY *is standing, enjoying the clearness of the June morning*

MOTHER   In a couple-a minutes nine o'clock Mass is gonna start—in a couple-a minutes . . . (*To passers-by off*) hallo, hallo . . . (*To* MARTY) Well, that was a nice girl last night, Marty. That was a nice girl.

MARTY   Yeah.

MOTHER   She wasn't a very good-looking girl, but she look like a nice girl. I said, she wasn't a very good-looking girl, not very pretty.

MARTY   I heard you, Ma.

MOTHER   She look a little old for you, about thirty-five, forty years old?

MARTY   She's twenny-nine, Ma.

MOTHER   She's more than twenny-nine years old, Marty. That's what she tells you. She looks thirty-five, forty. She didn't look Italian to me. I said, is she an Italian girl?

MARTY   I don't know. I don't think so.

MOTHER   She don't look like Italian to me. What kinda family she come from? There was something about her I don't like. It seems funny, the first time you meet her she comes to your empty house alone. These college girls, they all one step from the streets.

> MARTY *turns, frowning, to his* MOTHER

MARTY   What are you talkin' about? She's a nice girl.

MOTHER   I don't like her.

MARTY   You don't like her? You only met her for two minutes.

MOTHER   Don't bring her to the house no more.

MARTY   What didn't you like about her?

MOTHER   I don't know! She don't look like Italian to me, plenty nice Italian girls around.

MARTY   Well, let's not get into a fight about it, Ma. I just met the girl. I
    probably won't see her again.

> MARTY *leaves frame*

MOTHER   Eh, I'm no better than my sister Catherine.

> DISSOLVE TO: *Interior, the bar . . . about an hour later. The
> after-Mass crowd is there, about six men ranging from twenty to
> forty. A couple of women in the booths. One woman is holding a
> glass of beer in one hand and is gently rocking a baby carriage with
> the other.*
>
> *Sitting in the booth of Act One are* ANGIE *and three other
> fellows, ages twenty, thirty-two, and forty. One of the fellows, aged
> thirty-two, is giving a critical resumé of a recent work of literature by
> Mickey Spillane*

CRITIC   . . . So the whole book winds up, Mike Hammer, he's inna room
    there with this doll. So he says: "You rat, you are the murderer." So
    she begins to con him, you know? She tells him how she loves him.
    And then Bam! He shoots her in the stomach. So she's laying there,
    gasping for breath, and she says: "How could you do that?" And he
    says: "It was easy."

TWENTY-YEAR-OLD   Boy, that Mickey Spillane. Boy, he can write.

ANGIE (*leaning out of the booth and looking down the length of the bar, says with some
    irritation*)   What's keeping Marty?

CRITIC   What I like about Mickey Spillane is he knows how to handle
    women. In one book, he picks up a tomato who gets hit with a car, and
    she throws a pass at him. And then he meets two beautiful twins, and
    they throw passes at him. And then he meets some beautiful society
    leader, and she throws a pass at him, and . . .

TWENTY-YEAR-OLD   Boy, that Mickey Spillane, he sure can write . . .

ANGIE (*looking out, down the bar again*)   I don't know watsa matter with
    Marty.

FORTY-YEAR-OLD   Boy, Angie, what would you do if Marty ever died?
    You'd die right with him. A couple-a old bachelors hanging to each
    other like barnacles. There's Marty now.

> ANGIE *leans out of the booth*

ANGIE (*calling out*)   Hello, Marty, where you been?

> CUT TO: *Front end of the bar.* MARTY *has just come in. He waves
> back to* ANGIE, *acknowledges another hello from a man by the bar,
> goes over to the bar, and gets the bartender's attention*

MARTY   Hello, Lou, gimme change of a half and put a dime in it for a
    telephone call.

> *The* BARTENDER *takes the half dollar, reaches into his apron pocket
> for the change*

BARTENDER   I hear you was at the Waverly Ballroom last night.

MARTY   Yeah. Angie tell you?

BARTENDER (*picking out change from palm full of silver*)   Yeah, I hear you real-
    ly got stuck with a dog.

MARTY *looks at him*

MARTY   She wasn't so bad.

BARTENDER (*extending the change*)   Angie says she was a real scrawny-looking thing. Well, you can't have good luck alla time.

> MARTY *takes the change slowly and frowns down at it. He moves down the bar and would make for the telephone booth, but* ANGIE *hails him from the booth*

ANGIE   Who you gonna call, Marty?

MARTY   I was gonna call that girl from last night, take her to a movie tonight.

ANGIE   Are you kidding?

MARTY   She was a nice girl. I kinda liked her.

ANGIE (*indicating the spot in the booth vacated by the* FORTY-YEAR-OLD)   Sid-down. You can call her later.

> MARTY *pauses, frowning, and then shuffles to the booth where* ANGIE *and the other two sit. The* CRITIC *moves over for* MARTY. *There is an exchange of hellos*

TWENTY-YEAR-OLD   I gotta girl, she's always asking me to marry her. So I look at that face, and I say to myself: "Could I stand looking at that face for the resta my life?"

CRITIC   Hey, Marty, you ever read a book called *I, the Jury,* by Mickey Spillane?

MARTY   No.

ANGIE   Listen, Marty, I gotta good place for us to go tonight. The kid here, he says, he was downna bazaar at Our Lady of Angels last night and . . .

MARTY   I don't feel like going to the bazaar, Angie. I thought I'd take this girl to a movie.

ANGIE   Boy, you really musta made out good last night.

MARTY   We just talked.

ANGIE   Boy, she must be some talker. She musta been about fifty years old.

CRITIC   I always figger a guy oughtta marry a girl who's twenny years younger than he is, so that when he's forty, his wife is a real nice-looking doll.

TWENTY-YEAR-OLD   That means he'd have to marry the girl when she was one year old.

CRITIC   I never thoughta that.

MARTY   I didn't think she was so bad-looking.

ANGIE   She musta kept you inna shadows all night.

CRITIC   Marty, you don't wanna hang around with dogs. It gives you a bad reputation.

ANGIE   Marty, let's go downna bazaar.

MARTY   I told this dog I was gonna call her today.

ANGIE   Brush her.

> MARTY *looks questioningly at* ANGIE

MARTY   You didn't like her at all?

ANGIE   A nothing. A real nothing.

> MARTY *looks down at the dime he has been nervously turning between two fingers and then, frowning, he slips it into his jacket pocket. He lowers his face and looks down, scowling at his thoughts. Around him, the voices clip along*

CRITIC   What's playing on Fordham Road? I think there's a good picture in the Loew's Paradise.

ANGIE   Let's go down to Forty-second Street and walk around. We're sure to wind up with something.

> *Slowly* MARTY *begins to look up again. He looks from face to face as each speaks*

CRITIC   I'll never forgive La Guardia for cutting burlesque outta New York City.

TWENTY-YEAR-OLD   There's burlesque over in Union City. Let's go to Union City. . . .

ANGIE   Ah, they're always crowded on Sunday night.

CRITIC   So wadda you figure on doing tonight, Angie?

ANGIE   I don't know. Wadda you figure on doing?

CRITIC   I don't know. (*Turns to the* TWENTY-YEAR-OLD) Wadda you figure on doing?

> *The* TWENTY-YEAR-OLD *shrugs.*
>
> *Suddenly* MARTY *brings his fist down on the booth table with a crash. The others turn, startled, toward him.* MARTY *rises in his seat*

MARTY   "What are you doing tonight?" "I don't know, what are you doing?" Burlesque! Loew's Paradise! Miserable and lonely! Miserable and lonely and stupid! What am I, crazy or something?! I got something good! What am I hanging around with you guys for?!

> *He has said this in tones so loud that it attracts the attention of everyone in the bar. A little embarrassed,* MARTY *turns and moves quickly to the phone booth, pausing outside the door to find his dime again.* ANGIE *is out of his seat immediately and hurries after him*

ANGIE (*a little shocked at* MARTY'*s outburst*)   Watsa matter with you?

MARTY (*in a low, intense voice*)   You don't like her. My mother don't like her. She's a dog, and I'm a fat, ugly little man. All I know is I had a good time last night. I'm gonna have a good time tonight. If we have enough good times together, I'm going down on my knees and beg that girl to marry me. If we make a party again this New Year's, I gotta date for the party. You don't like her, that's too bad. (*He moves into the booth, sits, turns again to* ANGIE, *smiles*) When you gonna get married, Angie? You're thirty-four years old. All your kid brothers are married. You oughtta be ashamed of yourself.

> *Still smiling at his private joke, he puts the dime into the slot and then—with a determined finger—he begins to dial*

> FADE OUT

1. *Summarize the actions that move the plot forward.*

2. *List several complications.*

3. *What purpose is served by the subplot that involves Aunt Catherine?*

4. *By what means are the bartender, the stag, and the critic characterized? Explain their roles in the play.*

5. *What is the dramatic function of Angie?*

6. *What aspect of Marty's character is dramatized in Act One when he gives quick approval to Aunt Catherine's coming to live with him and his mother? Illustrate the consistency of this trait in Marty's future decisions or actions.*

7. *Identify speeches that help you "infer" the character of Clara Davis or Marty's mother.*

8. *What significance can you ascribe to Marty's final speech?*

Topics for Writing 1. *Characterize Marty by the actions he takes and the speeches he makes. Is he innocent? Stupid? Ugly? Weak? Good?*

2. *Discuss the following student's statement of theme: "How a bug and a dog can find love and happiness in a room full of tomatoes." Or express and discuss your version of the major theme of the play.*

Selected Bibliography Paddy Chayefsky

Goldstein, Malcolm. "Body and Soul on Broadway." *Modern Drama*, 7 (February 1965), 411–421.

Lewis, A. "Man's Relation to God—MacLeish, Chayefsky." *American Plays and Playwrights of the Contemporary Theatre*. New York: Crown Publishers, 1970. Pages 116–128.

Sayre, Nora, and Robert B. Silvers. "An Interview with Paddy Chayefsky." *Horizon*, 3 (September 1960), 50–56.

Weales, G. C. "The Video Boys." In *American Drama since World War II*. New York: Harcourt, Brace & World, 1962. Pages 57–75.

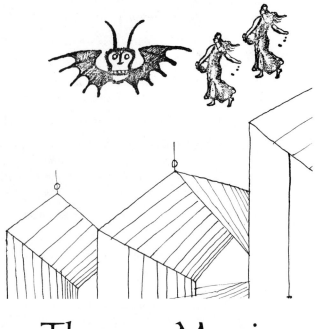

3 Theme or Meaning

The theme or meaning of a play—some truth about human life or experience—is contained mainly in and revealed chiefly by the actions and speeches of the characters. It exists in the dramatic story itself, not outside it.

Usually playwrights are avid readers and profound thinkers. Like most people they possess attitudes that make up a philosophy of life. Intentionally or not these attitudes invade the action and dialogue of the characters, and from those dialogues a reader or spectator derives meaning.

Concerned as playwrights are with people and problems, they serve us in their dramas the myriad issues and concerns and the innumerable complexities of life's imperishable diet. In most dramas that have endured the test of time, we discover dramatists pondering the themes of universal truth, the relationships and interrelationships of men and women, their society, and the forces in control of the universe. What the playwrights have to say about life may be far-reaching or piddling, true or false. And they may lead us to perceive these truths, half-truths, and lies by being glaringly obvious or deviously subtle.

Although drama seldom expresses a philosophy of life or a *modus vivendi* with society in a wholly systematic way, we can usually depend upon some element of plot, characterization, action, or all the elements together (the complete story itself) to give us glimpses of meaning, if not total meaning. In so many plays do we glean behind the action some code of psychological, moral, or ethical beliefs. Because the heart of drama beats with actions and words that exhibit human life, it must inevitably carry some conclusion about life. In searching for interpretation, we must, then, endeavor to make intelligible what that conclusion is.

Let us review several plays for the purpose of discovering theme through several elements of plot. Oedipus has vowed to appease the gods and end the pestilence in Thebes by bringing to justice the unpunished murderer of Laïos. Once he discovers the murderer to be himself and learns of his marriage to his mother, who bore him two sons and two daughters, he blinds himself and asks to be exiled. In the course of the action, Oedipus defies the gods and what they prophesied for him. Was Oedipus's arrogance a sin against the gods? Does one of the major themes, then, focus on a struggle that pits man against the gods?

We might also look at Keller, who, in *All My Sons*, has made his fortune by manufacturing airplane parts, some of which he delivered to the Air Force knowing full well that the parts were defective. When Keller is exposed for his crime, he commits suicide. This incident, the resolution in the play, suggests at least one important theme. That is, it points to the American dream of success, which, in this case, finds Keller irresponsible and deceived. His reckless pursuit of the mighty dollar-god and the trifles it can buy, his complete abandonment of humanistic values, have destroyed him. How could this theme be stated?

In *Tea and Sympathy*, Anderson shows us a conflict in which Tom Lee, a sensitive young man in a prep school, is believed to be a homosexual on the flimsiest of circumstantial evidence. His friends call him a queer because his hair is long and he walks funny. Immediately we are offered clues to possible interpretations. Should prejudice be the basis upon which a verdict is rendered? Should anyone be adjudged guilty without a substantiation of the facts? In this case what would your theme be? At the point of resolution in the play, Tom is afforded the opportunity he sought earlier with Ellie Martin. What has happened here? Has Tom found true love? Has he at last proved his manhood, at least to himself? Do you think the playwright intends to say that sexual love can be pure and spiritual outside the institution of marriage?

In *The Emperor Jones*, Jones, who has cheated, robbed, and killed during most of his adult life, now manages to fast-talk and slick-trick himself into the position of emperor of an island in the West Indies. The natives, who have reached the breaking point, pursue this tyrant, and shoot him. But what really destroys Jones are his own fears and superstitions. What likely themes does this play suggest? A person cannot escape his past. A person must repay society for the crimes he has committed against it. Would either of those statements represent fairly suitable, thematic capsules?

Finally, in the play by Chayevsky, when Marty makes a call to Clara Davis on the telephone, he is, in fact, rejecting the narrow-minded influences of his background; he is instead moving toward accepting the stranger he met in a dime-a-dance hall as his Cinderella. Why? Perhaps the playwright wishes to prove that it is possible for two lonely, physically unattractive people from two different worlds to find real, romantic love.

Sometimes a subplot will mirror the main plot, as in the Marie-Turk relationship in *Come Back, Little Sheba*, and so contribute to the meaning of the play. On other occasions the very forces in conflict with one another will shed light on what the playwright intends to say to us. If, for example, *Riders to the Sea* presents a conflict between people and the sea, a theme central to the story must consequently express something about people and the sea. Similarly, if *Romeo and Juliet* treats idealized love, surely the play must have something to say about idealized love. The drama may be saying that this kind of love is immortal.

Frequently, the study of main characters will lead us to discover meaning. Under the pressures of conflict a character speaks not only as a mouthpiece of the playwright, but more importantly, as a human being in the throes of developing new insights and attitudes as a consequence of actions taken or refused. The character of Oedipus, for example, is central to an understanding of this Sophoclean drama. Here is a strong human will arrogantly bent on challenging the will of the gods. Oedipus vows to bring to justice the murderer of Laïos; he persists in searching for his identity; he refuses to believe the prophecy; he did, in fact, murder his father and marry his mother; he blinds himself and demands exile. What is the nature of such a man? What motivates him? Could we not extract a theme from our understanding of this character?

In another cursory look at a protagonist, Maurya in *Riders to the Sea*, we must conclude that she is a dynamic character. She grows with the pain she must endure. At first she is clearly a mother, especially before Bartley leaves to do what he must, trying to keep her son from going to sea. But after her vision, she accepts Bartley's death as fact, and after her last dead son is brought into the shack, she surrenders almost stoically to her destiny. She will cry no more. She will at long last have peace of mind. Could you phrase a theme that encompasses Maurya's resignation?

We might also view the character of Keller as a killer. He is so caught up in the materialistic world and so insensitive to humanistic values that he needs to prevaricate, cheat, betray his partner, and kill his "sons." Therein lies one certain theme for *All My Sons*.

Like Keller, Jones is a liar, a cheat, and a murderer. He sits as a high panjandrum atop his little island empire. He has adopted the values of the white traders and their material-getting schemes. The strength of Jones's character lies in his fearlessness, overconfidence, and shrewdness. But it soon dissipates as he regresses into his own primitive origins and is overtaken by the fears and superstitions that ultimately destroy him.

Also, frequently the speeches that characters make will emit feelings, opinions, decisions, and conclusions that may serve to enlighten us. Some speeches focus directly upon thematic substance; in fact, they are explicit declarations of what the dramatist wishes to convey. But these instances are rare and not the rule.

The following examples are extracted from three plays: *Oedipus*, *Riders to the Sea*, and *All My Sons*. When, toward the end of the drama, the blind Oedipus gropes his way through the multitude, the Theban citizens offer this comment: "No man ever really finds happiness until he dies." Would you select this statement as an appropriate theme? Or is the theme explicitly stated here by the chorus: "O the generations of man!/ His life is vanity and nothingness"?

Perhaps Maurya's final sentence conveys succinctly and precisely the real message of the drama. She says, "No man at all can be living forever, and we must be satisfied."

Still another clue to meaning comes to us when Keller, discovering that his son has killed himself because of his father's crime, says: "Sure, he was my son. But I think to him they were all my sons. And I guess they were. I guess they were." Keller at this point reaches a moment of truth; he takes one long step toward understanding the nature of brotherly love. And, on considering the title of the play, we must be further convinced that this speech pinpoints one of the major themes of the play.

But in taking a statement by a character in a play as expressing our chosen theme, we must ascertain that it is fittingly consistent with the entire action of the play and verify that it represents a reasonable assessment of the total emphasis in the play.

Another element of plot worth considering as an avenue toward understanding is setting. Our knowledge of the sea, whose ferocious power has inflicted great human suffering, misery, and sacrifice in Maurya's life, is bound to lead us to several appropriate interpretations. We would derive similar results by reviewing the external setting of Jones's subconscious mind and their contribution to Jones's psychological disintegration.

Many other details—titles of plays, names of characters, perception of ironies, imagery, and symbols— may lead us to understand a playwright's purpose. Knowing how we are, all of us, "riders to the sea" will take us closer to the central meaning of *Riders to the Sea*. The titles *All My Sons*, *Tea and Sympathy*, and *Come Back, Little Sheba*, among the many, afford us meaningful hints.

Similarly useful are the names of characters. Consider these examples: Oedipus means "swollen foot' and also "on the tracks of knowledge"; Maurya means "goddess of fate"; Keller hints at killer; Marie suggests saintliness and Buckholder intimates wickedness; and how like Brutus might the Emperor Jones be?

Oedipus contains numerous ironies; *Riders to the Sea* is vivid with color imagery; *Romeo and Juliet* is made the more intense with body imagery; and *Come Back, Little Sheba* is enriched by the use of such symbols as Little Sheba and the final dream sequence. All these details are there to add dimension to our experience.

Finally, we may expand our understanding or even recognize some new aspect of theme by external means. That is, knowledge of the literary conventions, the social and historical backgrounds of the period in which a play was written, may provide us succor.

Numerous details, as well as plot, character, conflict, action, and speech, to mention only a few of the elements of the dramatic form, afford us various opportunities to discover theme or meaning in drama. But total meaning comes to us only as the by-product of the total impression we experience from seeing or reading a play.

ELIZABETHAN THEATER AND STAGE

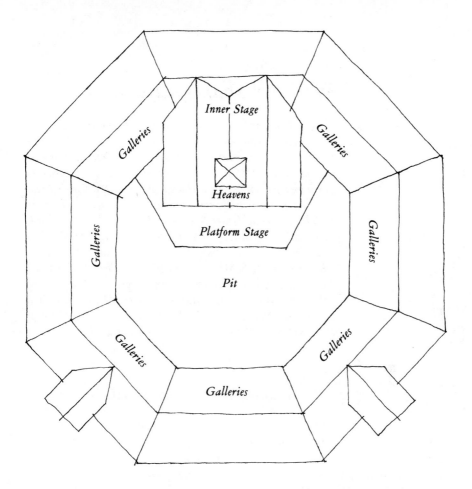

Inner stage	Acting area for intimate scenes; acting also done on one or two balconies above inner stage
Platform stage	Main acting area, raised several feet above pit
Heavens	Projecting roof, supported by pillars, half covering platform stage; underside often painted to resemble sky
Pit	Uncovered area for standing audience of about 600
Galleries	Three tiers of seats, topmost covered with a roof, seating 1,400 or more spectators

William Shakespeare *(1564–1616)*

Born in Stratford-on-Avon, son of a prosperous tradesman, he presumably completed grammar school, and married Anne Hathaway, a woman eight years his senior. Moving to London in the 1590s, he acted occasionally, wrote numerous plays and sonnets, and purchased shares in the King's Men, the most prosperous theatrical troupe in London, and in the fashionable Blackfriars Theatre. He retired at Stratford, apparently a relatively wealthy man, where he died. His better-known works include the following: Henry IV, Part I *(chronicle play),* A Midsummer Night's Dream *(fantasy),* The Merchant of Venice *(romantic comedy),* Romeo and Juliet *(romatic tragedy),* Julius Caesar *(tragedy),* Twelfth Night; or What You Will *(romantic comedy),* Hamlet *(tragedy),* Othello *(tragedy),* Macbeth *(tragedy).*

The Tragedy of Romeo and Juliet

[DRAMATIS PERSONAE

CHORUS

ESCALUS, *Prince of Verona*

PARIS, *a young nobleman, kinsman to the Prince*

MONTAGUE ⎤ *heads of two houses at variance with each*
CAPULET ⎦ *other*

An OLD MAN, *of the Capulet family*

ROMEO, *son to Montague*

MERCUTIO, *kinsman to the Prince, and friend to Romeo*

BENVOLIO, *nephew to Montague, and friend to Romeo*

TYBALT, *nephew to Lady Capulet*

PETRUCHIO, *a (mute) follower of Tybalt*

FRIAR LAWRENCE ⎤ *Franciscans*
FRIAR JOHN ⎦

BALTHASAR, *servant to Romeo*

ABRAM, *servant to Montague*

SAMPSON ⎤
GREGORY ⎥ *servants to Capulet*
CLOWN ⎦

PETER, *servant to Juliet's nurse*

PAGE *to Paris*

APOTHECARY

Three MUSICIANS

LADY MONTAGUE, *wife to Montague*

LADY CAPULET, *wife to Capulet*

JULIET, *daughter to Capulet*

NURSE *to Juliet*

CITIZENS *of Verona; several* GENTLEMEN *and* GENTLEWOMEN *of both houses;* MASKERS, TORCH-BEARERS, PAGES, GUARDS, WATCHMEN, SERVANTS, *and* ATTENDANTS

SCENE: *Verona; Mantua*]

PROLOGUE   [*Enter*] CHORUS
            Two households, both alike in dignity,
            In fair Verona, where we lay our scene,
            From ancient grudge break to new mutiny,
            Where civil blood makes civil hands unclean.
            From forth the fatal loins of these two foes   *5*
            A pair of star-cross'd lovers take their life;
            Whose misadventur'd piteous overthrows
            Doth with their death bury their parents' strife.
            The fearful passage of their death-mark'd love,
            And the continuance of their parents' rage,   *10*
            Which, but their children's end, nought could remove,
            Is now the two hours' traffic of·our stage;
            The which if you with patient ears attend,
            What here shall miss, our toil shall strive to mend.

                                                        [*Exit*]

[ACT ONE]   [*Scene One*]

            Enter SAMPSON *and* GREGORY, *with swords and bucklers, of the*
            house of Capulet

SAMPSON   Gregory, on my word, we'll not carry coals.
GREGORY   No, for then we should be colliers.
SAMPSON   I mean, and we be in choler, we'll draw.
GREGORY   Ay, while you live, draw your neck out of collar.
SAMPSON   I strike quickly, being mov'd.   *5*
GREGORY   But thou art not quickly mov'd to strike.
SAMPSON   A dog of the house of Montague moves me.
GREGORY   To move is to stir, and to be valiant is to stand; therefore, if
      thou art mov'd, thou run'st away.
SAMPSON   A dog of that house shall move me to stand! I will take the
      wall of any man or maid of Montague's.   *11*

Words and passages enclosed in square brackets in the text above are either
emendations of the copy text or additions to it. . . .

Pro. 1. *dignity:* rank
3. *mutiny:* strife
4. *civil blood:* the blood of civil strife.
civil hands: citizen's hands
6. *star-cross'd:* thwarted by the stars
12. *traffic:* business
14 *miss:* prove defective (in our performance). *mend:* i.e., mend in future
(as the result of knowing your judgment)
I.i. Location: Verona. ·A public place
1. *carry coals:* do menial work; figuratively, put up with insults, "eat dirt"

3. *and:* if. *choler:* anger. *draw:* draw
our swords
4. *draw . . . collar:* avoid hanging
5. *mov'd:* angered (with obvious punning in the following lines)
8. *stand:* make a stand, offer resistance
10–11. *take the wall:* the inner part of
the sidewalk being cleaner, it was
yielded out of courtesy to superiors;
to take it implied a claim to superiority

GREGORY   That shows thee a weak slave, for the weakest goes to the wall.

SAMPSON   'Tis true, and therefore women, being the weaker vessels, are ever thrust to the wall; therefore I will push Montague's men from the wall, and thrust his maids to the wall.   15

GREGORY   The quarrel is between our masters, and us their men.

SAMPSON   'Tis all one; I will show myself a tyrant: when I have fought with the men, I will be civil with the maids; I will cut off their heads.

GREGORY   The heads of the maids?

SAMPSON   Ay, the heads of the maids, or their maiden heads, take it in what sense thou wilt.   21

GREGORY   They must take it [in] sense that feel it.

SAMPSON   Me they shall feel while I am able to stand, and 'tis known I am a pretty piece of flesh.

GREGORY   'Tis well thou art not fish; if thou hadst, thou hadst been poor-John. Draw thy tool, here comes [two] of the house of Montagues.   27

                    Enter two other servingmen [ABRAM *and* BALTHASAR]

SAMPSON   My naked weapon is out. Quarrel, I will back thee.

GREGORY   How, turn thy back and run?

SAMPSON   Fear me not.

GREGORY   No, marry, I fear thee!

SAMPSON   Let us take the law of our sides, let them begin.

GREGORY   I will frown as I pass by, and let them take it as they list.

SAMPSON   Nay, as they dare. I will bite my thumb at them, which is disgrace to them if they bear it.   35

ABRAM   Do you bite your thumb at us, sir?

SAMPSON   I do bite my thumb, sir.

ABRAM   Do you bite your thumb at us, sir?

SAMPSON [*aside to* GREGORY]   Is the law of our side if I say ay?

GREGORY [*aside to* SAMPSON]   No.   40

SAMPSON   No, sir, I do not bite my thumb at you, sir, but I bite my thumb, sir.

GREGORY   Do you quarrel, sir?

ABRAM   Quarrel, sir? No, sir.

SAMPSON   But if you do, sir, I am for you. I serve as good a man as you.

ABRAM   No better?   46

12. *the weakest . . . wall:* the weakest must give way (proverbial)

13. *weaker vessels:* see 1 Peter 3:7

16. *between . . . men:* i.e., not with the maids

22. *They . . . feel it:* the ones who must take it in sense (= physical sensation) are those who feel it, i.e., the maids

23. *stand:* with bawdy pun

25. *fish:* with play on the slang sense "female"

26. *poor-John:* dried hake (a cheap fish). *tool:* weapon (with slang sexual reference that Sampson continues in *naked weapon,* line 28)

30. *Fear me not:* have no fears about me (deliberately misinterpreted by Gregory)

31. *marry:* indeed (originally, the name of the Virgin Mary used as an oath)

32. *take the law of:* have the law on

33. *list:* like

34. *bite my thumb:* considered an act of insolence or defiance

SAMPSON   Well, sir.

Enter BENVOLIO

GREGORY   Say "better," here comes one of my master's kinsmen.

SAMPSON   Yes, better, sir.

ABRAM   You lie.   50

SAMPSON   Draw, if you be men. Gregory, remember thy washing
   blow!   *They fight*

BENVOLIO   Part, fools!
   Put up your swords, you know not what you do.

                                              [*Beats down their swords*]
                                                        Enter TYBALT

TYBALT   What, art thou drawn among these heartless hinds?   55
   Turn thee, Benvolio, look upon thy death.

BENVOLIO   I do but keep the peace. Put up thy sword,
   Or manage it to part these men with me.

TYBALT   What, drawn and talk of peace? I hate the word
   As I hate hell, all Montagues and thee.   60
   Have at thee, coward!   [*They fight*]

                            Enter three or four CITIZENS *with clubs or partisans*

[CITIZENS]   Clubs, bills, and partisans! Strike! Beat them down!
   Down with the Capulets! Down with the Montagues!

                    Enter old CAPULET *in his gown, and his wife* [LADY CAPULET]

CAPULET   What noise is this? Give me my long sword ho!

LADY CAPULET   A crutch, a crutch! why call you for a sword?   65

CAPULET   My sword, I say! Old Montague is come,
   And flourishes his blade in spite of me.

                    Enter old MONTAGUE *and his wife* [LADY MONTAGUE]

MONTAGUE   Thou villain Capulet!—Hold me not, let me go.

LADY MONTAGUE   Thou shalt not stir one foot to seek a foe.

                              Enter PRINCE ESCALUS *with his* TRAIN

PRINCE   Rebellious subjects, enemies to peace,   70
   Profaners of this neighbor-stained steel—
   Will they not hear?—What ho, you men, you beasts!
   That quench the fire of your pernicious rage
   With purple fountains issuing from your veins—
   On pain of torture, from those bloody hands   75
   Throw your mistempered weapons to the ground,
   And hear the sentence of your moved prince.

---

51. *washing:* swashing, slashing
55. *heartless hinds:* cowardly servants;
with punning sense "female deer
without a stag [*hartless*]"
61. *Have at thee:* here I come at you
(formula for announcing attack). S.D.
partisans: broad-headed spears
62. *Clubs:* familiar London cry, calling apprentices armed with clubs to
riot or to suppress riot. *bills:* hooked
blades on long shafts
67. *spite:* defiance
68. *villain:* base, ignoble
71. *Profaners . . . steel:*   profaning
your weapons by staining them with
your neighbors' blood
76. *mistempered:* (1) angry; (2) tempered for use in a bad cause

Three civil brawls, bred of an airy word,
By thee, old Capulet, and Montague,
Have thrice disturb'd the quiet of our streets,   *80*
And made Verona's ancient citizens
Cast by their grave beseeming ornaments
To wield old partisans, in hands as old,
Cank'red with peace, to part your cank'red hate;
If ever you disturb our streets again   *85*
Your lives shall pay the forfeit of the peace.
For this time all the rest depart away.
You, Capulet, shall go along with me,
And, Montague, come you this afternoon,
To know our farther pleasure in this case,   *90*
To old Free-town, our common judgment-place.
Once more, on pain of death, all men depart.

> *Exeunt* [*all but* MONTAGUE, LADY MONTAGUE, *and*
> BENVOLIO]

MONTAGUE   Who set this ancient quarrel new abroach?
Speak, nephew, were you by when it began?

BENVOLIO   Here were the servants of your adversary,   *95*
And yours, close fighting ere I did approach.
I drew to part them. In the instant came
The fiery Tybalt, with his sword prepar'd,
Which, as he breath'd defiance to my ears,
He swung about his head and cut the winds,   *100*
Who, nothing hurt withal, hiss'd him in scorn.
While we were interchanging thrusts and blows,
Came more and more, and fought on part and part,
Till the Prince came, who parted either part.

LADY MONTAGUE   O, where is Romeo? Saw you him today?   *105*
Right glad I am he was not at this fray.

BENVOLIO   Madam, an hour before the worshipp'd sun
Peer'd forth the golden window of the east,
A troubled mind drive me to walk abroad,
Where, underneath the grove of sycamore   *110*
That westward rooteth from this city side,
So early walking did I see your son.

---

78. *airy:* light, insignificant
82. *Cast . . . ornaments:* throw aside appurtenances (like staffs) suitable for dignified age
84. *Cank'red . . . cank'red:* rusted . . . malignant
91. *Free-town:* Brooke's translation of *Villa franca,* the name of Capulet's residence in the Italian story. *common:* public

93. *abroach:* open, flowing (as of a barrel of liquor)
101. *nothing:* not at all. *withal:* therewith
103. *part and part:* one side or the other
104. *either part:* both sides
109. *drive:* drove (an archaic form, pronounced "driv")
111. *this city side:* the side of this city

Towards him I made, but he was ware of me,
And stole into the covert of the wood.
I, measuring his affections by my own,   *115*
Which then most sought where most might not be found,
Being one too many by my weary self,
Pursued my humor not pursuing his,
And gladly shunn'd who gladly fled from me.

MONTAGUE   Many a morning hath he there been seen,   *120*
With tears augmenting the fresh morning's dew,
Adding to clouds more clouds with his deep sighs,
But all so soon as the all-cheering sun
Should in the farthest east begin to draw
The shady curtains from Aurora's bed,   *125*
Away from light steals home my heavy son,
And private in his chamber pens himself,
Shuts up his windows, locks fair daylight out,
And makes himself an artificial night.
Black and portendous must this humor prove,   *130*
Unless good counsel may the cause remove.

BENVOLIO   My noble uncle, do you know the cause?

MONTAGUE   I neither know it, nor can learn of him.

BENVOLIO   Have you importun'd him by any means?

MONTAGUE   Both by myself and many other friends,   *135*
But he,[his] own affections' counsellor,
Is to himself (I will not say how true)
But to himself so secret and so close,
So far from sounding and discovery,
As is the bud bit with an envious worm,   *140*
Ere he can spread his sweet leaves to the air
Or dedicate his beauty to the [sun].
Could we but learn from whence his sorrows grow,
We would as willingly give cure as know.

                                                    Enter ROMEO

BENVOLIO   See where he comes. So please you step aside,   *145*
I'll know his grievance, or be much denied.

---

113. *ware:* (1) aware; (2) wary
115. *affections:* inclinations
116. *most sought . . . found:* wanted most to find somewhere to be solitary
118. *Pursued . . . his:* indulged my own mood by not following his moody self
119. *who:* him who
123. *all so:* just as
125. *Aurora:* goddess of dawn
126. *heavy:* sad
128. *windows:* shutters

130. *Black and portendous:* portentous of some dire event. *humor:* capricious or moody behavior
136. *counsellor:* confidential adviser, sharer of secrets
137. *true:* trustworthy, i.e., wise in his advice
139. *sounding:* being fathomed
140. *envious:* malicious
145. *So please you:* if you will be so good as to

MONTAGUE   I would thou wert so happy by thy stay
To hear true shrift. Come, madam, let's away.

Exeunt [MONTAGUE *and* LADY]

BENVOLIO   Good morrow, cousin.
ROMEO   Is the day so young?
BENVOLIO   But new strook nine.
ROMEO   Ay me, sad hours seem long.   *150*
Was that my father that went hence so fast?
BENVOLIO   It was. What sadness lengthens Romeo's hours?
ROMEO   Not having that which, having, makes them short.
BENVOLIO   In love?
ROMEO   Out—   *155*
BENVOLIO   Of love?
ROMEO   Out of her favor where I am in love.
BENVOLIO   Alas that love, so gentle in his view,
Should be so tyrannous and rough in proof!
ROMEO   Alas that love, whose view is muffled still,   *160*
Should, without eyes, see pathways to his will!
Where shall we dine? O me! what fray was here?
Yet tell me not, for I have heard it all:
Here's much to do with hate, but more with love.
Why then, O brawling love! O loving hate!   *165*
O any thing, of nothing first [create]!
O heavy lightness, serious vanity,
Misshapen chaos of well[-seeming] forms,
Feather of lead, bright smoke, cold fire, sick health,
Still-waking sleep, that is not what it is!   *170*
This love feel I, that feel no love in this.
Dost thou not laugh?
BENVOLIO   No, coz, I rather weep.
ROMEO   Good heart, at what?
BENVOLIO   At thy good heart's oppression.
ROMEO   Why, such is love's transgression.
Griefs of mine own lie heavy in my breast,   *175*

147. *would . . . happy:* hope that you
will be fortunate enough
148. *shrift:* confession
149. *cousin:* kinsman. Romeo and
Benvolio are cousins in the modern
sense, but the word was applied to
any collateral relative more distant
than a brother or sister
150. *strook:* struck
158. *his view:* its appearance
159. *in proof:* being experienced
160. *view . . . still:* eyes are always
blindfolded
161. *see . . . will:* find his way to get
what he wants

164. *to do:* ado, tumult
166. *create:* created. Romeo ironically justifies this string of paradoxes by
recalling the greatest of paradoxes—
God's creation of everything *ex nihilo,*
from nothing
167. *serious vanity:* heavy emptiness
168. *chaos . . . forms:* chaos, technically, is all matter and no form
170. *Still-waking:* constantly awake
172. *coz:* cousin, i.e., kinsman
174. *transgression:* overstepping of
limit

Which thou wilt propagate to have it press'd
With more of thine. This love that thou hast shown
Doth add more grief to too much of mine own.
Love is a smoke made with the fume of sighs,
Being purg'd, a fire sparkling in lovers' eyes,   *180*
Being vex'd, a sea nourish'd with loving tears.
What is it else? a madness most discreet,
A choking gall, and a preserving sweet.
Farewell, my coz.

BENVOLIO   Soft, I will go along;
And if you leave me so, you do me wrong.   *185*

ROMEO   Tut, I have lost myself, I am not here:
This is not Romeo, he's some other where.

BENVOLIO   Tell me in sadness, who is that you love?

ROMEO   What, shall I groan and tell thee?

BENVOLIO   Groan? why, no;
But sadly tell me, who?   *190*

ROMEO   [Bid] a sick man in sadness [make] his will—
A word ill urg'd to one that is so ill!
In sadness, cousin, I do love a woman.

BENVOLIO   I aim'd so near when I suppos'd you lov'd.

ROMEO   A right good mark-man! And she's fair I love.   *195*

BENVOLIO   A right fair mark, fair coz, is soonest hit.

ROMEO   Well, in that hit you miss: she'll not be hit
With Cupid's arrow, she hath Dian's wit;
And in strong proof of chastity well arm'd,
From Love's weak childish bow she lives uncharm'd.   *200*
She will not stay the siege of loving terms,
Nor bide th' encounter of assailing eyes,
Nor ope her lap to saint-seducing gold.
O, she is rich in beauty, only poor
That, when she dies, with beauty dies her store.   *205*

BENVOLIO   Then she hath sworn that she will still live chaste?

ROMEO   She hath, and in that sparing [makes] huge waste;
For beauty starv'd with her severity
Cuts beauty off from all posterity.

---

176. *propagate:* increase. *to have:* by
having. *press'd:* oppressed (with secondary sense "weighted down by a
lover," suggested by *propagate*)
180. *purg'd:* i.e., cleared of smoke
184. *Soft:* not so fast
185. *And if:* if
188. *sadness:* seriousness
198. *Dian's wit:* i.e., the good sense
to shun love. Diana was the goddess
of chastity
199. *proof:* armor of tested strength

200. *From . . . uncharm'd:* uncharmed
from = exempt from the spell of
201. *stay:* abide
203. *ope . . . gold:* like Danaë,
whom Jove visited in a shower of
gold
205. *store:* capital (of beauty, which
she should have perpetuated through
offspring
206. *still:* always
207. *sparing:* frugality

She is too fair, too wise, wisely too fair,   *210*
To merit bliss by making me despair.
She hath forsworn to love, and in that vow
Do I live dead that live to tell it now.
BENVOLIO   Be rul'd by me, forget to think of her.
ROMEO   O, teach me how I should forget to think.   *215*
BENVOLIO   By giving liberty unto thine eyes:
Examine other beauties.
ROMEO   'Tis the way
To call hers, exquisite, in question more.
These happy masks that kiss fair ladies' brows,
Being black, puts us in mind they hide the fair.   *220*
He that is strooken blind cannot forget
The precious treasure of his eyesight lost.
Show me a mistress that is passing fair,
What doth her beauty serve but as a note
Where I may read who pass'd that passing fair?   *225*
Farewell, thou canst not teach me to forget.
BENVOLIO   I'll pay that doctrine, or else die in debt.   *Exeunt*

[*Scene Two*]

Enter CAPULET, COUNTY PARIS, *and the Clown,* [*Capulet's*
SERVANT]
CAPULET   But Montague is bound as well as I,
In penalty alike, and 'tis not hard, I think,
For men so old as we to keep the peace.
PARIS   Of honorable reckoning are you both,
And pity 'tis you liv'd at odds so long.   *5*
But now, my lord, what say you to my suit?
CAPULET   But saying o'er what I have said before:
My child is yet a stranger in the world,
She hath not seen the change of fourteen years;
Let two more summers wither in their pride,   *10*
Ere we may think her ripe to be a bride.
PARIS   Younger than she are happy mothers made.
CAPULET   And too soon marr'd are those so early made.
Earth hath swallowed all my hopes but she;

---

211. *To . . . despair:* in earning salvation by chastity which drives me to
the dangerous sin of despair
218. *in question more:* all the more
acutely into consideration
225. *passing:* surpassingly
227. *I'll . . . debt:* I'll teach you that

lesson or feel that I haven't fulfilled a
friend's obligation
I.ii. Location: Verona. A street
O.S.D. *County:* count
4. *reckoning:* repute
8. *stranger:* newcomer

She's the hopeful lady of my earth. 15
But woo her, gentle Paris, get her heart,
My will to her consent is but a part;
And she agreed, within her scope of choice
Lies my consent and fair according voice.
This night I hold an old accustom'd feast, 20
Whereto I have invited many a guest,
Such as I love, and you, among the store
One more, most welcome, makes my number more.
At my poor house look to behold this night
Earth-treading stars that make dark heaven light. 25
Such comfort as do lusty young men feel
When well-apparell'd April on the heel
Of limping winter treads, even such delight
Among fresh fennel buds shall you this night
Inherit at my house; hear all, all see; 30
And like her most whose merit most shall be;
Which [on] more view of many, mine, being one,
May stand in number, though in reck'ning none.
Come go with me. [*To* SERVANT] Go, sirrah, trudge about
Through fair Verona, find those persons out 35
Whose names are written there, and to them say,
My house and welcome on their pleasure stay.   *Exit* [*with* PARIS]

SERVANT   Find them out whose names are written here! It is written that
the shoemaker should meddle with his yard and the tailor with his last,
the fisher with his pencil and the painter with his nets; but I am sent to
find those persons whose names are here writ, and can never find what
names the writing person hath here writ. I must to the learned. In
good time!   43

Enter BENVOLIO *and* ROMEO

BENVOLIO   Tut, man, one fire burns out another's burning,
[One] pain is less'ned by another's anguish;
Turn giddy, and be holp by backward turning;
One desperate grief cures with another's languish:
Take thou some new infection to thy eye,
And the rank poison of the old will die.

15. *the hopeful . . . earth:* (1) the hope
round which my world revolves; (2)
the heiress of my wealth
18. *agreed:* consenting
19. *according:* agreeing
29. *fennel:* a fragrant flowering plant
30. *Inherit:* possess, experience
32–33. *Which . . . none:* this obscure
passage seems to mean: "When you
have seen all of them, my daughter,
though one of the group, may no
longer have a place in your estimation

[*reckoning*]." There is punning on
reckoning in the sense "arithmetical
calculation" and on the proverbial
saying "One is no number"
34. *sirrah:* customary term of address
to an inferior
45. *another's anguish:* the anguish of
another pain
46. *holp:* helped, i.e., cured. *backward:* in reverse
47. *cures . . . languish:* is cured by the
distress of another grief

ROMEO   Your plantan leaf is excellent for that.   *50*
BENVOLIO   For what, I pray thee?
ROMEO   For your broken shin.
BENVOLIO   Why, Romeo, art thou mad?
ROMEO   Not mad, but bound more than a madman is;
    Shut up in prison, kept without my food,
    Whipt and tormented and—God-den, good fellow.   *55*
SERVANT   God gi' god-den. I pray, sir, can you read?
ROMEO   Ay, mine own fortune in my misery.
SERVANT   Perhaps you have learn'd it without book.
    But I pray, can you read any thing you see?
ROMEO   Ay, if I know the letters and the language.   *60*
SERVANT   Ye say honestly, rest you merry!
ROMEO   Stay, fellow, I can read.

    (*He reads the letter*)   "Signior Martino and his wife and daughters;
County Anselme and his beauteous sisters; the lady widow of
[Vitruvio]; Signior Placentio and his lovely nieces; Mercutio and his
brother Valentine; mine uncle Capulet, his wife, and daughters; my fair
niece Rosaline, [and] Livia; Signior Valentio and his cousin Tybalt;
Lucio and the lively Helena."

    A fair assembly. Whither should they come?
SERVANT   Up.   *70*
ROMEO   Whither? to supper?
SERVANT   To our house.
ROMEO   Whose house?
SERVANT   My master's.
ROMEO   Indeed I should have ask'd [thee] that before.   *75*
SERVANT   Now I'll tell you without asking. My master is the great rich
    Capulet, and if you be not of the house of Montagues, I pray come and
    crush a cup of wine. Rest you merry!   [*Exit*]
BENVOLIO   At this same ancient feast of Capulet's
    Sups the fair Rosaline whom thou so loves,   *80*
    With all the admired beauties of Verona.
    Go thither, and with unattainted eye
    Compare her face with some that I shall show,
    And I will make thee think thy swan a crow.
ROMEO   When the devout religion of mine eye   *85*
    Maintains such falsehood, then turn tears to [fires];

---

50. *plantan:* plantain, the leaf of which was applied to minor wounds
51. *broken shin:* broken skin on the shin
53–55.*bound . . . tormented:* the usual treatment of the insane
55. *God-den:* good evening (used after noon)

56. *gi':* give you
58. *without book:* by heart
61. *rest you merry:* conventional phrase of farewell
78. *crush:* drink
80. *loves:* lovest
82. *unattainted:* uninfected, unprejudiced

And these, who, often drown'd, could never die,
Transparent heretics, be burnt for liars!
One fairer than my love! The all-seeing sun
Ne'er saw her match since first the world begun. 90
BENVOLIO   Tut, you saw her fair, none else being by,
Herself pois'd with herself in either eye;
But in that crystal scales let there be weigh'd
Your lady's love against some other maid
That I will show you shining at this feast, 95
And she shall scant show well that now seems best.
ROMEO   I'll go along no such sight to be shown,
But to rejoice in splendor of mine own.   [Exeunt]

Scene Three

Enter CAPULET'S WIFE, and NURSE

LADY CAPULET   Nurse, where's my daughter? Call her forth to me.
NURSE   Now by my maidenhead at twelve year old,
I bade her come. What, lamb! What, ladybird!
God forbid! Where's this girl? What, Juliet!

Enter JULIET

JULIET   How now, who calls?
NURSE   Your mother.
JULIET   Madam, I am here, 5
What is your will?
LADY CAPULET   This is the matter. Nurse, give leave a while,
We must talk in secret. Nurse, come back again,
I have rememb'red me, thou s' hear our counsel.
Thou knowest my daughter's of a pretty age. 10
NURSE   Faith, I can tell her age unto an hour.
LADY CAPULET   She's not fourteen.
NURSE   I'll lay fourteen of my teeth—
And yet, to my teen be it spoken, I have but four—
She's not fourteen. How long is it now
To Lammas-tide?
LADY CAPULET   A fortnight and odd days. 15
NURSE   Even or odd, of all days in the year,
Come Lammas-eve at night shall she be fourteen,
Susan and she—God rest all Christian souls!—

87. *these:* i.e., my eyes
88. *Transparent:* (1) bright, clear; (2) manifest
92. *pois'd:* balanced
I.iii. Location: Verona. Capulet's house
4. *God forbid:* God forbid there

should be anything amiss (?) or God forbid I should call her "ladybird" (cant term for a prostitute)
9. *thou's:* thou shalt
13. *teen:* sorrow (*teen* and *four* echo fourteen)
15. *Lammas-tide:* August 1

Were of an age. Well, Susan is with God,
She was too good for me. But as I said,
On Lammas-eve at night shall she be fourteen,   *20*
That shall she, marry, I remember it well.
'Tis since the earthquake now aleven years,
And she was wean'd—I never shall forget it—
Of all the days of the year, upon that day;   *25*
For I had then laid wormwood to my 'dug,
Sitting in the sun under the dove-house wall.
My lord and you were then at Mantua—
Nay, I do bear a brain—but as I said,
When it did taste the wormwood on the nipple   *30*
Of my dug and felt it bitter, pretty fool,
To see it teachy and fall out wi' th' dug!
Shake, quoth the dove-house; 'twas no need, I trow,
To bid me trudge.
And since that time it is aleven years,   *35*
For then she could stand high-lone; nay, by th' rood,
She could have run and waddled all about;
For even the day before, she broke her brow,
And then my husband—God be with his soul!
'A was a merry man—took up the child.   *40*
"Yea," quoth he, "dost thou fall upon thy face?
Thou wilt fall backward when thou hast more wit,
Wilt thou not, Jule?" and by my holidam,
The pretty wretch left crying and said, "Ay."
To see now how a jest shall come about!   *45*
I warrant, and I should live a thousand years,
I never should forget it: 'Wilt thou not, Jule?' quoth he;
And, pretty fool, it stinted and said, "Ay."

LADY CAPULET   Enough of this, I pray thee hold thy peace.

NURSE   Yes, madam, yet I cannot choose but laugh   *50*
To think it should leave crying and say, "Ay."
And yet I warrant it had upon it brow
A bump as big as a young cock'rel's stone—

---

23. *aleven:* eleven
29. *bear a brain:* have a great memory
31. *fool:* here, a term of endearment, like wretch in line 44.
32. *teachy:* tetchy, fretful
33. *Shake . . . dove-house:* i.e., the dovecot, shaking, suggested it was time she should be off. *trow:* think, assure you
36. *stand high-lone:* stand upright along. *rood:* cross
38. *broke her brow:* (fell and) cut her forehead

40. *'A:* he
43. *holidam:* halidom, holiness; but, as the spelling shows, the word was sometimes understood as referring to the Virgin Mary
45. *how . . . about:* how something spoken in jest comes true
48. *stinted:* ceased (crying)
52. *it brow:* its brow
53. *stone:* testicle

A perilous knock—and it cried bitterly.
"Yea," quoth my husband, "fall'st upon thy face?   *55*
Thou wilt fall backward when thou comest to age,
Wilt thou not, Jule?" It stinted and said, "Ay."

JULIET   And stint thou too, I pray thee, nurse, say I.

NURSE   Peace, I have done. God mark thee to his grace!
Thou wast the prettiest babe that e'er I nurs'd.   *60*
And I might live to see thee married once,
I have my wish.

LADY CAPULET   Marry, that "marry" is the very theme
I came to talk of. Tell me, daughter Juliet,
How stands your dispositions to be married?   *65*

JULIET   It is an [honor] that I dream not of.

NURSE   An [honor]! were not I thine only nurse,
I would say thou hadst suck'd wisdom from thy teat.

LADY CAPULET   Well, think of marriage now; younger than you,
Here in Verona, ladies of esteem,   *70*
Are made already mothers. By my count,
I was your mother much upon these years
That you are now a maid. Thus then in brief:
The valiant Paris seeks you for his love.

NURSE   A man, young lady! Lady, such a man   *75*
As all the world—why, he's a man of wax.

LADY CAPULET   Verona's summer hath not such a flower.

NURSE   Nay, he's a flower, in faith, a very flower.

LADY CAPULET   What say you? can you love the gentleman?
This night you shall behold him at our feast;   *80*
Read o'er the volume of young Paris' face,
And find delight writ there with beauty's pen;
Examine every married lineament,
And see how one another lends content;
And what obscur'd in this fair volume lies   *85*
Find written in the margent of his eyes.
This precious book of love, this unbound lover,
To beautify him, only lacks a cover.
The fish lives in the sea, and 'tis much pride
For fair without the fair within to hide.   *90*

68. *thy teat:* the teat you sucked
72. *much . . . years:* at much the same age
76. *man of wax:* i.e., handsome as a wax figure
83. *married:* harmonious
86. *margent:* margin (which in early books frequently contained commentary on the adjacent text)
87. *unbound:* referring both to the book and to the unmarried man

88. *cover:* binding; but as Dover Wilson suggests, perhaps with quibble on the legal expression *femme couvert,* "married woman"
89. *The fish . . . sea:* i.e., the fish knows its proper habitat. The sense seems to be that Juliet would give Paris an equally suitable "outside"

That book in many's eyes doth share the glory,
That in gold clasps locks in the golden story;
So shall you share all that he doth possess,
By having him, making yourself no less.

NURSE   No less! nay, bigger: women grow by men.   *95*
LADY CAPULET   Speak briefly, can you like of Paris' love?
JULIET   I'll look to like, if looking liking move;
But no more deep will I endart mine eye
Than your consent gives strength to make [it] fly.   *99*

Enter SERVINGMAN

SERVINGMAN   Madam, the guests are come, supper serv'd up, you call'd,
my young lady ask'd for, the nurse curs'd in the pantry, and every thing
in extremity. I must hence to wait; I beseech you follow straight.

[*Exit*]

LADY CAPULET   We follow thee. Juliet, the County stays.
NURSE   Go, girl, seek happy nights to happy days.   *Exeunt*

[*Scene Four*]

Enter ROMEO, MERCUTIO, BENVOLIO, *with five or six other*
MASKERS; TORCH-BEARERS

ROMEO   What, shall this speech be spoke for our excuse?
Or shall we on without apology?
BENVOLIO   The date is out of such prolixity:
We'll have no Cupid hoodwink'd with a scarf,
Bearing a Tartar's painted bow of lath,   *5*
Scaring the ladies like a crow-keeper,
[Nor no without-book prologue, faintly spoke
After the prompter, for our entrance;]
But let them measure us by what they will,
We'll measure them a measure and be gone.   *10*

95. *grow:* i.e., become pregnant
97. *look:* expect (with obvious pun)
98. *endart:* shoot like a dart
101. *curs'd . . . pantry:* i.e., for not being on hand to help
102. *straight:* straightway
103. *stays:* waits
I.iv. Location: Verona. Before Capulet's house
1. *speech:* maskers, arriving thus to pay a compliment visit at some festivity, would usually preface their masked dance with a speech by the "presenter"
3. *The date . . . prolixity:* such long-winded preliminaries are out of fashion
4. *Cupid:* the presenter, often a boy, might well be dressed as Cupid. *hoodwink'd:* blindfolded (as part of the role)
5. *Tartar's painted bow:* the mounted Tartar archer presumably used a bow shorter and more curved than the English longbow, and hence closer in form to Cupid's lip-shaped bow
6. *crow-keeper:* scarecrow
7. *without-book:* memorized
10. *measure them a measure:* deal them out a dance

ROMEO   Give me a torch, I am not for this ambling;
Being but heavy, I will bear the light.

MERCUTIO   Nay, gentle Romeo, we must have you dance.

ROMEO   Not I, believe me. You have dancing shoes
With nimble soles, I have a soul of lead   15
So stakes me to the ground I cannot move.

MERCUTIO   You are a lover, borrow Cupid's wings,
And soar with them above a common bound.

ROMEO   I am too sore enpierced with his shaft
To soar with his light feathers, and so bound   20
I cannot bound a pitch above dull woe;
Under love's heavy burthen do I sink.

[MERCUTIO]   And, to sink in it, should you burthen love—
Too great oppression for a tender thing.

ROMEO   Is love a tender thing? It is too rough,   25
Too rude, too boist'rous, and it pricks like thorn.

MERCUTIO   If love be rough with you, be rough with love;
Prick love for pricking, and you beat love down.
Give me a case to put my visage in, [*puts on a mask*]
A visor for a visor! what care I   30
What curious eye doth cote deformities?
Here are the beetle brows shall blush for me.

BENVOLIO   Come knock and enter, and no sooner in,
But every man betake him to his legs.

ROMEO   A torch for me. Let wantons light of heart   35
Tickle the senseless rushes with their heels.
For I am proverb'd with a grandsire phrase,
I'll be a candle-holder and look on:
The game was ne'er so fair, and I am [done].

MERCUTIO   Tut, dun's the mouse, the constable's own word.   40
If thou art Dun, we'll draw thee from the mire

---

11. *torch:* as a torch-bearer, he would be disqualified from participation in the masking
12. *heavy:* low-spirited
18. *common bound:* ordinary leap (in dancing)
21. *pitch:* height (technical term in falconry)
23. *should . . . love:* i.e., you would have to make yourself a weight on the loved one
26. *rude:* rough
28. *Prick . . . pricking:* i.e., ease sexual desire by satisfying it
29. *case:* mask
30. *visor . . . visor:* mask . . . ugly face
31. *cote:* quote, note
34. *betake . . . legs:* join the dancing

36. *senseless:* without feeling. *rushes:* used for floor-covering
37. *grandsire phrase:* old proverb ("A good candle-holder [i.e., onlooker] proves a good gamester")
39. *The game . . . done:* alluding to another proverb, "He is wise who gives over when the game is fairest," i.e., when he is winning; but Romeo puns on *game* in the sense "quarry"
40. *dun's the mouse:* a proverb (arising as a quibble on Romeo's *done*) meaning "be silent and unseen"; hence the association with constables
41. *Dun . . . mire:* in the Christmas game "Dun is in the mire" a log representing a horse stuck in the mud was hauled out by the players

[Of this sir—]reverence love, wherein thou stickest
Up to the ears. Come, we burn daylight, ho!
ROMEO   Nay, that's not so.
MERCUTIO   I mean, sir, in delay   45
We waste our lights in vain, [like] lights by day!
Take our good meaning, for our judgment sits
Five times in that ere once in our [five] wits.
ROMEO   And we mean well in going to this mask,
But 'tis no wit to go.
MERCUTIO   Why, may one ask?
ROMEO   I dreamt a dream to-night.
MERCUTIO   And so did I.   50
ROMEO   Well, what was yours?
MERCUTIO   That dreamers often lie.
ROMEO   In bed asleep, while they do dream things true.
MERCUTIO   O then I see Queen Mab hath been with you.
She is the fairies midwife, and she comes
In shape no bigger than an agot-stone   55
On the forefinger of an alderman,
Drawn with a team of little atomi
Over men's noses as they lie asleep.
Her chariot is an empty hazel-nut,
Made by the joiner squirrel or old grub,   60
Time out a' mind the fairies' coachmakers.
Her waggon-spokes made of long spinners' legs,
The cover of the wings of grasshoppers,
Her traces of the smallest spider web,
Her collars of the moonshine's wat'ry beams,   65
Her whip of cricket's bone, the lash of film,
Her waggoner a small grey-coated gnat,
Not half so big as a round little worm
Prick'd from the lazy finger of a [maid].
And in this state she gallops night by night   70
Through lovers' brains, and then they dream of love;

42. *sir—reverence:* there is a pun on a euphemism for dung; but Mercutio's main point is to apply the notion of "Dun is in the mire" to Romeo's confessed immersion in love
43. *burn daylight:* waste time. Romeo pretends to take the phrase literally; hence Mercutio's injunction to him to take his "good meaning" (line 46), but Romeo continues his quibbling by taking this in the sense "meaning well"
46–47. *our . . . wits:* i.e., there is five times as much sense in what I mean as in what you hear me say (*five wits* = five senses)

49. *wit:* wisdom
53. *Queen Mab:* probably an invention of Shakespeare's, with play on *quean,* "slut." *Mab* was a stock name for a slut
54. *midwife:* in the sense that she delivers men's dreams
55. *agot-stone:* agate (often incised with figures and set in rings)
57. *atomi:* tiny creatures
62. *spinners':* spiders
68–69: *worm . . . maid:* an old wives' tale maintained that worms grew in the fingers of lazy girls
70. *state:* magnificence

[O'er] courtiers' knees, that dream on cur'sies straight;
O'er lawyers' fingers, who straight dream on fees;
O'er ladies' lips, who straight on kisses dream,
Which oft the angry Mab with blisters plagues,   *75*
Because their breath with sweetmeats tainted are.
Sometime she gallops o'er a courtier's nose,
And then dreams he of smelling out a suit;
And sometime comes she with a tithe-pig's tail
Tickling a parson's nose as 'a lies asleep,   *80*
Then he dreams of another benefice.
Sometime she driveth o'er a soldier's neck,
And then dreams he of cutting foreign throats,
Of breaches, ambuscadoes, Spanish blades,
Of healths five fadom deep; and then anon   *85*
Drums in his ear, at which he starts and wakes,
And being thus frighted, swears a prayer or two,
And sleeps again. This is that very Mab
That plats the manes of horses in the night,
And bakes the [elf-]locks in foul sluttish hairs,   *90*
Which, once untangled, much misfortune bodes.
This is the hag, when maids lie on their backs,
That presses them and learns them first to bear,
Making them women of good carriage.
This is she—

ROMEO   Peace, peace, Mercutio, peace!   *95*
Thou talk'st of nothing.

MERCUTIO   True, I talk of dreams,
Which are the children of an idle brain,
Begot of nothing but vain fantasy,
Which is as thin of substance as the air,
And more inconstant than the wind, who woos   *100*
Even now the frozen bosom of the north,
And, being anger'd, puffs away from thence,
Turning his side to the dew-dropping south.

BENVOLIO   This wind you talk of blows us from ourselves:
Supper is done, and we shall come too late.   *105*

---

72. *on:* of. *cur'sies:* curtsies, i.e., bows
78. *smelling . . . suit:* discovering a petitioner whose cause he can further at court in reward for a fee
79. *tithe-pig:* pig paid as part of parish dues
84. *breaches:* breaching fortifications. *ambuscadoes:* ambushes. *Spanish blades:* the best swords came from Toledo
85. *healths:* toasts. *fadom:* fathoms
90. *elf-locks:* the matted hair of slovenly people was thought to be the work of elves, who would take revenge if it were untangled
93. *learns:* teaches
94. *carriage:* (1) deportment; 2) supporting a lover's weight
102. *anger'd:* i.e., by his lack of success with the cold north

ROMEO   I fear, too early, for my mind misgives
Some consequence yet hanging in the stars
Shall bitterly begin his fearful date
With this night's revels, and expire the term
Of a despised life clos'd in my breast   *110*
By some vile forfeit of untimely death.
But He that hath the steerage of my course
Direct my [sail]! On, lusty gentlemen!
BENVOLIO   Strike, drum.

They march about the stage [and stand to one side]

[Scene Five]

And SERVINGMEN *come forth with napkins*

[FIRST] SERVINGMAN   Where's Potpan, that he helps not to take away?
He shift a trencher? he scrape a trencher?

[SECOND] SERVINGMAN   When good manners shall lie all in one or two
men's hands, and they unwash'd too, 'tis a foul thing.   *4*

[FIRST] SERVINGMAN   Away with the join-stools, remove the court-
cupboard, look to the plate. Good thou, save me a piece of marchpane,
and, as thou loves me, let the porter let in Susan Grindstone and Nell.
[*Exit* SECOND SERVANT.] Anthony and Potpan!

[Enter ANTHONY *and* POTPAN]

[ANTHONY]   Ay, boy, ready.   *9*

[FIRST] SERVINGMAN   You are look'd for and call'd for, ask'd for and
sought for, in the great chamber.

[POTPAN]   We cannot be here and there too. Cheerly, boys, be brisk a
while, and the longer liver take all.

Exeunt

*Enter [CAPULET, LADY CAPULET, JULIET, TYBALT, NURSE,
SERVINGMEN, and] all the GUESTS and GENTLEWOMEN to the
Maskers*

CAPULET   Welcome, gentlemen! Ladies that have their toes
Unplagu'd with corns will walk [a bout] with you.   *15*
Ah, my mistresses, which of you all
Will now deny to dance? She that makes dainty,
She I'll swear hath corns. Am I come near ye now?
Welcome, gentlemen! I have seen the day

108. *date:* appointed time
109. *expire the term:* terminate the du-
ration
111. *untimely:* premature
I.v. Location: Scene continues, now
as a hall in Capulet's house
2. *trencher:* wooden platter
5. *join-stools:* joint-stools, stools ex-
pertly made by joiners
5–6. *court-cupboard:* sideboard

6. *plate:* silverware. *marchpane:* mar-
zipan
13. *the longer . . . all:* the survivor
takes all (proverbial), i.e., live merrily, enjoy life while it lasts
15. *walk a bout:* dance a turn
17. *makes dainty:* behaves coyly (by
refusing to dance)
18. *come near ye:* hitting close to the
mark

That I have worn a visor and could tell   20
A whispering tale in a fair lady's ear,
Such as would please; 'tis gone, 'tis gone, 'tis gone.
You are welcome, gentlemen! Come, musicians, play.

> *Music plays, and they dance*

A hall, a hall! give room! and foot it, girls.
More light, you knaves, and turn the tables up;   25
And quench the fire, the room is grown too hot.
Ah, sirrah, this unlook'd-for sport comes well.
Nay, sit, nay, sit, good cousin Capulet,
For you and I are past our dancing days.
How long is't now since last yourself and I   30
Were in a mask?

SECOND CAPULET   By'r lady, thirty years.

CAPULET   What, man? 'tis not so much, 'tis not so much:
'Tis since the nuptial of Lucentio,
Come Pentecost as quickly as it will,
Some five and twenty years, and then we mask'd.   35

SECOND CAPULET   'Tis more, 'tis more. His son is elder, sir;
    His son is thirty.

CAPULET   Will you tell me that?
His son was but a ward two years ago.

ROMEO [*to a* SERVINGMAN]   What lady's that which doth enrich the hand
Of yonder knight?   40

SERVINGMAN   I know not, sir.

ROMEO   O, she doth teach the torches to burn bright!
It seems she hangs upon the cheek of night
As a rich jewel in an Ethiop's ear—
Beauty too rich for use, for earth too dear!   45
So shows a snowy dove trooping with crows,
As yonder lady o'er her fellows shows.
The measure done, I'll watch her place of stand,
And touching hers, make blessed my rude hand.
Did my heart love till now? Forswear it, sight!   50
For I ne'er saw true beauty till this night.

TYBALT   This, by his voice, should be a Montague.
Fetch me my rapier, boy. What dares the slave
Come hither, cover'd with an antic face,
To fleer and scorn at our solemnity?   55
Now, by the stock and honor of my kin,
To strike him dead I hold it not a sin.

CAPULET   Why, how now, kinsman, wherefore storm you so?

---

24. *A hall:* make room, clear the floor
38. *a ward:* under guardianship, not of age

49. *rude:* rough
53. *What:* i.e., how
54. *antic face:* grotesque mask
55. *fleer:* mock. *solemnity:* festivity

TYBALT   Uncle, this is a Montague, our foe;
A villain that is hither come in spite   *60*
To scorn at our solemnity this night.

CAPULET   Young Romeo is it?

TYBALT   'Tis he, that villain Romeo.

CAPULET   Content thee, gentle coz, let him alone,
'A bears him like a portly gentlemen;
And to say truth, Verona brags of him   *65*
To be a virtuous and well-govern'd youth.
I would not for the wealth of all this town
Here in my house do him disparagement;
Therefore be patient, take no note of him;
It is my will, the which if thou respect,   *70*
Show a fair presence and put off these frowns,
An ill-beseeming semblance for a feast.

TYBALT   It fits when such a villain is a guest.
I'll not endure him.

CAPULET   He shall be endured.
What, goodman boy? I say he shall, go to!   *75*
Am I the master here, or you? go to!
You'll not endure him! God shall mend my soul,
You'll make a mutiny among my guests!
You will set cock-a-hoop! you'll be the man!

TYBALT   Why, uncle, 'tis a shame.

CAPULET   Go to, go to,   *80*
You are a saucy boy. Is't so indeed?
This trick may chance to scath you, I know what.
You must contrary me! Marry, 'tis time.—
Well said, my hearts!—You are a princox, go,
Be quiet, or—More light, more light!—For shame,   *85*
I'll make you quiet, what!—Cheerly, my hearts!

TYBALT   Patience perforce with willful choler meeting
Makes my flesh tremble in their different greeting.

---

62. *villain:* base fellow
64. *'A bears him:* he conducts himself. *portly:* well-mannered
75. *goodman:* title accorded a yeoman, i.e., one below the rank of a gentleman. Hence *goodman boy* is a double barreled insult to Tybalt
78. *mutiny:* disturbance
79. *set cock-a-hoop:* cast off restraint (?). The phrase is explained as referring originally to unrestrained drinking, with the cock or tap removed from the barrel or turned on full. But possibly the notion of a cock crowing (whooping) to proclaim his dominance is also present. *be the man:* play at being a man

80. *shame:* insult
82. *trick:* foolish behavior. *scath:* scathe, harm (probably a personal threat, "damage your expectations from me"). *I know what:* i.e., I know what I'll do to make you feel my displeasure (?)
83. *contrary me:* go against my will. *'tis time:* i.e., to teach you a lesson
84. *Well said:* bravo (said to the dancers). *princox:* insolent boy
87. *Patience perforce:* enforced forbearance
88. *their different greeting:* the confrontation of these opposed states of mind

I will withdraw, but this intrusion shall,   89
Now seeming sweet, convert to bitt'rest gall.   *Exit*
ROMEO [*to* JULIET]   If I profane with my unworthiest hand
This holy shrine, the gentle sin is this,
My lips, two blushing pilgrims, ready stand
To smooth that rough touch with a tender kiss.
JULIET   Good pilgrim, you do wrong your hand too much,   95
Which mannerly devotion shows in this:
For saints have hands that pilgrims' hands do touch,
And palm to palm is holy palmers' kiss.
ROMEO   Have not saints lips, and holy palmers too?
JULIET   Ay, pilgrim, lips that they must use in pray'r.   100
ROMEO   O then, dear saint, let lips do what hands do,
They pray—grant thou, lest faith turn to despair.
JULIET   Saints do not move, though grant for prayers' sake.
ROMEO   Then move not while my prayer's effect I take.   104
Thus from my lips, by thine, my sin is purg'd.   [*Kissing her*]
JULIET   Then have my lips the sin that they have took.
ROMEO   Sin from my lips? O trespass sweetly urg'd!
Give me my sin again.   [*Kissing her again*]
JULIET   You kiss by th' book.
NURSE   Madam, your mother craves a word with you.
ROMEO   What is her mother?
NURSE   Marry, bachelor,   110
Her mother is the lady of the house,
And a good lady, and a wise and virtuous.
I nurs'd her daughter that you talk'd withal;
I tell you, he that can lay hold of her
Shall have the thinks.
ROMEO   Is she a Capulet?   115
O dear account! my life is my foe's debt.
BENVOLIO   Away, be gone, the sport is at the best.
ROMEO   Ay, so I fear, the more is my unrest.
CAPULET   Nay, gentlemen, prepare not to be gone,
We have a trifling foolish banquet towards.   120

91–104. These lines make a sonnet in
the Shakespearean form
92. *shrine:* image. *the gentle sin:* i.e.,
the sin gentlemen must commit
in wooing ladies (?). Most editors
emend *sin* to *fine* or *pain* (= penalty)
95. *you . . . much:* i.e., your touch
was not rough (and hence no kiss is
called for)
96. *mannerly devotion:* proper devout-
ness
97. *palmers':* pilgrims'
103. *move:* institute an action. *grant:*
they grant
104. *move not:* remain still

108. *by th' book:* methodically
110. *What:* who. *bachelor:* young
man
113. *withal:* with
115. *chinks:* money (probably, as Clifford Leech suggests in *TLS,* January
25, 1971, with an indecent pun)
116. *dear account:* heavy reckoning.
my foe's debt: in the power of my
enemy
117. *Away . . . best:* he reminds Romeo of his earlier remark (I.iv.39)
120. *banquet:* refreshments (wine,
fruit, etc.). *towards:* on the way

Is it e'en so? Why then I thank you all.
I thank you, honest gentlemen, good night.
More torches here! Come on, then let's to bed.
[*To* SECOND CAPULET] Ah, sirrah, by my fay, it waxes late,
I'll to my rest.   *125*

[*Exeunt all but* JULIET *and* NURSE]

JULIET   Come hither, nurse. What is yond gentleman?
NURSE   The son and heir of old Tiberio.
JULIET   What's he that now is going out of door?
NURSE   Marry, that, I think, be young Petruchio.
JULIET   What's he that follows here, that would not dance?   *130*
NURSE   I know not.
JULIET   Go ask his name.—If he be married,
    My grave is like to be my wedding-bed.
NURSE   His name is Romeo, and a Montague,
    The only son of your great enemy.   *135*
JULIET   My only love sprung from my only hate!
    Too early seen unknown, and known too late!
    Prodigious birth of love it is to me
    That I must love a loathed enemy.
NURSE   What's tis? what's tis?
JULIET   A rhyme I learnt even now   *140*
    Of one I danc'd withal.   *One calls within,* "Juliet!"
NURSE   Anon, anon!
    Come let's away, the strangers all are gone.   *Exeunt*

[ACT TWO]   [*Enter*] CHORUS
                 Now old desire doth in his death-bed lie,
                 And young affection gapes to be his heir;
                 That fair for which love groan'd for and would die,
                 With tender Juliet [match'd] is now not fair.
                 Now Romeo is belov'd and loves again,   *5*
                 Alike bewitched by the charm of looks;
                 But to his foe suppos'd he must complain,
                 And she steal love's sweet bait from fearful hooks.
                 Being held a foe, he may not have access
                 To breathe such vows as lovers use to swear,   *10*

122. *honest:* worthy   4. *match'd:* compared
124. *fay:* faith   5. *again:* in return
138. *Prodigious:* ominous   6. *Alike:* both lovers equally
140. *tis:* i.e., this   7. *complain:* i.e., of his love pains
141. *Anon:* right away, coming 8. *fearful:* causing fear, dangerous
II.Cho. 2. *gapes:* longs   10. *use:* are accustomed
3. *fair:* beautiful woman

And she as much in love, her means much less
To meet her new-beloved any where.
But passion lends them power, time means, to meet,
Temp'ring extremities with extreme sweet.   [*Exit*]

[*Scene One*]

Enter ROMEO *alone*

ROMEO   Can I go forward when my heart is here?
Turn back, dull earth, and find thy centre out.
                    Enter BENVOLIO *with* MERCUTIO. [ROMEO *withdraws*]
BENVOLIO   Romeo! my cousin Romeo! Romeo!
MERCUTIO   He is wise,
And, on my life, hath stol'n him home to bed.
BENVOLIO   He ran this way and leapt this orchard wall.   *5*
Call, good Mercutio.
MERCUTIO   Nay, I'll conjure too.
Romeo! humors! madman! passion! lover!
Appear thou in the likeness of a sigh!
Speak but one rhyme, and I am satisfied;
Cry but "Ay me!", [pronounce] but "love" and ["dove"],   *10*
Speak to my gossip Venus one fair word,
One nickname for her purblind son and [heir],
Young Abraham Cupid, he that shot so [trim],
When King Cophetua lov'd the beggar-maid!
He heareth not, he stirreth not, he moveth not,   *15*
The ape is dead, and I must conjure him.
I conjure thee by Rosaline's bright eyes,
By her high forehead and her scarlet lip,
By her fine foot, straight leg, and quivering thigh,
And the demesnes that there adjacent lie,   *20*
That in thy likeness thou appear to us!
BENVOLIO   And if he hear thee, thou wilt anger him.

14. *Temp'ring:* moderating. *extremities:* i.e., their plight
II.i. Location: Verona. Capulet's orchard
2. *dull earth:* i.e., his body. *centre:* Juliet is the core of his being, and he will move toward her as things on earth fall toward its centre
5. *orchard:* garden
6. *conjure:* call up a spirit (Romeo's)
11. *gossip:* crony (very familiar, suggesting that Venus is a garrulous old woman)
12. *purblind:* dim-sighted

13. *Abraham:* i.e., beggarly, thieving (alluding to the so-called "Abraham man," a beggar who wandered through the countryside half naked, picking up what he could). *trim:* adeptly, accurately. In the ballad of "King Cophetua and the Beggar Maid" Cupid is called "the blinded boy that shoots so trim"
16. *ape:* often used playfully or as a term of endearment
20. *demesnes:* estates
22. *And if:* if

MERCUTIO   This cannot anger him; 'twould anger him
        To raise a spirit in his mistress' circle,
        Of some strange nature, letting it there stand   25
        Till she had laid it and conjur'd it down.
        That were some spite. My invocation
        Is fair and honest; in his mistress' name
        I conjure only but to raise up him.
BENVOLIO   Come, he hath hid himself among these trees
        To be consorted with the humorous night.   30
        Blind is his love and best befits the dark.
MERCUTIO   If love be blind, love cannot hit the mark.
        Now will he sit under a medlar tree,
        And wish his mistress were that kind of fruit   35
        As maids call medlars, when they laugh alone.
        O, Romeo, that she were, O that she were
        An open[-arse], thou a pop'rin pear!
        Romeo, good night, I'll to my truckle-bed,
        This field-bed is too cold for me to sleep.   40
        Come, shall we go?
BENVOLIO   Go then, for 'tis in vain
        To seek him here that means not to be found.   *Exit* [*with* MERCUTIO]

                    [*Scene Two*]

                [ROMEO *advances*]
ROMEO   He jests at scars that never felt a wound.

                            [*Enter* JULIET *above at her window*]
        But soft, what light through yonder window breaks?
        It is the east, and Juliet is the sun.
        Arise, fair sun, and kill the envious moon,
        Who is already sick and pale with grief   5
        That thou, her maid, art far more fair than she.
        Be not her maid, since she is envious;
        Her vestal livery is but sick and green,
        And none but fools do wear it; cast it off.
        It is my lady, O, it is my love!   10
        O that she knew she were!

24. *spirit:* with pun on the sense
"semen," following a pun on *raise;*
the double-entendre continues in *circle* and in the next two lines
27. *spite:* vexation
31. *humorous:* (1) damp; (2) moody
34. *medlar:* apple-like fruit
38. *open-arse:* another name for the
medlar, with allusion to female pu-
denda. *pop'rin pear:* Flemish pear of
phallic shape

39. *truckle-bed:* low bed, made to fit
under a larger
II.ii. Location: Scene continues
7. *maid:* devotee (of the moon-
goddess Diana, patroness of virgins)
8. *sick and green:* alluding to a kind of
anemia called "the green-sickness,"
supposed to be found in unmarried
girls

She speaks, yet she says nothing; what of that?
Her eye discourses, I will answer it.
I am too bold, 'tis not to me she speaks.
Two of the fairest stars in all the heaven,   *15*
Having some business, [do] entreat her eyes
To twinkle in their spheres till they return.
What if her eyes were there, they in her head?
The brightness of her cheek would shame those stars,
As daylight doth a lamp; her [eyes] in heaven   *20*
Would through the airy region stream so bright
That birds would sing and think it were not night.
See how she leans her cheek upon her hand!
O that I were a glove upon that hand,
That I might touch that cheek!
JULIET   Ay me!
ROMEO   She speaks!   *25*
O, speak again, bright angel, for thou art
As glorious to this night, being o'er my head,
As is a winged messenger of heaven
Unto the white-upturned wond'ring eyes
Of mortals that fall back to gaze on him,   *30*
When he bestrides the lazy puffing clouds,
And sails upon the bosom of the air.
JULIET   O Romeo, Romeo, wherefore art thou Romeo?
Deny thy father and refuse thy name;
Or, if thou wilt not, be but sworn my love,   *35*
And I'll no longer be a Capulet.
ROMEO [*aside*]   Shall I hear more, or shall I speak at this?
JULIET   'Tis but thy name that is my enemy;
Thou art thyself, though not a Montague.
What's Montague? It is nor hand nor foot,   *40*
Nor arm nor face, [nor any other part]
Belonging to a man. O, be some other name!
What's in a name? That which we call a rose
By any other word would smell as sweet;
So Romeo would, were he not Romeo call'd,   *45*
Retain that dear perfection which he owes
Without that title. Romeo, doff thy name,
And for thy name, which is no part of thee,
Take all myself.

17. *spheres:* according to the Ptolema-
ic astronomy, the heavenly bodies
were fixed in concentric transparent
spheres that revolved around the
earth
21. *stream:* shine
29. *white-upturned:* turned upward so
that the whites are visible below the
irises
39. *Thou . . . Montague:* i.e., you
won't change yourself if you change
your name
46. *owes:* possesses
48. *for:* in exchange for

ROMEO   I take thee at thy word.
Call me but love, and I'll be new baptiz'd;   50
Henceforth I never will be Romeo.
JULIET   What man art thou that thus bescreen'd in night
So stumblest on my counsel?
ROMEO   By a name
I know not how to tell thee who I am.
My name, dear saint, is hateful to myself,   55
Because it is an enemy to thee;
Had I it written, I would tear the word.
JULIET   My ears have yet not drunk a hundred words
Of thy tongue's uttering, yet I know the sound.
Art thou not Romeo, and a Montague?   60
ROMEO   Neither, fair maid, if either thee dislike.
JULIET   How camest thou hither, tell me, and wherefore?
The orchard walls are high and hard to climb,
And the place death, considering who thou art,
If any of my kinsmen find thee here.   65
ROMEO   With love's light wings did I o'erperch these walls,
For stony limits cannot hold love out,
And what love can do, that dares love attempt;
Therefore thy kinsmen are no stop to me.
JULIET   If they do see thee, they will murther thee.   70
ROMEO   Alack, there lies more peril in thine eye
Than twenty of their swords! Look thou but sweet,
And I am proof against their enmity.
JULIET   I would not for the world they saw thee here.
ROMEO   I have night's cloak to hide me from their eyes,   75
And but thou love me, let them find me here;
My life were better ended by their hate,
Than death prorogued, wanting of thy love.
JULIET   By whose direction foundst thou out this place?
ROMEO   By love, that first did prompt me to inquire;   80
He lent me counsel, and I lent him eyes.
I am no pilot, yet, wert thou as far
As that vast shore [wash'd] with the farthest sea,
I should adventure for such merchandise.
JULIET   Thou knowest the mask of night is on my face,   85
Else would a maiden blush bepaint my cheek
For that which thou hast heard me speak to-night.

---

53. *counsel:* private thoughts   78. *prorogued:* put off. *wanting of:*
61. *dislike:* displease   lacking
66. *o'erperch:* fly over   83. *vast:* desolate
73. *proof:* armored   84. *adventure:* risk the voyage
76. *but:* unless

Fain would I dwell on form, fain, fain deny
What I have spoke, but farewell compliment!
Dost thou love me? I know thou wilt say, "Ay,"   *90*
And I will take thy word; yet, if thou swear'st,
Thou mayest prove false: at lovers' perjuries
They say Jove laughs. O gentle Romeo,
If thou dost love, pronounce it faithfully;
Of if thou thinkest I am too quickly won,   *95*
I'll frown and be perverse, and say thee nay,
So thou wilt woo, but else not for the world.
In truth, fair Montague, I am too fond,
And therefore thou mayest think my behavior light,
But trust me, gentleman, I'll prove more true   *100*
Than those that have [more] coying to be strange.
I should have been more strange, I must confess,
But that thou overheardst, ere I was ware,
My true-love passion; therefore pardon me,
And not impute this yielding to light love,   *105*
Which the dark night hath so discovered.

ROMEO   Lady, by yonder blessed moon I vow,
That tips with silver all these fruit-tree tops—

JULIET   O, swear not by the moon, th' inconstant moon,
That monthly changes in her [circled] orb,   *110*
Lest that thy love prove likewise variable.

ROMEO   What shall I swear by?

JULIET   Do not swear at all;
Or if thou wilt, swear by thy gracious self,
Which is the god of my idolatry,
And I'll believe thee.

ROMEO   If my heart's dear love—   *115*

JULIET   Well, do not swear. Although I joy in thee,
I have no joy of this contract to-night,
It is too rash, too unadvis'd, too sudden,
Too like the lightning, which doth cease to be
Ere one can say it lightens. Sweet, good night!   *120*
This bud of love, by summer's ripening breath,
May prove a beauteous flow'r when next we meet.
Good night, good night! as sweet repose and rest
Come to thy heart as that within my breast!

---

88. *Fain:* gladly. *dwell on form:* maintain formal behavior
89. *compliment:* social conventions
97. *So thou wilt:* i.e., in order to have
you
101. *coying:* skill at coquetry. *strange:*
aloof, standoffish
106. *discovered:* revealed

110. *circled orb:* sphere (see note on
line 17)
113. *gracious:* endowed with all graces
of mind and body
117. *contract:* exchange of promises
118. *rash:* hasty. *unadvis'd:* ill-con-
sidered

ROMEO	O, wilt thou leave me so unsatisfied?	125
JULIET	What satisfaction canst thou have to-night?	
ROMEO	Th' exchange of thy love's faithful vow for mine.	

JULIET   I gave thee mine before thou didst request it;
And yet I would it were to give again.

ROMEO   Wouldst thou withdraw it? for what purpose, love?   130

JULIET   But to be frank and give it thee again,
And yet I wish but for the thing I have.
My bounty is as boundless as the sea,
My love as deep; the more I give to thee,
The more I have, for both are infinite.   135

[NURSE calls within]

I hear some noise within; dear love, adieu!
Anon, good nurse! Sweet Montague, be true.
Stay but a little, I will come again.   [Exit above]

ROMEO   O blessed, blessed night! I am afeard,
Being in night, all this is but a dream,   140
Too flattering-sweet to be substantial.

[Enter JULIET above]

JULIET   Three words, dear Romeo, and good night indeed.
If that thy bent of love be honorable,
Thy purpose marriage, send me word to-morrow,
By one that I'll procure to come to thee,   145
Where and what time thou wilt perform the rite,
And all my fortunes at thy foot I'll lay,
And follow thee my lord throughout the world.

[NURSE within]   Madam!

JULIET   I come, anon.—But if thou meanest not well,   150
I do beseech thee—

[NURSE within]   Madam!

JULIET   By and by, I come—
To cease thy strife, and leave me to my grief.
To-morrow will I send.

ROMEO   So thrive my soul—

JULIET   A thousand times good night!   [Exit above]

ROMEO   A thousand times the worse, to want thy light.   155
Love goes toward love as schoolboys from their books,
But love from love, toward school with heavy looks.   [Retiring]

Enter JULIET again [above]

JULIET   Hist, Romeo, hist! O, for a falc'ner's voice,
To lure this tassel-gentle back again!

---

131. *frank:* generous
137. *Anon:* at once
143. *thy . . . love:* the intention of your love
151. *By and by:* immediately

152. *strife:* striving, endeavor
158. *Hist:* she calls him as a falconer calls his hawk
159. *tassel-gentle:* tercel-gentle, male falcon of a type reserved to princes

Bondage is hoarse, and may not speak aloud,   160
Else would I tear the cave where Echo lies,
And make her airy tongue more hoarse than [mine],
With repetition of my [Romeo's name.] Romeo!
ROMEO   It is my soul that calls upon my name.
How silver-sweet sound lovers' tongues by night,   165
Like softest music to attending ears!
JULIET   Romeo!
ROMEO   My [niesse]?
JULIET   What a' clock to-morrow
Shall I send to thee?
ROMEO   By the hour of nine.
JULIET   I will not fail, 'tis twenty year till then.
I have forgot why I did call thee back.   170
ROMEO   Let me stand here till thou remember it.
JULIET   I shall forget, to have thee still stand there,
Rememb'ring how I love thy company.
ROMEO   And I'll still stay, to have thee still forget,
Forgetting any other home but this.   175
JULIET   'Tis almost morning, I would have thee gone—
And yet no farther than a wanton's bird,
That lets it hop a little from his hand,
Like a poor prisoner in his twisted gyves,
And with a silken thread plucks it back again,   180
So loving-jealous of his liberty.
ROMEO   I would I were thy bird.
JULIET   Sweet, so would I,
Yet I should kill thee with much cherishing.
Good night, good night! Parting is such sweet sorrow,   184
That I shall say good night till it be morrow.   [Exit above]
[ROMEO]   Sleep dwell upon thine eyes, peace in thy breast!
Would I were sleep and peace, so sweet to rest!
Hence will I to my ghostly [sire's] close cell,
His help to crave, and my dear hap to tell.   Exit

[Scene Three]

Enter FRIAR [LAWRENCE] alone, with a basket
FRIAR LAWRENCE   The grey-ey'd morn smiles on the frowning night,
Check'ring the eastern clouds with streaks of light,

167. *niesse:* nestling hawk (disyllabic)
172. *to:* in order to. *still:* always
177. *wanton's:* spoiled child
179. *gyves:* fetters
181. *his:* its
188. *ghostly sire:* spiritual father, or

confessor. *close:* secluded (?) or narrow (?)
189. *dear hap:* good fortune
II.iii. Location: Verona. Friar Lawrence's cell

And fleckled darkness with a drunkard reels
From forth day's path and Titan's [fiery] wheels.
Now ere the sun advance his burning eye, 5
The day to cheer and night's dank dew to dry,
I must up-fill this osier cage of ours
With baleful weeds and precious-juiced flowers.
The earth that's nature's mother is her tomb;
What is her burying grave, that is her womb; 10
And from her womb children of divers kind
We sucking on her natural bosom find:
Many for many virtues excellent,
None but for some, and yet all different.
O, mickle is the powerful grace that lies 15
In plants, herbs, stones, and their true qualities;
For nought so vile that on the earth doth live
But to the earth some special good doth give;
Nor aught so good but, strain'd from that fair use,
Revolts from true birth, stumbling on abuse. 20
Virtue itself turns vice, being misapplied,
And vice sometime by action dignified.

Enter ROMEO

Within the infant rind of this weak flower
Poison hath residence and medicine power;
For this, being smelt, with that part cheers each part, 25
Being tasted, stays all senses with the heart.
Two such opposed kings encamp them still
In man as well as herbs, grace and rude will;
And where the worser is predominant,
Full soon the canker death eats up that plant. 30

ROMEO   Good morrow, father.

FRIAR LAWRENCE   *Benedicite!*
What early tongue so sweet saluteth me?
Young son, it argues a distempered head
So soon to bid good morrow to thy bed.
Care keeps his watch in every old man's eye, 35
And where care lodges, sleep will never lie;

3. *fleckled:* dappled
4. *From forth:* out of the way of. *Titan's fiery wheels:* the sun god's chariot wheels
7. *osier cage:* willow basket
13. *virtues:* properties, powers
14. *None . . . some:* none without some (virtue)
15. *mickle:* great. *powerful grace:* gracious (i.e., healing) power
16. *true:* inherent

20. *true birth:* innate goodness
21. *turns:* turns into
22. *by action dignified:* may in special circumstances have the quality of a virtue
25. *that part:* i.e., the odor. *each part:* i.e., of the body
26. *stays:* brings to a halt
30. *canker:* plant-destroying worm
31. *Benedicite:* bless you
33. *distempered:* disordered, disturbed

But where unbruised youth with unstuff'd brain
Doth couch his limbs, there golden sleep doth reign.
Therefore thy earliness doth me assure
Thou art up-rous'd with some distemp'rature;   *40*
Or if not so, then here I hit it right—
Our Romeo hath not been in bed to-night.

ROMEO   That last is true—the sweeter rest was mine.

FRIAR LAWRENCE   God pardon sin! Wast thou with Rosaline?

ROMEO   With Rosaline? my ghostly father, no;   *45*
I have forgot that name, and that name's woe.

FRIAR LAWRENCE   That's my good son, but where hast thou been then?

ROMEO   I'll tell thee ere thou ask it me again.
I have been feasting with mine enemy,
Where on a sudden one hath wounded me   *50*
That's by me wounded; both our remedies
Within thy help and holy physic lies.
I bear no hatred, blessed man, for lo
My intercession likewise steads my foe.

FRIAR LAWRENCE   Be plain, good son, and homely in thy drift, *55*
Riddling confession finds but riddling shrift.

ROMEO   Then plainly know my heart's dear love is set
On the fair daughter of rich Capulet.
As mine on hers, so hers is set on mine,
And all combin'd, save what thou must combine   *60*
By holy marriage. When and where and how
We met, we woo'd, and made exchange of vow,
I'll tell thee as we pass, but this I pray,
That thou consent to marry us to-day.

FRIAR LAWRENCE   Holy Saint Francis, what a change is here!   *65*
Is Rosaline, that thou didst love so dear,
So soon forsaken? Young men's love then lies
Not truly in their hearts, but in their eyes.
Jesu Maria, what a deal of brine
Hath wash'd thy sallow cheeks for Rosaline!   *70*
How much salt water thrown away in waste,
To season love, that of it doth not taste!
The sun not yet thy sighs from heaven clears,
Thy old groans yet ringing in mine ancient ears;
Lo here upon thy cheek the stain doth sit   *75*
Of an old tear that is not wash'd off yet.

---

37. *unbruised:* i.e., not yet injured in
life. *unstuff'd:* unburdened, carefree
52. *physic:* power to heal (by performing the marriage rite)
54. *intercession:* petition. *steads:* helps
55. *homely:* plain

56. *shrift:* absolution
63. *pass:* go along, proceed
72. *season:* preserve (with following
play on the sense "flavor")
73. *sighs:* thought of as producing
mist

If e'er thou wast thyself and these woes thine,
Thou and these woes were all for Rosaline.
And art thou chang'd? Pronounce this sentence then:
Women may fall, when there's no strength in men.   *80*

ROMEO   Thou chidst me oft for loving Rosaline.

FRIAR LAWRENCE   For doting, not for loving, pupil mine.

ROMEO   And badst me bury love.

FRIAR LAWRENCE   Not in a grave,
To lay one in, another out to have.

ROMEO   I pray thee chide me not. Her I love now   *85*
Doth grace for grace and love for love allow;
The other did not so.

FRIAR LAWRENCE   O, she knew well
Thy love did read by rote that could not spell.
But come, young waverer, come go with me,
In one respect I'll thy assistant be;   *90*
For this alliance may so happy prove
To turn your households' rancor to pure love.

ROMEO   O, let us hence, I stand on sudden haste.

FRIAR LAWRENCE   Wisely and slow, they stumble that run fast.   *Exeunt*

[*Scene Four*]

Enter BENVOLIO *and* MERCUTIO

MERCUTIO   Where the dev'l should this Romeo be?
Came he not home to-night?

BENVOLIO   Not to his father's, I spoke with his man.

MERCUTIO   Why, that same pale hard-hearted wench, that Rosaline,
Torments him so, that he will sure run mad.   *5*

BENVOLIO   Tybalt, the kinsman to old Capulet,
Hath sent a letter to his father's house.

MERCUTIO   A challenge, on my life.

BENVOLIO   Romeo will answer it.

MERCUTIO   Any man that can write may answer a letter.   *10*

BENVOLIO   Nay, he will answer the letter's master, how he dares, being
dar'd.

MERCUTIO   Alas, poor Romeo, he is already dead, stabb'd with a white
wench's black eye, run through the ear with a love-song, the very pin of

79. *sentence:* moral saying
86. *grace:* favor
88. *did . . . spell:* not being able to read, pretended to do so by reciting what it had learned by heart; i.e., Romeo had only imitated true love
90. *In one respect:* for one good reason
92. *To:* as to

93. *stand:* insist
II.iv. Location: Verona. A street
2. *to-night:* last night
9. *answer it:* accept the challenge
11. *how:* as
14. *pin:* peg in the centre of an archery target

his heart cleft with the blind bow-boy's butt-shaft; and is he a man to encounter Tybalt? _16_

[BENVOLIO]   Why, what is Tybalt?

MERCUTIO   More than Prince of Cats. O, he's the courageous captain of compliments. He fights as you sing prick-song, keeps time, distance, and proportion; he rests his minim rests, one, two, and the third in your bosom: the very butcher of a silk button, a duellist, a duellist; a gentleman of the very first house, of the first and second cause. Ah, the immortal _passado_, the _punto reverso_, the _hay_! _23_

BENVOLIO   The what?

MERCUTIO   The pox of such antic, lisping, affecting [phantasimes], these new tuners of accent! "By Jesu, a very good blade! a very tall man! a very good whore!" Why, is not this a lamentable thing, grandsire, that we should be thus afflicted with these strange flies, these fashion-mongers, these [pardon-]me's, who stand so much on the new form, that they cannot sit at ease on the old bench? O, their bones, their bones! _31_

Enter ROMEO

BENVOLIO   Here comes Romeo, here comes Romeo.

MERCUTIO   Without his roe, like a dried herring: O flesh, flesh, how art thou fishified! Now is he for the numbers that Petrarch flow'd in. Laura to his lady was a kitchen wench (marry, she had a better love to berhyme her), Dido a dowdy, Cleopatra a gipsy, Helen and Hero hildings and harlots, Thisby a grey eye or so, but not to the purpose. Signior Romeo, _bon jour!_ there's a French salutation to your French slop. You gave us the counterfeit fairly last night. _39_

ROMEO   Good morrow to you both. What counterfeit did I give you?

---

15. _butt-shaft:_ blunt arrow for practice, often assigned to Cupid, presumably because he was represented as a child
18. _Prince of Cats:_ in _Reynard the Fox_ the Prince of Cats is named Tibalt
18–19. _captain of compliments:_ master of dueling punctilio
19. _prick-song:_ printed music. Tybalt fights with studied accuracy, like singers who perform from printed music in contrast to those who sing by ear
20. _proportion:_ rhythm. _minim rests:_ the shortest rests in music
21. _butcher . . . button:_ an expert could strike any designated button on his opponent's clothing. _duellist:_ a word newly introduced into English
22. _first house:_ best school of fencing. _first . . . cause:_ these were occasions upon which a gentleman ought to take offense and require satisfaction
23. _passado:_ forward thrust. _punto reverso:_ backhanded thrust. _hay:_ home thrust (apparently a new term to Benvolio)

25. _affecting phantasimes:_ affected coxcombs
26. _new . . . accent:_ utterers of new-fangled phrases. _tall:_ brave
27. _grandsire:_ he addresses Benvolio, pretending they are old men complaining of the follies of the young
29. _pardon-me's:_ fellows of affected manners. _form:_ fashion (with following play on the sense "bench")
31. _bones:_ with pun on French _bons,_ "good" (plural)
33. _Without his roe:_ i.e., looking very thin (lovers were expected to have poor appetites); with play on the first syllable of "Romeo"
34. _numbers:_ verses
35. _Laura:_ beloved of Petrarch. All the ladies named in this passage were heroines of famous love stories. _to:_ in comparison with
37. _hildings:_ good-for-nothings. _to the purpose:_ worth mentioning
38–39. _French slop:_ loose breeches

MERCUTIO   The slip, sir, the slip, can you not conceive?

ROMEO   Pardon, good Mercutio, my business was great, and in such a case as mine a man may strain courtesy.

MERCUTIO   That's as much as to say, such a case as yours constrains a man to bow in the hams.   45

ROMEO   Meaning to cur'sy.

MERCUTIO   Thou hast most kindly hit it.

ROMEO   A most courteous exposition.

MERCUTIO   Nay, I am the very pink of courtesy.

ROMEO   Pink for flower.   50

MERCUTIO   Right.

ROMEO   Why then is my pump well flower'd.

MERCUTIO   Sure wit! Follow me this jest now, till thou hast worn out thy pump, that when the single sole of it is worn, the jest may remain, after the wearing, soly singular.   55

ROMEO   O single-sol'd jest, soly singular for the singleness!

MERCUTIO   Come between us, good Benvolio, my wits faints.

ROMEO   Swits and spurs, swits and spurs, or I'll cry a match.

MERCUTIO   Nay, if our wits run the wild-goose chase, I am done; for thou hast more of the wild goose in one of thy wits than, I am sure, I have in my whole five. Was I with you there for the goose?   61

ROMEO   Thou wast never with me for anything when thou wast not there for the goose.

MERCUTIO   I will bite thee by the ear for that jest.

ROMEO   Nay, good goose, bite not.   65

MERCUTIO   Thy wit is a very bitter sweeting, it is a most sharp sauce.

ROMEO   And is it not then well serv'd in to a sweet goose?

MERCUTIO   O, here's a wit of cheverel, that stretches from an inch narrow to an ell broad!

ROMEO   I stretch it out for that word "broad," which, added to the goose, proves thee far and wide a broad goose.   71

---

41. *The slip:* Counterfeit coins were called "slips." *can . . . conceive:* i.e., what's the matter with your brain
43. *strain courtesy:* transgress good manners. But Mercutio jocularly interprets Romeo's apology as a description of a man with a venereal infection
47. *kindly:* naturally, truly
50. *pink:* flower, i.e., acme
52. *pump:* shoe. *flower'd:* i.e., pinked, perforated in a decorative pattern
54. *single:* i.e., thin
55. *soly singular:* quite alone (*soly* is a variant of *solely*)
56. *single-sol'd:* i.e., feeble. *soly . . . singleness:* in a class by itself for silliness

58. *Swits and spurs:* switch and spurs, i.e., keep up the rapid pace. *cry a match:* claim the victory
59. *wild-goose chase:* mounted follow-the-leader. *done:* done for
61. *Was . . . goose:* did I score off you with that word *goose*
63. *for the goose:* (1) behaving like a goose; (2) looking for a prostitute (slang sense of *goose*)
66. *sweeting:* kind of apple
68. *cheverel:* kid leather, easily stretched
69. *ell:* 45 inches
71. *broad:* large, i.e., obvious; perhaps with a pun on the sense "indecent" (cf. *large* in line 78, which has this sense for one of its meanings)

MERCUTIO Why, is not this better now than groaning for love? Now art thou sociable, now art thou Romeo; now art thou what thou art, by art as well as by nature, for this drivelling love is like a great natural that runs lolling up and down to hide his bable in a hole. *75*

BENVOLIO Stop there, stop there.

MERCUTIO Thou desirest me to stop in my tale against the hair.

BENVOLIO Thou wouldst else have made thy tale large.

MERCUTIO O, thou art deceiv'd; I would have made it short, for I was come to the whole depth of my tale, and meant indeed to occupy the argument no longer. *81*

ROMEO Here's goodly gear!

Enter NURSE *and her man* [PETER]

A sail, a sail!

MERCUTIO Two, two: a shirt and a smock.

NURSE Peter! *85*

PETER Anon!

NURSE My fan, Peter.

MERCUTIO Good Peter, to hide her face, for her fan's the fairer face.

NURSE God ye good morrow, gentlemen.

MERCUTIO God ye good den, fair gentlewoman. *90*

NURSE Is it good den?

MERCUTIO 'Tis no less, I tell ye, for the bawdy hand of the dial is now upon the prick of noon.

NURSE Out upon you, what a man are you?

ROMEO One, gentlewoman, that God hath made, himself to mar. *95*

NURSE By my troth, it is well said; "for himself to mar," quoth 'a! Gentlemen, can any of you tell me where I may find the young Romeo?

ROMEO I can tell you, but young Romeo will be older when you have found him than he was when you sought him. I am the youngest of that name, for fault of a worse. *100*

NURSE You say well.

MERCUTIO Yea, is the worst well? Very well took, i' faith, wisely, wisely.

NURSE If you be he, sir, I desire some confidence with you.

BENVOLIO She will indite him to some supper. *105*

MERCUTIO A bawd, a bawd, a bawd! So ho!

---

74. *natural:* idiot
75. *lolling:* with his tongue hanging out. *bable:* bauble, stick carried by a court jester or "natural," with secondary meaning "penis," as also in *tale* (lines 77, 78) and *gear* (line 82). *Occupy* (line 80) is included in the wordplay
77. *against the hair:* against my wish (with sexual innuendo)
84. *shirt . . . smock:* man . . . woman
91. *Is . . . den:* i.e., is it already past noon

93. *prick:* mark on a sundial or clock (with another bawdy pun)
94. *what a man:* what kind of man
96. *troth:* faith
104. *confidence:* i.e., conference (malapropism)
105. *indite:* i.e., invite (intentional malapropism)
106. *So ho:* hunter's cry when sighting a hare. (*Bawd* is a dialect word for "hare," and *hare*, like *stale* in line 109 and *meat* in line 112, is slang for "prostitute")

ROMEO   What hast thou found?

MERCUTIO   No hare, sir, unless a hare, sir, in a lenten pie, that is something stale and hoar ere it be spent.   [*He walks by them and sings*]

An old hare hoar,   *110*

And an old hare hoar,

Is very good meat in Lent;

But a hare that is hoar

Is too much for a score,

When it hoars ere it be spent.   *115*

Romeo, will you come to your father's? We'll to dinner thither.

ROMEO   I will follow you.

MERCUTIO   Farewell, ancient lady, farewell, [*singing*] "lady, lady, lady."

Exeunt [MERCUTIO *and* BENVOLIO]

NURSE   I pray you, sir, what saucy merchant was this, that was so full of his ropery?   *120*

ROMEO   A gentleman, nurse, that loves to hear himself talk, and will speak more in a minute than he will stand to in a month.

NURSE   And 'a speak any thing against me, I'll take him down, and 'a were lustier than he is, and twenty such Jacks; and if I cannot, I'll find those that shall. Scurvy knave, I am none of his flirt-gills, I am none of his skains-mates. [*She turns to* PETER, *her man*] And thou must stand by too and suffer every knave to use me at his pleasure!   *127*

PETER   I saw no man use you at his pleasure; if I had, my weapon should quickly have been out. I warrant you, I dare draw as soon as another man, if I see occasion in a good quarrel, and the law on my side.

NURSE   Now, afore God, I am so vex'd that every part about me quivers. Scurvy knave! Pray you, sir, a word: and as I told you, my young lady bid me inquire you out; what she bid me say, I will keep to myself. But first let me tell ye, if ye should lead her in a fool's paradise, as they say, it were a very gross kind of behavior, as they say; for the gentlewoman is young; and therefore, if you should deal double with her, truly it were an ill thing to be off'red to any gentlewoman, and very weak dealing.   *138*

ROMEO   Nurse, commend me to thy lady and mistress. I protest unto thee—

NURSE   Good heart, and i' faith, I will tell her as much. Lord, Lord, she will be a joyful woman.

---

108. *lenten pie:* this should contain no meat; perhaps one might put in it an old poached hare from the black market (Mercutio is insulting the Nurse)
109. *hoar:* mouldy (with pun on "whore"). *spent:* eaten up
114. *too . . . score:* not worth paying for (*score* = reckoning, bill)
118. *lady, lady, lady:* a ballad refrain
119. *merchant:* fellow
120. *ropery:* knavery

123. *take him down:* humble him (with unintended bawdy second meaning)
124. *Jacks:* saucy fellows
125. *flirt-gills:* loose woman
126. *skains-mates:* derogatory term not occurring elsewhere
128–129. *I . . . out:* Peter joins in the indecent quibbling
137. *weak:* poor, mean
139. *commend me:* give my regards. *protest:* solemnly affirm

ROMEO   What wilt thou tell her, nurse? Thou dost not mark me.

NURSE   I will tell her, sir, that you do protest, which, as I take it, is a
gentleman-like offer.   145

ROMEO   Bid her devise

Some means to come to shrift this afternoon,

And there she shall at Friar Lawrence' cell

Be shriv'd and married. Here is for thy pains.

NURSE   No, truly, sir, not a penny.   150

ROMEO   Go to, I say you shall.

NURSE   This afternoon, sir? Well, she shall be there.

ROMEO   And stay, good nurse—behind the abbey wall

Within this hour my man shall be with thee,

And bring thee cords made like a tackled stair,   155

Which to the high top-gallant of my joy

Must be my convoy in the secret night.

Farewell, be trusty, and I'll quit thy pains.

Farewell, commend me to thy mistress.

NURSE   Now God in heaven bless thee! Hark you, sir.   160

ROMEO   What say'st thou, my dear nurse?

NURSE   Is your man secret? Did you ne'er hear say,

"Two may keep counsel, putting one away"?

ROMEO   'Warrant thee, my man's as true as steel.   164

NURSE   Well, sir, my mistress is the sweetest lady—Lord, Lord! when
'twas a little prating thing—O, there is a nobleman in town, one Paris,
that would fain lay knife aboard; but she, good soul, had as lieve see a
toad, a very toad, as see him. I anger her sometimes and tell her that
Paris is the properer man, but I'll warrant you, when I say so, she looks
as pale as any clout in the versal world. Doth not rosemary and Romeo
begin both with a letter?   171

ROMEO   Ay, nurse, what of that? Both with an R.

NURSE   Ah, mocker, that's the [dog's] name. R is for the—no, I know it
begins with some other letter—and she hath the prettiest sententious of
it, of you and rosemary, that it would do you good to hear it.

ROMEO   Commend me to thy lady.   176

NURSE   Ay, a thousand times. [*Exit* ROMEO] Peter!

143. *mark:* pay attention to
155. *tackled stair:* rope ladder
156. *top-gallant:* highest mast of a ship
157. *convoy:* means of passage (continuing the nautical figure)
158. *quit:* reward
162. *secret:* to be trusted with confidential information
163. *keep counsel:* keep a secret. *putting one away:* if one of them is away
167. *lay knife aboard:* i.e., press his claim. *lieve:* lief, willingly

169. *properer:* handsomer
170. *clout:* (white) cloth. *versal:* i.e., universal, entire
171. *a letter:* the same letter
173. *dog's name:* the letter r was called *littera canina,* "the dog's letter," because its sound was thought to resemble a dog's growl
174. *sententious:* i.e., sentences, sayings

PETER   Anon!

NURSE *[handing him her fan]*   Before, and apace.   *Exit [after* PETER]

[*Scene Five*]

Enter JULIET

JULIET   The clock strook nine when I did send the nurse;
In half an hour she promised to return.
Perchance she cannot meet him—that's not so.
O, she is lame! Love's heralds should be thoughts,
Which ten times faster glides than the sun's beams,   *5*
Driving back shadows over low'ring hills;
Therefore do nimble-pinion'd doves draw Love,
And therefore hath the wind-swift Cupid wings.
Now is the sun upon the highmost hill
Of this day's journey, and from nine till twelve   *10*
Is [three] long hours, yet she is not come.
Had she affections and warm youthful blood,
She would be as swift in motion as a ball;
My words would bandy her to my sweet love,
And his to me.   *15*
But old folks—many feign as they were dead,
Unwieldy, slow, heavy, and pale as lead.

Enter NURSE [*and* PETER]

O God, she comes! O honey nurse, what news?
Hast thou met with him? Send thy man away.

NURSE   Peter, stay at the gate.   *20*

[*Exit* PETER]

JULIET   Now, good sweet nurse—O Lord, why lookest thou sad?
Though news be sad, yet tell them merrily;
If good, thou shamest the music of sweet news
By playing it to me with so sour a face.

NURSE   I am a-weary, give me leave a while.   *25*
Fie, how my bones ache! What a jaunce have I!

JULIET   I would thou hadst my bones, and I thy news.
Nay, come, I pray thee speak, good, good nurse, speak.

NURSE   Jesu, what haste! Can you not stay a while?
Do you not see that I am out of breath?   *30*

JULIET   How art thou out of breath, when thou hast breath
To say to me that thou art out of breath?
The excuse that thou dost make in this delay

II.v. Location: Verona. Capulet's orchard
7. *draw Love:* pull Venus (in her
chariot)

14. *bandy:* toss
26. *jaunce:* jouncing, i.e., tiring
journey
29. *stay:* wait

Is longer than the tale thou dost excuse.
Is thy news good or bad? Answer to that.   35
Say either, and I'll stay the circumstance.
Let me be satisfied, is't good or bad?

NURSE   Well, you have made a simple choice, you know not how to
choose a man. Romeo! no, not he. Though his face be better than any
man's, yet his leg excels all men's, and for a hand and a foot and a body,
though they be not to be talk'd on, yet they are past compare. He is
not the flower of courtesy, but I'll warrant him, as gentle as a lamb. Go
thy ways, wench, serve God. What, have you din'd at home?

JULIET   No, no! But all this did I know before.
What says he of our marriage? what of that?   45

NURSE   Lord, how my head aches! What a head have I!
It beats as it would fall in twenty pieces.
My back a' t' other side—ah, my back, my back!
Beshrew your heart for sending me about
To catch my death with jauncing up and down!   50

JULIET   I' faith, I am sorry that thou art not well.
Sweet, sweet, sweet nurse, tell me, what says my love?

NURSE   Your love says, like an honest gentleman,
An' a courteous, and a kind, and a handsome,
And, I warrant, a virtuous— Where is your mother?   55

JULIET   Where is my mother! why, she is within,
Where should she be? How oddly thou repliest!
"Your love says, like an honest gentleman,
'Where is your mother?'"

NURSE   O God's lady dear!
Are you so hot? Marry, come up, I trow;   60
Is this the poultice for my aching bones?
Henceforward do your messages yourself.

JULIET   Here's such a coil! Come, what says Romeo?

NURSE   Have you got leave to go to shrift to-day?

JULIET   I have.   65

NURSE   Then hie you hence to Friar Lawrence' cell,
There stays a husband to make you a wife.
Now comes the wanton blood up in your cheeks,
They'll be in scarlet straight at any news.
Hie you to church, I must another way,   70

---

36. *stay the circumstance:* wait for the
details
38. *simple:* foolish
41. *be not . . . on:* are nothing to talk
about
48. *a' t':* on the
49. *Beshrew your heart:* a mild impre-
cation (literally, *beshrew* = a curse on)
53. *honest:* honorable

60. *hot:* impatient. *Marry, come up:* an
expression of reproof, implying that
Juliet is getting above herself
63. *coil:* fuss
66. *hie:* hasten
68. *wanton:* undisciplined, impetuous
69. *They'll . . . news:* i.e., you've always blushed easily

To fetch a ladder, by the which your love
Must climb a bird's nest soon when it is dark.
I am the drudge, and toil in your delight;
But you shall bear the burthen soon at night.
Go, I'll to dinner, hie you to the cell.   *75*

JULIET   Hie to high fortune! Honest nurse, farewell.   *Exeunt*

[Scene Six]

Enter FRIAR [LAWRENCE] *and* ROMEO

FRIAR LAWRENCE   So smile the heavens upon this holy act,
That after-hours with sorrow chide us not!

ROMEO   Amen, amen! but come what sorrow can,
It cannot countervail the exchange of joy
That one short minute gives me in her sight.   *5*
Do thou but close our hands with holy words,
Then love-devouring death do what he dare,
It is enough I may but call her mine.

FRIAR LAWRENCE   These violent delights have violent ends,
And in their triumph die, like fire and powder,   *10*
Which as they kiss consume. The sweetest honey
Is loathsome in his own deliciousness,
And in the taste confounds the appetite.
Therefore love moderately: long love doth so;
Too swift arrives as tardy as too slow.   *15*

Enter JULIET

Here comes the lady. O, so light a foot
Will ne'er wear out the everlasting flint;
A lover may bestride the gossamers
That idles in the wanton summer air,
And yet not fall; so light is vanity.   *20*

JULIET   Good even to my ghostly confessor.

FRIAR LAWRENCE   Romeo shall thank thee, daughter, for us both.

JULIET   As much to him, else is his thanks too much.

ROMEO   Ah, Juliet, if the measure of thy joy
Be heap'd like mine, and that thy skill be more   *25*
To blazon it, then sweeten with thy breath
This neighbor air, and let rich [music's] tongue

II.vi. Location: Verona. Friar Lawrence's cell
4. *countervail:* equal
13. *confounds:* destroys
18. *gossamers:* threads spun by spiders
19. *wanton:* sportive

20. *vanity:* transitory earthly joy
23. *As much:* the same greeting. She
returns Romeo's kiss
24–25. *if . . . that:* if . . . if
26. *blazon:* describe, proclaim

Unfold the imagin'd happiness that both
Receive in either by this dear encounter.

JULIET   Conceit, more rich in matter than in words,   *30*
Brags of his substance, not of ornament;
They are but beggars that can count their worth,
But my true love is grown to such excess
I cannot sum up sum of half my wealth.   *34*

FRIAR LAWRENCE   Come, come with me, and we will make short work,
For by your leaves, you shall not stay alone
Till Holy Church incorporate two in one.   *Exeunt*

[ACT THREE]   [*Scene One*]

Enter MERCUTIO, BENVOLIO, [PAGE,] *and* MEN

BENVOLIO   I pray thee, good Mercutio, let's retire.
The day is hot, the Capels [are] abroad,
And if we meet we shall not scape a brawl,
For now, these hot days, is the mad blood stirring.   *4*

MERCUTIO   Thou art like one of these fellows that, when he enters the
confines of a tavern, claps me his sword upon the table, and says, "God
send me no need of thee!" and by the operation of the second cup
draws him on the drawer, when indeed there is no need.

BENVOLIO   Am I like such a fellow?   *9*

MERCUTIO   Come, come, thou art as hot a Jack in thy mood as any in
Italy, and as soon mov'd to be moody, and as soon moody to be mov'd.

BENVOLIO   And what to?   *12*

MERCUTIO   Nay, and there were two such, we should have none shortly,
for one would kill the other. Thou? why, thou wilt quarrel with a man
that hath a hair more or a hair less in his beard than thou hast. Thou
wilt quarrel with a man for cracking nuts, having no other reason but
because thou hast hazel eyes. What eye but such an eye would spy out
such a quarrel? Thy head is as full of quarrels as an egg is full of meat,
and yet thy head hath been beaten as addle as an egg for quarrelling.
Thou hast quarrell'd with a man for coughing in the street, because he
hath waken'd thy dog that hath lain asleep in the sun. Didst thou not
fall out with a tailor for wearing his new doublet before Easter? with

28. *imagin'd:* felt within (but not expressed)
30. *Conceit:* understanding
31. *Brags of:* takes pride in
34. *sum up sum:* calculate the total
III.i. Location: Verona. A 'public
place
6. *claps me:* claps (a colloquialism)
8. *draws . . . drawer:* draws his sword
against the tapster

11. *moody:* angry
13. *two:* A quibble on Benvolio's *to*
18. *meat:* i.e., edible matter
19. *addle:* addled, i.e., muddled (with
reference to brains), rotten (with reference to eggs)
22. *doublet:* jacket

another for tying his new shoes with old riband? and yet thou wilt tutor
me from quarrelling!   24

BENVOLIO   And I were so apt to quarrel as thou art, any man should buy
the fee-simple of my life for an hour and a quarter.

MERCUTIO   The fee-simple! O simple!

                                Enter TYBALT, PETRUCHIO, *and others*

BENVOLIO   By my head, here comes the Capulets.

MERCUTIO   By my heel, I care not.   29

TYBALT   Follow me close, for I will speak to them. Gentlemen, good
den, a word with one of you.

MERCUTIO   And but one word with one of us? Couple it with something,
make it a word and a blow.

TYBALT   You shall find me apt enough to that, sir, and you will give me
occasion.   35

MERCUTIO   Could you not take some occasion without giving?

TYBALT   Mercutio, thou consortest with Romeo—

MERCUTIO   Consort! what, dost thou make us minstrels? And thou make
minstrels of us, look to hear nothing but discords. Here's my
fiddlestick, here's that shall make you dance. 'Zounds, consort!

BENVOLIO   We talk here in the public haunt of men.   41
Either withdraw unto some private place,
Or reason coldly of your grievances,
Or else depart; here all eyes gaze on us.

MERCUTIO   Men's eyes were made to look, and let them gaze;   45
I will not budge for no man's pleasure, I.

                                          Enter ROMEO

TYBALT   Well, peace be with you, sir, here comes my man.

MERCUTIO   But I'll be hang'd, sir, if he wear your livery.
Marry, go before to field, he'll be your follower;
Your worship in that sense may call him man.   50

TYBALT   Romeo, the love I bear thee can afford
No better term than this: thou art a villain.

ROMEO   Tybalt, the reason that I have to love thee
Doth much excuse the appertaining rage
To such a greeting. Villain am I none;   55
Therefore farewell, I see thou knowest me not.

---

23. *riband:* ribbon
23–24. *tutor me from:* instruct me
against
26. *fee-simple:* absolute ownership
38. *Consort:* Mercutio takes the word
in the sense "play music with." A
group of musicians was called a consort. *minstrels:* A disparaging term;
cf. IV.v.111
40. *fiddlestick:* i.e., rapier. *'Zounds:*
by God's (Christ's) wounds

43. *reason coldly of:* discuss calmly
44. *depart:* part company
48. *livery:* Mercutio pretends to interpret *my man* as "my servant."
Similarly, *follower* (line 49) plays on
the sense "attendant"
49. *field:* dueling-place
50. *man:* i.e., one worthy to be called
a man
54. *excuse . . . rage:* abate the angry
reaction appropriate

TYBALT   Boy, this shall not excuse the injuries
      That thou hast done me, therefore turn and draw.
ROMEO   I do protest I never injuried thee,
      But love thee better than thou canst devise,   60
      Till thou shalt know the reason of my love,
      And so, good Capulet—which name I tender
      As dearly as mine own—be satisfied.
MERCUTIO   O calm, dishonorable, vile submission!   64
      Alla stoccato carries it away.   [*Draws*]
      Tybalt, you rat-catcher, will you walk?
TYBALT   What wouldst thou have with me?
MERCUTIO   Good King of Cats, nothing but one of your nine lives; that I
      mean to make bold withal, and as you shall use me hereafter, dry-beat
      the rest of the eight. Will you pluck your sword out of his pilcher by
      the ears? Make haste, lest mine be about your ears ere it be out.
TYBALT   I am for you.   [*Drawing*]
ROMEO   Gentle Mercutio, put thy rapier up.   73
MERCUTIO   Come, sir, your *passado*.   [*They fight*]
ROMEO   Draw, Benvolio, beat down their weapons.
      Gentlemen, for shame, forbear this outrage!
      Tybalt, Mercutio, the Prince expressly hath
      Forbid this bandying in Verona streets.   [ROMEO *steps between them*]
      Hold, Tybalt! Good Mercutio!
                       [TYBALT *under* ROMEO's *arm thrusts* MERCUTIO *in*]
                                   Away TYBALT [*with his followers*]
MERCUTIO   I am hurt.
      A plague a' both houses! I am sped.   80
      Is he gone and hath nothing?
BENVOLIO   What, art thou hurt?
MERCUTIO   Ay, ay, a scratch, a scratch, marry, 'tis enough.
      Where is my page? Go, villain, fetch a surgeon.
                                              [*Exit* PAGE]
ROMEO   Courage, man, the hurt cannot be much.   84
MERCUTIO   No, 'tis not so deep as a well, nor so wide as a church-door,
      but 'tis enough, 'twill serve. Ask for me to-morrow, and you shall find

---

59. *protest:* affirm. *injuried:* injured
60. *devise:* understand
62. *tender:* value
65. *Alla stoccato:* literally, at the thrust (fencing term). Mercutio means that Tybalt's onslaught has apparently unarmed Romeo
66. *rat-catcher:* alluding to his name; see note on II.iv.18. *walk:* i.e., come outside
69. *as . . . hereafter:* according to your behavior to me in future. *dry-*

beat: thrash (without drawing blood)
70. *his pilcher:* its scabbard
70–71. *by the ears:* implying that the sword is reluctant to leave the scabbard
74. *passado:* lunge
78. *bandying:* exchanging blows
80. *sped:* dispatched
82. *a scratch:* another allusion to Tybalt's name
83. *villain:* fellow (not derogatory here)

me a grave man. I am pepper'd, I warrant, for this world. A plague a'
both your houses! 'Zounds, a dog, a rat, a mouse, a cat, to scratch a
man to death! a braggart, a rogue, a villain, that fights by the book of
arithmetic! Why the dev'l came you between us? I was hurt under
your arm.   91

ROMEO   I thought all for the best.

MERCUTIO   Help me into some house, Benvolio,
Or I shall faint. A plague a' both your houses!
They have made worms' meat of me. I have it,   95
And soundly too. Your houses!

Exeunt [MERCUTIO *and* BENVOLIO]

ROMEO   This gentleman, the Prince's near ally,
My very friend, hath got this mortal hurt
In my behalf; my reputation stain'd   100
With Tybalt's slander—Tybalt, that an hour
Hath been my cousin! O sweet Juliet,
Thy beauty hath made me effeminate,
And in my temper soft'ned valor's steel!

Enter BENVOLIO

BENVOLIO   O Romeo, Romeo, brave Mercutio is dead!   105
That gallant spirit hath aspir'd the clouds,
Which too untimely here did scorn the earth.

ROMEO   This day's black fate on moe days doth depend,
This but begins the woe others must end.

[*Enter* TYBALT]

BENVOLIO   Here comes the furious Tybalt back again.   110

ROMEO   He [gone] in triumph, and Mercutio slain!
Away to heaven, respective lenity,
And fire[-ey'd] fury be my conduct now!
Now, Tybalt, take the "villain" back again
That late thou gavest me, for Mercutio's soul   115
Is but a little way above our heads,
Staying for thine to keep him company.
Either thou or I, or both, must go with him.

TYBALT   Thou wretched boy, that didst consort him here,
Shalt with him hence.

ROMEO   This shall determine that.   120

They fight; TYBALT *falls*

BENVOLIO   Romeo, away, be gone!
The citizens are up, and Tybalt slain.

---

87. *for this world:* as far as this world is
concerned
97. *ally:* kinsman
98. *very:* true
104. *temper:* composition, nature
(with pun on the tempering of steel)

106. *aspir'd:* mounted to
108. *on . . . depend:* hangs over more
days than today
112. *respective:* considerate
113. *conduct:* guide
122. *up:* in arms

Stand not amazed, the Prince will doom thee death
If thou art taken. Hence be gone, away!
ROMEO   O, I am fortune's fool!
BENVOLIO   Why dost thou stay?   *125*

Exit ROMEO
Enter CITIZENS

[FIRST] CITIZEN   Which way ran he that kill'd Mercutio?
    Tybalt, that murtherer, which way ran he?
BENVOLIO   There lies that Tybalt.
[FIRST] CITIZEN   Up, sir, go with me;
    I charge thee in the Prince's name, obey.

Enter PRINCE, *old* MONTAGUE, CAPULET, *their* WIVES, *and all*

PRINCE   Where are the vile beginners of this fray?   *130*
BENVOLIO   O noble Prince, I can discover all
    The unlucky manage of this fatal brawl:
    There lies the man, slain by young Romeo,
    That slew thy kinsman, brave Mercutio.
LADY CAPULET   Tybalt, my cousin! O my brother's child!   *135*
    O Prince! O husband! O, the blood is spill'd
    Of my dear kinsman! Prince, as thou art true,
    For blood of ours, shed blood of Montague.
    O cousin, cousin!
PRINCE   Benvolio, who began this bloody fray?   *140*
BENVOLIO   Tybalt, here slain, whom Romeo's hand did slay!
    Romeo that spoke him fair, bid him bethink
    How nice the quarrel was, and urg'd withal
    Your high displeasure; all this, uttered
    With gentle breath, calm look, knees humbly bowed,   *145*
    Could not take truce with the unruly spleen
    Of Tybalt deaf to peace, but that he tilts
    With piercing steel at bold Mercutio's breast,
    Who, all as hot, turns deadly point to point,
    And, with a martial scorn, with one hand beats   *150*
    Cold death aside, and with the other sends
    It back to Tybalt, whose dexterity
    Retorts it. Romeo he cries aloud,
    "Hold, friends! friends, part!" and swifter than his tongue,
    His [agile] arm beats down their fatal points,   *155*
    And 'twixt them rushes; underneath whose arm
    An envious thrust from Tybalt hit the life
    Of stout Mercutio, and then Tybalt fled;

123. *amazed:* stupefied   143. *nice:* trivial
125. *fool:* plaything, dupe   157. *envious:* malicious
131. *discover:* reveal   158. *stout:* valorous
132. *manage:* conduct

But by and by comes back to Romeo,
Who had but newly entertain'd revenge, 160
And to't they go like lightning, for, ere I
Could draw to part them, was stout Tybalt slain;
And as he fell, did Romeo turn and fly.
This is the truth, or let Benvolio die.

LADY CAPULET   He is a kinsman to the Montague, 165
Affection makes him false, he speaks not true.
Some twenty of them fought in this black strife,
And all those twenty could but kill one life.
I beg for justice, which thou, Prince, must give:
Romeo slew Tybalt, Romeo must not live. 170

PRINCE   Romeo slew him, he slew Mercutio;
Who now the price of his dear blood doth owe?

[MONTAGUE]   Not Romeo, Prince, he was Mercutio's friend;
His fault concludes but what the law should end,
The life of Tybalt.

PRINCE   And for that offense 175
Immediately we do exile him hence.
I have an interest in your heart's proceeding;
My blood for your rude brawls doth lie a-bleeding;
But I'll amerce you with so strong a fine
That you shall all repent the loss of mine. 180
[I] will be deaf to pleading and excuses,
Nor tears nor prayers shall purchase out abuses;
Therefore use none. Let Romeo hence in haste,
Else, when he is found, that hour is his last.
Bear hence this body and attend our will; 185
Mercy but murders, pardoning those that kill.   *Exeunt*

[*Scene Two*]

Enter JULIET *alone*

[JULIET]   Gallop apace, you fiery-footed steeds,
Towards Phoebus' lodging; such a waggoner
As Phaëton would whip you to the west,

160. *entertain'd:* admitted the thought of
177. *interest:* participation, personal concern
178. *My blood:* Mercutio is his kinsman
179. *amerce:* punish by fine
182. *purchase out:* redeem
185. *attend our will:* come to hear my further judgment
186. *murders:* i.e., invites other murders by condoning them in advance

III.ii. Location: Verona. Capulet's house
1. *steeds:* the horses drawing the chariot of the sun god (here identified with Phoebus Appolo, not with the Titan Helios as at II.iii.4)
2. *lodging:* i.e., below the western horizon
3. *Phaëton:* Phaëthon, the sun god's son; when he drove the sun chariot he could not keep control and had to be killed by Zeus

And bring in cloudy night immediately.
Spread thy close curtain, love-performing night, 5
That [th'] runaway's eyes may wink, and Romeo
Leap to these arms untalk'd of and unseen!
Lovers can see to do their amorous rites
By their own beauties, or if love be blind,
It best agrees with night. Come, civil night, 10
Thou sober-suited matron all in black,
And learn me how to lose a winning match,
Play'd for a pair of stainless maidenhoods.
Hood my unmann'd blood, bating in my cheeks,
With thy black mantle; till strange love grow bold, 15
Think true love acted simple modesty.
Come, night, come, Romeo, come, thou day in night,
For thou wilt lie upon the wings of night,
Whiter than new snow upon a raven's back.
Come, gentle night, come, loving, black-brow'd night, 20
Give me my Romeo, and, when I shall die,
Take him and cut him out in little stars,
And he will make the face of heaven so fine
That all the world will be in love with night,
And pay no worship to the garish sun. 25
O, I have bought the mansion of a love,
But not possess'd it, and though I am sold,
Not yet enjoy'd. So tedious is this day
As is the night before some festival
To an impatient child that hath new robes 30
And may not wear them. O, here comes my nurse,

      Enter NURSE [*wringing her hands*], *with* [*the ladder of*] *cords* [*in
      her lap*]

And she brings news; and every tongue that speaks
But Romeo's name speaks heavenly eloquence.
Now, nurse, what news? What hast thou there? the cords 34
That Romeo bid thee fetch?

NURSE   Ay, ay, the cords.   [*Throws them down*]
JULIET   Ay me, what news? Why dost thou wring thy hands?

5. *close:* concealing
6. *runaway's:* unexplained; perhaps corrupt. Night must blind something or person that would comment harshly on their love. *wink:* be unable to see (?) or close, because night has come (?)
10. *civil:* grave
14. *Hood:* cover. *unmann'd:* untamed (with obvious pun). *bating:* fluttering. Like *Hood* and *unmann'd,* this

term is borrowed from falconry; a hawk "bates" when it attempts to escape from the falconer's wrist. It is controlled by means of a hood placed over its head
15. *strange:* reserved, diffident. *grow:* some editors read "grown"; without this emendation, "And" must be understood at the beginning of line 16
16. *modesty:* chastity

NURSE   Ah, weraday, he's dead, he's dead, he's dead!
　　　We are undone, lady, we are undone!
　　　Alack the day, he's gone, he's kill'd, he's dead!
JULIET   Can heaven be so envious?
NURSE   Romeo can,   40
　　　Though heaven cannot. O Romeo, Romeo!
　　　Who ever would have thought it? Romeo!
JULIET   What devil art thou that dost torment me thus?
　　　This torture should be roar'd in dismal hell.
　　　Hath Romeo slain himself? Say thou but ay,   45
　　　And that bare vowel *I* shall poison more
　　　Than the death[-darting] eye of cockatrice.
　　　I am not I, if there be such an ay,
　　　Or those eyes [shut], that makes thee answer ay.
　　　If he be slain, say ay, or if not, no.   50
　　　Brief sounds determine my weal or woe.
NURSE   I saw the wound, I saw it with mine eyes—
　　　God save the mark!—here on his manly breast.
　　　A piteous corse, a bloody piteous corse,
　　　Pale, pale as ashes, all bedaub'd in blood,   55
　　　All in gore blood; I sounded at the sight.
JULIET   O, break, my heart, poor bankrout, break at once!
　　　To prison, eyes, ne'er look on liberty!
　　　Vile earth, to earth resign, end motion here,
　　　And thou and Romeo press [one] heavy bier!   60
NURSE   O Tybalt, Tybalt, the best friend I had!
　　　O courteous Tybalt, honest gentleman,
　　　That ever I should live to see thee dead!
JULIET   What storm is this that blows so contrary?
　　　Is Romeo slaught'red? and is Tybalt dead?   65
　　　My dearest cousin, and my dearer lord?
　　　Then, dreadful trumpet, sound the general doom,
　　　For who is living, if those two are gone?
NURSE   Tybalt is gone, and Romeo banished,
　　　Romeo that kill'd him, he is banished.   70
JULIET   O God, did Romeo's hand shed Tybalt's blood?
[NURSE]   It did, it did, alas the day, it did!

37. *weraday:* alas
40. *envious:* malicious
47. *cockatrice:* basilisk, fabulous creature that killed by its glance
49. *Or . . . shut:* or if those eyes
(Romeo's) are shut in death
51. *determine:* put an end to (?) or
decide, settle(?)
53. *God . . . mark:* expression used
to avert ill omen

54. *corse:* corpse
56. *sounded:* swooned
57. *bankrout:* bankrupt (with play on
break = go bankrupt)
59. *Vile earth:* i.e., body. *resign:* surrender
67. *trumpet:* the "last trump," signaling the Day of Judgment

[JULIET]   O serpent heart, hid with a flow'ring face!
       Did ever dragon keep so fair a cave?
       Beautiful tyrant! fiend angelical!   75
       Dove-feather'd raven! wolvish ravening lamb!
       Despised substance of divinest show!
       Just opposite to what thou justly seem'st,
       A [damned] saint, an honorable villain!
       O nature, what hadst thou to do in hell   80
       When thou didst bower the spirit of a fiend
       In mortal paradise of such sweet flesh?
       Was ever book containing such vile matter
       So fairly bound? O that deceit should dwell
       In such a gorgeous palace!
NURSE   There's no trust,   85
       No faith, no honesty in men, all perjur'd,
       All forsworn, all naught, all dissemblers.
       Ah, where's my man? Give me some aqua-vitae;
       These griefs, these woes, these sorrows make me old.
       Shame come to Romeo!
JULIET   Blister'd be thy tongue   90
       For such a wish! he was not born to shame:
       Upon his brow shame is asham'd to sit;
       For 'tis a throne where honor may be crown'd
       Sole monarch of the universal earth.
       O, what a beast was I to chide at him!   95
NURSE   Will you speak well of him that kill'd your cousin?
JULIET   Shall I speak ill of him that is my husband?
       Ah, poor my lord, what tongue shall smooth thy name,
       When I, thy three-hours wife, have mangled it?
       But wherefore, villain, didst thou kill my cousin?   100
       That villain cousin would have kill'd my husband.
       Back, foolish tears, back to your native spring,
       Your tributary drops belong to woe,
       Which you, mistaking, offer up to joy.
       My husband lives that Tybalt would have slain,   105
       And Tybalt's dead that would have slain my husband.
       All this is comfort, wherefore weep I then?
       Some word there was, worser than Tybalt's death,

73. *flow'ring:* i.e., youthful and fair (?) or perhaps alluding to representations of the serpent in Eden with a human face encircled with flowers
74. *keep:* dwell in
77. *Despised:* despicable. *substance . . . show:* reality . . . appearance
78. *Just:* exactly. *what . . . seem'st:*

your semblance of truth
81. *bower:* lodge
87. *naught:* wicked
88. *aqua-vitae:* strong alcoholic spirits
103. *Your . . . woe:* your tears should be a tribute to woeful events
104. *joy:* i.e., the joyful event of Romeo's survival

That murd'red me; I would forget it fain,
But O, it presses to my memory   *110*
Like damned guilty deeds to sinners' minds:
"Tybalt is dead, and Romeo banished."
That "banished," that one word "banished,"
Hath slain ten thousand Tybalts. Tybalt's death
Was woe enough if it had ended there;   *115*
Or if sour woe delights in fellowship,
And needly will be rank'd with other griefs,
Why followed not, when she said, "Tybalt's dead,"
Thy father or thy mother, nay, or both,
Which modern lamentation might have moved?   *120*
But with a rearward following Tybalt's death,
"Romeo is banished," to speak that word,
Is father, mother, Tybalt, Romeo, Juliet,
All slain, all dead: "Romeo is banished"!
There is no end, no limit, measure, bound,   *125*
In that word's death, no words can that woe sound.
Where is my father and my mother, nurse?

NURSE   Weeping and wailing over Tybalt's corse.
Will you go to them? I will bring you thither.

JULIET   Wash they his wounds with tears? Mine shall be spent,   *130*
When theirs are dry, for Romeo's banishment.
Take up those cords. Poor ropes, you are beguil'd,
Both you and I, for Romeo is exil'd.
He made you for a highway to my bed,
But I, a maid, die maiden-widowed.   *135*
Come, cords, come, nurse, I'll to my wedding-bed,
And death, not Romeo, take my maidenhead!

NURSE   Hie to your chamber. I'll find Romeo
To comfort you, I wot well where he is.
Hark ye, your Romeo will be here at night.   *140*
I'll to him, he is hid at Lawrence' cell.

JULIET   O, find him! Give this ring to my true knight,
And bid him come to take his last farewell.   *Exeunt*

[*Scene Three*]

Enter FRIAR [LAWRENCE]

117. *needly:* necessarily. *rank'd:* in-   132. *beguil'd:* tricked, cheated
cluded in a series   139. *wot:* know
120. *modern:* ordinary   III.iii. Location: Verona. Friar Law-
121. *rearward:* rearguard   rence's cell
126. *sound:* (1) express; (2) fathom

FRIAR LAWRENCE   Romeo, come forth, come forth, thou fearful man:
    Affliction is enamor'd of thy parts,
    And thou art wedded to calamity.

                                                [Enter ROMEO]

ROMEO   Father, what news? What is the Prince's doom?
    What sorrow craves acquaintance at my hand,   5
    That I yet know not?
FRIAR LAWRENCE   Too familiar
    Is my dear son with such sour company!
    I bring thee tidings of the Prince's doom.
ROMEO   What less than dooms-day is the Prince's doom?
FRIAR LAWRENCE   A gentler judgment vanish'd from his lips—   10
    Not body's death, but body's banishment.
ROMEO   Ha, banishment? Be merciful, say "death";
    For exile hath more terror in his look,
    Much more than death. Do not say "banishment"!
FRIAR LAWRENCE   Here from Verona art thou banished.   15
    Be patient, for the world is broad and wide.
ROMEO   There is no world without Verona walls,
    But purgatory, torture, hell itself.
    Hence "banished" is banish'd from the world,
    And world's exile is death; then "banished"   20
    Is death misterm'd. Calling death "banished,"
    Thou cut'st my head off with a golden axe,
    And smilest upon the stroke that murders me.
FRIAR LAWRENCE   O deadly sin! O rude unthankfulness!
    Thy fault our law calls death, but the kind Prince,   25
    Taking thy part, hath rush'd aside the law,
    And turn'd that black word "death" to "banishment."
    This is dear mercy, and thou seest it not.
ROMEO   'Tis torture, and not mercy. Heaven is here
    Where Juliet lives, and every cat and dog   30
    And little mouse, every unworthy thing,
    Live here in heaven and may look on her,
    But Romeo may not. More validity,
    More honorable state, more courtship lives
    In carrion flies than Romeo; they may seize   35
    On the white wonder of dear Juliet's hand,

1. *fearful:* full of fear (but lines 2–3 suggest that the sense "evoking fear" may also be present)
2. *parts:* qualities
4. *doom:* judgment, sentence
9. *dooms-day:* i.e., death
10. *vanish'd:* issued without possibility of recall(?)
16. *Be patient:* compose yourself
17. *without:* outside
20. *world's exile:* exile from the world
25. *death:* i.e., a capital offense
26. *rush'd:* pushed
28. *dear:* precious, rare
33. *validity:* worth, dignity
34. *courtship:* courtly state (with play on "opportunity for wooing")

And steal immortal blessing from her lips,
Who, even in pure and vestal modesty,
Still blush, as thinking their own kisses sin;
But Romeo may not, he is banished.   40
Flies may do this, but I from this must fly;
They are free men, but I am banished:
And sayest thou yet that exile is not death?
Hadst thou no poison mix'd, no sharp-ground knife,
No sudden mean of death, though ne'er so mean,   45
But "banished" to kill me? "Banished"?
O friar, the damned use that word in hell;
Howling attends it. How hast thou the heart,
Being a divine, a ghostly confessor,
A sin-absolver, and my friend profess'd,   50
To mangle me with that word "banished"?

FRIAR LAWRENCE   [Thou] fond mad man, hear me a little speak.
ROMEO   O, thou wilt speak again of banishment.
FRIAR LAWRENCE   I'll give thee armor to keep off that word:
Adversity's sweet milk, philosophy,   55
To comfort thee though thou art banished.
ROMEO   Yet "banished"? Hang up philosophy!
Unless philosophy can make a Juliet,
Displant a town, reverse a prince's doom,
It helps not, it prevails not. Talk no more.   60
FRIAR LAWRENCE   O then I see that [madmen] have no ears.
ROMEO   How should they when that wise men have no eyes?
FRIAR LAWRENCE   Let me dispute with thee of thy estate.
ROMEO   Thou canst not speak of that thou dost not feel.
Wert thou as young as I, Juliet thy love,   65
An hour but married, Tybalt murdered,
Doting like me, and like me banished,
Then mightst thou speak, then mightst thou tear thy hair,
And fall upon the ground, as I do now,
Taking the measure of an unmade grave.   70

Enter NURSE [*within*] *and knock*

FRIAR LAWRENCE   Arise, one knocks. Good Romeo, hide thyself.
ROMEO   Not I, unless the breath of heart-sick groans
Mist-like infold me from the search of eyes.

Knock

FRIAR LAWRENCE   Hark how they knock!—Who's there?—Romeo,
arise,

---

39. *kisses:* i.e., contact with each   59. *Displant:* transplant
other   60. *prevails not:* is of no effect
45. *mean . . . mean:* means . . . base   63. *dispute:* discuss. *estate:* situation
52. *fond:* foolish

Thou wilt be taken.—Stay a while!—Stand up;   *75*

[*Loud*] *knock*

Run to my study.—By and by!—God's will,
What simpleness is this?—I come, I come!

Knock

Who knocks so hard? Whence come you? What's your will?
NURSE [*within*]   Let me come in, and you shall know my errant.
I come from Lady Juliet.
FRIAR LAWRENCE   Welcome then.   [*Unlocks the door*]

Enter NURSE

NURSE   O holy friar, O, tell me, holy friar,   *81*
Where's my lady's lord? where's Romeo?
FRIAR LAWRENCE   There on the ground, with his own tears made drunk.
NURSE   O, he is even in my mistress' case,
Just in her case. O woeful sympathy!   *85*
Piteous predicament! Even so lies she,
Blubb'ring and weeping, weeping and blubb'ring.
Stand up, stand up, stand, and you be a man.
For Juliet's sake, for her sake, rise and stand;
Why should you fall into so deep an O?   *90*
ROMEO   Nurse!   [*He rises*]
NURSE   Ah sir, ah sir, death's the end of all.
ROMEO   Spakest thou of Juliet? How is it with her?
Doth not she think me an old murtherer,
Now I have stain'd the childhood of our joy   *95*
With blood removed but little from her own?
Where is she? and how doth she? and what says
My conceal'd lady to our cancell'd love?
NURSE   O, she says nothing, sir, but weeps and weeps,
And now falls on her bed, and then starts up,   *100*
And Tybalt calls, and then on Romeo cries,
And then down falls again.
ROMEO   As if that name,
Shot from the deadly level of a gun,
Did murther her, as that name's cursed hand
Murder'd her kinsman. O, tell me, friar, tell me,   *105*
In what vile part of this anatomy
Doth my name lodge? Tell me, that I may sack
The hateful mansion.

[*He offers to stab himself, and the* NURSE *snatches the dagger away*]

FRIAR LAWRENCE   Hold thy desperate hand!
Art thou a man? Thy form cries out thou art;

75. *Stay a while:* wait a moment
77. *simpleness:* foolishness
79. *errant:* errand
85. *sympathy:* similarity of suffering

90. *O:* fit of groaning
94. *old:* inveterate, hardened
98. *conceal'd lady:* secret wife
103. *level:* aim

Thy tears are womanish, thy wild acts [denote]   *110*
The unreasonable fury of a beast.
Unseemly woman in a seeming man,
And ill-beseeming beast in seeming both,
Thou hast amaz'd me! By my holy order,
I thought thy disposition better temper'd.   *115*
Hast thou slain Tybalt? Wilt thou slay thyself,
And slay thy lady that in thy life [lives],
By doing damned hate upon thyself?
Why railest thou on thy birth? the heaven and earth?
Since birth, and heaven, and earth, all three do meet   *120*
In thee at once, which thou at once wouldst lose.
Fie, fie, thou shamest thy shape, thy love, thy wit,
Which like a usurer abound'st in all,
And usest none in that true use indeed
Which should bedeck thy shape, thy love, thy wit.   *125*
Thy noble shape is but a form of wax,
Digressing from the valor of a man;
Thy dear love sworn but hollow perjury,
Killing that love which thou hast vow'd to cherish;
Thy wit, that ornament to shape and love,   *130*
Misshapen in the conduct of them both,
Like powder in a skilless soldier's flask,
Is set afire by thine own ignorance,
And thou dismemb'red with thine own defense.
What, rouse thee, man! thy Juliet is alive,   *135*
For whose dear sake thou wast but lately dead:
There art thou happy. Tybalt would kill thee,
But thou slewest Tybalt: there art thou happy.
The law that threat'ned death becomes thy friend,
And turns it to exile: there art thou happy.   *140*
A pack of blessings light upon thy back,
Happiness courts thee in her best array,
But like a mishaved and sullen wench,
Thou [pouts upon] thy fortune and thy love.
Take heed, take heed, for such die miserable.   *145*

---

111. *unreasonable:* unreasoning
112. *Unseemly woman:* the Friar suggests that Romeo is behaving not simply like a woman but like a woman who offends good taste. Similarly, *Ill-beseeming beast* in line 113 suggests that he is acting in a way unbecoming even for a normal animal—that he is a sort of hybrid monster
115. *temper'd:* compounded
120. *heaven, and earth:* i.e., soul and body
122. *wit:* intellect

123. *Which:* (you) who. *usurer:* i.e., one who does not put his possessions to the proper use; a Shylock, not an Antonio who "ventures" in the world
126. *form of wax:* waxwork figure
131. *Misshapen:* deformed. *conduct:* guidance
132. *flask:* powder horn
134. *defense:* means of defense
137. *happy:* fortunate
143. *mishaved:* misbehaved

Go get thee to thy love as was decreed,
Ascend her chamber, hence and comfort her.
But look thou stay not till the watch be set,
For then thou canst not pass to Mantua,
Where thou shalt live till we can find a time   *150*
To blaze your marriage, reconcile your friends,
Beg pardon of the Prince, and call thee back
With twenty hundred thousand times more joy
Than thou went'st forth in lamentation.
Go before, nurse; commene me to thy lady,   *155*
And bid her hasten all the house to bed,
Which heavy sorrow makes them apt unto.
Romeo is coming.

NURSE   O Lord, I could have stay'd here all the night
To hear good counsel. O, what learning is!   *160*
My lord, I'll tell my lady you will come.

ROMEO   Do so, and bid my sweet prepare to chide.

> [NURSE *offers to go in, and turns again*]

NURSE   Here, sir, a ring she bid me give you, sir.
Hie you, make haste, for it grows very late.

ROMEO   How well my comfort is reviv'd by this!   *165*

> [*Exit* NURSE]

FRIAR LAWRANCE   Go hence, good night; and here stands all your state:
Either be gone before the watch be set,
Or by the break of day [disguis'd] from hence.
Sojourn in Mantua. I'll find out your man,
And he shall signify from time to time   *170*
Every good hap to you that chances here.
Give me thy hand. 'Tis late; farewell, good night.

ROMEO   But that a joy past joy calls out on me,
It were a grief, so brief to part with thee.
Farewell.   *Exeunt*

[*Scene Four*]

Enter old CAPULET, *his* WIFE *and* PARIS

CAPULET   Things have fall'n out, sir, so unluckily
That we have had no time to move our daughter.
Look you, she lov'd her kinsman Tybalt dearly,

---

146. *decreed:* appointed
148. *watch be set:* guard be posted.
The city gates would be closed at the
same time
151. *blaze:* make known. *friends:* relations

166. *here . . . state:* your situation depends on this
174. *brief:* hastily
III.iv. Location: Verona. Capulet's
house

And so did I. Well, we were born to die.
'Tis very late, she'll not come down to-night. 5
I promise you, but for your company,
I would have been a-bed an hour ago.

PARIS   These times of woe afford no times to woo.
Madam, good night, commend me to your daughter.

LADY CAPULET   I will, and know her mind early tomorrow; 10
To-night she's mewed up to her heaviness.

[PARIS *offers to go in, and* CAPULET *calls him again*]

CAPULET   Sir Paris, I will make a desperate tender
Of my child's love. I think she will [be] rul'd
In all respects by me; nay more, I doubt it not.
Wife, go you to her ere you go to bed, 15
Acquaint her here of my son Paris' love,
And bid her—mark you me?—on We'n'sday next—
But soft, what day is this?

PARIS   Monday, my lord.

CAPULET   Monday! ha, ha! Well, We'n'sday is too soon,
A' Thursday let it be—a' Thursday, tell her, 20
She shall be married to this noble earl.
Will you be ready? do you like this haste?
We'll keep no great ado—a friend or two,
For hark you, Tybalt being slain so late,
It may be thought we held him carelessly, 25
Being our kinsman, if we revel much:
Therefore we'll have some half a dozen friends,
And there an end. But what say you to Thursday?

PARIS   My lord, I would that Thursday were tomorrow.

CAPULET   Well, get you gone, a' Thursday be it then.— 30
Go you to Juliet ere you go to bed,
Prepare her, wife, against this wedding-day.
Farewell, my lord. Light to my chamber ho!
Afore me, it is so very late that we
May call it early by and by. Good night.   *Exeunt*

[*Scene Five*]

Enter ROMEO *and* JULIET *aloft* [*at the window*]

JULIET   Wilt thou be gone? it is not yet near day.
It was the nightingale, and not the lark,

6. *promise:* assure
11. *mew'd up to:* shut up with (a term
from falconry). *heaviness:* sorrow
12. *desperate tender:* bold offer
19. *ha, ha:* representing the sound he
utters as he considers the matter

20. *A':* on
32. *against:* in anticipation of
34. *Afore me:* a mild oath
III.v. Location: Verona. Capulet's
orchard

That pierc'd the fearful hollow of thine ear;
Nightly she sings on yond pomegranate tree.
Believe me, love, it was the nightingale.   *5*
ROMEO   It was the lark, the herald of the morn,
No nightingale. Look, love, what envious streaks
Do lace the severing clouds in yonder east.
Night's candles are burnt out, and jocund day
Stands tiptoe on the misty mountain tops.   *10*
I must be gone and live, or stay and die.
JULIET   Yond light is not day-light, I know it, I;
It is some meteor that the sun [exhal'd]
To be to thee this night a torch-bearer
And light thee on thy way to Mantua.   *15*
Therefore stay yet, thou need'st not to be gone.
ROMEO   Let me be ta'en, let me be put to death,
I am content, so thou wilt have it so.
I'll say yon grey is not the morning's eye,
'Tis but the pale reflex of Cynthia's brow;   *20*
Nor that is not the lark whose notes do beat
The vaulty heaven so high above our heads.
I have more care to stay than will to go.
Come, death, and welcome! Juliet wills it so.
How is't, my soul? Let's talk, it is not day.   *25*
JULIET   It is, it is! Hie hence, be gone, away!
It is the lark that sings so out of tune,
Straining harsh discords and unpleasing sharps.
Some say the lark makes sweet division;
This doth not so, for she divideth us.   *30*
Some say the lark and loathed toad change eyes;
O now I would they had change's voices too,
Since arm from arm that voice doth us affray,
Hunting thee hence with hunt's-up to the day.
O now be gone, more light and light it grows.   *35*
ROMEO   More light and light, more dark and dark our woes!

Enter NURSE [*hastily*]

NURSE   Madam!
JULIET   Nurse?

13. *exhal'd:* Meteors were thought to be vapors which had risen from the earth and been ignited by the sun's heat
20. *reflex:* reflection. *Cynthia's:* the moon's
23. *care:* concern, desire
28. *sharps:* high notes
29. *division:* florid variation on a melody

31. *change:* exchange
33. *arm from arm:* out of each other's arms. *affray:* frighten
34. *hunt's-up:* a song to waken hunters (with possible reference to the custom of singing and horn-playing outside the bridal chamber the morning after the wedding)

NURSE   Your lady mother is coming to your chamber.   *39*
          The day is broke, be wary, look about.   [*Exit*]
JULIET   Then, window, let day in, and let life out.
ROMEO   Farewell, farewell! One kiss, and I'll descend. [*He goeth down*]
JULIET   Art thou gone so, love, lord, ay, husband, friend!
          I must hear from thee every day in the hour,
          For in a minute there are many days.   *45*
          O, by this count I shall be much in years
          Ere I again behold my Romeo!
ROMEO [*from below*]   Farewell!
          I will omit no opportunity
          That may convey my greetings, love, to thee.   *50*
JULIET   O, think'st thou we shall ever meet again?
ROMEO   I doubt it not, and all these woes shall serve
          For sweet discourses in our times to come.
JULIET   O God, I have an ill-divining soul!
          Methinks I see thee now, thou art so low,   *55*
          As one dead in the bottom of a tomb.
          Either my eyesight fails, or thou lookest pale.
ROMEO   And trust me, love, in my eye so do you;
          Dry sorrow drinks our blood. Adieu, adieu!   *Exit.*
JULIET   O Fortune, Fortune, all men call thee fickle;   *60*
          If thou art fickle, what dost thou with him
          That is renowm'd for faith? Be fickle, Fortune:
          For then I hope thou wilt not keep him long,
          But send him back.
LADY CAPULET [*within*]   Ho, daughter, are you up?
JULIET   Who is't that calls? It is my lady mother.   *65*
          Is she not down so late, or up so early?
          What unaccustom'd cause procures her hither?

                                        [*She goeth down from the window*]
                                        Enter Mother [LADY CAPULET]

LADY CAPULET   Why, how now, Juliet?
JULIET   Madam, I am not well.
LADY CAPULET   Evermore weeping for your cousin's death?
          What, wilt thou wash him from his grave with tears?   *70*
          And if thou couldst, thou couldst not make him live;
          Therefore have done. Some grief shows much of love,
          But much of grief shows still some want of wit.

---

43. *friend:* ie., lover
46. *much in years:* old
54. *ill-divining:* premonitory of evil
59. *Dry . . . blood:* it was thought that sorrow gradually exhausted the blood. *Dry* = thirsty
61. *what dost thou:* what business have you

62. *renowm'd:* renowned
66. *not down:* not yet gone to bed
67. s.d. *She . . . window:* apparently she goes out above and re-enters below, the main stage ceasing to be the garden into which Romeo has descended and becoming a room in the house

JULIET   Yet let me weep for such a feeling loss.

LADY CAPULET   So shall you feel the loss, but not the friend   *75*
　　Which you weep for.

JULIET　　　　　　　　　Feeling so the loss,
　　I cannot choose but ever weep the friend.

LADY CAPULET   Well, girl, thou weep'st not so much for his death,
　　As that the villain lives which slaughter'd him.

JULIET   What villain, madam?

LADY CAPULET　　　　　　　That same villain Romeo.   *80*

JULIET [*aside*]   Villain and he be many miles asunder.—
　　God pardon [him]! I do with all my heart;
　　And yet no man like he doth grieve my heart.

LADY CAPULET   That is because the traitor murderer lives.

JULIET   Ay, madam, from the reach of these my hands.   *85*
　　Would none but I might venge my cousin's death!

LADY CAPULET   We will have vengeance for it, fear thou not.
　　Then weep no more. I'll send to one in Mantua,
　　Where that same banish'd runagate doth live,
　　Shall give him such an unaccustom'd dram   *90*
　　That he shall soon keep Tybalt company;
　　And then I hope thou wilt be satisfied.

JULIET   Indeed I never shall be satisfied
　　With Romeo, till I behold him—dead—
　　Is my poor heart, so for a kinsman vex'd.   *95*
　　Madam, if you could find out but a man
　　To bear a poison, I would temper it,
　　That Romeo should, upon receipt thereof,
　　Soon sleep in quiet. O how my heart abhors
　　To hear him nam'd, and cannot come to him   *100*
　　To wreak the love I bore my cousin
　　Upon his body that hath slaughter'd him!

LADY CAPULET   Find thou the means, and I'll find such a man.
　　But now I'll tell thee joyful tidings, girl.

JULIET   And joy comes well in such a needy time.   *105*
　　What are they, beseech your ladyship?

LADY CAPULET   Well, well, thou hast a careful father, child,
　　One who, to put thee from thy heaviness,
　　Hath sorted out a sudden day of joy,
　　That thou expects not, nor I look'd not for.   *110*

JULIET   Madam, in happy time, what day is that?

74. *feeling:* affecting
83. *like:* so much as
89. *runagate:* renegade
97. *temper:* mix (including the sense
"moderate, dilute")

102. *his body that:* the body of him
who
107. *careful:* i.e., concerned for your
welfare
109. *sudden:* soon to come

LADY CAPULET   Marry, my child, early next Thursday morn,
The gallant, young, and noble gentleman,
The County Paris, at Saint Peter's Church,
Shall happily make thee there a joyful bride.   *115*

JULIET   Now, by Saint Peter's Church and Peter too,
He shall not make me there a joyful bride.
I wonder at this haste, that I must wed
Ere he that should be husband comes to woo.
I pray you tell my lord and father, madam,   *120*
I will not marry yet, and when I do, I swear
It shall be Romeo, whom you know I hate,
Rather than Paris. These are news indeed!

LADY CAPULET   Here comes your father, tell him so yourself;
And see how he will take it at your hands.   *125*

                                Enter CAPULET *and* NURSE

CAPULET   When the sun sets, the earth doth drizzle dew,
But for the sunset of my brother's son
It rains downright.
How now, a conduit, girl? What, still in tears?
Evermore show'ring? In one little body   *130*
Thou counterfeits a bark, a sea, a wind:
For still thy eyes, which I may call the sea,
Do ebb and flow with tears; the bark thy body is,
Sailing in this salt flood; the winds, thy sighs,
Who, raging with thy tears, and they with them,   *135*
Without a sudden calm, will overset
Thy tempest-tossed body. How now, wife?
Have you delivered to her our decree?

LADY CAPULET   Ay, sir, but she will none, she [gives] you thanks.
I would the fool were married to her grave!   *140*

CAPULET   Soft, take me with you, take me with you, wife.
How, will she none? Doth she not give us thanks?
Is she not proud? Doth she not count her blest,
Unworthy as she is, that we have wrought
So worthy a gentleman to be her bride?   *145*

JULIET   Not proud you have, but thankful that you have.
Proud can I never be of what I hate,
But thankful even for hate that is meant love.

---

129. *conduit:* fountain
136. *Without . . . calm:* unless they abate very soon
139. *but . . . thanks:* but she says "No, thank you." In line 142 *Doth . . . thanks?* = isn't she grateful?
141. *take . . . you:* let me understand what you mean

143. *proud:* elated
144. *wrought:* secured
145. *bride:* bridegroom (a sense already rare in Shakespeare's day)
146. *thankful:* i.e., properly grateful for your solicitude

CAPULET   How how, how how, chopp'd logic! What is this?
    "Proud," and "I thank you," and "I thank you not,"   *150*
    And yet "not proud," mistress minion you?
    Thank me no thankings, nor proud me no prouds,
    But fettle your fine joints 'gainst Thursday next,
    To go with Paris to Saint Peter's Church,
    Or I will drag thee on a hurdle thither.   *155*
    Out, you green-sickness carrion! Out, you baggage!
    You tallow-face!
LADY CAPULET   Fie, fie, what, are you mad?
JULIET   Good father, I beseech you on my knees,
    Hear me with patience but to speak a word.   [*She kneels down*]
CAPULET   Hang thee, young baggage! disobedient wretch!   *160*
    I tell thee what: get thee to church a' Thursday,
    Or never after look me in the face.
    Speak not, reply not, do not answer me!
    My fingers itch. Wife, we scarce thought us blest
    That God had lent us but this only child,   *165*
    But now I see this one is one too much,
    And that we have a curse in having her.
    Out on her, hilding!
NURSE   God in heaven bless her!
    You are to blame, my lord, to rate her so.
CAPULET   And why, my Lady Wisdom? Hold your tongue,   *170*
    Good Prudence, smatter with your gossips, go.
NURSE   I speak no treason.
CAPULET   O, God-i-goden!
[NURSE]   May not one speak?
CAPULET   Peace, you mumbling fool!
    Utter your gravity o'er a gossip's bowl,
    For here we need it not.
LADY CAPULET   You are too hot.   *175*
CAPULET   God's bread, it makes me mad! Day, night, work, play,
    Alone, in company, still my care hath been
    To have her match'd; and having now provided
    A gentleman of noble parentage,

149. *chopp'd logic:* idle sophistry, or idle sophist
151. *minion:* spoiled child
153. *fettle:* prepare (normally a term of the stable)
155. *hurdle:* conveyance for dragging criminals to execution
156. *Out:* an exclamation of indignant reproach. *green-sickness:* alluding to Juliet's paleness (as is shown by *carrion,* implying that she is as pale as a corpse), but also to her reluctance to marry, since "the green-sickness" was a disease of unmarried girls. *baggage:* good-for-nothing
157. *Fie . . . mad:* addressed to Capulet
169. *rate:* berate
171. *smatter:* chatter
172. *God-i-goden:* here, an impatient exclamation equivalent to "for God's sake"

Of fair demesnes, youthful and nobly [lien'd],   *180*
Stuff'd, as they say, with honorable parts,
Proportion'd as one's thought would wish a man,
And then to have a wretched puling fool,
A whining mammet, in her fortune's tender,
To answer, "I'll not wed, I cannot love;   *185*
I am too young, I pray you pardon me."
But and you will not wed, I'll pardon you.
Graze where you will, you shall not house with me.
Look to't, think on't, I do not use to jest.
Thursday is near, lay hand on heart, advise.   *190*
And you be mine, I'll give you to my friend;
And you be not, hang, beg, starve, die in the streets,
For, by my soul, I'll ne'er acknowledge thee,
Nor what is mine shall never do thee good.
Trust to't, bethink you, I'll not be forsworn.   *Exit*

JULIET   Is there no pity sitting in the clouds,   *196*
That sees into the bottom of my grief?
O sweet my mother, cast me not away!
Delay this marriage for a month, a week,
Or if you do not, make the bridal bed   *200*
In that dim monument where Tybalt lies.

LADY CAPULET   Talk not to me, for I'll not speak a word.
Do as thou wilt, for I have done with thee.   *Exit*

JULIET   O God!—O nurse, how shall this be prevented?
My husband is on earth, my faith in heaven;   *205*
How shall that faith return again to earth,
Unless that husband send it me from heaven
By leaving earth? Comfort me, counsel me!
Alack, alack, that heaven should practice stratagems
Upon so soft a subject as myself!   *210*
What say'st thou? Hast thou not a word of joy?
Some comfort, nurse.

NURSE   Faith, here it is.
Romeo is banished, and all the world to nothing
That he dares ne'er come back to challenge you;
Or if he do, it needs must be by stealth.   *215*
Then, since the case so stands as now it doth,
I think it best you married with the County.

---

180. *demesnes:* estates. *nobly lien'd:*
well connected
184. *mammet:* doll. *in . . . tender:*
when good fortune is offered her
189. *do not use:* am not accustomed
190. *advise:* consider well
205. *my . . . heaven:* i.e., my marriage
vow sworn before God

206–208. *How . . . earth:* i.e., how
can I marry again unless Romeo dies
209. *practice:* devise
213. *all . . . nothing:* i.e., it is a perfectly safe bet
214. *challenge:* claim

O he's a lovely gentleman!
Romeo's a dishclout to him. An eagle, madam,
Hath not so green, so quick, so fair an eye   *220*
As Paris hath. Beshrow my very heart,
I think you are happy in this second match,
For it excells your first; or if it did not,
Your first is dead, or 'twere as good he were
As living here and you no use of him.   *225*

JULIET   Speak'st thou from thy heart?
NURSE   And from my soul too, else beshrew them both.
JULIET   Amen!
NURSE   What?
JULIET   Well, thou hast comforted me marvellous much.   *230*
Go in, and tell my lady I am gone,
Having displeas'd my father, to Lawrence' cell,
To make confession and to be absolv'd.
NURSE   Marry, I will, and this is wisely done.   [*Exit*]
JULIET [*she looks after* NURSE]   Ancient damnation! O most wicked fiend!
Is it more sin to wish me thus forsworn,   *236*
Or to dispraise my lord with that same tongue
Which she hath prais'd him with above compare
So many thousand times? Go, counsellor,
Thou and my bosom henceforth shall be twain.   *240*
I'll to the friar to know his remedy;
If all else fail, myself have power to die.   *Exit*

[ACT FOUR]   [*Scene One*]

                    Enter FRIAR [LAWRENCE] *and* COUNTY PARIS
FRIAR LAWRENCE   On Thursday, sir? The time is very short.
PARIS   My father Capulet will have it so,
And I am nothing slow to slack his haste.
FRIAR LAWRENCE   You say you do not know the lady's mind?
Uneven is the course, I like it not.   *5*
PARIS   Immoderately she weeps for Tybalt's death,
And therefore have I little [talk'd] of love,

---

219. *to:* in comparison with
221. *Beshrow:* beshrew (see note on
II.v.49)
225. *here:* i.e., on earth
228. *Amen:* i.e., may they be cursed
indeed. The Nurse, who has used
beshrew in the usual weakened sense,
does not follow
235. *Ancient damnation:* damned old
woman

240. *Bosom:* private thoughts. *twain:*
separated
IV.i. Location: Verona. Friar Lawrence's cell
3. *am nothing slow:* have no reluctance
of mind
5. *Uneven:* irregular

For Venus smiles not in a house of tears.
Now, sir, her father counts it dangerous
That she do give her sorrow so much sway;   10
And in his wisdom hastes our marriage,
To stop the inundation of her tears,
Which, too much minded by herself alone,
May be put from her by society.
Now do you know the reason of this haste.   15
FRIAR LAWRENCE [*aside*]   I would I knew not why it should be slowed.—
Look, sir, here comes the lady toward my cell.

                                                      Enter JULIET

PARIS   Happily met, my lady and my wife!
JULIET   That may be, sir, when I may be a wife.
PARIS   That may be must be, love, on Thursday next.   20
JULIET   What must be shall be.
FRIAR LAWRENCE   That's a certain text.
PARIS   Come you to make confession to this father?
JULIET   To answer that, I should confess to you.
PARIS   Do not deny to him that you love me.
JULIET   I will confess to you that I love him.   25
PARIS   So will ye, I am sure, that you love me.
JULIET   If I do so, it will be of more price,
Being spoke behind your back, than to your face.
PARIS   Poor soul, thy face is much abus'd with tears.
JULIET   The tears have got small victory by that,   30
For it was bad enough before their spite.
PARIS   Thou wrong'st it more than tears with that report.
JULIET   That is no slander, sir, which is a truth,
And what I spake, I spake it to my face.
PARIS   Thy face is mine, and thou hast sland'red it.   35
JULIET   It may be so, for it is not mine own.
Are you at leisure, holy father, now,
Or shall I come to you at evening mass?
FRIAR LAWRENCE   My leisure serves me, pensive daughter, now.
My lord, we must entreat the time alone.   40
PARIS   God shield I should disturb devotion!
Juliet, on Thursday early will I rouse ye;
Till then adieu, and keep this holy kiss.   *Exit*
JULIET   O, shut the door, and when thou hast done so,
Come weep with me, past hope, past [cure], past help!   45

---

13. *minded . . . alone:* thought about
by her in her solitude
34. *to my face:* (1) openly; (2) concerning my face

39. *pensive:* sad
41. *shield:* prevent, forbid

FRIAR LAWRENCE   O Juliet, I already know thy grief,
   It strains me past the compass of my wits.
   I hear thou must, and nothing may prorogue it,
   On Thursday next be married to this County.

JULIET   Tell me not, friar, that thou hearest of this,   *50*
   Unless thou tell me how I may prevent it.
   If in thy wisdom thou canst give no help,
   Do thou but call my resolution wise,
   And with this knife I'll help it presently.
   God join'd my heart and Romeo's, thou our hands,   *55*
   And ere this hand, by thee to Romeo's seal'd,
   Shall be the label to another deed,
   Or my true heart with treacherous revolt
   Turn to another, this shall slay them both.
   Therefore, out of thy long-experienc'd time,   *60*
   Give me some present counsel, or, behold,
   'Twixt my extremes and me this bloody knife
   Shall play the umpeer, arbitrating that
   Which the commission of thy years and art
   Could to no issue of true honor bring.   *65*
   Be not so long to speak, I long to die,
   If what thou speak'st speak not of remedy.

FRIAR LAWRENCE   Hold, daughter! I do spy a kind of hope,
   Which craves as desperate an execution
   As that is desperate which we would prevent.   *70*
   If rather than to marry County Paris,
   Thou hast the strength of will to [slay] thyself,
   Then is it likely thou wilt undertake
   A thing like death to chide away this shame,
   That cop'st with Death himself to scape from it;   *75*
   And if thou darest, I'll give thee remedy.

JULIET   O, bid me leap, rather than marry Paris,
   From off the battlements of any tower,
   Or walk in thievish ways, or bid me lurk
   Where serpents are; chain me with roaring bears,   *80*
   Or hide me nightly in a charnel-house,—
   O'ercover'd quite with dead men's rattling bones,
   With reeky shanks and yellow [chapless] skulls;

46. *thy grief:* the cause of your grief
47. *strains:* forces. *compass:* boundary, limits
54. *presently:* at once
57. *label:* i.e., seal (literally, a strip of material attached to a document to carry the seal)
62. *extremes:* desperate plight

63. *umpeer:* umpire
64. *commission:* authority. *art:* skill
75. *That cop'st with:* (you) who would encounter
79. *thievish:* infested with thieves
83. *reeky:* emitting foul vapor. *chapless:* without lower jaws

Or bid me go into a new-made grave,
And hide me with a dead man in his [shroud]—   *85*
Things that, to hear them told, have made me tremble—
And I will do it without fear or doubt,
To live an unstain'd wife to my sweet love.

FRIAR LAWRENCE   Hold then. Go home, be merry, give consent
To marry Paris. We'n'sday is to-morrow;   *90*
To-morrow night look that thou lie alone,
Let not the nurse lie with thee in thy chamber.
Take thou this vial, being then in bed,
And this distilling liquor drink thou off,
When presently through all thy veins shall run   *95*
A cold and drowsy humor; for no pulse
Shall keep his native progress, but surcease;
No warmth, no [breath] shall testify thou livest;
The roses in thy lips and cheeks shall fade
To [wanny] ashes, thy eyes' windows fall,   *100*
Like death when he shuts up the day of life;
Each part, depriv'd of supple government,
Shall, stiff and stark and cold, appear like death,
And in this borrowed likeness of shrunk death
Thou shalt continue two and forty hours,   *105*
And then awake as from a pleasant sleep.
Now when the bridegroom in the morning comes
To rouse thee from thy bed, there art thou dead.
Then, as the manner of our country is,
[In] thy best robes, uncovered on the bier,   *110*
Thou shall be borne to that same ancient vault
Where all the kindred of the Capulets lie.
In the mean time, against thou shalt awake,
Shall Romeo by my letters know our drift,
And hither shall he come, an' he and I   *115*
Will watch thy [waking], and that very night
Shall Romeo bear thee hence to Mantua.
And this shall free thee from this present shame,
If no inconstant toy, nor womanish fear,
Abate thy valor in the acting it.   *120*

JULIET   Give me, give me! O, tell not me of fear!

---

94. *distilling:* having the power to permeate the body
96. *humor:* fluid
97. *keep . . . progress:* maintain its natural progression. *surcease:* cease
100. *wanny:* pale. *windows:* shutters, i.e., lids
102. *supple government:* control of movement
113. *against:* in preparation for the time when
114. *drift:* intent
119. *inconstant toy:* capricious change of mind

FRIAR LAWRENCE   Hold, get you gone. Be strong and prosperous
    In this resolve. I'll send a friar with speed
    To Mantua, with my letters to thy lord.
JULIET   Love give me strength! and strength shall help afford.   *125*
    Farewell, dear father!   *Exeunt*

[*Scene Two*]

Enter FATHER CAPULET, *Mother* [LADY CAPULET], NURSE, *and*
    SERVINGMEN, *two or three*
CAPULET   So many guests invite as here are writ.

[*Exit* FIRST SERVANT]

    Sirrah, go hire me twenty cunning cooks.
SECOND SERVINGMAN   You shall have none ill, sir, for I'll try if they can
    lick their fingers.
CAPULET   How canst thou try them so?
SECOND SERVINGMAN   Marry, sir, 'tis an ill cook that cannot lick his own
    fingers; therefore he that cannot lick his fingers goes not with
    me.
CAPULET   Go, be gone.

[*Exit* SECOND SERVANT]

    We shall be much unfurnish'd for this time.   *10*
    What, is my daughter gone to Friar Lawrence?
NURSE   Ay forsooth.
CAPULET   Well, he may chance to do some good on her.
    A peevish self[-will'd] harlotry it is.

Enter JULIET

NURSE   See where she comes from shrift with merry look.   *15*
CAPULET   How now, my headstrong, where have you been gadding?
JULIET   Where I have learnt me to repent the sin
    Of disobedient opposition
    To you and your behests, and am enjoin'd
    By holy Lawrence to fall prostrate here   *20*
    To beg your pardon. [*She kneels down*] Pardon, I beseech you!
    Henceforward I am ever rul'd by you.
CAPULET   Send for the County, go tell him of this.
    I'll have this knot knit up to-morrow morning.
JULIET   I met the youthful lord at Lawrence' cell,   *25*
    And gave him what becomed love I might,
    Not stepping o'er the bounds of modesty.

122. *prosperous:* fortunate
IV.ii. Location: Verona. Capulet's
house
5. *try them so:* i.e., tell by that test
whether they are good cooks

6–7. *lick . . . fingers:* i.e., to show his
confidence in his own cooking
10. *unfurnish'd:* unprepared
14. *harlotry:* wench
26. *becomed:* befitting

CAPULET   Why, I am glad on't, this is well, stand up.
    This is as't should be. Let me see the County;
    Ay, marry, go, I say, and fetch him hither.   30
    Now, afore God, this reverend holy friar,
    All our whole city is much bound to him.
JULIET   Nurse, will you go with me into my closet
    To help me sort such needful ornaments
    As you think fit to furnish me to-morrow?   35
LADY CAPULET   No, not till Thursday, there is time enough.
CAPULET   Go, nurse, go with her, we'll to church to-morrow.

                                        Exeunt [JULIET *and* NURSE]
LADY CAPULET   We shall be short in our provision,
    'Tis now near night.
CAPULET   Tush, I will stir about,
    And all things shall be well, I warrant thee, wife;   40
    Go thou to Juliet, help to deck up her.
    I'll not to bed to-night; let me alone.
    I'll play the huswife for this once. What ho!
    They are all forth. Well, I will walk myself
    To County Paris, to prepare up him   45
    Against to-morrow. My heart is wondrous light,
    Since this same wayward girl is so reclaim'd.

                                                             Exeunt

                        [*Scene Three*]

                    Enter JULIET *and* NURSE
JULIET   Ay, those attires are best, but, gentle nurse,
    I pray thee leave me to myself to-night,
    For I have need of many orisons
    To move the heavens to smile upon my state,
    Which, well thou knowest, is cross and full of sin.   5
                                     Enter Mother [LADY CAPULET]
LADY CAPULET   What, are you busy, ho? Need you my help?
JULIET   No, madam, we have cull'd such necessaries
    As are behoofeful for our state to-morrow.
    So please you, let me now be left alone,
    And let the nurse this night sit up with you,   10
    For I am sure you have your hands full all,
    In this so sudden business.

---

33. *closet:* private room
34. *sort:* select
42. *let me alone:* leave everything to me

IV.iii. Location: Verona. Capulet's house
5. *cross:* perverse
8. *behoofeful:* needful. *state:* ceremony

LADY CAPULET   Good night.
   Get thee to bed and rest, for thou hast need.

                        Exeunt [LADY CAPULET *and* NURSE]

JULIET   Farewell! God knows when we shall meet again.

I have a faint cold fear thrills through my veins,	15
That almost freezes up the heat of life.	
I'll call them back again to comfort me.	
Nurse!—What should she do here?	
My dismal scene I needs must act alone.	
Come, vial.	20
What if this mixture do not work at all?	
Shall I be married then to-morrow morning?	
No, no, this shall forbid it. Lie thou there. *[Laying down her dagger]*	
What if it be a poison which the friar	
Subtilly hath minist'red to have me dead,	25
Lest in this marriage he should be dishonor'd	
Because he married me before to Romeo?	
I fear it is, and yet methinks it should not,	
For he hath still been tried a holy man.	
How if, when I am laid into the tomb,	30
I wake before the time that Romeo	
Come to redeem me? there's a fearful point!	
Shall I not then be stifled in the vault,	
To whose foul mouth no healthsome air breathes in,	
And there die strangled ere my Romeo comes?	35
Or if I live, is it not very like	
The horrible conceit of death and night,	
Together with the terror of the place—	
As in a vault, an ancient receptacle,	
Where for this many hundred years the bones	40
Of all my buried ancestors are pack'd,	
Where bloody Tybalt, yet but green in earth,	
Lie fest'ring in his shroud, where, as they say,	
At some hours in the night spirits resort—	
Alack, alack, is it not like that I,	45
So early waking—what with loathsome smells,	
And shrikes like mandrakes' torn out of the earth,	
That living mortals, hearing them, run mad—	
O, if I [wake], shall I not be distraught,	
Environed with all these hideous fears,	50

---

15. *faint cold:* producing faintness and coldness. *thrills:* that pierces
19. *dismal:* dreadful, fateful
29. *still:* always. *tried:* proved (by testing)
37. *conceit:* idea
42. *green in earth:* newly buried

47. *shrikes:* shrieks. *mandrakes':* the mandrake, a plant with a fleshy forked root, was thought to resemble a man. When pulled from the earth it supposedly uttered a shriek that caused anyone who heard it to run mad or die

And madly play with my forefathers' joints,
And pluck the mangled Tybalt from his shroud,
And in this rage, with some great kinsman's bone,
As with a club, dash out my desp'rate brains?
O, look! methinks I see my cousin's ghost   55
Seeking out Romeo, that did spit his body
Upon a rapier's point. Stay, Tybalt, stay!
Romeo, Romeo, Romeo! Here's drink—I drink to thee.

               [*She falls upon her bed, within the curtains*]

[*Scene Four*]

      Enter lady of the house [LADY CAPULET] *and* NURSE [*with herbs*]

LADY CAPULET   Hold, take these keys and fetch more spices, nurse.
NURSE   They call for dates and quinces in the pastry.

                     Enter old CAPULET

CAPULET   Come, stir, stir, stir! the second cock hath crowed,
The curfew-bell hath rung, 'tis three a' clock.
Look to the bak'd meats, good Angelica,   5
Spare not for cost.
NURSE   Go, you cot-quean, go,
Get you to bed. Faith, you'll be sick to-morrow
For this night's watching.
CAPULET   No, not a whit. What, I have watch'd ere now
All night for lesser cause, and ne'er been sick.   10
LADY CAPULET   Ay, you have been a mouse-hunt in your time,
But I will watch you from such watching now.

               Exeunt LADY [CAPULET] *and* NURSE

CAPULET   A jealous hood, a jealous hood!

      Enter three or four [SERVINGMEN] *with spits and logs and baskets.*
Now, fellow, what is there?
[FIRST SERVINGMAN]   Things for the cook, sir, but I know not what.   15
CAPULET   Make haste, make haste. Sirrah, fetch drier logs.

                   [*Exit* FIRST SERVANT]

Call Peter, he will show thee where they are.
[SECOND SERVINGMAN]   I have a head, sir, that will find out logs,
And never trouble Peter for the matter.

---

53. *rage:* insane fit. *great:* earlier by one or more generations, as in "great-grandfather"
57. *Stay:* stop
IV.iv. Location: Scene continues
2. *pastry:* pastry room
5. *Angelica:* i.e., the Nurse

6. *cot-quean:* man who plays house-wife
8. *watching:* staying awake
11. *mouse-hunt:* mouse-hunter, i.e., woman-chaser
13. *jealous hood:* jealous person (cf. "madcap," "bad hat")

CAPULET   Mass, and well said, a merry whoreson, ha!   20
Thou shalt be logger-head. Good [faith], 'tis day.

[*Exit* SECOND SERVANT.]

The County will be here with music straight,
For so he said he would. (*Play music* [*within*]) I hear him near.
Nurse! Wife! What ho! What, nurse, I say!

Enter NURSE

Go waken Juliet, go and trim her up,   25
I'll go and chat with Paris. Hie, make haste,
Make haste, the bridegroom he is come already,
Make haste, I say.   [*Exit*]

[*Scene Five*]

NURSE   Mistress! what, mistress! Juliet!—Fast, I warrant her, she.—
Why, lamb! why, lady! fie, you slug-a-bed!
Why, love, I say! madam! sweet heart! why, bride!
What, not a word? You take your pennyworths now;
Sleep for a week, for the next night, I warrant,   5
The County Paris hath set up his rest
That you shall rest but little. God forgive me!
Marry and amen! How sound is she asleep!
I needs must wake her. Madam, madam, madam!
Ay, let the County take you in your bed,   10
He'll fright you up, i' faith. Will it not be?   [*Draws back the curtains*]
What, dress'd, and in your clothes, and down again?
I must needs wake you. Lady, lady, lady!
Alas, alas! Help, help! my lady's dead!
O, weraday, that ever I was born!   15
Some aqua-vitae ho! My lord! my lady!

[*Enter Mother,* LADY CAPULET]

LADY CAPULET   What noise is here?
NURSE   O lamentable day!
LADY CAPULET   What is the matter?
NURSE   Look, look! O heavy day!
LADY CAPULET   O me, O me, my child, my only life!
Revive, look up, or I will die with thee!   20
Help, help! Call help.

Enter Father [CAPULET]

CAPULET   For shame, bring Juliet forth, her lord is come.

21. *logger-head:* blockhead   4. *pennyworths:* small quantities
IV.v. Location: Scene continues   6. *set . . . rest:* firmly resolved (a term
1. *Fast:* fast asleep   from the card game primero)

NURSE   She's dead, deceas'd, she's dead, alack the day!

LADY CAPULET   Alack the day, she's dead, she's dead, she's dead!

CAPULET   Hah, let me see her. Out alas, she's cold,   *25*
Her blood is settled, and her joints are stiff;
Life and these lips have long been separated.
Death lies on her like an untimely frost
Upon the sweetest flower of all the field.

NURSE   O lamentable day!

LADY CAPULET   O woeful time!   *30*

CAPULET   Death, that hath ta'en her hence to make me wail,
Ties up my tongue and will not let me speak.

> *Enter* FRIAR [LAWRENCE] *and the* COUNTY [PARIS *with the*
> MUSICIANS]

FRIAR LAWRENCE   Come, is the bride ready to go to church?

CAPULET   Ready to go, but never to return.—
O son, the night before thy wedding-day   *35*
Hath Death lain with thy wife. There she lies,
Flower as she was, deflowered by him.
Death is my son-in-law, Death is my heir,
My daughter he hath wedded. I will die,
And leave him all; life, living, all is Death's.   *40*

PARIS   Have I thought [long] to see this morning's face,
And doth it give me such a sight as this?

LADY CAPULET   Accurs'd, unhappy, wretched, hateful day!
Most miserable hour that e'er time saw
In lasting labor of his pilgrimage!   *45*
But one, poor one, one poor and loving child,
But one thing to rejoice and solace in,
And cruel Death hath catch'd it from my sight!

NURSE   O woe! O woeful, woeful, woeful day!
Most lamentable day, most woeful day   *50*
That ever, ever, I did yet behold!
O day, O day, O day, O hateful day!
Never was seen so black a day as this.
O woeful day, O woeful day!

PARIS   Beguil'd, divorced, wronged, spited, slain!   *55*
Most detestable Death, by thee beguil'd,
By cruel cruel thee quite overthrown!
O love, O life! not life, but love in death!

CAPULET   Despis'd, distressed, hated, martyr'd, kill'd!
Uncomfortable time, why cam'st thou now   *60*
To murther, murther our solemnity?

---

40. *living:* property
41. *thought long:* been impatient
45. *lasting:* ceaseless
48. *catch'd:* snatched
60. *Uncomfortable:* comfortless
61. *solemnity:* festivity

O child, O child! my soul, and not my child!
Dead art thou! Alack, my child is dead,
And with my child my joys are buried.   64

FRIAR LAWRENCE   Peace ho, for shame! Confusion's [cure] lives not
In these confusions. Heaven and yourself
Had part in this fair maid, now heaven hath all,
And all the better is it for the maid.
Your part in her you could not keep from death,
But heaven keeps his part in eternal life.   70
The most you sought was her promotion,
For 'twas your heaven she should be advanc'd,
And weep ye now, seeing she is advanc'd
Above the clouds, as high as heaven itself?
O, in this love, you love your child so ill   75
That you run mad, seeing that she is well.
She's not well married that lives married long,
But she's best married that dies married young.
Dry up your tears, and stick your rosemary
On this fair corse, and as the custom is,   80
And in her best array, bear her to church;
For though [fond] nature bids us all lament,
Yet nature's tears are reason's merriment.

CAPULET   All things that we ordained festival,
Turn from their office to black funeral: 85
Our instruments to melancholy bells,
Our wedding cheer to a sad burial feast;
Our solemn hymns to sullen dirges change;
Our bridal flowers serve for a buried corse;
And all things change them to the contrary.   90

FRIAR LAWRENCE   Sir, go you in, and, madam, go with him;
And go, Sir Paris. Every one prepare
To follow this fair corse unto her grave.
The heavens do low'r upon you for some ill;
Move them no more by crossing their high will.   95

            [*They all, but the* NURSE *and the* MUSICIANS, *go forth, casting
            rosemary on her, and shutting the curtains*]

[FIRST] MUSICIAN   Faith, we may put up our pipes and be gone.
NURSE   Honest good fellows, ah, put up, put up,
For well you know this is a pitiful case.   [*Exit*]

---

65. *Confusion's:* ruin's, loss's
66. *confusions:* disorderly outcries
71. *promotion:* advancement
75. *in this love:* i.e., by lamenting her
death
79. *rosemary:* herb signifying remembrance

83. *nature's . . . merriment:* that which
makes human nature mourn is cause
for joy to the reason
85. *office:* function
87. *cheer:* banquet
88. *sullen:* mournful
95. *Move:* anger

[FIRST MUSICIAN]   Ay, [by] my troth, the case may be amended.

Enter [PETER]

PETER   Musicians, O musicians, "Heart's ease," "Heart's ease"! O, and you will have me live, play "Heart's ease."   *101*

[FIRST MUSICIAN]   Why "Heart's ease"?

PETER   O musicians, because my heart itself plays "My heart is full." O, play me some merry dump to comfort me.

[FIRST MUSICIAN]   Not a dump we, 'tis no time to play now.

PETER   You will not then?   *106*

[FIRST MUSICIAN]   No.

PETER   I will then give it you soundly.

[FIRST MUSICIAN]   What will you give us?

PETER   No money, on my faith, but the gleek; I will give you the minstrel.   *111*

[FIRST MUSICIAN]   Then will I give you the serving-creature.

PETER   Then will I lay the serving-creature's dagger on your pate. I will carry no crotchets, I'll *re* you, I'll *fa* you. Do you note me?

[FIRST MUSICIAN]   And you *re* us and *fa* us, you note us.   *115*

SECOND MUSICIAN   Pray you put up your dagger, and put out your wit.

[PETER]   Then have at you with my wit! I will dry-beat you with an iron wit, and put up my iron dagger. Answer me like men:

> "When griping griefs the heart doth wound,
>> [And doleful dumps the mind oppress,]   *120*
> Then music with her silver sound"—

why "silver sound"? Why, "music with her silver sound"? What say you, Simon Catling?

[FIRST MUSICIAN]   Marry, sir, because silver hath a sweet sound.

PETER   [Pretty!] What say you, Hugh Rebeck?   *125*

SECOND MUSICIAN   I say, "silver sound," because musicians sound for silver.

PETER   [Pretty] too! What say you, James Soundpost?

THIRD MUSICIAN   Faith, I know not what to say.   *129*

---

99. *the case . . . amended:* (1) things could be better than they are; (2) the instrument case could well be repaired
100. *"Heart's ease":* a ballad tune; "My heart is full [of woe]" (line 103) is another
105. *dump:* mournful tune
110. *gleek:* gibe
110–111. *give . . . minstrel:* call you rogues
114. *carry:* (1) endure; (2) sing. *crotchets:* (1) whims; (2) quarter-notes. *re, fa:* notes of the scale (perhaps with puns on "ray" befoul and "fay" clean up)

114–115. *note . . . note:* heed . . . set to music
116. *put out:* display
117–118. *iron wit:* i.e., merciless wit
119–121, 133–135. These lines are from Richard Edwards' "In Commendation of Music."
123. *Catling:* name taken from that of a lute string
125. *Rebeck:* name based on that of a three-stringed violin
126. *sound:* play or sing
128. *Soundpost:* name based on that of the internal structural support of such instruments as the violin

PETER   O, I cry you mercy, you are the singer; I will say for you; it is "music with her silver sound," because musicians have no gold for sounding:

> "Then music with her silver sound
>> With speedy help doth lend redress."   *Exit*

[FIRST MUSICIAN]   What a pestilent knave is this same!   *135*

SECOND MUSICIAN   Hang him, Jack! Come, we'll in here, tarry for the mourners, and stay dinner.   *Exeunt*

[ACT FIVE]   [*Scene One*]

Enter ROMEO

ROMEO   If I may trust the flattering truth of sleep,
My dreams presage some joyful news at hand.
My bosom's lord sits lightly in his throne,
And all this day an unaccustom'd spirit
Lifts me above the ground with cheerful thoughts.   *5*
I dreamt my lady came and found me dead—
Strange dream, that gives a dead man leave to think!—
And breath'd such life with kisses in my lips
That I reviv'd and was an emperor.
Ah me, how sweet is love itself possess'd,   *10*
When but love's shadows are so rich in joy!

Enter ROMEO*'s man* [BALTHASAR, *booted*]

News from Verona! How now, Balthasar?
Dost thou not bring me letters from the friar?
How doth my lady? Is my father well?
How doth my Juliet? That I ask again,   *15*
For nothing can be ill if she be well.—

BALTHASAR   Then she is well and nothing can be ill:
Her body sleeps in Capel's monument,
And her immortal part with angels lives.
I saw her laid low in her kindred's vault,   *20*
And presently took post to tell it you.
O, pardon me for bringing these ill news,
Since you did leave it for my office, sir.

---

130. *cry you mercy:* beg your pardon. *singer:* implying that he can sing but not speak
131–132. *have . . . sounding:* (1) do not receive gold for playing; (2) possess no gold for jingling in their pockets
137. *stay:* wait for

V.i. Location: Mantua. A street
1. *flattering:* favorable, gratifying
3. *My bosom's lord:* i.e., love. *his throne:* i.e., my heart
21. *presently:* immediately. *took post:* hired post horses
23. *office:* duty

ROMEO   Is it [e'en] so? Then I [defy] you, stars!
         Thou knowest my lodging, get me ink and paper,   25
         And hire post-horses; I will hence to-night.
BALTHASAR   I do beseech you, sir, have patience.
         Your looks are pale and wild, and do import
         Some misadventure.
ROMEO   Tush, thou art deceiv'd.
         Leave me, and do the thing I bid thee do.   30
         Hast thou no letters to me from the friar?
BALTHASAR   No, my good lord.
ROMEO   No matter, get thee gone,
         And hire those horses; I'll be with thee straight.

                                                  Exit [BALTHASAR]

         Well, Juliet, I will lie with thee to-night.
         Let's see for means. O mischief, thou art swift   35
         To enter in the thoughts of desperate men!
         I do remember an apothecary—
         And hereabouts 'a dwells—which late I noted
         In tatt'red weeds, with overwhelming brows,
         Culling of simples; meagre were his looks,   40
         Sharp misery had worn him to the bones;
         And in his needy shop a tortoise hung,
         An alligator stuff'd, and other skins
         Of ill-shap'd fishes, and about his shelves
         A beggarly account of empty boxes,   45
         Green earthen pots, bladders, and musty seeds,
         Remnants of packthread, and old cakes of roses
         Were thinly scattered, to make up a show.
         Noting this penury, to myself I said,
         "An' if a man did need a poison now,   50
         Whose sale is present death in Mantua,
         Here lives a caitiff wretch would sell it him."
         O, this same thought did but forerun my need,
         And this same needy man must sell it me.
         As I remember, this should be the house.   55
         Being holiday, the beggar's shop is shut.
         What ho, apothecary!

                                                  [*Enter* APOTHECARY]

APOTHECARY   Who calls so loud?

35. *see for means:* think how to do it   47. *cakes of roses:* rose petals pressed
39. *weeds:* clothes. *overwhelming:* jut-   into cake form, for the perfume
ting, overhanging   50. *An' if:* if
40. *simples:* medicinal herbs   51. *present death:* punishable by im-
45. *beggarly account:* paltry lot   mediate execution

ROMEO   Come hither, man. I see that thou art poor.
    Hold, there is forty ducats; let me have
    A dram of poison, such soon-speeding gear   60
    As will disperse itself through all the veins
    That the life-weary taker may fall dead,
    And that the trunk may be discharg'd of breath
    As violently as hasty powder fir'd
    Doth hurry from the fatal cannon's womb.   65
APOTHECARY   Such mortal drugs I have, but Mantua's law
    Is death to any he that utters them.
ROMEO   Art thou so bare and full of wretchedness,
    And fearest to die? Famine is in thy cheeks,
    Need and oppression starveth in thy eyes,   70
    Contempt and beggary hangs upon thy back;
    The world is not thy friend, nor the world's law,
    The world affords no law to make thee rich;
    Then be not poor, but break it, and take this.
APOTHECARY   My poverty, but not my will, consents.   75
ROMEO   I [pay] thy poverty, and not thy will.
APOTHECARY   Put this in any liquid thing you will
    And drink it off, and if you had the strength
    Of twenty men, it would dispatch you straight.
ROMEO   There is thy gold, worse poison to men's souls,   80
    Doing more murther in this loathsome world,
    Than these poor compounds that thou mayest not sell.
    I sell thee poison, thou hast sold me none.
    Farewell! Buy food, and get thyself in flesh.

                              [*Exit* APOTHECARY]
    Come, cordial and not poison, go with me   85
    To Juliet's grave, for there must I use thee.   *Exit*

        [*Scene Two*]

              Enter FRIAR JOHN
FRIAR JOHN   Holy Franciscan friar! brother, ho!

                       Enter [FRIAR] LAWRENCE

---

59. *ducats:* gold coins
60. *soon-speeding gear:* quick-working stuff
67. *any he:* any man. *utters:* issues, sells
70. *Need and oppression:* i.e., oppressive need
71. *Contempt and beggary:* i.e., beggary that renders you contemptible

74. *it:* i.e., the law
84. *get . . . flesh:* grow fat
85. *cordial:* healing medicine, restorative
V.ii. Location: Verona. Friar Lawrence's cell

FRIAR LAWRENCE   This same should be the voice of Friar John.
Welcome from Mantua! What says Romeo?
Or, if his mind be writ, give me his letter.
FRIAR JOHN   Going to find a barefoot brother out,   5
One of our order, to associate me,
Here in this city visiting the sick,
And finding him, the searchers of the town,
Suspecting that we both were in a house
Where the infectious pestilence did reign,   10
Seal'd up the doors and would not let us forth,
So that my speed to Mantua there was stay'd.
FRIAR LAWRENCE   Who bare my letter then to Romeo?
FRIAR JOHN   I could not send it—here it is again—
Nor get a messenger to bring it thee,   15
So fearful were they of infection.
FRIAR LAWRENCE   Unhappy fortune! By my brotherhood,
The letter was not nice but full of charge,
Of dear import, and the neglecting it
May do much danger. Friar John, go hence,   20
Get me an iron crow, and bring it straight
Unto my cell.
FRIAR JOHN   Brother, I'll go and bring it thee.   *Exit*
FRIAR LAWRENCE   Now must I to the monument alone,
Within this three hours will fair Juliet wake.   25
She will beshrew me much that Romeo
Hath had no notice of these accidents;
But I will write again to Mantua,
And keep her at my cell till Romeo come—
Poor living corse, clos'd in a dead man's tomb!   *Exit*

[*Scene Three*]

Enter PARIS *and his* PAGE [*with flowers and sweet water and a torch*]

PARIS   Give me thy torch, boy. Hence, and stand aloof.
Yet put it out, for I would not be seen.
Under yond [yew] trees lay thee all along,
Holding thy ear close to the hollow ground,

---

6. *associate:* travel with. Franciscans journeyed in twos
8. *searchers:* health officers
18. *nice:* trivial. *charge:* weighty matter
19. *dear:* significant, urgent
21. *crow:* crowbar

26. *beshrew:* censure
27. *accidents:* events
V.iii. Location: Verona. A churchyard; in it a tomb belonging to the Capulets. O.S.D. *sweet:* perfumed
1. *aloof:* at a distance
3. *all along:* flat

So shall no foot upon the churchyard tread,   5
Being loose, unfirm, with digging up of graves,
But thou shalt hear it. Whistle then to me
As signal that thou hearest something approach.
Give me those flowers. Do as I bid thee, go.
PAGE [*aside*]   I am almost afraid to stand alone   10
Here in the churchyard, yet I will adventure.
                    [*Retires.* PARIS *strews the tomb with flowers*]
PARIS   Sweet flower, with flowers thy bridal bed I strew—
O woe, thy canopy is dust and stones!—
Which with sweet water nightly I will dew,
O wanting that, with tears distill'd by moans.   15
The obsequies that I for thee will keep
Nightly shall be to strew thy grave and weep.

                                                    Whistle BOY
The boy gives warning, something doth approach.
What cursed foot wanders this way to-night,
To cross my obsequies and true love's rite?   20
What, with a torch? Muffle me, night, a while.   [*Retires*]
                    Enter ROMEO *and* [BALTHASAR *with a torch, a mattock, and a*
                    crow of iron]
ROMEO   Give me that mattock and the wrenching iron.
Hold, take this letter; early in the morning
See thou deliver it to my lord and father.
Give me the light. Upon thy life I charge thee,   25
What e'er thou hearest or seest, stand all aloof,
And do not interrupt me in my course.
Why I descend into this bed of death
Is partly to behold my lady's face,
But chiefly to take thence from her dead finger   30
A precious ring—a ring that I must use
In dear employment—therefore hence be gone.
But if thou, jealous, dost return to pry
In what I farther shall intend to do,
By heaven, I will tear thee joint by joint,   35
And strew this hungry churchyard with thy limbs.
The time and my intents are savage-wild,
More fierce and more inexorable far
Than empty tigers or the roaring sea.
[BALTHASAR]   I will be gone, sir, and not trouble ye.   40
ROMEO   So shalt thou show me friendship. Take thou that;
Live and be prosperous, and farewell, good fellow.

---

6. *Being:* i.e., since the soil is   20. *cross:* interfere with
10. *stand:* stay   33. *jealous:* suspicious
16. *obsequies:* rites for the dead

[BALTHASAR] [*aside*]   For all this same, I'll hide me hereabout,
His looks I fear, and his intents I doubt.   [*Retires*]
ROMEO   Thou detestable maw, thou womb of death,   45
Gorg'd with the dearest morsel of the earth,
Thus I enforce thy rotten jaws to open,
And in despite I'll cram thee with more food.

[ROMEO *begins to open the tomb*]

PARIS   This is that banish'd haughty Montague,
That murd'red my love's cousin, with which grief   50
It is supposed the fair creature died,
And here is come to do some villainous shame
To the dead bodies. I will apprehend him.   [*Steps forth*]
Stop thy unhallowed toil, vile Montague!
Can vengeance be pursued further than death?   55
Condemned villain, I do apprehend thee.
Obey and go with me, for thou must die.
ROMEO   I must indeed, and therefore came I hither.
Good gentle youth, tempt not a desp'rate man.
Fly hence and leave me, think upon these gone,   60
Let them affright thee. I beseech thee, youth,
Put not another sin upon my head,
By urging me to fury: O, be gone!
By heaven, I love thee better than myself,
For I come hither arm'd against myself.   65
Stay not, be gone; live, and hereafter say
A madman's mercy bid thee run away.
PARIS   I do defy thy [conjuration],
And apprehend thee for a felon here.   69
ROMEO   Wilt thou provoke me? Then have at thee, boy!

[*They fight*]

[PAGE]   O Lord, they fight! I will go call the watch.   [*Exit*]
PARIS   O, I am slain! [*Falls*] If thou be merciful,
Open the tomb, lay me with Juliet.   [*Dies*]
ROMEO   In faith, I will. Let me peruse this face.
Mercutio's kinsman, noble County Paris!   75
What said my man, when my betossed soul
Did not attend him as we rode? I think
He told me Paris should have married Juliet.
Said he not so? or did I dream it so?
Or am I mad, hearing him talk of Juliet,   80
To think it was so? O, give me thy hand,

---

44. *fear:* am anxious about. *doubt:*   58. *conjuration:* appeal
suspect   78. *should have:* was to have
45. *womb:* belly
53. *apprehend:* arrest

One writ with me in sour misfortune's book!
I'll bury thee in a triumphant grave.
A grave? O no, a lanthorn, slaught'red youth;
For here lies Juliet, and her beauty makes   *85*
This vault a feasting presence full of light.
Death, lie thou there, by a dead man interr'd. [*Laying* PARIS *in the tomb*]
How oft when men are at the point of death
Have they been merry, which their keepers call
A lightning before death! O how may I   *90*
Call this a lightning? O my love, my wife,
Death, that hath suck'd the honey of thy breath,
Hath had no power yet upon thy beauty:
Thou art not conquer'd, beauty's ensign yet
Is crimson in thy lips and in thy cheeks,   *95*
And death's pale flag is not advanced there.
Tybalt, liest thou there in thy bloody sheet?
O, what more favor can I do to thee,
Than with that hand that cut thy youth in twain
To sunder his that was thine enemy?   *100*
Forgive me, cousin! Ah, dear Juliet,
Why art thou yet so fair? Shall I believe
That unsubstantial Death is amorous,
And that the lean abhorred monster keeps
Thee here in dark to be his paramour?   *105*
For fear of that, I still will stay with thee,
And never from this [palace] of dim night
Depart again. Here, here will I remain
With worms that are thy chambermaids; O, here
Will I set up my everlasting rest,   *110*
And shake the yoke of inauspicious stars
From this world-wearied flesh. Eyes, look your last!
Arms, take your last embrace! and, lips, O you
The doors of breath, seal with a righteous kiss
A dateless bargain to engrossing death!   *115*
Come, bitter conduct, come, unsavory guide!
Thou desperate pilot, now at once run on
The dashing rocks thy sea-sick weary bark!

83. *triumphant:* magnificent
84. *lanthorn:* lantern (variant spelling), i.e., a tower room glassed on all sides
86. *feasting presence:* festival presence chamber
89. *keepers:* jailers, or nurses
96. *advanced:* raised
100. *his:* i.e., Romeo's
106. *still:* forever

110. *set . . . rest:* make my firm resolution to repose forever (a telescoping of the literal sense of the words and the special use seen in IV.v.6)
115. *dateless bargain:* contract with no expiration date. *engrossing:* monopolizing (perhaps with pun on the sense "drawing up documents")
116. *conduct:* guide
118. *sea-sick:* weary of voyaging

Here's to my love! [*Drinks*] O true apothecary!   119
Thy drugs are quick. Thus with a kiss I die.   [*Dies*]
                    Enter FRIAR [LAWRENCE] *with lanthorn, crow, and spade*
FRIAR LAWRENCE   Saint Francis be my speed! how oft tonight
Have my old feet stumbled at graves! Who's there?
BALTHASAR   Here's one, a friend, and one that knows you well.
FRIAR LAWRENCE   Bliss be upon you! Tell me, good my friend,
What torch is yond, that vainly lends his light   125
To grubs and eyeless skulls? As I discern,
It burneth in the Capels' monument.
BALTHASAR   It doth so, holy sir, and there's my master,
One that you love.
FRIAR LAWRENCE   Who is it?
BALTHASAR   Romeo.
FRIAR LAWRENCE   How long hath he been there?
BALTHASAR   Full half an hour.   130
FRIAR LAWRENCE   Go with me to the vault.
BALTHASAR   I dare not, sir.
My master knows not but I am gone hence,
And fearfully did menace me with death
If I did stay to look on his intents.
FRIAR LAWRENCE   Stay then, I'll go alone. Fear comes upon me.   135
O, much I fear some ill unthrifty thing.
BALTHASAR   As I did sleep under this [yew] tree here,
I dreamt my master and another fought.
And that my master slew him.
FRIAR LAWRENCE   Romeo!
                    [FRIAR *stoops and looks on the blood and weapons*]
Alack, alack, what blood is this, which stains   140
The stony entrance of this sepulchre?
What mean these masterless and gory swords
To lie discolor'd by this place of peace?   [*Enters the tomb*]
Romeo, O, pale! Who else? What, Paris, too?
And steep'd in blood? Ah, what an unkind hour   145
Is guilty of this lamentable chance!
The lady stirs.

                                             [JULIET *rises*]

JULIET   O comfortable friar! where is my lord?
I do remember well where I should be,
And there I am. Where is my Romeo?   150
                                             [*Noise within*]
FRIAR LAWRENCE   I hear some noise, lady. Come from that nest
Of death, contagion, and unnatural sleep.

121. *speed:* aid   145. *unkind:* unnatural, cruel
136. *unthrifty:* unlucky   148. *comfortable:* providing comfort

A greater power than we can contradict
Hath thwarted our intents. Come, come away.
Thy husband in thy bosom there lies dead;   *155*
And Paris too. Come, I'll dispose of thee
Among a sisterhood of holy nuns.
Stay not to question, for the watch is coming.
Come go, good Juliet [*noise again*], I dare no longer stay.   *Exit*
JULIET   Go get thee hence, for I will not away.   *160*
What's here? A cup clos'd in my true love's hand?
Poison, I see, hath been his timeless end.
O churl, drunk all, and left no friendly drop
To help me after? I will kiss thy lips,
Haply some poison yet doth hang on them,   *165*
To make me die with a restorative.
Thy lips are warm.
[FIRST] WATCHMAN [*within*]   Lead, boy, which way?
JULIET   Yea, noise? Then I'll be brief. O happy dagger,
                                        [*Taking* ROMEO's *dagger*]
This is thy sheath [*stabs herself*]; there rust, and let me die.

                       [*Falls on* ROMEO's *body and dies*]
                    Enter [PARIS'] BOY *and* WATCH
PAGE   This is the place, there where the torch doth burn.
[FIRST] WATCHMAN   The ground is bloody, search about the churchyard.
Go, some of you, whoe'er you find attach.

                               [*Exeunt some*]

Pitiful sight! here lies the County slain,
And Juliet bleeding, warm, and newly dead,   *175*
Who here hath lain this two days buried.
Go tell the Prince, run to the Capulets,
Raise up the Montagues; some others search.

                              [*Exeunt others*]

We see the ground whereon these woes do lie,
But the true ground of all these piteous woes   *180*
We cannot without circumstance descry.
          Enter [*some of the* WATCH *with*] ROMEO's *man* [BALTHASAR]
[SECOND] WATCHMAN   Here's Romeo's man, we found him in the
    churchyard.
[FIRST] WATCHMAN   Hold him in safety till the Prince come hither.
              Enter FRIAR [LAWRENCE] *and another* WATCHMAN

---

162. *timeless:* untimely
163. *churl:* niggard
164. *after:* come after, follow
166. *with:* by means of. *a restorative:*
because it will restore her to him. Cf.
Romeo's "cordial and not poison,"
V.i.85
169. *happy:* opportune

170. *This:* i.e., her breast
173. *attach:* arrest
179. *ground . . . woes:* earth . . . woeful creatures
180. *ground . . . woes:* basis . . . woeful events
181. *circumstance:* details
183. *in safety:* securely

THIRD WATCHMAN   Here is a friar, that trembles, sighs, and weeps.
We took this mattock and this spade from him,   *185*
And he was coming from this churchyard's side.
[FIRST] WATCHMAN   A great suspicion. Stay the friar too.

Enter the PRINCE [*and* ATTENDANTS]

PRINCE   What misadventure is so early up,
That calls our person from our morning rest?

Enter Capels [CAPULET, LADY CAPULET, *and others*]

CAPULET   What should it be that is so [shrik'd] abroad?   *190*
LADY CAPULET   O, the people in the street cry "Romeo,"
Some "Juliet," and some "Paris," and all run
With open outcry toward our monument.
PRINCE   What fear is this which startles in your ears?
[FIRST] WATCHMAN   Sovereign, here lies the County Paris slain,   *195*
And Romeo dead, and Juliet, dead before,
Warm and new kill'd.
PRINCE   Search, seek, and know how this foul murder comes.
[FIRST] WATCHMAN   Here is a friar, and [slaughter'd] Romeo's man,
With instruments upon them, fit to open   *200*
These dead men's tombs.
CAPULET   O heavens! O wife, look how our daughter bleeds!
This dagger hath mista'en, for lo his house
Is empty on the back of Montague,
And it mis-sheathed in my daughter's bosom!   *205*
LADY CAPULET   O me, this sight of death is as a bell
That warns my old age to a sepulchre.

Enter MONTAGUE [*and others*]

PRINCE   Come, Montague, for thou art early up
To see thy son and heir now [early] down.
MONTAGUE   Alas, my liege, my wife is dead to-night;   *210*
Grief of my son's exile hath stopp'd her breath.
What further woe conspires against mine age?
PRINCE   Look and thou shalt see.
MONTAGUE   O thou untaught! what manners is in this,
To press before thy father to a grave?   *215*
PRINCE   Seal up the mouth of outrage for a while,
Till we can clear these ambiguities,
And know their spring, their head, their true descent,
And then will I be general of your woes,
And lead you even to death. Mean time forbear,   *220*

---

203. *house:* i.e., scabbard
210. *liege:* sovereign
216. *outrage:* impassioned grief
218. *spring:* source (of a stream); *head* is a synonym

219. *be general:* take command
220. *death:* i.e., the death of the guilty

And let mischance be slave to patience.
Bring forth the parties of suspicion.
FRIAR LAWRENCE   I am the greatest, able to do least,
  Yet most suspected, as the time and place
  Doth make against me, of this direful murther;   *225*
  And here I stand both to impeach and purge
  Myself condemned and myself excus'd.
PRINCE   Then say at once what thou dost know in this.
FRIAR LAWRENCE   I will be brief, for my short date of breath
  Is not so long as is a tedious tale.   *230*
  Romeo, there dead, was husband to that Juliet,
  And she, there dead, [that] Romeo's faithful wife.
  I married them, and their stol'n marriage-day
  Was Tybalt's dooms-day, whose untimely death
  Banish'd the new-made bridegroom from this city,   *235*
  For whom, and not for Tybalt, Juliet pin'd.
  You, to remove that siege of grief from her,
  Betroth'd and would have married her perforce
  To County Paris. Then comes she to me,
  And with wild looks bid me devise some mean   *240*
  To rid her from this second marriage,
  Or in my cell there would she kill herself.
  Then gave I her (so tutor'd by my art)
  A sleeping potion, which so took effect
  As I intended, for it wrought on her   *245*
  The form of death. Mean time I writ to Romeo,
  That he should hither come as this dire night
  To help to take her from her borrowed grave,
  Being the time the potion's force should cease.
  But he which bore my letter, Friar John,   *250*
  Was stayed by accident, and yesternight
  Return'd my letter back. Then all alone,
  At the prefixed hour of her waking,
  Came I to take her from her kindred's vault,
  Meaning to keep her closely at my cell,   *255*
  Till I conveniently could send to Romeo.
  But when I came, some minute ere the time
  Of her awakening, here untimely lay
  The noble Paris and true Romeo dead.
  She wakes, and I entreated her come forth   *260*

222. *of suspicion:* suspected
226–227. *both . . . excus'd:* both to
accuse myself and be found guilty,
and to exonerate myself and be excused

229. *my . . . breath:* the brief time I
have left to live
247. *as this:* this very
255. *closely:* secretly

And bear this work of heaven with patience.
But then a noise did scare me from the tomb,
And she, too desperate, would not go with me,
But as it seems, did violence on herself.
All this I know, and to the marriage   265
Her nurse is privy; and if aught in this
Miscarried by my fault, let my old life
Be sacrific'd some hour before his time,
Unto the rigor of severest law.
PRINCE   We still have known thee for a holy man.   270
Where's Romeo's man? what can he say to this?
BALTHASAR   I brought my master news of Juliet's death,
And then in post he came from Mantua
To this same place, to this same monument.
This letter he early bid me give his father,   275
And threat'ned me with death, going in the vault,
If I departed not and left him there.
PRINCE   Give me the letter, I will look on it.
Where is the County's page that rais'd the watch?
Sirrah, what made your master in this place?   280
PAGE   He came with flowers to strew his lady's grave,
And bid me stand aloof, and so I did.
Anon comes one with light to ope the tomb,
And by and by my master drew on him,
And then I ran away to call the watch.   285
PRINCE   This letter doth make good the friar's words,
Their course of love, the tidings of her death;
And here he writes that he did buy a poison
Of a poor apothecary, and therewithal
Came to this vault, to die and lie with Juliet.   290
Where be these enemies? Capulet! Montague!
See what a scourge is laid upon your hate,
That heaven finds means to kill your joys with love.
And I for winking at your discords too
Have lost a brace of kinsmen. All are punish'd.   295
CAPULET   O brother Montague, give me thy hand.
This is my daughter's jointure, for no more
Can I demand.
MONTAGUE   But I can give thee more,
For I will [raise] her statue in pure gold,
That whiles Verona by that name is known,   300

270. *still:* always
280. *made:* did
293. *kill your joys:* (1) turn your joys
to sorrows; (2) kill your children.
with: by means of

294. *winking at:* shutting my eyes to
295. *brace:* pair (Mercutio and Paris)
297. *jointure:* marriage portion

There shall no figure at such rate be set
As that of true and faithful Juliet.
CAPULET   As rich shall Romeo's by his lady's lie,
Poor sacrifices of our enmity!
PRINCE   A glooming peace this morning with it brings,   305
The sun, for sorrow, will not show his head.
Go hence to have more talk of these sad things;
Some shall be pardon'd, and some punished:
For never was a story of more woe
Than this of Juliet and her Romeo.   [*Exeunt omnes*]

Exercises   1. *Identify the protagonist and give reasons for your choice.*

2. *Where does the rising action begin and end? What is the turning point?*

3. *Summarize two or three speeches in Act One that characterize Romeo.*

4. *Summarize the action in Act Two that advances the plot. What does it accomplish?*

5. *The richness of language demands close attention to patterns of imagery and symbols. Some of the more important patterns have references to (1) the sun, moon, stars, heaven; (2) parts of the body such as lips, cheeks, hands; and (3) death and dying. How do these references contribute to meaning?*

6. *How do the suicides of Romeo and Juliet suggest triumph?*

7. *Explain the role of Fate in the play.*

8. *Interpret the following quotations:*

    a. Benvolio tells Romeo (I.ii.49–50):

Take thou some new infection to thy eye,
And the rank poison of the old will die.

    b. Romeo, alone, says (II.ii.156–157):

Love goes toward love as schoolboys from their books,
But love from love, toward school with heavy looks.

    c. Romeo speaks (III.i.102–104):

---

301. *rate:* value
304. *Poor sacrifices of:* (1) pitiful victims of; (2) inadequate atonement for
305. *glooming:* cloudy

O sweet Juliet,
Thy beauty hath made me effeminate,
And in my temper soft'ned valour's steel!

Topics for Writing

1. *Discuss how Romeo and Juliet and the actions they take all serve to develop one of these themes: "Love Conquers All" or "Great Love Is Immortal."*

2. *Write a theme on the nature of Romeo and Juliet's love.*

Selected Bibliography

William Shakespeare

Charleton, H. B. *Romeo and Juliet as an Experimental Tragedy.* London: Milford, 1939.

Erskine, John. "Romeo and Juliet." *Shakespearean Studies,* ed. B. Matthews and A. H. Thorndike. New York: Russell and Russell, 1916.

Gill, Brendan. "The Current Cinema." *The New Yorker,* 77 (1961), 196–197.

Granville-Barker, Harley. *Prefaces to Shakespeare.* 2 vols. Princeton: Princeton University Press, 1946–47.

Hart, John. "Romeo and Juliet." *Lovers' Meeting: Discussions of Five Plays by Shakespeare,* ed. by Donald M. Goodfellow. Pittsburgh: Carnegie Institute of Technology, 1964.

Hosley, Richard. "The Use of the Upper Stage in *Romeo and Juliet.*" *Shakespeare Quarterly,* 5 (1954), 375–379.

Knight, Arthur. "*SR* Goes to the Movies." *Saturday Review,* 14 October 1961, p. 40.

Levin, Harry. "Form and Formality in *Romeo and Juliet.*" *Modern Shakespearean Criticism,* ed. by Alvin B. Kernan. New York: Harcourt, Brace, and World, 1970.

Moore, O. H. "Shakespeare's Deviations from *Romeo and Juliet.*" *PMLA,* 52 (1937), 45.

———. "The Origins of the Legend of *Romeo and Juliet* in Italy. *Speculum,* 5 (1930), 264–277.

Muir, Kenneth. "Arthur Brooke and the Imagery of *Romeo and Juliet.*" *Notes and Queries,* 3 (1956), 241–243.

Stauffer, Donald A. "The School of Love: *Romeo and Juliet.*" *Shakespeare: The Tragedies,* ed. by Alfred Harbage. Englewood Cliffs, New Jersey: Prentice-Hall, Inc., 1964.

Stoll, Elmer Edgar. *Shakespeare's Young Lovers.* New York: A.M.S. Press, 1966.

Robert Anderson *(1917–   )*

Born in New York City, he received two degrees from Harvard University, taught playwriting for the American Theatre Wing and Actor's Studio, and wrote plays for radio and television. For Tea and Sympathy *(1954) he won the Drama Critics' Award. After adapting the play for motion pictures, he wrote two more screenplays,* The Nun's Story *(1958) and* The Sand Pebbles *(1966). Returning to Broadway, he produced* You Know I Can't Hear You When the Water's Running *(1967) and* I Never Sang for My Father *(1968). In 1969 he was appointed writer in residence at the University of North Carolina.*

Tea and Sympathy

CHARACTERS

LAURA REYNOLDS	STEVE
LILLY SEARS	BILL REYNOLDS
TOM LEE	PHIL
DAVID HARRIS	HERBERT LEE
RALPH	PAUL
AL	

ACT ONE   *The scene is a small old Colonial house which is now being used as a dormitory in a boys' school in New England.*

On the ground floor at stage right we see the housemaster's study. To stage left is a hall and stairway which leads up to the boys' rooms. At a half-level on stage left is one of the boys' rooms.

The housemaster's study is a warm and friendly room, rather on the dark side, but when the lamps are lighted, there are cheerful pools of light. There is a fireplace in the back wall, bookcases, and upstage right double doors leading to another part of the house. Since there is no common room for the eight boys in this house, there is considerable leniency in letting the boys use the study whenever the door is left ajar.

The boy's bedroom is small, containing a bed, a chair and a bureau. It was meant to be Spartan, but the present occupant has given it a few touches to make it a little more homelike: an Indian print on the bed, India print curtains for the dormer windows. There is a phonograph on the ledge of the window. The door to the room is presumed to lead to the sitting room which the roommates share. There is a door from the sitting room which leads to the stair landing. Thus, to get to the bedroom from the stairs, a person must go through the sitting room.

As the curtain rises, it is late afternoon of a day early in June. No lamps have been lighted yet so the study is in a sort of twilight.

Upstairs in his room, TOM LEE *is sitting on his bed playing the guitar and singing softly and casually, the plaintive song, "The Joys of Love"* . . . TOM *is going on eighteen.*

He is young and a little gangling, but intense. He is wearing faded khaki trousers, a white shirt open at the neck and white tennis sneakers.

Seated in the study listening to the singing are LAURA REYNOLDS *and* LILLY SEARS. LAURA *is a lovely, sensitive woman in her mid to late twenties. Her essence is gentleness. She is compassionate and tender. She is wearing a cashmere sweater and a wool skirt. As she listens to* TOM*'s singing, she is sewing on what is obviously a period costume.*

LILLY *is in her late thirties, and in contrast to the simple effectiveness of* LAURA*'s clothes, she is dressed a little too flashily for her surroundings. . . . It would be in good taste on East 57th Street, but not in a small New England town. . . . A smart suit and hat and a fur piece. As she listens to* TOM *singing, she plays with the martini glass in her hand.*

TOM (*singing*)   The joys of love
Are but a moment long . . .
The pains of love
Endure forever . . .
When he has finished, he strums on over the same melody very casually, and hums to it intermittently

LILLY (*while* TOM *is singing*)   Tom Lee?

LAURA   Yes.

LILLY   Doesn't he have an afternoon class?

LAURA   No. He's the only one in the house that doesn't.

LILLY (*when* TOM *has finished the song*)   Do you know what he's thinking of?

LAURA (*bites off a thread and looks up*)   What do you mean?

LILLY   What all the boys in this school are thinking about. Not only now in the spring, but all the time . . . Sex! (*She wags her head a little wisely, and smiles*)

LAURA   Lilly, you just like to shock people.

LILLY   Four hundred boys from the ages of thirteen to nineteen. That's the age, Laura. (*Restless, getting up*) Doesn't it give you the willies sometimes, having all these boys around?

LAURA   Of course not. I never think of it that way.

LILLY   Harry tells me they put saltpeter in their food to quiet them down. But the way they look at you, I can't believe it.

LAURA   At me?

LILLY   At any woman worth looking at. When I first came here ten years ago, I didn't think I could stand it. Now I love it. I love watching them look and suffer.

LAURA   Lilly.

LILLY   This is your first spring here, Laura. You wait.

LAURA   They're just boys.

LILLY   The authorities say the ages from thirteen to nineteen . . .

LAURA   Lilly, honestly!

LILLY   You sound as though you were in the grave. How old are you?

LAURA (*smiling*)   Over twenty-one.

LILLY   They come here ignorant as all get out about women and then spend the next four years exchanging misinformation. They're so cute, and so damned intense. (*She shudders again*)

LAURA   Most of them seem very casual to me.

LILLY   That's just an air they put on. This is the age Romeo should be played. You'd believe him! So intense! These kids would die for love, or almost anything else. Harry says all their themes end in death.

LAURA   That's boys.

LILLY   Failure; death! Dishonor; death! Lose their girls; death! It's gruesome.

LAURA   But rather touching too, don't you think?

LILLY   You won't tell your husband the way I was talking?

LAURA   Of course not.

LILLY   Though I don't know why I should care. All the boys talk about me. They have me in and out of bed with every single master in the school—and some married ones, too.

LAURA (*kidding her*)   Maybe I'd better listen to them.

LILLY   Oh, never with your husband, of course.

LAURA   Thanks.

LILLY   Even before he met you, Bill never gave me a second glance. He was all the time organizing teams, planning Mountain Club outings.

LAURA   Bill's good at that sort of thing; he likes it.

LILLY   And you? (LAURA *looks up at* LILLY *and smiles*) Not a very co-operative witness, are you? I know, mind my own business. But watch out he doesn't drag his usual quota of boys to the lodge in Maine this summer.

LAURA   I've got my own plans for him. (*She picks up some vacation folders*)

LILLY   Oh really? What?

LAURA   "Come to Canada" . . . I want to get him off on a trip alone.

LILLY   I don't blame you.

LAURA (*reflecting*)   Of course I'd really like to go back to Italy. We had a good time there last summer. It was wonderful then. You should have seen Bill.

LILLY   Look, honey, you married Bill last year on his sabbatical leave, and abroad to boot. Teachers on sabbatical leave abroad are like men in uniform during the war. They never look so good again.

LAURA   Bill looks all right to me.

LILLY   Did Bill ever tell you about the party we gave him before his sabbatical?

LAURA   Yes. I have a souvenir from it. (*She is wearing a rather large Woolworth's diamond ring on a gold chain around her neck . . . She now pulls it out from her sweater*)

LILLY   I never thought he'd use that five-and-dime engagement ring we gave him that night. Even though we gave him an awful ribbing, we all expected him to come back a bachelor.

LAURA   You make it sound as though you kidded him into marrying.

LILLY   Oh, no, honey, it wasn't that.

LAURA (*with meaning*)   No, it wasn't. (LAURA *laughs at* LILLY)

LILLY   Well, I've got to go. You know, Bill could have married any number of the right kind of girls around here. But I knew it would take more than the right kind of girl to get Bill to marry. It would take something special. And you're something special.

LAURA   How should I take that?

LILLY   As a compliment. Thanks for the drink. Don't tell Harry I had one when you see him at dinner.

LAURA   We won't be over to the hall. I've laid in a sort of feast for tonight.

LILLY   Celebrating something?

LAURA   No, just an impulse.

LILLY   Well, don't tell Harry anyway.

LAURA   You'd better stop talking the way you've been talking, or I won't have to tell him.

LILLY   Now, look, honey, don't you start going puritan on me. You're the only one in this school I can shoot my mouth off to, so don't change, baby. Don't change.

LAURA   I won't.

LILLY   Some day I'm going to wheedle out of you all the juicy stories you must have from when you were in the theater.

LAURA   Lilly, you would make the most hardened chorus girl blush.

LILLY (*pleased*)   Really?

LAURA   Really.

LILLY   That's the sweetest thing you've said to me in days. Good-bye.
         She goes out the door, and a moment later we hear the outside door close

LAURA (*sits for a moment, listening to* TOM's *rather plaintive whistling. She rises and looks at the Canada vacation literature on the desk, and then, looking at her watch, goes to the door, opens it, and calls up the stairway*)   Tom . . . Oh, Tom.

The moment TOM *hears his name, he jumps from the bed, and goes through the sitting room, and appears on the stairs*

TOM   Yes?

LAURA (*she is very friendly with him, comradely*)   If it won't spoil your supper, come on down for a cup of tea.

> TOM *goes back into his room and brushes his hair, then he comes on down the stairs, and enters the study. He enters this room as though it were something rare and special. This is where* LAURA *lives*

LAURA (*has gone out to the other part of the house. Comes to doorway for a moment pouring cream from bottle to pitcher*)   I've just about finished your costume for the play, and we can have a fitting.

TOM   Sure. That'd be great. Do you want the door open or shut?

LAURA (*goes off again*)   It doesn't make any difference.

> TOM *shuts the door. He is deeply in love with this woman, though he knows nothing can come of it. It is a sort of delayed puppy love. It is very touching and very intense. They are easy with each other, casual, though he is always trying in thinly veiled ways to tell her he loves her.* LAURA *enters with tea tray and sees him closing the door. She puts tray on table*

Perhaps you'd better leave it ajar, so that if some of the other boys get out of class early, they can come in too.

TOM (*is disappointed*)   Oh, sure.

LAURA (*goes off for the plate of cookies, but pauses long enough to watch* TOM *open the door the merest crack. She is amused. In a moment, she re-enters with a plate of cookies*)   Help yourself.

TOM   Thanks. (*He takes a cookie, and then sits on the floor, near her chair*)

LAURA   Are the boys warm enough in the rooms? They shut down the heat so early this spring, I guess they didn't expect this little chill.

TOM   We're fine. But this is nice. (*He indicates low fire in fireplace*)

LAURA (*goes back to her sewing*)   I heard you singing.

TOM   I'm sorry if it bothered you.

LAURA   It was very nice.

TOM   If it ever bothers you, just bang on the radiator.

LAURA   What was the name of the song? It's lovely.

TOM   It's an old French song . . . "The Joys of Love" . . . (*He speaks the lyric*)

> The joys of love
> Are but a moment long,
> The pain of love
> Endures forever.

LAURA   And is that true?

> TOM *shrugs his shoulders*

You sang as though you knew all about the pains of love.

TOM   And you don't think I do?

LAURA   Well . . .

TOM   You're right.

LAURA   Only the joys.

TOM   Neither, really.

Teapot whistles off stage

LAURA   Then you're a fake. Listening to you, one would think you knew everything there was to know. (*Rises and goes to next room for tea*) Anyway, I don't believe it. A boy like you.

TOM   It's true.

LAURA (*off stage*)   Aren't you bringing someone to the dance after the play Saturday?

TOM   Yes.

LAURA   Well, there.

TOM   You.

LAURA (*reappears in doorway with teapot*)   Me?

TOM   Yes, you're going to be a hostess, aren't you?

LAURA   Yes, of course, but . . .

TOM   As a member of the committee, I'm taking you. All the committee drew lots . . .

LAURA   And you lost.

TOM   I won.

LAURA (*a little embarrassed by this*)   Oh. My husband could have taken me. (*She sits down again in her chair*)

TOM   He's not going to be in town. Don't you remember, Mountain Climbing Club has its final outing this week-end.

LAURA   Oh, yes, of course. I'd forgotten.

TOM   He's out a lot on that kind of thing, isn't he?

LAURA ignores his probing

I hope you're not sorry that I'm to be your escort.

LAURA   Why, I'll be honored.

TOM   I'm supposed to find out tactfully and without your knowing it what color dress you'll be wearing.

LAURA   Why?

TOM   The committee will send you a corsage.

LAURA   Oh, how nice. Well, I don't have much to choose from, I guess my yellow.

TOM   The boy who's in charge of getting the flowers thinks a corsage should be something like a funeral decoration. So I'm taking personal charge of getting yours.

LAURA   Thank you.

TOM   You must have gotten lots of flowers when you were acting in the theater.

LAURA   Oh, now and then. Nothing spectacular.

TOM   I can't understand how a person would give up the theater to come and live in a school . . . I'm sorry. I mean, I'm glad you did, but, well . . .

LAURA   If you knew the statistics on unemployed actors, you might understand. Anyway, I was never any great shakes at it.

TOM   I can't believe that.

LAURA   Then take my word for it.

TOM (*after a moment, looking into the fire, pretending to be casual, but actually touching on his love for* LAURA)   Did you ever do any of Shaw's plays?

LAURA   Yes.

TOM   We got an assignment to read any Shaw play we wanted. I picked *Candida*.

LAURA   Because it was the shortest?

TOM (*laughs*)   No . . . because it sounded like the one I'd like the best, one I could understand. Did you ever play Candida?

LAURA   In stock—a very small stock company, way up in northern Vermont.

TOM   Do you think she did right to send Marchbanks away?

LAURA   Well, Shaw made it seem right. Don't you think?

TOM (*really talking about himself*)   That Marchbanks sure sounded off a lot. I could never sound off like that, even if I loved a woman the way he did. She could have made him seem awfully small if she'd wanted to.

LAURA   Well, I guess she wasn't that kind of woman. Now stand up. Let's see if this fits. (*She rises with dress in her hand*)

TOM (*gets up*)   My Dad's going to hit the roof when he hears I'm playing another girl.

LAURA   I think you're a good sport not to mind. Besides, it's a good part. Lady Teazle in *The School for Scandal*.

TOM (*puts on top of dress*)   It all started when I did Lady Macbeth last year. You weren't here yet for that. Lucky you.

LAURA   I hear it was very good.

TOM   You should have read a letter I got from my father. They printed a picture of me in the *Alumni Bulletin*, in costume. He was plenty peeved about it.

LAURA   He shouldn't have been.

TOM   He wrote me saying he might be up here today on Alumni Fund business. If he comes over here, and you see him, don't tell him about this.

LAURA   I won't . . . What about your mother? Did she come up for the play? (*She helps him button the dress*)

TOM   I don't see my mother. Didn't you know? (*He starts to roll up pants legs*)

LAURA   Why no. I didn't.

TOM   She and my father are divorced.

LAURA   I'm sorry.

TOM   You needn't be. They aren't. I was supposed to hold them together. That was how I happened to come into the world. I didn't work. That's a terrible thing, you know, to make a flop of the first job you've got in life.

LAURA   Don't you ever see her?

TOM   Not since I was five. I was with her till five, and then my father took me away. All I remember about my mother is that she was always telling me to go outside and bounce a ball.

LAURA (*handing him skirt of the dress*)   You must have done something before Lady Macbeth. When did you play that character named Grace?

TOM (*stiffens*)   I never played anyone called Grace.

LAURA   But I hear the boys sometimes calling you Grace. I thought . . . (*She notices that he's uncomfortable*) I'm sorry. Have I said something terrible?

TOM   No.

LAURA   But I have. I'm sorry.

TOM   It's all right. But it's a long story. Last year over at the movies, they did a revival of Grace Moore in *One Night of Love*. I'd seen the revival before the picture came. And I guess I oversold it, or something. But she was wonderful! . . . Anyway, some of the guys started calling me Grace. It was my own fault, I guess.

LAURA   Nicknames can be terrible. I remember at one time I was called "Beany." I can't remember why, now, but I remember it made me mad. (*She adjusts the dress a little*) Hold still a moment. We'll have to let this out around here. (*She indicates the bosom*) What size do you want to be?

TOM (*he is embarrassed, but rather nicely, not obviously and farcically. In his embarrassment he looks at* LAURA*'s bosom, then quickly away*)   I don't know. Whatever you think.

LAURA (*she indicates he is to stand on a small wooden footstool*)   I should think you would have invited some girl up to see you act, and then take her to the dance.

TOM (*gets on stool*)   There's nobody I could ask.

LAURA (*working on hem of dress*)   What do you mean?

TOM   I don't know any girls, really.

LAURA   Oh, certainly back home . . .

TOM   Last ten years I haven't been home, I mean really home. Summers my father packs me off to camps, and the rest of the time I've been at boarding schools.

LAURA   What about Christmas vacation, and Easter?

TOM   My father gets a raft of tickets to plays and concerts, and sends me and my aunt.

LAURA   I see.

TOM   So I mean it when I say I don't know any girls.

LAURA   Your roommate, Al, knows a lot of girls. Why not ask him to fix you up with a blind date?

TOM   I don't know . . . I can't even dance. I'm telling you this so you won't expect anything of me Saturday night.

LAURA   We'll sit out and talk.

TOM   Okay.

LAURA   Or I could teach you how to dance. It's quite simple.

TOM (*flustered*)   You?

LAURA   Why not?

TOM   I mean, isn't a person supposed to go to some sort of dancing class or something? (*He gets down from footstool*)

LAURA   Not necessarily. Look, I'll show you how simple it is. (*She assumes the dancing position*) Hold your left hand out this way, and put your right hand around my—(*She stops, as she sees him looking at her*) Oh, now you're kidding me. A boy your age and you don't know how to dance.

TOM   I'm not kidding you.

LAURA   Well, then, come on. I had to teach my husband. Put your arm around me. (*She raises her arms*)

TOM (*looks at her a moment, afraid to touch this woman he loves. Then to pass it off*)   We better put it off. We'd look kind of silly, both of us in skirts.

LAURA   All right. Take it off, then. No, wait a minute. Just let me stand off and take a look . . . (*She walks around him*) You're going to make a very lovely girl.

TOM   Thank you, ma'am . . .

> He kids a curtsy, like a girl, and starts out of his costume. MR. HARRIS, *a good-looking young master, comes in the hallway and starts up to* TOM'*s room. On the landing, he knocks on* TOM'*s door*

LAURA   I wonder who that is?

TOM   All the other fellows have late afternoon classes.

LAURA (*opens the door wider, and looks up the stairs*)   Yes? Oh, David.

HARRIS (*turns and looks down the stairs*)   Oh, hello, Laura.

LAURA   I just was wondering who was coming in.

> TOM *proceeds to get out of the costume*

HARRIS   I want to see Tom Lee.

LAURA   He's down here. I'm making his costume for the play.

HARRIS   I wonder if I could see him for a moment?

LAURA   Why yes, of course. Tom, Mr. Harris would like to see you. Do you want to use our study, David? I can go into the living room.

HARRIS   No, thanks. I'll wait for him in his room. Will you ask him to come up? (*He opens the door and goes in*)

LAURA (*is puzzled at his intensity, the urgency in his voice. Comes back in the study*)   Tom, Mr. Harris would like to see you in your room. He's gone along.

TOM   That's funny.

LAURA   Wait a minute . . . take this up with you, try it on in front of your mirror . . . see if you can move in it . . . (*She hands him skirt of costume*) When Mr. Harris is through, bring the costume back.

TOM (*anxious over what* HARRIS *wants to see him about*)   Yeah, sure. (*He starts out, then stops and picks up a cookie. He looks at her lovingly)* Thanks for tea.

LAURA   You're welcome.

> TOM *goes to the door as* LAURA *turns to the desk. He stands in the door a moment and looks at her back, then he turns and shuts the door and heads upstairs.* HARRIS *has come into* TOM's *bedroom, and is standing there nervously clenching and unclenching his hands*

TOM *(off stage, presumably in the study he shares with his roommate)*   Mr. Harris?

> LAURA *wanders off into the other part of the house after looking for a moment at the Canada vacation material on the desk*

HARRIS   I'm in here.

TOM *(comes in a little hesitantly)*   Oh. Hello, sir.

> HARRIS *closes the door to the bedroom.* TOM *regards this action with some nervousness*

HARRIS   Well?

TOM *(has dumped some clothes from a chair to his bed. Offers chair to* HARRIS*)* Sir?

HARRIS   What did you tell the Dean?

TOM   What do you mean, Mr. Harris?

HARRIS   What did you tell the Dean?

TOM   When? What are you talking about, sir?

HARRIS   Didn't the Dean call you in?

TOM   No. Why should he?

HARRIS   He didn't call you in and ask you about last Saturday afternoon?

TOM   Why should he? I didn't do anything wrong.

HARRIS   About being with me?

TOM   I'm allowed to leave town for the day in the company of a master.

HARRIS   I don't believe you. You must have said something.

TOM   About what?

HARRIS   About you and me going down to the dunes and swimming.

TOM   Why should I tell him about that?

HARRIS *(threatening)*   Why didn't you keep your mouth shut?

TOM   About what? What, for God's sake?

HARRIS   I never touched you, did I?

TOM   What do you mean, touch me?

HARRIS   Did you say to the Dean I touched you?

TOM *(turning away from* HARRIS*)*   I don't know what you're talking about.

HARRIS   Here's what I'm talking about. The Dean's had me on the carpet all afternoon. I probably won't be reappointed next year . . . and all because I took you swimming down off the dunes on Saturday.

TOM   Why should he have you on the carpet for that?

HARRIS   You can't imagine, I suppose.

TOM   What did you do wrong?

HARRIS   Nothing! Nothing, unless you made it seem like something wrong. Did you?

TOM   I told you I didn't see the Dean.

HARRIS   You will. He'll call for you. Bunch of gossiping old busy-bodies! Well . . . (*He starts for the door, stops, turns around and softens. He comes back to the puzzled* TOM) I'm sorry . . . It probably wasn't your fault. It was my fault. I should have been more . . . discreet . . . Good-bye. Good luck with your music.

> TOM *hasn't understood. He doesn't know what to say. He makes a helpless gesture with his hands.* HARRIS *goes into the other room on his way out. Three boys, about seventeen, come in from the downstairs hall door and start up the stairs. They're carrying books. All are wearing sport jackets, khaki or flannel trousers, white or saddle rubber-soled shoes*

AL   I don't believe a word of it.

RALPH (*he is large and a loud-mouthed bully*)   I'm telling you the guys saw them down at the dunes.

AL (*he is* TOM'*s roommate, an athlete*)   So what?

RALPH   They were bare-assed.

AL   Shut up, will you? You want Mrs. Reynolds to hear you?

RALPH   Okay. You watch and see. Harris'll get bounced, and I'm gonna lock my room at night as long as Tom is living in this house.

AL   Oh, dry up!

RALPH   Jeeze, you're his roommate and you're not worried.

HARRIS (*comes out the door and starts down the stairs*)   Hello. (*He goes down stairs and out*)

AL   Sir.

RALPH   Do you believe me now? You aren't safe. Believe me.

STEVE (*he is small,* RALPH'*s appreciative audience. He comes in the front door*)   Hey, Al, can I come in watch Mrs. Morrison nurse her kid?

RALPH   You're the loudest-mouthed bastard I ever heard. You want to give it away.

STEVE   It's time. How about it, Al?

AL (*grudgingly*)   Come on.

> TOM *hears them coming, and moves to bolt his door, but* STEVE *and* RALPH *break in before he gets to the door. He watches them from the doorway.* STEVE *rushes to bed and throws himself across it, looking out window next to bed.* RALPH *settles down next to him*

AL (*to* TOM *as he comes in*)   Hi. These horny bastards.

STEVE   Al, bring the glasses.

> AL *goes into sitting room*

RALPH   Some day she's going to wean that little bastard and spoil all our fun.

STEVE   Imagine sitting in a window . . .

TOM (*has been watching this with growing annoyance*)   Will you guys get out of here?

RALPH (*notices* TOM *for the first time*)   What's the matter with you, Grace?

TOM   This is my damned room.

RALPH   Gracie's getting private all of a sudden.

TOM   I don't want a lot of Peeping Toms lying on my bed watching a . . . a . . .

STEVE   You want it all for yourself, don't you?

RALPH   Or aren't you interested in women?

AL (*comes back in with field glasses*)   Shut up! (*Looks out window, then realizes* TOM *is watching him. Embarrassed*) These horny bastards.

STEVE (*looking*)   Geeze!

RALPH (*a bully, riding down on* TOM)   I thought you were going to play ball with us Saturday.

TOM   I didn't feel like it.

RALPH   What *did* you feel like doing, huh?

AL   Will you shut up?

STEVE   Hey, lookit. (*Grabs glasses from* AL. AL *leaves room*)

TOM (*climbing over* STEVE *and* RALPH *and trying to pull the shade*)   I told you to get out. I told you last time . . .

RALPH (*grabbing hold of* TOM, *and holding him down*)   Be still, boy, or she'll see, and you'll spoil everything.

TOM   Horny bastard. Get out of here.

RALPH   Who are you calling a horny bastard?

> He grabs hold of TOM more forcefully, and slaps him a couple of
> times across the face, not trying to hurt him, but just to humiliate him.
> STEVE gets in a few pokes and in a moment, it's not in fun, but
> verging on the serious

You don't mean that now, boy, do you . . . Do you Grace? (*He slaps him again*)

AL (*hearing the scuffle, comes in and hauls* RALPH *and* STEVE *off* TOM)   Come on, come on, break it up. Clear out. (*He has them both standing up now,* TOM *still on the bed*)

RALPH   I just don't like that son of a bitch calling me a horny bastard. Maybe if it was Dr. Morrison instead of Mrs. Morrison, he'd be more interested. Hey, wouldn't you, Grace?

> He tries to stick his face in front of TOM, but AL holds him back

AL   Come on, lay off the guy, will you? Go on. Get ready for supper.

> He herds them out during this. When they have left the room, TOM
> gets up and goes to bureau and gets a handkerchief. He has a bloody
> nose. He lies down on the bed, his head tilted back to stop the blood

AL (*in doorway*)   You all right?

TOM   Yeah.

> RALPH *and* STEVE *go up the stairway singing in raucous voices,*
> "One Night of Love." *The downstairs outside door opens, and* BILL
> REYNOLDS *enters the hall with a student,* PHIL. BILL *is* LAURA's
> *husband. He is large and strong with a tendency to be gruff. He's
> wearing gray flannel trousers, a tweed jacket, a blue button-down
> shirt. He is around forty*

BILL   Okay, boy, we'll look forward to— (*He notices* RALPH *still singing.
         He goes to bend in the stairs and calls*) Hey, Ralph . . . Ralph!
RALPH (*stops singing up out of sight*)   You calling me, Mr. Reynolds, sir?
BILL   Yeah. Keep it down to a shout, will you?
RALPH   Oh, *yes, sir.* Sorry, I didn't know I was disturbing you, Mr.
         Reynolds.
BILL (*comes back and talks with* PHIL *at the bend in the stairway*)   Phil, you come
         on up to the lodge around . . . Let's see . . . We'll open the lodge
         around July first, so plan to come up say, July third, and stay for two
         weeks. Okay?
PHIL   That'll be swell, sir.
BILL   Frank Hoctor's coming then. You get along with Frank, don't
         you? He's a regular guy.
PHIL   Oh, sure.
BILL   The float's all gone to pieces. We can make that your project to fix
         it up. Okay?
PHIL   Thanks a lot, Mr. Reynolds. (*He goes on up the stairs*)
BILL   See you. (*He comes in and crosses to phone and starts to call*)
LAURA (*off stage*)   Tom?
                    BILL *looks around in the direction of the voice, but says nothing*
LAURA (*comes on*)   Oh, Bill. Tom was down trying on his costume. I
         thought . . . You're early.
BILL   Yes. I want to catch the Dean before he leaves his office.
                    LAURA *goes up to him to be kissed, but he's too intent on the phone,
                    and she compromises by kissing his cheek*
         Hello, this is Mr. Reynolds. Is the Dean still in his office?
LAURA   What's the matter, Bill?
BILL   Nothing very pretty. Oh? How long ago? All right. Thanks. I'll
         give him a couple of minutes, then I'll call his home. (*Hangs up*) Well,
         they finally caught up with Harris. (*He goes into the next room to take off his
         jacket*)
LAURA   What do you mean, "caught up" with him?
BILL (*off stage*)   You're going to hear it anyhow . . . so . . . last Saturday
         they caught him down in the dunes, naked.
LAURA (*crosses to close door to hall*)   What's wrong with that?
BILL (*enters and crosses to fireplace and starts to go through letters propped there. He
         has taken off his jacket*)   He wasn't alone.
LAURA   Oh.
BILL   He was lying there naked in the dunes, and one of the students was
         lying there naked too. Just to talk about it is disgusting.
LAURA   I see.
BILL   I guess you'll admit that's something.
LAURA   I can't see that it's necessarily conclusive.
BILL   With a man like Harris, it's conclusive enough. (*Then casually*)
         The student with him was—

LAURA (*interrupting*)   I'm not sure I care to know.

BILL   I'm afraid you're going to have to know sooner or later, Laura. It was Tom Lee.

> TOM *rises from bed, grabs a towel and goes out up the stairs.* LAURA *just looks at* BILL *and frowns*

BILL   Some of the boys down on the Varsity Club outing came on them . . . or at least saw them . . . And Fin Hadley saw them too, and he apparently used his brains for once and spoke to the Dean.

LAURA   And?

BILL   He's had Harris on the carpet this afternoon. I guess he'll be fired. I certainly hope so. Maybe Tom too, I don't know.

LAURA   They put two and two together?

BILL   Yes, Laura.

LAURA   I suppose this is all over school by now.

BILL   I'm afraid so.

LAURA   And most of the boys know.

BILL   Yes.

LAURA   So what's going to happen to Tom?

BILL (*takes pipe from mantel piece and cleans it*)   I know you won't like this, Laura, but I think he should be kicked out. I think you've got to let people know the school doesn't stand for even a hint of this sort of thing. He should be booted.

LAURA   For what?

BILL   Look, a boy's caught coming out of Ellie Martin's rooms across the river. That's enough evidence. Nobody asks particulars. They don't go to Ellie's rooms to play Canasta. It's the same here.

LAURA (*hardly daring to suggest it*)   But, Bill . . . you don't think . . . I mean, you don't think Tom is . . .

> *She stops.* BILL *looks at her a moment, his answer is in his silence*

Oh, Bill!

BILL   And I'm ashamed and sorry as hell for his father. Herb Lee was always damned good to me . . . came down from college when I was playing football here . . . helped me get into college . . . looked after me when I was in college and he was in law school . . . And I know he put the boy in my house hoping I could do something with him. (*He dials number*)

LAURA   And you feel you've failed.

BILL   Yes. (*He pauses*) With your help, I might say. (*Busy signal. He hangs up*)

LAURA   How?

BILL   Because, Laura, the boy would rather sit around here and talk with you and listen to music and strum his guitar.

LAURA   Bill, I'm not to blame for everything. Everything's not my fault.

BILL (*disregarding this*)   What a lousy thing for Herb. (*He looks at a small picture of a team on his desk*) That's Herb. He was Graduate Manager of the team when I was a sophomore in college. He was always the manager of the teams, and he really wanted his son to be there in the center of the picture.

LAURA   Why are you calling the Dean?

BILL   I'm going to find out what's being done.

LAURA   I've never seen you like this before.

BILL   This is something that touches me very closely. The name of the school, its reputation, the reputation of all of us here. I went here and my father before me, and one day I hope our children will come here, when we have them. And, of course, one day I hope to be headmaster.

LAURA   Let's assume that you're right about Harris. It's a terrible thing to say on the evidence you've got, but let's assume you're right. Does it necessarily follow that Tom—

BILL   Tom was his friend. Everyone knew that.

LAURA   Harris encouraged him in his music.

BILL   Come on, Laura.

LAURA   What if Tom's roommate, Al, or some other great big athlete had been out with Harris?

BILL   He wouldn't have been.

LAURA   I'm saying what if he had been? Would you have jumped to the same conclusion?

BILL   It would have been different. Tom's always been an off-horse. And now it's quite obvious why. If he's kicked out, maybe it'll bring him to his senses. But he won't change if nothing's done about it.

LAURA *turns away.* BILL *starts to look over his mail again*

Anyway, why are you so concerned over what happens to Tom Lee?

LAURA   I've come to know him. You even imply that I am somewhat responsible for his present reputation.

BILL   All right. I shouldn't have said that. But you watch, now that it's out in the open. Look at the way he walks, the way he sometimes stands.

LAURA   Oh, Bill!

BILL   All right, so a woman doesn't notice these things. But a man knows a queer when he sees one. (*He has opened a letter. Reads*) The bookstore now has the book you wanted . . . *The Rose and The Thorn.* What's that?

LAURA   A book of poems. Do you know, Bill, I'll bet he doesn't even know the meaning of the word . . . queer.

BILL   What do you think he is?

LAURA   I think he's a nice sensitive kid who doesn't know the meaning of the word.

BILL   He's eighteen, or almost. I don't know.

LAURA   How much did you know at eighteen?

BILL   A lot. (*At the desk he now notices the Canada literature*) What are these?

LAURA   What?

BILL   These.

LAURA   Oh, nothing.

BILL (*he throws them in wastebasket, then notices her look*)   Well, they're obviously something. (*He takes them out of wastebasket*)

LAURA (*the joy of it gone for her*)   I was thinking we might take a motor trip up there this summer.

BILL (*dialing phone again*)   I wish you'd said something about it earlier. I've already invited some of the scholarship boys up to the lodge. I can't disappoint them.

LAURA   Of course not.

BILL   If you'd said something earlier.

LAURA   It's my fault.

BILL   It's nobody's fault, it's just—Hello, Fitz, Bill Reynolds—I was wondering if you're going to be in tonight after supper . . . Oh . . . oh, I see . . . Supper? Well, sure I could talk about it at supper. . . . Well, no, I think I'd better drop over alone. . . . All right. I'll see you at the house then . . . Good-bye.

> LAURA *looks at him, trying to understand him.* BILL *comes to her to speak softly to her. Seeing him come, she holds out her arms to be embraced, but he just takes her chin in his hand*

Look, Laura, when I brought you here a year ago, I told you it was a tough place for a woman with a heart like yours. I told you you'd run across boys, big and little boys, full of problems, problems which for the moment seem gigantic and heartbreaking. And you promised me then you wouldn't get all taken up with them. Remember?

LAURA   Yes.

BILL   When I was a kid in school here, I had my problems too. There's a place up by the golf course where I used to go off alone Sunday afternoons and cry my eyes out. I used to lie on my bed just the way Tom does, listening to phonograph records hour after hour.

> LAURA, *touched by this, kneels at his side*

But I got over it, Laura. I learned how to take it.

> LAURA *looks at him. This touches her*

When the headmaster's wife gave you this teapot, she told you what she tells all new masters' wives. You have to be an interested bystander.

LAURA   I know.

BILL   Just as she said, all you're supposed to do is every once in a while give the boys a little tea and sympathy. Do you remember?

LAURA   Yes, I remember. It's just that . . .

BILL   What?

LAURA   This age—seventeen, eighteen—it's so . . .

BILL   I know.

LAURA   John was this age when I married him.

BILL   Look, Laura . . .

LAURA   I know. You don't like me to talk about John, but . . .

BILL   It's not that. It's . . .

LAURA   He was just this age, eighteen or so, when I married him. We both were. And I know how this age can suffer. It's a heartbreaking time . . . no longer a boy . . . not yet a man . . . Bill? Bill?

BILL (*looks at her awkwardly a moment, then starts to move off*)   I'd better clean up if I'm going to get to the Dean's for supper. You don't mind, do you?

LAURA (*very quietly*)   I got things in for dinner here. But they'll keep.

BILL (*awkwardly*)   I'm sorry, Laura. But you understand, don't you? About this business?

> LAURA *shakes her head, "No." BILL stands over her, a little put out that she has not understood his reasoning. He starts to say something several times, then stops. Finally he notices the five-and-dime engagement ring around her neck. He touches it*

You're not going to wear this thing to the dining hall, are you?

LAURA   Why not?

BILL   It was just a gag. It means something to you, but to them . . .

LAURA (*bearing in, but gently*)   Does it mean anything to you, Bill?

BILL   Well, it did, but . . . (*He stops with a gesture, unwilling to go into it all*)

LAURA   I think you're ashamed of the night you gave it to me. That you ever let me see you needed help. That night in Italy, in some vague way you cried out . . .

BILL   What is the matter with you today? *Me* crying out for help. (*He heads for the other room. A knock on the study door is heard*) It's probably Tom.

> LAURA *goes to door*

HERB (*this is HERBERT LEE, TOM's father. He is a middle-sized man, fancying himself a man of the world and an extrovert. He is dressed as a conservative Boston businessman, but with still a touch of the collegiate in his attire—button-down shirt, etc.*)   Mrs. Reynolds?

LAURA   Yes?

BILL (*stopped by the voice, turns*)   Herb! Come in.

HERB (*coming in*)   Hiya, Bill. How are you, fella?

BILL (*taking his hand*)   I'm fine, Herb.

HERB (*poking his finger into BILL's chest*)   Great to see you. (*Looks around to LAURA*) Oh, uh . . .

BILL   I don't think you've met Laura, Herb. This is Laura. Laura this is Herb Lee, Tom's father.

HERB (*hearty and friendly, meant to put people at their ease*)   Hello, Laura.

LAURA   I've heard so much about you.

HERB (*after looking at her for a moment*)   I like her, Bill. I like her very much. (*LAURA blushes and is a little taken aback by this. To LAURA*) What I'd like to know is how did you manage to do it? (*Cuffing BILL*) I'll bet you make her life miserable . . . You look good, Bill.

BILL   You don't look so bad yourself. (*He takes in a notch in his belt*)

HERB   No, *you're* in shape. I never had anything to keep in shape, but you . . . You should have seen this boy, Laura.

LAURA   I've seen pictures.

HERB   Only exercise I get these days is bending the elbow.

LAURA   May I get you something? A drink?

HERB   No, thanks. I haven't got much time.

BILL   You drive out from Boston, Herb?

HERB   No, train. You know, Bill, I think that's the same old train you and I used to ride in when we came here.

BILL   Probably is.

HERB   If I don't catch the six-fifty-four, I'll have to stay all night, and I'd rather not.

BILL   We'd be glad to put you up.

HERB   No. You're putting me up in a couple of weeks at the reunion. That's imposing enough. (*There is an awkward pause. Both men sit down*) I . . . uh . . . was over at the Dean's this afternoon.

BILL   Oh, he called you?

HERB   Why, no. I was up discussing Alumni Fund matters with him . . .and . . . Do you know about it?

BILL   You mean about Tom?

HERB   Yes. (*Looks at* LAURA)

BILL   Laura knows too. (*He reaches for her to come to him, and he puts his arm around her waist*)

HERB   Well, after we discussed the Fund, he told me about that. Thought I ought to hear about it from him. Pretty casual about it, I thought.

BILL   Well, that's Fitz.

HERB   What I want to know is, what was a guy like Harris doing at the school?

BILL   I tried to tell them.

HERB   Was there anyone around like that in our day, Bill?

BILL   No. You're right.

HERB   I tried to find the guy. I wanted to punch his face for him. But he's cleared out. Is Tom around?

LAURA   He's in his room.

HERB   How'd he get mixed up with a guy like that?

BILL   I don't know, Herb . . .

HERB   I know. I shouldn't ask you. I know. Of course I don't believe Tom was really involved with this fellow. If I believed that, I'd . . . well, I don't know what I'd do. You don't believe it, do you, Bill?

BILL   Why . . . (*Looks at* LAURA)

HERB (*cutting in*)   Of course you don't. But what's the matter? What's happened, Bill? Why isn't my boy a regular fellow? He's had every chance to be since he was knee-high to a grasshopper—boys' camps every summer, boarding schools. What do you think, Laura?

LAURA   I'm afraid I'm not the one to ask, Mr. Lee. (*She breaks away from* BILL)

HERB   He's always been with men and boys. Why doesn't some of it rub off?

LAURA   You see, I feel he's a "regular fellow" . . . whatever that is.

HERB   You do?

LAURA   If it's sports that matter, he's an excellent tennis player.

HERB   But Laura, he doesn't even play tennis like a regular fellow. No hard drives and cannon-ball serves. He's a cut artist. He can put more damn twists on that ball.

LAURA   He wins. He's the school champion. And isn't he the champion of your club back home?

> TOM *comes down the stairs and enters his bedroom with the costume skirt and towel*

HERB   I'm glad you mentioned that . . . because that's just what I mean. Do you know, Laura, his winning that championship brought me one of my greatest humiliations? I hadn't been able to watch the match. I was supposed to be in from a round of golf in time, but we got held up on every hole . . . And when I got back to the locker room, I heard a couple of men talking about Tom's match in the next locker section. And what they said, cut me to the quick, Laura. One of them said, "It's a damn shame Tom Lee won the match. He's a good player, all right, but John Batty is such a regular guy." John Batty was his opponent. Now what pleasure was there for me in that?

BILL   I know what you mean.

HERB   I *want* to be proud of him. My God, that's why I had him in the first place. That's why I took him from his mother when we split up, but . . . Look, this is a terrible thing to say, but you know the scholarships the University Club sponsors for needy kids . . .

BILL   Sure.

HERB   Well, I contribute pretty heavily to it, and I happened to latch on to one of the kids we help—an orphan. I sort of talk to him like a father, go up to see him at his school once in a while, and that kid listens to me . . . and you know what, he's shaping up better than my own son.

> *There is an awkward pause. Upstairs* TOM *has put a record on the phonograph. It starts playing now*

BILL   You saw the Dean, Herb?

HERB   Yes.

BILL   And?

HERB   He told me the circumstances. Told me he was confident that Tom was innocently involved. He actually apologized for the whole thing. He did say that some of the faculty had suggested—though he didn't go along with this—that Tom would be more comfortable if I took him out of school. But I'm not going to. He's had nothing but comfort all his life, and look what's happened. My associates ask me what he wants to be, and I tell them he hasn't made up his mind. Because I'll be damned if I'll tell them he wants to be a singer of folk songs.

TOM *lies on the bed listening to the music*

BILL   So you're going to leave him in?

HERB   Of course. Let him stick it out. It'll be a good lesson.

LAURA   Mightn't it be more than just a lesson, Mr. Lee?

HERB   Oh, he'll take some kidding. He'll have to work extra hard to prove to them he's . . . well, manly. It may be the thing that brings him to his senses.

LAURA   Mr. Lee, Tom's a very sensitive boy. He's a very lonely boy.

HERB   Why should he be lonely? I've always seen to it that he's been with people . . . at camps, at boarding schools.

BILL   He's certainly an off-horse, Herb.

HERB   That's a good way of putting it, Bill. An off-horse. Well, he's going to have to learn to run with the other horses. Well, I'd better be going up.

LAURA   Mr. Lee, this may sound terribly naive of me, and perhaps a trifle indelicate, but I don't believe your son knows what this is all about. Why Mr. Harris was fired, why the boys will kid him.

HERB   You mean . . . (*Stops*)

LAURA   I'm only guessing. But I think when it comes to these boys, we often take too much knowledge for granted. And I think it's going to come as a terrible shock when he finds out what they're talking about. Not just a lesson, a shock.

HERB   I don't believe he's as naive as all that. I just don't. Well . . . (*He starts for the door*)

BILL (*takes* HERB's *arm and they go into the hall*)   I'm going over to the Dean's for supper, Herb. If you're through with Tom come by here and I'll walk you part way to the station.

HERB   All right. (*Stops on the stairs*) How do you talk to the boys, Bill?

BILL   I don't know. I just talk to them.

HERB   They're not your sons. I only talked with Tom, I mean, really talked with him, once before. It was after a Sunday dinner and I made up my mind it was time we sat in a room together and talked about important things. He got sick to his stomach. That's a terrible effect to have on your boy . . . Well, I'll drop down. (*He takes a roll of money from his pocket and looks at it, then starts up the stairs*)

BILL (*coming into his study*)   Laura, you shouldn't try to tell him about his own son. After all, if he doesn't know the boy, who does?

LAURA   I'm sorry.

> BILL *exits into the other part of the house, pulling off his tie.* HERB
> *has gone up the stairs. Knocks on the study door.* LAURA *settles
> down in her chair and eventually goes on with her sewing*

AL (*inside, calls*)   Come in.

HERB *goes in and shuts the door*

HERB (*opens* TOM's *bedroom door and sticks his head in*)   Hello, there.

TOM (*looks up from the bed, surprised*)   Oh . . . Hi . . .

HERB   I got held up at the Dean's.

TOM   Oh.

> *He has risen, and attempts to kiss his father on the cheek. But his father holds him off with a firm handshake*

HERB   How's everything? You look bushed.

TOM   I'm okay.

HERB (*looking at him closely*)   You sure?

TOM   Sure.

HERB (*looking around room*)   This room looks smaller than I remember. (*He throws on light switch*) I used to have the bed over here. Used to rain in some nights. (*Comes across phonograph*) This the one I gave you for Christmas?

TOM   Yeah. It works fine.

HERB (*turns phonograph off*)   You're neater than I was. My vest was always behind the radiator, or somewhere. (*Sees part of dress costume*) What's this?

TOM (*hesitates for a moment. Then*)   A costume Mrs. Reynolds made for me. I'm in the play.

HERB   You didn't write about it.

TOM   I know.

HERB   What are you playing? (*Looks at dress*)

TOM   You know *The School For Scandal*. I'm playing Lady Teazle.

HERB   Tom, I want to talk to you. Last time we tried to talk, it didn't work out so well.

TOM   What's up?

HERB   Tom, I'd like to be your friend. I guess there's something between fathers and sons that keeps them from being friends, but I'd like to try.

TOM (*embarrassed*)   Sure, Dad. (*He sits on the bed*)

HERB   Now when you came here, I told you to make friends slowly. I told you to make sure they were the right kind of friends. You're known by the company you keep. Remember I said that?

TOM   Yes.

HERB   And I told you if you didn't want to go out for sports like football, hockey . . . that was all right with me. But you'd get in with the right kind of fellow if you managed these teams. They're usually pretty good guys. You remember.

TOM   Yes.

HERB   Didn't you believe me?

TOM   Yes, I believed you.

HERB   Okay, then let's say you believed me, but you decided to go your own way. That's all right too, only you see what it's led to.

TOM   What?

HERB   You made friends with people like this Harris guy who got himself fired.

TOM   Why is he getting fired?

HERB   He's being fired because he was seen in the dunes with you.

TOM   Look, I don't—

HERB   Naked.

TOM   You too?

HERB   So you know what I'm talking about?

TOM   No, I don't.

HERB   You do too know. I heard my sister tell you once. She warned you about a janitor in the building down the street.

TOM (*incredulous*)   Mr. Harris . . . ?

HERB   Yes. He's being fired because he's been doing a lot of suspicious things around apparently, and this finished it. All right, I'll say it plain, Tom. He's a fairy. A homosexual.

TOM   Who says so?

HERB   Now, Tom—

TOM   And seeing us on the beach . . .

HERB   Yes.

TOM   And what does that make me?

HERB   Listen, I know you're all right.

TOM   Thanks.

HERB   Now wait a minute.

TOM   Look, we were just swimming.

HERB   All right, all right. So perhaps you didn't know.

TOM   What do you mean perhaps?

HERB   It's the school's fault for having a guy like that around. But it's your fault for being a damned fool in picking your friends.

TOM   So that's what the guys meant.

HERB   You're going to get a ribbing for a while, but you're going to be a man about it and you're going to take it and you're going to come through much more careful how you make your friends.

TOM   He's kicked out because he was seen with me on the beach, and I'm telling you that nothing, absolutely nothing . . . Look, I'm going to the Dean and tell him that Harris did nothing, that—

HERB (*stopping him*)   Look, don't be a fool. It's going to be hard enough for you without sticking your neck out, asking for it.

TOM   But, Dad!

HERB   He's not going to be reappointed next year. Nothing you can say is going to change anyone's mind. You got to think about yourself. Now, first of all, get your hair cut.

TOM *looks at father, disgusted*

Look, this isn't easy for me. Stop thinking about yourself, and give me a break.

TOM *looks up at this appeal*

I suppose you think it's going to be fun for *me* to have to live this down back home. It'll get around, and it'll affect me, too. So we've got to see this thing through together. You've got to do your part. Get your hair cut. And then . . . No, the first thing I want you to do is call whoever is putting on this play, and tell them you're not playing this lady whatever her name is.

TOM   Why shouldn't I play it? It's the best part in the play, and I was chosen to play it.

HERB   I should think you'd have the sense to see why you shouldn't.

TOM   Wait a minute. You mean . . . do you mean, you think I'm . . . whatever you call it? Do you, Dad?

HERB   I told you "no."

TOM   But the fellows are going to think that I'm . . . and Mrs. Reynolds?

HERB   Yes. You're going to have to fight their thinking it. Yes.

> TOM *sits on the bed, the full realization of it dawning*

RALPH (*sticks his head around the stairs from upstairs, and yells*)   Hey,   Grace, who's taking you to the dance Saturday night? Hey, Grace! (*He disappears again up the stairs*)

HERB   What's that all about?

TOM   I don't know.

> LAURA, *as the noise comes in, rises and goes to the door to stop it, but* AL *comes into the hall and goes upstairs yelling at the boys and* LAURA *goes back to her chair*

HERB (*looks at his watch*)   Now . . . Do you want me to stay over? If I'm not going to stay over tonight, I've got to catch the six-fifty-four.

TOM   Stay over?

HERB   Yes, I didn't bring a change of clothes along, but if you want me to stay over . . .

TOM   Why should you stay over?

HERB (*stung a little by this*)   All right. Now come on down to Bill's room and telephone this drama fellow. So I'll know you're making a start of it. And bring the dress.

TOM   I'll do it tomorrow.

HERB   I'd feel better if you did it tonight. Come on. I'm walking out with Bill. And incidentally, the Dean said if the ribbing goes beyond bounds . . . you know . . . you're to come to him and he'll take some steps. He's not going to do anthing now, because these things take care of themselves. They're better ignored . . .

> *They have both started out of the bedroom, but during the above* HERB *goes back for the dress.* TOM *continues out and stands on the stairs looking at the telephone in the hall*

HERB (*comes out of the study. Calls back*)   See you Al. Take good care of my boy here. (*Starts down stairs. Stops*) You need any money?

TOM   No.

HERB   I'm lining you up with a counselor's job at camp this year. If this thing doesn't spoil it. (*Stops*) You sure you've got enough money to come home?

TOM   Yes, sure. Look, Dad, let me call about the play from here. (*He takes receiver off hook*)

HERB   Why not use Bill's phone? He won't mind. Come on.

> TOM *reluctantly puts phone back on hook*

Look, if you've got any problems, talk them over with Bill—Mr. Reynolds. He's an old friend, and I think he'd tell you about what I'd tell you in a spot. (*Goes into master's study*) Is Bill ready?

LAURA   He'll be right down. How does the costume work?

TOM   I guess it's all right, only . . .

HERB   I'd like Tom to use your phone if he may—to call whoever's putting on the play. He's giving up the part.

LAURA   Giving up the part?

HERB   Yes. I've . . . I want him to. He's doing it for me.

LAURA   Mr. Lee, it was a great honor for him to be chosen to play the part.

HERB   Bill will understand. Bill! (*He thrusts costume into* LAURA's *hand and goes off through alcove*) Bill, what's the number of the man putting on the play. Tom wants to call him.

> LAURA *looks at* TOM, *who keeps his eyes from her. She makes a move towards him, but he takes a step away*

BILL (*off stage*)   Fred Mayberry . . . Three-two-six . . . You ready, Herb?

HERB (*off stage*)   Yes. You don't mind if Tom uses your phone, do you?

BILL   Of course not.

HERB (*comes in*)   When do you go on your mountain-climbing week-end, Bill?

BILL (*comes in*)   This week-end's the outing.

HERB   Maybe Tom could go with you.

BILL   He's on the dance committee, I think. Of course he's welcome if he wants to. Always has been.

HERB (*holding out phone to* TOM)   Tom.

> TOM *hesitates to cross to phone. As* LAURA *watches him with concern, he makes a move to escape out the door*

Three-two-six.

> TOM *slowly and painfully crosses the stage, takes the phone and sits*

BILL   Will you walk along with us as far as the dining hall, Laura?

LAURA   I don't think I feel like supper, thanks.

BILL (*looks from her to* TOM)   What?

HERB   I've got to get along if I want to catch my train.

> TOM *dials phone*

BILL   Laura?

> LAURA *shakes her head, tightlipped*

HERB   Well, then, good-bye, Laura . . . I still like you.

LAURA   Still going to the Dean's, Bill?

BILL   Yes. I'll be right back after supper. Sure you don't want to walk along with us to the dining hall?

> LAURA *shakes her head*

TOM   Busy.

HERB (*pats his son's arm*)   Keep trying him. We're in this together. Anything you want?

> TOM *shakes his head "no"*

Just remember, anything you want, let me know. (*To* LAURA) See you at reunion time . . . This'll all be blown over by then. (*He goes*)

BILL   Laura, I wish you'd . . . Laura! (*He is disturbed by her mood. He sees it's hopeless, and goes after* HERB, *leaving door open*)

TOM (*at phone*)   Hello, Mr. Mayberry . . . This is Tom Lee . . . Yes, I know it's time to go to supper, Mr. Mayberry . . . (*Looks around at open door.* LAURA *shuts it*) but I wanted you to know . . . (*This comes hard*) I wanted you to know I'm not going to be able to play in the play . . . No . . . I . . . well, I just can't. (*He is about to break. He doesn't trust himself to speak*)

LAURA (*quickly crosses and takes phone from* TOM)   Give it to me. Hello, Fred . . . Laura. Yes, Tom's father, well, he wants Tom—he thinks Tom is tired, needs to concentrate on his final exams. You had someone covering the part, didn't you? . . . Yes, of course it's a terrible disappointment to Tom. I'll see you tomorrow.

> *She hangs up.* TOM *is ashamed and humiliated. Here is the woman he loves, hearing all about him . . . perhaps believing the things . . .* LAURA *stands above him for a moment, looking at the back of his head with pity. Then he rises and starts for the door without looking at her.* RALPH *and* STEVE *come stampeding down the stairway*

RALPH (*as he goes*)   Okay, you can sit next to him if you want. Not me.

STEVE   Well, if you won't . . . why should I?

RALPH   Two bits nobody will.

> *They slam out the front door.* TOM *has shut the door quickly again when he has heard* RALPH *and* STEVE *start down. Now stands against the door listening*

AL (*comes out from his door, pulling on his jacket. Calls*)   Tom . . . Tom! (*Getting no answer, he goes down the stairs and out*)

LAURA   Tom . . .

TOM (*opens the study door*)   I'll bet my father thinks I'm . . . (*Stops*)

LAURA   Now, Tom! I thought I'd call Joan Harrison and ask her to come over for tea tomorrow. I want you to come too. I want you to ask her to go to the dance with you.

TOM (*turns in anguish and looks at her for several moments. Then*)   You were to go with me.

LAURA   I know, but . . .

TOM   Do you think so too, like the others? Like my father?

LAURA   Tom!

TOM   Is that why you're shoving me off on Joan?

LAURA (*moving toward him*)   Tom, I asked her over so that we could lick this thing.

TOM (*turns on her*)   What thing? What thing?

> *He looks at her a moment, filled with indignation, then he bolts up the stairs. But on the way up, PHIL is coming down. TOM feels like a trapped rat. He starts to turn down the stairs again, but he doesn't want to face LAURA, as he is about to break. He tries to hide his face and cowers along one side going up*

PHIL   What's the matter with you?

> *TOM doesn't answer. Goes on up and into the study door. PHIL shrugs his shoulders and goes on down the stairs and out. TOM comes into his own bedroom and shuts the door and leans against the doorjamb. LAURA goes to the partly opened door. Her impulse is to go up to TOM to comfort him, but she checks herself, and turns in the doorway and closes the door, then walks back to her chair and sits down and reaches out and touches the teapot, as though she were half-unconsciously rubbing out a spot. She is puzzled and worried. Upstairs we hear the first few sobs from TOM as the lights dim out, and*

THE CURTAIN FALLS

ACT TWO   *Scene One*

> *The scene is the same.*
>> *The time is two days later.*
>>> *As the curtain rises, AL is standing at the public telephone fastened to the wall on the first landing. He seems to be doing more listening than talking.*

AL   Yeah . . . (*He patiently waits through a long tirade*) Yeah, Dad. I know, Dad . . . No, I haven't done anything about it, yet . . . Yes, Mr. Hudson says he has a room in his house for me next year . . . But I haven't done anything about it here yet . . . Yeah, okay, Dad . . . I know what you mean . . . (*Gets angry*) I swear to God I don't . . . I lived with him a year, and I don't . . . All right, okay, Dad . . . No, don't *you* call. I'll do it. Right now. (*He hangs up. He stands and puts his hands in his pocket and tries to think this out. It's something he doesn't like*)

RALPH (*comes in the house door and starts up the steps*)   Hey, Al?

AL   Yeah?

RALPH   The guys over at the Beta house want to know has it happened yet?

AL   Has what happened?

RALPH   Has Tom made a pass at you yet?

AL (*reaches out to swat* RALPH)   For crying out loud!

RALPH   Okay, okay! You can borrow my chastity belt if you need it.

AL   That's not funny.

RALPH (*shifting his meaning to hurt* AL)   No, I know it's not. The guys on the ball team don't think it's funny at all.

AL   What do you mean?

RALPH   The guy they're supposed to elect captain rooming with a queer.

AL (*looks at him for a moment, then rejects the idea*)   Aw . . . knock it off, huh!

RALPH   So you don't believe me . . . Wait and see. (*Putting on a dirty grin*) Anyway, my mother said I should save myself for the girl I marry. Hell, how would you like to have to tell your wife, "Honey, I've been saving myself for you, except for one night when a guy—"

> AL *roughs* RALPH *up with no intention of hurting him*

Okay, okay. So you don't want to be captain of the baseball team. So who the hell cares. I don't, I'm sure.

AL   Look. Why don't you mind your own business?

RALPH   What the hell fun would there be in that?

AL   Ralph, Tom's a nice kid.

RALPH   Yeah. That's why all the guys leave the shower room at the gym when he walks in.

AL   When?

RALPH   Yesterday . . . Today. You didn't hear about it?

AL   No. What are they trying to do?

RALPH   Hell, they don't want some queer looking at them and—

AL   Oh, can it! Go on up and bury your horny nose in your *Art Models* magazine.

RALPH   At least I'm normal. I like to look at pictures of naked girls, not men, the way Tom does.

AL   Jeeze, I'm gonna push your face in a—

RALPH   Didn't you notice all those strong man poses he's got in his bottom drawer?

AL   Yes, I've noticed them. His old man wants him to be a muscle man, and he wrote away for this course in muscle building and they send those pictures. Any objections?

RALPH   Go on, stick up for him. Stick your neck out. You'll get it chopped off with a baseball bat, you crazy bastard.

> *Exits upstairs.* AL *looks at the phone, then up the way* RALPH *went. He is upset. He throws himself into a few push-ups, using the bannisters. Then still not happy with what he's doing, he walks down the stairs and knocks on the study door*

LAURA (*comes from inside the house and opens the door*)   Oh, hello, Al.

AL   Is Mr. Reynolds in?

LAURA   Why, no, he isn't. Can I do something?

AL   I guess I better drop down when he's in.

LAURA   All right. I don't really expect him home till after supper tonight.

AL (*thinks for a moment*)   Well . . . well, you might tell him just so he'll know and can make other plans . . . I won't be rooming in this house next year. This is the last day for changing, and I want him to know that.

LAURA (*moves into the room to get a cigarette*)   I see. Well, I know he'll be sorry to hear that, Al.

AL   I'm going across the street to Harmon House.

LAURA   Both you and Tom going over?

AL   No.

LAURA   Oh.

AL   Just me.

LAURA   I see. Does Tom know this?

AL   No. I haven't told him.

LAURA   You'll have to tell him, won't you, so he'll be able to make other plans.

AL   Yes, I suppose so.

LAURA   Al, won't you sit down for a moment, please? (AL *hesitates, but comes in and sits down. Offers* AL *a cigarette*) Cigarette?

AL (*reaches for one automatically, then stops*)   No, thanks. I'm in training. (*He slips a pack of cigarettes from his shirt pocket to his trousers pocket*)

LAURA   That's right. I'm going to watch you play Saturday afternoon.

> AL *smiles at her*

You're not looking forward to telling Tom, are you, Al?

> AL *shakes his head, "No"*

I suppose I can guess why you're not rooming with him next year.

> AL *shrugs his shoulders*

I wonder if you know how much it has meant for him to room with you this year. It's done a lot for him too. It's given him a confidence to know he was rooming with one of the big men of the school.

AL (*embarrassed*)   Oh . . .

LAURA   You wouldn't understand what it means to be befriended. You're one of the strong people. I'm surprised, Al.

AL (*blurting it out*)   My father's called me three times. How he ever found out about Harris and Tom, I don't know. But he did. And some guy called him and asked him, "Isn't that the boy your son is rooming with?" . . . and he wants me to change for next year.

LAURA   What did you tell your father?

AL   I told him Tom wasn't so bad, and . . . I'd better wait and see Mr. Reynolds.

LAURA   Al, you've lived with Tom. You know him better than anyone else knows him. If you do this, it's as good as finishing him so far as this school is concerned, and maybe farther.

AL (*almost whispering it*)   Well, he *does* act sort of queer, Mrs. Reynolds. He . . .

LAURA   You never said this before. You never paid any attention before. What do you mean, "queer"?

AL   Well, like the fellows say, he sort of walks lightly, if you know what I mean. Sometimes the way he moves . . . the things he talks about . . . long hair music all the time.

LAURA   All right. He wants to be a singer. So he talks about it.

AL   He's never had a girl up for any of the dances.

LAURA   Al, there are good explanations for all these things you're saying. They're silly . . . and prejudiced . . . and arguments all dug up to suit a point of view. They're all after the fact.

AL   I'd better speak to Mr. Reynolds. (*He starts for the door*)

LAURA   Al, look at me. (*She holds his eyes for a long time, wondering whether to say what she wants to say*)

AL   Yes?

LAURA (*she decides to do it*)   Al, what if I were to start the rumor tomorrow that you were . . . well, queer, as you put it.

AL   No one would believe it.

LAURA   Why not?

AL   Well, because . . .

LAURA   Because you're big and brawny and an athlete. What they call a top guy and a hard hitter?

AL   Well, yes.

LAURA   You've got some things to learn, Al. I've been around a little, and I've met men, just like you—same setup—who weren't men, some of them married and with children.

AL   Mrs. Reynolds, you wouldn't do a thing like that.

LAURA   No, Al, I probably wouldn't. But I could, and I almost would to show you how easy it is to smear a person, and once I got them believing it, you'd be surprised how quickly your . . . manly virtues would be changed into suspicious characteristics.

AL (*has been standing with his hands on his hips.* LAURA *looks pointedly at this stance.* AL *thrusts his hands down to his side, and then behind his back*) Mrs. Reynolds, I got a chance to be captain of the baseball team next year.

LAURA   I know. And I have no right to ask you to give up that chance. But I wish somehow or other you could figure out a way . . . so it wouldn't hurt Tom.

> TOM *comes in the hall and goes up the stairs. He's pretty broken up, and mad. After a few moments he appears in his room, shuts the door, and sits on the bed, trying to figure something out*

AL (*as* TOM *enters house*)   Well . . .

LAURA   That's Tom now.

> AL *looks at her, wondering how she knows*

I know all your footsteps. He's coming in for tea.

> AL *starts to move to door*)

Well, Al?

AL *makes a helpless motion*

You still want me to tell Mr. Reynolds about your moving next year?

AL (*after a moment*) No.

LAURA   Good.

AL   I mean, I'll tell him when I see him.

LAURA   Oh.

AL (*turns on her*)   What can I do?

LAURA   I don't know.

AL   Excuse me for saying so, but it's easy for you to talk the way you have. You're not involved. You're just a bystander. You're not going to be hurt. Nothing's going to happen to you one way or the other. I'm sorry.

LAURA   That's a fair criticism, Al. I'm sorry I asked you . . . As you say, I'm not involved.

AL   I'm sorry. I think you're swell, Mrs. Reynolds. You're the nicest housemaster's wife I've ever ran into . . . I mean . . . Well, you know what I mean. It's only that . . . (*He is flustered. He opens the door*) I'm sorry.

LAURA   I'm sorry too, Al.

> She smiles at him. AL *stands in the doorway for a moment, not knowing whether to go out the hall door or go upstairs. Finally, he goes upstairs, and into the study door.* LAURA *stands thinking over what* AL *has said, even repeating to herself, "I'm not involved." She then goes into the alcove and off*

AL (*outside* TOM's *bedroom door*)   Tom?

> TOM *moves quietly away from the door*

Tom? (*He opens the door*) Hey.

TOM   I was sleeping.

AL   Standing up, huh?

> TOM *turns away*

You want to be alone?

TOM   No. You want to look. Go ahead. (*He indicates the window*)

AL   No, I don't want to look, I . . . (*He looks at* TOM, *not knowing how to begin . . . He stalls . . . smiling*) Nice tie you got there.

TOM (*starts to undo tie*)   Yeah, it's yours. You want it?

AL   No. Why? I can only wear one tie at a time. (TOM *leaves it hanging around his neck. After an awkward pause*) I . . . uh . . .

TOM   I guess I don't need to ask you what's the matter?

AL   It's been rough today, huh?

TOM   Yeah. (*He turns away, very upset. He's been holding it in . . . but here's his closest friend asking him to open up*) Jesus Christ!

> AL *doesn't know what to say. He goes to* TOM's *bureau and picks up his hairbrush, gives his hair a few brushes*

Anybody talk to you?

AL   Sure. You know they would.

TOM   What do they say?

AL (*yanks his tie off*)   Hell, I don't know.

TOM   I went to a meeting of the dance committee. I'm no longer on the dance committee. Said that since I'd backed out of playing the part in the play, I didn't show the proper spirit. That's what they *said* was the reason.

AL (*loud*)   Why the hell don't you do something about it?

TOM (*yelling back*)   About what?

AL   About what they're saying.

TOM   What the hell can I do?

AL   Geez, you could . . . (*He suddenly wonders what* TOM *could do*) I don't know.

TOM   I tried to pass it off. Christ, you can't pass it off. You know, when I went into the showers today after my tennis match, everyone who was in there, grabbed a towel and . . . and . . . walked out.

AL   They're stupid. Just a bunch of stupid bastards. (*He leaves the room*)

TOM (*following him into sitting room*)   Goddamn it, the awful thing I found myself . . . Jesus, I don't know . . . I found myself self-conscious about things I've been doing for years. Dressing, undressing . . . I keep my eyes on the floor . . . (*Re-enters his own room*) Geez, if I even look at a guy that doesn't have any clothes on, I'm afraid someone's gonna say something, or . . . Jesus, I don't know.

AL (*during this,* AL *has come back into the room, unbuttoning his shirt, taking it off, etc. Suddenly he stops*) What the hell am I doing? I've had a shower today. (*He tries to laugh*)

TOM (*looks at him a moment*)   Undress in your own room, will ya? You don't want them talking about you too, do you?

AL   No I don't. (*He has said this very definitely and with meaning*)

TOM (*looks up at his tone of voice*)   Of course you don't. (*He looks at* AL *a long time. He hardly dares say this*) You . . . uh . . . you moving out?

AL (*doesn't want to answer*)   Look, Tom, do you mind if I try to help you?

TOM   Hell, no. How?

AL   I know this is gonna burn your tail, and I know it sounds stupid as hell. But it isn't stupid. It's the way people look at things. You could do a lot for yourself, just the way you talk and look.

TOM   You mean get my hair cut?

AL   For one thing.

TOM   Why the hell should a man with a crew cut look more manly than a guy who—

AL   Look, I don't know the reasons for these things. It's just the way they are.

TOM (*looking at himself in bureau mirror*)   I tried a crew cut a coupla times. I haven't got that kind of hair, or that kind of head. (*After a moment*) Sorry, I didn't mean to yell at you. Thanks for trying to help.

AL (*finds a baseball on the radiator and throws it at* TOM. TOM *smiles, and throws it back*)   Look, Tom, the way you walk . . .

TOM   Oh, Jesus.

AL (*flaring*)   Look, I'm only trying to help you.

TOM   No one gave a goddam about how I walked till last Saturday!

AL (*starts to go*)   Okay, okay. Forget it. (*He goes out*)

TOM (*stands there a few moments, then slams the baseball into the bed and walks out after* AL *into sitting room*)   Al?

AL (*off*)   Yeah?

TOM   Tell me about how I walk.

AL (*in the sitting room*)   Go ahead, walk!

TOM (*walks back into the bedroom.* AL *follows him, wiping his face on a towel and watching* TOM *walk. After he has walked a bit*)   Now I'm not going to be able to walk any more. Everything I been doing all my life makes me look like a fairy.

AL   Go on.

TOM   All right, now I'm walking. Tell me.

AL   Tom, I don't know. You walk sort of light.

TOM   Light? (*He looks at himself take a step*)

AL   Yeah.

TOM   Show me.

AL   No, I can't do it.

TOM   Okay. You walk. Let me watch you. I never noticed how you walked.

> AL *stands there for a moment, never having realized before how difficult it could be to walk if you think about it. Finally he walks*

Do it again.

AL   If you go telling any of the guys about this . . .

TOM   Do you think I would? . . .

> AL *walks again*

That's a good walk. I'll try to copy it. (*He tries to copy the walk, but never succeeds in taking even a step*) Do you really think that'll make any difference?

AL   I dunno.

TOM   Not now it won't. Thanks anyway.

AL (*comes and sits on bed beside* TOM. *Puts his arm around* TOM'S *shoulder and thinks this thing out*)   Look, Tom . . . You've been in on a lot of bull sessions. You heard the guys talking about stopping over in Boston on the way home . . . getting girls . . . you know.

TOM   Sure. What about it?

AL   You're not going to the dance Saturday night?

TOM   No. Not now.

AL   You know Ellie Martin. The gal who waits on table down at the soda joint?

TOM   Yeah. What about her?

AL   You've heard the guys talking about her.

TOM   What do you mean?

AL   Hell, do you want me to draw a picture?

TOM (*with disgust*)   Ellie Martin?

AL   Okay. I know she's a dog, but . . .

TOM   So what good's that going to do? I get caught there, I get thrown out of school.

AL   No one ever gets caught. Sunday morning people'd hear about it . . . not the Dean . . . I mean the fellows. Hell, Ellie tells and tells and tells . . . Boy, you'd be made!

TOM   Are you kidding?

AL   No.

TOM (*with disgust*)   Ellie Martin!

AL (*after a long pause*)   Look, I've said so much already, I might as well be a complete bastard . . . You ever been with a woman?

TOM   What do you think?

AL   I don't think you have.

TOM   So?

AL   You want to know something?

TOM   What?

AL   Neither have I. But if you tell the guys, I'll murder you.

TOM   All those stories you told . . .

AL   Okay, I'll be sorry I told you.

TOM   Then why don't you go see Ellie Martin Saturday night?

AL   Why the hell should I?

TOM   You mean you don't have to prove anything?

AL   Aw, forget it. It's probably a lousy idea anyway. (*He starts out*)

TOM   Yeah.

AL (*stops*)   Look, about next—(*Stops*)

TOM   Next year? Yes?

AL   Hap Hudson's asked me to come to his house. He's got a single there. A lot of the fellows from the team are over there, and . . . well . . . (*He doesn't look at* TOM)

TOM   I understand!

AL (*looks up at last. He hates himself but he's done it, and it's a load off his chest*)   See ya. (*He starts to go.*)

TOM (*as* AL *gets to door*)   Al . . . (AL *stops and looks back. Taking tie from around his neck*) Here.

AL (*looks at tie, embarrassed*)   I said wear it. Keep it.

TOM   It's yours.

AL (*looks at the tie for a long time, then without taking it, goes through the door*)   See ya.

> TOM *folds the tie neatly, dazed, then seeing what he's doing, he throws it viciously in the direction of the bureau, and turns and stares out the window. He puts a record on the phonograph*

BILL (*comes in to study from the hall, carrying a pair of shoes and a slim book. As he opens his study door, he hears the music upstairs. He stands in the door and listens, remembering his miserable boyhood. Then he comes in and closes the door*)   Laura. (*Throws shoes on floor near footstool*)

LAURA (*off stage, calling*)   Bill?

BILL   Yes.

LAURA (*coming in with tea things*)   I didn't think you'd be back before your class. Have some tea.

BILL   I beat young Harvey at handball.

LAURA   Good.

BILL   At last. It took some doing, though. He was after my scalp because of that D minus I gave him in his last exam. (*Gives her book*) You wanted this . . . book of poems.

LAURA (*looks at book. Her eyes shift quickly to the same book in the chair*)   Why yes. How did you know?

BILL (*trying to be offhand about it*)   The notice from the bookstore.

LAURA   That's very nice of you.

> She moves towards him to kiss him, but at this moment, in picking some wrapping paper from the armchair, he notices the duplicate copy

BILL (*a little angry*)   You've already got it.

LAURA   Why, yes . . . I . . . well, I . . .

> BILL *picking it up . . . opens it*

That is, someone gave it to me.

> BILL *reads the inscription*

Tom knew I wanted it, and . . .

BILL (*looks at her, a terrible look coming into his face. Then he slowly rips the book in two and hurls it into the fireplace*)   Damn!

LAURA   Bill!

> BILL *goes to footstool and sits down and begins to change his shoes*

Bill, what difference does it make that he gave me the book? He knew I wanted it too.

BILL   I don't know. It's just that every time I try to do something . . .

LAURA   Bill, how can you say that? It isn't so.

BILL   It is.

LAURA   Bill, this thing of the book is funny.

BILL   I don't think it's very funny.

LAURA (*going behind him, and kneeling by his side*)   Bill, I'm very touched that you should have remembered. Thank you.

> He turns away from her and goes on with his shoes

Bill, don't turn away. I want to thank you. (*As she gets no response from him, she rises*) Is it such a chore to let yourself be thanked? (*She puts her hands on his shoulders, trying to embrace him*) Oh, Bill, we so rarely touch any more. I keep feeling I'm losing contact with you. Don't you feel that?

BILL (*looking at his watch*)   Laura, I . . .

LAURA (*she backs away from him*)   I know, you've got to go. But it's just that, I don't know, we don't touch any more. It's a silly way of putting it, but you seem to hold yourself aloof from me. A tension seems to grow between us . . . and then when we do . . . touch . . . it's a violent thing . . . almost a compulsive thing.

BILL is uncomfortable at this accurate description of their relationship. He sits troubled. She puts her arms around his neck and embraces him, bending over him

You don't feel it? You don't feel yourself holding away from me until it becomes overpowering? There's no growing together any more . . . no quiet times, just holding hands, the feeling of closeness, like it was in Italy. Now it's long separations and then this almost brutal coming together, and . . . Oh, Bill, you do see, you do see.

BILL suddenly straightens up, toughens, and looks at her. LAURA repulsed, slowly draws her arms from around his shoulders

BILL   For God's sake, Laura, what are you talking about? (*He rises and goes to his desk*) It can't always be a honeymoon.

Upstairs in his room, TOM turns off the phonograph, and leaves the room, going out into the hall and up the stairs

LAURA   Do you think that's what I'm talking about?

BILL   I don't know why you chose a time like this to talk about things like . . .

LAURA   I don't know why, either. I just wanted to thank you for the book . . . (*Moves away and looks in book*) What did you write in it?

BILL (*starts to mark exam papers*)   Nothing. Why? Should I write in it? I just thought you wanted the book.

LAURA   Of course . . . Are you sure you won't have some tea? (*She bends over the tea things*)

BILL   Yes.

LAURA (*straightening up, trying another tack of returning to normality*)   Little Joan Harrison is coming over for tea.

BILL   No, she isn't.

LAURA looks inquiringly

I just saw her father at the gym. I don't think that was a very smart thing for you to do, Laura.

LAURA   I thought Tom might take her to the dance Saturday. He's on the committee, and he has no girl to take.

BILL   I understand he's no longer on the committee. You're a hostess, aren't you?

LAURA   Yes.

BILL   I've got the mountain-climbing business this week-end. Weather man predicts rain.

LAURA (*almost breaks. Hides her face in her hands. Then recovers*)   That's too bad. (*After a moment*) Bill?

BILL   Yes?

LAURA   I think someone should go to the Dean about Tom and the hazing he's getting.

BILL   What could the Dean do? Announce from chapel, "You've got to stop riding Tom. You've got to stop calling him Grace?" Is that what you'd like him to do?

LAURA   No. I suppose not.

BILL   You know we're losing Al next year because of Tom.

LAURA   Oh, you've heard?

BILL   Yes, Hudson tells me he's moving over to his house. He'll probably be captain of the baseball team. Last time we had a major sport captain was eight years ago.

LAURA   Yes, I'm sorry.

BILL   However, we'll also be losing Tom.

LAURA   Oh?

BILL (*noting her increased interest*)   Yes. We have no singles in this house, and he'll be rooming alone.

LAURA   I'm sorry to hear that.

BILL (*he turns to look at her*)   I knew you would be.

LAURA   Why should my interest in this boy make you angry?

BILL   I'm not angry.

LAURA   You're not only angry. It's almost as though you were, well, jealous.

BILL   Oh, come on now.

LAURA   Well, how else can you explain your . . . your vindictive attitude toward him?

BILL   Why go into it again? Jealous! (*He has his books together now. Goes to the door*) I'll go directly from class to the dining hall. All right?

LAURA   Yes, of course.

BILL   And please, please, Laura . . . (*He stops*)

LAURA   I'll try.

BILL   I know you like to be different, just for the sake of being different . . . and I like you for that . . . But this time, lay off. Show your fine free spirit on something else.

LAURA   On something that can't hurt us.

BILL   All right. Sure. I don't mind putting it that way. And Laura?

LAURA   Yes?

BILL   Seeing Tom so much . . . having him down for tea alone all the time . . .

LAURA   Yes?

BILL   I think you should have him down only when you have the other boys . . . for his own good. I mean that. Well, I'll see you in the dining hall. Try to be on time.

> He goes out. LAURA *brings her hands to her face, and cries, leaning against the back of the chair.* AL *has come tumbling out of the door to his room with books in hand, and is coming down the stairs. Going down the hall*

You going to class, Al?

AL   Hello, Mr. Reynolds. Yes I am.

BILL (*as they go*)   Let's walk together. I'm sorry to hear that you're moving across the street next year. (*And they are gone out the door*)

TOM (*has come down the stairs, and now stands looking at the hall telephone. He is carrying his coat. After a long moment's deliberation he puts in a coin and dials)* Hello, I'd like to speak to Ellie Martin, please.

> LAURA *has moved to pick up the torn book which her husband has thrown in the fireplace. She is smoothing it out, as she suddenly hears* TOM*'s voice in the hall. She can't help but hear what he is saying. She stands stock still and listens, her alarm and concern showing on her face*

Hello, Ellie? This is Tom Lee . . . Tom Lee. I'm down at the soda fountain all the time with my roommate, Al Thompson . . . Yeah, the guys do sometimes call me that . . . Well, I'll tell you what I wanted. I wondered if . . . you see, I'm not going to the dance Saturday night, and I wondered if you're doing anything? Yeah, I guess that is a hell of a way to ask for a date . . . but I just wondered if I could maybe drop by and pick you up after work on Saturday . . . I don't know what's *in* it for you, Ellie . . . but something I guess. I just thought I'd like to see you . . . What time do you get through work? . . . Okay, nine o'clock. (LAURA, *having heard this, goes out through the alcove. About to hang up)* Oh, thanks. *(He stands for a moment, contemplating what he's done, then he slips on his jacket, and goes to the study door and knocks. After a moment, he opens the door and enters)*

LAURA *(coming from the other room with a plate of cookies)* Oh, there you are. I've got your favorites today.

TOM Mrs. Reynolds, do you mind if I don't come to tea this afternoon?

LAURA Why . . . if you don't want to . . . How are you? *(She really means this question)*

TOM I'm okay.

LAURA Good.

TOM It's just I don't feel like tea.

LAURA Perhaps, it's just as well . . . Joan can't make it today, either.

TOM I didn't expect she would. She's nothing special; just a kid.

LAURA Something about a dentist appointment or something.

TOM It wouldn't have done any good anyway. I'm not going to the dance.

LAURA Oh?

TOM Another member of the committee will stop around for you.

LAURA What will you be doing?

TOM I don't know. I can take care of myself.

LAURA If you're not going, that gives me an easy out. I won't have to go.

TOM Just because I'm not going?

LAURA *(in an effort to keep him from going to Ellie)* Look, Tom . . . now that neither of us is going, why don't you drop down here after supper, Saturday night. We could listen to some records, or play gin, or we can just talk.

TOM I . . . I don't think you'd better count on me.

LAURA I'd like to.

TOM   No, really. I don't want to sound rude . . . but I . . . I may have another engagement.

LAURA   Oh?

TOM   I'd like to come. Please understand that. It's what I'd like to do . . . but . . .

LAURA   Well, I'll be here just in case, just in case you decide to come in. (LAURA *extends her hand*) I hope you'll be feeling better.

TOM (*hesitates, then takes her hand*)   Thanks.

LAURA   Maybe your plans will change.

> TOM *looks at her, wishing they would; knowing they won't. He runs out and down the hall as the lights fade out on* LAURA *standing at the door*

CURTAIN

Scene Two

> *The time is eight forty-five on Saturday night.*
>
> *In the study a low fire is burning. As the curtain rises, the town clock is striking the three quarter hour.* LAURA *is sitting in her chair sipping a cup of coffee. The door to the study is open slightly. She is waiting for* TOM. *She is wearing a lovely but informal dress, and a single flower. In his room,* TOM *listens to the clock strike. He has just been shaving. He is putting shaving lotion on his face. His face is tense and nervous. There is no joy in the preparations. In a moment, he turns and leaves the room, taking off his belt as he goes.*
>
> *After a moment,* LILLY *comes to the study door, knocks and comes in.*

LILLY   Laura?

LAURA   Oh; Lilly.

LILLY (*standing in the doorway, a raincoat held over her head. She is dressed in a low-cut evening gown, which she wears very well*)   You're not dressed yet. Why aren't you dressed for the dance?

LAURA (*still in her chair*)   I'm not going. I thought I told you.

LILLY (*deposits raincoat and goes immediately to look at herself in mirror next to the door*)   Oh, for Heaven's sake, why not? Just because Bill's away with his loathsome little mountain climbers?

LAURA   Well . . .

LILLY   Come along with us. It's raining on and off, so Harry's going to drive us in the car.

LAURA   No, thanks.

LILLY   If you come, Harry will dance with you all evening. You won't be lonely, I promise you.

> LAURA *shakes her head, ''no''*

You're the only one who can dance those funny steps with him.

LAURA   It's very sweet of you, but no.

LILLY (*at the mirror*)   Do you think this neck is too low?

LAURA   I think you look lovely.

LILLY   Harry says this neck will drive all the little boys crazy.

LAURA   I don't think so.

LILLY   Well, that's not very flattering.

LAURA   I mean, I think they'll appreciate it, but as for driving them crazy . . .

LILLY   After all I want to give them some reward for dancing their duty dances with me.

LAURA   I'm sure when they dance with you, it's no duty, Lilly. I've seen you at these dances.

LILLY   It's not this . . . (*indicating her bosom*) it's my line of chatter. I'm oh so interested in what courses they're taking, where they come from and where they learned to dance so divinely.

LAURA (*laughing*)   Lilly, you're lost in a boys' school. You were meant to shine some place much more glamorous.

LILLY   I wouldn't trade it for the world. Where else could a girl indulge in three hundred innocent flirtations a year?

LAURA   Lilly, I've often wondered what you'd do if one of the three hundred attempted to go, well, a little further than innocent flirtation.

LILLY   I'd slap him down . . . the little beast. (*She laughs and admires herself in mirror*) Harry says if I'm not careful I'll get to looking like Ellie Martin. You've seen Ellie.

LAURA   I saw her this afternoon for the first time.

LILLY   Really? The first time?

LAURA   Yes. I went into the place where she works . . . the soda shop . . .

LILLY   You!

LAURA   Yes . . . uh . . . for a package of cigarettes. (*After a moment she says with some sadness*) She's not even pretty, is she?

LILLY (*turns from admiring herself at the tone in* LAURA's *voice*)   Well, honey, don't sound so sad. What difference should it make to you if she's pretty or not?

LAURA   I don't know. It just seems so . . . they're so young.

LILLY   If they're stupid enough to go to Ellie Martin, they deserve whatever happens to them. Anyway, Laura, the boys *talk* more about Ellie than anything else. So don't fret about it.

LAURA (*arranges chair for* TOM *facing fireplace. Notices* LILLY *primping*)   You look lovely, Lilly.

LILLY   Maybe I'd better wear that corsage the dance committee sent, after all . . . right here. (*She indicates low point in dress*) I was going to carry it—or rather Harry was going to help me carry it. You know, it's like one of those things people put on Civil War monuments on Decoration Day.

LAURA   Yes, I've seen them.

LILLY (*indicating the flower* LAURA *is wearing*)   Now that's tasteful. Where'd you get that?

LAURA   Uh . . . I bought it for myself.

LILLY   Oh, now.

LAURA   It's always been a favorite of mine and I saw it in the florist's window.

LILLY   Well, Harry will be waiting for me to tie his bow tie. (*Starts towards door*) Will you be up when we get back?

LAURA (*giving* LILLY *her raincoat*)   Probably not.

LILLY   If there's a light on, I'll drop in and tell you how many I had to slap down . . . Night-night.

> *She leaves.* LAURA *stands at the closed door until she hears the outside door close. Then she opens her door a bit. She takes her cup of coffee and stands in front of the fireplace and listens*

TOM (*as* LILLY *goes, he returns to his room, dressed in a blue suit. He stands there deliberating a moment, then reaches under his pillow and brings out a pint bottle of whisky. He takes a short swig. It gags him. He corks it and puts it back under the pillow*)   Christ, I'll never make it. (*He reaches in his closet and pulls out a raincoat, then turns and snaps out the room light, and goes out. A moment later, he appears on the stairs. He sees* LAURA*'s door partly open, and while he is putting on his raincoat, he walks warily past it*)

LAURA (*when she hears* TOM*'s door close, she stands still and listens more intently. She hears him pass her door and go to the front door. She puts down the cup of coffee, and goes to the study door. She calls*)   Tom? (*After some moments,* TOM *appears in the door, and she opens it wide*) I've been expecting you.

TOM   I . . . I . . .

LAURA (*opening the door wide*)   Are you going to the dance, after all?

TOM (*comes in the door*)   No . . . You can report me if you want. Out after hours. *Or* . . . (*He looks up at her finally*) Or you can give me permission. Can I have permission to go out?

LAURA (*moving into the room, says pleasantly*)   I think I'd better get you some coffee.

TOM (*at her back, truculent*)   You can tell them that, too . . . that I've been drinking. There'll be lots to tell before—(*He stops*) I didn't drink much. But I didn't eat much either.

LAURA   Let me get you something to eat.

TOM (*as though convincing himself*)   No. I can't stay!

LAURA   All right. But I'm glad you dropped in. I was counting on it.

TOM (*chip on shoulder*)   I said I might not. When you invited me.

LAURA   I know. (*She looks at him a moment. He is to her a heartbreaking sight . . . all dressed up as though he were going to a prom, but instead he's going to Ellie . . . the innocence and the desperation touch her deeply . . . and this shows in her face as she circles behind him to the door*) It's a nasty night out, isn't it?

TOM   Yes.

LAURA   I'm just as glad I'm not going to the dance. (*She shuts the door gently.* TOM, *at the sound of the door, turns and sees what she has done*) It'll be nice just to stay here by the fire.

TOM   I wasn't planning to come in.

LAURA   Then why the flower . . . and the card? "For a pleasant evening?''

TOM   It was for the dance. I forgot to cancel it.

LAURA   I'm glad you didn't.

TOM   Why? (*He stops studying the curtains and looks at her*)

LAURA (*moving into the room again*)   Well, for one thing I like to get flowers. For another thing. . . .

> TOM *shakes his head a little to clear it*

Let me make you some coffee.

TOM   No. I'm just about right.

LAURA   Or you can drink this . . . I just had a sip. (*She holds up the cup.* TOM *looks at the proferred coffee*) You can drink from this side. (*She indicates the other side of the cup*)

TOM (*takes the cup, and looks at the side where her lips have touched and then slowly turns it around to the other and takes a sip*)   And for another thing?

LAURA   What do you mean?

TOM   For one thing you like to get flowers . . .

LAURA   For another it's nice to have flowers on my anniversary.

TOM   Anniversary?

LAURA   Yes.

TOM (*waving the cup and saucer around*)   And Mr. Reynolds on a mountain top with twenty stalwart youths, soaking wet . . . Didn't he remember?

LAURA (*rescues the cup and saucer*)   It's not that anniversary. (TOM *looks at her wondering. Seeing that she has interested him, she moves towards him*) Let me take your coat.

TOM (*definitely*)   I can't—

LAURA   I know. You can't stay. But . . . (*She comes up behind him and puts her hand on his shoulders to take off his coat. He can hardly stand her touch. She gently peels his coat from him and stands back to look at him*) How nice you look!

TOM (*disarranging his hair or tie*)   Put me in a blue suit and I look like a kid.

LAURA   How did you know I liked this flower?

TOM   You mentioned it.

LAURA   You're very quick to notice these things. So was he.

TOM (*after a moment, his curiosity aroused*)   Who?

LAURA   My first husband. That's the anniversary.

TOM   I didn't know.

LAURA (*she sits in her chair*)   Mr. Reynolds doesn't like me to talk about my first husband. He was, I'd say, about your age. How old are you, Tom?

TOM   Eighteen . . . tomorrow.

LAURA   Tomorrow . . . We must celebrate.

TOM   You'd better not make any plans.

LAURA   He was just your age then. (*She looks at him again with slight wonder*) It doesn't seem possible now, looking at you . . .

TOM   Why, do I look like such a child?

LAURA   Why no.

TOM   Men are married at my age.

LAURA   Of course, they are. *He* was. Maybe a few months older. Such a lonely boy, away from home for the first time . . . and . . . and going off to war.

TOM *looks up inquiringly*

Yes, he was killed.

TOM   I'm sorry . . . but I'm glad to hear about him.

LAURA   Glad?

TOM   Yes. I don't know . . . He sounds like someone you *should* have been married to, not . . . (*stops*) I'm sorry if I . . . (*stops*)

LAURA (*after a moment*)   He was killed being conspicuously brave. He had to be conspicuously brave, you see, because something had happened in training camp . . . I don't know what . . . and he was afraid the others thought him a coward . . . He showed them he wasn't.

TOM   He had that satisfaction.

LAURA   What was it worth if it killed him?

TOM   I don't know. But I can understand.

LAURA   Of course you can. You're very like him.

TOM   Me?

LAURA (*holding out the coffee cup*)   Before I finish it all?

TOM *comes over and takes a sip from his side of the cup*

He was kind and gentle, and lonely.

TOM *turns away in embarrassment at hearing himself so described*

We knew it wouldn't last . . . We sensed it . . . But he always said, "Why must the test of everything be its durability?"

TOM   I'm sorry he was killed.

LAURA   Yes, so am I. I'm sorry he was killed the way he was killed . . . trying to prove how brave he was. In trying to prove he was a man, he died a boy.

TOM   Still he must have died happy.

LAURA   Because he proved his courage?

TOM   That . . . and because he was married to you. (*Embarrassed, he walks to his coat which she has been holding in her lap*) I've got to go.

LAURA   Tom, please.

TOM   I've got to.

LAURA   It must be a very important engagement.

TOM   It is.

LAURA   If you go now, I'll think I bored you, talking all about myself.

TOM   You haven't.

LAURA   I probably shouldn't have gone on like that. It's just that I felt like it . . . a rainy night . . . a fire. I guess I'm in a reminiscent mood. Do you ever get in reminiscing moods on nights like this?

TOM   About what?

LAURA   Oh, come now . . . there must be something pleasant to remember, or someone.

> TOM *stands by the door beginning to think back, his raincoat in his hand, but still dragging on the floor*

Isn't there? . . . Of course there is. Who was it, or don't you want to tell?

TOM (*after a long silence*)   May I have a cigarette?

LAURA (*relieved that she has won another moment's delay*)   Yes, of course. (*Hands him a box, then lights his cigarette.*)

TOM   My seventh-grade teacher.

LAURA   What?

TOM   That's who I remember.

LAURA   Oh.

TOM   Miss Middleton . . .

LAURA   How sweet.

TOM (*drops the raincoat again, and moves into the room*)   It wasn't sweet. It was terrible.

LAURA   At that time, of course . . . Tell me about her.

TOM   She was just out of college . . . tall, blonde, honey-colored hair . . . and she wore a polo coat, and drove a convertible.

LAURA   Sounds very fetching.

TOM   Ever since then I've been a sucker for girls in polo coats.

LAURA (*smiling*)   I have one somewhere.

TOM   Yes, I know. (*He looks at her*)

LAURA   What happened?

TOM   What could happen? As usual I made a fool of myself. I guess everyone knew I was in love with her. People I like, I can't help showing it.

LAURA   That's a good trait.

TOM   When she used to go on errands and she needed one of the boys to go along and help carry something, there I was.

LAURA   She liked you too, then.

TOM   This is a stupid thing to talk about.

LAURA   I can see why she liked you.

TOM   I thought she . . . I thought she loved me. I was twelve years old.

LAURA   Maybe she did.

TOM   Anyway, when I was in eighth grade, she got married. And you know what they made me do? They gave a luncheon at school in her honor, and I had to be the toastmaster and wish her happiness and everything . . . I had to write a poem . . . (*He quotes*)

"Now that you are going to be married,
And away from us be carried,
Before you promise to love, honor and obey,
There are a few things I want to say."

(*He shakes his head as they both laugh*) From there on it turned out to be more of a love poem than anything else.

LAURA (*as she stops laughing*)   Puppy love can be heartbreaking.

TOM (*the smile dying quickly as he looks at her. Then after what seems like forever*)   I'm always falling in love with the wrong people.

LAURA   Who isn't?

TOM   You too?

LAURA   It wouldn't be any fun if we didn't. Of course, nothing ever comes of it, but there are bittersweet memories, and they can be pleasant. (*Kidding him as friend to friend, trying to get him to smile again*) Who else have you been desperately in love with?

TOM (*he doesn't answer. Then he looks at his watch*)   It's almost nine . . . I'm late. (*Starts to go*)

LAURA (*rising*)   I can't persuade you to stay?

                    TOM *shakes his head, "no"*

We were getting on so well.

TOM   Thanks.

LAURA   In another moment I would have told you all the deep, dark secrets of my life.

TOM   I'm sorry. (*He picks up his coat from the floor*)

LAURA (*desperately trying to think of something to keep him from going*)   Won't you stay even for a dance?

TOM   I don't dance.

LAURA   I was going to teach you. (*She goes over to the phonograph and snaps on the button*)

TOM (*opens the door*)   Some other time . . .

LAURA   Please, for me. (*She comes back*)

TOM (*after a moment he closes the door*)   Tell me something.

LAURA   Yes?

                    The record starts to play, something soft and melodic. It plays through to the end of the act

TOM   Why are you so nice to me?

LAURA   Why . . . I . . .

TOM   You're not this way to the rest of the fellows.

LAURA   No, I know I'm not. Do you mind my being nice to you?

TOM (*shakes his head, "no"*)   I just wondered why.

LAURA (*in a perfectly open way*)   I guess, Tom . . . I guess it's because I like you.

TOM   No one else seems to. Why do you?

LAURA   I don't know . . . I . . .

TOM   Is it *because* no one else likes me? Is it just pity?

LAURA   No, Tom, of course not . . . It's, well . . . it's because you've been very nice to me . . . very considerate. It wasn't easy for me, you know, coming into a school, my first year. You seemed to sense that. I don't know, we just seem to have hit it off. (*She smiles at him*)

TOM   Mr. Reynolds knows you like me.

LAURA   I suppose so. I haven't kept it a secret.

TOM   Is that why he hates me so?

LAURA   I don't think he hates you.

TOM   Yes, he hates me. Why lie? I think everyone here hates me but you. But they won't.

LAURA   Of course they won't.

TOM   He hates me because he made a flop with me. I know all about it. My father put me in this house when I first came here, and when he left me he said to your husband, "Make a man out of him." He's failed, and he's mad, and then you come along, and were nice to me . . . out of pity.

LAURA   No, Tom, not pity. I'm too selfish a woman to like you just out of pity.

TOM   (*he has worked himself up into a state of confusion, and anger, and desperation*)   There's so much I . . . there's so much I don't understand.

LAURA   (*reaches out and touches his arm*)   Tom, don't go out tonight.

TOM   I've got to. That's one thing that's clear. I've got to!

LAURA   (*holds up her arms for dancing*)   Won't you let me teach you how to dance?

TOM   (*suddenly and impulsively he throws his arms around her, and kisses her passionately, awkwardly, and then in embarrassment he buries his head in her shoulder*)   Oh, God . . . God.

LAURA   Tom . . . Tom . . .

          TOM *raises his face and looks at her, and would kiss her again*

No, Tom . . . No, I . . . (*At the first "No,"* TOM *breaks from her and runs out the door halfway up the stairs. Calling*) Tom! . . . Tom!

          TOM *stops at the sound of her voice and turns around and looks down the stairs.* LAURA *moves to the open door*

Tom, I . . .

          The front door opens and two of the mountain-climbing boys, PHIL *and* PAUL *come in, with their packs*

PHIL (*seeing* TOM *poised on the stairs*)   What the hell are you doing?

          TOM *just looks at him*

What's the matter with you? (*He goes on up the stairs*)

TOM   What are you doing back?

PAUL   The whole bunch is back. Who wants to go mountain climbing in the rain?

BILL (*outside his study door*)   Say, any of you fellows want to go across the street for something to eat when you get changed, go ahead.

PHIL *and* PAUL *go up the stairs past* TOM. BILL *goes into his own room, leaving door open*

Hi. (*He takes off his equipment and puts it on the floor*)

LAURA (*has been standing motionless where* TOM *has left her*)   Hello.

BILL (*comes to her and kisses her on the cheek*)   One lousy week-end a year we get to go climbing and it rains. (*Throws the rest of his stuff down*) The fellows are damned disappointed.

LAURA (*hardly paying any attention to him*)   That's too bad.

BILL (*going up to alcove*)   I think they wanted me to invite them down for a feed. But I didn't want to. I thought we'd be alone. Okay? (*He looks across at her*)

LAURA (*she is listening for footsteps outside*)   Sure.

BILL *goes out through alcove.* LAURA *stoops and picks up the raincoat which* TOM *has dropped and hides it in the cabinet by the fireplace*

BILL (*appears in door momentarily wiping his hands with towel*)   Boy it really rained.

He disappears again. LAURA *sadly goes to the door and slowly and gently closes it. When she is finished, she leans against the door, listening, hoping against hope that* TOM *will go upstairs. When* TOM *sees the door close, he stands there for a moment, then turns his coat collar up and goes down the hall and out. Off stage as* TOM *starts to go down the hall*

We never made it to the timberline. The rain started to come down. Another hour or so and we would have got to the hut and spent the night, but the fellows wouldn't hear of it . . . (*The door slams.* LAURA *turns away from the study door in despair. Still off stage*) What was that?

LAURA   Nothing . . . nothing at all.

BILL (*enters and gets pipe from mantelpiece*)   Good to get out, though. Makes you feel alive. Think I'll go out again next Saturday, alone. Won't be bothered by the fellows wanting to turn back.

He has settled down in the chair intended for TOM. *The school bells start to ring nine.* BILL *reaches out his hand for* LAURA. *Standing by the door, she looks at his outstretched hand, as the lights fade, and*

THE CURTAIN FALLS

ACT THREE   *The time is late the next afternoon.*

As the curtain rises, TOM *is in his room. His door is shut and bolted. He is lying on his back on the bed, staring up at the ceiling.*

RALPH (*he is at the phone*)   Hello, Mary . . . Ralph . . . Yeah, I just wanted you to know I'd be a little delayed picking you up . . . Yeah . . . everyone was taking a shower over here, and there's only one shower for eight guys . . . No it's not the same place as last night . . . The tea dance is at the Inn . . . (*He suddenly looks very uncomfortable*) Look, I'll tell you when I see you . . . Okay . . . (*almost whispers it*) I love you . . .

> STEVE, RALPH's *sidekick, comes running in from the outside. He's all dressed up and he's got something to tell*

Yeah, Mary. Well, I can't say it over again . . . Didn't you hear me the first time? (*Loud so she'll hear it*) Hi, Steve.

STEVE   Come on, get off. I got something to tell you.

RALPH   Mary—Mary, I'll get there faster if I stop talking now. Okay? Okay. See you a little after four. (*He hangs up*) What the hell's the matter with you?

STEVE   Have you seen Tom?

RALPH   No.

STEVE   You know what the hell he did last night?

RALPH   What?

STEVE   He went and saw Ellie.

RALPH   Who are you bulling?

STEVE   No, honest. Ellie told Jackson over at the kitchen. Everybody knows now.

RALPH   What did he want to go and do a thing like that for?

STEVE   But wait a minute. You haven't heard the half of it.

RALPH   Listen, I gotta get dressed. (*Starts upstairs*)

STEVE (*on the way up the stairs*)   The way Ellie tells it, he went there, all the hell dressed up like he was going to the dance, and . . .

> *They disappear up the stairs.* BILL *after a moment comes in the hall, and goes quickly up the stairs. He goes right into* AL *and* TOM's *main room without knocking. We then hear him try the handle of* TOM's *bedroom door.* TOM *looks at the door defiantly and sullenly*

BILL (*knocks sharply*)   Tom! (*Rattles door some more*) Tom, this is Mr. Reynolds. Let me in.

TOM   I don't want to see anyone.

BILL   You've got to see me. Come on. Open up! I've got to talk to the Dean at four, and I want to speak to you first.

TOM   There's nothing to say.

BILL   I can break the door down. Then your father would have to pay for a new door. Do you want that? Are you afraid to see me?

> TOM *after a moment, goes to the door and pulls back the bolt.* BILL *comes in quickly*

Well.

> TOM *goes back and sits on the bed. Doesn't look at* BILL

Now I've got to have the full story. All the details so that when I see the Dean . . .

TOM   You've got the full story. What the hell do you want?

BILL   We don't seem to have the full story.

TOM   When the school cops brought me in last night they told you I was with Ellie Martin.

BILL   That's just it. It seems you weren't *with* her.

TOM (*after a moment*)   What do you mean?

BILL   You weren't *with* her. You couldn't be *with* her. Do you understand what I mean?

TOM (*trying to brave it out*)   Who says so?

BILL   She says so. And she ought to know.

> TOM *turns away*

She says that you couldn't . . . and that you jumped up and grabbed a knife in her kitchen and tried to kill yourself . . . and she had to fight with you and that's what attracted the school cops.

TOM   What difference does it make?

BILL   I just wanted the record to be straight. You'll undoubtedly be expelled, no matter what . . . but I wanted the record straight.

TOM (*turning on him*)   You couldn't have stood it, could you, if I'd proved you wrong?

BILL   Where do you get off talking like that to a master?

TOM   You'd made up your mind long ago, and it would have killed you if I'd proved you wrong.

BILL   Talking like that isn't going to help you any.

TOM   Nothing's going to help. I'm gonna be kicked out, and then you're gonna be happy.

BILL   I'm not going to be happy. I'm going to be very sorry . . . sorry for your father.

TOM   All right, now you know. Go on, spread the news. How can you wait?

BILL   I won't tell anyone . . . but the Dean, of course.

TOM   And my father . . .

BILL   Perhaps . . .

TOM (*after a long pause*)   And Mrs. Reynolds.

BILL (*looks at* TOM)   Yes. I think she ought to know.

> *He turns and leaves the room. Goes through the sitting room and up the stairs, calling, "Ralph."* TOM *closes the door and locks it, goes and sits down in the chair*

LAURA (*as* BILL *goes upstairs to* RALPH, *she comes into the master's study. She is wearing a wool suit. She goes to the cupboard and brings out* TOM'*s raincoat. She moves with it to the door. There is a knock. She opens the door*)   Oh, hello, Mr. Lee.

HERB (*coming in, he seems for some reason rather pleased*)   Hello, Laura.

LAURA   Bill isn't in just now, though I'm expecting him any moment.

HERB   My train was twenty minutes late. I was afraid I'd missed him. We have an appointment with the Dean in a few minutes . . .

LAURA (*is coolly polite*)   Oh, I see.

HERB   Have I done something to displease you, Laura? You seem a little . . . (HERB *shrugs and makes a gesture with his hands meaning cool*)

LAURA   I'm sorry. Forgive me. Won't you sit down?

HERB   I remember that you were displeased at my leaving Tom in school a week ago. Well, you see I was right in a sense. Though, perhaps being a lady you wouldn't understand.

LAURA   I'm not sure that I do.

HERB   Well, now, look here. If I had taken Tom out of school after that scandal with Mr. . . . uh . . . what was his name?

LAURA   Mr. Harris.

HERB   Yes. If I'd taken Tom out then, he would have been marked for the rest of his life.

LAURA   You know that Tom will be expelled, of course.

HERB   Yes, but the circumstances are so much more normal.

LAURA (*after looking at him a moment*)   I think, Mr. Lee, I'm not quite sure, but I think, in a sense, you're proud of Tom.

HERB   Well.

LAURA   Probably for the first time you're proud of him because the school police found him out of bounds with a . . .

HERB   I shouldn't have expected you to understand. Bill will see what I mean.

> BILL *starts down the stairs*

LAURA   Yes. He probably will.

> BILL *comes in the room*

HERB   Bill.

BILL   Hello, Herb.

> HERB *looks from* LAURA *to* BILL. *Notices the coldness between them*

BILL   I was just seeing Tom.

HERB   Yes. I intend to go up after we've seen the Dean. How is he?

BILL   All right.

HERB (*expansive*)   Sitting around telling the boys all about it.

BILL   No, he's in his room alone. The others are going to the tea dance at the Inn. Laura . . . (*Sees* LAURA *is leaving the room*) Oh, Laura, I wish you'd stay.

> LAURA *takes one step back into the room*

HERB   I was telling your wife here, trying to make her understand the male point of view on this matter. I mean, how being kicked out for a thing like this, while not exactly desirable, is still not so serious. It's sort of one of the calculated risks of being a man. (*He smiles at his way of putting it*)

BILL (*preparing to tell* HERB)   Herb?

HERB   Yes, Bill. I mean, you agree with me on that, don't you?

BILL   Yes, Herb, only the situation is not exactly as it was reported to you over the phone. It's true that Tom went to this girl Ellie's place, and it's true that he went for the usual purpose. However . . . however, it didn't work out that way.

HERB   What do you mean?

BILL   Nothing happened.

HERB   You mean she . . . she wouldn't have him?

BILL   I mean, Tom . . . I don't know . . . he didn't go through with it. He couldn't. (*He looks at* LAURA) It's true. The girl says so. And when it didn't work, he tried to kill himself with a knife in the kitchen, and she struggled with him, and that brought the school cops, and that's that.

> LAURA *turns away, shocked and moved.* MR. LEE *sits down in a chair bewildered*

I'm sorry, Herb. Of course the fact that he was with Ellie at her place is enough to get him expelled.

HERB   Does everyone know this?

BILL   Well, Ellie talks. She's got no shame . . . and this is apparently something to talk about.

LAURA (*to* MR. LEE)   Do you still think it will make a good smoking-car story?

BILL   What do you mean?

HERB   Why did he do it? Before, maybe he could talk it down, but to go do a thing like this and leave no doubts.

LAURA   In whose mind?

BILL   Laura, please.

LAURA (*angry*)   You asked me to stay.

BILL (*flaring back at her*)   Well, now you've heard. We won't keep you.

LAURA (*knowing without asking*)   Why did you want me to hear?

BILL (*going to her*)   I wanted you to know the facts. That's all. The whole story.

> LAURA *stands in the alcove*

HERB   Bill, Bill! Maybe there's some way of getting this girl so she wouldn't spread the story.

BILL   I'm afraid it's too late for that.

HERB   I don't know. Some things don't make any sense. What am I going to do now?

LAURA (*re-entering*)   Mr. Lee, please don't go on drawing the wrong conclusions!

HERB   I'm drawing no conclusions. This sort of thing can happen to a normal boy. But it's what the others will think . . . Added to the Harris business. And that's all that's important. What they'll think.

LAURA   Isn't it important what Tom thinks?

BILL   Herb, we'd better be getting on over to the Dean's . . .

HERB (*indicating upstairs*)   Is he in his room?

BILL   Yes.

HERB   Packing?

BILL   No.

HERB   I told him to come to you to talk things over. Did he?

BILL   No.

HERB   What am I going to say to him now?

BILL   We're expected at four.

HERB   I know. But I've got to go up . . . Maybe I should have left him with his mother. She might have known what to do, what to say . . . (*He starts out*) You want to come along with me?

BILL (*moving to hall*)   All right.

LAURA (*serious*)   Bill, I'd like to talk with you.

BILL   I'll be back. (*Goes with* HERB *to the landing.* LAURA *exits, taking off her jacket*)

HERB   Maybe I ought to do this alone.

BILL   He's probably locked in his bedroom.

> HERB *goes up the stairs and inside the study.* BILL *stays in the hall.* TOM, *as he hears his father knocking on the bedroom door, stiffens.* HERB *tries the door handle*

HERB (*off, in the study*)   Tom . . . Tom . . . it's Dad.

> TOM *gets up, but just stands there*

Tom, are you asleep? (*After a few moments, he reappears on the landing. He is deeply hurt that his son wouldn't speak to him*) I think he's asleep.

BILL (*making a move to go in and get* TOM)   He can't be . . .

HERB (*stops*)   Yes, I think he is. He was always a sound sleeper. We used to have to drag him out of bed when he was a kid.

BILL   But he should see you.

HERB   It'll be better later, anyhow. (*He starts down the stairs, troubled, puzzled*)

BILL   I'll go right with you, Herb.

> They re-enter the study, and BILL goes out through the alcove. HERB stays in the master's study

TOM (*when his father is downstairs, he opens his bedroom door and faintly calls*)   Dad?

> HERB *looks up, thinking he's heard something but then figures it must have been something else.* RALPH, STEVE *and* PHIL *come crashing down the stairs, dressed for the tea dance, ad libbing comments about the girls at the dance.* TOM *closes his door. When they have gone, he opens it again and calls "Dad" faintly. When there is no response, he closes the door, and goes and lies on the bed*

BILL (*re-entering*)   Laura, I'm going to the Dean's now with Herb. I'm playing squash with the headmaster at five. So I'll see you at the dining room at six-thirty.

LAURA (*entering after him*)   I wish you'd come back here after.

BILL   Laura, I can't.

LAURA   Bill, I wish you would.

BILL (*sees that there is some strange determination in* LAURA's *face*)   Herb, I'll be with you in a minute. Why don't you walk along?

HERB   All right . . . Good-bye, Laura. See you again.

BILL   You'll see her in a couple of days at the reunion.

HERB   I may not be coming up for it now . . . Maybe I will. I don't know. I'll be walking along. Good-bye, Laura. Tell Tom I tried to see him. (*He goes out*)

BILL   Now, Laura, what's the matter? I've got to get to the Dean's
        rooms to discuss this matter.
LAURA   Yes, of course. But first I'd like to discuss the boys who made
        him do this . . . the men and boys who made him do this.
BILL   No one made him do anything.
LAURA   Is there to be no blame, no punishment for the boys and men
        who taunted him into doing this? What if he had succeeded in killing
        himself? What then?
BILL   You're being entirely too emotional about this.
LAURA   If he had succeeded in killing himself in Ellie's rooms, wouldn't
        you have felt some guilt?
BILL   I?
LAURA   Yes, you.
BILL   I wish you'd look at the facts and not be so emotional about this.
LAURA   The facts! What facts! an innocent boy goes swimming with an
        instructor . . . an instructor whom he likes because this instructor is
        one of the few who encourages him, who don't ride him . . . And
        because he's an off-horse, you and the rest of them are only too glad to
        put two and two together and get a false answer . . . anything which
        will let you go on and persecute a boy whom you basically don't like. If
        it had happened with Al or anybody else, you would have done
        nothing.
BILL   It would have been an entirely different matter. You can't escape
        from what you are . . . your character. Why do they spend so much
        time in the law courts on character witnesses? To prove this was the
        kind of man who could or couldn't commit such and such a crime.
LAURA   I resent this judgment by prejudice. He's not like me, there-
        fore, he is capable of all possible crimes. He's not one of us . . . a
        member of the tribe!
BILL   Now look, Laura, I know this is a shock to you, because you were
        fond of this boy. But you did all you could for him, more than anyone
        would expect. After all, your responsibility doesn't go beyond—
LAURA   I know. Doesn't go beyond giving him tea and sympathy on
        Sunday afternoons. Well, I want to tell you something. It's going to
        shock you . . . but I'm going to tell you.
BILL   Laura, it's late.
LAURA   Last night I knew what Tom had in mind to do. I heard him
        making the date with Ellie on the phone.
BILL   And you didn't stop him? Then you're the one responsible.
LAURA   Yes, I am responsible, but not as you think. I did try to stop
        him, but not by locking him in his room, or calling the school police. I
        tried to stop him by being nice to him, by being affectionate. By
        showing him that he was liked . . . yes, even loved. I knew what he
        was going to do . . . and why he was going to do it. He had to prove to
        you bullies that he was a man, and he was going to prove it with Ellie

Martin. Well . . . last night . . . last night, I wished he had proved it with me.

BILL   What in Christ's name are you saying?

LAURA   Yes, I shock you. I shock myself. But you are right. I am responsible here. I know what I should have done. I knew it then. My heart cried out for this boy in his misery . . . a misery imposed by my husband. And I wanted to help him as one human being to another . . . and I failed. At the last moment, I sent him away . . . sent him to . . .

BILL   You mean you managed to overcome your exaggerated sense of pity.

LAURA   No, it was not just pity. My heart in its loneliness . . . Yes, I've been lonely here, miserably lonely . . . and my heart in its loneliness cried out for this boy . . . cried out for the comfort he could give me too.

BILL   You don't know what you're saying.

LAURA   But I was a good woman. Good in what sense of the word? Good to whom . . . and for whom?

BILL   Laura, we'll discuss this, if we must, later on . . .

LAURA   Bill! There'll be no later on. I'm leaving you.

BILL   Over this thing?

LAURA (*after a moment*)   Yes, this *thing* and all the other *things* in our marriage.

BILL   For God's sake, Laura, what are you talking about?

LAURA   I'm talking about love and honor and manliness, and tenderness, and persecution. I'm talking about a lot. You haven't understood any of it.

BILL   Laura, you can't leave over a thing like this. You know what it means.

LAURA   I wouldn't worry too much about it. When I'm gone, it will probably be agreed by all that I was an off-horse too, and didn't really belong to the clan, and it's good riddance.

BILL   And you're doing this . . . all because of this . . . this fairy?

LAURA (*after a moment*)   This boy, Bill . . . this boy is more of a man than you are.

BILL   Sure. Ask Ellie.

LAURA   Because it was distasteful for him. Because for him there has to be love. He's more of a man than you are.

BILL   Yes, sure.

LAURA   Manliness is not all swagger and swearing and mountain climbing. Manliness is also tenderness, gentleness, consideration. You men think you can decide on who is a man, when only a woman can really know.

BILL   Ellie's a woman. Ask Ellie.

LAURA   I don't need to ask anyone.

BILL   What do you know about a man? Married first to that boy . . .
again, a pitiable boy . . . You want to mother a boy, not love a man.
That's why you never really loved me. Because I was not a boy you
could mother.

LAURA   You're quite wrong about my not loving you. I did love you.
But not just for your outward show of manliness, but because you
needed me . . . For one unguarded moment you let me know you
needed me, and I have tried to find that moment again the year we've
been married . . . Why did you marry me, Bill? In God's name, why?

BILL   Because I loved you. Why else?

LAURA   You've resented me . . . almost from the day you married me,
you've resented me. You never wanted to marry really . . . Did they
kid you into it? Does a would-be headmaster have to be married? Or
what was it, Bill? You would have been far happier going off on your
jaunts with the boys, having them to your rooms for feeds and bull
sessions . . .

BILL   That's part of being a master.

LAURA   Other masters and their wives do not take two boys always with
them whenever they go away on vacations or weekends.

BILL   They are boys without privileges.

LAURA   And I became a wife without privileges.

BILL   You became a wife . . . (*He stops*)

LAURA   Yes?

BILL   You did *not* become a wife.

LAURA   I know. I know I failed you. In some terrible way I've failed
you.

BILL   You were more interested in mothering that fairy up there than in
being my wife.

LAURA   But you wouldn't let me, Bill. You wouldn't let me.

BILL (*grabbing her by the shoulders*)   What do you mean I wouldn't let you?

LAURA (*quietly, almost afraid to say it*)   Did it ever occur to you that you
persecute in Tom, that boy up there, you persecute in him the thing
you fear in yourself?

> BILL *looks at her for a long moment of hatred. She has hit close to the
> truth he has never let himself be conscious of. There is a moment when
> he might hurt her, but then he draws away, still staring at her. He
> backs away, slowly, and then turns to the door*

Bill!

BILL (*not looking at her*)   I hope you will be gone when I come back from
dinner.

LAURA (*quietly*)   I will be . . . (*Going towards him*) Oh, Bill, I'm sorry. I
shouldn't have said that . . . it was cruel. (*She reaches for him as he goes
out the door*) This was the weakness you cried out for me to save you
from, wasn't it . . . And I have tried . . .

> He is gone

I have tried. (*Slowly she turns back into the room and looks at it*) I did try.

(For a few moments she stands stunned and tired from her outburst. Then she moves slowly to TOM's *raincoat, picks it up and turns and goes out of the room and to the stair-landing. She goes to the boy's study door and knocks)* Tom. *(She opens it and goes in out of sight. At* TOM's *door, she calls again)* Tom.

> TOM *turns his head slightly and listens.* LAURA *opens* TOM's *door and comes in*

Oh, I'm sorry. May I come in? *(She sees she's not going to get an answer from him, so she goes in)* I brought back your raincoat. You left it last night. *(She puts it on chair. She looks at him)* This is a nice room . . . I've never seen it before . . . As a matter of fact I've never been up here in this part of the house. *(Still getting no response, she goes on.* TOM *slowly turns and looks at her back, while she is examining something on the walls. She turns, speaking)* It's very cozy. It's really quite . . . *(She stops when she sees he has turned around looking at her)* Hello.

TOM *(barely audible)* Hello.

LAURA Do you mind my being here?

TOM You're not supposed to be.

LAURA I know. But everyone's out, and will be for some time . . . I wanted to return your raincoat.

TOM Thank you. *(After a pause he sits up on the bed, his back to her)* I didn't think you'd ever want to see me again.

LAURA Why not?

TOM After last night. I'm sorry about what happened downstairs.

LAURA *(she looks at him awhile, then)* I'm not.

TOM *(looks at her. Can't quite make it out)* You've heard everything I suppose.

LAURA Yes.

TOM Everything?

LAURA Everything.

TOM I knew your husband would be anxious to give you the details.

LAURA He did. *(She stands there quietly looking down at the boy)*

TOM So now you know too.

LAURA What?

TOM That everything they said about me is true.

LAURA Tom!

TOM Well, it is, isn't it?

LAURA Tom?

TOM I'm no man. Ellie knows it. Everybody knows it. It seems everybody knew it, except me. And now I know it.

LAURA *(moves toward him)* Tom . . . Tom . . . dear.

> TOM *turns away from her*

You don't think that just because . . .

TOM What else am I to think?

LAURA *(very gently)* Tom, that didn't work because you didn't believe in it . . . in such a test.

TOM *(with great difficulty)* I touched her, and there was nothing.

LAURA   You aren't in love with Ellie.

TOM   That's not supposed to matter.

LAURA   But it does.

TOM   I wish they'd let me kill myself.

LAURA   Tom, look at me.

> TOM *shakes his head*

Tom, last night you kissed me.

TOM   Jesus!

LAURA   Why did you kiss me?

TOM *(turns suddenly)*   And it made you sick, didn't it? Didn't it? *(Turns away from her again)*

LAURA   How can you think such a thing?

TOM   You sent me away . . . you . . . Anyway, when you heard this morning it must have made you sick.

LAURA *(sits on the edge of bed)*   Tom, I'm going to tell you something.

> TOM *won't turn*

Tom?

> *He still won't turn*

It was the nicest kiss I've ever had . . . from anybody.

> TOM *slowly turns and looks at her*

Tom, I came to say goodbye.

> TOM *shakes his head, looking at her*

I'm going away . . . I'll probably never see you again. I'm leaving Bill.

> TOM *knits his brows questioning*

For a lot of reasons . . . one of them, what he's done to you. But before I left, I wanted you to know, for your own comfort, you're more of a man now than he ever was or will be. And one day you'll meet a girl, and it will be right.

> TOM *turns away in disbelief*

Tom, believe me.

TOM   I wish I could. But a person knows . . . knows inside. Jesus, do you think after last night I'd ever . . . *(He stops. After a moment, he smiles at her)* But thanks . . . thanks a lot.

> *He closes his eyes.* LAURA *looks at him a long time. Her face shows the great compassion and tenderness she feels for this miserable boy. After some time, she gets up and goes out the door. A moment later she appears in the hall door. She pauses for a moment, then reaches out and closes it, and stays inside.*
>
> TOM, *when he hears the door close, his eyes open. He sees she has left his bedroom. Then in complete misery, he lies down on the bed, like a wounded animal, his head at the foot of the bed.*
>
> LAURA *in a few moments appears in the bedroom doorway. She stands there, and then comes in, always looking at the slender figure of the boy on the bed. She closes the bedroom door.*
>
> TOM *hears the sound and looks around. When he sees she has*

come back, he turns around slowly, wonderingly, and lies on his back, watching her.

LAURA, seeing a bolt on the door, slides it to. Then she stands looking at TOM, her hand at her neck. With a slight and delicate movement, she unbuttons the top button of her blouse, and moves towards TOM. When she gets alongside the bed, she reaches out her hand, still keeping one hand at her blouse. TOM makes no move. Just watches her.

LAURA makes a little move with the outstretched hand, asking for his hand. TOM slowly moves his hand to hers

LAURA (*stands there holding his hand and smiling gently at him. Then she sits and looks down at the boy, and after a moment, barely audible*)   And now . . . nothing?

TOM's other hand comes up and with both his hands he brings her hand to his lips

LAURA (*smiles tenderly at this gesture, and after a moment*)   Years   from   now . . . when you talk about this . . . and you will . . . be kind.

Gently she brings the boy's hands toward her opened blouse, as the lights slowly dim out . . . and . . .

THE CURTAIN FALLS

Exercises   1. *Characterize Tom Lee. What are his aesthetic and moral values?*

2. *What, specifically, is Tom seeking? Acceptance, love, manhood, or what?*

3. *Detail the subplots that involve Tom and Bill in one conflict and Tom and Herb in another. Identify the conflicts, tell how they are resolved, and explain their "dramatic" effectiveness.*

4. *How does Anderson manage to have us believe Tom, and not Bill and the boys who have labeled him a homosexual?*

5. *Bill rips apart the book of poems belonging to Laura and hurls it into the fireplace. What significance do you ascribe to this incident?*

6. *What are Tom's motives for making a date with Ellie Martin? Why does his mission fail, and why does he attempt to kill himself?*

7. *What comments does the play make about social acceptance in this society?*

8. *How does Laura lead us to an interpretation of the play?*

Topics for
Writing

1. The "appearance of things" and "circumstantial evidence" play important roles in Tom's alienation from society. Using the facts and details in the play, develop an indictment of society for its errors in judgment.

2. Laura tells Bill: "This boy is more of a man than you are." Discuss how Tom is more of a man than Bill.

Selected
Bibliography

Robert Anderson

Bentley, Eric. *The Dramatic Event.* New York: Horizon Press, 1954. Pages 150–153.

Gassner, John. *Theatre at the Crossroads.* New York: Holt, Rinehart & Winston. Pages 288–293.

Lewis, Allan. *American Plays and Playwrights of the Contemporary Theater.* New York: Crown, 1965. Pages 143–163.

Sieves, W. David. *Freud on Broadway.* New York: Cooper Square Publishers, 1971. Pages 410–411.

Tyman, K. *Curtains.* New York: Atheneum, 1961. Page 172.

Weales, Gerald. *American Drama since World War II.* New York: Harcourt, Brace & World, 1962. Pages 49–50, 51.

4　Dramatic Language

The study of language in drama deals almost exclusively with dramatic dialogue. Although dialogue is used sparingly in poetry and more freely in fiction, it is *all* the language in drama—it is the play. Only in stage directions does the playwright use other language.

Unlike the speeches of characters, written to be spoken and aimed primarily at argumentation, stage directions are written to be read and intended chiefly to inform. Older drama eschews stage directions; rarely are they used except to indicate entrances and exits. But modern drama makes ample use of stage directions, which serve many diverse functions especially valuable to the director, the actor, and the reader. In the main, they set mood and atmosphere, establish setting, describe character, interpret motivation, and editorialize.

Dramatic dialogue is concentrated, not desultory. It employs a pattern of affirmation and denial. The speech between characters proceeds by assents and dissents, by one speaker echoing or differing from another with all the harmony or discord between these extremes. Dialogue often involves a collision of opposed forces. It is scrappy, argumentative, and dramatic. It is the playwright's chief means of breathing life into a dramatic story. It is perhaps the one sacrosanct element of the play. Seldom will characters on stage remain stationary or speechless. They are continually on the move—opening and closing doors, sitting down and getting up, eating, drinking, dancing, swaggering, brandishing swords, swinging fists and hatchets—all the while talking. Nearly everything we know about characters, their backgrounds, their feelings, and their beliefs, we learn through dialogue.

Dramatic dialogue inherits special obligations as well as certain limitations. Of necessity, dialogue must be characteristic of the person speaking and appropriate to the situation in which that character is involved. Modern critics and readers may find fault with and be distracted by O'Neill's dialogue, particularly the dialect of Jones's Southern idiom and Smither's cockney, but it is nonetheless suited to the characters and their situations.

Further, dialogue must attend to one of three principal functions: delineate character, advance the plot, or explain motive. There is no room for palaver. Mainly because of the limitations of time playwrights must accomplish all that they can with a few, well-chosen words and well-turned phrases. They do not have the luxury that the novelist has of writing long, leisurely descriptive passages or philosophical treatises. Everything they say is vital; every bit of dialogue serves a purpose. And we might do well to remember that a speech during the performance of a play will be heard only one time. Moreover, dialogue must sound natural, even though it is paradoxically compounded of artifice like the magician's art and different from actual speech. How few people in the real world will speak as easily and eloquently—never at a loss to utter the right words at the right moment—as the characters who populate the make-believe world of the stage.

Consider the following sampling of speeches from *Riders to the Sea*. They are indeed eloquent and lyrical, lilting to the cadence of the islanders' spoken language; they exemplify thoughtful selectivity, achieve economy, compactness, and intensity, and emit crystallizations of wisdom.

What is the price of a thousand horses against a son where there is one son only? (Maurya)

In the big world the old people do be leaving things after them for their sons and children, but in this place it is the young men do be leaving things behind for them that do be old. (Maurya)

There does be a power of young men floating round in the sea . . . (Maurya)

Isn't it a pitiful thing when there is nothing left of a man who was a great rower and fisher, but a bit of an old shirt and a plain stocking? (Nora)

Poetic dramas naturally feature all the trappings of poetry; but prose drama, which comprises the bulk of modern drama, is not without its own kind of poetry. Let us examine for poetical effects excerpts from two Maurya speeches.

There were Stephen, and Shawn, were lost in the great wind, and found after in the Bay of Gregory of the Golden Mouth, and carried up the two of them on the one plank, and in by that door.

There was Sheamus and his father, and his own father again, were lost in a dark night, and not a stick or sign was seen of them when the sun went up. There was Patch after was drowned out of a curagh that turned over. I was sitting here with Bartley, and he a baby, lying on my two knees, and I seen two women, and three women, and four women coming in, and they crossing themselves, and not saying a word. . . .

Part of the poetry derives from the sound of unfamiliar words, names of people and places, the unusual syntax, and the rhythmic flow of the lines.

Imagery, too often considered the sole property of the poet, also enters the domain of drama. The playwright exhibits traditional images and invents others to compress meaning in a few, vivid word-pictures. Imagery heightens our intellectual and emotional awareness by appealing through our senses to something with which we are familiar.

The most obvious kind of imagery is visual as illustrated in the following example. Here Juliet, who is yearning for Romeo, describes the night. The appeal is chiefly to the eye through colors and contrasts of black and white.

Come, night, come Romeo, come, thou day in night;
For thou wilt lie upon the wings of night
Whiter than new snow on a raven's back.
Come, gentle night, come loving, black brow'd night,
Give me my Romeo; and, when he shall die,
Take him and cut him out in little stars,
And he will make the face of heaven so fine,
That all the world will be in love with night,
And pay no worship to the garish sun.

Imagery, often taken symbolically, is placed usually in a prominent position and referred to more than once to alert the reader to its importance. Symbols, like imagery, allow the playwright to communicate in a few words some complex idea.

Riders to the Sea contains much imagery that is also symbolic. Collectively, the color imagery of the grays, the blacks, and the reds embodies the concept of pain and suffering in life and heightens our awareness of man's perennial struggle with death. Similarly, the black pig's eating of the white rope and Bartley's wearing of Michael's shirt suggest death. Also, Maurya's cottage represents symbolically all the little shelters that impuissant man erects futilely as protection against nature's destructive forces. Furthermore, because of the impending immediacy of death, we might view the entire drama as symbolic, the brief stay of these islanders and their relentless contest against fear and suffering and grief and our brief, embattled tarry on our small island.

Another often used rhetorical device particularly effective in drama, especially in tragedy, is irony. Jones's situation in *Emperor Jones* is indeed ironic. Jones travels in a circle; he attempts to find a way out of the forest only to return to the spot where he had been earlier; he dies at dawn at the same place he had entered at twilight; and, at the end of the play, he has returned to his primitive origins, completing for all practical purposes, his circular journey.

This play also furnishes examples of dramatic irony, among them (1) Jones's good luck charm, the silver bullet, which was designed to save his life but instead kills him and (2) the fears and superstitions of the natives, which Jones had earlier found contemptible, now drive him into madness.

The master of tragic irony, however, is Sophocles. All three types of irony abound in *Oedipus*.

Examples of verbal irony: Oedipus curses the murderer of Laïos when, in effect, he is cursing himself; he vows to avenge the dead king "just as though I were his son," which, in fact, he is.

Examples of situation irony: Oedipus castigates Teiresias for his arrogance, a character trait he himself duly possesses; he berates the seer who is blind but knows the truth, when he himself has eyes to see but is blind to the truth; he is ingenious enough to solve the riddle of the Sphinx but not sufficiently clever to know his true identity; once again he saves Thebes by cleansing it of pollution (by bringing the murderer to justice), but in the process he discovers pollution in himself, and it destroys him.

Examples of dramatic irony: Oedipus curses the murderer of Laïos, whom we know to be Oedipus himself; he rejects the truth that the blind Teiresias imparts when he himself is blind and ignorant of the facts; he falsely charges Creon of treachery when he himself has been traiterous; he bitterly accuses Iocastâ of arrogance when she begs him not to pursue the matter of his parentage, and it is his own hubris that catapults his downfall; he shifts his search for the identity of the killer of Laïos to a search for his own identity when, in fact, his purpose has not changed; and finally, he compels the old shepherd to reveal his parentage, a fact we have known all along.

It is these tragic ironies that give the play *Oedipus* such power. The effects of the drama would have been lost had we been ignorant of the truth about Laïos' murderer.

All these features of language are available to the playwright. When they are so ordered as to work together—to react and interact with the other elements of drama—they produce powerful effects sure to reward us with a generous store of memorable experiences.

MODERN ARENA THEATER AND STAGE

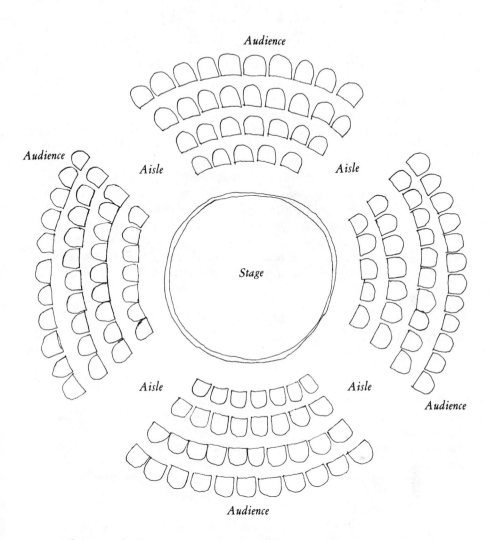

Stage	Acting area; may be any shape, round, oval, rectangular. Sets are simple, consisting primarily of props (furniture, rocks, etc.)
Audience	Seating area, raked upward away from the stage as in an amphitheater. Proximity to stage permits greater intimacy and immediacy than any other theater. Capacity is small
Aisles	Entrances and exits for performers, as well as audience; often on same level as stage

Eugene O'Neill *(1888–1953)*

Born in New York City, son of actor James O'Neill, he attended Princeton University, from which he was expelled because of a prank. Later he drifted as a prospector in Honduras, a sailor on voyages to Europe and South America, a bit actor, a cub reporter, and a waterfront bum. Two plays, which enjoyed great success in 1920, established him as America's leading playwright: Beyond the Horizon, *his first Broadway production, which won a Pulitzer Prize, and* The Emperor Jones. *He also won Pulitzer Prizes for* Annie Christie *(1921),* Strange Interlude *(1928), and* Long Day's Journey into Night *(1956), which was published and produced three years after his death from tuberculosis. In 1936 he was awarded the Nobel Prize for Literature, the first American author so honored.*

The Emperor Jones

CHARACTERS

BRUTUS JONES, *Emperor*

HENRY SMITHERS, *a Cockney trader*

AN OLD NATIVE WOMAN

LEM, *a native chief*

SOLDIERS, *adherents of Lem*

THE LITTLE FORMLESS FEARS

JEFF

THE NEGRO CONVICTS

THE PRISON GUARD

THE PLANTERS

THE AUCTIONEER

THE SLAVES

THE CONGO WITCH DOCTOR

THE CROCODILE GOD

SCENE *An island in the West Indies as yet not self-determined by white Marines. The form of native government is, for the time being, an empire.*

Scene One

The audience chamber in the palace of the Emperor—a spacious, high-ceilinged room with bare, whitewashed walls. The floor is of white tiles. In the rear, to the left of the center, a wide archway giving out on a portico with white pillars. The palace is evidently situated on high ground, for beyond the portico nothing can be seen but a vista of distant hills, their summits crowned with thick groves of palm trees. In the right wall, center, a smaller arched doorway leading to the living quarters of the palace. The room is bare of furniture with the exception of one huge chair made of uncut wood which stands at the center, its back to the rear. This is very apparently the Emperor's throne. It is painted a dazzling, eye-smiting scarlet. There is a brilliant orange cushion on the seat and another smaller one is placed on the floor to serve as a footstool. Strips of matting, dyed scarlet, lead from the foot of the throne to the two entrances.

It is late afternoon, but the sunlight still blazes yellowly beyond the portico and there is an oppressive burden of exhausting heat in the air.

As the curtain rises, a native Negro WOMAN *sneaks in cautiously from the entrance on the right. She is very old, dressed in cheap calico, barefooted, a red bandanna handkerchief covering all but a few stray wisps of white hair. A bundle bound in colored cloth is carried over her shoulder on the end of a stick. She hesitates beside the doorway, peering back as if in extreme dread of being discovered. Then she begins to glide noiselessly, a step at a time, toward the doorway in the rear. At this moment,* SMITHERS *appears beneath the portico.*

SMITHERS *is a tall, stoop-shouldered man about forty. His bald head, perched on a long neck with an enormous Adam's apple, looks like an egg. The tropics have tanned his naturally pasty face with its small, sharp features to a sickly yellow, and native rum has painted his pointed nose to a startling red. His little, washy-blue eyes are red-rimmed and dart about him like a ferret's. His expression is one of unscrupulous meanness, cowardly and dangerous. He is dressed in a worn riding suit of dirty white drill, puttees, spurs, and wears a white cork helmet. A cartridge belt with an automatic revolver is around his waist. He carries a riding whip in his hand. He sees the* WOMAN *and stops to watch her suspiciously. Then, making up his mind, he steps quickly on tiptoe into the room. The* WOMAN, *looking back over her shoulder continually, does not see him until it is too late. When she does* SMITHERS *springs forward and grabs her firmly by the shoulder. She struggles to get away, fiercely but silently.*

SMITHERS (*tightening his grasp—roughly*)   Easy! None o' that, me birdie. You can't wriggle out, now I got me ooks on yer.

WOMAN (*seeing the uselessness of struggling, gives way to frantic terror, and sinks to the ground, embracing his knees supplicatingly*)   No tell him! No tell him, mister!

SMITHERS (*with great curiosity*)   Tell 'im? (*Then scornfully*) Oh, you mean 'is bloomin' Majesty. What's the gaime, any'ow? What are you sneakin' away for? Been stealin' a bit, I s'pose. (*He taps her bundle with his riding whip significantly*)

WOMAN (*shaking her head vehemently*)   No, me no steal.

SMITHERS   Bloody liar! But tell me what's up. There's somethin' funny goin' on. I smelled it in the air first thing I got up this mornin'. You blacks are up to some devilment. This palace of 'is is like a bleedin' tomb. Where's all the 'ands?

> The woman keeps sullenly silent. SMITHERS *raises his whip threateningly*

Ow, yer won't, won't yer? I'll show yer what's what.

WOMAN (*coweringly*)   I tell, mister. You no hit. They go—all go. (*She makes a sweeping gesture toward the hills in the distance*)

SMITHERS   Run away—to the 'ills?

WOMAN   Yes, mister. Him Emperor—Great Father. (*She touches her forehead to the floor with a quick mechanical jerk*) Him sleep after eat. Then they go—all go. Me old woman. Me left only. Now me go too.

SMITHERS (*his astonishment giving way to an immense, mean satisfaction*)   Ow! So that's the ticket! Well, I know bloody well wot's in the air—when they runs orf to the 'ills. The tom-tom'll be thumpin' out there bloomin' soon. (*With extreme vindictiveness*) And I'm bloody glad of it, for one! Serve 'im right! Puttin' on airs, the stinkin' nigger! 'Is Majesty! Gawd blimey! I only 'opes I'm there when they takes 'im out to shoot 'im. (*Suddenly*) 'E's still 'ere all right, ain't 'e?

WOMAN   Him sleep.

SMITHERS   'E's bound to find out soon as 'e wakes up. 'E's cunnin' enough to know when 'is time's come.

> He goes to the doorway on the right and whistles shrilly with his fingers in his mouth. The old woman springs to her feet and runs out of the doorway at the rear. SMITHERS *goes after her, reaching for his revolver*

Stop or I'll shoot! (*Then, stopping—indifferently*) Pop orf, then, if yer like, yer black cow. (*He stands in the doorway, looking after her*)

> JONES *enters from the right. He is a tall, powerfully built, full-blooded Negro of middle age. His features are typically negroid, yet there is something decidedly distinctive about his face—an underlying strength of will, a hardy, self-reliant confidence in himself that inspires respect. His eyes are alive with a keen, cunning intelligence. In manner he is shrewd, suspicious, evasive. He wears a light-blue uniform coat sprayed with brass buttons, heavy gold chevrons on his shoulders, gold braid on the collar, cuffs, etc. His pants are bright-red with a light-blue stripe down the side. Patent-leather laced boots with brass spurs, and a belt with a long-barreled, pearl-handled revolver in a holster complete his make-up. Yet there is something not altogether ridiculous about his grandeur. He has a way of carrying it off*

JONES (*not seeing anyone—greatly irritated and blinking sleepily—shouts*) Who dare whistle dat way in my palace? Who dare wake up de Emperor? I'll git de hide frayled off some o' you niggers sho'!

SMITHERS (*showing himself—in a manner half afraid and half defiant*) It was me whistled to yer. (*As* JONES *frowns angrily*) I got news for yer.

JONES (*putting on his suavest manner, which fails to cover up his contempt for the white man*) Oh, it's you, Mr. Smithers. (*He sits down on his throne with easy dignity*) What news you got to tell me?

SMITHERS (*coming close to enjoy his discomfiture*) Don't yer notice nothin' funny today?

JONES (*coldly*) Funny? No. I ain't perceived nothin' of de kind!

SMITHERS Then yer ain't so foxy as I thought yer was. Where's all your court?—(*sarcastically*)—the Generals and the Cabinet Ministers and all?

JONES (*imperturbably*) Where dey mostly runs to minute I closes my eyes—drinkin' rum and talkin' big down in de town. (*Sarcastically*) How come you don't know dat? Ain't you sousin' with 'em most every day?

SMITHERS (*stung, but pretending indifference—with a wink*) That's part of the day's work. I got ter—ain't I—in my business?

JONES (*contemptuously*) Yo' business!

SMITHERS (*imprudently enraged*) Gawd blimey, you was glad enough for me ter take yer in on it when you landed here first. You didn' 'ave no 'igh and mighty airs in them days!

JONES (*his hand going to his revolver like a flash—menacingly*) Talk polite, white man! Talk polite, you heah me! I'm boss heah now, is you fergettin'?
> The Cockney seems about to challenge this last statement with the facts, but something in the other's eyes holds and cows him

SMITHERS (*in a cowardly whine*) No 'arm meant, old top.

JONES (*condescendingly*) I accepts yo' apology. (*Lets his hand fall from his revolver*) No use'n you rakin' up ole times. What I was den is one thing. What I is now's another. You didn't let me in on yo' crooked work out o' no kind feelin's dat time. I done de dirty work fo' you—and most o' de brainwork, too, fo' dat matter—and I was wu'th money to you, dat's de reason.

SMITHERS Well, blimey, I give yer a start, didn't I?—when no one else would. I wasn't afraid to 'ire you like the rest was—'count of the story about your breakin' jail back in the States.

JONES No, you didn't have no 'scuse to look down on me fo' dat. You been in jail you'self more'n once.

SMITHERS (*furiously*) It's a lie! (*Then trying to pass it off by an attempt at scorn*) Garn! Who told yer that fairy tale?

JONES Dey's some tings I ain't got to be tole. I kin see 'em in folks' eyes. (*Then after a pause—meditatively*) Yes, you sho' give me a start. And it didn't take long from dat time to git dese fool woods' niggers right where I wanted dem. (*With pride*) From stowaway to Emperor in two years! Dat's goin' some!

SMITHERS (*with curiosity*)   And I bet you got yer pile o' money 'id safe some place.

JONES (*with satisfaction*)   I sho' has! And it's in a foreign bank where no pusson don't ever git it out but me no matter what come. You didn't s'pose I was holdin' down dis Emperor job for de glory in it, did you? Sho'! De fuss and glory part of it, dat's only to turn de heads o' de low-flung bush niggers dat's here. Dey wants de big circus show for deir money. I gives it to 'em an' I gits de money. (*With a grin*) De long green, dat's me every time! (*Then rebukingly*) But you ain't got no kick agin me, Smithers. I'se paid you back all you done for me many times. Ain't I pertected you and winked at all de crooked tradin' you been doin' right out in de broad day? Sho' I has—and me makin' laws to stop it at de same time! (*He chuckles*)

SMITHERS (*grinning*)   But, meanin' no 'arm, you been grabbin' right and left yourself, ain't yer? Look at the taxes you've put on 'em! Blimey! You've squeezed 'em dry!

JONES (*chuckling*)   No, dey ain't *all* dry yet. I'se still heah, ain't I?

SMITHERS (*smiling at his secret thought*)   They're dry right now, you'll find out. (*Changing the subject abruptly*) And as for me breakin' laws, you've broke 'em all yerself just as fast as yer made 'em.

JONES   Ain't I de Emperor? De laws don't go for him. (*Judicially*) You heah what I tells you, Smithers. Dere's little stealin' like you does, and dere's big stealin' like I does. For de little stealin' dey gits you in jail soon or late. For de big stealin' dey makes you Emperor and puts you in de Hall o' Fame when you croaks. (*Reminiscently*) If dey's one thing I learns in ten years on de Pullman ca's listenin' to de white quality talk, it's dat same fact. And when I gits a chance to use it I winds up Emperor in two years.

SMITHERS (*unable to repress the genuine admiration of the small fry for the large*)   Yes, yer turned the bleedin' trick, all right. Blimey, I never seen a bloke 'as 'ad the bloomin' luck you 'as.

JONES (*severely*)   Luck? What you mean—luck?

SMITHERS   I suppose you'll say as that swank about the silver bullet ain't luck—and that was what first got the fool blacks on yer side the time of the revolution, wasn't it?

JONES (*with a laugh*)   Oh, dat silver bullet! Sho' was luck! But I makes dat luck, you heah? I loads de dice! Yessuh! When dat murderin' nigger ole Lem hired to kill me takes aim ten feet away and his gun misses fire and I shoots him dead, what you heah me say?

SMITHERS   You said yer'd got a charm so's no lead bullet'd kill yer. You was so strong only a silver bullet could kill yer, you told 'em. Blimey, wasn't that swank for yer—and plain, fat-'eaded luck?

JONES (*proudly*)   I got brains and I uses 'em quick. Dat ain't luck.

SMITHERS   Yer know they wasn't 'ardly liable to get no silver bullets. And it was luck 'e didn't 'it you that time.

JONES (*laughing*)   And dere all dem fool bush niggers was kneelin' down and bumpin' deir heads on de ground like I was a miracle out o' de Bible. Oh Lawd, from dat time on I has dem all eatin' out of my hand. I cracks de whip and dey jumps through.

SMITHERS (*with a sniff*)   Yankee bluff done it.

JONES   Ain't a man's talkin' big what makes him big—long as he makes folks believe it? Sho', I talks large when I ain't got nothin' to back it up, but I ain't talkin' wild just de same. I knows I kin fool 'em—I *knows* it—and dat's backin' enough fo' my game. And ain't I got to learn deir lingo and teach some of dem English befo' I kin talk to 'em? Ain't dat wuk? You ain't never learned ary word er it, Smithers, in de ten years you been heah, dough you knows it's money in yo' pocket tradin' wid 'em if you does. But you'se too shiftless to take de trouble.

SMITHERS (*flushing*)   Never mind about me. What's this I've 'eard about yer really 'avin' a silver bullet molded for yourself.

JONES   It's playin' out my bluff. I has de silver bullet molded and I tells 'em when de times comes I kills myself wid it. I tells 'em dat's 'cause I'm de on'y man in de world big enuff to git me. No use'n deir tryin'. And dey falls down and bumps deir heads. (*He laughs*) I does dat so's I kin take a walk in peace widout no jealous nigger gunnin' at me from behind de trees.

SMITHERS (*astonished*)   Then you 'ad it made—'onest?

JONES   Sho' did. Heah she be. (*He takes out his revolver, breaks it, and takes the silver bullet out of one chamber*) Five lead an' dis silver baby at de last. Don't she shine pretty? (*He holds it in his hand, looking at it admiringly, as if strangely fascinated*)

SMITHERS   Let me see. (*Reaches out his hand for it*)

JONES (*harshly*)   Keep yo' hands whar dey b'long, white man. (*He replaces it in the chamber and puts the revolver back on his hip*)

SMITHERS (*snarling*)   Gawd blimey! Think I'm a bleedin' thief, you would.

JONES   No, 'tain't dat. I knows you'se scared to steal from me. On'y I ain't 'lowin' nary body to touch dis baby. She's my rabbit's foot.

SMITHERS (*sneering*)   A bloomin' charm, wot? (*Venomously*) Well, you'll need all the bloody charms you 'as before long, s' 'elp me!

JONES (*judicially*)   Oh, I'se good for six months yit 'fore dey gits sick o' my game. Den, when I sees trouble comin', I makes my getaway.

SMITHERS   Ho! You got it all planned, ain't yer?

JONES   I ain't no fool. I knows dis Emperor's time is sho't. Dat why I make hay when de sun shine. Was you thinkin' I'se aimin' to hold down dis job for life? No, suh! What good is gittin' money if you stays back in dis raggedy country? I wants action when I spends. And when I sees dese niggers gittin' up deir nerve to tu'n me out, and I'se got all de money in sight, I resigns on de spot and beats it quick.

SMITHERS   Where to?

JONES   None o' yo' business.

SMITHERS   Not back to the bloody States, I'll lay my oath.

JONES (*suspiciously*)   Why don't I? (*Then with an easy laugh*) You mean 'count of dat story 'bout me breakin' from jail back dere? Dat's all talk.

SMITHERS (*skeptically*)   Ho, yes!

JONES (*sharply*)   You ain't 'sinuatin' I'se a liar, is you?

SMITHERS (*hastily*)   No, Gawd strike me! I was only thinkin' o' the bloody lies you told the blacks 'ere about killin' white men in the States.

JONES (*angered*)   How come dey're lies?

SMITHERS   You'd 'ave been in jail if you 'ad, wouldn't yer then? (*With venom*) And from what I've 'eard, it ain't 'ealthy for a black to kill a white man in the States. They burns 'em in oil, don't they?

JONES (*with cool deadliness*)   You mean lynchin' 'd scare me? Well, I tells you, Smithers, maybe I does kill one white man back dere. Maybe I does. And maybe I kills another right heah 'fore long if he don't look out.

SMITHERS (*trying to force a laugh*)   I was on'y spoofin' yer. Can't yer take a joke? And you was just sayin' you'd never been in jail.

JONES (*in the same tone—slightly boastful*)   Maybe I goes to jail dere for gettin' in an argument wid razors ovah a crap game. Maybe I gits twenty years when dat colored man die. Maybe I gits in 'nother argument wid de prison guard was overseer ovah us when we're wukin' de road. Maybe he hits me wid a whip and I splits his head wid a shovel and runs away and files de chain off my leg and gits away safe. Maybe I does all dat an' maybe I don't. It's a story I tells you so's you knows I'se de kind of man dat if you evah repeats one word of it, I ends yo' stealin' on dis yearth mighty damn quick!

SMITHERS (*terrified*)   Think I'd peach on yer? Not me! Ain't I always been yer friend?

JONES (*suddenly relaxing*)   Sho' you has—and you better be.

SMITHERS (*recovering his composure—and with it his malice*)   And just to show yer I'm yer friend, I'll tell yer that bit o' news I was going' to.

JONES   Go ahead! Shoot de piece. Must be bad news from de happy way you look.

SMITHERS (*warningly*)   Maybe it's gettin' time for you to resign—with that bloomin' silver bullet, wot? (*He finishes with a mocking grin*)

JONES (*puzzled*)   What's dat you say? Talk plain.

SMITHERS   Ain't noticed any of the guards or servants about the place today, I 'aven't.

JONES (*carelessly*)   Dey're all out in de garden sleepin' under de trees. When I sleeps, dey sneaks a sleep too, and I pretends I never suspicions it. All I got to do is to ring de bell and dey come flyin', makin' a bluff dey was wukin' all de time.

SMITHERS (*in the same mocking tone*)   Ring the bell now an' you'll bloody well see what I means.

JONES (*startled to alertness, but preserving the same careless tone*)   Sho' I rings. (*He reaches below the throne and pulls out a big, common dinner bell which is painted the same vivid scarlet as the throne. He rings this vigorously—then stops to listen. Then he goes to both doors, rings again, and looks out*)

SMITHERS (*watching him with malicious satisfaction, after a pause—mockingly*)   The bloody ship is sinkin' an' the bleedin' rats 'as slung their 'ooks.

JONES (*in a sudden fit of anger flings the bell clattering into a corner*)   Low-flung woods' niggers! (*Then catching SMITHERS' eye on him, he controls himself and suddenly bursts into a low chuckling laugh*)   Reckon I overplays my hand dis once! A man can't take de pot on a bobtailed flush all de time. Was I sayin' I'd sit in six months mo'? Well, I'se changed my mind den. I cashes in and resigns de job of Emperor right dis minute.

SMITHERS (*with real admiration*)   Blimey, but you're a cool bird, and no mistake.

JONES   No use'n fussin'. When I knows de game's up I kisses it good-by widout no long waits. Dey've all run off to de hills, ain't dey?

SMITHERS   Yes—every bleedin' man jack of 'em.

JONES   Den de revolution is at de post. And de Emperor better git his feet smokin' up de trail. (*He starts for the door in the rear*)

SMITHERS   Goin' out to look for your 'orse? Yer won't find any. They steals the 'orses first thing. Mine was gone when I went for 'im this mornin'. That's wot first give me a suspicion of wot was up.

JONES (*alarmed for a second, scratches his head, then, philosophically*)   Well, den I hoofs it. Feet, do yo' duty! (*He pulls out a gold watch and looks at it*) Three-thuty. Sundown's at six-thuty or dereabouts. (*Puts his watch back—with cool confidence*) I got plenty o' time to make it easy.

SMITHERS   Don't be so bloomin' sure of it. They'll be after you 'ot and 'eavy. Ole Lem is at the bottom o' this business an' 'e 'ates you like 'ell. 'E'd rather do for you than eat 'is dinner, 'e would!

JONES (*scornfully*)   Dat fool no-count nigger! Does you think I'se scared o' him? I stands him on his thick head more'n once befo' dis, and I does it again if he comes in my way— (*Fiercely*) And dis time I leave him a dead nigger fo' sho'!

SMITHERS   You'll 'ave to cut through the big forest—an' these blacks 'ere can sniff and follow a trail in the dark like 'ounds. You'd 'ave to 'ustle to get through that forest in twelve hours even if you knew all the bloomin' trails like a native.

JONES (*with indignant scorn*)   Look-a-heah, white man! Does you think I'se a natural bo'n fool? Give me credit fo' havin' some sense, fo' Lawd's sake! Don't you s'pose I'se looked ahead and made sho' of all de chances? I'se gone out in dat big forest, pretendin' to hunt, so many times dat I knows it high an' low like a book. I could go through dem trails wid my eyes shut. (*With great contempt*) Think dese ign'rent bush niggers dat ain't got brains enuff to know deir own names even can catch Brutus Jones? Huh, I s'pects not! Not on yo' life! Why, man, de white men went after me wid bloodhounds where I come from an' I jes' laughs at 'em. It's a shame to fool dese black trash around heah, dey're so easy. You watch me, man. I'll make dem look sick, I will. I'll be 'cross de plain to de edge of de forest by time dark comes. Once in de woods in de night, dey got a swell chance o' findin' dis baby! Dawn tomorrow I'll be out at de oder side and on de coast whar dat French gunboat is stayin'. She picks me up, takes me to Martinique when she go dar, and dere I is safe wid a mighty big bank roll in my jeans. It's easy as rollin' off a log.

SMITHERS (*maliciously*)   But s'posin somethin' 'appens wrong an' they do nab yer?

JONES (*decisively*)   Dey don't—dat's de answer.

SMITHERS   But, just for argyment's sake—what'd you do?

JONES (*frowning*)   I'se got five lead bullets in dis gun good enuff fo' common bush niggers—and after dat I got de silver bullet left to cheat 'em out o' gittin' me.

SMITHERS (*jeeringly*)   Ho, I was fergettin' that silver bullet. You'll bump yourself orf in style, won't yer? Blimey!

JONES (*gloomily*)   You kin bet yo' whole roll on one thing, white man. Dis baby plays out his string to de end and when he quits, he quits wid a bang de way he ought. Silver bullet ain't none too good for him when he go, dat's a fac'! (*Then, shaking off his nervousness—with a confident laugh*) Sho'! What is I talkin' about? Ain't come to dat yit and I never will—not wid trash niggers like dese yere. (*Boastfully*) Silver bullet bring me luck anyway. I kin outguess, outrun, outfight, an' outplay de whole lot o' dem all ovah de board any time o' de day er night! You watch me!

> From the distant hills comes the faint, steady thump of a tom-tom, low and vibrating. It starts at a rate exactly corresponding to normal pulse beat—72 to the minute—and continues at a gradually accelerating rate from this point uninterruptedly to the very end of the play

JONES (*starts at the sound; a strange look of apprehension creeps into his face for a moment as he listens; then he asks, with an attempt to regain his most casual manner*)   What's dat drum beatin' fo'?

SMITHERS (*with a mean grin*)   For you. That means the bleedin' ceremoney 'as started. I've 'eard it before and I knows.

JONES   Cer'money? What cer'money?

SMITHERS   The blacks is 'oldin' a bloody meetin', 'avin' a war dance, gettin' their courage worked up b'fore they starts after you.

JONES   Let dem! Dey'll sho' need it!

SMITHERS   And they're there 'oldin' their 'eathen religious service— makin' no end of devil spells and charms to 'elp 'em against your silver bullet. (*He guffaws loudly*) Blimey, but they're balmy as 'ell!

JONES (*a tiny bit awed and shaken in spite of himself*)   Huh! Takes more'n dat to scare dis chicken!

SMITHERS (*scenting the other's feeling—maliciously*)   Ternight when it's pitch-black in the forest, they'll 'ave their pet devils and ghosts 'oundin' after you. You'll find yer bloody 'air'll be standin' on end before termorrow mornin'. (*Seriously*) It's a bleedin' queer place, that stinkin' forest, even in daylight. Yer don't know what might 'appen in there, it's that rotten still. Always sends the cold shivers down my back minute I gets in it.

JONES (*with a contemptuous sniff*)   I ain't no chickenliver like you is. Trees an' me, we'se friends, and dar's a full moon comin' bring me light. And let dem po' niggers make all de fool spells dey'se a min' to. Does yo' s'pect I'se silly enuff to b'lieve in ghosts an' ha'nts an' all dat ole woman's talk? G'long, white man! You ain't talkin' to me. (*With a chuckle*) Doesn't you know dey's got to do wid a man was member in good standin' o' de Baptist Church? Sho' I was dat when I was porter on de Pullmans, befo' I gits into my little trouble. Let dem try deir heathen tricks. De Baptist Church done pertect me and land dem all in hell. (*Then with more confident satisfaction*) And I'se got little silver bullet o' my own, don't forgit!

SMITHERS   Ho! You 'aven't give much 'eed to your Baptist Church since you been down 'ere. I've 'eard myself you 'ad turned yer coat an' was takin' up with their blarsted witch doctors, or whatever the 'ell yer calls the swine.

JONES (*vehemently*)   I pretends to! Sho' I pretends! Dat's part o' my game from de fust. If I finds out dem niggers believes dat black is white, den I yells it out louder'n deir loudest. It don't git me nothin' to do missionary work for de Baptist Church. I'se after de coin, an' I lays my Jesus on de shelf for de time bein'. (*Stops abruptly to look at his watch—alertly*) But I ain't got de time to waste on no more fool talk wid you. I'se gwine away from heah dis secon'. (*He reaches in under the throne and pulls out an expensive panama hat with a bright multicolored band and sets it jauntily on his head*) So long, white man! (*With a grin*) See you in jail sometime, maybe!

SMITHERS   Not me, you won't. Well, I wouldn't be in yer bloody boots for no bloomin' money, but 'ere's wishin' yer luck just the same.

JONES (*contemptuously*)   You're de frightenedest man evah I see! I tells you I'se safe's 'f I was in New York City. It takes dem niggers from now to dark to git up de nerve to start somethin'. By dat time, I'se got a head start dey never kotch up wid.

SMITHERS (*maliciously*)   Give my regards to any ghosts yer meets up with.

JONES (*grinning*)   If dat ghost got money, I'll tell him never ha'nt you less'n he wants to lose it.

SMITHERS (*flattered*)   Garn! (*Then curiously*) Ain't yer takin' no luggage with yer?

JONES   I travels light when I wants to move fast. And I got tinned grub buried on de edge o' de forest. (*Boastfully*) Now say dat I don't look ahead an' use my brains! (*With a wide, liberal gesture*) I will all dat's left in de palace to you—and you better grab all you kin sneak away wid befo' dey gits here.

SMITHERS (*gratefully*)   Righto—and thanks ter yer. (*As* JONES *walks toward the door in the rear—cautioningly*) Say! Look 'ere, you ain't goin' out that way, are yer?

JONES   Does you think I'd slink out de back door like a common nigger? I'se Emperor yit, ain't I? And de Emperor Jones leaves de way he comes, and dat black trash don't dare stop him—not yit, leastways. (*He stops for a moment in the doorway, listening to the far-off but insistent beat of the tom-tom*) Listen to dat roll call, will you? Must be mighty big drum carry dat far. (*Then with a laugh*) Well, if dey ain't no whole brass band to see me off, I sho' got de drum part of it. So long, white man. (*He puts his hands in his pockets and with studied carelessness, whistling a tune, he saunters out of the doorway and off to the left*)

SMITHERS (*looks after him with a puzzled admiration*)   'E's got 'is bloomin' nerve with 'im, s'elp me! (*Then angrily*) Ho—the bleedin' nigger— puttin' on 'is bloody airs! I 'opes they nabs 'im an' gives 'im what's what!

Scene Two

The end of the plain where the Great Forest begins. The foreground is sandy, level ground dotted by a few stones and clumps of stunted bushes cowering close against the earth to escape the buffeting of the trade wind. In the rear the forest is a wall of darkness dividing the world. Only when the eye becomes accustomed to the gloom can the outlines of separate trunks of the nearest trees be made out, enormous pillars of deeper blackness. A somber monotone of wind lost in the leaves moans in the air. Yet this sound serves but to intensify the impression of the forest's relentless immobility, to form a background throwing into relief its brooding, implacable silence.

JONES enters from the left, walking rapidly. He stops as he nears the edge of the forest, looks around him quickly, peering into the dark as if searching for some familiar landmark. Then, apparently satisfied that he is where he ought to be, he throws himself on the ground, dog-tired.

JONES   Well, heah I is. In de nick o' time, too! Little mo' an' it'd be blacker'n de ace of spades heahabouts. (*He pulls a bandanna handkerchief from his hip pocket and mops off his perspiring face*) Sho'! Gimme air! I'se tuckered out sho' 'nuff. Dat soft Emperor job ain't no trainin' fo' a long hike ovah dat plain in de brilin' sun. (*Then with a chuckle*) Cheer up, nigger, de worst is yet to come. (*He lifts his head and stares at the forest. His chuckle peters out abruptly. In a tone of awe*) My goodness, look at dem woods, will you? Dat no-count Smithers said dey'd be black an' he sho' called de turn. (*Turning away from them quickly and looking down at his feet, he snatches at a chance to change the subject—solicitously*) Feet, you is holdin' up yo' end fine an' I sutinly hopes you ain't blisterin' none. It's time you git a rest. (*He takes off his shoes, his eyes studiously avoiding the forest. He feels the soles of his feet gingerly*) You is still in de pink—on'y a little mite feverish. Cool yo'selfs. Remember you done got a long journey yit befo' you. (*He sits in a weary attitude, listening to the rhythmic beating of the tom-tom. He grumbles in a loud tone to cover up a growing uneasiness*) Bush niggers! Wonder dey wouldn't git sick o' beatin' dat drum. Sound louder, seem like. I wonder if dey's startin' after me? (*He scrambles to his feet, looking back across the plain*) Couldn't see dem now, nohow, if dey was hundred feet away. (*Then, shaking himself like a wet dog to get rid of these depressing thoughts*) Sho', dey's miles an' miles behind. What you gittin' fidgety about? (*But he sits down and begins to lace up his shoes in great haste, all the time muttering reassuringly*) You know what? Yo' belly is empty, dat's what's de matter wid you. Come time to eat! Wid nothin' but wind on yo' stumach, o' course you feels jiggedy. Well, we eats right heah an' now soon's I gits dese pesky shoes laced up. (*He finishes lacing up his shoes*) Dere! Now le's see! (*Gets on his hands and knees and searches the ground around him with his eyes*) White stone, white stone, where is you? (*He sees the first white stone and crawls to it—with satisfaction*) Heah you is! I knowed dis was de right place. Box of grub, come to me. (*He turns over the stone and feels in under it—in a tone of dismay*) Ain't heah! Gorry, is I in de right place or isn't I? Dere's 'nother stone. Guess dat's it. (*He scrambles to the next stone and turns it over*) Ain't heah, neither! Grub, whar is you? Ain't heah. Gorry, has I got to go hungry into dem woods—all de night? (*While he is talking he scrambles from one stone to another, turning them over in frantic haste. Finally, he jumps to his feet excitedly*) Is I lost de place? Must have! But how dat happen when I was followin' de trail across de plain in broad daylight? (*Almost plaintively*) I'se hungry, I is! I gotta git my feed. Whar's my strength gonna come from if I doesn't? Gorry, I gotta find dat grub high an' low somehow! Why it come dark so quick like dat? Can't see nothin'. (*He scratches a match on his trousers and peers about him. The rate of the beat of the far-off tom-tom increases perceptibly as he does so. He mutters in a bewildered voice*) How come all dese white stones come heah when I only remembers one? (*Suddenly, with a frightened gasp, he flings the match on the ground and stamps on it*) Nigger, is you gone crazy mad? Is you lightin' matches to show dem whar you is? Fo' Lawd's sake, use yo' haid. Gorry, I'se got to be careful! (*He stares at the plain behind him apprehensively, his hand on his revolver*) But how come all dese white stones? And whar's dat tin box o' grub I hid all wrapped up in oilcloth?

While his back is turned, the LITTLE FORMLESS FEARS *creep out from the deeper blackness of the forest. They are black, shapeless, only their glittering little eyes can be seen. If they have any describable form at all it is that of a grubworm about the size of a creeping child. They move noiselessly, but with deliberate, painful effort, striving to raise themselves on end, failing and sinking prone again.* JONES *turns about to face the forest. He stares up at the trees, seeking vainly to discover his whereabouts by their conformation*

Can't tell nothin' from dem trees! Gorry, nothin' 'round heah looks like I evah seed it befo'. I'se done lost de place sho' 'nuff! (*With mournful foreboding*) It's mighty queer! It's mighty queer! (*With sudden forced defiance—in an angry tone*) Woods, is you tryin' to put somethin' ovah on me?

From the FORMLESS CREATURES *on the ground in front of him comes a tiny gale of low mocking laughter like a rustling of leaves. They squirm upward toward him in twisted attitudes.* JONES *looks down, leaps backward with a yell of terror, yanking out his revolver as he does so—in a quavering voice*

What's dat? Who's dar? What is you? Git away from me befo' I shoots you up! You don't?—

He fires. There is a flash, a loud report, then silence broken only by the far-off, quickened throb of the tom-tom. The FORMLESS CREATURES *have scurried back into the forest.* JONES *remains fixed in his position, listening intently. The sound of the shot, the reassuring feel of the revolver in his hand, have somewhat restored his shaken nerve. He addresses himself with renewed confidence*

Dey're gone. Dat shot fix 'em. Dey was only little animals—little wild pigs, I reckon. Dey've maybe rooted out yo' grub an' eat it. Sho', you fool nigger, what you think dey is—ha'nts? (*Excitedly*) Gorry, you give de game away when you fire dat shot. Dem niggers heah dat fo' sutin! Time you beat it in de woods widout no long waits. (*He starts for the forest—hesitates before the plunge—then urging himself in with manful resolution*) Git in, nigger! What you skeered at? Ain't nothin' dere but de trees! Git in! (*He plunges boldly into the forest*)

Scene Three

In the forest. The moon has just risen. Its beams, drifting through the canopy of leaves, make a barely perceptible, suffused, eerie glow. A dense low wall of underbrush and creepers is in the nearer foreground, fencing in a small triangular clearing. Beyond this is the massed blackness of the forest like an encompassing barrier. A path is dimly discerned leading down to the clearing from the left rear, and winding away from it again toward the right. As the scene opens nothing can be distinctly made out. Except for the beating of the tom-tom, which is a trifle louder and quicker than at the close of the previous scene, there is silence, broken every few seconds by a queer, clicking sound. Then gradually the figure of the Negro JEFF *can be discerned crouching on his haunches at the rear of the triangle. He is middle-aged, thin, brown in color, is dressed in a Pullman porter's uniform and cap. He is throwing a pair of dice on the ground before him, picking them up, shaking them, casting them out, with the regular, rigid, mechanical movements of an automaton. The heavy, plodding footsteps of someone approaching along the trail from the left are heard and* JONES' *voice, pitched on a slightly higher key and strained in a cheery effort to overcome its own tremors.*

JONES   De moon's rizen. Does you heah dat, nigger? You gits more light from dis out. No mo' buttin' yo' fool head agin de trunks an' scratchin' de hide off yo' legs in de bushes. Now you sees whar yo'se gwine. So cheer up! From now on you has a snap. (*He steps just to the rear of the triangular clearing and mops off his face on his sleeve. He has lost his panama hat. His face is scratched, his brilliant uniform shows several large rents*) What time's it gittin' to be, I wonder? I dassent light no match to find out. Phoo'. It's wa'm an' dat's a fac'! (*Wearily*) How long I been makin' tracks in dese woods? Must be hours an' hours. Seems like fo'evah! Yit can't be, when de moon's jes' riz. Dis am a long night fo' yo', yo' Majesty! (*With a mournful chuckle*) Majesty! Der ain't much majesty 'bout dis baby now. (*With attempted cheerfulness*) Never min'. It's all part o' de game. Dis night come to an end like everything else. And when you gits dar safe and has dat bankroll in yo' hands you laughs at all dis. (*He starts to whistle, but checks himself abruptly*) What yo' whistlin' for, you po' dope! Want all de worl' to heah you? (*He stops talking to listen*) Heah dat ole drum! Sho' gits nearer from de sound. Dey's packin' it along wid 'em. Time fo' me to move. (*He takes a step forward, then stops—worriedly*) What's dat odder queer clickety sound I heah? Dere it is! Sound close! Sound like— Sound like— Fo' God sake, sound like some nigger was shootin' crap! (*Frightenedly*) I better beat it quick when I gits dem notions. (*He walks quickly into the clear space—then stands transfixed as he sees* JEFF—*in a terrified gasp*) Who dar? Who dat? Is dat you, Jeff? (*Starting toward the other, forgetful for a moment of his surroundings and really believing it is a living man that he sees—in a tone of happy relief*) Jeff! I'se sho' mighty glad to see you! Dey tol' me you done died from dat razor cut I gives you. (*Stopping suddenly, bewilderedly*) But how you come to be heah, nigger? (*He stares fascinatedly at the other, who continues his mechanical play with the dice.* JONES' *eyes begin to roll wildly. He stutters*) Ain't you gwine—look up—can't you speak to me? Is you—is you—a ha'nt? (*He jerks out his revolver in a frenzy of terrified rage.*) Nigger, I kills you dead once. Has I got to kill you agin? You take it den. (*He fires. When the smoke clears away,* JEFF *has disappeared.* JONES *stands trem-*

bling—then with a certain reassurance) He's gone, anyway. Ha'nt or no ha'nt, dat shot fix him. (*The beat of the far-off tom-tom is perceptibly louder and more rapid.* JONES *becomes conscious of it—with a start, looking back, over his shoulder*) Dey's gittin' near! Dey's comin' fast! And heah I is shootin' shots to let 'em know jes' whar I is! Oh, Gorry, I'se got to run. (*Forgetting the path, he plunges wildly into the underbrush in the rear and disappears in the shadow*)

Scene Four

In the forest. A wide dirt road runs diagonally from the right front to the left rear. Rising sheer on both sides, the forest walls it in. The moon is now up. Under its light the road glimmers ghastly and unreal. It is as if the forest had stood aside momentarily to let the road pass through and accomplish its veiled purpose. This done, the forest will fold in upon itself again and the road will be no more. JONES *stumbles in from the forest on the right. His uniform is ragged and torn. He looks about him with numbed surprise when he sees the road, his eyes blinking in the bright moonlight. He flops down exhaustedly and pants heavily for a while. Then with sudden anger*

JONES   I'm meltin' wid heat! Runnin' an' runnin' an' runnin'! Damn dis heah coat! Like a strait jacket! (*He tears off his coat and flings it away from him, revealing himself stripped to the waist*) Dere! Dat's better! Now I kin breathe! (*Looking down at his feet, the spurs catch his eye*) And to hell wid dese high-fangled spurs. Dey're what's been a-trippin' me up an' breakin' my neck. (*He unstraps them and flings them away disgustedly*) Dere! I gits rid o' dem frippety Emperor trappin's an' I travels lighter. Lawd! I'se tired! (*After a pause, listening to the insistent beat of the tom-tom in the distance*) I must 'a' put some distance between myself an' dem—runnin' like dat—and yit—dat damn drum sounds jes' de same—nearer, even. Well, I guess I a'most holds my lead anyhow. Dey won't never catch up. (*With a sigh*) If on'y my fool legs stands up. Oh, I'se sorry I evah went in for dis. Dat Emperor job is sho' hard to shake. (*He looks around him suspiciously*) How'd dis road evah git heah? Good level road, too. I never remembers seein' it befo' (*Shaking his head apprehensively*) Dese woods is sho' full o' de queerest things at night. (*With a sudden terror*) Lawd God, don't let me see no more o' dem ha'nts! Dey gits my goat! (*Then, trying to talk himself into confidence*) Ha'nts! You fool nigger, dey ain't no such things. Don't de Baptist parson tell you dat many time? Is you civilized, or is you like dese ign'rent black niggers heah? Sho'! Dat was all in yo' own head. Wasn't nothin' dere. Wasn't no Jeff! Know what? You jes' get seein' dem things 'cause yo' belly's empty and you's sick wid hunger inside. Hunger 'fects yo' head and yo' eyes. Any fool know dat. (*Then, pleading fervently*) But bless God, I don't come across no more o' dem, whatever dey is! (*Then cautiously*) Rest! Don't talk! Rest! You needs it. Den you gits on yo' way again. (*Looking at the moon*) Night's half gone a'most. You hits de coast in de mawning! Den yo's all safe.

> *From the right forward a small gang of Negroes enter. They are dressed in striped convict suits, their heads are shaven, one leg drags limpingly, shackled to a heavy ball and chain. Some carry picks, the others shovels. They are followed by a white man dressed in the uniform of a* PRISON GUARD. *A Winchester rifle is slung across his shoulder and he carries a heavy whip. At a signal from the* GUARD *they stop on the road opposite where* JONES *is sitting.* JONES, *who has been staring up at the sky, unmindful of their noiseless approach, suddenly looks down and sees them. His eyes pop out, he tries to get to his feet and fly, but sinks back, too numbed by fright to move. His voice catches in a choking prayer*

Lawd Jesus!

> *The* PRISON GUARD *cracks his whip—noiselessly—and at that signal all the convicts start to work on the road. They swing their picks, they shovel, but not a sound comes from their labor. Their movements, like those of* JEFF *in the preceding scene, are those of automatons—rigid, slow, and mechanical. The* PRISON GUARD *points sternly at* JONES *with his whip, motions him to take his place among the other shovelers.* JONES *gets to his feet in a hypnotized stupor. He mumbles subserviently)*

Yes, suh! Yes, suh! I'se comin'. (*As he shuffles, dragging one foot, over to his place, he curses under his breath with rage and hatred*) God damn yo' soul, I gits even wid you yit, some time.

> *As if there were a shovel in his hands he goes through weary, mechanical gestures of digging up dirt, and throwing it to the roadside. Suddenly the* GUARD *approaches him angrily, threateningly. He raises his whip and lashes* JONES *viciously across the shoulders with it.* JONES *winces with pain and cowers abjectly. The* GUARD *turns his back on him and walks away contemptuously. Instantly* JONES *straightens up. With arms upraised as if his shovel were a club in his hands, he springs murderously at the unsuspecting* GUARD. *In the act of crashing down his shovel on the white man's skull,* JONES *suddenly becomes aware that his hands are empty. He cries despairingly*

Whar's my shovel? Gimme my shovel 'til I splits his damn head! (*Appealing to his fellow convicts*) Gimme a shovel, one o' you, fo' God sake!

> *They stand fixed in motionless attitudes, their eyes on the ground. The* GUARD *seems to wait expectantly, his back turned to the attacker.* JONES *bellows with baffled, terrified rage, tugging frantically at his revolver*

I kills you, you white debil, if it's de last thing I evah does! Ghost or debil, I kill you agin!

> *He frees the revolver and fires point-blank at the* GUARD's *back. Instantly the walls of the forest close in from both sides, the road and the figures of the convict gang are blotted out in an enshrouding darkness. The only sounds are a crashing in the underbrush as* JONES *leaps away in mad flight and the throbbing of the tom-tom, still far distant, but increased in volume of sound and rapidity of beat*

Scene Five

A large circular clearing, enclosed by the serried ranks of gigantic trunks of tall trees whose tops are lost to view. In the center is a big dead stump worn by time into a curious resemblance to an auction block. The moon floods the clearing with a clear light. JONES *forces his way through the forest on the left. He looks wildly about the clearing with hunted, fearful glances. His pants are in tatters, his shoes cut and misshapen, flapping about his feet. He slinks cautiously to the stump in the center and sits down in a tense position, ready for instant flight. Then he holds his head in his hands and rocks back and forth, moaning to himself miserably.*

JONES   Oh, Lawd, Lawd! Oh, Lawd, Lawd! (*Suddenly he throws himself on his knees and raises his clasped hands to the sky—in a voice of agonized pleading*) Lawd Jesus, heah my prayer! I'se a po' sinner, a po' sinner! I knows I done wrong, I knows it! When I cotches Jeff cheatin' wid loaded dice my anger overcomes me and I kills him dead! Lawd, I done wrong! When dat guard hits me wid de whip, my anger overcomes me, and I kills him dead. Lawd, I done wrong! And down heah whar dese fool bush niggers raises me up to de seat o' de mighty, I steals all I could grab. Lawd, I done wrong! I knows it! I'se sorry! Forgive me, Lawd! Forgive dis po' sinner! (*Then, beseeching terrifiedly*) And keep dem away, Lawd! Keep dem away from me! And stop dat drum soundin' in my ears! Dat begin to sound ha'nted, too. (*He gets to his feet, evidently slightly reassured by his prayer—with attempted confidence*) De Lawd'll preserve me from dem ha'nts after dis. (*Sits down on the stump again*) I ain't skeered o' real men. Let dem come. But dem odders— (*He shudders—then looks down at his feet, working his toes inside the shoes—with a groan*) Oh, my po' feet! Dem shoes ain't no use no more 'ceptin' to hurt. I'se better off widout dem. (*He unlaces them and pulls them off—holds the wrecks of the shoes in his hands and regards them mournfully*) You was real, A-one patin' leather, too. Look at you now. Emperor, you'se gittin' mighty low!

> *He sighs dejectedly and remains with bowed shoulders, staring down at the shoes in his hands as if reluctant to throw them away. While his attention is thus occupied, a crowd of figures silently enter the*

clearing from all sides. All are dressed in Southern costumes of the period of the 1850's. There are middle-aged men who are evidently well-to-do PLANTERS. *There is one spruce, authoritative individual—the* AUCTIONEER. *There is a crowd of curious spectators, chiefly young belles and dandies who have come to the slave market for diversion. All exchange courtly greetings in dumb show and chat silently together. There is something stiff, rigid, unreal, marionettish about their movements. They group themselves about the stump. Finally a batch of slaves is led in from the left by an attendant—three men of different ages, two women, one with a baby in her arms, nursing. They are placed to the left of the stump, beside* JONES. *The white planters look them over appraisingly as if they were cattle, and exchange judgments on each. The dandies point with their fingers and make witty remarks. The belles titter bewitchingly. All this in silence save for the ominous throb of the tom-tom. The* AUCTIONEER *holds up his hand, taking his place at the stump. The group strain forward attentively. He touches* JONES *on the shoulder peremptorily, motioning for him to stand on the stump—the auction block.* JONES *looks up, sees the figures on all sides, looks wildly for some opening to escape, sees none, screams, and leaps madly to the top of the stump to get as far away from them as possible. He stands there, cowering, paralyzed with horror. The* AUCTIONEER *begins his silent spiel. He points to* JONES, *appeals to the planters to see for themselves. Here is a good field hand, sound in wind and limb as they can see. Very strong still in spite of his being middle-aged. Look at that back. Look at those shoulders. Look at the muscles in his arms and his sturdy legs. Capable of any amount of hard labor. Moreover, of a good disposition, intelligent, and tractable. Will any gentleman start the bidding? The* PLANTERS *raise their fingers, make their bids. They are apparently all eager to possess* JONES. *The bidding is lively, the crowd interested. While this has been going on,* JONES *has been seized by the courage of desperation. He dares to look down and around him. Over his face abject terror gives way to mystification, to gradual realization—stutteringly*

What you all doin', white folks? What's all dis? What you all lookin' at me fo'? What you doin' wid me, anyhow? (*Suddenly convulsed with raging hatred and fear*) Is dis a auction? Is you sellin' me like dey uster befo' de war? (*Jerking out his revolver just as the* AUCTIONEER *knocks him down to one of the* PLANTERS*—glaring from him to the purchaser*) And *you* sells me? And *you* buys me? I shows you I'se a free nigger, damn yo' souls!

He fires at the AUCTIONEER *and at the* PLANTER *with such rapidity that the two shots are almost simultaneous. As if this were a signal the walls of the forest fold in. Only blackness remains and silence broken by* JONES *as he rushes off, crying with fear—and by the quickened, ever louder beat of the tom-tom*

Scene Six

A cleared space in the forest. The limbs of the trees meet over it, forming a low ceiling about five feet from the ground. The interlocked ropes of creepers reaching upward to entwine the tree trunks give an arched appearance to the sides. The space thus enclosed is like the dark, noisome hold of some ancient vessel. The moonlight is almost completely shut out and only a vague wan light filters through. There is the noise of someone approaching from the left, stumbling and crawling through the undergrowth. JONES' *voice is heard between chattering moans.*

JONES   Oh Lawd! What I gwine do now? Ain't got no bullet left on'y de silver one. If mo' o' dem ha'nts come after me, how I gwine skeer dem away? Oh Lawd, on'y de silver one left—an' I gotta save dat fo' luck. If I shoots dat one I'm a goner sho'! Lawd, it's black heah! Whar's de moon? Oh Lawd, don't dis night evah come to an end? (*By the sounds, he is feeling his way cautiously forward*) Dere! Dis feels like a clear space. I gotta lie down an' rest. I don't care if dem niggers does cotch me. I gotta rest.

> *He is well forward now where his figure can be dimly made out. His pants have been so torn away that what is left of them is no better than a breechcloth. He flings himself full length, face downward on the ground, panting with exhaustion. Gradually it seems to grow lighter in the enclosed space and two rows of seated figures can be seen behind* JONES. *They are sitting in crumpled, despairing attitudes, hunched, facing one another with their backs touching the forest walls as if they were shackled to them. All are Negroes, naked save for loincloths. At first they are silent and motionless. Then they begin to sway slowly forward toward each and back again in unison, as if they were laxly letting themselves follow the long roll of a ship at sea. At the same time a low, melancholy murmur rises among them, increasing gradually by rhythmic degrees which seem to be directed and controlled by the throb of the tom-tom in the distance, to a long, tremulous wail of despair that reaches a certain pitch, unbearably acute, then falls by slow gradations of tone into silence and is taken up again.* JONES *starts, looks up, sees the figures, and throws himself down again to shut out the sight. A shudder of terror shakes his whole body as the wail rises up about him again. But the next time, his voice, as if under some uncanny compulsion, starts with the others. As their chorus lifts he rises to a sitting posture similar to the others, swaying back and forth. His voice reaches the highest pitch of sorrow, of desolation. The light fades out, the other voices cease, and only darkness is left.* JONES *can be heard scrambling to his feet and running off, his voice sinking down the scale and receding as he moves*

farther and farther away in the forest. The tom-tom beats louder, quicker, with a more insistent, triumphant pulsation

Scene Seven

The foot of a gigantic tree by the edge of a great river. A rough structure of boulders, like an altar, is by the tree. The raised riverbank is in the nearer background. Beyond this the surface of the river spreads out, brilliant and unruffled in the moonlight, blotted out and merged into a veil of bluish mist in the distance. JONES' *voice is heard from the left rising and falling in the long, despairing wail of the chained slaves, to the rhythmic beat of the tom-tom. As his voice sinks into silence, he enters the open space. The expression of his face is fixed and stony, his eyes have an obsessed glare, he moves with a strange deliberation like a sleepwalker or one in a trance. He looks around at the tree, the rough stone altar, the moonlit surface of the river beyond, and passes his hand over his head with a vague gesture of puzzled bewilderment. Then, as if in obedience to some obscure impulse, he sinks into a kneeling, devotional posture before the altar. Then he seems to come to himself partly, to have an uncertain realization of what he is doing, for he straightens up and stares about him horrifiedly—in an incoherent mumble:*

JONES   What—what is I doin'? What is—dis place? Seems like I know dat tree—an' dem stones—an' de river. I remember—seems like I been heah befo'. (*Tremblingly*) Oh, Gorry, I'se skeered in dis place! I'se skeered. Oh Lawd, pertect dis sinner!

Crawling away from the altar, he cowers close to the ground, his face hidden, his shoulders heaving with sobs of hysterical fright. From behind the trunk of the tree, as if he had sprung out of it, the figure of the CONGO WITCH DOCTOR *appears. He is wizened and old, naked except for the fur of some small animal tied about his waist, its bushy tail hanging down in front. His body is stained all over a bright red. Antelope horns are on each side of his head, branching upward. In one hand he carries a bone rattle, in the other a charm stick with a bunch of white cockatoo feathers tied to the end. A great number of glass beads and bone ornaments are about his neck, ears, wrists, and ankles. He struts noiselessly with a queer prancing step to a position in the clear ground between* JONES *and the altar. Then with a preliminary, summoning stamp of his foot on the earth, he begins to dance and to chant. As if in response to his summons, the beating of the tom-tom grows to a fierce, exultant boom whose throbs seem to fill the air with vibrating rhythm.* JONES *looks up, starts to spring to his feet, reaches a half-kneeling, half-squatting position and remains rigidly fixed there, paralyzed with awed fascination by this new apparition. The* WITCH DOCTOR *sways, stamping with his foot, his bone rattle clicking the time. His voice rises and falls in a weird, monotonous croon, without articulate word divisions. Gradually his dance becomes clearly one of a narrative in pantomime, his croon is an incantation, a charm to allay the fierceness of some implacable deity demanding sacrifice. He flees, he is pursued by devils, he hides, he flees again. Ever wilder and wilder becomes his flight, nearer and nearer draws the pursuing evil, more and more the spirit of terror gains possession of him. His croon, rising to intensity, is punctuated by shrill cries.* JONES *has become completely hypnotized. His voice joins in the incantation, in the cries, he beats time with his hands and sways his body to and fro from the waist. The whole spirit and meaning of the dance has entered into him, has become his spirit. Finally the theme of the pantomime halts on a howl of despair, and is taken up again in a note of savage hope. There is a salvation. The forces of evil demand sacrifice. They must be appeased. The* WITCH DOCTOR *points with his wand to the sacred tree, to the river beyond, to the altar, and finally to* JONES, *with a ferocious command.* JONES *seems to sense the meaning of this. It is he who must offer himself for sacrifice. He beats his forehead abjectly on the ground, moaning hysterically*

Mercy, O Lawd! Mercy! Mercy on dis po' sinner.

The WITCH DOCTOR *springs to the riverbank. He stretches out his arms and calls to some god within its depths. Then he starts backward slowly, his arms remaining out. A huge head of a crocodile appears over the bank and its eyes, glittering greenly, fasten upon* JONES. *He stares into them fascinatedly. The* WITCH DOCTOR *prances up to him, touches him with his wand, motions with hideous command toward the waiting monster.* JONES *squirms on his belly nearer and nearer, moaning continually*

Mercy, Lawd! Mercy!

The crocodile heaves more of his enormous bulk onto the land. JONES *squirms toward him. The* WITCH DOCTOR'S *voice shrills out in furious exaltation, the tom-tom beats madly.* JONES *cries out in a fierce, exhausted spasm of anguished pleading*

Lawd, save me! Lawd Jesus, heah my prayer!

Immediately, in answer to his prayer, comes the thought of the one bullet left him. He snatches at his hip, shouting defiantly

De silver bullet! You don't git me yit!

He fires at the green eyes in front of him. The head of the crocodile sinks back behind the riverbank, the WITCH DOCTOR *springs behind the sacred tree and disappears.* JONES *lies with his face to the ground, his arms outstretched, whimpering with fear as the throb of the tom-tom fills the silence about him with a somber pulsation, a baffled but revengeful power*

Scene Eight

Dawn. Same as Scene Two, the dividing line of forest and plain. The nearest tree trunks are dimly revealed, but the forest behind them is still a mass of glooming shadow. The tom-tom seems on the very spot, so loud and continuously vibrating are its beats. LEM enters from the left, followed by a small squad of his soldiers, and by the Cockney trader, SMITHERS. LEM is a heavy-set, ape-faced old savage of the extreme African type, dressed only in a loincloth. A revolver and a cartridge belt are about his waist. His soldiers are in different degrees of rag-concealed nakedness. All wear broad palm-leaf hats. Each one carries a rifle. SMITHERS is the same as in Scene One. One of the soldiers, evidently a tracker, is peering about keenly on the ground. He points to the spot where JONES entered the forest. LEM and SMITHERS come to look.

SMITHERS (*after a glance, turns away in disgust*)   That's where 'e went in right enough. Much good it'll do yer. 'E's miles orf by this an' safe to the Coast, damn 's 'ide! I tole yer yer'd lose 'im, didn't I?—wastin' the 'ole bloomin' night beatin' yer bloody drum and castin' yer silly spells! Gawd blimey, wot a pack!

LEM (*gutturally*)   We cotch him. (*He makes a motion to his soldiers, who squat down on their haunches in a semicircle*)

SMITHERS (*exasperatedly*)   Well, ain't yer goin' in an' 'unt 'im in the woods? What the 'ell's the good of waitin'?

LEM (*imperturbably—squatting down himself*)   We cotch him.

SMITHERS (*turning away from him contemptuously*)   Aw! Garn! 'E's a better man than the lot o' you together. I 'ates the sight o' 'im but I'll say that for 'im.

> *A sound comes from the forest. The soldiers jump to their feet, cocking their rifles alertly. LEM remains sitting with an imperturbable expression, but listening intently. He makes a quick signal with his hand. His followers creep quickly into the forest, scattering so that each enters at a different spot*

SMITHERS   You ain't thinkin' that would be 'im, I 'ope?

LEM (*calmly*)   We cotch him.

SMITHERS   Blarsted fat'eads! (*Then after a second's thought—wonderingly*) Still an' all, it might 'appen. If 'e lost 'is bloody way in these stinkin' woods 'e'd likely turn in a circle without 'is knowin' it.

LEM (*peremptorily*)   Sssh!

> *The reports of several rifles sound from the forest, followed a second later by savage, exultant yells. The beating of the tom-tom abruptly ceases. LEM looks up at the white man with a grin of satisfaction*

We cotch him. Him dead.

SMITHERS (*with a snarl*)   'Ow d'yer know it's 'im an' 'ow d'yer know 'e's dead?

LEM   My mens dey got um silver bullets. Lead bullet no kill him. He got um strong charm. I cook um money, make um silver bullet, make um strong charm, too.

SMITHERS (*astonished*)   So that's wot you was up to all night, wot? You was scared to put after 'im till you'd molded silver bullets, eh?

LEM (*simply stating a fact*)   Yes. Him got strong charm. Lead no good.

SMITHERS (*slapping his thigh and guffawing*)   Hawhaw! If yer don't beat all 'ell. (*Then recovering himself—scornfully*) I'll bet yer it ain't 'im they shot at all, yer bleedin' looney!

LEM (*calmly*)   Dey come bring him now.

> *The soldiers come out of the forest, carrying* JONES' *limp body. He is dead. They carry him to* LEM, *who examines his body with great satisfaction*

SMITHERS (*leans over his shoulder—in a tone of frightened awe*)   Well, they did for yer right enough, Jonesy me lad! Dead as a 'erring! (*Mockingly*) Where's yer 'igh an' mighty airs now, yer bloomin' Majesty? (*Then with a grin*) Silver bullets! Gawd blimey, but yer died in the 'eighth o' style, any'ow!

CURTAIN

Exercises   1. *What does the opening scene between Smithers and the old black woman accomplish?*

2. *What function is served by Jones's divulging his earlier background to Smithers? By revealing his plans of escape?*

3. *What happens in Scene Two that points to the beginning of the end for Jones?*

4. *Two principal conflicts shape the structure of this play. One is external, the other is internal. What are they?*

5. *Why does O'Neill structure his scenes to parallel an orderly regression in Jones's mind?*

6. *What typifies the dialogue in this play?*

7. *Explain the prominent role of stage directions.*

8. *Cite examples of dramatic irony relating to the silver bullets.*

Topics for   1. *Analyze the means by which O'Neill has achieved sus-*
Writing   *pense.*

2. *Discuss the theme of the play.*

3. *The play has eight scenes. If you were preparing a production of the play, into how many acts would you divide it? Where would you have your act divisions, and why?*

Selected Bibliography   Eugene O'Neill

Adams, William J. "The Dramatic Structure of the Plays of O'Neill." *Dissertation Abstracts*, 17 (1957), 16 (Stanford).

Cargill, Oscar, N. Bryllion Fagin, and William J. Fisher, eds. *O'Neill and His Plays: Four Decades of Criticism*. New York: New York University Press, 1961.

Carpenter, Frederick L. *Eugene O'Neill*. New York: Twayne, 1964.

Engel, E. A. *Haunted Heroes of Eugene O'Neill*. Cambridge: Harvard University Press, 1953. Pages 48–53.

Falk, D. V. *Eugene O'Neil and the Tragic Tension*. New Brunswick: Rutgers University Press, 1958.

Gassner, John, ed. *O'Neill: A Collection of Critical Essays*. Englewood Cliffs: Prentice Hall, 1964.

Gelb, Arthur, and Barbara Gelt. *O'Neill*. New York: Harper and Row, 1962.

Lawson, John H. "Eugene O'Neill and His Plays." *Critical Quarterly* 3 (1961), 242–256; 339–353.

Leech, Clifford. *Eugene O'Neill*. New York: Grove, 1963.

Mais, S. P. B. *Some Modern Authors*. Freeport, N.Y.: Books for Libraries, 1923. Pages 296–302.

Mierow, Herbert E. "The Greeks Started It." *Catholic World*, 166 (October 1947), 65–66.

Skinner, Richard Dana. *Eugene O'Neill*. New York: Russell & Russell, 1964. Pages 85–91.

Stamm, R. "Dramatic Experiments of Eugene O'Neill." *English Studies*, 28 (February 1947), 11–12.

William Inge *(1913–1974)*

Born in Independence, Kansas, he received degrees from the University of Kansas and from George Peabody Teachers College. He taught English at Stephens College for Women and at Washington University in St. Louis and worked as a music and drama critic on The Saint Louis Star-Times. Come Back, Little Sheba *(1949), his first play produced on Broadway, won the George Jean Nathan and Theatre Times prizes. His best known works include* Picnic *(1953), which won the Drama Critics' Award, the Donaldson Award, and a Pulitzer Prize;* Bus Stop *(1955);* The Dark at the Top of the Stairs *(1957); and the screenplay* Splendor in the Grass *(1966), which won an Academy Award. He continued to write for films until his suicide in 1974.*

Come Back, Little Sheba

CAST

DOC	MILKMAN
MARIE	MESSENGER
LOLA	BRUCE
TURK	ED ANDERSON
POSTMAN	ELMO HUSTON
MRS. COFFMAN	

THE SCENE *An old house in a run-down neighborhood of a Midwestern city.*

ACT ONE   *Scene One*

The stage is empty.

It is the downstairs of an old house in one of those semi-respectable neighborhoods in a Midwestern city. The stage is divided into two rooms, the living room at right and the kitchen at left, with a stairway and a door between. At the foot of the stairway is a small table with a telephone on it. The time is about 8:00 A.M., a morning in the late spring.

At rise of curtain the sun hasn't come out in full force and outside the atmosphere is a little grey. The house is extremely cluttered and even dirty. The living room somehow manages to convey the atmosphere of the twenties, decorated with cheap pretense at niceness and respectability. The general effect is one of fussy awkwardness. The furniture is all heavy and rounded-looking, the chairs and davenport being covered with a shiny mohair. The davenport is littered and there are lace antimacassars on all the chairs. In such areas, houses are so close together, they hide each other from the sunlight. What sun could come through the window, at right, is dimmed by the smoky glass curtains. In the kitchen there is a table center. On it are piled dirty dishes from supper the night before. Woodwork in the kitchen is dark and grimy. No industry whatsoever has been spent in making it one of those white, cheerful rooms that we commonly think kitchens should be. There is no action on stage for several seconds.

    DOC comes downstairs to kitchen. Coat on back of chair center. Straightens chair. Takes roll from bag on drainboard. Folds bag, tucks behind sink. Lights stove. To table, fills dishpan there and takes it to sink. Turns on water. Tucks towel in vest for apron. To center chair, says prayer. To stove, takes fry pan to sink. Turns on water. MARIE, a young girl of 18 or 19 who rooms in the house, comes out of her bedroom (next to the living room), skipping airily into the kitchen. Her hair is piled in curls on top of her head and she wears a sheer dainty negligee and smart, feathery mules on her feet. She has the cheerfulness only youth can feel in the morning.

MARIE (*to chair right, opens pocketbook there*)   Hi!

DOC   Well, well, how is our star boarder this morning?

MARIE   Fine.

DOC   Want your breakfast now?

MARIE   Just my fruit juice. I'll drink it while I dress and have my breakfast later.

DOC (*two glasses to table*)   Up a little early, aren't you?

MARIE   I have to get to the library and check out some books before anyone else gets them.

DOC   Yes, you want to study hard, Marie. Learn to be a fine artist some day. Paint lots of beautiful pictures. I remember a picture my mother had over the mantelpiece at home, a picture of a cathedral in a sunset, one of those big cathedrals in Europe somewhere. Made you feel religious just to look at it.

MARIE   These books aren't for art, they're for biology. I have an exam.

DOC   Biology? Why do they make you take biology?

MARIE (*laughs*)   It's required. Didn't you have to take biology when you were in college?

DOC   Well—yes, but I was preparing to study medicine, so of course I *had* to take biology and things like that. You see—I was going to be a real doctor then—only I left college my third year.

MARIE   What's the matter? Didn't you like the pre-Med course?

DOC   Yes, of course—I had to give it up.

MARIE   Why?

DOC (*to stove with roll on plate. Evasive*)   I'll put your sweet roll in now, Marie, so it will be nice and warm for you when you want it.

MARIE   Dr. Delaney, you're so nice to your wife, and you're so nice to me; as a matter of fact, you're so nice to everyone. I hope my husband is as nice as you are. Most husbands would never think of getting their own breakfast.

DOC (*very pleased with this*)   —uh—you might as well sit down now and— yes, sit here and I'll serve you your breakfast now, Marie, and we can eat it together, the two of us.

MARIE (*a light little laugh as she starts dancing away from him*)   No. I like to bathe first and feel that I'm all fresh and clean to start the day. I'm going to hop into the tub now. See you later. (*She goes upstairs*)

DOC   Yes, fresh and clean—— (DOC *shows disappointment but goes on in businesslike way setting his breakfast on the table*)

MARIE (*off upstairs*)   Mrs. Delaney.

LOLA (*off upstairs*)   'Mornin', Honey.

> Then LOLA *comes downstairs. Enter* LOLA. *She is a contrast to* DOC'S *neat cleanliness, and* MARIE'S. *Over a nightdress she wears a lumpy kimono. Her eyes are dim with a morning expression of disillusionment, as though she had had a beautiful dream during the night and found on waking none of it was true. On her feet are worn, dirty comfies*

LOLA (*with some self-pity*)   I can't sleep late like I used to. It used to be I could sleep till noon if I wanted to, but I can't any more. I don't know why.

DOC   Habits change. Here's your fruit juice.

LOLA (*taking it*)   I oughta be gettin' your breakfast, Doc, instead of you gettin' mine.

DOC   I have to get up anyway, Baby.

LOLA (*sadly*)   I had another dream last night.

DOC (*pours coffee*)   About Little Sheba?

LOLA (*with sudden animation*)   It was just as real. I dreamt I put her on a leash and we walked down town—to do some shopping. All the people on the street turned around to admire her, and I felt so proud. Then we started to walk, and the blocks started going by so fast that Little Sheba couldn't keep up with me. Suddenly, I looked around and Little Sheba was gone. Isn't that funny? I looked everywhere for her but I couldn't find her. And I stood there feeling sort of afraid. (*Pause*) Do you suppose that means anything?

DOC   Dreams are funny.

LOLA   Do you suppose it means Little Sheba is going to come back?

DOC   I don't know, Baby.

LOLA (*petulant*)   I miss her so, Doc. She was such a cute little puppy. Wasn't she cute?

DOC (*smiles with the reminiscence*)   Yes, she was cute.

LOLA   Remember how white and fluffy she used to be after I gave her a bath? And how her little hind-end wagged from side to side when she walked?

DOC (*an appealing memory*)   I remember.

LOLA   She was such a cute little puppy. I hated to see her grow old, didn't you, Doc?

DOC   Yah. Little Sheba should have stayed young forever. Some things should never grow old. That's what it amounts to, I guess.

LOLA   She's been gone for such a long time. What do you suppose ever happened to her?

DOC   You can't ever tell.

LOLA (*with anxiety*)   Do you suppose she got run over by a car?—Or do you think that old Mrs. Coffman next door poisoned her? I wouldn't be a bit surprised.

DOC   No, Baby. She just disappeared. That's all we know.

LOLA (*redundantly*)   Just vanished one day—vanished into thin air. (*As though in a dream*)

DOC   I told you I'd find you another one, Baby.

LOLA (*pessimistically*)   You couldn't ever find another puppy as cute as Little Sheba.

DOC (*back to reality*)   Want an egg?

LOLA   No. Just this coffee. (*He pours coffee. Suddenly*) Have you said your prayer, Doc?

DOC   Yes, Baby.

LOLA   And did you ask God to be with you—all through the day, and keep you strong?

DOC   Yes, Baby.

LOLA   Then God will be with you, Docky. He's been with you almost a year now and I'm so proud of you.

DOC (*preening a little*)   Sometimes I feel sorta proud of myself.

LOLA   Say your prayer, Doc. I like to hear it.

DOC (*matter-of-factly*)   God grant me the serenity to accept the things I cannot change, courage to change the things I can, and wisdom always to tell the difference.

LOLA   That's nice. That's so pretty. When I think of the way you used to drink, always getting into fights, we had so much trouble. I was so scared! I never knew what was going to happen.

DOC   That was a long time ago, Baby.

LOLA   I know it, Daddy. I know how you're going to be when you come home now. (*She kisses him lightly*)

DOC   I don't know what I would have done without you.

LOLA   And now you've been sober almost a year.

DOC   Yep. A year next month. (*He rises and goes to the sink with coffee cup and two glasses, rinsing them*)

LOLA   Do you have to go to the meeting tonight?

DOC   No. I can skip the meetings now for a while.

LOLA   Oh, good! Then you can take me to a movie.

DOC   Sorry, Baby. I'm going out on some Twelfth Step work with Ed Anderson.

LOLA   What's that?

DOC (*drying the glasses*)   I showed you that list of twelve steps the Alcoholics Anonymous have to follow. This is the final one. After you learn to stay dry yourself, then you go out and help other guys that need it.

LOLA   Oh!

DOC (*to sink*)   When we help others, we help ourselves.

LOLA   I know what you mean. Whenever I help Marie in some way, it makes me feel good.

DOC   Yah. (LOLA *gives her cup to* DOC. *Washing it.*) Yes but this is a lot different, Baby. When I go out to help some poor drunk, I have to give him courage—to stay sober like I've stayed sober. Most alcoholics are disappointed men—They need courage——

LOLA   You weren't ever disappointed, were you, Daddy?

DOC (*after a pause*)   The important thing is to forget the past and live for the present. And stay sober doing it.

LOLA   Who do you have to help tonight?

DOC   Some guy they picked up on Skid Row last night. (*Gets his coat from back of chair*) They got him at the City Hospital. I kinda dread it.

LOLA   I thought you said it helped you.

DOC (*puts on coat*)   It does, if you can stand it. I did some Twelfth Step work down there once before. They put alcoholics right in with the crazy people. It's horrible—these men all twisted and shaking—eyes all foggy and full of pain. Some guy there with his fists clamped together, so he couldn't kill anyone. There was a young man, just a *young* man, had scratched his eyes out.

LOLA (*cringing*)   Don't, Daddy. Seems a shame to take a man there just cause he got drunk.

DOC   Well, they'll sober a man up. That's the important thing. Let's not talk about it any more.

LOLA (*with relief*)   Rita Hayworth's on tonight, out at the Plaza. Don't you want to see it?

DOC   Maybe Marie will go with you.

LOLA   Oh, no. She's probably going out with Turk tonight.

DOC   She's too nice a girl to be going out with a guy like Turk.

LOLA   I don't know why, Daddy. Turk's nice. (*Cuts coffee cake*)

DOC   A guy like that doesn't have any respect for *nice* young girls. You can tell that by looking at him.

LOLA   I never saw Marie object to any of the love-making.

DOC   A big, brawny bozo like Turk, he probably forces her to kiss him.

LOLA   Daddy, that's not so at all. I came in the back way once when they were in the living room, and she was kissing him like he was Rudolph Valentino.

DOC (*an angry denial*)   Marie is a nice girl.

LOLA   I know she's nice. I just said she and Turk were doing some tall spooning. It wouldn't surprise me any if——

DOC   Honey, I don't want to hear any more about it.

LOLA   You try to make out like every young girl is Jennifer Jones in the Song of Bernadette.

DOC   I do not. I just like to believe that young people like her are clean and decent——

MARIE (*comes down stairs*)   Hi! (*Gets cup and saucer from drain board*)

LOLA (*at stove*)   There's an extra sweet roll for you this morning, Honey. I didn't want mine.

MARIE   One's plenty, thank you.

DOC   How soon do you leave this morning?

MARIE (*eating*)   As soon as I finish my breakfast.

DOC   Well, I'll wait and we can walk to the corner together.

MARIE   Oh, I'm sorry, Doc. Turk's coming by. He has to go to the library, too.

DOC   Oh, well I'm not going to be competition with a football player. (*To* LOLA) It's a nice spring morning. Wanta walk to the office with me?

LOLA   I look too terrible, Daddy. I ain't even dressed.

DOC   Kiss Daddy goodbye.

LOLA (*gets up and kisses him softly*)   Bye, bye, Daddy. If you get hungry, come home and I'll have something for you.

MARIE (*joking*)   Aren't you going to kiss *me*, Dr. Delaney?

> LOLA *eggs* DOC *to go ahead*

DOC (*startled. Hesitates. Forces himself to realize she is only joking and manages to answer*)   Can't spend my time kissing *all* the girls.

> MARIE *laughs.* DOC *goes into living room while* LOLA *and* MARIE *continue talking.* MARIE'S *scarf is tossed over his hat on chair, so he picks it up, then looks at it fondly, holding it in the air, inspecting its delicate gracefulness. He drops it back on chair and starts out by front door*

MARIE   I think Dr. Delaney is so nice.

LOLA (*she is by the closet now, where she keeps a few personal articles. She is getting into a more becoming smock*)   When did you say Turk was coming by?

MARIE   Said he'd be here about 9:30.

> DOC *exits—hearing the line about* TURK

That's a pretty smock.

LOLA (*to table, sits center chair, changes shoes*)   It'll be better to work around the house in.

MARIE (*not sounding exactly cheerful*)   Mrs. Delaney, I'm expecting a telegram this morning. Would you leave it on my dresser for me when it comes?

LOLA   Sure, Honey. No bad news, I hope.

MARIE   Oh no!   It's from Bruce.

LOLA (MARIE'S *boy friends are one of her liveliest interests*)   Oh, your boy friend in Cincinnati. Is he coming to see you?

MARIE   I guess so.

LOLA   I'm just dying to meet him.

MARIE (*changing the subject*)   Really, Mrs. Delaney, you and Doc have been so nice to me. I just want you to know I appreciate it.

LOLA   Thanks, Honey.

MARIE   You've been like a father and mother to me. I appreciate it.

LOLA   Thanks, Honey.

MARIE   Turk was saying just the other night what good sports you both are.

LOLA (*brushing hair*)   That so?

MARIE   Honest. He said it was just as much fun being with you as with kids our own age.

LOLA (*couldn't be more flattered*)   Oh, I like that Turk. He reminds me of a boy I used to know in High School, Dutch McCoy. Where did you ever meet him?

MARIE   In art class.

LOLA   Turk take art?

MARIE (*laughs*)   No. It was in a life class. He was modeling. Lots of the athletes do that. It pays them a dollar an hour.

LOLA   That's nice.

MARIE   Mrs. Delaney? I've got some corrections to make in some of my drawings. Is it all right if I bring Turk home this morning to pose for me? It'll just take a few minutes.

LOLA   Sure, Honey.

MARIE   There's a contest on now. They're giving a prize for the best drawing to use for advertising the Spring Relays.

LOLA   And you're going to do a picture of Turk? That's nice. (*A sudden thought. A little secretively*) Doc's gonna be gone tonight. You and Turk can have the living room if you want to.

MARIE (*this is a temptation*)   O.K. Thanks. (*Exits to bedroom*)

LOLA   Tell me more about Bruce.

Follows right to bedroom door

MARIE (*off in bedroom. Remembering her affinity*)   Well, he comes from one of the best families in Cincinnati. And they have a great big house. And they have a maid, too. And he's got a wonderful personality. He makes $300 a month.

LOLA   That so?

MARIE   And he stays at the best hotels. His company insists on it. (*Enters*)

LOLA   Do you like him as well as Turk? (*Buttons up back of* MARIE'S *blouse*)

MARIE (*evasive*)   Bruce is so dependable, and—he's a gentleman, too.

LOLA   Are you goin' to marry him, Honey?

MARIE   Maybe, after I graduate from college and he feels he can support a wife and children. I'm going to have lots and lots of children.

LOLA   I wanted children, too. When I lost my baby and found out I couldn't have any more, I didn't know what to do with myself. I wanted to get a job, but Doc wouldn't hear of it.

MARIE   Bruce is going to come into a lot of money some day. His uncle made a fortune in men's garters. (*Exits into her room*)

LOLA (*leans on door frame*)   Doc was a rich boy when I married him. His mother left him $25,000 when she died. (*Disillusioned*) It took him a lot to get his office started and everything—then, he got sick. (*She makes a futile gesture; then on the bright side*) But Doc's always good to me—now.

MARIE (*re-enters*)   Oh, Doc's a peach.

LOLA   I used to be pretty, something like you. (*She gets her picture from table left*) I was Beauty Queen of the Senior Class in High School. My dad was awful strict, though. Once he caught me holding hands with that good-looking Dutch McCoy. Dad sent Dutch home, and wouldn't let me go out after supper for a whole month. Daddy would never let me go out with boys much. Just because I was pretty. He was afraid all the boys would get the wrong idea—*you* know. I never had any fun at all until I met Doc.

MARIE   Sometimes I'm glad I didn't know my father. Mom always let me do pretty much as I please.

LOLA   Doc was the first boy my dad ever let me go out with. We got married that spring.

> *Replaces picture.* MARIE *sits davenport, puts on shoes and socks*

MARIE   What did your father think of that?

LOLA   We came right to the city then. And, well, Doc gave up his pre-Med course, and went to Chiropractor School instead.

MARIE   You must have been married awful young.

LOLA   Oh yes. Eighteen.

MARIE   That must have made your father really mad.

LOLA   Yes, it did. I never went home after that, but my mother comes down here from Green Valley to visit me sometimes.

TURK (*bursts into the front room from outside. He is a young, big, husky, good-looking boy, nineteen or twenty. He has the openness, the generosity, vigor and health of youth. He's had a little time in the service, but he is not what one would call disciplined. He wears faded dungarees and a T-shirt. He always enters unannounced. He hollers for* MARIE)   Hey, Marie! Ready?

MARIE (*calling. Runs up center and exits bedroom, closing door*)   Just a minute, Turk.

LOLA (*confidentially*)   I'll entertain him until you're ready. (*She is by nature coy and kittenish with an attractive man. Picks up papers—stuffs under table right*) The house is such a mess, Turk! I'll bet you think I'm an awful housekeeper. Some day I'll surprise you. But you're like one of the family now. (*Pause*) My, you're an early caller.

TURK   Gotta get to the library. Haven't cracked a book for a biology exam and Marie's gotta help me.

LOLA (*unconsciously admiring his stature and physique and looking him over*)   My. I'd think you'd be chilly running around in just that thin little shirt.

TURK   Me? I go like this in the middle of winter.

LOLA   Well, you're a big husky man.

TURK (*laughs*)   Oh, I'm a brute, *I* am.

LOLA   You should be out in Hollywood making those Tarzan movies.

TURK   I had enough of that place when I was in the Navy.

LOLA   That so?

TURK (*calling*)   Hey, Marie, hurry up.

MARIE (*off*)   Oh, be patient, Turk.

TURK (*to* LOLA)   She doesn't realize how busy I am. I'll only have a half hour to study at most. I gotta report to the coach at 10:30.

LOLA   What are you in training for now?

TURK   Spring track. They got me throwing the javelin.

LOLA   The javelin? What's that?

TURK (*laughs at her ignorance*)   It's a big, long lance. (*Assumes the magnificent position*) You hold it like this, erect—then you let go and it goes singing through the air, and lands yards away, if you're any good at it, and sticks in the ground, quivering like an arrow. I won the State Championship last year.

LOLA (*she has watched as though fascinated*)   My!

TURK (*very generous*)   Get Marie to take you to the track field some afternoon, and you can watch me.

LOLA   That would be thrilling.

MARIE (*comes dancing in*)   Hi, Turk.

TURK   Hi, juicy.

LOLA (*as the* YOUNG COUPLE *move to the doorway*)   Remember, Marie, you and Turk can have the room tonight. All to yourselves. You can play the radio and dance and make a plate of fudge, or anything you want.

MARIE (*to* TURK)   O.K.?

TURK (*with eagerness*)   Sure.

MARIE   Let's go. (*Exits*)

LOLA   'Bye, kids.

TURK   'Bye, Mrs. Delaney. (*Gives her a chuck under the chin*) You're a swell skirt.

> LOLA *couldn't be more flattered. For a moment she is breathless. They speed out the door and* LOLA *stands, sadly watching them depart. Then a sad, vacant look comes over her face. Her arms drop in a gesture of futility. Slowly she walks out on the front porch and calls*

LOLA   Little Sheba! Come, Little She-ba. Come back—come back, Little Sheba! (*She waits for a few moments, then comes wearily back into the house, closing the door behind her. Now the morning has caught up with her. She goes to the kitchen, kicks off her pumps and gets back into comfies. The sight of the dishes on the drainboard depresses her. Clearly she is bored to death. Then the telephone rings with the promise of relieving her. She answers it)* Hello—— Oh no, you've got the wrong number—— Oh, that's all right. *(Again it looks hopeless. She hears the* POSTMAN. *Now her spirits are lifted. She runs to the front door, opens it and awaits him. When he's within distance, she lets loose a barrage of welcome)* 'Morning, Mr. Postman.

POSTMAN   'Morning, Ma'am.

LOLA   You better have something for me today. Sometimes I think you don't even know I live here. You haven't left me anything for two whole weeks. If you can't do better than that, I'll just have to get a new postman.

POSTMAN *(on the porch)*   You'll have to get someone to write you some letters, Lady. Nope, nothing for you.

LOLA   Well, I was only joking. You knew I was joking, didn't you? I'll bet you're thirsty. You come right in here and I'll bring you a glass of cold water. *(Enters living room)* Come in and sit down for a few minutes and rest your feet a while.

POSTMAN   I'll take you up on that, Lady. *(Coming in)* I've worked up quite a thirst.

LOLA   You sit down. I'll be back in just a minute. *(Goes to kitchen, gets pitcher out of refrigerator and brings it back)*

POSTMAN   Spring is turnin' into summer awful soon.

LOLA   You feel free to stop here and ask me for a drink of water any time you want to. *(Pouring drink)* That's what we're all here for, isn't it? To make each other comfortable?

POSTMAN   Thank you, Ma'am.

LOLA *(clinging, not wanting to be left alone so soon; she hurries her conversation to hold him)*   You haven't been our postman very long, have you?

POSTMAN *(she hands him a glass of water, stands holding pitcher as he drinks)* No.

LOLA   You postmen have things pretty nice, don't you? I hear you get nice pensions after you been working for the government twenty years. I think that's dandy. It's a *good* job, too. *(Pours him a second glass)* You may get tired but I think it's good for a man to be outside and get a lot of exercise. Keeps him strong and healthy. My husband, he's a doctor, a *chiro*practor; he has to stay inside his office all day long. The only exercise he gets is rubbin' people's backbones. *(They laugh.* LOLA *crosses left to table, leaves pitcher)* It makes his hands strong. He's got the strongest hands you ever did see. But he's got a poor digestion. I keep tellin' him he oughta get some fresh air once in a while and some exercise.

> POSTMAN *rises as if to go, and this hurries her into a more absorbing monologue*

You know what? My husband is an Alcoholics Anonymous. He doesn't care if I tell you that 'cause he's proud of it. He hasn't touched a drop in almost a year. All that time we've had a quart of whiskey in the pantry for company and he hasn't even gone near it. Doesn't even want to. You know, alcoholics can't drink like ordinary people; they're *allergic* to it. It affects them different. They get started drinking and can't stop. Liquor transforms them. Sometimes they get mean and violent and wanta fight—but if they let liquor alone, they're perfectly all right, just like you and me.

POSTMAN tries to leave

You should have seen Doc before he gave it up. He lost all his patients, wouldn't even go to the office; just wanted to stay drunk all day long and he'd come home at night and—— You just wouldn't believe it if you saw him now. He's got his patients all back, and he's just doing fine.

POSTMAN   Sure I know Dr. Delaney. I deliver his office mail. He's a fine man.

LOLA   Oh thanks. You don't ever drink, do you?

POSTMAN   Oh, a few beers once in a while. (*He is ready to go*)

LOLA   Well, I guess that stuff doesn't do any of us any good.

POSTMAN   No. (*Crosses down for mailbag on floor center*) Well, good day, Ma'am.

LOLA   Say, you got any kids?

POSTMAN   Three grandchildren.

LOLA (*getting it from table left*)   We don't have any kids, and we got this toy in a box of breakfast food. Why don't you take it home to them?

POSTMAN   Why, that's very kind of you, Ma'am. (*He takes it, and goes*)

LOLA   Goodbye, Mr. Postman.

POSTMAN (*on porch*)   I'll see that you get a letter, if I have to write it myself.

LOLA   Thanks. Goodbye. (*Left alone, she turns on radio. Then she goes to kitchen to start dishes, showing her boredom in the half-hearted way she washes them. Takes water back to ice box. Then she spies* MRS. COFFMAN *hanging baby clothes on lines just outside kitchen door. Goes to door*) My, you're a busy woman this morning, Mrs. Coffman.

MRS. COFFMAN (*German accent. She is outside, but sticks her head in for some of the following*)   Being busy is being happy.

LOLA   I guess so.

MRS. COFFMAN   I don't have it as easy as you. When you got seven kids to look after, you got no time to sit around the house, Mrs. Delaney.

LOLA   I s'pose not.

MRS. COFFMAN   But you don't hear me complain.

LOLA   Oh, no. You never complain. (*Pause*) I guess my little doggie's gone for good, Mrs. Coffman. I sure miss her.

MRS. COFFMAN   The only way to keep from missing one dog is to get another.

LOLA (*to sink, turns off water*)   Oh, I never could find another doggy as cute as Little Sheba.

MRS. COFFMAN   Did you put an ad in the paper?

LOLA   For two whole weeks. No one answered it. It's just like she vanished—into thin air. (*She likes this metaphor*) Every day, though, I go out on the porch and call her. You can't tell; she might be around. Don't you think?

MRS. COFFMAN   You should get busy and forget her. You should get busy, Mrs. Delaney.

LOLA   Yes, I'm going to. I'm going to start my spring house-cleaning one of these days real soon. Why don't you come in and have a cup of coffee with me, Mrs. Coffman, and we can chat a while?

MRS. COFFMAN   I got work to do, Mrs. Delaney. I got work. (*Exits*)
          LOLA *turns from the window, annoyed at her rejection. Is about to*
          start in on the dishes when the MILKMAN *arrives. She opens the*
          back door and detains him

MILKMAN   'Morning, Mrs. Coffman.

MRS. COFFMAN   'Morning.

LOLA   Hello there, Mr. Milkman. How are you today?

MILKMAN   'Morning, Lady.

LOLA   I think I'm going to want a few specials today. Can you come in a minute? (*To icebox*)

MILKMAN (*he probably is used to her. He is not a handsome man but husky and attractive in his uniform*)   What'll it be?

LOLA (*at icebox*)   Well, now, let's see. Have you got any cottage cheese?

MILKMAN   We always got cottage cheese, Lady. (*Showing her card*) All you gotta do is check the items on the card and we leave 'em. Now I gotta go back to the truck.

LOLA   Now, don't scold me. I always mean to do that but you're always here before I think of it. Now, I guess I'll need some coffee cream, too—half a pint.

MILKMAN   Coffee cream. O.K.

LOLA   Now let me see—— Oh, yes, I want a quart of buttermilk. My husband has liked buttermilk ever since he stopped drinking. My husband's an alcoholic. Had to give it up. Did I ever tell you?

MILKMAN   Yes, Lady. (*Starts to go. She follows*)

LOLA   Now he can't get enough to eat. Eats six times a day. He comes home in the middle of the morning, and I fix him a snack. In the middle of the afternoon he has a malted milk with an egg in it. And then another snack before he goes to bed.

MILKMAN   What'd ya know?

LOLA   Keeps his energy up.

MILKMAN   I'll bet. Anything else, lady?

LOLA   No, I guess not.

MILKMAN (*going out*)   Be back in a jiffy. (*Gives her slip. Exits*)

LOLA   I'm just so sorry I put you to so much extra work. (*He returns shortly with dairy products*) After this I'm going to do my best to remember to check the card. I don't think it's right to put people to extra work. (*To icebox, puts things away*)

MILKMAN (*smiles, is willing to forget*)   That's all right, Lady.

LOLA   Maybe you'd like a piece of cake or a sandwich. Got some awfully good cold cuts in the icebox.

MILKMAN   No, thanks, Lady.

LOLA   Or maybe you'd like a cup of coffee.

MILKMAN   No, thanks. (*He's checking the items, putting them on the bill*)

LOLA   You're just a young man. You oughta be going to college. I think everyone should have an education. Do you like your job?

MILKMAN   It's O.K. (*Looks at* LOLA)

LOLA   You're a husky young man. You oughta be out in Hollywood making those Tarzan movies.

MILKMAN (*steps back. Feels a little flattered*)   When I first began on this job I didn't get enough exercise, so I started working out on the bar bell.

LOLA   Bar bells?

MILKMAN   Keeps you in trim.

LOLA (*fascinated*)   Yes, I imagine.

MILKMAN   I sent my picture in to Strength and Health last month. (*Proudly*) It's a physique study! If they print it, I'll bring you a copy.

LOLA   Oh, will you? I think we should all take better care of ourselves, don't you?

MILKMAN   If you ask me, Lady, that's what's wrong with the world today. We're not taking care of ourselves.

LOLA   I wouldn't be surprised.

MILKMAN   Every morning I do forty push-ups before I eat my breakfast.

LOLA   Push-ups?

MILKMAN   Like this. (*He spreads himself on the floor and demonstrates, doing three rapid push-ups.* LOLA *couldn't be more fascinated. Then he springs to his feet*) That's good for shoulder development. Wanta feel my shoulders?

LOLA   Why—why, yes. (*He makes one arm tense and puts her hand on his shoulder*) Why, it's just like a rock.

MILKMAN   I can do seventy-nine without stopping.

LOLA   Seventy-nine!

MILKMAN   Now feel my arm.

LOLA (*does so*)   Goodness!

MILKMAN   You wouldn't believe what a puny kid I was. Sickly, no appetite.

LOLA   Is that a fact? And, my! Look at you now.

MILKMAN (*very proud*)   Shucks, any man could do the same—if he just takes care of himself.

LOLA   Oh sure, sure.

           A horn is heard offstage

MILKMAN   There's my buddy. I gotta beat it. (*Picks up his things, shakes hands, leaves hurriedly*) See you tomorrow, Lady.

LOLA   'Bye.

> *She watches him from kitchen window until he gets out of sight. There is a look of some wonder on her face, an emptiness, as though she were unable to understand anything that ever happened to her. She looks at clock, runs into living room, turns on radio. A pulsating tom-tom is heard as a theme introduction. Then the* ANNOUNCER

ANNOUNCER (*in dramatic voice*)   TA-BOOoooo! (*Now in a very soft, highly personalized voice.* LOLA *sits davenport, eats candy*) It's Ta-boo, radio listeners, your fifteen minutes of temptation. (*An alluring voice*) Won't you join me? (LOLA *swings feet up*) Won't you leave behind your routine, the dull cares that make up your day-to-day existence, the little worries, the uncertainties, the confusions of the work-a-day world and follow me where pagan spirits hold sway, where lithe natives dance on a moon-enchanted isle, where palm trees sway with the restless ocean tide, restless surging on the white shore. Won't you come along? (*More tom-tom. Now in an oily voice*) But remember, it's TA-BOOOOOooooo-OOO!

> *Now the tom-tom again, going into a sensual, primitive rhythm melody.* LOLA *has been transfixed from the beginning of the program. She lies down on the davenport, listening. Then, slowly, growing more and more comfortable*

WESTERN UNION BOY (*at door*)   Telegram for Miss Maria Buckholder.

LOLA   She's not here.

WESTERN UNION BOY   Sign here.

> LOLA *does, then she closes the door and brings the envelope into the house, looking at it wonderingly. This is a major temptation for her. She puts the envelope on the table down right, but can't resist looking at it. Finally she gives in and takes it to the kitchen to steam it open. Then* MARIE *and* TURK *burst into the room.* LOLA, *confused, wonders what to do with the telegram, then decides, just in the nick of time, to jam it in her apron pocket*

MARIE   Mrs. Delaney!

> *Turns off radio. At the sound of* MARIE'S *voice,* LOLA, *embarrassedly, runs in to greet them*

—mind if we turn your parlor into an art studio?

LOLA   Sure, go right ahead. Hi, Turk.

> TURK *gives a wave of his arm*

MARIE (*to* TURK, *indicating her bedroom*)   You can change in there, Turk.

> TURK *goes into bedroom*

LOLA   Change?

MARIE   He's gotta take off his clothes.

LOLA   Huh? (*Closes door*)

MARIE   These drawings are for my life class.

LOLA (*consoled but still mystified*)   Oh.

MARIE (*sits davenport*)   Turk's the best male model we've had all year. Lotsa athletes pose for us 'cause they've all got muscles. They're easier to draw.

LOLA   You mean—he's gonna pose *naked*?

MARIE (*laughs*)   No. The women do, but the men are always more proper. Turk's going to pose in his track suit.

LOLA   Oh. (*Almost to herself*) The women pose nude but the men don't. (*This strikes her as a startling inconsistency*) If it's all right for a woman, it oughta be for a man.

MARIE (*businesslike*)   The man always keeps covered. (*Calling to* TURK) Hurry up, Turk.

TURK (*with all his muscles in place, he comes out. He is not at all self-conscious about his semi-nudity. His body is something he takes very much for granted. LOLA is a little dazed by the spectacle of flesh*)   How do you want this lovely body? Same pose I took in Art Class?

MARIE   Yah. Over there where I can get more light on you.

TURK (*opens door. Starts pose*)   Anything in the house I can use for a javelin?

MARIE   Is there, Mrs. Delaney?

LOLA   How about the broom?

TURK   O.K.

> LOLA *runs out to get it.* TURK *goes to her in kitchen, takes it, returns to living room and resumes pose*

MARIE (*from davenport, studying* TURK *in relation to her sketch-pad. Moves his leg*)   Your left foot a little more this way. (*Studying it*) O.K., hold it. (*Starts sketching rapidly and industriously*)

LOLA (*looks on, lingeringly. Starts unwillingly into kitchen, changes her mind and returns to the scene of action.* MARIE *and* TURK *are too busy to comment.* LOLA *looks at sketch, inspecting it*)   Well—that's real pretty, Marie. (MARIE *is intent.* LOLA *moves closer to look at the drawing*) It—it's real artistic. (*Pause*) I wish *I* was artistic.

TURK   Baby, I can't hold this pose very long at a time.

MARIE   Rest whenever you feel like it.

TURK   O.K.!

MARIE (*to* LOLA)   If I make a good drawing, they'll use it for the posters for the Spring Relays.

LOLA   Ya. You told me.

MARIE (*to* TURK)   After I'm finished with these sketches I won't have to bother you any more.

TURK   No bother. (*Rubs his shoulder—he poses*)   Hard pose, though. Gets me in the shoulder.

> MARIE *pays no attention.* LOLA *peers at him so closely he becomes a little self-conscious and breaks pose. This also breaks* LOLA'S *concentration*

LOLA   I'll heat you up some coffee. (*Goes to kitchen*)

TURK (*crosses to* MARIE. *Softly to* MARIE)   Hey, can't you keep her out of here? She makes me feel naked.

MARIE (*laughs*)   I can't keep her out of her own house, can I?

TURK   Didn't she ever see a man before?

MARIE   Not a big, beautiful man like you, Turky.

> TURK *smiles, is flattered by any recognition of his physical worth, takes it as an immediate invitation to lovemaking. Pulling her up, he kisses her as* DOC *comes up on porch.* MARIE *pushes* TURK *away*

Turk, get back in your corner.

DOC (*comes in from outside. Cheerily*)   Hi, everyone.

MARIE   Hi.

TURK   Hi, Doc.

DOC (*sees* TURK, *feels immediate resentment. Goes into kitchen to* LOLA)   What's goin' on here?

LOLA (*getting cups*)   Oh, hello, Daddy. Marie's doin' a drawin'.

DOC (*trying to size the situation up.* MARIE *and* TURK *are too busy to speak*)   Oh.

LOLA   I've just heated up the coffee. Want some?

DOC   Yeah. What happened to Turk's clothes?

LOLA   Marie's doing some drawings for her *life* classes, Doc.

DOC   Can't she draw him with his clothes on?

LOLA (*crossing with coffee. Very professional now*)   No, Doc, it's not the same. See, it's a *life* class. They draw bodies. They all do it, right in the classroom.

DOC   Why, Marie's just a young girl; she shouldn't be drawing things like that. I don't care if they do teach it at college. It's not right.

LOLA (*disclaiming responsibility*)   I don't know, Doc.

TURK (*turns*)   I'm tired.

MARIE (*squats at his feet*)   Just let me finish the foot.

DOC   Why doesn't she draw something else—a bowl of flowers or a cathedral—or a sunset.

LOLA   All she told me, Doc, was if she made a good drawing of Turk, they'd use it for the posters for the Spring Relay. (*Pause*) So I guess they don't want sunsets.

DOC   What if someone walked into the house now? What would they think?

LOLA   Daddy, Marie just asked me if it was all right if Turk came and posed for her. Now that's all she said, and I said O.K. But if you think it's wrong, I won't let them do it again.

DOC   I just don't like it.

MARIE   Hold it a minute more.

TURK   O.K.

LOLA   Well, then you speak to Marie about it if——

DOC (*he'd never mention anything disapprovingly to* MARIE)   No, Baby. I couldn't do that.

LOLA   Well then——

DOC   Besides, it's not her fault. If those college people make her do drawings like that, I suppose she has to do them. I just don't think it's right she should have to, that's all.

LOLA   Well, if you think it's wrong——

DOC (*ready to dismiss it*)   Never mind.

LOLA   I don't see any harm in it, Daddy.

DOC   Forget it.

LOLA (*to ice box*)   Would you like some buttermilk?

DOC   Thanks.

MARIE (*finishes sketch*)   O.K. That's all I can do for today.

TURK   Is there anything I can do for *you*?

MARIE   Yes—get your clothes on.

TURK   O.K., Coach.

> TURK *exits to bedroom.* MARIE *sits down right*

LOLA   You know what Marie said, Doc? She said that the women posed naked, but the men don't.

DOC   Why, of course, Honey.

LOLA   Why is that?

DOC (*stumped*)   —well——

LOLA   If it's all right for a woman, it oughta be for a man. But the man always keeps covered. That's what she said.

DOC   Well, that's the way it should be, Honey. A man, after all, is a man, and he—well, he has to protect himself.

LOLA   And a woman doesn't?

DOC   It's different, Honey.

LOLA   Is it? I've got a secret, Doc. Bruce is comin'.

DOC   Is that so?

LOLA (*after a glum silence*)   You know—Marie's boy friend from Cincinnati. I promised Marie a long time ago, when her fiance came to town, dinner was on me. So I'm getting out the best china and cook the best meal you ever sat down to.

DOC   When did she get the news?

LOLA   The telegram came this morning.

DOC   That's fine. That Bruce sounds to me like just the fellow for her. I think I'll go in and congratulate her.

LOLA (*nervous*)   Not now, Doc.

DOC   Why not?

LOLA   Well, Turk's there. It might make him feel embarrassed.

DOC   Well, why doesn't Turk clear out now that Bruce is coming? What's he hanging around for? She's engaged to marry Bruce, isn't she?

> TURK *enters from bedroom and goes to* MARIE, *starting to make advances*

LOLA   Marie's just doing a picture of him, Doc.

DOC   You always stick up for him. You encourage him.

LOLA   Shhh, Daddy. Don't get upset.

DOC (*very angrily*)   All right, but if anything happens to the girl I'll never forgive you.

> DOC *goes upstairs.* TURK *then grabs* MARIE, *kisses her passionately*

CURTAIN

Scene Two

The same evening, after supper. Outside it is dark. There has been an almost miraculous transformation of the entire house. LOLA, *apparently, has been working hard and fast all day. The rooms are spotlessly clean and there are such additions as new lampshades, fresh curtains, etc. In the kitchen all the enamel surfaces glisten, and piles of junk that have lain around for months have been disposed of.*

> LOLA *and* DOC *are in the kitchen, he washing up the dishes and she puttering around putting the finishing touches on her housecleaning.*

LOLA (*at stove*)   There's still some beans left. Do you want them, Doc?

DOC   I had enough.

LOLA   I hope you got enough to eat tonight, Daddy. I been so busy cleaning I didn't have time to fix you much.

DOC   I wasn't very hungry.

LOLA (*to table, cleaning up*)   You know what? Mrs. Coffman said I could come over and pick all the lilacs I wanted for my centerpiece tomorrow. Isn't that nice? I don't think she poisoned Little Sheba, do you?

DOC   I never did think so, Baby. Where'd you get the new curtains?

LOLA   I went out and bought them this afternoon. Aren't they pretty? Be careful of the woodwork; it's been varnished.

DOC   How come, Honey?

LOLA (*gets broom and dust pan from closet*)   Bruce is comin'. I figured I had to do my spring house-cleaning sometime.

DOC   You got all this done in one day? The house hasn't looked like this in years.

LOLA   I can be a good housekeeper when I want to be, can't I, Doc?

DOC (*kneels, holding dustpan for* LOLA)   I never had any complaints. Where's Marie now?

LOLA   I don't know, Doc. I haven't seen her since she left here this morning with Turk.

DOC (*rises. A look of disapproval*)   Marie's too good to be wasting her time with him.

LOLA   Daddy, Marie can take care of herself. Don't worry. (*To closet—returns broom*)

DOC (*goes into living room*)   'Bout time for Fibber McGee and Molly.

LOLA (*untying apron. To closet and then to back door*)   Daddy, I'm gonna run over to Mrs. Coffman's and see if she's got any silver polish. I'll be right back.

> DOC *goes to radio.* LOLA *exits. At the radio* DOC *starts twisting the dial. He rejects one noisy program after another, then very unexpectedly he comes across a rendition of Schubert's famous "Ave Maria," sung in a high soprano voice. Probably he has encountered the piece before somewhere, but it is now making its first impression on him. Gradually he is transported into a world of ethereal beauty which he never knew existed. He listens intently. The music has expressed some ideal of beauty he never fully realized and he is even a little mystified. Then* LOLA *comes in the back door, letting it slam, breaking the spell, and announcing in a loud, energetic voice*

LOLA   Isn't it funny? I'm not a bit tired tonight. You'd think after working so hard all day I'd be pooped.

DOC (*he cringes*)   Baby, don't use that word.

LOLA (*sets silver polish down and joins* DOC *on davenport*)   I'm sorry, Doc. I hear Marie and Turk say it all the time, and I thought it was kinda cute.

DOC   It—it sounds vulgar.

LOLA (*kisses* DOC)   I won't say it again, Daddy. Where's Fibber McGee?

DOC   Not quite time yet.

LOLA   Let's get some peppy music.

DOC (*tuning in a sentimental dance band*)   That what you want?

LOLA   That's O.K.

> DOC *takes a pack of cards off radio, returns to davenport and starts shuffling them very deftly*

I love to watch you shuffle cards, Daddy. You use your hands so gracefully. (*She watches closely*) Do me one of your card tricks.

DOC   Baby, you've seen them all.

LOLA   But I never get tired of them.

DOC   O.K. Take a card.

> LOLA *does*

Keep it now. Don't tell me what it is.

LOLA   I won't.

DOC (*shuffling cards again*)   Now put it back in the deck. I won't look. (*He closes his eyes*)

LOLA (*with childish delight*)   All right.

DOC   Put it back.

LOLA   Uh-huh.

DOC   O.K. (*Shuffles cards again, cutting them, taking top half off, exposing* LOLA*'s card, to her astonishment*) That your card?

LOLA (*unbelievingly*)   Daddy, how did you do it?

DOC   Baby, I've pulled that trick on you dozens of times.

LOLA   But I never understand how you do it.

DOC   Very simple.

LOLA   Docky, show me how you do that.

DOC (*you can forgive him a harmless feeling of superiority*)   Try it for yourself.

LOLA   Doc, you're clever. I never could do it.

DOC   Nothing to it.

LOLA   There is *too*. Show me how you do it, Doc.

DOC   And give away all my secrets? It's a gift, Honey. A magic gift.

LOLA   Can't you give it to me?

DOC (*picks up newspaper*)   A man has to keep some things to himself.

LOLA   It's not a gift at all, it's just some trick you *learned*.

DOC   O.K., Baby, any way you want to look at it.

LOLA   Let's have some music. How soon do you have to meet Ed
    Anderson?

DOC (*turns on radio*)   I still got a little time. (*Pleased*)

LOLA   Marie's going to be awfully happy when she sees the house all
    fixed up. She can entertain Bruce here when he comes, and maybe we
    could have a little party here and you can do your card tricks.

DOC   O.K.

LOLA   I think a young girl should be able to bring her friends home.

DOC   Sure.

LOLA   We never liked to sit around the house 'cause the folks always
    stayed there with us. (*Rises—starts dancing alone*) Remember the
    dances we used to go to, Daddy?

DOC   Sure.

LOLA   We had awful good times—for a while, didn't we?

DOC   Yes, Baby.

LOLA   Remember the homecoming dance, when Charlie Kettlekamp and
    I won the Charleston Contest?

DOC   Yah. Please, Honey, I'm trying to read.

LOLA   And you got mad at him 'cause he thought he should take me
    home afterwards.

DOC   I did not.

LOLA   Yes, you did. Charlie was all right, Doc, really he was. You were
    just jealous.

DOC   I *wasn't* jealous.

LOLA (*she has become very coy and flirtatious now, an old dog playing old
    tricks*)   You got jealous. Every time we went out any place and I
    even looked at another boy. There was never anything between
    Charlie and me; there never was.

DOC   That was a long time ago——

LOLA   Lots of other boys called me up for dates—Sammy Knight—Hand
    Biederman—Dutch McCoy.

DOC   Sure, Baby. You were the "it" girl.

LOLA (*pleading for his attention now*)   But I saved all my dates for *you*, didn't
    I, Doc?

DOC (*trying to joke*)   As far as *I* know, Baby.

LOLA (*hurt*)   Daddy, I did. You *got* to believe that. I never took a date
    with any other boy but you.

DOC (*a little weary and impatient*)   That's all forgotten now. (*Turns off radio*)

LOLA   How can you talk that way, Doc? That was the happiest time of our lives. I'll never forget it.

DOC (*disapprovingly*)   Honey!

LOLA (*at the window*)   That was a nice spring. The trees were so heavy and green and the air smelled so sweet. Remember the walks we used to take, down to the old chapel, where it was so quiet and still? (*Sits davenport*)

DOC   In the spring a young man's fancy turns—pretty fancy.

LOLA (*in the same tone of reverie*)   I was pretty then, wasn't I, Doc? Remember the first time you kissed me? You were scared as a young girl, I believe, Doc; you trembled so. (*She is being very soft and delicate. Caught in the reverie, he chokes a little and cannot answer*) We'd been going together all year and you were always so shy. Then for the first time you grabbed me and kissed me. Tears came to your eyes, Doc, and you said you'd love me forever and ever. Remember? You said—if I didn't marry you, you wanted to die—I remember 'cause it scared me for anyone to say a thing like that.

DOC (*in a repressed tone*)   Yes, Baby.

LOLA   And when the evening came on, we stretched out on the cool grass and you kissed me all night long.

DOC (*opens door*)   Baby, you've got to forget those things. That was twenty years ago.

LOLA   I'll soon be forty. Those years have just vanished—vanished into thin air.

DOC   Yes.

LOLA   Just disappeared—like Little Sheba. (*Pause*) Maybe you're sorry you married me now. You didn't know I was going to get old and fat and sloppy——

DOC   Oh, Baby!

LOLA   It's the truth. That's what I am. But I didn't know it, either. Are you sorry you married me, Doc?

DOC   Of course not.

LOLA   I mean, are you sorry you *had* to marry me?

DOC (*onto porch*)   We were never going to talk about that, Baby.

LOLA (*following DOC out*)   You *were* the first one, Daddy, the *only* one. I'd just die if you didn't believe that.

DOC (*tenderly*)   I know, Baby.

LOLA   You were so nice and so proper, Doc; I thought nothing we could do together could ever be wrong—or make us unhappy. Do you think we did wrong, Doc?

DOC (*consoling*)   No, Baby, of course I don't.

LOLA   I don't think anyone knows about it except my folks, do you?

DOC (*crossing in to up right*)   Of course not, Baby.

LOLA (*follows in*)   I wish the baby had lived, Doc. I don't think that woman knew her business, do you, Doc?

DOC   I guess not.

LOLA   If we'd gone to a doctor, she would have lived, don't you think?

DOC   Perhaps.

LOLA   A doctor wouldn't have known we'd just got married, would he? Why were we so afraid?

DOC (*sits davenport*)   We were just kids. Kids don't know how to look after things.

LOLA (*sits davenport*)   If we'd had the baby she'd be a young girl now; then maybe you'd have *saved* your money, Doc, and she could be going to college—like Marie.

DOC   Baby, what's done is done.

LOLA   It must make you feel bad at times to think you had to give up being a doctor and to think you don't have any money like you used to.

DOC   No—no, Baby. We should never feel bad about what's past. What's in the past can't be helped. You—you've got to forget it and live for the present. If you can't forget the past, you stay in it and never get out. I might be a big M.D. today, instead of a chiropractor; we might have had a family to raise and be with us now; I might still have a lot of money if I'd used my head and invested it carefully, instead of gettin' drunk every night. We might have a nice house, and comforts, and friends. But we don't have any of those things. So what! We gotta keep on living, don't we? I can't stop just 'cause I made a few mistakes. I gotta keep goin'—somehow.

LOLA   Sure, Daddy.

DOC (*sighs and wipes brow*)   I—I wish you wouldn't ask me questions like that, Baby. Let's not talk about it any more. I gotta keep goin', and not let things upset me, or—or—*I* saw enough at the City Hospital to keep me sober for a long time.

LOLA   I'm sorry, Doc. I didn't mean to upset you.

DOC   I'm not upset.

LOLA   What time'll you be home tonight?

DOC   'Bout eleven o'clock.

LOLA   I wish you didn't have to go tonight. I feel kinda lonesome.

DOC   Ya, so do I, Baby, but sometime soon we'll go *out* together. I kinda hate to go to those night clubs and places since I stopped drinking, but some night I'll take you out to dinner.

LOLA   Oh, will you, Daddy?

DOC   We'll get dressed up and go to the Windermere and have a fine dinner, and dance between courses.

LOLA (*eagerly*)   Let's do, Daddy. I got a little money saved up. I got about forty dollars out in the kitchen. We can take that if you need it.

DOC   I'll have plenty of money the first of the month.

LOLA (*she has made a quick response to the change of mood, seeing a future evening of carefree fun*)   What are we sitting round here so serious for? (*To radio*) Let's have some music.

> LOLA *gets a lively foxtrot on the radio, dances with* DOC. *They begin dancing vigorously, as though to dispense with the sadness of the preceding dialogue, but slowly it winds them and leaves* LOLA *panting*

We oughta go dancing—all the time, Docky—It'd be good for us. Maybe if I danced more often I'd lose—some of—this fat. I remember—I used to be able to dance like this—all night—and not even notice—it. (LOLA *breaks into a Charleston routine as of yore*) Remember the Charleston, Daddy?

> DOC *is clapping his hands in rhythm. Then* MARIE *bursts in through the front door, the personification of the youth that* LOLA *is trying to recapture*

DOC   Hi, Marie!

MARIE   What are you trying to do, a jig, Mrs. Delaney?

> MARIE *doesn't intend her remark to be cruel, but it wounds* LOLA. LOLA *stops abruptly in her dancing, losing all the fun she has been able to create for herself. She feels she might cry, so to hide her feelings she hurries quietly out to kitchen.* DOC *and* MARIE *do not notice*

MARIE (*noticing the change in atmosphere*)   Hey, what's been happening around here?

DOC   Lola got to feeling industrious. You oughta see the kitchen.

MARIE (*running to kitchen, where she is too observant of the changes to notice* LOLA *is weeping in corner.* LOLA, *of course, straightens up as soon as* MARIE *enters*)   What got into you, Mrs. Delaney? You've done wonders with the house. It looks marvellous.

LOLA (*quietly*)   Thanks, Marie.

MARIE (*darting back into living room*)   I can hardly believe I'm in the same place.

DOC (*meaning* BRUCE)   Think your boy friend'll like it?

MARIE (*thinking of* TURK)   You know how men are. Turk never notices things like that.

> *Starts into her own room, blowing a kiss to* DOC *on her way.* LOLA *comes back in, dabbing at her eyes*

DOC   Turk? (MARIE *is gone; turning to* LOLA) What's the matter, Honey?

LOLA   I don't know.

DOC   Feel bad about something?

LOLA   I didn't want her to see me dancing that way. Makes me feel sorta silly.

DOC   Why, you're a fine dancer.

LOLA   I feel kinda silly.

MARIE (*jumps back into the room with her telegram*)   My telegram's here. When did it come?

LOLA   It came about an hour ago, Honey.

> LOLA *looks nervously at* DOC. DOC *looks puzzled and a little sore*

MARIE   Bruce is coming! "Arriving tomorrow 5:00 P.M. CST, Flight 22, Love, Bruce." When did the telegram come?

DOC   So it came an hour ago. (*Looks hopelessly at* LOLA, *then goes to kitchen*)

LOLA (*nervously*)   Isn't it nice I got the house all cleaned? Marie, you bring Bruce to dinner with us tomorrow night. It'll be a sort of wedding present.

MARIE   That would be wonderful, Mrs. Delaney, but I don't want you to go to any trouble.

LOLA   No trouble at all. Now I insist.

> *Front doorbell rings*

That must be Turk.

MARIE (*whispers*)   Don't tell *him*.

> *Goes to door.* LOLA *scampers to kitchen*

Hi, Turk. Come on in.

TURK (*entering. Stalks her*)   Hi. (*Looks around to see if anyone is present, then takes her in his arms and starts to kiss her*)

LOLA   I'm sorry, Doc. I'm sorry about the telegram.

DOC   Baby, people don't do things like that. Don't you understand? *Nice* people don't.

MARIE   Stop it!

TURK   What's the matter?

MARIE   They're in the kitchen.

> *Goes into bedroom.* TURK *sits with book*

DOC   Why didn't you give it to her when it came?

LOLA   Well, Doc, Turk was posing for Marie this morning, and I couldn't give it to her while he was here.

> TURK *listens at door*

DOC   Well, it just isn't nice to open other people's mail.

> TURK *crosses up to* MARIE'S *door*

LOLA   I guess I'm not nice, then. That what you mean?

MARIE   Turk, will you get away from that door?

DOC   No, Baby, but—

LOLA   I don't see any harm in it, Doc. I steamed it open and sealed it back.

> TURK *at switch in living room.*

She'll never know the difference. I don't see any harm in that, Doc.

DOC (*gives up*)   O.K., Baby, if you don't see any harm in it, I guess I can't explain it. (*Starts getting ready to go*)

LOLA   I'm sorry, Doc. Honest, I'll never do it again. Will you forgive me?

DOC (*giving her a peck of a kiss*)   I forgive you.

MARIE (*comes back with book*)   Let's look like we're studying.

TURK   Biology? Hot dog!

LOLA (*after* MARIE *leaves her room*)   Now I feel better. Do you have to go now?

DOC   Yah.

LOLA   Before you go why don't you show your tricks to Marie.

DOC (*reluctantly*)   Not now.

LOLA   Oh, please do. They'd be crazy about them.

DOC (*with pride*)   O.K. (*Preens himself a little*) If you think they'd enjoy them—

> LOLA, *starting to living room, stops suddenly upon seeing* MARIE *and* TURK *spooning behind a book. A broad, pleased smile breaks on her face and she stands silently watching.* DOC, *at sink*

Well—what's the matter, Baby?

LOLA (*soft voice*)   Oh—nothing—nothing—Doc.

DOC   Well, do you want me to show 'em my tricks or don't you?

LOLA (*coming back to center of kitchen; in a secretive voice with a little giggle*)   I guess they wouldn't be interested now.

DOC (*with injured pride. A little sore*)   Oh, very well.

LOLA   Come and look, Daddy.

DOC (*shocked and angry*)   No!

LOLA   Just one little look. They're just kids, Daddy. It's sweet. (*Drags him by arm*)

DOC (*jerking loose*)   Stop it, Baby. I won't do it. It's not decent to snoop around spying on people like that. It's cheap and mischievous and mean.

LOLA (*this had never occurred to her*)   Is it?

DOC   Of course it is.

LOLA   I don't spy on Marie and Turk to be mischievous and mean.

DOC   Then why *do* you do it?

LOLA   You watch young people make love in the movies, don't you, Doc? There's nothing wrong with that. And I *know* Marie and I like her, and Turk's nice, too. They're both so young and pretty. Why shouldn't I watch them?

DOC   I give up.

LOLA   Well, why shouldn't I?

DOC   I don't know, Baby, but it's not nice.

> TURK *kisses* MARIE'S *ear*

LOLA   I think it's one of the nicest things I know. (*Plaintive*)

MARIE   Let's go out on the porch. (*They steal out*)

DOC   It's not right for Marie to do that, particularly since Bruce is coming. We shouldn't allow it.

LOLA   Oh, they don't do any harm, Doc. I think it's all right.

DOC   It's not all right. I don't know why you encourage that sort of thing.

LOLA   I don't encourage it.

DOC   You do, too. You like that fellow Turk. You said so. And I say he's no good. Marie's sweet and innocent; she doesn't understand guys like him. I think I oughta run him outa the house.

LOLA   Daddy, you wouldn't do that.

DOC (*very heated*)   Then you talk to her and tell her how we feel.

LOLA   Hush, Daddy. They'll hear you.

DOC   I don't care if they do hear me.

LOLA (*to* DOC *at stove*)   Don't get upset, Daddy. Bruce is coming and Turk won't be around any longer. I promise you.

DOC   All right. I better go.

LOLA   I'll go with you, Doc. Just let me run up and get a sweater. Now wait for me.

DOC   Hurry, Baby.

> LOLA *goes upstairs.* DOC *is at platform when he hears* TURK *laugh on the porch. He goes down left to cabinet—sees whiskey bottle. Reaches for it and hears* MARIE *giggle. Turns away as* TURK *laughs again. Turns back to the bottle and hears* LOLA'S *voice from upstairs.* MARIE *and* TURK *return to living room.* TURK *takes* LOLA'S *picture from shelf up right*

LOLA   I'll be there in a minute, Doc. (*Enters downstairs*) I'm all ready.

> DOC *turns out kitchen lights and they go into living room*

I'm walking Doc down to the bus.

> DOC *sees* TURK *with* LOLA'S *picture. Takes it out of his hand, puts it on shelf up right as* LOLA *leads him out.* DOC *is off*

Come on, Dad, here's your hat. Then I'll go for a long walk in the moonlight. Have a good time. (*She exits*)

MARIE   'Bye, Mrs. Delaney.

TURK   He hates my guts. (*To front door*)

MARIE   Oh, he does not. (*Follows* TURK, *blocks his exit in door*)

TURK   Yes, he does. If you ask me, he's jealous.

MARIE   Jealous?

TURK   I've always thought he had a crush on you.

MARIE   Now, Turk, don't be silly. Doc is nice to me. It's just in a few little things he does, like fixing my breakfast, but he's nice to everyone.

TURK   He ever make a pass?

MARIE   No. He'd never get fresh.

TURK   He better not.

MARIE   Turk, don't be ridiculous. Doc's such a nice, quiet man; if he gets any fun out of being nice to me, why not?

TURK   He's got a wife of his own, hasn't he? Why doesn't he make a few passes at her.

MARIE   Things like that are none of our business.

TURK   O.K. How about a snuggle, Lovely?

MARIE (*a little prim and businesslike*)   No more for tonight, Turk.

TURK   Why's tonight different from any other night?

MARIE   I think we should make it a rule, every once in a while, just to sit and talk. (*Starts to sit davenport—crosses to chair down right*)

TURK (*restless. Sits davenport*)   O.K. What'll we talk about?

MARIE   Well—there's lotsa things.

TURK   O.K. Start in.

MARIE   A person doesn't start a conversation that way.

TURK   Start it any way you want to.

MARIE   Two people should have something to talk about, like politics or psychology or religion.

TURK   How 'bout sex?

MARIE   Turk!

TURK (*chases her around davenport*)   Have you read the Kinsey report, Miss Buckholder?

MARIE   I should say not.

TURK   How old were you when you had your first affair, Miss Buckholder?—and did you ever have relations with your grandfather?

MARIE   Turk, stop it.

TURK   You wanted to talk about something; I was only trying to please. Let's have a kiss.

MARIE   Not tonight.

TURK   Who you savin' it up for?

MARIE   Don't talk that way.

TURK (*yawns—crosses to door*)   Well, thanks, Miss Buckholder, for a nice evening. It's been a most enjoyable talk.

MARIE (*anxious*)   Turk, where are you going?

TURK   I guess I'm a man of action, Baby.

MARIE   Turk, don't go.

TURK   Why not? I'm not doin' any good here.

MARIE   Don't go.

TURK (*returns and she touches him*)   Now why didn't you think of this before? C'mon, let's get to work. (*They sit on davenport*)

MARIE   Oh Turk, this is all we ever do.

TURK   Are you complaining?

MARIE (*weakly*)   —no.

TURK   Then what do you want to put on such a front for?

MARIE   —it's not a front.

TURK   What else is it? (*Mimicking*) Oh, no, Turk. Not tonight, Turk. I want to talk about philosophy, Turk. (*Himself again*) When all the time you know that if I went outa here without givin' you a good lovin' up you'd be sore as hell—Wouldn't you?

MARIE (*she has to admit to herself it's true; she chuckles*)   Oh—Turk—

TURK   It's true, isn't it?

MARIE   Maybe.

TURK   How about tonight, Lovely; going to be lonesome?

MARIE   Turk, you have the Spring Relays.

TURK   What of it? I can throw that old javelin any old time, *any* old time. C'mon, Baby, we've got by with it before, haven't we?

MARIE   I'm not so sure.

TURK   What do you mean?

MARIE   Sometimes I think Mrs. Delaney knows.

TURK   Well, bring her along. I'll take care of her too, if it'll keep her quiet.

MARIE (*a pretense of being shocked*)   Turk!

TURK   What makes you think so?

MARIE   Women just sense those things. She asks so many questions.

TURK   She ever *say* anything?

MARIE   No.

TURK   Now *you're* imagining things.

MARIE   Maybe.

TURK   Well, stop it.

MARIE   O.K.

TURK (*rises—follows* MARIE)   Honey, I know I talk awful rough around you at times; I never was a very gentlemanly bastard, but you really don't mind it—do you? (*She only smiles mischievously*) Anyway, you know I'm nuts about you.

MARIE (*smug*)   Are you?

> *Now they engage in a little roughhouse, he cuffing her like an affectionate bear, she responding with "Stop it," "Turk, that hurt," etc. And she slaps him playfully. Then they laugh together at their own pretense. Now* LOLA *enters the back way very quietly, tiptoeing through the dark kitchen, standing by the doorway where she can peek at them. There is a quiet, satisfied smile on her face. She watches every move they make, alertly*

TURK   Now, Miss Buckholder, what is your opinion of the psychodynamic pressure of living in the atomic age?

MARIE (*playfully*)   Turk, don't make fun of me.

TURK   Tonight?

MARIE (*her eyes dance as she puts him off just a little longer*)   —well.

TURK   Tonight will never come again. (*This is true. She smiles*) O.K.?

MARIE   Tonight will never come again—O.K. (*They embrace and start to dance*) Let's go out somewhere first and have a few beers. We can't come back till they're asleep.

TURK   O.K.

> *They dance slowly out the door. Then* LOLA *moves quietly into the living room and out onto the porch. There she can be heard calling plaintively in a lost voice*

LOLA   Little Sheba—come back—Come back, Little Sheba. Come back.

CURTAIN

ACT TWO   *Scene One*

> *The next morning.*
>   LOLA *and* DOC *are at breakfast again.* LOLA *is rambling on while* DOC *sits meditatively, his head down, his face in his hands.*

LOLA (*in a light, humorous way, as though the faults of youth were as blameless as the uncontrollable actions of a puppy. Chuckles*) Then they danced for a while and went out together, arm in arm—

DOC (*left of table. Very nervous and tense*) I don't wanta hear any more about it, Baby.

LOLA What's the matter, Docky?

DOC Nothing.

LOLA You look like you didn't feel very good.

DOC I didn't sleep well last night.

LOLA You didn't take any of those sleeping pills, did you?

DOC No.

LOLA Well, don't. The doctors say they're terrible for you.

DOC I'll feel better after a while.

LOLA Of course you will.

DOC What time did Marie come in last night?

LOLA I don't know, Doc. I went to bed early and went right to sleep. Why?

DOC Oh—nothing.

LOLA You musta slept if you didn't hear her.

DOC I heard her; it was after midnight.

LOLA Then what did you ask me for?

DOC I wasn't sure it was her.

LOLA What do you mean?

DOC I thought I heard a man's voice.

LOLA Turk probably brought her inside the door.

DOC (*troubled*) I thought I heard someone laughing. A man's laugh—I guess I was just hearing things.

LOLA Say your prayer?

DOC (*gets up*) Yes.

LOLA Kiss me 'bye.

> He leans over and kisses her, then puts on his coat and starts to leave

Do you think you could get home a little early? I want you to help me entertain Bruce. Marie said he'd be here about 5:30. I'm going to have a lovely dinner: stuffed pork chops, twice-baked potatoes, and asparagus, and for dessert a big chocolate cake and maybe ice cream—

DOC Sounds fine.

LOLA So you get home and help me.

DOC O.K.

> DOC *leaves kitchen and goes into living room. Again on the chair down right is* MARIE's *scarf. He picks it up as before and fondles it. Then there is the sound of* TURK's *laughter, soft and barely audible. It sounds like the laugh of a sated Bacchus.* DOC's *body stiffens. It is a sickening fact he must face and it has been revealed to him in its ugliest light. The lyrical grace, the spiritual ideal of Ave Maria is shattered. He has been fighting the truth, maybe suspecting all along*

that he was deceiving himself. Now he looks as though he might vomit. All his blind confusion is inside him. With an immobile expression of blankness on his face, he stumbles into the table above the davenport

LOLA (*still in kitchen*)   Haven't you gone yet, Docky?

DOC (*dazed*)   No—no, Baby.

LOLA (*coming in doorway*)   Anything the matter?

DOC   No—no. I'm all right now.

> *Drops scarf, takes hat. He has managed to sound perfectly natural. He braces himself and goes out.* LOLA *stands a moment, looking after him with a little curiosity. Then* MRS. COFFMAN *enters, sticks her head in back door*

MRS. COFFMAN   Anybody home?

LOLA (*on platform*)   'Morning, Mrs. Coffman.

MRS. COFFMAN (*inspecting the kitchen's new look*)   So this is what you've been up to, Mrs. Delaney.

LOLA (*proud*)   Yes, I been busy.

> MARIE's *door opens and closes.* MARIE *sticks her head out of her bedroom door to see if the coast is clear, then sticks her head back in again to whisper to* TURK *that he can leave without being observed*

MRS. COFFMAN   Busy? Good Lord, I never seen such activity. What got into you, Lady?

LOLA   Company tonight. I thought I'd fix things up a little.

MRS. COFFMAN   You mean you done all this in one day?

LOLA (*with simple pride*)   I said I been busy.

MRS. COFFMAN   Dear God, you done your spring housecleaning all in one day.

> TURK *appears in living room*

LOLA (*appreciating this*)   I fixed up the living room a little, too.

MRS. COFFMAN   I must see it.

> *Goes into living room.* TURK *apprehends her and ducks back into* MARIE's *room, shutting the door behind himself and* MARIE

I declare! Overnight you turn the place into something really swanky.

LOLA   Yes, and I bought a few new things, too.

MRS. COFFMAN   Neat as a pin, and so warm and cozy. I take my hat off to you, Mrs. Delaney. I didn't know you had it in you. All these years, now, I been sayin' to myself, "That Mrs. Delaney is a good for nothing—sits around the house all day, and never so much as shakes a dust mop." I guess it just shows, we never really know what people are like.

LOLA   I still got some coffee, Mrs. Coffman.

MRS. COFFMAN   Not now, Mrs. Delaney. Seeing your house so clean makes me feel ashamed. I gotta get home and get to work. (*To kitchen*)

LOLA (*follows*)   I hafta get busy, too. I got to get out all the silver and china. I like to set the table early, so I can spend the rest of the day looking at it.

MRS. COFFMAN   Good day, Mrs. Delaney. (*Exits*)

> *Hearing the screen door slam,* MARIE *guards the kitchen door and* TURK *slips out the front. But neither has counted on* DOC's *reappearance. After seeing that* TURK *is safe,* MARIE *blows a good-bye kiss to him and joins* LOLA *in the kitchen. But* DOC *is coming in the front door just as* TURK *starts to go out. There is a moment of blind embarrassment, during which* DOC *only looks stupefied and* TURK, *after mumbling an unintelligible apology, runs out. First* DOC *is mystified, trying to figure it all out. His face looks more and more troubled. Meanwhile,* MARIE *and* LOLA *are talking in the kitchen*

MARIE   Boo! (*Sneaking up behind* LOLA *at back porch*)

LOLA (*jumping around*)   Heavens! You scared me, Marie. You up already?

MARIE   Yah.

LOLA   This is Saturday. You could sleep as late as you wanted.

MARIE   I thought I'd get up early and help you. (*Pouring a cup of coffee*)

LOLA   Honey, I'd sure appreciate it. You can put up the table in the living room, after you've had your breakfast. That's where we'll eat. Then you can help me set it.

> DOC *closes door*

MARIE   O.K.

LOLA   Want a sweet roll?

MARIE   I don't think so. Turk and I had so much beer last night. He got kinda tight.

LOLA   He shouldn't do that, Marie.

MARIE (*starts for living room*)   Just keep the coffee hot for me. I'll want another cup in a minute. (*Stops on seeing* DOC) Why, Dr. Delaney. I thought you'd gone.

DOC (*in his usual manner*)   Good morning, Marie. (*But not looking at her*)

MARIE (*she immediately wonders*)   Why—why—how long have you been here, Doc?

DOC   Just got here, just this minute.

LOLA   That you, Daddy? (*Comes in*)

DOC   It's me.

LOLA   What are you doing back?

DOC   I—I just thought I'd feel better—if I took a glass of soda water—

LOLA   I'm afraid you're not well, Daddy.

DOC   I'm all right. (*Starts for kitchen*)

LOLA (*helping* MARIE *move table from behind davenport to right center*)   The soda's on the drain board.

> DOC *goes to kitchen, fixes some soda, but stands a moment, just thinking. Then he sits sipping the soda, as though he were trying to make up his mind about something*

LOLA   Marie, would you help me move the table? It'd be nice now if we had a dining room, wouldn't it? But if we had a dining room, I guess we wouldn't have you, Marie. It was my idea to turn the dining room into a bedroom and rent it. I thought of lots of things to do for extra money—a few years ago—when Doc was so—so sick.

They set up table. LOLA *gets cloth from cabinet up left*

MARIE   This is a lovely tablecloth.

LOLA   Irish linen. Doc's mother gave it to us when we got married. She gave us all our silver and china, too. The china's Havelin. I'm so proud of it. It's the most valuable possession we own. I just washed it—Will you help me bring it in? (*Getting china from kitchen*) Doc was sortuva Mama's boy. He was an only child and his mother thought the sun rose and set in him. Didn't she, Docky? She brought Doc up like a real gentleman.

MARIE   Where are the napkins?

LOLA   Oh, I forgot them. They're so nice I keep them in my bureau drawer with my handkerchiefs. Come upstairs and we'll get them.

> LOLA *and* MARIE *go upstairs. Then,* DOC *listens to be sure* LOLA *and* MARIE *are upstairs, looks cautiously at the whiskey bottle on cabinet shelf, but manages to resist several times. Finally he gives in to temptation, grabs bottle off shelf, then starts wondering how to get past* LOLA *with it. Finally, it occurs to him to wrap it inside his trench coat, which he gets from closet and carries it over his arm.* LOLA *and* MARIE *are heard upstairs and they return to the living room and continue setting table as* DOC *enters from kitchen on his way out*

LOLA (*coming downstairs*)   Did you ever notice how nice he keeps his fingernails? Not many men think of things like that. And he used to take his mother to church every Sunday.

MARIE (*at table*)   Oh, Doc's a real gentleman.

LOLA   Treats women like they were all beautiful angels. We went together a whole year before he even kissed me.

> DOC *comes through the living room with coat and bottle, going to front door*

On your way back to the office now, Docky?

DOC (*his back to them*)   Yes.

LOLA   Aren't you going to kiss me goodbye before you go, Daddy?

> *She goes to him and kisses him.* MARIE *catches* DOC'*s eye and smiles. Then she exits to her room, leaving door open*

Get home early as you can. I'll need you. We gotta give Bruce a royal welcome.

DOC   Yes, Baby.

LOLA   Feeling all right?

DOC   Yes.

LOLA (*in doorway. He is on porch*)   Take care of yourself.

DOC (*toneless voice*)　　Goodbye. (*He goes*)

LOLA (*coming back to table with pleased expression, which changes to a puzzled look. Calls to* MARIE)　　Now that's funny. Why did Doc take his raincoat? It's a beautiful day. There isn't a cloud in sight.

CURTAIN

Scene Two

It is now 5:30.

> *The scene is the same as the preceding except that more finishing touches have been added and the* TWO WOMEN, *still primping the table, lighting the tapers, are dressed in their best.* LOLA *is arranging the centerpiece.*

LOLA (*above table, fixing flowers*)　　I just love lilacs, don't you, Marie? (*Takes one and studies it*) Mrs. Coffman was nice; she let me have all I wanted. (*Looks at it very closely*) Aren't they pretty? And they smell so sweet. I think they're the nicest flower there is.

MARIE　　They don't last long.

LOLA (*respectfully*)　　No. Just a few days. Mrs. Coffman's started blooming just day before yesterday.

MARIE　　By the first of the week they'll all be gone.

LOLA　　Vanish—they'll vanish into thin air. (*Gayer now*) Here, Honey, we have them to spare *now*. Put this in your hair. There. (MARIE *does*) Mrs. Coffman's been so nice lately. I didn't use to like her. Now where could Doc be? He didn't even come home for lunch.

MARIE (*gets two chairs from bedroom*)　　Mrs. Delaney, you're a peach to go to all this trouble.

LOLA (*gets salt and pepper*)　　Shoot, I'm gettin' more fun out of it than you are. Do you think Bruce is going to like us?

MARIE　　If he doesn't, I'll never speak to him again.

LOLA (*eagerly*)　　I'm just dying to meet him. But I feel sorta bad I never got to do anything nice for Turk.

MARIE (*carefully prying*)　　Did—Doc ever say anything to you about Turk—and me?

LOLA　　About Turk and you? No, Honey. Why?

MARIE　　I just wondered.

LOLA　　What if Bruce finds out that you've been going with someone else?

MARIE　　Bruce and I had a very businesslike understanding before I left for school that we weren't going to sit around lonely just because we were separated.

LOLA　　Aren't you being kind of mean to Turk?

MARIE　　I don't think so.

LOLA　　How's he going to feel when Bruce comes?

MARIE　　He may be sore for a little while. He'll get over it.

LOLA   Won't he feel bad?

MARIE   He's had his eye on a pretty little Spanish girl in his history class for a long time. I like Turk, but he's not the marrying kind.

LOLA   No! Really? (LOLA, *with a look of sad wonder on her face, sits right arm of couch. It's been a serious disillusionment*)

MARIE   What's the matter?

LOLA   I—I just felt kinda tired.

> *Sharp buzzing of doorbell.* MARIE *runs to answer it*

MARIE   That must be Bruce. (*She skips to the mirror, then to door*) Bruce!

BRUCE (*entering*)   How are you, Sweetheart?

MARIE   Wonderful.

BRUCE   Did you get my wire?

MARIE   Sure.

BRUCE   You're looking swell.

MARIE   Thanks. What took you so long to get here?

BRUCE   Well, Honey, I had to go to my hotel and take a bath.

MARIE   Bruce, this is Mrs. Delaney.

BRUCE (*now he gets the cozy quality out of his voice*)   How do you do, Ma'am?

LOLA   How d'ya do?

BRUCE   Marie has said some very nice things about you in her letters.

MARIE   Mrs. Delaney has fixed the grandest dinner for us.

BRUCE   Now that was to be my treat. I have a big expense account now, Honey. I thought we could all go down to the hotel and have dinner there, and celebrate first with a few cocktails.

LOLA   Oh, we can have cocktails, too. Excuse me just a minute.

> *She hurries to the kitchen and starts looking for the whiskey.* BRUCE *kisses* MARIE. *Then she whispers*

MARIE   Now, Bruce, she's been working on this dinner all day. She even cleaned the house for you.

BRUCE   Did she?

MARIE   And Doc's joining us. You'll like Doc.

BRUCE   Honey, are we going to have to stay here the whole evening?

MARIE   We just can't eat and run right away. We'll get away as soon as we can.

BRUCE   I hope so. I got the raise, Sweetheart. They're giving me new territory.

> LOLA *is frantic in the kitchen, having found the bottle missing. She hurries back into the living room*

LOLA   You kids are going to have to entertain yourselves a while 'cause I'm going to be busy in the kitchen. Why don't you turn on the radio, Marie? Get some dance music. I'll shut the door so—so I won't disturb you. (LOLA *does so. Then goes to the telephone*)

MARIE   Come and see my room, Bruce. I've fixed it up just darling. And I've got your picture in the prettiest frame right on my dresser.

> *They exit and their voices are heard from the bedroom while* LOLA *is telephoning*

LOLA (*at the telephone*)   This is Mrs. Delaney. Is—Doc there? Well, then, is Ed Anderson there? Well, would you give me Ed Anderson's telephone number? You see, he sponsored Doc into the club and helped him—you know—and—and I was a little worried tonight— Oh, thanks. Yes, I've got it. (*She writes down number*) Could you have Ed Anderson call me if he comes in? Thank you. (*She hangs up. On her face is a dismal expression of fear, anxiety, and doubt. She searches flour bin, icebox, closet. Then she goes into the living room, calling to* MARIE *and* BRUCE *as she comes*) I—I guess we'll go ahead without Doc, Marie.

MARIE (*enters from her room*)   What's the matter with Doc, Mrs. Delaney?

LOLA   Well—he got held up at the office—just one of those things, you know. It's too bad. It would have to happen when I needed him most.

MARIE   Sure you don't need any help?

LOLA   Huh? Oh, no. I'll make out. Everything's ready. I tell you what I'm going to do. Three's a crowd, so I'm going to be the butler and serve the dinner to you two young lovebirds—

> *The telephone rings.* MARIE *goes into bedroom*

Pardon me—pardon me just a minute. (*She rushes to telephone, closing the door behind her*) Hello? Ed? Have you seen Doc? He went out this morning and hasn't come back. We're having company for dinner and he was supposed to be home early— That's not all. This time we've had a quart of whiskey in the kitchen and Doc's never gone near it. I went to get it tonight. I was going to serve some cocktails. It was *gone*. Yes, I saw it there yesterday. No, I don't think so— He said this morning he had an upset stomach but— Oh would you?— Thank you, Mr. Anderson. Thank you a million times. And you let me know when you find out anything. Yes, I'll be here. Yes. (*Hangs up and crosses back to living room*) Well, I guess we're all ready.

> *Their voices continue in bedroom*

BRUCE   Aren't you going to look at your present?

MARIE   Oh sure; let's get some scissors. (*Enters with* BRUCE) Mrs. Delaney, we think you should eat with us.

LOLA   Oh, no, Honey. I'm not very hungry. Besides, this is the first time you've been together in months and I think you should be alone. Marie, why don't you light the candles, then we'll have just the right atmosphere.

> *She goes into kitchen, gets tomato juice glasses from ice box while* BRUCE *lights the candles*

BRUCE   Do we have to eat by candlelight? I won't be able to see.

LOLA (*returns*)   Now, Bruce, you sit here. (*He and* MARIE *sit*) Isn't that going to be cozy? Dinner for two. Sorry we won't have time for cocktails. Let's have a little music.

> *She turns on the radio and a Viennese waltz swells up as the Curtain falls, with* LOLA *looking at the young people eating*

CURTAIN

Scene Three

Funeral atmosphere. It is about 5:30 the next morning. The sky is just beginning to get light outside. While inside the room the shadows still cling heavily to the corners. The remains of last night's dinner clutter the table in the living room. The candles have guttered down to stubs amid the dirty dinner plates, and the lilacs in the centerpiece have wilted. LOLA is sprawled on the davenport, sleeping. Slowly she awakens and regards the morning light. She gets up and looks about strangely, beginning to show despair for the situation she is in. She wears the same spiffy dress she had on the night before, but it is wrinkled now, and her marcelled coiffure is awry. One silk stocking has twisted loose and falls around her ankle. When she is sufficiently awake to realize her situation, she rushes to the telephone and dials a number.

LOLA (*at telephone. She sounds frantic*)   Mr. Anderson? Mr. Anderson, this is Mrs. Delaney again. I'm sorry to call you so early, but I just *had* to— Did you find Doc?—No, he's not home yet. I don't suppose he'll come home till he's drunk all he can hold and wants to sleep— I don't know what else to think, Mr. Anderson. I'm scared, Mr. Anderson. I'm awful scared. Will you come right over?—Thanks, Mr. Anderson.

> *Hangs up and goes to kitchen to make coffee. She finds some left from the night before, so turns on the fire to warm it up. She wanders around vaguely, trying to get her thoughts in order, jumping at every sound. Pours herself a cup of coffee, then takes it to living room, sits down right and sips it. Very quietly DOC enters through the back way into the kitchen. He carries a big bottle of whiskey, which he carefully places back in the cabinet, not making a sound—hangs up overcoat, then puts suitcoat on back of chair. Starts to go upstairs. But LOLA speaks*

Doc? That you, Doc?

> *Then DOC quietly walks in from kitchen. He is staggering drunk, but he is managing for a few minutes to appear as though he were perfectly sober and nothing had happened. His steps, however, are not too sure and his eyes are like blurred ink pots. LOLA is too frightened to talk. Her mouth is gaping and she is breathless with fear*

DOC   Good morning, Honey.

LOLA   Doc! You all right?

DOC   The morning paper here? I wanta see the morning paper.

LOLA   Doc, we don't get a morning paper. *You* know that.

DOC   Oh, then I suppose I'm drunk or something. That what you're trying to say?

LOLA   No, Doc—

DOC   Then give me the morning paper.

LOLA (*scampering to get last night's paper from table left*)   Sure, Doc. Here it is. Now you just sit there and be quiet.

DOC (*resistance rising*)   Why shouldn't I be quiet?

LOLA   Nothin', Doc—

DOC (*has trouble unfolding paper. He places it before his face in order not to be seen. But he is too blind even to see. Mockingly*)   Nothing, Doc.

LOLA (*cautiously, after a few minute's silence*)   Doc, are you all right?

DOC   Of course I'm all right. Why shouldn't I be all right?

LOLA   Where you been?

DOC   What's it your business where I been? I been to London to see the Queen. What do you think of that?

> *Apparently she doesn't know what to think of it*

Just let me alone. That's all I ask. I'm all right.

LOLA (*whimpering*)   Doc, what made you do it? You said you'd be home last night—'cause we were having company. Bruce was here and I had a big dinner fixed—and you never came. What was the matter, Doc?

DOC (*mockingly*)   We had a big dinner for *Bruce.*

LOLA   Doc, it was for you, too.

DOC   Well—I don't want it.

LOLA   Don't get mad, Doc.

DOC (*threateningly*)   Where's Marie?

LOLA   I don't know, Doc. She didn't come in last night. She was out with Bruce.

DOC (*back to audience*)   I suppose you tucked them in bed together and peeked through the keyhole and applauded.

LOLA (*sickened*)   Doc, don't talk that way. Bruce is a nice boy. They're gonna get married.

DOC   He probably *has* to marry her, the poor bastard. Just 'cause she's pretty and he got amorous one day— Just like I had to marry *you.*

LOLA   Oh, Doc.

DOC   You and Marie are both a couple of sluts.

LOLA   Doc, please don't talk like that.

DOC   What are you good for? You can't even get up in the morning and cook my breakfast.

LOLA (*mumbling*)   I will, Doc. I will after this.

DOC   You won't even sweep the floor till some bozo comes along to make love to Marie, and then you fix things up like Buckingham Palace or a Chinese whorehouse with perfume on the lampbulbs, and flowers, and the gold-trimmed china *my mother* gave us. We're not going to use these any more. My mother didn't buy those dishes for whores to eat off of. (*Jerks the cloth off the table, sending the dishes rattling to the floor*)

LOLA   Doc! Look what you done.

DOC   Look what I *did*, not done. I'm going to get me a drink. (*To kitchen*)

LOLA (*follows to platform*)   Oh, no, Doc! You know what it does to you!

DOC   You're damn right I know what it does to me. It makes me willing
    to come home here and look at you, you two-ton old heifer. (*Gets
    bottle. Takes a long swallow*) There! And pretty soon I'm going to have
    another, then another.

LOLA (*with dread*)   Oh, Doc!

>   LOLA *takes phone. Doc sees this, rushes for the butcher-knife in
>   kitchen cabinet drawer. Not finding it, he gets a hatchet from the
>   back porch*

Mr. Anderson? Come quick, Mr. Anderson. He's back. He's *back*!
He's got a hatchet!

DOC   God damn you! Get away from that telephone. (*He chases her into
    living room, where she gets the davenport between them*) That's right, phone!
    Tell the world I'm drunk. Tell the whole damn world. Scream your
    head off, you fat slut. Holler till all the neighbors think I'm beatin' hell
    outuv you. Where's Bruce now—under Marie's bed? You got all
    fresh and pretty for him, didn't you? Combed your hair for once—
    You even washed the back of your neck, and put on a girdle. You were
    willing to harness all that fat into one bundle.

LOLA (*about to faint under the weight of the crushing accusations*)   Doc, don't say
    any more— I'd rather you hit me with an axe, Doc— Honest I would.
    But I can't stand to hear you talk like that.

DOC   I oughta hack off all that fat, and then wait for Marie and chop off
    those pretty ankles she's always dancing around on—then start lookin'
    for Turk and fix him too.

LOLA   Daddy, you're talking crazy!

DOC   I'm making sense for the first time in my life. You didn't know I
    knew about it, did you? But I saw him coming outa there. I saw him.
    You knew about it all the time and thought you were hidin' some-
    thing—

LOLA   Daddy, I didn't know anything about it at all. Honest, Daddy.

DOC   Then *you're* the one that's crazy, if you think I didn't know. You
    were running a regular house, weren't you? It's probably been going
    on for years, ever since we were married.

>   *He lunges for her. She breaks for kitchen. They struggle in front of
>   sink*

LOLA   Doc, it's not so; it's not so. You gotta believe me, Doc.

DOC   You're lyin'. But none a that's gonna happen any more. I'm
    gonna fix you now, once and for all—

LOLA   Doc—don't do that to me. (LOLA, *in a frenzy of fear clutches him
    around the neck, holding arm with axe by his side*) Remember, Doc. It's
    me, Lola! You said I was the prettiest girl you ever saw. Remember,
    Doc! It's me! Lola!

DOC (*the memory has overpowered him. He collapses, slowly mumbling*)   Lola—my
    pretty Lola.

>   *He passes out on the floor.* LOLA *stands, now, as though in a trance.
>   Quietly* MRS. COFFMAN *comes creeping in through the back way*

MRS. COFFMAN (*calling softly*)   Mrs. Delaney! (LOLA *doesn't even hear.* MRS. COFFMAN *comes on in*) Mrs. Delaney!—Here you are, Lady. I heard screaming and I was frightened for you.

LOLA   I—I'll be all right—some men are comin' pretty soon; everything'll be all right.

MRS. COFFMAN   I'll stay until they get here.

LOLA (*feeling a sudden need*)   Would you—would you *please*, Mrs. Coffman? (*Breaks into sobs*)

MRS. COFFMAN   Of course, Lady. (*Regarding* DOC) The Doctor got "sick" again?

LOLA (*mumbling*)   Some men—'ll be here pretty soon—

MRS. COFFMAN   I'll try to straighten things up before they get here—
     She rights chair, hangs up telephone and picks up the axe, which she is holding when ED ANDERSON *and* ELMO HUSTON *enter front door unannounced. They are experienced AA's. Neatly dressed businessmen approaching middle-age*

ED   Pardon us for walking right in, Mrs. Delaney, but I didn't want to waste a second. (*To kitchen. Kneels at* DOC)

LOLA (*weakly*)   —it's all right—
     Both MEN *observe* DOC *on the floor, and their expressions hold understanding mixed with a feeling of irony. There is even a slight smile of irony on* ED's *face. They have developed the surgeon's objectivity*

ED   Where is the hatchet? (*To* ELMO, *as though appraising* DOC's *condition*) What do you think, Elmo?

ELMO   We can't leave him here if he's gonna play around with hatchets.

ED   Give me a hand, Elmo. We'll get him to sit up and then try to talk some sense into him. (*They struggle with the lumpy body,* DOC *grunting his resistance*) Come on, Doc, old boy. It's Ed and Elmo. We're going to take care of you. (*They seat him at table*)

DOC (*through a thick fog*)   Lemme alone.

ED   Wake up. We're taking you away from here.

DOC   Lemme 'lone, God damn it. (*Falls forward—head on table*)

ELMO (*to* MRS. COFFMAN)   Is there any coffee?

MRS. COFFMAN   I think so. I'll see. (*To stove with cup from drainboard. Lights fire under coffee, and waits for it to get heated*)

ED   He's way beyond coffee.

ELMO   It'll help some. Get something hot into his stomach.

ED   —if we could get him to eat. How 'bout some hot food, Doc?
     DOC *gestures and they don't push the matter*

ELMO   City hospital, Ed?

ED   I guess that's what it will have to be.

LOLA   Where are you going to take him?
     ELMO *goes to telephone—speaks quietly to City Hospital*

ED   Don't know. Wanta talk to him first.

MRS. COFFMAN (*coming with the coffee*)   Here's the coffee.

ED (*taking cup*)   Hold him, Elmo, while I make him swallow this.

ELMO   Come on, Doc, drink your coffee.

DOC (*he only blubbers. After the coffee is down*)   Uh—what—what's goin' on here?

ED   It's me, Doc. Your old friend Ed. I got Elmo with me.

DOC (*twisting his face painfully*)   Get out, both of you. Lemme 'lone.

ED (*with certainty*)   We're takin' you with us, Doc.

DOC   Hell you are. I'm all right. I just had a little slip. We all have slips—

ED   Sometimes, Doc, but we gotta get over 'em.

DOC   I'll be O.K. Just gimme a day to sober up. I'll be as good as new.

ED   Remember the last time, Doc? You said you'd be all right in the morning and we found you with a broken collar bone. Come on.

DOC   Boys, I'll be all right. Now lemme alone.

ED   How much has he had, Mrs. Delaney?

LOLA   I don't know. He had a quart when he left here yesterday and he didn't get home till now.

ED   He's probably been through a *couple* of quarts. He's been dry for a long time. It's going to hit him pretty hard. Yah, he'll be a pretty sick man for a few days. (*Louder to* DOC, *as though he were talking to a deaf man*) Wanta go to the City Hospital, Doc?

DOC (*this has a sobering effect on him. He looks about him furtively for possible escape*)   No—no, boys. Don't take me there. That's a torture chamber. No, Ed. You wouldn't do that to me.

ED   They'll sober you up.

DOC   Ed, I been there; I've seen the place. That's where they take the crazy people. You can't do that to me, Ed.

ED   Well, *you're* crazy, aren't you? Goin' after your wife with a hatchet.

> They lift DOC *to his feet.* DOC *looks with dismal pleading in his eyes at* LOLA, *who has her face in her hands*

DOC (*so plaintive, a sob in his voice*)   Honey! Honey!

> LOLA *can't look at him. Now* DOC *tries to make a getaway, bolting blindly into the living room before the* TWO MEN *catch him and hold him in front of table*

Honey, don't let 'em take me there. They'll believe *you*. Tell 'em you won't *let* me take a drink.

LOLA   Isn't there any place else you could take him?

ED   Private sanitariums cost a lotta dough.

LOLA   I got forty dollars in the kitchen.

ED   That won't be near enough.

DOC   I'll be at the meeting tomorrow night sober as you are now.

ED (*to* LOLA)   All the king's horses couldn't keep him from takin' another drink now, Mrs. Delaney. He got himself into this; he's gotta sweat it out.

DOC   I won't go to the City Hospital. That's where they take the crazy people. (*Stumbles into chair down right*)

ED (*using all his patience now*)   Look, Doc. Elmo and I are your friends. You know that. Now if you don't come along peacefully, we're going to call the cops and you'll have to wear off this jag in the cooler. How'd you like that?

DOC *is as though stunned*

The important thing is for you to get sober.

DOC   I don't wanta go.

ED   The City Hospital or the City Jail. Take your choice. We're not going to leave you here. Come on, Elmo. (*They grab hold of him*)

DOC (*has collected himself and now given in*)   O.K., boys. Gimme another drink and I'll go.

LOLA   Oh no, Doc.

ED   Might as well humor him, Ma'am. Another few drinks couldn't make much difference now.

MRS. COFFMAN *runs for bottle and glass in cabinet, comes right back with them, hands them to* LOLA

ED   O.K., Doc, we're goin' to give you a drink. Take a good one; it's gonna be your last for a long time to come.

ED *takes the bottle, removes the cork and gives* DOC *a glass of whiskey.* DOC *takes his fill, straight, coming up once or twice for air. Then* ED *takes the bottle from him and hands it to* LOLA

They'll keep him three or four days, Mrs. Delaney; then he'll be home again, good as new. (*Modestly*) I—I don't want to pry into personal affairs, Ma'am—but he'll need you then, pretty bad—

LOLA   I know.

ED   Come on, Doc. Let's go.

ED *has a hold of* DOC's *coat sleeve, trying to maneuver him. A faraway look is in* DOC's *eyes, a dazed look containing panic and fear. He gets to his feet*

DOC (*struggling to sound reasonable*)   Just a minute, boys—

ED   What's the matter?

DOC   I—I wanta glass of water.

ED   You'll get a glass of water later. Come on.

DOC (*beginning to twist a little in* ED's *grasp*)   —a glass of water—that's all— (*One furious, quick twist of his body and he eludes* ED)

ED   Quick, Elmo.

ELMO *acts fast and they get* DOC *before he gets away. Then* DOC *struggles with all his might, kicking and screaming like a pampered child,* ED *and* ELMO *holding him tightly to usher him out*

DOC (*as he is led out*)   Don't let 'em take me there. Don't take me there. Stop them, somebody. Stop them. That's where they take the crazy people. Oh God, stop them, somebody. Stop them.

LOLA *looks on blankly while* ED *and* ELMO *depart with* DOC. *Sits down right. Now there are several moments of deep silence*

MRS. COFFMAN (*clears up. Very softly*)   Is there anything more I can do for you now, Mrs. Delaney?

LOLA   I guess not.

MRS. COFFMAN (*puts a hand on* LOLA's *shoulder*)   Get busy, Lady. Get busy and forget it.

LOLA   Yes—I'll get busy right away. Thanks, Mrs. Coffman.

MRS. COFFMAN   I better go. I've got to make breakfast for the children. If you want me for anything, let me know.

LOLA   Yes—yes— Goodbye, Mrs. Coffman.

> MRS. COFFMAN *exits back door.* LOLA *is too exhausted to move from the big chair. At first she can't even cry; then the tears come slowly, softly. In a few moments* BRUCE *and* MARIE *enter, bright and merry.* LOLA *turns her head slightly to regard them as creatures from another planet*

MARIE (*springing into room*)   Congratulate me, Mrs. Delaney.

> BRUCE *follows*

LOLA   Huh?

MARIE   We're going to be married.

LOLA   Married? (*It barely registers*)

MARIE (*showing ring*)   Here it is. My engagement ring.

> MARIE *and* BRUCE *are too engrossed in their own happiness to notice* LOLA's *stupor*

LOLA   That's lovely—lovely.

MARIE   We've had the most wonderful time. We danced all night and then drove out to the lake and saw the sun rise.

LOLA   That's nice.

MARIE   We've made all our plans. I'm quitting school and flying back to Cincinnati with Bruce this afternoon. His mother has invited me to visit them before I go home. Isn't that wonderful?

LOLA   Yes—yes, indeed.

MARIE   Going to miss me?

LOLA   Yes, of course, Marie. We'll miss you very much— Uh— congratulations.

MARIE   Thanks, Mrs. Delaney. (*Crosses up to bedroom door*) Come on, Bruce, help me get my stuff. Mrs. Delaney, would you throw everything into a big box and send it to me at home? We haven't had breakfast yet. We're going down to the hotel and celebrate.

BRUCE   I'm sorry we're in such a hurry, but we've got a taxi waiting. (*They go into bedroom*)

LOLA (*to telephone, dials*)   Long Distance? I want to talk to Green Valley 223. Yes. This is Delmar 1887.

> *She hangs up, crosses down. As she gets below table,* MARIE *comes from bedroom, followed by* BRUCE, *who carries suitcase*

MARIE   Mrs. Delaney, I sure hate to say goodbye to you. You've been so wonderful to me. But Bruce says I can come and visit you once in a while, didn't you, Bruce?

BRUCE   Sure thing.

LOLA   You're going?

MARIE   We're going downtown and have our breakfast, then do a little shopping and catch our plane. And thanks for everything, Mrs. Delaney.

BRUCE   It was very nice of you to have us to dinner.

LOLA   Dinner? Oh, don't mention it.

MARIE (*to* LOLA)   There isn't much time for goodbye now, but I just want you to know Bruce and I wish you the best of everything. You and Doc both. Tell Doc goodbye for me, will you, and remember, I think you're both a coupla peaches.

BRUCE   Hurry, Honey.

MARIE   'Bye, Mrs. Delaney! (*She goes out door*)

BRUCE   'Bye, Mrs. Delaney. Thanks for being nice to my girl. (*He goes out and off porch with* MARIE)

LOLA (*waves. The telephone rings. She goes to it quickly*)   Hello. Hello, Mom. It's Lola, Mom. How are you? Mom, Doc's sick again. Do you think Dad would let me come home for a while? I'm awfully unhappy, Mom. Do you think—just till I made up my mind?—All right. No, I guess it wouldn't do any good for you to come here— I—I'll let you know what I decide to do. That's all, Mom. Thanks. Tell Daddy hello. (*She hangs up*)

CURTAIN

Scene Four

It is morning, a week later. The house is neat again, as in Act One, Scene Two.

LOLA *is dusting in the living room as* MRS. COFFMAN *enters from back door.*

MRS. COFFMAN   Mrs. Delaney! Good morning, Mrs. Delaney.

LOLA   Come in, Mrs. Coffman.

MRS. COFFMAN (*coming in*)   It's a fine day for the games. I've got a box lunch ready, and I'm taking all the kids to the Stadium. My boy's got a ticket for you, too. You better get dressed and come with us.

LOLA   Thanks, Mrs. Coffman, but I've got work to do.

MRS. COFFMAN   But it's such a big day. The Spring Relays— All the athletes from the colleges are supposed to be there.

LOLA   Oh yes. You know that boy Turk who used to come here to see Marie—he's one of the big stars.

MRS. COFFMAN   Is that so? Come on—do. We've got a ticket for you—

LOLA   Oh no, I have to stay here and clean up the house. Doc may be coming home today. I talked to him on the phone. He wasn't sure what time they'd let him out, but I wanta have the place all nice for him.

MRS. COFFMAN   Well, I'll tell you all about it when I come home. Everybody and his brother will be there.

LOLA   Yes, do, and have a good time.

MRS. COFFMAN   'Bye, Mrs. Delaney.

LOLA   'Bye.

> MRS. COFFMAN *leaves, and* LOLA *goes into kitchen. The* MAIL-MAN *comes onto porch and leaves a letter, but* LOLA *doesn't even know he's there. Then the* MILKMAN *knocks on the back door*

LOLA   Come in.

MILKMAN (*entering with arm full of bottles, etc.*)   I see you checked the list, Lady. You've got a lot of extras.

LOLA   Ya—I think my husband's coming home.

MILKMAN (*he puts the supplies on table, then pulls out magazine*)   Remember, I told you my picture was going to appear in *Strength and Health*. (*Showing her magazine*) Well, see that pile of muscles? That's me.

LOLA (*totally without enthusiasm*)   My goodness. You got your picture in a magazine.

MILKMAN   Yes, Ma'am. See what it says about my chest development? For the greatest self-improvement in a three months' period.

LOLA   Goodness sakes. You'll be famous, won't you?

MILKMAN   If I keep busy on these bar-bells. I'm working now for "muscular separation."

LOLA   That's nice.

MILKMAN (*cheerily*)   Well, good day, Ma'am.

LOLA   You forgot your magazine.

MILKMAN   That's for you. (*Exits*)

> LOLA *puts away the supplies in the icebox. Then* DOC *comes in the front door carrying the little suitcase she previously packed for him.* DOC *is himself again. His quiet manner, his serious demeanor, are the same as before.* LOLA *is shocked by his sudden appearance. She jumps and can't help showing her fright*

LOLA   Docky!

> *Without thinking, she assumes an attitude of fear.* DOC *observes this and it obviously pains him*

DOC   Good morning, Honey. (*Pause*)

LOLA (*on platform*)   Are—are you all right, Doc?

DOC   Yes, I'm all right. (*An awkward pause. Then* DOC *tries to reassure her*) Honest, I'm all right, Honey. Please don't stand there like that—like I was gonna—gonna—

LOLA (*tries to relax*)   I'm sorry, Doc.

DOC   How you been?

LOLA   Oh, I been all right, Doc. Fine.

DOC   Any news?

LOLA   I told you about Marie—over the phone.

DOC   Yah.

LOLA   He was a very nice boy, Doc. Very nice.

DOC   That's good. I hope they'll be happy.

LOLA (*trying to sound bright*)   She said—maybe she'd come back and visit us sometime. That's what she *said*.

DOC (*pause*)   It—it's good to be home.

LOLA   Is it, Daddy?

DOC   Yah. (*Beginning to choke up just a little*)

LOLA   Did everything go all right— I mean—did they treat you well and—

DOC (*now loses control of his feelings. Tears in his eyes, he all but lunges at her, gripping her arms, drilling his head into her bosom*)   Honey, don't ever leave me. *Please* don't ever leave me. If you do, they'd have to keep me down at that place all the time. I don't know what I said to you or what I did. I can't remember hardly anything. But please forgive me—please—please— And I'll try to make everything up.

LOLA (*there is surprise on her face and new contentment. She becomes almost angelic in demeanor. Tenderly she places a soft hand on his head*)   Daddy! Why, of course I'll never leave you. (*A smile of satisfaction*) You're all I've got. You're all I ever had.

DOC (*collecting himself now. Very tenderly he kisses her.* LOLA *sits beside* DOC)   I—I feel better—already.

LOLA (*almost gay*)   So do I. Have you had your breakfast?

DOC   No. The food there was terrible. When they told me I could go this morning, I decided to wait and fix myself breakfast here.

LOLA (*happily*)   Come on out in the kitchen and I'll get you a nice, big breakfast. I'll scramble some eggs and— You see I've got the place all cleaned up just the way you like it. (DOC *goes to kitchen*) Now you sit down here and I'll get your fruit juice. (*He sits and she gets fruit juice from refrigerator*) I've got bacon this morning, too. My, it's expensive now. And I'll light the oven and make you some toast, and here's some orange marmalade, and—

DOC (*with a new feeling of control*)   Fruit juice. I'll need lots of it for a while. The doctor said it would restore the vitamins. You see, that damn whiskey kills all the vitamins in your system, eats up all the sugar in your kidneys. They came around every morning and shot vitamins in my arm. Oh, it didn't hurt. And the doctor told me to drink a quart of fruit juice every day. And you better get some candy bars for me at the grocery this morning. Doctor said to eat lots of candy, try to replace the sugar.

LOLA   I'll do that, Doc. Here's another glass of this pineapple juice now. I'll get some candy bars first thing.

DOC   The doctor said I should have a hobby. Said I should go out more. That's all that's wrong with me. I thought maybe I'd go hunting once in a while.

LOLA   Yes, Doc. And bring home lots of good things to eat.

DOC   I'll get a big bird dog, too. Would you like a sad-looking old bird dog around the house?

LOLA   Of course I would. (*All her life and energy have been restored*) You know what, Doc? I had another dream last night.

DOC   About Little Sheba?

LOLA   Oh, it was about everyone and everything. (*In a raptured tone. She gets bacon from ice box and starts to cook it*) Marie and I were going to the Olympics back in our old High School Stadium. There were thousands of people there. There was Turk out in the center of the field throwing the javelin. Every time he'd throw it, the crowd would roar—and you know who the man in charge was? It was my father. Isn't that funny?—but Turk kept changing into someone else all the time. And then my father disqualified him. So he had to sit on the sidelines—and guess who took his place, Daddy? You! You came trotting out there on the field just as big as you please—

DOC (*smilingly*)   How did I do, Baby?

LOLA   Fine. You picked the javelin up real careful, like it was awful heavy. But you threw it, Daddy, clear, *clear* up into the sky. And it never came down again.

> DOC *looks very pleased with himself.* LOLA *goes on*

Then it started to rain. And I couldn't find Little Sheba. I almost went crazy looking for her and there were so many people I didn't even know where to look. And you were waiting to take me home. And we walked and walked through the slush and mud, and people were hurrying all around us and—and— (*Leaves stove and sits. Sentimental tears come to her eyes*) But this part is sad, Daddy. All of a sudden I saw Little Sheba—she was lying in the middle of the field—dead— It made me cry, Doc. No one paid any attention— I cried and cried. It made me feel so bad, Doc. That sweet little puppy—her curly white fur all smeared with mud, and no one to stop and take care of her—

DOC   Why couldn't *you*?

LOLA   I wanted to, but you wouldn't let me. You kept saying, "We can't stay here, Honey; we gotta go on. We gotta go on." (*Pause*) Now, isn't that strange?

DOC   Dreams are funny.

LOLA   I don't think Little Sheba's ever coming back, Doc. I'm not going to call her any more.

DOC   Not much point in it, Baby. I guess she's gone for good.

LOLA   I'll fix your eggs.

> She gets up, embraces DOC, and goes to stove. DOC remains at table sipping his fruit juice. The Curtain comes slowly down

Exercises   1. *What does Doc's reaction to the mess in the kitchen, at the beginning of the play, point to?*

2. *Early in the play Lola considers the possibility that Mrs. Coffman has poisoned Little Sheba. Later in the play, after receiving an invitation from Mrs. Coffman to pick all the*

lilacs she needs, Lola changes her mind. What is revealed about Lola's character by this sudden change of heart?

3. *Giving incomplete information is a favorite device of playwrights to achieve suspense. In Act One, Scene One, Doc informs Marie that he had to forsake his premedical studies in his third year of college and avoids Marie's "why?" Cite other examples of purposely withheld information designed to sustain a reader's interest.*

4. *What is Marie to Doc?*

5. *How is Lola's character contrasted with Marie's?*

6. *What feelings in Lola are conveyed in the scenes with the postman and the milkman? What other purposes do these scenes serve?*

7. *Explain the plausibility of Doc's chasing Lola with a hatchet. (Exclude his drunkenness as a consideration.)*

8. *In Act Two, Scene Four, Lola suddenly becomes interested in good housekeeping. Why?*

9. *What does Little Sheba symbolize?*

Topics for Writing

1. *View Doc's prayer, taken from the creed of Alcoholics Anonymous—"God grant me the serenity to accept the things I cannot change, courage to change the things I can, and wisdom always to tell the difference"—as one of the major themes of the play.*

2. *Discuss the importance of Marie Buckholder's role in the play, especially in relation to Doc and Lola.*

Selected Bibliography

William Inge

Anonymous. "Picnic's Provider." *The New Yorker*, 29 (4 April 1953), 24–25.

Dusenbury, Winifred L. *The Theme of Loneliness in Modern American Drama*. Gainesville: University of Florida Press, 1960. Pages 9–16; 200–203.

Inge, William. "Schizophrenic Wonder." *Theatre Arts*, 34 (May 1950), 22–23.

Lumley, Frederick. *New Trends in Twentieth Century Drama*. New York: Oxford University Press, 1967. Pages 329–330.

Nathan, George Jean. *Theatre Book of the Year 1949–50*. New York: A. A. Knopf, 1943. Pages 232–236.

Shuman, R. Baird. *William Inge*. New York: Twayne, 1966. Pages 36–48.

Sieves, W. David. *Freud on Broadway*. New York: Cooper Square Publishers, 1971. Pages 352–354.

Weales, Gerald. *American Drama Since World War II*. New York: Harcourt, Brace & World, 1962. Pages 41, 43–47, 199.

Wolfson, Lester M. "Inge, O'Neill and the Human Condition." *Southern Speech Journal*, 22 (Summer 1957), 224–225.

Other Plays to Read

Ed Bullins (1935–   )

The Electronic Nigger

CHARACTERS

MR. JONES, *a light-brown-skinned man. Thirty years old. Hornrimmed glasses. Crewcut and small, smart mustache. He speaks in a clipped manner when in control of himself but is more than self-conscious, even from the beginning. Whatever, MR. JONES speaks as unlike the popular conception of how a negro speaks as is possible. Not even the fallacious accent acquired by many "cultured" or highly educated negroes should be sought, but that general cross-fertilized dialect found on various Ivy League and the campuses of the University of California. He sports an ascot.*

MR. CARPENTIER, *a large, dark man in his late thirties. He speaks in blustering orations, many times mispronouncing words. His tone is stentorian, and his voice has an absurdly ridiculous affected accent*

BILL, *twenty-two years old. Negro*

SUE, *twenty years old. White*

LENARD, *twenty-one. A fat white boy*

MISS MOSKOWITZ, *mid-thirties. An aging professional student*

MARTHA, *an attractive negro woman*

Any number of interracial STUDENTS *to supply background, short of the point of discouraging a producer*

SCENE: *A classroom of a Southern California junior college.*

Modern decor. New facilities: Light green blackboards, bright fluorescent lighting, elongated rectangular tables, seating four to eight students, facing each other, instead of the traditional rows of seats facing toward the instructor. The tables are staggered throughout the room and canted at angles impossible for the instructor to engage the eye of the student, unless the student turns toward him or the instructor leaves his small table and walks among the students.

It is seven o'clock by the wall-clock; twilight outside the windows indicates a fall evening. A NO SMOKING sign is beneath the clock, directly above the green blackboards, behind the instructor's table and rostrum.

The bell rings.

Half the STUDENTS *are already present.* MISS MOSKOWITZ *drinks coffee from a paper cup;* LENARD *munches an apple, noisily. More* STUDENTS *enter from the rear and front doors to the room and take seats. There is the general low buzz of activity and first night anticipation of a new evening class.*

BILL *comes in the back door to the room;* SUE *enters the other. They casually look about them for seats and indifferently sit next to each other.* JONES *enters puffing on his pipe and smoothing down his ascot.*

The bell rings.

MR. JONES (*exhaling smoke*)   Well . . . good evening . . . My name is Jones . . . ha ha . . . that won't be hard to remember, will it? I'll be your instructor this semester . . . ha ha . . . Now this is English 22E . . . Creative Writing.

LENARD   Did you say 22E?

MR. JONES   Yes, I did . . . Do all of you have that number on your cards? . . . Now look at your little I.B.M. cards and see if there is a little 22E in the upper left hand corner. Do you see it?

CARPENTIER *enters and looks over the class*

MISS MOSKOWITZ (*confused*)   Why . . . I don't see any numbers on my card.

MR. JONES (*extinguishing pipe*)   Good . . . now that everyone seems to belong here who is here, we can get started with our creativity . . . ha ha . . . If I sort of . . .

MISS MOSKOWITZ (*protesting*)   But I don't have a number!

LENARD (*ridicule*)   Yes, you do!

MISS MOSKOWITZ   Give that back to me . . . give that card back to me right now!

LENARD (*pointing to card*)   It's right here like he said . . . in the upper left-hand corner.

MISS MOSKOWITZ (*snatching card*)   I know where it is!

MR. JONES   Now that we all know our . . .

MR. CARPENTIER   Sir . . . I just arrived in these surroundings and I have not yet been oriented as to the primary sequence of events which have preceded my entrance.

MR. JONES   Well, nothing has . . .

MR. CARPENTIER (*cutting*)   If you will enlighten me I'll be eternally grateful for any communicative aid that you may render in your capacity as
professor *de la classe.*

MR. JONES   Well . . . well . . . I'm not a professor, I'm an instructor.

BILL   Just take a look at your card and see if . . .

MR. CARPENTIER   Didn't your mother teach you any manners, young
man?

BILL   What did you say, fellah?

MR. CARPENTIER   Don't speak until you're asked to . . .

MR. JONES   Now you people back there . . . pay attention.

MISS MOSKOWITZ   Why, I never in all my life . . .

MR. JONES   Now to begin with . . .

SUE   You've got some nerve speaking to him like that. Where did you
come from, mister?

MR. JONES   Class!

MR. CARPENTIER   Where I came from . . . *mon bonne femme* . . . has no
bearing on this situational conundrum . . . splendid word, conundrum,
heh, what? Jimmie Baldwin uses it brilliantly on occasion . . .

MR. JONES   I'm not going to repeat . . .

MR. CARPENTIER   But getting back to the matter at hand . . . I am here to
become acquainted with the formal aspects of authorcraft . . . Of
course I've been a successful writer for many years even though I
haven't taken the time for the past ten years to practice the art-forms of
fiction, drama or that very breath of the muse . . . poesy . . .

MR. JONES   Sir . . . please!

BILL   How do you turn it off?

LENARD   For christ sake!

MR. CARPENTIER   But you can find my name footnoted in numerous
professional sociological-psychological-psychiatric and psychedelic
journals . . .

MR. JONES   If you'll please . . .

MR. CARPENTIER   A. T. Carpentier is the name . . . notice the silent
T . . . My profession gets in the way of art, in the strict aesthetic
sense, you know . . . I'm a Sociological Data Research Analysis Tech-
nician Expert. Yes, penalology is my field, naturally, and I have been
in over thirty-three penal institutions across the country . . . in a
professional capacity, obviously . . . ha ho ho.

MR. JONES   Sir!

LENARD   Geez!

MR. CARPENTIER   Here are some of my random findings, conclusions,
etc. which I am re-creating into a new art-form . . .

SUE   A new art-form we have here already.

BILL   This is going to be one of those classes.

MR. CARPENTIER   Yes, young lady . . . Socio Drama . . .

MR. JONES   All right, Mr. Carpenter.

MR. CARPENTIER (*corrects*)   Carpentier! The T is silent.

MR. JONES   Okay. Complete what you were saying. . . .

MR. CARPENTIER   Thank you, sir.

MR. JONES   . . . and then . . .

MR. CARPENTIER   By the way, my good friend J. J. Witherthorn is already dickering with my agent for options on my finished draft for a pilot he is planning to shoot of *Only Corpses Beat the Big House* which, by the way, is the title of the first script, taken from an abortive *novella narratio* I had begun in my youth after a particularly torrid affair with one Eulah Mae Jackson . . .

MR. JONES   Good . . . now let's . . .

MR. CARPENTIER   Of course, after I read it some of you will say it resembles in some ways *The Quare Fellow*, but I have documented evidence that I've had this plot outlined since . . .

BILL   Question!

SUE   Won't somebody do something?

BILL   *Question!*

MR. JONES (*to* BILL)   Yes, what is it?

MR. CARPENTIER (*over*)   . . . Of course I'll finish it on time . . . the final draft, I mean . . . and have it to J. J. far ahead of the deadline but I thought that the rough edges could be chopped off here . . . and there . . .

MR. JONES (*approaching anger*)   Mr. Carpentier . . . if you'll please?

MR. CARPENTIER (*belligerent and glaring*)   I beg your pardon, sir?

MARTHA *enters*

MR. JONES   This class must get under way . . . immediately!

MARTHA (*to* MR. JONES)   Is this English 22E?

MR. CARPENTIER   Why, yes, you are in the correct locale, *mon jeune fil.*

MR. JONES   May I see your card, Miss?

MR. CARPENTIER (*mutters*)   Intrusion . . . non-equanimity . . .

MISS MOSKOWITZ   Are you speaking to me?

MR. JONES (*to* MARTHA)   I believe you're in the right class, miss.

MARTHA   Thank you.

MR. JONES (*clears throat*)   Hummp . . . huump . . . well, we can get started now.

MR. CARPENTIER   I emphatically agree with you, sir. In fact . . .

MR. JONES (*cutting*)   Like some of you, I imagine, this too is my first evening class . . . And I'd . . .

MISS MOSKOWITZ (*beaming*) . How nice!

LENARD   Oh . . . oh . . . we've got a green one.

MR. JONES   Well . . . I guess the first thing is to take the roll. I haven't the official roll sheet yet, so . . . please print your names clearly on this sheet of paper and pass it around so you'll get credit for being here tonight.

BILL   Question!

MR. JONES   Yes . . . you did have a question, didn't you?

BILL   Yeah . . . How will we be graded?

SUE   Oh . . . how square!

MR. JONES (*smiling*)   I'm glad you asked that.

MISS MOSKOWITZ   So am I.

LENARD   You are?

MR. JONES   Well . . . as of now everybody is worth an A. I see all students as A students until they prove otherwise . . .

MISS MOSKOWITZ   Oh, how nice.

MR. JONES   But tonight I'd like us to talk about story ideas. Since this is a writing class we don't wish to waste too much of our time on matters other than writing. And it is my conclusion that a story isn't a story without a major inherent idea which gives it substance . . .

MISS MOSKOWITZ   How true.

MR. JONES   And, by the way, that is how you are to retain your A's. By handing in all written assignments on time and doing the necessary outside work . . .

LENARD   Typewritten or in longhand, Mr. Jones?

MR. JONES   I am not a critic, so you will not be graded on how well you write but merely if you attempt to grow from the experience you have in this class . . . this class is not only to show you the fundamentals of fiction, drama and poetry but aid your productivity, or should I say creativity . . . ha ha . . .

MR. CARPENTIER (*admonishing*)   You might say from the standpoint of grammar that fundamentals are essential but . . .

MR. JONES (*piqued*)   Mr. Carpentier . . . I don't understand what point you are making!

MR. CARPENTIER (*belligerent*)   Why . . . why . . . you can say that without the basics of grammar, punctuation, spelling, etc. . . . . that these neophytes will be up the notorious creek without even the accommodation of a sieve.

SUE   *Jesus!*

LENARD (*scowling*)   Up the where, buddy?

MISS MOSKOWITZ   I don't think we should . . .

BILL   It's fantastic what you . . .

MARTHA   Is this really English 22E?

MR. JONES   Now wait a minute, class. Since this is the first night, I want everyone to identify themselves before they speak. All of you know my name . . .

MARTHA   I don't, sir.

MR. CARPENTIER   You might say they will come to grief . . . artistic calamity.

MR. JONES   Ohhh . . . It's Jones . . . Ray Jones.

LENARD   Didn't you just publish a novel, Mr. Jones?

MARTHA   Mine's Martha . . . Martha Butler.

MR. JONES   Oh, yes . . . yes, a first novel.

MR. CARPENTIER (*mutters*)   Cultural lag's the real culprit!

BILL (*to* SUE)   I'm Bill . . . Bill Cooper.

SUE   Pleased . . . just call me Sue. Susan Gold.

MR. JONES   Now . . . where were we? . . .

MR. CARPENTIER   In the time of classicism there wasn't this rampant commerce among Philistines . . .

MR. JONES   Does someone . . .

MISS MOSKOWITZ   Story ideas, Mr. Jones.

MR. JONES   Oh, yes.

Hands are raised. LENARD is pointed out

LENARD   I have an idea for a play.

MR. JONES   Your name, please.

LENARD   Lenard . . . Lenard Getz. I have an idea for a lavish stage spectacle using just one character.

MR. CARPENTIER   It won't work . . . it won't work!

SUE   How do you know?

MISS MOSKOWITZ   Let Lenard tell us, will ya?

MR. CARPENTIER (*indignant*)   Let him! Let him, you say!

MR. JONES (*annoyed*)   Please, Mr. Carpentier . . . please be . . .

MR. CARPENTIER (*glaring about the room*)   But I didn't say it had to be done as parsimoniously as a Russian play. I mean only as beginners you people should delve into the simplicity of the varied techniques of the visual communicative media and processes.

MR. JONES   For the last time . . .

MR. CARPENTIER   Now take for instance cinema . . . or a tele-drama . . . some of the integrative shots set the mood and that takes technique as well as craft.

MR. JONES   I have my doubts about all that . . . but it doesn't have anything to do with Lenard's idea, as I see it.

MR. CARPENTIER   I don't agree with you, sir.

MR. JONES   It's just as well that you don't. Lenard, will you go on, please?

LENARD   Ahhh . . . forget it.

MR. JONES   But, Lenard, won't you tell us your idea?

LENARD   No!

MISS MOSKOWITZ   Oh . . . Lenard.

MR. CARPENTIER   There is a current theory about protein variation . . .

MR. JONES   Not again!

SUE (*cutting*)   I have a story idea!

MISS MOSKOWITZ   Good!

MR. JONES   Can we hear it . . . Miss . . . Miss . . . ?

SUE   Miss Gold. Susan Gold.

MR. JONES   Thank you.

SUE   Well, it's about a story that I have in my head. It ends with a girl or woman, standing or sitting alone and frightened. It's weird. I don't know where I got *that* theme from! . . . There is just something about one person, alone, that is moving to me. It's the same thing in movies or in photography. Don't you think if it's two or more persons, it loses a dramatic impact?

MR. JONES   Why, yes, I do.

MISS MOSKOWITZ   It sounds so psychologically pregnant!

LENARD   It's my story of the stupendous one-character extravaganza!

A few in the class hesitantly clap

MR. CARPENTIER (*in a deep, pontifical voice*)   Loneliness! Estrangement! Alienation! The young lady's story should prove an interesting phenomena—it is a phenomena that we observe daily.

MISS MOSKOWITZ   Yes, it is one of the most wonderful things I've ever heard.

MR. JONES (*irritated*)   Well, now let's . . .

MR. CARPENTIER   The gist of that matter . . .

MR. JONES   I will not have any more interruptions, man. Are you all there!

MR. CARPENTIER   I mean only to say that it is strictly in a class of phenomenology in the classic ontonological sense.

MR. JONES   There are rules you must observe, Mr. Carpentier. Like our society, this school too has rules.

MR. CARPENTIER   Recidivism! Recidivism!

MARTHA   Re-sida-what?

MR. CARPENTIER (*explaining*)   Recidivism. A noted example of alienation in our society. We have tape-recorded AA meetings without the patients knowing that they were being recorded. In prison we pick up everything . . . from a con pacing his cell . . . down to the fights in the yard . . . and I can say that the milieu which creates loneliness is germane to the topic of recidivism.

MR. JONES   What? . . . You're a wire-tapper, Mr. Carpentier?

MR. CARPENTIER   Any method that deters crime in our society is most inadequate, old boy.

BILL   A goddamned fink!

LENARD   I thought I smelled somethin'.

MR. CARPENTIER   Crime is a most repetitive theme these days. . . . The primacy purpose of we law enforcement agents is to help stamp it out whatever the method.

MR. JONES   Carpentier!

MR. CARPENTIER   Let the courts worry about . . .

MR. JONES   But, sir, speaking man to man, how do you feel about your job? Doesn't it make you uneasy knowing that your race, I mean, our people, the Negro, is the most victimized by the police in this country? And you are using illegal and immoral methods to . . .

MR. CARPENTIER   Well, if you must personalize that's all right with me . . . but, really, I thought this was a class in creative writing, not criminology. I hesitate to say, Mr. Jones, that you are indeed out of your depth when you engage me on my own grounds . . . ha ha . . .

MR. JONES *has taken off his glasses and is looking at* MR.
CARPENTIER *strangely*

MARTHA (*rasing voice*)   I have a story idea . . . it's about this great dark
mass of dough . . .

BILL   Yeah . . . like a great rotten ham that strange rumbling and
bubbling noises come out of . . .

SUE   And it stinks something awful!

LENARD   Like horseshit!

MISS MOSKOWITZ   Oh, my.

MR. JONES   Class! Class!

MR. CARPENTIER (*oblivious*)   The new technology doesn't allow for the
weak tyranny of human attitudes.

MR. JONES   You are wrong, terribly wrong.

MR. CARPENTIER   This is the age of the new intellectual assisted by his
tool, the machine, I'll have you know!

MR. JONES (*furious*)   Carpentier! . . . That is what we are here in this
classroom to fight against . . . we are here to discover, to awaken, to
search out human values through art!

MR. CARPENTIER   Nonsense! Nonsense! Pure nonsense! All you pseu-
doartistic types and humanists say the same things when confronted by
truth. (*Prophetically*) This is an age of tele-symbology . . . phallic in
nature, oral in appearance.

MR. JONES   Wha' . . . I don't believe I follow you. Are you serious,
man?

MR. CARPENTIER   I have had more experience with these things so I can
say that the only function of cigarettes is to show the cigarette as a
symbol of gratification for oral types. . . . Tobacco, matches, Zig Zag
papers, etc. are all barter items in prison. There you will encounter a
higher incident of oral and anal specimens. I admit it is a liberal
interpretation, true, but I don't see how any other conclusion can be
drawn!

MR. JONES   You are utterly ineducable. I suggest you withdraw from this
class, Mr. Carpentier.

MISS MOSKOWITZ   Oh, how terrible.

BILL   Hit the road, Jack.

MR. CARPENTIER   If I must call it to your attention . . . in a tax-supported
institution . . . to whom does that institution belong?

LENARD   That won't save you, buddy.

MR. JONES   Enough of this! Are there any more story ideas, class?

MR. CARPENTIER (*mumbling*)   It's councilmatic . . . yes, councilmatic . . .

MISS MOSKOWITZ   My name is Moskowitz and I'd like to try a children's
story.

MR. CARPENTIER   Yes, yes, F. G. Peters once sold a story to the Howdie
Dowdie people on an adaptation of the *Cherry Orchard* theme . . . and
Jamie Judson, a good friend of mine . . .

MR. JONES   Mr. Carpentier . . . please. Allow someone else a chance.

MR. CARPENTIER   Why, all they have to do is speak up, Mr. Jones.

MR. JONES   Maybe so . . . but please let Mrs. Moskowitz . . .

MISS MOSKOWITZ (*coyly*)   That's Miss Moskowitz, Mr. Jones.

MR. JONES   Oh, I'm sorry, Miss Moskowitz.

MISS MOSKOWITZ   That's okay, Mr. Jones. . . . Now my story has an historical background.

MR. CARPENTIER   Which reminds me of a story I wrote which had a setting in colonial Boston . . .

LENARD   Not again. Not again, for chrissakes!

MR. CARPENTIER   Christopher Attucks was the major character . . .

SUE   Shhhhhh . . .

BILL   Shut up, fellow!

MR. CARPENTIER (*ignoring them*)   The whole thing was done in jest . . . the historical inaccuracies were most hilarious . . . ha ho ho . . .

MR. JONES   *Mr. Carpentier ! ! !*

MR. CARPENTIER *grumbles and glowers*

MISS MOSKOWITZ   Thank you, Mr. Jones.

MR. JONES   That's quite all right . . . go on, please.

MISS MOSKOWITZ   Yes, now this brother and sister are out in a park and they get separated from their mother and meet a lion escaped from the zoo and make friends with him.

LENARD   And they live happily ever afterwards.

MISS MOSKOWITZ   Why, no, not at all, Lenard. The national guard comes to shoot the lion but the children hide him up a tree.

BILL (*to* SUE)   I got the impression that it was a tall tale.

SUE   Not you too?

LENARD   I thought it had a historical background.

MARTHA   Can you convince children that they can easily make friends out of lions and then hide them up trees?

LENARD   I got that it's pretty clear what motivated the lion to climb the tree. If you had a hunting party after you wouldn't . . .

MR. CARPENTIER (*cutting*)   Unless you give the dear lady that liberty . . . you'll end up with merely thous and thees!

MR. JONES   What?

MISS MOSKOWITZ (*simpering*)   Oh, thank you, Mr. Carpentier.

MR. CARPENTIER (*Beau Brummel*)   Why, the pleasure is all mine, dear lady.

MR. JONES   Enough of this! Enough of this!

MISS MOSKOWITZ (*blushing*)   Why, Mr. Carpentier . . . how you go on.

MR. CARPENTIER   Not at all, my dear Miss Moskowitz . . .

MISS MOSKOWITZ   Call me Madge.

MR. JONES (*sarcastic*)   I'm sorry to interrupt this . . .

MR. CARPENTIER   A.T. to you . . . A.T. Booker Carpentier at your service.

MR. JONES   This is a college classroom . . . not a French boudoir.

MISS MOSKOWITZ (*to* JONES)   Watch your mouth, young man! There's ladies present.

MARTHA (*to* MOSKOWITZ)   Don't let that bother you, dearie.

LENARD   What kind of attitude must you establish with this type of story and do you create initial attitudes through mood?

MR. JONES (*confused*)   I beg your pardon?

MR. CARPENTIER (*answering*)   Why, young man, almost from the beginning the central motif should plant the atmosphere of . . .

MR. JONES   Thank you, Mr. Carpentier!

MR. CARPENTIER   But I wasn't . . .

BILL (*cutting*)   To what audience is it addressed?

SUE   Good for you!

MISS MOSKOWITZ   Why, young people, of course. In fact, for children.

MR. CARPENTIER   I hardly would think so!

MARTHA   Oh, what kinda stuff is this?

MISS MOSKOWITZ   Mr. Carpentier . . . I . . .

MR. JONES   Well, at least you're talking about something vaguely dealing with writing. Go on, Mr. Carpentier, try and develop your . . .

MR. CARPENTIER   A question of intellectual levels is being probed here. . . . The question is the adult or the child . . . hmm . . . *Robinson Crusoe, Gulliver's Travels, Alice in Wonderland, Animal Farm* can all be read by children, dear lady, but the works have added implication for the adult . . . in a word, they are potent!

MARTHA   You're talking about universality, man, not audience!

MR. CARPENTIER   Do you know the difference?

LENARD (*challenges* CARPENTIER)   What's the definition of audience?

MR. CARPENTIER   Of, course, I don't use myself as any type of criteria, but I don't see where that story would appeal to my sophisticated literary tastes, whereas . . .

MR. JONES   Now you are quite off the point, Mr. Carpentier.

BILL   He thinks we should all write like the Marquis de Sade.

SUE   Yeah, bedtime tales for tykes by Sade.

MISS MOSKOWITZ   I think you're trying to place an imposition of the adult world on the child's.

MR. JONES   The important thing is to write the story, class. To write the story!

MR. CARPENTIER   Well, I think that the story was not at all that emphatic . . . it didn't emote . . . it didn't elicite my . . .

MISS MOSKOWITZ (*confused*)   Why didn't it?

MR. CARPENTIER   I don't think the child would have the range of actual patterns for his peer group in this circumstantial instance.

MARTHA   What man?

LENARD   I got the impression that the protagonists are exempliar.

MR. JONES   Class, do you think this story line aids the writer in performing his functions? . . . The culture has values and the writer's duties are to . . .

MR. CARPENTIER   No, I don't think this story does it!

SUE   Why not?

MR. CARPENTIER   It is fallacious!

MISS MOSKOWITZ   But it's only a child's story, a fantasy, Mr. Carpentier!

MR. JONES   Yes, a child's story . . . for children, man!

MR. CARPENTIER   But it doesn't ring true, dear lady. The only way one can get the naturalistic speech and peer group patterns and mores of children recorded accurately . . .

MR. JONES (*begins a string of "Oh God's" rising in volume until* MR. CARPENTIER *finishes his speech*)   Oh God, Oh, God, *Oh, God, Oh, God,* OH, GOD!

MR. CARPENTIER   . . . is to scientifically eavesdrop on their peer group with electronic listening devices and get the actual evidence for any realistic fictionalizing one wishes to achieve.

MR. JONES (*scream*)   NO!!!

MR. CARPENTIER (*query*)   No?

MR. JONES (*in a tired voice*)   Thomas Wolfe once said . . .

MR. CARPENTIER (*ridicule*)   Thomas Wolfe!

MR. JONES   "I believe that we are lost here in America, but I believe we shall be found." . . . Mr. Carpentier . . . let's hope that we Black Americans can first find ourselves and perhaps be equal to the task . . . the burdensome and sometimes evil task, by the way . . . that being an American calls for in these days.

MR. CARPENTIER   Sir, I object!

MR. JONES   Does not the writer have some type of obligation to remove some of the intellectual as well as political, moral and social tyranny that infects this culture? What does all the large words in creation serve you, my Black brother, if you are a complete whitewashed man?

MR. CARPENTIER   Sir, I am not black nor your brother . . . There is a school of thought that is diametrically opposed to you and your black chauvinism. . . . You preach bigotry, black nationalism, and fascism! . . . The idea . . . black brother . . . intellectual barbarism! . . . Your statements should be reported to the school board—as well as your permitting smoking in your classroom.

SUE   Shut up, you Uncle Tom bastard!

BILL (*pulls her back*)   That's for me to do, not you, lady!

MR. JONES   Four hundred years. . . . Four hundred . . .

LENARD   We'll picket any attempt to have Mr. Jones removed!

MARTHA (*disgust*)   This is adult education?

MISS MOSKOWITZ (*to* MR. CARPENTIER)   I bet George Bernard Shaw would have some answers for you!

MR. CARPENTIER   Of course when examining G. B. Shaw you will discover he is advancing Fabian Socialism.

BILL   Who would picket a vacuum?

LENARD   Your levity escapes me.

SUE   Your what, junior?

MR. JONES   Let's try and go on, class. If you'll . . .

MR. CARPENTIER (*to* MISS MOSKOWITZ)   Your story just isn't professional, miss. It doesn't follow the Hitchcock formula . . . it just doesn't follow . . .

MISS MOSKOWITZ   Do you really think so?

MR. JONES   Somehow, I do now believe that you are quite real, Mr. Carpentier.

LENARD (*to* MR. CARPENTIER)   Have you read *The Invisible Man?*

BILL   Are you kidding?

MR. CARPENTIER   Socio Drama will be the new breakthrough in the theatrical-literary community.

MR. JONES   Oh, Lord . . . not again. This is madness.

MR. CARPENTIER   Combined with the social psychologist's case study, and the daily experiences of some habitant of a socio-economically depressed area, is the genius of the intellectual and artistic craftsman.

MR. JONES   Madness!

MISS MOSKOWITZ   Socio Drama . . . how thrilling.

MR. JONES   Don't listen to him, class . . . I'm the teacher, understand?

MR. CARPENTIER   Yes, yes . . . let me tell you a not quite unique but nevertheless interesting phenomenon . . .

MR. JONES   Now we know that there is realism, and naturalism and surrealism . . .

MR. CARPENTIER   . . . an   extremely   interesting   phenomenon . . . adolescent necrophilia!

MARTHA   Oh, shit!

MR. JONES   I have a degree. . . . I've written a book. . . . Please don't listen . . .

MISS MOSKOWITZ   It sounds fascinating, Mr. Carpentier.

MR. CARPENTIER   Yes, tramps will freeze to death and kids, children, will punch holes in the corpses . . .

LENARD   Isn't that reaching rather far just to prove that truth is stranger than fiction?

SUE   I have a story about crud and filth and disease . . .

MR. JONES   And stupidity and ignorance and vulgarity and despair . . .

MR. CARPENTIER   I go back to my original point . . . I go back to necrophilia!

BILL   And loneliness . . . and emptiness . . . and death.

MR. CARPENTIER   Cadavers! Cadavers! Yes, I come back to that! . . . Those findings could almost be case studies of true cases, they are so true in themselves, and that's where the real truth lies . . . Verily, social case histories of social psychologists . . .

MISS MOSKOWITZ (*enraptured*)   Never . . . never in all my experience has a class aroused such passionate response in my life!

LENARD   I don't believe it!

MR. JONES   But I have read Faulkner in his entirety . . .

MR. CARPENTIER   These people in New York, Philadelphia, Boston, Chicago, San Francisco . . . and places like that . . .

MR. JONES   I cut my teeth on Hemingway . . .

MR. CARPENTIER   . . . they just get drunk and die in the streets . . .

MR. JONES   *Leaves of Grass* is my Bible . . . and Emily Dickinson . . .

MR. CARPENTIER   . . . and then they are prone to suffer adolescent and urchin necrophilia!

MR. JONES (*frustrated*)   . . . Emily Dickinson has always been on my shelf beside *Mother Goose*.

MR. CARPENTIER   It's curiosity . . . not a sickness . . . curiosity!

MR. JONES   I don't want much . . . just to learn the meaning of life.

MARTHA   Will you discover it here, Ray?

LENARD   But how can anybody be so sure?

MR. CARPENTIER (*offhand*)   We happen to own some mortuaries . . . my family, that is . . . and it is our experience that children will disarrange a corpse . . . and if we don't watch them closely . . .

MR. JONES   Booker T. Washington walked barefooted to school! Think of that! Barefooted!

MR. CARPENTIER   Once as a case study in experimental methods I placed a microphone in a cadaver and gave some juvenile necrophilics unwitting access to my tramp.

> JONES *almost doubles over and clutches his stomach; his hands and feet twitch.*

MR. JONES   I'd like to adjourn class early tonight . . . will everyone please go home?

MR. CARPENTIER   What I'm saying is this . . . with our present cybernetic generation it is psycho-politically relevant to engage our socio-philosophical existence on a quanitatum scale which is, of course, pertinent to the outer-motivated migration of our inner-oriented social compact. Yes! Yes, indeed, I might add. A most visionary prognosis, as it were, but . . . ha ho ho . . . but we pioneers must look over our bifocals, I always say . . . ha ha ha . . . giving me added insight to perceive the political exiguousness of our true concomitant predicament. True, preclinical preconsciousness gives indication that our trivilization

LENARD   What's our assignment for next week, Mr. Jones?

MISS MOSKOWITZ   I have something to show you, Mr. Jones.

MARTHA   Are you okay, Mr. Jones?

MR. JONES   Ray . . . just Ray . . . okay?

SUE   Do you have office hours, Mr. Ray?

MR. JONES   I just want everybody to go home now and think about what has happened tonight . . . and if you want to be writers after this then please don't come back to this class.

I've just published an unsuccessful novel, as you know, and I thought I'd teach a while and finish my second one and eat a is vulva, but, owing to the press of the press our avowed aims are maleficent! True! Yes, true! And we are becoming more so. In areas of negative seeming communications probing our error factors are quite negligible. . . . For instance . . . Senator Dodd getting a pension for someone who has gotten abducted and initiated at a Ku Klux meeting . . . well . . . It's poesy! . . . Monochromatic!

bit. . . . But I think I'd rather not, eat well, that is, so you won't see me next week but if any of you'd like a good steady job I could recommend you . . .

MR. JONES   Reading is the answer. It must be . . . cultivating the sensibilities . . . Plato . . . Aristotle . . . Homer . . . Descartes. . . . And Jones. . . . I've always wanted to carry the Jones banner high.

BILL (*to* SUE)   Hey, I've got some pretty good grass that just came in from Mexico.

SUE   Yeah? You have, huh?

BILL   It's at my pad . . . would you like to stop by?

SUE   How far?

BILL   A couple of blocks.

SUE   Okay. It might be interesting.

MR. CARPENTIER (*to a* STUDENT)   Ubiquitous! A form of reference which exposes . . .

> BILL *and* SUE *exit.* STUDENTS *begin filing out.* MARTHA *walks over to* MR. JONES, *though the other students are gathered about* MR. CARPENTIER

MARTHA   You look tired, Ray.

MR. JONES   Yeah . . . yeah . . . I've been reading a lot. The classics are consuming.

MARTHA   Yes, I've heard. Why don't we stop by my place and I'll fix drinks and you can relax . . .

MR. JONES   Okay . . . okay . . . but my ulcer's bothering me. . . . Mind if I drink milk?

MARTHA   It's not my stomach.

> *She helps him off*

MR. CARPENTIER   Who's that French poet . . . Balu . . .

LENARD   Bouvier?

MR. CARPENTIER   . . . Bali . . . Blau? . . .

> MISS MOSKOWITZ *shows* MR. CARPENTIER *a bound manuscript as he deposits his own in his briefcase*

MISS MOSKOWITZ   Will you please look at my few labors of love when you find time, Mr. Carpentier?

> *He shoves it in the case beside his own*

LENARD (*gathering his books*)   Mr. Carpentier?

MR. CARPENTIER (*snapping clasps on his briefcase*)   Yes, Lenard.

LENARD (*pushing himself between* CARPENTIER *and other students*)   What weight does language have on the contemporary prevalence to act in existential terms?

MR. CARPENTIER (*leads them off*)   When the writer first named the crow "Caw Caw" it was onomatopoeia in practice, of course . . . but too it became the Egyptian symbol of death.

LENARD   The crow.

> MISS MOSKOWITZ *giggles.*
> *They all exit crowing: "Caw caw caw caw caw . . ."*

BLACKNESS

Carson McCullers *(1917–1967)*

The Member of the Wedding

ACT ONE   SCENE: *A part of a Southern back yard and kitchen. At stage left there is a scuppernong arbor. A sheet, used as a stage curtain, hangs raggedly at one side of the arbor. There is an elm tree in the yard. The kitchen has in the center a table with chairs. The walls are drawn with child drawings. There is a stove to the right and a small coal heating stove with coal scuttle in rear center of kitchen. The kitchen opens on the left into the yard. At the interior right a door leads to a small inner room. A door at the left leads into the front hall. The lights go on dimly, with a dreamlike effect, gradually revealing the family in the yard and* BERENICE SADIE BROWN *in the kitchen.* BERENICE, *the cook, is a stout, motherly Negro woman with an air of great capability and devoted protection. She is about forty-five years old. She has a quiet, flat face and one of her eyes is made of blue glass. Sometimes, when her socket bothers her, she dispenses with the false eye and wears a black patch. When we first see her she is wearing the patch and is dressed in a simple print work dress and apron.*

FRANKIE, *a gangling girl of twelve with blonde hair cut like a boy's, is wearing shorts and a sombrero and is standing in the arbor gazing adoringly at her brother* JARVIS *and his fiancée* JANICE. *She is a dreamy, restless girl, and periods of energetic activity alternate with a rapt attention to her inward world of fantasy. She is thin and awkward and very much aware of being too tall.* JARVIS, *a good-looking boy of twenty-one, wearing an army uniform, stands by* JANICE. *He is awkward when he first appears because this is his betrothal visit.* JANICE, *a young, pretty, fresh-looking girl of eighteen or nineteen is charming but rather ordinary, with brown hair done up in a small knot. She is dressed in her best clothes and is anxious to be liked by her new family.* MR. ADDAMS, FRANKIE'S *father, is a deliberate and absent-minded man of about forty-five. A widower of many years, he has become set in his habits. He is dressed conservatively, and there is about him an old-fashioned look and manner.* JOHN HENRY, FRANKIE'S *small cousin, aged seven, picks and eats any scuppernongs he can reach. He is a delicate, active boy and wears gold-rimmed spectacles which give him an oddly judicious look. He is blond and sunburned and when we first see him he is wearing a sun-suit and is barefooted.* BERENICE SADIE BROWN *is busy in the kitchen.*

JARVIS   Seems to me like this old arbor has shrunk. I remember when I was a child it used to seem absolutely enormous. When I was Frankie's age, I had a vine swing here. Remember, Papa?

FRANKIE   It don't seem so absolutely enormous to me, because I am so tall.

JARVIS   I never saw a human grow so fast in all my life. I think maybe we ought to tie a brick to your head.

FRANKIE (*hunching down in obvious distress*)   Oh, Jarvis! Don't.

JANICE   Don't tease your little sister. I don't think Frankie is too tall. She probably won't grow much more. I had the biggest portion of my growth by the time I was thirteen.

FRANKIE   But I'm just twelve. When I think of all the growing years ahead of me, I get scared.

>   JANICE *goes to* FRANKIE *and puts her arms around her comfortingly.* FRANKIE *stands rigid, embarrassed and blissful*

JANICE   I wouldn't worry.

>   BERENICE *comes from the kitchen with a tray of drinks.* FRANKIE *rushes eagerly to help her serve them*

FRANKIE   Let me help.

BERENICE   Them two drinks is lemonade for you and John Henry. The others got liquor in them.

FRANKIE   Janice, come sit on the arbor seat. Jarvis, you sit down too.

>   JARVIS *and* JANICE *sit close together on the wicker bench in the arbor.* FRANKIE *hands the drinks around, then perches on the ground before* JANICE *and* JARVIS *and stares adoringly at them*

FRANKIE   It was such a surprise when Jarvis wrote home you are going to be married.

JANICE   I hope it wasn't a bad surprise.

FRANKIE   Oh, Heavens no! (*With great feeling*) As a matter of fact . . . (*She strokes* JANICE'S *shoes tenderly and* JARVIS' *army boot*) If only you knew how I feel.

MR. ADDAMS   Frankie's been bending my ears ever since your letter came, Jarvis. Going on about weddings, brides, grooms, etc.

JANICE   It's lovely that we can be married at Jarvis' home.

MR. ADDAMS   That's the way to feel, Janice. Marriage is a sacred institution.

FRANKIE   Oh, it will be beautiful.

JARVIS   Pretty soon we'd better be shoving off for Winter Hill. I have to be back in barracks tonight.

FRANKIE   Winter Hill is such a lovely, cold name. It reminds me of ice and snow.

JANICE   You know it's just a hundred miles away, darling.

JARVIS   Ice and snow indeed! Yesterday the temperature on the parade ground reached 102.

> FRANKIE *takes a palmetto fan from the table and fans first* JANICE, *then* JARVIS

JANICE   That feels so good, darling. Thanks.

FRANKIE   I wrote you so many letters, Jarvis, and you never, never would answer me. When you were stationed in Alaska, I wanted so much to hear about Alaska. I sent you so many boxes of homemade candy, but you never answered me.

JARVIS   Oh, Frankie. You know how it is . . .

FRANKIE (*sipping her drink*)   You know this lemonade tastes funny. Kind of sharp and hot. I believe I got the drinks mixed up.

JARVIS   I was thinking my drink tasted mighty sissy. Just plain lemonade—no liquor at all. (FRANKIE *and* JARVIS *exchange their drinks.* JARVIS *sips his*) This is better.

FRANKIE   I drank a lot. I wonder if I'm drunk. It makes me feel like I had four legs instead of two. I think I'm drunk. (*She gets up and begins to stagger around in imitation of drunkenness.*) See! I'm drunk! Look, Papa, how drunk I am! (*Suddenly she turns a handspring; then there is a blare of music from the club-house gramophone off to the right.*)

JANICE   Where does the music come from? It sounds so close.

FRANKIE   It is. Right over there. They have club meetings and parties with boys on Friday nights. I watch them here from the yard.

JANICE   It must be nice having your club house so near.

FRANKIE   I'm not a member now. But they are holding an election this afternoon, and maybe I'll be elected.

JOHN HENRY   Here comes Mama.

> MRS. WEST, JOHN HENRY's *mother, crosses the yard from the right. She is a vivacious, blonde woman of about thirty-three. She is dressed in sleazy, rather dowdy summer clothes*

MR. ADDAMS   Hello, Pet. Just in time to meet our new family member.

MRS. WEST   I saw you out here from the window.

JARVIS (*rising, with* JANICE)   Hi, Aunt Pet. How is Uncle Eustace?

MRS. WEST   He's at the office.

JANICE (*offering her hand with the engagement ring on it*)   Look, Aunt Pet. May I call you Aunt Pet?

MRS. WEST (*hugging her*)   Of course, Janice. What a gorgeous ring!

JANICE   Jarvis just gave it to me this morning. He wanted to consult his father and get it from his store, naturally.

MRS. WEST   How lovely.

MR. ADDAMS   A quarter carat—not too flashy but a good stone.

MRS. WEST (*to* BERENICE, *who is gathering up the empty glasses*)   Berenice, what have you and Frankie been doing to my John Henry? He sticks over here in your kitchen morning, noon and night.

BERENICE   We enjoys him and Candy seems to like it over here.

MRS. WEST   What on earth do you do to him?

BERENICE   We just talks and passes the time of day. Occasionally plays cards.

MRS. WEST   Well, if he gets in your way just shoo him home.

BERENICE   Candy don't bother nobody.

JOHN HENRY (*walking around barefooted in the arbor*)   These grapes are so squelchy when I step on them.

MRS. WEST   Run home, darling, and wash your feet and put on your sandals.

JOHN HENRY   I like to squelch on the grapes.

> BERENICE *goes back to the kitchen*

JANICE   That looks like a stage curtain. Jarvis told me how you used to write plays and act in them out here in the arbor. What kind of shows do you have?

FRANKIE   Oh, crook shows and cowboy shows. This summer I've had some cold shows—about Esquimos and explorers—on account of the hot weather.

JANICE   Do you ever have romances?

FRANKIE   Naw . . . (*with bravado*) I had crook shows for the most part. You see I never believed in love until now. (*Her look lingers on* JANICE *and* JARVIS. *She hugs* JANICE *and* JARVIS, *bending over them from the back of the bench.*)

MRS. WEST   Frankie and this little friend of hers gave a performance of "The Vagabond King" out here last spring.

> JOHN HENRY *spreads out his arms and imitates the heroine of the play from memory, singing in his high childish voice*

JOHN HENRY   Never hope to bind me. Never hope to know. (*Speaking*) Frankie was the king-boy. I sold the tickets.

MRS. WEST   Yes, I have always said that Frankie has talent.

FRANKIE   Aw, I'm afraid I don't have much talent.

JOHN HENRY   Frankie can laugh and kill people good. She can die, too.

FRANKIE (*with some pride*)   Yeah, I guess I die all right.

MR. ADDAMS   Frankie rounds up John Henry and those smaller children, but by the time she dresses them in the costumes, they're worn out and won't act in the show.

JARVIS (*looking at his watch*)   Well, it's time we shove off for Winter Hill— Frankie's land of icebergs and snow—where the temperature goes up to 102. (JARVIS *takes* JANICE's *hand. He gets up and gazes fondly around the yard and the arbor. He pulls her up and stands with his arm around her, gazing around him at the arbor and yard*) It carries me back—this smell of mashed grapes and dust. I remember all the endless summer afternoons of my childhood. It does carry me back.

FRANKIE   Me too. It carries me back, too.

MR. ADDAMS (*putting one arm around* JANICE *and shaking* JARVIS' *hand*)   Merciful Heavens! It seems I have two Methuselahs in my family! Does it carry you back to your childhood too, John Henry?

JOHN HENRY   Yes, Uncle Royal.

MR. ADDAMS   Son, this visit was a real pleasure. Janice, I'm mighty pleased to see my boy has such lucky judgment in choosing a wife.

FRANKIE   I hate to think you have to go. I'm just now realizing you're here.

JARVIS   We'll be back in two days. The wedding is Sunday.

> *The family move around the house toward the street.* JOHN HENRY *enters the kitchen through the back door. There are the sounds of "good-byes" from the front yard*

JOHN HENRY   Frankie was drunk. She drank a liquor drink.

BERENICE   She just made out like she was drunk—pretended.

JOHN HENRY   She said, "Look, Papa, how drunk I am," and she couldn't walk.

FRANKIE'S VOICE   Good-bye, Jarvis. Good-bye, Janice.

JARVIS' VOICE   See you Sunday.

MR. ADDAMS' VOICE   Drive carefully, son. Good-bye, Janice.

JANICE'S VOICE   Good-bye and thanks, Mr. Addams. Good-bye, Frankie darling.

ALL THE VOICES   Good-bye! Good-bye!

JOHN HENRY   They are going now to Winter Hill.

> *There is the sound of the front door opening, then of steps in the hall.* FRANKIE *enters through the hall*

FRANKIE   Oh, I can't understand it! The way it all just suddenly happened.

BERENICE   Happened? Happened?

FRANKIE   I have never been so puzzled.

BERENICE   Puzzled about what?

FRANKIE   The whole thing. They are so beautiful.

BERENICE (*after a pause*)   I believe the sun done fried your brains.

JOHN HENRY (*whispering*)   Me too.

BERENICE   Look here at me. You jealous.

FRANKIE   Jealous?

BERENICE   Jealous because your brother's going to be married.

FRANKIE (*slowly*)   No. I just never saw any two people like them. When they walked in the house today it was so queer.

BERENICE   You jealous. Go and behold yourself in the mirror. I can see from the color of your eyes.

> FRANKIE *goes to the mirror and stares. She draws up her left shoulder, shakes her head, and turns away*

FRANKIE (*with feeling*)   Oh! They were the two prettiest people I ever saw. I just can't understand how it happened.

BERENICE   Whatever ails you?—actin' so queer.

FRANKIE   I don't know. I bet they have a good time every minute of the day.

JOHN HENRY   Less us have a good time.

FRANKIE   Us have a good time? Us? (*She rises and walks around the table*)

BERENICE   Come on. Less have a game of three-handed bridge.

> *They sit down to the table, shuffle the cards, deal, and play a game*

FRANKIE   Oregon, Alaska, Winter Hill, the wedding. It's all so queer.

BERENICE   I can't bid, never have a hand these days.

FRANKIE   A spade.

JOHN HENRY   I want to bid spades. That's what I was going to bid.

FRANKIE   Well, that's your tough luck. I bid them first.

JOHN HENRY   Oh, you fool jackass! It's not fair!

BERENICE   Hush quarreling, you two. (*She looks at both their hands*) To tell the truth, I don't think either of you got such a grand hand to fight over the bid about. Where is the cards? I haven't had no kind of a hand all week.

FRANKIE   I don't give a durn about it. It is immaterial with me. (*There is a long pause. She sits with her head propped on her hand, her legs wound around each other*) Let's talk about them—and the wedding.

BERENICE   What you want to talk about?

FRANKIE   My heart feels them going away—going farther and farther away—while I am stuck here by myself.

BERENICE   You ain't here by yourself. By the way, where's your Pa?

FRANKIE   He went to the store. I think about them, but I remembered them more as a feeling than as a picture.

BERENICE   A feeling?

FRANKIE   They were the two prettiest people I ever saw. Yet it was like I couldn't see all of them I wanted to see. My brains couldn't gather together quick enough to take it all in. And then they were gone.

BERENICE   Well, stop commenting about it. You don't have your mind on the game.

FRANKIE (*playing her cards, followed by* JOHN HENRY)   Spades are trumps and you got a spade. I have some of my mind on the game.

> JOHN HENRY *puts his donkey necklace in his mouth and looks away*

Go on, cheater.

BERENICE   Make haste.

JOHN HENRY   I can't. It's a king. The only spade I got is a king, and I don't want to play my king under Frankie's ace. And I'm not going to do it either.

FRANKIE (*throwing her cards down on the table*)   See, Berenice, he cheats!

BERENICE   Play your king, John Henry. You have to follow the rules of the game.

JOHN HENRY   My king. It isn't fair.

FRANKIE   Even with this trick, I can't win.

BERENICE   Where is the cards? For three days I haven't had a decent hand. I'm beginning to suspicion something. Come on less us count these old cards.

FRANKIE   We've worn these old cards out. If you would eat these old cards, they would taste like a combination of all the dinners of this summer together with a sweaty-handed, nasty taste. Why, the jacks and the queens are missing.

BERENICE   John Henry, how come you do a thing like that? So that's why you asked for the scissors and stole off quiet behind the arbor. Now Candy, how come you took our playing cards and cut out the pictures?

JOHN HENRY   Because I wanted them. They're cute.

FRANKIE   See? He's nothing but a child. It's hopeless. Hopeless!

BERENICE   Maybe so.

FRANKIE   We'll just have to put him out of the game. He's entirely too young.

> JOHN HENRY *whimpers*

BERENICE   Well, we can't put Candy out of the game. We gotta have a third to play. Besides, by the last count he owes me close to three million dollars.

FRANKIE   Oh, I am sick unto death.

> *She sweeps the cards from the table, then gets up and begins walking around the kitchen.* JOHN HENRY *leaves the table and picks up a large blonde doll on the chair in the corner*

I wish they'd taken me with them to Winter Hill this afternnon. I wish tomorrow was Sunday instead of Saturday.

BERENICE   Sunday will come.

FRANKIE   I doubt it. I wish I was going somewhere for good. I wish I had a hundred dollars and could just light out and never see this town again.

BERENICE   It seems like you wish for a lot of things.

FRANKIE   I wish I was somebody else except me.

JOHN HENRY (*holding the doll*)   You serious when you gave me the doll a while ago?

FRANKIE   It gives me a pain just to think about them.

BERENICE   It is a known truth that gray-eyed peoples are jealous.

> *There are sounds of children playing in the neighboring yard*

JOHN HENRY   Let's go out and play with the children.

FRANKIE   I don't want to.

JOHN HENRY   There's a big crowd, and they sound like they having a mighty good time. Less go.

FRANKIE   You got ears. You heard me.

JOHN HENRY   I think maybe I better go home.

FRANKIE   Why, you said you were going to spend the night. You just can't eat dinner and then go off in the afternoon like that.

JOHN HENRY   I know it.

BERENICE   Candy, Lamb, you can go home if you want to.

JOHN HENRY   But less go out, Frankie. They sound like they having a lot of fun.

FRANKIE   No, they're not. Just a crowd of ugly, silly children. Running and hollering and running and hollering. Nothing to it.

JOHN HENRY   Less go!

FRANKIE   Well, then I'll entertain you. What do you want to do? Would you like for me to read to you out of The Book of Knowledge, or would you rather do something else?

JOHN HENRY   I rather do something else.

> *He goes to the back door, and looks into the yard. Several young girls of thirteen or fourteen, dressed in clean print frocks, file slowly across the back yard*

Look. Those big girls.

FRANKIE (*running out into the yard*)   Hey, there. I'm mighty glad to see you. Come on in.

HELEN   We can't. We were just passing through to notify our new member.

FRANKIE (*overjoyed*)   Am I the new member?

DORIS   No, you're not the one the club elected.

FRANKIE   Not elected?

HELEN   Every ballot was unanimous for Mary Littlejohn.

FRANKIE   Mary Littlejohn! You mean that girl who just moved in next door? That pasty fat girl with those tacky pigtails? The one who plays the piano all day long?

DORIS   Yes. The club unanimously elected Mary.

FRANKIE   Why, she's not even cute.

HELEN   She is too; and, furthermore, she's talented.

FRANKIE   I think it's sissy to sit around the house all day playing classical music.

DORIS   Why, Mary is training for a concert career.

FRANKIE   Well, I wish to Jesus she would train somewhere else.

DORIS   You don't have enough sense to appreciate a talented girl like Mary.

FRANKIE   What are you doing in my yard? You're never to set foot on my Papa's property again. (FRANKIE *shakes* HELEN) Son-of-a-bitches. I could shoot you with my Papa's pistol.

JOHN HENRY (*shaking his fists*)   Son-of-a-bitches.

FRANKIE   Why didn't you elect me? (*She goes back into the house*) Why can't I be a member?

JOHN HENRY   Maybe they'll change their mind and invite you.

BERENICE   I wouldn't pay them no mind. All my life I've been wantin' things that I ain't been gettin'. Anyhow those club girls is fully two years older than you.

FRANKIE   I think they have been spreading it all over town that I smell bad. When I had those boils and had to use that black bitter-smelling ointment, old Helen Fletcher asked me what was that funny smell I had. Oh, I could shoot every one of them with a pistol.

> FRANKIE *sits with her head on the table.* JOHN HENRY *approaches and pats the back of* FRANKIE'S *neck*

JOHN HENRY   I don't think you smell so bad. You smell sweet, like a hundred flowers.

FRANKIE   The son-of-a-bitches. And there was something else. They were telling nasty lies about married people. When I think of Aunt Pet and Uncle Eustace! And my own father! The nasty lies! I don't know what kind of fool they take me for.

BERENICE   That's what I tell you. They too old for you.

> JOHN HENRY *raises his head, expands his nostrils and sniffs at himself.* Then FRANKIE *goes into the interior bedroom and returns with a bottle of perfume*

FRANKIE   Boy! I bet I use more perfume than anybody else in town. Want some on you, John Henry? You want some, Berenice? (*She sprinkles perfume*)

JOHN HENRY   Like a thousand flowers.

BERENICE   Frankie, the whole idea of a club is that there are members who are included and the nonmembers who are not included. Now what you ought to do is to round you up a club of your own. And you could be the president yourself. (*There is a pause*)

FRANKIE   Who would I get?

BERENICE   Why, those little children you hear playing in the neighborhood.

FRANKIE   I don't want to be the president of all those little young left-over people.

BERENICE   Well, then enjoy your misery. That perfume smells so strong it kind of makes me sick.

> JOHN HENRY *plays with the doll at the kitchen table and* FRANKIE *watches*

FRANKIE   Look here at me, John Henry. Take off those glasses.

> JOHN HENRY *takes off his glasses*

I bet you don't need those glasses. (*She points to the coal scuttle*) What is this?

JOHN HENRY   The coal scuttle.

FRANKIE (*taking a shell from the kitchen shelf*)   And this?

JOHN HENRY   The shell we got at Saint Peter's Bay last summer.

FRANKIE   What is that little thing crawling around on the floor?

JOHN HENRY   Where?

FRANKIE   That little thing crawling around near your feet.

JOHN HENRY   Oh. (*He squats down*) Why, it's an ant. How did that get in here?

FRANKIE   If I were you I'd just throw those glasses away. You can see good as anybody.

BERENICE   Now quit picking with John Henry.

FRANKIE   They don't look becoming.

> JOHN HENRY *wipes his glasses and puts them back on*

He can suit himself. I was only telling him for his own good. (*She walks restlessly around the kitchen*) I bet Janice and Jarvis are members of a lot of clubs. In fact, the army is kind of like a club.

> JOHN HENRY *searches through* BERENICE'*s pocketbook*

BERENICE   Don't root through my pocketbook like that, Candy. Ain't a wise policy to search folks' pocketbooks. They might think you trying to steal their money.

JOHN HENRY   I'm looking for your new glass eye. Here it is. (*He hands* BERENICE *the glass eye*) You got two nickels and a dime.

> BERENICE *takes off her patch, turns away and inserts the glass eye*

BERENICE   I ain't used to it yet. The socket bothers me. Maybe it don't fit properly.

JOHN HENRY   The blue glass eye looks very cute.

FRANKIE   I don't see why you had to get that eye. It has a wrong expression—let alone being blue.

BERENICE   Ain't anybody ask your judgment, wise-mouth.

JOHN HENRY   Which one of your eyes do you see out of the best?

BERENICE   The left eye, of course. The glass eye don't do me no seeing good at all.

JOHN HENRY   I like the glass eye better. It is so bright and shiny—a real pretty eye. Frankie, you serious when you gave me this doll a while ago?

FRANKIE   Janice and Jarvis. It gives me this pain just to think about them.

BERENICE   It is a known truth that gray-eyed people are jealous.

FRANKIE   I told you I wasn't jealous. I couldn't be jealous of one of them without being jealous of them both. I 'sociate the two of them together. Somehow they're just so different from us.

BERENICE   Well, I were jealous when my foster-brother, Honey, married Clorina. I sent a warning I could tear the ears off her head. But you see I didn't. Clorina's got ears just like anybody else. And now I love her.

FRANKIE (*stopping her walking suddenly*)   J.A.—Janice and Jarvis. Isn't that the strangest thing?

BERENICE   What?

FRANKIE   J.A.—Both their names begin with "J.A."

BERENICE   And? What about it?

FRANKIE (*walking around the kitchen table*)   If only my name was Jane. Jane or Jasmine.

BERENICE   I don't follow your frame of mind.

FRANKIE   Jarvis and Janice and Jasmine. See?

BERENICE   No. I don't see.

FRANKIE   I wonder if it's against the law to change your name. Or add to it.

BERENICE   Naturally. It's against the law.

FRANKIE (*impetuously*)   Well, I don't care. F. Jasmine Addams.

JOHN HENRY (*approaching with the doll*)   You serious when you give me this? (*He pulls up the doll's dress and pats her*) I will name her Belle.

FRANKIE   I don't know what went on in Jarvis' mind when he brought me that doll. Imagine bringing me a doll! I had counted on Jarvis bringing me something from Alaska.

BERENICE   Your face when you unwrapped that package was a study.

FRANKIE   John Henry, quit pickin' at the doll's eyes. It makes me so nervous. You hear me! (*He sits the doll up*) In fact, take the doll somewhere out of my sight.

JOHN HENRY   Her name is Lily Belle.

> JOHN HENRY *goes out and props the doll up on the back steps. There is the sound of an unseen Negro singing from the neighboring yard*

FRANKIE (*going to the mirror*)   The big mistake I made was to get this close crew cut. For the wedding, I ought to have long brunette hair. Don't you think so?

BERENICE   I don't see how come brunette hair is necessary. But I warned you about getting your head shaved off like that before you did it. But nothing would do but you shave it like that.

FRANKIE (*stepping back from the mirror and slumping her shoulders*)   Oh, I am so worried about being so tall. I'm twelve and five-sixths years old and already five feet five and three-fourths inches tall. If I keep on growing like this until I'm twenty-one, I figure I will be nearly ten feet tall.

JOHN HENRY (*reentering the kitchen*)   Lily Belle is taking a nap on the back steps. Don't talk so loud, Frankie.

FRANKIE (*after a pause*)   I doubt if they ever get married or go to a wedding. Those freaks.

BERENICE   Freaks. What freaks you talking about?

FRANKIE   At the fair. The ones we saw there last October.

JOHN HENRY   Oh, the freaks at the fair! (*He holds out an imaginary skirt and begins to skip around the room with one finger resting on the top of his head*) Oh, she was the cutest little girl I ever saw. I never saw anything so cute in my whole life. Did you, Frankie?

FRANKIE   No. I don't think she was cute.

BERENICE   Who is that he's talking about?

FRANKIE   That little old pin-head at the fair. A head no bigger than an orange. With the hair shaved off and a big pink bow at the top. Bow was bigger than the head.

JOHN HENRY   Shoo! She was too cute.

BERENICE   That little old squeezed-looking midget in them little trick evening clothes. And that giant with the hang-jaw face and them huge loose hands. And that morphidite! Half man—half woman. With that tiger skin on one side and that spangled skirt on the other.

JOHN HENRY   But that little-headed girl was cute.

FRANKIE   And that wild colored man they said came from a savage island and ate those real live rats. Do you think they make a very big salary?

BERENICE   How would I know? In fact, all them freak folks down at the fair every October just gives me the creeps.

FRANKIE (*after a pause, and slowly*)   Do I give you the creeps?

BERENICE   You?

FRANKIE   Do you think I will grow into a freak?

BERENICE   You? Why certainly not, I trust Jesus!

FRANKIE (*going over to the mirror, and looking at herself*)   Well, do you think I will be pretty?

BERENICE   Maybe. If you file down them horns a inch or two.

FRANKIE (*turning to face* BERENICE, *and shuffling one bare foot on the floor*) Seriously.

BERENICE   Seriously, I think when you fill out you will do very well. If you behave.

FRANKIE   But by Sunday, I want to do something to improve myself before the wedding.

BERENICE   Get clean for a change. Scrub your elbows and fix yourself nice. You will do very well.

JOHN HENRY   You will be all right if you file down them horns.

FRANKIE (*raising her right shoulder and turning from the mirror*)   I don't know what to do. I just wish I would die.

BERENICE   Well, die then!

JOHN HENRY   Die.

FRANKIE (*suddenly exasperated*)   Go home! (*There is a pause*) You heard me! (*She makes a face at him and threatens him with the fly swatter. They run twice around the table*)   Go home! I'm sick and tired of you, you little midget.

JOHN HENRY *goes out, taking the doll with him*

BERENICE   Now what makes you act like that? You are too mean to live.

FRANKIE   I know it. (*She takes a carving knife from the table drawer*) Something about John Henry just gets on my nerves these days. (*She puts her left ankle over her right knee and begins to pick with the knife at a splinter in her foot*) I've got a splinter in my foot.

BERENICE   That knife ain't the proper thing for a splinter.

FRANKIE   It seems to me that before this summer I used always to have such a good time. Remember this spring when Evelyn Owen and me used to dress up in costumes and go down town and shop at the five-and-dime? And how every Friday night we'd spend the night with each other either at her house or here? And then Evelyn Owen had to go and move away to Florida. And now she won't even write to me.

BERENICE   Honey, you are not crying, is you? Don't that hurt you none?

FRANKIE   It would hurt anybody else except me. And how the wisteria in town was so blue and pretty in April but somehow it was so pretty it made me sad. And how Evelyn and me put on that show the Glee Club did at the High School Auditorium? (*She raises her head and beats time with the knife and her fist on the table, singing loudly with sudden energy*) Sons of toil and danger! Will you serve a stranger! And bow down to Burgundy!

> BERENICE *joins in on "Burgundy."* FRANKIE *pauses, then begins to pick her foot again, humming the tune sadly*

BERENICE   That was a nice show you children copied in the arbor. You will meet another girl friend you like as well as Evelyn Owen. Or maybe Mr. Owen will move back into town. (*There is a pause*) Frankie, what you need is a needle.

FRANKIE   I don't care anything about my old feet. (*She stomps her foot on the floor and lays down the knife on the table*) It was just so queer the way it happened this afternoon. The minute I laid eyes on the pair of them I had this funny feeling. (*She goes over and picks up a saucer of milk near the cat-hole in back of the door and pours the milk in the sink*) How old were you, Berenice, when you married your first husband?

BERENICE   I were thirteen years old.

FRANKIE   What made you get married so young for?

BERENICE   Because I wanted to.

FRANKIE   You never loved any of your four husbands but Ludie.

BERENICE   Ludie Maxwell Freeman was my only true husband. The other ones were just scraps.

FRANKIE   Did you marry with a veil every time?

BERENICE   Three times with a veil.

FRANKIE (*pouring milk into the saucer and returning the saucer to the cat-hole*) If only I just knew where he is gone. Ps, ps, ps . . . Charles, Charles.

BERENICE   Quit worrying yourself about that old alley cat. He's gone off to hunt a friend.

FRANKIE   To hunt a friend?

BERENICE   Why certainly. He roamed off to find himself a lady friend.

FRANKIE   Well, why don't he bring his friend home with him? He ought to know I would be only too glad to have a whole family of cats.

BERENICE   You done seen the last of that old alley cat.

FRANKIE (*crossing the room*)   I ought to notify the police force. They will find Charles.

BERENICE   I wouldn't do that.

FRANKIE (*at the telephone*)   I want the police force, please . . . Police force? . . . I am notifying you about my cat . . . Cat! He's lost. He is almost pure Persian.

BERENICE   As Persian as I is.

FRANKIE   But with short hair. A lovely color of gray with a little white spot on his throat. He answers to the name of Charles, but if he don't answer to that, he might come if you call "Charlina." . . . My name is Miss F. Jasmine Addams and the address is 124 Grove Street.

BERENICE (*giggling as FRANKIE reenters*)   Gal, they going to send around here and tie you up and drag you off to Milledgeville. Just picture them fat blue police chasing tomcats around alleys and hollering, "Oh Charles! Oh come here, Charlina!" Merciful Heavens.

FRANKIE   Aw, shut up!

> *Outside a voice is heard calling in a drawn-out chant, the words almost indistinguishable: "Lot of okra, peas, fresh butter beans . . ."*

BERENICE   The trouble with you is that you don't have no sense of humor no more.

FRANKIE (*disconsolately*)   Maybe I'd be better off in jail.

> *The chanting voice continues and an ancient Negro woman, dressed in a clean print dress with several petticoats, the ruffle of one of which shows, crosses the yard. She stops and leans on a gnarled stick*

FRANKIE   Here comes the old vegetable lady.

BERENICE   Sis Laura is getting mighty feeble to peddle this hot weather.

FRANKIE   She is about ninety. Other old folks lose their faculties, but she found some faculty. She reads futures, too.

BERENICE   Hi, Sis Laura. How is your folks getting on?

SIS LAURA   We ain't much, and I feels my age these days. Want any peas today? (*She shuffles across the yard*)

BERENICE   I'm sorry, I still have some left over from yesterday. Good-bye, Sis Laura.

SIS LAURA   Good-bye.

> *She goes off behind the house to the right, continuing her chant. When the old woman is gone* FRANKIE *begins walking around the kitchen*

FRANKIE   I expect Janice and Jarvis are almost to Winter Hill by now.

BERENICE   Sit down. You make me nervous.

FRANKIE   Jarvis talked about Granny. He remembers her very good. But when I try to remember Granny, it is like her face is changing—like a face seen under water. Jarvis remembers Mother too, and I don't remember her at all.

BERENICE   Naturally! Your mother died the day that you were born.

FRANKIE (*standing with one foot on the seat of the chair, leaning over the chair back and laughing*)   Did you hear what Jarvis said?

BERENICE   What?

FRANKIE (*after laughing more*)   They were talking about whether to vote for C. P. MacDonald. And Jarvis said, "Why I wouldn't vote for that scoundrel if he was running to be dogcatcher." I never heard anything so witty in my life. (*There is a silence during which* BERENICE *watches* FRANKIE, *but does not smile*) And you know what Janice remarked. When Jarvis mentioned about how much I've grown, she said she didn't think I looked so terribly big. She said she got the major portion of her growth before she was thirteen. She said I was the right height and had acting talent and ought to go to Hollywood. She did, Berenice.

BERENICE   O.K. All right! She did!

FRANKIE   She said she thought I was a lovely size and would probably not grow any taller. She said all fashion models and movie stars . . .

BERENICE   She did not. I heard her from the window. She only remarked that you probably had already got your growth. But she didn't go on and on like that or mention Hollywood.

FRANKIE   She said to me . . .

BERENICE   She said to you! This is a serious fault with you, Frankie. Somebody just makes a loose remark and then you cozen it in your mind until nobody would recognize it. Your Aunt Pet happened to mention to Clorina that you had sweet manners and Clorina passed it on to you. For what it was worth. Then next thing I know you are going all around and bragging how Mrs. West thought you had the finest manners in town and ought to go to Hollywood, and I don't know what-all you didn't say. And that is a serious fault.

FRANKIE   Aw, quit preaching at me.

BERENICE   I ain't preaching. It's the solemn truth and you know it.

FRANKIE   I admit it a little. (*She sits down at the table and puts her forehead on the palms of her hands. There is a pause, and then she speaks softly*) What I need to know is this. Do you think I made a good impression?

BERENICE   Impression?

FRANKIE   Yes.

BERENICE   Well, how would I know?

FRANKIE   I mean, how did I act? What did I do?

BERENICE   Why, you didn't do anything to speak of.

FRANKIE   Nothing?

BERENICE   No. You just watched the pair of them like they was ghosts. Then, when they talked about the wedding, them ears of yours stiffened out the size of cabbage leaves . . .

FRANKIE (*raising her hand to her ear*)   They didn't!

BERENICE   They did.

FRANKIE   Some day you going to look down and find that big fat tongue of yours pulled out by the roots and laying there before you on the table.

BERENICE   Quit talking so rude.

FRANKIE (*after a pause*)   I'm so scared I didn't make a good impression.

BERENICE   What of it? I got a date with T. T. and he's supposed to pick me up here. I wish him and Honey would come on. You make me nervous.

> FRANKIE *sits miserably, her shoulders hunched. Then with a sudden gesture she bangs her forehead on the table. Her fists are clenched and she is sobbing*

Come on. Don't act like that.

FRANKIE (*her voice muffled*)   They were so pretty. They must have such a good time. And they went away and left me.

BERENICE   Sit up. Behave yourself.

FRANKIE   They came and went away, and left me with this feeling.

BERENICE   Hosee! I bet I know something. (*She begins tapping with her heel: one, two, three—bang! After a pause, in which the rhythm is established, she begins singing*) Frankie's got a crush! Frankie's got a crush! Frankie's got a crush on the *wedding*!

FRANKIE   Quit!

BERENICE   Frankie's got a crush! Frankie's got a crush!

FRANKIE   You better quit! (*She rises suddenly and snatches up the carving knife*)

BERENICE   You lay down that knife.

FRANKIE   Make me. (*She bends the blade slowly*)

BERENICE   Lay it down, *Devil*. (*There is a silence*) Just throw it! You just!

> After a pause FRANKIE *aims the knife carefully at the closed door leading to the bedroom and throws it. The knife does not stick in the wall*

FRANKIE   I used to be the best knife thrower in this town.

BERENICE   Frances Addams, you goin' to try that stunt once too often.

FRANKIE   I warned you to quit pickin' with me.

BERENICE   You are not fit to live in a house.

FRANKIE   I won't be living in this one much longer; I'm going to run away from home.

BERENICE   And a good riddance to a big old bag of rubbage.

FRANKIE   You wait and see. I'm leaving town.

BERENICE   And where do you think you are going?

FRANKIE (*gazing around the walls*)   I don't know.

BERENICE   You're going crazy. That's where you going.

FRANKIE.   No. (*Solemnly*) This coming Sunday after the wedding, I'm leaving town. And I swear to Jesus by my two eyes I'm never coming back here any more.

BERENICE (*going to* FRANKIE *and pushing her damp bangs back from her forehead*)   Sugar? You serious?

FRANKIE (*exasperated*)   Of course! Do you think I would stand here and say that swear and tell a story? Sometimes, Berenice, I think it takes you longer to realize a fact than it does anybody who ever lived.

BERENICE   But you say you don't know where you going. You going, but you don't know where. That don't make no sense to me.

FRANKIE (*after a long pause in which she again gazes around the walls of the room*)   I feel just exactly like somebody has peeled all the skin off me. I wish I had some good cold peach ice cream.

> BERENICE *takes her by the shoulders. During the last speech,* T. T. WILLIAMS *and* HONEY CAMDEN BROWN *have been approaching through the back yard.* T. T. *is a large and pompous-looking Negro man of about fifty. He is dressed like a church deacon, in a black suit with a red emblem in the lapel. His manner is timid and overpolite.* HONEY *is a slender, limber Negro boy of about twenty. He is quite light in color and he wears loud-colored, snappy clothes. He is brusque and there is about him an odd mixture of hostility and*

playfulness. He is very high-strung and volatile. They are trailed by JOHN HENRY. JOHN HENRY *is dressed for afternoon in a clean white linen suit, white shoes and socks.* HONEY *carries a horn. They cross the back yard and knock at the back door.* HONEY *holds his hand to his head*

FRANKIE   But every word I told you was the solemn truth. I'm leaving here after the wedding.

BERENICE (*taking her hands from* FRANKIE's *shoulders and answering the door*)   Hello, Honey and T. T. I didn't hear you coming.

T. T.   You and Frankie too busy discussing something. Well, your foster-brother, Honey, got into a ruckus standing on the sidewalk in front of the Blue Moon Café. Police cracked him on the haid.

BERENICE (*turning on the kitchen light*)   What! (*She examines* HONEY's *head*) Why, it's a welt the size of a small egg.

HONEY   Times like this I feel like I got to bust loose or die.

BERENICE   What were you doing?

HONEY   Nothing. I was just passing along the street minding my own business when this drunk soldier came out of the Blue Moon Café and ran into me. I looked at him and he gave me a push. I pushed him back and he raised a ruckus. This white M.P. came up and slammed me with his stick.

T. T.   It was one of those accidents can happen to any colored person.

JOHN HENRY (*reaching for the horn*)   Toot some on your horn, Honey.

FRANKIE   Please blow.

HONEY (*to* JOHN HENRY, *who has taken the horn*)   Now, don't bother my horn, Butch.

JOHN HENRY   I want to toot it some.

> JOHN HENRY *takes the horn, tries to blow it, but only succeeds in slobbering in it. He holds the horn away from his mouth and sings: "Too-ty-toot, too-ty-toot."* HONEY *snatches the horn away from him and puts it on the sewing table*

HONEY   I told you not to touch my horn. You got it full of slobber inside and out. It's ruined! (*He loses his temper, grabs* JOHN HENRY *by the shoulders and shakes him hard*)

BERENICE (*slapping* HONEY)   Satan! Don't you dare touch that little boy! I'm going to stomp out your brains!

HONEY   You ain't mad because John Henry is a little boy. It's because he's a white boy. John Henry knows he needs a good shake. Don't you, Butch?

BERENICE   Ornery—no good!

> HONEY *lifts* JOHN HENRY *and swings him, then reaches in his pocket and brings out some coins*

HONEY   John Henry, which would you rather have—the nigger money or the white money?

JOHN HENRY   I rather have the dime. (*He takes it*) Much obliged. (*He goes out and crosses the yard to his house*)

BERENICE   You troubled and beat down and try to take it out on a little boy. You and Frankie just alike. The club girls don't elect her and she turns on John Henry too. When folks are lonesome and left out, they turn so mean. T. T. do you wish a small little quickie before we start?

T. T. (*looking at* FRANKIE *and pointing toward her*)   Frankie ain't no tattletale. Is you?

BERENICE *pours a drink for* T. T.

FRANKIE (*disdaining his question*)   That sure is a cute suit you got on, Honey. Today I heard somebody speak of you as Lightfoot Brown. I think that's such a grand nickname. It's on account of your traveling—to Harlem, and all the different places where you have run away, and your dancing. Lightfoot! I wish somebody would call me Lightfoot Addams.

BERENICE   It would suit me better if Honey Camden had brick feets. As it is, he keeps me so anxious-worried. C'mon, Honey and T. T. Let's go!

HONEY *and* T. T. *go out*

FRANKIE   I'll go out into the yard.

FRANKIE, *feeling excluded, goes out into the yard. Throughout the act the light in the yard has been darkening steadily. Now the light in the kitchen is throwing a yellow rectangle in the yard*

BERENICE   Now Frankie, you forget all that foolishness we were discussing. And if Mr. Addams don't come home by good dark, you go over to the Wests'. Go play with John Henry.

HONEY AND T. T. (*from outside*)   So long!

FRANKIE   So long, you all. Since when have I been scared of the dark? I'll invite John Henry to spend the night with me.

BERENICE   I thought you were sick and tired of him.

FRANKIE   I am.

BERENICE (*kissing* FRANKIE)   Good night, Sugar!

FRANKIE   Seems like everybody goes off and leaves me. (*She walks towards the* WESTS' *yard, calling, with cupped hands*) John Henry. John Henry.

JOHN HENRY'S VOICE   What do you want, Frankie?

FRANKIE   Come over and spend the night with me.

JOHN HENRY'S VOICE   I can't.

FRANKIE   Why?

JOHN HENRY   Just because.

FRANKIE   Because why? (JOHN HENRY *does not answer*) I thought maybe me and you could put up my Indian tepee and sleep out here in the yard. And have a good time. (*There is still no answer*) Sure enough. Why don't you stay and spend the night?

JOHN HENRY (*quite loudly*)   Because, Frankie. I don't want to.

FRANKIE (*angrily*)   Fool Jackass! Suit yourself! I only asked you because you looked so ugly and so lonesome.

JOHN HENRY (*skipping toward the arbor*)   Why, I'm not a bit lonesome.

FRANKIE (*looking at the house*)   I wonder when that Papa of mine is coming home. He always comes home by dark. I don't want to go into that empty, ugly house all by myself.

JOHN HENRY   Me neither.

FRANKIE (*standing with outstretched arms, and looking around her*)   I think something is wrong. It is too quiet. I have a peculiar warning in my bones. I bet you a hundred dollars it's going to storm.

JOHN HENRY   I don't want to spend the night with you.

FRANKIE   A terrible, terrible dog-day storm. Or maybe even a cyclone.

JOHN HENRY   Huh.

FRANKIE   I bet Jarvis and Janice are now at Winter Hill. I see them just plain as I see you. Plainer. Something is wrong. It is too quiet.

> *A clear horn begins to play a blues tune in the distance*

JOHN HENRY   Frankie?

FRANKIE   Hush! It sounds like Honey.

> *The horn music becomes jazzy and spangling, then the first blues tune is repeated. Suddenly, while still unfinished, the music stops.*
> FRANKIE *waits tensely*

He has stopped to bang the spit out of his horn. In a second he will finish. (*After a wait*) Please, Honey, go on finish!

JOHN HENRY (*softly*)   He done quit now.

FRANKIE (*moving restlessly*)   I told Berenice that I was leavin' town for good and she did not believe me. Sometimes I honestly think she is the biggest fool that ever drew breath. You try to impress something on a big fool like that, and it's just like talking to a block of cement. I kept on telling and telling and telling her. I told her I had to leave this town for good because it is inevitable. Inevitable.

> MR. ADDAMS *enters the kitchen from the house, calling: "Frankie, Frankie"*

MR. ADDAMS (*calling from the kitchen door*)   Frankie, Frankie.

FRANKIE   Yes, Papa.

MR. ADDAMS (*opening the back door*)   You had supper?

FRANKIE   I'm not hungry.

MR. ADDAMS   Was a little later than I intended, fixing a timepiece for a railroad man. (*He goes back through the kitchen and into the hall, calling: "Don't leave the yard!"*)

JOHN HENRY   You want me to get the weekend bag?

FRANKIE   Don't bother me, John Henry. I'm thinking.

JOHN HENRY   What you thinking about?

FRANKIE   About the wedding. About my brother and the bride. Everything's been so sudden today. I never believed before about the fact that the earth turns at the rate of about a thousand miles a day. I didn't understand why it was that if you jumped up in the air you wouldn't land in Selma or Fairview or somewhere else instead of the same back yard. But now it seems to me I feel the world going around very fast.

FRANKIE *begins turning around in circles with arms outstretched.*
JOHN HENRY *copies her. They both turn*

I feel it turning and it makes me dizzy.

JOHN HENRY   I'll stay and spend the night with you.

FRANKIE (*suddenly stopping her turning*)   No. I just now thought of something.

JOHN HENRY   You just a little while ago was begging me.

FRANKIE   I know where I'm going.

There are sounds of children playing in the distance

JOHN HENRY   Let's go play with the children, Frankie.

FRANKIE   I tell you I know where I'm going. It's like I've known it all
my life. Tomorrow I will tell everybody.

JOHN HENRY   Where?

FRANKIE (*dreamily*)   After the wedding I'm going with them to Winter
Hill. I'm going off with them after the wedding.

JOHN HENRY   You serious?

FRANKIE   Shush, just now I realized something. The trouble with me is
that for a long time I have been just an "I" person. All other people
can say "we." When Berenice says "we" she means her lodge and
church and colored people. Soldiers can say "we" and mean the army.
All people belong to a "we" except me.

JOHN HENRY   What are we going to do?

FRANKIE   Not to belong to a "we" makes you too lonesome. Until this
afternoon I didn't have a "we," but now after seeing Janice and Jarvis I
suddenly realize something.

JOHN HENRY   What?

FRANKIE   I know that the bride and my brother are the "we" of me. So
I'm going with them, and joining with the wedding. This coming
Sunday when my brother and the bride leave this town, I'm going with
the two of them to Winter Hill. And after that to whatever place that
they will ever go. (*There is a pause*) I love the two of them so much and
we belong to be together. I love the two of them so much because they
are the *we* of me.

THE CURTAIN FALLS

ACT TWO   *The scene is the same: the kitchen of the* ADDAMS *home.* BERENICE
is cooking. JOHN HENRY *sits on the stool, blowing soap bubbles
with a spool. It is the afternoon of the next day. The front door
slams and* FRANKIE *enters from the hall*

BERENICE   I been phoning all over town trying to locate you. Where on
earth have you been?

FRANKIE   Everywhere. All over town.

BERENICE   I been so worried I got a good mind to be seriously mad with you. Your Papa came home to dinner today. He was mad when you didn't show up. He's taking a nap now in his room.

FRANKIE   I walked up and down Main Street and stopped in almost every store. Bought my wedding dress and silver shoes. Went around by the mills. Went all over the complete town and talked to nearly everybody in it.

BERENICE   What for, pray tell me?

FRANKIE   I was telling everybody about the wedding and my plans. (*She takes off her dress and remains barefooted in her slip*)

BERENICE   You mean just people on the street? (*She is creaming butter and sugar for cookies*)

FRANKIE   Everybody. Storekeepers. The monkey and monkey man. A soldier. Everybody. And you know the soldier wanted to join with me and asked me for a date this evening. I wonder what you do on dates.

BERENICE   Frankie, I honestly believe you have turned crazy on us. Walking all over town and telling total strangers this big tale. You know in your soul this mania of yours is pure foolishness.

FRANKIE   Please call me F. Jasmine. I don't wish to have to remind you any more. Everything good of mine has got to be washed and ironed so I can pack them in the suitcase. (*She brings in a suitcase and opens it*) Everybody in town believes that I'm going. All except Papa. He's stubborn as an old mule. No use arguing with people like that.

BERENICE   Me and Mr. Addams has some sense.

FRANKIE   Papa was bent over working on a watch when I went by the store. I asked him could I buy the wedding clothes and he said charge them at MacDougal's. But he wouldn't listen to any of my plans. Just sat there with his nose to the grindstone and answered with—kind of grunts. He never listens to what I say. (*There is a pause*) Sometimes I wonder if Papa loves me or not.

BERENICE   Course he loves you. He is just a busy widowman—set in his ways.

FRANKIE   Now I wonder if I can find some tissue paper to line this suitcase.

BERENICE   Truly, Frankie, what makes you think they want you taggin' along with them? Two is company and three is a crowd. And that's the main thing about a wedding. Two is company and three is a crowd.

FRANKIE   You wait and see.

BERENICE   Remember back to the time of the flood. Remember Noah and the Ark.

FRANKIE   And what has that got to do with it?

BERENICE   Remember the way he admitted them creatures.

FRANKIE   Oh, shut up your big old mouth!

BERENICE   Two by two. He admitted them creatures two by two.

FRANKIE (*after a pause*)   That's all right. But you wait and see. They will take me.

BERENICE   And if they don't?

FRANKIE (*turning suddenly from washing her hands at the sink*)   If they don't, I will kill myself.

BERENICE   Kill yourself, how?

FRANKIE   I will shoot myself in the side of the head with the pistol that Papa keeps under his handkerchiefs with Mother's picture in the bureau drawer.

BERENICE   You heard what Mr. Addams said about playing with that pistol. I'll just put this cookie dough in the icebox. Set the table and your dinner is ready. Set John Henry a plate and one for me.

> BERENICE *puts the dough in the icebox.* FRANKIE *hurriedly sets the table.* BERENICE *takes dishes from the stove and ties a napkin around* JOHN HENRY's *neck*

I have heard of many a peculiar thing. I have knew men to fall in love with girls so ugly that you wonder if their eyes is straight.

JOHN HENRY   Who?

BERENICE   I have knew women to love veritable satans and thank Jesus when they put their split hooves over the threshold. I have knew boys to take it into their heads to fall in love with other boys. You know Lily Mae Jenkins?

FRANKIE   I'm not sure. I know a lot of people.

BERENICE   Well, you either know him or you don't know him. He prisses around in a girl's blouse with one arm akimbo. Now this Lily Mae Jenkins fell in love with a man name Juney Jones. A man, mind you. And Lily Mae turned into a girl. He changed his nature and his sex and turned into a girl.

FRANKIE   What?

BERENICE   He did. To all intents and purposes. (BERENICE *is sitting in the center chair at the table. She says grace*) Lord, make us thankful for what we are about to receive to nourish our bodies. Amen.

FRANKIE   It's funny I can't think who you are talking about. I used to think I knew so many people.

BERENICE   Well, you don't need to know Lily Mae Jenkins. You can live without knowing him.

FRANKIE   Anyway, I don't believe you.

BERENICE   I ain't arguing with you. What was we speaking about?

FRANKIE   About peculiar things.

BERENICE   Oh, yes. As I was just now telling you I have seen many a peculiar thing in my day. But one thing I never knew and never heard tell about. No, siree. I never in all my days heard of anybody falling in love with a wedding. (*There is a pause*) And thinking it all over I have come to a conclusion.

JOHN HENRY   How? How did that boy change into a girl? Did he kiss his elbow? (*He tries to kiss his elbow*)

BERENICE   It was just one of them things, Candy Lamb. Yep, I have come to the conclusion that what you ought to be thinking about is a beau. A nice little white boy beau.

FRANKIE   I don't want any beau. What would I do with one? Do you mean something like a soldier who would maybe take me to the Idle Hour?

BERENICE   Who's talking about soldiers? I'm talking about a nice little white boy beau your own age. How 'bout that little old Barney next door?

FRANKIE   Barney MacKean! That nasty Barney!

BERENICE   Certainly! You could make out with him until somebody better comes along. He would do.

FRANKIE   You are the biggest crazy in this town.

BERENICE   The crazy calls the sane the crazy.

> BARNEY MACKEAN, *a boy of twelve, shirtless and wearing shorts, and* HELEN FLETCHER, *a girl of twelve or fourteen, cross the yard from the left, go through the arbor and out on the right.* FRANKIE *and* JOHN HENRY *watch them from the window*

FRANKIE   Yonder's Barney now with Helen Fletcher. They are going to the alley behind the Wests' garage. They do something bad back there. I don't know what it is.

BERENICE   If you don't know what it is, how come you know it is bad?

FRANKIE   I just know it. I think maybe they look at each other and peepee or something. They don't let anybody watch them.

JOHN HENRY   I watched them once.

FRANKIE   What do they do?

JOHN HENRY   I saw. They don't peepee.

FRANKIE   Then what do they do?

JOHN HENRY   I don't know what it was. But I watched them. How many of them did you catch, Berenice? Them beaus?

BERENICE   How many? Candy Lamb, how many hairs is in this plait? You're talking to Miss Berenice Sadie Brown.

FRANKIE   I think you ought to quit worrying about beaus and be content with T. T. I bet you are forty years old.

BERENICE   Wise-mouth. How do you know so much? I got as much right as anybody else to continue to have a good time as long as I can. And as far as that goes, I'm not so old as some peoples would try and make out. I ain't changed life yet.

JOHN HENRY   Did they all treat you to the picture show, them beaus?

BERENICE   To the show, or one thing or another. Wipe off your mouth.

> There is the sound of piano tuning

JOHN HENRY   The piano tuning man.

BERENICE   Ye Gods, I seriously believe this will be the last straw.

JOHN HENRY   Me too.

FRANKIE   It makes me sad. And jittery too. (*She walks around the room*) They tell me that when they want to punish the crazy people in

Milledgeville, they tie them up and make them listen to piano tuning. (*She puts the empty coal scuttle on her head and walks around the table*)

BERENICE   We could turn on the radio and drown him out.

FRANKIE   I don't want the radio on. (*She goes into the interior room and takes off her dress, speaking from inside*) But I advise you to keep the radio on after I leave. Some day you will very likely hear us speak over the radio.

BERENICE   Speak about what, pray tell me?

FRANKIE   I don't know exactly what about. But probably some eye witness account about something. We will be asked to speak.

BERENICE   I don't follow you. What are we going to eye witness? And who will ask us to speak?

JOHN HENRY (*excitedly*)   What, Frankie? Who is speaking on the radio?

FRANKIE   When I said *we*, you thought I meant you and me and John Henry West. To speak over the world radio. I have never heard of anything so funny since I was born.

JOHN HENRY (*climbing up to kneel on the seat of the chair*)   Who? What?

FRANKIE   Ha! Ha! Ho! Ho! Ho! Ho!

> FRANKIE *goes around punching things with her fist, and shadow boxing.* BERENICE *raises her right hand for peace. Then suddenly they all stop.* FRANKIE *goes to the windows, and* JOHN HENRY *hurries there also and stands on tiptoe with his hands on the sill.* BERENICE *turns her head to see what has happened. The piano is still. Three young girls in clean dresses are passing before the arbor.* FRANKIE *watches them silently at the window*

JOHN HENRY (*softly*)   The club of girls.

FRANKIE   What do you son-of-a-bitches mean crossing my yard? How many times must I tell you not to set foot on my Papa's property?

BERENICE   Just ignore them and make like you don't see them pass.

FRANKIE   Don't mention those crooks to me.

> T. T. *and* HONEY *approach by way of the back yard.* HONEY *is whistling a blues tune*

BERENICE   Why don't you show me the new dress? I'm anxious to see what you selected.

> FRANKIE *goes into the interior room.* T. T. *knocks on the door. He and* HONEY *enter*

Why T. T. what you doing around here this time of day?

T. T.   Good afternoon, Miss Berenice. I'm here on a sad mission.

BERENICE (*startled*)   What's wrong?

T. T.   It's about Sis Laura Thompson. She suddenly had a stroke and died.

BERENICE   What! Why she was by here just yesterday. We just ate her peas. They in my stomach right now, and her lyin' dead on the cooling board this minute. The Lord works in strange ways.

T. T.   Passed away at dawn this morning.

FRANKIE (*putting her head in the doorway*)   Who is it that's dead?

BERENICE   Sis Laura, Sugar. That old vegetable lady.

FRANKIE (*unseen, from the interior room*)   Just to think—she passed by yesterday.

T. T.   Miss Berenice, I'm going around to take up a donation for the funeral. The policy people say Sis Laura's claim has lapsed.

BERENICE   Well, here's fifty cents. The poor old soul.

T. T.   She was brisk as a chipmunk to the last. The Lord had appointed the time for her. I hope I go that way.

FRANKIE (*from the interior room*)   I've got something to show you all. Shut your eyes and don't open them until I tell you. (*She enters the room dressed in an orange satin evening dress with silver shoes and stockings*) These are the wedding clothes.

BERENICE, T. T. *and* JOHN HENRY *stare*

JOHN HENRY   Oh, how pretty!

FRANKIE   Now tell me your honest opinion. (*There is a pause*) What's the matter? Don't you like it, Berenice?

BERENICE   No. It don't do.

FRANKIE   What do you mean? It don't do.

BERENICE   Exactly that. It just don't do. (*She shakes her head while* FRANKIE *looks at the dress*)

FRANKIE   But I don't see what you mean. What is wrong?

BERENICE   Well, if you don't see it I can't explain it to you. Look there at your head, to begin with.

FRANKIE *goes to the mirror*

You had all your hair shaved off like a convict and now you tie this ribbon around this head without any hair. Just looks peculiar.

FRANKIE   But I'm going to wash and try to stretch my hair tonight.

BERENICE   Stretch your hair! How you going to stretch your hair? And look at them elbows. Here you got on a grown woman's evening dress. And that brown crust on your elbows. The two things just don't mix.

FRANKIE, *embarrassed, covers her elbows with her hands.*
BERENICE *is still shaking her head*

Take it back down to the store.

T. T.   The dress is too growny looking.

FRANKIE   But I can't take it back. It's bargain basement.

BERENICE   Very well then. Come here. Let me see what I can do.

FRANKIE (*going to* BERENICE, *who works with the dress*)   I think you're just not accustomed to seeing anybody dressed up.

BERENICE   I'm not accustomed to seein' a human Christmas tree in August.

JOHN HENRY   Frankie's dress looks like a Christmas tree.

FRANKIE   Two-faced Judas! You just now said it was pretty. Old double-faced Judas!

The sounds of piano tuning are heard again

Oh, that piano tuner!

BERENICE   Step back a little now.

FRANKIE (*looking in the mirror*)   Don't you honestly think it's pretty? Give me your candy opinion.

BERENICE   I never knew anybody so unreasonable! You ask me my candy opinion, I give you my candy opinion. You ask me again, and I give it to you again. But what you want is not my honest opinion, but my good opinion of something I know is wrong.

FRANKIE   I only want to look pretty.

BERENICE   Pretty is as pretty does. Ain't that right, T. T.? You will look well enough for anybody's wedding. Excepting your own.

MR. ADDAMS *enters through the hall door*

MR. ADDAMS   Hello, everybody. (*To* FRANKIE) I don't want you roaming around the streets all morning and not coming home at dinner time. Looks like I'll have to tie you up in the back yard.

FRANKIE   I had business to tend to. Papa, look!

MR. ADDAMS   What is it, Miss Picklepriss?

FRANKIE   Sometimes I think you have turned stone blind. You never even noticed my new dress.

MR. ADDAMS   I thought it was a show costume.

FRANKIE   Show costume! Papa, why is it you don't ever notice what I have on or pay any serious mind to me? You just walk around like a mule with blinders on, not seeing or caring.

MR. ADDAMS   Never mind that now. (*To* T. T. *and* HONEY.) I need some help down at my store. My porter failed me again. I wonder if you or Honey could help me next week.

T. T.   I will if I can, sir, Mr. Addams. What days would be convenient for you, sir?

MR. ADDAMS   Say Wednesday afternoon.

T. T.   Now, Mr. Addams, that's one afternoon I promised to work for Mr. Finny, sir. I can't promise anything, Mr. Addams. But if Mr. Finny change his mind about needing me, I'll work for you, sir.

MR. ADDAMS   How about you, Honey?

HONEY (*shortly*)   I ain't got the time.

MR. ADDAMS   I'll be so glad when the war is over and you biggety, worthless niggers get back to work. And, furthermore, you *sir* me! Hear me?

HONEY (*reluctantly*)   Yes,—sir.

MR. ADDAMS   I better go back to the store now and get my nose down to the grindstone. You stay home, Frankie. (*He goes out through the hall door*)

JOHN HENRY   Uncle Royal called Honey a nigger. Is Honey a nigger?

BERENICE   Be quiet now, John Henry. (*To* HONEY) Honey, I got a good mind to shake you till you spit. Not saying *sir* to Mr. Addams, and acting so impudent.

HONEY   T. T. said sir enough for a whole crowd of niggers. But for folks that calls me nigger, I got a real good nigger razor.

He takes a razor from his pocket. FRANKIE *and* JOHN HENRY *crowd close to look. When* JOHN HENRY *touches the razor* HONEY *says:*

Don't touch it, Butch, it's sharp. Liable to hurt yourself.

BERENICE   Put up that razor, Satan! I worry myself sick over you. You going to die before your appointed span.

JOHN HENRY   Why is Honey a nigger?

BERENICE   Jesus knows.

HONEY   I'm so tensed up. My nerves been scraped with a razor. Berenice, loan me a dollar.

BERENICE   I ain't handing you no dollar, worthless, to get high on them reefer cigarettes.

HONEY   Gimme, Berenice, I'm so tensed up and miserable. The nigger hole. I'm sick of smothering in the nigger hole. I can't stand it no more.

Relenting, BERENICE *gets her pocketbook from the shelf, opens it, and takes out some change*

BERENICE   Here's thirty cents. You can buy two beers.

HONEY   Well, thankful for tiny, infinitesimal favors. I better be dancing off now.

T. T.   Same here. I still have to make a good deal of donation visits this afternoon.

HONEY *and* T. T. *go to the door*

BERENICE   So long, T. T. I'm counting on you for tomorrow and you too, Honey.

FRANKIE AND JOHN HENRY   So long.

T. T.   Good-bye, you all. Good-bye. (*He goes out, crossing the yard*)

BERENICE   Poor ole Sis Laura. I certainly hope that when my time comes I will have kept up my policy. I dread to think the church would ever have to bury me. When I die.

JOHN HENRY   Are you going to die, Berenice?

BERENICE   Why, Candy, everybody has to die.

JOHN HENRY   Everybody? Are you going to die, Frankie?

FRANKIE   I doubt it. I honestly don't think I'll ever die.

JOHN HENRY   What is "die"?

FRANKIE   It must be terrible to be nothing but black, black, black.

BERENICE   Yes, baby.

FRANKIE   How many dead people do you know? I know six dead people in all. I'm not counting my mother. There's William Boyd who was killed in Italy. I knew him by sight and name. An' that man who climbed poles for the telephone company. An' Lou Baker. The porter at Finny's place who was murdered in the alley back of Papa's store. Somebody drew a razor on him and the alley people said that his cut throat shivered like a mouth and spoke ghost words to the sun.

JOHN HENRY   Ludie Maxwell Freeman is dead.

FRANKIE   I didn't count Ludie; it wouldn't be fair. Because he died just before I was born. (*To* BERENICE) Do you think very frequently about Ludie?

BERENICE   You know I do. I think about the five years when me and Ludie was together, and about all the bad times I seen since. Sometimes I almost wish I had never knew Ludie at all. It leaves you too lonesome afterward. When you walk home in the evening on the way from work, it makes a little lonesome quinch come in you. And you take up with too many sorry men to try to get over the feeling.

FRANKIE   But T. T. is not sorry.

BERENICE   I wasn't referring to T. T. He is a fine upstanding colored gentleman, who has walked in a state of grace all his life.

FRANKIE   When are you going to marry with him?

BERENICE   I ain't going to marry with him.

FRANKIE   But you were just now saying . . .

BERENICE   I was saying how sincerely I respect T. T. and sincerely regard T. T. (*There is a pause*) But he don't make me shiver none.

FRANKIE   Listen, Berenice, I have something queer to tell you. It's something that happened when I was walking around town today. Now I don't exactly know how to explain what I mean.

BERENICE   What is it?

FRANKIE (*now and then pulling her bangs or lower lip*)   I was walking along and I passed two stores with a alley in between. The sun was frying hot. And just as I passed this alley, I caught a *glimpse* of something in the corner of my left eye. A dark double shape. And this glimpse brought to my mind—so sudden and clear—my brother and the bride that I just stood there and couldn't hardly bear to look and see what it was. It was like they were there in that alley, although I knew that they are in Winter Hill almost a hundred miles away. (*There is a pause*) Then I turn slowly and look. And you know what was there? (*There is a pause*) It was just two colored boys. That was all. But it gave me such a queer feeling.

> BERENICE *has been listening attentively. She stares at* FRANKIE, *then draws a package of cigarettes from her bosom and lights one.*

BERENICE   Listen at me! Can you see through these bones in my forehead? (*She points to her forehead*) Have you, Frankie Addams, been reading my mind? (*There is a pause*) That's the most remarkable thing I ever heard of.

FRANKIE   What I mean is that . . .

BERENICE   I know what you mean. You mean right here in the corner of your eye. (*She points to her eye*) You suddenly catch something there. And this cold shiver run all the way down you. And you whirl around. And you stand there facing Jesus knows what. But not Ludie, not who you want. And for a minute you feel like you been dropped down a well.

FRANKIE   Yes. That is it. (FRANKIE *reaches for a cigarette and lights it, coughing a bit.*)

BERENICE   Well, that is mighty remarkable. This is a thing been happening to me all my life. Yet just now is the first time I ever heard it put into words. (*There is a pause*) Yes, that is the way it is when you are in love. A thing known and not spoken.

FRANKIE (*patting her foot*)   Yet I always maintained I never believed in love. I didn't admit it and never put any of it in my shows.

JOHN HENRY   I never believed in love.

BERENICE   Now I will tell you something. And it is to be a warning to you. You hear me, John Henry. You hear me, Frankie.

JOHN HENRY.   Yes. (*He points his forefinger.*) Frankie is smoking.

BERENICE (*squaring her shoulders*)   Now I am here to tell you I was happy. There was no human woman in all the world more happy than I was in them days. And that includes everybody. You listening to me, John Henry? It includes all queens and millionaires and first ladies of the land. And I mean it includes people of all color. You hear me, Frankie? No human woman in all the world was happier than Berenice Sadie Brown.

FRANKIE   The five years you were married to Ludie.

BERENICE   From that autumn morning when I first met him on the road in front of Campbell's Filling Station until the very night he died, November, the year 1933.

FRANKIE   The very year and the very month I was born.

BERENICE   The coldest November I ever seen. Every morning there was frost and puddles were crusted with ice. The sunshine was pale yellow like it is in winter time. Sounds carried far away, and I remember a hound dog that used to howl toward sundown. And everything I seen come to me as a kind of sign.

FRANKIE   I think it is a kind of sign I was born the same year and the same month he died.

BERENICE   And it was a Thursday towards six o'clock. About this time of day. Only November. I remember I went to the passage and opened the front door. Dark was coming on; the old hound was howling far away. And I go back in the room and lay down on Ludie's bed. I lay myself down over Ludie with my arms spread out and my face on his face. And I pray that the Lord would contage my strength to him. And I ask the Lord let it be anybody, but not let it be Ludie. And I lay there and pray for a long time. Until night.

JOHN HENRY   How? (*In a higher, wailing voice*) How, Berenice?

BERENICE   That night he died. I tell you he died. Ludie! Ludie Freeman! Ludie Maxwell Freeman died! (*She hums*)

FRANKIE (*after a pause*)   It seems to me I feel sadder about Ludie than any other dead person. Although I never knew him. I ought to cry sometimes about my mother, or anyhow Granny. But it looks like I can't. But Ludie—maybe it was because I was born so soon after Ludie died. But you were starting out to tell some kind of warning.

BERENICE (*looking puzzled for a moment*)   Warning? Oh, yes! I was going to tell you how this thing we was talking about applies to me.

> As BERENICE *begins to talk* FRANKIE *goes to a shelf above the refrigerator and brings back a fig bar to the table*

It was the April of the following year that I went one Sunday to the church where the congregation was strange to me. I had my forehead down on the top of the pew in front of me, and my eyes were open—not peeping around in secret, mind you, but just open. When suddenly this shiver ran all the way through me. I had caught sight of something from the corner of my eye. And I looked slowly to the left. There on the pew, just six inches from my eyes, was this *thumb.*

FRANKIE   What thumb?

BERENICE   Now I have to tell you. There was only one small portion of Ludie Freeman which was not pretty. Every other part about him was handsome and pretty as anyone would wish. All except this right thumb. This one thumb had a mashed, chewed appearance that was not pretty. You understand?

FRANKIE   You mean you suddenly saw Ludie's thumb when you were praying?

BERENICE   I mean I seen *this* thumb. And as I knelt there just staring at this thumb, I began to pray in earnest. I prayed out loud! Lord, manifest! Lord, manifest!

FRANKIE   And did He—manifest?

BERENICE   Manifest, my foot! (*Spitting*) You know who that thumb belonged to?

FRANKIE   Who?

BERENICE   Why, Jamie Beale. That big old no-good Jamie Beale. It was the first time I ever laid eyes on him.

FRANKIE   Is that why you married him? Because he had a mashed thumb like Ludie's?

BERENICE   Lord only knows. I don't. I guess I felt drawn to him on account of that thumb. And then one thing led to another. First thing I know I had married him.

FRANKIE   Well, I think that was silly. To marry him just because of that thumb.

BERENICE   I'm not trying to dispute with you. I'm just telling you what actually happened. And the very same thing occurred in the case of Henry Johnson.

FRANKIE   You mean to sit there and tell me Henry Johnson had one of those mashed thumbs too?

BERENICE   No. It was not the thumb this time. It was the coat.

> FRANKIE *and* JOHN HENRY *look at each other in amazement.*
> *After a pause* BERENICE *continues*

Now when Ludie died, them policy people cheated me out of fifty dollars so I pawned everything I could lay hands on, and I sold my coat and Ludie's coat. Because I couldn't let Ludie be put away cheap.

FRANKIE Oh! Then you mean Henry Johnson bought Ludie's coat and you married him because of it?

BERENICE Not exactly. I was walking down the street one evening when I suddenly seen this shape appear before me. Now the shape of this boy ahead of me was so similar to Ludie through the shoulders and the back of the head that I almost dropped dead there on the sidewalk. I followed and run behind him. It was Henry Johnson. Since he lived in the country and didn't come into town, he had chanced to buy Ludie's coat and from the back view it looked like he was Ludie's ghost or Ludie's twin. But how I married him I don't exactly know, for, to begin with, it was clear that he did not have his share of sense. But you let a boy hang around and you get fond of him. Anyway, that's how I married Henry Johnson.

FRANKIE He was the one went crazy on you. Had eatin' dreams and swallowed the corner of the sheet. (*There is a pause*) But I don't understand the point of what you was telling. I don't see how that about Jamie Beale and Henry Johnson applies to me.

BERENICE Why, it applies to everybody and it is a warning.

FRANKIE But how?

BERENICE Why, Frankie, don't you see what I was doing? I loved Ludie and he was the first man I loved. Therefore I had to go and copy myself forever afterward. What I did was to marry off little pieces of Ludie whenever I come across them. It was just my misfortune they all turned out to be the wrong pieces. My intention was to repeat me and Ludie. Now don't you see?

FRANKIE I see what you're driving at. But I don't see how it is a warning applied to me.

BERENICE You don't! Then I'll tell you.

> FRANKIE *does not nod or answer. The piano tuner plays an arpeggio*

You and that wedding tomorrow. That is what I am warning about. I can see right through them two gray eyes of yours like they was glass. And what I see is the saddest piece of foolishness I ever knew.

JOHN HENRY (*in a low voice*) Gray eyes is glass.

> FRANKIE *tenses her brows and looks steadily at* BERENICE

BERENICE I see what you have in mind. Don't think I don't. You see something unheard of tomorrow, and you right in the center. You think you going to march to the preacher right in between your brother and the bride. You think you going to break into that wedding, and then Jesus knows what else.

FRANKIE No. I don't see myself walking to the preacher with them.

BERENICE I see through them eyes. Don't argue with me.

JOHN HENRY (*repeating softly*)   Gray eyes is glass.

BERENICE   But what I'm warning is this. If you start out falling in love with some unheard-of thing like that, what is going to happen to you? If you take a mania like this, it won't be the last time and of that you can be sure. So what will become of you? Will you be trying to break into weddings the rest of your days?

FRANKIE   It makes me sick to listen to people who don't have any sense. (*She sticks her fingers in her ears and hums*)

BERENICE   You just settin' yourself this fancy trap to catch yourself in trouble. And you know it.

FRANKIE   They will take me. You wait and see.

BERENICE   Well, I been trying to reason seriously. But I see it is no use.

FRANKIE   You are just jealous. You are just trying to deprive me of all the pleasure of leaving town.

BERENICE   I am just trying to head this off. But I still see it is no use.

JOHN HENRY   Gray eyes is glass.

The piano is played to the seventh note of the scale and this is repeated

FRANKIE (*singing*)   Do, ray, mee, fa, sol, la, tee, do. Tee. Tee. It could drive you wild. (*She crosses to the screen door and slams it*) You didn't say anything about Willis Rhodes. Did he have a mashed thumb or a coat or something? (*She returns to the table and sits down*)

BERENICE   Lord, now that really was something.

FRANKIE   I only know he stole your furniture and was so terrible you had to call the Law on him.

BERENICE   Well, imagine this! Imagine a cold bitter January night. And me laying all by myself in the big parlor bed. Alone in the house because everybody else had gone for the Saturday night. Me, mind you, who hates to sleep in a big empty bed all by myself at any time. Past twelve o'clock on this cold, bitter January night. Can you remember winter time, John Henry? (JOHN HENRY *nods*) Imagine! Suddenly there comes a sloughing sound and a tap, tap, tap. So Miss Me . . . (*She laughs uproariously and stops suddenly, putting her hand over her mouth*)

FRANKIE   What? (*Leaning closer across the table and looking intently at* BERENICE) What happened?

BERENICE *looks from one to the other, shaking her head slowly. Then she speaks in a changed voice*

BERENICE   Why, I wish you would look yonder. I wish you would look.

FRANKIE *glances quickly behind her, then turns back to* BERENICE

FRANKIE   What? What happened?

BERENICE   Look at them two little pitchers and them four big ears. (BERENICE *gets up suddenly from the table*) Come on, chillin, less us roll out the dough for the cookies tomorrow. (BERENICE *clears the table and begins washing dishes at the sink*)

FRANKIE   If it's anything I mortally despise, it's a person who starts out to tell something and works up people's interest, and then stops.

BERENICE (*still laughing*)   I admit it. And I am sorry. But it was just one of them things I suddenly realized I couldn't tell you and John Henry.

JOHN HENRY *skips up to the sink*

JOHN HENRY (*singing*)   Cookies! Cookies! Cookies!

FRANKIE   You could have sent him out of the room and told me. But don't think I care a particle about what happened. I just wish Willis Rhodes had come in about that time and slit your throat. (*She goes out into the hall*)

BERENICE (*still chuckling*)   That is a ugly way to talk. You ought to be ashamed. Here, John Henry, I'll give you a scrap of dough to make a cookie man.

> BERENICE *gives* JOHN HENRY *some dough. He climbs up on a chair and begins to work with it.* FRANKIE *enters with the evening newspaper. She stands in the doorway, then puts the newspaper on the table*

FRANKIE   I see in the paper where we dropped a new bomb—the biggest one dropped yet. They call it a atom bomb. I intend to take two baths tonight. One long soaking bath and scrub with a brush. I'm going to try to scrape this crust off my elbows. Then let out the dirty water and take a second bath.

BERENICE   Hooray, that's a good idea. I will be glad to see you clean.

JOHN HENRY   I will take two baths.

> BERENICE *has picked up the paper and is sitting in a chair against the pale white light of the window. She holds the newspaper open before her and her head is twisted down to one side as she strains to see what is printed there*

FRANKIE   Why is it against the law to change your name?

BERENICE   What is that on your neck? I thought it was a head you carried on that neck. Just think. Suppose I would suddenly up and call myself Mrs. Eleanor Roosevelt. And you would begin naming yourself Joe Louis. And John Henry here tried to pawn himself off as Henry Ford.

FRANKIE   Don't talk childish; that is not the kind of changing I mean. I mean from a name that doesn't suit you to a name you prefer. Like I changed from Frankie to F. Jasmine.

BERENICE   But it would be a confusion. Suppose we all suddenly change to entirely different names. Nobody would ever know who anybody was talking about. The whole world would go crazy.

FRANKIE   I don't see what that has to do with it.

BERENICE   Because things accumulate around your name. You have a name and one thing after another happens to you and things have accumulated around the name.

FRANKIE   But what has accumulated around my old name? (BERENICE *does not reply*) Nothing! See! My name just didn't mean anything. Nothing ever happened to me.

BERENICE   But it will. Things will happen.

FRANKIE   What?

BERENICE   You pin me down like that and I can't tell you truthfully. If I could, I wouldn't be sitting here in this kitchen right now, but making a fine living on Wall Street as a wizard. All I can say is that things will happen. Just what, I don't know.

FRANKIE   Until yesterday, nothing ever happened to me.

> JOHN HENRY *crosses to the door and puts on* BERENICE*'s hat and shoes, takes her pocketbook and walks around the table twice*

BERENICE   John Henry, take off my hat and my shoes and put up my pocketbook. Thank you very much.

> JOHN HENRY *does so*

FRANKIE   Listen, Berenice. Doesn't it strike you as strange that I am I and you are you? Like when you are walking down a street and you meet somebody. And you are you. And he is him. Yet when you look at each other, the eyes make a connection. Then you go off one way. And he goes off another way. You go off into different parts of town, and maybe you never see each other again. Not in your whole life. Do you see what I mean?

BERENICE   Not exactly.

FRANKIE   That's not what I meant to say anyway. There are all these people here in town I don't even know by sight or name. And we pass alongside each other and don't have any connection. And they don't know me and I don't know them. And now I'm leaving town and there are all these people I will never know.

BERENICE   But who do you want to know?

FRANKIE   Everybody. Everybody in the world.

BERENICE   Why, I wish you would listen to that. How about people like Willis Rhodes? How about them Germans? How about them Japanese?

> FRANKIE *knocks her head against the door jamb and looks up at the ceiling*

FRANKIE   That's not what I mean. That's not what I'm talking about.

BERENICE   Well, what *is* you talking about?

> *A child's voice is heard outside, calling: "Batter up! Batter up!"*

JOHN HENRY (*in a low voice*)   Less play out, Frankie.

FRANKIE   No. You go. (*After a pause*) This is what I mean.

> BERENICE *waits, and when* FRANKIE *does not speak again, says*

BERENICE   What on earth is wrong with you?

FRANKIE (*after a long pause, then suddenly, with hysteria*)   Boyoman! Manoboy! When we leave Winter Hill we're going to more places than you ever thought about or even knew existed. Just where we will go first I don't know, and it don't matter. Because after we go to that place we're going on to another. Alaska, China, Iceland, South America. Travelling on trains. Letting her rip on motorcycles. Flying around all over the world in airplanes. Here today and gone tomorrow. All over the world. It's the damn truth. Boyoman! (*She runs around the table*)

BERENICE   Frankie!

FRANKIE   And talking of things happening. Things will happen so fast we won't hardly have time to realize them. Captain Jarvis Addams wins highest medals and is decorated by the President. Miss F. Jasmine Addams breaks all records. Mrs. Janice Addams elected Miss United Nations in beauty contest. One thing after another happening so fast we don't hardly notice them.

BERENICE   Hold still, fool.

FRANKIE (*her excitement growing more and more intense*)   And we will meet them. Everybody. We will just walk up to people and know them right away. We will be walking down a dark road and see a lighted house and knock on the door and strangers will rush to meet us and say: "Come in! Come in!" We will know decorated aviators and New York people and movie stars. We will have thousands and thousands of friends. And we will belong to so many clubs that we can't even keep track of all of them. We will be members of the whole world. Boyoman! Manoboy!

> FRANKIE *has been running round and round the table in wild excitement and when she passes the next time* BERENICE *catches her slip so quickly that she is caught up with a jerk*

BERENICE   *Is* you gone raving wild? (*She pulls* FRANKIE *closer and puts her arm around her waist*) Sit here in my lap and rest a minute.

> FRANKIE *sits in* BERENICE*'s lap.* JOHN HENRY *comes close and jealously pinches* FRANKIE

Leave Frankie alone. She ain't bothered you.

JOHN HENRY   I'm sick.

BERENICE   Now no, you ain't. Be quiet and don't grudge your cousin a little bit love.

JOHN HENRY (*hitting* FRANKIE)   Old mean bossy Frankie.

BERENICE   What she doing so mean right now? She just laying here wore out.

> *They continue sitting.* FRANKIE *is relaxed now*

FRANKIE   Today I went to the Blue Moon—this place that all the soldiers are so fond of and I met a soldier—a red-headed boy.

BERENICE   What is all this talk about the Blue Moon and soldiers?

FRANKIE   Berenice, you treat me like a child. When I see all these soldiers milling around town I always wonder where they came from and where they are going.

BERENICE   They were born and they going to die.

FRANKIE   There are so many things about the world I do not understand.

BERENICE   If you did understand you would be God. Didn't you know that?

FRANKIE   Maybe so. (*She stares and stretches herself on* BERENICE*'s lap, her long legs sprawled out beneath the kitchen table*) Anyway, after the wedding I won't have to worry about things any more.

BERENICE   You don't have to now. Nobody requires you to solve the riddles of the world.

FRANKIE (*looking at newspaper*)   The paper says this new atom bomb is worth twenty thousand tons of TNT.

BERENICE   Twenty thousand tons? And there ain't but two tons of coal in the coal house—all that coal.

FRANKIE   The paper says the bomb is a very important science discovery.

BERENICE   The figures these days have got too high for me. Read in the paper about ten million peoples killed. I can't crowd that many peoples in my mind's eye.

JOHN HENRY   Berenice, is the glass eye your mind's eye? (JOHN HENRY *has climbed up on the back rungs of* BERENICE's *chair and has been hugging her head. He is now holding her ears*)

BERENICE   Don't yank my head back like that, Candy. Me and Frankie ain't going to float up through the ceiling and leave you.

FRANKIE   I wonder if you have ever thought about this? Here we are—right now. This very minute. Now. But while we're talking right now, this minute is passing. And it will never come again. Never in all the world. When it is gone, it is gone. No power on earth could bring it back again.

JOHN HENRY (*beginning to sing*)

> I sing because I'm happy,
> I sing because I'm free,
> For His eye is on the sparrow,
> And I know He watches me.

BERENICE (*singing*)

> Why should I feel discouraged?
> Why should the shadows come?
> Why should my heart be lonely,
> Away from heaven and home?
> For Jesus is my portion,
> My constant friend is He,
> For His eye is on the sparrow,
> And I know He watches me.
> So, I sing because I'm happy.

JOHN HENRY *and* FRANKIE *join on the last three lines*

> I sing because I'm happy,
> I sing because I'm free,
> For His eye is on the sparrow,
> And I know He watches . . .

BERENICE   Frankie, you got the sharpest set of human bones I ever felt.

THE CURTAIN FALLS

ACT THREE   *Scene One*

> *The scene is the same: the kitchen. It is the day of the wedding. When the curtain rises* BERENICE, *in her apron, and* T. T.

WILLIAMS, *in a white coat, have just finished preparations for the wedding refreshments.* BERENICE *has been watching the ceremony through the half-open door leading into the hall. There are sounds of congratulations offstage, the wedding ceremony having just finished.*

BERENICE (*to* T. T. WILLIAMS)   Can't see much from this door. But I can see Frankie. And her face is a study. And John Henry's chewing away at the bubble gum that Jarvis bought him. Well, sounds like it's all over. They crowding in now to kiss the bride. We better take this cloth off the sandwiches. Frankie said she would help you serve.

T. T.   From the way she's been acting, I don't think we can count much on her.

BERENICE   I wish Honey was here. I'm so worried about him since what you told me. It's going to storm. It's a mercy they didn't decide to have the wedding in the back yard like they first planned.

T. T.   I thought I'd better not minch the matter. Honey was in a bad way when I saw him this morning.

BERENICE   Honey Camden don't have too large a share of judgment as it is, but when he gets high on them reefers, he's got no more judgment than a four-year-old child. Remember that time he swung at the police and nearly got his eyes beat out?

T. T.   Not to mention six months on the road.

BERENICE   I haven't been so anxious in all my life. I've got two people scouring Sugarville to find him. (*In a fervent voice*) God, you took Ludie but please watch over my Honey Camden. He's all the family I got.

T. T.   And Frankie behaving this way about the wedding. Poor little critter.

BERENICE   And the sorry part is that she's perfectly serious about all this foolishness.

FRANKIE *enters the kitchen through the hall door*

Is it all over?

T. T *crosses to the icebox with sandwiches*

FRANKIE   Yes. And it was such a pretty wedding I wanted to cry.

BERENICE   You told them yet?

FRANKIE   About my plans—no, I haven't yet told them.

JOHN HENRY *comes in and goes out*

BERENICE   Well, you better hurry up and do it, for they going to leave the house right after the refreshments.

FRANKIE   Oh, I know it. But something just seems to happen to my throat; every time I tried to tell them, different words came out.

BERENICE   What words?

FRANKIE   I asked Janice how come she didn't marry with a veil. (*With feeling*) Oh, I'm so embarrassed. Here I am all dressed up in this tacky evening dress. Oh, why didn't I listen to you! I'm so ashamed.

T. T. *goes out with a platter of sandwiches*

BERENICE   Don't take everything so strenuous like.

FRANKIE   I'm going in there and tell them now! (*She goes*)

JOHN HENRY (*coming out of the interior bedroom, carrying several costumes*) Frankie sure gave me a lot of presents when she was packing the suitcase. Berenice, she gave me all the beautiful show costumes.

BERENICE   Don't set so much store by all those presents. Come tomorrow morning and she'll be demanding them back again.

JOHN HENRY   And she even gave me the shell from the Bay. (*He puts the shell to his ear and listens*)

BERENICE   I wonder what's going on up there. (*She goes to the door and opens it and looks through*)

T. T. (*returning to the kitchen*)   They all complimenting the wedding cake. And drinking the wine punch.

BERENICE   What's Frankie doing? When she left the kitchen a minute ago she was going to tell them. I wonder how they'll take this total surprise. I have a feeling like you get just before a big thunder storm.

> FRANKIE *enters, holding a punch cup*

You told them yet?

FRANKIE   There are all the family around and I can't seem to tell them. I wish I had written it down on the typewriter beforehand. I try to tell them and the words just—die.

BERENICE   The words just die because the very idea is so silly.

FRANKIE   I love the two of them so much. Janice put her arms around me and said she had always wanted a little sister. And she kissed me. She asked me again what grade I was in in school. That's the third time she's asked me. In fact, that's the main question I've been asked at the wedding.

> JOHN HENRY *comes in, wearing a fairy costume, and goes out.*
> BERENICE *notices* FRANKIE's *punch and takes it from her*

FRANKIE   And Jarvis was out in the street seeing about this car he borrowed for the wedding. And I followed him out and tried to tell him. But while I was trying to reach the point, he suddenly grabbed me by the elbows and lifted me up and sort of swung me. He said: "Frankie, the lankie, the alaga fankie, the tee-legged, toe-legged, bow-legged Frankie." And he gave me a dollar bill.

BERENICE   That's nice.

FRANKIE   I just don't know what to do. I have to tell them and yet I don't know how to.

BERENICE   Maybe when they're settled, they will invite you to come and visit with them.

FRANKIE   Oh no! I'm going *with* them.

> FRANKIE *goes back into the house. There are louder sounds of voices from the interior.* JOHN HENRY *comes in again*

JOHN HENRY   The bride and the groom are leaving. Uncle Royal is taking their suitcases out to the car.

> FRANKIE *runs to the interior room and returns with her suitcase.*
> *She kisses* BERENICE

FRANKIE   Good-bye, Berenice. Good-bye, John Henry. (*She stands a moment and looks around the kitchen*) Farewell, old ugly kitchen.

> *She runs out. There are sounds of good-byes as the wedding party and the family guests move out of the house to the sidewalk. The voices get fainter in the distance. Then, from the front sidewalk there is the sound of disturbance. FRANKIE's voice is heard, diminished by distance, although she is speaking loudly*

FRANKIE'S VOICE   That's what I am telling you.

> *Indistinct protesting voices are heard*

MR. ADDAMS' VOICE (*indistinctly*)   Now be reasonable, Frankie.

FRANKIE'S VOICE (*screaming*)   I have to go. Take me! Take me!

JOHN HENRY (*entering excitedly*)   Frankie is in the wedding car and they can't get her out. (*He runs out but soon returns*) Uncle Royal and my Daddy are having to haul and drag old Frankie. She's holding onto the steering wheel.

MR. ADDAMS' VOICE   You march right along here. What in the world has come into you? (*He comes into the kitchen with FRANKIE who is sobbing*) I never heard of such an exhibition in my life. Berenice, you take charge of her.

> *FRANKIE flings herself on the kitchen chair and sobs with her head in her arms on the kitchen table*

JOHN HENRY   They put old Frankie out of the wedding. They hauled her out of the wedding car.

MR. ADDAMS (*clearing his throat*)   That's sufficient, John Henry. Leave Frankie alone. (*He puts a caressing hand on FRANKIE's head*) What makes you want to leave your old papa like this? You've got Janice and Jarvis all upset on their wedding day.

FRANKIE   I love them so!

BERENICE (*looking down the hall*)   Here they come. Now please be reasonable, Sugar.

> *The bride and groom come in. FRANKIE keeps her face buried in her arms and does not look up. The bride wears a blue suit with a white flower corsage pinned at the shoulder*

JARVIS   Frankie, we came to tell you good-bye. I'm sorry you're taking it like this.

JANICE   Darling, when we are settled we want you to come for a nice visit with us. But we don't yet have any place to live.

> *She goes to FRANKIE and caresses her head. FRANKIE jerks*

Won't you tell us good-bye now?

FRANKIE (*with passion*)   We! When you say *we*, you only mean you and Jarvis. And I am not included. (*She buries her head in her arms again and sobs*)

JANICE   Please, darling, don't make us unhappy on our wedding day. You know we love you.

FRANKIE   See! *We*—when you say we, I am not included. It's not fair.

JANICE   When you come visit us you must write beautiful plays, and we'll all act in them. Come, Frankie, don't hide your sweet face from us. Sit up.

>   FRANKIE *raises her head slowly and stares with a look of wonder and misery*

Good-bye, Frankie, darling.

JARVIS   So long, now, kiddo.

>   *They go out and* FRANKIE *still stares at them as they go down the hall. She rises, crosses towards the door and falls on her knees*

FRANKIE   Take me! Take me!

>   BERENICE *puts* FRANKIE *back on her chair*

JOHN HENRY   They put Frankie out of the wedding. They hauled her out of the wedding car.

BERENICE   Don't tease your cousin, John Henry.

FRANKIE   It was a frame-up all around.

BERENICE   Well, don't bother no more about it. It's over now. Now cheer up.

FRANKIE   I wish the whole world would die.

BERENICE   School will begin now in only three more weeks and you'll find another bosom friend like Evelyn Owen you so wild about.

JOHN HENRY (*seated below the sewing machine*)   I'm sick, Berenice. My head hurts.

BERENICE   No you're not. Be quiet, I don't have the patience to fool with you.

FRANKIE (*hugging her hunched shoulders*)   Oh, my heart feels so cheap!

BERENICE   Soon as you get started in school and have a chance to make these here friends, I think it would be a good idea to have a party.

FRANKIE   Those baby promises rasp on my nerves.

BERENICE   You could call up the society editor of the *Evening Journal* and have the party written up in the paper. And that would make the fourth time your name has been published in the paper.

FRANKIE (*with a trace of interest*)   When my bike ran into that automobile, the paper called me Fankie Addams, F-A-N-K-I-E. (*She puts her head down again*)

JOHN HENRY   Frankie, don't cry. This evening we can put up the teepee and have a good time.

FRANKIE   Oh, hush up your mouth.

BERENICE   Listen to me. Tell me what you would like and I will try to do it if it is in my power.

FRANKIE   All I wish in the world, is for no human being ever to speak to me as long as I live.

BERENICE   Bawl, then, misery.

>   MR. ADDAMS *enters the kitchen, carrying* FRANKIE'*s suitcase, which he sets in the middle of the kitchen fllor. He cracks his finger joints.* FRANKIE *stares at him resentfully then fastens her gaze on the suitcase*

MR. ADDAMS   Well, it looks like the show is over and the monkey's dead.

FRANKIE   You think it's over, but it's not.

MR. ADDAMS   You want to come down and help me at the store tomorrow? Or polish some silver with the shammy rag? You can even play with those old watch springs.

FRANKIE (*still looking at her suitcase*)   That's my suitcase I packed. If you think it's all over, that only shows how little you know.

> T. T. *comes in*

If I can't go with the bride and my brother as I was meant to leave this town, I'm going anyway. Somehow, anyhow, I'm leaving town. (FRANKIE *raises up in her chair*) I can't stand this existence—this kitchen—this town—any longer! I will hop a train and go to New York. Or hitch rides to Hollywood, and get a job there. If worse comes to worse, I can act in comedies. (*She rises*) Or I could dress up like a boy and join the Merchant Marines and run away to sea. Somehow, anyhow, I'm running away.

BERENICE   Now quiet down—

FRANKIE (*grabbing the suitcase and running into the hall*)   Please, Papa, don't try to capture me. (*Outside the wind starts to blow*)

JOHN HENRY (*from the doorway*)   Uncle Royal, Frankie's got your pistol in her suitcase.

> *There is the sound of running footsteps and of the screen door slamming*

BERENICE   Run catch her.

> T. T. *and* MR. ADDAMS *rush into the hall, followed by* JOHN HENRY

MR. ADDAMS VOICE   Frankie! Frankie! Frankie!

> BERENICE *is left alone in the kitchen. Outside the wind is higher and the hall door is blown shut. There is a rumble of thunder, then a loud clap. Thunder and flashes of lightning continue.* BERENICE *is seated in her chair, when* JOHN HENRY *comes in*

JOHN HENRY   Uncle Royal is going with my Daddy, and they are chasing her in our car.

> *There is a thunder clap*

The thunder scares me, Berenice.

BERENICE (*taking him in her lap*)   Ain't nothing going to hurt you.

JOHN HENRY   You think they're going to catch her?

BERENICE (*putting her hand to her head*)   Certainly. They'll be bringing her home directly. I've got such a headache. Maybe my eye socket and all these troubles.

JOHN HENRY (*with his arms around* BERENICE)   I've got a headache, too. I'm sick, Berenice.

BERENICE   No you ain't. Run along, Candy. I ain't got the patience to fool with you now.

> *Suddenly the lights go out in the kitchen, plunging it in gloom. The sound of wind and storm continues and the yard is a dark storm-green*

JOHN HENRY   Berenice!

BERENICE   Ain't nothing. Just the lights went out.

JOHN HENRY   I'm scared.

BERENICE   Stand still, I'll just light a candle. (*Muttering*) I always keep one around, for such like emergencies. (*She opens a drawer*)

JOHN HENRY   What makes the lights go out so scarey like this?

BERENICE   Just one of them things, Candy.

JOHN HENRY   I'm scared. Where's Honey?

BERENICE   Jesus knows. I'm scared, too. With Honey snow-crazy and loose like this—and Frankie run off with a suitcase and her Papa's pistol. I feel like every nerve been picked out of me.

JOHN HENRY (*holding out his seashell and stroking* BERENICE)   You want to listen to the ocean?

THE CURTAIN FALLS

Scene Two

The scene is the same. There are still signs in the kitchen of the wedding: punch glasses and the punch bowl on the drainboard. It is four o'clock in the morning. As the curtain rises, BERENICE *and* MR. ADDAMS *are alone in the kitchen. There is a crepuscular glow in the yard.*

MR. ADDAMS   I never was a believer in corporal punishment. Never spanked Frankie in my life, but when I lay my hands on her . . .

BERENICE   She'll show up soon—but I know how you feel. What with worrying about Honey Camden, John Henry's sickness and Frankie, I've never lived through such a anxious night. (*She looks through the window. It is dawning now*)

MR. ADDAMS   I'd better go and find out the last news of John Henry, poor baby.

He goes through the hall door. FRANKIE *comes into the yard and crosses to the arbor. She looks exhausted and almost beaten.* BERENICE *has seen her from the window, rushes into the yard and grabs her by the shoulders and shakes her*

BERENICE   Frankie Addams, you ought to be skinned alive. I been so worried.

FRANKIE   I've been so worried too.

BERENICE   Where have you been this night? Tell me everything.

FRANKIE   I will, but quit shaking me.

BERENICE   Now tell me the A and the Z of this.

FRANKIE   When I was running around the dark scarey streets, I begun to realize that my plans for Hollywood and the Merchant Marines were child plans that would not work. I hid in the alley behind Papa's store, and it was dark and I was scared. I opened the suitcase and took out Papa's pistol. (*She sits down on her suitcase*) I vowed I was going to shoot myself. I said I was going to count three and on three pull the trigger. I counted one—two—but I didn't count three—because at the last minute, I changed my mind.

BERENICE   You march right along with me. You going to bed.

FRANKIE   Oh, Honey Camden!

> HONEY CAMDEN BROWN, *who has been hiding behind the arbor, has suddenly appeared*

BERENICE   Oh, Honey, Honey. (*They embrace*)

HONEY   Shush, don't make any noise; the law is after me.

BERENICE (*in a whisper*)   Tell me.

HONEY   Mr. Wilson wouldn't serve me so I drew a razor on him.

BERENICE   You kill him?

HONEY   Didn't have no time to find out. I been runnin' all night.

FRANKIE   Lightfoot, if you drew a razor on a white man, you'd better not let them catch you.

BERENICE   Here's six dolla's. If you can get to Fork Falls and then to Atlanta. But be careful slippin' through the white folks' section. They'll be combing the county looking for you.

HONEY (*with passion*)   Don't cry, Berenice.

BERENICE   Already I feel that rope.

HONEY   Don't you dare cry. I know now all my days have been leading up to this minute. No more "boy this—boy that"—no bowing, no scraping. For the first time, I'm free and it makes me happy. (*He begins to laugh hysterically*)

BERENICE   When they catch you, they'll string you up.

HONEY (*beside himself, brutally*)   Let them hang me—I don't care. I tell you I'm glad. I tell you I'm happy. (*He goes out behind the arbor*)

FRANKIE (*calling after him*)   Honey, remember you are Lightfoot. Nothing can stop you if you want to run away.

> MRS. WEST, JOHN HENRY'S mother, *comes into the yard*

MRS. WEST   What was all that racket? John Henry is critically ill. He's got to have perfect quiet.

FRANKIE   John Henry's sick, Aunt Pet?

MRS. WEST   The doctors say he has meningitis. He must have perfect quiet.

BERENICE   I haven't had time to tell you yet. John Henry took sick sudden last night. Yesterday afternoon when I complained of my head, he said he had a headache too and thinking he copies me I said, "Run along, I don't have the patience to fool with you." Looks like a judgment on me. There won't be no more noise, Mrs. West.

MRS. WEST   Make sure of that. (*She goes away*)

FRANKIE (*putting her arm around* BERENICE)   Oh, Berenice, what can we do?

BERENICE (*stroking* FRANKIE'*s head*)   Ain't nothing we can do but wait.

FRANKIE   The wedding—Honey—John Henry—so much has happened that my brain can't hardly gather it in. Now for the first time I realize that the world is certainly—a sudden place.

BERENICE   Sometimes sudden, but when you are waiting, like this, it seems so slow.

THE CURTAIN FALLS

Scene Three

The scene is the same: the kitchen and arbor. It is months later, a November day, about sunset. The arbor is brittle and withered. The elm tree is bare except for a few ragged leaves. The yard is tidy and the lemonade stand and sheet stage curtain are now missing. The kitchen is neat and bare and the furniture has been removed. BERENICE, wearing a fox fur, is sitting in a chair with an old suitcase and doll at her feet. FRANKIE enters.

FRANKIE   Oh, I am just mad about these Old Masters.

BERENICE   Humph!

FRANKIE   The house seems so hollow. Now that the furniture is packed. It gives me a creepy feeling in the front. That's why I came back here.

BERENICE   Is that the only reason why you came back here?

FRANKIE   Oh, Berenice, you know. I wish you hadn't given quit notice just because Papa and I are moving into a new house with Uncle Eustace and Aunt Pet out in Limewood.

BERENICE   I respect and admire Mrs. West but I'd never get used to working for her.

FRANKIE   Mary is just beginning this Rachmaninoff Concerto. She may play it for her debut when she is eighteen years old. Mary playing the piano and the whole orchestra playing at one and the same time, mind you. Awfully hard.

BERENICE   Ma-ry Littlejohn.

FRANKIE   I don't know why you always have to speak her name in a tinged voice like that.

BERENICE   Have I ever said anything against her? All I said was that she is too lumpy and marshmallow white and it makes me nervous to see her just setting there sucking them pigtails.

FRANKIE   Braids. Furthermore, it is no use our discussing a certain party. You could never possibly understand it. It's just not in you.

BERENICE *looks at her sadly, with faded stillness, then pats and strokes the fox fur*

BERENICE   Be that as it may. Less us not fuss and quarrel this last afternoon.

FRANKIE   I don't want to fuss either. Anyway, this is not our last afternoon. I will come and see you often.

BERENICE   No, you won't, baby. You'll have other things to do. Your road is already strange to me.

>   FRANKIE *goes to* BERENICE, *pats her on the shoulder, then takes her fox fur and examines it*

FRANKIE   You still have the fox fur that Ludie gave you. Somehow this little fur looks so sad—so thin and with a sad little fox-wise face.

BERENICE (*taking the fur back and continuing to stroke it*)   Got every reason to be sad. With what has happened in these two last months. I just don't know what I have done to deserve it. (*She sits, the fur in her lap, bent over with her forearms on her knees and her hands limply dangling*) Honey gone and John Henry, my little boy gone.

FRANKIE   You did all you could. You got poor Honey's body and gave him a Christian funeral and nursed John Henry.

BERENICE   It's the way Honey died and the fact that John Henry had to suffer so. Little soul!

FRANKIE   It's peculiar—the way it all happened so fast. First Honey caught and hanging himself in the jail. Then later in that same week, John Henry died and then I met Mary. As the irony of fate would have it, we first got to know each other in front of the lipstick and cosmetics counter at Woolworth's. And it was the week of the fair.

BERENICE   The most beautiful September I ever seen. Countless white and yellow butterflies flying around them autumn flowers—Honey dead and John Henry suffering like he did and daisies, golden weather, butterflies—such strange death weather.

FRANKIE   I never believed John Henry would die. (*There is a long pause. She looks out the window*) Don't it seem quiet to you in here? (*There is another, longer pause*) When I was a little child I believed that out under the arbor at night there would come three ghosts and one of the ghosts wore a silver ring. (*Whispering*) Occasionally when it gets so quiet like this I have a strange feeling. It's like John Henry is hovering somewhere in this kitchen—solemn looking and ghost-grey.

A BOY'S VOICE (*from the neighboring yard*)   Frankie, Frankie.

FRANKIE (*calling to the boy*)   Yes, Barney. (*To* BERENICE) Clock stopped. (*She shakes the clock*)

THE BOY'S VOICE   Is Mary there?

FRANKIE (*to* BERENICE)   It's Barney MacKean. (*To the boy, in a sweet voice*) Not yet. I'm meeting her at five. Come on in, Barney, won't you?

BARNEY   Just a minute.

FRANKIE (*to* BERENICE)   Barney puts me in mind of a Greek god.

BERENICE   What? Barney puts you in mind of a what?

FRANKIE   Of a Greek god. Mary remarked that Barney reminded her of a Greek god.

BERENICE   It looks like I can't understand a thing you say no more.

FRANKIE   You know, those old-timey Greeks worship those Greek gods.

BERENICE   But what has that got to do with Barney MacKean?

FRANKIE   On account of the figure.

> BARNEY MACKEAN, *a boy of thirteen, wearing a football suit, bright sweater and cleated shoes, runs up the back steps into the kitchen*

BERENICE   Hi, Greek god Barney. This afternoon I saw your initials chalked down on the front sidewalk. M. L. loves B. M.

BARNEY   If I could find out who wrote it, I would rub it out with their faces. Did you do it, Frankie?

FRANKIE (*drawing herself up with sudden dignity*)   I wouldn't do a kid thing like that. I even resent you asking me. (*She repeats the phrase to herself in a pleased undertone*) Resent you asking me.

BARNEY   Mary can't stand me anyhow.

FRANKIE   Yes she can stand you. I am her most intimate friend. I ought to know. As a matter of fact she's told me several lovely compliments about you. Mary and I are riding on the moving van to our new house. Would you like to go?

BARNEY   Sure.

FRANKIE   O.K. You will have to ride back with the furniture 'cause Mary and I are riding on the front seat with the driver. We had a letter from Jarvis and Janice this afternoon. Jarvis is with the Occupation Forces in Germany and they took a vacation trip to Luxembourg. (*She repeats in a pleased voice*) Luxembourg. Berenice, don't you think that's a lovely name?

BERENICE   It's kind of a pretty name, but it reminds me of soapy water.

FRANKIE   Mary and I will most likely pass through Luxembourg when we—are going around the world together.

> FRANKIE *goes out followed by* BARNEY *and* BERENICE *sits in the kitchen alone and motionless. She picks up the doll, looks at it and hums the first two lines of "I Sing Because I'm Happy." In the next house the piano is heard again, as*

THE CURTAIN FALLS

WRITING
ABOUT
LITERATURE

The writing of an effective paper about literature must of necessity begin with precise reading. A close reading should produce the kinds of significant details about the structure and the overall effects of a story, a poem, or a play that ultimately lead to a better understanding of an author's work.

Careful reading should in time yield fuller understanding, deeper appreciation, and greater enjoyment of literature. To achieve this purpose we will read stories, poems, and plays of the first quality, literature more complex and more subtle than that with which we may have ever before kept company. We will be asked to expound on character or shed light on theme; but what may prove even more exacting will be justifying our analyses and interpretations in logical, well-organized, persuasive themes. Of course, the task need not be so massively difficult as one might imagine.

The combined exercises of reading literature and writing about it can be viewed as an inseparable process, a continuum; one activity merges into the other. Understanding one process, we understand the other. The intelligent reader who comprehends the structure of a literary piece, understands its meaning, and grasps the way in which theme manifests itself can easily—without torment—render an effective interpretation. Further, we are apt to recognize only negligible differences between a written composition and a well-conceived, oral discussion or composition. For in either situation we advance a thesis and give it support with relevant explanatory details.

A terse review of several necessary guidelines essential to the writing process may be useful:

Selecting a Topic   This initial exercise, sometimes a chore for students, has been eliminated here, at least for the nonresearch paper. A variety of topics suitable for essays based solely on students' observations are available throughout the book. You may, of course, want to modify a topic, consider the instructor's suggestions, or develop a personal line of thought.

1159

Limiting a Topic	Given a writing assignment that requires a limit of five hundred words, a writer could not, for example, summarize the main action, analyze the chief characters, discuss point of view, interpret symbols, and explicate the two or three significant themes in "Flowering Judas" and still produce a satisfactory paper. Obviously, the writer who attempts to cover so much material faces an impossible task. You could, however, limit the subject to one aspect of the story, let us say, to a view of Laura, the protagonist, as a betrayer of her own life.
Gathering Evidence	All the available evidence pertaining to a hypothesis or a thesis should be noted and examined carefully. Omitting certain information, for example, specifically disregarding Laura's final scene with Eugenio, would surely leave a wide gap in our understanding of her denunciation of life. Missing testimony will often destroy the complete truth or lead to misinterpretation. Such partial use of evidence might even destroy the credibility of a thesis.
Forming a Thesis	A simple, effective method of producing a thesis involves the posing of a specific question about a specific character or idea. For example: How is Laura a "Flowering Judas"? How are we, all of us, "Riders to the Sea"? Why is the "I" of Frost's poem "Stopping by Woods on a Snowy Evening"? What is the function of setting in "The Chrysanthemums"? Answers to these questions will inevitably yield one or more conclusions that can then be translated into the thesis proper. Our response to the question of the function of setting in "The Chrysanthemums" might well lead to the following determinations: it creates mood, foreshadows events, influences character, and symbolizes conflict. These elementary inferences will steer us to a clear affirmation of purpose, as well as guide us to the kind of organic structure and emphasis the paper should have. Most assuredly, it follows that if setting in the Steinbeck story functions in these four ways, the body of the paper will consist of and develop from these four characteristics. Thus, we might in the introduction state briefly and plainly what we propose to do: "The setting in 'The Chrysanthemums' contributes to creating mood, foreshadowing events, shaping character, and symbolizing conflict."

Having clearly stated our purpose, we need now to expand our generalizations and ask such questions as relate to the *specific* kind of mood created, the *specific* events foreshadowed, the *specific* influences shaping character, and the *specific* elements symbolizing conflict. Once this has been done, the collected information can be entered under its appropriate main heading; thus is formed the blueprint from which we can build our paper.

*Writing
the Paper*   a. Write a literary paper in a formal or semiformal style. Employ a standard usage of diction and grammar. (Usually, colloquialisms, slang expressions, and contractions are disallowed.)

b. Assume that your reader is reasonably familiar with the work you intend to discuss.

c. Use the present tense consistently. Say "Frost *uses* vivid imagery" not "used vivid imagery."

d. Maintain a proper balance. Give supportive evidence attention proportionate to its value, that is, give a lesser degree of emphasis to less significant matter than you would give to more important matter.

e. Summon details from the content of a selection to corroborate your statements. Meaning must continually emerge from the character, events, or issues contained in a story, play, or poem.

f. Adhere to the requirements of a well-organized, unified, logically-developed, coherent composition.

WRITING ABOUT PLOT

A straightforward summary, which merely sets down the dominant action of a story from beginning to end, fails as a satisfactory critique. An effective plot analysis not only recapitulates the prominent sequence of events, but does so in such a way as to lead conclusively to a sound evaluation of the significance of the story.

The ability to analyze a plot competently is indeed essential to the process of writing about literature because it is from this foundation that all other writing can spring. How can we write a cogent essay about any facet of literature without first having comprehended what we have read, that is, having recognized the essence of the story, uncovered its underlying logic, discerned its unity, perceived its vital details, and understood the nature, function, and interrelationship of the various parts that work together to convey the author's purpose or design? Obviously, we cannot.

A good approach to plot summary requires the reader to trace the pattern of a plot, as the eight-point analysis suggests.

Frequently a student asks, "What should an essay summarizing plot include or omit?" The correct reply can only be: "It should cover everything needed to produce a creditable job." In other words, an effective paper will depict the main characters, describe the world they live in, point out the forces in conflict, recount the principal action, and formulate some conclusion about what the author is attempting to do and say, as well as how the author is achieving his or her purpose. Always when writing a theme about plot, we should make clear not only *what* happens but also *how* and *why* things happen.

Of course, essays may deal with a complete plot summary or with only one feature of plot, perhaps setting. When dealing with setting in a literary paper, we should never be satisfied with mere description. There is more to the business office in "Bartleby" and the sea in "The Open Boat" than the vividness with which they are described. Setting often has a significance larger than itself and relates to the central meaning of the story. Its details an author chooses judiciously not only to prove its reality or create interest but also and frequently to unmask character, mirror conflict, or promote the theme of a story.

There is, of course, no single topic or set formula for writing a paper about setting. The possibilities abound. We might, for example, describe the general atmosphere of the race track at Saratoga in "I Want to Know Why" and explain the influence of that atmosphere on the emotions of the protagonist, the young boy. Or we might investigate the psychological effects of setting on the character of Miss Emily as revealed by her actions in "A Rose for Emily." Or, in another story, we might interpret the symbolic meaning of setting.

Plot in "A Hunger Artist"

The purpose of this paper is to summarize the plot of the short story "A Hunger Artist" by Franz Kafka. I will also point out a few similarities between the hunger artist and Christ.

"A Hunger Artist" is the unusual story of a man who fasted because he could not find any food he liked. The artist put on his black tights, climbed into a small barred cage, and sat down among the straw on the floor. Watchers were appointed by the public to watch the artist night and day in case he had somewhere hidden a supply of food. They did not understand the honor the artist placed in his profession. The guards even tempted and mocked the artist as they ate a large breakfast in his presence. The artist was not permitted to fast for more than forty days simply because public interest would lag after that length of time.

When interest in the act of fasting diminished, the show was taken to a large circus. The circus audience did not enjoy his performance either. Before long the only people who viewed his act were the ones on their way to see the animals; and they were in such a hurry that they hardly gave him a glance. Now the artist was able to fast as he had always wanted to; he felt that after forty days he was in his best fasting form. Hence he would not quit. Why should he not continue and break all fasting records? The act of fasting was of so little interest to the public, however, that the day-keeper forgot to change the record indicating the number of days the artist had been fasting.

One day an overseer saw the cage and wondered why a good cage was standing idle. The artist was found close to death but still fasting. Before he died he asked everyone to forgive him, admitting that he had always wanted them to admire his fasting. When they claimed they did admire his feat, he said that they should not, because it was something he had to do. Had he found some food to his liking he would have stuffed himself like a glutton. When he died they buried him with his straw.

Into his cage they put a young, healthy panther which everyone delighted in watching as he devoured everything put before him.

The hunger artist in this story could symbolize Christ in that both men lived secluded lives. Christ was absorbed in his religious duties and the artist in his fasting. Both men fasted for forty days and were tempted during their fast. Christ was tempted by the devil and replied that man did not live by bread alone; the artist may have been trying to prove that a man of faith could indeed live without bread. Unbelievers in the crowds followed both men; and both the artist and Christ, accused of tricking the public, were mocked and ridiculed. The hunger artist and

Christ both asked for forgiveness and both died for their cause. Jesus asked forgiveness for his murderers and the artist asked forgiveness for himself. He was his own murderer in that no one made him fast—he was fasting of his own free will.

I have tried to explain the plot and point out some of the similarities between the hunger artist and Christ. I have not gone into what each symbolizes because the word requirement of the paper does not permit it.

> Comment   *This paper represents a student's first attempt at writing a plot summary. It needs considerable revision—most importantly, a clear statement of thesis and a sharper focus on the main character's actions and thoughts if the writer is to lead us to the significance of the story.*

Plot and *Riders to the Sea*

Riders to the Sea sounds the knell of eternal death and grief. Often cited as the perfect one act play, Synge's masterpiece depends on a simple, fundamental plot with little action. A mother, mourning the loss and presumed drowning of one son, watches her last son make his final approach to the sea. She and her daughters learn the fate of the lost son, who has been buried in the far north, and the body of the last son is borne in, dripping the water which drowned him. This is a simple story, and the action that Synge chooses is equally sparce. Nora brings a bundle of clothes, possibly Michael's, which Cathleen hides as Maurya, their mother, enters. Bartley comes in for a rope for a halter that he needs for the horses he is taking to sea that day, and leaves again, receiving neither his bit of cake nor his mother's blessing. Maurya follows Bartley out with the cake, while the girls open the bundle, which proves to contain clothes of the dead Michael. Cake in hand, Maurya returns, keening, and tells of a horrible omen. Soon, keening women enter, and Bartley's body is carried in and prepared for burial.

Actually, then, the action is very simple. We do not see the critical moments of death, but are made aware of them through the bundle, through the bearing in of Bartley's body, and through exposition. Yet, Synge transforms this simple outline into a moving vehicle for his message. How does he do this?

First, Synge creates a primitive, elemental atmosphere through setting and character which makes the plot not only a basic story of human condition, but an archetype, an original pattern after which all such stories are patterned. The few incidental activities, such as cake-baking, fire-tending, and wool-spinning, all represent the basic, crudely necessary pursuits of man. There is also an aura of superstition in the play, partly created by the paganization of Christianity. The appeals that Maurya makes to "the Almighty God" are more like the invocation of some magical but useless charm than the invocation of the Christian God. In addition, Synge uses omens and archetypes himself, most notably in Maurya's vision of Michael riding behind Bartley, but also in the picture of the ship gliding up to the pier and "letting fall her sails." This is not only the ship that Bartley hopes to board and in which he hopes to brave the sea; it is the Death ship. Synge's archetypal plot, made somewhat mystical by superstition and made ancient by setting, character, and choice of stage activity, has thus gained the power to hold us in its universal net.

Because the activities and exposition that Synge employs are so carefully selected, every action intensifies and compacts the story, adding another dimension to the effectiveness of the plot. Most of the action is concerned in some way with the bundle of clothes and the cake, which is baking in the fire. The bundle of clothes is the spark that draws the audience immediately into the play, causing the suspension of disbelief to occur in a minimum amount of time. It also occasions the revelation of all we need to know, so that a clumsy exposition is avoided. Because of the bundle, the two girls express concern over Maurya, which immediately tells the audience that something is wrong. Furthermore, there is no need to tell the audience in narration that one son, Michael, has been lost and is presumed drowned; this information is skillfully woven into the dialogue. Finally, because the business with the bundle is picked up at several places in the play, a thread of unity is knitted into the fabric of the plot.

The use of the cake is a further stroke by Synge's brilliant brush, for the cake is a multiple symbol. First of all, it is food, nourishment. It is a life-symbol and, by being withheld from Bartley, foreshadows his death. Secondly, it is associated with Maurya's blessing, another needed thing that Bartley fails to take. Maurya exits with both, but the hope which lies in their power is frighteningly negated when Maurya, who is trying to give them to Bartley, is confronted instead with her chilling premonitory vision. The irony of this is compounded by the fact that the cake is shrouded in a cloth before Maurya takes it, just as the death-proclaiming clothes of Michael were wrapped in a bundle. There is a contrast between the meanings of the two bundles, yet together they portend death. Synge interweaves the two carefully, adding depth and irony to his plot.

Directly before Bartley's body is brought in, a bit of exposition is accomplished as Maurya narrates the story of her past tragedies. I have already mentioned how Synge avoids this in the beginning, but what would have stifled the play in the first moments now further intensifies the plot. First, little bits of the story have already come out, and foreshadow the story now told. Secondly, Synge's concern is with Maurya's mounting grief more than with the tragedy of the previous deaths.

She shows her grief by telling the story, and the effect is immediately multiplied by the entrance of the women, echoing again the past pattern of sorrow. The placement of this exposition is superb, for it adds much to the tension of the plot by appearing immediately before the climax. Synge paints another masterful stroke.

The power of the plot is skillfully enhanced by expert foreshadowing, some of which has been pointed out. The treatment of Michael's death prefigures Bartley's. This is established in many ways: Bartley, for instance, wears Michael's shirt, which is significantly out of the same flannel that Michael wore when he died. Michael also seems to have great importance as the hope of survival. His death establishes the archetype, not Bartley's. Cathleen remarks that Maurya was fonder of Michael, and the crutch she uses when she tries to give the cake to Bartley is a stick that Michael left. Furthermore, Michael's name is that of the Saint Michael who was a patron of mariners. Although the audience may not be aware of this, it nevertheless is a clue to the significance of the character. Michael's death as an omen of Bartley's is the substance of Maurya's vision, which is the single most important and effective piece of foreshadowing in the entire play. Every detail of the vision is perfect: Bartley, still living, rides the red horse, while Michael's is ghostly gray. Michael is dressed in new clothes, or burial clothes, while Bartley wears Michael's clothes. Bartley's death results from a freakish accident in which the gray horse, which Maurya saw Michael riding, pushes Bartley into the sea. Thus, although Bartley's death is not at sea, his delivery into the arms of the sea is nevertheless inevitable. The recounting of Patch's death and the mourning of the women then is the last, most chilling, and most immediate foreshadowing of the final blow to Maurya.

Synge has admirably transformed his sparse plot. The simple actions of the plot are skillfully intertwined into a complex web, which is intensified by the use of mystic foreshadowing. The supernatural flavor of the vision establishes an atmosphere of impending and inevitable doom which, along with the bleak, primordial setting and symbols makes the tale an archetype of human suffering. The portrait is masterfully painted with sharp, brilliant strokes by a fine and sensitive hand. Synge's plot becomes a great tolling of the bell, a keening for human death and grief.

Comment　　　*This student was asked to write an original paper that summarized the plot in such a way as to indicate that she had grasped the essential details in the play and understood Synge's theme. The synopsis is an adequate enough account of the main action, some of the observations made are astute, but the focus on theme is grossly neglected. The paper fails to deliver the total meaning of the play, particularly as it relates to Maurya: the suffering, the vision, the moment of truth, and the stoical acceptance of her fate.*

WRITING ABOUT CHARACTER

One of the most interesting writing exercises involves the analysis of principal characters. The aim of a paper addressing itself to the study of character should be to discover *who* the character under consideration is, *what*, and *why*. To achieve this end we must give due consideration to what the character does, says, and thinks, how other characters see that one, and what we ourselves can infer from all the perceptible evidence in the story.

The type of questions almost certain to require our attention before we can begin to write may be illustrated by the following: Is this character one-dimensional or three-dimensional? An inveterate liar, an impossible dreamer, a cynic, a romantic, an eccentric? What motivates his or her behavior? What aspect of human nature is exemplified? Answers to these questions should provide an ample range of interest and emphasis readily adaptable to nearly any kind of paper.

A paper, then, might trace the development or growth of a character, describe an author's attitude toward a central character, explain a character's perverted behavior, indicate the influences that shape a character, or declare the flaw in character that causes a protagonist's downfall.

Other investigations might lead to an analysis of one of the following situations: Two central figures whose character traits may be regarded as the dual personality of one "real" character (Bartleby and the lawyer in "Bartleby"); several characters whose relationship to each other may be seen as more significant than what each character individually represents (the four men typifying man in "The Open Boat"); and one or more minor characters whose function in a story contributes to a fuller understanding of plot, some other character, or theme. Here are two examples:

Fallen Monument

In a characterization of Emily Grierson, from William Faulkner's "A Rose for Emily," a woman of inherited and enforced grandeur is banished by time and circumstance from her position. Unable to cope with this turn of fate, she is forced to lose touch with reality in order to maintain her dignity.

The social position of the Grierson family was of long standing; they held themselves to be a cut above others in the town. The two female cousins who came to counsel Emily on the error of her ways were, in the words of the author, "more Grierson than Miss Emily had ever been." Public opinion, with its candid play-by-play commentary, held her to her *noblesse oblige* by expecting a socially advantageous marriage. Even Miss Emily's father demanded compliance with heritage—in life, with a horse whip, and in death, with his gaze from a crayon portrait.

As the years fell away, Emily's chances for marriage faded; the gentry wondered if indeed there had been chances or only wishful thoughts. Then the father, who had thwarted all aspirations, died leaving her only the house and faded splendor. Miss Emily was now a person to be pitied; she was alone, unchampioned, compelled to the same harsh lot as the rest.

During a prolonged sickness, Emily regained a shadow of that which she had lost in the form of a tragic and angelic-looking serenity.

The first brush with loss of reality occurred when Emily refused to give her father up to death in the finality of burial. This loss of reality was countered by a last desperate attempt at marriage in the form of an affair with Homer Barron. Miss Emily's choice of a suitor was in itself a necessary loss of reality in that Homer was a day laborer and not a part of her world; but any suitor would enable her to hold up her head in public.

With public opinion brought to bear and culminating in the visit of her relatives, Emily is once again forced out of touch with reality. She buys men's clothing, toileteries, and poison.

Miss Emily completely loses touch with the real world when Homer Barron is seen no more. She remains shut up in the house for the next few years and only touches reality on rare occasions. The night men sprinkled lime around her house, in an attempt to dispel the mysterious odor, she caught a fleeting glimpse of the real world.

Emily made a last feeble attempt at reality by giving china-painting lessons. As her clientele left her, not to be replaced, the lessons themselves proved to be a farewell to reality.

Events from this point on only serve to illustrate the total and complete loss of reality: the postal service and the taxes which had been remitted out of a sense of obligation by the older generation. These forgotten burdens were imposed again by a younger generation and subsequently ignored by Emily until the end.

Death for Emily revealed a certain victory for her that had been hidden from public view. In the faded bridal chamber—in the fleshless bones of her lover—there was dignity. Even though Homer Barron was dead, Emily still had a lover; the only thing that mattered was his being there.

The past splendor and the great lengths to which Emily went to preserve the things of value in her way of life are not by any means the only approach to a study of character in this short story. An equally interesting view is a parallel to the history of the South: great defeat in the Civil War, the destruction of a way of life, and the tenacious preservation of dignity and honor.

> **Comment** *On the whole this paper represents a satisfactory response to an assignment on character analysis. The student establishes a valid thesis and draws upon sufficient evidence to support his conclusion.*

The Human Being Inside Marty

What makes Marty Piletti a sympathetic character? What makes us cry in pity and joy? Well, Marty is a "human being" without someone to be close to. Were Marty not so kind, were he cruel, sarcastic, or temperamental, his lack of companionship would not move a reader to tears. It is the average reader—with a matchmaker's heart and mother's desire to see everyone paired off—that first sparks an interest in Marty. It is this observer who would say "Why 'The Human Being Inside Marty'? It is evident in everything he says and does; he is outwardly human." Perhaps this is true, considering the connotation of the words "human being"—a person capable of great joy and sorrow but with kindness for all. Yes, to the reader this is clear, but apparently by some of the other characters the point was missed. Some of Marty's deepest emotions are overlooked by his "friends and relations," and it is because of these insensitive fools that we give our hearts to Marty—we who see deeper.

It is not the average person, but rather the one who is less than attractive or the one who has often been left clinging to the wall watching couples dance by who identifies with Marty and thereby feels his hurt the most. To the young the future seems bright and full of opportunity; everything promising abounds. But, as the years pass one by one and acquaintances pass two by two, fear overtakes the early optimism, anxiety shadows the bright promises, and empty hearts yield to lost opportunity. Before long all that is left is quiet toleration of sorrow. This is Marty.

If one is reminded too often of his situation, very many times, as in Marty's case, it becomes a source of irritation and boredom. Marty is forced into embarrassment constantly with reminders of his nil marital prospects. His mother and all the curious friends may mean well, but apparently they overlook the fact that love or, especially the lack of it, is a most sensitive area. As a child the teasing one receives about boyfriends or girlfriends is a little embarrassing or painful if there is no such friend, but as this condition is prolonged it is the worst kind of hurt one can endure.

Marty has had thirty-six years of rejection. His troubles are rooted in his appearance. Were his problem personality, a change could be the road to a new life, but there is very little hope for the correction of "fat ugliness." At least this is how Marty views the situation each year as the dateless New Year's Eve rolls around. There comes a time when one can sink no farther into his problems, and he sees that there is no turning around or getting out by repeating the same motions he has been going through before. Marty realizes this when he calls Mary Feeney and is rejected. At this time, Marty faces the truth. He is prepared for Clara's arrival on the scene.

Clara may be a "dog" by all standard conceptions of beauty, but those who criticize first and loudest are usually those with problems of their own and with no real feeling and understanding for others. Angie would not be sitting in a bar with the guys on Saturday night asking what everyone feels like doing if he did not have some sort of problem himself.

It is the person inside the physical shell that is given a title like "human being." Marty has a self-realization of just what he is. He accepts it with Clara. More importantly, he accepts what she is—a dog—a dog that could possibly love the mutt he is.

It is his acceptance of life as it is, the ability he has for disguising hurt with toleration, and his determination to seize an opportunity both for himself and another, ignoring harmful influence that show us Marty's inner heart and pulls the tears from all the Martys who recognize themselves and wish for a Clara of their own.

Comment   *Asked to write an original essay about the character of Marty which would reveal who he is, what he is, and why, this drama student has satisfactorily handled the assignment. She establishes a valid controlling idea and draws sufficient evidence from the play to prove her thesis. But the paper contains flaws, including, among the more serious ones, a propensity for oversentimentalizing and editorializing.*

WRITING ABOUT POINT OF VIEW

The bare definition of point of view and sheer identification of the narrator in a story hardly fulfills the requirements of a paper on this subject.

A good analysis of point of view conveys a keen perception of the total emotional and intellectual effects a distinct narrative style produces. It informs us about the advantages and disadvantages of one method of narration over another; it reveals what the author expects to accomplish through the eyes of the narrator; it furnishes reasons for the author's choice; it illustrates the effectiveness of the narration; and it discloses more specifically how a particular point of view contributes explicitly to an understanding of tone, character, and the interpretation of a story.

Beyond the conspicuous indispensability of defining point of view and characterizing the narrator through whose consciousness we attend to the action of a story, we might further want to investigate the following:

1. the reliability of the narrator

2. the impression a special point of view makes on the reader

3. the contribution of the narrator's attitude, his or her objectivity or lack of it, to an appreciation of a story

4. the degree of success with which an author's narrative technique achieves reality or authenticity

Why "I Want to Know Why" Works

A young boy of fifteen decides to fulfill his lifelong dream of going to a big horse race. Along with three of his friends he jumps a freight to Saratoga. While there, he observes a man whom he admires very much, acting in a most disgraceful fashion in a "house of bad women." Through this and other experiences, he learns that people are not always what they should be or what we would like them to be. This realization is the beginning of his maturation.

* * *

The examination of point of view in a piece of literature must always be a two part project. It is important to know why the particular point of view was chosen, as well as how it is used to enhance the story. Therefore, the most logical point to launch such a study from would be a general discussion of the advantages and the disadvantages of the point of view chosen.

The first person is the most intimate point of view an author can use. It allows the reader access to all the feelings, thoughts, opinions, and reactions of the character chosen to be the narrator. By having the story related first-hand, the feeling of being within the situation and living it with the characters becomes much more vivid. The reader can much more readily identify with an "I that *is seeing*" than a "he or she that *has seen"*. The illusion of the story happening in the present, as it is being read, promotes sympathy as well as suspense in the mind of the reader.

The disadvantages of the first person stem from the limited source of information. The reader learns everything from the narrator. If he should have an incorrect opinion or be deceived, then the reader has the same distorted view of the situation that the narrator does. One can only see what the narrator sees as he sees it. In addition, the reader is unaware of what is going on in the minds of other characters.

I feel, however, that in spite of the disadvantages, the first person is the ideal choice for this story. The only significance of the other characters in the story is in how the boy relates and reacts to them. Therefore, what they are thinking is of no importance. We are left, then, with the problem of imperfect knowledge—which is what the story is all about. No one person can ever possibly know why other people behave as they do.

In turning to a discussion of how the author uses the point of view within the story, I find that it operates on two levels. The most obvious, of course, is that it serves as a vehicle for telling the story. One might say that the boyish dialect and the meandering plot-line are merely tools for the author to establish the credibility of the narrator—to make the reader believe that a fifteen-year-old boy is really telling the story. However, I feel that these tools have other, more important functions.

The dialect sets the tone of the story. The reader reaches greater insights through its presence in the story. It serves to develop the character much more than a third person narrative ever could. The boy is fresh and honest, but has a haunting concern over something that happened to him on his trip to Saratoga. His enthusiasm and trusting nature must be established so that the reader can understand how an incident that might have been a small moment in the life of someone else was to him traumatic. The author, then, through the use of the first person, builds up the reader's sympathy for the boy and sensitivity to his plight.

The wandering plot line also has an additional meaning, other than the fact that boys are always getting sidetracked when they tell stories. It serves as a means of mixing the narrative with the exposition in a very interesting fashion. It also gives the reader important information he needs to know about the boy. The information about his father reveals that these two have a trusting relationship, which, I feel, gave the boy the self-confidence necessary to face this step in his development. To those readers who have no knowledge of horseracing or horse tracks, the information the boy provides on the paddocks, the niggers, and how he feels about horses is crucial to their understanding of what is going on. Certain things need to be felt and discovered before the actual incident is told. So the author keeps alluding to the incident to keep the reader's interest mounting, while letting the boy wander off to give us some necessary information.

The most important function of this point of view

relates to the theme of the story. The boy is at that stage where he is beginning to recognize the inconsistency of human nature. He does not understand it. He wants to understand why people are the way they are and behave as they do. Throughout the story the reader is constantly being made aware of the boy's new awareness through cleverly placed asides. Quite often he says: "That's the way I feel about it" or "I don't know why." So the author brilliantly uses his first person narrator again and again to bring his theme back to the reader.

Obviously no other character in the story and no third person outside this cast of characters could tell this story without damaging its total effect. Anderson has taken a simple element and made it into the foundation of the story itself. In short, the first person narrative in this story is the pivotal point around which the style, plot development, characterization, and theme are neatly balanced.

Comment *This paper reflects a mature and perceptive discussion of point of view. Certainly, despite several flaws, the student has grasped the essential functions of the first person point of view and communicated their significance to this story.*

WRITING ABOUT THEME

A popular writing assignment often calls for treating the central thematic idea or one of the major themes of a literary work. The initial step in the process of writing such a paper involves a search for the meaning which will logically form the basis of our topic. Having discovered and isolated that idea, we can proceed to define our thesis and state our intentions in the opening paragraph or paragraphs. Having done this, we are ready to organize and develop the body of the paper with what supportive evidence the title, setting, character, conflict, thought revelations, direct statements by the author, prominent actions, and other data may suggest to us.

As always, what we claim to be a valid summing up of any meaning that a story, poem, or play communicates must be strengthened by textual proof, manifest or implied. We can be certain that the more thoughtfully we scrutinize the emotional and intellectual content of a selection, the more explicit our thesis statement is likely to become and the more convincing our interpretation of any portion of the piece is likely to be.

A paper discussing theme may have a variety of purposes: it may divulge how setting points to theme, how character, action, or specific episodes disclose certain truths about the human experience, or how an author's style ministers to the expression of meaning in a story.

A Critique of Crane's "The Open Boat"

This paper intends to discuss the main theme of the short story "The Open Boat" which is: throughout the following paragraphs, the indifference of nature toward the existence of man.

Throughout this story one sees four ship-wrecked men struggling against the forces of nature for their own survival. The reader can easily sense the terrible state that these men are in from the opening sentence: "None of them knew the color of the sky." These men, a captain, an oiler, a cook, and a correspondent (thought to be Crane himself), had been dazed by the storm.

Quite frequently one of the four would ask: "If I am going to be drowned, why, in the name of the seven mad gods who rule the sea, was I allowed to come thus far and contemplate sand and trees?" Here, it is shown that nature is indifferent to man. Man must face nature. He must show his power to struggle; however, in the end, nature will prevail. The characters then question Fate, the old "ninny-woman." "Just you drown me, now, and then hear what I call you!" Seemingly, man has enough intellect to one day conquer Fate, which is death. This same quotation shows the absurdity of man and the ridiculousness of life. Perhaps, the human race will one day overcome death. But to do this man may have to achieve a tragic death.

As one continues to read, he can feel man being tossed about on the sea of life: "The billows that came at this time were more formidable. They seem always just about to break and roll over the little boat in a turmoil of foam." In everyday life there is nothing that can possibly be done to combat the forces of nature. Man has always had to change to fit the law of nature. As man travels through life, he is always tempted. Certain temptations may endanger his life and the life of his fellow comrades. Notice the symbolism exhibited in the story when sea gulls fly around the dinghy in which the men are sailing. One bird attempts to light on the top of the captain's head. If he had yielded to his temptation of knocking the bird away with the oar, he would have capsized the boat. Instead, he gently waved it away.

The reader can see the four men as united for one cause, which is survival for each one. All men are dependent on others for a while; however, when death enters the scene, it is every man for himself. There it can be seen how impersonal death is. When nature strikes and the boat is capsized by a wave, each man is forced to protect himself. Instead of worrying about his survival, the correspondent is troubled about the coldness of the water which surrounded him. As the correspondent reaches shore, he sees the oiler lying face down upon the sand. Here we come to learn that man needs others if he is to survive. One might also question the absurdity of life. The oiler was intellectual and powerful. This meant nothing to the forces of nature. His death, consequently, points to the ironic situation of the fittest man not surviving but dying.

In conclusion, nature has been shown to be indifferent toward the existence of man. When nature, fate, and death combine forces, man is doomed no matter how hard he might struggle. Thus, we know that man will continue to combat the forces of nature to no avail. These forces have remained the same throughout history and will probably remain indifferent to the end of time.

> *Comment*   *Note this student's simple, clear expression of thesis. He does prove his point but not so convincingly because of his predilection to digress and editorialize. Further, the paper would gain strength with additional examples of nature's indifference to man.*

Significance of Lola's Dreams in *Come Back, Little Sheba*

Come Back, Little Sheba is a tale of personal failure, frustration, and loss. Much of the symbolism in the play can be found in Lola's dreams.

The first dream the audience is told about is a recurrent one concerning the loss of Lola's little dog Sheba. In this dream, Sheba is the symbolic representation of Lola's youth, and the loss of the dog is synonymous with the passing of her youth. Lola dreams that she puts Sheba on a leash and takes her downtown: "All the people on the street turned around to admire her, and I felt so proud"; and Lola was much admired in her own youth because of her beauty. "Then we started to walk, and the blocks started going by so fast that Little Sheba couldn't keep up with me. Suddenly I looked around and Little Sheba was gone. Isn't that funny? I looked everywhere for her but couldn't find her. And I stood there feeling sort of afraid." In this speech, the blocks are symbolic of the passing years in Lola's life, for which she really has nothing to show. Her most noteworthy achievement has been in keeping Doc away from the bottle; but there is not a line in the play that would indicate that she has ever experienced anything which might legitimately be called fulfillment.

In this same speech, Lola indicates that she is looking for her lost youth and that her failure in finding it has caused her to be afraid. She is afraid because she is not able to have any stable relationship with another human being. Lola and Doc have each robbed the other of any chance of finding a satisfactory human relationship; and an almost hysterical fear becomes the only bond between then.

Lola is unable to believe that her loss of years is permanent, for she asks Doc, "Do you suppose it means Little Sheba is going to come back?" Lola is looking to Doc for hope that some of the joy and affection that she had in her youth will return. She tells Doc, "Remember how white and fluffy she used to be after I gave her a bath? And how her little hind-end wagged from side to side when she walked?" In those youthful days, Lola was pure (just as Sheba was white) and feminine (just as Sheba was fluffy). And we assume from her comments that she was a flirt and very much desired then (just as Sheba wagged her tail, Lola probably swung her hips to attract boys). Lola tells Doc that she hated to see Little Sheba grow old and he replies, "Little Sheba should have stayed young forever. Some things should never grow old." Again, the dog represents Lola since what Doc is really doing is expressing his inner wish that Lola could still be as lovely and passionate as she once was.

Lola's final dream is a very significant one, which contains the heart of the play. In the closing minutes of the play, after Doc has returned home from the hospital, he tells Lola that he might take up hunting and get a bird dog to replace Sheba. Then Lola says that she has had another dream "about everyone and everything." The dream has taken her back to a scene of her youth, her high school, where she and Marie are going to the Olympics. She makes a point of saying that there were thousands of people there and that Turk was out in the field throwing the javelin. Perhaps the fact that thousands of people were watching helps to assuage Lola's guilt feeling at having watched throughout the play Marie and Turk at various stages of their lovemaking, an action for which Doc has chided her.

A pervasive symbol in Lola's final dream is the symbol of the javelin. Turk, whose sexuality is emphasized throughout the play, is in training for a spring track season. He tells Lola early in the play, "They got me throwing the javelin." Lola does not know what a javelin is, and Turk tells her, "It's a big, long lance. You hold it like this, erect—then you let go and it goes singing through the air, and lands yards away, if you're any good at it, and sticks in the ground, quivering like an arrow." The sexual connotations of this speech are very obvious. Lola has a basic phallic fascination for Turk, indicating that Lola, who was forced into marriage with her bashful suitor, has always secretly hoped for the sheer animal pleasure that a brute like Turk could provide. Lola, who has been essentially a pure woman all her life, now feels somewhat cheated at never having known any other man than Doc. But this feeling is something that she cannot even acknowledge to herself, except in her dreams.

The man in charge of the games in this dream is Lola's father. In the dream, Turk kept changing into someone else all the time, indicating Lola's desire for acceptance and love. But Lola's father finally disqualifies Turk, as he had disqualified all of Lola's would-be suitors; and Turk is replaced on the field by Doc. In her youth, Lola had been protected by an overly suspicious father, who approved of none of her suitors except Doc. But when Lola ended up pregnant by Doc, her father rejected her and would not let her return home again. Her guilt feelings about her pregnancy and her father's reaction to it are coming through in this dream.

Then Lola's dream brings from deep within her subconscious the memory of what Doc once was to her: "You picked up the javelin real careful like it was awful heavy. But you threw it, Daddy, clear, clear up into the sky. And it never came down again. Then it started to rain." Doc, who courted Lola for a year before he dared to kiss her, is not as impetuous as Turk, who did not share Doc's reluctance to pick up the javelin. But having sufficiently overcome his basic shyness to kiss Lola, Doc proceeded with great dispatch to get her pregnant and then to marry her. The rain in this speech indicates that with Lola's pregnancy and their marriage, their lives were washed away. Doc's dreams of becoming a great doctor and Lola's need for fulfillment were both lost when they were forced into marriage.

At this point in the dream Lola misses Little Sheba. She searches for her in the crowd and "all of a sudden I saw Little Sheba . . . she was lying in the middle of the field . . . dead. . . . It made me cry. . . . It made me feel so bad, Doc." Here, Little Sheba represents Doc and Lola's baby that died, apparently because the delivery of the child was botched by a midwife to whom Lola went because she felt too guilty to go to a regular obstetrician. This baby, the result of its parents' affair, was not to blame for their sin, so Lola feels much guilt about its death. When Lola says, "That sweet little puppy . . . her curly white [virginal] fur all smeared with mud [loss of innocence], and no one to stop and take care of her [parental rejection]," she is actually referring to herself. Doc considers Lola dirty because of their affair, even though he is just as guilty as she is. He seems to be rationalizing his own failures by convincing himself that Lola is to blame for them.

But as the play closes, Lola gives some indication that she is ready to face life on more realistic terms than before. Now she tells Doc, "I don't think Little Sheba's ever coming back, Doc. I'm not going to call her any more." This final dream causes her to bring to surface many of her subconscious guilt feelings, and in relating them to Doc, she realizes at last that these feelings are from the past and that they must be abandoned in order to make a new life with Doc.

Comment   *The assignment here required the student to write a theme interpreting symbolic content in* Come Back, Little Sheba. *The paper correctly identifies the major symbols and interprets them consistently with the facts and theme of the play. Also, the quotations, which were carefully selected, give significant insight into their meaning. The obvious faults of the paper include an unclear statement of purpose, and an inadequate conclusion, as well as grammatical errors.*

Social Acceptance in *Tea and Sympathy*

Human beings, the social animals, reap the rewards and the innate evils of the society they create. One of the most insidious dangers of a community is the prevalent attitude of conformity, and Robert Anderson concentrates on this conformity and acceptance in *Tea and Sympathy*. He poignantly traces the pressure of social acceptance in Tom Lee's life, revealing the devastating effect on the boy who does not conform.

Tom's naive outlook on life is the most dominant, contributing factor to the anguish he suffers. At the beginning of the play, when confronted by Mr. Harris, the teacher with whom he has been swimming, the boy is entirely unaware of the imminent danger in that event. He innocently questions his teacher: "What did you do wrong?" And Harris replies: "Nothing! Nothing, unless you made it seem like something wrong."

When Herb approaches his son about the swimming incident, his father must literally spell out the implications of his son's actions. Even then Tom is painfully slow to realize what is suggested. Tom's naiveté about homosexuality, when all the other characters seem well aware of all the ensuing consequences, is a direct indication to the reader that the boy does not fit readily into the social atmosphere of his associates. He is a misfit, and soon the emerging social pressure to fit in will begin to affect him more directly.

Tom is not actually a part of the rigorous physical fitness emphasis in his house. When Bill Reynolds is planning his annual mountain-climbing weekend, Tom cannot go because he is a member of the dance committee. In defense Laura alludes to Tom's tennis championships, and Herb acknowledges his son's prowess there. However, he is quick to qualify that skill in a derogatory manner. "But Laura, he doesn't even play tennis like a regular fellow. No hard drives and cannon-ball serves. He's a cut artist." Even his tennis playing is suspect. Because he does not perform like a "regular fellow" according to society's definition, there is something wrong.

Anderson does not fail to include as many details as he can about Tom's personality to build up a negative but circumstantial case. The past year he had played Lady Macbeth in the school play, and when we first meet him, he is being fitted for his costume as Lady Teazle in *The School for Scandal*. After finding out about this latter role, Herb not only insists on Tom's refusing the part, but also coerces him to do so in the presence of

Bill and Laura. Tom's nickname, Grace, adds a further humiliation to his social status at the school.

As the pressure to "be like everyone else" descends full force onto Tom, he becomes almost paranoid about his behavior everywhere. He feels that the boys are avoiding him entirely, thus convicting him surely. Yet, when his roommate attempts to help him surmount the spreading rumors, Al can only vaguely suggest a shorter haircut and new style of walking. Even Al admits that these external mannerisms are trivial and will probably not alter the existing opinions.

The other boys have also been brain-washed by their society's code, which dictates that the only way to prove conclusively your masculinity is to make it with a girl. Though Tom was not acquainted with any girls well enough to ask them to the dance, he is still teased about his failure to get a date or to go out with girls. Thus, Al's counseling of his friend leads to the ultimate test—an encounter with Ellie Martin. This will successfully discredit any of the current rumors and set Tom's feet on the path to being a "regular fellow."

Tom does not fail with Ellie because he is not a man. He fails because the society he strives so hard to conform to puts more emphasis on actions than feelings. He has feelings for Ellie, so he cannot pretend. Tom's attempted suicide after his traumatic failure is the futile action of a boy who has, according to society, failed the last exam.

The society that rejects this sensitive boy does not comprehend the struggle inside of its victim. Herb is ashamed and humiliated because this incident appears to prove his worse suspicions. He extends no understanding to his son. Initially Bill is most upset because Al, the potential baseball captain, will be moving to another house because of Tom. This injures the status of the whole house. After the suicide attempt, Bill's smug I-told-you-so attitude proceeds directly from the insensitivity he has projected throughout the drama.

The infectious disease of social pressure to conform to certain standards has almost killed Tom. Though he is physically alive, his spirit and will to exist as a man has been destroyed. The single remedy for him is the understanding of a sensitive person who will accept him and his feelings. This person is Laura.

Tom is beyond a verbal confirmation now, so Laura realizes that she must use the norms of the society that has rejected him. She assures him that he is more of a man than her husband and that he can love if it is with the right person. Laura's sensitivity to Tom's feelings is the only saving factor in the young boy's life.

Robert Anderson deals with the social pressure of acceptance in a gentle, understanding way. He shows how insensitivity can condemn in circumstantial situations and almost destroy the person involved. Through Laura he concludes that only by attempting to understand the feelings of others do we ever help them to reach their full potential in society.

WRITING ABOUT STYLE

A critical paper that analyzes an author's style may well prove to be the most intellectually demanding and the most rewarding of all writing assignments in literature.

A paper on style may focus on a great variety of literary matters. We may inspect the complexity, simplicity, or subtlety of an author's way of telling a story; assess a writer's powers of description or use of dialogue; test the atmosphere or mood of a poem; explore the symbolic meaning of an individual character, action, or setting; inquire into the relationship of one or all parts to the unified whole; or investigate any other distinct feature of an author's artistic talent.

A Brief Analysis of Henry James's "The Real Thing"

Whenever Henry James's name is brought up, one is almost certain that a lively discussion will follow, for most students of literature have strong opinions about him. Numerous books and articles have been written concerning his works. They range from explications of specific works to analyses of themes throughout his writings to discussions of his imagery and symbolism. The following is one student's brief analysis of one of James's short stories "The Real Thing".

As the title suggests, the theme is concerned with the real and the unreal. The author demonstrates that the real thing can be much less precious than the unreal. He uses Major and Mrs. Monarch, an artist narrator, and two models from the lower class to carry out his theme. In addition, he emphasizes both title and theme with frequent allusions to "the real thing."

The Monarchs, whose name seems representative of the type of society in which they have been living, request employment as models from the artist who relates the story in the first person. They have emphasized that they are the real thing from society and as such will be a great advantage to the artist. However, the artist gradually recognizes that the real "society" models are inflexible; thus he uses his imitative models from the lower classes more and more until he finally dismisses the Monarchs. Consequently, the "real" people find themselves less valuable than the "unreal."

Though the theme centers upon people in the world of art, it finds application to numerous situations outside the artistic world. One such application is the retreat from reality that most people escape to at some time. For many, this retreat leads them to a world of dreams and plans for the future which provides a healthy outlet for frustrations and perhaps a stimulus to harder work; for others, it involves a complete divorce from the real world.

That the narrator is an artist and the setting is an art studio proves significant because the world of art is often considered an unreal one. The value of the "real" Monarchs is lessened in this world where the necessity of suggesting a situation is greater than that of illustrating it exactly.

Henry James uses mainly an expository or summary method of revealing action in his story. The reader is aware of the narrator's thoughts and of the internal conflict he faces in trying to be true to his artistic standards and sympathetic to his chief characters the Monarchs. He is also aware of the thoughts and motivations of the Monarchs because of the way their actions are described.

Much of James's art is in his style. He uses irony throughout the narration. At one point in the story the artist asks the unsophisticated Miss Churm to serve tea (not an unusual task for her) while the Monarchs are sitting for a picture. Although she performs the task willingly enough, she later complains about being asked to serve the Monarchs. Later when Oronte and Miss Churm are posing, the proper Mrs. Monarch is asked to serve tea. This is something of a blow to her ego, but she serves admirably. This scene also seems to introduce another irony: When the Monarchs realize that their services as models are to be taken by the artist's servants, then they become his servants for a brief time.

The reader can easily assess the author's descriptive powers. He is immediately struck by the nobility of Mrs. Monarch's rearranging of Miss Churm's curls while the latter is sitting for a picture. He feels the hesitancy present at the first meeting of the artist and the Monarchs. The description of this situation is aided by the author's complex sentence structure (a technique he often uses). James's long sentences are interrupted frequently with parentheses and contain independent clauses that are loosely connected with conjunctions and punctuation. An example of this type sentence occurs in the following paragraph: "They were visibly shy; they stood there letting me take them in—which as I afterward perceived, was the most practical thing they could have done."

Another technique is the author's frequent use of italics. Occasionally the reason for their use is obvious when the artist cries, "Oh, my dear Major—I can't be ruined for *you*!" At other times italics are used for less obvious reasons. Often a person places a slight emphasis on the word in a speech, as in the artist's comment relating to a facial expression of Mrs. Monarch: "I should have liked to have been able to paint *that* . . ."

Throughout the story there are italicized pronouns and verbs that emphasize the relationship of the characters in the story and the fact that the Monarchs represent the "real" thing.

Finally, James's belief in the importance of experience is clearly seen when the artist comments in the person of Jack Hawley, that though the Monarchs did permanent damage to his work, the memory is nevertheless well worth it.

> *Comment* *This paper, written interestingly enough and grammatically satisfactory, has several weaknesses: the introduction, though arresting, lacks a clear statement of purpose; the analysis of James' style begins midway in the paper; and the conclusion loses effectiveness by failing to tie it in to the central purpose.*

Polarity and Contrast in *Come Back, Little Sheba*

One of the characteristics of a good drama is difference or contrast. William Inge's *Come Back, Little Sheba* contains many such contrasts, both of situation, and of the very personalities of the characters themselves. Polarity of situation may be seen in the relationship between Lola and Marie, between Mrs. Coffman and Lola, and between the Doc/Lola relationship and the Turk/Marie relationship. Certain contrasts of the personalities of the characters are also apparent, such as those between Lola and Marie, between Marie and Doc's daughter image, Turk and Doc, as well as Doc and Lola. These contrasts make the drama more powerful and give the characters emphasis. The play is written so as to let the contrasts flow and intermingle until in the end they all seem to move together, somewhat merging. This makes for a very effective drama.

The logical starting point of the drama or the basic skeleton is the basic situation in which the characters are found. This varies with each character and differs from the others. In *Come Back, Little Sheba* the first situation contrast encountered is that of Marie and Lola. Lola has lost her youth; indeed even in her youth she never had the freedom that Marie has. Marie is busy, always in a hurry; she rises early to get to the library before anyone else. Lola begins her day listless, lonely, and bored, wishing she could sleep until noon. Marie will not even eat her breakfast before she bathes so that she will be fresh and clean to start the day. Lola is the absolute antithesis as she moves in her lumpy kimono, "morning disillusionment," and "worn dirty comfies."

The adjectives "sad," "vacant," "bored," "clinging,"

and "futile" are appropriately used to describe Lola and her day. She tries desperately to detain the postman and the milkman, for although the rooms of her house are in various stages of disarray, *she can find nothing to do*. Mrs. Coffman, on the other hand, is *always* busy at something; in fact, her motto is "Being busy is being happy." We get the feeling that Lola, whose one baby died, is envious or even jealous of Mrs. Coffman's seven children, who keep her so busy.

Another contrast is that between the relationship of Doc and Lola and the relationship of Turk and Marie. Doc and Lola's relationship seems to exist without something for which Lola apparently craves. On the other hand, Marie and Turk's relationship is purely physical, nothing but sex. This is illustrated when they try to sit and talk and are both dissatisfied.

Other contrasts in *Come Back, Little Sheba* are contrasts in the characters themselves, not just their circumstances. Lola is a meek person, and she has let both herself and the house go to ruin, probably out of her dejection in old age. She is easily hurt, and has a strong fear of rejection. Marie is strong, vivacious and hurts Lola without meaning to. It is obvious that she is looking out for herself and would never find herself in such a situation as that in which young Lola found herself.

Doc and Turk are another marked contrast. Doc cannot cope with his problems alone; he needs something to help him, Alcoholics Anonymous, or the Bible. He once makes the statement, "Alcoholics need courage," and this he at least certainly needs.

Turk, on the other hand, needs only himself. He would not feel the loss of Marie; instead he would promptly find someone else. He is sure of himself. The reason for Doc's drinking is the loss of his daughter. What drives Doc to drink in the play is the realization that Marie is not the embodiment of this daughter, but an exact opposite. He sees Marie as "nice" and "decent." Once he says, "I just like to believe that young people like her are clean and decent," and another time he refers to her as "sweet and innocent." So much does he believe this of Marie that, when he finds out the truth, he cannot handle it and must go back to his old crutch. Doc's ideas are also quite different from Lola's on a number of subjects, including letter-opening, spying, and lovemaking. These basic polarities make up the texture over which the whole drama moves.

As situations change within the plot, the various relationships and contrasts seem to flow under and over one another, some merging, others breaking away. Toward the end of the play, at least Doc is more able to cope with his situation and indicates his dependency upon Lola. Lola, now needed, has become busy, assumed a closer identity with Mrs. Coffman, and established a more stable relationship with Doc. Turk has ceased to be the villain, and Marie will now settle into a marital relationship.

All the polarities and contrasts, both those of character personality and those of character situation, play an important role in the vitality of the drama. William Inge has used both with maximum effectiveness in moving the play to its natural end.

<table>
<tr><td>Comment</td><td>This student was asked to prepare an original paper dealing with any facet of style. She chose to treat contrasts of characters and of situations. The essay contains good material, but the organization and emphasis are poorly managed. If the purpose of the essay is to show that "contrasts" make for good drama, then it fails miserably, and the conclusion is woefully inadequate. Furthermore, the writer says too little about the Doc/Turk contrast in character, referring only to one aspect of character, and she too quickly abandons that subject to explore, in the same paragraph, a contrast of character between Doc and Marie.</td></tr>
</table>

"Carrion Comfort"

Not, I'll not, carrion comfort, Despair, not feast on
    thee;
Not untwist—slack they may be—these last strands of
    man
In me or, most weary, cry I CAN NO MORE. I can;
Can something, hope, wish day come, not choose not to
    be.
But ah, but O thou terrible, why wouldst thou rude on
    me
Thy wring-world right foot rock? lay a lionlimb against
    me? scan
With darksome devouring eyes my bruised bones: and
    fan,
O in turns of tempest, me heaped there; me frantic to
    avoid thee and flee?

Why? That my chaff might fly; my grain lie, sheer and
    clear.
Nay in all that toil, that coil, since (seems) I kissed the
    rod,
Hand rather, my heart lo! lapped strength, stole joy,
    would laugh, cheer.
Cheer whom though? the hero whose heaven-handling
    flung me, foot trod
Me? or me that fought him? O which one? is it each
    one? That night, that year
Of now done darkness I wretch lay wrestling with (my
    God!) my God.

One of the main signposts in this poem is the sonnet form itself. For although Hopkins is an innovator with meter, he does not violate the sonnet's basic structure. In "Carrion Comfort" the rhymes, the grammar, and the very physical appearance of the poem clearly point to the Italian sonnet with its primary division of octave and sestet. Within each of these divisions the rhyme and grammar indicate a further division into equal parts, so that what we have structurally is a pair of quatrains and a pair of tercets.

Between the first and second quatrains exists a seeming inconsistency; that of being devoured in the latter countered by the feasting image of the former. Both can be resolved by analysis of Hopkins' use of the word "carrion." As a noun it is "lifeless, rotting flesh." Adjectivally, however, it becomes "eating lifeless, rotting flesh." A case could probably be made for "carrion" both as a descriptive adjective and as an adjective restricting the comprehension of "comfort" (since "Despair," its appositive, is used as a proper noun), but it's easier to simply look to the two meanings of the epithet "carrion comfort": "comfort for lifeless flesh" and "comfort that comes from feeding on lifeless flesh." Not only are both meanings pertinent to the first quatrain, but the ambiguity also explains the shift from the tempting feast in the first quatrain to the threat of being devoured in the second as a change of imagery rather than a change of metaphorical meaning.

There is an awkwardness, however, if "Despair" is taken exclusively as appositive to "carrion comfort": "Not, I'll not . . . not feast on thee." But because we are inclined to read "Despair" also as a verb (to feast on despair is, in effect, to despair), the repetition of "not" before "feast" is smooth enough and emphasizes the determination to resist. Hopkins is in a sense defining "Despair" through its consequences or physical manifestations; that is, he is calling "Despair" a comfort for lifeless flesh and a comfort consisting of feeding on lifeless flesh. He is resisting both.

Because of Hopkins' religious orientation, it is easy to assume that the despair of which he speaks is not only a state of mind, but the sin for which heaven supposedly holds no forgiveness, the sin against the Holy Spirit, and the force being resisted in the first quatrain is the temptations of the flesh. (Obviously, this is not the same thing as sensuality; it may be acute sensuousness, self-love, or attachment to worldly values—the more subtle elements of Christian warfare, that between the flesh and the spirit.) Thus the first person of the poem, the "I," is really the spirit of the poet and the "thou," although it immediately refers to "Despair," is really addressed to the forces tempting the spirit to despair, the flesh itself.

The conjunction "But" which begins the second quatrain is appropriate because it connects the opposite ideas of the firm resisting of the inclination toward despair (which seems to imply victory) in the first quatrain, and the painful awareness that his temptation is continuing, that the war is not yet won. The "ah" and "O" in the fifth line are examples of the interjections that emphasize the pathos of the speaker's plight. Dramatically, he has refused the comfort that flesh has to offer and now the tempter has fallen back on violence. This has been prepared for by the ambiguity of "carrion," which evokes images both of the flesh being offered to the speaker as enticement and of the speaker becoming lifeless flesh and therefore likely to be devoured by some carrion animal. The shift from the first quatrain to the second, then, far from violating unity, achieves a powerful dramatic and psychological realism. Promise is replaced by threat.

The questions in the second quatrain may be interpreted as the poet's questionings of his own mind. They are not altogether logical, but are descriptive and sincere. The description is, at first, of something indistinct, something that wrings the world with its right foot. Then it takes on more definite shape with the word "lionlimb." The beast is glaring "with darksome devouring eyes" at the speaker's "bruised bones" and is described as "turns of tempest," which in turn suggests the emotional turmoil within the poet. Whatever may be the habits of real carrion beasts or birds, this creature in the poem is not standing by idly waiting for the man to die; it is tormenting him and he is struggling to escape from it. The octave ends: "me frantic to avoid thee and flee."

The "Why" of the sestet seems to echo the "why wouldst thou" of the second quatrain. But there is another question suggested by the last words of the octave. Why is the speaker anxious to avoid the temptations of the flesh? So that his soul will shine in its purity, "that my chaff might fly; my grain lie, sheer and clear." Not only ("Nay"), but his "heart" (his soul, spirit) "would" (wishes to) "laugh, cheer" in (be full of gladness about) all that "toil, that coil" (turmoil) which was suffered since he "kissed the rod,/Hand rather" (submitted to the will of his God), and received "strength" and "joy" of spirit.

This would seem to be a contradiction: the poet submitted to the will of God and yet the "toil" and "coil" have existed since that submission. But Hopkins explains this apparent contradiction with his "(seems)". It indicates that his submission was only a superficial one. Indeed, because the "Hand rather" is a correction too emphatic to be disregarded, the reader is encouraged to distinguish between the greater degree of submission in kissing the rod (a willing submission to authority). The issue of that former struggle, then, was something less than complete submission to the will of God and for some time afterwards the poet suffered an agony of spirit along with joy that was stolen (not honestly acquired) and strength that was "lapped." So, in the first three lines of the sestet, the poet may be explaining that he wants to flee from the temptations of the flesh so that his soul will shine in its purity and in order to "cheer" in that torment he had suffered for a time when he first imperfectly submitted to the will of God. In other words, if he gives in to the flesh, either by submitting to its temptations or by suicide, all his previous suffering will have been in vain.

The final three lines of the sestet take up the word "cheer" in a new sense to raise yet another question: which of the former antagonists is to be cheered, applauded, in the event of a successful termination of this new struggle: The last sentence of the poem defines the "toil" and "coil" of the sestet; it is a period during which the poet wrestled with God instead of completely submitting to His will. That struggle is now over ("now done darkness"); he wants to avoid the temptations of the flesh in order to reap the rewards of that earlier struggle. But who, he wonders, is the real victor of that struggle? Is it God, whose "heaven-handling flung" him down, whose "foot trod" him into submission? Or is it the speaker himself who resisted God? When the poet finally reaps his reward (his "Cheer"), will applause be due to God or to himself? The answer is put in the form of a question, "is it each?" It will be due to both God and man; for the soul, when it achieves complete success, will have won through defeat, through submission to God. Both God and man will deserve the applause.

Hopkins' familiarity with the "Spiritual Exercises" of St. Ignatius as well as the sonnet form itself support this literal interpretation. The octave presents the situation: the speaker resolutely refuses to take the comfort, despair, which flesh has to offer in this struggle between the flesh and the spirit, and he defiantly cries out against these terrible temptations from which he is anxious to escape. The sestet gives the reason for the refusal to despair and for the desire to flee from the temptations of the flesh; the poet wishes for a successful resolution of his struggle with his God, a struggle which is now over and done with (the struggle of faith) but which cannot be rewarded unless the new struggle (with the flesh) is victoriously concluded.

In the first quatrain the spirit in turmoil says "No" to the comfort offered by the flesh even though it sees very little comfort ahead. The speaker can at least "hope, wish day come, not choose not to be." He is left in a horrible world with the monster raging around him. How can he avoid it? Why, after all, had he resisted? By shifting his attention from the temptations to the motives for his resistance, he manages to emerge victorious. Thus the poem moves from preoccupation with the temptation to the thoughts of the reward that will crown the final victory. In the process the mind of the speaker recalls the path he has already trod and through this intellectual contemplation the emotional turmoil is dissipated. The parenthetical ejaculation at the end—"(my God!)"—indicating a sudden awakening to the real nature of his former antagonist, and a final complete submission to God's will, dramatically represents the triumph of the spirit over the flesh.

Robert Bridges' choice of "Carrion Comfort" for the title of this sonnet is a particularly felicitous one. In its denotative and connotative ambiguities, the phrase well covers the turns of thought from despair, to the struggle against the force arguing for despair (the flesh), and to the spiritual comfort that mortal flesh can take from the anticipation of "cheer." Its suggestive ambiguity, moreover, is the very stuff out of which the poem objectifies the way in which the mind debates with itself.

<blockquote>
Comment   *This student's strategy was one of a close textual analysis. By paying very close attention to the structure of Hopkins' "Carrion Comfort," the student had a viable starting point to keep him from going astray in his reading. In the reading itself, meanwhile, the student confined himself to the poet's words. There was certainly interpretation, but the student allowed each potential ambiguity to have its day. The result is admirable because of the student's willingness to be flexible and as objective as possible.*
</blockquote>

The Penultimate Lines of John Keats's "Ode on a Grecian Urn"

John Keats's "Ode on a Grecian Urn" is perhaps the most famous of his poems, and certainly the best known of his odes. The poem presents a contrast between the permanence of art and the transiency of life. The penultimate line of the poem, however, presents a definite problem in relation to the ultimate meaning of the ode. It is the relationship of the final lines and the importance placed upon the Beauty-Truth concept of the poem that I wish to deal with in my paper. Before beginning, an explanation of the poem should be given and its theme incorporated into the final lines.

Keats knew the classics well and was acquainted with Grecian works of art. Speculation that he had a specific urn in mind when writing his ode is certainly far-fetched since no amount of research has revealed an urn with the same three scenes. He had also studied Homer's *Iliad*, *Odyssey*, and *Hymns*, and a translation of Ovid's *Metamorphoses*.

In Arthur Swanson's essay on "Form and Content," he states that "Keats, a Romantic poet, contemplates a Classical Greek urn; his Romantic reaction to Classical balance results in a poem whose form is Classical and whose content is Romantic."[1] Because Keats is a Romantic poet and artist, he is able to allow his reader to complete the art work by using his creative imagination. This type of vague, allusive poetry enables the reader to recognize and apply the "unheard" part to which the allusion is made.[2]

Keats' "Ode" is an art work about an art work. The significance of the poem, its ultimate meaning, lies in the specific relationship between the art work Keats was creating and the already created art work of the urn.

We can say with assurance that "the poem's the thing"; paradoxically the urn becomes less important as an art work than the poem, despite the imaginative rendering of the urn, the tale it has to tell. Paradoxically the beauty of the urn enhances the poem rather than the urn until in the closing stanza the beauty of the urn is secondary to the more significant and meaningful beauty of the poem. What becomes more important than the urn and its message, an integral part of its beauty, is what the poem has made of the urn—something more than a beautiful piece of pottery.[3]

The poem is about a Grecian urn, any urn, with bas reliefs superimposed on the surface. There are three main impressions on the urn: One of lovers chasing each other, a piper playing his instrument, and a priest leading a heifer to the sacrifice.

Verse one is an introduction to the three images on the urn. Keats has personified the urn and calls it an "unravish'd bride of quietness" as if it were virginal in essence. Although the urn does not speak directly to the viewer and is considered a "foster-child of silence," it conveys its ideas through visual images. The final six lines make up a series of questions, each beginning with the interrogative word "what." Each question is related to events occuring on the urn.

In each one of the above instances Keats is trying—and succeeding—to show the reader or give him an aesthetic experience toward art by relating it to an immortal, momentary experience with the eternal. He reveals to us that art is transitory. His words "Heard melodies are sweet, but those unheard are sweeter" reflect a harmony from the work of art that plays to the spirit.

The final six lines of stanza two show us a picture of love exemplified in youth and nature. Even though the piper can never stop playing, he will not tire of his song. Just as the leaves can never fall from the trees so will the lovers be forever pursuing one another. He will never be able to obtain a kiss "though winning near the goal." This is an idealized love with no change in it; it is almost as if it were immortal. Their beauty cannot fade because it has been wrought on the urn which (in my estimation) is also a symbol of immortality. This brings to mind Hopkins' poem "The Leaden Echo and the Golden Echo," in which he assures the reader that by giving over one's soul and spiritual being to God early in life, despairing is, or should be, erased from the heart and mind of the believer.

In stanza three Keats repeats the state of the piper, spring, and the lovers, but adds to it the adjective "happy." His repetition of the word is not meant to be sentimental or sickening to the reader's ears. He uses it as a linking word, or feeling, to tie together three different images, all of which should be happy events.

> All breathing human passion far above,
> That leaves a heart high-sorrowful and cloy'd,
> A burning forehead, and a parching tongue.

These last three lines would seem to indicate that art is above life and our sources.

Stanza four begins in the same manner that stanza one ends—questioning. A description of the city and sacrifice is given in the midst of all the questioning. The altar is described as green and the heifer as having silken flanks, indicating fertility and plenty. The town is by a river or sea shore or mountain. Why then is there no one in the town? Why are the streets silent and empty? Why is everything so desolate? Pictured on the urn is the priest leading a heifer to the sacrifice. The town is not even pictured on the urn at all; it is to be imagined. Everyone is attending the sacrifice. Here again we have the blending or combining of human and divine. And here again we are asked to use our imaginations to create the art work.

The final stanza again gives a brief description of the urn and its impressions. In line forty-four it is a "silent form" that "dost tease us out of thought/ As doth eternity: Cold Pastoral." This could possibly mean that we are brought into a world of imagination that is only momentary and we get only a small glimpse of the eternal.

We are now, finally, brought to the last few lines of the poem. Naturally, some critics will feel that these lines were added to give an aesthetic viewpoint to the poem or to make a highly moral statement about beauty and truth. Several articles relating to the concept will now be discussed and analyzed and my own interpretation rendered.

In his article "Keats' 'Ode on a Grecial Urn,'" Wayne Warncke states:

> In demanding that we be always aware, agonizingly aware, of the large discrepancy between an imaginative-ly perceived beauty and the reality of which it is a part, the poem actually relates itself to reality and thus identifies art with reality. In fact the poem constantly asks us to think, as well as to feel—to be teased "out of thought" but, at the same time, to be aware of the conflict between the ideal and the real.
>
> The poem's truth is that art is not simply ideal beauty, but more important, art *is* a reality in the world, a friend to man in the midst of his woe to which man can come generation upon generation for sustenance, for

the human experience of beauty that gives life meaning and makes life worthwhile here and now.[4]

In reading poetry it is not necessary to be able to perceive what the poet has intended. The reader should use his imagination and glean everything he can out of a line of verse or one word. Hopkins' poetry is a supreme example of this very idea. Why then should the poem have to relate itself to reality and identify art with reality? Anyone but a fool, idealist, or Romantic is aware of the conflicts between the ideal and the real. And by the way, what is the definition of real and ideal? Real: Having no imaginary part; not artificial, fraudulent, illusory, or apparent; of or relating to fixed, permanent, or immovable things. Ideal: Existing as a mere mental image or in fancy or imagination only; lacking practicality. Now, of course we know that art is a reality in the world. Why then, did Keats title his poem "Ode *on* a Grecial Urn" instead of substituting the word *to* in its place? Because the urn is relating a message to us through our imaginations and Keats is not seen through the poem.

Virgil Hutton has this to say of the Beauty-Truth Concept:

> For the urn and its "overwrought" figures, "Beauty is truth, truth beauty," and that is all they know or need to know in their static world of beauty. But, the last line implies, man, because of his own and his world's mutability, knows that beauty is only a part of his truth. The urn befriends man by incarnating what he himself can attain so rarely: the enigma of beauty.
>
> Thus, the urn, where beauty and truth become one, offers its beauty-truth jingle to man not as a cryptic philosophical insight but as a feeble, slightly mocking consolation. And thus, as usual, an explication of the Ode's beginning has merely served as an excuse for discussing its close, which, when recognized as the culminating tragic contrast of the poem, attains a power similar to Swift's "serene peaceful state, of being a fool among knaves."[5]

The last lines of this statement ring true for most critics. There is no need to ruin a beautiful poem (up to this point) for the sake of a last "touch-up." Possibly the reader could *imagine* someone holding a gun to Keats's head and forcing him to write the last two lines—"Don't be a nerd. Your lines or your life!" Who would be so bold as to assault Keats?

Again, let me refer back to Swanson's essay for another encounter with the Classical and Romantic. When an aesthetically pleasing object stimulates a type of pure contemplation and a creation that is independent of the senses and, as Plato suggests in the *Symposium*, "the love of beauty, i.e., in a beautiful object, gives rise to the love of birth in beauty—then the derived pleasure is sweeter insofar as it is more abstract and less bound to sense."[6] Perhaps instead of "real" and "imaginary" we should use such concrete terms as "symmetry" and "asymmetry." In great art works, form and content coalesce, as one thing and another thing become the same thing: sound becomes silence, thought becomes experience, symmetry becomes asymmetry, the tangible becomes intangible, sculpture becomes literature, humanity becomes art, Classicism becomes Romanticism.[7] This is a truly great concept of the poem. Although art is reality, it can come alive in the mind of the artist and viewer.

We must, in studying the final lines of the poem, take into consideration its ultimate meaning. The intention of the poem should be to view art as the highest form of wisdom. A wisdom of the mortal and eternal. Earl Wasserman states that all man needs to know is: "The sum of earthly wisdom is that in this world of pain and decay, where love cannot be forever warm and where even the highest pleasures necessarily leave a burning forehead and a parching tongue, art remains, immutable in its essence because that essence is captured in a "Cold Pastoral," a form which has not been created for the destiny of progressing to a heaven-alter, as warm and passionate man is."[8]

Keats was a true artist. An artist in the sense of creating for us a tangible reality: poetry that we can comprehend, and the ability to imagine what we cannot. Keats wrote to Bailey on November 22, 1817, "I am certain of nothing but of the holiness of the Heart's affections, and the truth of Imagination—What the imagination seizes as Beauty must be truth—whether it existed before or not—for I have the same Idea of all our Passions as of Love they are all in their sublime, creative of essential Beauty."[9] As an artist, Keats has created for us a "thing of beauty."

NOTES

[1]Roy Arthur Swanson, "Form and Content in Keats' 'Ode on a Grecian Urn'," *College English*, 23 (1962), 302.

[2]Ibid., p. 304.

[3]Wayne Warncke, "Keats' 'Ode on a Grecian Urn'," *The Explicator*, 24, (1966), item 40.

[4]Ibid., p. 38.

[5]Virgil Hutton, "Keats' 'Ode on A Grecian Urn'," *The Explicator*, 19 (1961), item 40.

[6]Roy Arthur Swanson, "Form and Content in Keats' 'Ode on a Grecian Urn'," *College English*, 23 (1962), 304.

[7]Ibid., p. 304.

[8]Walter Jackson Bate, *Keats: A Collection of Critical Essays*, Englewood Cliffs, N.J.: Prentice-Hall (1964), p. 140.

BIBLIOGRAPHY

Bate, Walter Jackson, *Keats: A Collection of Critical Essays.* Englewood Cliffs, N.J.: Prentice-Hall, 1964.

Hutton, Virgil. "Keats' 'Ode on a Grecian Urn'." *The Explicator*, 19 (1961), item 40.

Swanson, Roy Arthur. "Form and Content in Keats' 'Ode on a Grecian Urn'." *College English*, 23 (1962).

Warncke, Wayne. "Keats' 'Ode on A Grecian Urn'." *The Explicator*, 24 (1966), item 40.

> Comment   *This is a good example of a research-oriented student paper. A problem is set up early in the study, and the rest of the paper is devoted to the solving of this problem. The student is careful to include appropriate comments from outside sources and to give full credit for these comments in her Notes and Bibliography. The basic fault in this paper is a nebulous quality, a tendency to drift away from the original problem. This weakens the argument.*

Bibliography

FICTION

History and
Criticism

Bader, A. L. "The Structure of the Modern Short Story." *College English*, 7 (November 1945), 86–92.

Baker, Howard. "The Contemporary Short Story." *The Southern Review*, vol. 3, no. 3 (1937-1938), 576–596.

Bates, H. E. *The Modern Short Story: A Critical Survey*. Boston: The Writer, 1961. (This volume was originally published in 1941.)

Canby, Henry Seidel. *The Short Story in English*. New York: Holt, Rinehart and Winston, 1909.

Gold, Herbert, ed. *Fiction of the Fifties: A Decade of American Writing*. New York: Doubleday, 1959. Pages 7–15.

Maugham, W. Somerset. "The Short Story." *Points of View: Five Essays*. Garden City, N.Y.: Doubleday, 1959. Pages 163–212.

O'Connor, Frank. *The Lonely Voice: A Study of the Short Story*. Cleveland and New York: World, 1963.

O'Faolain, Sean. *The Short Story*. New York: Devin-Adair, 1951.

Peden, William. *The American Short Story: Front Line in the National Defense of Literature*. Boston: Houghton Mifflin, 1964.

Ross, Danforth. *The American Short Story*. Minneapolis: University of Minnesota Press, 1961.

Welty, Eudora. *Short Stories.* New York: Harcourt, Brace and World, 1949.

West, Ray B., Jr. *The Short Story in America: 1900–1950.* Chicago: Regnery, 1952.

Wright, Austin McGiffert. *The American Short Story in the Twenties.* Chicago: University of Chicago Press, 1961.

Other References

Jones, Howard Mumford. *Guide to American Literature and Its Backgrounds since 1890.*

Leary, Lewis. *Articles on American Literature, 1900-1950.*

Millett, Fred B. *Contemporary American Authors: A Critical Survey and 219 Bio-Bibliographies.*

Smith, Frank R. "Periodical Articles on the American Short Story: A Selected, Annotated Bibliography."

Walker, Warren S. *Twentieth-Century Short Story Explication: Interpretations, 1900-1966.*

Woodress, James, ed. *American Literary Scholarship: An Annual.*

Periodicals

Abstracts of English Studies
American Literature
The Explicator
Modern Language Quarterly
Modern Philology
Nineteenth Century Fiction
Philological Quarterly
PMLA: Publications of the Modern Language Association of America
Studies in Short Fiction

POETRY

History and Theory

Bodkin, Maud. *Archetypal Patterns in Poetry.* London, 1934, 1965. Oxford Paperbacks, No. 66.

Brooks, Cleanth. *Modern Poetry and the Tradition.* Chapel Hill, N.C., 1939; New York, 1965. Galaxy Books, GB-150.

———. *The Well-Wrought Urn: Studies in the Structure of Poetry.* New York, 1947, 1964. Harvest Books, HB-11.

Burke, Kenneth. *A Grammar of Motives.* Englewood Cliffs, N.J.: Prentice-Hall, 1945.

Bush, Douglas. *Mythology and the Renaissance Tradition in English Poetry.* London, 1932; New York, 1963. Norton Library, N-187.

————. *Mythology and the Romantic Tradition in English Poetry.* Cambridge, Mass., 1937, 1969. Norton Library, N–186.

Collingwood, R. G. *Essays in the Philosophy of Art.* Bloomington: University of Indiana Press, 1964.

Daiches, David. *Poetry and the Modern World: A Study of Poetry in England between 1900 and 1939.* New York: Biblo and Tannen, 1969.

Deutsch, Babette. *Poetry in Our Time.* 2d ed., Garden City, N.Y.: Doubleday (Anchor), 1963.

Dubos, René. *So Human an Animal.* New York: Scribners, 1969.

Empson, William. *Seven Types of Ambiguity.* New York: New Directions, 1949.

Frye, Northrop. *Anatomy of Criticism.* Princeton: Princeton University Press, 1971.

Pearce, Roy Harvey. *The Continuity of American Poetry.* Princeton: Princeton University Press, 1961.

Ransom, John Crowe. *The World's Body.* New York: Scribners, 1938, 1968.

Richards, I. A. *Practical Criticism: A Study of Literary Judgement.* London and New York, 1929, 1962. Harvest Books, HB–16.

————. *Science and Poetry.* New York: Norton, 1926.

Shapiro, Karl, and Robert Beum. *A Prosody Handbook.* New York: 1965.

Waggoner, Hyatt H. *American Poets: From the Puritans to the Present.* Boston: Houghton Mifflin 1968.

Individual Figures

Blackmur, R. P. *Form and Value in Modern Poetry.* Garden City, N.Y.: Doubleday (Anchor), 1957.

Eliot, T. S. *On Poetry and Poets.* New York: Farrar, Straus, 1957.

————. *Selected Essays.* New York: Harcourt Brace Jovanovich, 1950.

Jarrell, Randall. *Poetry and the Age.* New York, 1953, 1955. Vintage Books, K-12.

Leavis, F. R. *New Bearings in English Poetry.* London, 1932; New York, 1950. Ann Arbor Paperbacks, AA–36.

Miller, J. Hillis. *Poets of Reality: Six 20th-Century Writers.* New York: Atheneum, 1965.

Rosenthal, M. L. *The Modern Poets.* New York: Oxford University Press, 1960.

Wilson, Edmund. *Axel's Castle.* New York: Scribners, 1950.

Winters, Yvor. *In Defense of Reason.* Denver: Swallow, 1943.

Other
References

Halle, Morris, and Samuel Jay Keyser. *English Stress: Its Form, Its Growth and Its Role in Verse.*

Kuntz, Joseph M. *Poetry Explication: A Checklist of Interpretation Since 1925 of British and American Poems Past and Present.*

Preminger, Alex, ed. *Princeton Encyclopedia of Poetry and Poetics.*

Shapiro, Karl. *Prose Keys to Modern Poetry.*

Periodicals

American Poetry Review
The Atlantic
Berkeley Poets Cooperative
Kenyon Review
The Massachusetts Review
New York Quarterly
New York Review of Books
Paris Review

DRAMA

Theory

Bentley, Eric. *The Life of the Drama.* New York: Atheneum, 1964.

Brooks, Cleanth, and Robert B. Heilman. *Understanding Drama: Twelve Plays.* New York: Holt, 1948.

Cole, Toby, ed. *Playwrights on Playwriting: The Meaning and Making of Modern Drama from Ibsen to Ionesco.* New York: Hill and Wang (Dramabook), 1960.

Corrigan, Robert W., ed. *Comedy: Meaning and Form.* San Francisco: Chandler, 1965.

———, ed. *Tragedy: Vision and Form.* San Francisco: Chandler, 1965.

——— and James L. Rosenberg, eds. *The Context and Craft of Drama.* San Francisco: Chandler, 1964.

Downer, Alan S. *The Art of the Play: An Anthology of Nine Plays.* New York: Holt, 1955.

Drew, Elizabeth. *Discovering Drama.* New York: Norton, 1937.

Fergusson, Francis. *The Human Image in Dramatic Literature.* Garden City, N.Y.: Doubleday (Anchor), 1957.

———. *The Idea of a Theater.* Garden City, N.Y.: Doubleday (Anchor), 1949.

Kerr, Walter. *Tragedy and Comedy.* New York: Simon and Schuster, 1967.

Nicoll, Allardyce. *The Theatre and Dramatic Theory*. New York: Barnes and Noble, 1962.
———. *The Theory of Drama*. London: Harrap, 1937.

History and Criticism

Bentley, Eric. *In Search of Theater*. New York: Knopf, 1953.
———. *The Playwright as Thinker*. New York: Meridian, 1957.

Bogard, Travis, and William I. Oliver, eds. *Modern Drama: Essays in Criticism*. New York: Oxford University Press, 1965.

Clark, Barrett H., and George Freedley, eds. *A History of Modern Drama*. New York: Appleton-Century, 1947.

Corrigan, Robert W., ed. *Theatre in the Twentieth Century*. New York: Grove Press, 1963.

Downer, Alan S. *Fifty Years of American Drama*. Chicago: Regnery 1951.

Esslin, Martin. *The Theatre of the Absurd*. Garden City, N.Y.: Doubleday (Anchor), 1961.

Freedman, Morris, ed. *Essays in the Modern Drama*. Boston: Heath, 1964.

———. *The Moral Impulse: Modern Drama from Ibsen to the Present*. Carbondale: Southern Illinois University Press, 1967.

Gassner, John. *Form and Idea in Modern Theatre*. New York: Dryden Press, 1956.

———. *Masters of the Drama*. 3d rev. ed. New York: Dover, 1954.

———. *The Theatre in Our Times*. New York: Crown, 1954.

Krutch, Joseph Wood. *"Modernism" in Modern Drama*. Ithaca, N.Y.: Cornell University Press, 1953.

Lumley, Frederick. *Trends in Twentieth Century Drama*. New York: Oxford University Press (Essential Books), 1960.

Nicoll, Allardyce. *World Drama from Aeschylus to Anouilh*. London: Harrap, 1949.

Williams, Raymond. *Drama from Ibsen to Eliot*. London: Chatto & Windus, 1952.

Periodicals

Drama Survey
Educational Theatre Journal
Plays and Players
The Drama Review
World Theatre

Glossary

Alliteration	the repetition of initial sounds in words, e.g., "*w*eary *w*anderer"
Allusion	a device whereby the writer refers to or plays upon a personage or event usually biblical, classical, literary, or historical in nature. The reference can aid the reader in his understanding of the piece, but is not absolutely essential to such understanding. Allusions, then, are often indirect and can pass unnoticed by the inexperienced reader. Once recognized, allusions can be easily understood, and thus they are more literal than figurative in application
Ambiguity	see *Irony*
Anapestic foot	two unstressed syllables followed by one stressed one
Antagonist	the character or group of characters against whom the protagonist struggles
Antithesis	a figure of speech embodying a marked contrast in words, word groups, or thoughts. Alexander Pope's "Man proposes, God disposes" is an example
Apostrophe	a figure of speech in which a person, subject, or quality is addressed as though it were a person, and present. An example is Michael Drayton's line, "Stay, stay, sweet Time . . ."

1199

Artistic unity	that quality of a literary work in which each part develops logically and works intentionally with every other part to achieve the author's desired effects
Aside	an utterance by a character who is addressing another character or the audience
Assonance	the close repetition of the same vowels followed by different consonants, such as "rolled over"
Ballad stanza	a quatrain with the first and third lines in iambic tetrameter and the second and fourth in iambic trimeter; the second and fourth being rhymed
Blank verse	unrhymed iambic pentameter; used most often in long serious poems
Caesura	a rest or pause in the metrical progression of a line
Climax	the point at which the opposing forces reach the apex of their struggle; the highest emotional peak; the moment of truth
Complication	a moment of crisis; an occurrence that makes the conflict more difficult to resolve
Conceit	a variety of metaphor in which the objects compared are particularly dissimilar. The figure of speech thus aims at highlighting a striking parallel, like that in George Herbert's "The Windows," in which the poet compares a minister to a stained-glass window through which God's light shines
Conflict	a clash between opposing forces resulting in opposition to the desires of the protagonist
Connotations	the meanings and associations that a word suggests to the reader in addition to the literal meaning (or denotation)
Consistency	a quality of behavior that corresponds to the dictates of a character's established nature
Consonance	the repetition of consonant sounds without corresponding repetition of vowel sounds "A heavyhanded hundredfold" from "The Leader Echo and the Golden Echo" by Gerard Manley Hopkins
Controlling image	one that throughout an entire passage dominates the responses evoked
Context	the passages surrounding a word, phrase, or section that can illuminate meaning

Couplet	a pair of lines that are rhymed at the end of each line
Dactylic foot	one stressed syllable followed by two unstressed
Denotations	see *Connotations* and *Literal meaning*
Dialogue	the speech of characters; their conversations
Diction	the author's choice of words
Dimeter	a line of poetry with two feet
Dramatic irony	the reader or spectator's awareness of the truth regarding a speech or an incident about which the characters remain ignorant
Dramatic point of view	the telling of a story objectively without access to the consciousness of any character
Dynamic character	a developing character whose conflict brings about a lasting change in personality, basic values, or concept of human nature
Epiphany	a moment of awareness, revelation, or insight for the reader and sometimes for the characters that usually occurs near the end of a story
Exposition	the technique of furnishing background information necessary to an understanding of a story or play
Figurative image	an image that involves a shift in the literal meaning of a word or group of words
Figurative language	language that involves an alteration of the normal, literal meaning or use of words. One or more of the figures of speech is employed
Figures of speech	the various types of alteration in the normal literal meanings of words used to create an effect
First-person point of view	the telling of a story through the "I" of the story
Fixed image	an image for which the association and meanings are approximately the same for all readers. A fixed image is designed to evoke a predictable response. See *Free image*
Flat character	a character drawn with only surface facts and details
Foot	a group of two, three, or more syllables; the basic metrical unit
Foreshadowing	a device achieved by a particular speech, action, or symbol that permits a reader or viewer to anticipate a happening

Free image	an image open to various responses and having a variety of meanings. In contrast to a fixed image, it requires considerable use of the reader's imagination; if extremely free, the image becomes almost no image
Free verse	poetry that does not conform to any predetermined configurations based on accents or syllables
Hexameter	a six-foot poetic line
Heroic couplet	a couplet of iambic pentameter lines that are end-stopped, that is, finished with a strong punctuation mark like a period or colon. Each line is usually balanced with a caesura, or rest, somewhere in the middle
Hyperbole	a figure of speech employing exaggeration, for the purpose of creating an effect rather than persuading literally
Iambic foot	one unstressed syllable followed by a stressed one
Image	a word or group of words that causes the reader to experience sensory impressions. As a literary term, "image" is not limited to visual impressions, but includes all sensory experience, such as that caused by sound, taste, smell, touch, temperature, distance, and movement
Image cluster	a grouping of similar images in a short passage
Image pattern	an arrangement, perhaps created subconsciously by the writer, of images in such a relationship with each other and with the action of the work as to suggest particular meanings. The recurrence of one or more images is a simple image pattern
Imagery	a group of single images
Internal rhyme	the repetition of terminal sounds in words, like "c*at*", and "r*at*," when they occur within a line of poetry rather than at the end
Irony	a figure of speech in which the intended meaning is just the opposite of the stated meaning. Irony is sometimes a matter of context, i.e., the situation surrounding the statement. For example, the simple statement "It is very sunny outside" would be ironic if it were actually pouring at the time the statement was made. Ambiguity is a situation wherein a word might have more than one meaning, and thus it lends itself to ironic statement.

If irony is saying one thing and meaning another, then ambiguity is saying one thing and meaning it, but meaning another as well. Paradox is the intellectual result of extended ironic discourse and ambiguous phrasing. A paradoxical statement can seem to be inherently contradictory or contrary to fact and experience. Usually, however, the paradox is resolved by logically considering the statement from another angle of experience. For example, a statement that is a contradiction according to physical law may be true according to religious metaphor: "Adam fell so that he might rise." Even when a paradoxical statement insists on nonsense logically, it may nevertheless resolve itself into emotional sense

Literal image an image that involves no change or turn in meaning

Literal meaning the standard, dictionary meaning (or denotation)

Metaphor a figure of speech in which an implied comparison between two unlike subjects is expressed. The major subject is the tenor and the secondary subject that is identified with it is the vehicle. These lines by Milton contain a metaphor in which the morning (the tenor) is identified with a pilgrim (the vehicle):

Thus passed the night so foul till morning fair
Came forth with pilgrim steps in amice gray.

A *simple metaphor* is one in which only a single correlation between the tenor and vehicle is intended. An *extended metaphor* incorporates multiple similarities

Meter the regular rhythm of poetry

Monometer a line of poetry with only one foot

Mood see *Voice*

Motivation that which causes a character to behave as he or she does

Narrator one who recounts the events or experiences of a story, poem, novel, or play

Obstacle the force opposing the protagonist—other human beings, society, environment, fate, or some aspect of the self

Octave an eight-line stanza

Omniscient point of view a God-like omniscience and "all-knowing" position from which a story is told

One-dimensional character	a person whom the author sketches simply as a flat, stock or stereotyped, static, or unchanging character
Ottava rima	a stanza consisting of eight lines of iambic pentameter with a rhyme scheme of *abababcc*
Paradox	see *Irony*
Pathetic fallacy	a variation of personification ascribing to any nonhuman subject human emotions. George Herbert employs the pathetic fallacy in the following lines from "Virtue":

> Sweet day, so cool, so calm, so bright
>   The bridal of the earth and sky;
> The dew shall weep they fall tonight,
>   For thou must die.

Pentameter	a line of poetry with five feet
Persona	see *Voice*
Personification	a figure of speech that metaphorically endows anything nonhuman with human form or any human qualities. A slight personification involves a single correlation; a more complete personification involves multiple correlations
Plausibility	the quality that permits the acceptance of a character, an action, or speech as true
Plot	the sequence of interrelated actions and events that make up a story or drama
Point of attack	the incident or initial complication that introduces the conflict
Point of view	the eyes and mind through which the reader views the unfolding of events in a story
Prize	the goal of the protagonist; what the protagonist wants or strives to achieve or overcome
Prologue	an introductory part to a poem, play or novel, which gives background information
Protagonist	the chief character who generally controls or forces most of the important action
Quatrain	any stanza or poem of four lines
Resolution	the settling or the outcome of the conflict
Retrospection	a flashback in which the action shifts to something that happened earlier

Rhyme	the correspondence of terminal sounds in words, e.g., the repetition of the *ong* sound in "strong" and "along"
Rhythm	patterns of intonation and stress that are found in all language forms
Round character	a fully developed character as opposed to a flat or stock character
Scanning	analyzing a line of poetry in order to determine its meter
Sestet	a six-line stanza
Setting	the elements of time and place
Simile	a figure of speech employing a directly stated comparison between two unlike subjects; the tenor and vehicle are clearly stated and are usually connected by *like* or *as*. Similes are simple if a single similarity is intended, and extended if many relevant similarities exist
Situation irony	the effects achieved by the discrepancy between what one expects to happen and what actually does happen
Soliloquy	an utterance by a character who is talking to himself
Sonnet	a fourteen-line poem written in iambic pentameter with a specific rhyme scheme. The Italian or Petrarchan sonnet is divided into two parts, an octave usually rhymed *abbaabba* and a sestet rhyming much as the poet chooses. The English or Shakespearean sonnet is divided into three quatrains and ends with a rhymed couplet. The rhyme scheme is *ababcdcd efefgg*
Spencerian stanza	a nine-line stanza, with eight lines of iambic pentameter and a last line of iambic hexameter, called an *alexandrine*. The rhyme scheme is *ababbcbcc*
Sprung rhythm	a theory of prosody developed by Gerard Manley Hopkins. According to Hopkins, the basis for the organization of the poetic lines is a fixed number of stressed syllables in the line with no regard for the unstressed syllables
Stage directions	information about character and action especially valuable to the director, the actor, and the reader
Stanza	a group of lines organized into a regular pattern, usually involving both meter and rhyme
Static character	a minor character who rarely revises his essential nature

Stereotyped or stock character	a character sketched lightly with one or two easily recognizable traits
Style	an author's distinct manner of writing a story, a poem, or a play
Suspense	the curiosity or anxiety the reader feels about what will happen next
Symbol	a person, place, action, or object in which a multitude of possible meanings inhere. Symbols are artificial referents that the mind makes on the basis of associations and resemblances, either drawn from common personal experiences or based on established literary conventions. A river is like time; a lion acts like a king; a flower is fragile and beautiful like youth and love. Every symbolic statement implies a metaphor and relies heavily upon the connotative quality of words
Syntax	the arrangement and interrelationship of words in phrases and sentences
Tenor	one of the two essential elements of a metaphor or simile. The tenor constitutes the major subject and is compared with the vehicle, or secondary subject. See metaphor
Tercet	a three-line stanza
Terza rima	three-line stanzas rhyming *aba*, *bcb*, *cdc*, *ded*, etc., to provide an interlocking rhyme scheme
Tetrameter	a line of poetry with four feet
Theme	the central meaning, thesis, premise, or significance of a literary work
Three-dimensional character	a person whom the author delineates fully as a round, dynamic, or developing character
Tone	an author's attitude toward material and audience
Trimeter	a line of poetry with three feet
Trochaic foot	a stressed syllable followed by an unstressed one
Vehicle	the secondary subject in a metaphor or simile. See metaphor
Verbal irony	the effects achieved when a speaker says one thing but means the opposite
Vers libre	French for *Free verse*

Villanelle a poetic form made up of five tercets rhyming *aba* with a quatrain at the end rhyming *abaa*

Voice the total effect of the poet's words. *Mood* constitutes the speaker's attitude toward the subject. *Tone* is the attitude toward the reader that the poet's style suggests. *Persona* is the combination of those two attitudes, constituting the speaker's mask. The poet-as-speaker can assume the expressive "I" persona or mask of lyric poetry or can play a character, as in dramatic poetry ("The Passionate Shepherd to His Love," "Andrea del Sarto") or can tell us a story without being personally involved in the action, as in narrative poetry ("The Rape of the Lock"). Whatever role the speaker assumes, voice gives us a sense of the poet's attitude toward subject and reader and allows him or her to indicate how literally and on what level the poetic statements are to be taken

Indexes

AUTHORS' NAMES, TITLES, AND
FIRST LINES OF POEMS

Names of authors appear in capitals, titles in italics, and first lines of poems in
roman. Numbers in roman type indicate pages where authors and their selections
appear; numbers in italics indicate discussion of story, poem, or play.

We caught the tread of dancing feet, 696

Wednesday morning at five o'clock as the day begins, 426

Weep you no more, sad fountains, 559

Well then; I now do plainly see, 585

WELTY, EUDORA, 254–262

What dire offense from amorous causes springs, 644

What happens to a dream deferred, 611

What passing-bells for these who die as cattle, 637

When a man hath no freedom, 579

Whenever Richard Cory went down town, 665

When I am dead, my dearest, 483

When I consider how my light is spent, 632–633

When I heard the learn'd astronomer, 694

When, in disgrace with fortune and men's eyes, 673

When in the chronicle of wasted time, 493

When I see birches bend to left and right, 598

When I survey the wondrous cross, 693

Where the quiet-colored end of evening smiles, 570

Where true Love burns Desire is Love's pure flame, 584

White House, The, 433

WHITMAN, WALT, 457, 486, 526–527, 693–695

Who has ever stopped to think of the divinity of Lamont Cranston?, 521

Whose woods these are I think I know, 598

Why have such scores of lovely, gifted girls, 600

WILBUR, RICHARD, 695–696

WILDE, OSCAR, 696–698

WILLIAMS, WILLIAM CARLOS, 478, 531–532

WILLIS, NATHANIEL, 429

Windhover, The, 479

Windows, The, 604

Winter, 449–450

Wish, The, 585

Woof of the sun, ethereal gauze, 473

WOOLF, VIRGINIA, 362–364

WORDSWORTH, WILLIAM, 463, 502, 698–701

World, The, 455

World is too much with us, The, 699

Worn Path, A, 6, 14, 147–148, 199, 203, 254–261, 261–262

WRIGHT, RICHARD, 326–336

WYATT, THOMAS, 476–477

WYLIE, ELINOR, 448–449

YEATS, WILLIAM BUTLER, 439–440, 446–447, 509–510, 523

You, Andrew Marvell, 628–629

"You are old, father William," 582

You do not do, you do not do, 518

YOUNG, AL, 428

Your door is shut against my tightened face, 433